Praise for *OpenGL® Shading Language*

"As the 'Red Book' is known to be the gold standard for OpenGL, the 'Orange Book' is considered to be the gold standard for the OpenGL Shading Language. With Randi's extensive knowledge of OpenGL and GLSL, you can be assured you will be learning from a graphics industry veteran. Within the pages of the second edition you can find topics from beginning shader development to advanced topics such as the spherical harmonic lighting model and more."

—David Tommeraasen
CEO/Programmer
Plasma Software

"This will be the definitive guide for OpenGL shaders; no other book goes into this detail. Rost has done an excellent job at setting the stage for shader development, what the purpose is, how to do it, and how it all fits together. The book includes great examples and details, as well as good additional coverage of 2.0 changes!"

—Jeffery Galinovsky
Director of Emerging Market
Platform Development
Intel Corporation

"The coverage in this new edition of the book is pitched just right to help many new shader-writers get started, but with enough deep information for the 'old hands.'"

—Marc Olano
Assistant Professor
University of Maryland

"This is a really great book on GLSL—well written and organized, very accessible, and with good real-world examples and sample code. The topics flow naturally and easily, explanatory code fragments are inserted in very logical places to illustrate concepts, and, all in all, this book makes an excellent tutorial as well as a reference."

—John Carey
Chief Technology Officer
C.O.R.E. Feature Animation

"*OpenGL® Shading Language* provides a timely, thorough, and entertaining introduction to the only OpenGL ARB-approved high-level shading language in existence. Whether an expert or a novice, there are gems to be discovered throughout the book, and the reference pages will be your constant companion as you dig into the depths of the shading APIs. From algorithms to APIs, this book has you covered."

—Bob Kuehne
CEO, Blue Newt Software

"Computer graphics and rendering technologies just took a giant leap forward with hardware vendors rapidly adopting the new OpenGL Shading Language. This book presents a detailed treatment of these exciting technologies in a way that is extremely helpful for visualization and game developers."

—Andy McGovern
Founder
Virtual Geographics, Inc.

"The OpenGL Shading Language is at the epicenter of the programmable graphics revolution, and Randi Rost has been at the center of the development of this significant new industry standard. If you need the inside track on how to use the OpenGL Shading Language to unleash new visual effects and unlock the supercomputer hiding inside the new generation of graphics hardware, then this is the book for you."

—Neil Trevett
Senior Vice President
Market Development
3Dlabs

OpenGL® Shading Language
Third Edition

OpenGL®
Shading
Language
Third Edition

Randi J. Rost
Bill Licea-Kane

With contributions by
Dan Ginsburg,
John M. Kessenich,
Barthold Lichtenbelt,
Hugh Malan, and
Mike Weiblen

✦Addison-Wesley

Upper Saddle River, NJ • Boston • Indianapolis • San Francisco
New York • Toronto • Montreal • London • Munich • Paris • Madrid
Capetown • Sydney • Tokyo • Singapore • Mexico City

Many of the designations used by manufacturers and sellers to distinguish their products are claimed as trademarks. Where those designations appear in this book, and the publisher was aware of a trademark claim, the designations have been printed with initial capital letters or in all capitals.

The authors and publisher have taken care in the preparation of this book, but make no expressed or implied warranty of any kind and assume no responsibility for errors or omissions. No liability is assumed for incidental or consequential damages in connection with or arising out of the use of the information or programs contained herein.

The publisher offers excellent discounts on this book when ordered in quantity for bulk purchases or special sales, which may include electronic versions and/or custom covers and content particular to your business, training goals, marketing focus, and branding interests. For more information, please contact:

U.S. Corporate and Government Sales
(800) 382-3419
corpsales@pearsontechgroup.com

For sales outside the United States, please contact:

International Sales
international@pearsoned.com

Visit us on the Web: informit.com/aw

Library of Congress Cataloging-in-Publication Data

Rost, Randi J., 1960-
  OpenGL shading language / Randi J. Rost, Bill Licea-Kane ; with contributions by Dan Ginsburg ... [et al.]. — 3rd ed.
      p.   cm.
  Includes bibliographical references and index.
  ISBN 978-0-321-63763-5 (pbk. : alk. paper) 1. Computer graphics. I. Licea-Kane, Bill. II. Title.
  T385.R665 2009
  006.6'86—dc22

                                                                        2009019529

ISBN-13: 978-0-321-63763-5
ISBN-10:   0-321-63763-1
Text printed in the United States on recycled paper at Edwards Brothers in Ann Arbor, Michigan.
First printing, July 2009

*To Baby Cakes, Baby Doll, Love Bug, and
Little Zooka—thanks for your love and support*

To Mom and Pop—my first and best teachers

Contents

Foreword to the Second Edition

To me, graphics shaders are about the coolest things to ever happen in computer graphics. I grew up in graphics in the 1970s, watching the most amazing people do the most amazing things with the mathematics of graphics. I remember Jim Blinn's bump-mapping technique, for instance, and what effects it was able to create. The method was deceptively simple, but the visual impact was momentous. True, it took a substantial amount of time for a computer to work through the pixel-by-pixel software process to make that resulting image, but we cared about that only a little bit. It was the effect that mattered.

My memory now fast-forwards to the 1980s. Speed became a major issue, with practitioners like Jim Clark working on placing graphics algorithms in silicon. This resulted in the blossoming of companies such as Evans & Sutherland and Silicon Graphics. They brought fast, interactive 3D graphics to the masses, but the compromise was that they forced us into doing our work using standard APIs that could easily be hardware supported. Deep-down procedural techniques such as bump mapping could not follow where the hardware was leading.

But the amazing techniques survived in software. Rob Cook's classic paper on shade trees brought attention to the idea of using software "shaders" to perform the pixel-by-pixel computations that could deliver the great effects. This was embodied by the Photorealistic RenderMan rendering software. The book *RenderMan Companion* by Steve Upstill is still the first reference that I point my students to when they want to learn about the inner workings of shaders. The ability to achieve such fine-grained control over the graphics rendering process gave RenderMan users the ability to create the dazzling, realistic effects seen in Pixar animation shorts and TV commercials. The process was still miles away from real time, but the seed of the idea of giving an *interactive* application developer that type of control was planted. And it was such a powerful idea that it was only a matter of time until it grew.

Now, fast-forward to the start of the new millennium. The major influence on graphics was no longer science and engineering applications. It had become games and other forms of entertainment. (Nowhere has this been more obvious than in the composition of the SIGGRAPH Exhibition.) Because games live and die by their ability to deliver realistic effects at interactive speeds, the shader seed planted a few years earlier was ready to flourish in this new domain. The capacity to place procedural graphics rendering algorithms into the graphics hardware was definitely an idea whose time had come. Interestingly, it brought the graphics community full circle. We searched old SIGGRAPH proceedings to see how pixel-by-pixel scene control was performed in software then, so we could "re-invent" it using interactive shader code.

So, here we are in the present, reading Randi Rost's *OpenGL Shading Language*. This is the next book I point my shader-intrigued students to, after Upstill's. It is also the one that I, and they, use most often day to day. By now, my first edition is pretty worn.

But great news—I have an excuse to replace it! This second edition is a *major* enhancement over the first. This is more than just errata corrections. There is substantial new material in this book. New chapters on lighting, shadows, surface characteristics, and RealWorldz are essential for serious effects programmers. There are also 18 new shader examples. The ones I especially like are shadow mapping, vertex noise, image-based lighting, and environmental mapping with cube maps. But they are all really good, and you will find them all useful.

The OpenGL Shading Language is now part of standard OpenGL. It will be used everywhere. There is no reason not to. Anybody interested in effects graphics programming will want to read this book cover to cover. There are many nuggets to uncover. But GLSL is useful even beyond those borders. For example, we use it in our visualization research here at OSU (dome transformation, line integral convolution, image compression, terrain data mapping, etc.). I know that GLSL will find considerable applications in many other non-game areas as well.

I want to express my appreciation to Randi, who obviously started working on the first edition of this book even before the GLSL specification was fully decided upon. This must have made the book extra difficult to write, but it let the rest of us jump on the information as soon as it was stable. Thanks, too, for this second edition. It will make a significant contribution to the shader-programming community, and we appreciate it.

—Mike Bailey, Ph.D.
Professor, Computer Science
Oregon State University

Foreword to the First Edition

This book is an amazing measure of how far and how fast interactive shading has advanced. Not too many years ago, procedural shading was something done only in offline production rendering, creating some of the great results we all know from the movies, but were not anywhere close to interactive. Then a few research projects appeared, allowing a slightly modified but largely intact type of procedural shading to run in real time. Finally, in a rush, widely accessible commercial systems started to support shading. Today, we've come to the point where a real-time shading language developed by a cross-vendor group of OpenGL participants has achieved official designation as an OpenGL Architecture Review Board approved extension. This book, written by one of those most responsible for spearheading the development and acceptance of the OpenGL shading language, is your guide to that language and the extensions to OpenGL that let you use it.

I came to my interest in procedural shading from a strange direction. In 1990, I started graduate school at the University of North Carolina in Chapel Hill because it seemed like a good place for someone whose primary interest was interactive 3D graphics. There, I started working on the Pixel-Planes project. This project had produced a new graphics machine with several interesting features beyond its performance at rendering large numbers of polygons per second. One feature in particular had an enormous impact on the research directions I've followed for the past 13 years. Pixel-Planes 5 had programmable pixel processors—lots of them. Programming these processors was similar in many ways to the assembly-language fragment programs that have burst onto the graphics scene in the past few years.

Programming them was exhilarating, yet also thoroughly exasperating.

I was far from the only person to notice both the power and pain of writing low-level code to execute per-pixel. Another group within the Pixel-Planes team built an assembler for shading code to make it a little easier to write, although it was still both difficult to write a good shader and ever-so-rewarding once you had it working. The shaders produced will be familiar to anyone who has seen demos of any of the latest graphics products, and not surprisingly you'll find versions of many of them in this book: wood, clouds, brick, rock, reflective wavy water, and (of course) the Mandelbrot fractal set.

The rewards and difficulties presented by Pixel-Planes 5 shaders guided many of the design decisions behind the next machine, PixelFlow. PixelFlow was designed and built by a university/industry partnership with industrial participation first by Division, then by Hewlett-Packard. The result was the first interactive system capable of running procedural shaders compiled from a high-level shading language. PixelFlow was demonstrated at the SIGGRAPH conference in 1997. For a few years thereafter, if you were fortunate enough to be at UNC-Chapel Hill, you could write procedural shaders and run them in real time when no one else could. And, of course, the only way to see them in action was to go there.

I left UNC for a shading project at SGI, with the hopes of providing a commercially supported shading language that could be used on more than just one machine at one site. Meanwhile, a shading language research project started up at Stanford, with some important results for shading on PC-level graphics hardware. PC graphics vendors across the board started to add low-level shading capabilities to their hardware. Soon, people everywhere could write shading code similar in many ways to that which had so inspired me on the Pixel-Planes 5 machine. And, not surprisingly, soon people everywhere also knew that we were going to need a higher-level language for interactive shading.

Research continues into the use, improvement, and abuse of these languages at my lab at University of Maryland, Baltimore County; and at many, many others. However, the mere existence of real-time high-level shading languages is no longer the subject of that research. Interactive shading languages have moved from the research phase to wide availability. There are a number of options for anyone wanting to develop an application using the shading capabilities of modern graphics hardware. The principal choices are Cg, HLSL, and the OpenGL Shading Language. The last of which has the distinction of being the only one that has been through a rigorous multivendor review process. I participated in that process, as did more than two dozen representatives from a dozen companies and universities.

This brings us back full circle to this book. If you are holding this book now, you are most likely interested in some of the same ideals that drove the creation of the OpenGL Shading Language, the desire for a cross-OS, cross-platform, robust and standardized shading language. You want to learn how to use all of that? Open up and start reading. Then get shading!

—Marc Olano
University of Maryland
Baltimore County, MD
September 2003

Preface

For just about as long as there has been graphics hardware, there has been programmable graphics hardware. Over the years, building flexibility into graphics hardware designs has been a necessary way of life for hardware developers. Graphics APIs continue to evolve, and because a hardware design can take two years or more from start to finish, the only way to guarantee a hardware product that can support the then current graphics APIs at its release is to build in some degree of programmability from the very beginning.

Until recently, the realm of programming graphics hardware belonged to just a few people, mainly researchers and graphics hardware driver developers. Research into programmable graphics hardware has been taking place for many years, but the point of this research has not been to produce viable hardware and software for application developers and end users. The graphics hardware driver developers have focused on the immediate task of providing support for the important graphics APIs of the time: PHIGS, PEX, Iris GL, OpenGL, Direct3D, and so on. Until recently, none of these APIs exposed the programmability of the underlying hardware, so application developers have been forced into using the fixed functionality provided by traditional graphics APIs.

Hardware companies have not exposed the programmable underpinnings of their products because of the high cost of educating and supporting customers to use low-level, device-specific interfaces and because these interfaces typically change quite radically with each new generation of graphics hardware. Application developers who use such a device-specific interface to a piece of graphics hardware face the daunting task of updating their software for each new generation of hardware that comes along. And forget about supporting the application on hardware from multiple vendors!

As we moved into the 21st century, some of these fundamental tenets about graphics hardware were challenged. Application developers pushed the envelope as never before and demanded a variety of new features in hardware in order to create more and more sophisticated onscreen effects. As a result, new graphics hardware designs became more programmable than ever before. Standard graphics APIs were challenged to keep up with the pace of hardware innovation. For OpenGL, the result was a spate of extensions to the core API as hardware vendors struggled to support a range of interesting new features that their customers were demanding.

The creation of a standard, cross-platform, high-level shading language for commercially available graphics hardware was a watershed event for the graphics industry. A paradigm shift occurred, one that took us from the world of rigid, fixed functionality graphics hardware and graphics APIs to a brave new world where the graphics processing unit, or GPU (i.e., graphics hardware), is as important as the central processing unit, or CPU. The GGU is optimized for processing dynamic media such as 3D graphics and video. Highly parallel processing of floating-point data is the primary task for GPUs, and the flexibility of the GPU means that it can also be used to process data other than a stream of traditional graphics commands. Applications can take advantage of the capabilities of both the CPU and the GPU, using the strengths of each to optimally perform the task at hand.

This book describes how graphics hardware programmability is exposed through a high-level language in the leading cross-platform 3D graphics API: OpenGL. This language, the OpenGL Shading Language, lets applications take total control over the most important stages of the graphics processing pipeline. No longer restricted to the graphics rendering algorithms and formulas chosen by hardware designers and frozen in silicon, software developers are beginning to use this programmability to create stunning effects in real time.

Intended Audience

The primary audience for this book is application programmers who want to write shaders. This book can be used as both a tutorial and a reference book by people interested in learning to write shaders with the OpenGL Shading Language. Some will use the book in one fashion, and some in the other. The organization is amenable to both uses and is based on the assumption that most people won't read the book in sequential order from back to front (but some intrepid readers of the first edition reported that they did just that!).

Readers do not need previous knowledge of OpenGL to absorb the material in this book, but such knowledge is very helpful. A brief review of OpenGL is included, but this book does not attempt to be a tutorial or reference book for OpenGL. Anyone attempting to develop an OpenGL application that uses shaders should be armed with OpenGL programming documentation in addition to this book.

Computer graphics has a mathematical basis, so some knowledge of algebra, trigonometry, and calculus will help readers understand and appreciate some of the details presented. With the advent of programmable graphics hardware, key parts of the graphics processing pipeline are once again under the control of software developers. To develop shaders successfully in this environment, developers must understand the mathematical basis of computer graphics.

About This Book

This book has three main parts. Chapters 1 through 8 teach the reader about the OpenGL Shading Language and how to use it. This part of the book covers details of the language and details of the OpenGL commands that create and manipulate shaders. To supply a basis for writing shaders, Chapters 9 through 19 contain a gallery of shader examples and some explanation of the underlying algorithms. This part of the book is both the baseline for a reader's shader development and a springboard for inspiring new ideas. Finally, Chapter 20 compares other notable commercial shading languages, and Appendixes A and B contain reference material for the language and the API entry points that support it.

The chapters are arranged to suit the needs of the reader who is least familiar with OpenGL and shading languages. Certain chapters can be skipped by readers who are more familiar with both topics. This book has somewhat compartmentalized chapters in order to allow such usage.

- Chapter 1 reviews the fundamentals of the OpenGL API. Readers already familiar with OpenGL may skip to Chapter 2.

- Chapter 2 introduces the OpenGL Shading Language and the OpenGL entry points that have been added to support it. If you want to know what the OpenGL Shading Language is all about and you have time to read only two chapters of this book, this chapter and Chapter 3 are the ones to read.

- Chapter 3 thoroughly describes the OpenGL Shading Language. This material is organized to present the details of a programming language. This section serves as a useful reference section for readers who have developed a general understanding of the language.

- Chapter 4 discusses how the newly defined programmable parts of the rendering pipeline interact with each other and with OpenGL's fixed functionality. This discussion includes descriptions of the built-in variables defined in the OpenGL Shading Language.

- Chapter 5 describes the built-in functions that are part of the OpenGL Shading Language. This section is a useful reference section for readers with an understanding of the language.

- Chapter 6 presents and discusses a fairly simple shader example. People who learn best by diving in and studying a real example will benefit from the discussion in this chapter.

- Chapter 7 describes the entry points that have been added to OpenGL to support the creation and manipulation of shaders. Application programmers who want to use shaders in their application must understand this material.

- Chapter 8 presents some general advice on shader development and describes the shader development process. It also describes tools that are currently available to aid the shader development process.

- Chapter 9 begins a series of chapters that present and discuss shaders with a common characteristic. In this chapter, shaders that duplicate some of the fixed functionality of the traditional OpenGL pipeline are presented.

- Chapter 10 presents a few shaders that are based on the capability to store data in and retrieve data from texture maps.

- Chapter 11 is devoted to shaders that are procedural in nature; that is, effects are computed algorithmically rather than being based on information stored in textures.

- Chapter 12 presents several alternative lighting models that can be implemented with OpenGL shaders.

- Chapter 13 discusses algorithms and shaders for producing shadows.

- Chapter 14 delves into the details of shaders that implement more realistic surface characteristics, including refraction, diffraction, and more realistic reflection.

- Chapter 15 describes noise and the effects that can be achieved with its proper use.

- Chapter 16 contains examples of how shaders can create rendering effects that vary over time.

- Chapter 17 contains a discussion of the aliasing problem and how shaders can be written to reduce the effects of aliasing.

- Chapter 18 illustrates shaders that achieve effects other than photorealism. Such effects include technical illustration, sketching or hatching effects, and other stylized rendering.

- Chapter 19 presents several shaders that modify images as they are being drawn with OpenGL.

- Chapter 20 compares the OpenGL Shading Language with other notable commercial shading languages.

- Appendix A contains the language grammar that more clearly specifies the OpenGL Shading Language.

- Appendix B contains reference pages for the API entry points that are related to the OpenGL Shading Language.

- Finally, the Glossary collects terms defined in the book, Further Reading gathers all the chapter references and adds more, and the Index ends the book.

About the Shader Examples

The shaders contained in this book are primarily short programs that illustrate the capabilities of the OpenGL Shading Language. None of the example shaders should be presumed to illustrate the "best" way of achieving a particular effect. (Indeed, the "best" way to implement certain effects may have yet to be discovered through the power and flexibility of programmable graphics hardware.) Performance improvements for each shader are possible for any given hardware target. For most of the shaders, image quality may be improved if greater care is taken to reduce or eliminate causes of aliasing.

The source code for these shaders is written in a way that I believe represents a reasonable trade-off between source code clarity, portability, and performance. Use them to learn the OpenGL Shading Language, and improve on them for use in your own projects.

I have taken as much care as possible to present shaders that are done "the right way" for the OpenGL Shading Language rather than those with idiosyncrasies from their development on specific implementations of the OpenGL Shading Language. Electronic versions of most of these shaders are available through a link at this book's Web site at http://3dshaders.com.

Errata

I know that this book contains some errors, but I've done my best to keep them to a minimum. If you find any errors, please report them to me (randi@3dshaders.com), and I will keep a running list on this book's Web site at http://3dshaders.com.

Typographical Conventions

This book contains a number of typographical conventions to enhance readability and understanding.

- SMALL CAPS are used for the first occurrence of defined terms.

- *Italics* are used for emphasis, document titles, and coordinate values such as *x*, *y*, and *z*.

- **Bold serif** is used for language keywords.

- Sans serif is used for macros and symbolic constants that appear in the text.

- **Bold sans serif** is used for function names.

- *Italic sans serif* is used for variables, parameter names, spatial dimensions, and matrix components.

- `Fixed width` is used for code examples.

About the Authors

Randi Rost is currently the external manager at Intel Corporation, where he manages relationships with a variety of game developers and other software developers. He also directs Intel's visual computing university research program.

Before joining Intel, Randi was the director of developer relations at 3Dlabs. In this role, he led a team that educated developers and helped them take advantage of the new graphics hardware technology. He led a team that produced development tools, documentation, and white papers; and contributed to standards and open source efforts.

Before his developer relations role, Randi was the manager of 3Dlabs' Fort Collins, Colorado, graphics software team. This group drove the definition of the OpenGL 2.0 standard and implemented OpenGL drivers for 3Dlabs' graphics products. Before joining 3Dlabs, Randi was a graphics software architect for Hewlett-Packard's Graphics Software Lab and the chief architect for graphics software at Kubota Graphics Corporation.

Randi has been involved in the graphics industry for more than twenty-five years and has participated in emerging graphics standards efforts for more than twenty years. He has been involved with the design and evolution of OpenGL since before version 1.0 was released in 1992. He is one of the few people credited as a contributor for each major revision of OpenGL, up through and including OpenGL 2.0. He was one of the chief architects and the specification author for PEX, and he was a member of the Graphics Performance Characterization (GPC) Committee during the development of the Picture-Level Benchmark (PLB). He served as 3Dlabs' representative to the Khronos Group from the time the group started in 1999 until the OpenML 1.0 specification was released, and he chaired the graphics subcommittee of that organization during this time. He received the National Computer Graphics Association (NCGA) 1993 Achievement Award for the Advancement of Graphics Standards.

Randi has participated in or organized numerous graphics tutorials at SIGGRAPH, Eurographics, and the Game Developer's conference since 1990. He has given tutorials on the OpenGL Shading Language at SIGGRAPH 2002 and SIGGRAPH 2003 and made presentations on this topic at the Game Developer's Conference in 2002 and 2003. In 2004, Randi taught OpenGL Shading Language MasterClasses across North America, Europe, and Japan.

Randi received his B.S. in computer science and mathematics from Minnesota State University, Mankato, in 1981 and his M.S. in computing science from the University of California, Davis, in 1983.

On a dreary winter day, you might find Randi in a desolate region of southern Wyoming, following a road less traveled.

Bill Licea-Kane is currently a principal member of technical staff at AMD. There he is a contributor to the OpenGL ARB and is chair of the OpenGL Shading Language Technical Subcommittee. Prior to his work at AMD, Bill worked at Digital Equipment Corporation (DEC), Compaq, 3Dlabs, and ATI. Bill has a B.S. in mechanical engineering from Cornell University.

About the Contributors

Dan Ginsburg has been working on developing 3D computer graphics software for more than ten years. He is currently a software engineer at Still River Systems where he is developing OpenGL-based image registration software for the Monarch250 proton beam radiotherapy system. Before joining Still River Systems, Dan was a senior member of technical staff at AMD where he worked in a variety of roles including developing OpenGL drivers, creating desktop and handheld 3D demos, and leading the development of handheld GPU developer tools. Prior to working for AMD, he worked for n-Space, Inc., an Orlando-based game development company. Dan has a B.S. in computer science from Worcester Polytechnic Institute and an MBA from Bentley College.

John Kessenich, a Colorado native, has worked in Fort Collins as a software architect in a variety of fields including CAD applications, operating system kernels, and 3D graphics. He received a patent for using Web browsers to navigate through huge collections of source code and another for processor architecture. John studied mathematics and its application to computer graphics, computer languages, and compilers at Colorado State University, receiving a bachelor's degree in applied mathematics in 1985. Later, while working at Hewlett-Packard, he earned his master's degree in applied mathematics in 1988. John has been working on OpenGL drivers since 1999 at 3Dlabs and led the 3Dlabs shading language compiler development effort. John was the lead author for the OpenGL Shading Language specification, and in this role he was one of the leaders of the technical effort to finalize and standardize it as part of core OpenGL. Currently, John is a senior staff architect at Intel, and he continues to work as spec editor for the OpenGL Shading Language.

Barthold Lichtenbelt received his master's degree in electrical engineering in 1994 from the University of Twente in the Netherlands. From 1994 to 1998, he worked on volume rendering techniques at Hewlett-Packard Company, first at Hewlett-Packard Laboratories in Palo Alto, California, and later at Hewlett-Packard's graphics software lab in Fort Collins, Colorado. During that time, he coauthored the book *Introduction to Volume Rendering*, and wrote several papers on the subject. He was awarded four patents in the field of volume rendering. In 1998, Barthold joined Dynamic Pictures (subsequently acquired by 3Dlabs), where he worked on both Direct3D and OpenGL drivers for professional graphics accelerators. Since 2001, he has been heavily involved in efforts to extend the OpenGL API and was the lead author of the three ARB extensions that support the OpenGL Shading Language. Barthold also led the implementation of 3Dlabs' first drivers that use these extensions. He is currently a senior OpenGL manager at NVIDIA and is also chair of the OpenGL Architecture Review Board.

Hugh Malan is a computer graphics programmer currently working for Real Time Worlds in Dundee, Scotland. In 1997, he received B.S. degrees in mathematics and physics from Victoria University in Wellington, New Zealand, and followed that with a year in the honors program for mathematics. He subsequently received an M.S. in computer graphics from Otago University in Dunedin, New Zealand. After receiving his M.S., Hugh worked on 3D paint and UV mapping tools at Right Hemisphere, then joined Pandromeda, Inc., and currently works at Realtime Worlds.

Michael Weiblen received his B.S. in electrical engineering from the University of Maryland, College Park, in 1989. Mike began exploring computer graphics in the 1980s and developed 3D renderers for the TRS-80 Model 100 laptop and Amiga 1000. Using OpenGL and IrisGL since 1993, he has developed global-scale synthetic environments, visual simulations, and virtual reality applications, which have been presented at such venues as the United States Capitol, EPCOT Center, DARPA, NASA, and SIGGRAPH. He has been awarded two U.S. patents and has published several papers and articles. In 2003, Mike joined 3Dlabs in Fort Collins, Colorado, where he was an engineer with the 3Dlabs Developer Relations group, focusing on applications of hardware-accelerated rendering using the OpenGL Shading Language. Mike is currently senior software engineer at Zebra Imaging, and he contributes to several open source software projects, including spearheading the integration of OpenGL Shading Language support into OpenSceneGraph.

Acknowledgments

John Kessenich of Intel was the primary author of the OpenGL Shading Language specification document and the author of Chapter 3 of this book. Some of the material from the OpenGL Shading Language specification document was modified and included in Chapters 3, 4, and 5, and the OpenGL Shading Language grammar written by John for the specification is included in its entirety in Appendix A. John worked tirelessly throughout the standardization effort discussing, resolving, and documenting language and API issues; updating the specification through numerous revisions; and providing insight and education to many of the other participants in the effort. John also did some of the early shader development, including the very first versions of the wood, bump map, and environment mapping shaders discussed in this book. Since August 2005, John has been working at Intel, where he is editor of the OpenGL Shading Language Specification and is active in several standardization efforts at the Khronos Group.

Barthold Lichtenbelt of Nvidia was the primary author and document editor of the OpenGL extension specifications that defined the OpenGL Shading Language API. Some material from those specifications has been adapted and included in Chapter 7. Barthold worked tirelessly updating the specifications; discussing, resolving, and documenting issues; and guiding the participants of the ARB-GL2 working group to consensus. Barthold is also the coauthor of Chapter 4 of this book. Since August 2005, Barthold has been working at NVIDIA, where he is involved in OpenGL standardization efforts.

The industrywide initiative to define a high-level shading effort for OpenGL was ignited by a white paper called *The OpenGL 2.0 Shading Language*, written by Dave Baldwin (2001) of 3Dlabs. Dave's ideas provided the basic framework from which the OpenGL Shading Language has evolved. Publication of this white paper occurred almost a year before any publication of information on competing, commercially viable, high-level shading languages. In this respect, Dave deserves credit as the trailblazer for a standard high-level shading language. Dave continued to be heavily involved in the design of the language and the API during its formative months. His original white paper also included code for a variety of shaders. This code served as the starting point for several of the shaders in this book: notably, the brick shaders presented in Chapter 6 and Chapter 17, the traditional shaders presented in Chapter 9, the antialiased checkerboard shader in Chapter 17, and the Mandelbrot shader in Chapter 18. Steve Koren of 3Dlabs was responsible for getting the aliased brick shader and the Mandelbrot shader working on real hardware for the first time.

Mike Weiblen developed and described the GLSL diffraction shader in Chapter 14, contributed a discussion of scene graphs and their uses in Chapter 8, and contributed to the shadow volume shader in Section 13.3. Philip Rideout was instrumental in developing frameworks for writing and testing shaders. Many of the illustrations in this book were generated with Philip's **GLSLdemo** and **deLight** applications. Philip also contributed several of the shaders in this book, including the shadow shaders in Chapter 13 and the sphere morph and vertex noise shaders in Chapter 16. Joshua Doss developed the initial version of the glyph bombing shader described in Chapter 10. He and Inderaj Bains were the coauthors of **ShaderGen**, a tool that verified the fixed functionality code segments presented in Chapter 9 and that can automatically generate working shaders from current fixed functionality state. Teri Morrison contributed the OpenGL 1.5 to 2.0 migration guide that appears in Appendix B. Barthold Lichtenbelt took the pictures that were used to create the Old Town Square environment maps.

Hugh Malan of Realtime Worlds contributed the initial version of the shadow volume shader discussed in Section 13.3.

Bert Freudenberg of the University of Magdeburg developed the hatching shader described in Chapter 18. As part of this effort, Bert also explored some of the issues involved with analytic antialiasing with programmable graphics hardware. I have incorporated some of Bert's diagrams and results in Chapter 17. The stripe shader included in Chapter 11 was implemented by LightWork Design, Ltd. Antonio Tejada of 3Dlabs conceived and implemented the wobble shader presented in Chapter 16.

William "Proton" Vaughn of Newtek provided a number of excellent models for use in this book. I thank him for the use of his Pug model that appears in Color Plates 19 and 22 and the Drummer model that appears in Color Plate 20. Christophe Desse of xtrm3D.com also allowed me to use some of his great models. I used his Spaceman model in Color Plate 17, his Scout-walker model in Color Plate 18, and his Orc model in Color Plate 21. Thanks are owed to William and Christophe not only for allowing me to use their models in this book, but for also contributing these models and many others for public use.

I would like to thank my colleagues at 3Dlabs for their assistance with the OpenGL 2.0 effort in general and for help in developing this book. Specifically, the 3Dlabs compiler team has been doing amazing work implementing the OpenGL Shading Language compiler, linker, and object support in the 3Dlabs OpenGL implementation. Dave Houlton and Mike Weiblen worked on RenderMonkey and other shader development tools. Dave also worked closely with companies such as SolidWorks and LightWork Design to enable them to take full advantage of the OpenGL Shading Language. Teri Morrison and Na Li implemented and tested the original OpenGL Shading Language extensions, and Teri, Barthold, and Matthew Williams implemented the official OpenGL 2.0 API support in the 3Dlabs drivers. This work has made it possible to create the code and images that appear in this book. The Fort Collins software team, which I was privileged to lead for several years, was responsible for producing the publicly available specifications and source code for the OpenGL Shading Language and OpenGL Shading Language API.

Dale Kirkland, Jeremy Morris, Phil Huxley, and Antonio Tejada of 3Dlabs were involved in many of the OpenGL 2.0 discussions and provided a wealth of good ideas and encouragement as the effort moved forward. Antonio also implemented the first parser for the OpenGL Shading Language. Other members of the 3Dlabs driver development teams in Fort Collins, Colorado; Egham, U.K.; Madison, Alabama; and Austin, Texas have contributed to the effort as well. The 3Dlabs executive staff should be commended for having the vision to move forward with the OpenGL 2.0 proposal and the courage to allocate resources to its development. Thanks to Osman Kent, Hock Leow, Neil Trevett, Jerry Peterson, Jeff Little, and John Schimpf in particular.

Numerous other people have been involved in the OpenGL 2.0 discussions. I would like to thank my colleagues and fellow ARB representatives at ATI, SGI, NVIDIA, Intel, Microsoft, Evans & Sutherland, IBM, Sun Microsystems, Apple, Imagination Technologies, Dell, Compaq, and HP for contributing to discussions and for helping to move the process along. Evan Hart, Jeremy

Sandmel, Benjamin Lipchak, and Glenn Ortner of ATI also provided insightful review and studious comments for both the OpenGL Shading Language and the OpenGL Shading Language API. Steve Glanville and Cass Everitt of NVIDIA were extremely helpful during the design of the OpenGL Shading Language, and Pat Brown of NVIDIA contributed enormously to the development of the OpenGL Shading Language API. Others with notable contributions to the final specifications include Marc Olano of the University of Maryland/Baltimore County; Jon Leech of SGI; Folker Schamel of Spinor; Matt Cruikshank, Steve Demlow, and Karel Zuiderveld of Vital Images; Allen Akin, contributing as an individual; and Kurt Akeley of NVIDIA. Numerous others provided review or commentary that helped improve the specification documents.

I think that special recognition should go to people who were not affiliated with a graphics hardware company and still participated heavily in the ARB-GL2 working group. When representatives from a bunch of competing hardware companies get together in a room and try to reach agreement on an important standard that materially affects each of them, there is often squabbling over details that will cause one company or another extra grief in the short term. Marc Olano and Folker Schamel contributed enormously to the standardization effort as "neutral" third parties. Time and time again, their comments helped lead the group back to a higher ground. Allen Akin and Matt Cruikshank also contributed in this regard. Thanks, gentlemen, for your technical contributions and your valuable but underappreciated work as "referees."

A big thank you goes to the software developers who have taken the time to talk with us, send us e-mail, or answer survey questions on http://opengl.org. Our ultimate aim is to provide you with the best possible API for doing graphics application development, and the time that you have spent telling us what you need has been invaluable. A few ISVs lobbied long and hard for certain features, and they were able to convince us to make some significant changes to the original OpenGL 2.0 proposal. Thanks, all you software developers, and keep telling us what you need!

A debt of gratitude is owed to the designers of the C programming language, the designers of RenderMan, and the designers of OpenGL, the three standards that have provided the strongest influence on our efforts. Hopefully, the OpenGL Shading Language will continue their traditions of success and excellence.

The reviewers of various drafts of this book have helped greatly to increase its quality. Thanks to John Carey, Steve Cunningham, Bert Freudenberg, Michael Garland, Jeffrey Galinovsky, Dave Houlton, John Kessenich, Slawek

Kilanowski, Bob Kuehne, Na Li, Barthold Lichtenbelt, Andy McGovern, Teri Morrison, Marc Olano, Brad Ritter, Philip Rideout, Teresa Rost, Folker Schamel, Maryann Simmons, Mike Weiblen, and two anonymous reviewers for reviewing some or all of the material in this book. Your comments have been greatly appreciated! Clark Wolter worked with me on the design of the cover image, and he improved and perfected the original concepts.

Thanks go to my three children, Rachel, Hannah, and Zachary, for giving up some play time with Daddy for a while, and for the smiles, giggles, hugs, and kisses that helped me get through this project. Finally, thank you, Teresa, the love of my life, for the support you've given me in writing this book. These have been busy times in our personal lives too, but you have had the patience, strength, and courage to see it through to completion. Thank you for helping me make this book a reality.

Chapter 1

Review of OpenGL Basics

This chapter briefly reviews the OpenGL application programming interface to lay the foundation for the material in subsequent chapters. It is not an exhaustive overview. If you are already extremely familiar with OpenGL, you can safely skip ahead to the next chapter. If you are familiar with another 3D graphics API, you can glean enough information here about OpenGL to begin using the OpenGL Shading Language for shader development.

Unless otherwise noted, descriptions of OpenGL functionality in this book are based on the OpenGL 3.1 specification. However, in this chapter, we will also include OpenGL functionality included in the ARB_compatibility extension.

1.1 OpenGL History

OpenGL is an industry-standard, cross-platform APPLICATION PROGRAMMING INTERFACE (API). The specification for this API was finalized in 1992, and the first implementations appeared in 1993. It was largely compatible with a proprietary API called Iris GL (Graphics Library) that was designed and supported by Silicon Graphics, Inc. To establish an industry standard, Silicon Graphics collaborated with various other graphics hardware companies to create an open standard, which was dubbed "OpenGL."

The evolution of OpenGL is controlled by the OpenGL Architecture Review Board, or ARB, created by Silicon Graphics in 1992. This group is governed by a set of by-laws, and its primary task is to guide OpenGL by controlling the specification and conformance tests. In September

1

2006 the OpenGL ARB became a workgroup of the Khronos Group. This enabled closer working opportunities with the OpenGL ES workgroup. The original ARB contained representatives from SGI, Intel, Microsoft, Compaq, Digital Equipment Corporation, Evans & Sutherland, and IBM. The ARB currently has as active promoters and contributors AMD, Apple, ARM, Blizzard, IBM, Intel, NVIDIA, S3 Graphics, and TransGaming.

OpenGL shares many of Iris GL's design characteristics. Its intention is to provide access to graphics hardware capabilities at the lowest possible level that still provides hardware independence. It is designed to be the lowest-level interface for accessing graphics hardware. OpenGL has been implemented in a variety of operating environments, including Macs, PCs, UNIX-based systems, game consoles, and phones. It has been supported on a variety of hardware architectures, from those that support little in hardware other than the framebuffer itself to those that accelerate virtually everything in hardware.

Since the release of the initial OpenGL specification (version 1.0) in June 1992, nine revisions have added new functionality to the API. The current version of the OpenGL specification is 3.1. The first conformant implementations of OpenGL 1.0 began appearing in 1993.

- Version 1.1 was finished in 1997 and added support for two important capabilities—vertex arrays and texture objects.

- The specification for OpenGL 1.2 was released in 1998 and added support for 3D textures and an optional set of imaging functionality.

- The OpenGL 1.3 specification was completed in 2001 and added support for cube map textures, compressed textures, multitextures, and other things.

- OpenGL 1.4 was completed in 2002 and added automatic mipmap generation, additional blending functions, internal texture formats for storing depth values for use in shadow computations, support for drawing multiple vertex arrays with a single command, more control over point rasterization, control over stencil wrapping behavior, and various additions to texturing capabilities.

- The OpenGL 1.5 specification was published in October 2003. It added support for vertex buffer objects, shadow comparison functions, occlusion queries, and nonpower-of-2 textures.

- OpenGL 2.0 was finished in September 2004. In addition to OpenGL Shading Language Version 110 for programmable vertex and fragment shading, OpenGL 2.0 added multiple render targets, nonpower-of-2 textures, point sprites, separate blend equation, and separate stencil.

- Version 2.1 was released in August 2006. OpenGL Shading Language Version 120 added support for nonsquare matrices, promoted arrays to first class objects, allowed limited type conversion, and introduced centroid and invariant qualifiers. OpenGL 2.1 also added support for nonsquare matrices, pixel buffer objects, and sRGB textures.

- OpenGL 3.0 was released in August 2008. OpenGL Shading Language 130 added many new features including the following:

  - Native signed and unsigned integer

  - Texture functions for size query, explicit LOD, offset, and gradient

  - Texture arrays

  - Switch/case/default

  - In, out, centroid, flat, smooth, invariant, noperspective

  - Special variables *gl_VertexID, gl_ClipDistance*

  - Hyperbolic, **isinf**, **isnan**, and additional rounding functions

  OpenGL 3.0 also added integer and unsigned integer texture formats, conditional rendering, buffer object subrange mapping and flushing, float-point color and depth formats for textures and renderbuffers, framebuffer objects, half-float vertex array and pixel data formats, multisample stretch blit, nonnormalized integer color internal formats, one-dimensional and two-dimensional texture arrays, packed depth-stencil formats, separate blend enables, RGTC compressed textures, one and two channel texture formats (R and RG), transform feedback, vertex array objects, and sRGB framebuffer.

- OpenGL 3.1 followed shortly after in March 2009. OpenGL Shading Language 140 added uniform blocks, rectangular textures, texture buffers and gl_InstanceID. OpenGL 3.1 also added instanced rendering, copying data between buffer objects, primitive restart, texture buffer objects, rectangle textures, uniform buffer objects, and signed normalized texture formats.

All versions of OpenGL from 1.0 through 1.5 were based on a fixed-function configurable pipeline—the user could control various parameters, but the underlying functionality and order of processing were fixed.

OpenGL 2.0, finalized in September 2004, opened up the processing pipeline for user control by providing programmability for both vertex processing and fragment processing as part of the core OpenGL specification. With this version of OpenGL, application developers have been able to implement their own rendering algorithms, using a high-level shading language. The addition of programmability to OpenGL represents a fundamental shift in its design, which is why the version number changed from 1.5 to 2.0.

OpenGL 3.0, finalized in August 2008, brought another fundamental shift in its design. For the first time, portions of OpenGL were marked "deprecated," setting the stage for future streamlined specifications. In March 2009, OpenGL 3.1 moved much of the deprecated functions into the ARB_compatibility extension.

1.2 OpenGL Evolution

Because of its fundamental design as a fixed-function state machine, before OpenGL 2.0, the only way to modify OpenGL was to define extensions to it. Therefore, a great deal of functionality is available in various OpenGL implementations in the form of extensions that expose new hardware functionality. OpenGL has a well-defined extension mechanism, and hardware vendors are free to define and implement features that expose new hardware functionality. Since only OpenGL implementors can implement extensions, there was previously no way for applications to extend the functionality of OpenGL beyond what was provided by their OpenGL provider.

To date, more than 400 extensions have been defined. Extensions that are supported by only one vendor are identified by a short prefix unique to that vendor (e.g., SGI for extensions developed by Silicon Graphics, Inc.). Extensions that are supported by more than one vendor are denoted by the prefix EXT in the extension name. Extensions that have been thoroughly reviewed by the ARB are designated with an ARB prefix in the extension name to indicate that they have a special status as a recommended way of exposing a certain piece of functionality. Extensions that achieve the ARB designation are candidates to be added to standard OpenGL. Published specifications for OpenGL extensions are available at the OpenGL extension registry at www.opengl.org/registry/.

The extensions supported by a particular OpenGL implementation can be determined by calling the OpenGL **glGetStringi** function with the symbolic constant GL_EXTENSIONS with an index indicating which extension to query. The returned string contains the name of the extension supported by the implementation. Some vendors currently support more than 100 separate OpenGL extensions. It can be a little bit daunting for an application to try to determine whether the needed extensions are present on a variety of implementations and what to do if they're not. The proliferation of extensions has been primarily a positive factor for the development of OpenGL, but in a sense, it has become a victim of its own success. It allows hardware vendors to expose new features easily, but it presents application developers with a dizzying array of nonstandard options. Like any standards body, the ARB is cautious about promoting functionality from extension status to standard OpenGL.

Before version 2.0 of OpenGL, none of the underlying programmability of graphics hardware was exposed. The original designers of OpenGL, Mark Segal and Kurt Akeley, stated, "One reason for this decision is that, for performance reasons, graphics hardware is usually designed to apply certain operations in a specific order; replacing these operations with arbitrary algorithms is usually infeasible." This statement may have been mostly true when it was written in 1994 (there were programmable graphics architectures even then). But today, all of the graphics hardware that is being produced is programmable. Because of the proliferation of OpenGL extensions and the need to support Microsoft's DirectX API, hardware vendors have no choice but to design programmable graphics architectures. As discussed in the remaining chapters of this book, providing application programmers with access to this programmability is the purpose of the OpenGL Shading Language.

1.3 Execution Model

The OpenGL API is focused on drawing graphics into framebuffer memory and, to a lesser extent, in reading back values stored in that framebuffer. It is somewhat unique in that its design includes support for drawing three-dimensional geometry (such as points, lines, and polygons, collectively referred to as PRIMITIVES) as well as for drawing images and bitmaps.

The execution model for OpenGL can be described as client-server. An application program (the client) issues OpenGL commands that are interpreted and processed by an OpenGL implementation (the server). The application program and the OpenGL implementation can execute on a single computer or on two different computers. Some OpenGL state is stored in the address space of the application (client state), but the majority of it is stored in the address space of the OpenGL implementation (server state).

OpenGL commands are always processed in the order in which they are received by the server, although command completion may be delayed because of intermediate operations that cause OpenGL commands to be buffered. Out-of-order execution of OpenGL commands is not permitted. This means, for example, that a primitive will not be drawn until the previous primitive has been completely drawn. This in-order execution also applies to queries of state and framebuffer read operations. These commands return results that are consistent with complete execution of all previous commands.

Data binding for OpenGL occurs when commands are issued, not when they are executed. Data passed to an OpenGL command is interpreted when the command is issued and copied into OpenGL memory if needed. Subsequent changes to this data by the application have no effect on the data that is now stored within OpenGL.

1.4   The Framebuffer

OpenGL is an API for drawing graphics, and so the fundamental purpose for OpenGL is to transform data provided by an application into something that is visible on the display screen. This processing is often referred to as RENDERING. Typically, this processing is accelerated by specially designed hardware, but some or all operations of the OpenGL pipeline can be performed by a software implementation running on the CPU. It is transparent to the user of the OpenGL implementation how this division among the software and hardware is handled. The important thing is that the results of rendering conform to the results defined by the OpenGL specification.

The hardware that is dedicated to drawing graphics and maintaining the contents of the display screen is often called the GRAPHICS ACCELERATOR. Graphics accelerators typically have a region of memory that is dedicated to maintaining the contents of the display. Every visible picture element (pixel) of the display is represented by several bytes of memory on the graphics accelerator. A color display might have a byte of memory for each of red, green, and blue in order to represent the color value for each pixel. This so-called DISPLAY MEMORY is scanned (refreshed) a certain number of times per second in order to maintain a flicker-free representation on the display. Graphics accelerators also typically have a region of memory called OFFSCREEN MEMORY that is not displayable and is used to store things that aren't visible.

OpenGL assumes that allocation of the display memory and offscreen memory is handled by the window system. The window system decides which portions of memory may be accessed by OpenGL and how these portions are structured. In each environment in which OpenGL is supported, a small set of function calls tie OpenGL into that particular environment. In the Microsoft Windows environment, this set of routines is called WGL (pronounced "wiggle"). In the X Window System environment, this set of routines is called GLX. In the Macintosh environment, this set of routines is called NSOpenGL, CGL, or AGL. In each environment, this set of calls supports such things as allocating and deallocating regions of graphics memory, allocating and deallocating data structures called GRAPHICS CONTEXTS that maintain OpenGL state, selecting the current graphics context, selecting the region of graphics memory in which to draw, and synchronizing commands between OpenGL and the window system.

The region of graphics memory that is modified as a result of OpenGL rendering is called the FRAMEBUFFER. In a windowing system, the OpenGL notion of a default framebuffer corresponds to a window. Facilities in window-system-specific OpenGL routines let users select the default framebuffer characteristics for the window. The windowing system typically also clarifies how the OpenGL default framebuffer behaves when windows overlap. In a nonwindowed system, the OpenGL default framebuffer corresponds to the entire display.

A window that supports OpenGL rendering (i.e., a default framebuffer) may consist of some combination of the following:

* Up to four color buffers

* A depth buffer

* A stencil buffer

* A multisample buffer

* One or more auxiliary buffers

Most graphics hardware supports both a front buffer and a back buffer in order to perform DOUBLE BUFFERING. This allows the application to render into the (offscreen) back buffer while displaying the (visible) front buffer. When rendering is complete, the two buffers are swapped so that the completed rendering is now displayed as the front buffer and rendering can begin anew in the back buffer. When double buffering is used, the end user never sees the graphics when they are in the process of being drawn, only the finished image. This technique allows smooth animation at interactive rates.

Stereo viewing is supported by having a color buffer for the left eye and one for the right eye. Double buffering is supported by having both a front and a back buffer. A double-buffered stereo window will therefore have four color buffers: front left, front right, back left, and back right. A normal (non-stereo) double-buffered window will have a front buffer and a back buffer. A single-buffered window will have only a front buffer.

If 3D objects are to be drawn with hidden-surface removal, a DEPTH BUFFER is needed. This buffer stores the depth of the displayed object at each pixel. As additional objects are drawn, a depth comparison can be performed at each pixel to determine whether the new object is visible or obscured.

A STENCIL BUFFER is used for complex masking operations. A complex shape can be stored in the stencil buffer, and subsequent drawing operations can use the contents of the stencil buffer to determine whether to update each pixel.

Normally, when objects are drawn, a single decision is made as to whether the graphics primitive affects a pixel on the screen. The MULTISAMPLE BUFFER is a buffer that allows everything that is rendered to be sampled multiple times within each pixel in order to perform high-quality full-screen anti-aliasing without rendering the scene more than once. Each sample within a pixel contains color, depth, and stencil information, and the number of samples per pixel can be queried. When a window includes a multisample buffer, it does not include separate depth or stencil buffers. As objects are rendered, the color samples are combined to produce a single color value, and that color value is passed on to be written into the color buffer. Because multisample buffers contain multiple samples (often 2, 4, 8, or 16) of color, depth, and stencil for every pixel in the window, they can use up large amounts of offscreen graphics memory.

AUXILIARY BUFFERS are offscreen memory buffers that can store arbitrary data such as intermediate results from a multipass rendering algorithm. A framebuffer may have 1, 2, 3, 4, or even more associated auxiliary buffers.

In addition to the default framebuffer, OpenGL provides framebuffer objects. These are application-created framebuffers and are much more flexible than the window system default framebuffer. Framebuffer objects may have several buffers of different formats, including normalized formats (storing numbers in the range 0.0 to 1.0), signed normalized formats (storing numbers in the range –1.0 to 1.0), signed and unsigned integers, and floating-point numbers.

1.5 State

OpenGL was designed as a state machine for updating the contents of a framebuffer. The process of turning geometric primitives, images, and bit-maps into pixels on the screen is controlled by a fairly large number of state settings. These state settings are orthogonal to one another—setting one piece of state does not affect the others. Cumulatively, the state settings define the behavior of the OpenGL rendering pipeline and the way in which primitives are transformed into pixels on the display device.

OpenGL state is collected into a data structure called a GRAPHICS CONTEXT. Window-system-specific functions create and delete graphics contexts. Another window-system-specific call designates a graphics context and an OpenGL framebuffer that are used as the targets for subsequent OpenGL commands.

Quite a few server-side state values in OpenGL have just two states: on or off. To turn a mode on, you must pass the appropriate symbolic constant to the OpenGL command **glEnable**. To turn a mode off, you pass the symbolic constant to **glDisable**. You enable client-side state (such as pointers that define vertex arrays) with **glEnableClientState** and disable it with **glDisableClientState**.

glGet is a generic function that can query many of the components of a graphics context. Symbolic constants are defined for simple state items (e.g., GL_CURRENT_COLOR and GL_LINE_WIDTH), and these values can be passed as arguments to **glGet** to retrieve the current value of the indicated component of a graphics context. Variants of **glGet** return the state value as an integer, float, double, or boolean. More complex state values are returned by "get" functions that are specific to those state values, for instance, **glGetTexParameter**. Error conditions can be detected with the **glGetError** function.

1.6 Processing Pipeline

For specifying the behavior of OpenGL, the various operations are defined to be applied in a particular order, so we can also think of OpenGL as a GRAPHICS PROCESSING PIPELINE.

Let's start by looking at a block diagram of how OpenGL was defined up through OpenGL 1.5. Figure 1.1 is a diagram of the so-called FIXED FUNCTIONALITY of OpenGL. This diagram shows the fundamentals of how OpenGL has worked since its inception and is a simplified representation of how OpenGL still works with the ARB_compatibility extension. It shows the main features of the OpenGL pipeline for the purposes of this overview. Some new features were added to OpenGL in versions 1.1 through 1.5, but the basic architecture of OpenGL remained unchanged through OpenGL 3.0. We use the term *fixed functionality* because every OpenGL implementation supporting the ARB_compatibility extension is required to have the same functionality and a result that is consistent with the OpenGL specification for a given set of inputs. Both the set of operations and the order in which they occur are defined (fixed) by the OpenGL specification.

It is important to note that OpenGL implementations are not required to match precisely the order of operations shown in Figure 1.1. Implementations are free to modify the order of operations as long as the rendering results are consistent with the OpenGL specification. Many innovative software and hardware architectures have been designed to implement OpenGL, and most block diagrams of those implementations look nothing like Figure 1.1. However, the diagram does ground our discussion of the way the rendering process *appears* to work in OpenGL, even if the underlying implementation does things a bit differently.

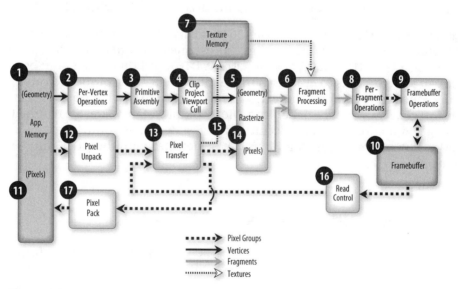

Figure 1.1   Overview of OpenGL operation

1.7 Drawing Geometry

As you can see from Figure 1.1, data for drawing geometry (points, lines, and polygons) starts off in application-controlled memory (1). This memory may be on the host CPU, or, with the help of some recent additions to OpenGL or under-the-covers data caching by the OpenGL implementation, it may actually reside in video memory on the graphics accelerator. Either way, the fact is that it is memory that contains geometry data that the application can cause to be drawn.

1.7.1 Geometry Specification

The geometric primitives supported in OpenGL are points, lines, line strips, line loops, polygons, triangles, triangle strips, triangle fans, quadrilaterals, and quadrilateral strips. There are four main ways to send geometry data to OpenGL. The first is the deprecated, but still available with ARB_compatibility, vertex-at-a-time method, which calls **glBegin** to start a primitive and calls **glEnd** to end it. In between are commands that set specific VERTEX ATTRIBUTES such as vertex position, color, normal, texture coordinates, secondary color, edge flags, and fog coordinates, using calls such as **glVertex**, **glColor**, **glNormal**, and **glTexCoord**. (A number of variants of these function calls allow the application to pass these values with various data types as well as to pass them by value or by reference.) Up through version 1.5 of OpenGL, there was no way to send arbitrary (user-defined) per-vertex data. The only per-vertex attributes allowed were those specifically defined in the OpenGL specification. OpenGL 2.0 added a method for sending arbitrary per-vertex data; that method is described in Section 7.7.

When the vertex-at-a-time method is used, the call to **glVertex** signals the end of the data definition for a single vertex, and it may also define the completion of a primitive. After **glBegin** is called and a primitive type is specified, a graphics primitive is completed whenever **glVertex** is called enough times to completely specify a primitive of the indicated type. For independent triangles, a triangle is completed every third time **glVertex** is called. For triangle strips, a triangle is completed when **glVertex** is called for the third time, and an additional connecting triangle is completed for each subsequent call to **glVertex**.

The second deprecated method of drawing primitives is to use vertex arrays. With this method, applications store vertex attributes in user-defined arrays, set up pointers to the arrays, and use **glDrawArrays**, **glMultiDrawArrays**,

glDrawElements, **glMultiDrawElements**, **glDrawRangeElements**, or **glInterleavedArrays** to draw a large number of primitives at once. Because these entry points can efficiently pass large amounts of geometry data to OpenGL, application developers are encouraged to use them for portions of code that are extremely performance critical. Using **glBegin** and **glEnd** requires a function call to specify each attribute of each vertex, so the function call overhead can become substantial when objects with thousands of vertices are drawn. In contrast, vertex arrays can be used to draw a large number of primitives with a single function call after the vertex data is organized into arrays. Processing the array data in this fashion can be faster because it is often more efficient for the OpenGL implementation to deal with data organized in this way. The current array of color values is specified with **glColorPointer**, the current array of vertex positions is specified with **glVertexPointer**, the current array of normal vectors is specified with **glNormalPointer**, and so on. The function **glInterleavedArrays** can specify and enable several interleaved arrays simultaneously (e.g., each vertex might be defined with three floating-point values representing a normal followed by three floating-point values representing a vertex position.)

The preceding two methods are referred to as drawing in IMMEDIATE MODE because primitives are rendered as soon as they have been specified. The third deprecated method involves storing either the vertex-at-a-time function calls or the vertex array calls in a DISPLAY LIST, an OpenGL-managed data structure that stores commands for later execution. Display lists can include commands to set state as well as commands to draw geometry. Display lists are stored on the server side and can be processed later with **glCallList** or **glCallLists**. This is not illustrated in Figure 1.1, but it is another way that data can be provided to the OpenGL processing pipeline. The definition of a display list is initiated with **glNewList**, and the display list definition is completed with **glEndList**. All the commands issued between those two calls become part of the display list, although certain OpenGL commands are not allowed within display lists. Depending on the implementation, DISPLAY LIST MODE can provide a performance advantage over immediate mode. Storing commands in a display list gives the OpenGL implementation an opportunity to optimize the commands in the display list for the underlying hardware. It also gives the implementation the chance to store the commands in a location that enables better drawing performance, perhaps even in memory on the graphics accelerator. Of course, some extra computation or data movement is usually required to implement these optimizations, so applications will typically see a performance benefit only if the display list is executed more than once.

The fourth method, now strongly preferred, added in version 1.5 of OpenGL permitted vertex array data to be stored in server-side memory. This mechanism typically provides the highest performance rendering because the data can be stored in memory on the graphics accelerator and need not be transferred over the I/O bus each time it is rendered. The API also supports the concept of efficiently streaming data from client to server. The **glBindBuffer** command creates a buffer object, and **glBufferData** and **glBufferSubData** specify the data values in such a buffer. **glMapBuffer** can map a buffer object into the client's address space and obtain a pointer to this memory so that data values can be specified directly. The command **glUnmapBuffer** must be called before the values in the buffer are accessed by subsequent GL rendering commands. **glBindBuffer** can also make a particular buffer object part of current state. If buffer object 0 is bound when calls are made to vertex array pointer commands such as **glColorPointer**, **glNormalPointer**, **glVertexPointer**, and so on, the pointer parameter to these calls is understood to be a pointer to client-side memory. When a buffer object other than 0 is bound, the pointer parameter is understood to be an offset into the currently bound buffer object. Subsequent calls to one of the vertex array drawing commands (e.g., **glMultiDrawArrays**) can thus obtain their vertex data from either client- or server-side memory or a combination thereof.

OpenGL supports the rendering of curves and surfaces with evaluators. Evaluators use a polynomial mapping to produce vertex attributes such as color, normal, and position that are sent to the vertex processing stage just as if they had been provided by the client. See the OpenGL specification for a complete description of this deprecated functionality.

1.7.2 Per-Vertex Operations

No matter which of these methods is used, the net result is that geometry data is transferred into the first stage of processing in OpenGL, VERTEX PROCESSING (2). Fixed-function vertex processing is deprecated but still available with the ARB_compatibility extension. At this point, vertex positions are transformed by the modelview and projection matrices, normals are transformed by the inverse transpose of the upper leftmost 3×3 matrix taken from the modelview matrix, texture coordinates are transformed by the texture matrices, lighting calculations are applied to modify the base color, texture coordinates may be automatically generated, color material state is applied, and point sizes are computed. All of these things are rigidly defined by the OpenGL specification. They are performed in a specific order, according to specific formulas, with specific items of OpenGL state controlling the process.

Because the most important things that occur in this stage are transformation and lighting, the vertex processing stage is sometimes called TRANSFORMATION AND LIGHTING, or, more familiarly, T&L. There is no application control to this process other than modifying OpenGL state values: turning lighting on or off with **glEnable/glDisable**; changing lighting attributes with **glLight** and **glLightModel**; changing material properties with **glMaterial**; or modifying the modelview matrix by calling matrix manipulation functions such as **glMatrixMode**, **glLoadMatrix**, **glMultMatrix**, **glRotate**, **glScale**, **glTranslate**. At this stage of processing, each vertex is treated independently. The vertex position computed by the transformation stage is used in subsequent clipping operations. The transformation process is discussed in detail in Section 1.9.

Lighting effects in OpenGL are controlled by manipulation of the attributes of one or more of the simulated light sources defined in OpenGL. The number of light sources supported by an OpenGL implementation is specifically limited to GL_MAX_LIGHTS. This value can be queried with **glGet** and must be at least 8. Each simulated light source in OpenGL has attributes that cause it to behave as a directional light source, a point light source, or a spotlight. Light attributes that can be adjusted by an application include the color of the emitted light, defined as ambient, diffuse, and specular RGBA intensity values; the light source position; attenuation factors that define how rapidly the intensity drops off as a function of distance; and direction, exponent, and cutoff factors for spotlights. These attributes can be modified for any light with **glLight**. Individual lights can be turned on or off by a call to **glEnable/glDisable** with a symbolic constant that specifies the affected light source.

Lighting produces a primary and secondary color for each vertex. The entire process of lighting can be turned on or off by a call to **glEnable/glDisable** with the symbolic constant GL_LIGHTING. If lighting is disabled, the values of the primary and secondary color are taken from the last color value set with the **glColor** command and the last secondary color set with the **glSecondaryColor** command.

The effects from enabled light sources are used in conjunction with surface material properties to determine the lit color at a particular vertex. Materials are characterized by the color of light they emit; the color of ambient, diffuse, and specular light they reflect; and their shininess. Material properties can be defined separately for front-facing surfaces and for back-facing surfaces and are specified with **glMaterial**.

Global lighting parameters are controlled with **glLightModel**. You can use this function to

- Set the value used as the global ambient lighting value for the entire scene.

- Specify whether the lighting calculations assume a local viewer or one positioned at infinity. (This affects the computation of specular reflection angles.)

- Indicate whether one- or two-sided lighting calculations are performed on polygons. (If one-sided, only front material properties are used in lighting calculations. Otherwise, normals are reversed on back-facing polygons and back material properties are used to perform the lighting computation.)

- Specify whether a separate specular color component is computed. (This specular component is later added to the result of the texturing stage to provide specular highlights.)

1.7.3 Primitive Assembly

After vertex processing, all the attributes associated with each vertex are completely determined. The vertex data is then sent on to a stage called PRIMITIVE ASSEMBLY (3). At this point the vertex data is collected into complete primitives. Points require a single vertex, lines require two, triangles require three, quadrilaterals require four, and general polygons can have an arbitrary number of vertices. For the vertex-at-a-time API, an argument to **glBegin** specifies the primitive type; for vertex arrays, the primitive type is passed as an argument to the function that draws the vertex array. The primitive assembly stage effectively collects enough vertices to construct a single primitive, and then this primitive is passed on to the next stage of processing. The reason this stage is needed is that at the very next stage, operations are performed on a set of vertices, and the operations depend on the type of primitive. In particular, clipping is done differently, depending on whether the primitive is a point, line, or polygon.

1.7.4 Primitive Processing

The next stage of processing (4), actually consists of several distinct steps that have been combined into a single box in Figure 1.1 just to simplify the diagram. The first step that occurs is clipping. This operation compares each primitive to the view volume, and with the ARB_compatibility extension, any user-defined clipping planes set by calling **glClipPlane**. If the primitive is completely within the view volume and the user-defined clipping planes, it is passed on for subsequent processing. If it is completely outside the view volume or the user-defined clipping planes, the primitive is rejected, and no further processing is required. If the primitive is partially in and partially out, it is divided (CLIPPED) in such a way that only the portion within the clip volume and the user-defined clipping planes is passed on for further processing.

Another operation that occurs at this stage is perspective projection. If the current view is a perspective view, each vertex has its x, y, and z components divided by its homogeneous coordinate w. Following this, each vertex is transformed by the current viewport transformation (set with **glDepthRange** and **glViewport**) to generate window coordinates. Certain OpenGL states can be set to cause an operation called CULLING to be performed on polygon primitives at this stage. With the computed window coordinates, each polygon primitive is tested to see whether it is facing away from the current viewing position. The culling state can be enabled with **glEnable**, and **glCullFace** can be called to specify that back-facing polygons will be discarded (culled), front-facing polygons will be discarded, or both will be discarded.

1.7.5 Rasterization

Geometric primitives that are passed through the OpenGL pipeline contain a set of data at each of the vertices of the primitive. At the next stage (5), primitives (points, lines, or polygons) are decomposed into smaller units corresponding to pixels in the destination framebuffer. This process is called RASTERIZATION. Each of these smaller units generated by rasterization is referred to as a FRAGMENT. For instance, a line might cover five pixels on the screen, and the process of rasterization converts the line (defined by two vertices) into five fragments. A fragment comprises a window coordinate and depth and other associated attributes such as color, texture coordinates, and so on. The values for each of these attributes are determined by interpolation between the values specified (or computed) at the vertices of the primitive. At the time they are rasterized, vertices have a primary color and a secondary color. The **glShadeModel** function specifies whether these color values are interpolated between the vertices (SMOOTH SHADING) or whether the color values for the last vertex of the primitive are used for the entire primitive (FLAT SHADING).

Each type of primitive has different rasterization rules and different OpenGL state. Points have a width controlled by **glPointSize** and other rendering attributes that are defined by **glPointParameter**. OpenGL 2.0 added the ability to draw an arbitrary shape at each point position by means of a texture called a POINT SPRITE. Lines have a width that is controlled with **glLineWidth** and a stipple pattern that is set with **glLineStipple**. Polygons have a stipple pattern that is set with **glPolygonStipple**. Polygons can be drawn as filled, outline, or vertex points depending only on the value set with **glPolygonMode**. The depth values for each fragment in a polygon can be modified by a value that is computed with the state set with **glPolygonOffset**. The orientation of polygons that are to be considered front facing can be set with **glFrontFace**. The process of smoothing the jagged appearance of a primitive is called ANTIALIASING. Primitive antialiasing can be enabled with **glEnable** and the appropriate symbolic constant: GL_POINT_SMOOTH, GL_LINE_SMOOTH, or GL_POLYGON_SMOOTH.

1.7.6 Fragment Processing

After fragments have been generated by rasterization, a number of operations occur on fragments. Collectively, these operations are called FRAGMENT PROCESSING (6). Fixed-function fragment processing has been deprecated, but remains available with the ARB_compatibility extensions. Perhaps the most important operation that occurs at this point is called TEXTURE MAPPING. In this operation, the texture coordinates associated with the fragment are used to access a region of graphics memory called TEXTURE MEMORY (7). OpenGL defines a lot of state values that affect how textures are accessed as well as how the retrieved values are applied to the current fragment. Many extensions have been defined to this area that is rather complex to begin with. We spend some time talking about texturing operations in Section 1.10.

Other operations that occur at this point are FOG (modifying the color of the fragment depending on its distance from the view point) and COLOR SUM (combining the values of the fragment's primary color and secondary color). Fog parameters are set with **glFog**, and secondary colors are vertex attributes that can be passed in with the vertex attribute command **glSecondaryColor** or that can be computed by the lighting stage.

1.7.7 Per-Fragment Operations

After fragment processing, fragments are submitted to a set of fairly simple operations called PER-FRAGMENT OPERATIONS (8). These include tests like the following:

- PIXEL OWNERSHIP TEST—Determines whether the destination pixel is visible or obscured by an overlapping window

- SCISSOR TEST—Clips fragments against a rectangular region set with **glScissor**

- ALPHA TEST—Decides whether to discard the fragment on the basis of the fragment's ALPHA value and the function set with **glAlphaFunc**

- STENCIL TEST—Compares the value in the stencil buffer with a reference value, using a comparison set with **glStencilFunc** and **glStencilOp**, by which it decides the fate of the fragment

- DEPTH TEST—Uses the function established with **glDepthFunc** to compare the depth of the incoming fragment to the depth stored in the frame-buffer

Blending, dithering, and logical operations are also considered per-fragment operations. The blending operation calculates the color to be written into the framebuffer using a blend of the fragment's color, the color stored in the framebuffer, and the blending state as established by **glBlendFunc**, **glBlendColor**, and **glBlendEquation**. Dithering is a method of trading spatial resolution for color resolution, but today's graphics accelerators contain enough framebuffer memory to make this trade-off unnecessary. The final fragment value is written into the framebuffer with the logical operation set by **glLogicOp**.

Each of the per-fragment operations is conceptually simple and nowadays can be implemented efficiently and inexpensively in hardware. Some of these operations also involve reading values from the framebuffer (i.e., color, depth, or stencil). With today's hardware, all these back-end rendering operations can be performed at millions of pixels per second, even those that require reading from the framebuffer.

1.7.8 Framebuffer Operations

Things that control or affect the whole framebuffer are called FRAMEBUFFER OPERATIONS (9). Certain OpenGL state controls the region of the framebuffer into which primitives are drawn. OpenGL supports display of stereo images as well as double buffering, so a number of choices are available for the rendering destination. Regions of the framebuffer are called BUFFERS and are referred to as the front, back, left, right, front left, front right, back left, back right, front and back, and aux0, aux1, and so on, up to the number of auxiliary buffers supported minus 1. Any of these buffers can be set as the destination for subsequent rendering operations with **glDrawBuffer**. Multiple buffers can be established as the destination for rendering with **glDrawBuffers**. Regions within the draw buffer(s) can be write protected. The **glColorMask** function determines whether writing is allowed to the red, green, blue, or alpha components of the destination buffer. The **glDepthMask** function determines whether the depth components of the destination buffer can be modified. The **glStencilMask** function controls the writing of particular bits in the stencil components of the destination buffer. Values in the framebuffer can be initialized with **glClear**. Values that will be used to initialize the color components, depth components, stencil components, and accumulation buffer components are set with **glClearColor**, **glClearDepth**, **glClearStencil**, and **glClearAccum**, respectively. The accumulation buffer operation can be specified with **glAccum**.

For performance, OpenGL implementations often employ a variety of buffering schemes in order to send larger batches of graphics primitives to the 3D graphics hardware. To make sure that all graphics primitives for a specific rendering context are progressing toward completion, an application should call **glFlush**. To make sure that all graphics primitives for a particular rendering context have finished rendering, an application should call **glFinish**. This command blocks until the effects of all previous commands have been completed. Blocking can be costly in terms of performance, so **glFinish** should be used sparingly.

The overall effect of these stages is that graphics primitives defined by the application are converted into pixels in the framebuffer for subsequent display. But so far, we have discussed only geometric primitives such as points, lines, and polygons. OpenGL also renders bitmap and image data.

1.8 Drawing Images

As mentioned previously, OpenGL has a great deal of support for drawing images in addition to its support for drawing 3D geometry. Although deprecated, they remain in the ARB_compatibility extension. In OpenGL parlance, images are called PIXEL RECTANGLES. The values that define a pixel rectangle start out in application-controlled memory, as shown in Figure 1.1 (11). Color or grayscale pixel rectangles are rendered into the framebuffer with **glDrawPixels**, and bitmaps are rendered into the framebuffer with **glBitmap**. Images that are destined for texture memory are specified with **glTexImage** or **glTexSubImage**. Up to a point, the same basic processing is applied to the image data supplied with each of these commands.

1.8.1 Pixel Unpacking

OpenGL reads image data provided by the application in a variety of formats. Parameters that define how the image data is stored in memory (length of each pixel row, number of rows to skip before the first one, number of pixels to skip before the first one in each row, etc.) can be specified with **glPixelStore**. So that operations on pixel data can be defined more precisely, pixels read from application memory are converted into a coherent stream of pixels by an operation referred to as PIXEL UNPACKING (12). When a pixel rectangle is transferred to OpenGL by a call like **glDrawPixels**, this operation applies the current set of pixel unpacking parameters to determine how the image data should be read and interpreted. As each pixel is read from memory, it is converted to a PIXEL GROUP that contains either a color, a depth, or a stencil value. If the pixel group consists of a color, the image data is destined for the color buffer in the framebuffer. If the pixel group consists of a depth value, the image data is destined for the depth buffer. If the pixel group consists of a stencil value, the image data is destined for the stencil buffer. Color values are made up of a red, a green, a blue, and an alpha component (i.e., RGBA) and are constructed from the input image data according to a set of rules defined by OpenGL. The result is a stream of RGBA values that are sent to OpenGL for further processing.

1.8.2 Pixel Transfer

After a coherent stream of image pixels is created, pixel rectangles undergo a series of operations called PIXEL TRANSFER (13). These operations are applied whenever pixel rectangles are transferred from the application to OpenGL (**glDrawPixels**, **glTexImage**, **glTexSubImage**), from OpenGL back to the application (**glReadPixels**), or when they are copied within OpenGL (**glCopyPixels**, **glCopyTexImage**, **glCopyTexSubImage**).

The behavior of the pixel transfer stage is modified with **glPixelTransfer**. This command sets state that controls whether red, green, blue, alpha, and depth values are scaled and biased. It can also set state that determines whether incoming color or stencil values are mapped to different color or stencil values through the use of a lookup table. The lookup tables used for these operations are specified with the **glPixelMap** command.

Some additional operations that occur at this stage are part of the OpenGL IMAGING SUBSET, which is an optional part of OpenGL. Hardware vendors that find it important to support advanced imaging capabilities will support the imaging subset in their OpenGL implementations, and other vendors will not support it. To determine whether the imaging subset is supported, applications need to call **glGetString** with the symbolic constant GL_EXTENSIONS. This returns a list of extensions supported by the implementation; the application should check for the presence of the string "ARB_imaging" within the returned extension string.

The pixel transfer operations that are defined to be part of the imaging subset are convolution, color matrix, histogram, min/max, and additional color lookup tables. Together, they provide powerful image processing and color correction operations on image data as it is being transferred to, from, or within OpenGL.

1.8.3 Rasterization and Back-End Processing

Following the pixel transfer stage, fragments are generated through rasterization of pixel rectangles in much the same way as they are generated from 3D geometry (14). This process, along with the current OpenGL state, determines where the image will be drawn in the framebuffer. Rasterization takes into account the current RASTER POSITION, which can be set with **glRasterPos** or **glWindowPos**, and the current zoom factor, which can be set with **glPixelZoom** and which causes an image to be magnified or reduced in size as it is drawn.

After fragments have been generated from pixel rectangles, they undergo the same set of fragment processing operations as geometric primitives (6) and then go on to the remainder of the OpenGL pipeline in exactly the same manner as geometric primitives, all the way until pixels are deposited in the framebuffer (8, 9, 10).

Pixel values provided through a call to **glTexImage** or **glTexSubImage** do not go through rasterization or the subsequent fragment processing but directly update the appropriate portion of texture memory (15).

1.8.4 Read Control

Pixel rectangles are read from the framebuffer and returned to application memory with **glReadPixels**. They can also be read from the framebuffer and written to another portion of the framebuffer with **glCopyPixels**, or they can be read from the framebuffer and written into texture memory with **glCopyTexImage** or **glCopyTexSubImage**. In all of these cases, the portion of the framebuffer that is to be read is controlled by the READ CONTROL stage of OpenGL and set with the **glReadBuffer** command (16).

The values read from the framebuffer are sent through the pixel transfer stage (13) in which various image processing operations can be performed. For copy operations, the resulting pixels are sent to texture memory or back into the framebuffer, depending on the command that initiated the transfer. For read operations, the pixels are formatted for storage in application memory under the control of the PIXEL PACKING stage (17). This stage is the mirror of the pixel unpacking stage (12), in that parameters that define how the image data is to be stored in memory (length of each pixel row, number of rows to skip before the first one, number of pixels to skip before the first one in each row, etc.) can be specified with **glPixelStore**. Thus, application developers enjoy a lot of flexibility in determining how the image data is returned from OpenGL into application memory.

1.9 Coordinate Transforms

The purpose of the OpenGL graphics processing pipeline is to convert three-dimensional descriptions of objects into a two-dimensional image that can be displayed. The ARB_compatibility extension retains many of the transformation functions. In many ways, this process is similar to using a camera to convert a real-world scene into a two-dimensional print. To accomplish the transformation from three dimensions to two, OpenGL defines several coordinate spaces and transformations between those spaces. Each coordinate space has some properties that make it useful for some part of the rendering process. The transformations defined by OpenGL afford applications a great deal of flexibility in defining the 3D-to-2D mapping. For success at writing shaders in the OpenGL Shading Language, understanding the various transformations and coordinate spaces used by OpenGL is essential.

In computer graphics, MODELING is the process of defining a numerical representation of an object that is to be rendered. For OpenGL, this usually means creating a polygonal representation of an object so that it can be drawn with the polygon primitives built into OpenGL. At a minimum, a polygonal representation of an object needs to include the coordinates of each vertex in each polygon and the connectivity information that defines the polygons. Additional data might include the color of each vertex, the surface normal at each vertex, one or more texture coordinates at each vertex, and so on.

In the past, modeling an object was a painstaking effort, requiring precise physical measurement and data entry. (This is one of the reasons the Utah teapot, modeled by Martin Newell in 1975, has been used in so many graphics images. It is an interesting object, and the numerical data is freely available. Several of the shaders presented in this book are illustrated with this object; see, for example, Color Plate 24.) More recently, a variety of modeling tools have become available, both hardware and software, and this has made it relatively easy to create numerical representations of three-dimensional objects that are to be rendered.

Three-dimensional object attributes, such as vertex positions and surface normals, are defined in OBJECT SPACE. This coordinate space is one that is convenient for describing the object that is being modeled. Coordinates are specified in units that are convenient to that particular object. Microscopic objects may be modeled in units of angstroms, everyday objects may be modeled in inches or centimeters, buildings might be modeled in feet or meters, planets could be modeled in miles or kilometers, and galaxies might be modeled in light years or parsecs. The origin of this coordinate system (i.e., the point (0, 0, 0)) is also something that is convenient for the object being modeled. For some objects, the origin might be placed at one corner of the object's three-dimensional bounding box. For other objects, it might be more convenient to define the origin at the centroid of the object. Because of its intimate connection with the task of modeling, this coordinate space is also often referred to as MODEL SPACE or the MODELING COORDINATE SYSTEM. Coordinates are referred to equivalently as object coordinates or modeling coordinates.

To compose a scene that contains a variety of three-dimensional objects, each of which might be defined in its own unique object space, we need a common coordinate system. This common coordinate system is called WORLD SPACE or the WORLD COORDINATE SYSTEM, and it provides a common frame of reference for all objects in the scene. Once all the objects in the scene are transformed into a single coordinate system, the spatial relationships between all the objects, the light sources, and the viewer are known. The units of this coordinate system are chosen in a way that is convenient for describing a scene. You might choose feet or meters if you are composing a scene that represents one of the rooms in your house, but you might choose city blocks as your units if you are composing a scene that represents a city skyline. The choice for the origin of this coordinate system is also arbitrary. You might define a three-dimensional bounding box for your scene and set the origin at the corner of the bounding box such that all of the other coordinates of the bounding box have positive values. Or you may want to pick an important point in your scene (the corner of a building, the location of a key character, etc.) and make that the origin.

After world space is defined, all the objects in the scene must be transformed from their own unique object coordinates into world coordinates. The transformation that takes coordinates from object space to world space is called the MODELING TRANSFORMATION. If the object's modeling coordinates are in feet but the world coordinate system is defined in terms of inches, the object coordinates must be scaled by a factor of 12 to produce world coordinates. If the object is defined to be facing forward but in the scene it needs to be facing backwards, a rotation must be applied to the object coordinates. A translation is also typically required to position the object at its desired location in world coordinates. All of these individual transformations can be put together into a single matrix, the MODEL TRANSFORMATION MATRIX, that represents the transformation from object coordinates to world coordinates.

After the scene has been composed, the viewing parameters must be specified. One aspect of the view is the vantage point (i.e., the eye or camera position) from which the scene will be viewed. Viewing parameters also include the focus point (also called the LOOKAT POINT or the direction in which the camera is pointed) and the up direction (e.g., the camera may be held sideways or upside down).

The viewing parameters collectively define the VIEWING TRANSFORMATION, and they can be combined into a matrix called the VIEWING MATRIX. A coordinate multiplied by this matrix is transformed from world space into EYE SPACE, also called the EYE COORDINATE SYSTEM. By definition, the origin of this coordinate system is at the viewing (or eye) position. Coordinates in this space are called EYE COORDINATES. The spatial relationships in the scene remain unchanged, but orienting the coordinate system in this way makes it easy to determine the distance from the viewpoint to various objects in the scene.

Although some 3D graphics APIs allow applications to separately specify the modeling matrix and the viewing matrix, OpenGL combines them into a single matrix called the MODELVIEW MATRIX. This matrix is defined to transform coordinates from object space into eye space (see Figure 1.2).

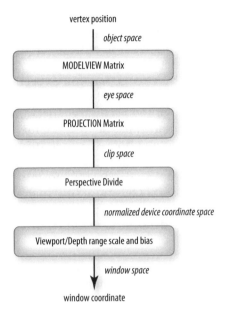

Figure 1.2   Coordinate spaces and transforms in OpenGL

You can manipulate a number of matrices in OpenGL. Call the **glMatrixMode** function to select the modelview matrix or one of OpenGL's other matrices. Load the current matrix with the identity matrix by calling **glLoadIdentity**, or replace it with an arbitrary matrix by calling **glLoadMatrix**. Be sure you know what you're doing if you specify an arbitrary matrix—the transformation might give you a completely incomprehensible image! You can also multiply the current matrix by an arbitrary matrix by calling **glMultMatrix**.

Applications often start by setting the current modelview matrix to the view matrix and then add on the necessary modeling matrices. You can set the modelview matrix to a reasonable viewing transformation with the **gluLookAt** function. (This function is not part of OpenGL proper but is part of the OpenGL utility library that is provided with every OpenGL implementation.) OpenGL actually supports a stack of modelview matrices, and you can duplicate the topmost matrix and copy it onto the top of the stack with **glPushMatrix**. When this is done, you can concatenate other transformations to the topmost matrix with the functions **glScale**, **glTranslate**, and **glRotate** to define the modeling transformation for a particular three-dimensional object in the scene. Then, pop this topmost matrix off the stack with **glPopMatrix** to get back to the original view transformation matrix. Repeat the process for each object in the scene.

At the time light source positions are specified with the **glLight** function, they are transformed by the current modelview matrix. Therefore, light positions are stored within OpenGL as eye coordinates. You must set up the modelview matrix to perform the proper transformation before light positions are specified, or you won't get the lighting effects that you expect. The lighting calculations that occur in OpenGL are defined to happen on a per-vertex basis in the eye coordinate system. For the necessary reflection computations, light positions and surface normals must be in the same coordinate system. OpenGL implementations often choose to do lighting calculations in eye space; therefore, the incoming surface normals have to be transformed into eye space as well. You accomplish this by transforming surface normals by the inverse transpose of the upper leftmost 3×3 matrix taken from the modelview matrix. At that point, you can apply the per-vertex lighting formulas defined by OpenGL to determine the lit color at each vertex.

After coordinates have been transformed into eye space, the next thing is to define a viewing volume. This is the region of the three-dimensional scene that is visible in the final image. The transformation that takes the objects in the viewing volume into CLIP SPACE (also known as the CLIPPING COORDINATE SYSTEM, a coordinate space that is suitable for clipping) is called the PROJECTION TRANSFORMATION. In OpenGL, you establish the projection transformation by calling **glMatrixMode** to select the projection matrix and then setting this matrix appropriately. Parameters that may go into creating an appropriate projection matrix are the field of view (how much of the scene is visible), the aspect ratio (the horizontal field of view may differ from the vertical field of view), and near and far clipping planes to eliminate things that are too far away or too close (for perspective projections, weirdness will occur if you try to draw things that are at or behind the viewing position). Three utility functions set the projection matrix: **glOrtho**, **glFrustum**, and **gluPerspective**. The difference between these functions is that **glOrtho** defines a parallel projection (i.e., parallel lines in the scene are projected to parallel lines in the final two-dimensional image), whereas **glFrustum** and **gluPerspective** define perspective projections (i.e., parallel lines in the scene are foreshortened to produce a vanishing point in the image, such as railroad tracks converging to a point in the distance).

FRUSTUM CLIPPING is the process of eliminating any graphics primitives that lie outside an axis-aligned cube in clip space. This cube is defined such that the x, y, and z components of the clip space coordinate are less than or equal to the w component for the coordinate, and greater than or equal to $-w$ (i.e., $-w \le x \le w$, $-w \le y \le w$, and $-w \le z \le w$). Graphics primitives (or portions thereof) that lie outside this cube are discarded. Frustum clipping is always performed on all incoming primitives in OpenGL. USER CLIPPING, on the other hand, is a feature that can be enabled or disabled by the application. Applications can call **glClipPlane** to specify one or more clipping planes that further restrict the size of the viewing volume, and each clipping plane can be individually enabled with **glEnable**. At the time user clipping planes are specified, OpenGL transforms them into eye space using the inverse of the current modelview matrix. Each plane specified in this manner defines a half-space, and only the portions of primitives that lie within the intersection of the view volume and all of the enabled half-spaces defined by user clipping planes are drawn.

The next step in the transformation of vertex positions is the perspective divide. This operation divides each component of the clip space coordinate by the homogeneous coordinate w. The resulting x, y, and z components range from [–1,1], and the resulting w coordinate is always 1, so it is no longer needed. In other words, all the visible graphics primitives are transformed into a cubic region between the point (–1, –1, –1) and the point (1, 1, 1). This is the NORMALIZED DEVICE COORDINATE SPACE, which is an intermediate space that allows the viewing area to be properly mapped onto a viewport of arbitrary size and depth.

Pixels within a window on the display device aren't referred to with floating-point coordinates from –1 to 1; they are usually referred to with coordinates defined in the WINDOW COORDINATE SYSTEM, where x values range from 0 to the width of the window minus 1, and y values range from 0 to the height of the window minus 1. Therefore, one more transformation step is required. The VIEWPORT TRANSFORMATION specifies the mapping from normalized device coordinates into window coordinates. You specify this mapping by calling the OpenGL functions **glViewport**, which specifies the mapping of the x and y coordinates, and **glDepthRange**, which specifies the mapping of the z coordinate. Graphics primitives are rasterized in the window coordinate system.

1.10 Texturing

The area of texture mapping is one of the more complex areas of the OpenGL API. It has been extended more often than most of the other areas of OpenGL primarily because this was the area of graphics for which hardware was the least mature when OpenGL was defined in the early 1990s. The programmability added through the OpenGL Shading Language in OpenGL 2.0 makes this area much more straightforward, but the existing OpenGL APIs are still used to create, modify, and define the behavior of textures. This section describes the texturing functionality as it existed for OpenGL 1.5. Some significant changes have been made to this model by OpenGL 2.0, particularly to the concept of texture units, and are described later in this book. Additional texture maps were added in OpenGL 2.1, OpenGL 3.0, and OpenGL 3.1.

OpenGL currently supports eight basic types of texture maps: one-dimensional, two-dimensional, three-dimensional, cube maps, one-dimensional array, two-dimensional array, texture buffer, and rectangle. (Only one- and two-dimensional textures were supported in OpenGL 1.0.) A 1D TEXTURE is an array containing *width* pixel values, a 2D TEXTURE is an array containing *width* × *height* pixel values, and a 3D TEXTURE is an array containing *width* × *height* × *depth* pixel values. A CUBE MAP TEXTURE contains six two-dimensional textures: one for each major axis direction (i.e., ±*x*, ±*y*, and ±*z*).

OpenGL has the notion of a TEXTURE UNIT. A texture unit corresponds to the underlying piece of graphics hardware that performs the various texturing operations. With OpenGL 1.3, support was added for multiple texture units. Each texture unit maintains the following state for performing texturing operations:

- Enabled/disabled state of the texture unit

- Texture matrix stack that for transforming incoming texture coordinates

- State used for automatic texture coordinate generation

- Texture environment state

- Current 1D texture

- Current 2D texture

- Current 3D texture

- Current cube map texture

Commands to set the state in the preceding list operate on the ACTIVE TEXTURE UNIT. Texture units are numbered from 0 to GL_MAX_TEXTURE_UNITS – 1 (a value that can be queried with **glGet**), and the active texture unit can be set with **glActiveTexture** with a symbolic constant indicating the desired texture unit. Subsequent commands to set state in the preceding list operate on only the active texture unit. A texture unit can be enabled for 1D, 2D, 3D, or cube map texturing by calling **glEnable** with the appropriate symbolic constant.

The active texture unit specifies the texture unit accessed by commands involving texture coordinate processing. Such commands include those accessing the current texture matrix stack (if GL_MATRIX_MODE is GL_TEXTURE), **glTexGen**, and **glEnable/glDisable** (if any enumerated value for texture coordinate generation is selected), as well as queries of the current texture coordinates and current raster texture coordinates. The active texture unit selector also selects the texture unit accessed by commands involving texture image processing. Such commands include all variants of **glTexEnv**, **glTexParameter**, and **glTexImage** commands; **glBindTexture**; **glEnable/glDisable** for any texture target (e.g., GL_TEXTURE_2D); and queries of all such state.

A TEXTURE OBJECT is created as follows: call **glBindTexture** and provide a texture target (a symbolic constant that indicates whether the texture will be a 1D, 2D, 3D, or cube map texture) and a previously unused texture name (an integer other than zero) that can be used to refer to the newly created texture object. The newly created texture object also becomes active and is used in subsequent texturing operations. If **glBindTexture** is called with a texture name that has already been used, that previously created texture becomes active. In this way, an application can create any number of textures and switch between them easily.

After a texture object has been created, the pixel values that define the texture can be provided. Pixel values for a 3D texture can be supplied by **glTexImage3D**, pixel values for 2D or cube map textures can be provided by **glTexImage2D**, and pixel values for a 1D texture can be specified by **glTexImage1D**. In versions 1.0–1.5 of OpenGL, when any of these three commands was used, each dimension of the texture map had to be a size that was a power of 2 (including the border width). OpenGL 2.0 allows textures to have sizes that are not restricted to being powers of 2. These functions all work in the same way as **glDrawPixels**, except that the pixels constituting a texture are deposited into texture memory before rasterization. If only a portion of a texture needs to be respecified, the **glTexSubImage1D/2D/3D** functions can be used. When any of these three commands is used, there is no power-of-2 restriction on the texture size. Textures can be created or modified with values copied from framebuffer memory by **glCopyTexImage1D/2D** or **glCopyTexSubImage1D/2D/3D**.

OpenGL also provides a method for specifying textures with compressed image formats. Applications can use the commands **glCompressedTexImage1D/2D/3D** and **glCompressedTexSubImage1D/2D/3D** to create and store compressed textures in texture memory. Compressed textures may use significantly less memory on the graphics accelerator and thereby enhance an application's functionality or performance. Standard

OpenGL does not define any particular compressed image formats, so applications need to query the extension string in order to determine the compressed texture formats supported by a particular implementation.

Each of the preceding texture creation commands includes a LEVEL-OF-DETAIL argument that supports the creation of MIPMAP TEXTURES. A mipmap texture is an ordered set of arrays representing the same image. Each array has a resolution that is half the previous one in each dimension. The idea behind mipmaps is that more pleasing final images will result if the texture to be used has roughly the same resolution as the object being drawn on the display. If a mipmap texture is supplied, OpenGL can automatically choose the appropriately sized texture (i.e., MIPMAP LEVEL) for use in drawing the object on the display. Interpolation between the TEXELS (pixels that comprise a texture) of two mipmap levels can also be performed. Objects that are textured with mipmap textures can therefore be rendered with high quality, no matter how they change size on the display.

After a texture object has been defined and bound to a texture unit, properties other than the pixels that define the texture can be modified with the command **glTexParameter**. This command sets parameters that control how the texture object is treated when it is specified, changed, or accessed. Texture object parameters include

- The wrapping behavior in each dimension—Whether the texture repeats, clamps, or is mirrored when texture coordinates go outside the range [0,1]

- The minification filter—How the texture is to be sampled if the mapping from texture space to window space causes the texture image to be made smaller than a one-to-one pixel mapping in order to be mapped onto the surface

- The magnification filter—How the texture is to be sampled if the mapping from texture space to window space causes the texture image to be made larger than a one-to-one pixel mapping in order to be mapped onto the surface

- The border color to be used if the wrapping behavior indicates clamping to a border color

- The priority to be assigned to the texture—A value from [0,1] that tells OpenGL the importance of performance for this texture

- Values for clamping and biasing the level-of-detail value that is automatically computed by OpenGL

- The level that is defined as the base (highest-resolution) level for a mipmap texture

- The level that is defined as the maximum (lowest-resolution) level for a mipmap texture

- Depth comparison values—Whether a comparison operation should be performed when the texture is accessed, what type of comparison operation should be performed, and how to treat the result of the comparison (these values are used with depth textures to implement shadowing)

- A value that signifies whether mipmap levels are to be computed automatically by OpenGL whenever the base level is specified or modified

The manner in which a texture value is applied to a graphics primitive is controlled by the parameters of the texture environment, which are set with the **glTexEnv** function. The set of fixed formulas for replacing an object color with a value computed through texture access is rather lengthy. Suffice it to say that texture functions include replacement, modulation, decal application, blending, adding, enabling point sprites, and even more complex combining of red, green, blue, and alpha components. A wide variety of texturing effects can be achieved with the flexibility provided by the **glTexEnv** function. This function can also specify an additional per-texture-unit level-of-detail bias that is added to the per-texture-object level-of-detail bias previously described.

OpenGL supports the concept of multitexturing, by which the results of more than one texture access are combined to determine the value of the fragment. Each texture unit has a texture environment function. Texture units are connected serially. The first texture unit computes a fragment value by using the texture value that it reads from texture memory and its texture environment function, and passes on the result to be used as the input fragment value for the second texture unit. This fragment value is used together with the texture environment function for the second texture unit and the texture value read from texture memory by the second texture unit to provide the input fragment value for the third texture unit. This process is repeated for all enabled texture units.

After texture objects have been defined and one or more texture units have been properly set up and enabled, texturing is performed on all subsequent graphics primitives. Texture coordinates are supplied at each vertex with **glTexCoord** or **glMultiTexCoord** (for use with vertex-at-a-time entry points) or as an array indicated by **glTexCoordPointer** (for use with vertex array commands). The **glMultiTexCoord** command specifies texture coordinates that are to be operated on by a specific texture unit. This command specifies the texture unit as well as the texture coordinates to be used. The command **glTexCoord** is equivalent to the command **glMultiTexCoord** with its texture parameter set to GL_TEXTURE0. For vertex arrays, it is necessary to call **glClientActiveTexture** between each call to **glTexCoordPointer** in order to specify different texture coordinate arrays for different texture units.

Texture coordinates can also be generated automatically by OpenGL. Parameters for controlling automatic texture coordinate generation are set on a per-texture unit basis with the **glTexGen** command. This function lets the application select a texture generation function and supply coefficients for that function for the currently active texture unit. Supported texture generation functions are object linear (useful for automatically generating texture coordinates for terrain models), eye linear (useful for producing dynamic contour lines on moving objects), and sphere map (useful for a type of environment mapping that requires just one texture).

When texture coordinates have been sent to OpenGL or generated by the texture unit's texture generation function, they are transformed by the texture unit's current texture transformation matrix. The **glMatrixMode** command selects the texture matrix stack for modification, and subsequent matrix commands modify the texture matrix stack of the currently active texture unit. The current texture transformation matrix can translate the texture across the object, rotate it, stretch it, shrink it, and so on. Both texture generation and texture transformation are defined by OpenGL to occur as part of vertex processing (i.e., they are performed once per-vertex before rasterization).

TEXTURE ACCESS is the process by which the texture coordinates are used by a texture unit to access the enabled texture for that unit. It occurs after rasterization of the graphics primitive and interpolation of the transformed texture coordinates. The texture access is performed according to the bound texture object's parameters for filtering, wrapping, computed level-of-detail, and so on.

After a texture value has been retrieved, it is combined with the incoming color value according to the texture function established by calling **glTexEnv**. This operation is called TEXTURE APPLICATION. This computation produces a new fragment color value that is used for all subsequent processing of the fragment. Both texture access and texture application are defined to occur on every fragment that results from the rasterization process.

1.11 Summary

This chapter has briefly reviewed the fundamentals of the OpenGL API. In it, we've touched on some of the deprecated OpenGL function calls still available with the ARB_compatibility extension. If you haven't used OpenGL for quite some time, the hope is that this review chapter has been enough to orient you properly for the task of using the OpenGL Shading Language to write shaders. If you have been using another 3D graphics programming API, the hope is that this short overview is enough to get you started using OpenGL and writing your own shaders. If not, the next section lists a number of resources for learning more about OpenGL.

1.12 Further Information

The Web site http://opengl.org has the latest information for the OpenGL community, forums for developers, and links to a variety of demos and technical information. OpenGL developers should bookmark this site and visit it often.

The standard reference book for the OpenGL API is the *OpenGL Programming Guide, Seventh Edition* (2010) by Dave Shreiner and the Khronos OpenGL ARB Working Group. Another useful OpenGL book is *OpenGL SuperBible, Fourth Edition,* by Richard S. Wright Jr., Benjamin Lipchak, and Nicholas Haemel (2008).

A good overview of OpenGL is provided in the technical paper *The Design of the OpenGL Graphics Interface* by Mark Segal and Kurt Akeley (1994). Of course, the definitive document on OpenGL is the specification itself, *The OpenGL Graphics System: A Specification (Version 3.1),* by Mark Segal and Kurt Akeley, edited by Jon Leech (2009).

The OpenGL.org Web site, http://opengl.org, is also a good source for finding source code for OpenGL example programs. Another useful site is Tom Nuyden's site at http://delphi3d.net. The hardware vendors that support OpenGL typically provide lots of example programs, especially for newer OpenGL functionality and extensions. The AMD and NVIDIA Web sites are particularly good in this regard.

[1] *AMD developer Web site.* http://developer.amd.com

[2] *NVIDIA developer Web site.* http://developer.nvidia.com

[3] *Delphi3D Web site.* http://delphi3d.net

[4] OpenGL Architecture Review Board, *OpenGL Reference Manual, Fourth Edition: The Official Reference to OpenGL, Version 1.4*, Editor: Dave Shreiner, Addison-Wesley, Reading, Massachusetts, 2004.

[5] *OpenGL, official Web site.* http://opengl.org

[6] Segal, Mark, and Kurt Akeley, *The OpenGL Graphics System: A Specification (Version 2.0)*, Editor (V1.1): Chris Frazier, (V1.2–V3.1): Jon Leech, (V2.0): Jon Leech and Pat Brown, March 2009. www.opengl.org/documentation/specs/

[7] Segal, Mark, and Kurt Akeley, *The Design of the OpenGL Graphics Interface*, Silicon Graphics Inc., 1994. wwws.sun.com/software/graphics/opengl/OpenGLdesign.pdf

[8] Shreiner, Dave, and the Khronos OpenGL ARB Working Group, *OpenGL Programming Guide, Seventh Edition: The Official Guide to Learning OpenGL, Versions 3.0 and 3.1*, Addison-Wesley, Boston, Massachusetts, 2010.

[9] Wright, Richard, Benjamin Lipchak, and Nicholas Haemel, *OpenGL SuperBible, Fourth Edition*, Sams Publishing, 2008. www.starstonesoftware.com/OpenGL/opengl_superbbile.htm

Chapter 2

Basics

This chapter introduces the OpenGL Shading Language to get you started writing your own shaders as quickly as possible. When you finish reading this chapter, you should understand how programmability has been added to OpenGL and be ready to tackle the details of the shading language description in the next three chapters and the simple example in Chapter 6. After that, you can learn more details about the API that supports the shading language or explore the examples contained in the later chapters.

2.1 Introduction to the OpenGL Shading Language

This book helps you learn and use a high-level graphics programming language formally called the OPENGL SHADING LANGUAGE. Informally, this language is sometimes referred to as GLSL. This language has been made part of the OpenGL standard as of OpenGL 2.0 and has since further evolved through OpenGL 3.0.

The recent trend in graphics hardware has been to replace fixed functionality with programmability in areas that have grown exceedingly complex. Two such areas are vertex processing and fragment processing. Vertex processing involves the operations that occur at each vertex, most notably transformation and lighting. Fragments are per-pixel data structures that are created by the rasterization of graphics primitives. A fragment contains all the data necessary to update a single location in the framebuffer. Fragment processing consists of the operations that occur on a per-fragment basis, most notably reading from texture memory and applying the texture value(s) at each fragment. With the OpenGL Shading Language, the fixed functionality stages for vertex processing and fragment processing have been replaced with programmable stages that can do everything the fixed functionality stages could do—and a whole lot more. The OpenGL Shading Language allows application programmers to express the processing that occurs at those programmable points of the OpenGL pipeline.

The OpenGL Shading Language code that is intended for execution on one of the OpenGL programmable processors is called a SHADER. The term OPENGL SHADER is sometimes used to differentiate a shader written in the OpenGL Shading Language from a shader written in another shading language such as RenderMan. Because two programmable processors are defined in OpenGL, there are two types of shaders: VERTEX SHADERS and FRAGMENT SHADERS. OpenGL provides mechanisms for compiling shaders and linking them to form executable code called a PROGRAM. A program contains one or more EXECUTABLES that can run on the programmable processing units.

The OpenGL Shading Language has its roots in C and has features similar to RenderMan and other shading languages. The language has a rich set of types, including vector and matrix types to make code more concise for typical 3D graphics operations. A special set of type qualifiers manages the unique forms of input and output needed by shaders. Some mechanisms from C++, such as function overloading based on argument types and the capability to declare variables where they are first needed instead of at the beginning of blocks, have also been borrowed. The language includes support for loops, subroutine calls, and conditional expressions. An extensive set of built-in functions provides many of the capabilities needed for implementing shading algorithms. In brief,

- The OpenGL Shading Language is a high-level procedural language.

- As of OpenGL 2.0, it is part of standard OpenGL, the leading cross-platform, operating-environment-independent API for 3D graphics and imaging.

- The same language, with a small set of differences, is used for both vertex and fragment shaders.

- It is based on C and C++ syntax and flow control.

- It natively supports vector and matrix operations since these are inherent to many graphics algorithms.

- It is stricter with types than C and C++, and functions are called by value-return.

- It uses type qualifiers rather than reads and writes to manage input and output.

- It imposes no practical limits to a shader's length, nor does the shader length need to be queried.

The following sections contain some of the key concepts that you will need to understand in order to use the OpenGL Shading Language effectively. The concepts are covered in much more detail later in the book, but this introductory chapter should help you understand the big picture.

2.2 Why Write Shaders?

Until recently, OpenGL has presented application programmers with a configurable but static interface for putting graphics on the display device. As described in Chapter 1, you could think of OpenGL as a sequence of operations that occurred on geometry or image data as it was sent through the graphics hardware to be displayed on the screen. Various parameters of these pipeline stages could be configured to select variations on the processing that occurred for that pipeline stage. But neither the fundamental operation of the OpenGL graphics pipeline nor the order of operations could be changed through the OpenGL API.

By exposing support for traditional rendering mechanisms, OpenGL has evolved to serve the needs of a fairly broad set of applications. If your particular application was well served by the traditional rendering model presented by OpenGL, you may never have felt the need to write shaders. But if you have ever been frustrated because OpenGL did not allow you to define area lights or because lighting calculations are performed per-vertex rather than per-fragment or, if you have run into any of the many limitations of the traditional OpenGL rendering model, you may need to write your own OpenGL shader.

The OpenGL Shading Language and its supporting OpenGL API entry points allows *application developers* to define the processing that occurs at key points in the OpenGL processing pipeline by using a high-level programming language specifically designed for this purpose. These key points in the pipeline are defined to be programmable in order to give developers complete freedom to define the processing that occurs. This lets developers utilize the underlying graphics hardware to achieve a much wider range of rendering effects.

To get an idea of the range of effects possible with OpenGL shaders, take a minute to browse through the color images that are included in this book. This book presents a variety of shaders that only begin to scratch the surface of what is possible. With each new generation of graphics hardware, more complex rendering techniques can be implemented as OpenGL shaders and can be used in real-time rendering applications. Here's a brief list of what's possible with OpenGL shaders:

- Increasingly realistic materials—metals, stone, wood, paints, and so on

- Increasingly realistic lighting effects—area lights, soft shadows, and so on

- Natural phenomena—fire, smoke, water, clouds, and so on

- Advanced rendering effects—global illumination, ray-tracing, and so on

- Nonphotorealistic materials—painterly effects, pen-and-ink drawings, simulation of illustration techniques, and so on

- New uses for texture memory—storage of normals, gloss values, polynomial coefficients, and so on

- Procedural textures—dynamically generated 2D and 3D textures, not static texture images

- Image processing—convolution, unsharp masking, complex blending, and so on

- Animation effects—key frame interpolation, particle systems, procedurally defined motion

- User programmable antialiasing methods

- General computation—sorting, mathematical modeling, fluid dynamics, and so on

Many of these techniques have been available before now only through software implementations. If they were at all possible through OpenGL, they were possible only in a limited way. The fact that these techniques can now be implemented with hardware acceleration provided by dedicated graphics hardware means that rendering performance can be increased dramatically and at the same time the CPU can be off-loaded so that it can perform other tasks.

2.3 OpenGL Programmable Processors

The introduction of programmable vertex and fragment processors is the biggest change to OpenGL since its inception and is the reason a high-level shading language is needed. In Chapter 1, we discussed the OpenGL pipeline and the fixed functionality that implements vertex processing and fragment processing. With the introduction of programmability, the fixed functionality vertex processing and fixed functionality fragment processing are disabled when an OpenGL Shading Language program is made current (i.e., made part of the current rendering state).

Figure 2.1 shows the OpenGL processing pipeline when the programmable processors are active. In this case, the fixed functionality vertex and fragment processing shown in Figure 1.1 are replaced by programmable vertex and fragment processors, as shown in Figure 2.1. All other parts of the OpenGL processing pipeline remain the same.

This diagram illustrates the stream processing nature of OpenGL made possible by the programmable processors that are defined as part of the OpenGL Shading Language. Data flows from the application to the vertex processor, on to the fragment processor, and ultimately to the framebuffer. The OpenGL Shading Language was carefully designed to allow hardware implementations to perform parallel processing of both vertices and fragments. This gives graphics hardware vendors the opportunity to produce faster graphics hardware with more parallel processors with each new generation of hardware.

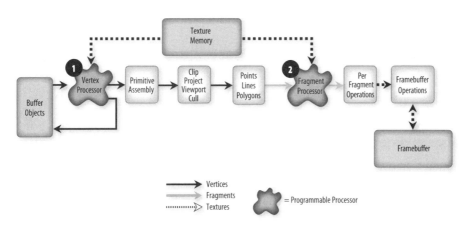

Figure 2.1   OpenGL logical diagram showing programmable processors for vertex and fragment shaders rather than fixed functionality

2.3.1 Vertex Processor

The traditional VERTEX PROCESSOR is a configurable unit that operates on incoming vertex values and their associated data. The vertex processor usually performs traditional graphics operations such as the following:

- Vertex transformation

- Normal transformation and normalization

- Texture coordinate generation

- Texture coordinate transformation

- Lighting

- Color material application

The vertex processor has evolved from a configurable unit into a programmable unit. Because of its general-purpose programmability, this processor can also be used to perform a variety of other computations. Shaders that are intended to run on this processor are called VERTEX SHADERS. Vertex shaders can specify a completely general sequence of operations to be applied to each vertex and its associated data. Vertex shaders that perform some of the computations in the preceding list must contain the code for all desired functionality from the preceding list. For instance, it is not possible to have the existing fixed functionality perform the vertex and normal transformation but to have a vertex shader perform a specialized lighting function. The vertex shader must be written to perform all three functions.

The vertex processor does not replace graphics operations that require knowledge of several vertices at a time or that require topological knowledge. OpenGL operations that remain as fixed functionality in between the vertex processor and the fragment processor include perspective divide and viewport mapping, primitive assembly, frustum and user clipping, frontface/backface determinaton, culling, polygon mode, polygon offset, and depth range.

Figure 2.2 shows the data values that are used as inputs to the vertex processor and the data values that are produced by the vertex processor. Vertex shaders express the algorithm that executes on the vertex processor to produce output values based on the provided input values. Type qualifiers that are defined as part of the OpenGL Shading Language manage the input to the vertex processor and the output from it.

Global variables defined in a vertex shader can be qualified as IN VARIABLES. These represent values that are frequently passed from the application to the

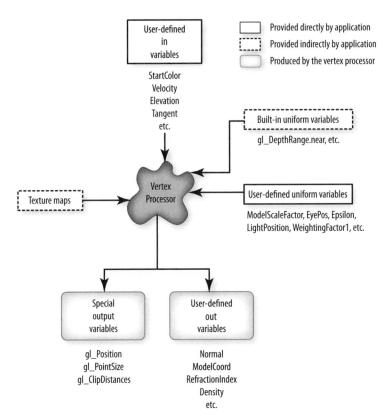

Figure 2.2   Vertex processor inputs and outputs

vertex processor. Because this type of variable is used only for data from the application that defines vertices, it is permitted only as part of a vertex shader.

In the OpenGL API these are called GENERIC VERTEX attributes. (Historically, generic vertex attributes replaced the now deprecated SPECIALIZED vertex attributes such as **glColor, glNormal, glMultiTexCoord,** and **glVertex**.) Applications can provide attribute values with vertex array calls, so they can change as often as every vertex. Generic vertex attributes are defined and referenced by numbers from 0 up to some implementation-dependent maximum value. The command **glVertexAttrib** sends generic vertex attributes to OpenGL by specifying the index of the generic attribute to be modified and the value for that generic attribute.

Vertex shaders can access these generic vertex attributes through user-defined in variables. Another OpenGL command, **glBindAttribLocation**, allows an application to tie together the index of a generic vertex attribute to the user-defined in variable.

Global variables that are available to either the vertex processor or the fragment processor are UNIFORM VARIABLES. Uniform variables typically provide values that change relatively infrequently. A shader can be written so that it is parameterized with uniform variables. The application can provide initial values for these uniform variables, and the end user can manipulate them through a graphical user interface to achieve a variety of effects with a single shader. But uniform variables cannot be specified within **glDrawArrays** or other OpenGL drawing commands, so they can change at most once per primitive.

The OpenGL Shading Language supports user-defined uniform variables. Applications can make arbitrary data values available directly to a shader through user-defined uniform variables. **glGetUniformLocation** obtains the location of a user-defined uniform variable that has been defined as part of a shader. Data can be loaded into this location with another new OpenGL command, **glUniform**. Variations of this command facilitate loading of floating-point, integer, Boolean, and matrix values, as well as arrays of these.

Another new feature is the capability of vertex processors to read from texture memory. This allows vertex shaders to implement displacement mapping algorithms, among other things. For accessing mipmap textures, level of detail can be specified directly in the shader. Existing OpenGL parameters for texture maps define the behavior of the filtering operation, borders, and wrapping.

Conceptually, the vertex processor operates on one vertex at a time (but an implementation may have multiple vertex processors that operate in parallel). The vertex shader is executed once for each vertex passed to OpenGL. The design of the vertex processor is focused on the functionality needed to transform and light a single vertex. Output from the vertex shader is accomplished partly with special output variables. Vertex shaders must compute the homogeneous position of the coordinate in clip space and store the result in the special output variable *gl_Position*. Values to be used during user clipping and point rasterization can be stored in the special output variables *gl_ClipDistances* and *gl_PointSize*.

Global variables that define data that is passed from the vertex processor to the rasterizer are called OUT VARIABLES. They may be further qualified with one of the interpolation qualifiers smooth, noperspective, and flat. If qualified smooth (the default), the out values are gathered together by the rasterizer, and perspective-correct interpolation is performed to provide a value at each fragment for use by the fragment shader. For noperspective, the values are interpolated without perspective correction. A flat qualified out tells the rasterizer to pass only the value of the provoking vertex to the fragment shader. A vertex shader can use a user-defined varying variable to pass along anything that needs to be interpolated: colors, normals (useful for per-fragment lighting computations), texture coordinates, model coordinates, and other arbitrary values.

There is actually no harm (other than a possible loss of performance) in having a vertex shader calculate more varying variables than are needed by the fragment shader. A warning may be generated if the fragment shader consumes fewer varying variables than the vertex shader produces. But you may have good reasons to use a somewhat generic vertex shader with a variety of fragment shaders. The fragment shaders can be written to use a subset of the varying variables produced by the vertex shader. Developers of applications that manage a large number of shaders may find that reducing the costs of shader development and maintenance is more important than squeezing out a tiny bit of additional performance.

The vertex processor output (special output variables and user-defined out variables) is sent to subsequent stages of processing that are defined exactly the same as they are for fixed-function processing: primitive assembly, user clipping, frustum clipping, perspective divide, viewport mapping, polygon offset, polygon mode, and culling.

2.3.2 Fragment Processor

The FRAGMENT PROCESSOR is a programmable unit that operates on fragment values and their associated data. The fragment processor usually performs traditional graphics operations such as the following:

- Operations on interpolated values

- Texture access

- Texture application

- Fog

- Color sum

- Alpha Test

A wide variety of other computations can be performed on this processor. It is easy to implement some traditional vertex operations such as lighting in a fragment shader. Shaders that are intended to run on this processor are called FRAGMENT SHADERS. Fragment shaders express the algorithm that executes on the fragment processor and produces output values based on the input values that are provided. A fragment shader cannot change a fragment's x/y position. Fragment shaders that perform some of the computations from the preceding list must perform all desired functionality from the preceding list. For instance, it is not possible to use the existing fixed functionality to compute fog but have a fragment shader perform specialized texture access and texture application. The fragment shader must be written to perform all three functions.

The fragment processor does not replace graphics operations that require knowledge of several fragments at a time. To support parallelism at the fragment-processing level, fragment shaders are written in a way that expresses the computation required for a single fragment, and direct access to neighboring fragments is not allowed. An implementation may have multiple fragment processors that operate in parallel.

The fragment processor can perform operations on each fragment that is generated by the rasterization of points, lines, and polygons. If images are first downloaded into texture memory, the fragment processor can also be used for pixel processing that requires access to a pixel and its neighbors. A rectangle can be drawn with texturing enabled, and the fragment processor can read the image from texture memory and apply it to the rectangle while performing traditional operations such as the following:

- Pixel zoom
- Scale and bias
- Color table lookup
- Convolution
- Color matrix

The fragment processor does not replace the fixed functionality graphics operations that occur at the back end of the OpenGL pixel processing pipeline such as coverage, pixel ownership test, scissor test, depth test, stencil test, alpha blending, logical operations, dithering, and plane masking.

Figure 2.3 shows the values that provide input to the fragment processor and the data values that are produced by the fragment processor.

The primary inputs to the fragment processor are the interpolated varying variables (both built in and user defined) that are the results of rasterization. User-defined varying variables must be defined in a fragment shader, and their types must match those defined in the vertex shader.

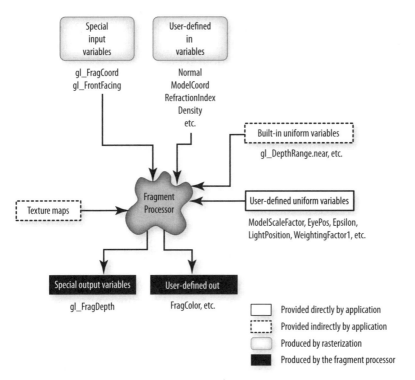

Figure 2.3   Fragment processor inputs and outputs

Values computed by fixed functionality between the vertex processor and the fragment processor are made available through special input variables. The window coordinate position of the fragment is communicated through the special input variable *gl_FragCoord*. An indicator of whether the fragment was generated by rasterizing a front-facing primitive is communicated through the special input variable *gl_FrontFacing*. The point sprite coordinate position of the fragment is communicated through the special input variable *gl_PointCoord*.

Global variables that define data that is passed from the vertex processor through the rasterizer into the fragment processor are called IN VARIABLES. They may be further qualified with one of the interpolation qualifiers smooth, noperspective, and flat. The name, type and interpolation qualifier of the fragment shader's IN VARIABLE must match the corresponding vertex shader's OUT VARIABLE. A fragment shader can use a user-defined in variable to read interpolated: colors, normals (useful for per-fragment lighting computations), texture coordinates, model coordinates, and other arbitrary values.

User-defined uniform variables allow the application to pass relatively infrequently changing values to a fragment shader. The same uniform variable can be accessed by both a vertex shader and a fragment shader if both shaders declare the variable using the same data type.

A small amount of OpenGL state for depth range is accessible to a fragment shader through built-in uniform variable *gl_DepthRange*. This OpenGL state is available to both vertex and fragment shaders.

One of the biggest advantages of the fragment processor is that it can access texture memory an arbitrary number of times and combine in arbitrary ways the values that it reads. A fragment shader is free to read multiple values from a single texture or multiple values from multiple textures. The result of one texture access can be used as the basis for performing another texture access (a DEPENDENT TEXTURE READ). There is no inherent limitation on the number of such dependent reads that are possible, so ray-casting algorithms can be implemented in a fragment shader.

The OpenGL parameters for texture maps continue to define the behavior of the filtering operation, borders, wrapping, and texture comparison modes. These operations are applied when a texture is accessed from within a shader. The shader is free to use the resulting value however it chooses. The shader can read multiple values from a texture and perform a custom filtering operation. It can also use a texture to perform a lookup table operation.

The fragment processor defines almost all the capabilities necessary to implement the fixed-function pixel transfer operations defined in OpenGL, including those in the imaging subset. This means that advanced pixel processing is supported with the fragment processor. Lookup table operations can be done with 1D texture accesses, allowing applications to fully control their size and format. Scale and bias operations are easily expressed through the programming language. The color matrix can be accessed through a built-in uniform variable. Convolution and pixel zoom are supported by accessing a texture multiple times to compute the proper result. Histogram and minimum/maximum operations are left to be defined as extensions because these prove to be quite difficult to support at the fragment level with high degrees of parallelism.

For each fragment, the fragment shader may also compute a replacement depth writing to the special output variable *gl_FragDepth*, or completely discard the fragment. If the fragment is not discarded, the results of the fragment shader are sent on for further processing.

Global variables that define data that is passed from the fragment processor to the fixed-function per-fragment pipeline are called OUT VARIABLES. Another OpenGL command, **glBindFragDataLocation**, allows an application to tie together the user-defined out variable to an index of a drawbuffer.

The remainder of the OpenGL pipeline remains as defined for fixed-function processing. Fragments are submitted to coverage application, pixel ownership testing, scissor testing, stencil testing, depth testing, blending, dithering, logical operations, and masking before ultimately being written into the framebuffer. The back end of the processing pipeline remains as fixed functionality because it is easy to implement in nonprogrammable hardware. Making these functions programmable is more complex because read/modify/write operations can introduce significant instruction scheduling issues and pipeline stalls. Most of these fixed functionality operations can be disabled, and alternative operations can be performed within a fragment shader if desired (albeit with possibly lower performance).

2.4 Language Overview

Because of its success as a standard, OpenGL has been the target of our efforts to define an industry-standard, high-level shading language. The shading language that has been defined as a result of the efforts of OpenGL ARB members is called the OpenGL Shading Language. This language has been designed to be forward looking and to eventually support programmability in other areas as well.

This section provides a brief overview of the OpenGL Shading Language. For a complete discussion of the language, see Chapter 3, Chapter 4, and Chapter 5.

2.4.1 Language Design Considerations

In the past few years, semiconductor technology has progressed to the point at which the levels of computation that can be done per vertex or per fragment have gone beyond what is feasible to describe by the traditional OpenGL mechanisms of setting state to influence the action of fixed pipeline stages. A natural way of taming this complexity and the proliferation of OpenGL extensions is to replace parts of the pipeline with user-programmable stages. This has been done in some recent OpenGL extensions, but the programming is done in assembly language. It can be difficult and time-consuming to write shaders in such low-level languages, and maintaining such code can be costly. As programmable graphics hardware evolves, the current crop of shader assembly languages may also prove to be cumbersome and inefficient to support in hardware.

The ideal solution to these issues was to define a forward-looking, hardware-independent, high-level language that would be easy to use and powerful enough to stand the test of time and that would drastically reduce the need for extensions. These desires were tempered by the need for fast implementations within a generation or two of hardware.

The following design goals were fundamental to the design of the OpenGL Shading Language.

Define a language that works well with OpenGL—The OpenGL Shading Language is designed specifically for use within the OpenGL environment. It provides programmable alternatives to certain parts of the fixed functionality of OpenGL. Therefore, the language itself and the programmable processors it defines must have at least as much functionality as what they replace. Furthermore, by design, it is quite easy to refer to existing OpenGL state from within a shader. By design, it is also quite easy to use fixed functionality in one part of the OpenGL processing pipeline and programmable processing in another.

Expose the flexibility of near-future hardware—Graphics hardware has been changing rapidly to a model that allows general programmability for vertex and fragment processing. To expose this programmability, the shading language is high level, with appropriate abstractions for the graphics problem domain. The language includes a rich set of built-in functions that allow expression of operations on vectors as easily as on scalars. Exposing hardware capabilities through a high-level programming language also obviates the need for OpenGL extensions that define small changes to the fixed functionality behavior. Exposing an abstraction that is independent of the actual underlying hardware eliminates the plethora of piecemeal extensions to OpenGL.

Provide hardware independence—As previously mentioned, the first attempts at exposing the programmability of graphics hardware focused on assembly language interfaces. This was a dangerous direction for software developers to take because it results in software that is inherently nonportable. The goal of a high-level shading language is for the abstraction level to be high enough that application developers can code in a portable way and that hardware vendors have plenty of room to provide innovative hardware architectures and compiler technology.

Define a language that exposes the performance of the underlying graphics hardware—Today's graphics hardware is based on programmable processor technology. It is an established fact nowadays that compiler technology can generate extremely high-performance executable code. With the complexity of today's CPUs, it is difficult to manually generate code that can surpass the performance of code generated by a compiler. It is the intent that the object code generated for a shader be independent of other OpenGL state, so that recompiles or managing multiple copies of object code are not necessary.

Define a language that is easy to use—One of the considerations here is that writing shaders should be simple and easy. Since most graphics application programmers are familiar with C and C++, this led us to adopt the salient features of these languages as the basis for the OpenGL Shading Language. We also believed that compilers, not application programmers, should perform difficult tasks. We concluded that a single language (with very minor variations) should be the basis for programming all the programmable processors that we were defining, as well as those we envisioned adding in future versions of OpenGL. This allows application programmers to become familiar with the basic shading language constructs and apply them to all programming tasks involving the programmable processors in OpenGL.

Define a language that will stand the test of time—This design consideration also led us to base the design of the OpenGL Shading Language on previously successful programming languages such as C and RenderMan. Our hope is that programs written when the OpenGL Shading Language was first defined will still be valid in ten years. Longevity also requires standardization of some sort, so we expended a great deal of effort both in making hardware vendors happy with the final language specification and in pushing the specification through the approval process of OpenGL's governing body, the OpenGL Architecture Review Board (ARB).

Don't preclude higher levels of parallel processing—Newer graphics hardware architectures are providing more and more parallelism at both the vertex and the fragment processing levels. So we took great care with the definition of the OpenGL Shading Language to allow for even higher levels of parallel processing. This consideration has shaped the definition of the language in some subtle but important ways.

Don't include unnecessary language features—Some features of C have made implementing optimizing compilers difficult. Some OpenGL Shading Language features address this issue. For example, C allows hidden aliasing of memory by using pointers and passing pointers as function arguments, which may give multiple names to the same memory. These potential aliases handicap the optimizer, leading to complexity or less optimized code. The OpenGL Shading language does not allow pointers, and it calls by value-return to prevent such aliasing. In general, aliasing is disallowed, simplifying the job of the optimizer.

2.4.2 C Basis

As stated previously, the OpenGL Shading Language is based on the syntax of the ANSI C programming language, and at first glance, programs written in this language look very much like C programs. This is intentional, to make the language easier to use for those most likely to be using it, namely, those developing graphics applications in C or C++.

The basic structure of programs written in the OpenGL Shading Language is the same as it is for programs written in C. The entry point of a set of shaders is the function **void main()**; the body of this function is delimited by curly braces. Constants, identifiers, operators, expressions, and statements are basically the same for the OpenGL Shading Language as they are for C. Control flow for looping, if-then-else, and function calls are virtually identical to C.

2.4.3 Additions to C

The OpenGL Shading Language has a number of language features that have been added because of its special-purpose nature as a language for encoding graphics algorithms. Here are some of the main things that have been added to the OpenGL Shading Language that are different from ANSI C.

Vector types are supported for floating-point, integer, and Boolean values. For floating-point values, these vector types are referred to as **vec2** (two floats), **vec3** (three floats), and **vec4** (four floats). Operators work as readily on vector types as they do on scalars. To sum vectors *v1* and *v2*, you simply would say *v1* + *v2*. Individual components of a vector can be accessed either with array syntax or as fields of a structure. Color values can be accessed by appending .r to the name of a vector variable to access the first component, .g to access the second component, .b to access the third, and .a to access the fourth. Position values can be accessed with .x, .y, .z, and .w, and texture values can be accessed with .s, .t, .p, and .q. Multiple components can be selected by specification of multiple names, like .xy.

Floating-point matrix types are also supported as basic types. The data type **mat2** refers to a 2×2 matrix of floating-point values, **mat3** refers to a 3×3 matrix, **mat4** refers to a 4×4 matrix, and **mat***mxn* refers to an *m* column by *n* row matrix. Matrices are a convenient type for expressing the linear transformations common in 3D graphics. Columns of a matrix can be selected with array syntax, yielding a vector whose components can be accessed as just described.

A set of basic types called SAMPLERS has also been added to create the mechanism by which shaders access texture memory. Samplers are a special type of opaque variable that access a particular texture map. A variable of type **sampler1D** can be used to access a 1D texture map, a variable of type **sampler2D** can be used to access a 2D texture map, and so on. Shadow and cube map textures are also supported through this mechanism.

Qualifiers to global variables have been added to manage the input and output of shaders. The **in**, **uniform**, and **out** qualifiers specify what type of input or output a variable serves. In variables communicate frequently changing values from the application or prior processing stage to a shader, uniform variables communicate infrequently changing values from the application to any shader, and out variables communicate frequently changing values from a shader to a subsequent processing stages.

Shaders written in the OpenGL Shading Language can use built-in variables that begin with the reserved prefix "gl_" in order to access existing OpenGL state and to communicate with the fixed functionality of OpenGL. Both vertex and fragment shaders can access built-in uniform variables that contain state values that are available within the current rendering context. The few built-in uniforms are *gl_DepthRange.near*, *gl_DepthRange.far*, and *gl_DepthRange.diff*. The vertex shader must write the special variable *gl_Position* in order to provide necessary information to the fixed functionality stages between vertex processing and fragment processing, namely, primitive assembly, clipping, culling, and rasterization. A fragment shader may optionally write *gl_FragDepth* to replace the depth produced by rasterization.

A variety of built-in functions is also provided in the OpenGL Shading Language in order to make coding easier and to take advantage of possible hardware acceleration for certain operations. The language defines built-in functions for a variety of operations:

- Trigonometric operations—sine, cosine, tangent, and so on

- Exponential operations—power, exponential, logarithm, square root, and inverse square root

- Common math operations—absolute value, floor, ceiling, fractional part, modulus, and so on

- Geometric operations—length, distance, dot product, cross product, normalization, and so on

- Relational operations based on vectors—component-wise operations such as greater than, less than, equal to, and so on

- Specialized fragment shader functions for computing derivatives and estimating filter widths for antialiasing

- Functions for accessing values in texture memory

- Functions that return noise values for procedural texturing effects

2.4.4 Additions from C++

The OpenGL Shading Language also includes a few notable language features from C++. In particular, it supports function overloading to make it easy to define functions that differ only in the type or number of arguments being passed. This feature is heavily used by the built-in functions. For instance, the dot product function is overloaded to deal with arguments that are types **float**, **vec2**, **vec3**, and **vec4**.

The concept of constructors also comes from C++. Initializers are done only with constructors in the OpenGL Shading Language. Using constructors allows for more than one way of initializing variables.

Another feature borrowed from C++ is that variables can be declared when they are needed; they do not have to be declared at the beginning of a basic block. The basic type **bool** is supported as in C++.

As in C++, functions must be declared before being used. This can be accomplished either with the function's definition (its body) or just with a prototype.

2.4.5 C Features Not Supported

Unlike ANSI C, the OpenGL Shading Language supports limited implicit conversion of data types. Scalar and vector expressions of integer or unsigned integer may be implicitly converted to the equivalent scalar or vector float expression. Otherwise, compiler errors are generated if variables used in an expression are of different types. For instance, an error is generated for the statement int i = 0.0; but not for the statement float f = 0;. This approach might seem like a bit of a nuisance, but it simplifies the language by eliminating ambiguous circular promotion rules.

The OpenGL Shading Language does not support pointers, strings, or characters, or any operations based on these. It is fundamentally a language for processing numerical data, not for processing character or string data, so there is no need for these features to complicate the language. To lower the implementation burden (both for the compiler and for the graphics hardware), there is no support for byte, short, or long integers.

A few other C language features that were eliminated from consideration in order to simplify the OpenGL Shading Language (or because there was no compelling need for them at the time) are unions, enumerated types, and bit fields in structures. Finally, the language is not file based, so you won't see any **#include** directives or other references to filenames.

2.4.6 Other Differences

There are a few areas in which the OpenGL Shading Language provides the same functionality as C but does so in a different way. One of these is that constructors, rather than type casts, are used for data type conversion. Constructors, not C-style initializers, are also used for variable initialization. There is no support at all for type casting without conversion, so constructors keep the language type safe. Constructors use the syntax of a function call, where the function name is the name of the desired type and the arguments are the values that will be used to construct the desired value.

Constructors allow a much richer set of operations than simple type casts or C-style initializers, and the flexibility that this richness provides comes in quite handy for dealing with vector and matrix data types. In addition to converting from one scalar type to another, constructors can create a larger type out of a smaller type or reduce a larger type to a smaller type. For instance, the constructor vec3(1.0, 2.0, 3.0) constructs a **vec3** data type out of three scalar values, and the constructor `vec3 (myVec4)` strips the fourth component from *myVec4* to create a **vec3** value.

The other area of difference is that, unlike the call-by-value calling convention used by C, the OpenGL Shading Language uses CALL BY VALUE-RETURN. Input parameters are copied into the function at call time, and output parameters are copied back to the caller before the function exits. Because the function deals only with copies of the function parameters, there are no issues regarding aliasing of variables within a function. Function parameters are identified as input parameters with the qualifier **in**, they are identified as output parameters with the qualifier **out**, and they are identified as both input and output parameters with the qualifier **inout**; if no qualifier is present, they are identified as input parameters.

2.5 System Overview

We have already described briefly some of the pieces that provide applications with access to the programmability of underlying graphics hardware. This section briefly describes how these pieces go together in a working system.

2.5.1 Driver Model

A piece of software that controls a piece of hardware and manages shared access to that piece of hardware is commonly called a DRIVER. No matter what environment OpenGL is implemented in, it falls into the driver category because OpenGL manages shared access to the underlying graphics hardware. Some of its tasks must also be coordinated with, or supervised by, facilities in the operating system.

Figure 2.4 illustrates how OpenGL shaders are handled in the execution environment of OpenGL. Applications communicate with OpenGL by calling functions that are part of the OpenGL API. A new OpenGL function, **glCreateShader**, allows applications to allocate within the OpenGL driver the data structures that are necessary for storing an OpenGL shader. These data structures are called SHADER OBJECTS. After a shader object has been created, the application can provide the source code for the shader by calling **glShaderSource**. This command provides to OpenGL the character strings containing the shader source code.

As you can see from Figure 2.4, the compiler for the OpenGL Shading Language is actually part of the OpenGL driver environment. This is one of the

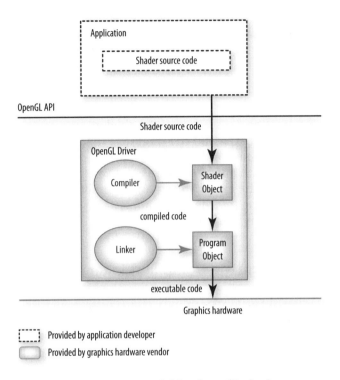

Figure 2.4 Execution model for OpenGL shaders

key differences between the OpenGL Shading Language and other shading language designs, such as the Stanford Shading Language, High-Level Shader Language (HLSL) from Microsoft, or Cg from NVIDIA. In these other languages, the high-level shading language compiler sits above the graphics API and translates the high-level shading language into something that can be consumed by the underlying graphics API. (See Chapter 17 for more details.) With the OpenGL Shading Language, the source code for shaders is passed to the OpenGL driver, and in that environment, the shaders are compiled to the native machine code as efficiently as possible. After source code for a shader has been loaded into a shader object in the OpenGL driver environment, it can be compiled with **glCompileShader.**

A PROGRAM OBJECT is an OpenGL-managed data structure that acts as a container for shader objects. Applications are required to attach shader objects to a program object by using the command **glAttachShader**. When attached to a program object, the compiled shader objects can be linked with **glLinkProgram**. Support for multiple shader objects (and the subsequent need for a linker built into OpenGL) is a key difference between the OpenGL Shading Language and assembly-level APIs such as those provided by the OpenGL extensions *ARB_vertex_program* and *ARB_fragment_program*. For more complex shading tasks, separately compiled shader objects are a much more attractive alternative than a single, monolithic block of assembly-level code.

The link step resolves external references between the shaders, checks the compatibility between the vertex shader and the fragment shader, assigns memory locations to uniform variables, and so on. The result is one or more executables that can be installed with **glUseProgram** as part of OpenGL's current state. This command installs the executables on the vertex processor, the fragment processor, or both. The installed executables are responsible for processing all subsequent graphics primitives.

2.5.2 OpenGL Shading Language Compiler/Linker

The source for a single shader is an array of strings of characters, and a single shader is made from the concatenation of these strings. There is no inherent connection between strings and the lines of code in a shader. A shader may be entirely represented by a single string, or each line of shader source code may be contained in a separate string. Each string can contain multiple lines, separated by new-lines. No new-lines need be present in a string; a single line can be formed from multiple strings. No new-lines or other characters are inserted by the OpenGL implementation when it concatenates the strings to form a single shader. It is entirely up to the application programmer to provide shader source code to OpenGL with new-lines between each line of source code.

Diagnostic messages returned from compiling a shader must identify both the line number within a string and the source string to which the diagnostic message applies. Source strings are counted sequentially with the first string counted as string 0. For source code parsing, the current line number is one more than the number of new-lines that have been processed.

The front end of the OpenGL Shading Language compiler has been released as open source by 3Dlabs and can be used by anyone interested in writing his or her own compiler. This publicly available front end performs lexical analysis of OpenGL Shading Language source code to produce a token stream and then performs syntactic and semantic analysis of this token stream to produce a binary, high-level representation of the language. This front end acts as a reference implementation of the OpenGL Shading

Language, and therefore it goes hand-in-hand with the language specification to define the language clearly. Another advantage to using this publicly available front end in an OpenGL Shading Language compiler implementation is that the syntax and semantics for shaders are checked consistently by all implementations that use this front end. More consistency among compiler implementations makes it easier for developers to write shaders that work as intended across a variety of implementations.

It is assumed that the back end of the OpenGL Shading Language compiler will be implemented differently on different platforms. Each implementation must take the high-level representation produced by the publicly available front end and produce optimized machine code for a particular hardware target. This is an area in which individual hardware vendors can add value to their shading language implementation by figuring out ways to map the high-level representation onto the actual machine instructions found in their hardware. Likewise, the linking stage is also highly hardware dependent because it involves operations like assigning variables to actual memory locations in the hardware. A variety of global optimizations may also be performed as part of linking.

The net result of this assumption is that graphics hardware vendors will implement the majority of the OpenGL Shading Language compiler and linker. Along with the OpenGL driver itself, this software will typically be included as part of the graphics driver installation package that is provided by a graphics hardware vendor.

2.5.3 OpenGL Shading Language API

As of OpenGL 2.0, support for the OpenGL Shading Language is available as part of standard OpenGL. The following OpenGL entry points support the OpenGL Shading Language:

- **glAttachShader**—Attach a shader object to a program object

- **glBindAttribLocation**—Specify the generic vertex attribute index to be used for a particular user-defined attribute variable in a vertex shader

- **glCompileShader**—Compile a shader

- **glCreateProgram**—Create a program object

- **glCreateShader**—Create a shader object

- **glDeleteProgram**—Delete a program object

- **glDeleteShader**—Delete a shader object

- **glDetachShader**—Detach a shader object from a program object

- **glDisableVertexAttribArray**—Disable a generic vertex attribute from being sent to OpenGL with vertex arrays

- **glEnableVertexAttribArray**—Enable a generic vertex attribute to be sent to OpenGL with vertex arrays

- **glGetActiveAttrib**—Obtain the name, size, and type of an active attribute variable for a program object

- **glGetActiveUniform**—Obtain the name, size, and type of an active uniform variable for a program object

- **glGetAttachedShaders**—Get the list of shader objects attached to a program object

- **glGetAttribLocation**—Return the generic vertex attribute index that is bound to a specified user-defined attribute variable

- **glGetProgram**—Query one of the parameters of a program object

- **glGetProgramInfoLog**—Obtain the information log for a program object

- **glGetShader**—Query one of the parameters of a shader object

- **glGetShaderInfoLog**—Obtain the information log for a shader object

- **glGetShaderSource**—Get the source code for a specific shader object

- **glGetUniform**—Query the current value of a uniform variable

- **glGetUniformLocation**—Query the location assigned to a uniform variable by the linker

- **glGetVertexAttrib**—Return current state for the specified generic vertex attribute

- **glGetVertexAttribPointer**—Return the vertex array pointer value for the specified generic vertex attribute

- **glIsProgram**—Determine if an object name corresponds to a program object

- **glIsShader**—Determine if an object name corresponds to a shader object

- **glLinkProgram**—Link a program object to create executable code

- **glShaderSource**—Load source code strings into a shader object

- **glUniform**—Set the value of a uniform variable

- **glUseProgram**—Install a program object's executable code as part of current state

- **glValidateProgram**—Return validation information for a program object

- **glVertexAttrib**—Send generic vertex attributes to OpenGL one vertex at a time

- **glVertexAttribPointer**—Specify location and organization of generic vertex attributes to be sent to OpenGL with vertex arrays

These new entry points are all discussed in more detail in Chapter 7. Reference pages for all of the OpenGL Shading Language API entry points defined by these extensions are included in Appendix B at the back of this book.

2.6 Key Benefits

The following key benefits are derived from the choices that were made during the design of the OpenGL Shading Language:

Tight integration with OpenGL—The OpenGL Shading Language was designed for use in OpenGL. It is designed in such a way that an existing, working OpenGL application can easily be modified to take advantage of the capabilities of programmable graphics hardware. Built-in access to existing OpenGL state, reuse of API entry points that are already familiar to application developers, and a close coupling with the existing architecture of OpenGL are all key benefits of using the OpenGL Shading Language for shader development.

Runtime compilation—Source code stays as source code, in its easiest-to-maintain form, for as long as possible. An application passes source code to any conforming OpenGL implementation that supports the OpenGL Shading Language, and it will be compiled and executed properly. There is no need for a multitude of binaries for a multitude of different platforms.[1]

---

1. At the time of this writing, the OpenGL ARB is still considering the need for an API that allows shaders to be specified in a form other than source code. The primary issues are the protection of intellectual property that may be embedded in string-based shader source code and the performance that would be gained by allowing shaders to be at least partially precompiled. When such an API is defined, shader portability may be reduced, but application developers will have the option of getting better code security and better performance.

No reliance on cross-vendor assembly language—Both DirectX and OpenGL have widespread support for assembly language interfaces to graphics programmability. High-level shading languages could be (and have been) built on top of these assembly language interfaces, and such high-level languages can be translated into these assembly language interfaces completely outside the environment of OpenGL or DirectX. This does have some advantages, but relying on an assembly language interface as the primary interface to hardware programmability restricts innovation by graphics hardware designers. Hardware designers have many more choices for acceleration of an expressive high-level language than they do for a restrictive assembly language. It is much too early in the development of programmable graphics hardware technology to establish an assembly language standard for graphics programmability. C, on the other hand, was developed long before any CPU assembly languages that are in existence today, and it is still a viable choice for application development.

Unconstrained opportunities for compiler optimization plus optimal performance on a wider range of hardware—As we've learned through experience with CPUs, compilers are much better at quickly generating efficient code than humans are. By allowing high-level source code to be compiled within OpenGL, rather than outside of OpenGL, individual hardware vendors have the best possible opportunity to deliver optimal performance on their graphics hardware. In fact, compiler improvements can be made with each OpenGL driver release, and the applications won't need to change any application source code, recompile the application, or even relink it. Furthermore, most of the current crop of assembly language interfaces are string based. This makes them inefficient for use as intermediate languages for compilation because two string translations are required. First, the string-based, high-level source must be translated into string-based assembly language, and then that string-based assembly language must be passed to OpenGL and translated from string-based assembly language to machine code.

A truly open, cross-platform standard—No other high-level graphics shading language has been approved as part of an open, multivendor standard. Like OpenGL itself, the OpenGL Shading Language will be implemented by a variety of different vendors for a variety of different environments.

One high-level language for all programmable graphics processing—The OpenGL Shading Language is used to write shaders for both the vertex processor and the fragment processor in OpenGL, with very small differences in the language for the two types of shaders. In the future, it is intended that the OpenGL Shading Language will bring programmability to other areas of OpenGL as well. Areas that have already received some discussion include programmability for packing/unpacking arbitrary image formats and support for programmable tessellation of higher-order surfaces in the graphics hardware.

Support for modular programming—By defining compilation and linking as two separate steps, shader writers have a lot more flexibility in how they choose to implement complex shading algorithms. Rather than implement a complex algorithm as a single, monolithic shader, developers are free to implement it as a collection of shaders that can be independently compiled and attached to a program object. Shaders can be designed with common interfaces so that they are interchangeable, and a link operation joins them to create a program.

No additional libraries or executables—The OpenGL Shading Language and the compiler and linker that support it are defined as part of OpenGL. Applications need not worry about linking against any additional runtime libraries. Compiler improvements are delivered as part of OpenGL driver updates.

2.7 Summary

Here are the key points to understand about how all the pieces fit together at execution time:

- When installed as part of current state, the executable created for the vertex processor is executed once for every vertex provided to OpenGL.

- When installed as part of current state, the executable created for the fragment processor is executed once for every fragment that is produced by rasterization.

- When vertex or fragment shaders are used, the corresponding fixed functionality is disabled. Shaders must implement such functionality themselves if it is desired.

- In variables defined in a vertex shader are per-vertex values that are output from the vertex processor. Rasterization is the process that causes the per-vertex values to be interpolated and per-fragment values to be generated. The per-fragment values become the input to the fragment processor and are accessed in the fragment shader with the same varying variable name as was used in the vertex shader.

- An application can communicate directly with a vertex shader in two ways: by using attribute variables and by using uniform variables.

- Attribute variables are expected to change frequently and may be supplied by the application as often as every vertex.

- Applications can pass arbitrary vertex data to a vertex shader with user-defined attribute variables.

- Applications can pass standard vertex attributes (color, normal, texture coordinates, position, etc.) to a vertex shader with built-in attribute variables.

- An application communicates directly with a fragment shader with uniform variables.

- Uniform variables are expected to change relatively infrequently (at a minimum, they are constant for an entire graphics primitive).

- The compiler and linker for the language are contained within OpenGL, but tools for compiling, linking, and debugging shaders can exist outside of OpenGL as well.

To summarize, the following are the most important points about the OpenGL Shading Language:

- The language is based on the syntax of C.

- Basic structure and many keywords are the same as in C.

- Vectors and matrices are included in the language as basic types.

- Global type qualifiers **in**, **uniform**, and **out** are added to describe variables that manage shader I/O.

  - Variables of type **in** allow the communication of frequently changing values from the application to the vertex shader, or from fixed-function rasterization to the fragment shader.

  - Variables of type **out** allow the communication of frequently changing values to be output from a vertex shader or fragment shader.

  - Variables of type **uniform** allow the application to provide relatively infrequently changing values to both vertex shaders and fragment shaders.

- The data type **sampler** is added for accessing textures.

- Built-in variable names can be used to access standard OpenGL state and to communicate with OpenGL fixed functionality.

- A variety of built-in functions perform common graphics operations.

- Function declarations are required, and overloading based on number and type of arguments is supported as in C++.

- Variables can be declared when needed.

To install and use OpenGL shaders, do the following:

1. Create one or more (empty) shader objects by calling **glCreateShader**.

2. Provide source code for these shaders by calling **glShaderSource**.

3. Compile each of the shaders by calling **glCompileShader**.

4. Create a program object by calling **glCreateProgram**.

5. Attach all the shader objects to the program object by calling **glAttachShader**.

6. Link the program object by calling **glLinkProgram**.

7. Install the executable program as part of OpenGL's current state by calling **glUseProgram**.

After these steps, subsequent graphics primitives will be drawn with the shaders you've provided rather than with OpenGL's defined fixed functionality pipeline.

2.8 Further Information

Just keep reading this book and you'll get to all of the really good stuff! If you really must have more technical details, here are pointers to the official specification documents. The 3Dlabs Web site also has additional material, including slide presentations, demos, example shaders, and source code.

[1] Kessenich, John, Dave Baldwin, and Randi Rost, *The OpenGL Shading Language, Version 1.40*, 3Dlabs/Intel March 2009. www.opengl.org/documentation/specs/

[2] Segal, Mark, and Kurt Akeley, *The OpenGL Graphics System: A Specification (Version 3.1)*, Editor (v1.1): Chris Frazier, (v1.2–3.1): Jon Leech, (v2.0): Jon Leech and Pat Brown, March 2009. www.opengl.org/documentation/spec.html

[3] GLSL Compiler Front-End. Now at http://3dshaders.com.

Chapter 3

Language Definition

by John Kessenich

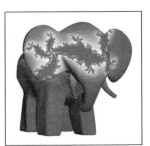

In this chapter, we present the language features of the OpenGL Shading Language. We start with a simple example of a working pair of vertex and fragment shaders to show their basic structure and interfaces. Each aspect of the language is then discussed in turn.

The OpenGL Shading Language syntax comes from the C family of programming languages. Tokens, identifiers, semicolons, nesting with curly braces, control-flow, and many keywords look like C. Both comment styles, // ... and /* ... */, are accepted. Much is also different, though, and all important differences from C are discussed.

Each shader example is presented as it might appear in a file or onscreen. However, as explained in Chapter 7, the OpenGL API passes shaders as strings, not files, because OpenGL does not consider shaders file based.

3.1 Example Shader Pair

A program typically contains two shaders: one vertex shader and one fragment shader. More than one shader of each type can be present, but there must be exactly one function **main** between all the fragment shaders and exactly one function **main** between all the vertex shaders. Frequently, it's easiest to just have one shader of each type.

The following is a simple vertex and fragment shader pair that can smoothly express a surface temperature with color. The range of temperatures and their colors are parameterized. First, we show the vertex shader. It is executed once for each vertex.

```
#version 140
// Global variables

// uniform qualified variables are changed at most once per primitive
uniform float CoolestTemp;
uniform float TempRange;
uniform mat4  MVPMatrix;

// in qualified variables are typically changed per vertex
in   vec4  mcVertex;
in   float VertexTemp;



// out qualified variables communicate from the vertex shader to
// the fragment shader
out float Temperature;

void main()
{
    // compute a temperature to be interpolated per fragment,
    // in the range [0.0, 1.0]
    Temperature = (VertexTemp - CoolestTemp) /  TempRange;
    gl_Position = MVPMatrix * mcVertex;
}
```

That's it for the vertex shader. Primitive assembly follows the preceding vertex processing, providing the rasterizer with enough information to create fragments. The rasterizer interpolates the *Temperature* values written per vertex to create values per fragment. Each fragment is then delivered to a single execution of the fragment shader, as follows:

```
#version 140
// Global variables

// uniform qualified variables are changed at most once per primitive
// by the application, and vec3 declares a vector of three
// floating-point numbers
uniform vec3 CoolestColor;
uniform vec3 HottestColor;

// Temperature contains the now interpolated per-fragment
// value of temperature set by the vertex shader
in float Temperature;

// out qualified global variables communicate from the fragment shader
// to per-fragment operations (blending) and the framebuffer
out vec4 FragmentColor;
```

```
void main()
{
    // get a color between coolest and hottest colors, using
    // the mix() built-in function
    vec3 color = mix(CoolestColor, HottestColor, Temperature);

    // make a vector of 4 floating-point numbers by appending an
    // alpha of 1.0, and set this fragment's color
    FragmentColor = vec4(color, 1.0);
}
```

Both shaders receive user-defined state from the application through the declared **uniform** qualified variables. The vertex shader gets information associated with each vertex through the **in** qualified variables. Information is passed from the vertex shader's **out** qualified variables to the fragment shader's **in** qualified variables. The **out** declarations in the vertex shader must match the **in** declarations in the fragment shader. The fixed functionality located between the vertex and fragment processors will interpolate the per-vertex values written to each **out** variable. When the fragment shader reads this same **in** variable, it reads the value interpolated for the location of the fragment being processed.

Shaders interact with the fixed functionality OpenGL pipeline by writing built-in variables. OpenGL prefixes built-in variables with "gl_". In the preceding examples, writing to *gl_Position* tells the OpenGL pipeline where the transformed vertices are located.

Shaders may also interact with the fixed functionality by reading or writing user-defined variables. In the preceding examples, mcVertex and VertexTemp read from generic vertex attributes. Writing FragmentColor outputs to the fixed-function per-fragment operations (blending) and, from there, to the framebuffer.

Execution of the preceding shaders occurs multiple times to process a single primitive, once per vertex for the vertex shader and once per fragment for the fragment shader. Many such executions of the same shader can happen in parallel. In general, there is no direct tie or ordering between shader executions. Information can be communicated neither from vertex to vertex nor from fragment to fragment.

3.2 Data Types

We saw vectors of floating-point numbers in the example in the previous section. Many other built-in data types are available to ease the expression of graphical operations. Booleans, integers, matrices, vectors of other types, structures, and arrays are all included. Each is discussed in the following sections. Notably missing are string and character types, since there is little use for them in processing vertex and fragment data.

3.2.1 Scalars

The scalar types available are

float	declares a single floating-point number
int	declares a single integer number
uint	declares a single unsigned integer number
bool	declares a single Boolean number

These declare variables, as is familiar from C/C++.

```
float f;
float g, h = 2.4;
uint NumTextures = 4;
bool skipProcessing;
```

Unlike the original C, the OpenGL Shading Language requires you to provide the type name because there are no default types. As in C++, declarations may appear when needed, not just after an open curly brace ({).

Literal floating-point numbers are also specified as in C, except the only permitted suffixes to specify precision are **f** and **F** since there is only one floating-point type. (Unlike in C, if no suffix is specified, it is implicitly **f**.)

```
3.14159
3.
0.2f
.609F
1.5e10
0.4E-4
etc.
```

In general, floating-point values and operations act as they do in C.

Starting with OpenGL 3.0, integers and unsigned integers are fully supported. Signed ints are 32 bits, including a sign bit, in two's complement form. Unsigned ints must have exactly 32 bits of precision. Arithmetic overflows or underflows will not cause any exception, nor will they saturate; they will simply "wrap," producing the low-order 32 bits of the result.

Bit-wise operations like left-shift (<<) and bit-wise and (&) are supported.

Literal integers can be given as decimal values, octal values, or hexadecimal values, as in C. They may also be suffixed with either **u** or **U**.

```
15u    // a literal decimal unsigned integer
42     // a literal decimal integer
052    // a literal octal integer
0x2A   // a literal hexadecimal integer
```

Boolean variables are as **bool** in C++. They can have only one of two values: true or false. Literal Boolean constants **true** and **false** are provided. Relational operators like less-than (<) and logical operators like logical and (&&) always result in Boolean values. Flow-control constructs like **if-else** accept only Boolean-typed expressions. In these regards, the OpenGL Shading Language is more restrictive than C++.

3.2.2 Vectors

Vectors of **float**, **int**, or **bool** are built-in basic types. They can have two, three, or four components and are named as follows:

vec2	Vector of two floating-point numbers
vec3	Vector of three floating-point numbers
vec4	Vector of four floating-point numbers
ivec2	Vector of two integers
ivec3	Vector of three integers
ivec4	Vector of four integers
uvec2	Vector of two unsigned integers
uvec3	Vector of three unsigned integers
uvec4	Vector of four unsigned integers
bvec2	Vector of two Booleans
bvec3	Vector of three Booleans
bvec4	Vector of four Booleans

Vectors are quite useful. They conveniently store and manipulate colors, positions, texture coordinates, and so on. Built-in variables and built-in functions make heavy use of these types. Also, special operations are supported. Finally, hardware is likely to have vector-processing capabilities that mirror vector expressions in shaders.

Note that the language does not distinguish between a color vector and a position vector or other uses of a floating-point vector. These are all just floating-point vectors from the language's perspective.

Special features of vectors include component access that can be done either through field selection (as with structures) or as array accesses. For example, if *position* is a **vec3**, it can be considered as the vector (x, y, z), and *position.x* will select the first component of the vector.

In all, the following names are available for selecting components of vectors:

x, y, z, w	Treat a vector as a position or direction
r, g, b, a	Treat a vector as a color
s, t, p, q	Treat a vector as a texture coordinate

There is no explicit way of stating that a vector is a color, a position, a coordinate, and so on. Rather, these component selection names are provided simply for readability in a shader. The only compile-time checking done is that the vector is large enough to provide a specified component. Also, if multiple components are selected (swizzling, discussed in Section 3.7.2), all the components are from the same family.

Vectors can also be indexed as a zero-based array to obtain components. For instance, *position[2]* returns the third component of *position*. Variable indices are allowed, making it possible to loop over the components of a vector. Multiplication takes on special meaning when operating on a vector since linear algebraic multiplies with matrices are understood. Swizzling, indexing, and other operations are discussed in detail in Section 3.7.

3.2.3 Matrices

Built-in types are available for matrices of floating-point numbers. There are nonsquare matrices and square matrices up to 4×4 in size.

mat2	2×2 matrix of floating-point numbers
mat3	3×3 matrix of floating-point numbers
mat4	4×4 matrix of floating-point numbers
mat*mxn*	$m \times n$ matrix of floating point numbers (column × row)

These are useful for storing linear transforms or other data. They are treated semantically as matrices, particularly when a vector and a matrix are multiplied together, in which case the proper linear-algebraic computation is performed. When relevant, matrices are organized in column major order, as is the tradition in OpenGL.

You may access a matrix as an array of column vectors—that is, if *transform* is a **mat4**, *transform[2]* is the third column of *transform*. The resulting type of *transform[2]* is **vec4**. Column 0 is the first column. Because *transform[2]* is a vector and you can also treat vectors as arrays, *transform[3][1]* is the second component of the vector forming the fourth column of *transform*. Hence, it ends up looking as if *transform* is a two-dimensional array. Just remember that the first index selects the column, not the row, and the second index selects the row.

3.2.4 Samplers

Texture lookups require some indication as to which texture or texture unit will do the lookup. The OpenGL Shading Language doesn't really care about the underlying implementation of texture units or other forms of organizing texture lookup hardware. Hence, it provides a simple opaque handle to encapsulate what to look up. These handles are called SAMPLERS. The sampler types available are

sampler1D	Accesses a one-dimensional texture
sampler2D	Accesses a two-dimensional texture
sampler3D	Accesses a three-dimensional texture
samplerCube	Accesses a cube-map texture
sampler2DRect	Accesses a two-dimensional rectangle texture
sampler1DShadow	Accesses a one-dimensional depth texture with comparison
sampler2DShadow	Accesses a two-dimensional depth texture with comparison
sampler2DRectShadow	Accesses a two-dimensional rectangle depth texture with comparison
sampler1DArray	Accesses a one-dimensional texture array
sampler2DArray	Accesses a two-dimensional texture array
sampler1DArrayShadow	Accesses a one-dimensional depth texture array with comparison

sampler2DArrayShadow	Accesses a two-dimensional depth texture array with comparison
samplerBuffer	Accesses a texture buffer
isampler1D	Accesses a one-dimensional integer texture
isampler2D	Accesses a two-dimensional integer texture
isampler3D	Accesses a three-dimensional integer texture
isamplerCube	Accesses a cube-map integer texture
isampler2DRect	Accesses a two-dimensional integer rectangle texture
isampler1DArray	Accesses a two-dimensional integer texture array
isampler2DArray	Accesses a two-dimensional integer texture array
isamplerBuffer	Accesses an integer texture buffer
usampler1D	Accesses a one-dimensional unsigned integer texture
usampler2D	Accesses a two-dimensional unsigned integer texture
usampler3D	Accesses a three-dimensional unsigned integer texture
usamplerCube	Accesses a cube-map unsigned integer texture
usampler2DRect	Accesses a two-dimensional unsigned integer rectangle texture
usampler1DArray	Accesses a one-dimensional unsigned integer texture array
usampler2DArray	Accesses a two-dimensional unsigned integer texture array
usamplerBuffer	Accesses an unsigned integer texture buffer

When the application initializes a sampler, the OpenGL implementation stores into it whatever information is needed to communicate which texture to access. Shaders cannot themselves initialize samplers. They can only receive them from the application, through a **uniform** qualified sampler, or pass them on to user-defined or built-in functions. As a function parameter, a sampler cannot be modified, so there is no way for a shader to change a sampler's value.

For example, a sampler could be declared as

```
uniform sampler2D Grass;
```

(Uniform qualifiers are discussed in more detail in Section 3.5.2.)

This variable can then be passed into a corresponding texture lookup function to access a texture:

```
vec4 color = texture(Grass, coord);
```

where *coord* is a **vec2** holding the two-dimensional position used to index the grass texture, and *color* is the result of doing the texture lookup. Together, the compiler and the OpenGL driver validate that *Grass* really references a two-dimensional texture and that *Grass* is passed only into texture lookups.

Shaders may not manipulate sampler values. For example, the expression `Grass + 1` is not allowed. Arrays of samplers are considered archaic and, if used, should be indexed with integral constant expressions. (Arrays of samplers indexed with nonconstant expressions are at best implemented inefficiently by fetching from every sampler that might have been needed in the array.) The new **sampler*n*DArray** types allow for efficient access of sampler arrays, although with the restriction that the texture formats and texture sizes are constant across the sampler array.

3.2.5 Structures

The OpenGL Shading Language provides user-defined structures similar to C. For example,

```
struct light
{
    vec3 position;
    vec3 color;
};
```

As in C++, the name of the structure is the name of this new user-defined type. No **typedef** is needed. In fact, the **typedef** keyword is still reserved because there is not yet a need for it. A variable of type *light* from the preceding example is simply declared as

```
light ceilingLight;
```

Most other aspects of structures mirror C. They can be embedded and nested. Embedded structure type names have the same scope as the structure in which they are declared. However, embedded structures must be named. Structure members can also be arrays. Finally, each level of structure has its own name space for its members' names, as is familiar.

Bit-fields (the capability to declare an integer with a specified number of bits) are not supported.

Currently, structures are the only user-definable type. The keywords **union**, **enum**, and **class** are reserved for possible future use.

3.2.6 Arrays

Arrays of any type can be created. The declaration

```
vec4 points[10];
```

creates an array of ten **vec4** variables, indexed starting with zero. There are no pointers; the only way to declare an array is with square brackets. Declaring an array as a function parameter also requires square brackets and a size because, currently, array arguments are passed as if the whole array is a single object, not as if the argument is a pointer.

Arrays, unless they are function parameters, do not have to be declared with a size. A declaration like

```
vec4 points[];
```

is allowed, as long as *either* of the following two cases is true:

1. Before the array is referenced, it is declared again with a size, with the same type as the first declaration. For example,

```
vec4 points[];    // points is an array of unknown size
vec4 points[10];  // points is now an array of size 10
```

This cannot be followed by another declaration:

```
vec4 points[];    // points is an array of unknown size
vec4 points[10];  // points is now an array of size 10
vec4 points[20];  // this is illegal
vec4 points[];    // this is also illegal
```

2. All indices that statically reference the array are compile-time
   constants. In this case, the compiler will make the array large enough
   to hold the largest index it sees used. For example,

```
vec4 points[];          // points is an array of unknown size
points[2] = vec4(1.0);  // points is now an array of size 3
points[7] = vec4(2.0);  // points is now an array of size 8
```

In this case, at runtime the array has only one size, determined by the
largest index the compiler sees. Such automatically sized arrays cannot be
passed as function arguments.

Multiple shaders sharing the same array must declare it with the same size.
The linker verifies this.

3.2.7 Void

The type **void** declares a function that returns no value. For example, the
function **main** returns no value and must be declared as type **void**.

```
void main()
{
    ...
}
```

Other than for functions that return nothing, the **void** type is not useful.

3.2.8 Declarations and Scope

Variables are declared quite similarly to the way they are declared in C++.
They can be declared where needed and have scope as in C++. For example,

```
float f;

f = 3.0;

vec4 u, v;

for (int i = 0; i < 10; ++i)
    v = f * u + v;
```

The scope of a variable declared in a **for** statement ends at the end of
the loop's substatement. However, variables may not be declared in an

if statement. This simplifies implementation of scoping across the **else** sub-statement, with little practical cost.

As in C, variable names are case sensitive, must start with a letter or underscore (_), and contain only letters, numbers, and underscores (_). User-defined variables cannot start with the string "gl_" because those names are reserved for future use by OpenGL. Names containing consecutive underscores (__) are also reserved.

3.2.9 Type Matching and Promotion

The OpenGL Shading Language is fairly strict with type matching. In general, types being assigned must match, argument types passed into functions must match formal parameter declarations, and types being operated on must match the requirements of the operator.

There are no automatic promotions from one type to another. There are, however, limited implicit conversions. A scalar integer or scalar unsigned integer may be implicitly converted to a scalar float. A vector integer or vector unsigned integer may be implicitly converted to a vector float of the same number of elements.

This fairly strict type matching may occasionally make a shader have an extra explicit conversion. However, it also simplifies the language, preventing some forms of obfuscated code and some classes of defects. For example, there are no ambiguities in which overloaded function should be chosen for a given function call.

3.3 Initializers and Constructors

A shader variable may be initialized when it is declared. As is familiar from C, the following example initializes *b* at declaration time and leaves *a* and *c* undefined:

```
float a, b = 3.0, c;
```

Constant qualified variables must be initialized.

```
const int Size = 4;  // initializer is required
```

Global variables qualified with in or out may not be initialized. Global variables qualified with uniform, however, may be initialized.

```
in float Temperature;        // No initializer allowed
uniform int Size;            // Initializer allowed, but not required
out float density;           // No initializer allowed
```

To initialize aggregate types, at either declaration time or elsewhere, CONSTRUCTORS are used. No initializer uses the brace syntax "{...}" from C. Syntactically, constructors look like function calls that have a type name where the function name would go—for example, to initialize a **vec4** with the values (1.0, 2.0, 3.0, 4.0), use

```
vec4 v = vec4(1.0, 2.0, 3.0, 4.0);
```

Or, because constructor syntax is the same whether it's in an initializer or not, use

```
vec4 v;
v = vec4(1.0, 2.0, 3.0, 4.0);
```

There are constructors for all the built-in types (except samplers) as well as for structures and arrays. Some examples:

```
vec4 v = vec4(1.0, 2.0, 3.0, 4.0);
ivec2 c = ivec2(3, 4);
vec3 color = vec3(0.2, 0.5, 0.8);
vec4 color4 = vec4(color, 1.0)
struct light
{
    vec4 position;
    struct tLightColor
    {
        vec3 color;
        float intensity;
    } lightColor;
} light1 = light(v, tLightColor(color, 0.9));
float a[4] = float[4](1.0, 1.0, 0.0, 1.0 );
```

For matrices, the components are written in column major order. For example,

```
mat2 Matrix0 = mat2( 1.0, 2.0, 3.0, 4.0 );
mat2 Matrix1 = mat2( 1.0, 2.0,
                     3.0, 4.0 ); // Same matrix as above.
```

results in the following matrix:

$$\begin{bmatrix} 1.0 & 3.0 \\ 2.0 & 4.0 \end{bmatrix}$$

So far, we've only shown constructors taking one argument for each component being constructed. Built-in constructors for vectors can also take a single argument, which is replicated into each component.

```
vec3 v = vec3(0.6);
```

is equivalent to

```
vec3 v = vec3(0.6, 0.6, 0.6);
```

This is true only for vectors. Structure constructors must receive one argument per member being constructed.

Matrix constructors also have a single argument form, but in this case it initializes just the diagonal of the matrix. The remaining components are initialized to 0.0.

```
mat2 m = mat2(1.0);  // makes a 2 x 2 identity matrix
```

is equivalent to

```
mat2 m = mat2(1.0, 0.0, 0.0, 1.0);     // makes a 2 x 2 identity matrix
```

Constructors can also have vectors and matrices as arguments. However, constructing matrices from other matrices is reserved for future definition.

```
vec4 v = vec4(1.0);
vec2 u = vec2(v);  // the first two components of v initialize u
mat2 m = mat2(v);
```

Matrix components are read out of arguments in column major order and written in column major order.

Extra components within a single constructor argument are silently ignored. Normally, this is useful for shrinking a value, like eliminating *alpha* from a color or *w* from a position. It is an error to have completely unused arguments passed to a constructor.

```
vec2 t = vec2(1.0, 2.0, 3.0);  // illegal; third argument is unused
```

3.4 Type Conversions

Explicit type conversions are performed with constructors. For example,

```
float f = 2.3;
bool b = bool(f);
```

sets b to **true**. This is useful for flow-control constructs, like **if**, which require Boolean values. Boolean constructors convert nonzero numeric values to **true** and zero numeric values to false.

The OpenGL Shading Language does not provide C-style typecast syntax, which can be ambiguous as to whether a value is converted to a different type or is simply reinterpreted as a different type. In fact, there is no way of reinterpreting a value as a different type in the OpenGL Shading Language. There are no pointers, no type unions, no implicit type changes, and no reinterpret casts. Instead, constructors perform conversions. The arguments to a constructor are converted to the type they are constructing. Hence, the following are allowed:

```
float f = float(3);   // convert integer 3 to floating-point 3.0
float g = float(b);   // convert Boolean b to floating point
vec4 v = vec4(2);     // set all components of v to 2.0
```

For conversion from a Boolean, **true** is converted to 1 or 1.0, and **false** is converted to a zero.

3.5 Qualifiers and Interface to a Shader

Qualifiers prefix both variables and formal function parameters. The qualifiers that modify formal function parameters (**const**, **in**, **out**, and **inout**) are discussed in Section 3.6.2. This section focuses on the other qualifiers, most of which form the interfaces of the shaders to their outside world. The following is the complete list of qualifiers (used outside of formal function parameters):

in	For frequently changing information, from the application to a vertex shader and for interpolated values read in a fragment shader
uniform	For infrequently changing information, from the application to either a vertex shader or a fragment shader
out	For interpolated information passed from a vertex shader to a fragment shader, and for output from a fragment shader
const	For declaring nonwritable, compile-time constant variables, as in C

Getting information into and out of a shader is quite different from more typical programming environments. Information is transferred to and from a shader by reading and writing built-in special variables and user-defined **in**, **uniform**, and **out** global variables. One of the most common built-in special variables was shown in the example at the beginning of this chapter. The special variable *gl_Position* is used for output of the homogeneous coordinates of the vertex position. The complete set of built-in special variables is provided in Chapter 4. Examples of **in**, **uniform**, and **out** qualified variables were seen briefly in the opening example for getting other information into and out of shaders. Each is discussed in this section.

Global variables may be qualified as **in**, **uniform**, or **out**. This is sensible since they are visible outside of shaders in the OpenGL API and, for a single program, they all share a single name space.

Qualifiers are always specified before the type of a variable, and because there is no default type, the form of a qualified variable declaration always includes a type.

```
in float Temperature;
const int NumLights = 3;
uniform vec4 LightPosition[NumLights];
out float LightIntensity;
```

3.5.1 Uniform Qualifiers

Uniform qualified variables (or uniforms) are set only outside a shader and are intended for data that changes less frequently. They can be changed at most once per primitive. All data types and arrays of all data types are supported for uniform qualified variables. All the vertex and fragment shaders forming a single program share a single global name space for uniforms. Hence, uniforms of the same name in a vertex and fragment program will be the same uniform variable.

Uniforms cannot be written to in a shader. This is sensible because an array of processors may be sharing the same resources to hold uniforms and other language semantics break down if uniforms could be modified.

Recall that unless a sampler (e.g., **sampler2D**) is a function parameter, the **uniform** qualifier must be used when it is declared. This is because samplers are opaque, and making them uniforms allows the OpenGL driver to validate that the application initializes a sampler with a texture and texture unit consistent with its use in the shader.

3.5.2 Uniform Blocks

Uniform qualified global variables, except for samplers, may be grouped together into named uniform blocks. The declaration is an optional layout qualifier, the **uniform** keyword, a uniform block name, and a member list similar to a structure definition. Unlike structures, each element in the list directly joins the global namespace. The OpenGL API uses the uniform block name to bind an appropriate uniform buffer object.

The uniform block may also be optionally qualified with a layout qualifier.

The default layout qualifier is **shared**, which prohibits dead-storage elimination of any unused members in the uniform block but otherwise permits the implementation control over the layout. This enables an OpenGL application to share the same uniform buffer object with multiple shader programs.

The **packed** layout qualifier allows dead-storage elimination. It is unlikely that such a buffer can be shared between multiple shader programs, but for large uniform blocks dead-storage elimination might significantly reduce the uniform buffer size.

A standard layout qualifier **std140** prohibits dead-storage elimination and also defines implementation-independent rules for how the elements are to be laid out in the uniform buffer. This may cost some storage space and/or performance but has the advantage of a portable layout across multiple OpenGL implementations.

Finally, matrix layout qualifiers **column_major** (the default) and **row_major** affect *only* the storage of matrices in a buffer object.

Some examples:

```
layout( std140 ) uniform; // provide an alternative default qualifier

uniform xform {
   uniform mat4 MVMatrix;
   uniform mat4 MVPMatrix;
   uniform mat3 NormalMatrix;
};

uniform skinning {
   layout( row_major ) mat4x3 SkinningMatrix[20];
}

layout( packed ) uniform surfaceProperties {
   vec4 BaseColor;
   vec4 RustColor;
};
```

3.5.3 In Qualifiers (Vertex Shader)

The **in** qualifier forms the input interface between the previous stages of the OpenGL pipeline and the shader. For each shader type, they have slightly different properties and limitations.

For vertex shaders, in-qualified global variables form the interface between the OpenGL API's generic vertex attributes and the vertex shader. This enables an application to pass frequently modified data into a vertex shader. They can be changed as often as once per vertex, either directly or indirectly by the application.

Vertex inputs are limited to floating-point scalars, integer scalars, unsigned integer scalars, floating-point vectors, integer vectors, and unsigned integer vectors, and matrices. In-qualified Boolean scalars, Boolean vectors, structures, or arrays are not permitted. This is, in part, a result of encouraging high-performance frequent changing of attributes in hardware implementations of the OpenGL system.

3.5.4 Out Qualifiers (Vertex Shader)

Out-qualified variables are the only way a vertex shader can communicate results through the rasterizer to a fragment shader. The intention is that each vertex in a drawing primitive might have a different value and the rasterizer will create many fragments (perhaps millions) each with unique interpolated values. The vertex shader writes the per-vertex values to be interpolated to an **out** variable.

Vertex shader out variables may be further qualified with interpolation qualifiers.

The default interpolation qualifier is **smooth out**, which interpolates the values of several vertices in a perspective-correct manner. However, there are times when the shader writer does not want perspective-correct interpolation. The interpolation qualifier **noperspective out** provides this control. Finally, it is possible to pass a single value from a single vertex in a primitive (called the PROVOKING VERTEX) to all fragments being rasterized. This is done with the qualifier **flat out**.

Vertex outputs are generally limited to floating-point scalars, floating-point vectors, matrices, and arrays of these. If the output is qualified **flat out**, then integer scalars, unsigned integer scalars, integer vectors, unsigned integer vectors, and arrays of these are also permitted. Structures cannot be output from a vertex shader.

3.5.5   In Qualifiers (Fragment Shader)

In-qualified variables are the way the fragment shader communicates with the rasterizer. Each named in variable must match in type, size, and interpolation qualifier with the out variables of the vertex shader.

3.5.6   Out Qualifiers (Fragment Shader)

Fragment shader out-qualified variables output data to the subsequent per-fragment fixed-function stage. They may not be further qualified. They can apply to floating-point scalars, floating-point vectors, integer scalars, integer vectors, unsigned integer scalars, unsigned integer vectors, and arrays of these. Matrices and structures cannot be output from a fragment shader.

3.5.7   Constant Qualifiers

Variables qualified as **const** (except for formal function parameters) are compile-time constants and are not visible outside the shader that declares them. Both scalar and nonscalar constants are supported. Structure fields may not be qualified with **const**, but structure variables can be declared as **const** and initialized with a structure constructor. Initializers for **const** declarations must be formed from literal values, other **const** qualified variables (not including function call parameters), or expressions of these.

Some examples:

```
const int numIterations = 10;
const float pi = 3.14159;
const vec2 v = vec2(1.0, 2.0);
const vec3 u = vec3(v, pi);
const struct light
{
    vec3 position;
    vec3 color;
} fixedLight = light(vec3(1.0, 0.5, 0.5), vec3(0.8, 0.8, 0.5));
```

All the preceding variables are compile-time constants. The compiler may propagate and fold constants at compile time, using the precision of the processor executing the compiler, and need not allocate any runtime resources to **const** qualified variables.

3.5.8 Absent Qualifier

If no qualifier is specified when a variable (not a function parameter) is declared, the variable can be both read and written by the shader. Nonqualified variables declared at global scope can be shared between shaders of the same type that are linked in the same program. Vertex shaders and fragment shaders each have their own separate global name space for nonqualified globals. However, nonqualified user-defined variables are not visible outside a program.

Unqualified variables have a lifetime limited to a single run of a shader. There is also no concept corresponding to a **static** variable in a C function that would allow a variable to be set to a value and have its shader retain that value from one execution to the next. Implementation of such variables is made difficult by the parallel processing nature of the execution environment, in which multiple instantiations run in parallel, sharing much of the same memory. In general, writable variables must have unique instances per processor executing a shader and therefore cannot be shared.

Because unqualified global variables have a different name space for vertex shaders than that for fragment shaders, it is not possible to share information through such variables between vertex and fragment shaders. Read-only variables can be shared if declared as **uniform**, and variables written by a vertex shader can be read by the fragment shader only through the **in** and **out** mechanism.

3.6 Flow Control

Flow control is very much like that in C++. The entry point into a shader is the function **main**. A program containing both vertex and fragment shaders has two functions named **main**, one for entering a vertex shader to process each vertex and one to enter a fragment shader to process each fragment. Before **main** is entered, any initializers for global variable declarations are executed.

Looping can be done with **for, while,** and **do-while,** just as in C++. Variables can be declared in **for** and **while** statements, and their scope lasts until the end of their substatements. The keywords **break** and **continue** also exist and behave as in C.

Selection can be done with **if** and **if-else**, just as in C++, with the exception that a variable cannot be declared in the **if** statement. Selection by means of the selection operator (**?:**) is also available, with the extra constraint that the second and third operands must have exactly the same type.

The type of the expression provided to an **if** statement or a **while** statement, or to terminate a **for** statement, must be a scalar Boolean. As in C, the right-hand operand to logical and (**&&**) is not evaluated (or at least appears not to be evaluated) if the left-hand operand evaluates to false, and the right-hand operand to logical or (**||**) is not evaluated if the left-hand operand evaluates to true. Similarly, only one of the second or third operands in the selection operator (**:?**) will be evaluated. A logical exclusive or (**^^**) is also provided, for which both sides are always evaluated.

A special branch, **discard**, can prevent a fragment from updating the framebuffer. When a fragment shader executes the **discard** keyword, the fragment being processed is marked to be discarded. An implementation might or might not continue executing the shader, but it is guaranteed that there is no effect on the framebuffer.

A **goto** keyword or equivalent is not available, nor are labels. Switching with **switch** is also not provided.

3.6.1 Functions

Function calls operate much as in C++. Function names can be overloaded by parameter type but not solely by return type. Either a function definition (body) or declaration must be in scope before a function is called. Parameter types are always checked. This means an empty parameter list () in a function declaration is not ambiguous, as in C, but rather explicitly means that the function accepts no arguments. Also, parameters must have exact matches since no automatic promotions are done, so selection of over-loaded functions is quite straightforward.

Exiting from a function with **return** operates the same as in C++. Functions returning nonvoid types must return values whose type must exactly match the return type of the function.

Functions may not be called recursively, either directly or indirectly.

3.6.2 Calling Conventions

The OpenGL Shading Language uses call by value-return as its calling convention. The call by value part is familiar from C: Parameters qualified as input parameters are copied into the function and not passed as a reference. Because there are no pointers, a function need not worry about its parameters being aliases of some other memory. The return part of call by value-return means parameters qualified as output parameters are returned to the caller by being copied back from the called function to the caller when the function returns.

To specify which parameters are copied when, prefix them with the qualifier keywords **in**, **out**, or **inout**. For something that is just copied into the function but not returned, use **in**. The **in** qualifier is also implied when no qualifiers are specified. To say a parameter is not to be copied in but is to be set and copied back on return, use the qualifier **out**. To say a parameter is copied both in and out, use the qualifier **inout**.

in	Copy in but don't copy back out; still writable within the function
out	Only copy out; readable, but undefined at entry to function
inout	Copy in and copy out

The **const** qualifier can also be applied to function parameters. Here, it does not mean the variable is a compile-time constant, but rather that the function is not allowed to write it. Note that an ordinary, nonqualified input-only parameter can be written to; it just won't be copied back to the caller. Hence, there is a distinction between a parameter qualified as **const in** and one qualified only as **in** (or with no qualifier). Of course, **out** and **inout** parameters cannot be declared as **const**.

Some examples:

```
void ComputeCoord(in vec3 normal,  // Parameter 'normal' is copied in,
                                    // can be written to, but will not be
                                    // copied back out.
                  vec3 tangent,     // Same behavior as if "in" was used.
                  inout vec3 coord)// Copied in and copied back out.
```

Or,

```
vec3 ComputeCoord(const vec3 normal,// normal cannot be written to
                  vec3 tangent,
                  in vec3 coord)    //the function will return the result
```

The following are not legal:

```
void ComputeCoord(const out vec3 normal, //not legal; can't write normal
                  const inout vec3 tang, //not legal; can't write tang
                  in out vec3 coord)     //not legal; use inout
```

Structures and arrays can also be passed as arguments to a function. Keep in mind, though, that these data types are passed by value and there are no references, so it is possible to cause some large copies to occur at function call time. Array parameters must be declared with their size, and only arrays of matching type and size can be passed to an array parameter.

Functions can either return a value or return nothing. If a function returns nothing, it must be declared as type **void**. If a function returns a value, the type can be any type, including struct.

3.6.3 Built-in Functions

A large set of built-in functions is available. Built-in functions are documented in full in Chapter 5.

A shader can override these functions, providing its own definition. To override a function, provide a prototype or definition that is in scope at call time. The compiler or linker then looks for a user-defined version of the function to resolve that call. For example, one of the built-in sine functions is declared as

```
float sin(float x);
```

If you want to experiment with performance or accuracy trade-offs in a sine function or specialize it for a particular domain, you can override the built-in function with your own function.

```
float sin(float x)
{
    return <.. some function of x..>
}

void main()
{
    // call the sin function above, not the built-in sin function
    float s = sin(x);
}
```

This is similar to the typical language linking techniques of using libraries of functions and to having more locally scoped function definitions satisfy references before the library is checked. If the definition is in a different shader, just make sure a prototype is visible before calling the function. Otherwise, the built-in version is used.

3.7 Operations

Table 3.1 includes the operators, in order of precedence, available in the OpenGL Shading Language. The precedence and associativity are consistent with C.

Table 3.1   Operators, in order of precedence

Operator	Description
()	Parenthetical grouping
[ ]	Index
()	Function call and constructor
.	Member selection and swizzle
++ --	Postfix increment/decrement
++ --	Prefix increment/decrement
+ - ~ !	Unary
* / %	Multiplicative
+ −	Additive
<< >>	Bit-wise shift
< > <= >=	Relational
== !=	Equality
&	Bit-wise and
^	Bit-wise exclusive or
|	Bit-wise inclusive or
&&	Logical and

Table 3.1 Operators, in order of precedence, *continued*

Operator	Description
^^	Logical exclusive or
||	Logical inclusive or
?:	Selection
=	Assignment
+= -= *= /= %= <<= >>= &= ^= |=	Arithmetic assignment
,	Sequence

3.7.1 Indexing

Vectors, matrices, and arrays can be indexed with the index operator ([ ]). All indexing is zero based; the first element is at index 0. Indexing an array operates just as in C.

Indexing a vector returns scalar components. This allows giving components numerical names of 0, 1, … and also enables variable selection of vector components, should that be needed. For example,

```
vec4 v = vec4(1.0, 2.0, 3.0, 4.0);
float f = v[2];  // f takes the value 3.0
```

Here, *v[2]* is the floating-point scalar 3.0, which is then assigned into *f*.

Indexing a matrix returns columns of the matrix as vectors. For example,

```
mat4 m = mat4(3.0);  // initializes the diagonal to all 3.0
vec4 v;
v = m[1];    // places the vector (0.0, 3.0, 0.0, 0.0) into v
```

Here, the second column of *m, m[1]* is treated as a vector that is copied into *v.*

Behavior is undefined if an array, vector, or matrix is accessed with an index that is less than zero or greater than or equal to the size of the object.

3.7.2 Swizzling

The normal structure-member selector (.) is also used to SWIZZLE components of a vector—that is, select or rearrange components by listing their names after the swizzle operator (.). Examples:

```
vec4 v4;
v4.rgba;  // is a vec4 and the same as just using v4,
v4.rgb;   // is a vec3,
v4.b;     // is a float,
v4.xy;    // is a vec2,
v4.xgba;  // is illegal - the component names do not come from
          // the same set.
```

The component names can be out of order to rearrange the components, or they can be replicated to duplicate the components.

```
vec4 pos = vec4(1.0, 2.0, 3.0, 4.0);
vec4 swiz = pos.wzyx; // swiz = (4.0, 3.0, 2.0, 1.0)
vec4 dup = pos.xxyy;  // dup = (1.0, 1.0, 2.0, 2.0)
```

At most, four component names can be listed in a swizzle; otherwise, they would result in a nonexistent type. The rules for swizzling are slightly different for R-VALUES (expressions that are read from) and L-VALUES (expressions that say where to write to). R-values can have any combination and repetition of components. L-values must not have any repetition. For example,

```
vec4 pos = vec4(1.0, 2.0, 3.0, 4.0);
pos.xw = vec2(5.0, 6.0); // pos = (5.0, 2.0, 3.0, 6.0)
pos.wx = vec2(7.0, 8.0); // pos = (8.0, 2.0, 3.0, 7.0)
pos.xx = vec2(3.0, 4.0); // illegal - 'x' used twice
```

For R-values, this syntax can be used on any expression whose resultant type is a vector. For example, getting a two-component vector from a texture lookup can be done as

```
vec2 v = texture(sampler, coord).xy;
```

where the built-in function **texture** returns a **vec4**.

3.7.3 Component-wise Operation

With a few important exceptions, when an operator is applied to a vector, it behaves as if it were applied independently to each component of the vector. We refer to this behavior as COMPONENT-WISE for short.

For example,

```
vec3 v, u;
float f;
v = u + f;
```

is equivalent to

```
v.x = u.x + f;
v.y = u.y + f;
v.z = u.z + f;
```

and

```
vec3 v, u, w;
w = v + u;
```

is equivalent to

```
w.x = v.x + u.x;
w.y = v.y + u.y;
w.z = v.z + u.z;
```

If a binary operation operates on a vector and a scalar, the scalar is applied to each component of the vector. If two vectors are operated on, their sizes must match.

Exceptions are multiplication of a vector times a matrix and a matrix times a matrix, which perform standard linear-algebraic multiplies, not component-wise multiplies.

Increment and decrement operators (++ and --) and unary negation (–) behave as in C. When applied to a vector or matrix, they increment or decrement each component. They operate on integer and floating-point-based types.

Arithmetic operators of addition (+), subtraction (–), multiplication (*), and division (/) behave as in C, or component-wise, with the previously described exception of using linear-algebraic multiplication on vectors and matrices.

```
vec4 v, u;
mat4 m;
v * u;  // This is a component-wise multiply
v * m;  // This is a linear-algebraic row-vector times matrix multiply
m * v;  // This is a linear-algebraic matrix times column-vector multiply
m * m;  // This is a linear-algebraic matrix times matrix multiply
```

All other operations are performed component by component.

Logical not (!), logical and (&&), logical or (||), and logical inclusive or (^^) operate only on expressions that are typed as scalar Booleans, and they result in a Boolean. These cannot operate on vectors. A built-in function, **not**, computes the component-wise logical not of a vector of Booleans.

Relational operations (<, >, <=, and >=) operate only on floating-point and integer scalars and result in a scalar Boolean. Certain built-in functions, for instance, **lessThanEqual**, compute a Boolean vector result of component-wise comparisons of two vectors.

The equality operators (== and !=) operate on all types except arrays. They compare every component or structure member across the operands. This results in a scalar Boolean, indicating whether the two operands were equal. For two operands to be equal, their types must match, and each of their components or members must be equal. To compare two vectors in a component-wise fashion, call the built-in functions **equal** and **notEqual**.

Scalar Booleans are produced by the operators equal (==), not equal (!=), relational (<, >, <=, and >=), and logical not (!) because flow-control constructs (**if**, **for**, and so on) require a scalar Boolean. If built-in functions like **equal** are called to compute a vector of Booleans, such a vector can be turned into a scalar Boolean with the built-in functions **any** or **all**. For example, to do something if any component of a vector is less than the corresponding component of another vector, the code would be

```
vec4 u, v;
...
if (any(lessThan(u, v)))
    ...
```

Assignment (=) requires exact type match between the left- and right-hand side. Any type, except for arrays, can be assigned. Other assignment operators (+=, -=, *=, and /=) are similar to C but must make semantic sense when expanded, as in

```
a *= b   ⇒   a = a * b
```

where the expression *a * b* must be semantically valid, and the type of the expression *a * b* must be the same as the type of *a*. The other assignment operators behave similarly.

The ternary selection operator (?:) operates on three expressions: *exp1* ? *exp2* : *exp3*. This operator evaluates the first expression, which must result in a scalar Boolean. If the result is true, the operator selects to evaluate the second expression; otherwise, it selects to evaluate the third expression. Only one of the second and third expressions will appear to be evaluated. The second and third expressions must be the same type, but they can be of any type other than an array. The resulting type is the same as the type of the second and third expressions.

The sequence operator (,) operates on expressions by returning the type and value of the rightmost expression in a comma-separated list of expressions. All expressions are evaluated, in order, from left to right.

3.8 Preprocessor

The preprocessor is much like that in C. Support for

```
#
#define
#undef
#if
#ifdef
#ifndef
#else
#elif
#endif
```

as well as the `defined` and ## operators are exactly as in standard C. This includes macros with arguments and macro expansion. Built-in macros are

```
__LINE__
__FILE__
__VERSION__
```

`__LINE__` substitutes a decimal integer constant that is one more than the number of preceding new-lines in the current source string.

`__FILE__` substitutes a decimal integer constant that says which source string number is currently being processed.

`__VERSION__` substitutes a decimal integer reflecting the version number of the OpenGL Shading Language. The version of the shading language described in this document has `__VERSION__` defined as the decimal integer 140.

Macro names containing two consecutive underscores (__) are reserved for future use as predefined macro names, as are all macro names prefixed with "GL_".

There is also the usual support for

```
#error message
#line
#pragma
```

`#error` puts *message* into the shader's information log. The compiler then proceeds as if a semantic error has been encountered.

`#line` must have, after macro substitution, one of the following two forms:

```
#line line
#line line source-string-number
```

where *line* and *source-string-number* are constant integer expressions. After processing this directive (including its new-line), the implementation behaves as if it were compiling at line number *line+1* and source string number *source-string-number*. Subsequent source strings are numbered sequentially until another `#line` directive overrides that numbering.

`#pragma` is implementation dependent. Tokens following `#pragma` are not subject to preprocessor macro expansion. If an implementation does not recognize the tokens specified by the pragma, the pragma is ignored. However, the following pragmas are defined as part of the language.

```
#pragma STDGL
```

The STDGL pragma reserves pragmas for use by future revisions of the OpenGL Shading Language. No implementation may use a pragma whose first token is STDGL.

Use the optimize pragma

```
#pragma optimize(on)
#pragma optimize(off)
```

to turn optimizations on or off as an aid in developing and debugging shaders. The optimize pragma can occur only outside function definitions. By default, optimization is turned on for all shaders.

The debug pragma

```
#pragma debug(on)
#pragma debug(off)
```

enables compiling and annotating a shader with debug information so that it can be used with a debugger. The debug pragma can occur only outside function definitions. By default, debug is set to off.

Shaders should declare the version of the language to which they are written by using

```
#version number
```

If the targeted version of the language is the version that was approved in conjunction with OpenGL 3.1, then a value of 140 should be used for *number.* Any value less than 110 causes an error to be generated. Any value greater than the latest version of the language supported by the compiler also causes an error to be generated. Version 110 of the language does not require shaders to include this directive, and shaders without this directive are assumed to target version 110 of the OpenGL Shading Language. This directive, when present, must occur in a shader before anything else except comments and white space.

By default, compilers must issue compile-time syntactic, grammatical, and semantic errors for shaders that do not conform to the OpenGL Shading Language specification. Any extended behavior must first be enabled through a preprocessor directive. The behavior of the compiler with respect to extensions is declared with the `#extension` directive.

```
#extension extension_name : behavior
#extension all : behavior
```

extension_name is the name of an extension. The token `all` means that the specified behavior should apply to all extensions supported by the compiler. The possible values for behavior and their corresponding effects are shown in Table 3.2. A shader could check for the existence of a built-in function named **foo** defined by a language extension named *GL_ARB_foo* in the following way:

```
#ifdef GL_ARB_foo
    #extension GL_ARB_foo : enable
 // use the built-in function fooARB()
#else
    vec4 fooARB(); // provide a fallback for fooARB()
                   // with a user-defined function prototype
#endif
```

Directives that occur later override those that occur earlier. The `all` token sets the behavior for all extensions, overriding all previously issued `#extension` directives, but only for behaviors `warn` and `disable`.

The initial state of the compiler is as if the directive

```
#extension all : disable
```

were issued, telling the compiler that all error and warning reporting must be done according to the nonextended version of the OpenGL Shading Language that is being targeted (i.e., all extensions are ignored).

Macro expansion is not done on lines containing `#extension` and `#version` directives.

Table 3.2 Permitted values for the *behavior* expression in the #extension directive

Value of *behavior*	Effect
require	Behave as specified by the extension extension_name. The compiler reports an error on the #extension directive if the specified extension is not supported or if the token all is used instead of an extension name.
enable	Behave as specified by the extension extension_name. The compiler provides a warning on the #extension directive if the specified extension is not supported, and it reports an error if the token all is used instead of an extension name.
warn	Behave as specified by the extension extension_name, except cause the compiler to issue warnings on any detectable use of the specified extension, unless such use is supported by other enabled or required extensions. If all is specified, then the compiler warns on all detectable uses of any extension used.
disable	Behave (including errors and warnings) as if the extension specified by extension_name is not part of the language definition. If all is specified, then behavior must revert to that of the nonextended version of the language that is being targeted. The compiler warns if the specified extension is not supported.

The number sign (#) on a line by itself is ignored. Any directive not described in this section causes the compiler to generate an error message. The shader is subsequently treated as ill-formed.

3.9 Preprocessor Expressions

Preprocessor expressions can contain the operators listed in Table 3.3.

Preprocessor expressions have precedence, associativity, and behavior matching the standard C preprocessor.

Table 3.3   Preprocessor operators

Operator	Description
+ - ~ ! **defined**	Unary
* / %	Multiplicative
+ -	Additive
<< >>	Bit-wise shift
< > <= >=	Relational
== !=	Equality
& ^ |	Bit-wise
&& ||	Logical

Preprocessor expressions can be executed on the processor running the compiler and not on the graphics processor that executes the shader. Precision is allowed to be this host processor's precision and hence will likely be different from the precision available when expressions are executed in the core language.

As with the core language, string types and operations are not provided. None of the hash-based operators (#, ##, and so on) are provided, nor is a preprocessor **sizeof** operator.

3.10   Error Handling

Compilers accept some ill-formed programs because it is impossible to detect all ill-formed programs. For example, completely accurate detection of usage of an uninitialized variable is not possible. Such ill-formed shaders may execute differently on different platforms. Therefore, the OpenGL Shading Language specification states that portability is ensured only for well-formed programs.

OpenGL Shading Language compilers should detect ill-formed programs and issue diagnostic messages but are not required to do so for all cases. Compilers are required to return messages regarding shaders that are lexically, grammatically, or semantically incorrect. Shaders that generate such error messages cannot be executed. The OpenGL entry points for obtaining any diagnostic messages are discussed in Section 7.6.

3.11 Summary

The OpenGL Shading Language is a high-level procedural language designed specifically for the OpenGL environment. This language allows applications to specify the behavior of programmable, highly parallel graphics hardware. It contains constructs that allow succinct expression of graphics shading algorithms in a way that is natural for programmers experienced in C and C++.

The OpenGL Shading Language includes support for scalar, vector, and matrix types; structures and arrays; sampler types that access textures; data type qualifiers that define shader input and output; constructors for initialization and type conversion; and operators and flow-control statements like those in C and C++.

3.12 Further Information

The OpenGL Shading Language is defined in *The OpenGL Shading Language, Version 1.40*, by Kessenich, Baldwin, and Rost (2009). The grammar for the OpenGL Shading Language is included in its entirety in Appendix A. These two documents can be consulted for additional details about the language itself.

The functionality of the OpenGL Shading Language is augmented by the OpenGL extensions that were designed to support it. Read the specifications for these extensions and the OpenGL specification itself to gain further clarity on the behavior of a system that supports the OpenGL Shading Language. You can also consult the OpenGL books referenced at the conclusion of Chapter 1 for a better overall understanding of OpenGL.

The standard reference for the C programming language is *The C Programming Language* by the designers of the language, Brian Kernighan and Dennis Ritchie (1988). Likewise, the standard for the C++ programming language is *The C++ Programming Language*, written by the designer of C++, Bjarne Stroustrup (2000). Numerous other books on both languages are available.

[1] Kernighan, Brian, and Dennis Ritchie, *The C Programming Language, Second Edition*, Prentice Hall, Englewood Cliffs, New Jersey, 1988.

[2] Kessenich, John, Dave Baldwin, and Randi Rost, *The OpenGL Shading Language, Version 1.40*, 3Dlabs/Intel, March 2009. www.opengl.org/documentation/specs/

[3] Segal, Mark, and Kurt Akeley, *The OpenGL Graphics System: A Specification (Version 3.1)*, Editor (v1.1): Chris Frazier, (v1.2–3.1): Jon Leech, (v2.0): Jon Leech and Pat Brown, March 2009. www.opengl.org/documentation/specs/Stroustrup, Bjarne, *The C++ Programming Language (Special 3rd Edition)*, Addison-Wesley, Reading, Massachusetts, 2000.

Chapter 4

The OpenGL Programmable Pipeline

With contributions by Barthold Lichtenbelt

The OpenGL Shading Language is designed specifically for use with OpenGL. Vertex shader and fragment shader input and output are tied into the standard OpenGL pipeline in a well-defined manner. The basics of how the programmable processors fit into the OpenGL pipeline were covered in Section 2.3. This chapter discusses the details of that integration and the language mechanisms used to achieve it.

Applications can provide data to shaders with user-defined attribute variables and user-defined uniform variables. The OpenGL Shading Language also provides special built-in variables that can communicate between the programmable processors and the surrounding fixed functionality in the following ways:

- Limited OpenGL state is accessible from either vertex shaders or fragment shaders by means of built-in uniform variables.

- Vertex shaders communicate to subsequent processing in OpenGL through the use of special built-in vertex shader output variables and user-defined out variables.

- Fragment shaders obtain the results from the preceding processing through special built-in fragment shader input variables and user-defined in variables.

- Fragment shaders communicate results to subsequent processing stages of OpenGL through special fragment shader output variables and user-defined out variables.

- Built-in constants are accessible from within both types of shaders and define some of the same implementation-dependent constants that are accessible with OpenGL's **glGet** function.

All the built-in identifiers begin with the reserved prefix "gl_" to set them apart.

4.1   The Vertex Processor

The vertex processor executes a vertex shader and replaces the fixed functionality OpenGL per-vertex operations. Specifically, the following fixed functionality operations are removed:

- The transformation of vertex coordinates by the modelview matrix.
- The transformation of the vertex coordinates by the projection matrix.
- The transformation of the texture coordinates by the texture matrices.
- The transformation of normals to eye coordinates.
- Rescaling and normalization of normals.
- Texture coordinate generation.
- Per-vertex lighting computations.
- Color material computations.
- Point size distance attenuation.

The following fixed functionality operations are applied to vertex values that are the result of executing the vertex shader:

- Perspective division on clip coordinates
- Viewport mapping
- Depth range scaling
- View frustum clipping
- Front face determination
- Culling
- Flat-shading
- Associated data clipping
- Final color processing

The basic operation of the vertex processor was discussed in Section 2.3.1. As shown in Figure 2.2, data can come into the vertex shader through user-defined in variables, uniform variables (built in or user defined), or texture maps. Data exits the vertex processor through built-in special variables, user-defined varying variables, and special vertex shader output variables. Built-in constants (described in Section 4.4) are also accessible from within a vertex shader. A vertex shader has no knowledge of the primitive type for the vertex it is working on.

4.1.1 Vertex Attributes

To draw things with OpenGL, applications must provide vertex information such as normal, color, texture coordinates, and so on. These are called generic vertex attributes by the OpenGL API and may be specified outside of draw commands with the OpenGL function **glVertexAttrib**. When set with these function calls, the generic vertex attributes become part of OpenGL's current state.

Geometry can also be drawn with vertex buffers. With this method, applications arrange generic vertex attributes in separate arrays containing positions, normals, colors, texture coordinates, and so on. By calling **glDrawArrays**, applications can send a large number of generic vertex attributes to OpenGL in a single function call.

Generic vertex attributes are connected to the user-defined vertex shader in variables through binding. For example:

```
//
// Vertex Attributes
//
// in qualified global variables are typically changed per vertex
in  vec4  mcVertex;
in  vec3  mcBiNormal;
in  vec3  mcTangentNormal;

in  vec2  mcTexCoord;
in  vec2  mcDetailTexCoord;

in  float PointSize
```

Details on binding generic vertex attributes to a vertex shader through the OpenGL Shading Language API are provided in Section 7.7.

The number of generic vertex attributes a vertex shader can use is limited. This limit is implementation specific and can be queried with **glGet** with the symbolic constant GL_MAX_VERTEX_ATTRIBS. Every OpenGL implementation is required to support at least 16 generic vertex attributes in a vertex shader.

4.1.2 Special Input Variables

There are two special vertex shader inputs, *gl_VertexID* and *gl_InstanceID*. The variable *gl_VertexID* contains the implict vertex index passed by DrawArrays or one of the other drawing commands. The variable *gl_InstanceID* holds the implicit primitive index passed by instanced draw commands.

```
int gl_VertexID;          // may be read
int gl_InstanceID;        // may be read
```

4.1.3 Uniform Variables

Shaders can access limited OpenGL state through built-in uniform variables containing the reserved prefix "gl_". This limited OpenGL state used by the shader is automatically tracked and made available to the shader. This automatic state-tracking mechanism enables the application to use existing OpenGL state commands for state management and have the current values of such state automatically available for use in the shader.

OpenGL state is accessible to both vertex shaders and fragment shaders by means of the built-in uniform variables defined in Section 4.3.

Applications can also define their own uniform variables in a vertex shader and use OpenGL API calls to set their values (see Section 7.8 for a complete description). There is an implementation-dependent limit on the amount of storage allowed for uniform variables in a vertex shader. The limit refers to the storage for the combination of built-in uniform variables and user-defined uniform variables that are actually used in a vertex shader. It is defined in terms of components, where a component is the size of a **float**. Thus, a **vec2** takes up two components, a **vec3** takes three, and so on. This value can be queried with **glGet** with the symbolic constant GL_MAX_VERTEX_UNIFORM_COMPONENTS.

4.1.4 User-Defined Out Variables

Vertex shaders can also define out variables to pass arbitrary values to the fragment shader. Such values are not clamped, but they are subjected to subsequent fixed functionality processing such as clipping and interpolation. The vertex shader may control interpolation with interpolation qualifiers. The **smooth** qualifier will interpolate the output with perspective-correction (the default). The **noperspective** qualifier eliminates the perspective divide during interpolation. The **flat** qualifier selects the value of a provoking vertex. There is an implementation-dependent limit to the number of floating-point values that can be interpolated. This limit can be queried with **glGet** with the symbolic constant GL_MAX_VARYING_FLOATS.

4.1.5 Special Output Variables

Earlier we learned that results from the vertex shader are sent on for additional processing by fixed functionality within OpenGL, including primitive assembly and rasterization. Several special built-in variables are defined as part of the OpenGL Shading Language to allow the vertex shader to pass information to these subsequent processing stages. The built-in variables discussed in this section are available only from within a vertex shader.

The variable *gl_Position* writes the vertex position in clipping coordinates after it has been computed in a vertex shader. Results of primitive assembly and rasterization are undefined if a vertex shader is executed and it does not store a value into *gl_Position*.

The built-in variable *gl_PointSize* writes the size (diameter) of a point primitive. It is measured in pixels. This allows a vertex shader to compute a screen size that is related to the distance to the point, for instance. Results of rasterizing points are undefined if a vertex shader is executed and it does not store a value into *gl_PointSize*. Section 4.5.1 provides more details on using *gl_PointSize*.

If user clipping is enabled, it occurs as a fixed functionality operation after the vertex shader has been executed. For user clipping to function properly in conjunction with the use of a vertex shader, the vertex shader must compute clip distances. These values must then be stored in the built-in variable *gl_ClipDistance*. It is up to the application and shader writer to ensure that the clip distance values are computed in the desired coordinate space. Clip distances work properly in linear (or locally near linear) coordinate spaces. Results of user clipping are undefined if user clipping is enabled and a vertex shader does not store a value into *gl_ClipDistance*. More details on using *gl_ClipDistance* are contained in Section 4.5.2.

These variables each have global scope. They can be written to at any time during the execution of the vertex shader, and they can be read back after they have been written. Reading them before writing them results in undefined behavior. If they are written more than once, the last value written will be the one that is consumed by the subsequent operations.

These variables can be referenced only from within a vertex shader and are intrinsically declared with the following types:

```
vec4  gl_Position;        // may be written to
float gl_PointSize;       // may be written to
float gl_ClipDistances[]; // may be written to
```

4.2 The Fragment Processor

The fragment processor executes a fragment shader and replaces fixed functionality OpenGL fragment operations. Specifically, the following fixed functionality OpenGL operations are removed:

- Texture environments and texture functions
- Texture application
- Color sum
- Fog

The behavior of the following operations does not change:

- Texture image specification
- Alternate texture image specification
- Compressed texture image specification
- Texture parameters that behave as specified even when a texture is accessed from within a fragment shader
- Texture state and proxy state
- Texture object specification
- Texture comparison modes

The basic operation of the fragment processor was discussed in Section 2.3.2. As shown in Figure 2.3, data can come into the fragment shader through user-defined in variables, uniform variables (built in or user defined), special input variables, or texture maps. Data exits the fragment processor through special fragment shader output variables or user-defined output variables Built-in constants (described in Section 4.4) are also accessible from within a fragment shader.

4.2.1 User-Defined In Variables

Fragment shaders can also define in variables to receive arbitrary interpolated values from the vertex shader. The fragment shader may control interpolation with interpolation qualifiers. The *smooth* qualifier will interpolate the output with perspective-correction (the default). The *noperspective* qualifier eliminates the perspective divide during interpolation. The *flat* qualifier selects the value of a provoking vertex. The interpolation qualifiers of a fragment shader must match the interpolation qualifiers of the vertex shader. There is an implementation-dependent limit to the number of floating-point values that can be interpolated. This limit can be queried with **glGet** with the symbolic constant GL_MAX_VARYING_FLOATS.

4.2.2 Special Input Variables

The variable *gl_FragCoord* is available as a variable from within fragment shaders, and it holds the window relative coordinates x, y, z, and $1/w$ for the fragment. This window position value is the result of the fixed functionality that interpolates primitives after vertex processing to generate fragments. The z component contains the depth value as modified by the polygon offset calculation. This built-in variable allows implementation of window position-dependent operations such as screen-door transparency (e.g., use **discard** on any fragment for which *gl_FragCoord.x* is odd or *gl_FragCoord.y* is odd, but not both).

The fragment shader also has access to the built-in variable *gl_FrontFacing* whose value is true if the fragment belongs to a front-facing primitive, and false otherwise. This value can be used to select between two colors calculated by the vertex shader to emulate two-sided lighting, or it can be used to apply completely different shading effects to front and back surfaces. A fragment derives its facing direction from the primitive that generates the fragment. All fragments generated by primitives other than polygons are considered to be front facing. For all other fragments (including fragments resulting from polygons drawn with a polygon mode of GL_POINT or GL_LINE), the determination is made by examination of the sign of the area of the primitive in window coordinates. This sign can possibly be reversed, depending on the last call to **glFrontFace**. If the sign is positive, the fragments are front facing; otherwise, they are back facing.

The special variable *gl_PointCoord* contains a two-dimensional coordinate whose values are in the range 0.0 to 1.0 when a fragment belongs to a point (including fragments resulting from polygons drawn with a polygon mode of GL_POINT); otherwise, the values are undefined.

These special input variables have global scope and can be referenced only from within a fragment shader. They are intrinsically declared with the following types:

```
vec4  gl_FragCoord;
bool  gl_FrontFacing;
vec2  gl_PointCoord;
```

4.2.3 Uniform Variables

As described in Section 4.1.3, OpenGL state is available to both vertex shaders and fragment shaders through built-in uniform variables that begin with the reserved prefix "gl_". The list of uniform variables that can be used to access OpenGL state is provided in Section 4.3.

User-defined uniform variables can be defined and used within fragment shaders in the same manner as they are used within vertex shaders. OpenGL API calls are provided to set their values (see Section 7.8 for complete details).

The implementation-dependent limit that defines the amount of storage available for uniform variables in a fragment shader can be queried with **glGet** with the symbolic constant GL_MAX_FRAGMENT_UNIFORM_COMPONENTS. This limit refers to the storage for the combination of built-in uniform variables and user-defined uniform variables that are actually used in a fragment shader. It is defined in terms of components, where a component is the size of a **float**.

4.2.4 User-Defined Out Variables

The primary purpose of a fragment shader is to compute values that will ultimately be written into the framebuffer. Unless the keyword **discard** is encountered, the output of the fragment shader goes on to be processed by the fixed-function operations at the back end of the OpenGL pipeline.

User-defined out variables in the fragment shader link the fragment outputs to fixed-function per-fragment operations, and from there to the framebuffer. Each output may be a float, an integer, an unsigned integer, vectors, and arrays of that type. They may not be matrices or structures.

Details on binding fragment shader out variables to the fixed-function per-fragment operations through the OpenGL Shading Language API are provided in Section 7.10.

4.2.5 Special Output Variables

Fragment shaders send some of their results on to the back end of the OpenGL pipeline by using the built-in special output variable *gl_FragDepth*. This built-in fragment shader variable has global scope and may be written more than once by a fragment shader. If written more than once, the last value assigned is the one used in the subsequent operations. It can also be read back after it has been written. Reading before writing results in undefined behavior.

If a shader does not write *gl_FragDepth*, the fixed-function value for depth is used as the fragment's depth value. Otherwise, writing to *gl_FragDepth* establishes the depth value for the fragment being processed. As it exits the fragment processor, this value is clamped to the range [0,1] and converted to fixed point with at least as many bits as are in the depth component in the destination framebuffer. Fragment shaders that write to *gl_FragDepth* should take care to write to it for every execution path through the shader. If it is written in one branch of a conditional statement but not the other, the depth value will be undefined for some execution paths.

The *z* component of *gl_FragCoord* contains the depth value resulting from the preceding fixed-function processing. It contains the value that would be used for the fragment's depth if the shader contained no writes to *gl_FragDepth*. This component can be used to achieve an invariant result if a fragment shader conditionally computes *gl_FragDepth* but otherwise wants the fixed functionality fragment depth.

The value *gl_FragDepth* does not need to be clamped within a shader. The fixed functionality pipeline following the fragment processor clamps the value, if needed, to the range required by the buffer into which the fragment will be written.

The fragment shader output variable has global scope, can be referenced only from within a fragment shader, and is intrinsically declared with the following type:

```
float gl_FragDepth;
```

4.3 Built-in Uniform Variables

OpenGL was originally designed as a configurable state machine. It had a large variety of state that could be set. At the time graphics primitives are provided to OpenGL for rendering, the current state settings affect how the graphics primitives are treated and ultimately how they are rendered into the framebuffer.

OpenGL has replaced much of the configurable state machine with programmable processors. The state associated with much of the configurable state machine is deprecated in 3.0. (It had already been removed in OpenGL ES 2.0.)

The built-in uniform variables in Listing 4.1 allow shaders to access limited current OpenGL state. These variables can be accessed from within either vertex shaders or fragment shaders. If an OpenGL state value has not been modified by an application, it contains the default value as defined by OpenGL, and the corresponding built-in uniform variable is also equal to that value.

Listing 4.1   Built-in uniform variables

```
//
// Depth range in window coordinates
//
struct gl_DepthRangeParameters
{
    float near;         // n
    float far;          // f
    float diff;         // f - n
};
uniform gl_DepthRangeParameters gl_DepthRange;
```

4.4 Built-in Constants

The OpenGL Shading Language defines a number of built-in constants. These values can be accessed from within either vertex shaders or fragment shaders. Values for lights, clip planes, and texture units are values that are equivalent to those that would be returned by OpenGL's **glGet** function for the underlying implementation. Implementation-dependent values that are new with the OpenGL Shading Language are the number of floating-point values that could be stored as uniform values accessible by the vertex shader and by the fragment shader, the number of floating-point values that could be defined as varying variables, the number of texture image units that are accessible by the vertex processor and by the fragment processor, the total number of texture image units available to the vertex processor and the fragment processor combined, the number of texture coordinates sets that are supported, and the number of draw buffers that are accessible. All these new implementation-dependent constants can also be obtained in application code with the OpenGL **glGet** function (see Section 7.12).

OpenGL defines minimum values for each implementation-dependent constant. The minimum value informs application writers of the lowest value that is permissible for a conforming OpenGL implementation. The minimum value for each of the built-in constants is shown here:

```
//
// Implementation-dependent constants.  The following values
// are the minimum values allowed for these constants.
//
const int   gl_MaxVertexAttribs            =   16;
const int   gl_MaxVertexUniformComponents  = 1024;
const int   gl_MaxVaryingComponents        =   64;
const int   gl_MaxVertexTextureImageUnits  =   16;
const int   gl_MaxCombinedTextureImageUnits =  16;
const int   gl_MaxTextureImageUnits        =   16;
const int   gl_MaxFragmentUniformComponents = 1024;
const int   gl_MaxDrawBuffers              =    8;
const int   gl_MaxClipDistances            =    8;
```

4.5 Interaction with OpenGL Fixed Functionality

This section offers a little more detail to programmers who are intimately familiar with OpenGL operations and need to know precisely how the programmable capabilities introduced by the OpenGL Shading Language interact with the rest of the OpenGL pipeline. This section is more suitable for seasoned OpenGL programmers than for OpenGL novices.

4.5.1 Point Size Mode

Vertex shaders can operate in point size mode. A vertex shader can compute a point size in pixels and assign it to the built-in variable $gl\_PointSize$. If point size mode is enabled, the point size is taken from this variable and used in the rasterization stage; otherwise, it is taken from the value set with the **glPointSize** command. If $gl\_PointSize$ is not written while vertex shader point size mode is enabled, the point size used in the rasterization stage is undefined. Vertex shader point size mode is enabled and disabled with **glEnable** or **glDisable** with the symbolic value GL_VERTEX_PROGRAM_POINT_SIZE.

This point size enable is convenient for the majority of applications that do not change the point size within a vertex shader. By default, this mode is disabled, so most vertex shaders for which point size doesn't matter need not write a value to *gl_PointSize*. The value set by calls to **glPointSize** is always used by the rasterization stage.

If the primitive is clipped and vertex shader point size mode is enabled, the point size values are also clipped in a manner analogous to color clipping. The potentially clipped point size is used by the fixed functionality part of the pipeline as the derived point size (the distance attenuated point size). Thus, if the application wants points farther away to be smaller, it should compute some kind of distance attenuation in the vertex shader and scale the point size accordingly. If vertex shader point size mode is disabled, the derived point size is taken directly from the value set with the **glPointSize** command and no distance attenuation is performed. The derived point size is then used, as usual, optionally to alpha-fade the point when multi-sampling is also enabled. Again, see the OpenGL specification for details.

Distance attenuation should be computed in a vertex shader and cannot be left to the fixed functionality distance attenuation algorithm. This fixed functionality algorithm computes distance attenuation as a function of the distance between the eye at (0, 0, 0, 1) and the vertex position, in eye coordinates. However, the vertex position computed in a vertex shader might not have anything to do with locations in eye coordinates. Therefore, when a vertex shader is active, this fixed functionality algorithm is skipped. A point's alpha-fade, on the other hand, can be computed correctly only with the knowledge of the primitive type. That information is not available to a vertex shader, because it executes before primitive assembly. Consider the case of rendering a triangle and having the back polygon mode set to GL_POINT and the front polygon mode to GL_FILL. The vertex shader should fade only the alpha if the vertex belongs to a back facing triangle. But it cannot do that because it does not know the primitive type.

4.5.2 Clipping

User clipping can be used in conjunction with a vertex shader. The vertex shader must provide the clip distances (typically, by taking the dot product of the vertex in eye space with clip planes in eye space). It does that by writing this location to the output variable *gl_ClipDistances*. If *gl_ClipDistances* is not specified and user clipping is enabled, the results are undefined. When a vertex shader that mimics OpenGL's fixed functionality is used, the vertex shader should compute the clip distances of the vertex and store it in *gl_ClipDistance*. For example,

```
in vec4 MCVertex;
uniform mat4 MVMatrix;
uniform vec4 ECClipPlane[6];
// ...
vec4 ECVertex = MVMatrix * MCVertex;
int i;
for (i=0 ; i<6 ; i++ )
{
    gl_ClipDistance[i] = dot( ECVertex, ECClipPlane[i] );

}
```

After user clipping, vertices are clipped against the view volume, as usual. In this operation, the value specified by *gl_Position* (i.e., the homogeneous vertex position in clip space) is evaluated against the view volume.

4.5.3 Position Invariance

For multipass rendering, several vertex shaders may perform one or more passes positional invariance is important. This means that the vertex shaders must compute the exact same vertex position in clip coordinates. Positional invariance can be achieved with the **invariant** qualifier in a vertex shader as follows:

```
invariant gl_Position;
```

The use of the invariant qualifier prevents the compiler optimizer from reordering calculations used in the calculation of *gl_Position*. If each of the shaders in a family of vertex shaders computes *gl_Position* in the same manner, then no matter what other independent operations in the vertex shader differ, those operations cannot directly or indirectly effect the result.

4.5.4 Texturing

One of the major improvements to OpenGL made by the OpenGL Shading Language is in the area of texturing. For one thing, texturing operations can be performed in a vertex shader. But the fragment side of the pipeline has improved as well. The number of texture image units has grown dramatically with fragment shaders. This means that more independent texture lookups can be performed in a single rendering pass. And with programmability, the results of all those texture lookups can be combined in any way the shader writer sees fit. The symbolic constant GL_MAX_TEXTURE_IMAGE_UNITS can be queried with **glGet** to obtain a number of texture image units accessible to shaders.

Three different limits related to texture mapping should be taken into account.

*   For a vertex shader, the maximum number of available texture image units is given by GL_MAX_VERTEX_TEXTURE_IMAGE_UNITS.

*   For a fragment shader, the maximum number of available texture image units is given by GL_MAX_TEXTURE_IMAGE_UNITS.

*   The combined number of texture image units used in the vertex and the fragment processing parts of OpenGL (either a fragment shader or fixed function) cannot exceed the limit GL_MAX_COMBINED_TEXTURE_ IMAGE_UNITS. If a vertex shader and the fragment processing part of OpenGL both use the same texture image unit, that counts as two units against this limit. This rule exists because an OpenGL implemen- tation might have only GL_MAX_COMBINED_TEXTURE_IMAGE_UNITS actual texture image units implemented, and it might share those units between the vertex and fragment processing parts of OpenGL.

The somewhat confusing (and often error prone) fixed-function hierarchy of texture-enables (GL_TEXTURE_CUBE_MAP, GL_TEXTURE_3D, GL_TEXTURE_2D, and GL_TEXTURE_1D) is gone. A sampler bound to a texture image unit determines which target will be sampled. (However, samplers of different dimensions may not be bound to the same texture image unit.)

Samplers of type **sampler1DShadow** or **sampler2DShadow** must be used to access depth textures (textures with a base internal format of GL_DEPTH_ COMPONENT). The texture comparison mode requires the shader to use one of the variants of the **shadow** built-in functions for accessing the texture (see Section 5.7). If these built-in functions are used to access a texture with a base internal format other than GL_DEPTH_COMPONENT, the result is unde- fined. Similarly, if a texture access function other than one of the shadow variants is used to access a depth texture, the result is undefined.

If a shader uses a sampler to reference a texture object that is not complete (e.g., one of the textures in a mipmap has a different internal format or bor- der width than the others, see the OpenGL specification for a complete list), the texture image unit returns (R, G, B, A) = (0, 0, 0, 1).

4.6 Summary

Two new programmable units have been added to OpenGL: the vertex processor and the fragment processor. The same language, with minor differences, expresses algorithms intended to run on either processor. The vertex processor replaces the fixed functionality vertex processing of OpenGL, and a shader intended for execution on this processor is called a vertex shader. The vertex shader is executed once for each vertex that is processed by OpenGL. The fragment processor replaces the fixed functionality fragment processing of OpenGL, and a shader that is intended for execution on this processor is called a fragment shader. The fragment shader is executed once for each fragment that arises from rasterization.

Great care was taken to define the interfaces between the programmable stages of OpenGL and the intervening fixed functionality. They also allow a shader to communicate with the preceding and following fixed functionality stages of the graphics-processing pipeline.

4.7 Further Information

The built-in variables defined in this chapter are used in various examples throughout this book. The OpenGL Shading Language specification and the OpenGL specification can be consulted for additional details. The OpenGL books referenced at the conclusion of Chapter 1 can also be consulted for a better understanding of the OpenGL state that is referenced through built-in variables. Parts of the paper *Integrating the OpenGL Shading Language* by Barthold Lichtenbelt have been adapted for inclusion in this book.

[1] Kessenich, John, Dave Baldwin, and Randi Rost, *The OpenGL Shading Language, Version 1.40*, 3Dlabs/Intel, March 2008. www.opengl.org/documentation/specs/

[2] Lichtenbelt, Barthold, *Integrating the OpenGL Shading Language*, 3Dlabs internal white paper, July 2003.

[3] Segal, Mark, and Kurt Akeley, *The OpenGL Graphics System: A Specification (Version 3.1)*, Editor (v1.1): Chris Frazier, (v1.2–3.1): Jon Leech, (v2.0): Jon Leech and Pat Brown, March 2008. www.opengl.org/documentation/specs/

Chapter 5

Built-in Functions

This chapter provides the details of the functions that are defined as part of the OpenGL Shading Language. Feel free to skip ahead to the next chapter if you want to get down to the nitty-gritty of writing your own shaders. This chapter can be useful as a reference after you are well on your way to writing OpenGL shaders for your own application.

The OpenGL Shading Language defines an assortment of built-in convenience functions for scalar and vector operations. The reasons for providing built-in functions for the OpenGL Language include

- Making shaders simpler to develop and easier to understand and maintain.

- Exposing some necessary hardware functionality in a convenient way such as accessing a texture map. The language for these functions cannot be emulated by a shader.

- Representing a trivial operation (clamp, mix, etc.) that is simple for a user to write but that is common and may have direct hardware support. Providing a built-in function makes it much easier for the compiler to map such expressions to complex hardware instructions.

- Representing an operation that graphics hardware is likely to accelerate at some point. The trigonometry functions fall into this category.

Many of the functions are similar to the same named ones in common C libraries, but they support vector input as well as the more traditional scalar input. Because the OpenGL Shading Language supports function overloading, the built-in functions usually have several variants, all with the same name. The difference in the functions is in the type of arguments and the type of the value returned. Quite a few of the built-in functions have four variants: one that takes **float** parameters and returns a **float**, one that takes **vec2** parameters and returns a **vec2**, one that takes **vec3** parameters and returns a **vec3**, and one that takes **vec4** parameters and returns a **vec4**.

Whenever possible, you should use the built-in functions rather than do the equivalent computations in your own shader code. It is expected that the built-in functions will be implemented in an optimal way, perhaps even supported directly in hardware. Almost all the built-in functions can be used in either a vertex shader or a fragment shader, but a few are available only for a specific type of shader. You can write a shader to replace a built-in function with your own code simply by redeclaring and defining the same function name and argument list.

Graphical representations of some of the functions are shown for clear illustration. The functions are generally simple ones, and most readers would have no trouble constructing such diagrams themselves. But as we see in later chapters, many of the built-in functions can be used in unconventional ways to achieve interesting effects in shaders. When you are developing a shader, it is often helpful to draw a simple function diagram to clearly envision the value of a variable at a particular spot in a shader. By seeing a pictorial representation of some of these functions, you may find it easier to draw such diagrams yourself and to gain some insight about how you might use them in procedural shaders. Some common uses for these functions are pointed out along the way, and some are illustrated by shader examples in the later chapters of this book.

5.1 Angle and Trigonometry Functions

Trigonometry functions can be used within either vertex shaders or fragment shaders. Function parameters specified as *angle* are assumed to be in units of radians. In no case do any of these functions result in a divide-by-zero error. If the divisor of a ratio is 0, results are undefined.

These functions all operate component-wise (see Table 5.1). The description column specifies the operation on each component.

In addition to their usefulness as trigonometric functions, **sin** and **cos** can be used in a variety of ways as the basis for a smoothly varying function with no cusps or discontinuities (see Figure 5.1). Such a function can be used to model waves on the surface of an object, to change periodically between two materials, to introduce a rocking motion to an object, or to achieve many other effects.

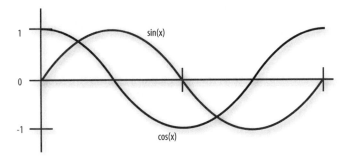

Figure 5.1 The **sin** and **cos** functions

Table 5.1 Angle and trigonometry functions

Syntax	Description
float **radians** (float *degrees*) vec2 **radians** (vec2 *degrees*) vec3 **radians** (vec3 *degrees*) vec4 **radians** (vec4 *degrees*)	Converts *degrees* to radians and returns the result, i.e., result = $\pi/180 \cdot$ *degrees*.
float **degrees** (float *radians*) vec2 **degrees** (vec2 *radians*) vec3 **degrees** (vec3 *radians*) vec4 **degrees** (vec4 *radians*)	Converts *radians* to degrees and returns the result, i.e., result = $180/\pi \cdot$ *radians*.
float **sin** (float *radians*) vec2 **sin** (vec2 *radians*) vec3 **sin** (vec3 *radians*) vec4 **sin** (vec4 *radians*)	The standard trigonometric sine function. The values returned by this function are in the range [–1,1].
float **cos** (float *radians*) vec2 **cos** (vec2 *radians*) vec3 **cos** (vec3 *radians*) vec4 **cos** (vec4 *radians*)	The standard trigonometric cosine function. The values returned by this function are in the range [–1,1].
float **tan** (float *radians*) vec2 **tan** (vec2 *radians*) vec3 **tan** (vec3 *radians*) vec4 **tan** (vec4 *radians*)	The standard trigonometric tangent function.

(continues)

Table 5.1   Angle and trigonometry functions, *continued*

Syntax	Description
float **asin** (float *x*) vec2 **asin** (vec2 *x*) vec3 **asin** (vec3 *x*) vec4 **asin** (vec4 *x*)	Arc sine. Returns an angle whose sine is *x*. The range of values returned by this function is $[-\pi/2, \pi/2]$. Results are undefined if $|x| > 1$.
float **acos** (float *x*) vec2 **acos** (vec2 *x*) vec3 **acos** (vec3 *x*) vec4 **acos** (vec4 *x*)	Arc cosine. Returns an angle whose cosine is *x*. The range of values returned by this function is $[0, \pi]$. Results are undefined if $|x| > 1$.
float **atan** (float *y*, float *x*) vec2 **atan** (vec2 *y*, vec2 *x*) vec3 **atan** (vec3 *y*, vec3 *x*) vec4 **atan** (vec4 *y*, vec4 *x*)	Arc tangent. Returns an angle whose tangent is *y/x*. The signs of *x* and *y* determine what quadrant the angle is in. The range of values returned by this function is $[-\pi, \pi]$. Results are undefined if *x* and *y* are both 0.
float **atan** (float *y_over_x*) vec2 **atan** (vec2 *y_over_x*) vec3 **atan** (vec3 *y_over_x*) vec4 **atan** (vec4 *y_over_x*)	Arc tangent. Returns an angle whose tangent is *y_over_x*. The range of values returned by this function is $[-\pi/2, \pi/2]$.
float **sinh** (float *x*) vec2 **sinh** (vec2 *x*) vec3 **sinh** (vec3 *x*) vec4 **sinh** (vec4 *x*)	Hyperbolic sine. Returns $(e^x-e^{-x})/2$.
float **cosh** (float *x*) vec2 **cosh** (vec2 *x*) vec3 **cosh** (vec3 *x*) vec4 **cosh** (vec4 *x*)	Hyperbolic cosine. Returns $(e^x+e^{-x})/2$.
float **tanh** (float *x*) vec2 **tanh** (vec2 *x*) vec3 **tanh** (vec3 *x*) vec4 **tanh** (vec4 *x*)	Hyperbolic tangent. Returns $(e^x-e^{-x})/(e^x+e^{-x})$.

Table 5.1 Angle and trigonometry functions, *continued*

Syntax	Description
float **asinh** (float *x*) vec2 **asinh** (vec2 *x*) vec3 **asinh** (vec3 *x*) vec4 **asinh** (vec4 *x*)	Arc hyperbolic sine. Returns the inverse of **sinh**.
float **acosh** (float *x*) vec2 **acosh** (vec2 *x*) vec3 **acosh** (vec3 *x*) vec4 **acosh** (vec4 *x*)	Arc hyperbolic cosine. Returns the non-negative inverse of **cosh**. Results are undefined if *x* < 1.0.
float **atanh** (float *x*) vec2 **atanh** (vec2 *x*) vec3 **atanh** (vec3 *x*) vec4 **atanh** (vec4 *x*)	Arc hyperbolic tangent. Returns the inverse of **tanh**. Results are undefined if |*x*| >= 1.0.

5.2 Exponential Functions

Exponential functions can be used within either vertex shaders or fragment shaders. These all operate component-wise (see Table 5.2). The description column specifies the operation on each component.

Table 5.2 Exponential functions

Syntax	Description
float **pow** (float *x*, float *y*) vec2 **pow** (vec2 *x*, vec2 *y*) vec3 **pow** (vec3 *x*, vec3 *y*) vec4 **pow** (vec4 *x*, vec4 *y*)	Returns *x* raised to the *y* power, i.e., x^y. Results are undefined if *x* < 0. Results are undefined if *x* = 0 and *y* = 0.
float **exp** (float *x*) vec2 **exp** (vec2 *x*) vec3 **exp** (vec3 *x*) vec4 **exp** (vec4 *x*)	Returns the natural exponentiation of *x*, i.e., e^x.

(continues)

Table 5.2   Exponential functions, *continued*

Syntax	Description
float **log** (float x) vec2 **log** (vec2 x) vec3 **log** (vec3 x) vec4 **log** (vec4 x)	Returns the natural logarithm of x, i.e., returns the value y, which satisfies the equation $x = e^y$. Results are undefined if $x <= 0$.
float **exp2** (float x) vec2 **exp2** (vec2 x) vec3 **exp2** (vec3 x) vec4 **exp2** (vec4 x)	Returns 2 raised to the x power, i.e., 2^x.
float **log2** (float x) vec2 **log2** (vec2 x) vec3 **log2** (vec3 x) vec4 **log2** (vec4 x)	Returns the base 2 log of x, i.e., returns the value y, which satisfies the equation $x = 2^y$. Results are undefined if $x <= 0$.
float **sqrt** (float x) vec2 **sqrt** (vec2 x) vec3 **sqrt** (vec3 x) vec4 **sqrt** (vec4 x)	Returns the positive square root of x. Results are undefined if $x < 0$.
float **inversesqrt** (float x) vec2 **inversesqrt** (vec2 x) vec3 **inversesqrt** (vec3 x) vec4 **inversesqrt** (vec4 x)	Returns the reciprocal of the positive square root of x. Results are undefined if $x <= 0$.

5.3   Common Functions

Common functions can be used within either vertex shaders or fragment shaders. These functions all operate in a component-wise fashion (see Table 5.3) The description column specifies the operation on each component.

Table 5.3 Common functions

Syntax	Description
float **abs** (float *x*) vec2 **abs** (vec2 *x*) vec3 **abs** (vec3 *x*) vec4 **abs** (vec4 *x*) int **abs** (int x) ivec2 **abs** (ivec2 x) ivec3 **abs** (ivec3 x) ivec4 **abs** (ivec4 x)	Returns *x* if *x* >= 0; otherwise, it returns –*x*.
float **sign** (float *x*) vec2 **sign** (vec2 *x*) vec3 **sign** (vec3 *x*) vec4 **sign** (vec4 *x*) int **sign** (int *x*) ivec2 **sign** (ivec2 *x*) ivec3 **sign** (ivec3 *x*) ivec4 **sign** (ivec4 *x*)	Returns 1.0 if *x* > 0, 0.0 if *x* = 0, or –1.0 if *x* < 0.
float **floor** (float *x*) vec2 **floor** (vec2 *x*) vec3 **floor** (vec3 *x*) vec4 **floor** (vec4 *x*)	Returns a value equal to the nearest integer that is less than or equal to *x*.
float **trunc** (float *x*) vec2 **trunc** (vec2 *x*) vec3 **trunc** (vec3 *x*) vec4 **trunc** (vec4 *x*)	Returns a value equal to the nearest integer to *x* whose absolute value is not larger than the absolute value of *x*.
float **round** (float *x*) vec2 **round** (vec2 *x*) vec3 **round** (vec3 *x*) vec4 **round** (vec4 *x*)	Returns a value equal to the nearest integer of *x*. A fractional part of 0.5 will round in an implementation direction.

(continues)

Table 5.3   Common functions, *continued*

Syntax	Description
float **roundEven** (float *x*) vec2 **roundEven** (vec2 *x*) vec3 **roundEven** (vec3 *x*) vec4 **roundEven** (vec4 *x*)	Returns a value equal to the nearest integer to *x*. A fractional part of 0.5 will round toward the nearest even integer. (Example: Both 3.5 and 4.5 for *x* will return 4.0.)
float **ceil** (float *x*) vec2 **ceil** (vec2 *x*) vec3 **ceil** (vec3 *x*) vec4 **ceil** (vec4 *x*)	Returns a value equal to the nearest integer that is greater than or equal to *x*.
float **fract** (float *x*) vec2 **fract** (vec2 *x*) vec3 **fract** (vec3 *x*) vec4 **fract** (vec4 *x*)	Returns *x* – **floor** (*x*).
float **mod** (float *x*, float *y*) vec2 **mod** (vec2 *x*, float *y*) vec3 **mod** (vec3 *x*, float *y*) vec4 **mod** (vec4 *x*, float *y*)	Modulus. Returns *x* – *y* ∗ **floor** (*x*/*y*) for each component in *x* using the floating-point value *y*.
vec2 **mod** (vec2 *x*, vec2 *y*) vec3 **mod** (vec3 *x*, vec3 *y*) vec4 **mod** (vec4 *x*, vec4 *y*)	Modulus. Returns *x* – *y* ∗ **floor** (*x*/*y*) for each component in *x* using the corresponding component of *y*.
float **min** (float *x*, float *y*) vec2 **min** (vec2 *x*, vec2 *y*) vec3 **min** (vec3 *x*, vec3 *y*) vec4 **min** (vec4 *x*, vec4 *y*) int **min** (int *x*, int *y*) ivec2 **min** (ivec2 *x*, ivec2 *y*) ivec3 **min** (ivec3 *x*, ivec3 *y*) ivec4 **min** (ivec4 *x*, ivec4 *y*) uint **min** (uint *x*, uint *y*) uvec2 **min** (uvec2 *x*, uvec2 *y*) uvec3 **min** (uvec3 *x*, uvec3 *y*) uvec4 **min** (uvec4 *x*, uvec4 *y*)	Returns *y* if *y* < *x*; otherwise, it returns *x*.

Table 5.3 Common functions, *continued*

Syntax	Description
vec2 **min** (vec2 *x*, float *y*) vec3 **min** (vec3 *x*, float *y*) vec4 **min** (vec4 *x*, float *y*) ivec2 **min** (ivec2 *x*, int *y*) ivec3 **min** (ivec3 *x*, int *y*) ivec4 **min** (ivec4 *x*, int *y*) uvec2 **min** (uvec2 *x*, uint *y*) uvec3 **min** (uvec3 *x*, uint *y*) uvec4 **min** (uvec4 *x*, uint *y*)	Returns minimum for each component of *x* compared with the scalar value *y*.
float **max** (float *x*, float *y*) vec2 **max** (vec2 *x*, vec2 *y*) vec3 **max** (vec3 *x*, vec3 *y*) vec4 **max** (vec4 *x*, vec4 *y*) int **max** (int *x*, int *y*) ivec2 **max** (ivec2 *x*, ivec2 *y*) ivec3 **max** (ivec3 *x*, ivec3 *y*) ivec4 **max** (ivec4 *x*, ivec4 *y*) uint **max** (uint *x*, uint *y*) uvec2 **max** (uvec2 *x*, uvec2 *y*) uvec3 **max** (uvec3 *x*, uvec3 *y*) uvec4 **max** (uvec4 *x*, uvec4 *y*)	Returns *y* if $x < y$; otherwise, it returns *x*.
vec2 **max** (vec2 *x*, float *y*) vec3 **max** (vec3 *x*, float *y*) vec4 **max** (vec4 *x*, float *y*) ivec2 **max** (ivec2 *x*, int *y*) ivec3 **max** (ivec3 *x*, int *y*) ivec4 **max** (ivec4 *x*, int *y*) uvec2 **max** (uvec2 *x*, uint *y*) uvec3 **max** (uvec3 *x*, uint *y*) uvec4 **max** (uvec4 *x*, uint *y*)	Returns maximum for each component of *x* compared with the scalar value *y*.

(continues)

Table 5.3 Common functions, *continued*

Syntax	Description
float **clamp** (float *x*, float *minVal*, float *maxVal*) vec2 **clamp** (vec2 *x*, float *minVal*, float *maxVal*) vec3 **clamp** (vec3 *x*, float *minVal*, float *maxVal*) vec4 **clamp** (vec4 *x*, float *minVal*, float *maxVal*) int **clamp** (int *x*, int *minVal*, int *maxVal*) ivec2 **clamp** (ivec2 *x*, int *minVal*, int *maxVal*) ivec3 **clamp** (ivec3 *x*, int *minVal*, int *maxVal*) ivec4 **clamp** (ivec4 *x*, int *minVal*, int *maxVal*) uint **clamp** (uint *x*, uint *minVal*, uint *maxVal*) uvec2 **clamp** (uvec2 *x*, uint *minVal*, uint *maxVal*) uvec3 **clamp** (uvec3 *x*, uint *minVal*, uint *maxVal*) uvec4 **clamp** (uvec4 *x*, uint *minVal*, uint *maxVal*)	Returns **min** (**max** (*x*, *minVal*), *maxVal*) for each component in *x* using the scalar values *minVal* and *maxVal*. Results are undefined if *minVal* > *maxVal*.

Table 5.3 Common functions, *continued*

Syntax	Description
vec2 **clamp** (vec2 *x*, vec2 *minVal*, vec2 *maxVal*) vec3 **clamp** (vec3 *x*, vec3 *minVal*, vec3 *maxVal*) vec4 **clamp** (vec4 *x*, vec4 *minVal*, vec4 *maxVal*) ivec2 **clamp** (ivec2 *x*, ivec2 *minVal*, ivec2 *maxVal*) ivec3 **clamp** (ivec3 *x*, ivec3 *minVal*, ivec3 *maxVal*) ivec4 **clamp** (ivec4 *x*, ivec4 *minVal*, ivec4 *maxVal*) uvec2 **clamp** (uvec2 *x*, uvec2 *minVal*, uvec2 *maxVal*) uvec3 **clamp** (uvec3 *x*, uvec3 *minVal*, uvec3 *maxVal*) uvec4 **clamp** (uvec4 *x*, uvec4 *minVal*, uvec4 *maxVal*)	Returns the component-wise result of **min** (**max** (*x*, *minVal*), *maxVal*). Results are undefined if *minVal* > *maxVal*.
float **mix** (float *x*, float *y*, float *a*) vec2 **mix** (vec2 *x*, vec2 *y*, float *a*) vec3 **mix** (vec3 *x*, vec3 *y*, float *a*) vec4 **mix** (vec4 *x*, vec4 *y*, float *a*)	Returns $x * (1.0 - a) + y * a$, i.e., the linear blend of *x* and *y* using the floating-point value *a*. The value for *a* is not restricted to the range [0,1].
vec2 **mix** (vec2 *x*, vec2 *y*, vec2 *a*) vec3 **mix** (vec3 *x*, vec3 *y*, vec3 *a*) vec4 **mix** (vec4 *x*, vec4 *y*, vec4 *a*)	Returns the component-wise result of $x * (1.0 - a) + y * a$, i.e., the linear blend of vectors *x* and *y* using the vector *a*. The value for *a* is not restricted to the range [0,1].
float **step** (float *edge*, float *x*) vec2 **step** (vec2 *edge*, vec2 *x*) vec3 **step** (vec3 *edge*, vec3 *x*) vec4 **step** (vec4 *edge*, vec4 *x*) float **step** (float *edge*, float *x*)	Returns 0.0 if *x* < *edge;* otherwise, it returns 1.0.

(continues)

Table 5.3 Common functions, *continued*

Syntax	Description
vec2 **step** (float *edge*, vec2 *x*) vec3 **step** (float *edge*, vec3 *x*) vec4 **step** (float *edge*, vec4 *x*)	Returns 0.0 for each component in *x* if *x* < the scalar *edge*; otherwise, it returns 1.0.
float **smoothstep** (float *edge0*, float *edge1*, float *x*) vec2 **smoothstep** (vec2 *edge0*, vec2 *edge1*, vec2 *x*) vec3 **smoothstep** (vec3 *edge0*, vec3 *edge1*, vec3 *x*) vec4 **smoothstep** (vec4 *edge0*, vec4 *edge1*, vec4 *x*)	Returns 0.0 if *x* <= *edge0* and 1.0 if *x* >= *edge1* and performs smooth Hermite interpolation between 0.0 and 1.0 when *edge0* < *x* < *edge1*. Results are undefined if *edge0* >= *edge1*.
vec2 **smoothstep** (float *edge0*, float *edge1*, vec2 *x*) vec3 **smoothstep** (float *edge0*, float *edge1*, vec3 *x*) vec4 **smoothstep** (float *edge0*, float *edge1*, vec4 *x*)	Returns 0.0 for each component in *x* if *x* <= the scalar *edge0* and 1.0 if *x* >= the scalar *edge1* and performs smooth Hermite interpolation between 0.0 and 1.0 when *edge0* < *x* < *edge1*. Results are undefined if *edge0* >= *edge1*.
bool **isnan** (float *x*) bvec2 **isnan** (vec2 *x*) bvec3 **isnan** (vec3 *x*) bvec4 **isnan** (vec4 *x*)	Returns **true** if *x* holds a **NaN** (not a number), **false** otherwise. (Implementations that do not support **NaN** always return **false**.)
bool **isinf** (float *x*) bvec2 **isinf** (vec2 *x*) bvec3 **isinf** (vec3 *x*) bvec4 **isinf** (vec4 *x*)	Returns **true** if *x* holds an **INF** (infinity, positive or negative), **false** otherwise. (Implementations that do not support **INF** always return **false**.)

Aside from their general usefulness as math functions, many of these functions are useful in creating interesting shaders, as we see in subsequent chapters. The **abs** function can ensure that a particular function never produces negative values. It can also introduce a discontinuity in an otherwise smooth function. As we see in Section 15.5, this property of the **abs** function is used to introduce discontinuities in a noise function to produce an effect that looks like turbulence. A graphical representation of the **abs** function is shown in Figure 5.2.

The **sign** function simply maps the incoming value to –1, 0, or 1, depending on its sign. This results in a discontinuous function, as shown in Figure 5.3.

The **floor** function produces a discontinuous stair-step pattern, as shown in Figure 5.4. The fractional part of each incoming value is dropped, so the output value is always the integer value that is closest to but less than or equal to the input value.

The **ceil** function is almost the same as the **floor** function, except that the value returned is always the integer value that is closest to but greater than

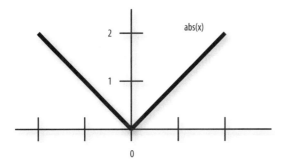

Figure 5.2   The **abs** function

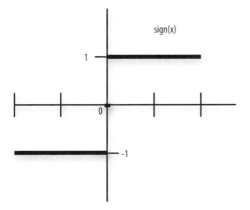

Figure 5.3   The **sign** function

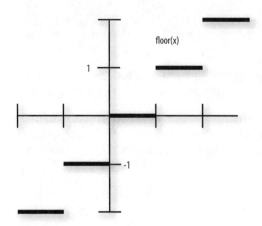

Figure 5.4   The **floor** function

or equal to the input value. This function is shown in Figure 5.5. As you can see, this function looks the same as Figure 5.4 except that the output values are shifted up by one. (Although **ceil** and **floor** always produce integer values, the functions are defined to return floating-point data types.)

The **fract** function produces a discontinuous function where each segment has a slope of 1.0 (see Figure 5.6).

The **mod** function is very similar to **fract**. In fact, if we divide the result of **mod**(*x*, *y*) by *y*, the result is very nearly the same. The only difference is the period of the discontinuous segments (see Figure 5.7).

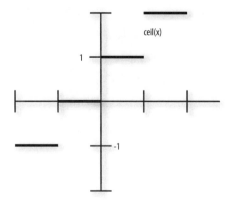

Figure 5.5   The **ceil** function

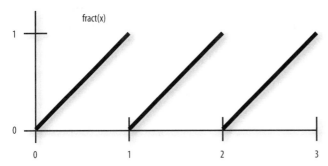

Figure 5.6   The **fract** function

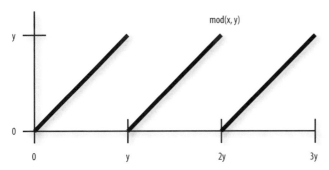

Figure 5.7   The periodic function **mod**(*x, y*)

The **clamp** function is useful for making sure that a value is within a particular range. A common operation is

```
clamp(x, 0.0, 1.0);
```

which clamps the variable x to the range [0,1]. Because two comparisons are necessary for this function, you should use it only when there is a chance that the tested value could be outside either end of the specified range. For the **min** and **max** functions, only one comparison is necessary. If you know a value will not be less than 0, using

```
min(x, 1.0);
```

will likely be faster and may use fewer machine instructions than

```
clamp(x, 0.0, 1.0);
```

because there is no point in testing to see whether the final value is less than 0. Keep in mind that there is no need to clamp the final color and depth values computed by a fragment shader because they are clamped automatically by the back-end fixed functionality processing.

The **min**, **max**, and **clamp** functions are shown in Figure 5.8, Figure 5.9, and Figure 5.10. The **min**(x, y) function has a slope of 1 where x is less than y, and a slope of 0 where x is greater than y. This function is often used to put an upper bound on a value, for instance, to make sure the computed result never exceeds 1.0.

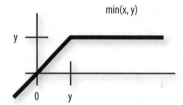

Figure 5.8   The **min** function

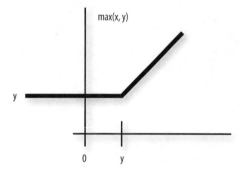

Figure 5.9   The **max** function

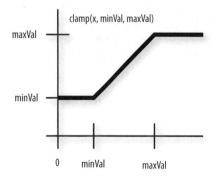

Figure 5.10   The **clamp** function

The **max**(*x, y*) function has a slope of 0 where *x* is less than *y*, and a slope of 1 where *x* is greater than *y*. This function is often used to put a lower bound on a value, for instance, to make sure the computed result never goes below 0.

The **clamp**(*x, minVal, maxVal*) function has a slope of 0 where *x* is less than *minVal* and where *x* is greater than *maxVal*, and it has a slope of 1 in between where *x* is greater than *minVal* and less than *maxVal*. It is functionally equivalent to the expression **min**(**max**(*x, minVal*), *maxVal*).

The **step** function creates a discontinuous jump at an arbitrary point (see Figure 5.11). We use this function to create a simple procedural brick shader in Chapter 6.

The **smoothstep** function (see Figure 5.12) is useful in cases where you want a threshold function with a smooth transition. For the case in which *t* is a **float**, this is equivalent to

```
float t;
t = clamp((x - edge0) / (edge1 - edge0), 0.0, 1.0);
return t * t * (3.0 - 2.0 * t);
```

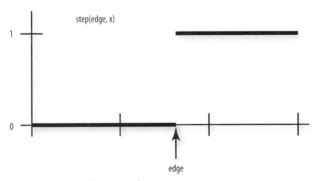

Figure 5.11   The **step** function

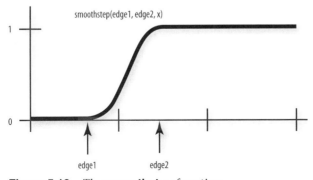

Figure 5.12   The **smoothstep** function

The cases for **vec2**, **vec3**, and **vec4** differ from the preceding example only in the data type used to declare *t*.

5.4 Geometric Functions

Except for **ftransform**, geometric functions can be used within either vertex shaders or fragment shaders. These functions operate on vectors as vectors, not in a component-wise fashion (see Table 5.4).

Table 5.4 Geometric functions

Syntax	Description
float **length** (float *x*) float **length** (vec2 *x*) float **length** (vec3 *x*) float **length** (vec4 *x*)	Returns the length of vector *x*, i.e., **sqrt**($x[0] * x[0] + x[1] * x[1] + ...$).
float **distance** (float *p0*, float *p1*) float **distance** (vec2 *p0*, vec2 *p1*) float **distance** (vec3 *p0*, vec3 *p1*) float **distance** (vec4 *p0*, vec4 *p1*)	Returns the distance between *p0* and *p1*, i.e., **length**(*p0* – *p1*).
float **dot** (float *x*, float *y*) float **dot** (vec2 *x*, vec2 *y*) float **dot** (vec3 *x*, vec3 *y*) float **dot** (vec4 *x*, vec4 *y*)	Returns the dot product of *x* and *y*, i.e., result = $x[0] * y[0] + x[1] * y[1] + ...$
vec3 **cross** (vec3 *x*, vec3 *y*)	Returns the cross product of *x* and *y*, i.e., result[0] = $x[1] * y[2] - y[1] * x[2]$ result[1] = $x[2] * y[0] - y[2] * x[0]$ result[2] = $x[0] * y[1] - y[0] * x[1]$
float **normalize** (float *x*) vec2 **normalize** (vec2 *x*) vec3 **normalize** (vec3 *x*) vec4 **normalize** (vec4 *x*)	Returns a vector in the same direction as *x* but with a length of 1.

Table 5.4 Geometric functions, *continued*

Syntax	Description
float **faceforward** (float *N*, float *I*, float *Nref*) vec2 **faceforward** (vec2 *N*, vec2 *I*, vec2 *Nref*) vec3 **faceforward** (vec3 *N*, vec3 *I*, vec3 *Nref*) vec4 **faceforward** (vec4 *N*, vec4 *I*, vec4 *Nref*)	If **dot** (*Nref*, *I*) < 0.0, return *N*; otherwise, return –*N*.
float **reflect** (float *I*, float *N*) vec2 **reflect** (vec2 *I*, vec2 *N*) vec3 **reflect** (vec3 *I*, vec3 *N*) vec4 **reflect** (vec4 *I*, vec4 *N*)	For the incident vector *I* and surface orientation *N*, returns the reflection direction: result = *I* – 2.0 ∗ **dot** (*N*, *I*) ∗ *N* *N* must already be normalized to achieve the desired result. *I* need not be normalized.

float **refract** (float *I*, float *N*, float *eta*)
vec2 **refract** (vec2 *I*, vec2 *N*, float *eta*)
vec3 **refract** (vec3 *I*, vec3 *N*, float *eta*)
vec4 **refract** (vec4 *I*, vec4 *N*, float *eta*)
	For the incident vector *I* and surface normal *N* and the ratio of indices of refraction *eta*, returns the refraction vector. The returned result is computed as
	k = 1.0 – *eta* * *eta* * (1.0 – **dot** (*N*, *I*) * **dot** (*N*, *I*))
	if (k < 0.0)
	   result = 0.0;
	   // result type is float or vec2/3/4
	else
	   result = *eta* * *I*–
	      (*eta* * **dot** (*N*, *I*) * **sqrt** (k)) * *N*
	The input parameters for the incident vector *I* and surface normal *N* must already be normalized to achieve the desired result.

The **float** version of the **distance** function may not seem terribly useful (it's the same as the absolute value of the difference), but the vector forms compute the Euclidean distance between two points. Similarly, the **float** version of **normalize** always returns 1, and the **float** version of **length** always returns the absolute value of the input argument as the result. These scalar forms are useful in that the data type of the argument can be changed without the need to change the code that calls the built-in function.

You can use the **ftransform** function to transform the incoming vertex position:

```
gl_Position = ftransform()
```

It transforms the value of *gl_Vertex* by the current modelview-projection matrix to produce a value for *gl_Position* that is identical to what would have been computed by the fixed functionality pipeline. This function should be used, for example, when an application is rendering the same geometry in separate passes, where one pass uses the fixed functionality path to render and another pass uses the programmable processors.

5.5 Matrix Functions

Matrix functions can be used within either vertex shaders or fragment shaders (see Table 5.5).

Table 5.5   Matrix functions

Syntax	Description
mat2 **matrixCompMult** (mat2 *x*, mat2 *y*) mat3 **matrixCompMult** (mat3 *x*, mat3 *y*) mat4 **matrixCompMult** (mat4 *x*, mat4 *y*)	Multiply matrix *x* by matrix *y* component-wise, i.e., *result*[i][j] is the scalar product of *x*[i][j] and *y*[i][j]. Note: To get linear-algebraic matrix multiplication, use the multiply operator (*).
mat2 **transpose** (mat2 *m*) mat3 **transpose** (mat3 *m*) mat4 **transpose** (mat4 *m*) mat2x3 **transpose** (mat3x2 *m*) mat3x2 **transpose** (mat2x3 *m*) mat2x4 **transpose** (mat4x2 *m*) mat4x2 **transpose** (mat2x4 *m*) mat3x4 **transpose** (mat4x3 *m*) mat4x3 **transpose** (mat3x4 *m*)	Returns a matrix that is the transpose of *m*. The input matrix is not modified.

Table 5.5 Matrix functions, *continued*

Syntax	Description
mat2 **inverse** (mat2 *m*) mat3 **inverse** (mat3 *m*) mat4 **inverse** (mat4 *m*)	Returns a matrix that is the inverse of *m*. The input matrix is not modified. The values in the returned matrix are undefined if the input matrix is singular or poorly conditioned (nearly singular).
mat2 **outerProduct** (vec2 *c*, vec2 *r*) mat3 **outerProduct** (vec3 *c*, vec3 *r*) mat4 **outerProduct** (vec4 *c*, vec4 *r*) mat2x3 **outerProduct** (vec2 *c*, vec3 *r*) mat3x2 **outerProduct** (vec3 *c*, vec2 *r*) mat2x4 **outerProduct** (vec2 *c*, vec4 *r*) mat4x2 **outerProduct** (vec4 *c*, vec2 *r*) mat3x4 **outerProduct** (vec3 *c*, vec4 *r*) mat4x3 **outerProduct** (vec4 *c*, vec3 *r*)	Returns the outer product. Treats the first parameter as a column vector and the second parameter as a row vector and performs a linear algebra matrix multipy *c**r yielding a matrix.

These functions produce the component-wise multiplication of two matrices. For instance, the result of calling **matrixCompMult** with two 3D matrices *x* and *y* looks like this:

```
mat3 x, y, newmat;
. . .
newmat = matrixCompMult(x, y);
```

$$\begin{bmatrix} x_{00} & x_{01} & x_{02} \\ x_{10} & x_{11} & x_{12} \\ x_{20} & x_{21} & x_{22} \end{bmatrix} \begin{bmatrix} y_{00} & y_{01} & y_{02} \\ y_{10} & y_{11} & y_{12} \\ y_{20} & y_{21} & y_{22} \end{bmatrix} = \begin{bmatrix} x_{00}y_{00} & x_{01}y_{01} & x_{02}y_{02} \\ x_{10}y_{10} & x_{11}y_{11} & x_{12}y_{12} \\ x_{20}y_{20} & x_{21}y_{21} & x_{22}y_{22} \end{bmatrix}$$

This is not usually what you want if you are using matrices to represent transformation steps. In this case, you would use the multiply operator (*) to perform the linear-algebraic matrix multiplication

```
mat3 x, y, newmat;
. . .
newmat = x * y;
```

which performs the following operation:

$$
\begin{bmatrix} x_{00} & x_{01} & x_{02} \\ x_{10} & x_{11} & x_{12} \\ x_{20} & x_{21} & x_{22} \end{bmatrix}
\begin{bmatrix} y_{00} & y_{01} & y_{02} \\ y_{10} & y_{11} & y_{12} \\ y_{20} & y_{21} & y_{22} \end{bmatrix} =
$$

$$
\begin{bmatrix}
x_{00}y_{00} + x_{01}y_{10} + x_{02}y_{20} & x_{00}y_{01} + x_{01}y_{11} + x_{02}y_{21} & x_{00}y_{02} + x_{01}y_{12} + x_{02}y_{22} \\
x_{10}y_{00} + x_{11}y_{10} + x_{12}y_{20} & x_{10}y_{01} + x_{11}y_{11} + x_{12}y_{21} & x_{10}y_{02} + x_{11}y_{12} + x_{12}y_{22} \\
x_{20}y_{00} + x_{21}y_{10} + x_{22}y_{20} & x_{20}y_{01} + x_{21}y_{11} + x_{22}y_{21} & x_{20}y_{02} + x_{21}y_{12} + x_{22}y_{22}
\end{bmatrix}
$$

5.6 Vector Relational Functions

Relational and equality operators (<, <=, >, >=, ==, !=) are defined to produce scalar Boolean results and can be used within either vertex shaders or fragment shaders. For vector results, use the built-in functions in Table 5.6.

Table 5.6 Vector relational functions

Syntax	Description
bvec2 **lessThan**(vec2 x, vec2 y) bvec3 **lessThan**(vec3 x, vec3 y) bvec4 **lessThan**(vec4 x, vec4 y) bvec2 **lessThan**(ivec2 x, ivec2 y) bvec3 **lessThan**(ivec3 x, ivec3 y) bvec4 **lessThan**(ivec4 x, ivec4 y)	Returns the component-wise compare of $x < y$.
bvec2 **lessThanEqual**(vec2 x, vec2 y) bvec3 **lessThanEqual**(vec3 x, vec3 y) bvec4 **lessThanEqual**(vec4 x, vec4 y) bvec2 **lessThanEqual**(ivec2 x, ivec2 y) bvec3 **lessThanEqual**(ivec3 x, ivec3 y) bvec4 **lessThanEqual**(ivec4 x, ivec4 y)	Returns the component-wise compare of $x <= y$.

Table 5.6 Vector relational functions, *continued*

Syntax	Description
bvec2 **greaterThan**(vec2 *x*, vec2 *y*) bvec3 **greaterThan**(vec3 *x*, vec3 *y*) bvec4 **greaterThan**(vec4 *x*, vec4 *y*) bvec2 **greaterThan**(ivec2 *x*, ivec2 *y*) bvec3 **greaterThan**(ivec3 *x*, ivec3 *y*) bvec4 **greaterThan**(ivec4 *x*, ivec4 *y*)	Returns the component-wise compare of *x* > *y*.
bvec2 **greaterThanEqual**(vec2 *x*, vec2 *y*) bvec3 **greaterThanEqual**(vec3 *x*, vec3 *y*) bvec4 **greaterThanEqual**(vec4 *x*, vec4 *y*) bvec2 **greaterThanEqual**(ivec2 *x*, ivec2 *y*) bvec3 **greaterThanEqual**(ivec3 *x*, ivec3 *y*) bvec4 **greaterThanEqual**(ivec4 *x*, ivec4 *y*)	Returns the component-wise compare of *x* >= *y*.
bvec2 **equal**(vec2 *x*, vec2 *y*) bvec3 **equal**(vec3 *x*, vec3 *y*) bvec4 **equal**(vec4 *x*, vec4 *y*) bvec2 **equal**(ivec2 *x*, ivec2 *y*) bvec3 **equal**(ivec3 *x*, ivec3 *y*) bvec4 **equal**(ivec4 *x*, ivec4 *y*) bvec2 **equal**(bvec2 *x*, bvec2 *y*) bvec3 **equal**(bvec3 *x*, bvec3 *y*) bvec4 **equal**(bvec4 *x*, bvec4 *y*)	Returns the component-wise compare of *x* == *y*.
bvec2 **notEqual**(vec2 *x*, vec2 *y*) bvec3 **notEqual**(vec3 *x*, vec3 *y*) bvec4 **notEqual**(vec4 *x*, vec4 *y*) bvec2 **notEqual**(ivec2 *x*, ivec2 *y*) bvec3 **notEqual**(ivec3 *x*, ivec3 *y*) bvec4 **notEqual**(ivec4 *x*, ivec4 *y*) bvec2 **notEqual**(bvec2 *x*, bvec2 *y*) bvec3 **notEqual**(bvec3 *x*, bvec3 *y*) bvec4 **notEqual**(bvec4 *x*, bvec4 *y*)	Returns the component-wise compare of *x* != *y*.

(continues)

Table 5.6 Vector relational functions, *continued*

Syntax	Description
bool **any**(bvec2 *x*) bool **any**(bvec3 *x*) bool **any**(bvec4 *x*)	Returns true if any component of *x* is **true**.
bool **all**(bvec2 *x*) bool **all**(bvec3 *x*) bool **all**(bvec4 *x*)	Returns true only if all components of *x* are **true**.
bvec2 **not**(bvec2 *x*) bvec3 **not**(bvec3 *x*) bvec4 **not**(bvec4 *x*)	Returns the component-wise logical complement of *x*.

5.7 Texture Access Functions

Texture access functions are available to both vertex and fragment shaders. Each of these functions takes as its first argument a variable of type **sampler**. If a variable qualified by **sampler1D** is used, then the texture access operation reads from the 1D texture that has previously been associated with that sampler by the application. Similarly, a **sampler2D** variable is used to access a 2D texture, and so on. The texture precedence rules for OpenGL fixed functionality are ignored. It is up to the application to set up texture state before the shader executes in order to get the expected results (see Section 7.9).

The texture access functions obtain texture values from either mipmapped or non-mipmapped textures. However, implicit derivatives and level-of-detail are not computed for vertex shaders since each vertex is processed in isolation and there is no local neighborhood. For fragment shaders, there is limited access to neighboring fragments sufficient to calculate implicit derivatives and level of detail. So, there are some differences in operation between vertex and fragment texture access functions. Texture properties such as size, pixel format, number of dimensions, filtering method, number of mipmap levels, depth comparison, and so on, are also defined by OpenGL API calls. Such properties are taken into account as the texture is accessed through the built-in functions defined in this section.

The built-in functions use suffixes to indicate modifications to the texture function.

The built-in functions suffixed with "Proj" can perform projective texturing. This allows a texture to be projected onto an object in much the same way that a slide projector projects an image onto a surface. Functions suffixed with "Proj" can compute shadow maps for rendering shadows, among other things.

The suffix "Lod" is used to specify an explicit level of detail and may be used in either the vertex or fragment shader.

The suffix "Grad" is used to specify an explicit derivative and may be used in either the vertex or fragment shader.

The suffix "Offset" adds an offset to the u and v values used to select texels in the texture image. The offset can be useful for computing custom filter kernels on texture images.

The suffixes can be combined together (though only one of "Lod" or "Grad" can be used in any given function) to combine modifications for the texture function.

The *bias* parameter is optional for fragment shaders. The *bias* parameter is not accepted in a vertex shader. For a fragment shader, if *bias* is present, it is added to the calculated level of detail before the texture access operation is performed. If the *bias* parameter is not provided, the implementation automatically selects level of detail. For a texture that is not mipmapped, the texture is used directly. If a mipmap texture is accessed from a fragment shader, the level of detail may be computed by the implementation for use during the texture lookup.

A number of examples in later sections illustrate the use of these functions. With the programmability available with the OpenGL Shading Language, texture memory can store much more than just image data. These texture access functions provide fast, flexible access to such data in order to achieve a wide variety of effects (see Table 5.7).

Texturing results are undefined if

- A texture function that requires an implicit derivative is called in the vertex shader, or

- A texture function that requires an implicit derivative is called inside nonuniform control flow, or

- A **shadow** sampler is not specified for a depth format texture with depth comparisons enabled, or

- A **shadow** sampler is specified for a depth format texture with depth comparisons disabled, or

- A **shadow** sampler is specified for a texture that is not a depth format.

Table 5.7 Texture access functions

Syntax	Description
int **textureSize** (sampler1D *sampler*, int *lod*)	Returns the width of level *lod* of the 1D texture currently specified by *sampler*.
vec4 **texture** (sampler1D *sampler*, float *coord* [, float *bias*]) vec4 **textureProj** (sampler1D *sampler*, vec2 *coord* [, float *bias*]) vec4 **textureProj** (sampler1D *sampler*, vec4 *coord* [, float *bias*]) vec4 **textureLod** (sampler1D *sampler*, float *coord*, float *lod*) vec4 **textureGrad** (sampler1D *sampler*, float *coord*, float *dPdx*, float *dPdy*) vec4 **textureOffset** (sampler1D *sampler*, float *coord*, int *offset*, [, float *bias*])	Use the texture coordinate *coord* to access the 1D texture currently specified by *sampler*. Unsuffixed access the texture (with optional lod *bias*). **Proj** suffix accesses the texture with projection (with optional lod *bias*) **Lod** suffix accesses the texture with explict *lod*. **Grad** suffix accesses the texture with explicit partial derivatives *dPdx* and *dPdy*. **Offset** suffix accesses the texture (with optional lod *bias*) with the *offset* added to the *u* texel coordinate before looking up each texel.
vec4 **texelFetch** (sampler1D *sampler*, int *coord*, int *lod*) vec4 **texelFetchOffset** (sampler1D *sampler*, int *coord*, int *lod*, int *offset*)	Use the texel integer *coord* to lookup a single texel of the explicit *lod* to access the 1D texture currently specified by *sampler*. **Offset** suffix accesses the texture (with optional lod *bias*) with the *offset* added to the *u* texel coordinate before looking up each texel.

Table 5.7 Texture access functions, *continued*

Syntax	Description
vec4 **textureProjLod** (sampler1D *sampler*, vec2 *coord* , float *lod*)	Use the texture coordinate *coord* to access the 1D texture currently specified by *sampler*.
vec4 **textureProjLod** (sampler1D *sampler*, vec4 *coord* , float *lod*)	Combinations of the suffixes **Proj**, **Lod**, **Grad**, and **Offset** are as described earlier.
vec4 **textureProjGrad** (sampler1D *sampler*, vec2 *coord*, float *dPdx*, float *dPdy*)	
vec4 **textureProjGrad** (sampler1D *sampler*, vec4 *coord*, float *dPdx*, float *dPdy*)	
vec4 **textureProjOffset** (sampler1D *sampler*, vec2 *coord*, int *offset* [, float *bias*])	
vec4 **textureProjOffset** (sampler1D *sampler*, vec4 *coord*, int *offset* [, float *bias*])	
vec4 **textureLodOffset** (sampler1D *sampler*, float *coord*, float *lod*, int *offset*)	
vec4 **textureGradOffset** (sampler1D *sampler*, float *coord*, float *dPdx*, float *dPdy*, int *offset*)	
vec4 **textureProjLodOffset** (sampler1D *sampler*, vec2 *coord*, float *lod*, int *offset*)	Use the texture coordinate *coord* to access the 1D texture currently specified by *sampler*.
vec4 **textureProjLodOffset** (sampler1D *sampler*, vec4 *coord*, float *lod*, int *offset*)	Combinations of the suffixes **Proj**, **Lod**, **Grad**, and **Offset** are as described earlier.
vec4 **textureProjGradOffset** (sampler1D *sampler*, vec2 *coord*, float *dPdx*, float *dPdy*, int *offset*)	
vec4 **textureProjGradOffset** (sampler1D *sampler*, vec4 *coord*, float *dPdx*, float *dPdy*, int *offset*)	
int **textureSize** (isampler1D *sampler*, int *lod*)	Returns the width of level *lod* of the 1D texture currently specified by *sampler*.

(continues)

Table 5.7 Texture access functions, *continued*

Syntax	Description
ivec4 **texture** (isampler1D *sampler*, float *coord*[, float *bias*])	Use the texture coordinate *coord* to access the 1D texture currently specified by *sampler*.
ivec4 **textureProj** (isampler1D *sampler*, vec2 *coord*[, float *bias*])	Unsuffixed access the texture (with optional lod *bias*).
ivec4 **textureProj** (isampler1D *sampler*, vec4 *coord*[, float *bias*])	
ivec4 **textureLod** (isampler1D *sampler*, float *coord*, float *lod*)	**Proj** suffix accesses the texture with projection (with optional lod *bias*).
ivec4 **textureGrad** (isampler1D *sampler*, float *coord*, float *dPdx*, float *dPdy*)	**Lod** suffix accesses the texture with explicit *lod*.
ivec4 **textureOffset** (isampler1D *sampler*, float *coord*, int *offset*, [, float *bias*])	**Grad** suffix accesses the texture with explicit partial derivatives *dPdx* and *dPdy*.
	Offset suffix accesses the texture (with optional lod *bias*) with the *offset* added to the *u* texel coordinate before looking up each texel.
ivec4 **texelFetch** (isampler1D *sampler*, int *coord*, int *lod*)	Use the texel integer *coord* to look up a single texel of the explicit *lod* to access the 1D texture currently specified by *sampler*.
ivec4 **texelFetchOffset** (isampler1D *sampler*, int *coord*, int *lod*, int *offset*)	**Offset** suffix accesses the texture (with optional lod *bias*) with the *offset* added to the *u* texel coordinate before looking up each texel.

Table 5.7 Texture access functions, *continued*

Syntax	Description
ivec4 **textureProjLod** (isampler1D *sampler*, vec2 *coord* , float *lod*) ivec4 **textureProjLod** (isampler1D *sampler*, vec4 *coord* , float *lod*)	Use the texture coordinate *coord* to access the 1D texture currently specified by *sampler*.
ivec4 **textureProjGrad** (isampler1D *sampler*, vec2 *coord*, float *dPdx*, float *dPdy*)	Combinations of the suffixes **Proj**, **Lod**, **Grad**, and **Offset** are as described earlier.
ivec4 **textureProjGrad** (isampler1D *sampler*, vec4 *coord*, float *dPdx*, float *dPdy*)	
ivec4 **textureProjOffset** (isampler1D *sampler*, vec2 *coord*, int *offset* [, float *bias*])	
ivec4 **textureProjOffset** (isampler1D *sampler*, vec4 *coord*, int *offset* [, float *bias*])	
ivec4 **textureLodOffset** (isampler1D *sampler*, float *coord*, float *lod*, int *offset*)	
ivec4 **textureGradOffset** (isampler1D *sampler*, float *coord*, float *dPdx*, float *dPdy*, int *offset*)	
ivec4 **textureProjLodOffset** (isampler1D *sampler*, vec2 *coord*, float *lod*, int *offset*)	Use the texture coordinate *coord* to access the 1D texture currently specified by *sampler*.
ivec4 **textureProjLodOffset** (isampler1D *sampler*, vec4 *coord*, float *lod*, int *offset*)	Combinations of the suffixes **Proj**, **Lod**, **Grad**, and **Offset** are as described earlier.
ivec4 **textureProjGradOffset** (isampler1D *sampler*, vec2 *coord*, float *dPdx*, float *dPdy*, int *offset*)	
ivec4 **textureProjGradOffset** (isampler1D *sampler*, vec4 *coord*, float *dPdx*, float *dPdy*, int *offset*)	

(continues)

Table 5.7 Texture access functions, *continued*

Syntax	Description
int **textureSize** (usampler1D *sampler*, int *lod*)	Returns the width of level *lod* of the 1D texture currently specified by *sampler*.
uvec4 **texture** (usampler1D *sampler*, float *coord* [, float *bias*])	Use the texture coordinate *coord* to access the 1D texture currently specified by *sampler*.
uvec4 **textureProj** (usampler1D *sampler*, vec2 *coord* [, float *bias*])	Unsuffixed access the texture (with optional lod *bias*).
uvec4 **textureProj** (usampler1D *sampler*, vec4 *coord* [, float *bias*])	**Proj** suffix accesses the texture with projection (with optional lod *bias*).
uvec4 **textureLod** (usampler1D *sampler*, float *coord*, float *lod*)	**Lod** suffix accesses the texture with explicit *lod*.
uvec4 **textureGrad** (usampler1D *sampler*, float *coord*, float *dPdx*, float *dPdy*)	**Grad** suffix accesses the texture with explicit partial derivatives *dPdx* and *dPdy*.
uvec4 **textureOffset** (usampler1D *sampler*, float *coord*, int *offset*, [, float *bias*])	**Offset** suffix accesses the texture (with optional lod *bias*) with the *offset* added to the *u* texel coordinate before looking up each texel.
uvec4 **texelFetch** (usampler1D *sampler*, int *coord*, int *lod*)	Use the texel integer *coord* to look up a single texel of the explicit *lod* to access the 1D texture currently specified by *sampler*.
uvec4 **texelFetchOffset** (usampler1D *sampler*, int *coord*, int *lod*, int *offset*)	**Offset** suffix accesses the texture (with optional lod *bias*) with the *offset* added to the *u* texel coordinate before looking up each texel.

Table 5.7 Texture access functions, *continued*

Syntax	Description

uvec4 **textureProjLod** (usampler1D *sampler*, vec2 *coord* , float *lod*)
uvec4 **textureProjLod** (usampler1D *sampler*, vec4 *coord* , float *lod*)
uvec4 **textureProjGrad** (usampler1D *sampler*, vec2 *coord*,
    float *dPdx*, float *dPdy*)
uvec4 **textureProjGrad** (usampler1D *sampler*, vec4 *coord*,
    float *dPdx*, float *dPdy*)
uvec4 **textureProjOffset** (usampler1D *sampler*, vec2 *coord*,
    int *offset*[, float *bias*])
uvec4 **textureProjOffset** (usampler1D *sampler*, vec4 *coord*,
    int *offset*[, float *bias*])
uvec4 **textureLodOffset** (usampler1D *sampler*, float *coord*,
    float *lod*, int *offset*)
uvec4 **textureGradOffset** (usampler1D *sampler*, float *coord*,
    float *dPdx*, float *dPdy*, int *offset*)
	Use the texture coordinate *coord* to access the 1D texture currently specified by *sampler*.
	Combinations of the suffixes **Proj**, **Lod**, **Grad**, and **Offset** are as described earlier.

uvec4 **textureProjLodOffset** (usampler1D *sampler*, vec2 *coord*,
    float *lod*, int *offset*)
uvec4 **textureProjLodOffset** (usampler1D *sampler*, vec4 *coord*,
    float *lod*, int *offset*)
uvec4 **textureProjGradOffset** (usampler1D *sampler*, vec2 *coord*,
    float *dPdx*, float *dPdy*, int *offset*)
uvec4 **textureProjGradOffset** (usampler1D *sampler*, vec4 *coord*,
    float *dPdx*, float *dPdy*, int *offset*)
	Use the texture coordinate *coord* to access the 1D texture currently specified by *sampler*.
	Combinations of the suffixes **Proj**, **Lod**, **Grad**, and **Offset** are as described earlier.

(continues)

Table 5.7 Texture access functions, *continued*

Syntax	Description
ivec2 **textureSize** (sampler2D *sampler*, int *lod*)	Returns the width and height of level *lod* of the 2D texture currently specified by *sampler*.
vec4 **texture**(sampler2D *sampler*, vec2 *coord* [, float *bias*]) vec4 **textureProj** (sampler2D *sampler*, vec3 *coord* [, float *bias*]) vec4 **textureProj** (sampler2D *sampler*, vec4 *coord* [, float *bias*]) vec4 **textureLod** (sampler2D *sampler*, vec2 *coord*, float *lod*) vec4 **textureGrad** (sampler2D *sampler*, vec2 *coord*, vec2 *coord*, vec2 *dPdx*, vec2 *dPdy*) vec4 **textureOffset** (sampler2D *sampler*, vec2 *coord*, ivec2 *offset*, [, float *bias*])	Use the texture coordinate *coord* to access the 2D texture currently specified by *sampler*. Unsuffixed access the texture (with optional lod *bias*). **Proj** suffix accesses the texture with projection (with optional lod *bias*). **Lod** suffix accesses the texture with explicit *lod*. **Grad** suffix accesses the texture with explicit partial derivatives *dPdx* and *dPdy*. **Offset** suffix accesses the texture (with optional lod *bias*) with the *offset* added to the *u* and *v* texel coordinates before looking up each texel.
vec4 **texelFetch** (sampler2D *sampler*, ivec2 *coord*, int *lod*) vec4 **texelFetchOffset** (sampler2D *sampler*, ivec2 *coord*, int *lod*, ivec2 *offset*)	Use the texel integer *coord* to look up a single texel of the explicit *lod* to access the 2D texture currently specified by *sampler*. **Offset** suffix accesses the texture (with optional lod *bias*) with the *offset* added to the *u* and *v* texel coordinate before looking up each texel.

Table 5.7 Texture access functions, *continued*

Syntax	Description

vec4 **textureProjLod** (sampler2D *sampler*, vec3 *coord* , float *lod*)
vec4 **textureProjLod** (sampler2D *sampler*, vec4 *coord*, float *lod*)
vec4 **textureProjGrad** (sampler2D *sampler*, vec3 *coord*,
    vec2 *dPdx*, vec2 *dPdy*)
vec4 **textureProjGrad** (sampler2D *sampler*, vec4 *coord*,
    vec2 *dPdx*, vec2 *dPdy*)
vec4 **textureProjOffset** (sampler2D *sampler*, vec3 *coord*,
    ivec2 *offset* [, float *bias*])
vec4 **textureProjOffset** (sampler2D *sampler*, vec4 *coord*,
    ivec2 *offset* [, float *bias*])
vec4 **textureLodOffset** (sampler2D *sampler*, vec2 *coord*,
    float *lod*, ivec2 *offset*)
vec4 **textureGradOffset** (sampler2D *sampler*, vec2 *coord*,
    vec2 *dPdx*, vec2 *dPdy*, ivec2 *offset*)
	Use the texture coordinate *coord* to access the 2D texture currently specified by *sampler*.
	Combinations of the suffixes **Proj**, **Lod**, **Grad**, and **Offset** are as described earlier.

vec4 **textureProjLodOffset** (sampler2D *sampler*, vec3 *coord*,
    float *lod*, ivec2 *offset*)
vec4 **textureProjLodOffset** (sampler2D *sampler*, vec4 *coord*,
    float *lod*, ivec2 *offset*)
vec4 **textureProjGradOffset** (sampler2D *sampler*, vec3 *coord*,
    vec2 *dPdx*, vec2 *dPdy*, ivec2 *offset*)
vec4 **textureProjGradOffset** (sampler2D *sampler*, vec4 *coord*,
    vec2 *dPdx*, vec2 *dPdy*, ivec2 *offset*)
	Use the texture coordinate *coord* to access the 2D texture currently specified by *sampler*.
	Combinations of the suffixes **Proj**, **Lod**, **Grad**, and **Offset** are as described earlier.

(continues)

Table 5.7 Texture access functions, *continued*

Syntax	Description
ivec2 **textureSize** (isampler2D *sampler*, int *lod*)	Returns the width and height of level *lod* of the 2D texture currently specified by *sampler*.
ivec4 **texture** (isampler2D *sampler*, vec2 *coord* [, float *bias*]) ivec4 **textureProj** (isampler2D *sampler*, vec3 *coord* [, float *bias*]) ivec4 **textureProj** (isampler2D *sampler*, vec4 *coord* [, float *bias*]) ivec4 **textureLod** (isampler2D *sampler*, vec2 *coord*, float *lod*) ivec4 **textureGrad** (isampler2D *sampler*, vec2 *coord*,vec2 *dPdx*, vec2 *dPdy*) ivec4 **textureOffset** (isampler2D *sampler*, vec2 *coord*, ivec2 *offset*, [, float *bias*])	Use the texture coordinate *coord* to access the 2D texture currently specified by *sampler*. Unsuffixed access the texture (with optional lod *bias*). **Proj** suffix accesses the texture with projection (with optional lod *bias*). **Lod** suffix accesses the texture with explicit *lod*. **Grad** suffix accesses the texture with explicit partial derivatives *dPdx* and *dPdy*. **Offset** suffix accesses the texture (with optional lod *bias*) with the *offset* added to the *u* and *v* texel coordinates before looking up each texel.
ivec4 **texelFetch** (isampler2D *sampler*, ivec2 *coord*, int *lod*) ivec4 **texelFetchOffset** (isampler2D *sampler*, ivec2 *coord*, int *lod*, ivec2 *offset*)	Use the texel integer *coord* to look up a single texel of the explicit *lod* to access the 2D texture currently specified by *sampler*. **Offset** suffix accesses the texture (with optional lod *bias*) with the *offset* added to the *u* and *v* texel coordinate before looking up each texel.

Table 5.7 Texture access functions, *continued*

Syntax	Description

ivec4 **textureProjLod** (isampler2D *sampler*, vec3 *coord* , float *lod*)
ivec4 **textureProjLod** (isampler2D *sampler*, vec4 *coord* , float *lod*)
ivec4 **textureProjGrad** (isampler2D *sampler*, vec3 *coord*,
    vec2 *dPdx*, vec2 *dPdy*)
ivec4 **textureProjGrad** (isampler2D *sampler*, vec4 *coord*,
    vec2 *dPdx*, vec2 *dPdy*)
ivec4 **textureProjOffset** (isampler2D *sampler*, vec3 *coord*,
    ivec2 *offset* [, float *bias*])
ivec4 **textureProjOffset** (isampler2D *sampler*, vec4 *coord*,
    ivec2 *offset* [, float *bias*])
ivec4 **textureLodOffset** (isampler2D *sampler*, vec2 *coord*,
    float *lod*, ivec2 *offset*)
ivec4 **textureGradOffset** (isampler2D *sampler*, vec2 *coord*,
    vec2 *dPdx*, vec2 *dPdy*, ivec2 *offset*)
	Use the texture coordinate *coord* to access the 2D texture currently specified by *sampler*.
	
	Combinations of the suffixes **Proj**, **Lod**, **Grad**, and **Offset** are as described earlier.

ivec4 **textureProjLodOffset** (isampler2D *sampler*, vec3 *coord*,
    float *lod*, ivec2 *offset*)
ivec4 **textureProjLodOffset** (isampler2D *sampler*, vec4 *coord*,
    float *lod*, ivec2 *offset*)
ivec4 **textureProjGradOffset** (isampler2D *sampler*, vec3 *coord*,
    vec2 *dPdx*, vec2 *dPdy*, ivec2 *offset*)
ivec4 **textureProjGradOffset** (isampler2D *sampler*, vec4 *coord*,
    vec2 *dPdx*, vec2 *dPdy*, ivec2 *offset*)
	Use the texture coordinate *coord* to access the 2D texture currently specified by *sampler*.
	
	Combinations of the suffixes **Proj**, **Lod**, **Grad**, and **Offset** are as described earlier.

(continues)

Table 5.7 Texture access functions, *continued*

Syntax	Description
ivec2 **textureSize** (usampler2D *sampler*, int *lod*)	Returns the width and height of level *lod* of the 2D texture currently specified by *sampler.*
uvec4 **texture** (usampler2D *sampler*, vec2 *coord* [, float *bias*])	Use the texture coordinate *coord* to access the 2D texture currently specified by *sampler:*
uvec4 **textureProj** (usampler2D *sampler*, vec3 *coord* [, float *bias*])	Unsuffixed access the texture (with optional lod *bias*).
uvec4 **textureProj** (usampler2D *sampler*, vec4 *coord* [, float *bias*])	**Proj** suffix accesses the texture with projection (with optional lod *bias*).
uvec4 **textureLod** (usampler2D *sampler*, vec2 *coord*, float *lod*)	**Lod** suffix accesses the texture with explicit *lod.*
uvec4 **textureGrad** (usampler2D *sampler*, vec2 *coord*, vec2 *dPdx*, vec2 *dPdy*)	**Grad** suffix accesses the texture with explicit partial derivatives *dPdx* and *dPdy*.
uvec4 **textureOffset** (usampler2D *sampler*, vec2 *coord*, ivec2 *offset*, [, float *bias*])	**Offset** suffix accesses the texture (with optional lod *bias*) with the *offset* added to the *u* and *v* texel coordinates before looking up each texel.
uvec4 **texelFetch** (usampler2D *sampler*, ivec2 *coord*, int *lod*)	Use the texel integer *coord* to look up a single texel of the explicit *lod* to access the 2D texture currently specified by *sampler:*
uvec4 **texelFetchOffset** (usampler2D *sampler*, ivec2 *coord*, int *lod*, ivec2 *offset*)	**Offset** suffix accesses the texture (with optional lod *bias*) with the *offset* added to the *u* and *v* texel coordinate before looking up each texel.

Table 5.7 Texture access functions, *continued*

Syntax	Description
uvec4 **textureProjLod** (usampler2D *sampler*, vec3 *coord*, float *lod*) uvec4 **textureProjLod** (usampler2D *sampler*, vec4 *coord*, float *lod*) uvec4 **textureProjGrad** (usampler2D *sampler*, vec3 *coord*, vec2 *dPdx*, vec2 *dPdy*) uvec4 **textureProjGrad** (usampler2D *sampler*, vec4 *coord*, vec2 *dPdx*, vec2 *dPdy*) uvec4 **textureProjOffset** (usampler2D *sampler*, vec3 *coord*, ivec2 *offset* [, float *bias*]) uvec4 **textureProjOffset** (usampler2D *sampler*, vec4 *coord*, ivec2 *offset* [, float *bias*]) uvec4 **textureLodOffset** (usampler2D *sampler*, vec2 *coord*, float *lod*, ivec2 *offset*) uvec4 **textureGradOffset** (usampler2D *sampler*, vec2 *coord*, vec2 *dPdx*, vec2 *dPdy*, ivec2 *offset*)	Use the texture coordinate *coord* to access the 2D texture currently specified by *sampler*. Combinations of the suffixes **Proj**, **Lod**, **Grad**, and **Offset** are as described earlier.
uvec4 **textureProjLodOffset** (usampler2D *sampler*, vec3 *coord*, float *lod*, ivec2 *offset*) uvec4 **textureProjLodOffset** (usampler2D *sampler*, vec4 *coord*, float *lod*, ivec2 *offset*) uvec4 **textureProjGradOffset** (usampler2D *sampler*, vec3 *coord*, vec2 *dPdx*, vec2 *dPdy*, ivec2 *offset*) uvec4 **textureProjGradOffset** (usampler2D *sampler*, vec4 *coord*, vec2 *dPdx*, vec2 *dPdy*, ivec2 *offset*)	Use the texture coordinate *coord* to access the 2D texture currently specified by *sampler*. Combinations of the suffixes **Proj**, **Lod**, **Grad**, and **Offset** are as described earlier.

(continues)

Table 5.7 Texture access functions, *continued*

Syntax	Description
ivec2 **textureSize** (sampler2DRect *sampler*)	Returns the width and height of the rectangle texture currently specified by *sampler*.
vec4 **texture** (sampler2DRect *sampler*, vec2 *coord*)	Use the unnormalized texture coordinate *coord* to access the rectangle texture currently specified by *sampler*:
vec4 **textureProj** (sampler2DRect *sampler*, vec3 *coord*)	Unsuffixed access the texture.
vec4 **textureProj** (sampler2DRect *sampler*, vec4 *coord*)	**Proj** suffix accesses the texture with projection.
vec4 **textureGrad** (sampler2DRect *sampler*, vec2 *coord*, vec2 *dPdx*, vec2 *dPdy*)	**Grad** suffix accesses the texture with explicit partial derivatives *dPdx* and *dPdy*.
vec4 **textureOffset** (sampler2DRect *sampler*, vec2 *coord*, ivec2 *offset*)	**Offset** suffix accesses the texture with the *offset* added to the *u* and *v* texel coordinates before looking up each texel.
vec4 **texelFetch** (sampler2DRect *sampler*, ivec2 *coord*)	Use the texel integer *coord* to look up a single texel of the rectangle texture currently specified by *sampler*:
vec4 **texelFetchOffset** (sampler2DRect *sampler*, ivec2 *coord*, ivec2 *offset*)	**Offset** suffix accesses the texture with the *offset* added to the *u* and *v* texel coordinate before looking up each texel.

Table 5.7 Texture access functions, *continued*

Syntax	Description
vec4 **textureProjGrad** (sampler2DRect *sampler*, vec3 *coord*, vec2 *dPdx*, vec2 *dPdy*) vec4 **textureProjGrad** (sampler2DRect *sampler*, vec4 *coord*, vec2 *dPdx*, vec2 *dPdy*) vec4 **textureProjOffset** (sampler2DRect *sampler*, vec3 *coord*, ivec2 *offset*) vec4 **textureProjOffset** (sampler2DRect *sampler*, vec4 *coord*, ivec2 *offset*) vec4 **textureProjGradOffset** (sampler2DRect *sampler*, vec3 *coord*, vec2 *dPdx*, vec2 *dPdy*, ivec2 *offset*) vec4 **textureProjGradOffset** (sampler2DRect *sampler*, vec4 *coord*, vec2 *dPdx*, vec2 *dPdy*, ivec2 *offset*)	Use the unnormalized texture coordinate *coord* to access the rectangle texture currently specified by *sampler.* Combination of the suffixes **Proj**, **Grad** and **Offset** are as described earlier.
ivec2 **textureSize** (isampler2DRect *sampler*)	Returns the width and height of the rectangle texture currently specified by *sampler.*
ivec4 **texture** (isampler2DRect *sampler*, vec2 *coord*) ivec4 **textureProj** (isampler2DRect *sampler*, vec3 *coord*) ivec4 **textureProj** (isampler2DRect *sampler*, vec4 *coord*) ivec4 **textureGrad** (isampler2DRect *sampler*, vec2 *coord*, vec2 *dPdx*, vec2 *dPdy*) ivec4 **textureOffset** (isampler2DRect *sampler*, vec2 *coord*, ivec2 *offset*)	Use the unnormalized texture coordinate *coord* to access the rectangle texture currently specified by *sampler:* Unsuffixed access the texture. **Proj** suffix accesses the texture with projection. **Grad** suffix accesses the texture with explicit partial derivatives *dPdx* and *dPdy.* **Offset** suffix accesses the texture with the *offset* added to the *u* and *v* texel coordinates before looking up each texel.

(continues)

Table 5.7 Texture access functions, *continued*

Syntax	Description
ivec4 **texelFetch** (isampler2DRect *sampler*, ivec2 *coord*) ivec4 **texelFetchOffset** (isampler2DRect *sampler*, ivec2 *coord*, ivec2 *offset*)	Use the texel integer *coord* to look up a single texel of the rectangle texture currently specified by *sampler*. **Offset** suffix accesses the texture with the *offset* added to the *u* and *v* texel coordinate before looking up each texel.
ivec4 **textureProjGrad** (isampler2DRect *sampler*, vec3 *coord*, vec2 *dPdx*, vec2 *dPdy*) ivec4 **textureProjGrad** (isampler2DRect *sampler*, vec4 *coord*, vec2 *dPdx*, vec2 *dPdy*) ivec4 **textureProjOffset** (isampler2DRect *sampler*, vec3 *coord*, ivec2 *offset*) ivec4 **textureProjOffset** (isampler2DRect *sampler*, vec4 *coord*, ivec2 *offset*) ivec4 **textureProjGradOffset** (isampler2DRect *sampler*, vec3 *coord*, vec2 *dPdx*, vec2 *dPdy*, ivec2 *offset*) ivec4 **textureProjGradOffset** (isampler2DRect *sampler*, vec4 *coord*, vec2 *dPdx*, vec2 *dPdy*, ivec2 *offset*)	Use the unnormalized texture coordinate *coord* to access the rectangle texture currently specified by *sampler*. Combination of the suffixes **Proj**, **Grad** and **Offset** are as described earlier.
ivec2 **textureSize** (usampler2DRect *sampler*)	Returns the width and height of the rectangle texture currently specified by *sampler*.

Table 5.7 Texture access functions, *continued*

Syntax	Description
uvec4 **texture** (usampler2DRect *sampler*, vec2 *coord*)	Use the unnormalized texture coordinate *coord* to access the rectangle texture currently specified by *sampler*.
uvec4 **textureProj** (usampler2DRect *sampler*, vec3 *coord*)	Unsuffixed access the texture.
uvec4 **textureProj** (usampler2DRect *sampler*, vec4 *coord*)	**Proj** suffix accesses the texture with projection.
uvec4 **textureGrad** (usampler2DRect *sampler*, vec2 *coord*, vec2 *dPdx*, vec2 *dPdy*)	**Grad** suffix accesses the texture with explicit partial derivatives *dPdx* and *dPdy*.
uvec4 **textureOffset** (usampler2DRect *sampler*, vec2 *coord*, ivec2 *offset*)	**Offset** suffix accesses the texture with the *offset* added to the *u* and *v* texel coordinates before looking up each texel.
uvec4 **texelFetch** (usampler2DRect *sampler*, ivec2 *coord*)	Use the texel integer *coord* to look up a single texel of the rectangle texture currently specified by *sampler*.
uvec4 **texelFetchOffset** (usampler2DRect *sampler*, ivec2 *coord*, ivec2 *offset*)	**Offset** suffix accesses the texture with the *offset* added to the *u* and *v* texel coordinate before looking up each texel.

(continues)

Table 5.7 Texture access functions, *continued*

Syntax	Description
uvec4 **textureProjGrad** (usampler2DRect *sampler*, vec3 *coord*, vec2 *dPdx*, vec2 *dPdy*)	Use the unnormalized texture coordinate *coord* to access the rectangle texture currently specified by *sampler*.
uvec4 **textureProjGrad** (usampler2DRect *sampler*, vec4 *coord*, vec2 *dPdx*, vec2 *dPdy*)	Combination of the suffixes **Proj**, **Grad** and **Offset** are as described earlier.
uvec4 **textureProjOffset** (usampler2DRect *sampler*, vec3 *coord*, ivec2 *offset*)	
uvec4 **textureProjOffset** (usampler2DRect *sampler*, vec4 *coord*, ivec2 *offset*)	
uvec4 **textureProjGradOffset** (usampler2DRect *sampler*, vec3 *coord*, vec2 *dPdx*, vec2 *dPdy*, ivec2 *offset*)	
uvec4 **textureProjGradOffset** (uusampler2DRect *sampler*, vec4 *coord*, vec2 *dPdx*, vec2 *dPdy*, ivec2 *offset*)	
ivec3 **textureSize** (sampler3D *sampler*, int *lod*)	Returns the width, height and depth of level *lod* of the 3D texture currently specified by *sampler*.
vec4 **texture** (sampler3D *sampler*, vec3 *coord*[, float *bias*])	Use the texture coordinate *coord* to access the 3D texture currently specified by *sampler*.
vec4 **textureProj** (sampler3D *sampler*, vec4 *coord*[, float *bias*])	Unsuffixed access the texture (with optional lod *bias*).
vec4 **textureLod** (sampler3D *sampler*, vec3 *coord*, float *lod*)	**Proj** suffix accesses the texture with projection (with optional lod *bias*).
vec4 **textureGrad** (sampler3D *sampler*, vec3 *coord*,vec3 *dPdx*, vec3 *dPdy*)	**Lod** suffix accesses the texture with explicit *lod*.
vec4 **textureOffset** (sampler3D *sampler*, vec3 *coord*, ivec3 *offset*, [, float *bias*])	**Grad** suffix accesses the texture with explicit partial derivatives *dPdx* and *dPdy*.
	Offset suffix accesses the texture (with optional lod *bias*) with the *offset* added to the *u*, *v*, and *w* texel coordinates before looking up each texel.

Table 5.7 Texture access functions, *continued*

Syntax	Description
vec4 **texelFetch** (sampler3D *sampler*, ivec3 *coord*, int *lod*) vec4 **texelFetchOffset** (sampler3D *sampler*, ivec3 *coord*, int *lod*, ivec3 *offset*)	Use the texel integer *coord* to look up a single texel of the explicit *lod* of the 3D texture currently specified by *sampler*. **Offset** suffix accesses the texture (with optional lod *bias*) with the *offset* added to the *u*, *v*, and *w* texel coordinate before looking up each texel.

vec4 **textureProjLod** (sampler3D *sampler*, vec4 *coord*, float *lod*)
 	
vec4 **textureProjGrad** (sampler3D *sampler*, vec4 *coord*, vec3 *dPdx*,
               vec3 *dPdy*)
 	
vec4 **textureProjOffset** (sampler3D *sampler*, vec4 *coord*, ivec3 *offset*
               [, float *bias*])
 	
vec4 **textureLodOffset** (sampler3D *sampler*, vec3 *coord*, float *lod*,
               ivec3 *offset*)
 	
vec4 **textureGradOffset** (sampler3D *sampler*, vec3 *coord*, vec3 *dPdx*,
               vec3 *dPdy*, ivec3 *offset*)
	Use the texture coordinate *coord* to access the 3D texture currently specified by *sampler*.
	
	Combinations of the suffixes **Proj**, **Lod**, **Grad**, and **Offset** are as described earlier.

vec4 **textureProjLodOffset** (sampler3D *sampler*, vec4 *coord*, float *lod*,
               ivec3 *offset*)
 	
vec4 **textureProjGradOffset** (sampler3D *sampler*, vec4 *coord*, vec3 *dPdx*,
               vec3 *dPdy*, ivec3 *offset*)
	Use the texture coordinate *coord* to access the 3D texture currently specified by *sampler*.
	
	Combinations of the suffixes **Proj**, **Lod**, **Grad**, and **Offset** are as described earlier.

ivec3 **textureSize** (isampler3D *sampler*, int *lod*)	Returns the width, height and depth of level *lod* of the 3D texture currently specified by *sampler*.

(continues)

Table 5.7 Texture access functions, *continued*

Syntax	Description
ivec4 **texture** (isampler3D *sampler*, vec3 *coord* [, float *bias*])	Use the texture coordinate *coord* to access the 3D texture currently specified by *sampler*.
ivec4 **textureProj** (isampler3D *sampler*, vec4 *coord* [, float *bias*])	Unsuffixed access the texture (with optional lod *bias*).
ivec4 **textureLod** (isampler3D *sampler*, vec3 *coord*, float *lod*)	**Proj** suffix accesses the texture with projection (with optional lod *bias*).
ivec4 **textureGrad** (isampler3D *sampler*, vec3 *coord*, vec3 *dPdx*, vec3 *dPdy*)	**Lod** suffix accesses the texture with explicit *lod*.
ivec4 **textureOffset** (isampler3D *sampler*, vec3 *coord*, ivec3 *offset*, [, float *bias*])	**Grad** suffix accesses the texture with explicit partial derivatives *dPdx* and *dPdy*.
	Offset suffix accesses the texture (with optional lod *bias*) with the *offset* added to the *u*, *v*, and *w* texel coordinates before looking up each texel.
ivec4 **texelFetch** (isampler3D *sampler*, ivec3 *coord*, int *lod*)	Use the texel integer *coord* to look up a single texel of the explicit *lod* to access the 3D texture currently specified by *sampler*.
ivec4 **texelFetchOffset** (isampler3D *sampler*, ivec3 *coord*, int *lod*, ivec3 *offset*)	**Offset** suffix accesses the texture (with optional lod *bias*) with the *offset* added to the *u* and *v* texel coordinate before looking up each texel.

Table 5.7 Texture access functions, *continued*

Syntax	Description
ivec4 **textureProjLod** (isampler3D *sampler*, vec4 *coord* , float *lod*) ivec4 **textureProjGrad** (isampler3D *sampler*, vec4 *coord*, vec3 *dPdx*, vec3 *dPdy*) ivec4 **textureProjOffset** (isampler3D *sampler*, vec4 *coord*, ivec3 *offset* [, float *bias*]) ivec4 **textureLodOffset** (isampler3D *sampler*, vec3 *coord*, float *lod*, ivec3 *offset*) ivec4 **textureGradOffset** (isampler3D *sampler*, vec3 *coord*, vec3 *dPdx*, vec3 *dPdy*, ivec3 *offset*)	Use the texture coordinate *coord* to access the 3D texture currently specified by *sampler*. Combinations of the suffixes **Proj**, **Lod**, **Grad**, and **Offset** are as described earlier.
ivec4 **textureProjLodOffset** (isampler3D *sampler*, vec4 *coord*, float *lod*, ivec3 *offset*) ivec4 **textureProjGradOffset** (isampler3D *sampler*, vec4 *coord*, vec3 *dPdx*, vec3 *dPdy*, ivec3 *offset*)	Use the texture coordinate *coord* to access the 3D texture currently specified by *sampler*. Combinations of the suffixes **Proj**, **Lod**, **Grad**, and **Offset** are as described earlier.
ivec3 **textureSize** (usampler3D *sampler*, int *lod*)	Returns the width, height and depth of level *lod* of the 3D texture currently specified by *sampler*.

(continues)

Table 5.7 Texture access functions, *continued*

Syntax	Description
uvec4 **texture** (usampler3D *sampler*, vec3 *coord* [, float *bias*])	Use the texture coordinate *coord* to access the 3D texture currently specified by *sampler*.
uvec4 **textureProj** (usampler3D *sampler*, vec4 *coord* [, float *bias*])	Unsuffixed access the texture (with optional lod *bias*).
uvec4 **textureLod** (usampler3D *sampler*, vec3 *coord*, float *lod*)	**Proj** suffix accesses the texture with projection (with optional lod *bias*).
uvec4 **textureGrad** (usampler3D *sampler*, vec3 *coord*, vec3 *dPdx*, vec3 *dPdy*)	**Lod** suffix accesses the texture with explicit *lod*.
uvec4 **textureOffset** (usampler3D *sampler*, vec3 *coord*, ivec3 *offset*, [, float *bias*])	**Grad** suffix accesses the texture with explicit partial derivatives *dPdx* and *dPdy*. **Offset** suffix accesses the texture (with optional lod *bias*) with the *offset* added to the *u* and *v* texel coordinates before looking up each texel.
uvec4 **texelFetch** (usampler3D *sampler*, ivec3 *coord*, int *lod*)	Use the texel integer *coord* to look up a single texel of the explicit *lod* to access the 3D texture currently specified by *sampler*.
uvec4 **texelFetchOffset** (usampler3D *sampler*, ivec3 *coord*, int *lod*, ivec3 *offset*)	**Offset** suffix accesses the texture (with optional lod *bias*) with the *offset* added to the *u*, *v*, and *w* texel coordinate before looking up each texel.

Table 5.7 Texture access functions, *continued*

Syntax	Description
uvec4 **textureProjLod** (usampler3D *sampler*, vec4 *coord* , float *lod*)	Use the texture coordinate *coord* to access the 3D texture currently specified by *sampler*.
uvec4 **textureProjGrad** (usampler3D *sampler*, vec4 *coord*, vec3 *dPdx*, vec3 *dPdy*)	Combinations of the suffixes **Proj, Lod, Grad**, and **Offset** are as described earlier.
uvec4 **textureProjOffset** (usampler3D *sampler*, vec4 *coord*, ivec3 *offset*[, float *bias*])	
uvec4 **textureLodOffset** (usampler3D *sampler*, vec3 *coord*, float *lod*, ivec3 *offset*)	
uvec4 **textureGradOffset** (usampler3D *sampler*, vec3 *coord*, vec3 *dPdx*, vec3 *dPdy*, ivec3 *offset*)	
uvec4 **textureProjLodOffset** (usampler3D *sampler*, vec4 *coord*, float *lod*, ivec3 *offset*)	Use the texture coordinate *coord* to access the 3D texture currently specified by *sampler*.
uvec4 **textureProjGradOffset** (usampler3D *sampler*, vec4 *coord*, vec3 *dPdx*, vec3 *dPdy*, ivec3 *offset*)	Combinations of the suffixes **Proj, Lod, Grad**, and **Offset** are as described earlier.
ivec2 **textureSize** (samplerCube *sampler*, int *lod*)	Returns the width and height of level *lod* of the cube map texture currently specified by *sampler*.
vec4 **texture** (samplerCube *sampler*, vec3 *coord*[, float *bias*])	Use the texture coordinate *coord* to access the cube map texture currently specified by *sampler*.
vec4 **textureLod** (samplerCube *sampler*, vec3 *coord*, float *lod*)	Unsuffixed access the texture (with optional lod *bias*).
vec4 **textureGrad** (samplerCube *sampler*, vec3 *coord*, vec3 *dPdx*, vec3 *dPdy*)	**Lod** suffix accesses the texture with explicit *lod*. **Grad** suffix accesses the texture with explicit partial derivatives *dPdx* and *dPdy*.

(continues)

Table 5.7 Texture access functions, *continued*

Syntax	Description
vec4 **texelFetch** (samplerCube *sampler*, ivec3 *coord*, int *lod*)	Use the texel integer *coord* to look up a single texel of the explicit *lod* to access the cube map texture currently specified by *sampler*.
ivec2 **textureSize** (isamplerCube *sampler*, int *lod*)	Returns the width and height of level *lod* of the cube map texture currently specified by *sampler*.
ivec4 **texture** (isamplerCube *sampler*, vec3 *coord*[, float *bias*]) ivec4 **textureLod** (isamplerCube *sampler*, vec3 *coord*, float *lod*) ivec4 **textureGrad** (isamplerCube *sampler*, vec3 *coord*, vec3 *dPdx*, vec3 *dPdy*)	Use the texture coordinate *coord* to access the cube map texture currently specified by *sampler*: Unsuffixed access the texture (with optional lod *bias*). **Lod** suffix accesses the texture with explicit *lod*. **Grad** suffix accesses the texture with explicit partial derivatives *dPdx* and *dPdy*.
ivec4 **texelFetch** (isamplerCube *sampler*, ivec3 *coord*, int *lod*)	Use the texel integer *coord* to look up a single texel of the explicit *lod* to access the cube map texture currently specified by *sampler*.
ivec2 **textureSize** (usamplerCube *sampler*, int *lod*)	Returns the width and height of level *lod* of the cube map texture currently specified by *sampler*.

Table 5.7 Texture access functions, *continued*

Syntax	Description
uvec4 **texture** (usamplerCube *sampler*, vec3 *coord* [, float *bias*]) uvec4 **textureLod** (usamplerCube *sampler*, vec3 *coord*, float *lod*) uvec4 **textureGrad** (usamplerCube *sampler*, vec3 *coord*, vec3 *dPdx*, vec3 *dPdy*)	Use the texture coordinate *coord* to access the cube map texture currently specified by *sampler*. Unsuffixed access the texture (with optional lod *bias*). **Lod** suffix accesses the texture with explicit *lod*. **Grad** suffix accesses the texture with explicit partial derivatives *dPdx* and *dPdy*.
uvec4 **texelFetch** (usamplerCube *sampler*, ivec3 *coord*, int *lod*)	Use the texel integer *coord* to look up a single texel of the explicit *lod* to access the cube map texture currently specified by *sampler*.
int **textureSize** (sampler1DArray *sampler*, int *lod*)	Returns the width of level *lod* of the 1D texture array currently specified by *sampler*.

vec4 **texture** (sampler1DArray *sampler*, vec2 *coord* [, float *bias*])
vec4 **textureLod** (sampler1DArray *sampler*, vec2 *coord*, float *lod*)
vec4 **textureGrad** (sampler1DArray *sampler*, vec2 *coord*, float *dPdx*,
    float *dPdy*)
vec4 **textureOffset** (sampler1DArray *sampler*, vec2 *coord*, int *offset*,
    [, float *bias*])
	Use the texture coordinate *coord* to access the 1D texture array currently specified by *sampler*.
	
	Unsuffixed access the texture (with optional lod *bias*).
	
	Lod suffix accesses the texture with explicit *lod*.
	
	Grad suffix accesses the texture with explicit partial derivatives *dPdx* and *dPdy*.
	
	Offset suffix accesses the texture (with optional lod *bias*) with the *offset* added to the *u* texel coordinate before looking up each texel.

(continues)

Table 5.7 Texture access functions, *continued*

Syntax	Description
vec4 **texelFetch** (sampler1DArray *sampler*, ivec2 *coord*, int *lod*) vec4 **texelFetchOffset** (sampler1DArray *sampler*, ivec2 *coord*, int *lod*, int *offset*)	Use the texel integer *coord* to look up a single texel of the explicit *lod* to access the 1D texture currently specified by *sampler*. **Offset** suffix accesses the texture (with optional lod *bias*) with the *offset* added to the *u* texel coordinate before looking up each texel.
vec4 **textureLodOffset** (sampler1DArray *sampler*, vec2 *coord*, float *lod*, int *offset*) vec4 **textureGradOffset** (sampler1DArray *sampler*, vec2 *coord*, float *dPdx*, float *dPdy*, int *offset*)	Use the texture coordinate *coord* to access the 1D texture currently specified by *sampler*. Combinations of the suffixes **Lod**, **Grad**, and **Offset** are as described earlier.
int **textureSize** (isampler1DArray *sampler*, int *lod*)	Returns the width of level *lod* of the 1D texture array currently specified by *sampler*.
ivec4 **texture** (isampler1DArray *sampler*, vec2 *coord* [, float *bias*]) ivec4 **textureLod** (isampler1DArray *sampler*, vec2 *coord*, float *lod*) ivec4 **textureGrad** (isampler1DArray *sampler*, vec2 *coord*, float *dPdx*, float *dPdy*) ivec4 **textureOffset** (isampler1DArray *sampler*, vec2 *coord*, int *offset*, [, float *bias*])	Use the texture coordinate *coord* to access the 1D texture array currently specified by *sampler*. Unsuffixed access the texture (with optional lod *bias*). **Lod** suffix accesses the texture with explicit *lod*. **Grad** suffix accesses the texture with explicit partial derivatives *dPdx* and *dPdy*. **Offset** suffix accesses the texture (with optional lod *bias*) with the *offset* added to the *u* texel coordinate before looking up each texel.

Table 5.7 Texture access functions, *continued*

Syntax	Description
ivec4 **texelFetch** (isampler1DArray *sampler*, ivec2 *coord*, int *lod*) ivec4 **texelFetchOffset** (isampler1DArray *sampler*, ivec2 *coord*, int *lod*, int *offset*)	Use the texel integer *coord* to look up a single texel of the explicit *lod* of the 1D texture array currently specified by *sampler*. **Offset** suffix accesses the texture (with optional lod *bias*) with the *offset* added to the *u* texel coordinate before looking up each texel.
ivec4 **textureLodOffset** (isampler1DArray *sampler*, vec2 *coord*, float *lod*, int *offset*) ivec4 **textureGradOffset** (isampler1DArray *sampler*, fvec2 *coord*, float *dPdx*, float *dPdy*, int *offset*)	Use the texture coordinate *coord* to access the 1D texture array currently specified by *sampler*. Combinations of the suffixes **Lod**, **Grad**, and **Offset** are as described earlier.
int **textureSize** (usampler1DArray *sampler*, int *lod*)	Returns the width of level *lod* of the 1D texture array currently specified by *sampler*.
uvec4 **texture** (usampler1DArray *sampler*, vec2 *coord* [, float *bias*]) uvec4 **textureLod** (usampler1DArray *sampler*, vec2 *coord*, float *lod*) uvec4 **textureGrad** (usampler1DArray *sampler*, vec2 *coord*, float *dPdx*, float *dPdy*) uvec4 **textureOffset** (usampler1DArray *sampler*, vec2 *coord*, int *offset*, [, float *bias*])	Use the texture coordinate *coord* to access the 1D texture array currently specified by *sampler*. Unsuffixed access the texture (with optional lod *bias*). **Lod** suffix accesses the texture with explicit *lod*. **Grad** suffix accesses the texture with explicit partial derivatives *dPdx* and *dPdy*. **Offset** suffix accesses the texture (with optional lod *bias*) with the *offset* added to the *u* texel coordinate before looking up each texel.

(continues)

Table 5.7 Texture access functions, *continued*

Syntax	Description
uvec4 **texelFetch** (usampler1DArray *sampler*, ivec2 *coord*, int *lod*) uvec4 **texelFetchOffset** (usampler1DArray *sampler*, ivec2 *coord*, int *lod*, int *offset*)	Use the texel integer *coord* to look up a single texel of the explicit *lod* to access the 1D texture array currently specified by *sampler*. **Offset** suffix accesses the texture (with optional lod *bias*) with the *offset* added to the *u* texel coordinate before looking up each texel.
uvec4 **textureLodOffset** (usampler1DArray *sampler*, vec2 *coord*, float *lod*, int *offset*) uvec4 **textureGradOffset** (usampler1DArray *sampler*, vec2 *coord*, float *dPdx*, float *dPdy*, int *offset*)	Use the texture coordinate *coord* to access the 1D texture array currently specified by *sampler*. Combinations of the suffixes **Lod**, **Grad**, and **Offset** are as described earlier.
ivec2 **textureSize** (sampler2DArray *sampler*, int *lod*)	Returns the width and height of level *lod* of the 1D texture array currently specified by *sampler*.
vec4 **texture** (sampler2DArray *sampler*, vec3 *coord*[, float *bias*]) vec4 **textureLod** (sampler2DArray *sampler*, vec3 *coord*, float *lod*) vec4 **textureGrad** (sampler2DArray *sampler*, vec3 *coord*, vec2 *dPdx*, vec2 *dPdy*) vec4 **textureOffset** (sampler2DArray *sampler*, vec3 *coord*, vec2 *offset*, [, float *bias*])	Use the texture coordinate *coord* to access the 1D texture array currently specified by *sampler*. Unsuffixed access the texture (with optional lod *bias*). **Lod** suffix accesses the texture with explicit *lod*. **Grad** suffix accesses the texture with explicit partial derivatives *dPdx* and *dPdy*. **Offset** suffix accesses the texture (with optional lod *bias*) with the *offset* added to the *u* texel coordinate before looking up each texel.

Table 5.7 Texture access functions, *continued*

Syntax	Description
vec4 **texelFetch** (sampler2DArray *sampler*, ivec3 *coord*, int *lod*) vec4 **texelFetchOffset** (sampler2DArray *sampler*, ivec3 *coord*, int *lod*, ivec2 *offset*)	Use the texel integer *coord* to look up a single texel of the explicit *lod* of the 1D texture array currently specified by *sampler*. **Offset** suffix accesses the texture (with optional lod *bias*) with the *offset* added to the *u* texel coordinate before looking up each texel.
vec4 **textureLodOffset** (sampler2DArray *sampler*, vec3 *coord*, float *lod*, int *offset*) vec4 **textureGradOffset** (sampler2DArray *sampler*, vec3 *coord*, vec2 *dPdx*, vec2 *dPdy*, ivec2 *offset*)	Use the texture coordinate *coord* to access the 1D texture array currently specified by *sampler*. Combinations of the suffixes **Lod**, **Grad**, and **Offset** are as described earlier.
ivec2 **textureSize** (isampler2DArray *sampler*, int *lod*)	Returns the width and height of level *lod* of the 1D texture array currently specified by *sampler*.
ivec4 **texture** (isampler2DArray *sampler*, vec3 *coord* [, float *bias*]) ivec4 **textureLod** (isampler2DArray *sampler*, vec3 *coord*, float *lod*) ivec4 **textureGrad** (isampler2DArray *sampler*, vec3 *coord*, vec2 *dPdx*, vec2 *dPdy*) ivec4 **textureOffset** (isampler2DArray *sampler*, vec3 *coord*, vec2 *offset*, [, float *bias*])	Use the texture coordinate *coord* to access the 1D texture array currently specified by *sampler*. Unsuffixed access the texture (with optional lod *bias*). **Lod** suffix accesses the texture with explicit *lod*. **Grad** suffix accesses the texture with explicit partial derivatives *dPdx* and *dPdy*. **Offset** suffix accesses the texture (with optional lod *bias*) with the *offset* added to the *u* texel coordinate before looking up each texel.

(continues)

Table 5.7 Texture access functions, *continued*

Syntax	Description
ivec4 **texelFetch** (isampler2DArray *sampler*, ivec3 *coord*, int *lod*) ivec4 **texelFetchOffset** (isampler2DArray *sampler*, ivec3 *coord*, int *lod*, ivec2 *offset*)	Use the texel integer *coord* to look up a single texel of the explicit *lod* to access the 1D texture array currently specified by *sampler*. **Offset** suffix accesses the texture (with optional lod *bias*) with the *offset* added to the *u* texel coordinate before looking up each texel.
ivec4 **textureLodOffset** (isampler2DArray *sampler*, vec3 *coord*, float *lod*, int *offset*) ivec4 **textureGradOffset** (isampler2DArray *sampler*, vec3 *coord*, vec2 *dPdx*, vec2 *dPdy*, ivec2 *offset*)	Use the texture coordinate *coord* to access the 1D texture array currently specified by *sampler*. Combinations of the suffixes **Lod**, **Grad**, and **Offset** are as described earlier.
ivec2 **textureSize** (usampler2DArray *sampler*, int *lod*)	Returns the width and height of level *lod* of the 1D texture array currently specified by *sampler*.
uvec4 **texture** (usampler2DArray *sampler*, vec3 *coord* [, float *bias*]) uvec4 **textureLod** (usampler2DArray *sampler*, vec3 *coord*, float *lod*) uvec4 **textureGrad** (usampler2DArray *sampler*, vec3 *coord*, vec2 *dPdx*, vec2 *dPdy*) uvec4 **textureOffset** (usampler2DArray *sampler*, vec3 *coord*, vec2 *offset*, [, float *bias*])	Use the texture coordinate *coord* to access the 1D texture array currently specified by *sampler*. Unsuffixed access the texture (with optional lod *bias*). **Lod** suffix accesses the texture with explicit *lod*. **Grad** suffix accesses the texture with explicit partial derivatives *dPdx* and *dPdy*. **Offset** suffix accesses the texture (with optional lod *bias*) with the *offset* added to the *u* and *v* texel coordinate before looking up each texel.

Table 5.7 Texture access functions, *continued*

Syntax	Description
uvec4 **texelFetch** (usampler2DArray *sampler*, ivec3 *coord*, int *lod*) uvec4 **texelFetchOffset** (usampler2DArray *sampler*, ivec3 *coord*, int *lod*, ivec2 *offset*)	Use the texel integer *coord* to look up a single texel of the explicit *lod* to access the 1D texture array currently specified by *sampler*. **Offset** suffix accesses the texture (with optional lod *bias*) with the *offset* added to the *u* and *v* texel coordinate before looking up each texel.

uvec4 **textureLodOffset** (usampler2DArray *sampler*, vec3 *coord*, float *lod*,
       int *offset*)
uvec4 **textureGradOffset** (usampler2DArray *sampler*, vec3 *coord*,
       vec2 *dPdx*, vec2 *dPdy*, ivec2 *offset*)
	Use the texture coordinate *coord* to access the 1D texture array currently specified by *sampler*.
	Combinations of the suffixes **Lod**, **Grad**, and **Offset** are as described earlier.

int **textureSize** (samplerBuffer *sampler*)	Returns the size of the buffer texture currently specified by *sampler*.
vec4 **texelFetch** (samplerBuffer *sampler*, int *coord*, int *lod*)	Use the texel integer *coord* to look up a single texel of the buffer texture currently specified by *sampler*.
int **textureSize** (isamplerBuffer *sampler*)	Returns the size of the buffer texture currently specified by *sampler*.
ivec4 **texelFetch** (isamplerBuffer *sampler*, int *coord*, int *lod*)	Use the texel integer *coord* to look up a single texel of the buffer texture currently specified by *sampler*.

(continues)

Table 5.7 Texture access functions, *continued*

Syntax	Description
int **textureSize** (usamplerBuffer *sampler*)	Returns the size of the buffer texture currently specified by *sampler*.
uvec4 **texelFetch** (usamplerBuffer *sampler*, int *coord*, int *lod*)	Use the texel integer *coord* to look up a single texel of the buffer texture currently specified by *sampler*.
int **textureSize** (sampler1DShadow *sampler*, int *lod*)	Returns the width of level *lod* of the 1D shadow texture currently specified by *sampler*.
float **texture** (sampler1DShadow *sampler*, vec3 *coord* [, float *bias*]) float **textureProj** (sampler1DShadow *sampler*, vec4 *coord* [, float *bias*]) float **textureLod** (sampler1DShadow *sampler*, vec3 *coord*, float *lod*) float **textureGrad** (sampler1DShadow *sampler*, vec3 *coord*, float *dPdx*, float *dPdy*) float **textureOffset** (sampler1DShadow *sampler*, vec3 *coord*, int *offset*, [, float *bias*])	Use the texture coordinate *coord* to access the 1D shadow texture currently specified by *sampler*: Unsuffixed access the texture (with optional lod *bias*). **Proj** suffix accesses the texture with projection (with optional lod *bias*). **Lod** suffix accesses the texture with explicit *lod*. **Grad** suffix accesses the texture with explicit partial derivatives *dPdx* and *dPdy*. **Offset** suffix accesses the texture (with optional lod *bias*) with the *offset* added to the *u* texel coordinate before looking up each texel.

Table 5.7 Texture access functions, *continued*

Syntax	Description
float **textureProjLod** (sampler1DShadow *sampler*, vec4 *coord* , float *lod*) float **textureProjGrad** (sampler1DShadow *sampler*, vec4 *coord*, float *dPdx*, float *dPdy*)	Use the texture coordinate *coord* to access the 1D shadow texture currently specified by *sampler*.
float **textureProjOffset** (sampler1DShadow *sampler*, vec4 *coord*, int *offset*[, float *bias*])	Combinations of the suffixes **Proj**, **Lod**, **Grad**, and **Offset** are as described earlier.
float **textureLodOffset** (sampler1DShadow *sampler*, vec3 *coord*, float *lod*, int *offset*)	
float **textureGradOffset** (sampler1DShadow *sampler*, vec3 *coord*, float *dPdx*, float *dPdy*, int *offset*)	
float **textureProjLodOffset** (sampler1DShadow *sampler*, vec4 *coord*, float *lod*, int *offset*)	Use the texture coordinate *coord* to access the 1D shadow texture currently specified by *sampler*.
float **textureProjGradOffset** (sampler1DShadow *sampler*, vec4 *coord*, float *dPdx*, float *dPdy*, int *offset*)	Combinations of the suffixes **Proj**, **Lod**, **Grad**, and **Offset** are as described earlier.
ivec2 **textureSize** (sampler2DShadow *sampler*, int *lod*)	Returns the width and height of level *lod* of the 2D shadow texture currently specified by *sampler*.

(continues)

Table 5.7 Texture access functions, *continued*

Syntax	Description
float **texture** (sampler2DShadow *sampler*, vec3 *coord* [, float *bias*]) float **textureProj** (sampler2DShadow *sampler*, vec4 *coord* [, float *bias*]) float **textureLod** (sampler2DShadow *sampler*, vec3 *coord*, float *lod*) float **textureGrad** (sampler2DShadow *sampler*, vec3 *coord*, vec2 *dPdx*, vec2 *dPdy*) float **textureOffset** (sampler2DShadow *sampler*, vec3 *coord*, ivec2 *offset*, [, float *bias*])	Use the texture coordinate *coord* to access the 2D shadow texture currently specified by *sampler*. Unsuffixed access the texture (with optional lod *bias*). **Proj** suffix accesses the texture with projection (with optional lod *bias*). **Lod** suffix accesses the texture with explicit *lod*. **Grad** suffix accesses the texture with explicit partial derivatives *dPdx* and *dPdy*. **Offset** suffix accesses the texture (with optional lod *bias*) with the *offset* added to the *u* and *v* texel coordinate before looking up each texel.
float **textureProjLod** (sampler2DShadow *sampler*, vec4 *coord* , float *lod*) float **textureProjGrad** (sampler2DShadow *sampler*, vec4 *coord*, vec2 *dPdx*, vec2 *dPdy*) float **textureProjOffset** (sampler2DShadow *sampler*, vec4 *coord*, ivec2 *offset* [, float *bias*]) float **textureLodOffset** (sampler2DShadow *sampler*, vec3 *coord*, float *lod*, ivec2 *offset*) float **textureGradOffset** (sampler2DShadow *sampler*, vec3 *coord*, vec2 *dPdx*, vec2 *dPdy*, ivec2 *offset*)	Use the texture coordinate *coord* to access the 2D shadow texture currently specified by *sampler*. Combinations of the suffixes **Proj, Lod, Grad,** and **Offset** are as described earlier.
float **textureProjLodOffset** (sampler2DShadow *sampler*, vec4 *coord*, float *lod*, ivec2 *offset*) float **textureProjGradOffset** (sampler2DShadow *sampler*, vec4 *coord*, vec2 *dPdx*, vec2 *dPdy*, ivec2 *offset*)	Use the texture coordinate *coord* to access the 2D shadow texture currently specified by *sampler*. Combinations of the suffixes **Proj, Lod, Grad,** and **Offset** are as described earlier.

Table 5.7 Texture access functions, *continued*

Syntax	Description
ivec2 **textureSize** (sampler2DRectShadow *sampler*, int *lod*)	Returns the width and height of level *lod* of the rect shadow texture currently specified by *sampler*.
float **texture** (sampler2DRectShadow *sampler*, vec3 *coord*) float **textureProj** (sampler2DRectShadow *sampler*, vec4 *coord*) float **textureGrad** (sampler2DRectShadow *sampler*, vec3 *coord*, vec2 *dPdx*, vec2 *dPdy*) float **textureOffset** (sampler2DRectShadow *sampler*, vec3 *coord*, ivec2 *offset*)	Use the texture coordinate *coord* to access the rect shadow texture currently specified by *sampler*: Unsuffixed access the texture. **Proj** suffix accesses the texture with projection. **Grad** suffix accesses the texture with explicit partial derivatives *dPdx* and *dPdy*. **Offset** suffix accesses the texture with the *offset* added to the *u* and *v* texel coordinate before looking up each texel.
float **textureProjGrad** (sampler2DRectShadow *sampler*, vec4 *coord*, vec2 *aPdx*, vec2 *dPdy*) float **textureProjOffset** (sampler2DRectShadow *sampler*, vec4 *coord*, ivec2 *offset*) float **textureGradOffset** (sampler2DRectShadow *sampler*, vec3 *coord*, vec2 *dPdx*, vec2 *dPdy*, ivec2 *offset*)	Use the texture coordinate *coord* to access the rect shadow texture currently specified by *sampler*: Combinations of the suffixes **Proj**, **Grad**, and **Offset** are as described earlier.
float **textureProjGradOffset** (sampler2DShadow *sampler*, vec4 *coord*, vec2 *dPdx*, vec2 *dPdy*, ivec2 *offset*)	Use the texture coordinate *coord* to access the rect shadow texture currently specified by *sampler*: Combinations of the suffixes **Proj**, **Grad**, and **Offset** are as described earlier.

(continues)

5.8 Fragment Processing Functions

Fragment processing functions are available only in shaders intended for use on the fragment processor. Fragment shaders have limited access to neighboring fragments sufficient to calculate derivatives. Two fragment processing functions obtain derivatives, and the other fragment processing estimates the filter width used to antialias procedural textures based on those derivatives.

The derivative functions, **dFdx** and **dFdy**, determine the rate of change of an expression. The function **dFdx**(p) evaluates the derivative of the expression p in the x direction in window coordinates, and the function **dFdy**(p) evaluates the derivative of the expression p in the y direction in window coordinates. These values indicate how fast the expression is changing in window space, and this information can be used to take steps to prevent aliasing. For instance, if texture coordinates are changing rapidly, it may be better to set the resulting color to the average color for the texture in order to avoid aliasing.

It only makes sense to apply these functions to expressions that vary from one fragment to the next. Because the value of a uniform variable does not change from one pixel to the next, its derivative in x and in y is always 0. See Table 5.8.

Table 5.8   Fragment processing functions

Syntax	Description
float **dFdx** (float p) vec2 **dFdx** (vec2 p) vec3 **dFdx** (vec3 p) vec4 **dFdx** (vec4 p)	Returns the derivative in x for the input argument p
float **dFdy** (float p) vec2 **dFdy** (vec2 p) vec3 **dFdy** (vec3 p) vec4 **dFdy** (vec4 p)	Returns the derivative in y for the input argument p
float **fwidth** (float p) vec2 **fwidth** (vec2 p) vec3 **fwidth** (vec3 p) vec4 **fwidth** (vec4 p)	Returns the sum of the absolute derivative in x and y for the input argument p, i.e., return = **abs** (**dFdx** (p)) + **abs** (**dFdy** (p));

5.9 Noise Functions

Noise functions (see Table 5.9) are available to both fragment and vertex shaders. These stochastic functions, first described by Ken Perlin, increase visual complexity. Values returned by the following noise functions give the appearance of randomness, but they are not truly random. A more complete description of and motivation for the noise function can be found in Chapter 15.

Table 5.9 Noise Functions

Syntax	Description
float **noise1** (float *x*) float **noise1** (vec2 *x*) float **noise1** (vec3 *x*) float **noise1** (vec4 *x*)	Returns a 1D noise value based on the input value *x*
vec2 **noise2** (float *x*) vec2 **noise2** (vec2 *x*) vec2 **noise2** (vec3 *x*) vec2 **noise2** (vec4 *x*)	Returns a 2D noise value based on the input value *x*
vec3 **noise3** (float *x*) vec3 **noise3** (vec2 *x*) vec3 **noise3** (vec3 *x*) vec3 **noise3** (vec4 *x*)	Returns a 3D noise value based on the input value *x*
vec4 **noise4** (float *x*) vec4 **noise4** (vec2 *x*) vec4 **noise4** (vec3 *x*) vec4 **noise4** (vec4 *x*)	Returns a 4D noise value based on the input value *x*

The built-in noise functions are defined to have the following characteristics:

- The return values are always in the range [–1,1] and cover at least the range [–0.6,0.6] with a Gaussian-like distribution.

- The return values have an overall average of 0.

- The functions are repeatable, in that a particular input value always produces the same return value.

- They are statistically invariant under rotation; that is, no matter how the domain is rotated, it has the same statistical character.

- They have a statistical invariance under translation; that is, no matter how the domain is translated, it has the same statistical character.

- They typically give different results under translation.

- The spatial frequency is narrowly concentrated, centered somewhere between 0.5 and 1.0.

- They are C^1 continuous everywhere; that is the first derivative is continuous.

5.10 Summary

The OpenGL Shading Language contains a rich set of built-in functions. Some of these functions are similar to those found in C and C++, and others are similar to those found in RenderMan. These functions expose hardware functionality (e.g., texture access) or support common operations (e.g., square root, clamp), or they represent operations likely to be accelerated in future generations of graphics hardware (trigonometry functions, noise, etc.).

Function overloading is used extensively because many of these functions operate on either vectors or scalars. Vendors that support the OpenGL Shading Language are expected to provide optimal implementations of these functions, so the built-in functions should be used whenever possible.

The built-in mathematical functions can be used in some unique and perhaps unexpected ways to create procedural textures. Shader examples throughout the rest of this book illustrate this. Visualizing the function needed to achieve a particular effect can be a vital part of the shader development process.

5.11 Further Information

Many of the built-in functions described in this chapter are used in example shaders in the remainder of this book. All you need to do is keep reading to see them in action.

Some additional detail on the built-in functions can be found in the *The OpenGL Shading Language, Version 1.40,* by John Kessenich, Dave Baldwin, and Randi Rost (2008).

Various OpenGL Shading Language built-in functions, including the derivative and filter width functions, were inspired by similar functions in RenderMan. Motivation for some of these functions is discussed in *The RenderMan Companion: A Programmer's Guide to Realistic Computer Graphics* by Steve Upstill (1990) and *Advanced RenderMan: Creating CGI for Motion Pictures* by Anthony A. Apodaca and Larry Gritz (1999). For additional details on noise functions, see the papers by Perlin and the references provided at the end of Chapter 15.

[1] Apodaca, Anthony A., and Larry Gritz, *Advanced RenderMan: Creating CGI for Motion Pictures*, Morgan Kaufmann Publishers, San Francisco, 1999. www.renderman.org/RMR/Books/arman/materials.html

[2] Kessenich, John, Dave Baldwin, and Randi Rost, *The OpenGL Shading Language, Version 1.40*, 3Dlabs/Intel, March 2008. www.opengl.org/documentation/specs/

[3] Perlin, Ken, *An Image Synthesizer*, Computer Graphics (SIGGRAPH '85 Proceedings), pp. 287–296, July 1985.

[4] Perlin, Ken, *Improving Noise*, Computer Graphics (SIGGRAPH 2002 Proceedings), pp. 681–682, July 2002. http://mrl.nyu.edu/perlin/paper445.pdf

[5] Pixar, *The RenderMan Interface Specification*, Version 3.2, Pixar, July 2000. https://renderman.pixar.com/products/rispec/index.htm

[6] Segal, Mark, and Kurt Akeley, *The OpenGL Graphics System: A Specification (Version 3.1)*, Editor (v1.1): Chris Frazier, (v1.2–3.1): Jon Leech, (v2.0): Jon Leech and Pat Brown, March 2008. www.opengl.org/documentation/spec.html

[7] Upstill, Steve, *The RenderMan Companion: A Programmer's Guide to Realistic Computer Graphics*, Addison-Wesley, Reading, Massachusetts, 1990.

[8] Zwillinger, Dan, *CRC Standard Mathematical Tables and Formulas*, 30th Edition, CRC Press, 1995. www.geom.uiuc.edu/docs/reference/CRC-formulas/

Chapter 6

Simple Shading Example

Now that we've described the OpenGL Shading Language, let's look at a simple example. In this example, we apply a brick pattern to an object. The brick pattern is calculated entirely within a fragment shader. If you'd prefer to skip ahead to the next chapter for a more in-depth discussion of the API that allows shaders to be defined and manipulated, feel free to do so.

The shader for rendering a procedural brick pattern was the first interesting shader ever executed by the OpenGL Shading Language on programmable graphics hardware. It ran for the first time in March 2002, on the 3Dlabs Wildcat VP graphics accelerator. Dave Baldwin published the first GLSL brick fragment shader in a white paper that described the language destined to become the OpenGL Shading Language. His GLSL shader was based on a RenderMan shader by Darwyn Peachey that was published in the book *Texturing and Modeling: A Procedural Approach*. Steve Koren and John Kessenich adapted Dave's shader to get it working on real hardware for the first time, and it has subsequently undergone considerable refinement for inclusion in this book.

This example, like most of the others in this book, consists of three essential components: the source code for the vertex shader, the source code for the fragment shader, and the application code that initializes and uses these shaders. This chapter focuses on the vertex and fragment shaders. The application code for using these shaders is discussed in Section 7.13, after the details of the OpenGL Shading Language API have been discussed.

With this first example, we take a little more time discussing the details in order to give you a better grasp of what's going on. In examples later in the book, we focus mostly on the details that differ from previous examples.

6.1 Brick Shader Overview

One approach to writing shaders is to come up with a description of the effect that you're trying to achieve and then decide which parts of the shader need to be implemented in the vertex shader, which need to be implemented in the fragment shader, and how the application will tie everything together.

In this example, we develop a shader that applies a computed brick pattern to all objects that are drawn. We don't attempt the most realistic-looking brick shader, but rather a fairly simple one that illustrates many of the concepts we introduced in the previous chapters. We don't use textures for this brick pattern; the pattern itself is generated algorithmically. We can build a lot of flexibility into this shader by parameterizing the different aspects of our brick algorithm.

Let's first come up with a description of the overall effect we're after. We want

- A single light source

- Diffuse and specular reflection characteristics

- A brick pattern based on the position in modeling coordinates of the object being rendered—where the *x* coordinate is related to the brick horizontal position and the *y* coordinate is related to the brick vertical position

- Alternate rows of bricks offset by one-half the width of a single brick

- Easy-to-modify colors and ratios: brick color, mortar color, brick-to-brick horizontal distance, brick-to-brick vertical distance, brick width fraction (ratio of the width of a brick to the overall horizontal distance between two adjacent bricks), and brick height fraction (ratio of the height of a brick to the overall vertical distance between two adjacent bricks)

The brick geometry parameters that we use to control geometry and color are illustrated in Figure 6.1. Brick size and brick percentage parameters are both stored in user-defined uniform variables of type **vec2**. The horizontal distance between two bricks, including the width of the mortar, is provided by *BrickSize.x*. The vertical distance between two rows of bricks, including the height of the mortar, is provided by *BrickSize.y*. These two values are given in units of modeling coordinates. The fraction of *BrickSize.x* represented by the brick only is provided by *BrickPct.x*. The fraction of *BrickSize.y* represented by the brick only is provided by *BrickPct.y*. These two values are in the range [0,1]. Finally, the brick color and the mortar color are represented by the variables *BrickColor* and *MortarColor*.

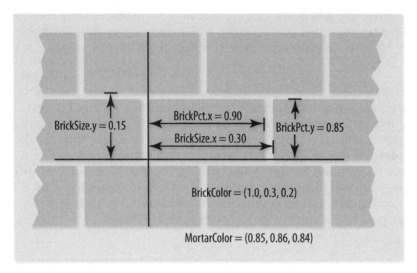

Figure 6.1   Parameters for defining brick

Now that we're armed with a firm grasp of our desired outcome, we'll design our vertex shader, then our fragment shader, and then the application code that will tie it all together.

6.2 Vertex Shader

The vertex shader embodies the operations that occur on each vertex that is provided to OpenGL. To define our vertex shader, we need to answer three questions.

- What data must be passed to the vertex shader for every vertex (i.e., generic attribute variables or in variables)?

- What global state is required by the vertex shader (i.e., uniform variables)?

- What values are computed by the vertex shader (i.e., out variables)?

Let's look at these questions one at a time.

We can't draw any geometry at all without specifying a value for each vertex position. Furthermore, we can't do any lighting unless we have a surface normal for each location for which we want to apply a lighting computation. So at the very least, we need a vertex position and a normal for every incoming vertex. We'll define a global in-qualified variable to hold the MCvertex (vertex in model coordinates), and a global in-qualified variable to hold the MCnormal (normal in model coordinates):

```
in vec4    MCvertex;
in vec3    MCnormal;
```

We need access to several matrices for our brick algorithm. We need to access the current modelview-projection matrix (*MVPMatrix*) in order to transform our vertex position into the clipping coordinate system. We need to access the current modelview matrix (*MVMatrix*) in order to transform the vertex position into eye coordinates for use in the lighting computation. And we also need to transform our incoming normals into eye coordinates by using OpenGL's normal transformation matrix (*NormalMatrix*, which is just the inverse transpose of the upper-left 3 × 3 subset of *MVMatrix*).

```
uniform mat4 MVMatrix;
uniform mat4 MVPMatrix;
uniform mat3 NormalMatrix;
```

In addition, we need the position of a single light source. We define the light source position as a uniform variable like this:[1]

```
uniform vec3 LightPosition;
```

We also need values for the lighting calculation to represent the contribution from specular reflection and the contribution from diffuse reflection. We could define these as uniform variables so that they could be changed dynamically by the application, but to illustrate some additional features of the language, we define them as constants like this:

```
const float SpecularContribution = 0.3;
const float DiffuseContribution  = 1.0 - SpecularContribution;
```

Finally, we need to define the values that are passed on to the fragment shader. Every vertex shader must compute the homogeneous vertex position and store its value in the standard variable *gl_Position*, so we know that our brick vertex shader must do likewise. On the fly, we compute the brick pattern in the fragment shader as a function of the incoming geometry's *x* and *y* values in modeling coordinates, so we define an out variable called *MCposition* for this purpose. To apply the lighting effect on top of our brick, we do part of the lighting computation in the fragment shader and apply

---

1. The shaders in this book observe the convention of capitalizing the first letter of user-specified uniform, in, out, and nonqualified global variable names to set them apart from local variables.

the final lighting effect after the brick/mortar color has been computed in the fragment shader. We do most of the lighting computation in the vertex shader and simply pass the computed light intensity to the fragment shader in an out variable called *LightIntensity*. These two out variables are defined like this:

```
out float    LightIntensity;
out vec2     MCposition;
```

We're now ready to get to the meat of our brick vertex shader. We begin by declaring a main function for our vertex shader and computing the vertex position in eye coordinates:

```
void main()
{
    vec3 ecPosition = vec3(MVMatrix * MCvertex);;
```

In this first line of code, our vertex shader defines a variable called *ecPosition* to hold the eye coordinate position of the incoming vertex. We compute the eye coordinate position by transforming the vertex position (*MCvertex*) by the current modelview matrix (*MVMatrix*). Because one of the operands is a matrix and the other is a vector, the * operator performs a matrix multiplication operation rather than a component-wise multiplication.

The result of the matrix multiplication is a **vec4**, but *ecPosition* is defined as a **vec3**. There is no automatic conversion between variables of different types in the OpenGL Shading Language, so we convert the result to a **vec3** by using a constructor. This causes the fourth component of the result to be dropped so that the two operands have compatible types. (Constructors provide an operation that is similar to type casting, but it is much more flexible, as discussed in Section 3.3.) As we'll see, the eye coordinate position is used a couple of times in our lighting calculation.

The lighting computation that we perform is a simple one. Some light from the light source is reflected in a diffuse fashion (i.e., in all directions). Where the viewing direction is very nearly the same as the reflection direction from the light source, we see a specular reflection. To compute the diffuse reflection, we need to compute the angle between the incoming light and the surface normal. To compute the specular reflection, we need to compute the angle between the reflection direction and the viewing direction. First, we transform the incoming normal:

```
    vec3 tnorm     = normalize(NormalMatrix * MCnormal);
```

This line defines a new variable called *tnorm* for storing the transformed normal (remember, in the OpenGL Shading Language, variables can be declared when needed). The incoming surface normal (*MCnormal*, a user-defined in variable for accessing the normal value through a generic vertex attribute) is transformed by the current normal transformation matrix (*NormalMatrix*). The resulting vector is normalized (converted to a vector of unit length) by the built-in function **normalize**, and the result is stored in *tnorm*.

Next, we need to compute a vector from the current point on the surface of the three-dimensional object we're rendering to the light source position. Both of these should be in eye coordinates (which means that the value for our uniform variable *LightPosition* must be provided by the application in eye coordinates). The light direction vector is computed as follows:

```
vec3 lightVec   = normalize(LightPosition - ecPosition);
```

The object position in eye coordinates was previously computed and stored in *ecPosition*. To compute the light direction vector, we subtract the object position from the light position. The resulting light direction vector is also normalized and stored in the newly defined local variable *lightVec*.

The calculations we've done so far have set things up almost perfectly to call the built-in function **reflect**. Using our transformed surface normal and the computed incident light vector, we can now compute a reflection vector at the surface of the object; however, **reflect** requires the incident vector (the direction from the light to the surface), and we've computed the direction to the light source. Negating *lightVec* gives us the proper vector:

```
vec3 reflectVec = reflect(-lightVec, tnorm);
```

Because both vectors used in this computation were unit vectors, the resulting vector is a unit vector as well. To complete our lighting calculation, we need one more vector—a unit vector in the direction of the viewing position. Because, by definition, the viewing position is at the origin (i.e., (0,0,0)) in the eye coordinate system, we can simply negate and normalize the computed eye coordinate position, *ecPosition*:

```
vec3 viewVec    = normalize(-ecPosition);
```

With these four vectors, we can perform a per-vertex lighting computation. The relationship of these vectors is shown in Figure 6.2.

The modeling of diffuse reflection is based on the assumption that the incident light is scattered in all directions according to a cosine distribution function. The reflection of light is strongest when the light direction vector and the surface normal are coincident. As the difference between the two angles increases to 90°, the diffuse reflection drops off to zero. Because both vectors have been normalized to produce unit vectors, we can determine the cosine of the angle between *lightVec* and *tnorm* by performing a dot

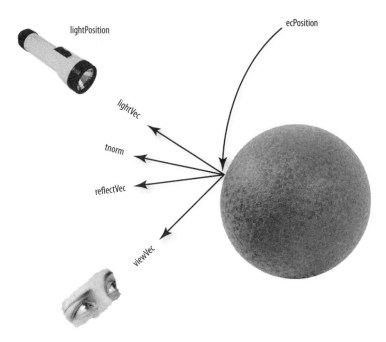

Figure 6.2 Vectors involved in the lighting computation for the brick vertex shader

product operation between those vectors. We want the diffuse contribution to be 0 if the angle between the light and the surface normal is greater than 90° (there should be no diffuse contribution if the light is behind the object), and the **max** function accomplishes this:

```
float diffuse = max(dot(lightVec, tnorm), 0.0);
```

The specular component of the light intensity for this vertex is computed by

```
float spec = 0.0;
if (diffuse > 0.0)
{
    spec = max(dot(reflectVec, viewVec), 0.0);
    spec = pow(spec, 16.0);
}
```

The variable for the specular reflection value is defined and initialized to 0. We compute a specular value other than 0 only if the angle between the light direction vector and the surface normal is less than 90° (i.e., the diffuse value is greater than 0) because we don't want any specular highlights if the light source is behind the object. Because both *reflectVec* and *viewVec* are normalized, computing the dot product of these two vectors gives us the cosine of the angle between them. If the angle is near zero (i.e., the reflection vector and the viewing vector are almost the same), the resulting value is near 1.0. By raising the result to the 16th power in the subsequent line of code, we effectively "sharpen" the highlight, ensuring that we have a specular highlight only in the region where the reflection vector and the view vector are almost the same. The choice of 16 for the exponent value is arbitrary. Higher values produce more concentrated specular highlights, and lower values produce less concentrated highlights. This value could also be passed in as a uniform variable so that it can be easily modified by the end user.

All that remains is to multiply the computed diffuse and specular reflection values by the *diffuseContribution* and *specularContribution* constants and sum the two values:

```
LightIntensity = DiffuseContribution * diffuse +
                 SpecularContribution * spec;
```

This value will be assigned to the out variable *LightIntensity* and interpolated between vertices. We also have one other out variable to compute, and we can do that quite easily.

```
MCposition = MCvertex.xy;
```

When the brick pattern is applied to a geometric object, we want the brick pattern to remain constant with respect to the surface of the object, no matter how the object is moved. We also want the brick pattern to remain constant with respect to the surface of the object, no matter what the viewing position. To generate the brick pattern algorithmically in the fragment shader, we need to provide a value at each fragment that represents a location on the surface. For this example, we provide the modeling coordinate at each vertex by setting our out variable *MCposition* to the same value as our incoming vertex position (which is, by definition, in modeling coordinates).

We don't need the *z* or *w* coordinate in the fragment shader, so we need a way to select just the *x* and *y* components of *MCvertex*. We could have used a constructor here (e.g., **vec2**(*MCvertex*)), but to show off another language feature, we use the component selector **.xy** to select the first two components of *MCvertex* and store them in our out variable *MCposition*.

All that remains to be done is what all vertex shaders must do: compute the homogeneous vertex position. We do this by transforming the incoming vertex value by the current modelview-projection matrix:

```
    gl_Position    = MVPMatrix * MCvertex;
}
```

For clarity, the code for our vertex shader is provided in its entirety in
Listing 6.1.

Listing 6.1   Source code for brick vertex shader

```
#version 140

in vec4      MCvertex;
in vec3      MCnormal;

uniform mat4 MVMatrix;
uniform mat4 MVPMatrix;
uniform mat3 NormalMatrix;

uniform vec3 LightPosition;

const float SpecularContribution = 0.3;
const float DiffuseContribution  = 1.0 - SpecularContribution;

out float    LightIntensity;
out vec2     MCposition;

void main()
{
    vec3 ecPosition = vec3(MVMatrix * MCvertex);
    vec3 tnorm      = normalize(NormalMatrix * MCnormal);
    vec3 lightVec   = normalize(LightPosition - ecPosition);
    vec3 reflectVec = reflect(-lightVec, tnorm);
    vec3 viewVec    = normalize(-ecPosition);
    float diffuse   = max(dot(lightVec, tnorm), 0.0);
    float spec      = 0.0;

    if (diffuse > 0.0)
    {
        spec = max(dot(reflectVec, viewVec), 0.0);
        spec = pow(spec, 16.0);
    }

    LightIntensity  = DiffuseContribution * diffuse +
                      SpecularContribution * spec;

    MCposition      = MCvertex.xy;
    gl_Position     = MVPMatrix * MCvertex;
}
```

6.3 Fragment Shader

The typical purpose of a fragment shader is to compute the color to be
applied to a fragment or to compute the depth value for the fragment or

both. In this case (and indeed with most fragment shaders), we're concerned only about the color of the fragment. We're perfectly happy using the depth value that's been computed by the OpenGL rasterization stage. Therefore, the entire purpose of this shader is to compute the color of the current fragment.

Our brick fragment shader starts off by defining a few more uniform variables than did the vertex shader. The brick pattern that will be rendered on our geometry is parameterized to make it easier to modify. The parameters that are constant across an entire primitive can be stored as uniform variables and initialized (and later modified) by the application. This makes it easy to expose these controls to the end user for modification through user interface elements such as sliders and color pickers. The brick fragment shader uses the parameters that are illustrated in Figure 6.1. These are defined as uniform variables as follows:

```
uniform vec3   BrickColor, MortarColor;
uniform vec2   BrickSize;
uniform vec2   BrickPct;
```

We want our brick pattern to be applied consistently to our geometry in order to have the object look the same no matter where it is placed in the scene or how it is rotated. The key to determining the placement of the brick pattern is the modeling coordinate position that is computed by the vertex shader and passed in the in variable *MCposition*:

```
in vec2        MCposition;
```

This variable was computed at each vertex by the vertex shader in the previous section, and it is interpolated across the primitive and made available to the fragment shader at each fragment location. Our fragment shader can use this information to determine where the fragment location is in relation to the algorithmically defined brick pattern. The other in variable that is provided as input to the fragment shader is defined as follows:

```
in float       LightIntensity;
```

This in variable contains the interpolated value for the light intensity that we computed at each vertex in our vertex shader. Note that both of the in variables in our fragment shader are defined with the same type that was used to define them in our vertex shader. A link error would be generated if this were not the case.

The purpose of this fragment shader is to calculate the fragment color. We define an out variable ***FragColor***.

```
out vec4       FragColor;
```

With our uniform, in, and out variables defined, we can begin with the actual code for the brick fragment shader.

```
void main()
{
    vec3  color;
    vec2  position, useBrick;
```

In this shader, we do things more like we would in C and define all our local variables before they're used at the beginning of our **main** function. In some cases, this can make the code a little cleaner or easier to read, but it is mostly a matter of personal preference and coding style. The first actual line of code in our brick fragment shader computes values for the local **vec2** variable *position*:

```
    position = MCposition / BrickSize;
```

This statement divides the fragment's *x* position in modeling coordinates by the brick column width and the *y* position in modeling coordinates by the brick row height. This gives us a "brick row number" (*position.y*) and a "brick number" within that row (*position.x*). Keep in mind that these are signed, floating-point values, so it is perfectly reasonable to have negative row and brick numbers as a result of this computation.

Next, we use a conditional to determine whether the fragment is in a row of bricks that is offset (see Figure 6.3):

```
    if (fract(position.y * 0.5) > 0.5)
        position.x += 0.5;
```

The "brick row number" (*position.y*) is multiplied by 0.5, the integer part is dropped by the **fract** function, and the result is compared to 0.5. Half the time (or every other row), this comparison is true, and the "brick number" value (*position.x*) is incremented by 0.5 to offset the entire row by half the width of a brick. This is illustrated by the graph in Figure 6.3.

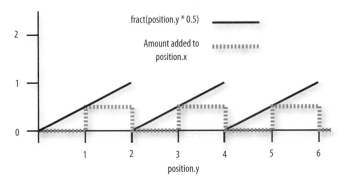

Figure 6.3 A graph of the function **fract**(*position.y* * 0.5) shows how the even/odd row determination is made. The result of this function is compared against 0.5. If the value is greater than 0.5, a value of 0.5 is added to *position.x*; otherwise, nothing is added. The result is that rows whose integer values are 1, 3, 5, …, are shifted half a brick position to the right.

Following this, we compute the fragment's location within the current brick.

```
position = fract(position);
```

This computation gives us the vertical and horizontal position within a single brick. This position serves as the basis for determining whether to use the brick color or the mortar color.

Figure 6.4 shows how we might visualize the results of the fragment shader to this point. If we were to apply this shader to a square with modeling coordinates of (–1.0, –1.0) at the lower-left corner and (1.0, 1.0) at the upper right, our partially completed shader would show the beginnings of the brick pattern we're after. Because the overall width of the square is 2.0 units in modeling coordinates, our division of *MCposition.x* by *BrickSize.x* gives us 2.0 / 0.3, or roughly six and two-thirds bricks across, as we see in Figure 6.4. Similarly, the division of *MCposition.y* by *BrickSize.y* gives us 2.0 / 0.15, or roughly thirteen and two-thirds rows of bricks from top to bottom. For this illustration, we shaded each fragment by summing the fractional part of *position.x* and *position.y*, multiplying the result by 0.5, and then storing this value in the red, green, and blue components of *FragColor*.

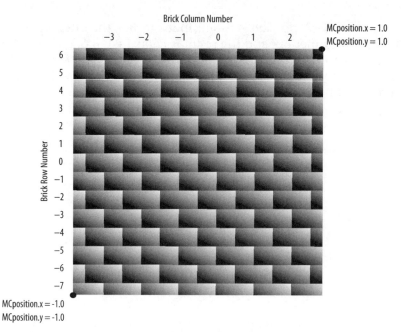

Figure 6.4   Intermediate results of brick fragment shader

To complete our brick shader, we need a function that gives us a value of 1.0 when the brick color should be used and 0 when the mortar color should be used. If we can achieve this, we can end up with a simple way to choose the appropriate color. We know that we're working with a horizontal component of the brick texture function and a vertical component. If we can create the desired function for the horizontal component and the desired function for the vertical component, we can just multiply the two values together to get our final answer. If the result of either of the individual functions is 0 (mortar color), the multiplication causes the final answer to be 0; otherwise, it is 1.0, and the brick color is used.

We use the **step** function to achieve the desired effect. The **step** function takes two arguments, an edge (or threshold) and a parameter to test against that edge. If the value of the parameter to be tested is less than the edge value, the function returns 0; otherwise, it returns 1.0. (Refer to Figure 5.11 for a graph of this function.) In typical use, the **step** function produces a pattern of pulses (i.e., a square wave) whereby the function starts at 0 and rises to 1.0 when the threshold is reached. We can get a function that starts at 1.0 and drops to 0 just by reversing the order of the two arguments provided to this function.

```
useBrick = step(position, BrickPct);
```

In this line of code, we compute two values that tell us whether we are in the brick or in the mortar in the horizontal direction (*useBrick.x*) and in the vertical direction (*useBrick.y*). The built-in function **step** produces a value of 0 when *BrickPct.x* < *position.x* and a value of 1.0 when *BrickPct.x* >= *position.x*. Because of the **fract** function, we know that *position.x* varies from (0,1). The variable *BrickPct* is a uniform variable, so its value is constant across the primitive. This means that the value of *useBrick.x* is 1.0 when the brick color should be used and 0 when the mortar color should be used as we move horizontally. The same thing is done in the vertical direction, with *position.y* and *BrickPct.y* computing the value for *useBrick.y*. By multiplying *useBrick.x* by *useBrick.y*, we can get a value of 0 or 1.0 that lets us select the appropriate color for the fragment. The periodic step function for the horizontal component of the brick pattern is illustrated in Figure 6.5.

The values of *BrickPct.x* and *BrickPct.y* can be computed by the application to give a uniform mortar width in both directions based on the ratio of column width to row height, or the values can be chosen arbitrarily to give a mortar appearance that looks right.

All that remains is to compute our final color value and store it in the out variable *FragColor*.

```
color  = mix(MortarColor, BrickColor, useBrick.x * useBrick.y);
color *= LightIntensity;
FragColor = vec4(color, 1.0);
}
```

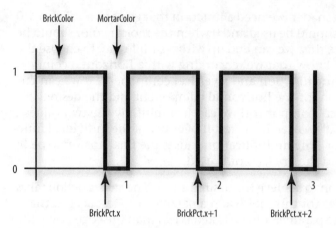

Figure 6.5   The periodic step function that produces the horizontal component of the procedural brick pattern

Here we compute the color of the fragment and store it in the local variable *color.* We use the built-in function **mix** to choose the brick color or the mortar color, depending on the value of *useBrick.x * useBrick.y.* Because *useBrick.x* and *useBrick.y* can have values of only 0 (mortar) or 1.0 (brick), we choose the brick color only if both values are 1.0; otherwise, we choose the mortar color.

The resulting value is then multiplied by the light intensity, and that result is stored in the local variable *color.* This local variable is a **vec3**, and *FragColor* is defined as a **vec4**, so we create our final color value by using a constructor to add a fourth component (alpha) equal to 1.0 and assign the result to the out variable *FragColor.*

The source code for the complete fragment shader is shown in Listing 6.2.

Listing 6.2   Source code for brick fragment shader

```
#version 140

uniform vec3   BrickColor, MortarColor;
uniform vec2   BrickSize;
uniform vec2   BrickPct;

in vec2        MCposition;
in float       LightIntensity;

out vec4       FragColor;

void main()
{
    vec3  color;
    vec2  position, useBrick;
```

```
    position = MCposition / BrickSize;

    if (fract(position.y * 0.5) > 0.5)
        position.x += 0.5;

    position = fract(position);

    useBrick = step(position, BrickPct);
//
    color  = mix(MortarColor, BrickColor, useBrick.x * useBrick.y);
    color *= LightIntensity;
    FragColor = vec4(color, 1.0);
}
```

When comparing this shader to the vertex shader in the previous example, we notice one of the key features of the OpenGL Shading Language, namely, that the language used to write these two shaders is almost identical. Both shaders have a main function, some uniform variables, and some local variables; expressions are the same; built-in functions are called in the same way; constructors are used in the same way; and so on. The only perceptible differences exhibited by these two shaders are (A) the vertex shader accesses generic attribute variables through user-defined in variables, such as *MCvertex* and *MCnormal*, (B) the vertex shader writes to the built-in variable *gl_Position*, whereas the fragment shader writes to the user-defined out variable *FragColor*, and (C) the out variables **LightIntensity** and **MCposition** are written by the vertex shader, and the fragment shader reads the in variables **LightIntensity** and **MCposition**.

The application code to create and use these shaders is shown in Section 7.13, after the OpenGL Shading Language API has been presented. The result of rendering some simple objects with these shaders is shown in Figure 6.6. A color version of the result is shown in Color Plate 34.

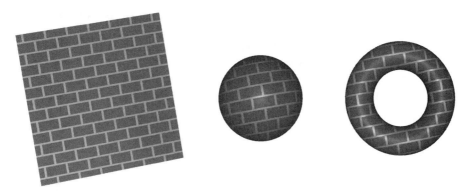

Figure 6.6   A flat polygon, a sphere, and a torus rendered with the brick shaders

6.4 Observations

A couple of problems with our shader make it unfit for anything but the simplest cases. Because the brick pattern is computed with the modeling coordinates of the incoming object, the apparent size of the bricks depends on the size of the object in modeling coordinates. The brick pattern might look fine with some objects, but the bricks may turn out much too small or much too large on other objects. At the very least, we should probably have a uniform variable in the vertex shader to scale the modeling coordinates. The application could allow the end user to adjust the scale factor to make the brick pattern look good on the object being rendered.

Another potential issue is that we've chosen to base the brick pattern on the object's x and y coordinates in modeling space. This can result in some unrealistic-looking effects on objects that aren't as regular as the objects shown in Figure 6.6. By using only the x and y coordinates of the object, we end up modeling bricks that are infinitely deep. The brick pattern looks fine when viewed from the front of the object, but when you look at it from the side, you'll be able to see how the brick extends in depth. To get a truly three-dimensional brick shader, we'd need to add a third dimension to our procedural texture calculation and use the z component of the position in modeling coordinates to determine whether we were in brick or mortar in the z dimension as well (see if you can modify the shaders to do this).

If we look closely at our brick pattern, we also notice aliasing artifacts (jaggies) along the transition from brick color to mortar color. These artifacts are due to the **step** function causing an instantaneous change from 0 to 1.0 (or from 1.0 to 0) when we cross the transition point between brick color and mortar color. Our shader has no alternative but to pick one color or the other for each fragment, and, because we cannot sample at a high enough frequency to represent this instantaneous change at the brick/mortar border, aliasing artifacts occur. Instead of using the **step** function, we could have used the built-in **smoothstep** function. This function is like the **step** function, except that it defines two edges and a smooth interpolation between 0 and 1.0 between those two edges. This would have the effect of blurring the transition between the brick color and the mortar color, thus making the aliasing artifacts much less noticeable. A method for analytically antialiasing the procedural brick texture is described in Section 17.4.5.

Despite these shortcomings, our brick shaders are perfectly good examples of a working OpenGL shader. Together, our brick vertex and fragment shaders illustrate a number of the interesting features of the OpenGL Shading Language.

6.5 Summary

This chapter has applied the language concepts from previous chapters to the development of working shaders that create a procedurally defined brick pattern. The vertex shader is responsible for transforming the vertex position, passing along the modeling coordinate position of the vertex, and computing a light intensity value at each vertex, using a single simulated light source. The fragment shader is responsible for determining whether each fragment should be brick color or mortar color. Once this determination is made, the light intensity value is applied to the chosen color, and the final color value is passed from the fragment shader so that it can ultimately be written in the framebuffer. The source code for these two shaders was discussed line by line to explain clearly how they work. This pair of shaders illustrates many of the features of the OpenGL Shading Language and can be used as a springboard for doing bigger and better things with the language.

6.6 Further Information

This shader and others are available from the 3Dlabs developer Web site. Source code for getting started with OpenGL shaders is also available.

[1] *Former 3Dlabs developer Web site*. Now at http://3dshaders.com.

[2] Baldwin, Dave, *OpenGL 2.0 Shading Language White Paper, Version 1.0*, 3Dlabs, October, 2001.

[3] Ebert, David S., John Hart, Bill Mark, F. Kenton Musgrave, Darwyn Peachey, Ken Perlin, and Steven Worley, *Texturing and Modeling: A Procedural Approach, Third Edition*, Morgan Kaufmann Publishers, San Francisco, 2002. www.texturingandmodeling.com

[4] Kessenich, John, Dave Baldwin, and Randi Rost, *The OpenGL Shading Language, Version 1.40*, 3Dlabs/Intel, March 2008. www.opengl.org/documentation/specs/

[5] Segal, Mark, and Kurt Akeley, *The OpenGL Graphics System: A Specification (Version 3.1)*, Editor (v1.1): Chris Frazier, (v1.2–3.1): Jon Leech, (v2.0): Jon Leech and Pat Brown, March 2008. www.opengl.org/documentation/specs/

Chapter 7

OpenGL Shading Language API

In support of the OpenGL Shading Language, more than 40 entry points were added to OpenGL starting in version 2.0. This set of API calls is referred to throughout this book as the OPENGL SHADING LANGUAGE API. In this chapter, we look at the OpenGL entry points that have been added to create, load, compile, and link shaders, as well as the entry points that have been added for passing generic vertex attributes and uniform variables to shaders. Reference pages for all of the OpenGL Shading Language API entry points are found in Appendix B.

At the end of this chapter, we discuss the application code that is needed to create and use the brick shader presented in Chapter 6. If you just can't wait, go ahead and sneak a peek at Section 7.13, and then come back here to learn the details of the API.

Here is an overview of creating and using OpenGL shaders:

1. Create one or more (empty) shader objects with **glCreateShader.**

2. Provide source code for these shaders with **glShaderSource.**

3. Compile each of the shaders with **glCompileShader.**

4. Create a program object with **glCreateProgram.**

5. Attach all the shader objects to the program object with **glAttachShader.**

6. Link the program object with **glLinkProgram.**

7. Install the executable program as part of OpenGL's current state with **glUseProgram.**

8. If the shaders uses the default uniform block, query the locations of uniform variables with **glGetUniformLocation** and then set their values with **glUniform**.

9. If the shaders use named uniform blocks, query the uniform block information with **glGetUniformBlockIndex** and **glGetActiveUniformBlockiv**. Query the offsets of the uniform variables within the uniform block with **glGetActiveUniformsiv**. The uniform blocks are associated with buffer object binding points with **glUniformBlockBinding**, and buffer objects are bound to those binding points with **glBindBufferRange**.

10. If the vertex shader uses user-defined in variables, the application must provide values for them, using OpenGL API calls that place attribute values in generic, numbered vertex attribute locations. Before such attribute data is passed to the shader, the index of the generic vertex attribute should be associated with an in variable in a vertex shader in one of two ways. Applications can create this association explicitly by calling **glBindAttribLocation** before linking. Alternatively, if no explicit association is made, OpenGL makes these associations automatically during linking. An application can query the assignment that was made with **glGetAttribLocation**. Thereafter, generic vertex attributes can be passed to a vertex shader with **glVertexAttrib** or with **glVertexAttribPointer** and **glEnableVertexArrayPointer** in conjunction with standard OpenGL commands to draw vertex arrays.

11. If the fragment shader uses user-defined out variables, the application may create an association between a user-defined out variable and a fragment data index with **glBindFragDataLocation** before linking. Alternatively, if no explicit association is made, OpenGL makes these associations automatically during linking. An application can query the assignment that was made with **glGetFragDataLocation**.

12. An application may optionally record vertex shader out variables to one or more transform feedback buffers. Before vertex shader out variables are recorded, the vertex shader out variables are associated with feedback buffer binding points with **glTransformFeedbackVarying**, and buffer objects are bound to those binding points with **glBindBufferRange**.

7.1 Obtaining Version Information

With the addition of the OpenGL Shading Language, the OpenGL version number was changed from 1.5 to 2.0. The number before the period is referred to as the MAJOR VERSION NUMBER, and the number after the period is referred to as the MINOR VERSION NUMBER. This did not reflect a change in compatibility, as is often the case when a product's major version number is changed. Instead, the OpenGL ARB believed that inclusion of a high-level shading language was a major addition to OpenGL. To call attention to this important capability, the committee decided that a change to OpenGL's major version number was warranted.

This caused some incompatibility with applications that were written assuming that OpenGL would never have a major version number greater than 1. The OpenGL Shading Language also has a version number since it is expected that it too will have additional features added over time. Both of these values can be queried with the OpenGL function **glGetString**.

To write applications that will work properly in a variety of OpenGL environments and that will stand the test of time, be sure to properly query and parse the OpenGL and OpenGL Shading Language version strings. Both strings are defined as

<version number><space><vendor-specific information>

The version number is defined to be either

majorVersionNumber.minorVersionNumber

or

majorVersionNumber.minorVersionNumber.releaseNumber

where each component contains one or more digits. The vendor specification information and the release number are optional and might not appear in the version string. The version number is not a floating-point number, but a series of integers separated by periods.

To determine the OpenGL version number, call **glGetString** with the symbolic constant GL_VERSION. To determine the OpenGL Shading Language version, call **glGetString** with the symbolic constant GL_SHADING_LANGUAGE_VERSION. The shading language version that was approved at the time OpenGL 2.0 was approved was 1.10.

Listing 7.1 contains code for C functions that query and parse the OpenGL and OpenGL Shading Language version strings. Both functions assume that a valid OpenGL context already exists, and both return 0 for the major and minor number if an error is encountered. Values returned by these functions can be tested to see if the underlying implementation provides the necessary support.

Listing 7.1 C functions to obtain OpenGL and OpenGL Shading Language version information

```
void getGlVersion(int *major, int *minor)
{
    const char *verstr = (const char *) glGetString(GL_VERSION);
    if ((verstr == NULL) || (sscanf(verstr,"%d.%d", major, minor) != 2))
    {
        *major = *minor = 0;
        fprintf(stderr, "Invalid GL_VERSION format!!!\n");
    }
}

void getGlslVersion(int *major, int *minor)
{
    int gl_major, gl_minor;
    getGlVersion(&gl_major, &gl_minor);

    *major = *minor = 0;
    if(gl_major == 1)
    {
        /* GL v1.x can provide GLSL v1.00 only as an extension */
        const char *extstr = (const char *) glGetString(GL_EXTENSIONS);
        if ((extstr != NULL) &&
            (strstr(extstr, "GL_ARB_shading_language_100") != NULL))
        {
            *major = 1;
            *minor = 0;
        }
    }
    else if (gl_major >= 2)
    {
        /* GL v2.0 and greater must parse the version string */
        const char *verstr =
            (const char *) glGetString(GL_SHADING_LANGUAGE_VERSION);

        if((verstr == NULL) ||
            (sscanf(verstr, "%d.%d", major, minor) != 2))
        {
            *major = *minor = 0;
            fprintf(stderr,
                "Invalid GL_SHADING_LANGUAGE_VERSION format!!!\n");
        }
    }
}
```

7.2 Creating Shader Objects

The design of the OpenGL Shading Language API mimics the process of developing a C or C++ application. The first step is to create the source code. The source code must then be compiled, the various compiled modules must be linked, and finally the resulting code can be executed by the target processor.

To support the concept of a high-level shading language within OpenGL, the design must provide storage for source code, compiled code, and executable code. The solution to this problem is to define two new OpenGL-managed data structures, or objects. These objects provide the necessary storage, and operations on these objects have been defined to provide functionality for specifying source code and then compiling, linking, and executing the resulting code. When one of these objects is created, OpenGL returns a unique identifier for it. This identifier can be used to manipulate the object and to set or query the parameters of the object.

The first step toward utilizing programmable graphics hardware is to create a shader object. This creates an OpenGL-managed data structure that can store the shader's source code. The command to create a shader is

---

GLuint **glCreateShader**(GLenum *shaderType*)

Creates an empty shader object and returns a nonzero value by which it can be referenced. A shader object maintains the source code strings that define a shader. *shaderType* specifies the type of shader to be created. Two types of shaders are supported. A shader of type GL_VERTEX_SHADER is a shader that runs on the programmable vertex processor; it replaces the fixed functionality vertex processing in OpenGL. A shader of type GL_FRAGMENT_SHADER is a shader that runs on the programmable fragment processor; it replaces the fixed functionality fragment processing in OpenGL.

When created, a shader object's GL_SHADER_TYPE parameter is set to either GL_VERTEX_SHADER or GL_FRAGMENT_SHADER, depending on the value of *shaderType*.

After a shader object is created, strings that define the shader's source code must be provided. The source code for a shader is provided as an array of strings. The command for defining a shader's source code is

---

void **glShaderSource**(GLuint *shader,*

GLsizei *count,*

const GLchar ****string,*

const GLint **length*)

Sets the source code in *shader* to the source code in the array of strings specified by *string.* Any source code previously stored in the shader object is completely replaced. The number of strings in the array is specified by *count.* If *length* is NULL, then each string is assumed to be null terminated. If *length* is a value other than NULL, it points to an array containing a string length for each of the corresponding elements of *string.* Each element in the *length* array can contain the length of the corresponding string (the null character is not counted as part of the string length) or a value less than 0 to indicate that the string is null terminated. The source code strings are not scanned or parsed at this time; they are simply copied into the specified shader object. An application can modify or free its copy of the source code strings immediately after the function returns.

The multiple strings interface provides a number of benefits, including

- A way to organize common pieces of source code (for instance, the in variable definitions and out variable definitions that are shared between a vertex shader and a fragment shader)

- A way to share prefix strings (analogous to header files) between shaders

- A way to share **#define** values to control the compilation process

- A way to include user-defined or third-party library functions

7.3 Compiling Shader Objects

After the source code strings have been loaded into a shader object, the source code must be compiled to check its validity. The result of compilation remains as part of the shader object until another compilation operation occurs or until the shader object itself is deleted. The command to compile a shader object is

---

void **glCompileShader**(GLuint *shader*)

Compiles the source code strings that have been stored in the shader object specified by *shader*.

The compilation status is stored as part of the shader object's state. This value is set to GL_TRUE if the shader was compiled without errors and is ready for use, and GL_FALSE otherwise. It can be queried by calling **glGetShader** with arguments *shader* and GL_COMPILE_STATUS.

A shader will fail to compile if it is lexically, grammatically, or semantically incorrect. Whether or not the compilation was successful, information about the compilation can be obtained from the shader object's information log with **glGetShaderInfoLog**.

The OpenGL Shading Language has compilation rules that are slightly different depending on the type of shader being compiled, and so the compilation takes into consideration whether the shader is a vertex shader or a fragment shader.

Information about the compile operation can be obtained by calling **glGetShaderInfoLog** (described in Section 7.6) with *shader*, but the information log should not be used as an indication of whether the compilation was successful. If the shader object was compiled successfully, either the information log is an empty string or it contains information about the compile operation. If the shader object was not compiled successfully, the information log contains information about any lexical, grammatical, or semantic errors that occurred, along with warning messages and any other information the compiler deems pertinent.

7.4 Linking and Using Shaders

Each shader object is compiled independently. To create a program, applications need a mechanism for specifying a list of shader objects to be linked. You can specify the list of shaders objects to be linked by creating a program object and attaching to it all the shader objects needed to create the program.

To create a program object, use the following command:

GLuint **glCreateProgram**(void)

Creates an empty program object and returns a nonzero value by which it can be referenced. A program object is an object to which shader objects can be attached. This provides a mechanism to specify the shader objects that will be linked to create a program. It also provides a means for checking the compatibility between shaders that will be used to create a program (for instance, checking the compatibility between a vertex shader and a fragment shader). When no longer needed as part of a program object, shader objects can be detached.

After the program object has been defined, shader objects can be attached to it. Attaching simply means creating a reference to the shader object so that it will be included when an attempt to link a program object is made. This is the application's way of describing the recipe for creating a program. The command to attach a shader object to a program object is

---

void **glAttachShader**(GLuint *program*,

GLuint *shader*)

Attaches the shader object specified by *shader* to the program object specified by *program*. This indicates that *shader* will be included in link operations that are performed on *program*.

There is no inherent limit on the number of shader objects that can be attached to a program object. All operations that can be performed on a shader object are valid whether or not the shader object is attached to a program object. It is permissible to attach a shader object to a program object before source code has been loaded into the shader object or before the shader object has been compiled. It is also permissible to attach a shader object to more than one program object. In other words, **glAttachShader** simply specifies the set of shader objects to be linked.

To create a valid program, all the shader objects attached to a program object must be compiled, and the program object itself must be linked. The link operation assigns locations for uniform variables, initializes user-defined uniform variables, resolves references between independently compiled shader objects, and checks to make sure the vertex and fragment shaders are compatible with one another. To link a program object, use the command

---

void **glLinkProgram**(GLuint *program*)

Links the program object specified by *program*. If any shader objects of type GL_VERTEX_SHADER are attached to *program*, they are used to create an executable that will run on the programmable vertex processor. If any shader objects of type GL_FRAGMENT_SHADER are attached to *program*, they are used to create an executable that will run on the programmable fragment processor.

The status of the link operation is stored as part of the program object's state. This value is set to GL_TRUE if the program object was linked without errors and is ready for use and set to GL_FALSE otherwise. It can be queried by calling **glGetProgram** with arguments *program* and GL_LINK_STATUS.

As a result of a successful link operation, all active user-defined uniform variables (see Section 7.8) belonging to *program* are initialized to 0, and each of the program object's active uniform variables is assigned a location that can be queried with **glGetUniformLocation**. Also, any active user-defined attribute variables (see Section 7.7) that have not been bound to a generic vertex attribute index are bound to one at this time.

If *program* contains shader objects of type GL_VERTEX_SHADER but it does not contain shader objects of type GL_FRAGMENT_SHADER, the vertex shader is linked to the implicit interface for fixed functionality fragment processing. Similarly, if *program* contains shader objects of type GL_FRAGMENT_SHADER but it does not contain shader objects of type GL_VERTEX_SHADER, the fragment shader is linked to the implicit interface for fixed functionality vertex processing.

glLinkProgram also installs the generated executables as part of the current rendering state if the link operation was successful and the specified program object is already currently in use as a result of a previous call to **glUseProgram**. If the program object currently in use is relinked unsuccessfully, its link status is set to GL_FALSE, but the previously generated executables and associated state remain part of the current state until a subsequent call to **glUseProgram** removes them. After they are removed, they cannot be made part of current state until the program object has been successfully relinked.

Linking of a program object can fail for a number of reasons.

- The number of active attribute variables supported by the implementation has been exceeded.

- The number of active uniform variables supported by the implementation has been exceeded.

- The **main** function is missing for the vertex shader or the fragment shader.

- An in variable actually used in the fragment shader is not declared as an out variable with the same type (or is not declared at all) in the vertex shader.

- A reference to a function or variable name is unresolved.

- A shared global is declared with two different types or two different initial values.

- One or more of the attached shader objects has not been successfully compiled.

- Binding a generic attribute matrix caused some rows of the matrix to fall outside the allowed maximum of GL_MAX_VERTEX_ATTRIBS.

- Not enough contiguous vertex attribute slots could be found to bind attribute matrices.

The program object's information log is updated at the time of the link operation. If the link operation is successful, a program is generated. It may contain an executable for the vertex processor, an executable for the fragment processor, or both. Whether the link operation succeeds or fails, the information and executables from the previous link operation will be lost. After the link operation, applications are free to modify attached shader objects, compile attached shader objects, detach shader objects, and attach additional shader objects. None of these operations affect the information log or the program that is part of the program object until the next link operation on the program object.

Information about the link operation can be obtained by calling **glGetProgramInfoLog** (described in Section 7.6) with *program*. If the program object was linked successfully, the information log either is an empty string or contains information about the link operation. If the program object was not linked successfully, the information log contains information about any link errors that occurred, along with warning messages and any other information the linker chooses to provide.

When the link operation has completed successfully, the program it contains can be installed as part of the current rendering state. The command to install the program as part of the rendering state is

---

void **glUseProgram**(GLuint *program*)

Installs the program object specified by *program* as part of current rendering state.

A program object contains an executable that will run on the vertex processor if it contains one or more shader objects of type GL_VERTEX_SHADER that have been successfully compiled and linked. Similarly, a program object contains an executable that will run on the fragment processor if it contains one or more shader objects of subtype GL_FRAGMENT_SHADER that have been successfully compiled and linked.

If *program* contains shader objects of type GL_VERTEX_SHADER but it does not contain shader objects of type GL_FRAGMENT_SHADER, an executable is installed on the vertex processor but fixed functionality is used for fragment processing. Similarly, if *program* contains shader objects of type GL_FRAGMENT_SHADER but it does not contain shader objects of type GL_VERTEX_SHADER, an executable is installed on the fragment processor but fixed functionality is used for vertex processing. If *program* is 0, the programmable processors are disabled, and fixed functionality is used for both vertex and fragment processing.

Successfully installing an executable on a programmable processor causes the corresponding fixed functionality of OpenGL to be disabled. Specifically, if an executable is installed on the vertex processor, the OpenGL fixed functionality is disabled as described in Section 4.1. Similarly, if an executable is installed on the fragment processor, the OpenGL fixed functionality is disabled as described in Section 4.2.

While a program object is in use, applications are free to modify attached shader objects, compile attached shader objects, attach additional shader objects, detach shader objects, delete any shader objects attached, or delete the program object itself. None of these operations affect the executables that are part of the current state. However, relinking the program object that is currently in use installs the program as part of the current rendering state if the link operation was successful. While a program object is in use, the state that controls the disabled fixed functionality can also be updated with the normal OpenGL calls.

7.5 Cleaning Up

Objects should be deleted when they are no longer needed, and deletion
can be accomplished with the following commands:

---

void **glDeleteShader**(GLuint *shader*)

Frees the memory and invalidates the name associated with the shader
object specified by *shader*. This command effectively undoes the effects of
a call to **glCreateShader**.

If a shader object to be deleted is attached to a program object, it will be
flagged for deletion, but it will not be deleted until it is no longer attached
to any program object for any rendering context (i.e., it must be detached
from wherever it was attached before it can be deleted). A value of 0 for
shader is silently ignored.

To determine whether a shader object has been flagged for deletion, call
glGetShader with arguments *shader* and GL_DELETE_STATUS.

---

void **glDeleteProgram**(GLuint *program*)

Frees the memory and invalidates the name associated with the program
object specified by *program*. This command effectively undoes the effects
of a call to **glCreateProgram**.

If a program object is in use as part of a current rendering state, it will be
flagged for deletion, but it will not be deleted until it is no longer part of
current state for any rendering context. If a program object to be deleted
has shader objects attached to it, those shader objects are automatically
detached but not deleted unless they have already been flagged for deletion
by a previous call to **glDeleteShader**.

To determine whether a program object has been flagged for deletion, call
glGetProgram with arguments *program* and GL_DELETE_STATUS.

When a shader object no longer needs to be attached to a program object,
it can be detached with the command

---

void **glDetachShader**(GLuint *program*, GLuint *shader*)

Detaches the shader object specified by *shader* from the program object
specified by *program*. This command undoes the effect of the command
glAttachShader.

If *shader* has already been flagged for deletion by a call to **glDeleteShader**
and it is not attached to any other program object, it is deleted after it has
been detached.

A programming tip that might be useful in keeping things orderly is to delete shader objects as soon as they have been attached to a program object. They won't be deleted at this time, but they will be flagged for deletion when they are no longer referenced. To clean up later, the application only needs to delete the program object. All the attached shader objects will be automatically detached, and, because they are flagged for deletion, they will be automatically deleted at that time as well.

7.6 Query Functions

The OpenGL Shading Language API contains several functions for querying object state. To obtain information about a shader object, use the following command:

---

void **glGetShaderiv**(GLuint *shader*,

GLenum *pname*,

GLint **params*)

Returns in *params* the value of a parameter for a specific shader object. This function returns information about a shader object. Permitted parameters and their meanings are described in Table 7.1. In this table, the value for *pname* is shown on the left, and the operation performed is shown on the right.

Table 7.1 Queriable shader object parameters

Parameter	Operation
GL_SHADER_TYPE	*params* returns a value of either GL_VERTEX_SHADER or GL_FRAGMENT_SHADER, depending on whether *shader* is the name of a vertex shader object or a fragment shader object.
GL_DELETE_STATUS	*params* returns GL_TRUE if *shader* is currently flagged for deletion, and GL_FALSE otherwise.
GL_COMPILE_STATUS	*params* returns GL_TRUE if the last compile operation on *shader* was successful, and GL_FALSE otherwise.

(continues)

Table 7.1 Queriable shader object parameters, *continued*

Parameter	Operation
GL_INFO_LOG_LENGTH	*params* returns the number of characters in the information log for *shader*, including the null termination character. If the object has no information log, a value of 0 is returned.
GL_SHADER_SOURCE_LENGTH	*params* returns the length of the concatenation of the source strings that make up the shader source for *shader*, including the null termination character. If no source code exists, 0 is returned.

A similar function is provided for querying the state of a program object: the status of an operation on a program object, the number of attached shader objects, the number of active attributes (see Section 7.7), the number of active uniform variables (see Section 7.8), or the length of any of the strings maintained by a program object. The command to obtain information about a program object is

void **glGetProgramiv**(GLuint *program*,
GLenum *pname*,
GLint **params*)

Returns in *params* the value of a parameter for a particular program object. This function returns information about a program object. Permitted parameters and their meanings are described in Table 7.2. In this table, the value for *pname* is shown on the left, and the operation performed is shown on the right.

Table 7.2 Queriable program object parameters

Parameter	Operation
GL_DELETE_STATUS	*params* returns GL_TRUE if *program* is currently flagged for deletion, and GL_FALSE otherwise.
GL_LINK_STATUS	*params* returns GL_TRUE if the last link operation on *program* was successful, and GL_FALSE otherwise.

Table 7.2 Queriable program object parameters, *continued*

Parameter	Operation
GL_VALIDATE_STATUS	*params* returns GL_TRUE if the last validation operation on *program* was successful, and GL_FALSE otherwise.
GL_INFO_LOG_LENGTH	*params* returns the number of characters in the information log for *program*, including the null termination character. If the object has no information log, a value of 0 is returned.
GL_ATTACHED_SHADERS	*params* returns the number of shader objects attached to *program*.
GL_ACTIVE_ATTRIBUTES	*params* returns the number of active attribute variables for *program*.
GL_ACTIVE_ATTRIBUTE_MAX_LENGTH	*params* returns the length of the longest active attribute variable name for *program*, including the null termination character. If no active attribute variables exist, 0 is returned.
GL_ACTIVE_UNIFORMS	*params* returns the number of active uniform variables for *program*.
GL_ACTIVE_UNIFORM_MAX_LENGTH	*params* returns the length of the longest active uniform variable name for *program*, including the null termination character. If no active uniform variables exist, 0 is returned.

The command to obtain the current shader string from a shader object is

---

void **glGetShaderSource**(GLuint *shader*

GLsizei *bufSize*,

GLsizei **length*,

GLchar **source*)

Returns a concatenation of the source code strings from the shader object specified by *shader*. The source code strings for a shader object are the result of a previous call to **glShaderSource**. The string returned by the function is null terminated.

glGetShaderSource returns in *source* as much of the source code string as
it can, up to a maximum of *bufSize* characters. The number of characters
actually returned, excluding the null termination character, is specified by
length. If the length of the returned string is not required, a value of NULL
can be passed in the *length* argument. The size of the buffer required to store
the returned source code string can be obtained by calling **glGetShader**
with the value GL_SHADER_SOURCE_LENGTH.

Information about the compilation operation is stored in the information
log for a shader object. Similarly, information about the link and validation
operations is stored in the information log for a program object. The information log is a string that contains diagnostic messages and warnings. The
information log may contain information useful during application development even if the compilation or link operation was successful. The information log is typically useful only during application development, and an
application should not expect different OpenGL implementations to produce identical descriptions of error. To obtain the information log for a
shader object, call

---

void **glGetShaderInfoLog**(GLuint *shader*,

GLsizei *maxLength*,

GLsizei **length*,

GLchar **infoLog*)

Returns the information log for the specified shader object. The information
log for a shader object is modified when the shader is compiled. The string
that is returned is null terminated.

glGetShaderInfoLog returns in *infoLog* as much of the information log
as it can, up to a maximum of *maxLength* characters. The number of
characters actually returned, excluding the null termination character, is
specified by *length*. If the length of the returned string is not required, a
value of NULL can be passed in the *length* argument. The size of the buffer
required to store the returned information log can be obtained by calling
glGetShader with the value GL_INFO_LOG_LENGTH.

The information log for a shader object is a string that may contain
diagnostic messages, warning messages, and other information about the
last compile operation. When a shader object is created, its information log
is a string of length 0.

To obtain the information log for a program object, call

---

void **glGetProgramInfoLog**(GLuint *program*,

GLsizei *maxLength*,

GLsizei **length*,

GLchar **infoLog*)

Returns the information log for the specified program object. The information log for a program object is modified when the program object is linked or validated. The string that is returned is null terminated.

glGetProgramInfoLog returns in *infoLog* as much of the information log as it can, up to a maximum of *maxLength* characters. The number of characters actually returned, excluding the null termination character, is specified by *length*. If the length of the returned string is not required, a value of NULL can be passed in the *length* argument. The size of the buffer required to store the returned information log can be obtained by calling **glGetProgram** with the value GL_INFO_LOG_LENGTH.

The information log for a program object is an empty string, a string containing information about the last link operation, or a string containing information about the last validation operation. It may contain diagnostic messages, warning messages, and other information. When a program object is created, its information log is a string of length 0.

The way the API is set up, you first need to perform a query to find out the length of the information log (number of characters in the string). After allocating a buffer of the appropriate size, you can call **glGetShaderInfoLog** or **glGetProgramInfoLog** to put the information log string into the allocated buffer. You can then print it if you want to do so. Listing 7.2 shows a C function that does all this for a shader object. The code for obtaining the information log for a program object is almost identical.

Listing 7.2 C function to print the information log for an object

```
void printShaderInfoLog(GLuint shader)
{
    int infologLen = 0;
    int charsWritten = 0;
    GLchar *infoLog;

    glGetShaderiv(shader, GL_INFO_LOG_LENGTH, &infologLen);

    printOpenGLError();  // Check for OpenGL errors

    if (infologLen > 0)
    {
        infoLog = (GLchar*) malloc(infologLen);
        if (infoLog == NULL)
```

```
        {
            printf("ERROR: Could not allocate InfoLog buffer\n");
            exit(1);
        }
        glGetShaderInfoLog(shader, infologLen, &charsWritten, infoLog);
        printf("InfoLog:\n%s\n\n", infoLog);
        free(infoLog);
    }
    printOpenGLError();  // Check for OpenGL errors
}
```

You can obtain the program object that is currently in use by calling **glGet** with the symbolic constant GL_CURRENT_PROGRAM.

The command to query a list of shader objects attached to a particular program object is

---

void **glGetAttachedShaders**(GLuint *program*,

GLsizei *maxCount*,

GLsizei **count*,

GLuint **shaders*)

Returns the handles of the shader objects attached to *program*. It returns in *shaders* as many of the handles of these shader objects as it can, up to a maximum of *maxCount*. The number of handles actually returned is specified by *count*. If the number of handles actually returned is not required (for instance, if it has just been obtained with **glGetProgram**), a value of NULL may be passed for *count*. If no shader objects are attached to *program*, a value of 0 is returned in *count*. The actual number of attached shaders can be obtained by calling **glGetProgram** with the value GL_ATTACHED_ SHADERS.

Two new functions have been added to determine whether an object is a shader object or a program object. These functions may be useful if you have to process an object (for instance, to print its information log) without knowing whether it is a valid shader or program object. These two functions are defined as

---

GLboolean **glIsShader**(GLuint *shader*)

Returns GL_TRUE if *shader* is the name of a shader object. If *shader* is zero or a nonzero value that is not the name of a shader object, **glIsShader** returns GL_FALSE.

GLboolean **glIsProgram**(GLuint *program*)

Returns GL_TRUE if *program* is the name of a program object. If *program* is zero or a nonzero value that is not the name of a program object, **glIsProgram** returns GL_FALSE.

7.7 Specifying Vertex Attributes

The brave new world of programmability means that applications no longer need to be limited to the standard vertex attributes like normal or color once defined by OpenGL. There are many per-vertex attributes that applications might like to pass into a vertex shader. It is easy to imagine that, in addition to normal or color, applications will want to specify per-vertex data such as tangents, temperature, pressure, and who knows what else. How do we allow applications to pass nontraditional attributes to OpenGL and operate on them in vertex shaders?

The answer is that OpenGL provides a small number of generic locations, sometimes called CURRENT VERTEX STATE, for passing in vertex attributes. Each location is numbered and has room to store up to four floating-point components (i.e., it is a **vec4**). An implementation that supports 16 attribute locations will have them numbered from 0 to 15. An application can pass a vertex attribute into any of the generic numbered slots by using one of the following functions:

void **glVertexAttrib{1|2|3|4}{s|f|d}**(GLuint *index*, *TYPE v*)

void **glVertexAttrib{1|2|3}{s|f|d}v**(GLuint *index*, const *TYPE *v*)

void **glVertexAttrib4{b|s|i|f|d|ub|us|ui}v**(GLuint *index*, const *TYPE *v*)

Sets the generic vertex attribute specified by *index* to the value specified by *v.* This command can have up to three suffixes that differentiate variations of the parameters accepted. The first suffix can be 1, 2, 3, or 4 to specify whether *v* contains 1, 2, 3, or 4 components. If the second and third components are not provided, they are assumed to be 0, and if the fourth component is not provided, it is assumed to be 1. The second suffix indicates the data type of *v* and may specify byte (**b**), short (**s**), int (**i**), float (**f**), double (**d**), unsigned byte (**ub**), unsigned short (**us**), or unsigned int (**ui**). The third suffix is an optional **v** meaning that *v* is a pointer to an array of values of the specified data type.

This set of commands has a certain set of rules for converting data to the floating-point internal representation specified by OpenGL. Floats and doubles are mapped into OpenGL internal floating-point values as you would expect, and integer values are converted to floats by a decimal point added to the right of the value provided. Thus, a value of 27 for a byte, int, short, unsigned byte, unsigned int, or unsigned short becomes a value of 27.0 for computation within OpenGL.

Another set of entry points supports the passing of normalized values as generic vertex attributes:

---

void **glVertexAttrib4Nub**(GLuint *index*, *TYPE v*)

void **glVertexAttrib4N{b|s|i|f|d|ub|us|ui}v**(GLuint *index*, const *TYPE *v*)

Sets the generic vertex attribute specified by *index* to the normalized value specified by *v*. In addition to **N** (to indicate normalized values), this command can have two suffixes that differentiate variations of the parameters accepted. The first suffix indicates the data type of *v* and specifies byte (**b**), short (**s**), int (**i**), float (**f**), double (**d**), unsigned byte (**ub**), unsigned short (**us**), or unsigned int (**ui**). The second suffix is an optional **v** meaning that *v* is a pointer to an array of values of the specified data type.

N in a command name indicates that, for data types other than float or double, the arguments will be linearly mapped to a normalized range in the same way as data provided to the integer variants of **glColor** or **glNormal**— that is, for signed integer variants of the functions, the most positive, representable value maps to 1.0, and the most negative representable value maps to –1.0. For the unsigned integer variants, the largest representable value maps to 1.0, and the smallest representable value maps to 0.

Attribute variables are allowed to be of type **mat2**, **mat3**, or **mat4**. Attributes of these types can be loaded with the **glVertexAttrib** entry points. Matrices must be loaded into successive generic attribute slots in column major order, with one column of the matrix in each generic attribute slot. Thus, to load a **mat4** attribute, you would load the first column in generic attribute slot *i*, the second in slot *i* + 1, the third in slot *i* + 2, and the fourth in slot *i* + 3.

Applications more commonly specify vertices with the vertex array interface instead. This interface allows you to store vertex data in vertex buffers and set offsets to those buffers. Instead of sending one vertex at a time to OpenGL, you can send a whole set of primitives at a time. With vertex buffer objects, it is even possible that vertex data is stored in memory on the graphics board to exact maximum performance.

When a vertex buffer is sent to OpenGL, the vertex data in the vertex buffer is processed one vertex at a time, with each generic vertex attribute copied to an in variable in the vertex shader.

The vertex array API allows generic vertex attributes to be specified as vertex arrays. The following call establishes the vertex array pointer for a generic vertex attribute:

---

void **glVertexAttribPointer**(GLuint *index*,

GLint *size*,

GLenum *type*,

GLboolean *normalized*,

GLsizei *stride*,

const GLvoid **pointer*)

Specifies the location and data format of an array of generic vertex attribute values to use when rendering. The generic vertex attribute array to be specified is indicated by *index*. *size* specifies the number of components per attribute and must be 1, 2, 3, or 4. *type* specifies the data type of each component (GL_BYTE, GL_UNSIGNED_BYTE, GL_SHORT, GL_UNSIGNED_SHORT, GL_INT, GL_UNSIGNED_INT, GL_FLOAT, or GL_DOUBLE). *stride* specifies the byte stride from one attribute to the next, allowing attribute values to be intermixed with other attribute values or stored in a separate array. A value of 0 for *stride* means that the values are stored sequentially in memory with no gaps between successive elements. If set to GL_TRUE, *normalize* specifies that values stored in an integer format are to be mapped to the range [–1.0,1.0] (for signed values) or [0.0,1.0] (for unsigned values) when they are accessed and converted to floating point. Otherwise, values are converted to floats directly without normalization. *pointer* is the memory address of the first generic vertex attribute in the vertex array.

After the vertex array information has been specified for a generic vertex attribute array, the array needs to be enabled. When enabled, the generic vertex attribute data in the specified array is provided along with other enabled vertex array data when vertex array drawing commands such as **glDrawArrays** are called. To enable or disable a generic vertex attribute array, use the commands

---

void **glEnableVertexAttribArray**(GLuint *index*)

void **glDisableVertexAttribArray**(GLuint *index*)

Enables or disables the generic vertex attribute array specified by *index*. By default, all client-side capabilities are disabled, including all generic vertex attribute arrays. If enabled, the values in the generic vertex attribute array are accessed and used for rendering when calls are made to vertex array commands such as **glArrayElement**, **glDrawArrays**, **glDrawElements**, **glDrawRangeElements**, **glMultiDrawArrays**, or **glMultiDrawElements**.

This solves the question of how generic vertex data is passed into OpenGL, but how do we access that data from within a vertex shader? We don't want to refer to these numbered locations in our shader, because this approach is not very descriptive and is prone to errors. The OpenGL Shading Language API provides two ways for associating generic vertex indices with vertex shader attribute variables.

The first way is to let the linker assign the bindings automatically. In this case, the application would need to query OpenGL after linking to determine the generic vertex indices that were assigned and then would use these indices when passing the attributes to OpenGL.

The second way is for the application to choose the index value of the generic vertex attribute to be used and explicitly bind it to a specific attribute variable in the vertex shader by using the following function before linking occurs:

---

void **glBindAttribLocation**(GLuint *program*,

GLuint *index*,

const GLchar **name*)

Associates a user-defined attribute variable in the program object specified by *program* with a generic vertex attribute index. The name of the user-defined attribute variable is passed as a null-terminated string in *name*. If *name* was bound previously, that information is lost. Thus, you cannot bind one user-defined attribute variable to multiple indices, but you can bind multiple user-defined attribute variables to the same index. The generic vertex attribute index to be bound to this variable is specified by *index*. When *program* is made part of current state, values provided through the generic vertex attribute *index* modify the value of the user-defined attribute variable specified by *name*.

If *name* refers to a matrix attribute variable, *index* refers to the first column of the matrix. Other matrix columns are then automatically bound to locations *index+1* for a matrix of type **mat2**; *index+1* and *index+2* for a matrix of type **mat3**; and *index+1*, *index+2*, and *index+3* for a matrix of type **mat4**.

Applications are not allowed to bind any of the standard OpenGL vertex attributes with this command because they are bound automatically when needed. Any attribute binding that occurs after the program object has been linked does not take effect until the next time the program object is linked.

glBindAttribLocation can be called before any vertex shader objects are attached to the specified program object. It is also permissible to bind an attribute variable name that is never used in a vertex shader to a generic attribute index.

Applications are allowed to bind more than one vertex shader attribute name to the same generic vertex attribute index. This is called ATTRIBUTE ALIASING, and it is allowed only if just one of the aliased attributes is active in the executable program or if no path through the shader consumes more than one attribute of a set of attributes aliased to the same location. Another way of saying this is that more than one attribute name may be bound to a generic attribute index if, in the end, only one name is used to access the generic attribute in the vertex shader. The compiler and linker are allowed to assume that no aliasing is done and are free to employ optimizations that work only in the absence of aliasing. OpenGL implementations are not required to do error checking to detect attribute aliasing.

The binding between an attribute variable name and a generic attribute index can be specified at any time with **glBindAttribLocation**. Attribute bindings do not go into effect until **glLinkProgram** is called, so any attribute variables that need to be bound explicitly for a particular use of a shader should be bound before the link operation occurs. After a program object has been linked successfully, the index values for attribute variables remain fixed (and their values can be queried) until the next link command occurs. To query the attribute binding for a named vertex shader attribute variable, use **glGetAttribLocation**. It returns the binding that actually went into effect the last time **glLinkProgram** was called for the specified program object. Attribute bindings that have been specified since the last link operation are not returned by **glGetAttribLocation**.

GLint **glGetAttribLocation**(GLuint *program*,
                 const GLchar **name*)

Queries the previously linked program object specified by *program* for the attribute variable specified by *name* and returns the index of the generic vertex attribute that is bound to that attribute variable. If *name* is a matrix attribute variable, the index of the first column of the matrix is returned. If the named attribute variable is not an active attribute in the specified program object or if *name* starts with the reserved prefix "*gl_*", a value of –1 is returned.

Using these functions, we can create a vertex shader that contains a user-defined attribute variable named *Opacity* that is used directly in the lighting calculations. We can decide that we want to pass per-vertex opacity values in generic attribute location 1 and set up the proper binding with the following line of code:

```
glBindAttribLocation(myProgram, 1, "Opacity");
```

Subsequently, we can call **glVertexAttrib** to pass a single opacity value to every vertex:

```
glVertexAttrib1f(1, opacity);
```

Or we can call **glEnableVertexAttribArray** to pass potentially different opacity values to every vertex:

```
glEnableVertexAttribArray(1);
```

The jargon in this section can get a little confusing, so let's look at a diagram to make sure we have things straight. Let's look at the case of generic vertex attributes as illustrated in Figure 7.1. A user-defined in variable must be bound to a generic vertex attribute index. This binding can be done with **glBindAttribLocation**, or it can happen implicitly at link time.

Let's assume we have a vertex shader that uses three user-defined in variables: *Opacity*, *Binormal*, and *MyData*. These are shown on the right side of Figure 7.1. These user-defined in variables can each be bound to a generic vertex attribute index as follows:

```
glBindAttribLocation(myProgram, 1, "Opacity");
glBindAttribLocation(myProgram, 2, "Binormal");
glBindAttribLocation(myProgram, 3, "MyData");
```

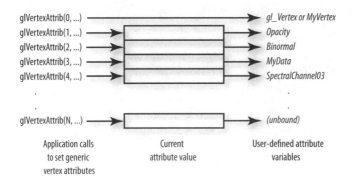

Figure 7.1 Mapping of generic vertex attribute commands to user-defined attribute variables

This sets up the mapping so that values written into generic vertex attribute locations 1, 2, and 3 will modify the values of the in variables *Opacity*, *Binormal*, and *MyData* in the vertex shader. The diagram shows that generic vertex attribute index *N* is not currently bound to any user-defined in variable.

As mentioned, each of the generic attribute locations has enough room for four floating-point components. Applications are permitted to store 1, 2, 3, or 4 components in each location. A vertex shader may access a single location by using a user-defined in variable that is a **float**, a **vec2**, a **vec3**, or a **vec4**. It may access two consecutive locations by using a user-defined in variable that is a **mat2**, three using a **mat3**, and four using a **mat4**.

The bindings between generic attribute index values and user-defined in variables (i.e., the arrows on the right side of Figure 7.1) are part of the state maintained within a program object, whereas the contents of the attribute array itself is considered current attribute state. The application can provide a different program object and specify different names and mappings for attribute variables in the vertex shader, and if no calls have been made to update the attribute values in the interim, the attribute variables in the new vertex shader get the values left behind by the previous one.

Attribute variables that can be accessed when a vertex shader is executed are called ACTIVE ATTRIBUTES. To obtain information about an active attribute, use the following command:

---

void **glGetActiveAttrib**(GLuint *program*,

GLuint *index*,

GLsizei *bufSize*,

GLsizei **length*,

GLint **size*,

GLenum **type*,

GLchar **name*)

Returns information about an active attribute variable in the program object specified by *program*. The number of active attributes in a program object can be obtained by calling **glGetProgram** with the value GL_ ACTIVE_ATTRIBUTES. A value of 0 for *index* causes information about the first active attribute variable to be returned. Permissible values for *index* range from 0 to the number of active attributes minus 1.

A vertex shader can use built-in attribute variables, user-defined attribute variables, or both. Built-in attribute variables have a prefix of "*gl_*" and reference conventional OpenGL vertex attributes (e.g., *gl_Vertex*, *gl_Normal*, etc.; see Section 4.1.1 for a complete list). User-defined attribute variables have arbitrary names and obtain their values through numbered generic vertex attributes. An attribute variable (either built-in or user-defined) is considered active if it is determined during the link operation that it can be accessed during program execution. Therefore, *program* should have previously been the target of a call to **glLinkProgram,** but it is not necessary for it to have been linked successfully.

The size of the character buffer needed to store the longest attribute variable name in *program* can be obtained by calling **glGetProgram** with the value GL_ACTIVE_ATTRIBUTE_MAX_LENGTH. This value should be used to allocate a buffer of sufficient size to store the returned attribute name. The size of this character buffer is passed in *bufSize*, and a pointer to this character buffer is passed in *name*.

glGetActiveAttrib returns the name of the attribute variable indicated by *index*, storing it in the character buffer specified by *name*. The string returned is null terminated. The actual number of characters written into this buffer is returned in *length*, and this count does not include the null termination character. If the length of the returned string is not required, a value of NULL can be passed in the *length* argument.

The *type* argument returns a pointer to the attribute variable's data type. The symbolic constants GL_FLOAT, GL_FLOAT_VEC2, GL_FLOAT_VEC3, GL_FLOAT_VEC4, GL_FLOAT_MAT2, GL_FLOAT_MAT3, and GL_FLOAT_MAT4 may be returned. The *size* argument returns the size of the attribute in units of the type returned in *type*.

The list of active attribute variables may include both built-in attribute variables (which begin with the prefix "*gl_*") as well as user-defined attribute variable names.

This function returns as much information as it can about the specified active attribute variable. If no information is available, *length* is 0 and *name* is an empty string. This situation could occur if this function is called after a link operation that failed. If an error occurs, the return values *length*, *size*, *type*, and *name* are unmodified.

The **glGetActiveAttrib** command can be useful in an environment in which shader development occurs separately from application development. If some attribute-naming conventions are agreed to between the shader writers and the application developers, the latter could query the program object at runtime to determine the attributes that are actually needed and could pass those down. This approach can provide more flexibility in the shader development process.

To query the state of a particular generic vertex attribute, call one of the following commands:

---

void **glGetVertexAttribfv**(GLuint *index*,

GLenum *pname*,

GLfloat **params*)

void **glGetVertexAttribiv**(GLuint *index*,

GLenum *pname*,

GLint **params*)

void **glGetVertexAttribdv**(GLuint *index*,

GLenum *pname*,

GLdouble **params*)

Returns in *params* the value of a generic vertex attribute parameter. The generic vertex attribute to be queried is specified by *index*, and the parameter to be queried is specified by *pname*. Parameters and return values are summarized in Table 7.3. All the parameters except GL_CURRENT_VERTEX_ATTRIB represent client-side state.

Table 7.3 Generic vertex attribute parameters

Parameter	Operation
GL_VERTEX_ATTRIB_ARRAY_ENABLED	*params* returns a single value that is nonzero (true) if the vertex attribute array for *index* is enabled and 0 (false) if it is disabled. The initial value is GL_FALSE.
GL_VERTEX_ATTRIB_ARRAY_SIZE	*params* returns a single value, the size of the vertex attribute array for *index*. The size is the number of values for each element of the vertex attribute array, and it is 1, 2, 3, or 4. The initial value is 4.
GL_VERTEX_ATTRIB_ARRAY_STRIDE	*params* returns a single value, the array stride (number of bytes between successive elements) for the vertex attribute array for *index*. A value of 0 indicates that the array elements are stored sequentially in memory. The initial value is 0.
GL_VERTEX_ATTRIB_ARRAY_TYPE	*params* returns a single value, a symbolic constant indicating the array type for the vertex attribute array for *index*. Possible values are GL_BYTE, GL_UNSIGNED_BYTE, GL_SHORT, GL_UNSIGNED_SHORT, GL_INT, GL_UNSIGNED_INT, GL_FLOAT, and GL_DOUBLE. The initial value is GL_FLOAT.

(continues)

Table 7.3 Generic vertex attribute parameters, *continued*

Parameter	Operation
GL_VERTEX_ATTRIB_ARRAY_NORMALIZED	*params* returns a single value that is nonzero (true) if fixed-point data types for the vertex attribute array indicated by *index* are normalized when they are converted to floating point and 0 (false) otherwise. The initial value is GL_FALSE.
GL_CURRENT_VERTEX_ATTRIB	*params* returns four values that represent the current value for the generic vertex attribute specified by *index*. Generic vertex attribute 0 is unique in that it has no current state, so an error is generated if *index* is 0. The initial value for all other generic vertex attributes is (0, 0, 0, 1).

---

void **glGetVertexAttribPointerv**(GLuint *index*,

GLenum *pname*,

GLvoid ***pointer)

Returns pointer information. *index* is the generic vertex attribute to be queried, *pname* is a symbolic constant specifying the pointer to be returned, and *params* is a pointer to a location in which to place the returned data. The only accepted value for *pname* is GL_VERTEX_ATTRIB_ARRAY_POINTER. This causes *params* to return a single value that is a pointer to the vertex attribute array for the generic vertex attribute specified by *index*.

7.8 Specifying Uniform Variables

As described in the previous section, attribute variables provide frequently modified data to the vertex shader. Less frequently changing data can be specified using uniform variables. Uniform variables are declared within a shader and can be loaded directly by the application. This lets applications provide any type of arbitrary data to a shader. Applications can modify these values as often as every primitive in order to modify the behavior of the shader (although performance may suffer if this is done). Typically, uniform variables are used to supply state that stays constant for many primitives.

The basic model for specifying uniform variables is different from the model for specifying attribute variables. As discussed in the preceding section, for attribute variables, the application can specify the attribute location before linking occurs. In contrast, the locations or offsets of uniform variables cannot be specified by the application. Instead, they are always determined by OpenGL at link time. As a result, applications need to query the uniform location or offset after linking occurs.

Uniforms are gathered together into uniform blocks. There are two types of uniform blocks in OpenGL, the default uniform block and named uniform blocks.

7.8.1 Default Uniform Block

The default uniform block contains all the uniform variables that are declared outside of named uniform blocks. Any uniforms may be in the default uniform block, though any uniform of sampler type must be in the default uniform block.

One advantage of the default uniform block is that the uniform storage is associated with the program object, so the default uniform block is best for uniforms closely associated with an individual shader. One disadvantage of the default uniform block is that changing a uniform value is relatively expensive, so uniforms in the default uniform block are best reserved for infrequently changing uniform values.

To update the value of a user-defined uniform variable, an application needs to determine its location and then specify its value. The locations of uniform variables are assigned at link time and do not change until the next link operation occurs. Each time linking occurs, the locations of uniform variables may change, and so the application must query them again before setting them. The locations of the user-defined uniform variables in a program object can be queried with the following command:

GLint **glGetUniformLocation**(GLuint *program*,

const GLchar **name*)

Returns an integer that represents the location of a specific uniform variable within a program object. *name* must be a null-terminated string that contains no white space. *name* must be an active uniform variable name in *program* that is not a structure, an array of structures, or a subcomponent of a vector or a matrix. This function returns –1 if *name* does not correspond to an active uniform variable in *program*, if *name* is associated with a named uniform block, or if *name* starts with the reserved prefix "*gl_*".

Uniform variables that are structures or arrays of structures can be queried with **glGetUniformLocation** for each field within the structure. The array element operator "[]" and the structure field operator "." can be used in *name* to select elements within an array or fields within a structure. The result of using these operators is not allowed to be another structure, an array of structures, or a subcomponent of a vector or a matrix. Except if the last part of *name* indicates a uniform variable array, the location of the first element of an array can be retrieved with the name of the array or with the name appended by "[0]".

The actual locations assigned to uniform variables are not known until the program object is linked successfully. After linking has occurred, the command **glGetUniformLocation** can obtain the location of a uniform variable. This location value can then be passed to **glUniform** to set the value of the uniform variable or to **glGetUniform** in order to query the current value of the uniform variable. After a program object has been linked successfully, the index values for uniform variables remain fixed until the next link command occurs. Uniform variable locations and values can be queried after a link only if the link was successful.

Loading of user-defined uniform values is possible only for the program object that is currently in use. All user-defined uniform variables are initialized when a program object is successfully linked, either to an explicit default or to 0. User-defined uniform values are part of the state of a program object. Their values can be modified only when the program object is part of current rendering state, but the values of uniform variables are preserved as the program object is swapped in and out of current state. The following commands load uniform variables into the program object that is currently in use:

---

void **glUniform{1|2|3|4}{f|i}**(GLint *location*, *TYPE v*)

Sets the user-defined uniform variable or uniform variable array specified by *location* to the value specified by *v*. The suffix **1**, **2**, **3**, or **4** indicates whether *v* contains 1, 2, 3, or 4 components. This value should match the number of components in the data type of the specified uniform variable (e.g., **1** for **float**, **int**, **bool**; **2** for **vec2**, **ivec2**, **bvec2**, etc.). The suffix **f** indicates that floating-point values are being passed, and the suffix **i** indicates that integer values are being passed; this type should also match the data type of the specified uniform variable. The **i** variants of this function should be used to provide values for uniform variables defined as **int**, **ivec2**, **ivec3**, and **ivec4**, or arrays of these. The **f** variants should be used to provide values for uniform variables of type **float**, **vec2**, **vec3**, or **vec4**, or arrays of these. Either the **i** or the **f** variants can be used to provide values for uniform variables of type **bool**, **bvec2**, **bvec3**, and **bvec4** or arrays of these. The uniform variable is set to **false** if the input value is 0 or 0.0f, and it is set to **true** otherwise.

void **glUniform{1|2|3|4}{f|i}v**(GLint *location*,

　　　　　　　　　GLuint *count*,

　　　　　　　　　const *TYPE v*)

Sets the user-defined uniform variable or uniform variable array specified by *location* to the values specified by *v*. These commands pass a count and a pointer to the values to be loaded into a uniform variable or a uniform variable array. A count of 1 should be used for modifying the value of a single uniform variable, and a count of 1 or greater can be used to modify an array. The number specified in the name of the command specifies the number of components for each element in *v*, and it should match the number of components in the data type of the specified uniform variable (e.g., **1** for **float**, **int**, **bool**; **2** for **vec2**, **ivec2**, **bvec2**, etc.). The **v** in the command name indicates that a pointer to a vector of values is being passed. The **f** and **i** suffixes are defined in the same way as for the nonvector variants of **glUniform**.

For uniform variable arrays, each element of the array is considered to be of the type indicated in the name of the command (e.g., **glUniform3f** or **glUniform3fv** can be used to load a uniform variable array of type **vec3**). The number of elements of the uniform variable array to be modified is specified by *count*.

void **glUniformMatrix{2|3|4}fv**(GLint *location*,

　　　　　　　　　　　GLuint *count*,

　　　　　　　　　　　GLboolean *transpose*,

　　　　　　　　　　　const GLfloat **v*)

Sets the user-defined uniform matrix variable or uniform matrix array variable specified by *location* to the values specified by *v*. The number in the command name is interpreted as the dimensionality of the matrix. The number **2** indicates a 2×2 matrix (i.e., 4 values), the number **3** indicates a 3×3 matrix (i.e., 9 values), and the number **4** indicates a 4×4 matrix (i.e., 16 values). If *transpose* is GL_FALSE, each matrix is assumed to be supplied in column major order. If transpose is GL_TRUE, each matrix is assumed to be supplied in row major order. The *count* argument specifies the number of matrices to be passed. A count of 1 should be used for modifying the value of a single matrix, and a count greater than 1 can be used to modify an array of matrices.

glUniform1i and **glUniform1iv** are the only two functions that can be used to load uniform variables defined as sampler types (see Section 7.9). Attempting to load a sampler with any other function results in an error.

Errors can also be generated by **glUniform** for any of the following reasons:

*   If there is no current program object

*   If *location* is an invalid uniform variable location for the current program object

*   If the number of values specified by *count* would exceed the declared extent of the indicated uniform variable or uniform variable array

*   Other than the preceding exceptions noted, if the type and size of the uniform variable as defined in the shader do not match the type and size specified in the name of the command used to load its value

In all of these cases, the indicated uniform variable will not be modified.

When the location of a user-defined uniform variable has been determined, the following command can be used to query its current value:

---

void **glGetUniformfv**(GLuint *program*,

GLint *location*,

GLfloat **params*)

void **glGetUniformiv**(GLuint *program*,

GLint *location*,

GLint **params*)

Return in *params* the value(s) of the specified uniform variable. The type of the uniform variable specified by *location* determines the number of values returned. If the uniform variable is defined in the shader as a **bool**, **int**, or **float**, a single value is returned. If it is defined as a **vec2**, **ivec2**, or **bvec2**, two values are returned. If it is defined as a **vec3**, **ivec3**, or **bvec3**, three values are returned, and so on. To query values stored in uniform variables declared as arrays, call **glGetUniform** for each element of the array. To query values stored in uniform variables declared as structures, call **glGetUniform** for each field in the structure. The values for uniform variables declared as a matrix are returned in column major order.

The locations assigned to uniform variables are not known until the program object is linked. After linking has occurred, the command **glGetUniformLocation** can obtain the location of a uniform variable. This location value can then be passed to **glGetUniform** to query the current value of the uniform variable. After a program object has been linked successfully, the index values for uniform variables remain fixed until the next link command occurs. The uniform variable values can be queried after a link only if the link was successful.

The location of a uniform variable cannot be used for anything other than specifying or querying that particular uniform variable. Say you declare a uniform variable as a structure that has three fields in succession that are defined as floats. If you call **glGetUniformLocation** to determine that the first of those three floats is at location *n*, do not assume that the next one is at location *n* + 1. It is possible to query the location of the *i*th element in an array. That value can then be passed to **glUniform** to load one or more values into the array, starting at the *i*th element of the array. It is not possible to take *i* and add an integer *N* and use the result to try to modify element *i* + *N* in the array. The location of array element *i* + *N* should be queried specifically before any attempt to set its value. These location values do not necessarily represent real memory locations. Applications that assume otherwise will not work.

For example, consider the following structure defined within a shader:

```
uniform struct
{
    struct
    {
        float a;
        float b[10];
    } c[2];
    vec2 d;
}  e;
```

and consider the following API calls that attempt to determine locations within that structure:

```
loc1 = glGetUniformLocation(progObj, "e.d");       // is valid
loc2 = glGetUniformLocation(progObj, "e.c[0]");    // is not valid
loc3 = glGetUniformLocation(progObj, "e.c[0].b") ; // is valid
loc4 = glGetUniformLocation(progObj, "e.c[0].b[2]"); // is valid
```

The location *loc2* cannot be retrieved because *e.c[0]* references a structure.

Now consider the following commands to set parts of the uniform variable:

```
glUniform2f(loc1, 1.0f, 2.0f);     // is valid
glUniform2i(loc1, 1, 2);           // is not valid
glUniform1f(loc1, 1.0f);           // is not valid
glUniform1fv(loc3, 10, floatPtr);  // is valid
glUniform1fv(loc4, 10, floatPtr);  // is not valid
glUniform1fv(loc4, 8, floatPtr);   // is valid
```

The second command in the preceding list is invalid because *loc1* references a uniform variable of type **vec2**, not **ivec2**. The third command is invalid because *loc1* references a **vec2**, not a **float**. The fifth command in the preceding list is invalid because it attempts to set values that will exceed the length of the array.

Uniform variables (either built in or user defined) that can be accessed when a shader is executed are called ACTIVE UNIFORMS. You can think of this as though the process of compiling and linking is capable of deactivating uniform variables that are declared but never used. This provides more flexibility in coding style—modular code can define lots of uniform variables, and those that can be determined to be unused are typically optimized away.

To obtain the list of active uniform variables from a program object, use **glGetActiveUniform**. This command can be used by an application to query the uniform variables in a program object and set up user interface elements to allow direct manipulation of all the user-defined uniform values.

---

void **glGetActiveUniform**(GLuint *program,*

GLuint *index,*

GLsizei *bufSize,*

GLsizei **length,*

GLint **size,*

GLenum **type,*

GLchar **name*)

Returns information about an active uniform variable in the program object specified by program. The number of active uniform variables can be obtained by calling **glGetProgram** with the value GL_ACTIVE_UNIFORMS. A value of 0 for *index* selects the first active uniform variable. Permissible values for *index* range from 0 to the number of active uniform variables minus 1.

Shaders may use built-in uniform variables, user-defined uniform variables, or both. Built-in uniform variables have a prefix of "*gl_*" and reference existing OpenGL state or values derived from such state (e.g., *gl_Fog*, *gl_ModelViewMatrix*, etc.; see Section 4.3 for a complete list). User-defined uniform variables have arbitrary names and obtain their values from the application through calls to **glUniform.** A uniform variable (either built in or user defined) is considered active if it is determined during the link operation that it can be accessed during program execution. Therefore, *program* should have previously been the target of a call to **glLinkProgram,** but it is not necessary for it to have been linked successfully.

The size of the character buffer required to store the longest uniform variable name in *program* can be obtained by calling **glGetProgram** with the value GL_ACTIVE_UNIFORM_MAX_LENGTH. This value should be used to allocate a buffer of sufficient size to store the returned uniform variable name. The size of this character buffer is passed in *bufSize*, and a pointer to this character buffer is passed in *name*.

glGetActiveUniform returns the name of the uniform variable indicated by *index*, storing it in the character buffer specified by *name*. The string returned is null terminated. The actual number of characters written into this buffer is returned in *length*, and this count does not include the null termination character. If the length of the returned string is not required, a value of NULL can be passed in the *length* argument.

The *type* argument returns a pointer to the uniform variable's data type. One of the following symbolic constants may be returned: GL_FLOAT, GL_FLOAT_VEC2, GL_FLOAT_VEC3, GL_FLOAT_VEC4, GL_INT, GL_INT_VEC2, GL_INT_VEC3, GL_INT_VEC4, GL_BOOL, GL_BOOL_VEC2, GL_BOOL_VEC3, GL_BOOL_VEC4, GL_FLOAT_MAT2, GL_FLOAT_MAT3, GL_FLOAT_MAT4, GL_SAMPLER_1D, GL_SAMPLER_2D, GL_SAMPLER_3D, GL_SAMPLER_CUBE, GL_SAMPLER_1D_SHADOW, or GL_SAMPLER_2D_SHADOW.

If one or more elements of an array are active, the name of the array is returned in *name*, the type is returned in *type*, and the *size* parameter returns the highest array element index used, plus one, as determined by the compiler and linker. Only one active uniform variable will be reported for a uniform array.

Uniform variables that are declared as structures or arrays of structures are not returned directly by this function. Instead, each of these uniform variables is reduced to its fundamental components containing the "." and "[]" operators such that each of the names is valid as an argument to **glGetUniformLocation**. Each of these reduced uniform variables is counted as one active uniform variable and is assigned an index. A valid name cannot be a structure, an array of structures, or a subcomponent of a vector or matrix.

The size of the uniform variable is returned in *size*. Uniform variables other than arrays have a size of 1. Structures and arrays of structures are reduced as described earlier, such that each of the names returned will be a data type in the earlier list. If this reduction results in an array, the size returned is as described for uniform arrays; otherwise, the size returned is 1.

The list of active uniform variables may include both built-in uniform variables (which begin with the prefix "*gl_*") as well as user-defined uniform variable names.

This function returns as much information as it can about the specified active uniform variable. If no information is available, *length* is 0, and *name* is an empty string. This situation could occur if this function is called after a link operation that failed. If an error occurs, the return values *length*, *size*, *type*, and *name* are unmodified.

Using **glGetActiveUniform**, the application developer can programmatically query the uniform variables actually used in a shader and automatically create a user interface that allows the end user to modify those uniform variables. If among the shader writers there were some convention concerning the names of uniform variables, the user interface could be even more specific. For instance, any uniform variable name that ended with "Color" would be edited with the color selection tool. This function can also be useful when mixing and matching a set of vertex and fragment shaders designed to play well with each other, using a subset of known uniform variables. It can be much safer and less tedious to programmatically determine which uniform variables to send down than to hardcode all the combinations.

7.8.2 Named Uniform Blocks

OpenGL 3.1 adds named uniform blocks and the OpenGL Shading Language API to support them. Named uniform blocks are backed by uniform buffer objects. They can therefore be updated far more efficiently with buffer data commands or by mapping the buffer object. An entire uniform buffer object can also be changed rapidly by changing the buffer object bound to a uniform buffer binding point.

Sets of uniform variables (except uniforms of type sampler) can be grouped into named uniform blocks. For example, consider this named uniform block:

```
uniform MatrixBlock
{
    uniform mat4 MVmatrix;
    uniform mat4 MVPmatrix;
    uniform mat3 NormalMatrix;
};
```

The named uniform block is named **MatrixBlock**. It contains three uniforms added directly to the global namespace, **MVmatrix**, **MVPmatrix**, and **NormalMatrix**.

To update the value of a user-defined uniform variable in a named uniform block, an application needs to determine its offset and then specify its value. The offsets of uniform variables are assigned at link time and do not change until the next link operation occurs. Each time linking occurs, the locations of uniform variables may change, and so the application must query them again before setting them. First, the index of a named uniform block can be queried with the following command:

GLuint **glGetUniformBlockIndex**(GLuint *program*,

const GLchar **name*)

Returns the uniform block index for the uniform block named by *name* of
the program object specified by *program*. If *name* does not identify an active
uniform block, then GL_INVALID_INDEX is returned.

Information about the named uniform block can also be queried, including
the number of active uniforms in the named uniform block, the indices of
the active uniforms, and the size of the uniform buffer needed to back the
named uniform block.

GLuint **glGetUniformBlockiv**(GLuint *program*,

GLuint *index*,

GLenum *pname*,

GLint **params*)

Returns in *params* the value of a uniform block parameter of the program
object specified by *program*. Parameters and return values are summarized
in Table 7.4. The uniform block to be queried is specified by *index*, and the
parameter to be queried is specified by *pname*.

Table 7.4 Named uniform block parameters

Parameter	Operation
GL_UNIFORM_BLOCK_ BINDING	*params* returns a single value that is the index of the uniform buffer binding point. The initial value is 0.
GL_UNIFORM_BLOCK_DATA_ SIZE	*params* returns a single value that is the implementation-dependent minimum total buffer size in basic machine units.
GL_UNIFORM_BLOCK_ NAME_LENGTH	*params* returns a single value that is the total length (including the null terminator) of the name of the uniform block.
GL_UNIFORM_BLOCK_ ACTIVE_UNIFORMS	*params* returns a single value that is the number of active uniforms of the uniform block.
GL_UNIFORM_BLOCK_ ACTIVE_UNIFORM_INDICES	*params* returns a list of the active uniform indices for the uniform block.

(continues)

Table 7.4 Named uniform block parameters, *continued*

Parameter	Operation
GL_UNIFORM_BLOCK_ REFERENCED_BY_VERTEX_ SHADER	*params* returns a single value that is nonzero (true) if the uniform block is referenced by the vertex shader and 0 (false) if it is not.
GL_UNIFORM_BLOCK_ REFERENCED_BY_ FRAGMENT_SHADER	*params* returns a single value that is nonzero (true) if the uniform block is referenced by the fragment shader and 0 (false) if it is not.

Information about each uniform in the named uniform block can then be queried, including their names and offsets. The application can collect the information needed to update the values of a buffer object.

GLuint **glGetActiveUniformsiv**(GLuint *program*,
GLsizei *count*,
const GLuint **indices*,
GLenum *pname*,
GLint **params*)

Returns in *params* information about the uniforms selected by *indices* of the program object specified by *program*. Parameters and return values are summarized in Table 7.5. The uniforms to be queried is specified by *pname*, and the parameter to be queried is specified by *pname*.

Table 7.5 Queriable active uniform parameters

Parameter	Operation
GL_UNIFORM_TYPE	*params* returns an array identifying the types of the uniforms specified by indices.
GL_UNIFORM_SIZE	*params* returns an array identifying the sizes of the uniforms specified by indices.
GL_UNIFORM_NAME_ LENGTH	*params* returns an array identifying the lengths of the uniform names specified by indices.

Table 7.5 Queriable active uniform parameters, *continued*

Parameter	Operation
GL_UNIFORM_BLOCK_ INDEX	*params* returns an array identifying the uniform block index uniforms specified by indices. For uniforms in the default uniform block, –1 is returned.
GL_UNIFORM_OFFSET	*params* returns an array of uniform buffer offsets, in basic machine units, of the uniforms specified by indices. For uniforms in the default uniform block, –1 is returned.
GL_UNIFORM_ARRAY_ STRIDE	*params* returns an array identifying the stride between elements, in basic machine units, of the uniforms specified by indices. For uniforms in the default uniform block, –1 is returned. For uniforms that are not arrays, 0 is returned.
GL_UNIFORM_MATRIX_ STRIDE	*params* returns an array identifying the stride between elements, in basic machine units, of the uniforms specified by indices. For uniforms in the default uniform block, –1 is returned. For uniforms that are not matrices, 0 is returned.
GL_UNIFORM_MATRIX_IS_ ROW_MAJOR	*params* returns an array identifying whether the matrix is a row-major matrix. A value of 1 indicates a row-major matrix. A value of 0 indicates a column-major matrix, a matrix in the default uniform block, or a nonmatrix.

After linking a shader, each named uniform block may be bound to a uniform buffer binding point.

---

void **glUniformBlockBinding**(GLuint *program*,

GLuint *index*,

GLuint binding)

The binding point *bind* is assigned to the named uniform block selected by *index* of the program object specified by *program*. The *index* must be an active named uniform block of the program object, otherwise INVALID_ VALUE is generated.

7.9 Samplers

glUniform1i and **glUniform1iv** load uniform variables defined as sampler types (i.e., uniform variables of type **sampler1D**, **sampler2D**, **sample3D**, **samplerCube**, **sampler1DShadow**, or **sampler2DShadow**). They may be declared within either vertex shaders or fragment shaders.

The value contained in a sampler is used within a shader to access a particular texture map. The value loaded into the sampler by the application should be the number of the texture unit to be used to access the texture. For vertex shaders, this value should be less than the implementation-dependent constant GL_MAX_VERTEX_TEXTURE_IMAGE_UNITS, which can be queried with **glGet**. For fragment shaders, this value should be less than the implementation-dependent constant GL_MAX_TEXTURE_IMAGE_UNITS.

The suffix on the sampler type indicates the texture type to be accessed: 1D, 2D, 3D, cube map, 1D shadow, or 2D shadow. In OpenGL, a texture object of each of the first four texture types can be bound to a single texture unit, and this suffix allows the desired texture object to be chosen. A 1D shadow sampler is used to access the 1D texture when depth comparisons are enabled, and a 2D shadow sampler is used to access the 2D texture when depth comparisons are enabled. If two uniform variables of different sampler types contain the same value, an error is generated when the next rendering command is issued. Attempting to load a sampler with any command other than **glUniform1i** or **glUniform1iv** results in an error being generated.

From within a shader, samplers should be considered an opaque data type. The current API provides a way of specifying an integer representing the texture image unit to be used. In the future, the API may be extended to allow a sampler to refer directly to a texture object.

Samplers that can be accessed when a program is executed are called ACTIVE SAMPLERS. The link operation fails if it determines that the number of active samplers exceeds the maximum allowable limits. The number of active samplers permitted on the vertex processor is specified by GL_MAX_VERTEX_TEXTURE_IMAGE_UNITS, the number of active samplers permitted on the fragment processor is specified by GL_MAX_TEXTURE_IMAGE_UNITS, and the number of active samplers permitted on both processors combined is GL_COMBINED_TEXTURE_IMAGE_UNITS.

More detail on using samplers within a shader is provided in Section 10.1.

7.10 Multiple Render Targets

Another feature added to OpenGL in version 2.0 was the ability to render into multiple buffers simultaneously. The OpenGL Shading Language makes provisions for this capability with user-defined fragment shader out variables. The number of data buffers that may be written by a fragment shader is implementation dependent but must be at least 4.

With this capability, applications can develop fragment shaders that compute multiple values for each fragment and store them in offscreen memory. These values can be accessed during a future rendering pass. Among other things, this lets applications implement complex multipass algorithms and use the graphics hardware for general-purpose computation.

To set up OpenGL for rendering into multiple target buffers, use

---

void **glDrawBuffers**(GLsizei *n*,

const GLenum *bufs)

Defines an array of buffers into which fragment color values or fragment data will be written. If a fragment shader is active and it writes values to the user-defined out variables, then those values are written into the buffers specified by *bufs*.

The symbolic constants contained in *bufs* are defined in Table 7.6. Except for GL_NONE, none of the symbolic constants may appear more than once in *bufs*. The maximum number of draw buffers supported is implementation dependent and can be queried by calling **glGet** with the argument GL_MAX_DRAW_BUFFERS.

Table 7.6 Buffer names for use with the **glDrawBuffers** call

Parameter	Operation
GL_NONE	The fragment color/data value is not written into any color buffer.
GL_COLOR_ ATTACHMENT*i*	The fragment color/data value is written into the draw buffer specified by GL_COLOR_ATTACHMENT*i*.

An error is generated if **glDrawBuffers** specifies a buffer that does not exist in the current GL context.

User-defined fragment shader out variables may be bound to data buffers with the following command:

---

void **glBindFragDataLocation**(GLuint *program,*

GLuint *index,*

const GLchar **name*)

The user-defined out variable *name* is assigned to the draw buffer selected by *index* of the program object specified by *program.* The *index* must be an active user-defined out variable of the program object, otherwise INVALID_ VALUE is generated.

---

void **glDrawBuffers**(GLsizei *n,*

const GLenum **bufs*)

Defines an array of buffers into which fragment color values or fragment data will be written. If a fragment shader is active and it writes values to the user-defined out variables, then those values are written into the buffers specified by *bufs.*

The symbolic constants contained in *bufs* are defined in Table 7.6. Except for GL_NONE, none of the symbolic constants may appear more than once in *bufs.* The maximum number of draw buffers supported is implementation dependent and can be queried by calling **glGet** with the argument GL_MAX_DRAW_BUFFERS.

7.11 Development Aids

A situation that can be difficult to diagnose is one in which a program may fail to execute because of the value of a sampler variable. These variables can be changed anytime between linking and program execution. To ensure robust behavior, OpenGL implementations must do some runtime checking just before the shader is executed (i.e., when a rendering operation is about to occur). At this point, the only way to report an error is to set the OpenGL error flag, and this is not usually something that applications check at this performance-critical juncture.

To provide more information when these situations occur, the OpenGL Shading Language API defines a new function that can be called to perform this runtime check explicitly and provide diagnostic information.

---

void **glValidateProgram**(GLuint *program*)

Checks whether the executables contained in *program* can execute given the current OpenGL state. The information generated by the validation process is stored in *program*'s information log. The validation information may consist of an empty string, or it may be a string containing information about how the current program object interacts with the rest of current OpenGL state. This function provides a way for OpenGL implementors to convey more information about why the current program is inefficient, suboptimal, failing to execute, and so on.

The status of the validation operation is stored as part of the program object's state. This value is set to GL_TRUE if the validation succeeded and GL_FALSE otherwise. It can be queried by calling **glGetProgram** with arguments *program* and GL_VALIDATE_STATUS. If validation is successful, *program* is guaranteed to execute given the current state. Otherwise, *program* is guaranteed to not execute.

This function is typically useful only during application development. The informational string stored in the information log is completely implementation dependent. Therefore, an application should not expect different OpenGL implementations to produce identical information strings.

Because the operations described in this section can severely hinder performance, they should be used only during application development and removed before shipment of the production version of the application.

7.12 Implementation-Dependent API Values

Some of the features we've described in previous sections have implementation-dependent limits. All of the implementation-dependent values in the OpenGL Shading Language API are defined in the list that follows, and all of them can be queried with **glGet**. Several implementation-dependent values were raised in OpenGL 3.0.

GL_MAX_COMBINED_TEXTURE_IMAGE_UNITS—Defines the total number of hardware units that can be used to access texture maps from the vertex processor and the fragment processor combined. The minimum legal value is 32.

GL_MAX_DRAW_BUFFERS—Defines the maximum number of buffers that can be written into from within a single fragment shader using out variables. The minimum legal value is 8. (The limit prior to OpenGL 3.0 was 1.)

GL_MAX_FRAGMENT_UNIFORM_COMPONENTS—Defines the number of components (i.e., floating-point values) that are available for fragment shader uniform variables. The minimum legal value is 1024 (was 64).

GL_MAX_TEXTURE_IMAGE_UNITS—Defines the total number of hardware units that can be used to access texture maps from the fragment processor. The minimum legal value is 16 (was 2).

GL_MAX_VARYING_COMPONENTS—Defines the number of components available for varying variables, the out variables in the vertex shader, and the matching in variables in the fragment shader. The minimum legal value is 64 (was 32 floating-point values).

GL_MAX_VERTEX_ATTRIBS—Defines the number of active vertex attributes that are available. The minimum legal value is 16.

GL_MAX_VERTEX_TEXTURE_IMAGE_UNITS—Defines the number of hardware units that can be used to access texture maps from the vertex processor. The minimum legal value is 16 (was 0).

GL_MAX_VERTEX_UNIFORM_COMPONENTS—Defines the number of components (i.e., floating-point values) that are available for vertex shader default uniform block. The minimum legal value is 1024 (was 512).

Several implementation-dependent values are new in OpenGL 3.1.

GL_MAX_CLIP_DISTANCES—Defines the number of clip distances that are available per program. The minimum legal value is 8.

GL_MAX_COMBINED_UNIFORM_BLOCKS—Defines the number of uniform blocks that are available per program. The minimum legal value is 24.

GL_MAX_FRAGMENT_UNIFORM_BLOCKS—Defines the number of fragment uniform blocks that are available per program. The minimum legal value is 12.

GL_MAX_VERTEX_UNIFORM_BLOCKS—Defines the number of vertex uniform blocks that are available per program. The minimum legal value is 12.

GL_MAX_UNIFORM_BLOCK_SIZE—Defines the size in basic-machine units (usually bytes) of a uniform block. The minimum legal value is 16384.

7.13 Application Code for Brick Shaders

Each shader is going to be a little bit different. Each vertex shader may use a different set of attribute variables or different uniform variables, attribute variables may be bound to different generic vertex attribute index values, and so on. One of the demo programs whose source code is available for download from the 3Dlabs Web site is called **ogl2brick**. It is a small, clear example of how to create and use a vertex shader and a fragment shader. The code in **ogl2brick** was derived from an earlier demo program called **ogl2demo**, written primarily by Barthold Lichtenbelt with contributions from several others. In **ogl2brick** an "install" function installs the brick shaders that were presented in Chapter 6. We discuss that shader installation function, but first we define a simple function that make it a little easier to set the values of uniform variables.

```
GLint getUniLoc(GLuint program, const GLchar *name)
{
    GLint loc;

    loc = glGetUniformLocation(program, name);

    if (loc == -1)
        printf("No such uniform named \"%s\"\n", name);

    printOpenGLError();  // Check for OpenGL errors
    return loc;
}
```

Shaders are passed to OpenGL as strings. For our shader installation function, we assume that each of the shaders has been defined as a single string, and pointers to those strings are passed to the following function. This function does all the work to load, compile, link, and install our brick shaders. The function definition and local variables for this function are declared as follows:

```
int installBrickShaders(const GLchar *brickVertex,
                        const GLchar *brickFragment)
{
    GLuint brickVS, brickFS, brickProg;   // handles to objects
    GLint  vertCompiled, fragCompiled;    // status values
    GLint  linked;
```

The argument *brickVertex* contains a pointer to the string containing the source code for the brick vertex shader, and the argument *brickFragment* contains a pointer to the source code for the brick fragment shader. Next, we declare variables to refer to three OpenGL objects: a shader object that stores and compiles the brick vertex shader, a second shader object that stores and compiles the brick fragment shader, and a program object to which the shader objects will be attached. Flags to indicate the status of the compile and link operations are defined next.

The first step is to create two empty shader objects, one for the vertex shader and one for the fragment shader.

```
brickVS = glCreateShader(GL_VERTEX_SHADER);
brickFS = glCreateShader(GL_FRAGMENT_SHADER);
```

Source code can be loaded into the shader objects after they have been created. The shader objects are empty, and we have a single null-terminated string containing the source code for each shader, so we can call **glShaderSource** as follows:

```
glShaderSource(brickVS, 1, &brickVertex, NULL);
glShaderSource(brickFS, 1, &brickFragment, NULL);
```

The shaders are now ready to be compiled. For each shader, we call **glCompileShader** and then call **glGetShader** to see what transpired. **glCompileShader** sets the shader object's GL_COMPILE_STATUS parameter to GL_TRUE if it succeeded and GL_FALSE otherwise. Regardless of whether the compilation succeeded or failed, we print the information log for the shader. If the compilation was unsuccessful, this log will have information about the compilation errors. If the compilation was successful, this log may still have useful information that would help us improve the shader in some way. You would typically check the info log only during application development or after running a shader for the first time on a new platform. The function exits if the compilation of either shader fails.

```
glCompileShader(brickVS);
printOpenGLError();  // Check for OpenGL errors
glGetShaderiv(brickVS, GL_COMPILE_STATUS, &vertCompiled);
printShaderInfoLog(brickVS);

glCompileShader(brickFS);
printOpenGLError();  // Check for OpenGL errors
glGetShaderiv(brickFS, GL_COMPILE_STATUS, &fragCompiled);
printShaderInfoLog(brickFS);

if (!vertCompiled || !fragCompiled)
    return 0;
```

This section of code uses the **printShaderInfoLog** function that we defined previously.

At this point, the shaders have been compiled successfully, and we're almost ready to try them out. First, the shader objects need to be attached to a program object so that they can be linked.

```
brickProg = glCreateProgram();
glAttachShader(brickProg, brickVS);
glAttachShader(brickProg, brickFS);
```

The program object is linked with **glLinkProgram**. Again, we look at the information log of the program object regardless of whether the link succeeded or failed. There may be useful information for us if we've never tried this shader before.

```
glLinkProgram(brickProg);
printOpenGLError();  // Check for OpenGL errors
glGetProgramiv(brickProg, GL_LINK_STATUS, &linked);
printProgramInfoLog(brickProg);

if (!linked)
    return 0;
```

If we make it to the end of this code, we have a valid program that can become part of current state simply by calling **glUseProgram**.

```
glUseProgram(brickProg);
```

Before returning from this function, we also want to initialize the values of the uniform variables used in the two shaders. To obtain the location that was assigned by the linker, we query the uniform variable by name, using the **getUniLoc** function defined previously. Then we use that location to immediately set the initial value of the uniform variable.

```
glUniform3f(getUniLoc(brickProg, "BrickColor"), 1.0, 0.3, 0.2);
glUniform3f(getUniLoc(brickProg, "MortarColor"), 0.85, 0.86, 0.84);
glUniform2f(getUniLoc(brickProg, "BrickSize"), 0.30, 0.15);
glUniform2f(getUniLoc(brickProg, "BrickPct"), 0.90, 0.85);
glUniform3f(getUniLoc(brickProg, "LightPosition"), 0.0, 0.0, 4.0);

    return 1;
}
```

When this function returns, the application is ready to draw geometry that will be rendered with our brick shaders. The result of rendering some simple objects with this application code and the shaders described in Chapter 6 is shown in Figure 6.6. The complete C function is shown in Listing 7.3.

Listing 7.3 C function for installing brick shaders

```
int installBrickShaders(const GLchar *brickVertex,
                        const GLchar *brickFragment)
{

    GLuint brickVS, brickFS, brickProg;   // handles to objects
    GLint  vertCompiled, fragCompiled;    // status values
    GLint  linked;

    // Create a vertex shader object and a fragment shader object
```

```
brickVS = glCreateShader(GL_VERTEX_SHADER);
brickFS = glCreateShader(GL_FRAGMENT_SHADER);

// Load source code strings into shaders

glShaderSource(brickVS, 1, &brickVertex, NULL);
glShaderSource(brickFS, 1, &brickFragment, NULL);

// Compile the brick vertex shader and print out
// the compiler log file.

glCompileShader(brickVS);
printOpenGLError();  // Check for OpenGL errors
glGetShaderiv(brickVS, GL_COMPILE_STATUS, &vertCompiled);
printShaderInfoLog(brickVS);

// Compile the brick fragment shader and print out
// the compiler log file.

glCompileShader(brickFS);
printOpenGLError();  // Check for OpenGL errors
glGetShaderiv(brickFS, GL_COMPILE_STATUS, &fragCompiled);
printShaderInfoLog(brickFS);

if (!vertCompiled || !fragCompiled)
    return 0;

// Create a program object and attach the two compiled shaders

brickProg = glCreateProgram();
glAttachShader(brickProg, brickVS);
glAttachShader(brickProg, brickFS);

// Bind user-defined in variable to vertex attribute

glBindVertexAttrib( brickProg, 1, "MCvertex");
glBindVertexAttrib( brickProg, 2, "MCnormal");

// Bind user-defined out variable to data buffer

glBindFragData( brickProg, 0, "FragColor");"

// Link the program object and print out the info log

glLinkProgram(brickProg);
printOpenGLError();  // Check for OpenGL errors
glGetProgramiv(brickProg, GL_LINK_STATUS, &linked);
printProgramInfoLog(brickProg);

if (!linked)
    return 0;
```

```
// Install program object as part of current state

glUseProgram(brickProg);

// Set up initial uniform values

glUniform3f(getUniLoc(brickProg, "BrickColor"), 1.0, 0.3, 0.2);
glUniform3f(getUniLoc(brickProg, "MortarColor"), 0.85, 0.86, 0.84);
glUniform2f(getUniLoc(brickProg, "BrickSize"), 0.30, 0.15);
glUniform2f(getUniLoc(brickProg, "BrickPct"), 0.90, 0.85);
glUniform3f(getUniLoc(brickProg, "LightPosition"), 0.0, 0.0, 4.0);

return 1;
}
```

7.14 Summary

The set of function calls added to OpenGL to create and manipulate shaders is actually quite small. The interface mimics the software development process followed by a C/C++ programmer. To install and use OpenGL shaders, do the following:

1. Create one or more (empty) shader objects with **glCreateShader**.

2. Provide source code for these shaders with **glShaderSource**.

3. Compile each of the shaders with **glCompileShader**.

4. Create a program object with **glCreateProgram**.

5. Attach all the shader objects to the program object with **glAttachShader**.

6. Link the program object with **glLinkProgram**.

7. Install the executable program as part of OpenGL's current state with **glUseProgram**.

8. If the shaders uses the default uniform block, query the locations of uniform variables with **glGetUniformLocation** and then set their values with **glUniform**.

9. If the shaders use named uniform blocks, query the uniform block information with **glGetUniformBlockIndex** and **glGetActiveUniformBlockiv**. Query the offsets of the uniform variables within the uniform block with **glGetActiveUniformsiv**. The uniform blocks are associated with buffer object binding points with **glUniformBlockBinding**, and buffer objects are bound to those binding points with **glBindBufferRange**.

10. If the vertex shader uses user-defined in variables, the application must provide values for them, using OpenGL API calls that place attribute values in generic, numbered vertex attribute locations. Before such attribute data is passed to the shader, the index of the generic vertex attribute should be associated with an in variable in a vertex shader in one of two ways. Applications can create this association explicitly by calling **glBindAttribLocation** before linking. Alternatively, if no explicit association is made, OpenGL makes these associations automatically during linking. An application can query the assignment that was made with **glGetAttribLocation**. Thereafter, generic vertex attributes can be passed to a vertex shader with **glVertexAttrib** or with **glVertexAttribPointer** and **glEnableVertexArrayPointer** in conjunction with standard OpenGL commands to draw vertex arrays.

11. If the fragment shader uses user-defined out variables, the application may create an association between a user-defined out variable and a fragment data index with **glBindFragDataLocation** before linking. Alternatively, if no explicit association is made, OpenGL makes these associations automatically during linking. An application can query the assignment that was made with **glGetFragDataLocation**.

12. An application may optionally record vertex shader out variables to one or more transform feedback buffers. Before vertex shader out variables are recorded, the vertex shader out variables are associated with feedback buffer binding points with **glTransformFeedbackVarying**, and buffer objects are bound to those binding points with **glBindBufferRange**.

A number of query functions obtain information about shader and program objects.

7.15 Further Information

Reference pages for the OpenGL Shading Language API can be found in Appendix B. Source code for the example in this chapter can be found at the 3Dlabs developer Web site. More complex source code examples and a variety of shaders can be found there as well.

[1] *Former 3Dlabs developer Web site.* Now at http://3dshaders.com.

[2] Ebert, David S., John Hart, Bill Mark, F. Kenton Musgrave, Darwyn Peachey, Ken Perlin, and Steven Worley, *Texturing and Modeling: A Procedural Approach, Third Edition*, Morgan Kaufmann Publishers, San Francisco, 2002. www.texturingandmodeling.com

[3] Kessenich, John, Dave Baldwin, and Randi Rost, *The OpenGL Shading Language, Version 1.40*, 3Dlabs/Intel, March 2008. http://www.opengl.org/documentation/specs/

[4] OpenGL Architecture Review Board, *OpenGL Reference Manual, Fourth Edition: The Official Reference to OpenGL, Version 1.4*, Editor: Dave Shreiner, Addison-Wesley, Reading, Massachusetts, 2004.

[5] Segal, Mark, and Kurt Akeley, *The OpenGL Graphics System: A Specification (Version 3.1)*, Editor (v1.1): Chris Frazier, (v1.2–3.1): Jon Leech, (v2.0): Jon Leech and Pat Brown, March 2008. www.opengl.org/documentation/spec.html

[6] Shreiner, Dave, and the Khronos OpenGL ARB Working Group, *OpenGL Programming Guide, Seventh Edition: The Official Guide to Learning OpenGL, Versions 3.0 and 3.1*, Addison-Wesley, Boston, Massachusetts, 2010.

Chapter 8

Shader Development

At the time of this writing, several shader development tools for the OpenGL Shading Language are available. There are some specialized tools for shader development, notably, AMD's RenderMonkey and Apple's GLSLEditorSample. More generalized tools for OpenGL development such as Graphic Remedy's gDEBugger are now adding significant support for debugging shaders. A whole ecosystem of tools for shader development is beginning to arise.

This chapter sets forth some ideas on the shader development process and describes the tools that are currently available. Both general software development techniques and techniques that are unique to shader development are discussed.

8.1 General Principles

Shader development can be thought of as another form of software engineering; therefore, existing software engineering principles and practices should be brought into play when you are developing shaders. Spend some time designing the shader before writing any code. The design should aim to keep things as simple as possible while still getting the job done. If the shader is part of a larger shader development effort, take care to design the shader for reliability and reuse.

In short, you should treat shader development the same as you would any other software development tasks, allocating appropriate amounts of time for design, implementation, testing, and documentation.

Here are a few more useful thoughts for developing shaders. Consider these to be friendly advice and not mandates. There will be situations in which some of these shader development suggestions make sense and others in which they do not.

8.1.1 Understand the Problem

It is worth reminding yourself periodically that you will be most successful at developing shaders if you understand the problem before you write any of the shader code. The first step is to make sure you understand the rendering algorithm you plan on implementing. If your aim is to develop a shader for bump mapping, make sure you understand the necessary mathematics before plunging into coding. It is usually easier to think things through with a pencil and paper and get the details straight in your mind before you begin to write code.

Because the tools for developing shaders are currently less powerful than those for developing code intended to run on the CPU, you might consider implementing a simulation of your algorithm on the CPU before coding it in the OpenGL Shading Language. Doing this will let you use the powerful debugging tools available for typical software development, single-step through source code, set breakpoints, and really watch your code in action.

8.1.2 Add Complexity Progressively

Many shaders depend on a combination of details to achieve the desired effect. Develop your shader in such a way that you implement and test the largest and most important details first and add progressive complexity after the basic shader is working. For instance, you may want to develop a shader that combines effects from noise with values read from several texture maps and then performs some unique lighting effects. You can approach this task in a couple of different ways. One way would be to get your unique lighting effects working first with a simple shading model. After testing this part of the shader, you can add the effects from reading the texture maps and thoroughly test again. After this, you can add the noise effects, again, testing as you proceed.

In this way, you have reduced a large development task into several smaller ones. After a task has been successfully completed and tested, move on to the next task.

8.1.3 Test and Iterate

Sometimes it is impossible to visualize ahead of time the effect a shader will have. This is particularly true when you are dealing with mathematical functions that are complex or hard to visualize, such as noise. In this case, you may want to parameterize your algorithm and modify the parameters systematically. You can take notes as you modify the parameters and observe the effect. These observations will be useful comments in the shader source, providing insight for someone who might come along later and want to tweak the shader in a different direction.

After you have found a set of parameters that gives you the desired effect, you can consider simplifying the shader by removing some of the "tweakable" parameters and replacing them with constants. This may make your shader less flexible, but it may make it easier for someone coming along later to understand.

8.1.4 Strive for Simplicity

There's a lot to be said for simplicity. Simple shaders are easier to understand and easier to maintain. There's often more than one algorithm for achieving the effect you want. Have you chosen the simplest one? There's often more than one way to implement a particular algorithm. Have you chosen the language features that let you express the algorithm in the simplest way possible?

8.1.5 Exploit Modularity

The OpenGL Shading Language and its API support modular shaders, so take advantage of this capability. Use the principle of "divide and conquer" to develop small, simple modules that are designed to work together. Your lighting modules might all be interchangeable and offer support for standard light source types as well as custom lighting modules. You may also have fog modules that offer a variety of fog effects. If you do things right, you can mix and match any of your lighting modules with any of your fog modules. You can apply this principle to other aspects of shader computation, both for vertex shaders and for fragment shaders.

8.2 Performance Considerations

After you have done all the right things from a software engineering stand-point, your shader may or may not have acceptable performance. Here are some ideas for eking out better performance from your carefully crafted shader.

8.2.1 Consider Computational Frequency

Shading computations can occur in three areas: on the CPU, on the vertex processor, and on the fragment processor. It is tempting to put most of your shader computation in the fragment shader because this is executed for every pixel that is drawn, and you will, therefore, get the highest-quality image. But if performance is a concern, you may be able to identify computations that can be done with acceptable quality per vertex instead of per fragment. By moving the computation to the vertex shader, you can make your fragment shader faster. In some cases, there may be no visible difference between doing the computation in the vertex shader versus doing it in the fragment shader. This might be the case with fog computations, for example.

One way to think about the problem is to implement rapidly changing characteristics in the fragment shader and to implement characteristics that don't change as rapidly in the vertex shader. For instance, diffuse lighting effects change slowly over a surface and so can usually be computed with sufficient quality in the vertex shader. Specular lighting effects might need to be implemented in the fragment shader to achieve high quality. If a particular value changes linearly across an object's surface, you can get the same result by computing the value per vertex and interpolating it as you would by computing the value at each fragment. In this case, you may as well have the vertex shader do the computation. Unless you are rendering very small triangles, your fragment shader will execute far more times than your vertex shader will, so it is more efficient to do the computation in the vertex shader.

Similarly, you may be able to find computations that can be done once on the CPU and remain constant for a great many executions of your vertex shader or fragment shader. You can often save shader instruction space or improve shader performance (or both) by precomputing values in your application code and passing them to your shader as uniform variables. Sometimes you can spot these things by analyzing your shader code. If you pass *length* in as a uniform variable and your shader always computes

sqrt(*length*), you're better off doing the computation once on the host CPU and passing that value to your shader rather than computing the value for every execution of your shader. If your shader needs both *length* and **sqrt**(*length*), you can pass both values in as uniform variables.

Deciding where to perform computation also involves knowing where the computational bottleneck occurs for a particular rendering operation. You just need to speed up the slowest part of the system to see an improvement in performance. Conversely, you shouldn't spend time improving the performance of something that isn't a bottleneck, because you won't see the gain in performance anyway.

8.2.2 Analyze Your Algorithm

You can often make your shader more efficient just by understanding the math it uses. For instance, you might want to limit the range of the variable *finalcolor* to [0,1]. But if you know that you are adding values only to compute this variable and the values that you're adding are always positive, there's really no need to check the result against 0. An instruction like **min**(*finalcolor*, 1.0) clamps the result at 1.0, and this instruction likely has higher performance than an instruction like **clamp**(*finalcolor*, 0.0, 1.0) because it needs only to compare values against one number instead of two. If you define the valid range of all the variables in your shader, you can more easily see the boundary conditions that you need to handle.

8.2.3 Use the Built-in Functions

Whenever possible, use the built-in functions to implement the effect that you're trying to achieve. Built-in functions are intended to be implemented in an optimal way by the graphics hardware vendor. If your shader hand-codes the same effect as a built-in function, there's little chance that it will be faster than the built-in function but a good chance that it will be slower.

8.2.4 Use Vectors

The OpenGL Shading Language lets you express vector computations naturally, and underlying graphics hardware is often built to operate simultaneously on a vector of values. Therefore, you should take advantage of this and use vectors for calculations whenever possible. On the other hand, you shouldn't use vectors that are bigger than the computations require. Such use can waste registers, hardware interpolators (in the case of varying variables), processing bandwidth, or memory bandwidth.

8.2.5 Use Textures to Encode Complex Functions

Because fragment processing is now programmable, textures can be used for a lot more than just image data. You might want to consider storing a complex function in a texture and doing a single lookup rather than a complex computation within the fragment shader. This is illustrated in Chapter 15, in which we encode a noise function as a 3D texture. This approach takes advantage of the specialized high-performance hardware that performs texture access, and it can also take advantage of texture filtering hardware to interpolate between values encoded in the texture.

8.2.6 Review the Information Logs

One of the main ways that an OpenGL implementation can provide feedback to an application developer is through the shader object and program object information logs (see Section 7.6). During shader development, you should review the messages in the information logs for compiler and linker errors, but you should also review them to see if they include any performance or functionality warnings or other descriptive messages. These information logs are one of the primary ways for OpenGL implementations to convey implementation-dependent information about performance, resource limitations, and so on.

8.3 Shader Debugging

Shader development tools are in their infancy, so debugging shaders can be a difficult task. Here are a few practical tips that may be helpful as you try to debug your shaders.

8.3.1 Use the Vertex Shader Output

To determine whether vertex shader code is behaving as expected, you can use conditionals to test intermediate values to see if a value is something unexpected. If it is, you can modify one of the shader's output values so that a visually distinct change occurs. For instance, if you think that the value *foo* should never be greater than 5.0, you can set the color values that are being passed to the fragment shader to magenta or neon green if the value of *foo* exceeds 5.0. If that's not distinctive enough and you've already computed the transformed homogeneous position, you can do something like this:

```
if (foo > 5.0)
    gl_Position += 1.0;
```

This code adds 1 to each component of the transformed position for which *foo* was greater than 5. When it is executed, you should see the object shift on the screen. With this approach, you can systematically check your assumptions about the intermediate values being generated by the vertex shader.

8.3.2 Use the Fragment Shader Output

Fragment shaders can produce a fragment color, a fragment depth, or an array of fragment data values. You can use the **discard** keyword to prevent the computed fragment value from updating the framebuffer. The depth value may not be helpful during debugging, but you can either color-code your fragment colors or use the **discard** keyword to discard fragments with certain qualities. These techniques provide you with visual feedback about what's going on within the shader.

For instance, if you're not quite sure if your 2D texture coordinates span the whole range from 0 to 1.0, you could put an **if** test in the shader and discard fragments with certain qualities. You can discard all the fragments for which both *s* and *t* texture coordinates are greater than 0.5 or for which either coordinate is greater than 0.99, and so on. The model will be drawn with "missing" pixels where fragments were discarded. The **discard** keyword is quite useful because it can appear anywhere in a fragment shader. You can put the discard statement near the beginning of a complex fragment shader and gradually move it down in the code as you verify that things are working properly.

Similarly, you can assign values to *FragColor* that convey debugging information. If you have a mathematical function in your shader that is expected to range from [0,1] and average 0.5, you can assign solid green to *FragColor* if the value is less than 0, solid red if it is between 0 and 0.5, solid blue if it is between 0.5 and 1.0, and solid white if it is greater than 1.0. This kind of debugging information can quickly tell you whether a certain computation is going astray.

8.3.3 Use Simple Geometry

For debugging texture computations, it may be useful to render a single large rectangle with identity matrices for the modeling, viewing, and projection matrices and to look carefully at what is occurring. Use a distinct texture image, for example, color bars or a simple color gradient ramp (yellow to blue perhaps), so that you can visually verify that the texturing operation is occurring as you expect it to.

8.4 Shader Development Tools

In coming years, we should see some exciting advances in the area of tools for shader development. This section briefly describes shader development tools available at the time of this writing.

8.4.1 RenderMonkey

As the era of programmable graphics hardware has unfolded, we've learned that there is more to developing shaders than just developing the code for the shaders themselves. Shaders can be highly customized to the point that they may work as intended only on a single model. Shader source code, textures, geometry, and initial values for uniform variables are all important parts of a production-quality shader. Shader development tools must capture all the essential elements of a shader and allow these elements to easily be modified and maintained.

Another factor in shader development is that the person writing the shader is not necessarily the same person developing the application code that deploys the shader. Often, an artist will be employed to design textures and contribute to or even control the shader development process. The collaboration between the artist and programmer is an important one for entertainment-based applications and must be supported by shader development tools.

An integrated development environment (IDE) allows programmers and artists to develop and experiment with shaders outside the environment of the application. This reduces the complexity of the shader development task and encourages rapid prototyping and experimentation. Finished shaders are a form of intellectual property, and maintenance, portability, and easy deployment to a variety of platforms are essential to maximizing the benefit of this type of company asset. The idea behind an IDE is that all the essential elements of the finished shader can be encapsulated, managed, shared, and exported for use in the final application.

ATI first released an IDE called RenderMonkey in 2002. In its initial release, RenderMonkey supported shader development for DirectX vertex shaders and pixel shaders. However, RenderMonkey was architected in such a way that it could easily be extended to support other shader programming languages. In 2004, ATI and 3Dlabs collaborated to produce the first version of RenderMonkey that added support for high-level shader development in OpenGL with the OpenGL Shading Language. In 2006, AMD and ATI merged, and RenderMonkey continues to evolve, adding OpenGL ES Shading Language development. The RenderMonkey IDE is currently available for free from AMD's developer Web site, http://developer.amd.com/.

RenderMonkey was designed for extensibility. At its core is a flexible framework that allows easy incorporation of shading languages. It is an environment that is language agnostic, allowing any high-level shading language to be supported by means of plug-ins. It currently supports the pixel shaders and vertex shaders defined in Microsoft's DirectX 8.1 and 9.0, the High-Level Shader Language (HLSL) defined in DirectX 9.0, the OpenGL Shading Language, and the OpenGL ES Shading Language.

In RenderMonkey, the encapsulation of all the information necessary to re-create a shading effect is called an EFFECT WORKSPACE. An effect workspace consists of effects group nodes, variable nodes, and stream mapping nodes. Each effects group is made up of one or more effect nodes, and each effect node is made up of one or more rendering passes. Each rendering pass may contain rendering state, source code for a vertex shader, source code for a fragment shader, geometry, and textures. All the effect data is organized into a tree hierarchy that is visible in the workspace viewer.

Effects group nodes collect related effects into a single container. This is sometimes handy for taming the complexity of dealing with lots of different effects. You might also use an effects group as a container for several similar effects with different performance characteristics (for instance, "best quality," "fast," and "fastest"). The criteria for grouping things within effects groups is entirely up to you.

Effect nodes encompass all the information needed to implement a real-time visual effect. The effect may be composed of multiple passes. Starting state is inherited from a default effect to provide a known starting state for all effects. The default effect can store effect data that is common to all shading effects.

Pass nodes define a drawing operation (i.e., a rendering pass). Each pass inherits data from previous passes within the effect, and the first pass inherits from the default effect. A typical pass contains a vertex shader and fragment shader pair, a render state block, textures, geometry, and nodes of other types (for example, variable nodes). Different geometry can be used in each pass to render effects like fur.

Variable nodes define the parameters that are available from within a shader. For the OpenGL Shading Language, variable nodes are the mechanisms for defining uniform variables. Intuitive names and types can be assigned to variable nodes, and the contents of a variable node can be manipulated with a GUI widget.

RenderMonkey is built completely out of plug-ins. Source code for some plug-ins is available, and you are encouraged to write your own plug-ins to perform tasks necessary for your workflow or to support importing and exporting your data with proprietary formats. Existing RenderMonkey modules are listed here:

- Shader editors—These are modeled on the interface of Microsoft's Visual Studio to provide an intuitive interface. They support editing of vertex and fragment shaders; syntax coloring; and creation of OpenGL, HLSL, and assembly language shaders.

- Variable editors—Shader parameters can be edited with GUI widgets that "know" the underlying data type for editing; editors exist for colors, vectors, matrices, and scalars; and custom widgets can be created.

- Artist editor—Shader parameters relevant to the art designer can be presented in an artist-friendly fashion so that they can be viewed and modified; programmers can select which parameters are artist-editable; and changes can be seen in real time.

- Previewers—These allow real-time viewing of the shading effect; changes to the shader source code or its parameters are immediately reflected in the preview window; view settings are customizable; views (front, back, side, etc.) are preset; and DirectX 9.0 and OpenGL Shading Language/OpenGL previews are available.

- Exporter—Everything required to re-create a shading effect is encapsulated and written into a single XML file.

- Importer—Everything required to re-create a shading effect is read back from an XML file.

- COLLADA viewer—This is an open source COLLADA effects previewer.

The XML file format was chosen as the basis for encapsulating shader information in RenderMonkey because it is an industry standard, it has a user-readable file format, it is user extensible, and it works with the many free parsers that are available. It is relatively easy to adapt an existing XML parser for your own use or to write a new one. The XML file that encapsulates a shader effect contains all shader source code, all render states, all models, and all texture information. This makes it straightforward to create, manage, and share shader assets.

8.4.2   Apple GLSLEditorSample

This small free gem is included in Apple's developer tools for Mac OS X. This sample application is an Xcode project with complete source code, so it is highly customizable. But even for casual use, it has all the basics for a simple shader developer environment. Like RenderMonkey, it has shader editor windows for vertex and fragment shaders, windows to set uniform variables and other OpenGL state, simple and intuitive texture setup, and diagnostic windows for error messages.

8.4.3   Graphic Remedy gDEBugger

This broad OpenGL debugging environment is available on Windows, Mac OS X, and Linux. At the time of this writing, it already fully supports OpenGL 3.0. Particularly significant for OpenGL 3.0 are the tools it provides to aid in identifying deprecated OpenGL functions. The debugging environment lets you easily view all of the programs and shaders used by an application and adds "edit on the fly" to replace selected shaders during a debugging session.

8.4.4   OpenGL Shading Language Compiler Front End

In June 2003, 3Dlabs released an open source version of its lexical analyzer, parser, and semantic checker (i.e., an OpenGL Shading Language COMPILER

FRONT END). This code reads an OpenGL shader and turns it into a token stream. This process is called LEXICAL ANALYSIS. The token stream is then processed to ensure that the program consists of valid statements. This process is referred to as SYNTACTIC ANALYSIS, or parsing. SEMANTIC ANALYSIS is then performed to determine whether the shader conforms to the semantic rules defined or implied by the OpenGL Shading Language specification. The result of this processing is turned into a high-level representation of the original source code. This high-level intermediate language (HIL) is a binary representation of the original source code that can be further processed by a target-specific back end to provide machine code for a particular type of graphics hardware.

It is anticipated that individual hardware vendors will implement the back end needed for their particular hardware. The compiler back end will typically include intellectual property and hardware-specific information that is proprietary to the graphics hardware vendor. It is not anticipated that 3Dlabs or other hardware vendors will make public the source code for their compiler back ends.

Still, the compiler front end provided by 3Dlabs has been, and will continue to be, a useful tool for the development of the OpenGL Shading Language, and it will be useful for other organizations that want to develop an OpenGL Shading Language compiler or tools for shader development. As the language specification was nearing completion, the compiler front end was being developed. Except for the preprocessor (which was derived from another open source preprocessor), it was implemented from scratch with the publicly available system utilities *flex* and *bison*. It was not derived from existing code. This made it a clean way to double-check the specification and discover language flaws before the specification was released. Indeed, a number of such flaws were discovered through this effort, and, as a result, the specification was improved before its release.

Because of its clean implementation, the OpenGL Shading Language compiler front end also serves as additional technical documentation about the language. The specification should be your first stop, but if you really want to know the details of what's allowed in the language and what's not, studying the compiler front end will provide a definitive answer.

OpenGL implementors that base their compiler on the compiler front end from 3Dlabs will also be doing a big favor to their end users: The semantics of the OpenGL Shading Language will be checked in the same way for all implementations that use this front end. This will benefit developers as they encounter consistent error-checking between different implementations.

Although few readers of this book will likely end up developing an OpenGL Shading Language compiler, this resource is nevertheless a useful one to know about. The source code for the compiler front end is available for download at the former 3Dlabs Web site (now at http://3dshaders.com).

Using the GLSL compiler front end, 3Dlabs has also written a tool called GLSLvalidate. This tool reads a file containing a shader and uses the compiler front end to parse it. Errors are reported in the output window. This tool can be executed on any platform; an OpenGL 2.0 driver is not required. This tool is provided as open source by 3Dlabs.

Another tool from 3Dlabs, GLSLParserTest, determines whether your OpenGL implementation properly supports the OpenGL Shading Language specification. It attempts to compile some 200 shaders and compares the results against the reference compiler. Some shaders should compile, and some should not. Results are printed, and the information log for any shader can be examined. Again, this tool is provided as open source (see the former 3Dlabs developer Web site, now at http://3dshaders.com).

8.5 Scene Graphs

by Mike Weiblen

A SCENE GRAPH is a hierarchical data structure containing a description of a scene to be rendered. Rather than explicitly coding a scene to be rendered as OpenGL API calls, an application builds a scene graph and then calls the scene graph rendering engine to do the actual rendering by traversing the data structure. In this way, a scene graph allows a developer to focus on what to draw, rather than on the details of how to draw. In typical terminology, the term *scene graph* is often used to describe the toolkit for both the data structure itself and the rendering engine that traverses the data structure to render the scene.

Scene graphs make it possible for a developer of visualization applications to leverage the performance of OpenGL without necessarily being an expert in all the details of OpenGL; the scene graph itself encapsulates OpenGL best practices. Because a scene graph is a toolkit layer on top of OpenGL, it raises the programming abstractions closer to the application domain.

As a tree, a scene graph consists of nodes that have one or more children. Since OpenGL state often has a hierarchical nature (such as the modelview matrix stack), that state can easily be mapped to nodes in the tree.

The following are some of the attributes and benefits of scene graphs:

- Encapsulation of best practices for rendering OpenGL, such as optimized GL state control; optimized internal data representations; and minimal geometry sent for rendering based on camera visibility.

- Implementation of sophisticated rendering architectures for performance, for example, pervasive multithreading, multi-CPU, multi-graphics pipe, or synchronized multisystem clustering.

- Definition of the output viewports. For complex display systems such as multiprojector domes, the scene graph can provide support for nonlinear distortion compensation.

- Hierarchical in-memory representation, for example, a tree of nodes with child nodes or a directed acyclic graph (DAG).

- OpenGL state control. By associating GL state with nodes in the graph, the scene graph renderer collects those state requests and applies them efficiently to the OpenGL pipeline. The scene graph can implement a form of lazy state application, by which it avoids forcing state changes down the pipe if no geometry actually requires it for rendering. State can be inherited from parents down to children.

- View culling, by which the spatial position of scene graph nodes are tested against the position of a camera's view volume; only if a node will actually contribute to visible pixels will its geometry be sent to the pipe for rendering. (There is no reason to send vertices to the pipe for geometry that is behind the eyepoint.)

- Instancing of assets. One model of a tire can be referenced four times on a single car; a single car can be instanced many times to create a parking lot full of cars.

The typical application code for a scene graph–based rendering application is conceptually not much more than

```
build the scene graph (loading files from disc at startup, etc.)
do forever
{
    update the camera position
    update other time-varying entities in the scene (such as vehicles
    or particle effects)

    draw the scene
}
```

Although a scene graph allows a visualization developer to focus on what to draw rather than on the details of how to draw it, that does not mean the developer is isolated from direct OpenGL control. In fact, the developer could define custom rendering methods. But for many common rendering tasks, the scene graph renderer already provides a complete solution and acts as a reusable toolkit for leveraging that capability. As expected from a well-designed toolkit, there are no inviolate rules; if you as the developer really need to do something out of the ordinary, the toolkit provides the avenues necessary.

The palette of nodes available for constructing the scene graph provides ways to apply attributes to be inherited by the children of that node. Here are some examples (certainly not an exhaustive list) of scene graph nodes:

- Parent node—Multiple child nodes can be attached.

- Transform nodes—The children are transformed by the parent's transformation matrix.

- Switch nodes—Only one child of the parent will be rendered, governed by a switching condition.

- Level-of-detail node (a specialized switch node)—Only one child is rendered, according to the distance of the node from the camera.

- Billboard node—Its children are automatically oriented toward the camera.

- Light node—Other nodes in the scene are illuminated by lights at the position and with the attributes contained here.

By helping the developer focus on "what" rather than "how," a scene graph can simplify the use of shaders. For example, using the hierarchical nature of a scene graph, a developer can compose a scene that has a shader with default values for uniform variables near the root of the scene graph, so it affects much of the scene. Alternative values for uniform variables attached at lower nodes can specialize the shader for a particular piece of geometry. The scene graph rendering engine can take over the tasks of determining if or when to compile or link the components of the shader and when to actually send updates for uniform variables to the pipeline, depending on visibility.

Several OpenGL scene graph products are currently available. OpenScene-Graph (or OSG, www.openscenegraph.org/) is an open source project that also has recently included support for OpenGL and the OpenGL Shading Language. OpenSG (www.opensg.org) is another open source OpenGL scene graph. Depending on your application, any one of these could save you a great deal of time and application development effort.

8.6 Summary

Writing shaders is similar in many ways to other software engineering tasks. A good dose of common sense can go a long way. Software engineering principles should be applied just as for any other software engineering task. This is especially true in these early generations of programmable graphics hardware. Shader development is more challenging because early OpenGL Shading Language implementations might be incomplete in some ways, compilers will be immature, performance characteristics may differ widely between vendors, and tools to aid shader development are in their infancy. RenderMonkey, GLSLEditorSample and gDEBugger are shader development tools that are available now. Perhaps others will be following.

On the other hand, writing shaders for programmable graphics hardware presents some unique challenges. Good decisions need to be made about how to split the computation between the CPU, the vertex processor, and the fragment processor. It is useful to have a solid foundation in mathematics and computer graphics before attempting to write shaders. Thorough knowledge of how OpenGL works is also a key asset, and having some understanding of the underlying graphics hardware can be helpful. It often pays to collaborate with an artist when developing a shader. This can help you develop a shader that is parameterized in such a way that it can be put to a variety of uses in the final application.

8.7 Further Information

Numerous books describe sound software engineering principles and practices. Two that describe tactics specific to developing shaders are *Texturing and Modeling: A Procedural Approach* by David X. Ebert et al. (2002) and *Advanced RenderMan: Creating CGI for Motion Pictures* by Anthony A. Apodaca and Larry Gritz (1999). Some of the shader development discussion in these books is specific to RenderMan, but many of the principles are also relevant to developing shaders with the OpenGL Shading Language.

For performance tuning, the best advice I have right now is to become good friends with the developer relations staff at your favorite graphics hardware company (or companies). These are the people who can provide you with additional insight or information about the underlying graphics hardware architecture and the relative performance of various aspects of the hardware. Until we go through another generation or two of programmable graphics hardware development (and perhaps even longer), performance differences between various hardware architectures will depend on the trade-offs made by the hardware architects and the driver developers. Scour the Web sites of these companies, attend their presentations at trade shows, and ask lots of questions.

The ATI developer Web site contains a number of presentations on Render-Monkey. The RenderMonkey IDE and documentation can be downloaded from either the ATI Web site or the 3Dlabs Web site. The 3Dlabs Web site contains the open source GLSL compiler front end, the GLSLvalidate tool, and other useful tools and examples.

[1] *3Dlabs developer Web site*. Now at http://3dshaders.com.

[2] Apodaca, Anthony A., and Larry Gritz, *Advanced RenderMan: Creating CGI for Motion Pictures*, Morgan Kaufmann Publishers, San Francisco, 1999. www.renderman.org/RMR/Books/ arman/ materials.html

[3] *AMD developer Web site*. http://developer.amd.com/

[4] *Apple developer Web site*. http://developer.apple.com/

[5] Ebert, David S., John Hart, Bill Mark, F. Kenton Musgrave, Darwyn Peachey, Ken Perlin, and Steven Worley, *Texturing and Modeling: A Procedural Approach, Third Edition*, Morgan Kaufmann Publishers, San Francisco, 2002. www.texturingandmodeling.com/

[6] *Graphic Remedy Web site*. www.gremedy.com/

[7] *NVIDIA developer Web site*. http://developer.nvidia.com/

[8] *OpenSceneGraph Web site*. www.openscenegraph.org/

[9] *OpenSG Web site*. www.opensg.org/

Chapter 9

Emulating OpenGL
Fixed Functionality

The programmability of OpenGL opens many new possibilities for never-before-seen rendering effects. Programmable shaders can provide results that are superior to OpenGL fixed functionality, especially in the area of realism. Nevertheless, it can still be instructive to examine how some of OpenGL's fixed functionality rendering steps could be implemented with OpenGL shaders. While simplistic, these code snippets may be useful as stepping stones to bigger and better things.

This chapter describes OpenGL shader code that mimics the behavior of the OpenGL fixed functionality vertex, fragment, and matrix processing. The shader code snippets are derived from the Full OpenGL Pipeline and Pixel Pipeline shaders developed by Dave Baldwin for inclusion in the white paper *OpenGL 2.0 Shading Language*. Further refinement of this shader code occurred for the first edition of this book. These code snippets were then verified and finalized with a tool called **ShaderGen** that takes a description of OpenGL's fixed functionality state and automatically generates the equivalent shaders. **ShaderGen** was implemented by Inderaj Bains and Joshua Doss while at 3Dlabs.

The goal of the shader code in this chapter is to faithfully represent OpenGL fixed functionality. The code examples in this chapter reference OpenGL state wherever possible through user-defined variables. By doing this, these examples are "forward looking." But don't get too enamored with the shaders presented in this chapter. In later chapters of this book, we explore a variety of shaders that provide more flexible or more efficient results than those discussed in this chapter.

We need to provide a small warning, however. Matrix operations, especially matrix concatenation and matrix inversion, are not that cheap. So in Chapter 16, we will show a technique for running these matrix shader functions less often than once a vertex.

9.1 Transformation

The features of the OpenGL Shading Language make it very easy to express transformations between the coordinate spaces defined by OpenGL. We've already seen the transformation that will be used by almost every vertex shader. The incoming vertex position must be transformed into clipping coordinates for use by the fixed functionality stages that occur after vertex processing. This is done in one of two ways, either this:

```
uniform mat4 MVPmatrix; // modelview-projection matrix
// ...

in vec4 MCVertex;
// ...

a(); // A function that does not modify gl_Position, MVP, or MCVertex

// ...
// Transform vertex to clip space
gl_Position = MVP * MCVertex;
```

or this:

```
uniform mat4 MVPmatrix; // modelview-projection matrix
// ...

invariant gl_Position;
in vec4 MCVertex;
// ...

a(); // A function that does not modify gl_Position, MVP or MCVertex

// ...
// Transform vertex to clip space
gl_Position = MVPmatrix * MCVertex;
```

The only difference between these two methods is the **invariant** qualifier modifying **gl_Position**. The first case may or may not compute the transformed positions in exactly the same way no matter what unrelated function or expression is linked to the shader. This can cause problems in rendering if a multipass algorithm is used to render the same geometry more than once. The **invariant** qualifier instructs the compiler and linker to ignore expressions and functions that are not directly related to the computation of the output. The second case must compute the transformed positions in exactly the same way no matter what unrelated function or expression is linked to the shader. For multipass algorithms, the second method is preferred because it produces the same transformed position for a family of shaders.

OpenGL specifies that light positions are transformed by the modelview matrix when they are provided to OpenGL. This means that they are stored in eye coordinates. It is often convenient to perform lighting computations in eye space, so it is often necessary to transform the incoming vertex position into eye coordinates as shown in Listing 9.1.

Listing 9.1 Computation of eye coordinate position

```
uniform mat4 MVMatrix;
// ...

vec4 ecPosition;
vec3 ecPosition3;    // in 3 space
// ...

// Transform vertex to eye coordinates
if (NeedEyePosition)
{
    ecPosition  = MVMatrix * MCVertex;
    ecPosition3 = (vec3(ecPosition)) / ecPosition.w;
}
```

This snippet of code computes the homogeneous point in eye space (a **vec4**) as well as the nonhomogeneous point (a **vec3**). Both values are useful as we shall see.

To perform lighting calculations in eye space, incoming surface normals must also be transformed. A user-defined uniform variable is available to store the normal transformation matrix, as shown in Listing 9.2.

Listing 9.2 Transformation of normal

```
uniform mat3 NormalMatrix;
// ...

in vec3 MCNormal;
// ...

vec3 normal;

normal = NormalMatrix * MCNormal;
```

In many cases, the application may not know anything about the characteristics of the surface normals that are being provided. For the lighting computations to work correctly, each incoming normal must be normalized so that it is unit length. In an OpenGL shader, if normalization is required, we do it as shown in Listing 9.3.

Listing 9.3 Normalization of normal

```
normal = normalize(normal);
```

Sometimes an application will always be sending normals that are unit length and the modelview matrix is always one that does uniform scaling. In this case, rescaling can be used to avoid the possibly expensive square root operation that is a necessary part of normalization. If the rescaling factor is supplied by the application through the OpenGL API, the normal can be rescaled as shown in Listing 9.4.

Listing 9.4 Normal rescaling

```
uniform float NormalScale;
// ...

normal = normal * NormalScale;
```

The rescaling factor is stored as state within OpenGL and can be accessed from within a shader by the user-defined uniform variable *NormalScale*.

Texture coordinates can also be transformed. A texture matrix is defined for each texture coordinate set in OpenGL and can be accessed with the user-defined uniform matrix array variable *TextureMatrix*. Incoming texture coordinates can be transformed in the same manner as vertex positions, as shown in Listing 9.5.

Listing 9.5 Texture coordinate transformation

```
uniform TextureMatrix[MaxTextureCoords];
// ...

in vec4 MultiTexCoord0;
out vec4 TexCoord[MaxTexCoord];

TexCoord[0] = TextureMatrix[0] * MultiTexCoord0;
```

9.2 Light Sources

The lighting computations defined by OpenGL are somewhat involved. Let's start by defining a function for each of the types of light sources defined by OpenGL: directional lights, point lights, and spotlights. We pass in variables that store the total ambient, diffuse, and specular contributions from all light sources. These must be initialized to 0 before any of the light source computation routines are called.

9.2.1 Directional Lights

A directional light is assumed to be at an infinite distance from the objects being lit. According to this assumption, all light rays from the light source are parallel when they reach the scene. Therefore, a single direction vector can be used for every point in the scene. This assumption simplifies the math, so the code to implement a directional light source is simpler and typically runs faster than the code for other types of lights. Because the light source is assumed to be infinitely far away, the direction of maximum highlights is the same for every point in the scene. This direction vector can be computed ahead of time for each light source *i* and stored in *LightSource[i].halfVector*. This type of light source is useful for mimicking the effects of a light source like the sun.

The directional light function shown in Listing 9.6 computes the cosine of the angle between the surface normal and the light direction, as well as the cosine of the angle between the surface normal and the half angle between the light direction and the viewing direction. The former value is multiplied by the light's diffuse color to compute the diffuse component from the light. The latter value is raised to the power indicated by *FrontMaterial.shininess* before being multiplied by the light's specular color.

The only way either a diffuse reflection component or a specular reflection component can be present is if the angle between the light source direction and the surface normal is in the range [−90°,90°]. We determine the angle by examining *nDotVP*. This value is set to the greater of 0 and the cosine of the angle between the light source direction and the surface normal. If this value ends up being 0, the value that determines the amount of specular reflection is set to 0 as well. Our directional light function assumes that the vectors of interest are normalized, so the dot product between two vectors results in the cosine of the angle between them.

Listing 9.6 Directional light source computation

```
void DirectionalLight(const in int   i,
                      const in vec3 normal,
                      inout    vec4 ambient,
                      inout    vec4 diffuse,
                      inout    vec4 specular)
{
    float nDotVP; // normal . light direction
    float nDotHV; // normal . light half vector
    float pf; // power factor

    nDotVP = max(0.0, dot(normal,
                normalize(vec3(LightSource[i].position))));
    nDotHV = max(0.0, dot(normal, vec3(LightSource[i].halfVector)));

    if (nDotVP == 0.0)
        pf = 0.0;
    else
        pf = pow(nDotHV, FrontMaterial.shininess);

    ambient  += LightSource[i].ambient;
    diffuse  += LightSource[i].diffuse * nDotVP;
    specular += LightSource[i].specular * pf;
}
```

9.2.2 Point Lights

Point lights mimic lights that are near the scene or within the scene, such as lamps or ceiling lights or street lights. There are two main differences between point lights and directional lights. First, with a point light source, the direction of maximum highlights must be computed at each vertex rather than with the precomputed value from *LightSource[i].halfVector.* Second, light received at the surface is expected to decrease as the point light source gets farther and farther away. This is called ATTENUATION. Each light source has constant, linear, and quadratic attenuation factors that are taken into account when the lighting contribution from a point light is computed.

These differences show up in the first few lines of the point light function (see Listing 9.7). The first step is to compute the vector from the surface to the light position. We compute this distance by using the length function. Next, we normalize *VP* so that we can use it in a dot product operation to compute a proper cosine value. We then compute the attenuation factor and the direction of maximum highlights as required. The remaining code is the same as for our directional light function except that the ambient, diffuse, and specular terms are multiplied by the attenuation factor.

One optimization that we could make is to have two point light functions, one that computes the attenuation factor and one that does not. If the values for the constant, linear, and quadratic attenuation factors are (1, 0, 0) (the default values), we could use the function that does not compute attenuation and get better performance.

Listing 9.7   Point light source computation

```
void PointLight(const in int   i,
                const in vec3 eye,
                const in vec3 ecPosition3,
                const in vec3 normal,
                inout    vec4 ambient,
                inout    vec4 diffuse,
                inout    vec4 specular)
{
    float nDotVP;        // normal . light direction
    float nDotHV;        // normal . light half vector
    float pf;            // power factor
    float attenuation;   // computed attenuation factor
    float d;             // distance from surface to light source
    vec3  VP;            // direction from surface to light position
    vec3  halfVector;    // direction of maximum highlights

    // Compute vector from surface to light position
    VP = vec3(LightSource[i].position) - ecPosition3;

    // Compute distance between surface and light position
    d = length(VP);

    // Normalize the vector from surface to light position
    VP = normalize(VP);

    // Compute attenuation

    attenuation = 1.0 / (LightSource[i].constantAttenuation +
                    LightSource[i].linearAttenuation * d +
                    LightSource[i].quadraticAttenuation * d * d);

    halfVector = normalize(VP + eye);

    nDotVP = max(0.0, dot(normal, VP));
    nDotHV = max(0.0, dot(normal, halfVector));

    if (nDotVP == 0.0)
       pf = 0.0;
    else
       pf = pow(nDotHV, FrontMaterial.shininess);

    ambient  += LightSource[i].ambient * attenuation;
    diffuse  += LightSource[i].diffuse * nDotVP * attenuation;
    specular += LightSource[i].specular * pf * attenuation;
}
```

9.2.3 Spotlights

In stage and cinema, spotlights project a strong beam of light that illuminates a well-defined area. The illuminated area can be further shaped through the use of flaps or shutters on the sides of the light. OpenGL includes light attributes that simulate a simple type of spotlight. Whereas point lights are modeled as sending light equally in all directions, OpenGL models spotlights as light sources that are restricted to producing a cone of light in a particular direction.

The first and last parts of our spotlight function (see Listing 9.8) look the same as our point light function (shown earlier in Listing 9.7). The differences occur in the middle of the function. A spotlight has a focus direction (*LightSource[i].spotDirection*), and this direction is dotted with the vector from the light position to the surface (*−VP*). The resulting cosine value is compared to the precomputed cosine cutoff value (*LightSource[i].spotCosCutoff*) to determine whether the position on the surface is inside or outside the spotlight's cone of illumination. If it is outside, the spotlight attenuation is set to 0; otherwise, this value is raised to a power specified by *LightSource[i].spotExponent.* The resulting spotlight attenuation factor is multiplied by the previously computed attenuation factor to give the overall attenuation factor. The remaining lines of code are the same as they were for point lights.

Listing 9.8 Spotlight computation

```
void SpotLight(const in int   i,
               const in vec3 eye,
               const in vec3 ecPosition3,
               const in vec3 normal,
               inout    vec4 ambient,
               inout    vec4 diffuse,
               inout    vec4 specular)
{
    float nDotVP;          // normal . light direction
    float nDotHV;          // normal . light half vector
    float pf;              // power factor
    float spotDot;         // cosine of angle between spotlight
    float spotAttenuation; // spotlight attenuation factor
    float attenuation;     // computed attenuation factor
    float d;               // distance from surface to light source
    vec3 VP;               // direction from surface to light position
    vec3 halfVector;       // direction of maximum highlights

    // Compute vector from surface to light position
    VP = vec3(LightSource[i].position) - ecPosition3;

    // Compute distance between surface and light position
    d = length(VP);
```

```
// Normalize the vector from surface to light position
VP = normalize(VP);

// Compute attenuation
attenuation = 1.0 / (LightSource[i].constantAttenuation +
                     LightSource[i].linearAttenuation * d +
                     LightSource[i].quadraticAttenuation * d * d);

// See if point on surface is inside cone of illumination
spotDot = dot(-VP, normalize(LightSource[i].spotDirection));
if (spotDot < LightSource[i].spotCosCutoff)
    spotAttenuation = 0.0; // light adds no contribution
else
    spotAttenuation = pow(spotDot, LightSource[i].spotExponent);

// Combine the spotlight and distance attenuation.
attenuation *= spotAttenuation;

halfVector = normalize(VP + eye);

nDotVP = max(0.0, dot(normal, VP));
nDotHV = max(0.0, dot(normal, halfVector));

if (nDotVP == 0.0)
    pf = 0.0;
else
    pf = pow(nDotHV, FrontMaterial.shininess);

ambient  += LightSource[i].ambient * attenuation;
diffuse  += LightSource[i].diffuse * nDotVP * attenuation;
specular += LightSource[i].specular * pf * attenuation;
}
```

9.3 Material Properties and Lighting

OpenGL lighting calculations require knowing the viewing direction in the eye coordinate system in order to compute specular reflection terms. By default, the view direction is assumed to be parallel to and in the direction of the $-z$ axis. OpenGL also has a mode that requires the viewing direction to be computed from the origin of the eye coordinate system (local viewer). To compute this, we can transform the incoming vertex into eye space by using the current modelview matrix. The x, y, and z coordinates of this point are divided by the homogeneous coordinate w to get a **vec3** value that can be used directly in the lighting calculations. The computation of this eye coordinate position (*ecPosition3*) was illustrated in Section 9.10. To get a unit vector corresponding to the viewing direction, we normalize and negate the eye space position. Shader code to implement these computations is shown in Listing 9.9.

Listing 9.9 Local viewer computation

```
if (NeedLocalViewer)
    eye = -normalize(ecPosition3);
else
    eye = vec3(0.0, 0.0, 1.0);
```

With the viewing direction calculated, we can initialize the variables that accumulate the ambient, diffuse, and specular lighting contributions from all the light sources in the scene. We can then call the functions defined in the previous section to compute the contributions from each light source. In the code in Listing 9.10, we assume that all lights with an index less than the constant NumEnabledLights are enabled. Directional lights are distinguished by having a position parameter with a homogeneous (*w*) coordinate equal to 0 at the time they were provided to OpenGL. (These positions are transformed by the modelview matrix when the light is specified, so the *w* coordinate remains 0 after transformation if the last column of the modelview matrix is the typical (0 0 0 1)). Point lights are distinguished by having a spotlight cutoff angle equal to 180.

Listing 9.10 Loop to compute contributions from all enabled light sources

```
// Clear the light intensity accumulators
amb  = vec4(0.0);
diff = vec4(0.0);
spec = vec4(0.0);

// Loop through enabled lights, compute contribution from each
for (int i = 0; i < NumEnabledLights; i++)
{
    if (LightSource[i].position.w == 0.0)
        DirectionalLight(i, normal, amb, diff, spec);
    else if (LightSource[i].spotCutoff == 180.0)
        PointLight(i, eye, ecPosition3, normal, amb, diff, spec);
    else
        SpotLight(i, eye, ecPosition3, normal, amb, diff, spec);
}
```

One of the changes made to OpenGL in version 1.2 was to add functionality to compute the color at a vertex in two parts: a primary color that contains the combination of the emissive, ambient, and diffuse terms as computed by the usual lighting equations; and a secondary color that contains just the specular term as computed by the usual lighting equations. If this mode is not enabled (the default case), the primary color is computed with the combination of emissive, ambient, diffuse, and specular terms.

Computing the specular contribution separately allows specular highlights to be applied after texturing has occurred. The specular value is added to the computed color after texturing has occurred to allow the specular highlights to be the color of the light source rather than the color of the surface. Listing 9.11 shows how to compute the surface color (according to OpenGL rules) with everything but the specular contribution:

Listing 9.11 Surface color computation, omitting the specular contribution

```
FrontLightModelProduct.sceneColor +
       amb  * FrontMaterial.ambient +
       diff * FrontMaterial.diffuse;
```

We use a user-defined uniform variable (*FrontLightModelProduct.sceneColor*) to contain the emissive material property for front-facing surfaces plus the product of the ambient material property for front-facing surfaces and the global ambient light for the scene (i.e., *FrontMaterial.emission + FrontMaterial.ambient * LightModel.ambient*). We can add this together with the intensity of reflected ambient light and the intensity of reflected diffuse light. Next, we can do the appropriate computations, depending on whether the separate specular color mode is indicated, as shown in Listing 9.12.

Listing 9.12 Final surface color computation

```
if (NeedSeparateSpecular)
    FrontSecondaryColor = vec4( spec.rgb *
                               FrontMaterial.specular.rgb, 1.0);
else
    color += spec * FrontMaterial.specular;

FrontColor = clamp(color, 0.0, 1.0);
```

9.4 Two-Sided Lighting

To mimic OpenGL's two-sided lighting behavior, you need to invert the surface normal and perform the same computations as defined in the preceding section, using the back-facing material properties. You can probably do it more cleverly than this, but it might look like Listing 9.13. The functions **DirectionalLight**, **PointLight**, and **SpotLight** that are referenced in this code segment are identical to the functions described in Section 9.2 except that the value *BackMaterial.shininess* is used in the computations instead of the value *FrontMaterial.shininess*.

Listing 9.13 Two-sided lighting computation

```
normal = -normal;

// Clear the light intensity accumulators
amb =  vec4(0.0);
diff = vec4(0.0);
spec = vec4(0.0);

// Loop through enabled lights, compute contribution from each
for (int i = 0; i < NumEnabledLights; i++)
{
    if (LightSource[i].position.w == 0.0)
        DirectionalLight(i, normal, amb, diff, spec);
    else if (LightSource[i].spotCutoff == 180.0)
        PointLight(i, eye, ecPosition3, normal, amb, diff, spec);
    else
        SpotLight(i, eye, ecPosition3, normal, amb, diff, spec);
}

color = BackLightModelProduct.sceneColor +
        amb  * BackMaterial.ambient +
        diff * BackMaterial.diffuse;

if (NeedSeparateSpecular)
    BackSecondaryColor = vec4( spec.rgb *
                               BackMaterial.specular.rgb, 1.0);
else
    color += spec * BackMaterial.specular;

BackColor = clamp(color, 0.0, 1.0);
```

9.5 No Lighting

If no enabled lights are in the scene, it is a simple matter to pass the per-vertex color and secondary color for further processing with the commands shown in Listing 9.14.

Listing 9.14 Setting final color values with no lighting

```
if (NeedSecondaryColor)
    FrontSecondaryColor = clamp(SecondaryColor, 0.0, 1.0);

FrontColor = clamp(color;, 0.0, 1.0);
```

9.6 Fog

In OpenGL, DEPTH-CUING and fog effects are controlled by fog parameters. A fog factor is computed according to one of three equations, and this fog factor performs a linear blend between the fog color and the computed color for the fragment. The depth value to be used in the fog equation can be either the fog coordinate passed in as a user-defined vertex attribute (*FogCoord*) or the eye-coordinate distance from the eye. In the latter case, it is usually sufficient to approximate the depth value as the absolute value of the *z*-coordinate in eye space (i.e., **abs**(*ecPosition.z*)). When there is a wide angle of view, this approximation may cause a noticeable artifact (too little fog) near the edges. If this is the case, you could compute *z* as the true distance from the eye to the fragment with **length**(*ecPosition*). (This method involves a square root computation, so the code may run slower as a result.) The choice of which depth value to use would normally be done in the vertex shader as follows:

```
in float FogCoord;
out float FogFragCoord;
//...

if (UseFogCoordinate)
    FogFragCoord = FogCoord;
else
    FogFragCoord = abs(ecPosition.z);;
```

A linear computation (which corresponds to the traditional computer graphics operation of depth-cuing) can be selected in OpenGL with the symbolic constant GL_LINEAR. For this case, the fog factor *f* is computed with the following equation:

$$f = \frac{end - z}{end - start}$$

start, *end*, and *z* are all distances in eye coordinates. *start* is the distance to the start of the fog effect, *end* is the distance to the end of the effect, and *z* is the value stored in *FogFragCoord*. We can explicitly provide the start and end positions as uniform variables, or we can access the current values in OpenGL state by using the user-defined uniform variables *Fog.start* and *Fog.end*. The shader code to compute the fog factor with the built-in variables for accessing OpenGL state is shown in Listing 9.15.

Listing 9.15 GL_LINEAR fog computation

```
in float FogFragCoord;
// ...

float fog;
fog = (Fog.end - FogFragCoord) * Fog.scale;
```

Because 1.0 / (*Fog.end – Fog.start)* doesn't depend on any per-vertex or per-fragment state, this value is precomputed and stored in the user-defined uniform variable *Fog.scale*.

We can achieve a more realistic fog effect with an exponential function. With a negative exponent value, the exponential function will model the diminishing of the original color as a function of distance. A simple exponential fog function can be selected in OpenGL with the symbolic constant GL_EXP. The formula corresponding to this fog function is

$$f = e^{-(density \cdot z)}$$

The *z* value is computed as described for the previous function, and *density* is a value that represents the density of the fog. The user-defined uniform variable *Fog.density* can be used to store the density. The larger this value becomes, the "thicker" the fog becomes. For this function to work as intended, *density* must be greater than or equal to 0.

The OpenGL Shading Language has a built-in **exp** (base *e*) function that we can use to perform this calculation. Our OpenGL shader code to compute the preceding equation is shown in Listing 9.16.

Listing 9.16 GL_EXP fog computation

```
fog = exp(-Fog.density * FogFragCoord);
```

The final fog function defined by OpenGL is selected with the symbolic constant GL_EXP2 and is defined as

$$f = e^{-(density \cdot z)^2}$$

This function changes the slope of the exponential decay function by squaring the exponent. The OpenGL shader code to implement it is similar to the previous function (see Listing 9.17).

Listing 9.17 GL_EXP2 fog computation

```
fog = exp(-Fog.density * Fog.density *
          FogFragCoord * FogFragCoord);
```

OpenGL also requires the final value for the fog factor to be limited to the range [0,1]. We can accomplish this with the statement in Listing 9.18.

Listing 9.18 Clamping the fog factor

```
fog = clamp(fog, 0.0, 1.0);
```

Any of these three fog functions can be computed in either a vertex shader or a fragment shader. Unless you have very large polygons in your scene, you probably won't see any difference if the fog factor is computed in the vertex shader and passed to the fragment shader as a varying variable. This will probably also give you better performance overall, so it's generally the preferred approach. In the fragment shader, when the (almost) final color is computed, the fog factor can be used to compute a linear blend between the fog color and the (almost) final fragment color. The OpenGL shader code in Listing 9.19 does the trick by using the fog color saved as part of current OpenGL state.

Listing 9.19 Applying fog to compute final color value

```
color = mix(vec3(Fog.color), color, fog);
```

The code presented in this section achieves the same results as OpenGL's fixed functionality. But with programmability, you are free to use a completely different approach to compute fog effects.

9.7 Texture Coordinate Generation

OpenGL can be set up to compute texture coordinates automatically, based only on the incoming vertex positions. Five methods are defined, and each can be useful for certain purposes. The texture generation mode specified by GL_OBJECT_LINEAR is useful for cases in which a texture is to remain fixed to a geometric model, such as in a terrain modeling application. GL_EYE_LINEAR is useful for producing dynamic contour lines on an object. Examples of this usage include a scientist studying isosurfaces or a geologist interpreting seismic data. GL_SPHERE_MAP can generate texture coordinates for simple environment mapping. GL_REFLECTION_MAP and GL_NORMAL_MAP can work in conjunction with cube map textures. GL_REFLECTION_MAP passes the reflection vector as the texture coordinate. GL_NORMAL_MAP simply passes the computed eye space normal as the texture coordinate.

A function that generates sphere map coordinates according to the OpenGL specification is shown in Listing 9.20.

Listing 9.20 GL_SPHERE_MAP computation

```
vec2 SphereMap(const in vec3 ecPosition3,
               const in vec3 normal)
{
    float m;
    vec3 r, u;
    u = normalize(ecPosition3);
    r = reflect(u, normal);
    r.z += 1.0;
    m = 0.5 * inversesqrt( dot(r,r) );
    return r.xy * m + 0.5;
}
```

A function that generates reflection map coordinates according to the OpenGL specification looks almost identical to the function shown in Listing 9.20. The difference is that it returns the reflection vector as its result (see Listing 9.21).

Listing 9.21 GL_REFLECTION_MAP computation

```
vec3 ReflectionMap(const in vec3 ecPosition3,
                   const in vec3 normal)
{
    float NdotU, m;
    vec3 u;
    u = normalize(ecPosition3);
    return (reflect(u, normal));
}
```

Listing 9.22 shows the code for selecting between the five texture generation methods and computing the appropriate texture coordinate values.

Listing 9.22 Texture coordinate generation computation

```
// Compute sphere map coordinates if needed
if (TexGenSphere)
    sphereMap = SphereMap(ecPosition3, normal);

// Compute reflection map coordinates if needed
if (TexGenReflection)
    reflection = ReflectionMap(ecPosition3, normal);

// Compute texture coordinate for each enabled texture unit
for (int i = 0; i < NumEnabledTextureUnits; i++)

{
    if (TexGenObject)
    {
```

```
        TexCoord[i].s = dot(MCvertex, ObjectPlaneS[i]);
        TexCoord[i].t = dot(MCvertex, ObjectPlaneT[i]);
        TexCoord[i].p = dot(MCvertex, ObjectPlaneR[i]);
        TexCoord[i].q = dot(MCvertex, ObjectPlaneQ[i]);
    }

    if (TexGenEye)
    {
        TexCoord[i].s = dot(ecPosition, EyePlaneS[i]);
        TexCoord[i].t = dot(ecPosition, EyePlaneT[i]);
        TexCoord[i].p = dot(ecPosition, EyePlaneR[i]);
        TexCoord[i].q = dot(ecPosition, EyePlaneQ[i]);
    }

    if (TexGenSphere)
        TexCoord[i] = vec4(sphereMap, 0.0, 1.0);

    if (TexGenReflection)
        TexCoord[i] = vec4(reflection, 1.0);

    if (TexGenNormal)
        TexCoord[i] = vec4(normal, 1.0);
}
```

In this code, we assume that each texture unit less than *NumEnabledTexture-Units* is enabled. If this value is 0, the whole loop is skipped. Otherwise, each texture coordinate that is needed is computed in the loop.

Because the sphere map and reflection computations do not depend on any of the texture unit state, they can be performed once, and the result is used for all texture units. For the GL_OBJECT_LINEAR and GL_EYE_LINEAR methods, there is a plane equation for each component of each set of texture coordinates. For the former case, we generate the components of *TexCoord[0]* by multiplying the plane equation coefficients for the specified component by the incoming vertex position. For the latter case, we compute the components of *TexCoord[0]* by multiplying the plane equation coefficients by the eye coordinate position of the vertex. Depending on what type of texture access is done during fragment processing, it may not be necessary to compute the *t*, *p*, or *q* texture component,[1] so these computations could be eliminated.

---

1. For historical reasons, the OpenGL texture coordinate components are named *s*, *t*, *r*, and *q*. Because of the desire to have single-letter, component-selection names in the OpenGL Shading Language, components for textures are named *s*, *t*, *p*, and *q*. This lets us avoid using *r*, which is needed for selecting color components as *r*, *g*, *b*, and *a*.

9.8 User Clipping

To take advantage of OpenGL's user clipping (which remains as fixed functionality between vertex processing and fragment processing in programmable OpenGL), a vertex shader must calculate the distances between clip planes and the vertex. The shader writer can choose to transform either the clip planes or the vertex, or both, to a convenient space. The example shader in Listing 9.23 performs user clipping in eye space.

Listing 9.23   User-clipping computation

```
uniform vec4 ClipPlane[MaxClipPlanes];
// ...

for ( int i=0; i<MaxClipPlanes; i++ )
{
    gl_ClipDistance[i] = dot( ClipPlane[i], ecPosition );
}
```

9.9 Texture Application

The built-in texture functions read values from texture memory. The values read from texture memory are used in a variety of ways. OpenGL fixed functionality includes support for texture application formulas enabled with the symbolic constants GL_REPLACE, GL_MODULATE, GL_DECAL, GL_BLEND, and GL_ADD. These modes operate differently, depending on the format of the texture being accessed. The following code illustrates the case in which an RGBA texture is accessed with the sampler *tex0*. The variable *color* is initialized to be *Color* and then modified as needed so that it contains the color value that results from texture application.

GL_REPLACE is the simplest texture application mode of all. It simply replaces the current fragment color with the value read from texture memory. See Listing 9.24.

Listing 9.24   GL_REPLACE computation

```
color = texture(tex0, TexCoord[0].xy);
```

GL_MODULATE causes the incoming fragment color to be multiplied by the value retrieved from texture memory. This is a good texture function to use if lighting is computed before texturing (e.g., the vertex shader performs the lighting computation, and the fragment shader does the texturing). White can be used as the base color for an object rendered with this technique, and the texture then provides the diffuse color. This technique is illustrated with the OpenGL shader code in Listing 9.25.

Listing 9.25 GL_MODULATE computation

```
color *= texture(tex0, TexCoord[0].xy);
```

GL_DECAL is useful for applying an opaque image to a portion of an object. For instance, you might want to apply a number and company logos to the surfaces of a race car or tattoos to the skin of a character in a game. When an RGBA texture is accessed, the alpha value at each texel linearly interpolates between the incoming fragment's RGB value and the texture's RGB value. The incoming fragment's alpha value is used as is. The code for implementing this mode is in Listing 9.26.

Listing 9.26 GL_DECAL computation

```
vec4 texel = texture(tex0, TexCoord[0].xy);
vec3 col = mix(color.rgb, texel.rgb, texel.a);
color = vec4(col, color.a);
```

GL_BLEND is the only texture application mode that takes the current texture environment color into account. The RGB values read from the texture linearly interpolate between the RGB values of the incoming fragment and the texture environment color. We compute the new alpha value by multiplying the alpha of the incoming fragment by the alpha read from the texture. The OpenGL shader code is shown in Listing 9.27.

Listing 9.27 GL_BLEND computation

```
vec4 texel = texture(tex0, TexCoord[0].xy);
vec3 col = mix(color.rgb, TextureEnvColor[0].rgb, texel.rgb);
color = vec4(col, color.a * texel.a);;
```

GL_ADD computes the sum of the incoming fragment color and the value read from the texture. The two alpha values are multiplied together to compute the new alpha value. This is the only traditional texture application mode for which the resulting values can exceed the range [0,1], so we clamp the final result (see Listing 9.28).

Listing 9.28 GL_ADD computation

```
vec4 texel = texture(tex0, TexCoord[0].xy);
color.rgb += texel.rgb;
color.a   *= texel.a;
color = clamp(color, 0.0, 1.0);
```

The texture-combine environment mode that was added in OpenGL 1.3 and extended in OpenGL 1.4 defines a large number of additional simple ways to perform texture application. A variety of new formulas, source values, and operands were defined. The mapping of these additional modes into OpenGL shader code is straightforward but tiresome, so it is omitted here.

9.10 Matrices

The features of the OpenGL Shading Language make it very easy to build the transformation matrices that were provided by OpenGL matrix commands. We've already seen the transformation matrices will be used by almost every vertex shader. In this section, we'll cover these functions, staring with the basic building blocks of computing matrices.

9.10.1 Identity Matrix

This is very simple (see Listing 9.29), but still surprisingly useful.

Listing 9.29 Identity matrix computation

```
mat4 IdentityMatrix( void )
{
    return mat4( 1.0 );
}
```

9.10.2 Scale

Nearly as simple, the **ScaleMatrix** function in Listing 9.30 computes a matrix that scales each of *x*, *y*, and *z* independently. It is a generalization of **IdentityMatrix**.

Listing 9.30 Scale matrix computation

```
mat4 ScaleMatrix( const in vec3 s )
{
    return mat4( s.x, 0.0, 0.0, 0.0,
                 0.0, s.y, 0.0, 0.0,
                 0.0, 0.0, s.z, 0.0,
                 0.0, 0.0, 0.0, 1.0 );
}
```

9.10.3 Translate

The **TranslateMatrix** function computes a transformation matrix.

One thing we need to remember is that matrices are specified in column major order, as is the tradition in OpenGL. The OpenGL specification and the OpenGL Reference Manual follow the linear algebra convention that vectors are columns. We need to "read" the matrices column by column. The first four elements are the first column, even though they show up in the first row of the constructor. While at first glance it might look like the matrix in Listing 9.31 has been transposed, it has not.

Listing 9.31 Translation matrix computation

```
mat4 TranslateMatrix( const in vec3 t )
{
    return mat4( 1.0, 0.0, 0.0, 0.0,
                 0.0, 1.0, 0.0, 0.0,
                 0.0, 0.0, 1.0, 0.0,
                 t.x, t.y, t.z, 1.0 );
}
```

9.10.4 Rotate

The *Rotate* command in OpenGL takes an angle in degrees and an axis that may be unnormalized. We convert the angle in degrees to radians, and we also normalize the axis in the shader function. One optimization that we could make to the shader in Listing 9.32 is to have multiple rotate functions, versions that convert the angle and normalize the axis, and versions that do not.

Listing 9.32 Rotation matrix computation

```
mat4 RotateMatrix( const in float angle,
                   const in vec3  axis )
{
    vec3 n = normalize( axis );
    float theta = radians( angle );
    float c = cos( theta );
    float s = sin( theta );
    mat3 R;
    R[0] = n.xyz*n.x*(1.0-c) + vec3(       c,  n.z*s, -n.y*s );
    R[1] = n.xyz*n.y*(1.0-c) + vec3( -n.z*s,      c,  n.x*s );
    R[2] = n.xyz*n.z*(1.0-c) + vec3(  n.y*s, -n.x*s,      c );
    return mat4( R[0],          0.0,
                 R[1],          0.0,
                 R[2],          0.0,
                 0.0, 0.0, 0.0, 1.0 );
}
```

9.10.5 Ortho

Orthographic projection is not very photorealistic but has a long tradition in several areas, including mechanical engineering, architecture, and even early "3D" video games. It is also the view of a very powerful telescope looking at objects far, far away.

The OpenGL command Ortho takes the left, right, top and bottom clipping planes and projects them orthogonally along the z axis, with the near and far clipping planes capping the view volume (see Listing 9.33).

Listing 9.33 Orthographic matrix projection

```
mat4 OrthoMatrix( const in float     left, const in float right,
                  const in float bottom, const in float    top,
                  const in float  zNear, const in float   zFar )
{
    vec3 delta = vec3( right,    top,   zFar )
               - vec3(  left, bottom, zNear )
               ;
    vec3 sum   = vec3( right,    top,   zFar )
               + vec3(  left, bottom, zNear );

    vec3 ratio = sum / delta;
    vec3 twoRatio = 2.0 / delta;

    return mat4( twoRatio.x,          0.0,           0.0, 0.0,
                        0.0,   twoRatio.y,           0.0, 0.0,
                        0.0,          0.0,   -twoRatio.z, 0.0,
                   -ratio.x,     -ratio.y,      -ratio.z, 1.0 );

}
```

9.10.6 Frustum

Perspective projection was rediscovered during the Renaissance. The OpenGL command *Frustum* computes a simple version, an extension of Ortho. Instead of projecting orthogonally along the z axis, the four corners of the front image plane are projected along each direction from the origin (eye) to the corner. The view volume is truncated by the near and far planes, or looks like a truncated pyramid—a frustum. The OpenGL shader code is shown in Listing 9.34.

Listing 9.34 Frustum matrix computation

```
mat4 FrustumMatrix( const in float     left, const in float right,
                    const in float bottom, const in float    top,
                    const in float  zNear, const in float   zFar )
```

```
{
    vec3 delta = vec3( right,      top,   zFar )
               - vec3(  left, bottom, zNear );

    vec3 sum   = vec3( right,      top,   zFar )
               + vec3(  left, bottom, zNear );

    vec3 ratio = sum / delta;
    vec3 twoRatio = 2.0 * zNear / delta;

    return mat4( twoRatio.x,          0.0,              0.0,  0.0,
                       0.0,  twoRatio.y,              0.0,  0.0,
                   ratio.x,     ratio.y,        -ratio.z, -1.0,
                       0.0,         0.0,  -zNear*twoRatio.z,  0.0 );

}
```

9.11 Operating on the Current Matrices

We have laid the foundation of the core OpenGL matrix computation functions. But the OpenGL matrix commands operate on a current matrix, selected by MatrixMode. We'll ignore the texture matrices and the rarely used color matrices for now.

In Listing 9.35 we put them together into operations on a current matrix.

Listing 9.35 Matrix operations

```
const int MODELVIEW = 0;
const int PROJECTION =1;

int  CurrentMode = MODELVIEW;
mat4 ModelviewMatrix = mat4( 1.0 );
mat4 ProjectionMatrix = mat4( 1.0 );
mat4 CurrentMatrix = mat4( 1.0 );

void MatrixMode ( const in int mode )
{
    if ( mode != CurrentMode )
    {
        switch (mode)
        {
            case MODELVIEW:
            {
                ProjectionMatrix = CurrentMatrix;
                CurrentMatrix = ModelviewMatrix;
                CurrentMode = MODELVIEW;
                break;
            }
            case PROJECTION:
```

```
            {
                ModelviewMatrix = CurrentMatrix;
                CurrentMatrix = ProjectionMatrix;
                CurrentMode = PROJECTION;
                break;
            }
            default:
            {
                break;
            }
        }
    }
    return;
}

void LoadIdentity( void )
{
    CurrentMatrix = IdentityMatrix();
}
void LoadMatrix( const in mat4 m )
{
    CurrentMatrix = m;
}
void MultMatrix( const in mat4 m )
{
    CurrentMatrix = m
                * CurrentMatrix;
}
void Scale( const in vec3 s )
{
    CurrentMatrix = ScaleMatrix( s )
                * CurrentMatrix;
}
void Translate( const in vec3 t )
{
    CurrentMatrix = TranslateMatrix( t )
                * CurrentMatrix;
}


void Rotate( const in float angle,
            const in vec3   axis )
{
    CurrentMatrix = RotateMatrix( angle, axis )
                * CurrentMatrix;
}
void Ortho( const in float    left, const in float right,
            const in float bottom, const in float    top,
            const in float  zNear, const in float   zFar )
{
    CurrentMatrix = OrthoMatrix( left, right, bottom, top,
                                    zNear, zFar )
                * CurrentMatrix;
}
```

```
void Frustum( const in float    left, const in float right,
              const in float bottom, const in float    top,
              const in float  zNear, const in float   zFar )
{
    CurrentMatrix = FrustumMatrix( left, right, bottom, top,
                                   zNear, zFar )
              * CurrentMatrix;
}
```

9.11.1 A Simple Matrix Transformation Example

We can now "port" a transformation sequence from OpenGL to the
OpenGL Shading Language. This simple example in Listing 9.36 will
scale, rotate, and translate a model from model coordinates into world
coordinates.

We need to provide the warning again. Matrix operations, especially matrix
concatentations, are not that cheap. There are more efficient ways to
accomplish this in a vertex shader.

Listing 9.36 Simple matrix transformation

```
// Shading Language Equivalent  // Original OpenGL code
uniform float MCscale;          // float MCscale;
uniform float MCangle;          // float MCangle;
uniform vec3  MCaxis;           // float MCaxis[3];
uniform vec3  WCtranslate;      // float WCtranslate[3];

// ...

void ModelCoordinates2WorldCoordinates( void )
{
    MatrixMode( MODELVIEW );    // glMatrixMode( GL_MODELVIEW );
    LoadIdentity();             // glLoadIdentity;
    Scale( vec3(MCscale) );     // glScalef( MCscale,
                                //           MCscale,
                                //           MCscale );
    Rotate( MCangle, MCaxis );  // glRotatef( MCangle,
                                //            MCaxis[0],
                                //            MCaxis[1],
                                //            MCaxis[2] );
    Translate( WCtranslate );   // glTranslatef( WCtranslate[0],
                                //               WCtranslate[1],
                                //               WCtranslate[2] );
// ...
}
```

9.12 Summary

The rendering formulas specified by OpenGL have been reasonable ones to implement in fixed functionality hardware for the past decade or so, but they are not necessarily the best ones to use in your shaders. We look at better-performing and more realistic shaders in subsequent chapters. Still, it can be instructive to see how these formulas can be expressed in shaders written in the OpenGL Shading Language. The shader examples presented in this chapter demonstrate the expression of these fixed functionality transformation formulas, but they should not be considered optimal implementations. Take the ideas and the shading code illustrated in this chapter and adapt them to your own needs.

9.13 Further Information

The *OpenGL Programming Guide, Seventh Edition* (2010) by Dave Shreiner and the Khronos OpenGL ARB Working Group, contains more complete descriptions of the various formulas presented in this chapter. The functionality is defined in the OpenGL specification, *The OpenGL Graphics System: A Specification Version 3.0*, by Mark Segal and Kurt Akeley, edited by Jon Leech and Pat Brown (2008). Basic graphics concepts like transformation, lighting, fog, and texturing are also covered in standard graphics texts such as *Introduction to Computer Graphics* by J.D. Foley et al. (1994). *Real-Time Rendering* by Tomas Akenine-Möller and E. Haines (2002) also contains good descriptions of these basic topics.

[1] Akenine-Möller, Tomas, E. Haines, *Real-Time Rendering, Second Edition*, A K Peters, Ltd., Natick, Massachusetts, 2002. www.realtimerendering.com

[2] Baldwin, Dave, *OpenGL 2.0 Shading Language White Paper, Version 1.0*, 3Dlabs, October, 2001.

[3] Foley, J.D., A. van Dam, S.K. Feiner, J.H. Hughes, and R.L. Philips, *Introduction to Computer Graphics*, Addison-Wesley, Reading, Massachusetts, 1994.

[4] Foley, J.D., A. van Dam, S.K. Feiner, and J.H. Hughes, *Computer Graphics: Principles and Practice, Second Edition in C, Second Edition*, Addison-Wesley, Reading, Massachusetts, 1996.

[5] OpenGL Architecture Review Board, *OpenGL Reference Manual, Fourth Edition: The Official Reference to OpenGL, Version 1.4*, Editor: Dave Shreiner, Addison-Wesley, Reading, Massachusetts, 2004.

[6] Segal, Mark, and Kurt Akeley, *The OpenGL Graphics System: A Specification (Version 3.1)*, Editor (v1.1): Chris Frazier, (v1.2–3.1): Jon Leech, (v2.0): Jon Leech and Pat Brown, March 2009. www.opengl.org/documentation/specs/

[7] Shreiner, Dave, and the Khronos OpenGL ARB Working Group, *OpenGL Programming Guide, Seventh Edition: The Official Guide to Learning OpenGL, Versions 3.0 and 3.1*, Addison-Wesley, Boston, Massachusetts, 2010.

Chapter 10

Stored Texture Shaders

Texture mapping is a powerful mechanism built into OpenGL. At the time OpenGL was initially defined (1992), texture-mapping hardware was just starting to be available on commercial products. Nowadays, texture mapping is available on graphics hardware at all price points, even entry-level consumer graphics boards.

When OpenGL 1.0 was defined, texture mapping had a fairly narrow definition. It was simply a way to apply an image to the surface of an object. Since then, hardware has become capable of doing much more in this area, and researchers have come up with a lot of interesting things to do with textures other than just plastering images on surfaces. The scope of texture mapping has also been extended in OpenGL. Texture objects were one of the key additions in OpenGL 1.1. Three-dimensional textures were made part of the standard in OpenGL 1.2. The capability of hardware to access two or more textures simultaneously was exposed in OpenGL 1.3, along with cube map textures and a framework for supporting compressed textures formats. OpenGL 1.4 added support for depth textures and shadows, automatic mipmap generation, and another texture wrap mode (mirrored repeat). If you need a quick review of how texturing works in OpenGL, refer to Section 1.10.

The programmability introduced with the OpenGL Shading Language allows for a much broader definition of texture mapping. With programmable shaders, an application can read values from any number of textures and use them in any way that makes sense. This includes supporting sophisticated algorithms that use the results of one texture access to define the parameters of another texture access. Textures can also store intermediate rendering results; they can serve as lookup tables for complex functions;

they can store normals, normal perturbation factors, gloss values, visibility information, and polynomial coefficients; and they can do many other things. These things could not be done nearly as easily, if at all, in unextended OpenGL, and this flexibility means that texture maps are coming closer to being general-purpose memory that can be used for arbitrary purposes. (Filtering and wrapping behavior still differentiate texture-map access from normal memory access operations.)

This chapter describes several shaders that, at their core, rely on looking up values in texture memory and using those values to achieve interesting effects. We start by talking a little bit about how textures are accessed from within a shader, and then we look at several examples of shaders that access texture memory for various purposes other than just the straightforward application of an image to the surface of a 3D object.

10.1 Access to Texture Maps from a Shader

Applications are required to set up and initialize texturing state properly before executing a shader that accesses texture memory. An application must perform the following steps to set up a texture for use within a shader:

1. Select a specific texture unit, and make it active by calling **glActiveTexture**.

2. Create a texture object, and bind it to the active texture unit by calling **glBindTexture**.

3. Set various parameters (wrapping, filtering, etc.) of the texture object by calling **glTexParameter**.

4. Define the texture by calling **glTexImage**.

It is quite straightforward to access textures from within a shader after texture state has been set up properly by the application. The OpenGL Shading Language has built-in data types (see Section 3.2.4) and built-in functions (see Section 5.7) to accomplish this task.

A uniform variable of type **sampler** must be used to access a texture from within a shader. Within a shader, a sampler is considered an opaque data type containing a value that can access a particular texture. The shader is responsible for declaring such a uniform variable for each texture that it wants to access. The application must provide a value for the sampler before execution of the shader, as described in Section 7.9.

The type of the sampler indicates the type of texture that is to be accessed. A variable of type **sampler1D** accesses a 1D texture; a variable of type

sampler2D accesses a 2D texture; a variable of type **sampler3D** accesses a 3D texture; a variable of type **samplerCube** accesses a cube map texture; and variables of type **samplerShadow1D** and **samplerShadow2D** access 1D and 2D depth textures. For instance, if the application intends to use texture unit 4 to store a 2D texture, the shader must declare a uniform variable of type **sampler2D**, and the application must load a value of 4 into this variable before executing the shader.

The built-in function **texture** performs texture access within a shader. The first argument in each of these built-in functions is a sampler.

The built-in texture-access function also takes a texture coordinate as an argument. Hardware uses this texture coordinate to determine which locations in the texture map are to be accessed. A 1D texture is accessed with a single floating-point texture coordinate. A 2D texture is accessed with a **vec2**, and a 3D texture is accessed with a **vec3**. A projective version of the texture access function, **textureProj**, is also provided. In this function, the individual components of the texture coordinate are divided by the last component of the texture coordinate, and the result is used in the texture access operation.

There are some differences between accessing a texture from a vertex shader and accessing a texture from a fragment shader (the OpenGL Shading Language allows both). The level of detail to be used for accessing a mipmap texture is calculated with implicit derivatives. Derivatives are available in the fragment shader but not in the vertex shader. For this reason, the OpenGL Shading Language includes a built-in texture function that can be used to allow the level of detail to be expressed directly as a function argument, **textureLOD**, and a built-in texture function that allows explicit derivatives as function arguments, **textureGrad**. These may be used in either the vertex or the fragment shader. The OpenGL Shading Language also includes built-in functions that can be used only in a fragment shader that allows a level-of-detail bias to be passed in. This bias value is added to the mechanically computed level-of-detail value. In this way, a shader writer can add a little extra sharpness or blurriness to the texture mapping function, depending on the situation. If any of these functions is used with a texture that is not a mipmap texture, the level-of-detail bias value is ignored.

The built-in functions to access cube maps operate in the same way as defined for fixed functionality. The texture coordinate that is provided is treated as a direction vector that emanates from the center of a cube. This value selects one of the cube map's 2D textures, based on the coordinate with the largest magnitude. The other two coordinates are divided by the absolute value of this coordinate and scaled and biased to calculate a 2D coordinate that will be used to access the chosen face of the cube map.

The built-in functions to access depth textures also operate in the same way as defined for fixed functionality. The texture accessed by one of these functions must have a base internal format of GL_DEPTH_COMPONENT. The value that is returned when this type of texture is accessed depends on the texture-comparison mode, the texture-comparison function, and the depth texture mode. Each of these values can be set with **glTexParameter**.

The built-in texture access functions operate according to the current state of the texture unit that is being accessed and according to the parameters of the texture object that is bound to that texture unit. In other words, the value returned by the built-in texture access functions take into consideration the texturing state that has already been established for the texture unit and the texture object, including wrap mode, minification filter, magnification filter, border color, minimum/maximum level of detail, texture comparison mode, and so on.

10.2 Simple Texturing Example

With these built-in functions for accessing textures, it's easy to write a simple shader that does texture mapping. Our goal is to create a texture-mapped sphere by using a realistic texture of the earth's surface. Application code described in this chapter came from **ogl2demo**, written primarily by Barthold Lichtenbelt. Similar code is available in **GLSLdemo**, written by Philip Rideout.

To achieve good results, it helps to start with excellent textures. Color Plate 3 shows an example of a two-dimensional texture map, a cylindrical projection of the earth's surface, including clouds. This image, and other images in this section, were obtained from the NASA Web site and were created by Reto Stöckli of the NASA/Goddard Space Flight Center. These images of Earth are part of a series of consistently processed data sets (land, sea ice, and clouds) from NASA's remote sensing satellite, the Moderate Resolution Imaging Spectroradiometer, or MODIS. Data from this satellite was combined with other related data sets (topography, land cover, and city lights), all at 1 kilometer resolution. The resulting series of images is extremely high resolution (43200×21600 pixels). For our purposes, we can get by with a much smaller texture, so we use versions that have been sampled down to 2048×1024.

10.2.1 Application Setup

We assume that the image data has been read into our application and that the image width, image height, a pointer to the image data, and a texture name generated by OpenGL can be passed to our texture initialization function.

```
init2DTexture(GLint texName, GLint texWidth,
            GLint texHeight, GLubyte *texPtr)
{
    glBindTexture(GL_TEXTURE_2D, texName);
    glTexParameteri(GL_TEXTURE_2D, GL_TEXTURE_WRAP_S, GL_REPEAT);
    glTexParameteri(GL_TEXTURE_2D, GL_TEXTURE_WRAP_T, GL_REPEAT);
    glTexParameteri(GL_TEXTURE_2D, GL_TEXTURE_MAG_FILTER, GL_LINEAR);
    glTexParameteri(GL_TEXTURE_2D, GL_TEXTURE_MIN_FILTER, GL_LINEAR);
    glTexImage2D(GL_TEXTURE_2D, 0, GL_RGB, texWidth, texHeight, 0,
                GL_RGB, GL_UNSIGNED_BYTE, texPtr);
}
```

This initialization function creates a texture object named *texName*. Calls to **glTexParameter** set the wrapping behavior and filtering modes. We've chosen to use repeat as our wrapping behavior and to do linear filtering. We specify the data for the texture by calling **glTexImage2D** (the values passed to this function depend on how the image data has been stored in memory).

When we're ready to use this texture, we can use the following OpenGL calls:

```
    glActiveTexture(GL_TEXTURE0);
    glBindTexture(GL_TEXTURE_2D, earthTexName);
```

This sequence of calls sets the active texture unit to texture unit 0, binds our earth texture to this texture unit, and makes it active. We need to provide the values for two uniform variables. The vertex shader needs to know the light position, and the fragment shader needs to know the texture unit that is to be accessed. We define the light position as a **vec3** in the vertex shader named *lightPosition* and the texture unit as a **sampler2D** in the fragment shader named *EarthTexture*. Our application code needs to determine the location of these uniform variables and then provide appropriate values. We assume that our shaders have been compiled, linked using a program object whose handle is *programObj*, and installed as part of current state. We can make the following calls to initialize the uniform variables:

```
lightLoc = glGetUniformLocation(programObj, "LightPosition");
glUniform3f(lightLoc, 0.0, 0.0, 4.0);
texLoc   = glGetUniformLocation(programObj, "EarthTexture");
glUniform1i(texLoc, 0);
```

The light source position is set to a point right in front of the object along the viewing axis. We plan to use texture unit 0 for our earth texture, so that is the value loaded into our sampler variable.

The application can now make appropriate OpenGL calls to draw a sphere, and the earth texture will be applied. A surface normal, a 2D texture coordinate, and a vertex position must be specified for each vertex.

10.2.2 Vertex Shader

The vertex shader for our simple texturing example is similar to the simple brick vertex shader described in Section 6.2. The main difference is that a texture coordinate is passed in as a vertex attribute, and it is passed on as a user-defined out variable name *TexCoord* (see Listing 10.1).

Listing 10.1 Vertex shader for simple texturing

```
#version 140
in  vec4  MCVertex;
in  vec3  MCNormal;
out vec2  TexCoord;

out float LightIntensity;
out vec4  TexCoord;

uniform mat4 MVMatrix;
uniform mat4 MVPMatrix;
uniform mat3 NormalMatrix;

uniform vec3 LightPosition;

const float specularContribution = 0.1;
const float diffuseContribution  = 1.0 - specularContribution;

void main()
{
    vec3 ecPosition = vec3(MVMatrix * MCVertex);
    vec3 tnorm      = normalize(NormalMatrix * MCNormal);
    vec3 lightVec   = normalize(LightPosition - ecPosition);
    vec3 reflectVec = reflect(-lightVec, tnorm);
    vec3 viewVec    = normalize(-ecPosition);

    float spec      = clamp(dot(reflectVec, viewVec), 0.0, 1.0);
    spec            = pow(spec, 16.0);

    LightIntensity  = diffuseContribution
                        * max(dot(lightVec, tnorm), 0.0)
                        + specularContribution * spec;

    TexCoord        = TexCoord0.st;
    gl_Position     = MVPMatrix * MCVertex;
}
```

10.2.3 Fragment Shader

The fragment shader shown in Listing 10.2 applies the earth texture to the incoming geometry. So, for instance, if we define a sphere where the *s* texture coordinates are related to longitude (e.g., 0° longitude is *s* = 0, and 360° longitude is *s* = 1.0) and *t* texture coordinates are related to latitude (90° south latitude is *t* = 0.0, and 90° north latitude is *t* = 1.0), then we can apply the texture map to the sphere's geometry as shown in Color Plate 6.

In the following fragment shader, the incoming *s* and *t* texture coordinate values (part of the user-defined in variable *TexCoord*) are used to look up a value from the texture currently bound to texture unit 0. The resulting value is multiplied by the light intensity computed by the vertex shader and passed as an in variable. The color is then clamped, and an alpha value of 1.0 is added to create the final fragment color, which is sent on for further processing, including depth testing. The resulting image as mapped onto a sphere is shown in Color Plate 6.

Listing 10.2 Fragment shader for simple texture mapping example

```
#version 140
in float LightIntensity;
in vec2  TexCoord;

out vec4 FragColor;

uniform sampler2D EarthTexture;

void main()
{
    vec3 lightColor = vec3(texture(EarthTexture, TexCoord));
    FragColor    = vec4(lightColor * LightIntensity, 1.0);
}
```

10.3 Multitexturing Example

The resulting image looks pretty good, but with a little more effort we can get it looking even better. For one thing, we know that there are lots of man-made lights on our planet, so when it's nighttime, major towns and cities can be seen as specks of light, even from space. So we use the angle between the light direction and the normal at each surface location to determine whether that location is in "daytime" or "nighttime." For points that are in daytime, we access the texture map that contains daylight colors and do an appropriate lighting calculation. For points in the nighttime region of the planet, we do no lighting and access a texture that shows the earth as illuminated at night. The daytime and nighttime textures are shown in Color Plate 4 and Color Plate 5.

Another somewhat unrealistic aspect to our simple approach is the reflection of sunlight off the surface of oceans and large lakes. Water is a very good reflective surface, and when our viewpoint is nearly the same as the reflection angle for the light source, we should see a specular reflection. But we know that desert, grass, and trees don't have this same kind of reflective property, so how can we get a nice specular highlight on the water but not on the land?

The answer is a technique called a GLOSS MAP. We make a single channel (i.e., grayscale) version of our original texture and assign values of 1.0 for areas that represent water and 0 for everything else. At each fragment, we read this gloss texture and multiply its value by the specular illumination portion of our lighting equation. It's fairly simple to create the gloss map in an image-editing program. The easiest way to do this is by editing the red channel of the cloudless daytime image. In this channel, all the water areas appear black or nearly black because they contain very little red information. We use a selection tool to select all the black (water) areas and then fill the selected area (water regions) with white. We invert the selection and fill the land areas with black. The result is a texture that contains a value of 1.0 (white) for areas in which we want a specular highlight, and a value of 0 (black) for areas in which we don't. We use this "gloss" value as a multiplier in our specular reflection calculation, so areas that represent water include a specular reflection term, and areas that represent land don't. Our gloss map is shown in Figure 10.1.

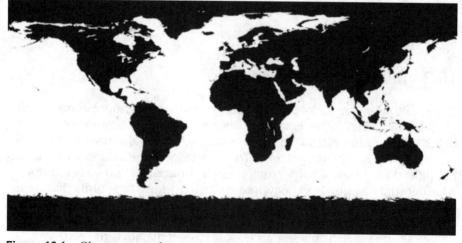

Figure 10.1   Gloss map used to create specular reflections from water surfaces

As you saw in Color Plate 4 and Color Plate 5, our daytime and nighttime textures no longer include cloud cover. So we store our cloud texture as a single channel (i.e., grayscale) texture as shown in Figure 10.2. By doing this, we have more flexibility about how we combine the cloud image with the images of the Earth's surface. For daytime views, we want the clouds to have diffuse reflection but no specular reflection. Furthermore, clouds obscure the surface, so a value of 1.0 for the cloud cover indicates that the earth's surface at that location is completely obscured by clouds. For night-time views, we don't want any light reflecting from the clouds, but we do want them to obscure the surface below. For convenience, we've stored our single channel cloud image into the red channel of an RGB texture, and we've stored our gloss map as the green channel. The blue channel is unused. (Another choice would be to store the gloss map as the alpha channel for our daytime image and the cloud texture as the alpha channel in our nighttime image.)

10.3.1 Application Setup

The setup required for multitexturing is about the same as it was for the simple texturing example, except that we need to set up three textures instead of one. We can call the **init2Dtexture** function described in Section 10.2.1 three times, once each for the daytime earth texture, the nighttime earth texture,

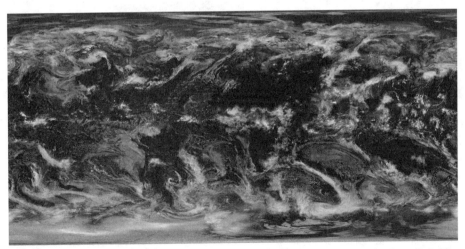

Figure 10.2   Texture map showing cloud cover (Blue Marble image by Reto Stöckli, NASA Goddard Space Flight Center)

and the cloud/gloss texture. We can activate these textures with the following OpenGL calls:

```
glActiveTexture(GL_TEXTURE0);
glBindTexture(GL_TEXTURE_2D, earthDayTexName);

glActiveTexture(GL_TEXTURE1);
glBindTexture(GL_TEXTURE_2D, earthNightTexName);

glActiveTexture(GL_TEXTURE2);
glBindTexture(GL_TEXTURE_2D, earthCloudsTexName);
```

The necessary uniform variables can be initialized as follows:

```
lightLoc = glGetUniformLocation(programObj, "LightPosition");
glUniform3f(lightLoc, 0.0, 0.0, 4.0);
texLoc   = glGetUniformLocation(programObj, "EarthDay");
glUniform1i(texLoc, 0);
texLoc   = glGetUniformLocation(programObj, "EarthNight");
glUniform1i(texLoc, 1);
texLoc   = glGetUniformLocation(programObj, "EarthCloudGloss");
glUniform1i(texLoc, 2);
```

The application can now make appropriate OpenGL calls to draw a sphere. A surface normal, a 2D texture coordinate, and a vertex position must be specified for each vertex.

10.3.2 Vertex Shader

The vertex shader for this multitexturing example is similar to the one described for the simple texturing example in Section 10.2.2, except that the diffuse and specular factors are computed by the vertex shader and passed as separate out variables to the fragment shader. The computed specular value is multiplied by the constant vector (1.0, 0.941, 0.898) to approximate the color of sunlight (see Listing 10.3).

Listing 10.3 Vertex shader for multitexturing

```
#version 140
in   vec4  MCVertex;
in   vec3  MCNormal;
in   vec4  TexCoord0;

out  float  Diffuse;
out  vec3   Specular;
out  vec2   TexCoord;

uniform vec3 LightPosition;
```

```
uniform mat4 MVMatrix;
uniform mat4 MVPMatrix;
uniform mat3 NormalMatrix;

void main()
{
    vec3 ecPosition = vec3(MVMatrix * MCVertex);
    vec3 tnorm      = normalize(NormalMatrix * MCNormal);
    vec3 lightVec   = normalize(LightPosition - ecPosition);
    vec3 reflectVec = reflect(-lightVec, tnorm);
    vec3 viewVec    = normalize(-ecPosition);

    float spec      = clamp(dot(reflectVec, viewVec), 0.0, 1.0);
    spec            = pow(spec, 8.0);
    Specular        = spec * vec3(1.0, 0.941, 0.898) * 0.3;

    Diffuse         = max(dot(lightVec, tnorm), 0.0);

    TexCoord        = TexCoord0.st;
    gl_Position     = MVPMatrix * MCVertex;
}
```

10.3.3 Fragment Shader

The fragment shader that performs the desired multitexturing is shown in
Listing 10.4. The application has loaded the daytime texture in the texture
unit specified by *EarthDay*, the nighttime texture into the texture unit specified by *EarthNight*, and the cloud/gloss texture into the texture unit specified by *EarthCloudGloss*. The lighting computation is done in a vertex shader
that computes diffuse and specular reflection factors and passes them to the
fragment shader independently. The texture coordinates supplied by the
application are also passed to the fragment shader and form the basis of our
texture lookup operation.

In our fragment shader, the first thing we do is access our cloud/gloss texture because its values will be used in the computations that follow. Next,
we look up the value from our daytime texture, multiply it by our diffuse
lighting factor, and add to it the specular lighting factor multiplied by the
gloss value. If the fragment is unobscured by clouds, our computation gives
us the desired effect of diffuse lighting over the whole surface of the earth
with specular highlights from water surfaces. This value is multiplied by 1.0
minus the cloudiness factor. Finally, we add the cloud effect by multiplying
our cloudiness factor by the diffuse lighting value and adding this to our
previous result.

The nighttime calculation is simpler. Here, we just look up the value from our nighttime texture and multiply that result by 1.0 minus the cloudiness factor. Because this fragment will be in shadow, the diffuse and specular components are not used.

With these values computed, we can determine the value to be used for each fragment. The key is our diffuse lighting factor, which is greater than zero for areas in sunlight, equal to zero for areas in shadow, and near zero for areas near the terminator. The color value ends up being the computed *daytime* value in the sunlit areas, the computed *nighttime* value in the areas in shadow, and a mix of the two values to make a gradual transition near the terminator.

An alpha value of 1.0 is added to produce our final fragment color. Several views from the final shader are shown in Color Plate 7. You can see the nice specular highlight off the Gulf of Mexico in the first image. If you look closely at the third (nighttime) image, you can see the clouds obscuring the central part of the east coast of the United States and the northwestern part of Brazil.

It is worth pointing out that this shader should not be considered a general-purpose shader because it has some built-in assumptions about the type of geometry that will be drawn. It will look "right" only when used with a sphere with proper texture coordinates. More can be done to make the shader even more realistic. The color of the atmosphere actually varies, depending on the viewing position and the position of the sun. It is redder when near the shadow boundary, a fact that we often notice near sunrise and sunset. See the references at the end of the chapter for more information about achieving realistic effects such as Rayleigh scattering.

Listing 10.4 "As the world turns" fragment shader

```
uniform sampler2D EarthDay;
uniform sampler2D EarthNight;
uniform sampler2D EarthCloudGloss;

in float Diffuse;
in vec3  Specular;
in vec2  TexCoord;

out vec4 FragColor;

void main()
{
    // Monochrome cloud cover value will be in clouds.r
    // Gloss value will be in clouds.g
    // clouds.b will be unused
```

```
vec2 clouds    = texture(EarthCloudGloss, TexCoord).rg;
vec3 daytime   = (texture(EarthDay, TexCoord).rgb * Diffuse +
                     Specular * clouds.g) * (1.0 - clouds.r) +
                     clouds.r * Diffuse;
vec3 nighttime = texture(EarthNight, TexCoord).rgb *
                     (1.0 - clouds.r) * 2.0;

vec3 color = daytime;

if (Diffuse < 0.1)
    color = mix(nighttime, daytime, (Diffuse + 0.1) * 5.0);

FragColor = vec4(color, 1.0);
}
```

10.4 Cube Mapping Example

A technique called ENVIRONMENT MAPPING models reflections in a complex environment without resorting to ray-tracing. In this technique, one or more texture maps simulate the environment's reflections. This technique is best used for rendering objects that have some mirrorlike qualities.

The fundamental idea behind environment mapping is that we use the reflection vector from the surface of an object to look up the reflection color from an "environment" that is stored in a texture map. If environment mapping is done properly, the result looks as if the object being rendered is shiny and is reflecting its environment.

There are several ways to do environment mapping, including SPHERE MAPPING and CUBE MAPPING, both of which are supported in standard OpenGL. An example cube map is shown in Color Plate 10.

In this section, we describe OpenGL shaders that use a cube map to perform environment mapping on an object. The object is assumed to have an underlying layer that acts as a diffuse reflector. The result from the diffuse portion is combined with the environment reflection to produce a final value at each pixel.

A cube map is a texture that has six 2D textures that are organized to represent the faces of a cube. Cube maps are accessed with three texture coordinates that are treated as a direction vector emanating from the center of the cube. The cube map faces are differentiated by the sign along each of the three major axis directions. Think of the faces this way: The positive and negative *x* faces are the right and left sides of the cube; positive and negative *y* faces are the top and bottom sides of the cube; and positive and negative *z* faces are the back and front sides of the cube. Graphics hardware can use the three texture coordinates as a direction vector and automatically select the proper face and return a texel value where the direction vector intersects that face of the cube map.

10.4.1 Application Setup

The application needs to do very little to set up this shader. We use a simple lighting model, so the only lighting state that we need to pass in is a single light source position. We access the cube map through texture unit 4. *baseColor* defines the color of the diffuse underlayer of our object, and *mixRatio* sets the ratio of base color to environment map reflection. Here are the definitions for the uniform variables that we use:

```
LightPosition   0.0, 0.0, 4.0
BaseColor       0.4, 0.4, 1.0
MixRatio        0.8
EnvMap          4
```

After the shaders have been installed and the uniform variables have been provided, the application is expected to send a normal and the vertex position for each vertex that is to be drawn. The current values for the model-view matrix, the modelview-projection matrix, and the normal matrix are all accessed from within the vertex shader.

10.4.2 Vertex Shader

Listing 10.5 comprises the vertex shader that is used to do environment mapping with a cube map.

Listing 10.5 Vertex shader used for environment mapping with a cube map

```
#version 140

in   vec4  MCVertex;
in   vec3  MCNormal;

out float LightIntensity;
out vec3  ReflectDir;

uniform vec3 LightPosition;

uniform mat4 MVMatrix;
uniform mat4 MVPMatrix;
uniform mat3 NormalMatrix;
```

```
void main()
{
    gl_Position      = MVPMatrix * MCVertex;
    vec3 normal      = normalize(NormalMatrix * MCNormal);
    vec4 pos         = MVMatrix * MCVertex;
    vec3 eyeDir      = pos.xyz;
    ReflectDir       = reflect(eyeDir, normal);
    vec3 lightDir    = normalize(LightPosition - eyeDir);
    LightIntensity   = max(dot(lightDir, normal),0.0);
}
```

The goal of this vertex shader is to produce two values that will be interpolated across each primitive: a diffuse lighting value and a reflection direction. The reflection direction is used as the texture coordinate for accessing the cube map in the fragment shader.

We compute the transformed position of the vertex in the first line of the program in the usual way. We transform and normalize the incoming normal, and then we compute the eye direction, based on the current modelview matrix and the incoming vertex value. We pass these two values to the built-in function **reflect** to compute the reflection direction vector. Finally, we compute a diffuse lighting value in the same manner that we've done in previous examples.

10.4.3 Fragment Shader

Listing 10.6 contains the fragment shader that performs environment mapping with a cube map.

Listing 10.6 Fragment shader for doing environment mapping with a cube map

```
#version 140

uniform vec3  BaseColor;
uniform float MixRatio;

uniform samplerCube EnvMap;

in vec3  ReflectDir;
in float LightIntensity;

out vec4 FragColor;

void main()
{
    // Look up environment map value in cube map

    vec3 envColor = vec3(texture(EnvMap, ReflectDir));
```

```
// Add lighting to base color and mix

vec3 base = LightIntensity * BaseColor;
envColor  = mix(envColor, base, MixRatio);

FragColor = vec4(envColor, 1.0);
}
```

The fragment shader for cube map environment mapping does three things. First, the computed and interpolated in variable *ReflectDir* is used to access our cube map texture and return the texel value that is used to simulate the reflection from a shiny surface. Second, the base color of the object is modulated by the interpolated light intensity value. Finally, these two values are combined in the ratio defined by the uniform variable *MixRatio*. This uniform variable can be modified by the user to make the object vary between completely shiny and completely diffuse.

10.5 Another Environment Mapping Example

Another option for environment mapping is to use photographic methods to create a single 2D texture map, called an EQUIRECTANGULAR TEXTURE MAP or a LAT-LONG TEXTURE MAP. This type of texture can be obtained from a real-world environment by photography techniques, or it can be created to represent a synthetic environment. An example is shown in Color Plate 9.

Whatever means are used to obtain an image, the result is a single image that spans 360° horizontally and 180° vertically. The image is also distorted as you move up or down from the center of the image. This distortion is done deliberately so that you will see a reasonable representation of the environment if you "shrink-wrap" this texture around the object that you're rendering.

The key to using an equirectangular texture as the environment map is to produce a pair of angles that index into the texture. We compute an altitude angle by determining the angle between the reflection direction and the *XZ* plane. This altitude angle varies from 90° (reflection is straight up) to –90° (reflection is straight down). The sine of this angle varies from 1.0 to –1.0, and we use this fact to get a texture coordinate in the range of [0,1].

We determine an azimuth angle by projecting the reflection direction onto the *XZ* plane. The azimuth angle varies from 0° to 360°, and this gives us the key to get a second texture coordinate in the range of [0,1].

The following OpenGL shaders work together to perform environment mapping on an object by using an equirectangular texture map. These shaders are derived from a "bumpy/shiner" shader pair that was developed with John Kessenich and presented at SIGGRAPH 2002. The altitude and azimuth angles are computed to determine *s* and *t* values for indexing into our 2D environment texture. This texture's wrapping behavior is set so that it wraps in both *s* and *t*. (This supports a little trick that we do in the fragment shader.) Otherwise, the initial conditions are the same as described for the cube map environment mapping example.

10.5.1 Vertex Shader

Listing 10.7 comprises the vertex shader that does environment mapping with an equirectangular texture map. The only real difference between this shader and the one described in Section 10.4.2 is that this one computes *Normal* and *EyeDir* and passes them to the fragment shader as in variables so that the reflection vector can be computed in the fragment shader.

Listing 10.7 Vertex shader used for environment mapping

```
#version 140

in   vec4  MCVertex;
in   vec3  MCNormal;

out vec3  Normal;
out vec3  EyeDir;
out float LightIntensity;

uniform vec3 LightPosition;

uniform mat4 MVMatrix;
uniform mat4 MVPMatrix;
uniform mat3 NormalMatrix;

void main()
{
    gl_Position   = MVPMatrix * MCVertex;
    Normal        = normalize(NormalMatrix * MCNormal);
    vec4 pos      = MVMatrix * MCVertex;
    EyeDir        = pos.xyz;
    vec3 LightDir = normalize(LightPosition - EyeDir);
    LightIntensity = max(dot(LightDir, Normal), 0.0);
}
```

10.5.2 Fragment Shader

Listing 10.8 contains the fragment shader that does environment mapping by using an equirectangular texture map.

Listing 10.8 Fragment shader for doing environment mapping with an equirectangular texture map

```
#version 140

const vec3 Xunitvec = vec3(1.0, 0.0, 0.0);
const vec3 Yunitvec = vec3(0.0, 1.0, 0.0);

uniform vec3  BaseColor;
uniform float MixRatio;

uniform sampler2D EnvMap;   // = 4

in vec3  Normal;
in vec3  EyeDir;
in float LightIntensity;

out vec4 FragColor;

void main()
{
    // Compute reflection vector

    vec3 reflectDir = reflect(EyeDir, Normal);

    // Compute altitude and azimuth angles

    vec2 index;

    index.t = dot(normalize(reflectDir), Yunitvec);
    reflectDir.y = 0.0;
    index.s = dot(normalize(reflectDir), Xunitvec) * 0.5;

    // Calculate gradiants before discontinuous changes to index

    vec2 dPdx = dFdx( index );
    vec2 dPdy = dFdy( index );

    // Translate index values into proper range

    if (reflectDir.z >= 0.0)
        index = (index + 1.0) * 0.5;
    else
    {
```

```
        index.t = (index.t + 1.0) * 0.5;
        index.s = (-index.s) * 0.5 + 1.0;
    }


    // if reflectDir.z >= 0.0, s will go from 0.25 to 0.75
    // if reflectDir.z <  0.0, s will go from 0.75 to 1.25, and
    // that's OK, because we've set the texture to wrap.

    // Do a lookup into the environment map.

    vec3 envColor = vec3(textureGrad(EnvMap, index, dPdx, dPdy)););

    // Add lighting to base color and mix

    vec3 base = LightIntensity * BaseColor;
    envColor = mix(envColor, base, MixRatio);

    FragColor = vec4(envColor, 1.0);
}
```

The in variables *Normal* and *EyeDir* are the values generated by the vertex shader and then interpolated across the primitive. To get truly precise results, these values should be normalized again in the fragment shader. However, for this shader, skipping the normalization gives us a little better performance, and the quality is acceptable for certain objects.

The constants *Xunitvec* and *Yunitvec* have been set up with the proper values for computing our altitude and azimuth angles. First, we compute our altitude angle by normalizing the *reflectionDir* vector and performing a dot product with the *Yunitvec* constant. Because both vectors are unit vectors, this dot product computation gives us a cosine value for the desired angle that ranges from [–1,1]. Setting the *y* component of our reflection vector to 0 causes it to be projected onto the *XZ* plane. We normalize this new vector to get the cosine of our azimuth angle. Again, this value ranges from [–1,1]. Because the horizontal direction of our environment texture spans 360°, we multiply by 0.5 so that we get a value that maps into half of our environment map. Then we need to do a little more work to determine which half this is.

If the *z* portion of our reflection direction is positive, we know that the reflection direction is "toward the front" and we use the computed texture map indices directly. The index values are scaled and biased so that when we access the environment map texture, we get *s* values that range from [0.25,0.75] and *t* values that range from [0,1].

If *z* is negative, we do our calculations a little differently. The *t* value is still computed the same way, but the *s* value is scaled and biased so that it ranges from [0.75,1.25]. We can use these values directly because we've set our texture wrap modes to GL_REPEAT. *s* values between 1.0 and 1.25 will map to *s* values from 0 to 0.25 in our actual texture (the trick alluded to earlier). In this way, we can properly access the entire environment texture, depending on the reflection direction. We could compare *s* to 1.0 and subtract 1.0 if its value is greater than 1.0, but this would end up requiring additional instructions in the machine code, and hence the performance would be reduced. By using the repeat mode trick, we get the hardware to take care of this for free.

With our index values set, all we need to do is look up the value in the texture map. We compute a diffusely lit base color value by multiplying our incoming light intensity by *BaseColor*. We mix this value with our environment map value to create a ceramic effect. We then create a **vec4** by adding an alpha value of 1.0 and send the final fragment color on for further processing. The final result is shown in Color Plate 11A. You can see the branches from the tree in the environment on the back and rear of the triceratops. For this example, we used a color of (0.4, 0.4, 1.0) (i.e., light blue) and a mix ratio of 0.8 (i.e., 80% diffuse color, 20% environment map value).

An example of environment mapping that assumes a mirrorlike surface and adds procedural bumps is shown in Color Plate 11B.

10.6 Glyph Bombing

In this section, we develop a shader that demonstrates a couple of different uses for textures. In *Texturing and Modeling: A Procedural Approach*, Darwyn Peachy described a process called TEXTURE BOMBING that creates an irregular texture pattern. The idea is to divide a surface into a grid and then draw a decorative element or image (e.g., a star, a polka dot, or some other shape) within each cell. By applying some randomness to the placement, scaling, or rotation of each texture element, you can easily create an interesting pattern that is suitable for objects such as wallpaper, gift wrap, clothing, and the like. Peachey described a RenderMan shader to perform texture bombing, and in *GPU Gems*, Steve Glanville described a method for texture bombing in Cg.

The basic concept of texture bombing can be taken a bit further. Joshua Doss developed a GLSL shader that randomly selects from several collections of related character glyphs. Two textures are used for the so-called GLYPH BOMBING shader—a single texture that stores character glyphs and a texture that stores random values. Let's examine how this shader works.

10.6.1 Application Setup

The first step is to create a 2D texture that contains the glyphs that will be used. To set this up, you just need to carefully draw characters on a 10 × 10 grid, using a 2D image-editing program like Photoshop. Each row should have a common theme like the image shown in Figure 10.3. A single uniform variable (*ColAdjust*) is used to select the row to be accessed. Within this row, a glyph is chosen at random, and when it is drawn, it can also be optionally scaled and rotated. Thus, we can easily choose a pattern from a collection snowflakes, musical symbols, animal silhouettes, flower dingbats, and so on. Applying a random color and placing the glyph randomly within the cell add even more irregularity and interest to the final result.

The second texture that this shader uses contains random values in the range of [0,1.0] for each component. We access this texture to obtain a **vec4** containing random numbers and use these values to apply randomness to several computations within the fragment shader.

Figure 10.3 Texture map showing a collection of character glyphs that are used with the glyph bombing shader

Just like the brick shader discussed in Chapter 6, this shader needs a frame of reference for creating the cells in which we draw our glyphs. In this case, we use the object's texture coordinates to establish the reference frame. We can scale the texture coordinates with a uniform variable (*ScaleFactor*) to make the cells larger or smaller. Our glyph texture map contains only levels of gray. We use the value obtained from the glyph texture map to linearly interpolate between a default object color (*ModelColor*) and a random color that is generated when a glyph is drawn.

Because we are allowing random offsets and random rotation, we need to take care of some complications in our shader. Each of these effects can cause the object we are drawing to extend into neighboring cells.

Let's first consider the case of random offsets. When each glyph is drawn, our shader offsets the glyph by adding a value in the range [0,1.0] for each of x and y. This means that the glyph can be shifted over and up by some amount, possibly contributing to the contents of pixel locations in three neighboring cells to the right and above. Figure 10.4 illustrates the possibilities.

Consequently, as we consider how to compute the value at one particular pixel location, we must consider the possibility that the glyphs to be drawn

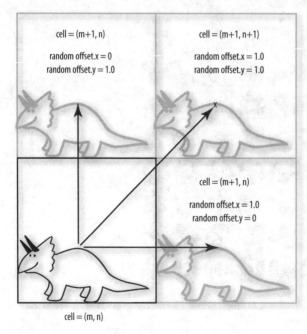

Figure 10.4   Depending on the random offset for a particular cell, a glyph may contribute to any one of four cells.

in cells to the left and below the current cell may be contributing to the fragment. For instance, the spot marked by the × in Figure 10.4 might actually have contributions from the glyphs in cells (*m*, *n*), (*m*+1, *n*), (*m*, *n*+1) in addition to the glyph contained in the cell (*m*+1, *n*+1).

Things get even more interesting when we allow for a random angle of rotation. Now the offset combined with rotation can cause our glyph to extend into any of nine cells, as shown in Figure 10.5. For this case, as we render fragments we must consider all eight surrounding cells in addition to the cell containing the fragment being rendered. We use a Boolean uniform variable, *RandomRotate*, to determine whether we need to loop over four cells or nine.

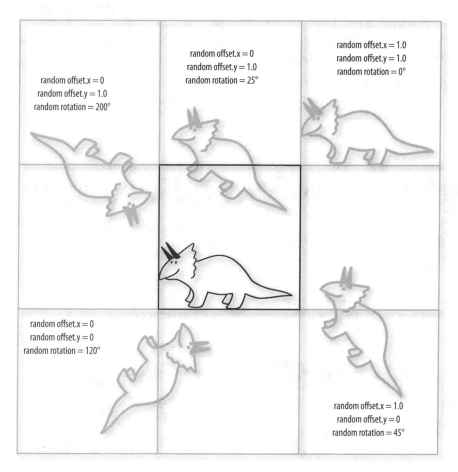

Figure 10.5   Depending on a random offset and a random angle of rotation, a glyph may contribute to fragments in any of nine adjacent cells.

We use a few additional uniform variables to offer more control over the number of glyphs and their placement and to give an even greater appearance of randomness to the final pattern. *RandomScale* is a Boolean value that causes the size of the glyph to be scaled in both x and y by random values in the range [0,1.0]. (This has no effect on the cells that are affected, because the glyph can only be made smaller by this operation.) Another uniform variable, *Percentage*, indicates the probability that a glyph will be drawn in each cell. Lowering this value increases the number of empty cells in the final image.

We can even include a loop in the shader so that we can apply more than one glyph per cell. The number of glyphs drawn per cell is set with *SamplesPerCell*. Setting this value to increasingly higher values will bring any graphics hardware to its knees. If random rotation is enabled, the fragment shader will need to iterate over nine cells and within each of these cells loop *SamplesPerCell* times in order to draw all the glyphs. This is a lot of computation at every fragment!

Some images that demonstrate different values for *RandomRotate*, *RandomScale*, and *SamplesPerCell* are shown in Figure 10.6, Figure 10.7, and Color Plate 8.

Figure 10.6   Normal glyph bombing, glyph bombing with random scaling, with random rotation, and with both random scaling and rotation

Figure 10.7   Glyph bombing with 2, 3, 4, and 5 glyphs per cell

The uniform variables for this shader and their initial values are

SpecularContribution	`0.2`
LightPosition	`4.0, 14.0, 4.0`
ScaleFactor	`10.0`
ModelColor	`1.0, 1.0, 1.0, 1.0`
GlyphTex	`0`
RandomTex	`1`
ColAdjust	`0.75`
Percentage	`1.0`
SamplesPerCell	`1.0`
R01	`0.29`
RandomScale	`false`
RandomRotate	`false`

10.6.2 Vertex Shader

Listing 10.9 contains the vertex shader for glyph bombing. The only differences between this shader and the vertex shader for bricks discussed in Chapter 6 are that the diffuse factor is multiplied by a somewhat arbitrary factor of two and that the scaled texture coordinates are passed to the fragment shader to form the frame of reference for defining the cells into which glyphs will be drawn.

Listing 10.9 Vertex shader for doing glyph bombing

```
#version 140

in   vec4   MCVertex;
in   vec3   MCNormal;

out vec3   Normal;
out vec2   TexCoord;
out float LightIntensity;

uniform float   SpecularContribution;
uniform vec3    LightPosition;
uniform float   ScaleFactor;

uniform mat4 MVMatrix;
uniform mat4 MVPMatrix;
uniform mat3 NormalMatrix;

void main()
{
    vec3   ecPosition = vec3(MVMatrix * MCVertex);
    vec3   tnorm      = normalize(NormalMatrix * MCNormal);
    vec3   lightVec   = normalize(LightPosition - ecPosition);
    vec3   reflectVec = reflect(-lightVec, tnorm);
    vec3   viewVec    = normalize(-ecPosition);
```

```
float diffuse     = max(dot(lightVec, tnorm), 0.0);
float spec        = 0.0;

if(diffuse > 0.0)
   {
      spec = max(dot(reflectVec, viewVec), 0.0);
      spec = pow(spec, 16.0);
   }

float diffusecontribution  = 1.0 - SpecularContribution;
LightIntensity = diffusecontribution * diffuse * 2.0 +
                      SpecularContribution * spec;

TexCoord = TexCoord0.st * ScaleFactor;

gl_Position = MVPMatrix * MCVertex;
}
```

10.6.3 Fragment Shader

Listing 10.10 contains the fragment shader for glyph bombing. As you can see, this shader makes heavy use of looping. The first step is to assign the base color for the fragment and then compute the fragment's cell and position within the cell. As we iterate through the loops, the value for color accumulates the color for the current fragment, which may be covered by multiple glyphs of different colors. A double for-next loop lets us iterate across four cells if *RandomRotate* is false (0) and across nine cells if it is true (1). This double loop determines whether any of the neighboring cells contain a glyph that contributes to the fragment currently being computed.

For each iteration of the inner loop, we need to determine whether the glyph in the neighboring cell affects the fragment that is being rendered. This requires that we compute the cell number for each neighboring cell as well the offset from the lower-left corner of the neighboring cell to the current fragment.

We use the cell value to compute the initial index value used to access our random number texture. This provides the beginning of a repeatable sequence of random numbers used for the calculations within that cell. This means that whenever we consider the contents of this cell, we always compute the same random glyph, the same random offset, and so on.

To start the random number sequence in a different location for each of the cells, during each loop iteration we compute the index into our random texture by multiplying the current cell value by a uniform variable (*RO1*) that a user can adjust to achieve pleasing results.

At this point, we enter yet another loop. This loop iterates over the number of samples per cell. Within this loop, the first thing we do is access our random number texture to obtain four random numbers in the range [0,1.0]. The result of this operation is a variable (*random*) that we use in performing a number of computations that require an element of randomness. To avoid using the same random number for each iteration of this loop, we add the third and fourth components of the random number to our random texture index. We use this value to access the texture in the next iteration of the loop. Now we get to the heart of the glyph bombing algorithm.

If the first component of the random number we've obtained is greater than or equal to *Percentage*, we exit the loop, use the color value computed thus far as the value for the fragment, and are done with the computation concerning this particular cell. Otherwise, we must generate a value that can index into our glyph texture. The first steps are to use *ColAdjust* to select the row of our glyph texture (*index.t*) and then select a random glyph within that row (*index.s*). Multiplying by 10 and using the floor function divides the texture into 10 sections in each direction. This gives us access to the 100 separate glyphs.

The next thing we need to do is compute a value that can access the proper texel in the glyph for this particular cell (*glyphIndex*). Here the offset, rotation, and scaling factors come into play. If *RandomRotate* is true, we generate a random angle of rotation, compute the corresponding rotation matrix, and use this matrix to transform the texture coordinates for accessing the glyph. This value is then combined with the random offset for the glyph. If we're not doing rotation, we just apply the random offset.

(Interestingly, the fragment shader for drawing glyphs never actually has to add the random offsets for drawing glyphs. Instead, the fragment shader assumes that the random offsets have been added and computes whether a glyph in a neighboring cell contributes to the current fragment by subtracting the random offset and then doing a texture lookup for the glyph in the neighboring cell. This is an example of the type of logic that is sometimes needed to convert a rendering algorithm into a fragment shader.)

The next step is to apply random scaling to the texture coordinates. *random.r* is a value in the range [0, 1.0]. If we divide our glyph index by this value, the glyph index values (i.e., the coordinates used to access the glyph) get larger. And if the coordinates used to access the glyph get larger, the apparent size of the glyph that is drawn gets smaller. By multiplying *random.r* by 0.5 and adding 0.5, we constrain the random scaling to be between 50% and 100% of the original size.

The resulting texture coordinates are clamped to the range [0,1.0], added to the index of the glyph that is rendered, divided by 10, and then used to access the glyph texture. All the glyphs in our glyph texture have at least one pixel of white along each edge. By clamping the values to the range [0,1.0], we effectively say "no contribution for this glyph" whenever the glyph index values exceed the range [0,1.0]. If the glyph value obtained is a color other than white, we use the resulting texture value to linearly interpolate between the color value computed thus far and a random color. Because the glyph texture contains only levels of gray, the comparison is only true for texels other than pure white. The **mix** function gives us a smoothly antialiased edge when the glyph is drawn, and it allows us to properly layer multiple glyphs of different colors, one on top of the other.

Listing 10.10   Fragment shader for doing glyph bombing

```
#version 140

#define TWO_PI 6.28318

uniform vec4       ModelColor;

uniform sampler2D GlyphTex;
uniform sampler2D RandomTex;

uniform float      ColAdjust;
uniform float      ScaleFactor;
uniform float      Percentage;
uniform float      SamplesPerCell;
uniform float      RO1;

uniform bool       RandomScale;
uniform bool       RandomRotate;

in vec2      TexCoord;
in float     LightIntensity;

out vec4     FragColor;

void main()
{
    vec4 color  = ModelColor;
    vec2 cell   = floor(TexCoord);
    vec2 offset = fract(TexCoord);

    vec2 dPdx = dFdx( TexCoord )/ScaleFactor;
    vec2 dPdy = dFdy( TexCoord )/ScaleFactor;

    for (int i = -1; i <= int (RandomRotate); i++)
    {
        for (int j = -1; j <= int (RandomRotate); j++)
        {
            vec2 currentCell   = cell + vec2(float(i), float(j));
            vec2 currentOffset = offset - vec2(float(i), float(j));
```

```
        vec2 randomUV = currentCell * vec2(RO1);

        for (int k = 0; k < int (SamplesPerCell); k++)
        {
            vec4 random = textureGrad(RandomTex, randomUV,
                                      dPdx, dPdy);
            randomUV   += random.ba;

            if (random.r < Percentage)
            {
                vec2 glyphIndex;
                mat2 rotator;
                vec2 index;
                float rotationAngle, cosRot, sinRot;

                index.s = floor(random.b * 10.0);
                index.t = floor(ColAdjust * 10.0);

                if (RandomRotate)
                {
                  rotationAngle = TWO_PI * random.g;
                    cosRot = cos(rotationAngle);
                    sinRot = sin(rotationAngle);
                    rotator[0] = vec2(cosRot, sinRot);
                    rotator[1] = vec2(-sinRot, cosRot);
                    glyphIndex = -rotator *
                          (currentOffset - random.rg);
                }
                else
                {
                    glyphIndex = currentOffset - random.rg;
                }

                if (RandomScale)
                    glyphIndex /= vec2(0.5 * random.r + 0.5);

                glyphIndex =
                    (clamp(glyphIndex, 0.0, 1.0) + index) * 0.1;

                vec4 image = textureGrad(GlyphTex, glyphIndex,
                                         dPdx, dPdy);

                if (image.r != 1.0)
                    color.rgb = mix(random.rgb * 0.7, color.rgb,
                                    image.r);
            }
        }
    }
}
FragColor   = color * LightIntensity;
}
```

This particular shader was designed for flexibility in operation, not performance. Consequently, there are enormous opportunities for making it run faster. There are two texture accesses per iteration of the innermost loop, so enabling rotation and having five samples per cell implies 90 texture accesses per fragment. Still, there are times when some of the techniques demonstrated by this shader come in handy.

10.7 Summary

This chapter discussed several shaders that rely on information stored in texture maps. The programmability of OpenGL opens up all sorts of new uses for texture memory. In the first example, we used two typical color images as texture maps, and we also used one texture as an opacity map and another as a gloss map. In the second example, we accessed a cube map from within a shader. In the third example, we used a typical color image as a texture, but the shader accessed it in a unique manner. In the final example, we used one texture to store small images for rendering and another texture to store random numbers that added irregularity and interest to the final result.

In examples later in this book, you'll see how textures can be used to store normal maps, noise functions, and polynomial coefficients. There is really no end to the possibilities for creating unique effects with stored textures when your mind is free to think of texture memory as storage for things other than color images.

10.8 Further Information

The basics of OpenGL texture mapping are explained in much more detail in *OpenGL Programming Guide, Seventh Edition* (2010), by Dave Shreiner et al. from Addison-Wesley.

More information about the earth images used in Section 10.2 can be found at the NASA Web site at http://earthobservatory.nasa.gov/Newsroom/BlueMarble.

Papers regarding the realistic rendering of planets include Jim Blinn's 1982 SIGGRAPH paper *Light Reflection Functions for Simulation of Clouds and Dusty Surfaces,* the 1993 SIGGRAPH paper *Display of the Earth Taking into Account Atmospheric Scattering* by Tomoyuki Nishita et al., and the 2002 paper

Physically-based Simulation: A Survey of the Modelling and Rendering of the Earth's Atmosphere by Jaroslav Sloup.

Mipmapping was first described by Lance Williams in his classic 1983 paper *Pyramidal Parametrics*. A good overview of environment mapping techniques is available in the paper *Environment Maps and Their Applications* by Wolfgang Heidrich. This paper was part of the course notes for SIGGRAPH 2000 Course 27, entitled *Procedural Shading on Graphics Hardware*. This material, and a thorough treatment of reflectance and lighting models, can be found in the book *Real-Time Shading*, by Marc Olano et al. (2002).

Texture bombing is described by Darwyn Peachey in *Texturing and Modeling: A Procedural Approach, Third Edition*. The book *GPU Gems* also has a chapter by Steve Glanville on this topic.

[1] Blinn, James, *Light Reflection Functions for Simulation of Clouds and Dusty Surfaces*, Computer Graphics (SIGGRAPH '82 Proceedings), pp. 21–29, July 1982.

[2] Ebert, David S., John Hart, Bill Mark, F. Kenton Musgrave, Darwyn Peachey, Ken Perlin, and Steven Worley, *Texturing and Modeling: A Procedural Approach, Third Edition*, Morgan Kaufmann Publishers, San Francisco, 2002. www.texturingandmodeling.com

[3] Glanville, Steve, *Texture Bombing*, in *GPU Gems: Programming Techniques, Tips, and Tricks for Real-Time Graphics*, Editor: Randima Fernando, Addison-Wesley, Reading, Massachusetts, 2004. http://developer.nvidia.com/object/gpu_gems_home.html

[4] Heidrich, Wolfgang, and Hans-Peter Seidel, *View-Independent Environment Maps*, ACM SIGGRAPH/Eurographics Workshop on Graphics Hardware, pp. 39–45, August 1998.

[5] Heidrich, Wolfgang, *Environment Maps and Their Applications*, SIGGRAPH 2000, Course 27, course notes. www.csee.umbc.edu/~olano/s2000c27/envmap.pdf

[6] NASA, *Earth Observatory*, Web site. http://earthobservatory.nasa.gov/Newsroom/BlueMarble

[7] Nishita, Tomoyuki, Takao Sirai, Katsumi Tadamura, and Eihachiro Nakamae, *Display of the Earth Taking Into Account Atmospheric Scattering*, Computer Graphics (SIGGRAPH '93 Proceedings), pp. 175–182, August 1993. http://nis-lab.is.s.u-tokyo.ac.jp/~nis/abs_sig.html#sig93

[8] OpenGL Architecture Review Board, *OpenGL Reference Manual, Fourth Edition: The Official Reference to OpenGL, Version 1.4*, Editor: Dave Shreiner, Addison-Wesley, Reading, Massachusetts, 2004.

[9] Rost, Randi J., *The OpenGL Shading Language*, SIGGRAPH 2002, Course 17, course notes. http://3dshaders.com/pubs

[10] Shreiner, Dave, and the Khronos OpenGL ARB Working Group, *OpenGL Programming Guide, Seventh Edition: The Official Guide to Learning OpenGL, Versions 3.0 and 3.1*, Addison-Wesley, Boston, Massachusetts, 2010.

[11] Sloup, Jaroslav, *Physically-based Simulation: A Survey of the Modeling and Rendering of the Earth's Atmosphere*, Proceedings of the 18th Spring Conference on Computer Graphics, pp. 141–150, April 2002. http://sgi.felk.cvut.cz/~sloup/html/research/project

[12] Williams, Lance, *Pyramidal Parametrics*, Computer Graphics (SIGGRAPH '83 Proceedings), pp. 1–11, July 1983.

Chapter 11

Procedural Texture Shaders

The fact that we have a full-featured, high-level programming language to express the processing at each fragment means that we can algorithmically compute a pattern on an object's surface. We can use this new freedom to create a wide variety of rendering effects that wouldn't be possible otherwise.

In the previous chapter, we discussed shaders that achieve their primary effect by reading values from texture memory. This chapter focuses on shaders that do interesting things primarily by means of an algorithm defined by the shader. The results from such a shader are synthesized according to the algorithm rather than being based primarily on precomputed values such as a digitized painting or photograph. This type of shader is sometimes called a PROCEDURAL TEXTURE SHADER, and the process of applying such a shader is called PROCEDURAL TEXTURING. Often the texture coordinate or the object coordinate position at each point on the object is the only piece of information needed to shade the object with a shader that is entirely procedural.

In principle, procedural texture shaders can accomplish many of the same tasks as shaders that access stored textures. In practice, there are times when it is more convenient or feasible to use a procedural texture shader and times when it is more convenient or feasible to use a stored texture shader. When deciding whether to write a procedural texture shader or one that uses stored textures, keep in mind some of the main advantages of procedural texture shaders.

- Textures generated procedurally have very low memory requirements compared with stored textures. The only representation of the texture is in the algorithm defined by the code in the procedural texture shader. This representation is extremely compact compared with the size of stored 2D textures. Typically, it is a couple of orders of magnitude smaller (e.g., a few kilobytes for the code in a procedural shader versus a few hundred kilobytes or more for a high-quality 2D texture). This means procedural texture shaders require far less memory on the graphics accelerator. Procedural texture shaders have an even greater advantage when the desire is to have a 3D (solid) texture applied to an object (a few kilobytes versus tens of megabytes or more for a stored 3D texture).

- Textures generated by procedural texture shaders have no fixed area or resolution. They can be applied to objects of any scale with precise results because they are defined algorithmically rather than with sampled data, as in the case of stored textures. There are no decisions to be made about how to map a 2D image onto a 3D surface patch that is larger or smaller than the texture, and there are no seams or unwanted replication. As your viewpoint gets closer and closer to a surface rendered with a procedural texture shader, you won't see reduced detail or sampling artifacts like you might with a shader that uses a stored texture.

- Procedural texture shaders can be written to parameterize key aspects of the algorithm. These parameters can easily be changed, allowing a single shader to produce an interesting variety of effects. Very little can be done to alter the effect from a stored texture after it has been created.

Some of the disadvantages of using procedural shaders rather than stored textures are as follows:

- Procedural texture shaders require the algorithm to be encoded in a program. Not everyone has the technical skills needed to write such a program, whereas it is fairly straightforward to create a 2D or 3D texture with limited technical skills.

- Performing the algorithm embodied by a procedural texture shader at each location on an object can be a lot slower than accessing a stored texture.

- Procedural texture shaders can have serious aliasing artifacts that can be difficult to overcome. Today's graphics hardware has built-in capabilities for antialiasing stored textures (e.g., filtering methods and mipmaps).

- Because of differences in arithmetic precision and differences in implementations of built-in functions such as **noise**, procedural texture shaders could produce somewhat different results on different platforms.

The ultimate choice of whether to use a procedural shader or a stored texture shader should be made pragmatically. Things that would be artwork in the real world (paintings, billboards, anything with writing, etc.) are good candidates for rendering with stored textures. Objects that are extremely important to the final "look" of the image (character faces, costumes, important props) can also be rendered with stored textures because this presents the easiest route for an artist to be involved. Things that are relatively unimportant to the final image and yet cover a lot of area are good candidates for rendering with a procedural shader (walls, floors, ground).

Often, a hybrid approach is the right answer. A golf ball might be rendered with a base color, a hand-painted texture map that contains scuff marks, a texture map containing a logo, and a procedurally generated dimple pattern. Stored textures can also control or constrain procedural effects. If our golf ball needs grass stains on certain parts of its surface and it is important to achieve and reproduce just the right look, an artist could paint a grayscale map that would direct the shader to locations where grass smudges should be applied on the surface (for instance, black portions of the grayscale map) and where they should not be applied (white portions of the grayscale map). The shader can read this CONTROL TEXTURE and use it to blend between a grass-smudged representation of the surface and a pristine surface.

All that said, let's turn our attention to a few examples of shaders that are entirely procedural.

11.1   Regular Patterns

In Chapter 6, we examined a procedural shader for rendering bricks. Our first example in this chapter is another simple one. We try to construct a shader that renders stripes on an object. A variety of man-made objects can be rendered with such a shader: children's toys, wallpaper, wrapping paper, flags, fabrics, and so on.

The object in Figure 11.1 is a partial torus rendered with a stripe shader. The stripe shader and the application in which it is shown were both developed in 2002 by LightWork Design, a company that develops software to provide photorealistic views of objects created with commercial CAD/CAM packages. The application developed by LightWork Design contains a graphical user interface that allows the user to interactively modify the shader's parameters. The various shaders that are available are accessible on the upper-right portion of the user interface, and the modifiable parameters for the current shader are accessible in the lower-right portion of the user interface. In this case, you can see that the parameters for the stripe shader include the stripe color (blue), the background color (orange), the stripe scale (how many stripes there will be), and the stripe width (the ratio of stripe to background; in this case, it is 0.5 to make blue and orange stripes of equal width).

For our stripe shader to work properly, the application needs to send down only the geometry (vertex values) and the texture coordinate at each vertex. The key to drawing the stripe color or the background color is the t texture coordinate at each fragment (the s texture coordinate is not used at all). The application must also supply values that the vertex shader uses to perform a lighting computation. And the aforementioned stripe color, background color, scale, and stripe width must be passed to the fragment shader so that our procedural stripe computation can be performed at each fragment.

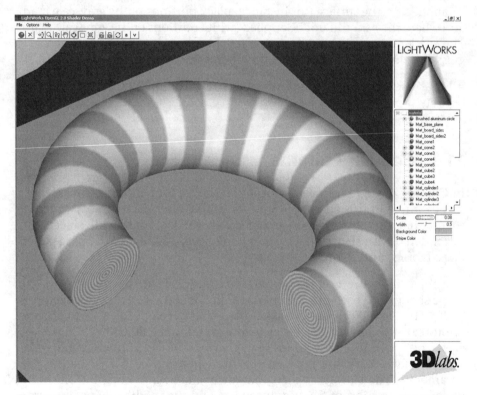

Figure 11.1   Close-up of a partial torus rendered with the stripe shader described in Section 11.1 (courtesy of LightWork Design)

11.1.1 Stripes Vertex Shader

The vertex shader for our stripe effect is shown in Listing 11.1.

Listing 11.1 Vertex shader for drawing stripes

```
#version 140

uniform vec3  LightPosition;
uniform vec3  LightColor;
uniform vec3  EyePosition;
uniform vec3  Specular;
uniform vec3  Ambient;
uniform float Kd;

uniform mat4 MVMatrix;
uniform mat4 MVPMatrix;
uniform mat3 NormalMatrix;

in  vec4  MCVertex;
in  vec3  MCNormal;
in  vec2  TexCoord0;

out vec3  DiffuseColor;
out vec3  SpecularColor;
out float TexCoord;

void main()
{
    vec3 ecPosition = vec3(MVMatrix * MCVertex);
    vec3 tnorm      = normalize(NormalMatrix * MCNormal);
    vec3 lightVec   = normalize(LightPosition - ecPosition);
    vec3 viewVec    = normalize(EyePosition - ecPosition);
    vec3 hvec       = normalize(viewVec + lightVec);

    float spec = clamp(dot(hvec, tnorm), 0.0, 1.0);
    spec = pow(spec, 16.0);

    DiffuseColor    = LightColor * vec3(Kd * dot(lightVec, tnorm));
    DiffuseColor    = clamp(Ambient + DiffuseColor, 0.0, 1.0);
    SpecularColor   = clamp((LightColor * Specular * spec), 0.0, 1.0);

    TexCoord   = TexCoord0.t;
    gl_Position     = MVPMatrix * MCVertex;
}
```

There are some nice features to this particular shader. Nothing in it really makes it specific to drawing stripes. It provides a good example of how we might do the lighting calculation in a general way that would be compatible with a variety of fragment shaders.

As we mentioned, the values for doing the lighting computation (*LightPosition, LightColor, EyePosition, Specular, Ambient*, and *Kd*) are all passed in by the application as uniform variables. The purpose of this shader is to compute *DiffuseColor* and *SpecularColor,* two out variables that will be interpolated across each primitive and made available to the fragment shader at each fragment location. These values are computed in the typical way. A small optimization is that *Ambient* is added to the value computed for the diffuse reflection so that we send one less value to the fragment shader as an out variable. The incoming texture coordinate is passed down to the fragment shader as the out variable *TexCoord,* and the vertex position is transformed in the usual way.

11.1.2 Stripes Fragment Shader

The fragment shader contains the algorithm for drawing procedural stripes. It is shown in Listing 11.2.

Listing 11.2 Fragment shader for drawing stripes

```
#version 140

uniform vec3   StripeColor;
uniform vec3   BackColor;
uniform float Width;
uniform float Fuzz;
uniform float Scale;

in vec3  DiffuseColor;
in vec3  SpecularColor;
in float TexCoord;

out vec4 FragColor;

void main()
{
    float scaledT = fract(TexCoord * Scale);

    float frac1 = clamp(scaledT / Fuzz, 0.0, 1.0);
    float frac2 = clamp((scaledT - Width) / Fuzz, 0.0, 1.0);

    frac1 = frac1 * (1.0 - frac2);
    frac1 = frac1 * frac1 * (3.0 - (2.0 * frac1));

    vec3 finalColor = mix(BackColor, StripeColor, frac1);
    finalColor = finalColor * DiffuseColor + SpecularColor;

    FragColor = vec4(finalColor, 1.0);
}
```

The application provides one other uniform variable, called *Fuzz*. This value controls the smooth transitions (i.e., antialiasing) between stripe color and background color. With a *Scale* value of 10.0, a reasonable value for *Fuzz* is 0.1. It can be adjusted as the object changes size to prevent excessive blurriness at high magnification levels. It shouldn't really be set to a value higher than 0.5 (maximum blurriness of stripe edges).

The first step in this shader is to multiply the incoming *t* texture coordinate by the stripe scale factor and take the fractional part. This computation gives the position of the fragment within the stripe pattern. The larger the value of *Scale*, the more stripes we have as a result of this calculation. The resulting value for the local variable *scaledT* is in the range from [0,1].

We'd like to have nicely antialiased transitions between the stripe colors. One way to do this would be to use **smoothstep** in the transition from *StripeColor* to *BackColor* and use it again in the transition from *BackColor* to *StripeColor*. But this shader uses the fact that these transitions are symmetric to combine the two transitions into one.

So, to get our desired transition, we use *scaledT* to compute two other values, *frac1* and *frac2*. These two values tell us where we are in relation to the two transitions between *BackColor* and *StripeColor*. For *frac1*, if *scaledT*/*Fuzz* is greater than 1, that indicates that this point is not in the transition zone, so we clamp the value to 1. If *scaledT* is less than *Fuzz*, *scaledT*/*Fuzz* specifies the fragment's relative distance into the transition zone for one side of the stripe. We compute a similar value for the other edge of the stripe by subtracting *Width* from *scaledT*, dividing by *Fuzz*, clamping the result, and storing it in *frac2*.

These values represent the amount of fuzz (blurriness) to be applied. At one edge of the stripe, *frac2* is 0 and *frac1* is the relative distance into the transition zone. At the other edge of the stripe, *frac1* is 1 and *frac2* is the relative distance into the transition zone. Our next line of code (*frac1 = frac1 * (1.0 – frac2)*) produces a value that can be used to do a proper linear blend between *BackColor* and *StripeColor*. But we'd actually like to perform a transition that is smoother than a linear blend. The next line of code performs a Hermite interpolation in the same way as the **smoothstep** function. The final value for *frac1* performs the blend between *BackColor* and *StripeColor*.

The result of this effort is a smoothly "fuzzed" boundary in the transition region between the stripe colors. Without this fuzzing effect, we would have abrupt transitions between the stripe colors that would flash and pop as the object is moved on the screen. The fuzzing of the transition region eliminates those artifacts. A close-up view of the fuzzed boundary is shown in Figure 11.2. (More information about antialiasing procedural shaders can be found in Chapter 17.)

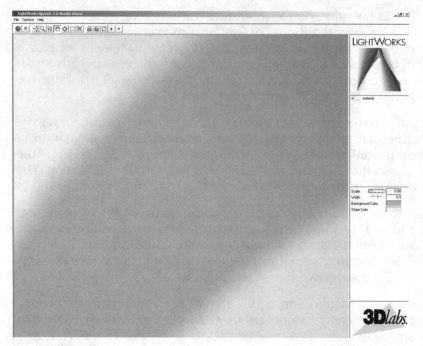

Figure 11.2   Extreme close-up view of one of the stripes that shows the effect of the "fuzz" calculation from the stripe shader (courtesy of LightWork Design)

Now all that remains to be done is to apply the diffuse and specular lighting effects computed by the vertex shader and supply an alpha value of 1.0 to produce our final fragment color. By modifying the five basic parameters of our fragment shader, we can create a fairly interesting number of variations of our stripe pattern, using the exact same shader.

11.2 Toy Ball

Programmability is the key to procedurally defining all sorts of texture patterns. This next shader takes things a bit further by shading a sphere with a procedurally defined star pattern and a procedurally defined stripe. This shader was inspired by the ball in one of Pixar's early short animations, *Luxo Jr.* This shader is quite specialized. It shades any surface as long as it's a sphere. The reason is that the fragment shader exploits the following property of the sphere: The surface normal for any point on the surface points in the same direction as the vector from the center of the sphere to that point on the surface. This property is used to analytically compute the surface normal used in the shading calculations within the fragment shader.

The key to this shader is that the star pattern is defined by the coefficients for five half-spaces that define the star shape. These coefficients were chosen to make the star pattern an appropriate size for the ball. Points on the sphere are classified as "in" or "out," relative to each half space. Locations in the very center of the star pattern are "in" with respect to all five half-spaces. Locations in the points of the star are "in" with respect to four of the five half-spaces. All other locations are "in" with respect to three or fewer half-spaces.

Fragments that are in the stripe pattern are simpler to compute. After we have classified each location on the surface as "star," "stripe," or "other," we can color each fragment appropriately. The color computations are applied in an order that ensures a reasonable result even if the ball is viewed from far away. A surface normal is calculated analytically (i.e., exactly) within the fragment shader. A lighting computation that includes a specular highlight calculation is also applied at every fragment.

11.2.1 Application Setup

The application needs only to provide vertex positions for this shader to work properly. Both colors and normals are computed algorithmically in the fragment shader. The only catch is that for this shader to work properly, the vertices must define a sphere. The sphere can be of arbitrary size because the fragment shader performs all the necessary computations, based on the known geometry of a sphere.

A number of parameters to this shader are specified with uniform variables. The values that produce the images shown in the remainder of this section are summarized in Listing 11.3.

Listing 11.3 Values for uniform variables used by the toy ball shader

```
HalfSpace[0]        1.0,           0.0,           0.0, 0.2
HalfSpace[1]        0.309016994,   0.951056516,   0.0, 0.2
HalfSpace[2]       -0.809016994,   0.587785252,   0.0, 0.2
HalfSpace[3]       -0.809016994,  -0.587785252,   0.0, 0.2
HalfSpace[4]        0.309016994,  -0.951056516,   0.0, 0.2

StripeWidth         0.3

InOrOutInit        -3.0
FWidth              0.005

StarColor           0.6, 0.0, 0.0, 1.0
StripeColor         0.0, 0.3, 0.6, 1.0
BaseColor           0.6, 0.5, 0.0, 1.0

BallCenter          0.0, 0.0, 0.0, 1.0
```

```
LightDir          0.57735, 0.57735, 0.57735, 0.0
HVector           0.32506, 0.32506, 0.88808, 0.0

SpecularColor     1.0, 1.0, 1.0, 1.0
SpecularExponent 200.0

Ka                0.3
Kd                0.7
Ks                0.4
```

11.2.2 Vertex Shader

The fragment shader is the workhorse for this shader duo, so the vertex shader needs only to compute the ball's center position in eye coordinates, the eye-coordinate position of the vertex, and the clip space position at each vertex. The application could provide the ball's center position in eye coordinates, but our vertex shader doesn't have much to do, and doing it this way means the application doesn't have to keep track of the modelview matrix. This value could easily be computed in the fragment shader, but the fragment shader will likely have a little better performance if we leave the computation in the vertex shader and pass the result as a flat interpolated out variable (see Listing 11.4).

Listing 11.4 Vertex shader for drawing a toy ball

```
#version 140
uniform vec4 MCBallCenter;

uniform mat4 MVMatrix;
uniform mat4 MVPMatrix;
uniform mat3 NormalMatrix;

in vec4 MCVertex;

    out vec3 OCPosition;
    out vec4 ECPosition;
flat out vec4 ECBallCenter;

void main (void)
{

   OCPosition = MCVertex.xyz;
   ECPosition = MVMatrix * MCVertex;
   ECBallCenter = MVMatrix * MCBallCenter;

   gl_Position = MVPMatrix * MCVertex;
}
```

11.2.3 Fragment Shader

The toy ball fragment shader is a little bit longer than some of the previous examples, so we build it up a few lines of code at a time and illustrate some intermediate results. Here are the definitions for the local variables that are used in the toy ball fragment shader:

```
vec3  normal;        // Analytically computed normal
vec4  pShade;        // Point in shader space
vec4  surfColor;     // Computed color of the surface
float intensity;     // Computed light intensity
vec4  distance;      // Computed distance values
float inorout;       // Counter for classifying star pattern
```

The first thing we do is turn the surface location that we're shading into a point on a sphere with a radius of 1.0. We can do this with the **normalize** function:

```
pShade.xyz  = normalize(OCPosition.xyz);
pShade.w    = 1.0;
```

We don't want to include the *w* coordinate in the computation, so we use the component selector *.xyz* to select the first three components of *OCposition.* This normalized vector is stored in the first three components of *pShade*. With this computation, *pShade* represents a point on the sphere with radius 1, so all three components of *pShade* are in the range [–1,1]. The *w* coordinate isn't really pertinent to our computations at this point, but to make subsequent calculations work properly, we initialize it to a value of 1.0.

We are always going to be shading spheres with this fragment shader, so we analytically calculate the surface normal of the sphere:

```
normal     = normalize(ECPosition.xyz-ECBallCenter.xyz);
```

Next, we perform our half-space computations. We initialize a counter called *inorout* to a value of –3.0. We increment the counter each time the surface location is "in" with respect to a half-space. Because five half-spaces are defined, the final counter value will be in the range [–3,2]. Values of 1 or 2 signify that the fragment is within the star pattern. Values of 0 or less signify that the fragment is outside the star pattern.

```
inorout = InOrOutInit;     // initialize inorout to -3
```

We have defined the half-spaces as an array of five **vec4** values, done our "in" or "out" computations, and stored the results in an array of five **float** values. But we can take a little better advantage of the parallel nature of the underlying graphics hardware if we do things a bit differently. You'll see how in a minute. First, we compute the distance between *pShade* and the first four half-spaces by using the built-in dot product function:

```
distance[0] = dot(p, HalfSpace[0]);
distance[1] = dot(p, HalfSpace[1]);
distance[2] = dot(p, HalfSpace[2]);
distance[3] = dot(p, HalfSpace[3]);
```

The results of these half-space distance calculations are visualized in (A)–(D) of Figure 11.3. Surface locations that are "in" with respect to the half-space are shaded in gray, and points that are "out" are shaded in black.

You may have been wondering why our counter was defined as a **float** instead of an **int**. We're going to use the counter value as the basis for a smoothly antialiased transition between the color of the star pattern and the color of the rest of the ball's surface. To this end, we use the **smoothstep** function to set the distance to 0 if the computed distance is less than –*FWidth*, to 1 if the computed distance is greater than *FWidth*, and to a smoothly interpolated value between 0 and 1 if the computed distance is in between those two values. By defining *distance* as a **vec4**, we can perform the smooth step computation on four values in parallel. **smoothstep** implies a divide operation, and because *FWidth* is a float, only one divide operation is necessary. This makes it all very efficient.

```
distance    = smoothstep(-FWidth, FWidth, distance);
```

Now we can quickly add the values in *distance* by performing a dot product between *distance* and a **vec4** containing all 1s:

```
inorout     += dot(distance, vec4(1.0));
```

Because we initialized *inorout* to –3, we add the result of the dot product to the previous value of *inorout*. This variable now contains a value in the range [–3,1], and we have one more half-space distance to compute. We compute the distance to the fifth half-space, and we do the computation

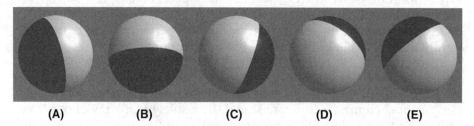

(A)   **(B)**   **(C)**   **(D)**   **(E)**

Figure 11.3 Visualizing the results of the half-space distance calculations (courtesy of AMD)

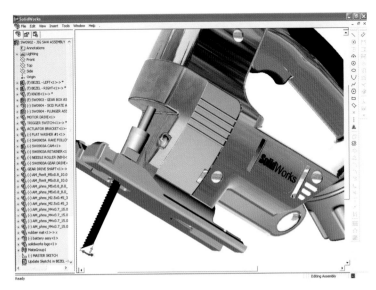

Color Plate 1 Screen shot of the SolidWorks application, showing a jigsaw rendered with OpenGL shaders to simulate a chrome body, galvanized steel housing, and cast iron blade. (Courtesy of Solid-Works Corporation)

Color Plate 2 Screen shots illustrating realistic material shaders developed by LightWork Design. Upper-left and lower-left images use complex OpenGL shaders for accurately visualizing real-world GE Plastics materials. Upper-right image illustrates the real-world visualization of Milliken carpets using the LightWork Archive (LWA) format. Lower-right image illustrates high-quality lighting created using materials in the LWA format. LightWork Design provides the shaders, materials, and information about the LWA format at http://www.lightworks-user.com. (Created using the LightWork rendering engine. Copyright LightWork Design)

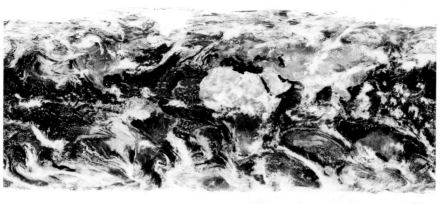

Color Plate 3
A full-color image of Earth that is used as a texture map for the shader discussed in Section 10.2. (Blue Marble image by Reto Stöckli, NASA Goddard Space Flight Center)

Color Plate 4
"Daytime" texture map used in the fragment shader described in Section 10.3. (Blue Marble images by Reto Stöckli, NASA Goddard Space Flight Center)

Color Plate 5
"Nighttime" texture map used in the fragment shader described in Section 10.3. (Blue Marble images by Reto Stöckli, NASA Goddard Space Flight Center)

Color Plate 6 Earth image texture mapped onto a sphere using the fragment shader described in Section 10.2. (3Dlabs, Inc./Blue Marble image by Reto Stöckli, NASA Goddard Space Flight Center)

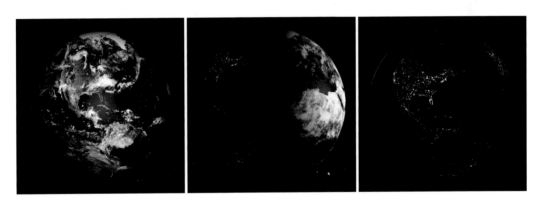

Color Plate 7 As the world turns—daytime, dawn, and nighttime views of Earth, rendered by the shaders discussed in Section 10.3. (3Dlabs, Inc./Blue Marble image by Reto Stöckli, NASA Goddard Space Flight Center)

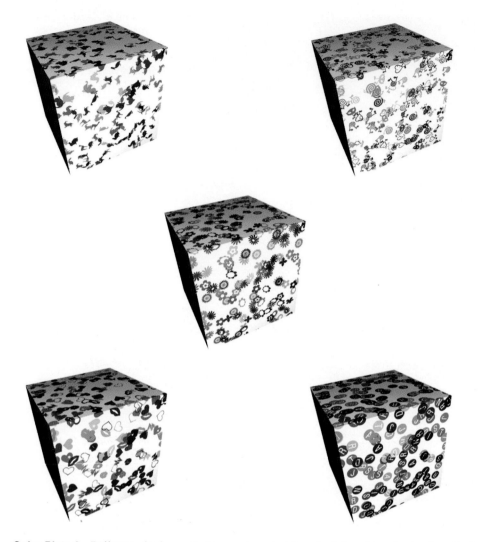

Color Plate 8 Different glyphs applied to a cube using the glyph bombing shader described in Section 10.6. (3Dlabs, Inc.)

Color Plate 9 An equirectangular (or latlong) texture map of Old Town Square, Fort Collins, Colorado. This image is used as the environment map for the shader presented in Section 10.5. (3Dlabs, Inc.)

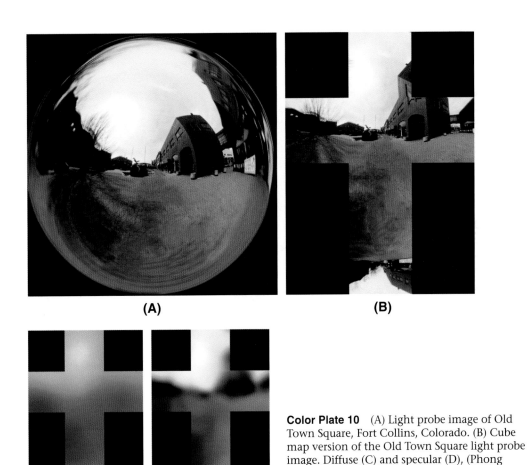

(A)

(B)

(C)

(D)

Color Plate 10 (A) Light probe image of Old Town Square, Fort Collins, Colorado. (B) Cube map version of the Old Town Square light probe image. Diffuse (C) and specular (D), (Phong exponent = 50) environment maps created with HDRshop. (3Dlabs, Inc.)

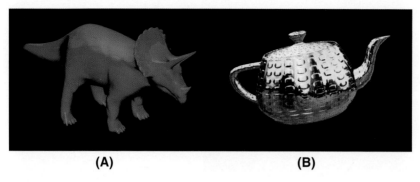

(A)   **(B)**

Color Plate 11   Environment mapped shader examples. (A) The cube map shown in Color Plate 10 is used together with the environment mapping shaders discussed in Section 10.4. (B) Environment mapping a mirror-like surface with procedural bumps using the environment map shown in Color Plate 9. The bumps are applied using the technique described in Section 11.4. (3Dlabs, Inc.)

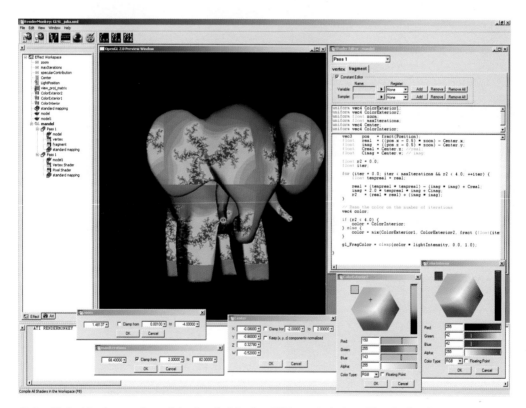

Color Plate 12   Screen shot of the RenderMonkey IDE user interface. The shader that is procedurally generating a Julia set on the surface of the elephant is shown in the source code window. Color selection tools and user interface elements for manipulating user-defined uniform variables are also shown.

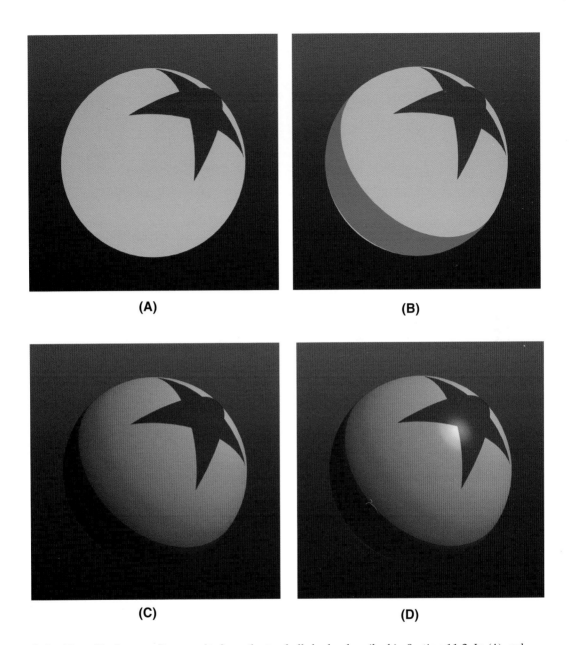

Color Plate 13 Intermediate results from the toy ball shader described in Section 11.2. In (A), red is applied to the procedurally defined star pattern and yellow to the rest of the sphere. In (B), the blue stripe is added. In (C), diffuse lighting is applied. In (D), the analytically defined normal is used to apply a specular highlight. (Courtesy of ATI Research, Inc.)

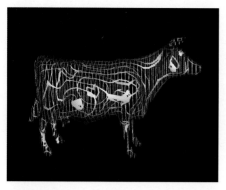

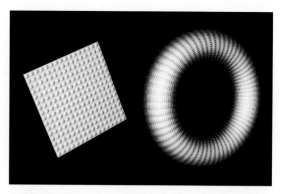

Color Plate 14 The lattice shader presented in Section 11.3 is applied to the cow model. (3Dlabs, Inc.)

Color Plate 15 A simple box and a torus that have been bump-mapped using the procedural method described in Section 11.4. (3Dlabs, Inc.)

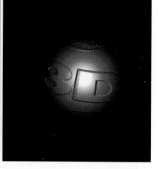

Color Plate 16 A normal map (left) and the rendered result on a simple box and a sphere using the techniques described in Section 11.4.4. (3Dlabs, Inc.)

Color Plate 17 The reflection/refraction shader from Section 14.1 used to render a model with chromatic aberration (middle) and without (left). On the middle image, notice the color fringing on the knees, chest, and tops of the arms. On the right, three orientations of an object rendered with the diffraction shader from Section 14.2. (3Dlabs, Inc.)

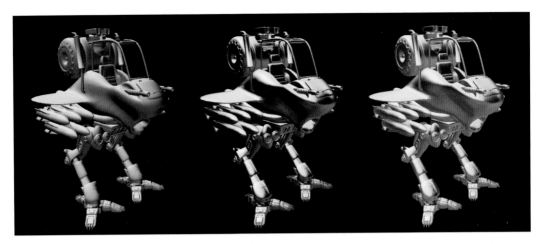

Color Plate 18 The image-based lighting shader described in Section 12.2 can produce a variety of effects using the Old Town Square diffuse and specular environment maps shown in Color Plate 9. Left: *BaseColor* set to (1.0, 1.0, 1.0), *SpecularPercent* is 0, and *DiffusePercent* is 1.0. Middle: *BaseColor* is set to (0, 0, 0), *SpecularPercent* is set to 1.0, and *DiffusePercent* is set to 0. Right: *BaseColor* is set to (0.35, 0.29, 0.09), *SpecularPercent* is set to 0.75, and *DiffusePercent* is set to 0.5. (3Dlabs, Inc.)

Color Plate 19 The spherical harmonics lighting shader described in Section 12.3 is used as the sole lighting for a model with a base color of white (RGB=1.0, 1.0, 1.0). The coefficients from Table 12.1 that are used to create these images are from left: Old Town Square, Grace Cathedral, Galileo's Tomb, Campus Sunset, and St. Peter's Basilica. Ambient occlusion factors are also applied (see Section 13.1). (3Dlabs, Inc.)

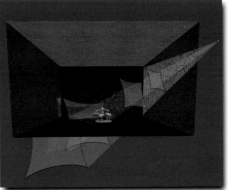

Color Plate 20 Effects of the überlight shader (see Section 12.4) and a user interface for manipulating its controls. (3Dlabs, Inc.)

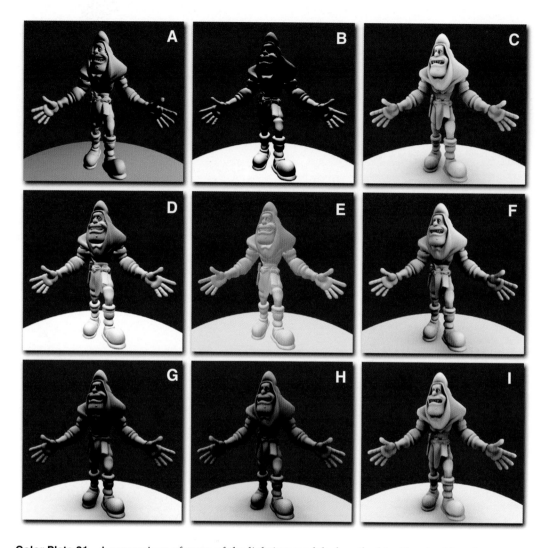

Color Plate 21 A comparison of some of the lighting models described in Chapter 12 and Chapter 13. The model uses a base color of white (RGB=1.0, 1.0, 1.0) to emphasize areas of light and shadow. (A) uses fixed functionality lighting with a light above and to the right of the model. (B) uses fixed functionality with a light directly above the model. These two images illustrate the difficulties with the traditional lighting model. Detail is lost in areas of shadow. (C) multiplies the ambient occlusion value by the model color to achieve quite pleasing results. (D) illustrates hemisphere lighting while (G) illustrates hemisphere lighting plus ambient occlusion. (E) illustrates spherical harmonic lighting using the Old Town Square coefficients, while (H) uses spherical harmonic lighting plus ambient occlusion. (F) is simple diffuse lighting attenuated by the ambient occlusion factor. (I) uses ambient occlusion and the bent normal to access the Old Town Square environment map to determine the color of the light reaching the surface. (3Dlabs, Inc.)

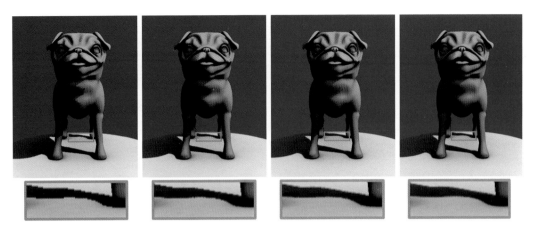

Color Plate 22 Comparing the shadow-generation techniques described in Section 13.2. From left, accessing the shadow map with one sample per pixel, with four samples per pixel, with four dithered samples per pixel, and with 16 samples per pixel. (3Dlabs, Inc.)

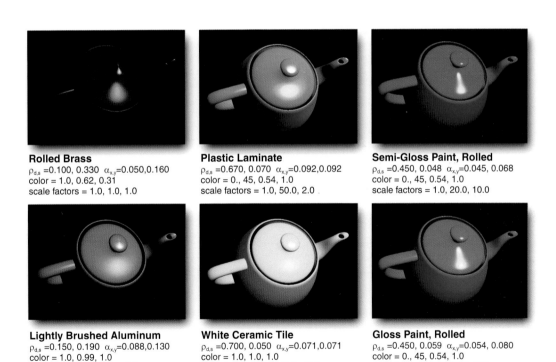

Rolled Brass
$\rho_{d,s}$ =0.100, 0.330 $\alpha_{x,y}$=0.050,0.160
color = 1.0, 0.62, 0.31
scale factors = 1.0, 1.0, 1.0

Plastic Laminate
$\rho_{d,s}$ =0.670, 0.070 $\alpha_{x,y}$=0.092,0.092
color = 0., 45, 0.54, 1.0
scale factors = 1.0, 50.0, 2.0

Semi-Gloss Paint, Rolled
$\rho_{d,s}$ =0.450, 0.048 $\alpha_{x,y}$=0.045, 0.068
color = 0., 45, 0.54, 1.0
scale factors = 1.0, 20.0, 10.0

Lightly Brushed Aluminum
$\rho_{d,s}$ =0.150, 0.190 $\alpha_{x,y}$=0.088,0.130
color = 1.0, 0.99, 1.0
scale factors = 2.0, 2.0, 2.0

White Ceramic Tile
$\rho_{d,s}$ =0.700, 0.050 $\alpha_{x,y}$=0.071,0.071
color = 1.0, 1.0, 1.0
scale factors = 1.0, 10.0, 10.0

Gloss Paint, Rolled
$\rho_{d,s}$ =0.450, 0.059 $\alpha_{x,y}$=0.054, 0.080
color = 0., 45, 0.54, 1.0
scale factors = 1.0, 20.0, 10.0

Color Plate 23 A variety of materials rendered with Ward's BRDF model (see Section 14.3) and his measured/fitted material parameters. Note the difference in the shapes of the specular highlights, particularly on the knob of the teapot. The metals and paints exhibit anisotropic reflection while the plastic and tile materials are isotropic. (3Dlabs, Inc.)

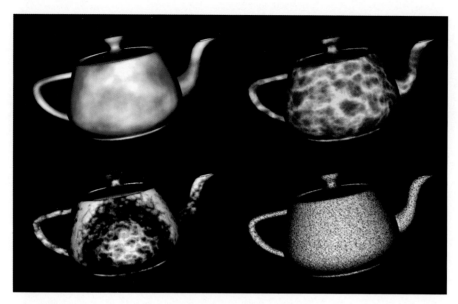

Color Plate 24 Teapots rendered with noise shaders, as described in Chapter 15. Clockwise from upper left: a cloud shader that sums four octaves of noise and uses a blue-to-white color gradient to code the result; a sun surface shader that uses the absolute value function to introduce discontinuities (turbulence); a granite shader that uses a single high-frequency noise value to modulate between white and black; a marble shader that uses noise to modulate a sine function to produce alternating "veins" of color. (3Dlabs, Inc.)

Color Plate 25 A bust of Beethoven rendered with the wood shader described in Section 15.7. (3Dlabs, Inc.)

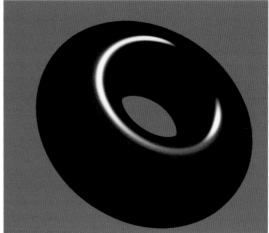

Color Plate 26 Left: The difference between a conventional texture map (lower left) and a polynomial texture map (PTM) (upper right). The conventional texture looks flat and unrealistic as the light source is moved, while the PTM faithfully reproduces changing specular highlights and self-shadowing. Right: A torus rendered using the BRDF PTM shaders described in Section 14.4. Although the paint is basically black, note the change in the highlight color (from bluish-purple in the back to reddish-brown in the front) as the reflection angle changes. (© Copyright 2003 Hewlett-Packard Development Company, L.P., Reproduced with Permission)

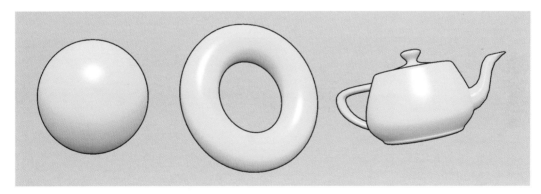

Color Plate 27 Gooch shading applied to three objects (see Section 18.2). Background color (gray), warm color (yellow), and cool color (blue) are chosen in order so that they do not impede the clarity of the outline color (black) or highlight color (white). Details are still visible in this rendering that would be lost in shadow using traditional shading. (3Dlabs, Inc.)

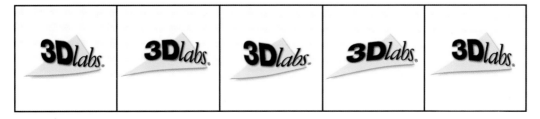

Color Plate 28 Several frames from the animated sequence produced by the wobble shader described in Section 16.8. (3Dlabs, Inc.)

Color Plate 29 Results of the image brightness shader discussed in Section 19.5.1 with *alpha* equal to 0.4, 0.6, 0.8, 1.0, and 1.2 from left to right. The image with *alpha* = 1.0 is the same as the unmodified source image.

Color Plate 30 Results of the image contrast shader discussed in Section 19.5.2 with *alpha* equal to 0.4, 0.6, 0.8, 1.0, and 1.2 from left to right. The image with *alpha* = 1.0 is the same as the unmodified source image.

Color Plate 31 Results of the image saturation shader discussed in Section 19.5.3 with *alpha* equal to 0.0, 0.5, 0.75, 1.0, and 1.25 from left to right. The image with *alpha* = 0.0 is the same as the unmodified target image. The image with *alpha* = 1.0 is the same as the unmodified source image.

Color Plate 32 Results of the image sharpness shader discussed in Section 19.5.4 with *alpha* equal to 0.0, 0.5, 1.0, 1.5, and 2.0 from left to right. The image with *alpha* = 0.0 is the same as the unmodified target image. The image with *alpha* = 1.0 is the same as the unmodified source image.

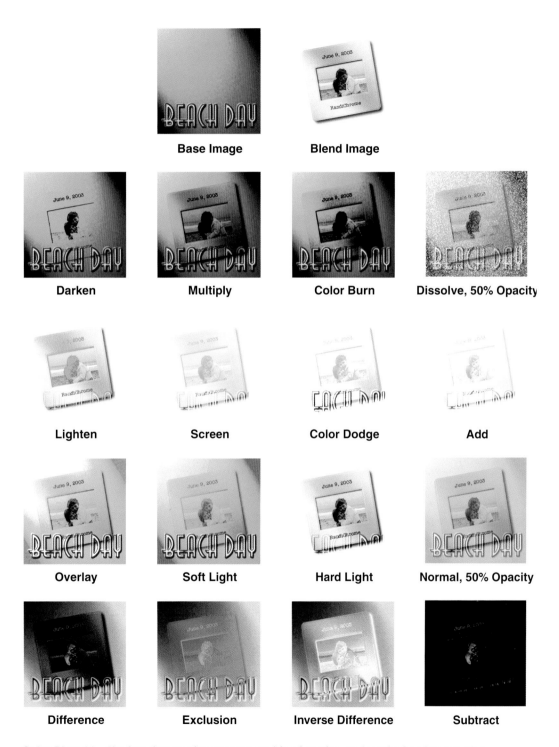

Color Plate 33 Shaders that implement various blend modes, as described in Section 19.6.

Color Plate 34 Brick shader with and without antialiasing. On the left, the results of the brick shader presented in Chapter 6. On the right, results of antialiasing by analytic integration using the brick shader described in Section 17.4.5. (3Dlabs, Inc.)

to determine whether we're "in" or "out" of the stripe around the ball. We call the **smoothstep** function to do the same operation on these two values as was performed on the previous four half-space distances. We update the *inorout* counter by adding the result from the distance computation with the final half-space. The distance computation with respect to the fifth half-space is illustrated in (E) of Figure 11.3.

```
distance.x  = dot(pShade, HalfSpace[4]);
distance.y  = StripeWidth - abs(pShade.z);
distance.xy = smoothstep(-FWidth, FWidth, distance.xy);
inorout     += distance.x;
```

(In this case, we're performing a smooth step operation only on the *x* and *y* components.)

The value for *inorout* is now in the range [–3,2]. This intermediate result is illustrated in Figure 11.4 (A). By clamping the value of *inorout* to the range [0,1], we obtain the result shown in Figure 11.4 (B).

```
inorout     = clamp(inorout, 0.0, 1.0);
```

At this point, we can compute the surface color for the fragment. We use the computed value of *inorout* to perform a linear blend between yellow and red to define the star pattern. If we were to stop here, the result would look like Color Plate 13A. If we take the results of this calculation and do a linear blend with the color of the stripe, we get the result shown in Color Plate 13B. Because we used **smoothstep**, the values of *inorout* and *distance.y* provide a nicely antialiased edge at the border between colors.

```
surfColor   = mix(BaseColor, StarColor, inorout);
surfColor   = mix(surfColor, StripeColor, distance.y);
```

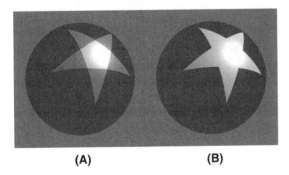

(A)   **(B)**

Figure 11.4 Intermediate results from "in" or "out" computation. Surface points that are "in" with respect to all five half-planes are shown in white, and points that are "in" with respect to four half-planes are shown in gray (A). The value of *inorout* is clamped to the range [0,1] to produce the result shown in (B). (Courtesy of AMD.)

The result at this stage is flat and unrealistic. Performing a lighting calculation will fix this. The first step is to analytically compute the normal for this fragment, which we can do because we know the eye-coordinate position of the center of the ball (it's provided in the in variable *ECballCenter*) and we know the eye-coordinate position of the fragment (it's passed in the in variable *ECposition*). (This approach could have been used with the earth shader discussed in Section 10.2 to avoid passing the surface normal as an in variable and using the interpolated results.)

```
// Calculate analytic normal of a sphere
normal     = normalize(ECPosition.xyz - ECBallCenter.xyz);
```

The diffuse part of the lighting equation is computed with these three lines of code:

```
// Per-fragment diffuse lighting
intensity  = Ka; // ambient
intensity += Kd * clamp(dot(LightDir.xyz, normal), 0.0, 1.0);
surfColor *= intensity;
```

The result of diffuse-only lighting is shown in Color Plate 13C. The final step is to add a specular contribution with these three lines of code:

```
// Per-fragment specular lighting
intensity  = clamp(dot(HVector.xyz, normal), 0.0, 1.0);
intensity  = Ks * pow(intensity, SpecularExponent);
surfColor.rgb += SpecularColor.rgb * intensity;
```

Notice in Color Plate 13D that the specular highlight is perfect! Because the surface normal at each fragment is computed exactly, there is no misshapen specular highlight caused by tesselation facets like we're used to seeing. The resulting value is written to *gl_FragColor* and sent on for final processing before ultimately being written into the framebuffer.

```
FragColor = surfColor;
```

Voila! Your very own toy ball, created completely out of thin air! The complete listing of the toy ball fragment shader is shown in Listing 11.5.

Listing 11.5 Fragment shader for drawing a toy ball

```
#version 140
uniform vec4   HalfSpace[5]; // half-spaces used to define star pattern
uniform float  StripeWidth;

uniform float  InOrOutInit;   // -3.0
uniform float  FWidth;        // = 0.005

uniform vec4   StarColor;
uniform vec4   StripeColor;
uniform vec4   BaseColor;
```

```
uniform vec4  LightDir;     // light direction, should be normalized
uniform vec4  HVector;      // reflection vector for infinite light


uniform vec4  SpecularColor;
uniform float SpecularExponent;
uniform float Ka;
uniform float Kd;
uniform float Ks;

     in vec4  ECPosition;   // surface position in eye coordinates
     in vec3  OCPosition;   // surface position in object coordinates
flat in vec4  ECBallCenter; // ball center in eye coordinates

out vec4 FragColor;

void main()
{
    vec3  normal;       // Analytically computed normal
    vec4  pShade;       // Point in shader space
    vec4  surfColor;    // Computed color of the surface
    float intensity;    // Computed light intensity
    vec4  distance;     // Computed distance values
    float inorout;      // Counter for classifying star pattern

    pShade.xyz = normalize(OCPosition.xyz);
    pShade.w   = 1.0;

    inorout    = InOrOutInit;     // initialize inorout to -3.0

    distance[0] = dot(pShade, HalfSpace[0]);
    distance[1] = dot(pShade, HalfSpace[1]);
    distance[2] = dot(pShade, HalfSpace[2]);
    distance[3] = dot(pShade, HalfSpace[3]);

    //float FWidth = fwidth(pShade);
    distance    = smoothstep(-FWidth, FWidth, distance);

    inorout     += dot(distance, vec4(1.0));

    distance.x  = dot(pShade, HalfSpace[4]);
    distance.y  = StripeWidth - abs(pShade.z);
    distance.xy = smoothstep(-FWidth, FWidth, distance.xy);
    inorout     += distance.x;

    inorout     = clamp(inorout, 0.0, 1.0);

    surfColor   = mix(BaseColor, StarColor, inorout);
    surfColor   = mix(surfColor, StripeColor, distance.y);

    // Calculate analytic normal of a sphere
    normal      = normalize(ECPosition.xyz-ECBallCenter.xyz);
```

```
    // Per-fragment diffuse lighting
    intensity  = Ka; // ambient
    intensity += Kd * clamp(dot(LightDir.xyz, normal), 0.0, 1.0);
    surfColor *= intensity;

    // Per-fragment specular lighting
    intensity  = clamp(dot(HVector.xyz, normal), 0.0, 1.0);
    intensity  = Ks * pow(intensity, SpecularExponent);
    surfColor.rgb += SpecularColor.rgb * intensity;

    FragColor = surfColor;
}
```

11.3 Lattice

Here's a little bit of a gimmick. In this example, we show how *not* to draw the object procedurally.

In this example, we look at how the **discard** command can be used in a fragment shader to achieve some interesting effects. The **discard** command causes fragments to be discarded rather than used to update the framebuffer. We use this to draw geometry with "holes." The vertex shader is the exact same vertex shader used for stripes (Section 11.1.1). The fragment shader is shown in Listing 11.6.

Listing 11.6 Fragment shader for procedurally discarding part of an object

```
in vec3  DiffuseColor;
in vec3  SpecularColor;
in vec2  TexCoord

out vec3 FragColor;

uniform vec2  Scale;
uniform vec2  Threshold;
uniform vec3  SurfaceColor;

void main()
{
    float ss = fract(TexCoord.s * Scale.s);
    float tt = fract(TexCoord.t * Scale.t);

    if ((ss > Threshold.s) && (tt > Threshold.t)) discard;

    vec3 finalColor = SurfaceColor * DiffuseColor + SpecularColor;
    FragColor = vec4(finalColor, 1.0);
}
```

The part of the object to be discarded is determined by the values of the *s* and *t* texture coordinates. A scale factor is applied to adjust the frequency of the lattice. The fractional part of this scaled texture-coordinate value is computed to provide a number in the range [0,1]. These values are compared with the threshold values that have been provided. If both values exceed the threshold, the fragment is discarded. Otherwise, we do a simple lighting calculation and render the fragment.

In Color Plate 14, the threshold values were both set to 0.13. This means that more than three-quarters of the fragments were being discarded! And that's what I call a "holy cow!"

11.4 Bump Mapping

We have already seen procedural shaders that modified color (*brick, stripes*) and opacity (*lattice*). Another whole class of interesting effects can be applied to a surface with a technique called BUMP MAPPING. Bump mapping involves modulating the surface normal before lighting is applied. We can perform the modulation algorithmically to apply a regular pattern, we can add noise to the components of a normal, or we can look up a perturbation value in a texture map. Bump mapping has proved to be an effective way of increasing the apparent realism of an object without increasing the geometric complexity. It can be used to simulate surface detail or surface irregularities.

The technique does not truly alter the surface being shaded; it merely "tricks" the lighting calculations. Therefore, the "bumping" does not show up on the silhouette edges of an object. Imagine modeling a planet as a sphere and shading it with a bump map so that it appears to have mountains that are quite large relative to the diameter of the planet. Because nothing has been done to change the underlying geometry, which is perfectly round, the silhouette of the sphere always appears perfectly round, even if the mountains (bumps) go right up to the silhouette edge. In real life, you would expect the mountains on the silhouette edges to prevent the silhouette from looking perfectly round. For this reason, it is a good idea to use bump mapping to apply only "small" effects to a surface (at least relative to the size of the surface). Wrinkles on an orange, embossed logos, and pitted bricks are all good examples of things that can be successfully bump-mapped.

Bump mapping adds apparent geometric complexity during fragment processing, so once again the key to the process is our fragment shader. This implies that the lighting operation must be performed by our fragment shader instead of by the vertex shader where it is often handled. Again, this points out one of the advantages of the programmability that is available through the OpenGL Shading Language. We are free to perform whatever operations are necessary, in either the vertex shader or the fragment shader. We don't need to be bound to the fixed functionality ideas of where things like lighting are performed.

The key to bump mapping is that we need a valid surface normal at each fragment location, and we also need a light source and viewing direction vectors. If we have access to all these values in the fragment shader, we can procedurally perturb the normal prior to the light source calculation to produce the appearance of "bumps." In this case, we really are attempting to produce bumps or small spherical nodules on the surface being rendered.

The light source computation is typically performed with dot products. For the result to have meaning, all the components of the light source calculation must be defined in the same coordinate space. So if we used the vertex shader to perform lighting, we would typically define light source positions or directions in eye coordinates and would transform incoming normals and vertex values into this space to do the calculation.

However, the eye-coordinate system isn't necessarily the best choice for doing lighting in the fragment shader. We could normalize the direction to the light and the surface normal after transforming them to eye space and then pass them to the fragment shader as out variables. However, the light direction vector would need to be renormalized after interpolation to get accurate results. Moreover, whatever method we use to compute the perturbation normal, it would need to be transformed into eye space and added to the surface normal; that vector would also need to be normalized. Without renormalization, the lighting artifacts would be quite noticeable. Performing these operations at every fragment might be reasonably costly in terms of performance. There is a better way.

Let us look at another coordinate space called the SURFACE-LOCAL COORDINATE SPACE. This coordinate system varies over a rendered object, and it assumes that each point is at (0, 0, 0) and that the unperturbed surface normal at each point is (0, 0, 1). This would be a pretty convenient coordinate system in which to do our bump mapping calculations. But, to do our lighting computation, we need to make sure that our light direction, viewing direction, and the computed perturbed normal are all defined in the same coordinate system. If our perturbed normal is defined in surface-local coordinates, that means we need to transform our light direction and viewing direction into surface-local space as well. How is that accomplished?

What we need is a transformation matrix that transforms each incoming vertex into surface-local coordinates (i.e., incoming vertex (x, y, z) is transformed to $(0, 0, 0)$). We need to construct this transformation matrix at each vertex. Then, at each vertex, we use the surface-local transformation matrix to transform both the light direction and the viewing direction. In this way, the surface local coordinates of the light direction and the viewing direction are computed at each vertex and interpolated across the primitive. At each fragment, we can use these values to perform our lighting calculation with the perturbed normal that we calculate.

But we still haven't answered the real question. How do we create the transformation matrix that transforms from object coordinates to surface-local coordinates? An infinite number of transforms will transform a particular vertex to $(0, 0, 0)$. To transform incoming vertex values, we need a way that gives consistent results as we interpolate between them.

The solution is to require the application to send down one more attribute value for each vertex, a tangent value. Furthermore, we require the application to send us tangents that are consistently defined across the surface of the object. By definition, this tangent vector is in the plane of the surface being rendered and perpendicular to the incoming surface normal. If defined consistently across the object, it serves to orient consistently the coordinate system that we derive. If we perform a cross-product between the tangent vector and the surface normal, we get a third vector that is perpendicular to the other two. This third vector is called the BINORMAL, and it's something that we can compute in our vertex shader. Together, these three vectors form an orthonormal basis, which is what we need to define the transformation from object coordinates into surface-local coordinates. Because this particular surface-local coordinate system is defined with a tangent vector as one of the basis vectors, this coordinate system is sometimes referred to as TANGENT SPACE.

The transformation from object space to surface-local space is shown in Figure 11.5. We transform the object space vector (O_x, O_y, O_z) into surface-local space by multiplying it by a matrix that contains the tangent vector

$$\begin{bmatrix} S_x \\ S_y \\ S_z \end{bmatrix} = \begin{bmatrix} T_x & T_y & T_z \\ B_x & B_y & B_z \\ N_x & N_y & N_z \end{bmatrix} \begin{bmatrix} O_x \\ O_y \\ O_z \end{bmatrix}$$

Figure 11.5 Transformation from object space to surface-local space

(T_x, T_y, T_z) in the first row, the binormal vector (B_x, B_y, B_z) in the second row, and the surface normal (N_x, N_y, N_z) in the third row. We can use this process to transform both the light direction vector and the viewing direction vector into surface-local coordinates. The transformed vectors are interpolated across the primitive, and the interpolated vectors are used in the fragment shader to compute the reflection with the procedurally perturbed normal.

11.4.1 Application Setup

For our procedural bump map shader to work properly, the application must send a vertex position, a surface normal, and a tangent vector in the plane of the surface being rendered. The application passes the tangent vector as a generic vertex attribute and binds the index of the generic attribute to be used to the vertex shader variable *tangent* by calling **glBindAttribLocation**. The application is also responsible for providing values for the uniform variables *LightPosition*, *SurfaceColor*, *BumpDensity*, *BumpSize*, and *SpecularFactor*.

You must be careful to orient the tangent vectors consistently between vertices; otherwise, the transformation into surface-local coordinates will be inconsistent, and the lighting computation will yield unpredictable results. Consistent tangents can be computed algorithmically for mathematically defined surfaces. Consistent tangents for polygonal objects can be computed with neighboring vertices and by application of a consistent ordering with respect to the object's texture coordinates.

The problem with inconsistently defined normals is illustrated in Figure 11.6. This diagram shows two triangles, one with consistently defined tangents and one with inconsistently defined tangents. The gray arrowheads indicate the tangent and binormal vectors (the surface normal is pointing straight out of the page). The white arrowheads indicate the direction toward the light source (in this case, a directional light source is illustrated).

When we transform vertex 1 to surface-local coordinates, we get the same initial result in both cases. When we transform vertex 2, we get a large difference because the tangent vectors are very different between the two vertices. If tangents were defined consistently, this situation would not occur unless the surface had a high degree of curvature across this polygon. And if that were the case, we would really want to tessellate the geometry further to prevent this from happening.

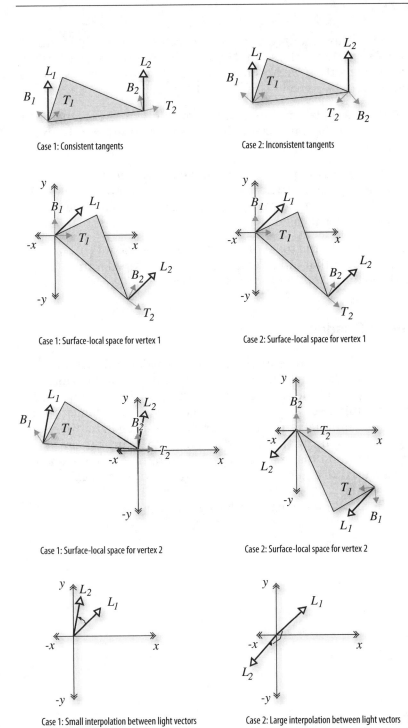

Figure 11.6 Inconsistently defined tangents can lead to large lighting errors.

The result is that in case 1, our light direction vector is smoothly interpolated from the first vertex to the second, and all the interpolated vectors are roughly the same length. If we normalize this light vector at each vertex, the interpolated vectors are very close to unit length as well.

But in case 2, the interpolation causes vectors of wildly different lengths to be generated, some of them near zero. This causes severe artifacts in the lighting calculation.

OpenGL does not have a defined vertex attribute for a tangent vector. The best choice is to use a generic vertex attribute to pass in the tangent value. We don't need to compute the binormal in the application; we have the vertex shader compute it automatically.

The shaders described in the following section are descendants of the "bumpy/shiny" shader that John Kessenich and I developed for the SIGGRAPH 2002 course, *State of the Art in Hardware Shading*.

11.4.2 Vertex Shader

The vertex shader for our procedural bump map shader is shown in Listing 11.7. This shader is responsible for computing the surface-local direction to the light and the surface-local direction to the eye. To do this, it accepts the incoming vertex position, surface normal, and tangent vector; computes the binormal; and transforms the eye space light direction and viewing direction, using the created surface-local transformation matrix. The texture coordinates are also passed on to the fragment shader because they are used to determine the position of our procedural bumps.

Listing 11.7   Vertex shader for doing procedural bump mapping

```
#version 140

uniform vec3 LightPosition;

uniform mat4 MVMatrix;
uniform mat4 MVPMatrix;
uniform mat3 NormalMatrix;

in   vec4 MCVertex;
in   vec3 MCNormal;
in   vec3 MCTangent;
in   vec2 TexCoord0;

out vec3 LightDir;
out vec3 EyeDir;
out vec2 TexCoord;
```

```
void main()
{
    gl_Position     = MVPMatrix * MCVertex;

    EyeDir          = vec3(MVMatrix * MCVertex);
    TexCoord        = TexCoord0.st;

    vec3 n = normalize(NormalMatrix * MCNormal);
    vec3 t = normalize(NormalMatrix * MCTangent);
    vec3 b = cross(n, t);

    vec3 v;
    v.x = dot(LightPosition, t);
    v.y = dot(LightPosition, b);
    v.z = dot(LightPosition, n);
    LightDir = normalize(v);

    v.x = dot(EyeDir, t);
    v.y = dot(EyeDir, b);
    v.z = dot(EyeDir, n);
    EyeDir = normalize(v);
}
```

11.4.3 Fragment Shader

The fragment shader for doing procedural bump mapping is shown in
Listing 11.8. A couple of the characteristics of the bump pattern are parameterized by being declared as uniform variables, namely, *BumpDensity* (how
many bumps per unit area) and *BumpSize* (how wide each bump will be).
Two of the general characteristics of the overall surface are also defined as uniform variables: *SurfaceColor* (base color of the surface) and *SpecularFactor*
(specular reflectance property).

The bumps that we compute are round. Because the texture coordinate is
used to determine the positioning of the bumps, the first thing we do is
multiply the incoming texture coordinate by the *density* value. This controls whether we see more or fewer bumps on the surface. Using the resulting grid, we compute a bump located in the center of each grid square. The
components of the perturbation vector *p* are computed as the distance from
the center of the bump in the *x* direction and the distance from the center
of the bump in the *y* direction. (We only perturb the normal in the *x* and *y*
directions. The *z* value for our perturbation normal is always 1.0.) We compute a "pseudodistance" *d* by squaring the components of *p* and summing
them. (The real distance could be computed at the cost of doing another
square root, but it's not really necessary if we consider *BumpSize* to be a relative value rather than an absolute value.)

To perform a proper reflection calculation later on, we really need to normalize the perturbation normal. This normal must be a unit vector so that we can perform dot products and get accurate cosine values for use in the lighting computation. We normalize a vector by multiplying each component of the normal by $1.0 / \mathbf{sqrt}(x^2 + y^2 + z^2)$. Because of our computation for d, we've already computed part of what we need (i.e., $x^2 + y^2$). Furthermore, because we're not perturbing z at all, we know that z^2 will always be 1.0. To minimize the computation, we just finish computing our normalization factor at this point in the shader by computing $1.0 / \mathbf{sqrt}(d + 1.0)$.

Next, we compare d to *BumpSize* to see if we're in a bump or not. If we're not, we set our perturbation vector to 0 and our normalization factor to 1.0. The lighting computation happens in the next few lines. We compute our normalized perturbation vector by multiplying through with the normalization factor f. The diffuse and specular reflection values are computed in the usual way, except that the interpolated surface-local coordinate light and view direction vectors are used. We get decent results without normalizing these two vectors as long as we don't have large differences in their values between vertices.

Listing 11.8 Fragment shader for procedural bump mapping

```
#version 140

uniform vec4  SurfaceColor;     // = (0.7, 0.6, 0.18, 1.0)
uniform float BumpDensity;      // = 16.0
uniform float BumpSize;         // = 0.15
uniform float SpecularFactor;   // = 0.5

in  vec3 LightDir;
in  vec3 EyeDir;
in  vec2 TexCoord;

out vec4 FragColor;

void main()
{
    vec3 litColor;
    vec2 c = BumpDensity * TexCoord.st;
    vec2 p = fract(c) - vec2(0.5);

    float d, f;
    d = dot(p,p);
    f = inversesqrt(d + 1.0);

    if (d >= BumpSize)
        { p = vec2(0.0); f = 1.0; }
```

```
    vec3 normDelta = vec3(p.x, p.y, 1.0) * f;
    litColor = SurfaceColor.rgb * max(dot(normDelta, LightDir), 0.0);
    vec3 reflectDir = reflect(LightDir, normDelta);

    float spec = max(dot(EyeDir, reflectDir), 0.0);
    spec = pow(spec, 6.0);
    spec *= SpecularFactor;
    litColor = min(litColor + spec, vec3(1.0));

    FragColor = vec4(litColor, SurfaceColor.a);
}
```

The results from the procedural bump map shader are shown applied to two objects, a simple box and a torus, in Color Plate 15. The texture coordinates are used as the basis for positioning the bumps, and because the texture coordinates go from 0.0 to 1.0 four times around the diameter of the torus, the bumps look much closer together on that object.

11.4.4 Normal Maps

It is easy to modify our shader so that it obtains the normal perturbation values from a texture rather generating them procedurally. A texture that contains normal perturbation values for the purpose of bump mapping is called a BUMP MAP or a NORMAL MAP.

An example of a normal map and the results applied to our simple box object are shown in Color Plate 16. Individual components for the normals can be in the range [–1,1]. To be encoded into an RGB texture with 8 bits per component, they must be mapped into the range [0,1]. The normal map appears chalk blue because the default perturbation vector of (0,0,1) is encoded in the normal map as (0.5,0.5,1.0). The normal map could be stored in a floating-point texture. Today's graphics hardware supports textures with 16-bit floating-point values per color component and textures with 32-bit floating-point values per color component. If you use a floating-point texture format for storing normals, your image quality tends to increase (for instance, reducing banding effects in specular highlights). Of course, textures that are 16 bits per component require twice as much texture memory as 8-bit per component textures, and performance might be reduced.

The vertex program is identical to the one described in Section 11.4.2. The fragment shader is almost the same, except that instead of computing the perturbed normal procedurally, the fragment shader obtains it from a normal map stored in texture memory.

11.5 Summary

A master magician can make it look like something is created out of thin air. With procedural textures, you, as a shader writer, can express algorithms that turn flat gray surfaces into colorful, patterned, bumpy, or reflective ones. The trick is to come up with an algorithm that expresses the texture you envision. By coding this algorithm as an OpenGL shader, you too can create something out of thin air.

In this chapter, we only scratched the surface of what's possible. We created a stripe shader, but grids and checkerboards and polka dots are no more difficult. We created a toy ball with a star, but we could have created a beach ball with snowflakes. Shaders can be written to procedurally include or exclude geometry or to add bumps or grooves. Additional procedural texturing effects are illustrated later in this book. Chapter 15 shows how an irregular function (noise) can achieve a wide range of procedural texturing effects. Shaders for generating procedural textures with a more complex mathematical function (the Mandelbrot and Julia sets) and for creating non-photorealistic effects are also described later in the book.

Procedural textures are mathematically precise, are easy to parameterize, and don't require large amounts of texture memory. The end goal of a vertex shader/fragment shader pair is to produce a color value (and possibly a depth value) that will be written into the framebuffer. Because the OpenGL Shading Language is a procedural programming language, the only limit to this computation is your imagination.

11.6 Further Information

The book *Texturing and Modeling: A Procedural Approach, Third Edition*, by David S. Ebert et al. (2002) is entirely devoted to creating images procedurally. This book contains a wealth of information and inspires a ton of ideas for the creation and use of procedural models and textures.

The shaders written in the RenderMan Shading Language are often procedural in nature, and *The RenderMan Companion* by Steve Upstill (1990) and *Advanced RenderMan: Creating CGI for Motion Pictures* by Anthony A. Apodaca and Larry Gritz (1999) contain some notable examples.

Bump mapping was invented by Jim Blinn and described in his 1978 SIGGRAPH paper, *Simulation of Wrinkled Surfaces*. A very good overview of bump mapping techniques can be found in a paper titled *A Practical and Robust Bump-mapping Technique for Today's GPUs* by Mark Kilgard (2000).

A Photoshop plug-in for creating a normal map from an image is available at NVIDIA's developer Web site at http://developer.nvidia.com/object/ photoshop_dds_plugins.html.

[1] *AMD developer Web site.* http://developer.amd.com/

[2] Apodaca, Anthony A., and Larry Gritz, *Advanced RenderMan: Creating CGI for Motion Pictures*, Morgan Kaufmann Publishers, San Francisco, 1999. www.renderman.org/RMR/Books/arman/materials.html

[3] Blinn, James, *Simulation of Wrinkled Surfaces*, Computer Graphics (SIGGRAPH '78 Proceedings), pp. 286–292, August 1978.

[4] Ebert, David S., John Hart, Bill Mark, F. Kenton Musgrave, Darwyn Peachey, Ken Perlin, and Steven Worley, *Texturing and Modeling: A Procedural Approach, Third Edition*, Morgan Kaufmann Publishers, San Francisco, 2002. www.texturingandmodeling.com

[5] Kilgard, Mark J., *A Practical and Robust Bump-mapping Technique for Today's GPUs*, Game Developers Conference, NVIDIA White Paper, 2000. http://developer.nvidia.com/object/Practical_ Bumpmapping_Tech.html

[6] *NVIDIA developer Web site.* http://developer.nvidia.com

[7] Rost, Randi J., *The OpenGL Shading Language*, SIGGRAPH 2002, Course 17, course notes. http://3dshaders.com/pubs

[8] Upstill, Steve, *The RenderMan Companion: A Programmer's Guide to Realistic Computer Graphics*, Addison-Wesley, Reading, Massachusetts, 1990.

Chapter 12

Lighting

In the real world, we see things because they reflect light from a light source or because they are light sources themselves. In computer graphics, just as in real life, we won't be able to see an object unless it is illuminated or emits light. To generate more realistic images, we need to have more realistic models for illumination, shadows, and reflection than those we've discussed so far.

In this chapter and the next two, we explore how the OpenGL Shading Language can help us implement such models so that they can execute at interactive rates on programmable graphics hardware. In this chapter, we look at some lighting models that provide more flexibility and give more realistic results than those built into OpenGL's fixed functionality rendering pipeline. Much has been written on the topic of lighting in computer graphics. We examine only a few methods in this chapter. Ideally, you'll be inspired to try implementing some others on your own.

12.1 Hemisphere Lighting

In Chapter 9, we looked carefully at the fixed functionality lighting model built into OpenGL and developed shader code to mimic the fixed functionality behavior. However, this model has a number of flaws, and these flaws become more apparent as we strive for more realistic rendering effects. One problem is that objects in a scene do not typically receive all their illumination from a small number of specific light sources. Interreflections between objects often have noticeable and important contributions to objects in the scene. The traditional computer graphics illumination model attempts to account for this phenomena through an ambient light term. However, this ambient light term is usually applied equally across an object or an entire scene. The result is a flat and unrealistic look for areas of the scene that are not affected by direct illumination.

Another problem with the traditional illumination model is that light sources in real scenes are not point lights or even spotlights—they are area lights. Consider the indirect light coming in from the window and illuminating the floor and the long fluorescent light bulbs behind a rectangular translucent panel. For an even more common case, consider the illumination outdoors on a cloudy day. In this case, the entire visible hemisphere is acting like an area light source. In several presentations and tutorials, Chas Boyd, Dan Baker, and Philip Taylor of Microsoft described this situation as HEMISPHERE LIGHTING and discussed how to implement it in DirectX. Let's look at how we might create an OpenGL shader to simulate this type of lighting environment.

The idea behind hemisphere lighting is that we model the illumination as two hemispheres. The upper hemisphere represents the sky, and the lower hemisphere represents the ground. A location on an object with a surface normal that points straight up gets all of its illumination from the upper hemisphere, and a location with a surface normal pointing straight down gets all of its illumination from the lower hemisphere (see Figure 12.1). By picking appropriate colors for the two hemispheres, we can make the sphere look as though locations with normals pointing up are illuminated and those with surface normals pointing down are in shadow.

To compute the illumination at any point on the surface, we must compute the integral of the illumination received at that point:

$$Color = a \cdot SkyColor + (1 - a) \cdot GroundColor$$

where

$$a = 1.0 - (0.5 \cdot \sin(\theta)) \quad \text{for } \theta \leq 90°$$
$$a = 0.5 \cdot \sin(\theta) \quad \text{for } \theta > 90°$$
$$\theta = \text{angle between surface normal and north pole direction}$$

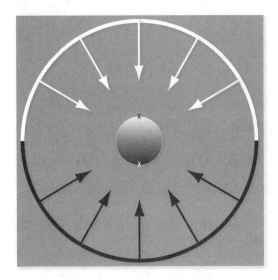

Figure 12.1 A sphere illuminated using the hemisphere lighting model. A point on the top of the sphere (the black "x") receives illumination only from the upper hemisphere (i.e., the sky color). A point on the bottom of the sphere (the white "x") receives illumination only from the lower hemisphere (i.e., the ground color). A point right on the equator would receive half of its illumination from the upper hemisphere and half from the lower hemisphere (e.g., 50% sky color and 50% ground color).

But we can actually calculate a in another way that is simpler but roughly equivalent:

$$a = 0.5 + (0.5 \cdot \cos(\theta))$$

This approach eliminates the need for a conditional. Furthermore, we can easily compute the cosine of the angle between two unit vectors by taking the dot product of the two vectors. This is an example of what Jim Blinn likes to call "the ancient Chinese art of *chi ting.*" In computer graphics, if it looks good enough, it is good enough. It doesn't really matter whether your calculations are physically correct or a colossal cheat. The difference between the two functions is shown in Figure 12.2. The shape of the two curves is similar. One is the mirror of the other, but the area under the curves is the same. This general equivalency is good enough for the effect we're after, and the shader is simpler and will likely execute faster as well.

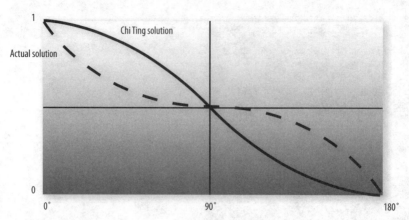

Figure 12.2 Comparing the actual analytic function for hemisphere lighting to a similar but higher-performance function

For the hemisphere shader, we need to pass in uniform variables for the sky color and the ground color. We can also consider the "north pole" to be our light position. If we pass this in as a uniform variable, we can light the model from different directions.

Listing 12.1 shows a vertex shader that implements hemisphere lighting. As you can see, the shader is quite simple. The main purpose of the shader is to compute the diffuse color value and pass it on to fixed functionality fragment processing so that it can be written into the framebuffer. We accomplish this purpose by storing the computed color value in the user-defined out variable *Color*. Results for this shader are shown in Color Plate 21D and G. Compare this to the results of shading with a single directional light source shown in Color Plate 21A and B. Not only is the hemisphere shader simpler and more efficient, it produces a much more realistic lighting effect too! This lighting model can be utilized for tasks like model preview, where it is important to examine all the details of a model. It can also be used in conjunction with the traditional computer graphics illumination model. Point, directional, or spot lights can be added on top of the hemisphere lighting model to provide more illumination to important parts of the scene.

Listing 12.1 Vertex shader for hemisphere lighting

```
#version 140

uniform vec3 LightPosition;
uniform vec3 SkyColor;
uniform vec3 GroundColor;
```

```
uniform mat4 MVMatrix;
uniform mat4 MVPMatrix;
uniform mat3 NormalMatrix;

in vec4      MCVertex;
in vec3      MCNormal;

out vec3     Color;

void main()
{
    vec3 ecPosition = vec3(MVMatrix * MCVertex);
    vec3 tnorm = normalize(NormalMatrix * MCNormal);
    vec3 lightVec = normalize(LightPosition - ecPosition);
    float costheta = dot(tnorm, lightVec);
    float a = costheta * 0.5 + 0.5;
    Color = mix(GroundColor, SkyColor, a);
    gl_Position = MVPMatrix * MCvertex;
}
```

One of the issues with this model is that it doesn't account for self-occlusion. Regions that should really be in shadow because of the geometry of the model appear too bright. We remedy this in Chapter 13.

12.2 Image-Based Lighting

Back in Chapter 10 we looked at shaders to perform environment mapping. If we're trying to achieve realistic lighting in a computer graphics scene, why not just use an environment map for the lighting? This approach to illumination is called IMAGE-BASED LIGHTING; it has been popularized in recent years by researcher Paul Debevec at the University of Southern California. Churches and auditoriums may have dozens of light sources on the ceiling. Rooms with many windows also have complex lighting environments. It is often easier and much more efficient to sample the lighting in such environments and store the results in one or more environment maps than it is to simulate numerous individual light sources.

The steps involved in image-based lighting are

1. Use a LIGHT PROBE (e.g., a reflective sphere) to capture (e.g., photograph) the illumination that occurs in a real-world scene. The captured omnidirectional, high-dynamic range image is called a LIGHT PROBE IMAGE.

2. Use the light probe image to create a representation of the environment (e.g., an environment map).

3. Place the synthetic objects to be rendered inside the environment.

4. Render the synthetic objects by using the representation of the environment created in step 2.

On his Web site (www.debevec.org), Debevec offers a number of useful things to developers. For one, he has made available a number of images that can be used as high-quality environment maps to provide realistic lighting in a scene. These images are high dynamic range (HDR) images that represent each color component with a 32-bit floating-point value. Such images can represent a much greater range of intensity values than can 8-bit-per-component images. For another, he makes available a tool called HDRShop that manipulates and transforms these environment maps. Through links to his various publications and tutorials, he also provides step-by-step instructions on creating your own environment maps and using them to add realistic lighting effects to computer graphics scenes.

Following Debevec's guidance, I purchased a 2-inch chrome steel ball from McMaster-Carr Supply Company (www.mcmaster.com). We used this ball to capture a light probe image from the center of the square outside our office building in downtown Fort Collins, Colorado (Color Plate 10A). We then used HDRShop to create a lat-long environment map (Color Plate 9) and a cube map (Color Plate 10B) of the same scene. The cube map and lat-long map can be used to perform environment mapping as described in Chapter 10. That shader simulated a surface with an underlying base color and diffuse reflection characteristics that was covered by a transparent mirror-like layer that reflected the environment flawlessly.

We can simulate other types of objects if we modify the environment maps before they are used. A point on the surface that reflects light in a diffuse fashion reflects light from all the light sources that are in the hemisphere in the direction of the surface normal at that point. We can't really afford to access the environment map a large number of times in our shader. What we can do instead is similar to what we discussed for hemisphere lighting. Starting from our light probe image, we can construct an environment map for diffuse lighting. Each texel in this environment map will contain the weighted average (i.e., the convolution) of other texels in the visible hemisphere as defined by the surface normal that would be used to access that texel in the environment.

Again, HDRShop has exactly what we need. We can use HDRShop to create a lat-long image from our original light probe image. We can then use a command built into HDRShop that performs the necessary convolution. This operation can be time-consuming, because at each texel in the image, the contributions from half of the other texels in the image must be considered. Luckily, we don't need a very large image for this purpose. The effect is essentially the same as creating a very blurry image of the original light probe image. Since there is no high-frequency content in the computed image, a cube map with faces that are 64×64 or 128×128 works just fine. An example of a diffuse environment map is shown in Color Plate 10C.

A single texture access into this diffuse environment map provides us with the value needed for our diffuse reflection calculation. What about the specular contribution? A surface that is very shiny will reflect the illumination from a light source just like a mirror. This is what we saw in the environment mapping shader from Chapter 10. A single point on the surface reflects a single point in the environment. For surfaces that are rougher, the highlight defocuses and spreads out. In this case, a single point on the surface reflects several points in the environment, though not the whole visible hemisphere like a diffuse surface. HDRShop lets us blur an environment map by providing a Phong exponent—a degree of shininess. A value of 1.0 convolves the environment map to simulate diffuse reflection, and a value of 50 or more convolves the environment map to simulate a somewhat shiny surface. An example of the Old Town Square environment map that has been convolved with a Phong exponent value of 50 is shown in Color Plate 10D.

The shaders that implement these concepts end up being quite simple and quite fast. In the vertex shader, all that is needed is to compute the reflection direction at each vertex. This value and the surface normal are sent to the fragment shader as out variables. They are interpolated across each polygon, and the interpolated values are used in the fragment shader to access the two environment maps in order to obtain the diffuse and the specular components. The values obtained from the environment maps are combined with the object's base color to arrive at the final color for the fragment. The shaders are shown in Listing 12.2 and Listing 12.3. Examples of images created with this technique are shown in Color Plate 18.

Listing 12.2   Vertex shader for image-based lighting

```
#version 140

uniform mat4 MVMatrix;
uniform mat4 MVPMatrix;
uniform mat3 NormalMatrix;

in  vec4  MCVertex;
in  vec3  MCNormal;
```

```
out vec3  ReflectDir;
out vec3  Normal;

void main()
{
    gl_Position = MVPMatrix * MCVertex;
    Normal = normalize(NormalMatrix * MCNormal);
    vec4 pos = MVMatrix * MCvertex;
    vec3 eyeDir = pos.xyz;
    ReflectDir = reflect(eyeDir, Normal);
}
```

Listing 12.3 Fragment shader for image-based lighting

```
#version 140

uniform vec3  BaseColor;
uniform float SpecularPercent;
uniform float DiffusePercent;

uniform samplerCube SpecularEnvMap;
uniform samplerCube DiffuseEnvMap;

in  vec3  ReflectDir;
in  vec3  Normal;

out vec4  FragColor;

void main()
{
    // Look up environment map values in cube maps
    vec3 diffuseColor =
        vec3(texture(DiffuseEnvMap, normalize(Normal)));

    vec3 specularColor =
        vec3(texture(SpecularEnvMap, normalize(ReflectDir)));

    // Add lighting to base color and mix

    vec3 color = mix(BaseColor, diffuseColor*BaseColor, DiffusePercent);
    color = mix(color, specularColor + color, SpecularPercent);

    FragColor = vec4(color, 1.0);
}
```

The environment maps that are used can reproduce the light from the whole scene. Of course, objects with different specular reflection properties require different specular environment maps. And producing these environment maps requires some manual effort and lengthy preprocessing. But the resulting quality and performance make image-based lighting a great choice in many situations.

12.3 Lighting with Spherical Harmonics

In 2001, Ravi Ramamoorthi and Pat Hanrahan presented a method that uses spherical harmonics for computing the diffuse lighting term. This method reproduces accurate diffuse reflection, based on the content of a light probe image, without accessing the light probe image at runtime. The light probe image is preprocessed to produce coefficients that are used in a mathematical representation of the image at runtime. The mathematics behind this approach is beyond the scope of this book (see the references at the end of this chapter if you want all the details). Instead, we lay the necessary groundwork for this shader by describing the underlying mathematics in an intuitive fashion. The result is remarkably simple, accurate, and realistic, and it can easily be codified in an OpenGL shader. This technique has already been used successfully to provide real-time illumination for games and has applications in computer vision and other areas as well.

Spherical harmonics provides a frequency space representation of an image over a sphere. It is analogous to the Fourier transform on the line or circle. This representation of the image is continuous and rotationally invariant. Using this representation for a light probe image, Ramamoorthi and Hanrahan showed that you could accurately reproduce the diffuse reflection from a surface with just nine spherical harmonic basis functions. These nine spherical harmonics are obtained with constant, linear, and quadratic polynomials of the normalized surface normal.

Intuitively, we can see that it is plausible to accurately simulate the diffuse reflection with a small number of basis functions in frequency space since diffuse reflection varies slowly across a surface. With just nine terms used, the average error over all surface orientations is less than 3 percent for any physical input lighting distribution. With Debevec's light probe images, the average error was shown to be less than 1 percent, and the maximum error for any pixel was less than 5 percent.

Each spherical harmonic basis function has a coefficient that depends on the light probe image being used. The coefficients are different for each color channel, so you can think of each coefficient as an RGB value. A preprocessing step is required to compute the nine RGB coefficients for the light probe image to be used. Ramamoorthi makes the code for this preprocessing step available for free on his Web site. I used this program to compute the coefficients for all the light probe images in Debevec's light probe gallery as well as the Old Town Square light probe image and summarized the results in Table 12.1.

Table 12.1 Spherical harmonic coefficients for light probe images

Coefficient	Old Town Square	Grace Cathedral	Eucalyptus Grove	St. Peter's Basilica	Uffizi Gallery
L00	.87 .88 .86	.79 .44 .54	.38 .43 .45	.36 .26 .23	.32 .31 .35
L1m1	.18 .25 .31	.39 .35 .60	.29 .36 .41	.18 .14 .13	.37 .37 .43
L10	.03 .04 .04	-.34 -.18 -.27	.04 .03 .01	-.02 -.01 .00	.00 .00 .00
L11	-.00 -.03 -.05	-.29 -.06 .01	-.10 -.10 -.09	.03 .02 .00	-.01 -.01 -.01
L2m2	-.12 -.12 -.12	-.11 -.05 .12	-.06 -.06 -.04	.02 .01 .00	-.02 -.02 -.03
L2m1	.00, .00 .01	-.26 -.22 -.47	.01 -.01 -.05	-.05 -.03 -.01	-.01 -.01 -.01
L20	-.03 -.02 -.02	-.16 -.09 -.15	-.09 -.13 -.15	-.09 -.08 -.07	-.28 -.28 -.32
L21	-.08 -.09 -.09	.56 .21 .14	-.06 -.05 -.04	.01 .00 .00	.00 .00 .00
L22	-.16 -.19 -.22	.21 -.05 -.30	.02 .00 -.05	-.08 -.03 .00	-.24 -.24 -.28

Coefficient	Galileo's Tomb	Vine Street Kitchen	Breezeway	Campus Sunset	Funston Beach Sunset
L00	1.04 .76 .71	.64 .67 .73	.32 .36 .38	.79 .94 .98	.68 .69 .70
L1m1	.44 .34 .34	.28 .32 .33	.37 .41 .45	.44 .56 .70	.32 .37 .44
L10	-.22 -.18 -.17	.42 .60 .77	-.01 -.01 -.01	-.10 -.18 -.27	-.17 -.17 -.17
L11	.71 .54 .56	-.05 -.04 -.02	-.10 -.12 -.12	.45 .38 .20	-.45 -.42 -.34
L2m2	.64 .50 .52	-.10 -.08 -.05	-.13 -.15 -.17	.18 .14 .05	-.17 -.17 -.15
L2m1	-.12 -.09 -.08	.25 .39 .53	-.01 -.02 .02	-.14 -.22 -.31	-.08 -.09 -.10
L20	-.37 -.28 -.29	.38 .54 .71	-.07 -.08 -.09	-.39 -.40 -.36	-.03 -.02 -.01
L21	-.17 -.13 -.13	.06 .01 -.02	.02 .03 0.03	.09 .07 .04	.16 .14 .10
L22	.55 .42 .42	-.03 -.02 -.03	-.29 -.32 -.36	.67 .67 .52	.37 .31 .20

The equation for diffuse reflection using spherical harmonics is

$$Diffuse = c_1 L_{22}(x^2 - y^2) + c_3 L_{20}z^2 + c_4 L_{20} - c_5 L_{20} +$$
$$2c_1(L_{2-2}xy + L_{21}xz + L_{2-1}yz) + 2c_2(L_{11}x + L_{1-1}y + L_{10}z)$$

The constants *c1–c5* result from the derivation of this formula and are shown in the vertex shader code in Listing 12.4. The *L* coefficients are the nine basis function coefficients computed for a specific light probe image in the preprocessing phase. The *x*, *y*, and *z* values are the coordinates of the normalized surface normal at the point that is to be shaded. Unlike low dynamic range images (e.g., 8 bits per color component) that have an implicit minimum value of 0 and an implicit maximum value of 255, high dynamic range images represented with a floating-point value for each color component don't contain well-defined minimum and maximum values. The minimum and maximum values for two HDR images may be quite different from each other, unless the same calibration or creation process was used to create both images. It is even possible to have an HDR image that contains negative values. For this reason, the vertex shader contains an overall scaling factor to make the final effect look right.

The vertex shader that encodes the formula for the nine spherical harmonic basis functions is actually quite simple. When the compiler gets hold of it, it becomes simpler still. An optimizing compiler typically reduces all the operations involving constants. The resulting code is quite efficient because it contains a relatively small number of addition and multiplication operations that involve the components of the surface normal.

Listing 12.4 Vertex shader for spherical harmonics lighting

```
#version 140

uniform mat4 MVMatrix;
uniform mat4 MVPMatrix;
uniform mat3 NormalMatrix;

uniform float ScaleFactor;

const float C1 = 0.429043;
const float C2 = 0.511664;
const float C3 = 0.743125;
const float C4 = 0.886227;
const float C5 = 0.247708;

// Constants for Old Town Square lighting
const vec3 L00  = vec3( 0.871297,  0.875222,  0.864470);
const vec3 L1m1 = vec3( 0.175058,  0.245335,  0.312891);
const vec3 L10  = vec3( 0.034675,  0.036107,  0.037362);
const vec3 L11  = vec3(-0.004629, -0.029448, -0.048028);
const vec3 L2m2 = vec3(-0.120535, -0.121160, -0.117507);
const vec3 L2m1 = vec3( 0.003242,  0.003624,  0.007511);
const vec3 L20  = vec3(-0.028667, -0.024926, -0.020998);
const vec3 L21  = vec3(-0.077539, -0.086325, -0.091591);
const vec3 L22  = vec3(-0.161784, -0.191783, -0.219152);
```

```
in  vec4  MCVertex;
in  vec3  MCNormal;

out vec3  DiffuseColor;

void main()
{
   vec3 tnorm    = normalize(NormalMatrix * MCNormal);

   DiffuseColor = C1 * L22 * (tnorm.x * tnorm.x - tnorm.y * tnorm.y) +
                  C3 * L20 *  tnorm.z * tnorm.z +
                  C4 * L00 -
                  C5 * L20 +
                  2.0 * C1 * L2m2 * tnorm.x * tnorm.y +
                  2.0 * C1 * L21  * tnorm.x * tnorm.z +
                  2.0 * C1 * L2m1 * tnorm.y * tnorm.z +
                  2.0 * C2 * L11  * tnorm.x +
                  2.0 * C2 * L1m1 * tnorm.y +
                  2.0 * C2 * L10  * tnorm.z;

   DiffuseColor *= ScaleFactor;

   gl_Position = MVPMatrix * MCVertex;
```

Listing 12.5 Fragment shader for spherical harmonics lighting

```
#version 140

in vec3       DiffuseColor;

out vec4      FragColor;

void main()
{
    FragColor = vec4(DiffuseColor, 1.0);
}
```

Our fragment shader, shown in Listing 12.5, has very little work to do.
Because the diffuse reflection typically changes slowly, for scenes without
large polygons we can reasonably compute it in the vertex shader and
interpolate it during rasterization. As with hemispherical lighting, we can
add procedurally defined point, directional, or spotlights on top of the
spherical harmonics lighting to provide more illumination to important
parts of the scene. Results of the spherical harmonics shader are shown in
Color Plate 19. Compare Color Plate 19A with the Old Town Square environment map in Color Plate 9. Note that the top of the dog's head has a
bluish cast, while there is a brownish cast on his chin and chest. Coefficients for some of Paul Debevec's light probe images provide even greater
color variations. We could make the diffuse lighting from the spherical

harmonics computation more subtle by blending it with the object's base color.

The trade-offs in using image-based lighting versus procedurally defined lights are similar to the trade-offs between using stored textures versus procedural textures, as discussed in Chapter 11. Image-based lighting techniques can capture and re-create complex lighting environments relatively easily. It would be exceedingly difficult to simulate such an environment with a large number of procedural light sources. On the other hand, procedurally defined light sources do not use up texture memory and can easily be modified and animated.

12.4 The Überlight Shader

So far in this chapter we've discussed lighting algorithms that simulate the effect of global illumination for more realistic lighting effects. Traditional point, directional, and spotlights can be used in conjunction with these global illumination effects. However, the traditional light sources leave a lot to be desired in terms of their flexibility and ease of use.

Ronen Barzel of Pixar Animation Studios wrote a paper in 1997 that described a much more versatile lighting model specifically tailored for the creation of computer-generated films. This lighting model has so many features and controls compared to the traditional graphics hardware light source types that its RenderMan implementation became known as the "überlight" shader (i.e., the lighting shader that has everything in it except the proverbial kitchen sink). Larry Gritz wrote a public domain version of this shader that was published in *Advanced RenderMan: Creating CGI for Motion Pictures*, which he coauthored with Anthony A. Apodaca. A Cg version of this shader was published by Fabio Pellacini and Kiril Vidimice of Pixar in the book *GPU Gems*, edited by Randima Fernando. The full-blown überlight shader has been used successfully in a variety of computer-generated films, including *Toy Story, Monsters, Inc.*, and *Finding Nemo*. Because of the proven usefulness of the überlight shader, this section looks at how to implement its essential features in the OpenGL Shading Language.

12.4.1 Überlight Controls

In movies, lighting helps to tell the story in several different ways. Sharon Calahan gives a good overview of this process in the book *Advanced RenderMan: Creating CGI for Motion Pictures*. This description includes five important fundamentals of good lighting design that were derived from the book *Matters of Light & Depth* by Ross Lowell:

- Directing the viewer's eye
- Creating depth
- Conveying time of day and season
- Enhancing mood, atmosphere, and drama
- Revealing character personality and situation

Because of the importance of lighting to the final product, movies have dedicated lighting designers. To light computer graphics scenes, lighting designers must have an intuitive and versatile lighting model to use.

For the best results in lighting a scene, it is crucial to make proper decisions about the shape and placement of the lights. For the überlight lighting model, lights are assigned a position in world coordinates. The überlight shader uses a pair of superellipses to determine the shape of the light. A SUPERELLIPSE is a function that varies its shape from an ellipse to a rectangle, based on the value of a roundness parameter. By varying the roundness parameter, we can shape the beam of illumination in a variety of ways (see Figure 12.3 for some examples). The superellipse function is defined as

$$\left(\frac{x}{a}\right)^{\frac{2}{d}} + \left(\frac{y}{b}\right)^{\frac{2}{d}} = 1$$

As the value for *d* nears 0, this function becomes the equation for a rectangle, and when *d* is equal to 1, the function becomes the equation for an ellipse. Values in between create shapes in between a rectangle and an ellipse, and these shapes are also useful for lighting. This is referred to in the shader as BARN SHAPING since devices used in the theater for shaping light beams are referred to as BARN DOORS.

It is also desirable to have a soft edge to the light, in other words, a gradual drop-off from full intensity to zero intensity. We accomplish this by defining a pair of nested superellipses. Inside the innermost superellipse, the light has full intensity. Outside the outermost superellipse, the light has zero intensity. In between, we can apply a gradual transition by using the **smoothstep** function. See Figure 12.3 for examples of lights with and without such soft edges.

Two more controls that add to the versatility of this lighting model are the near and far distance parameters, also known as the CUTON and CUTOFF

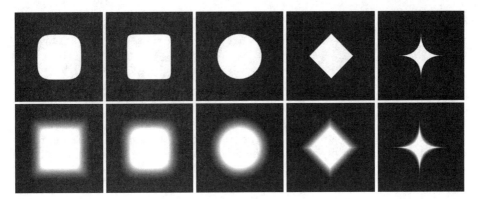

Figure 12.3 A variety of light beam shapes produced with the überlight shader. We enabled barn shaping and varied the roundness and edge width parameters of the superellipse shaping function. The top row uses edge widths of 0, and the bottom row uses 0.3. From left to right, the roundness parameter is set to 0.2, 0.5, 1.0, 2.0, and 4.0.

values. These define the region of the beam that actually provides illumination (see Figure 12.4). Again, smooth transition zones are desired so that the lighting designer can control the transition. Of course, this particular control has no real-world analogy, but it has proved to be useful for softening the lighting in a scene and preventing the light from reaching areas where no light is desired. See Figure 12.5 for an example of the effect of modifying these parameters.

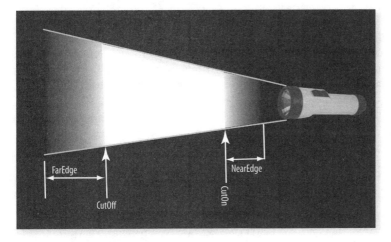

Figure 12.4 Effects of the near and far distance parameters for the überlight shader

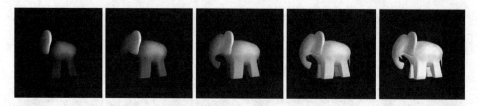

Figure 12.5 Dramatic lighting effects achieved by alteration of the depth cutoff parameters of the überlight shader. In the first frame, the light barely reaches the elephant model. By simply adjusting the far depth edge value, we can gradually bathe our model in light.

12.4.2 Vertex Shader

Listing 12.6 shows the code for the vertex shader for the überlight model. The main purpose of the vertex shader is to transform vertex positions, surface normals, and the viewing (camera) position into the lighting coordinate system. In this coordinate system the light is at the origin, and the z axis is pointed toward the origin of the world coordinate system. This allows us to more easily perform the lighting computations in the fragment shader. The computed values are passed to the fragment shader in the form of the out variables *LCpos*, *LCnorm*, and *LCcamera*.

To perform these calculations, the application must provide *ViewPosition*, the position of the camera in world space, and *WCLightPos*, the position of the light source in world coordinates.

To do the necessary transformations, we need matrices that transform points from modeling coordinates to world coordinates (*MCtoWC*) and from world coordinates to the light coordinate system (*WCtoLC*). The corresponding matrices for transforming normals between the same coordinate systems are the inverse transpose matrices (*MCtoWCit* and *WCtoLCit*).

Listing 12.6 Überlight vertex shader

```
#version 140

uniform mat4 MVMatrix;
uniform mat4 MVPMatrix;
uniform mat3 NormalMatrix;

uniform vec3 WCLightPos;     // Position of light in world coordinates
uniform vec4 ViewPosition;   // Position of camera in world space
uniform mat4 WCtoLC;         // World to light coordinate transform
uniform mat4 WCtoLCit;       // World to light inverse transpose
```

```
uniform mat4 MCtoWC;        // Model to world coordinate transform
uniform mat4 MCtoWCit;      // Model to world inverse transpose

in   vec4  MCVertex;
in   vec3  MCNormal;

out vec3  LCpos;            // Vertex position in light coordinates
out vec3  LCnorm;           // Normal in light coordinates
out vec3  LCcamera;         // Camera position in light coordinates

void main()
{
    gl_Position = MVPMatrix * MCVertex;

    // Compute world space position and normal
    vec4 wcPos  = MCtoWC * MCVertex;
    vec3 wcNorm = (MCtoWCit * vec4(MCNormal, 0.0)).xyz;

    // Compute light coordinate system camera position,
    // vertex position and normal
    LCcamera = (WCtoLC * ViewPosition).xyz;
    LCpos    = (WCtoLC * wcPos).xyz;
    LCnorm   = (WCtoLCit * vec4(wcNorm, 0.0)).xyz;
}
```

12.4.3 Fragment Shader

With the key values transformed into the lighting coordinate system for the specified light source, the fragment shader (Listing 12.7) can perform the necessary lighting computations. One subroutine in this shader (**superEllipseShape**) computes the attenuation factor of the light across the cross section of the beam. This value is 1.0 for fragments within the inner superellipse, 0 for fragments outside the outer superellipse, and a value between 0 and 1.0 for fragments between the two superellipses. Another subroutine (**distanceShape**) computes a similar attenuation factor along the direction of the light beam. These two values are multiplied together to give us the illumination factor for the fragment.

The computation of the light reflection is done in a manner similar to shaders we've examined in previous chapters. Because the computed normals may become denormalized by linear interpolation, we must renormalize them in the fragment shader to obtain more accurate results. After the attenuation factors are computed, we perform a simple reflection computation that gives a plastic appearance. You could certainly modify these computations to simulate the reflection from some other type of material.

Listing 12.7 Überlight fragment shader

```
#version 140

uniform vec3 SurfaceColor;

// Light parameters
uniform vec3  LightColor;
uniform vec3  LightWeights;

// Surface parameters
uniform vec3  SurfaceWeights;
uniform float SurfaceRoughness;
uniform bool  AmbientClamping;

// Super ellipse shaping parameters
uniform bool  BarnShaping;
uniform float SeWidth;
uniform float SeHeight;
uniform float SeWidthEdge;
uniform float SeHeightEdge;
uniform float SeRoundness;

// Distance shaping parameters
uniform float DsNear;
uniform float DsFar;
uniform float DsNearEdge;
uniform float DsFarEdge;

in  vec3 LCpos;     // Vertex position in light coordinates
in  vec3 LCnorm;    // Normal in light coordinates
in  vec3 LCcamera;  // Camera position in light coordinates

out vec4 FragColor;

float superEllipseShape(vec3 pos)
{
   if (!BarnShaping)
      return 1.0;
   else
   {
      // Project the point onto the z = 1.0 plane
      vec2 ppos = pos.xy / pos.z;
      vec2 abspos = abs(ppos);

      float w = SeWidth;
      float W = SeWidth + SeWidthEdge;
      float h = SeHeight;
      float H = SeHeight + SeHeightEdge;

      float exp1 = 2.0 / SeRoundness;
      float exp2 = -SeRoundness / 2.0;
```

```
      float inner = w * h * pow(pow(h * abspos.x, exp1) +
                               pow(w * abspos.y, exp1), exp2);

      float outer = W * H * pow(pow(H * abspos.x, exp1) +
                               pow(W * abspos.y, exp1), exp2);

      return 1.0 - smoothstep(inner, outer, 1.0);
   }
}

float distanceShape(vec3 pos)
{
   float depth;

   depth = abs(pos.z);

   float dist = smoothstep(DsNear - DsNearEdge, DsNear, depth) *
                (1.0 - smoothstep(DsFar, DsFar + DsFarEdge, depth));
   return dist;
}

void main()
{
   vec3 tmpLightColor = LightColor;

   vec3 N = normalize(LCnorm);
   vec3 L = -normalize(LCpos);
   vec3 V = normalize(LCcamera-LCpos);
   vec3 H = normalize(L + V);

   vec3 tmpColor = tmpLightColor;

   float attenuation = 1.0;
   attenuation *= superEllipseShape(LCpos);
   attenuation *= distanceShape(LCpos);

   float ndotl = dot(N, L);
   float ndoth = dot(N, H);

   vec3 litResult;
   litResult[0] = AmbientClamping ? max(ndotl, 0.0) : 1.0;
   litResult[1] = max(ndotl, 0.0);
   litResult[2] = litResult[1] * max(ndoth, 0.0) * SurfaceRoughness;
   litResult *= SurfaceWeights * LightWeights;

   vec3 ambient = tmpLightColor * SurfaceColor * litResult[0];
   vec3 diffuse = tmpColor * SurfaceColor * litResult[1];
   vec3 specular = tmpColor * litResult[2];
   FragColor = vec4(attenuation *
                    (ambient + diffuse + specular), 1.0);
}
```

An example of using this shader is shown in Color Plate 20, along with a screenshot of a user interface designed by Philip Rideout for manipulating its controls. The überlight shader as described by Barzel and Gritz actually has several additional features. It can support multiple lights, but our example shader showed just one for simplicity. The key parameters can be defined as arrays, and a loop can be executed to perform the necessary computations for each light source. In the following chapter, we show how to add shadows to this shader.

12.5 Summary

The summary of this chapter is "Just say no!" to the traditional computer graphics lighting model." Now that programmable graphics hardware has freed us from the shackles of the traditional hardware lighting equations, we are free to implement and experiment with a variety of new techniques. Some of the techniques we explored are both faster and more realistic than the traditional methods.

Hemisphere lighting is a simple way to approximate global illumination in a scene. Environment maps are very useful tools for simulating complex lighting environments. It is neither expensive nor difficult to capture images of real-world lighting conditions. Such light probe images can be preprocessed and used to perform image-based lighting directly, or they can be preprocessed to compute spherical harmonic basis function coefficients that can be used for simple and high-performance lighting.

We've also seen that the traditional OpenGL fixed functionality lighting model leaves a lot to be desired in terms of flexibility and ease of use. Lighting models such as the one defined by the überlight shader are much more versatile and easier for artists to use.

12.6 Further Information

Hemisphere lighting has been popularized by Microsoft and is described in several presentations on DirectX. An online article, *Per-Pixel Lighting*, by Microsoft's Phil Taylor describes this technique. Material in this article was derived from a talk given by Dan Baker and Chas Boyd at Meltdown 2001.

Image-based lighting builds on the foundations of texture mapping and reflection mapping first discussed by Jim Blinn and Martin Newell in 1976.

Paul Debevec has recently popularized this area and maintains a Web site (www.debevec.org) with lots of useful information on this topic, including a gallery of light probe images, the history of reflection mapping, electronic versions of his publications, and much more. A related Web site is www.hdrshop.com from which you can download the free (for personal and educational use) version of HDRShop or obtain the commercial version. There are also tutorials that helped me create the light probe images and environment maps described in this chapter.

Spherical harmonic lighting was described by Ravi Ramamoorthi and Pat Hanrahan in their 2001 SIGGRAPH paper. A lengthy and more tractable discussion of the details of this approach is available in a white paper by Robin Green of Sony.

The überlight shader for RenderMan is discussed in the book *Advanced RenderMan: Creating CGI for Motion Pictures* by Apodaca and Gritz. A Cg version of this shader is described by Fabio Pellacini and Kiril Vidimice in the book *GPU Gems*, edited by Randima Fernando.

[1] Apodaca, Anthony A., and Larry Gritz, *Advanced RenderMan: Creating CGI for Motion Pictures*, Morgan Kaufmann Publishers, San Francisco, 1999. www.renderman.org/RMR/Books/arman/materials.html

[2] Baker, Dan, and C. Boyd, *Advanced Shading and Lighting*, Microsoft Corp. Meltdown 2001 Presentation. www.microsoft.com/mscorp/corpevents/meltdown2001/ppt/DXGLighting.ppt

[3] Barzel, Ronen, *Lighting Controls for Computer Cinematography*, Journal of Graphics Tools, 2(1), 1997, pp. 1–20.

[4] Blinn, James, and M.E. Newell, *Texture and Reflection in Computer Generated Images*, Communications of the ACM, vol. 19, no. 10, pp. 542–547, October 1976.

[5] Debevec, Paul, Image-Based Lighting, IEEE Computer Graphics and Applications, vol. 22, no 2, pp. 26-34. www.debevec.org/CGAIBL2/ibl-tutorial-cga2002.pdf

[6] Debevec, Paul, personal Web site. www.debevec.org

[7] Debevec, Paul, and J. Malik, *Recovering High Dynamic Range Radiance Maps from Photographs*, Computer Graphics (SIGGRAPH '97 Proceedings), pp. 369–378. www.debevec.org/Research/HDR/

[8] Debevec, Paul, Rendering Synthetic Objects into Real Scenes: Bridging Traditional and Image-Based Graphics with Global Illumination and High Dynamic Range Photography, Computer Graphics (SIGGRAPH '98 Proceedings), pp. 189–198. http://athens.ict.usc.edu/Research/IBL/

[9] *GPU Gems: Programming Techniques, Tips, and Tricks for Real-Time Graphics*, Editor: Randima Fernando, Addison-Wesley, Reading, Massachusetts, 2004. http://developer.nvidia.com/object/gpu_gems_home.html

[10] Green, Robin, *Spherical Harmonic Lighting: The Gritty Details*, GDC 2003 Presentation. www.research.scea.com/gdc2003/spherical-harmonic-lighting.html

[11] Lowell, Ross, *Matters of Light & Depth*, Lowel-Light Manufacturing, 1992.

[12] Ramamoorthi, Ravi, and P. Hanrahan, *An Efficient Representation for Irradiance Environment Maps*, Computer Graphics (SIGGRAPH 2001 Proceedings), pp. 497–500. http://www1.cs.columbia.edu/~ravir/papers/envmap/index.html

[13] Taylor, Philip, *Per-Pixel Lighting*, Microsoft Corp., Nov. 2001.

Chapter 13

Shadows

I have a little shadow that goes in and out with me
And what can be the use of him is more than I can see.

—From *My Shadow* by Robert Louis Stevenson

Like Robert Louis Stevenson, have you ever wondered what shadows are good for? The previous chapter discussed lighting models, and wherever there is light, there are also shadows. Well, maybe this is true in the real world, but it is not always true in computer graphics. We have talked a lot about illumination already and have developed a variety of shaders that simulate light sources. But so far we have not described any shaders that generate shadows. This lack of shadows is part of the classic computer graphics "look" and is one obvious clue that a scene is synthetic rather than real.

What are shadows good for? Shadows help define the spatial relationships between objects in a scene. Shadows tell us when a character's feet make contact with the floor as he is running. The shape and movement of a bouncing ball's shadow gives us a great deal of information about the ball's location at any point in time. Shadows on objects help reveal shape and form. In film and theater, shadows play a vital role in establishing mood. And in computer graphics, shadows help enhance the apparent realism of the scene.

Although computing shadows adds complexity and slows performance, the increase in comprehension and realism is often worth it. In this chapter, we explore some relatively simple techniques that produce shadows and shadow effects.

13.1 Ambient Occlusion

The lighting model built into OpenGL that we explored in Chapter 9 has a simple assumption for ambient light, namely, that it is constant over the entire scene. But if you look around your current location, you will probably see that this is almost always a bad assumption as far as generating a realistic image is concerned. Look underneath the table, and you will see an area that is darker than other areas. Look at the stack of books on the table, and you will see that there are dark areas between the books and probably a darker area near the base of the books. Almost every scene in real life contains a variety of complex shadows.

The alternative lighting models described in the previous chapter are an improvement over OpenGL's fixed-function lighting model, but they still fall short. If you look carefully at Color Plate 21D, you can see that the lighting still does not look completely realistic. The area under the chin, the junctions of the legs and the boots, and the creases in the clothing are brightly lit. If this were a real scene, we know that these areas would be darker because they would be obscured by nearby parts of the model. Hence, this object looks fake.

A relatively simple way to add realism to computer-generated imagery is a technique called AMBIENT OCCLUSION. This technique uses a precomputed occlusion (or accessibility) factor to scale the calculated direct diffuse illumination factor. It can be used with a variety of illumination methods, including hemisphere lighting and image-based lighting, as discussed in the preceding chapter. It results in soft shadows that darken parts of the object that are only partially accessible to the overall illumination in a scene.

The basic idea with ambient occlusion is to determine, for each point on an object, how much of the potentially visible hemisphere is actually visible and how much is obstructed by nearby parts of the object. The hemisphere that is considered at each point on the surface is in the direction of the surface normal at that point. For instance, consider the venerable teapot in Figure 13.1. The top of the knob on the teapot's lid receives illumination from the entire visible hemisphere. But a point partway down inside the teapot's spout receives illumination only from a very small percentage of the visible hemisphere, in the direction of the small opening at the end of the spout.

For a specific model we can precompute these occlusion factors and save them as per-vertex attribute values. Alternatively, we can create a texture map that stores these values for each point on the surface. One method for computing occlusion factors is to cast a large number of rays from each vertex and keep track of how many intersect another part of the object and how many do not. The percentage of such rays that are unblocked is the

Figure 13.1   A 2D representation of the process of computing occlusion (accessibility) factors. A point on the top of the knob on the teapot's lid has nothing in the way of the visible hemisphere (accessibility = 1.0), while a point inside the spout has its visible hemisphere mostly obscured (accessibility nearer to 0).

accessibility factor. The top of the lid on the teapot has a value of 1 since no other part of the model blocks its view of the visible hemisphere. A point partway down the spout has an accessibility value near 0, because its visible hemisphere is almost completely obscured.

We then multiply the computed accessibility (or occlusion) factor by our computed diffuse reflection value. This has the effect of darkening areas that are obscured by other parts of the model. It is simple enough to use this value in conjunction with our other lighting models. For instance, the hemisphere lighting vertex shader that we developed in Section 12.1 can incorporate ambient occlusion with a few simple changes, as shown in Listing 13.1.

Listing 13.1   Vertex shader for hemisphere lighting with ambient occlusion

```
#version 140

uniform mat4 MVMatrix;
uniform mat4 MVPMatrix;
uniform mat3 NormalMatrix;

uniform vec3 LightPosition;
uniform vec3 SkyColor;
uniform vec3 GroundColor;

in vec4  MCVertex;
in vec3  MCNormal;
in float Accessibility;
```

```
out vec3  DiffuseColor;

void main()
{
    vec3 ecPosition = vec3(MVMatrix  * MCVertex);
    vec3 tnorm      = normalize(NormalMatrix * MCNormal);
    vec3 lightVec   = normalize(LightPosition - ecPosition);
    float costheta  = dot(tnorm, lightVec);
    float a         = 0.5 + 0.5 * costheta;

    DiffuseColor = mix(GroundColor, SkyColor, a) * Accessibility;

    gl_Position     = MVPMatrix * MCVertex;
}
```

The only change made to this shader is to pass in the accessibility factor as
an in variable and use this to attenuate the computed diffuse color value.
The results are quite a bit more realistic, as you can see by comparing Color
Plate 21D and G. The overall appearance is too dark, but this can be reme-
died by choosing a mid-gray for the ground color rather than black. Color
Plate 21F shows ambient occlusion with a simple diffuse lighting model.

The same thing can be done to the image-based lighting shader that we
developed in Section 12.2 (see Listing 13.2) and to the spherical harmonic
lighting shader that we developed in Section 12.3 (see Listing 13.3). In the
former case, the lighting is done in the fragment shader, so the per-vertex
accessibility factor must be passed to the fragment shader as an out variable.
(Alternatively, the accessibility values could be stored in a texture that could
be accessed in the fragment shader.)

Listing 13.2 Fragment shader for image-based lighting

```
#version 140

uniform vec3  BaseColor;
uniform float SpecularPercent;
uniform float DiffusePercent;

uniform samplerCube SpecularEnvMap;
uniform samplerCube DiffuseEnvMap;

in  vec3  ReflectDir;
in  vec3  Normal;
in  float Accessibility;

out vec4  FragColor;

void main()
{
```

```
    // Look up environment map values in cube maps

    vec3 diffuseColor  =
        vec3(texture(DiffuseEnvMap,  normalize(Normal)));

    vec3 specularColor =
        vec3(texture(SpecularEnvMap, normalize(ReflectDir)));

    // Add lighting to base color and mix

    vec3 color = mix(BaseColor, diffuseColor*BaseColor, DiffusePercent);
    color     *= Accessibility;
    color      = mix(color, specularColor + color, SpecularPercent);

    FragColor = vec4(color, 1.0);
}
```

Listing 13.3 Vertex shader for spherical harmonic lighting

```
#version 140

uniform mat4 MVMatrix;
uniform mat4 MVPMatrix;
uniform mat3 NormalMatrix;

uniform float ScaleFactor;

const float C1 = 0.429043;
const float C2 = 0.511664;
const float C3 = 0.743125;
const float C4 = 0.886227;
const float C5 = 0.247708;

// Constants for Old Town Square lighting
const vec3 L00  = vec3( 0.871297,  0.875222,  0.864470);
const vec3 L1m1 = vec3( 0.175058,  0.245335,  0.312891);
const vec3 L10  = vec3( 0.034675,  0.036107,  0.037362);
const vec3 L11  = vec3(-0.004629, -0.029448, -0.048028);
const vec3 L2m2 = vec3(-0.120535, -0.121160, -0.117507);
const vec3 L2m1 = vec3( 0.003242,  0.003624,  0.007511);
const vec3 L20  = vec3(-0.028667, -0.024926, -0.020998);
const vec3 L21  = vec3(-0.077539, -0.086325, -0.091591);
const vec3 L22  = vec3(-0.161784, -0.191783, -0.219152);

in  vec4  MCVertex;
in  vec3  MCNormal;
in  float Accessibility;

out vec3  DiffuseColor;

void main()
{
```

```
foo();
vec3 tnorm    = normalize(NormalMatrix * MCNormal);

DiffuseColor = C1 * L22 * (tnorm.x * tnorm.x - tnorm.y * tnorm.y) +
               C3 * L20 *  tnorm.z * tnorm.z +
               C4 * L00 -
               C5 * L20 +
               2.0 * C1 * L2m2 * tnorm.x * tnorm.y +
               2.0 * C1 * L21  * tnorm.x * tnorm.z +
               2.0 * C1 * L2m1 * tnorm.y * tnorm.z +
               2.0 * C2 * L11  * tnorm.x +
               2.0 * C2 * L1m1 * tnorm.y +
               2.0 * C2 * L10  * tnorm.z;

DiffuseColor *= ScaleFactor;
DiffuseColor *= Accessibility;

gl_Position = MVPMatrix * MCVertex;
}
```

Results for ambient occlusion shaders are shown in Color Plate 21 C, F, G, H, and I. These images come from a GLSL demo program called **deLight**, written by Philip Rideout. Philip also wrote the ray-tracer that generated per-vertex accessibility information for a number of different models.

Ambient occlusion is a view-independent technique, but the computation of the occlusion factors assumes that the object is rigid. If the object has moving parts, the occlusion factors would need to be recomputed for each position. Work has been done recently on methods for computing the occlusion factors in real time (see *Dynamic Ambient Occlusion and Indirect Lighting* by Michael Bunnell in the book *GPU Gems 2*).

During the preprocessing stage, we can also compute an attribute called a BENT NORMAL. We obtain this value by averaging all the nonoccluded rays from a point on a surface. It represents the average direction of the available light arriving at that particular point on the surface. Instead of using the surface normal to access an environment map, we use the bent normal to obtain the color of the light from the appropriate portion of the environment map. We can simulate a soft fill light with a standard point or spotlight by using the bent normal instead of the surface normal and then multiplying the result by the occlusion factor.

Occlusion factors are not only useful for lighting but are also useful for reducing reflections from the environment in areas that are occluded. Hayden Landis of Industrial Light & Magic has described how similar techniques have been used to control reflections in films such as *Pearl Harbor* and *Jurassic Park III*. The technique is modified still further to take into account the type of surface that is reflecting the environment. Additional rays used along the main reflection vector provide an average (blurred) reflection. For diffuse surfaces (e.g., rubber), the additional rays are spread out more widely from the main reflection vector so that the reflection appears more diffuse. For more specular surfaces, the additional rays are nearer the main reflection vector, so the reflection is more mirrorlike.

13.2   Shadow Maps

Ambient occlusion is quite useful for improving the realism of rigid objects under diffuse lighting conditions, but often a scene will need to incorporate lighting from one or more well-defined light sources. In the real world, we know that strong light sources cause objects to cast well-defined shadows. Producing similar shadows in our computer-generated scenes will make them seem more realistic. How can we accomplish this?

The amount of computer graphics literature that discusses generation of shadows is vast. This is partly because no single shadowing algorithm is optimal for all cases. There are numerous trade-offs in performance, quality, and simplicity. Some algorithms work well for only certain types of shadow-casting objects or shadow-receiving objects. Some algorithms work for certain types of light sources or lighting conditions. Some experimentation and adaptation may be needed to develop a shadow-generation technique that is optimal for a specific set of conditions.

OpenGL and the OpenGL Shading Language include facilities for a generally useful shadowing algorithm called SHADOW MAPPING. In this algorithm, the scene is rendered multiple times—once for each light source that is capable of causing shadows and once to generate the final scene, including shadows. Each of the per-light passes is rendered from the point of view of the light source. The results are stored in a texture that is called a SHADOW MAP or a DEPTH MAP. This texture is essentially a visible surface representation from the point of view of the light source. Surfaces that are visible from the point of view of this light source are fully illuminated by the light source. Surfaces that are not visible from the point of view of this light source are in shadow. Each of the textures so generated is accessed during the final rendering pass to create the final scene with shadows from one or more light sources. During the final rendering pass, the distance from the fragment to each light is computed and compared to the depth value in the shadow map for that light. If the distance from the fragment to the light is greater than the depth value in the shadow map, the fragment receives no contribution from that light source (i.e., it is in shadow);

otherwise, the fragment is subjected to the lighting computation for that particular light source.

Because this algorithm involves an extra rendering pass for each light source, performance is a concern if a large number of shadow-casting lights are in the scene. But for interactive applications, it is quite often the case that shadows from one or two lights add sufficiently to the realism and comprehensibility of a scene. More than that and you may be adding needless complexity. And, just like other algorithms that use textures, shadow mapping is prone to severe aliasing artifacts unless proper care is taken.

The depth comparison can also lead to problems. Since the values being compared were generated in different passes with different transformation matrices, it is possible to have a small difference in the values. Therefore, you must use a small epsilon value in the comparison. You can use the **glPolygonOffset** command to bias depth values as the shadow map is being created. You must be careful, though, because too much bias can cause a shadow to become detached from the object casting the shadow.

A way to avoid depth precision problems with illuminated faces is to draw backfaces when you are building the shadow map. This avoids precision problems with illuminated faces because the depth value for these surfaces is usually quite different from the shadow map depth, so there is no possibility of precision problems incorrectly darkening the surface.

Precision problems are still possible on surfaces facing away from the light. You can avoid these problems by testing the surface normal—if it points away from the light, then the surface is in shadow. There will still be problems when the back and front faces have similar depth values, such as at the edge of the shadow. A carefully weighted combination of normal test plus depth test can provide artifact-free shadows even on gently rounded objects. However, this approach does not handle occluders that aren't simple closed geometry.

Despite its drawbacks, shadow mapping is still a popular and effective means of generating shadows. A big advantage is that it can be used with arbitrarily complex geometry. It is supported in RenderMan and has been used to generate images for numerous movies and interactive games. OpenGL supports shadow maps (they are called DEPTH COMPONENT TEXTURES in OpenGL) and a full range of depth comparison modes that can be used with them. Shadow mapping can be performed in OpenGL with either fixed functionality or the programmable processing units. The OpenGL Shading Language contains corresponding functions for accessing shadow maps from within a shader (**texture**, **textureProj**, and the like).

13.2.1 Application Setup

As mentioned, the application must create a shadow map for each light source by rendering the scene from the point of view of the light source. For objects that are visible from the light's point of view, the resulting texture map contains depth values representing the distance to the light. (The source code for the example program deLight available from the 3dshaders.org Web site illustrates specifically how this is done.)

For the final pass of shadow mapping to work properly, the application must create a matrix that transforms incoming vertex positions into projective texture coordinates for each light source. The vertex shader is responsible for performing this transformation, and the fragment shader uses the interpolated projective coordinates to access the shadow map for each light source. To keep things simple, we look at shaders that deal with just a single light source. (You can use arrays and loops to extend the basic algorithm to support multiple light sources.)

We construct the necessary matrix by concatenating

- The modeling matrix (M) that transforms modeling coordinates into world coordinates

- A view matrix (V_{light}) that rotates and translates world coordinates into a coordinate system that has the light source at the origin and is looking at the point (0, 0, 0) in world coordinates

- A projection matrix (P_{light}) that defines the frustum for the view from the light source (i.e., field of view, aspect ratio, near and far clipping planes)

- A scale and bias matrix that takes the clip space coordinates (i.e., values in the range [–1,1]) from the previous step into values in the range [0,1] so that they can be used directly as the index for accessing the shadow map.

The equation for the complete transformation looks like this:

$$\begin{bmatrix} 0.5 & 0 & 0 & 0.5 \\ 0 & 0.5 & 0 & 0.5 \\ 0 & 0 & 0.5 & 0.5 \\ 0 & 0 & 0 & 1 \end{bmatrix} M V_{light} P_{light} \begin{bmatrix} x \\ y \\ z \\ w \end{bmatrix} = \begin{bmatrix} s \\ t \\ r \\ q \end{bmatrix}$$

By performing this transformation in a vertex shader, we can have shadows and can add any desired programmable functionality as well. Let's see how this is done in a vertex shader. Philip Rideout developed some shaders for the deLight demo that use shadow mapping. They have been adapted slightly for inclusion in this book.

13.2.2 Vertex Shader

The vertex shader in Listing 13.4 shows how this is done. We use ambient occlusion in this shader, so these values are passed in as vertex attributes through the attribute variable *Accessibility*. These values attenuate the incoming per-vertex color values after a simple diffuse lighting model has been applied. The alpha value is left unmodified by this process. The matrix that transforms modeling coordinates to light source coordinates is stored in *MCtoLightMatrix*. This matrix transforms the incoming vertex and writes to the out variable *ShadowCoord*.

Listing 13.4 Vertex shader for generating shadows

```
#version 140

uniform mat4 MVMatrix;
uniform mat4 MVPMatrix;
uniform mat3 NormalMatrix;
uniform mat4 MCtoLightMatrix;

uniform vec3 LightPosition;

// Ambient and diffuse scale factors.
const float As = 1.0 / 1.5;
const float Ds = 1.0 / 3.0;

in  float Accessibility;
in  vec4  MCVertex;
in  vec4  MCNormal;
in  vec4  MColor;

out vec4  ShadowCoord;
out vec4  Color;


void main()
{
    vec4 ecPosition = MVMatrix * MCVertex;
    vec3 ecPosition3 = (vec3(ecPosition)) / ecPosition.w;
    vec3 VP = LightPosition - ecPosition3;
    VP = normalize(VP);
    vec3 normal = normalize(NormalMatrix * MCNormal);
    float diffuse = max(0.0, dot(normal, VP));
```

```
      float scale = min(1.0, Accessibility * As + diffuse * Ds);

      vec4 texCoord = MCtoLightMatrix * MCVertex;
      ShadowCoord   = texCoord;

      Color  = vec4(scale * MColor.rgb, MColor.a);
      gl_Position    = MVPMatrix * MCVertex;
}
```

13.2.3 Fragment Shader

A simple fragment shader for generating shadows is shown in Listing 13.5.
When **textureProj** is used to access a texture of a shadow sampler, the third
component of the texture index (i.e., *ShadowCoord.p*) is compared with the
depth value stored in the shadow map. The comparison function is the one
specified for the texture object indicated by *ShadowMap*. For nearest filtering, if the comparison results in a value of true, **textureProj** returns 1.0;
otherwise, it returns 0.0. For linear filtering, more than one texel is compared to *ShadowCoord.p* (probably four texels). If all comparisons are true,
textureProj returns 1.0; if all comparisons are false, it returns 0.0; otherwise,
it returns a value between 0.0 and 1.0. (OpenGL gives a lot of flexibility
here. It may return a weighted average of the results, so the value can be any
value between 0.0 and 1.0. It may return a strict percent closer filter [PCF]
value resulting in values of 0.0, 0.25, 0.5, 0.75, and 1.0 if there were four
comparisons.) We scale and bias this result so that the result ranges from
0.75 (fully shadowed) to 1.0 (fully illuminated). (This shader instruction
emulates the ARB_shadow_ambient extension.) Fragments that are fully
illuminated are unchanged, fragments that are fully shadowed are multiplied by a factor of 0.75 to make them darker, and fragments that are partially shadowed are multiplied by a value between 0.75 and 1.0.

Listing 13.5 Fragment shader for generating shadows

```
#version 140

uniform sampler2DShadow ShadowMap;

in  vec4 ShadowCoord;
in  vec4 Color;
out vec4 FragColor;

void main()
{
    float shadeFactor = textureProj(ShadowMap, ShadowCoord);
    shadeFactor = shadeFactor * 0.25 + 0.75;
    FragColor = vec4(shadeFactor * Color.rgb, Color.a);
}
```

Chances are that as soon as you execute this shader, you will be disappointed by the aliasing artifacts that appear along the edges of the shadows. This is because there is either only one depth comparison (for nearest filtering) to four depth comparisons (for linear filtering). We can do something about this, and we can customize the shader for a specific viewing situation to get a more pleasing result. Michael Bunnell and Fabio Pellacini describe a method for doing this in an article called *Shadow Map Antialiasing* in the book *GPU Gems*. Philip Rideout implemented this technique in GLSL, as shown in Listing 13.6 and Listing 13.7.

The shader in Listing 13.6 adds a couple of things. The first thing is an additional flat in variable, ShadowScaleBias. The vertex shader essentially distinguishes between two types of shadows—those that are generated by the object itself and those that are generated by another object in the scene. The self-shadows are made a little lighter than other cast shadows for aesthetic reasons. The result is that where the object shadows itself, the shadows are relatively light. And where the object's shadow falls on the floor, the shadows are darker. (See Color Plate 22.)

The second difference is that the shadow map is sampled 16 times (for linear sampling). The purpose of sampling multiple times is to try to do better at determining the shadow boundary. This lets us apply a smoother transition between shadowed and unshadowed regions, thus reducing the jagged edges of the shadow.

Listing 13.6 Fragment shader for generating shadows with antialiased edges, using sixteen samples per fragment (four texture fetches with four depth comparisons each)

```
#version 140

uniform sampler2DShadow ShadowMap;

flat in  vec2   ShadowScaleBias;
     in  vec4   ShadowCoord;
     in  vec4   Color;

     out vec4   FragColor;

void main()
{
    float sum;

    sum  = textureProjOffset(ShadowMap, ShadowCoord, ivec2(-1, -1));
    sum += textureProjOffset(ShadowMap, ShadowCoord, ivec2( 1, -1));
    sum += textureProjOffset(ShadowMap, ShadowCoord, ivec2(-1,  1));
    sum += textureProjOffset(ShadowMap, ShadowCoord, ivec2( 1,  1));
```

```
    sum = sum * ShadowScaleBias.x + ShadowScaleBias.y;

    FragColor = vec4(sum * 0.25 * Color.rgb, Color.a);
}
```

This shader can be extended in the obvious way to perform even more samples per fragment and thus improve the quality of the shadow boundaries even more. However, the more texture lookups that we perform in our shader, the slower it will run.

Using a method akin to dithering, we can actually use four texture fetches that are spread somewhat farther apart to achieve a quality of antialiasing that is similar to that of using quite a few more than four texture fetches per fragment. In Listing 13.7 we include code for computing offsets in x and y from the current fragment location. These offsets form a regular dither pattern that is used to access the shadow map. The results of using four dithered texture fetches per fragment trades off a noisy sampling of a larger area.

Listing 13.7 Fragment shader for generating shadows, using four dithered texture fetches (sixteen depth comparisons for linear filtering)

```
#version 140

uniform sampler2DShadow ShadowMap;

     in  vec4  ShadowCoord;
     in  vec4  Color;
flat in  vec2  ShadowScaleBias;

     out vec4  FragColor;

void main()
{

    float sum;

    // use modulo to vary the sample pattern
    ivec2 o = ivec2(mod(floor(gl_FragCoord.xy), 2.0));

    sum  = textureProjOffset(ShadowMap, ShadowCoord, ivec2(-1, -1)+o);
    sum += textureProjOffset(ShadowMap, ShadowCoord, ivec2( 1, -1)+o);
    sum += textureProjOffset(ShadowMap, ShadowCoord, ivec2(-1,  1)+o);
    sum += textureProjOffset(ShadowMap, ShadowCoord, ivec2( 1,  1)+o);

    sum = sum * ShadowScaleBias.x + ShadowScaleBias.y;

    FragColor = vec4(sum * 0.25 * Color.rgb, Color.a);
}
```

Sample images using these shaders are shown in Color Plate 22. A small area of the shadow has been enlarged by 400 percent to show the differences in quality at the edge of the shadow.

13.3 Deferred Shading for Volume Shadows

With contributions by Hugh Malan and Mike Weiblen

One of the disadvantages of shadow mapping as discussed in the previous section is that the performance depends on the number of lights in the scene that are capable of casting shadows. With shadow mapping, a rendering pass must be performed for each of these light sources. These shadow maps are utilized in a final rendering pass. All these rendering passes can reduce performance, particularly if a great many polygons are to be rendered.

It is possible to do higher-performance shadow generation with a rendering technique that is part of a general class of techniques known as DEFERRED SHADING. With deferred shading, the idea is to first quickly determine the surfaces that will be visible in the final scene and apply complex and time-consuming shader effects only to the pixels that make up those visible surfaces. In this sense, the shading operations are deferred until it can be established just which pixels contribute to the final image. A very simple and fast shader can render the scene into an offscreen buffer with depth buffering enabled. During this initial pass, the shader stores whatever information is needed to perform the necessary rendering operations in subsequent passes. Subsequent rendering operations are applied only to pixels that are determined to be visible in the high-performance initial pass. This technique ensures that no hardware cycles are wasted performing shading calculations on pixels that will ultimately be hidden.

To render soft shadows with this technique, we need to make two passes. In the first pass, we perform the following two tasks:

1. We use a shader to render the geometry of the scene without shadows or lighting into the framebuffer.

2. We use the same shader to store a normalized camera depth value for each pixel in a separate buffer. (This separate buffer is accessed as a texture in the second pass for the shadow computations.)

In the second pass, the shadows are composited with the existing contents of the framebuffer. To do this compositing operation, we render the shadow volume (i.e., the region in which the light source is occluded) for each shadow casting object. In the case of a sphere, computing the shadow volume is relatively easy. The sphere's shadow is in the shape of a truncated cone, where the apex of the cone is at the light source. One end of the truncated cone is at the center of the sphere (see Figure 13.2). (It is somewhat more complex to compute the shadow volume for an object defined by polygons, but the same principle applies.)

We composite shadows with the existing geometry by rendering the polygons that define the shadow volume. This allows our second pass shader to be applied only to regions of the image that might be in shadow.

To draw a shadow, we use the texture map shown in Figure 13.3. This texture map expresses how much a visible surface point is in shadow relative to a shadow-casting object (i.e., how much its value is attenuated) based on a function of two values: 1) the squared distance from the visible surface point to the central axis of the shadow volume, and 2) the distance from the visible surface point to the center of the shadow-casting object. The first value is used as the s coordinate for accessing the shadow texture, and the second value is used as the t coordinate. The net result is that shadows are

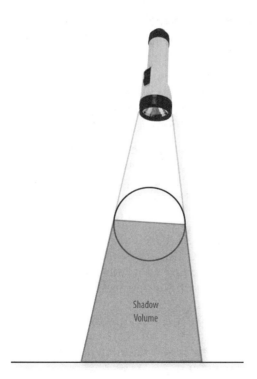

Figure 13.2   The shadow volume for a sphere

relatively sharp when the shadow-casting object is very close to the fragment being tested and the edges become softer as the distance increases.

In the second pass of the algorithm, we do the following:

1. Draw the polygons that define the shadow volume. Only the fragments that could possibly be in shadow are accessed during this rendering operation.

2. For each fragment rendered,

    a. Look up the camera depth value for the fragment as computed in the first pass.

    b. Calculate the coordinates of the visible surface point in the local space of the shadow volume. In this space, the z axis is the axis of the shadow volume, and the origin is at the center of the shadow-casting object. The x component of this coordinate corresponds to the distance from the center of the shadow-casting object and is used directly as the second coordinate for the shadow texture lookup.

    c. Compute the squared distance between the visible surface point and the z axis of the shadow volume. This value becomes the first coordinate for the texture lookup.

    d. Access the shadow texture by using the computed index values to retrieve the light attenuation factor and store this in the output fragment's alpha value. The red, green, and blue components of the output fragment color are each set to 0.

    e. Compute for the fragment the light attenuation factor that will properly darken the existing framebuffer value. For the computation, enable fixed functionality blending, set the blend mode source function to GL_SRC_ALPHA, and set the blend destination function to GL_ONE.

Because the shadow (second pass) shader is effectively a 2D compositing operation, the texel it reads from the depth texture must exactly match the pixel in the framebuffer it affects. So, the texture coordinate and other quantities must be bilinearly interpolated without perspective correction. We interpolate by ensuring that w is constant across the polygon—dividing $x, y,$ and z by w and then setting w to 1.0 does the job. Another issue is that when the viewer is inside the shadow volume, all faces are culled. We handle this special case by drawing a screen-sized quadrilateral since the shadow volume would cover the entire scene.

Figure 13.3 A texture map used to generate soft shadows

13.3.1 Shaders for First Pass

The shaders for the first pass of the volume shadow algorithm are shown in Listings 13.8 and 13.9. In the vertex shader, to accomplish the standard rendering of the geometry (which in this specific case is all texture mapped), we just transform the vertex and pass along the texture coordinate. The other lines of code compute the normalized value for the depth from the vertex to the camera plane. The computed value, *CameraDepth*, is stored in an out variable so that it can be interpolated and made available to the fragment shader.

To render into two buffers by using a fragment shader, the application must call **glDrawBuffers** and pass it a pointer to an array containing symbolic constants that define the two buffers to be written. With framebuffer objects we can bind *FragData[0]* to one renderable color format texture and *FragData[1]* to another renderable depth format texture. Thus, the fragment shader for the first pass of our algorithm contains just two lines of code (Listing 13.9).

Listing 13.8 Vertex shader for first pass of soft volume shadow algorithm

```
#version 140

uniform mat4 MVPMatrix;

uniform vec3  CameraPos;
uniform vec3  CameraDir;
uniform float DepthNear;
uniform float DepthFar;
```

```
in   vec4   MCVertex;
in   vec2   TexCoord0;

out float CameraDepth;   // normalized camera depth
out vec2   TexCoord;

void main()
{
    // offset = vector to vertex from camera's position
    vec3 offset = (MCVertex.xyz / MCVertex.w) - CameraPos;

    // z = distance from vertex to camera plane
    float z = -dot(offset, CameraDir);

    // Depth from vertex to camera, mapped to [0,1]
    CameraDepth = (z - DepthNear) / (DepthFar - DepthNear);

    // typical interpolated coordinate for texture lookup
    TexCoord = TexCoord0;

    gl_Position = MVPMatrix * MCVertex;
}
```

Listing 13.9 Fragment shader for first pass of soft volume shadow algorithm

```
#version 140;

uniform sampler2D TextureMap;

in   float CameraDepth;
in   vec2   TexCoord;

out vec4   FragData[2];

void main()
{
    // draw the typical textured output to visual framebuffer
    FragData[0] = texture(TextureMap, TexCoord);

    // write "normalized vertex depth" to the depth map's alpha.
    FragData[1] = vec4(vec3(0.0), CameraDepth);
}
```

13.3.2 Shaders for Second Pass

The second pass of our shadow algorithm is responsible for compositing
shadow information on top of what has already been rendered. After the
first pass has been completed, the application must arrange for the depth

information rendered into the depth format renderable texture to be made accessible for use as a texture by binding the texture object to the appropriate texture unit.

In the second pass, the only polygons rendered are the ones that define the shadow volumes for the various objects in the scene. We enable blending by calling **glEnable** with the symbolic constant GL_BLEND, and we set the blend function by calling **glBlendFunc** with a source factor of GL_ONE and a destination factor of GL_SRC_ALPHA. The fragment shader outputs the shadow color and an alpha value obtained from a texture lookup operation. This alpha value blends the shadow color value into the framebuffer.

The vertex shader for the second pass (see Listing 13.10) is responsible for computing the coordinates for accessing the depth values that were computed in the first pass. We accomplish the computation by transforming the incoming vertex position, dividing the x, y, and z components by the w component, and then scaling and biasing the x and y components to transform them from the range [–1,1] into the range [0,1]. Values for *ShadowNear* and *ShadowDir* are also computed. These are used in the fragment shader to compute the position of the fragment relative to the shadow-casting object.

Listing 13.10 Vertex shader for second pass of soft volume shadow algorithm

```
#version 140

uniform mat4 MVPMatrix;
uniform mat3 WorldToShadow;
uniform vec3 SphereOrigin;

uniform vec3 CameraPos;
uniform vec3 CameraDir;
uniform float DepthNear;
uniform float DepthFar;

in   vec4  MCVertex;

noperspective out vec2   DepthTexCoord;
noperspective out vec3   ShadowNear;
noperspective out vec3   ShadowDir;

void main()
{
    gl_Position = MVPMatrix * MCVertex;

    // Grab the transformed vertex's XY components as a texcoord
    // for sampling from the depth texture from pass 1.
    // Normalize them from [0,0] to [1,1]
```

```
        DepthTexCoord = gl_Position.xy * 0.5 + 0.5;

        // offset = vector to vertex from camera's position
        vec3 offset = (MCVertex.xyz / MCVertex.w) - CameraPos;

        // z = distance from vertex to camera plane
        float z = -dot(offset, CameraDir);

        vec3 shadowOffsetNear = offset * DepthNear / z;
        vec3 shadowOffsetFar  = offset * DepthFar / z;

        vec3 worldPositionNear = CameraPos + shadowOffsetNear;
        vec3 worldPositionFar  = CameraPos + shadowOffsetFar;

        vec3 shadowFar  = WorldToShadow * (worldPositionFar - SphereOrigin);
        ShadowNear = WorldToShadow * (worldPositionNear - SphereOrigin);
        ShadowDir  = shadowFar - ShadowNear;
    }
```

The fragment shader for the second pass is shown in Listing 13.11. In this shader, we access the *cameraDepth* value computed by the first pass by performing a texture lookup. We then map the fragment's position into the local space of the shadow volume. The mapping from world to shadow space is set up so that the center of the occluding sphere maps to the origin, and the circle of points on the sphere at the terminator between light and shadow maps to a circle in the *YZ* plane.

The variables *d* and *l* are, respectively, the distance along the shadow axis and the squared distance from it. These values are used as texture coordinates for the lookup into the texture map defining the shape of the shadow.

With the mapping described earlier, points on the terminator map to a circle in the *YZ* plane. The texture map has been painted with the transition from light to shadow occurring at *s*=0.5; to match this, the mapping from world to shadow is set up so that the terminator circle maps to a radius of **sqrt**(0.5).

Finally, the value retrieved from the shadow texture is used as the alpha value for blending the shadow color with the geometry that has already been rendered into the framebuffer.

Listing 13.11 Fragment shader for second pass of soft volume shadow algorithm

```
#version 140

uniform sampler2D DepthTexture;
uniform sampler2D ShadowTexture;
```

```
noperspective in vec2 DepthTexCoord;
noperspective in vec3 ShadowNear;
noperspective in vec3 ShadowDir;

out vec4 FragColor;

const vec3 shadowColor = vec3(0.0);

void main()
{
    // read from DepthTexture
    // (depth is stored in texture's alpha component)
    float cameraDepth = texture(DepthTexture, DepthTexCoord).a;

    vec3 shadowPos = (cameraDepth * ShadowDir) + ShadowNear;
    float l = dot(shadowPos.yz, shadowPos.yz);
    float d = shadowPos.x;

    // k = shadow density: 0=opaque, 1=transparent
    // (use texture's red component as the density)
    float k = texture(ShadowTexture, vec2(l, d)).r;

    FragColor = vec4(shadowColor, k);
}
```

Figure 13.4 shows the result of this multipass shading algorithm in a scene with several spheres. Note how the shadows for the four small spheres get progressively softer edges as the spheres increase in distance from the checkered floor. The large sphere that is farthest from the floor casts an especially soft shadow.

The interesting part of this deferred shading approach is that the volumetric effects are implemented by rendering geometry that bounds the volume of the effect. This almost certainly means processing fewer vertices and fewer fragments. The shaders required are relatively simple and quite fast. Instead of rendering the geometry once for each light source, the geometry is rendered just once, and all the shadow volumes due to all light sources can be rendered in a single compositing pass. Localized effects such as shadow maps, decals, and projective textures can be accomplished easily. Instead of having to write tricky code to figure out the subset of the geometry to which the effect applies, you write a shader that is applied to each pixel and use that shader to render geometry that bounds the effect. This technique can be extended to render a variety of different effects—volumetric fog, lighting, and improved caustics, to name a few.

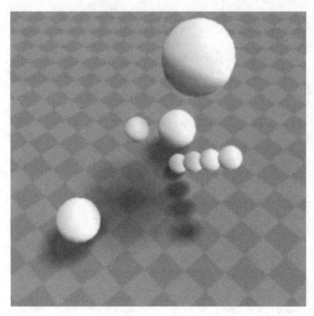

Figure 13.4 Screenshot of the volume shadows shader in action. Notice that spheres that are farther from the surface have shadows with softer edges.

13.4 Summary

There are a number of techniques for generating shadows, and this chapter described several that particularly lend themselves to real-time usage. Ambient occlusion is a technique that complements the global illumination techniques described in Chapter 12 by adding soft shadows that would naturally appear in the corners and crevices of objects in a scene. Shadow mapping is a technique that is well suited to implementation with OpenGL shaders on today's graphics hardware. A number of variations to shadow mapping can be used to improve its quality. We looked at a couple of methods that produce antialiased shadow edges. Finally, we also looked at a method that uses a deferred shading approach to render shadow volumes in order to produce soft shadows.

13.5 Further Information

The SIGGRAPH 2002 course notes are contained the article *Production-Ready Global Illumination* by Hayden Landis. This document describes ambient environments, reflection occlusion, and ambient occlusion, and it explains how they are used in the ILM computer graphics production environment. The article *Ambient Occlusion* by Matt Pharr and Simon Green provides further details about the preprocessing step and gives example shaders written in Cg. The *GPU Gems 2* book contains an article by Michael Bunnell that describes efforts to compute occlusion factors in real time.

Frank Crow pioneered the development of shadow algorithms for computer graphics. Mark Segal and others described the basics of using texture mapping hardware to generate shadows in a 1992 SIGGRAPH paper. Randima Fernando and Mark Kilgard discuss a Cg implementation of these techniques in the book *The Cg Tutorial*. Eric Haines wrote a survey of real-time shadow algorithms and presented this information at GDC in 2001. Some of this material is also in the book *Real-Time Rendering* by Tomas Akenine-Möller and E. Haines.

Deferred shading has recently been a hot topic in computer games development. In the book *GPU Gems 2*, Oles Shishkovtsov discusses how this approach was used for the computer game *S.T.A.L.K.E.R.* His article also mentions presentations from the 2004 Game Developer's Conference.

[1] Akenine-Möller, Tomas, and E. Haines, *Real-Time Rendering, Second Edition*, AK Peters, Ltd., Natick, Massachusetts, 2002. www.realtimerendering.com

[2] Bunnell, Michael, *Dynamic Ambient Occlusion and Indirect Lighting*, in *GPU Gems 2: Programming Techniques for High-Performance Graphics and General-Purpose Computation*, Editor: Matt Pharr, Addison-Wesley, Reading, Massachusetts, 2005. http://download.nvidia.com/developer/GPU_Gems_2/GPU_Gems2_ch14.pdf

[3] Bunnell, Michael, and Fabio Pellacini, *Shadow Map Antialiasing*, in *GPU Gems: Programming Techniques, Tips, and Tricks for Real-Time Graphics*, Editor: Randima Fernando, Addison-Wesley, Reading, Massachusetts, 2004. http://developer.nvidia.com/object/gpu_gems_home.html

[4] Crow, Franklin C., *Shadow Algorithms for Computer Graphics*, Computer Graphics (SIGGRAPH '77 Proceedings), vol. 11, no. 2, pp. 242–248, July 1977.

[5] Fernando, Randima, and Mark J. Kilgard, *The Cg Tutorial: The Definitive Guide to Programmable Real-Time Graphics*, Addison-Wesley, Boston, Massachusetts, 2003.

[6] Haines, Eric, *Real-Time Shadows*, GDC 2001 Presentation. www.gdconf.com/archives/2001/haines.pdf

[7] Landis, Hayden, *Production-Ready Global Illumination*, SIGGRAPH 2002 Course Notes, course 16, RenderMan In Production. www.debevec.org/HDRI2004/landis-S2002-course16-prodreadyGI.pdf

[8] Pharr, Matt and Simon Green, *Ambient Occlusion*, in *GPU Gems: Programming Techniques, Tips, and Tricks for Real-Time Graphics*, Editor: Randima Fernando, Addison-Wesley, Reading, Massachusetts, 2004. http://developer.nvidia.com/object/gpu_gems_home.html

[9] Reeves, William T., David H. Salesin, and Robert L. Cook, *Rendering Antialiased Shadows with Depth Maps*, Computer Graphics (SIGGRAPH '87 Proceedings), vol. 21, no. 4, pp. 283–291, July 1987.

[10] Segal, Mark, C. Korobkin, R. van Widenfelt, J. Foran, and P. Haeberli, *Fast Shadows and Lighting Effects Using Texture Mapping*, Computer Graphics (SIGGRAPH '92 Proceedings), vol. 26, no. 2, pp. 249–252, July 1992.

[11] Shishkovtsov, Oles, *Deferred Shading in S.T.A.L.K.E.R.*, in *GPU Gems 2: Programming Techniques for High-Performance Graphics and General-Purpose Computation*, Editor: Matt Pharr, Addison-Wesley, Reading, Massachusetts, 2005. http://developer.nvidia.com/object/gpu_gems_2_home.html

[12] Woo, Andrew, P. Poulin, and A. Fournier, *A Survey of Shadow Algorithms*, IEEE Computer Graphics and Applications, vol. 10, no. 6, pp.13–32, November 1990.

[13] Zhukov, Sergei, A. Iones, G. Kronin, *An Ambient Light Illumination Model*, Proceedings of Eurographics Rendering Workshop '98.

Chapter 14

Surface Characteristics

Up to this point, we have primarily been modeling surface reflection in a simplistic way. The traditional reflection model is simple enough to compute and gives reasonable results, but it reproduces the appearance of only a small number of materials. In the real world, there is enormous variety in the way objects interact with light. To simulate the interaction of light with materials such as water, metals, metallic car paints, CDs, human skin, butterfly wings, and peacock feathers, we need to go beyond the basics.

One way to achieve greater degrees of realism in modeling the interaction between light and surfaces is to use models that are more firmly based on the physics of light reflection, absorption, and transmission. Such models have been the pursuit of graphics researchers since the 1970s. With the programmable graphics hardware of today, we are now at a point where such models can be used in real-time graphics applications to achieve unprecedented realism. A performance optimization that is often employed is to precompute these functions and store the results in textures that can be accessed from within a shader. A second way to achieve greater degrees of realism is to measure or photograph the characteristics of real materials and use these measurements in our shading algorithms. In this chapter, we look at shaders based on both approaches.

In addition, we have not yet looked at any shaders that allow for the transmission of light through a surface. This is our first example as we look at several shaders that model materials with differing surface characteristics.

14.1 Refraction

Refraction is the bending of light as it passes through a boundary between surfaces with different optical densities. You can easily see this effect by looking through the side of an aquarium or at a straw in a glass of water. Light bends by different amounts as it passes from one material to another, depending on the materials that are transmitting light. This effect is caused by light traveling at different speeds in different types of materials. This characteristic of a material is called its INDEX OF REFRACTION, and this value has been determined for many common materials that transmit light. It is easy to model refraction in our shaders with the built-in function **refract**. The key parameter that is required is the ratio of the index of refraction for the two materials forming a boundary where refraction occurs. The application can compute this ratio and provide it to the OpenGL shader as a uniform variable. Given a surface normal, an angle of incidence, and the aforementioned ratio, the **refract** function applies Snell's law to compute the refracted vector. We can use the refracted vector in a fragment shader to access a cube map to determine the surface color for a transparent object.

Once again, our goal is to produce results that are "good enough." In other words, we're after a refraction effect that looks plausible, rather than a physically accurate simulation. One simplification that we make is that we model the refraction effect at only one surface boundary. When light goes from air through glass, it is refracted once at the air-glass boundary, transmitted through the glass, and refracted again at the glass-air boundary on the other side. We satisfy ourselves with simulating the first refraction effect. The results of refraction are complex enough that most people would not be able to tell the difference in the final image.

If we go ahead and write a shader that performs refraction, we will likely be somewhat disappointed in the results. It turns out that most transparent objects exhibit both reflection and refraction. The surface of a lake reflects the mountains in the distance if you are looking at the lake from one side. But if you get into your boat and go out into the lake and look straight down, you may see fish swimming around underneath the surface. This is known as the FRESNEL EFFECT. The Fresnel equations describe the reflection and refraction that occur at a material boundary as a function of the angle of incidence, the polarization and wavelength of the light, and the indices of refraction of the materials involved. It turns out that many materials exhibit a higher degree of reflectivity at extremely shallow (grazing) angles. Even a material such as nonglossy paper exhibits this phenomenon. For instance, hold a sheet of paper (or a book) so that you are looking at a page at a grazing angle and looking toward a light source. You will see a specular (mirrorlike) reflection from the paper, something you wouldn't see at steeper angles.

Because the Fresnel equations are relatively complex, we make the simplifying assumptions that (A) the light in our scene is not polarized, (B) all light is of the same wavelength (but we loosen this assumption later in this section), and (C) it is sufficient to use an approximation to the Fresnel equations rather than the exact equations themselves. An approximation for the ratio between reflected light and refracted light created by Christophe Schlick is

$$F = f + (1 - f)(1 - V \bullet N)^5$$

In this equation, V is the direction of view, N is the surface normal, and f is the reflectance of the material when θ is 0 given by

$$f = \frac{\left(1.0 - \frac{n_1}{n_2}\right)^2}{\left(1.0 + \frac{n_1}{n_2}\right)^2}$$

where n_1 and n_2 are the indices of refraction for materials 1 and 2.

Let's put this together in a shader. Figure 14.1 shows the relevant parameters in two dimensions. For the direction of view V, we want to compute a reflected ray and a refracted ray. We use each of these to access a texture in a cube map. We linearly blend the two values with a ratio we compute using the Fresnel approximations described earlier.

In *The Cg Tutorial*, Randima Fernando and Mark Kilgard describe Cg shaders for refraction that can easily be implemented in GLSL. The code for our vertex shader is shown in Listing 14.1. The ratio of indices of refraction for the two materials is precomputed and stored in the constant *Eta*. A value of 0.66 represents a boundary between air (index of refraction 1.000293) and glass (index of refraction 1.52). We can allow the user to control the amount of reflectivity at grazing angles by using a variable for the Fresnel power. Lower values provide higher degrees of reflectivity at grazing angles, whereas

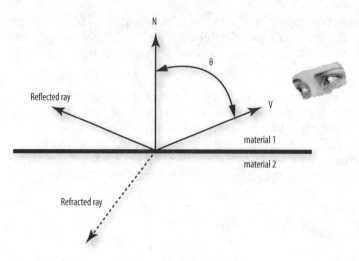

Figure 14.1   The geometry of refraction

higher values reduce this effect. The value for *f* in the previous equations is also stored as a constant. (We could have the application provide *Eta* and *FresnelPower* as uniform variables. This would then require the application to compute and pass *F* as well.)

The vertex shader uses the viewing position and the surface normal to compute a reflected ray and a refracted ray. The vertex position is transformed into eye coordinates. The **reflect** and **refract** functions both require an incident vector. This is just the vector going in the direction opposite of *V* in Figure 14.1. We compute this vector (*i*) by subtracting the viewing position (which is defined as being at (0, 0, 0) in the eye coordinate system) from the eye coordinate position and normalizing the result. We also transform the surface normal into the eye coordinate system and normalize it (*n*).

To compute the angle θ, we really need the vector *V* as shown in Figure 14.1 instead of *i* so that we can perform a dot product operation. We get this vector by negating *i*. We plug the values into the Fresnel approximation equation to get the ratio between the reflective and refractive components.

The values for *i* and *n* are sent to the built-in functions **reflect** and **refract** to compute a reflected vector and a refracted vector. These are used in the fragment shader to access the environment map. The application that uses these shaders allows the environment map to be rotated independently of the geometry. This transformation is stored in one of OpenGL's texture matrices. The resulting rays must be transformed with this matrix to access the proper location in the rotated environment.

Listing 14.1 Vertex shader for Fresnel reflection/refraction effect

```
#version 140

in vec4      MCvertex;
in vec3      MCnormal;

uniform mat4 MVMatrix;
uniform mat4 MVPMatrix;
uniform mat3 NormalMatrix;
uniform mat4 TextureMatrix;

const float Eta = 0.66; // Ratio of indices of refraction
const float FresnelPower = 5.0;

const float F = ((1.0-Eta) * (1.0-Eta)) / ((1.0+Eta) * (1.0+Eta));

out vec3  Reflect;
out vec3  Refract;
out float Ratio;

void main()
{
   vec4 ecPosition  = MVMatrix * MCvertex;
   vec3 ecPosition3 = ecPosition.xyz / ecPosition.w;

   vec3 i = normalize(ecPosition3);
   vec3 n = normalize(NormalMatrix * MCnormal);

   Ratio    = F + (1.0 - F) * pow((1.0 - dot(-i, n)), FresnelPower);

   Refract = refract(i, n, Eta);
   Refract = vec3(TextureMatrix * vec4(Refract, 1.0));

   Reflect = reflect(i, n);
   Reflect = vec3(TextureMatrix * vec4(Reflect, 1.0));

   gl_Position = MVPMatrix * MCvertex;
}
```

The corresponding fragment shader is shown in Listing 14.2. All the hard work has been done in the vertex shader. All that remains for the fragment shader is to perform the two environment map lookups and to use the computed ratio to blend the two values.

Listing 14.2 Fragment shader for Fresnel reflection/refraction effect

```
#version 140

uniform samplerCube Cubemap;

in vec3  Reflect;
in vec3  Refract;
in float Ratio;

out vec4 FragColor;

void main()
{
    vec3 refractColor = vec3(texture(Cubemap, Refract));
    vec3 reflectColor = vec3(texture(Cubemap, Reflect));

    vec3 color = mix(refractColor, reflectColor, Ratio);

    FragColor = vec4(color, 1.0);
}
```

With a small modification, we can get our reflection/refraction shader to perform another cool effect, although we stray a bit further from realistic physics. As stated earlier, the refraction of light is wavelength dependent. We made the simplifying assumption that all our light was a single wavelength, and this allowed us to compute a single refracted ray. In reality, there would be a continuum of refracted rays, one for each constituent wavelength of the light source. The breaking up of a light source into its constituent components, for example, with a prism, is called CHROMATIC DISPERSION. In camera lenses, this effect is undesirable and is called CHROMATIC ABERRATION.

We can model our light as though it contains three wavelengths of light: red, green, and blue. By providing a slightly different index of refraction for each of red, green, and blue, we can compute three slightly different refraction rays (see Listing 14.3). These three rays are passed to the fragment shader, where they perform three environment map accesses. The *RefractR* ray obtains just the red component of the final refracted color, and *RefractG* and *RefractB* obtain the green and blue components similarly. The result is used as the refracted color value. The remainder of the fragment shader is the same (see Listing 14.4).

Listing 14.3 Vertex shader for chromatic aberration effect

```
#version 140

uniform mat4 MVMatrix;
uniform mat4 MVPMatrix;
uniform mat3 NormalMatrix;
uniform mat4 TextureMatrix;

in vec4     MCVertex;
in vec3     MCNormal;

const float EtaR = 0.65;
const float EtaG = 0.67; // Ratio of indices of refraction
const float EtaB = 0.69;
const float FresnelPower = 5.0;

const float F = ((1.0-EtaG) * (1.0-EtaG)) / ((1.0+EtaG) * (1.0+EtaG));

out vec3 Reflect;
out vec3 RefractR;
out vec3 RefractG;
out vec3 RefractB;
out float Ratio;

void main()
{
    vec4 ecPosition  = MVMatrix * MCVertex;
    vec3 ecPosition3 = ecPosition.xyz / ecPosition.w;

    vec3 i = normalize(ecPosition3);
    vec3 n = normalize(NormalMatrix * MCNormal);

    Ratio   = F + (1.0 - F) * pow((1.0 - dot(-i, n)), FresnelPower);

    RefractR = refract(i, n, EtaR);
    RefractR = vec3(TextureMatrix * vec4(RefractR, 1.0));

    RefractG = refract(i, n, EtaG);
    RefractG = vec3(TextureMatrix * vec4(RefractG, 1.0));

    RefractB = refract(i, n, EtaB);
    RefractB = vec3(TextureMatrix * vec4(RefractB, 1.0));

    Reflect = reflect(i, n);
    Reflect = vec3(TextureMatrix * vec4(Reflect, 1.0));

    gl_Position = MVPMatrix * MCVertex;
}
```

Listing 14.4 Fragment shader for chromatic aberration effect

```
#version 140

uniform samplerCube Cubemap;

in vec3  Reflect;
in vec3  RefractR;
in vec3  RefractG;
in vec3  RefractB;
in float Ratio;

out vec4 FragColor;

void main()
{
    vec3 refractColor, reflectColor;

    refractColor.r = vec3(texture(Cubemap, RefractR)).r;
    refractColor.g = vec3(texture(Cubemap, RefractG)).g;
    refractColor.b = vec3(texture(Cubemap, RefractB)).b;

    reflectColor = vec3(texture(Cubemap, Reflect));

    vec3 color = mix(refractColor, reflectColor, Ratio);

    FragColor = vec4(color, 1.0);
}
```

Results of these shaders are shown in Color Plate 17. Notice the color fringes that occur on the character's knee and chest and on the top of his arm.

14.2 Diffraction

by Mike Weiblen

DIFFRACTION is the effect of light bending around a sharp edge. A device called a DIFFRACTION GRATING leverages that effect to efficiently split white light into the rainbow of its constituent colors. Jos Stam described how to approximate this effect, first with assembly language shaders (in a SIGGRAPH '99 paper) and then with Cg (in an article in the book *GPU Gems*). Let's see how we can approximate the behavior of a diffraction grating with an OpenGL shader.

First, let's quickly review the wave theory of light and diffraction gratings. One way of describing the behavior of visible light is as waves of electromagnetic radiation. The distance between crests of those waves is called the WAVELENGTH, usually represented by the Greek letter lambda (λ).

The wavelength is what determines the color we perceive when the light hits the sensing cells on the retina of the eye. The human eye is sensitive to the range of wavelengths beginning from about 400 nanometers (nm) for deep violet up to about 700nm for dark red. Within that range are what humans perceive as all the colors of the rainbow.

A diffraction grating is a tool for separating light based on its wavelength, similar in effect to a prism but using diffraction rather than refraction. Diffraction gratings typically are very closely spaced parallel lines in an opaque or reflective material. They were originally made with a mechanical engine that precisely scribed parallel lines onto the surface of a mirror. Modern gratings are usually created with photographic processes.

The lines of a grating have a spacing roughly on the order of the wavelengths of visible light. Because of the difference in path length when white light is reflected from adjacent mirrored lines, the different wavelengths of reflected light interfere and reinforce or cancel, depending on whether the waves constructively or destructively interfere.

For a given wavelength, if the path length of light reflecting from two adjacent lines differs by an integer number of wavelengths (meaning that the crests of the waves reflected from each line coincide), that color of light constructively interferes and reinforces in intensity. If the path difference is an integer number of wavelengths plus half a wavelength (meaning that crests of waves from one line coincide with troughs from the other line), those waves destructively interfere and extinguish at that wavelength. That interference condition varies according to the wavelength of the light, the spacing of the grating lines, and the angle of the light's path (both incident and reflected) with respect to the grating surface. Because of that interference, white light breaks into its component colors as the light source and eyepoint move with respect to the diffracting surface.

Everyday examples of diffraction gratings include compact discs, novelty "holographic" gift-wrapping papers, and the rainbow logos on modern credit cards used to discourage counterfeiting.

To demonstrate this shader, we use the everyday compact disc as a familiar example; extending this shader for other applications is straightforward.

While everyone is familiar with the overall physical appearance of a CD, let's look at the microscopic characteristics that make it a functional diffraction grating. A CD consists of one long spiral of microscopic pits embossed onto one side of a sheet of mirrored plastic. The dimensions of those pits is on the order of several hundred nanometers or the same order of magnitude as the wavelengths of visible light. The track pitch of the spiral of pits (i.e., the spacing between each winding of the spiral) is nominally 1600 nanometers. The range of those dimensions, being so close to visible wavelengths, is what gives a CD its rainbow light-splitting qualities.

Our diffraction shader computes two independent output color components per vertex:

- An anisotropic glint that reflects the color of the light source

- A color based on accumulation of the wavelengths that constructively interfere for the given light source and eyepoint locations

We can do this computation just by using a vertex shader. The vertex shader writes to the out variable *Color* and the special output variable *gl_Position*, and no programmable fragment processing is necessary. The fragment shader simply passes the in variable *Color* to the out variable *FragColor*.

The code for the diffraction vertex shader is shown in Listing 14.5. To render the diffraction effect, the shader requires the application to send a normal and tangent for each vertex. For this shader, the tangent is defined to be parallel to the orientation of the simulated grating lines. In the case of a compact disc (which has a spiral of pits on its mirrored surface), the close spacing of that spiral creates a diffraction grating of basically concentric circles, so the tangent is tangent to those circles.

Since the shader uses wavelength to compute the constructive interference, we need to convert wavelength to OpenGL's RGB representation of color. We use the function **lambda2rgb**, which approximates the conversion of wavelength to RGB by using a bump function. We begin the conversion by mapping the range of visible wavelengths to a normalized 0.0 to 1.0 range. From that normalized wavelength, we create a **vec3** by subtracting an offset for each of the red/green/blue bands. Then for each color component, we compute the contribution with the bump expression $1 - cx^2$ clamped to the range of [0,1]. The c term controls the width of the bump and is selected for best appearance by allowing the bumps to overlap somewhat, approximating a relatively smooth rainbow spread. This bump function is quick and easy to implement, but we could use another approach to the wavelength-to-RGB conversion, for example, using the normalized wavelength to index into a lookup table or using a 1D texture, which would be tuned for enhanced spectral qualities.

More than one wavelength can satisfy the constructive interference condition at a vertex for a given set of lighting and viewing conditions, so the shader must accumulate the contribution from each of those wavelengths. Using the condition that constructive interference occurs at path differences of integer wavelength, the shader iterates over those integers to determine the reinforced wavelength. That wavelength is converted to an RGB value by the **lambda2rgb** function and accumulated in *diffColor*.

A specular glint of *HighlightColor* is reflected from the grating lines in the region where diffractive interference does not occur. The *SurfaceRoughness* term controls the width of that highlight to approximate the scattering of light from the microscopic pits.

The final steps of the shader consist of the typical vertex transformation to compute *gl_Position* and the summing of the lighting contributions to determine *Color*. The *diffAtten* term attenuates the diffraction color slightly to prevent the colors from being too intensely garish.

A simplification we made in this shader is this: Rather than attempt to represent the spectral composition of the *HighlightColor* light source, we assume the incident light source is a flat spectrum of white light.

Being solely a vertex shader, the coloring is computed only at vertices. Since diffraction gratings can produce dramatic changes in color for a small displacement, there is an opportunity for artifacts caused by insufficient tessellation. Depending on the choice of performance trade-offs, this shader could easily be ported to a fragment shader if per-pixel shading is preferred.

Results from the diffraction shader are shown in Figure 14.2 and Color Plate 17.

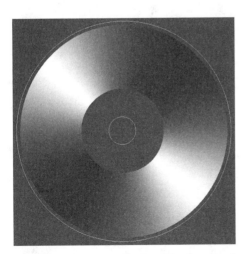

Figure 14.2 The diffraction shader simulates the look of a vinyl phonograph record (3Dlabs, Inc.).

Listing 14.5 Vertex shader for diffraction effect

```glsl
#version 140


uniform mat4 MVMatrix;
uniform mat4 MVPMatrix;
uniform mat3 NormalMatrix;

uniform vec3  LightPosition;
uniform float GratingSpacing;
uniform float SurfaceRoughness;
uniform vec4  HighlightColor;

in  vec4  MCVertex;
in  vec3  MCNormal;
in  vec3  MCTangent; // parallel to grating lines at each vertex

out vec4  Color;

// map a visible wavelength [nm] to OpenGL's RGB representation

vec3 lambda2rgb(float lambda)
{
    const float ultraviolet = 400.0;
    const float infrared     = 700.0;

    // map visible wavelength range to 0.0 -> 1.0
    float a = (lambda-ultraviolet) / (infrared-ultraviolet);

    // bump function for a quick/simple rainbow map
    const float C = 7.0;          // controls width of bump
    vec3 b = vec3(a) - vec3(0.75, 0.5, 0.25);
    return max((1.0 - C * b * b), 0.0);
}

void main()
{
    // extract positions from input uniforms
    vec3 lightPosition = LightPosition.xyz;
    vec3 eyePosition   = -MVMatrix[3].xyz / MVMatrix[3].w;

    // H = halfway vector between light and viewer from vertex
    vec3 P = vec3(MVMatrix * MCVertex);
    vec3 L = normalize(lightPosition - P);
    vec3 V = normalize(eyePosition - P);
    vec3 H = L + V;

    // accumulate contributions from constructive interference
    // over several spectral orders.
    vec3  T = NormalMatrix * MCTangent;
    float u = abs(dot(T, H));
```

```
vec3 diffColor = vec3(0.0);

const int numSpectralOrders = 3;
for (int m = 1; m <= numSpectralOrders; ++m)
{
    float lambda = GratingSpacing * u / float(m);
    diffColor += lambda2rgb(lambda);
}

// compute anisotropic highlight for zero-order (m = 0) reflection.
vec3  N = NormalMatrix * MCNormal;
float w = dot(N, H);
float e = SurfaceRoughness * u / w;
vec3 hilight = exp(-e * e) * HighlightColor.rgb;

// write the values required for fixed-function fragment processing
const float diffAtten = 0.8; // attenuation of the diffraction color
Color = vec4(diffAtten * diffColor + hilight, 1.0);
gl_Position = MVPMatrix * MCVertex;
}
```

14.3 BRDF Models

The traditional OpenGL reflectance model and the one that we have been using for most of the previous shader examples in this book (see, for example, Section 6.2) consists of three components: ambient, diffuse, and specular. The ambient component is assumed to provide a certain level of illumination to everything in the scene and is reflected equally in all directions by everything in the scene. The diffuse and specular components are directional in nature and are due to illumination from a particular light source. The diffuse component models reflection from a surface that is scattered in all directions. The diffuse reflection is strongest where the surface normal points directly at the light source, and it drops to zero where the surface normal is pointing 90° or more away from the light source. Specular reflection models the highlights caused by reflection from surfaces that are mirrorlike or nearly so. Specular highlights are concentrated on the mirror direction.

But relatively few materials have perfectly specular (mirrorlike) or diffuse (Lambertian) reflection characteristics. To model more physically realistic surfaces, we must go beyond the simplistic lighting/reflection model that is built into OpenGL. This model was developed empirically and is not physically accurate. Furthermore, it can realistically simulate the reflection from only a relatively small class of materials.

For more than two decades, computer graphics researchers have been rendering images with more realistic reflection models called BIDIRECTIONAL REFLECTANCE DISTRIBUTION FUNCTIONS, or BRDFs. A BRDF model for computing the reflection from a surface takes into account the input direction of incoming light and the outgoing direction of reflected light. The elevation and azimuth angles of these direction vectors are used to compute the relative amount of light reflected in the outgoing direction (the fixed functionality OpenGL model uses only the elevation angle). A BRDF model renders surfaces with ANISOTROPIC reflection properties (i.e., surfaces that are not rotationally invariant in their surface reflection properties). Instruments have been developed to measure the BRDF of real materials. In some cases, the measured data has been used to create a function with a few parameters that can be modified to model the reflective characteristics of a variety of materials. In other cases, the measured data has been sampled to produce texture maps that reconstruct the BRDF function at runtime. A variety of different measuring, sampling, and reconstruction methods have been devised to use BRDFs in computer graphics, and this is still an area of active research.

Generally speaking, the amount of light that is reflected to a particular viewing position depends on the position of the light, the position of the viewer, and the surface normal and tangent. If any of these changes, the amount of light reflected to the viewer may also change. The surface characteristics also play a role because different wavelengths of light may be reflected, transmitted, or absorbed, depending on the physical properties of the material. Shiny materials have concentrated, near-mirrorlike specular highlights. Rough materials have specular highlights that are more spread out. Metals have specular highlights that are the color of the metal rather than the color of the light source. The color of reflected light may change as the reflection approaches a grazing angle with the surface. Materials with small brush marks or grooves reflect light differently as they are rotated, and the shapes of their specular highlights also change. These are the types of effects that BRDF models are intended to accurately reproduce.

A BRDF is a function of two pairs of angles as well as the wavelength and polarization of the incoming light. The angles are the altitude and azimuth of the incident light vector (θ_i, ϕ_i) and the altitude and azimuth of the reflected light vector (θ_r, ϕ_r). Both sets of angles are given with respect to a given tangent vector. For simplicity, some BRDF models omit polarization effects and assume that the function is the same for all wavelengths. Because the incident and reflected light vectors are measured against a fixed tangent vector in the plane of a surface, BRDF models can reproduce the reflective characteristics of anisotropic materials such as brushed or rolled metals. And because both the incident and reflected light vectors are considered, BRDF models can also reproduce the changes in specular highlight shapes or colors that occur when an object is illuminated by a light source at a grazing angle.

BRDF models can be either theoretical or empirical. Theoretical models attempt to model the physics of light and materials in order to reproduce the observed reflectance properties. In contrast, an empirical model is a function with adjustable parameters that is designed to fit measured reflectance data for a certain class of materials. The volume of measured data typically prohibits its direct use in a computer graphics environment, and this data is often imperfect or incomplete. Somehow, the measured data must be boiled down to a few useful values that can be plugged into a formula or used to create textures that can be accessed during rendering. A variety of methods for reducing the measured data have been developed.

One such model was described by Greg Ward in a 1992 SIGGRAPH paper. He and his colleagues at Lawrence Berkeley Laboratory built a device that was relatively efficient in collecting reflectance data from a variety of materials. The measurements were the basis for creating a mathematical reflectance model that provided a reasonable approximation to the measured data. Ward's goal was to produce a simple empirical formula that was physically valid and fit the measured reflectance data for a variety of different materials. Ward measured the reflectivity of various materials to determine a few key values with physical meaning and plugged those values into the formula he developed to replicate the measured data in a computer graphics environment.

To understand Ward's model, we should first review the geometry involved, as shown in Figure 14.3. This diagram shows a point on a surface and the relevant direction vectors that are used in the reflection computation:

- N is the unit surface normal.

- L is the unit vector in the direction of the simulated light source.

- V is the unit vector in the direction of the viewer.

- R is the unit vector in the direction of reflection from the simulated light source.

- H is the unit angular bisector of V and L (sometimes called the halfway vector).

- T is a unit vector in the plane of the surface that is perpendicular to N (i.e., the tangent).

- B is a unit vector in the plane of the surface that is perpendicular to both N and T (i.e., the binormal).

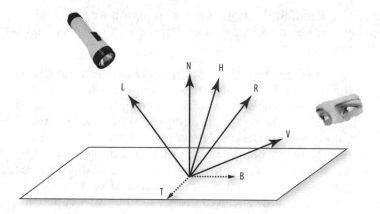

Figure 14.3 The geometry of reflection

The formula developed by Ward is based on a Gaussian reflectance model. The key parameters of the formula are the diffuse reflectivity of the surface (ρ_d), the specular reflectivity of the surface (ρ_s), and the standard deviation of the surface slope (α). The final parameter is a measure of the roughness of a surface. The assumption is that a surface is made up of tiny microfacets that reflect in a specular fashion. For a mirrorlike surface, all the microfacets line up with the surface. For a rougher surface, some random orientation of these microfacets causes the specular highlight to spread out more. The fraction of facets that are oriented in the direction of H is called the FACET SLOPE DISTRIBUTION FUNCTION, or the SURFACE SLOPE. Several possibilities for this function have been suggested.

With but a single value for the surface slope, the mathematical model is limited in its ability to reproduce materials exhibiting anisotropic reflection. To deal with this, Ward's model includes two α values, one for the standard deviation of the surface slope in the x direction (i.e., in the direction of the surface tangent vector T) and one for the standard deviation of the surface slope in the y direction (i.e., in the direction of the surface binormal value B). The formula used by Ward to fit his measured reflectance data and the key parameters derived from that data is

$$\rho_{bd}(\theta_i, \phi_i, \theta_r, \phi_r) = \frac{\rho_d}{\pi} + \rho_s \cdot \frac{1}{\sqrt{\cos\theta_i \cos\theta_r}} \cdot \frac{1}{4\pi\alpha_x\alpha_y} \cdot \exp\left[-2\frac{\left[\frac{H \bullet T}{\alpha_x}\right]^2 + \left[\frac{H \bullet B}{\alpha_y}\right]^2}{1 + H \bullet N}\right]$$

This formula looks a bit onerous, but Ward has supplied values for ρ_d, ρ_s, α_x, and α_y for several materials, and all we need to do is code the formula in the OpenGL Shading Language. The result of this BRDF is plugged into the overall equation for illumination, which looks like this:

$$L(\theta_r, \phi_r) = I\frac{\rho_d}{\pi} + L_s\rho_s + \sum_{i=1}^{N} L_i\omega_i \cos\theta_i\rho_{bd}(\theta_i, \phi_i, \theta_r, \phi_r)$$

This formula basically states that the reflected radiance is the sum of a general indirect radiance contribution, plus an indirect semispecular contribution, plus the radiance from each of N light sources in the scene. I is the indirect radiance, L_s is the radiance from the indirect semispecular contribution, and L_i is the radiance from light source i. For the remaining terms, ω_i is the solid angle in steradians of light source i, and ρ_{bd} is the BRDF defined in the previous equation.

This all translates quite easily into OpenGL Shading Language code. To get higher-quality results, we compute all the vectors in the vertex shader, interpolate them, and then perform the reflection computations in the fragment shader.

The application is expected to provide four attributes for every vertex. The four attributes are a vertex coordinate, a normal, a tangent vector, and a binormal vector, which the application computes. These four attributes should be provided to OpenGL with a generic vertex array. The location to be used for these generic attributes can be bound to the appropriate attribute in our vertex shader with **glBindAttribLocation**. For instance, if we choose to pass the vertex values in vertex attribute location 1, the normal in vertex attribute location 2, the tangent values in vertex attribute location 3, and the binormal values in vertex attribute location 4, we would set up the binding with these lines of code:

```
glBindAttribLocation(programObj, 1, "MCvertex");
glBindAttribLocation(programObj, 2, "MCNormal");
glBindAttribLocation(programObj, 3, "MCTangent");
glBindAttribLocation(programObj, 4, "MCBinormal");
```

Listing 14.6 contains the vertex shader. Its primary job is to compute and normalize the vectors shown in Figure 14.3, namely, the unit vectors *N*, *L*, *V*, *H*, *R*, *T*, and *B*. We compute the values for *N*, *T*, and *B* by transforming the application-supplied normal, tangent, and binormal into eye coordinates. We compute the reflection vector *R* by using the built-in function **reflect**.

We determine *L* by normalizing the direction to the light source. Because the viewing position is defined to be at the origin in eye coordinates, we compute *V* by transforming the viewing position into eye coordinates and subtracting the surface position in eye coordinates. *H* is the normalized sum of *L* and *V*. All seven of these values are stored in out variables that will be interpolated and made available to the fragment shader.

Listing 14.6   Vertex shader for rendering with Ward's BRDF model

```
#version 140

uniform mat4 MVMatrix;
uniform mat4 MVPMatrix;
uniform mat3 NormalMatrix;

uniform vec3 LightDir; // Light direction in eye coordinates
uniform vec4 ViewPosition;

in   vec4   MCvertex;
in   vec3   MCnormal;
in   vec3   MCTangent;
in   vec3   MCBinormal;
*/
out vec3   N, L, H, R, T, B;

void main()
{
    vec3 V, eyeDir;
    vec4 pos;

    pos    = MVPMatrix * MCVertex;
    eyeDir = pos.xyz;

    N = normalize(NormalMatrix * MCNormal);
    L = normalize(LightDir);
    V = normalize((MVMatrix * ViewPosition).xyz - pos.xyz);
    H = normalize(L + V);
    R = normalize(reflect(eyeDir, N));
    T = normalize(NormalMatrix * MCTangent);
    B = normalize(NormalMatrix * MCBinormal);

    gl_Position = MVPMatrix * MCVertex;
}
```

It is then up to the fragment shader to implement the equations defined previously. The values that parameterize a material (ρ_d, ρ_s, α_x, α_y) are passed as the uniform variables *P* and *A*. We can use the values from the table published in Ward's paper or try some values of our own. The base color of the surface is also passed as a uniform variable (Ward's measurements did not include color for any of the materials). Instead of dealing with the radiance and solid angles of light sources, we just use a uniform variable to supply coefficients that manipulate these terms directly.

The vectors passed as out variables become denormalized during interpolation, but if the polygons in the scene are all relatively small, this effect is hard to notice. For this reason, we can usually skip the step of renormalizing these values in the fragment shader. The first three lines of code in the fragment shader (Listing 14.7) compute the expression in the *exp* function from Ward's BRDF. The next two lines obtain the necessary cosine values by computing the dot product of the appropriate vectors. We then use these values to compute the value for *brdf*, which is the same as ρ_{bd} in the earlier equations. The next equation puts it all together into an intensity value that attenuates the base color for the surface. The attenuated value becomes the final color for the fragment.

Listing 14.7 Fragment shader for rendering with Ward's BRDF model

```
#version 140

const float PI = 3.14159;
const float ONE_OVER_PI = 1.0 / PI;

uniform vec4 SurfaceColor; // Base color of surface
uniform vec2 P; // Diffuse (x) and specular reflectance (y)
uniform vec2 A; // Slope distribution in x and y
uniform vec3 Scale; // Scale factors for intensity computation

in  vec3  N, L, H, R, T, B;

out vec4  FragColor;

void main()
{
    float e1, e2, E, cosThetaI, cosThetaR, brdf, intensity;

    e1 = dot(H, T) / A.x;
    e2 = dot(H, B) / A.y;
    E = -2.0 * ((e1 * e1 + e2 * e2) / (1.0 + dot(H, N)));

    cosThetaI = dot(N, L);
    cosThetaR = dot(N, R);

    brdf = P.x * ONE_OVER_PI +
           P.y * (1.0 / sqrt(cosThetaI * cosThetaR)) *
           (1.0 / (4.0 * PI * A.x * A.y)) * exp(E);
```

```
    intensity = Scale[0] * P.x * ONE_OVER_PI +
                Scale[1] * P.y * cosThetaI * brdf +
                Scale[2] * dot(H, N) * P.y;

    vec3 color = intensity * SurfaceColor.rgb;

    FragColor = vec4(color, 1.0);
}
```

Some results from this shader are shown in Color Plate 23. It certainly would be possible to extend the formula and surface parameterization values to operate on three channels instead of just one. The resulting shader could be used to simulate materials whose specular highlight changes color depending on the viewing angle.

14.4 Polynomial Texture Mapping with BRDF Data

This section describes the OpenGL Shading Language BRDF shaders that use the Polynomial Texture Mapping technique developed by Hewlett-Packard. The shaders presented are courtesy of Brad Ritter, Hewlett-Packard. The BRDF data is from Cornell University. It was obtained by measurement of reflections from several types of automotive paints that were supplied by Ford Motor Co.

One reason this type of rendering is important is that it achieves realistic rendering of materials whose reflection characteristics vary as a function of view angle and light direction. Such is the case with these automotive paints. To a car designer, it is extremely important to be able to visualize the final "look" of the car, even when it is painted with a material whose reflection characteristics vary as a function of view angle and light direction. One of the paint samples tested by Cornell, Mystique Lacquer, has the peculiar property that the color of its specular highlight color changes as a function of viewing angle. This material cannot be adequately rendered if only conventional texture-mapping techniques are used.

The textures used in this example are called POLYNOMIAL TEXTURE MAPS, or PTMs. PTMs are essentially light-dependent texture maps; PTMs are described in a 2001 SIGGRAPH paper by Malzbender, Gelb, and Wolters. PTMs reconstruct the color of a surface under varying lighting conditions. When a surface is rendered with a PTM, it takes on different illumination characteristics depending on the direction of the light source. As with bump mapping, this behavior helps viewers by providing perceptual clues about the surface geometry. But PTMs go beyond bump maps in that they capture surface variations resulting from self-shadowing and interreflections. PTMs are generated from real materials and preserve the visual characteristics of the actual materials. Polynomial texture mapping is an image-based technique that does not require bump maps or the modeling of complex geometry.

The image in Color Plate 26 (left) shows two triangles from a PTM demo developed by Hewlett-Packard. The triangle on the upper right has been rendered with a polynomial texture map, and the triangle on the lower left has been rendered with a conventional 2D texture map. The objects that were used in the construction of the texture maps were a metallic bezel with the Hewlett-Packard logo on it and a brushed metal notebook cover with an embossed 3Dlabs logo. As you move the simulated light source in the demo, the conventional texture looks flat and somewhat unrealistic, whereas the PTM texture faithfully reproduces the highlights and surface shadowing that occur on the real-life objects. In the image captured here, the light source is a bit in front and above the two triangles. The PTM shows realistic reflections, but the conventional texture can reproduce the lighting effect only from a single lighting angle (in this case, as if the light were directly in front of the object).

The PTM technique developed by HP requires as input a set of images of the desired object, with the object illuminated by a light source of a different known direction for each image, all captured from the same viewpoint. For each texel of the PTM, these source images are sampled and a least-squares biquadric curve fit is performed to obtain a polynomial that approximates the lighting function for that texel. This part of the process is partly science and partly art (a bit of manual intervention can improve the end results). The biquadric equation generated in this manner allows runtime reconstruction of the lighting function for the source material. The coefficients stored in the PTM are A, B, C, D, E, and F, as shown in this equation:

$$Au^2 + Bv^2 + Cuv + Du + Ev + F$$

One use of PTMs is for representing materials with surface properties that vary spatially across the surface. Materials such as brushed metal, woven fabric, wood, and stone all reflect light differently depending on the viewing angle and light source direction. They may also have interreflections and self-shadowing. The PTM technique captures these details and reproduces them at runtime. There are two variants for PTMs: luminance (LRGB) and RGB. An LRGB PTM uses the biquadric polynomials to determine the brightness of each rendered pixel. Because each texel in an LRGB PTM has its own biquadric polynomial function, the luminance or brightness characteristics of each texel can be unique. An RGB PTM uses a separate biquadric polynomial for each of the three colors: red, green, and blue. This allows objects rendered with an RGB PTM to vary in color as the light position shifts. Thus, color-shifting materials such as holograms can be accurately reconstructed with an RGB PTM.

The key to creating a PTM for these types of spatially varying materials is to capture images of them as lit from a variety of light source directions. Engineers at Hewlett-Packard have developed an instrument—a dome with multiple light sources and a camera mounted at the top—to do just that. This device can automatically capture 50 images of the source material from a single fixed camera position as illuminated by light sources in different positions. A photograph of this picture-taking device is shown in Figure 14.4.

The image data collected with this device is the basis for creating a PTM for the real-world texture of a material (e.g., automobile paints). These types of PTMs have four degrees of freedom. Two of these represent the spatially varying characteristics of the material. These two degrees of freedom are controlled by the 2D texture coordinates. The remaining two degrees of freedom represent the light direction. These are the two independent variables in the biquadric polynomial.

Figure 14.4   A device for capturing images for the creation of polynomial texture maps (Copyright © 2003, Hewlett-Packard Development Company, L.P., reproduced with permission)

A BRDF PTM is slightly different from a spatially varying PTM. BRDF PTMs model homogeneous materials—that is, they do not vary spatially. BRDF PTMs use two degrees of freedom to represent the light direction, and the remaining two degrees of freedom represent the view direction. The parameterized light direction (Lu, Lv) is used for the independent variables of the biquadric polynomial, and the parameterized view direction (Vu, Vv) is used as the 2D texture coordinate.

No single parameterization works well for all BRDF materials. A further refinement to enhance quality for BRDF PTMs for the materials we are trying to reproduce is to reparameterize the light and view vectors as half angle and difference vectors (Hu, Hv) and (Du, Dv). In the BRDF PTM shaders discussed in the next section, Hu and Hv are the independent variables of the biquadric polynomial, and (Du, Dv) is the 2D texture coordinate. A large part of the vertex shader's function is to calculate (Hu, Hv) and (Du, Dv).

BRDF PTMs can be created as either LRGB or RGB PTMs. The upcoming example shows how an RGB BRDF PTM is rendered with OpenGL shaders. RGBA textures with 8 bits per component are used because the PTM file format and tools developed by HP are based on this format.

14.4.1 Application Setup

To render BRDF surfaces using the following shaders, the application must set up a few uniform variables. The vertex shader must be provided with values for uniform variables that describe the eye direction (i.e., an infinite viewer) and the position of a single light source (i.e., a point light source). The fragment shader requires the application to provide values for scaling and biasing the six polynomial coefficients. (These values were prescaled when the PTM was created to preserve precision, and they must be rescaled with the scale and bias factors that are specific to that PTM.)

The application is expected to provide the surface normal, vertex position, tangent, and binormal in exactly the same way as the BRDF shader discussed in the previous section. Before rendering, the application should also set up seven texture maps: three 2D texture maps to hold the A, B, and C coefficients for red, green, and blue components of the PTM; three 2D texture maps to hold the D, E, and F coefficients for red, green, and blue components of the PTM; and a 1D texture map to hold a lighting function.

This last texture is set up by the application whenever the lighting state is changed. The light factor texture solves four problems:

- The light factor texture is indexed with *LdotN*, which is positive for front-facing vertices and negative for back-facing vertices. As a first level of complexity, the light texture can solve the front-facing/back-facing discrimination problem by being 1.0 for positive index values and 0.0 for back-facing values.

- We'd like to be able to light BRDF PTM shaded objects with colored lights. As a second level of complexity, the light texture (which has three channels, R, G, and B) uses a light color instead of 1.0 for positive index values.

- An abrupt transition from front-facing to back-facing looks awkward and unrealistic on rendered images. As a third level of complexity, we apply a gradual transition in the light texture values from 0 to 1.0. We use a sine or cosine curve to determine these gradual texture values.

- There is no concept of ambient light for PTM rendering. It can look very unrealistic to render back-facing pixels as (0,0,0). Instead of using 0 values for negative indices, we use values such as 0.1.

14.4.2 Vertex Shader

The BRDF PTM vertex shader is shown in Listing 14.8. This shader produces five out values:

- *gl_Position*, as required by every vertex shader

- *TexCoord*, which is used to access our texture maps to get the two sets of polynomial coefficients

- *Du*, a float that contains the cosine of the angle between the light direction and the tangent vector

- *Dv*, a float that contains the cosine of the angle between the light direction and the binormal vector

- *LdotN*, a float that contains the cosine of the angle between the incoming surface normal and the light direction

The shader assumes a viewer at infinity and one point light source.

Listing 14.8 Vertex shader for rendering BRDF-based polynomial texture maps

```
#version 140
//
// PTM vertex shader by Brad Ritter, Hewlett-Packard
// and Randi Rost, 3Dlabs.
//
// © Copyright 2003 3Dlabs, Inc., and
// Hewlett-Packard Development Company, L.P.,
// Reproduced with Permission
//

uniform mat4 MVPMatrix;

uniform vec3 LightPos;
uniform vec3 EyeDir;

in   vec4   MCvertex;
in   vec3   MCnormal;
in   vec3   MCTangent;
in   vec3   MCBinormal;

out float Du;
out float Dv;
out float LdotN;
out vec2  TexCoord;

void main()
{
    vec3 lightTemp;
    vec3 halfAngleTemp;
    vec3 tPrime;
    vec3 bPrime;

    // Transform vertex
    gl_Position = MVPMatrix * MCVertex;
    lightTemp = normalize(LightPos - MCVertex.xyz);

    // Calculate the Half Angle vector
    halfAngleTemp = normalize(EyeDir + lightTemp);

    // Calculate T' and B'
    // T' = |T - (T.H)H|
    tPrime = MCTangent - (halfAngleTemp * dot(MCTangent, halfAngleTemp));
    tPrime = normalize(tPrime);

    // B' = H x T'
    bPrime = cross(halfAngleTemp, tPrime);
    Du = dot(lightTemp, tPrime);
    Dv = dot(lightTemp, bPrime);
```

```
// Multiply the Half Angle vector by NOISE_FACTOR
// to avoid noisy BRDF data
halfAngleTemp = halfAngleTemp * 0.9;

// Hu = Dot(HalfAngle, T)
// Hv = Dot(HalfAngle, B)
// Remap [-1.0..1.0] to [0.0..1.0]
TexCoord.s = dot(MCTangent, halfAngleTemp) * 0.5 + 0.5;
TexCoord.t = dot(MCBinormal, halfAngleTemp) * 0.5 + 0.5;

// "S" Text Coord3: Dot(Light, Normal);
LdotN = dot(lightTemp, MCNormal) * 0.5 + 0.5;
}
```

The light source position and eye direction are passed in as uniform variables by the application. In addition to the standard OpenGL vertex and normal vertex attributes, the application is expected to pass in a tangent and a binormal per vertex, as described in the previous section. These two generic attributes are defined with appropriate names in our vertex shader.

The first line of the vertex shader transforms the incoming vertex value by the current modelview-projection matrix. The next line computes the light source direction for our positional light source by subtracting the vertex position from the light position. Because *LightPos* is defined as a **vec3** and the user defined in variable *MCVertex* is defined as a **vec4**, we must use the **.xyz** component selector to obtain the first three elements of *MCVertex* before doing the vector subtraction operation. The result of the vector subtraction is then normalized and stored as our light direction.

The following line of code computes the half angle by summing the eye direction vector and the light direction vector and normalizing the result.

The next few lines of code compute the 2D parameterization of our half angle and difference vector. The goal here is to compute values for *u* (*Du*) and *v* (*Dv*) that can be plugged into the biquadric equation in our fragment shader. The technique we use is called Gram-Schmidt orthonormalization. *H* (half angle), *T'*, and *B'* are the orthogonal axes of a coordinate system. *T'* and *B'* maintain a general alignment with the original *T* (tangent) and *B* (binormal) vectors. Where *T* and *B* lie in the plane of the triangle being rendered, *T'* and *B'* are in a plane perpendicular to the half angle vector. More details on the reasons for choosing *H*, *T'*, and *B'* to define the coordinate system are available in the paper *Interactive Rendering with Arbitrary BRDFs Using Separable Approximations* by Jan Kautz and Michael McCool (1999).

BRDF data often has noisy data values for extremely large incidence angles (i.e., close to 180°), so in the next line of code, we avoid the noisy data in a somewhat unscientific manner by applying a scale factor to the half angle. This effectively causes these values to be ignored.

Our vertex shader code then computes values for *Hu* and *Hv* and places them in the out variable *TexCoord*. These are plugged into our biquadric equation in the fragment shader as the *u* and *v* values. These values hold our parameterized difference vector and are used to look up the required polynomial coefficients from the texture maps, so they are mapped into the range [0,1].

Finally, we compute a value that applies the lighting effect. This value is simply the cosine of the angle between the surface normal and the light direction. It is also mapped into the range [0,1] because it is the texture coordinate for accessing a 1D texture to obtain the lighting factor that is used.

14.4.3 Fragment Shader

The fragment shader for our BRDF PTM surface rendering is shown in Listing 14.9.

Listing 14.9 Fragment shader for rendering BRDF-based polynomial texture maps

```
#version 140
//
// PTM fragment shader by Brad Ritter, Hewlett-Packard
// and Randi Rost, 3Dlabs.
//
// © Copyright 2003 3Dlabs, Inc., and
// Hewlett-Packard Development Company, L.P.,
// Reproduced with Permission
//
uniform sampler2D ABCred;        // = 0
uniform sampler2D DEFred;        // = 1
uniform sampler2D ABCgrn;        // = 2
uniform sampler2D DEFgrn;        // = 3
uniform sampler2D ABCblu;        // = 4
uniform sampler2D DEFblu;        // = 5
uniform sampler1D Lighttexture;  // = 6

uniform vec3 ABCscale, ABCbias;
uniform vec3 DEFscale, DEFbias;

in  float Du;        // passes the computed L*tPrime value
in  float Dv;        // passes the computed L*bPrime value
in  float LdotN;     // passes the computed L*Normal value
in  vec2  TexCoord;  // passes s, t, texture coords
```

```
out vec4  FragColor;

void main()
{
    vec3 ABCcoef, DEFcoef;
    vec3 ptvec;

    // Read coefficient values for red and apply scale and bias factors
    ABCcoef = (texture(ABCred, TexCoord).rgb - ABCbias) * ABCscale;
    DEFcoef = (texture(DEFred, TexCoord).rgb - DEFbias) * DEFscale;

    // Compute red polynomial
    ptvec.r = ABCcoef[0] * Du * Du +
              ABCcoef[1] * Dv * Dv +
              ABCcoef[2] * Du * Dv +
              DEFcoef[0] * Du +
              DEFcoef[1] * Dv +
              DEFcoef[2];

    // Read coefficient values for green and apply scale and bias factors
    ABCcoef = (texture(ABCgrn, TexCoord).rgb - ABCbias) * ABCscale;
    DEFcoef = (texture(DEFgrn, TexCoord).rgb - DEFbias) * DEFscale;

    // Compute green polynomial
    ptvec.g = ABCcoef[0] * Du * Du +
              ABCcoef[1] * Dv * Dv +
              ABCcoef[2] * Du * Dv +
              DEFcoef[0] * Du +
              DEFcoef[1] * Dv +
              DEFcoef[2];

    // Read coefficient values for blue and apply scale and bias factors
    ABCcoef = (texture(ABCblu, TexCoord).rgb - ABCbias) * ABCscale;
    DEFcoef = (texture(DEFblu, TexCoord).rgb - DEFbias) * DEFscale;

    // Compute blue polynomial
    ptvec.b = ABCcoef[0] * Du * Du +
              ABCcoef[1] * Dv * Dv +
              ABCcoef[2] * Du * Dv +
              DEFcoef[0] * Du +
              DEFcoef[1] * Dv +
              DEFcoef[2];

    // Multiply result * light factor
    ptvec *= texture(Lighttexture, LdotN).rgb;

    // Assign result to FragColor
    FragColor = vec4(ptvec, 1.0);
}
```

This shader is relatively straightforward if you've digested the information in the previous three sections. The values in the *s* and *t* components of

TexCoord hold a 2D parameterization of the difference vector. *TexCoord* indexes into each of our coefficient textures and retrieves the values for the A, B, C, D, E, and F coefficients. The BRDF PTMs are stored as mipmap textures, and, because we're not providing a *bias* argument, the computed level-of-detail bias is just used directly. Using vector operations, we scale and bias the six coefficients by using values passed from the application through uniform variables.

We then use these scaled, biased coefficient values together with our parameterized half angle (*Du* and *Dv*) in the biquadric polynomial to compute the red value for the surface. We repeat the process to compute the green and blue values as well. We compute the lighting factor by accessing the 1D light texture, using the cosine of the angle between the light direction and the surface normal. Finally, we multiply the lighting factor by our polynomial vector and use an alpha value of 1.0 to produce the final fragment color.

The image in Color Plate 26 (right) shows our BRDF PTM shaders rendering a torus with the BRDF PTM created for the Mystique Lacquer automotive paint. The basic color of this paint is black, but, in the orientation captured for the still image, the specular highlight shows up as mostly white with a reddish-brown tinge on one side of the highlight and a bluish tinge on the other. As the object is moved around or as the light is moved around, our BRDF PTM shaders properly render the shifting highlight color.

14.5 Summary

This chapter looked at how shaders model the properties of light that arrives at a particular point on a surface. Light can be transmitted, reflected, or absorbed. We developed shaders that model the reflection and refraction of light based on an approximation to the Fresnel equations, a shader that simulates diffraction, and shaders that implement a bidirectional reflectance distribution function. Finally, we studied a shader that uses image-based methods to reproduce varying lighting conditions and self-shadowing for a variety of materials.

Pardon the pun, but the shaders presented in this chapter (as well as in the preceding two chapters) only begin to scratch the surface of the realistic rendering effects that are possible with the OpenGL Shading Language. The hope is that by developing shaders to implement a few examples of lighting, shadows, and reflection, you will be equipped to survey the literature and implement a variety of similar techniques. The shaders we've developed can be further streamlined and optimized for specific purposes.

14.6 Further Information

A thorough treatment of reflectance and lighting models can be found in the book *Real-Time Shading* by Marc Olano et al. (2002). *Real-Time Rendering* by Tomas Akenine-Möller and E. Haines also contains discussions of Fresnel reflection and the theory and implementation of BRDFs. The paper discussing the Fresnel approximation we've discussed was published by Christophe Schlick as part of Eurographics '94. Cg shaders that utilize this approximation are described in the *Cg Tutorial* and *GPU Gems* books. The diffraction shader is based on work presented by Jos Stam in a 1999 SIGGRAPH paper called *Diffraction Shaders*. Stam later developed a diffraction shader in Cg and discussed it in the book *GPU Gems*.

The specific paper that was drawn upon heavily for the BRDF reflection section was Gregory Ward's *Measuring and Modeling Anisotropic Reflection*, which appeared in the 1992 SIGGRAPH conference proceedings. A classic early paper that set the stage for this work was the 1981 SIGGRAPH paper, *A Reflectance Model for Computer Graphics* by Robert L. Cook and Kenneth E. Torrance.

The SIGGRAPH 2001 proceedings contain the paper *Polynomial Texture Maps* by Tom Malzbender, Dan Gelb, and Hans Wolters. Additional information is available at the Hewlett-Packard Laboratories Web site, www.hpl.hp.com/ptm/. At this site, you can find example data files, a PTM viewing program, the PTM file format specification, and utilities to assist in creating PTMs.

The book *Physically-Based Rendering: From Theory to Implementation* by Matt Pharr and Greg Humphreys is a thorough treatment of techniques for achieving realism in computer graphics.

[1] Akenine-Möller, Tomas, and E. Haines, *Real-Time Rendering, Second Edition*, AK Peters, Ltd., Natick, Massachusetts, 2002. www.realtimerendering.com

[2] Cook, Robert L., and Kenneth E. Torrance, *A Reflectance Model for Computer Graphics*, Computer Graphics (SIGGRAPH '81 Proceedings), pp. 307–316, July 1981.

[3] Fernando, Randima, and Mark J. Kilgard, *The Cg Tutorial: The Definitive Guide to Programmable Real-Time Graphics*, Addison-Wesley, Boston, Massachusetts, 2003.

[4] Hewlett-Packard, *Polynomial Texture Mapping*, Web site. www.hpl.hp.com/ptm

[5] Kautz, Jan, and Michael D. McCool, *Interactive Rendering with Arbitrary BRDFs Using Separable Approximations*, 10th Eurographics Workshop on Rendering, pp. 281–292, June 1999. www.mpi-sb.mpg.de/~jnkautz/publications

[6] Malzbender, Tom, Dan Gelb, and Hans Wolters, *Polynomial Texture Maps*, Computer Graphics (SIGGRAPH 2001 Proceedings), pp. 519–528, August 2001. www.hpl.hp.com/research/ptm/papers/ptm.pdf

[7] Olano, Marc, John Hart, Wolfgang Heidrich, and Michael McCool, *Real-Time Shading*, AK Peters, Ltd., Natick, Massachusetts, 2002.

[8] Pharr, Matt, and Greg Humphreys, *Physically Based Rendering: From Theory to Implementation*, Morgan Kaufmann, San Francisco, 2004. http://pbrt.org/

[9] Schlick, Christophe, *An Inexpensive BRDF Model for Physically Based Rendering*, Eurographics '94, published in Computer Graphics Forum, vol. 13., no. 3, pp. 149–162, September, 1994.

[10] Stam, Jos, *Diffraction Shaders*, Computer Graphics (SIGGRAPH '99 Proceedings, pp. 101–110, August 1999. www.dgp.toronto.edu/people/stam/reality/Research/pdf/diff.pdf

[11] Stam, Jos, *Simulating Diffraction*, in *GPU Gems: Programming Techniques, Tips, and Tricks for Real-Time Graphics*, Editor: Randima Fernando, Addison-Wesley, Reading, Massachusetts, 2004. http://developer.nvidia.com/object/gpu_gems_home.html

[12] Ward, Gregory, *Measuring and Modeling Anisotropic Reflection*, Computer Graphics (SIGGRAPH '92 Proceedings), pp. 265–272, July 1992. http://radsite.lbl.gov/radiance/papers/sg92/paper.html

Chapter 15

Noise

In computer graphics, it's easy to make things look good. By definition, geometry is drawn and rendered precisely. However, when realism is a goal, perfection isn't always such a good thing. Real-world objects have dents and dings and scuffs. They show wear and tear. Computer graphics artists have to work hard to make a perfectly defined bowling pin look like it has been used and abused for 20 years in a bowling alley or to make a space ship that seems a little worse for wear after many years of galactic travel.

This was the problem that Ken Perlin was trying to solve when he worked for a company called Magi in the early 1980s. Magi was working with Disney on a feature film called *Tron* that was the most ambitious film in its use of computer graphics until that time. Perlin recognized the "imperfection" of the perfectly rendered objects in that film, and he resolved to do something about it.

In a seminal paper published in 1985, Perlin described a renderer that he had written that used a technique he called NOISE. His definition of noise was a little different from the everyday definition of noise. Normally, when we refer to noise, we're referring to something like a random pattern of pixels on a television channel with no signal (also called SNOW) or to static on the radio on a frequency that doesn't have any nearby station broadcasting.

But a truly random function like this isn't that useful for computer graphics. For computer graphics, we need a function that is repeatable so that an object can be drawn from different view angles. We also need the ability to draw the object the same way, frame after frame, in an animation. Truly random functions do not depend on any input values, so an object rendered with such a function would look different each time it was drawn.

The visual artifacts caused by this type of rendering would look horrible as the object was moved around the screen. What is needed is a function that produces the same output value for a given input value every time and yet gives the appearance of randomness. This function also needs to be continuous at all levels of detail.

Perlin was the first to come up with a usable function for that purpose. Since then, a variety of similar noise functions have been defined and used in combinations to produce interesting rendering effects such as

- Rendering natural phenomena (clouds, fire, smoke, wind effects, etc.)

- Rendering natural materials (marble, granite, wood, mountains, etc.)

- Rendering man-made materials (stucco, asphalt, cement, etc.)

- Adding imperfections to perfect models (rust, dirt, smudges, dents, etc.)

- Adding imperfections to perfect patterns (wiggles, bumps, color variations, etc.)

- Adding imperfections to time periods (time between blinks, amount of change between successive frames, etc.)

- Adding imperfections to motion (wobbles, jitters, bumps, etc.)

Actually, the list is endless. Today, most rendering libraries include support for Perlin noise or something nearly equivalent. It is a staple of realistic rendering, and it's been heavily used in the generation of computer graphics images for the movie industry. For his groundbreaking work in this area, Perlin was presented with an Academy Award for technical achievement in 1997.

Because noise is such an important technique, it is included as a built-in function in the OpenGL Shading Language. There are several ways to make use of noise within a fragment shader. After laying the groundwork for noise, we take a look at several shader examples that depend on noise to achieve an interesting effect.

15.1 Noise Defined

The purpose of this section is not to explain the mathematical underpinnings of noise but to provide enough of an intuitive feel that you can grasp the noise-based OpenGL shaders presented in the chapter and then use the OpenGL Shading Language to create additional noise-based effects. For a deeper understanding of noise functions, consult the references listed at the end of this chapter, especially *Texturing and Modeling: A Procedural Approach, Third Edition* by David S. Ebert et al., which contains several significant discussions of noise, including a description by Perlin of his original noise function. In that book, Darwyn Peachey also provides a taxonomy of noise functions called *Making Noises*. The application of different noise functions and combinations of noise functions are discussed by Ken Musgrave in his section on building procedural planets.

As Perlin describes it, you can think of noise as "seasoning" for graphics. It often helps to add a little noise, but noise all by itself isn't all that appealing. A perfect model looks a little less perfect and, therefore, a little more realistic if some subtle noise effects are applied.

The ideal noise function has some important qualities.

- It is a continuous function that gives the appearance of randomness.

- It is a function that is repeatable (i.e., it generates the same value each time it is presented with the same input).

- It has a well-defined range of output values (usually the range is [–1,1] or [0,1]).

- It results in values that do not show obvious regular patterns or periods.

- It is a function whose small-scale form is roughly independent of large-scale position.

- It is a function that is isotropic (i.e., its statistical character is rotationally invariant).

- It can be defined for 1, 2, 3, 4, or even more dimensions.

This definition of noise provides an irregular primitive that adds variety or an apparent element of "randomness" to a regular pattern or period. It can be used as part of modeling, rendering, or animation. Its characteristics make it a valuable tool for creating a variety of interesting effects. Algorithms for creating noise functions make various trade-offs in quality and performance, so they meet the preceding criteria with varying degrees of success.

We can construct a simple noise function (called VALUE NOISE by Peachey) by first assigning a pseudorandom number in the range [–1,1] to each integer value along the x axis, as shown in Figure 15.1, and then smoothly interpolating between these points, as shown in Figure 15.2. The function is repeatable in that, for a given input value, it always returns the same output value.

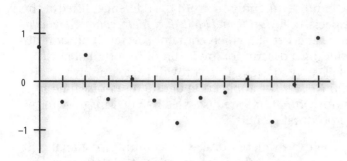

Figure 15.1   A discrete 1D noise function

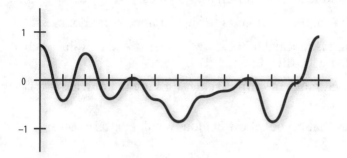

Figure 15.2   A continuous 1D noise function

A key choice to be made in this type of noise function is the method used to interpolate between successive points. Linear interpolation is not good enough, because the resulting noise pattern shows obvious artifacts. A cubic interpolation method is usually used to produce smooth-looking results.

By varying the frequency and the amplitude, you can get a variety of noise functions (see Figure 15.3).

As you can see, the "features" in these functions get smaller and closer together as the frequency increases and the amplitude decreases. When two frequencies are related by a ratio of 2:1, it's called an OCTAVE. Figure 15.3 illustrates five octaves of the 1D noise function. These images of noise don't look all that useful, but by themselves they can provide some interesting characteristics to shaders. If we add the functions at different frequencies (see Figure 15.4), we start to see something that looks even more interesting.

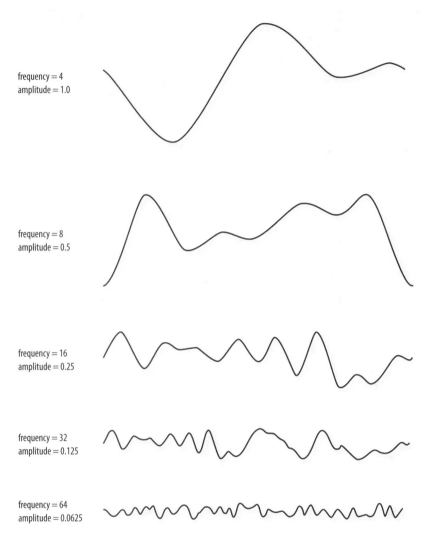

frequency = 4
amplitude = 1.0

frequency = 8
amplitude = 0.5

frequency = 16
amplitude = 0.25

frequency = 32
amplitude = 0.125

frequency = 64
amplitude = 0.0625

Figure 15.3   Varying the frequency and the amplitude of the noise function

The result is a function that contains features of various sizes. The larger bumps from the lower-frequency functions provide the overall shape, whereas the smaller bumps from the higher-frequency functions provide detail and interest at a smaller scale. The function that results from summing the noise of consecutive octaves, each at half the amplitude of the previous octave, was called 1/f noise by Perlin, but the terms "fractional Brownian motion" and "fBm" are used more commonly today.

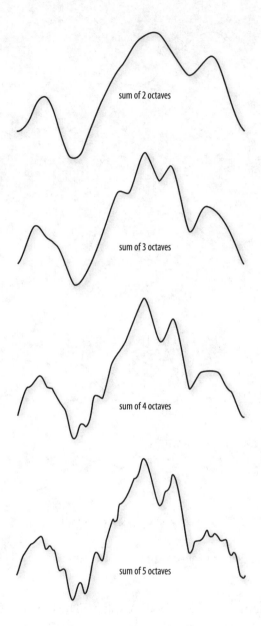

sum of 2 octaves

sum of 3 octaves

sum of 4 octaves

sum of 5 octaves

Figure 15.4   Result of summing noise functions of different amplitude and frequency

If you sum octaves of noise in a procedural shader, at some point you will begin to add frequencies that cause aliasing artifacts. Algorithms for anti-aliasing noise functions typically stop adding detail (higher-frequency noise) before this occurs. This is another key aspect of the noise function—it can be faded to the average value at the point at which aliasing artifacts would begin to occur.

The noise function defined by Perlin (PERLIN NOISE) is sometimes called GRADIENT NOISE. It is defined as a function whose value is 0 at each integer input value, and its shape is created by defining a pseudorandom gradient vector for the function at each of these points. The characteristics of this noise function make it a somewhat better choice, in general, for the effects we're after (see Ebert et al. [2002] for details). It is used for the implementation of the noise function in RenderMan, and it is also intended to be used for implementations of the **noise** function built into the OpenGL Shading Language.

Lots of other noise functions have been defined, and there are many ways to vary the basic ideas. The examples of Perlin noise shown previously have a frequency multiplier of 2, but it can be useful to use a frequency multiplier, such as 2.21, that is not an integer value. This frequency multiplier is called the LACUNARITY of the function. The word comes from the Latin word *lacuna*, which means *gap*. Using a value larger than 2 allows us to build up more "variety" more quickly (e.g., by summing fewer octaves to achieve the same apparent visual complexity). Similarly, it is not necessary to divide the amplitude of each successive octave by 2.

Summed noise functions are the basis for the terrain and features found in the planet-building software package *MojoWorld* from Pandromeda. In *Texturing and Modeling: A Procedural Approach*, Ken Musgrave defines a fractal as "a geometrically complex object, the complexity of which arises through the repetition of a given form over a range of scales." The relationship between the change in frequency and the change in amplitude determines the fractal dimension of the resulting function. If we use a noise function as the basis for generating a terrain model, we can take steps to make it behave differently at different locations. For instance, natural terrain has plains, rolling hills, foothills, and mountains. Varying the fractal dimension based on location can create a similar appearance—such a function is called a MULTIFRACTAL.

You can achieve interesting effects by using different noise functions for different situations or by combining noise functions of different types. It's not that easy to visualize in advance the results of calculations that depend on noise values, so varied experience will be a key ally as you try to achieve the effect you're after.

15.1.1 2D Noise

Armed with a basic idea of what the noise function looks like in one dimension, we can take a look at two-dimensional noise. Figure 15.5 contains images of 2D Perlin noise at various frequencies mapped into the range [0,1] and displayed as a grayscale image. Each successive image is twice the frequency of the previous one. In each image, the contrast has been enhanced to make the peaks brighter and the valleys darker. In actual use, each subsequent image has an average that is half the previous one and an amplitude that is half the previous one. If we were to print images of the actual values, the images would be much grayer, and it would be harder to see what 2D noise really looks like.

As in the 1D case, adding the different frequency functions provides more interesting results (Figure 15.6).

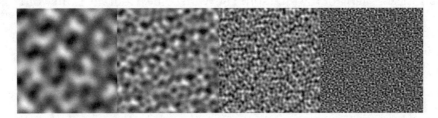

Figure 15.5   Basic 2D noise, at frequencies 4, 8, 16, and 32 (contrast enhanced)

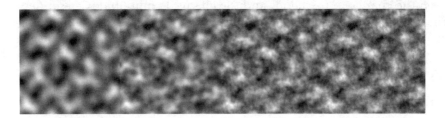

Figure 15.6   Summed noise, at 1, 2, 3, and 4 octaves (contrast enhanced)

The first image in Figure 15.6 is exactly the same as the first image in Figure 15.5. The second image in Figure 15.6 is the sum of the first image in Figure 15.6 plus half of the second image in Figure 15.5 shifted so that its average intensity value is 0. This causes intensity to be increased in some areas and decreased in others. The third image in Figure 15.6 adds the third octave of noise to the first two, and the fourth image in Figure 15.6 adds the fourth octave. The fourth picture is starting to look a little bit like clouds in the sky.

15.1.2 Higher Dimensions of Noise

3D and 4D noise functions are obvious extensions of the 1D and 2D functions. It's a little hard to generate pictures of 3D noise, but the images in Figure 15.5 can be thought of as 2D slices out of a 3D noise function. Neighboring slices have continuity between them.

Often, a higher dimension of noise is used to control the time aspect of the next lower-dimension noise function. For instance, 1D noise can add some wiggle to otherwise straight lines in a drawing. If you have a 2D noise function, one dimension can control the wiggle, and the second dimension can animate the effect (i.e., make the wiggles move in successive frames). Similarly, a 2D noise function can create a 2D cloud pattern, whereas a 3D noise function can generate the 2D cloud pattern and animate it in a realistic way. With a 4D noise function, you can create a 3D object like a planet and use the fourth dimension to watch it evolve in "fits and starts."

15.1.3 Using Noise in OpenGL Shaders

You include noise in an OpenGL shader in three ways:

1. Use the OpenGL Shading Language built-in **noise** functions.

2. Write your own noise function in the OpenGL Shading Language.

3. Use a texture map to store a previously computed noise function.

With today's graphics hardware, option 3 typically gives the best performance, so in this chapter, we look at some shaders based on this approach. In the next chapter, we look at a shader that uses the built-in **noise** functions to animate geometry. The important thing is to realize the usefulness of noise in computer-generated imagery.

15.2 Noise Textures

The programmability offered by the OpenGL Shading Language lets us use values stored in texture memory in new and unique ways. We can pre-compute a noise function and save it in a 1D, 2D, or 3D texture map. We can then access this texture map (or texture maps) from within a shader. Because textures can contain up to four components, we can use a single texture map to store four octaves of noise or four completely separate noise functions.

Listing 15.1 shows a C function that generates a 3D noise texture. This function creates an RGBA texture with the first octave of noise stored in the red texture component, the second octave stored in the green texture component, the third octave stored in the blue component, and the fourth octave stored in the alpha component. Each octave has twice the frequency and half the amplitude as the previous one.

This function assumes the existence of a **noise3** function that can generate 3D noise values in the range [–1,1]. If you want, you can start with Perlin's C implementation (available from www.texturingandmodeling.com/ CODE/PERLIN/PERLIN.C). John Kessenich made some small changes to this code (adding a **setNoiseFrequency** function) to produce noise values that wrap smoothly from one edge of the array to the other. This means we can use the texture with the wrapping mode set to GL_REPEAT, and we won't see any discontinuities in the function when it wraps. The revised version of the code is in a program from 3Dlabs called **GLSLdemo**, and the source code for this example program can be downloaded from the 3Dlabs Web site at http://developer.3dlabs.com.

Listing 15.1   C function to generate a 3D noise texture

```
int noise3DTexSize = 128;
GLuint noise3DTexName = 0;
GLubyte *noise3DTexPtr;

void make3DNoiseTexture(void)
{
    int f, i, j, k, inc;
    int startFrequency = 4;
    int numOctaves = 4;
    double ni[3];
    double inci, incj, inck;
    int frequency = startFrequency;
    GLubyte *ptr;
    double amp = 0.5;
```

```
    if ((noise3DTexPtr = (GLubyte *) malloc(noise3DTexSize *
                                            noise3DTexSize *
                                            noise3DTexSize * 4)) == NULL)
    {
        fprintf(stderr,"ERROR: Could not allocate 3D noise texture\n");
        exit(1);
    }

    for (f = 0, inc = 0; f < numOctaves;
         ++f, frequency *= 2, ++inc, amp *= 0.5)
    {
        setNoiseFrequency(frequency);
        ptr = noise3DTexPtr;
        ni[0] = ni[1] = ni[2] = 0;

        inci = 1.0 / (noise3DTexSize / frequency);
        for (i = 0; i < noise3DTexSize; ++i, ni[0] += inci)
        {
            incj = 1.0 / (noise3DTexSize / frequency);
            for (j = 0; j < noise3DTexSize; ++j, ni[1] += incj)
            {
                inck = 1.0 / (noise3DTexSize / frequency);
                for (k = 0; k < noise3DTexSize; ++k, ni[2] += inck, ptr+= 4)
                {
                    *(ptr+inc) = (GLubyte)(((noise3(ni)+1.0) * amp)*128.0);
                }
            }
        }
    }
}
```

This function computes noise values for four octaves of noise and stores them in a 3D RGBA texture of size $128 \times 128 \times 128$. This code also assumes that each component of the texture is stored as an 8-bit integer value. The first octave has a frequency of 4 and an amplitude of 0.5. In the innermost part of the loop, we call the **noise3** function to generate a noise value based on the current value of *ni*. The **noise3** function returns a value in the range [−1,1], so by adding 1, we end up with a noise value in the range [0,2]. Multiplying by our amplitude value of 0.5 gives a value in the range [0,1]. Finally, we multiply by 128 to give us an integer value in the range [0,128] that can be stored in the red component of a texture. (When accessed from within a shader, the value is a floating-point value in the range [0,0.5].)

The amplitude value is cut in half and the frequency is doubled in each pass through the loop. The result is that integer values in the range [0,64] are stored in the green component of the noise texture, integer values in the range [0,32] are stored in the blue component of the noise texture, and integer values in the range [0,16] are stored in the alpha component of the texture. We generated the images in Figure 15.5 by looking at each of these channels independently after scaling the values by a constant value that allowed them to span the maximum intensity range (i.e., integer values in the range [0,255] or floating-point values in the range [0,1]).

After the values for the noise texture are computed, the texture can be provided to the graphics hardware with the code in Listing 15.2. First, we pick a texture unit and bind to it the 3D texture we've created. We set up its wrapping parameters so that the texture wraps in all three dimensions. This way, we always get a valid result for our noise function no matter what input values are used. We still have to be somewhat careful to avoid using the texture in a way that makes obvious repeating patterns. The next two lines set the texture filtering modes to linear because the default is mipmap linear and we're not using mipmap textures here. (Using a mipmap texture might be appropriate in some circumstances, but we are controlling the scaling factors from within our noise shaders, so a single texture is sufficient.) When all the parameters are set up, we can download the noise texture to the hardware by using the **glTexImage3D** function.

Listing 15.2   A function for activating the 3D noise texture

```
void init3DNoiseTexture()
{
    glGenTextures(1, &noise3DTexName);

    glActiveTexture(GL_TEXTURE6);
    glBindTexture(GL_TEXTURE_3D, noise3DTexName);
    glTexParameterf(GL_TEXTURE_3D, GL_TEXTURE_WRAP_S, GL_REPEAT);
    glTexParameterf(GL_TEXTURE_3D, GL_TEXTURE_WRAP_T, GL_REPEAT);
    glTexParameterf(GL_TEXTURE_3D, GL_TEXTURE_WRAP_R, GL_REPEAT);
    glTexParameterf(GL_TEXTURE_3D, GL_TEXTURE_MAG_FILTER, GL_LINEAR);
    glTexParameterf(GL_TEXTURE_3D, GL_TEXTURE_MIN_FILTER, GL_LINEAR);

    glTexImage3D(GL_TEXTURE_3D, 0, GL_RGBA, noise3DTexSize,
                 noise3DTexSize, noise3DTexSize, 0, GL_RGBA,
                 GL_UNSIGNED_BYTE, noise3DTexPtr);
}
```

This is an excellent approach if the period of repeatability can be avoided in the final rendering. One way to avoid it is to make sure that no texture value is accessed more than once when the target object is rendered. For instance, if a $128 \times 128 \times 128$ texture is being used and the position on the object is used as the input to the noise function, the repeatability won't be visible if the entire object fits within the texture.

15.3 Trade-offs

As previously mentioned, three methods can be used to generate noise values in a shader. How do you know which is the best choice for your application? A lot depends on the underlying implementation, but generally speaking, if we assume a hardware computation of noise that does not use texturing, the points favoring usage of the OpenGL Shading Language built-in **noise** function are the following:

- It doesn't consume any texture memory (a $128 \times 128 \times 128$ texture map stored as RGBA with 8 bits per component uses 8MB of texture memory).

- It doesn't use a texture unit.

- It is a continuous function rather than a discrete one, so it does not look "pixelated" no matter what the scaling is.

- The repeatability of the function should be undetectable, especially for 2D and 3D noise (but it depends on the hardware implementation).

- Shaders written with the built-in **noise** function don't depend on the application to set up appropriate textures.

The advantages of using a texture map to implement the noise function are as follows:

- Because the noise function is computed by the application, the application has total control of this function and can ensure matching behavior on every hardware platform.

- You can store four noise values (i.e., one each for the R, G, B, and A values of the texture) at each texture location. This lets you precompute four octaves of noise, for instance, and retrieve all four values with a single texture access.

- Accessing a texture map may be faster than calling the built-in **noise** function.

User-defined functions can implement noise functions that provide a different appearance from that of the built-in **noise** functions. A user-defined function can also provide matching behavior on every platform, whereas the built-in **noise** functions cannot (at least not until all graphics hardware developers support the **noise** function in exactly the same way). But hardware developers will optimize the built-in **noise** function, perhaps accelerating it with special hardware, so it is apt to be faster than user-defined noise functions.

In the long run, using the built-in **noise** function or user-defined noise functions will be the way to go for most applications. This will result in noise that doesn't show a repetitive pattern, has greater numerical precision, and doesn't use up any texture resources. Applications that want full control over the noise function and can live within the constraints of a fixed-size noise function can be successful using textures for their noise. With current generation hardware, noise textures may also provide better performance and require fewer instructions in the shader.

15.4   A Simple Noise Shader

Now we put all these ideas into some OpenGL shaders that do some interesting rendering for us. The first shader we look at uses noise in a simple way to produce a cloud effect.

15.4.1   Application Setup

Very little needs to be passed to the noise shaders discussed in this section and in Section 15.5 and Section 15.6. The vertex position must be passed in as always, and the surface normal is needed for performing lighting computations. Colors and scale factors are parameterized as uniform variables for the various shaders.

15.4.2   Vertex Shader

The code shown in Listing 15.3 is the vertex shader that we use for the four noise fragment shaders that follow. It is fairly simple because it really only needs to accomplish three things.

- As in all vertex shaders, our vertex shader transforms the incoming vertex value and stores it in the built-in special variable *gl_Position*.

- Using the incoming normal and the uniform variable *LightPos*, the vertex shader computes the light intensity from a single white light source and applies a scale factor of 1.5 to increase the amount of illumination.

- The vertex shader scales the incoming vertex value and stores it in the out variable *MCposition*. This value is available to us in our fragment shader as the modeling coordinate position of the object at every fragment. It is an ideal value to use as the input for our 3D texture lookup.

No matter how the object is drawn, fragments always produce the same position values (or very close to them); therefore, the noise value obtained for each point on the surface is also the same (or very close to it). The application can set a uniform variable called *Scale* to optimally scale the object in relationship to the size of the noise texture.

Listing 15.3   Cloud vertex shader

```
#version 140

uniform mat4 MVMatrix;
uniform mat4 MVPMatrix;
uniform mat3 NormalMatrix;

uniform vec3 LightPos;
uniform float Scale;

in  vec4  MCvertex;
in  vec3  MCnormal;

out float LightIntensity;
out vec3  MCposition;

void main()
{
    vec3 ECposition = vec3(MVMatrix * MCVertex);
    MCposition      = vec3(MCVertex) * Scale;
    vec3 tnorm      = normalize(vec3(NormalMatrix * MCNormal));
    LightIntensity  = dot(normalize(LightPos - ECposition), tnorm);
    LightIntensity *= 1.5;
    gl_Position     = MVPMatrix * MCVertex;
}
```

15.4.3 Fragment Shader

After we've computed a noise texture and used OpenGL calls to download it to the graphics card, we can use a fairly simple fragment shader together with the vertex shader described in the previous section to make an interesting "cloudy sky" effect (see Listing 15.4). This shader results in something that looks like the sky on a mostly cloudy day. You can experiment with the color values to get a result that is visually pleasing.

This fragment shader receives as input the two in variables—*LightIntensity* and *MCposition*—that were computed by the vertex shader shown in the previous section. These values were computed at each vertex by the vertex shader and then interpolated across the primitive by the rasterization hardware. Here, in our fragment shader, we have access to the interpolated value of each of these variables at every fragment.

The first line of code in the shader performs a 3D texture lookup on our 3D noise texture to produce a four-component result. We compute the value of *intensity* by summing the four components of our noise texture. This value is then scaled by 1.5 and used to perform a linear blend between two colors: white and sky blue. The four channels in our noise texture have mean values of 0.25, 0.125, 0.0625, and 0.03125. An additional 0.03125 term is added to account for the average values of all the octaves at higher frequencies. You can think of this as fading to the average values of all the higher frequency octaves that aren't being included in the calculation, as described earlier in Section 15.1. Scaling the sum by 1.5 stretches the resulting value to use up more of the range from [0,1].

The computed color is then scaled by *LightIntensity* value to simulate a diffuse surface lit by a single light source. The result is assigned to the out variable *FragColor* with an alpha value of 1.0 to produce the color value that is used by the remainder of the OpenGL pipeline. An object rendered with this shader is shown in Color Plate 24. Notice that the texture on the teapot looks a lot like the final image in Figure 15.6.

Listing 15.4   Fragment shader for cloudy sky effect

```
#version 140

uniform sampler3D Noise;
uniform vec3 SkyColor;      // (0.0, 0.0, 0.8)
uniform vec3 CloudColor;    // (0.8, 0.8, 0.8)

in   float LightIntensity;
in   vec3  MCposition;

out vec4  FragColor;

void main()
{
    vec4 noisevec = texture(Noise, MCposition);

    float intensity = (noisevec[0] + noisevec[1] +
                      noisevec[2] + noisevec[3] + 0.03125) * 1.5;

    vec3 color = mix(SkyColor, CloudColor, intensity) * LightIntensity;
    FragColor = vec4(color, 1.0);
}
```

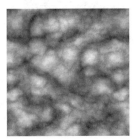

Figure 15.7   Absolute value noise or "turbulence"

15.5 Turbulence

We can obtain some additional interesting effects by taking the absolute value of the noise function. This technique introduces a discontinuity of the derivative because the function folds on itself when it reaches 0 (see Figure 5.2 for an illustration of the absolute value function). When this folding is done to noise functions at several frequencies and the results are summed, the result is cusps or creases in the texture at various scales. Perlin started referring to this type of noise as TURBULENCE because it is reminiscent of turbulent flow. It shows up in a variety of places in nature, so this type of noise can be used to simulate various things like flames or lava. The two-dimensional appearance of this type of noise is shown in Figure 15.7.

15.5.1 Sun Surface Shader

We can achieve an effect that looks like a pit of hot molten lava or the surface of the sun by using the same vertex shader as the cloud shader and a slightly different fragment shader. The main difference is that we scale each noise value and shift it over so that it is centered at 0; then we take its absolute value. After summing the values, we scale the result again to occupy nearly the full range of [0,1]. We clamp this value and use it to mix between yellow and red to get the result shown in Color Plate 24 (see Listing 15.5). (In Chapter 16, we examine some ways of animating these textures to make them more interesting.)

Listing 15.5   Sun surface fragment shader

```
#version 140

in float LightIntensity;
in vec3 MCposition;
```

```
uniform sampler3D Noise;
uniform vec3  Color1;        // (0.8, 0.7, 0.0)
uniform vec3  Color2;        // (0.6, 0.1, 0.0)
uniform float NoiseScale;    // 1.2

out vec4 FragColor;

void main()
{
    vec4 noisevec = texture(Noise, MCposition * NoiseScale);

    float intensity = abs(noisevec[0] - 0.25) +
                      abs(noisevec[1] - 0.125) +
                      abs(noisevec[2] - 0.0625) +
                      abs(noisevec[3] - 0.03125);

    intensity = clamp(intensity * 6.0, 0.0, 1.0);
    vec3 color = mix(Color1, Color2, intensity) * LightIntensity;
    FragColor = vec4(color, 1.0);
}
```

15.5.2 Marble

Yet another variation on the noise function is to use it as part of a periodic function such as sine. By adding noise to the input value for the sine function, we get a "noisy" oscillating function. We use this to create a look similar to the alternating color veins of some types of marble. Listing 15.6 shows the fragment shader to do it. Again, we use the same vertex shader. Results of this shader are also shown in Color Plate 24.

Listing 15.6   Fragment shader for marble

```
#version 140

uniform sampler3D Noise;

uniform vec3 MarbleColor;
uniform vec3 VeinColor;

in float LightIntensity;
in vec3  MCposition;

out vec4 FragColor;

void main()
{
    vec4 noisevec = texture(Noise, MCposition);
```

```
float intensity = abs(noisevec[0] - 0.25) +
                  abs(noisevec[1] - 0.125) +
                  abs(noisevec[2] - 0.0625) +
                  abs(noisevec[3] - 0.03125);

float sineval = sin(MCposition.y * 6.0 + intensity * 12.0) * 0.5
                + 0.5;
vec3 color    = mix(VeinColor, MarbleColor, sineval)
                  * LightIntensity;
FragColor     = vec4(color, 1.0);
}
```

15.6 Granite

With noise, it's also easy just to try to make stuff up. In this example,
I wanted to simulate a grayish rocky material with small black specks. To
generate a relatively high-frequency noise texture, I used only the fourth
component (the highest frequency one). I scaled it by an arbitrary amount
to provide an appropriate intensity level and then used this value for each
of the red, green, and blue components. The shader in Listing 15.7 generates an appearance similar to granite, as shown in Color Plate 24.

Listing 15.7   Granite fragment shader

```
#version 140

uniform sampler3D Noise;

uniform float NoiseScale;

in float LightIntensity;
in vec3  MCposition;

out vec4 FragColor;

void main()
{
    vec4 noisevec   = texture(Noise, NoiseScale * MCposition);
    float intensity = min(1.0, noisevec[3] * 18.0);
    vec3 color      . = vec3(intensity * LightIntensity);
    FragColor       = vec4(color, 1.0);
}
```

15.7 Wood

We can do a fair approximation of wood with this approach as well. In *Advanced Renderman*, Anthony A. Apodaca and Larry Gritz describe a model for simulating the appearance of wood. We can adapt their approach to create wood shaders in the OpenGL Shading Language. Here are the basic ideas behind the wood fragment shader shown in Listing 15.8:

- The wood is composed of light and dark areas alternating in concentric cylinders surrounding a central axis.

- Noise is added to warp the cylinders to create a more natural-looking pattern.

- The center of the "tree" is taken to be the y axis.

- Throughout the wood, a high-frequency grain pattern gives the appearance of wood that has been sawed, exposing the open grain nature of the wood.

The wood shader uses the same vertex shader as the other noise-based shaders discussed in this chapter.

15.7.1 Application Setup

The wood shaders don't require too much from the application. The application is expected to pass in a vertex position and a normal per vertex, using the usual OpenGL entry points. In addition, the vertex shader takes a light position and a scale factor that are passed in as uniform variables. The fragment shader takes a number of uniform variables that parameterize the appearance of the wood.

The uniform variables needed for the wood shaders are initialized as follows:

LightPos	0.0, 0.0, 4.0
Scale	2.0
LightWood	0.6, 0.3, 0.1
DarkWood	0.4, 0.2, 0.07
RingFreq	4.0
LightGrains	1.0
DarkGrains	0.0
GrainThreshold	0.5
NoiseScale	0.5, 0.1, 0.1
Noisiness	3.0
GrainScale	27.0

15.7.2 Fragment Shader

Listing 15.8 shows the fragment shader for procedurally generated wood.

Listing 15.8 Fragment shader for wood

```
#version 140

uniform sampler3D Noise;

uniform vec3 LightWood;
uniform vec3 DarkWood;
uniform float RingFreq;
uniform float LightGrains;
uniform float DarkGrains;
uniform float GrainThreshold;
uniform vec3 NoiseScale;
uniform float Noisiness;
uniform float GrainScale;

in  float LightIntensity;
in  vec3  MCposition;

out vec4  FragColor;

void main()
{
    vec3 noisevec = vec3(texture(Noise, MCposition * NoiseScale) *
                                        Noisiness);
    vec3 location = MCposition + noisevec;

    float dist = sqrt(location.x * location.x + location.z * location.z);
    dist *= RingFreq;

    float r = fract(dist + noisevec[0] + noisevec[1] + noisevec[2])
            * 2.0;

    if (r > 1.0)
       r = 2.0 - r;

    vec3 color = mix(LightWood, DarkWood, r);

    r = fract((MCposition.x + MCposition.z) * GrainScale + 0.5);
    noisevec[2] *= r;
    if (r < GrainThreshold)
       color += LightWood * LightGrains * noisevec[2];
    else
       color -= LightWood * DarkGrains * noisevec[2];

    color *= LightIntensity;
    FragColor = vec4(color, 1.0);
}
```

As you can see, we've parameterized quite a bit of this shader through the use of uniform variables to make it easy to manipulate through the application's user interface. As in many procedural shaders, the object position is the basis for computing the procedural texture. In this case, the object position is multiplied by *NoiseScale* (a **vec3** that allows us to scale the noise independently in the *x*, *y*, and *z* directions), and the computed value is used as the index into our 3D noise texture. The noise values obtained from the texture are scaled by the value *Noisiness*, which allows us to increase or decrease the contribution of the noise.

Our tree is assumed to be a series of concentric rings of alternating light wood and dark wood. To give some interest to our grain pattern, we add the noise vector to our object position. This has the effect of adding our low frequency (first octave) noise to the *x* coordinate of the position and the third octave noise to the *z* coordinate (the *y* coordinate won't be used). The result is rings that are still relatively circular but have some variation in width and distance from the center of the tree.

To compute where we are in relation to the center of the tree, we square the *x* and *z* components and take the square root of the result. This gives us the distance from the center of the tree. The distance is multiplied by *RingFreq*, a scale factor that gives the wood pattern more rings or fewer rings.

Following this, we attempt to create a function that goes from 0 up to 1.0 and then back down to 0. We add three octaves of noise to the distance value to give more interest to the wood grain pattern. We could compute different noise values here, but the ones we've already obtained will do just fine. Taking the fractional part of the resulting value gives us a function in the range [0.0, 1.0]. Multiplying this value by 2.0 gives us a function in the range [0.0, 2.0). And finally, by subtracting 1.0 from values that are greater than 1.0, we get our desired function that varies from 0 to 1.0 and back to 0.

We use this "triangle" function to compute the basic color for the fragment, using the built-in **mix** function. The **mix** function linearly blends *LightWood* and *DarkWood* according to our computed value *r*.

At this point, we would have a pretty nice result for our wood function, but we attempt to make it a little better by adding a subtle effect to simulate the look of open-grain wood that has been sawed. (You may not be able to see this effect on the object shown in Color Plate 25.)

Our desire is to produce streaks that are roughly parallel to the *y* axis. So we add the *x* and *z* coordinates, multiply by the *GrainScale* factor (another uniform variable that we can adjust to change the frequency of this effect), add 0.5, and take the fractional part of the result. Again, this gives us a function that varies from [0.0, 1.0), but for the default values for *GrainScale* (27.0) and *RingFreq* (4.0), this function for *r* goes from 0 to 1.0 much more often than our previous function for *r*.

We could just make our "grains" go linearly from light to dark, but we try something a little more subtle. We multiply the value of *r* by our third octave noise value to produce a value that increases nonlinearly. Finally, we compare our value of *r* to the *GrainThreshold* value (the default is 0.5). If the value of *r* is less than *GrainThreshold*, we modify our current color by adding to it a value we computed by multiplying the *LightWood* color, the *LightGrains* color, and our modified noise value. Conversely, if the value of *r* is greater than *GrainThreshold*, we modify our current color by subtracting from it a value we computed by multiplying the *DarkWood* color, the *DarkGrains* color, and our modified noise value. (By default, the value of *LightGrains* is 1.0, and the value of *DarkGrains* is 0, so we don't actually see any change if *r* is greater than *GrainThreshold*.)

You can play around with this effect and see if it really does help the appearance. It seemed to me that it added to the effect of the wood texture for the default settings I've chosen, but there probably is a way to achieve a better effect more simply.

With our final color computed, all that remains is to multiply the color by the interpolated diffuse lighting factor and add an alpha value of 1.0 to produce our final fragment value. The results of our shader are applied to a bust of Beethoven in Color Plate 25.

15.8 Summary

This chapter introduced noise, an incredibly useful function for adding irregularity to procedural shaders. After a brief description of the mathematical definition of this function, we used it as the basis for shaders that simulated clouds, turbulent flow, marble, granite, and wood. The noise function is available as a built-in function in the OpenGL Shading Language. Noise functions can also be created with user-defined shader functions or textures. However it is implemented, noise can increase the apparent realism of an image or an animation by adding imperfections, complexity, and an element of apparent randomness.

15.9 Further Information

Ken Perlin has a tutorial and history of the noise function as well as a recent reference implementation in the Java programming language at his Web site (www.noisemachine.com). A lot of other interesting things are available on Ken's home page at NYU (http://mrl.nyu.edu/~perlin). His paper, *An Image Synthesizer*, appeared in the 1985 SIGGRAPH proceedings, and his improvements to the original algorithm were published in the paper *Improving Noise* as part of SIGGRAPH 2002. He also described a clever method for combining two small 3D textures to get a large 3D Perlin-like noise function in the article *Implementing Improved Perlin Noise* in the book *GPU Gems*.

The book *Texturing & Modeling: A Procedural Approach, Third Edition*, by David S. Ebert et al. (2000) contains several excellent discussions on noise, and that book's Web site, www.texturingandmodeling.com contains C source code for a variety of noise functions that appear in the book, including Perlin's original noise function. Perlin has written a chapter for that book that provides more depth on his noise algorithm, and Ken Musgrave explores breathtakingly beautiful mathematical worlds based on a variety of noise functions. Planet-building software built on these ideas is available from Musgrave's company, Pandromeda, at www.pandromeda.com. In Chapter 2 of that book, Darwyn Peachey describes a variety of noise functions, and in Chapter 7, David Ebert describes an approach similar to the 3D texturing approach described previously. *Advanced RenderMan: Creating CGI for Motion Pictures* by Anthony A. Apodaca and Larry Gritz (1999) also contains a discussion of noise and presents some excellent noise-based RenderMan shaders.

[1] Apodaca, Anthony A., and Larry Gritz, *Advanced RenderMan: Creating CGI for Motion Pictures*, Morgan Kaufmann Publishers, San Francisco, 1999. www.renderman.org/RMR/Books/arman/materials.html

[2] Ebert, David S., John Hart, Bill Mark, F. Kenton Musgrave, Darwyn Peachey, Ken Perlin, and Steven Worley, *Texturing and Modeling: A Procedural Approach, Third Edition*, Morgan Kaufmann Publishers, San Francisco, 2002. www.texturingandmodeling.com

[3] Hart, John C., *Perlin Noise Pixel Shaders*, ACM SIGGRAPH/Eurographics Workshop on Graphics Hardware, pp. 87–94, August 2001. http://graphics.cs.uiuc.edu/~jch/papers/pixelnoise.pdf

[4] Perlin, Ken, *An Image Synthesizer*, Computer Graphics (SIGGRAPH '85 Proceedings), pp. 287–296, July 1985.

[5] Perlin, Ken, *Implementing Improved Perlin Noise* in *GPU Gems: Programming Techniques, Tips, and Tricks for Real-Time Graphics*, Editor: Randima Fernando, Addison-Wesley, Reading, Massachusetts, 2004. http://developer.nvidia.com/object/gpu_gems_home.html

[6] Perlin, Ken, *Improving Noise*, Computer Graphics (SIGGRAPH 2002 Proceedings), pp. 681–682, July 2002. http://mrl.nyu.edu/perlin/paper445.pdf

[7] Perlin, Ken, personal Web site. www.noisemachine.com

[8] Perlin, Ken, personal Web site. http://mrl.nyu.edu/~perlin

Chapter 16

Animation

Animation can explain whatever the mind of man can conceive. This facility makes it the most versatile and explicit means of communication yet devised for quick mass appreciation.

—Walt Disney

As Walt Disney noted, animation is largely about explanation. Rotating an object provides information about shape and form. Doing a simulated walk-through of a building gives a sense of how it would feel to be inside the building. Watching a character's facial expressions provides insight into the emotions the character is feeling.

With the latest graphics hardware and the OpenGL Shading Language, we can do even more realistic rendering in real time on low-cost graphics hardware. I was somewhat surprised when I found out how easy it was to animate programmable shaders. By developing shaders that modify their behavior over time, we can turn over even more of the rendering task to the graphics hardware.

This chapter describes how a shader can be written to produce an animation effect. Typically, the animation effect is controlled by one or more uniform variables that convey an application's sense of time. These variables pass a frame count, an elapsed time value, or some other value that can be used as the basis for chronology. If there are multiple objects in a scene and they are expected to animate in different ways, each object is rendered with its own unique shader. If objects have identical characteristics other than the animation effect, the source code for each of the shaders can be the same except for the portion that defines the animation effect.

A shader can be written to behave differently depending on these control values, and so, if they are updated at each frame, the scene is drawn slightly differently in each frame to produce the animation effect. Discontinuities in cyclical motion can be avoided by design, with a smooth overlap whereby the end of the cycle wraps back to the beginning. By controlling the animation effect in an OpenGL shader, the application need not perform any complex computations to achieve this motion. All it needs to do is update the control value(s) of each frame and redraw the object. However, the application can perform animation computations in addition to the animation effects built into a shader to produce extremely interesting effects.

Interesting animation effects can be created with stored textures, procedural textures, noise, and other mechanisms. In this chapter, we describe simple animation effects and discuss shaders for modifying the shape and position of an object and for simulating an oscillating motion.

16.1 On/Off

Suppose you have an object in the scene that must be drawn two different ways, such as a neon restaurant sign saying "OPEN" that repeatedly flashes on and off. It would certainly be possible to write two different shaders for rendering this object, one for when the sign is "on" and one for when the sign is "off." However, in a situation like this, it may actually be easier to write a single shader that takes a control variable specifying whether the object is to be drawn as on or off. The shader can be written to render one way if the control variable is on and another way if it is off.

To do this, the application would set up a uniform variable that indicates the on/off state. The application would update this variable as needed. To achieve a sequence of three seconds on and one second off, the application would write the variable with the value for on, update the value to off three seconds later, update the value to on one second later, and repeat this sequence. In the interim, the application just continually redraws the geometry every frame. The decoupling of the rendering from the animation effect might make the application a little simpler and a little more maintainable as a result.

16.2 Threshold

An improvement to the "on/off" animation is to have the application pass the shader one or more values that are tested against one or more threshold values within the shader. Using one control value and two threshold values, you could write a shader with three behaviors: one for when the control value is less than the first threshold value, one for when the control value is between the two threshold values, and one for when the control value is greater than the second threshold value.

In the case just described, you actually may have a transition period when the neon light is warming up to full brightness or dissipating to its off condition. This type of transition helps to "soften" the change between two states so that the transition appears more natural. The **smoothstep** function is handy for calculating such a transition.

16.3 Translation

We can achieve a simple animation effect for stored textures or procedural textures just by adding an offset to the texture access calculation. For instance, if we wanted to have procedural clouds that drift slowly across the sky, we could make a simple change to the cloud shader that we discussed in Section 15.4. Instead of using the object position as the index into our 3D noise texture, we add an offset value. The offset is defined as a uniform variable and can be updated by the application at each frame. If we want the clouds to drift slowly from left to right, we just subtract a small amount from the *x* component of this uniform variable each frame. If we want the clouds to move rapidly from bottom to top, we just subtract a larger amount from the *y* component of this value. To achieve a more complex effect, we might modify all three coordinates each frame. We could use a noise function in computing this offset to make the motion more natural and less like a scrolling effect.

The cloud shader as modified so as to be animatable is shown in Listing 16.1.

Listing 16.1   Animatable fragment shader for cloudy sky effect

```
#version 140

uniform sampler3D Noise;
uniform vec3 SkyColor;      // (0.0, 0.0, 0.8)
uniform vec3 CloudColor;    // (0.8, 0.8, 0.8)
```

```
uniform vec3 Offset;        // updated each frame by the application

in  float LightIntensity;
in  vec3  MCPosition;
out vec4  FragColor;

void main()
{
    vec4  noisevec  = texture(Noise, MCPosition + Offset);

    float intensity = (noisevec[0] + noisevec[1] +
                        noisevec[2] + noisevec[3]) * 0.33;

    vec3 color = mix(SkyColor, CloudColor, intensity) * LightIntensity;
    FragColor = vec4(color, 1.0);
}
```

16.4 Morphing

Another cool animation effect, called MORPHING, gradually blends between
two things. This could be used to mix two effects over a sequence of frames.
A complete animation sequence can be created by performing KEY-FRAME
INTERPOLATION. Important frames of the animation are identified, and the
frames in between them can be generated with substantially less effort.
Instead of the application doing complex calculations to determine the
proper way to render the "in between" object or effect, it can all be done
automatically within the shader.

You can blend between the geometry of two objects to create a TWEENED
(INBETWEEN) version or do a linear blend between two colors, two textures,
two procedural patterns, and so on. All it takes is a shader that uses a control
value that is the ratio of the two items being blended and that is updated
each frame by the application. In some cases, a linear blend is sufficient. For
an oscillating effect, you'll probably want to have the application compute
the interpolation factor by using a spline function to avoid jarring discontinuities in the animation. (You could have the shader compute the interpolation value, but it's better to have the application compute it once per
frame rather than have the vertex shader compute it once per vertex or have
the fragment shader compute it needlessly at every fragment.)

For instance, using generic vertex attributes, you can actually pass the
geometry for two objects at a time. The geometry for the first object would
be passed through a second of generic vertex attributes 0, 2, 4. A second set

of vertex information can be passed by means of generic vertex attributes 1, 3, 5, etc. The application can provide a blending factor through a uniform variable, and the vertex shader can use this blending factor to do a weighted average of the two sets of vertex data. The tweened vertex position is the one that actually gets transformed, the tweened normal is the one actually used for lighting calculations, and so on.

To animate a character realistically, you need to choose the right number of key frames as well as the proper number of inbetweens to use. In their classic book, *Disney Animation—The Illusion of Life,* Frank Thomas and Ollie Johnston (1995, pp. 64–65) describe this concept as "Timing" and explain it in the following way:

Just two drawings of a head, the first showing it leaning toward the right shoulder and the second with it over on the left and its chin slightly raised, can be made to communicate a multitude of ideas, depending entirely on the Timing used. Each inbetween drawing added between these two "extremes" gives a new meaning to the action.

No inbetweens	*The character has been hit by a tremendous force. His head is nearly snapped off.*
One inbetween	*. . . has been hit by a brick, rolling pin, frying pan.*
Two inbetweens	*. . . has a nervous tic, a muscle spasm, an uncontrollable twitch.*
Three inbetweens	*. . . is dodging the brick, rolling pin, frying pan.*
Four inbetweens	*. . . is giving a crisp order, "Get going!" "Move it!"*
Five inbetweens	*. . . is more friendly, "Over here." "Come on—hurry!"*
Six inbetweens	*. . . sees a good-looking girl, or the sports car he has always wanted.*
Seven inbetweens	*. . . tries to get a better look at something.*
Eight inbetweens	*. . . searches for the peanut butter on the kitchen shelf.*
Nine inbetweens	*. . . appraises, considering thoughtfully.*
Ten inbetweens	*. . . stretches a sore muscle.*

16.4.1 Sphere Morph Vertex Shader

The shader in Listing 16.2, developed by Philip Rideout, morphs between
two objects—a square that is generated by the application and a sphere that
is procedurally generated in the vertex shader. The sphere is defined
entirely by a single value—its radius—provided by the application through
a uniform variable. The application passes the geometry defining the square
to the vertex shader with the user-defined in variables *MCNormal* and
MCVertex. The vertex shader computes the corresponding vertex and normal on the sphere with a subroutine called **sphere**. The application provides
a time-varying variable (*Blend*) for morphing between these two objects.
Because we are using the two input vertex values to compute a third,
in-between, value, we cannot use the **ftransform** function. We'll transform
the computed vertex directly within the vertex shader.

Listing 16.2   Vertex shader for morphing between a plane and a sphere

```
#version 140

uniform mat4 MVPMatrix;
uniform mat4 MVMatrix;
uniform mat3 NormalMatrix;

uniform vec3 LightPosition;
uniform vec3 SurfaceColor;

uniform float Radius;
uniform float Blend;

const float PI = 3.14159;
const float TWO_PI = PI * 2.0;

in   vec4  MCVertex;
in   vec4  MCNormal;

out  vec4  Color;

vec3 sphere(vec2 domain)
{
    vec3 range;
    range.x = Radius * cos(domain.y) * sin(domain.x);
    range.y = Radius * sin(domain.y) * sin(domain.x);
    range.z = Radius * cos(domain.x);
    return range;
}

void main()
{
```

```
vec2 p0 = MCVertex.xy * TWO_PI;
vec3 normal = sphere(p0);;
vec3 r0 = Radius * normal;
vec3 vertex = r0;

normal = mix(MCNormal, normal, abs(Blend));
vertex = mix(MCVertex.xyz, vertex, abs(Blend));

normal = normalize(NormalMatrix * normal);
vec3 position = vec3(MVMatrix * vec4(vertex, 1.0));

vec3 lightVec = normalize(LightPosition - position);
float diffuse = max(dot(lightVec, normal), 0.0);

if (diffuse < 0.125)
    diffuse = 0.125;

Color = vec4(SurfaceColor * diffuse, 1.0);
gl_Position = MVPMatrix * vec4(vertex,1.0);
}
```

In this shader, a simple lighting model is used. The color value that is generated by the vertex shader is simply passed through the fragment shader to be used as our final fragment color.

The sphere is somewhat unique in that it can be procedurally generated. Another way to morph between two objects is to specify the geometry for one object and to specify the geometry for the second object, using generic vertex attributes. The shader then just has to blend between the two sets of geometry in the same manner as described for the sphere morph shader.

16.5 Other Blending Effects

Another blending effect gradually causes an object to disappear over a sequence of frames. The control value could be used as the alpha value to cause the object to be drawn totally opaque (alpha is 1.0), totally invisible (alpha is 0), or partially visible (alpha is between 0 and 1.0).

You can also fade something in or out by using the **discard** keyword. The lattice shader described in Section 11.3 discards a specific percentage of pixels in the object each time it is drawn. You could vary this percentage from 0 to 1.0 to make the object appear, or vary from 1.0 to 0 to make the object disappear. Alternatively, you could evaluate a noise function at each location on the surface and compare with this value instead. In this way, you can cause an object to erode or rust away over time.

16.6 Vertex Noise

In the previous chapter, we talked about some of the interesting and useful things that can be done with noise. Listing 16.3 shows a vertex shader by Philip Rideout that calls the built-in **noise3** function in the vertex shader and uses it to modify the shape of the object over time. The result is that the object changes its shape irregularly.

Listing 16.3   Vertex shader using noise to modify and animate an object's shape

```
#version 140

uniform vec3   LightPosition;
uniform vec3   SurfaceColor;
uniform vec3   Offset;
uniform float  ScaleIn;
uniform float  ScaleOut;

uniform mat4   MVMatrix;
uniform mat4   MVPMatrix;
uniform mat3   NormalMatrix;

in   vec4   MCVertex;
in   vec3   MCNormal;

out vec4   Color;

void main()
{
    vec3 normal = MCNormal;
    vec3 vertex = MCVertex.xyz
                + noise3(Offset + MCVertex.xyz * ScaleIn) * ScaleOut;

    normal = normalize(NormalMatrix * normal);
    vec3 position = vec3(MVMatrix * vec4(vertex,1.0));
    vec3 lightVec = normalize(LightPosition - position);
    float diffuse = max(dot(lightVec, normal), 0.0);

    if (diffuse < 0.125)
        diffuse = 0.125;

    Color = vec4(SurfaceColor * diffuse, 1.0);
    gl_Position = MVPMatrix * vec4(vertex,1.0);
}
```

The key to this shader is the call to **noise3** with a value (*Offset*) that changes over time. The vertex itself is also used as input to the **noise3** function so that the effect is repeatable. The *ScaleIn* and *ScaleOut* factors control the amplitude of the effect. The result of this computation is added to the incoming vertex position to compute a new vertex position.

16.7 Particle Systems

A new type of rendering primitive was invented by Bill Reeves and his colleagues at Lucasfilm in the early 1980s as they struggled to come up with a way to animate the fire sequence called "The Genesis Demo" in the motion picture *Star Trek II: The Wrath of Khan*. Traditional rendering methods were more suitable for rendering smooth, well-defined surfaces. What Reeves was after was a way to render a class of objects he called "fuzzy"—things like fire, smoke, liquid spray, comet tails, fireworks, and other natural phenomena. These things are fuzzy because none of them has a well-defined boundary and the components typically change over time.

The technique that Reeves invented to solve this problem was described in the 1983 paper *Particle Systems—A Technique for Modeling a Class of Fuzzy Objects*. PARTICLE SYSTEMS had been used in rendering before, but Reeves realized that he could get the particles to behave the way he wanted them to by giving each particle its own set of initial conditions and by establishing a set of probabilistic rules that governed how particles would change over time.

There are three main differences between particle systems and traditional surface-based rendering techniques. First, rather than an object being defined with polygons or curved surfaces, it is represented by a cloud of primitive particles that define its volume. Second, the object is considered dynamic rather than static. The constituent particles come into existence, evolve, and then die. During their lifetime, they can change position and form. Finally, objects defined in this manner are not completely specified. A set of initial conditions are specified, along with rules for birth, death, and evolution. Stochastic processes are used to influence all three stages, so the shape and appearance of the object is nondeterministic.

Some assumptions are usually made to simplify the rendering of particle systems, among them,

- Particles do not collide with other particles.

- Particles do not reflect light; they emit light.

- Particles do not cast shadows on other particles.

Particle attributes often include position, color, transparency, velocity, size, shape, and lifetime. For rendering a particle system, each particle's attributes are used along with certain global parameters to update its position and appearance at each frame. Each particle's position might be updated on the basis of the initial velocity vector and the effects from gravity, wind, friction, and other global factors. Each particle's color (including transparency), size, and shape can be modified as a function of global time, the age of the particle, its height, its speed, or any other parameter that can be calculated.

What are the benefits of using particle systems as a rendering technique? For one thing, complex systems can be created with little human effort. For another, the complexity can easily be adjusted. And as Reeves says in his 1983 paper, "The most important thing about particle systems is that they move: good dynamics are quite often the key to making things look real."

16.7.1 Application Setup

For this shader, my goal was to produce a shader that acted like a "confetti cannon"—something that spews out a large quantity of small, brightly colored pieces of paper. They don't come out all at once, but they come out in a steady stream until none are left. Initial velocities are somewhat random, but there is a general direction that points up and away from the origin. Gravity influences these particles and eventually brings them back to earth.

The code in Listing 16.4 shows the C subroutine that I used to create the initial values for my particle system. To accomplish the look I was after, I decided that for each particle I needed its initial position, a randomly generated color, a randomly generated initial velocity (with some constraints), and a randomly generated start time.

The subroutine **createPoints** lets you create an arbitrary-sized, two-dimensional grid of points for the particle system. There's no reason for a two-dimensional grid, but I was interested in seeing the effect of particles "popping off the grid" like pieces of popcorn. It would be even easier to define the particle system as a 1D array, and all of the vertex positions could have exactly the same initial value (for instance (0,0,0)).

But I set it up as a 2D array, and so you can pass in a width and height to define the number of particles to be created. After the memory for the arrays is allocated, a nested loop computes the values for each of the particle attributes at each grid location. Each vertex position has a y-coordinate value of 0, and the x and z coordinates vary across the grid. Each color component is assigned a random number in the range [0.5,1.0] so that mostly bright pastel colors are used. The velocity vectors are assigned random numbers to which I gave a strong upward bias by multiplying the y coordinate by 10. The general direction of the particles is aimed away from the origin by the addition of 3 to both the x and the z coordinates. Finally, each particle is given a start-time value in the range [0,10].

Listing 16.4   C subroutine to create vertex data for particles

```c
static GLint arrayWidth, arrayHeight;
static GLfloat *verts = NULL;
static GLfloat *colors = NULL;
static GLfloat *velocities = NULL;
static GLfloat *startTimes = NULL;

void createPoints(GLint w, GLint h)
{
    GLfloat *vptr, *cptr, *velptr, *stptr;
    GLfloat i, j;

    if (verts != NULL)
        free(verts);

    verts  = malloc(w * h * 3 * sizeof(float));
    colors = malloc(w * h * 3 * sizeof(float));
    velocities = malloc(w * h * 3 * sizeof(float));
    startTimes = malloc(w * h * sizeof(float));

    vptr = verts;
    cptr = colors;
    velptr = velocities;
    stptr  = startTimes;

    for (i = 0.5 / w - 0.5; i < 0.5; i = i + 1.0/w)
        for (j = 0.5 / h - 0.5; j < 0.5; j = j + 1.0/h)
        {
            *vptr       = i;
            *(vptr + 1) = 0.0;
            *(vptr + 2) = j;
            vptr += 3;

            *cptr       = ((float) rand() / RAND_MAX) * 0.5 + 0.5;
            *(cptr + 1) = ((float) rand() / RAND_MAX) * 0.5 + 0.5;
            *(cptr + 2) = ((float) rand() / RAND_MAX) * 0.5 + 0.5;
            cptr += 3;

            *velptr       = (((float) rand() / RAND_MAX)) + 3.0;
            *(velptr + 1) =  ((float) rand() / RAND_MAX) * 10.0;
            *(velptr + 2) = (((float) rand() / RAND_MAX)) + 3.0;
            velptr += 3;

            *stptr = ((float) rand() / RAND_MAX) * 10.0;
            stptr++;
        }

    arrayWidth  = w;
    arrayHeight = h;
}
```

We need to use generic vertex attributes to specify the particle's position, color, initial velocity, and start time. Let's pick indices 3 and 4 and define the necessary constants:

```
#define VERTEX_ARRAY 1
#define COLOR_ARRAY 2
#define VELOCITY_ARRAY 3
#define START_TIME_ARRAY 4
```

After we have created a program object, we can bind a generic vertex attribute index to a vertex shader attribute variable name. (We can do this even before the vertex shader is attached to the program object.) These bindings are checked and go into effect at the time **glLinkProgram** is called. To bind the generic vertex attribute index to a vertex shader variable name, we do the following:

```
glBindAttribLocation(ProgramObject, VERTEX_ARRAY, "MCVertex");
glBindAttribLocation(ProgramObject, COLOR_ARRAY, "MColor");
glBindAttribLocation(ProgramObject, VELOCITY_ARRAY, "Velocity");
glBindAttribLocation(ProgramObject, START_TIME_ARRAY, "StartTime");
```

After the shaders are compiled, attached to the program object, and linked, we're ready to draw the particle system. All we need to do is call the **drawPoints** function shown in Listing 16.5. In this function, we set the point size to 2 to render somewhat larger points. The next four lines of code set up pointers to the vertex arrays that we're using. In this case, we have four: one for vertex positions (i.e., initial particle position), one for particle color, one for initial velocity, and one for the particle's start time (i.e., birth). After that, we enable the arrays for drawing by making calls to **glEnableVertexAttribArray** for the generic vertex attributes. Next we call **glDrawArrays** to render the points, and finally, we clean up by disabling each of the enabled vertex arrays.

Listing 16.5 C subroutine to draw particles as points

```
void drawPoints()
{

    glPointSize(2.0);

    glVertexAttribPointer(VERTEX_ARRAY,      3, GL_FLOAT,
                            GL_FALSE, 0, verts);
    glVertexAttribPointer(COLOR_ARRAY,       3, GL_FLOAT,
                            GL_FALSE, 0, colors);
    glVertexAttribPointer(VELOCITY_ARRAY,    3, GL_FLOAT,
                            GL_FALSE, 0, velocities);
```

```
glVertexAttribPointer(START_TIME_ARRAY, 1, GL_FLOAT,
                      GL_FALSE,  0, startTimes);

glEnableVertexAttribArray(VERTEX_ARRAY);
glEnableVertexAttribArray(COLOR_ARRAY);
glEnableVertexAttribArray(VELOCITY_ARRAY);
glEnableVertexAttribArray(START_TIME_ARRAY);

glDrawArrays(GL_POINTS, 0, arrayWidth * arrayHeight);

glDisableVertexAttribArray(VERTEX_ARRAY);
glDisableVertexAttribArray(COLOR_ARRAY);
glDisableVertexAttribArray(VELOCITY_ARRAY);
glDisableVertexAttribArray(START_TIME_ARRAY);
}
```

To achieve the animation effect, the application must communicate its notion of time to the vertex shader, as shown in Listing 16.6. Here, the variable *ParticleTime* is incremented once each frame and loaded into the uniform variable *Time*. This allows the vertex shader to perform computations that vary (animate) over time.

Listing 16.6   C code snippet to update the time variable each frame

```
if (DoingParticles)
{
    location = glGetUniformLocation(ProgramObject, "Time");
    ParticleTime += 0.001f;
    glUniform1f(location, ParticleTime);
    CheckOglError();
}
```

16.7.2 Confetti Cannon Vertex Shader

The vertex shader (see Listing 16.7) is the key to this example of particle system rendering. Instead of simply transforming the incoming vertex, we use it as the initial position to compute a new position based on a computation involving the uniform variable *Time*. It is this newly computed position that is actually transformed and rendered.

This vertex shader defines the in variables *MCVertex*, *MColor*, *Velocity*, and *StartTime*. In the previous section, we saw how generic vertex attribute arrays were defined and bound to these vertex shader attribute variables. As a result of this, each vertex has an updated value for the in variables *MCVertex*, *MColor*, *Velocity*, and *StartTime*.

The vertex shader starts by computing the age of the particle. If this value is less than zero, the particle has not yet been born. In this case, the particle is just assigned the color provided through the uniform variable *Background*. (If you actually want to see the grid of yet-to-be-born particles, you could provide a color value other than the background color. And if you want to be a bit more clever, you could pass the value *t* as a varying variable to the fragment shader and let it discard fragments for which *t* is less than zero. For our purposes, this wasn't necessary.)

If a particle's start time is less than the current time, the following kinematic equation is used to determine its current position:

$$P = P_i + vt + \frac{1}{2}at^2$$

In this equation P_i represents the initial position of the particle, *v* represents the initial velocity, *t* represents the elapsed time, *a* represents the acceleration, and *P* represents the final computed position. For acceleration, we use the value of acceleration due to gravity on Earth, which is 9.8 meters per second^2. In our simplistic model, we assume that gravity affects only the particle's height (*y* coordinate) and that the acceleration is negative (i.e., the particle is slowing down and falling back to the ground). The coefficient for the t^2 term in the preceding equation therefore appears in our code as the constant –4.9, and it is applied only to *vert.y*.

After this, all that remains is to transform the computed vertex and store the result in *gl_Position*.

Listing 16.7   Confetti cannon (particle system) vertex shader

```
#version 140

uniform float Time;                 // updated each frame by the application
uniform vec4  Background;           // constant color equal to background

uniform mat4  MVPMatrix;

in   vec4  MCVertex;
in   vec4  MColor;

in   vec3  Velocity;        // initial velocity
in   float StartTime;       // time at which particle is activated

out vec4  Color;
```

```
void main()
{
    vec4   vert;
    float t = Time - StartTime;

    if (t >= 0.0)
    {
        vert    = MCVertex + vec4(Velocity * t, 0.0);
        vert.y -= 4.9 * t * t;
        Color   = MColor;
    }
    else
    {
        vert  = MCVertex;         // Initial position
        Color = Background;       // "pre-birth" color
    }

    gl_Position  = MVPMatrix * vert;
}
```

The value computed by the vertex shader is simply passed through the fragment shader to become the final color of the fragment to be rendered. Some frames from the confetti cannon animation sequence are shown in Figure 16.1.

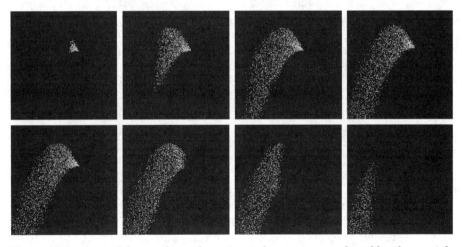

Figure 16.1   Several frames from the animated sequence produced by the particle system shader. In this animation, the particle system contains 10,000 points with randomly assigned initial velocities and start times. The position of the particle at each frame is computed entirely in the vertex shader according to a formula that simulates the effects of gravity. (3Dlabs, Inc.)

16.7.3 Further Enhancements

There's a lot that you can do to make this shader more interesting. You might pass the *t* value from the vertex shader to the fragment shader as suggested earlier and make the color of the particle change over time. For instance, you could make the color change from yellow to red to black to simulate an explosion. You could reduce the alpha value over time to make the particle fade out. You might also provide a "time of death" and extinguish the particle completely at a certain time or when a certain distance from the origin is reached. Instead of drawing the particles as points, you might draw them as short lines so that you could blur the motion of each particle. You could also vary the size of the point (or line) over time to create particles that grow or shrink. You can make the physics model a lot more sophisticated than the one illustrated. To make the particles look better, you could render them as point sprites. A point sprite is a point that is rendered as a textured quadrilateral that always faces the viewer.

The real beauty in doing particle systems within a shader is that the computation is done completely in graphics hardware rather than on the host CPU. If the particle system data is stored in a vertex buffer object, there's a good chance that it will be stored in the on-board memory of the graphics hardware, so you won't even be using up any I/O bus bandwidth as you render the particle system each frame. With the OpenGL Shading Language, the equation for updating each particle can be arbitrarily complex. And, because the particle system is rendered like any other 3D object, you can rotate it around and view it from any angle while it is animating. There's really no end to the effects (and the fun!) that you can have with particle systems.

16.8 Wobble

The previous three examples discussed animating the geometry of an object and used the vertex processor to achieve this animation (because the geometry of an object cannot be modified by the fragment processor). The fragment processor can also create animation effects. The main purpose of most fragment shaders is to compute the fragment color, and any of the factors that affect this computation can be varied over time. In this section, we look at a shader that perturbs the texture coordinates in a time-varying way to achieve an oscillating or wobbling effect. With the right texture, this effect can make it very simple to produce an animated effect to simulate a gelatinous surface or a "dancing" logo.

This shader was developed to mimic the wobbly 2D effects demonstrated in some of the real-time graphics demos that are available on the Web (see www.scene.org for some examples). Its author, Antonio Tejada, wanted to use the OpenGL Shading Language to create a similar effect.

The central premise of the shader is that a sine function is used in the fragment shader to perturb the texture coordinates before the texture lookup operation. The amount and frequency of the perturbation can be controlled through uniform variables sent by the application. Because the goal of the shader was to produce an effect that looked good, the accuracy of the sine computation was not critical. For this reason and because the sine function had not been implemented at the time he wrote this shader, Antonio chose to approximate the sine value by using the first two terms of the Taylor series for sine. The fragment shader would have been simpler if the built-in **sin** function had been used, but this approach demonstrates that numerical methods can be used as needed within a shader. (As to whether using two terms of the Taylor series would result in better performance than using the built-in **sin** function, it's hard to say. It probably varies from one graphics hardware vendor to the next, depending on how the **sin** function is implemented.)

For this shader to work properly, the application must provide the frequency and amplitude of the wobbles, as well as a light position. In addition, the application increments a uniform variable called *StartRad* at each frame. This value is used as the basis for the perturbation calculation in the fragment shader. By incrementing the value at each frame, we animate the wobble effect. The application must provide the vertex position, the surface normal, and the texture coordinate at each vertex of the object to be rendered.

The vertex shader for the wobble effect is responsible for a simple lighting computation based on the surface normal and the light position provided by the application. It passes along the texture coordinate without modification. This is exactly the same as the functionality of the earth vertex shader described in Section 10.2.2, so we can simply use that vertex shader.

The fragment shader to achieve the wobbling effect is shown in Listing 16.8. It receives as input the varying variable *LightIntensity* as computed by the vertex shader. This variable is used at the very end to apply a lighting effect to the fragment. The uniform variable *StartRad* provides the starting point for the perturbation computation in radians, and it is incremented by the application at each frame to animate the wobble effect. We can make the wobble effect go faster by using a larger increment value, and we can make it go slower by using a smaller increment amount. We found that an increment value of about 1° gave visually pleasing results.

The frequency and amplitude of the wobbles can be adjusted by the application with the uniform variables *Freq* and *Amplitude*. These are defined as **vec2** variables so that the *x* and *y* components can be adjusted independently. The final uniform variable defined by this fragment shader is *WobbleTex*, which specifies the texture unit to be used for accessing the 2D texture that is to be wobbled.

For the Taylor series approximation for sine to give more precise results, it is necessary to ensure that the value for which sine is computed is in the range [−π/2,π/2]. The constants C_PI (π), C_2PI (2π), C_2PI_I (1/2π), and C_PI_2 (π/2) are defined to assist in this process.

The first half of the fragment shader computes a perturbation factor for the *x* direction. We want to end up with a perturbation factor that depends on both the *s* and the *t* components of the texture coordinate. To this end, the local variable *rad* is computed as a linear function of the *s* and *t* values of the texture coordinate. (A similar but different expression computes the *y* perturbation factor in the second half of the shader.) The current value of *StartRad* is added. Finally, the *x* component of *Freq* is used to scale the result.

The value for *rad* increases as the value for *StartRad* increases. As the scaling factor *Freq.x* increases, the frequency of the wobbles also increases. The scaling factor should be increased as the size of the texture increases on the screen to keep the apparent frequency of the wobbles the same at different scales. You can think of the *Freq* uniform variable as the Richter scale for wobbles. A value of 0 results in no wobbles whatsoever. A value of 1.0 results in gentle rocking, a value of 2.0 causes jiggling, a value of 4.0 results in wobbling, and a value of 8.0 results in magnitude 8.0 earthquakelike effects.

The next seven lines of the shader bring the value of *rad* into the range [−π/2,π/2]. When this is accomplished, we can compute **sin**(*rad*) by using the first two terms of the Taylor series for sine, which is just $x - x^3/3!$ The result of this computation is multiplied by the *x* component of *Amplitude*. The value for the computed sine value will be in the range [−1,1]. If we just add this value to the texture coordinate as the perturbation factor, it will *really* perturb the texture coordinate. We want a wobble, not an explosion! Multiplying the computed sine value by a value of 0.05 results in reasonably sized wobbles. Increasing this scale factor makes the wobbles bigger, and decreasing it makes them smaller. You can think of this as how far the texture coordinate is stretched from its original value. Using a value of

0.05 means that the perturbation alters the original texture coordinate by no more than ±0.05. A value of 0.5 means that the perturbation alters the original texture coordinate by no more than ±0.5.

With the *x* perturbation factor computed, the whole process is repeated to compute the *y* perturbation factor. This computation is also based on a linear function of the *s* and *t* texture coordinate values, but it differs from that used for the *x* perturbation factor. Computing the *y* perturbation value differently avoids symmetries between the *x* and *y* perturbation factors in the final wobbling effect, which doesn't look as good when animated.

With the perturbation factors computed, we can finally do our (perturbed) texture access. The color value that is retrieved from the texture map is multiplied by *LightIntensity* to compute the final color value for the fragment. Several frames from the animation produced by this shader are shown in Color Plate 28. These frames show the shader applied to a logo to illustrate the perturbation effects more clearly in static images. But the animation effect is also quite striking when the texture used looks like the surface of water, lava, slime, or even animal/monster skin.

Listing 16.8   Fragment shader for wobble effect

```
#version 140

// Constants
const float C_PI    = 3.1415;
const float C_2PI   = 2.0 * C_PI;
const float C_2PI_I = 1.0 / (2.0 * C_PI);
const float C_PI_2  = C_PI / 2.0;

uniform float StartRad;
uniform vec2  Freq;
uniform vec2  Amplitude;

uniform sampler2D WobbleTex;

in   float LightIntensity;
in   vec2  TexCoord;

out vec4  FragColor;

void main()
{
    vec2  perturb;
    float rad;
    vec3  color;
```

```
// Compute a perturbation factor for the x direction
rad = (TexCoord.s + TexCoord.t - 1.0 + StartRad) * Freq.x;

// Wrap to -2.0*PI, 2*PI
rad = rad * C_2PI_I;
rad = fract(rad);
rad = rad * C_2PI;

// Center in -PI, PI
if (rad >  C_PI) rad = rad - C_2PI;
if (rad < -C_PI) rad = rad + C_2PI;

// Center in -PI/2, PI/2
if (rad >  C_PI_2) rad =  C_PI - rad;
if (rad < -C_PI_2) rad = -C_PI - rad;

perturb.x = (rad - (rad * rad * rad / 6.0)) * Amplitude.x;

// Now compute a perturbation factor for the y direction
rad = (TexCoord.s - TexCoord.t + StartRad) * Freq.y;

// Wrap to -2*PI, 2*PI
rad = rad * C_2PI_I;
rad = fract(rad);
rad = rad * C_2PI;

// Center in -PI, PI
if (rad >  C_PI) rad = rad - C_2PI;
if (rad < -C_PI) rad = rad + C_2PI;

// Center in -PI/2, PI/2
if (rad >  C_PI_2) rad =  C_PI - rad;
if (rad < -C_PI_2) rad = -C_PI - rad;

perturb.y = (rad - (rad * rad * rad / 6.0)) * Amplitude.y;

color = vec3(texture(WobbleTex, perturb + TexCoord.st));

FragColor = vec4(color * LightIntensity, 1.0);
}
```

16.9 Animating Once per Frame

If you are mulling over what it means to combine animation in shaders, such as the confetti cannon, with some of the effects we covered earlier, such as shadowing, you might begin to worry about what such combinations imply. We would have to animate the confetti for each cannon, for each of several lights, and then finally from the eye view. Suddenly it seems that doing animation in vertex shaders can be fairly expensive. It can be so expensive in some cases that perhaps it is better to keep the animation with the application on the host CPU.

The answer to this dilemma is fairly simple. Animate only once per frame. OpenGL 3.0 introduces Transform Feedback, which allows the application to capture vertex shader out variables in buffer objects. The vertex animation pass can be done once per frame to capture the transformed vertices and attributes in buffer objects. The buffer objects can then be used in subsequent light and eye passes. Brilliant!

We can make some very small changes in the confetti cannon vertex shader in Listing 16.7:

```
out vec4 Position;
// ...
// gl_Position = MVPMatrix * vert;
Position = MCtoWorldMatrix * vert;
```

The vertex shader no longer must write the special out variable *gl_Position*. And instead of transforming the position to clip space, which is specific to a specific view and projection, the vertex shader transforms the position to world coordinates.

16.9.1 Application Setup

There are four simple steps to enable transform feedback. First, the application must specify what out variables to record in the transform feedback buffer. In this example, we will be recording *Position* and *Color* into separate feedback buffers:

```
GLchar outStrings[2] = { "Position", "Color" };
glTransformFeedbackVaryings(ProgramObject, 2,
                        outStrings, GL_SEPARATE_ATTRIBS )
```

These bindings are checked and go into effect at the time **glLinkProgram** is called.

Next, the application must bind buffer objects of the appropriate size to the transform feedback buffer binding points:

```
glBindBufferBase(GL_TRANSFORM_FEEDBACK_BUFFER, 0, BufferObjectPosition);
glBindBufferBase(GL_TRANSFORM_FEEDBACK_BUFFER, 1, BufferObjectColor);
```

A small modification to the original draw call is all that is needed to record the vertex out variables to the transform feedback buffer:

```
glBeginTransformFeedback(GL_POINTS);
glDrawArrays(GL_POINTS, 0, arrayWidth * arrayHeight);
glEndTransformFeedback();
```

Finally, unbind the buffer objects from the transform feedback binding points, and bind them to vertex array binding points. But to avoid undefined behavior, be careful not to leave buffer objects bound to both transform feedback binding points and vertex array binding points.

16.9.2 Updating Matrices Once per Frame

Related to animating models, animating the camera and lights involves updating several common matrices. These need to be updated only once per frame, yet with user-defined uniforms they need to be updated for each and every program.

OpenGL 3.1 adds named uniform blocks. These named uniform blocks are backed by buffer objects. We can use a transform feedback buffer to record the output of a vertex shader. This vertex shader is designed to output to a single transform feedback buffer (with the buffer mode **GL_INTERLEAVED_ATTRIBUTES**). The recording rules for output to a transform feedback buffer coincidentally match the layout rule "std140" for named uniform blocks. (For details of the layout rule "std140," see the OpenGL Shading Language specification.)

We can render a single point to record to a transform feedback buffer and then bind that buffer object to a uniform buffer. All shaders that use that named uniform buffer are updated only once per frame.

This simple example takes two uniform matrices, *MVMatrix* and *PMatrix* as inputs, and it outputs the original *MVMatrix* as well as the derived matrices *MVPMatrix* and *NormalMatrix*:

```
#version 140

uniform mat4 MVMatrix;
uniform mat4 PMatrix;

out mat4    MV;
out mat4    MVP;
out mat3x4  N;

//
```

```
// Vertex shader that records transform feedback buffer
// that can be used with this named uniform block:
//
// layout (std140,column_major) uniform TransformBlock
// {
//      uniform mat4 MVMatrix;
//      uniform mat4 MVPmatrix;
//      uniform mat3 NormalMatrix;
// }
//
void main()
{
   MV = MVMatrix;
   MVP = PMatrix*MV;
   mat4 MVI = inverse(MV);
   mat4 MVIT = transpose(MVI);
   N = mat3x4(MVIT); // the last element of each column is a pad
}
```

This simple example can be readily extended. Many of the transformation functions in Chapter 9 can be combined in useful ways here.

16.10 Summary

With the fixed functionality in previous versions of OpenGL, animation effects were strictly in the domain of the application and had to be computed on the host CPU. With programmability, it has become easy to specify animation effects within a shader and let the graphics hardware do this work. Just about any aspect of a shader—position, shape, color, texture coordinates, and lighting, to name just a few—can be varied according to a global definition of current time.

When you develop a shader for an object that will be in motion, you should also consider how much of the animation effect you can encode within the shader. Encoding animation effects within a shader can offload the CPU and simplify the code in the application. This chapter described some simple ways for doing this. On and off, scrolling, and threshold effects are quite easy to do within a shader. Key-frame interpolation can be supported in a simple way through the power of programmability. Particles can be animated, including their position, color, velocity, and any other important attributes. Objects and textures can be made to oscillate, move, grow, or change based on mathematical expressions. "Cameras" and "lights" can move in ways natural for the application and derive the matrices necessary for efficient operation.

Animation is a powerful tool for conveying information, and the OpenGL Shading Language provides another avenue for expressing animation effects.

16.11 Further Information

If you're serious about animated effects, you really should read *Disney Animation: The Illusion of Life* by two of the "Nine Old Men" of Disney animation fame, Frank Thomas and Ollie Johnston (1981). This book is loaded with color images and insight into the development of the animation art form at Disney Studios. It contains several decades worth of information about making great animated films. If you can, try to find a used copy of the original printing from Abbeville Press rather than the reprint by Hyperion. A softcover version was also printed by Abbeville, but this version eliminates much of the history of Disney Studios. A brief encapsulation of some of the material in this book can be found in the 1987 SIGGRAPH paper *Principles of Traditional Animation Applied to 3D Computer Animation* by John Lasseter.

Rick Parent's 2001 book, *Computer Animation: Algorithms and Techniques*, contains descriptions of a variety of algorithms for computer animation. The book *Game Programming Gems*, edited by Mark DeLoura (2000), also has several pertinent sections on animation.

Particle systems were first described by Bill Reeves in his 1983 SIGGRAPH paper, *Particle Systems—A Technique for Modeling a Class of Fuzzy Objects*. In 1998, Jeff Lander wrote an easy-to-follow description of particle systems, titled "The Ocean Spray in Your Face," in his column for *Game Developer Magazine*. He also made source code available for a simple OpenGL-based particle system demonstration program that he wrote.

[1] DeLoura, Mark, ed., *Game Programming Gems*, Charles River Media, Hingham, Massachusetts, 2000.

[2] Lander, Jeff, *The Ocean Spray in Your Face*, Game Developer Magazine, vol. 5, no. 7, pp. 13–19, July 1998. www.darwin3d.com/gdm1998.htm

[3] Lasseter, John, *Principles of Traditional Animation Applied to 3D Computer Animation*, Computer Graphics, (SIGGRAPH '87 Proceedings), pp. 35–44, July 1987.

[4] Parent, Rick, *Computer Animation: Algorithms and Techniques*, Morgan Kaufmann Publishers, San Francisco, 2001.

[5] Reeves, William T., *Particle Systems—A Technique for Modeling a Class of Fuzzy Objects*, ACM Transactions on Graphics, vol. 2, no. 2, pp. 91–108, April 1983.

[6] Reeves, William T., and Ricki Blau, *Approximate and Probabilistic Algorithms for Shading and Rendering Structured Particle Systems*, Computer Graphics (SIGGRAPH '85 Proceedings), pp. 313–322, July 1985.

[7] Thomas, Frank, and Ollie Johnston, *Disney Animation—The Illusion of Life,* Abbeville Press, New York, 1981.

[8] Thomas, Frank, and Ollie Johnston, *The Illusion of Life—Disney Animation, Revised Edition*, Hyperion, 1995.

[9] Watt, Alan H., and Mark Watt, *Advanced Animation and Rendering Techniques: Theory and Practice,* Addison-Wesley, Reading, Massachusetts, 1992.

Chapter 17

Antialiasing
Procedural Textures

Jaggies, popping, sparkling, stair steps, strobing, and marching ants. They're all names used to describe the anathema of computer graphics—ALIASING. Anyone who has used a computer has seen it. For still images, it's not always that noticeable or objectionable. But as soon as you put an object in motion, the movement of the jagged edges catches your eye and distracts you. From the early days of computer graphics, the fight to eliminate these nasty artifacts has been called ANTIALIASING.

This chapter does not contain a thorough description of the causes of aliasing, nor the methods used to combat it. But it does introduce the reasons the problem occurs and the facilities within the OpenGL Shading Language for antialiasing. Armed with this knowledge, you should be well on your way to fighting the jaggies in your own shaders.

17.1 Sources of Aliasing

The human eye is extremely good at noticing edges. This is how we comprehend shape and form and how we recognize letters and words. Our eye is naturally good at it, and we spend our whole lives practicing it, so naturally it is something we do very, very well.

A computer display is limited in its capability to present an image. The display is made up of a finite number of discrete elements called PIXELS. At a given time, each pixel can produce only one color. This makes it impossible for a computer display to accurately represent detail that is smaller than one pixel in screen space, such as an edge.

When you combine these two things, the human eye's ability to discern edges and the computer graphics display's limitations in replicating them, you have a problem, and this problem is known as aliasing. In a nutshell, aliasing occurs when we try to reproduce a signal with an insufficient sampling frequency. With a computer graphics display, we'll always have a fixed number of samples (pixels) with which to reconstruct our image, and this will always be insufficient to provide adequate sampling, so we will always have aliasing. We can reduce it to the point that it's not noticeable, or we can transform it into some other problem that is less objectionable, like blurriness or noise.

The problem is illustrated in Figure 17.1. In this diagram, we show the results of trying to draw a gray object. The intended shape is shown in Figure 17.1 (A). The computer graphics display limits us to a discrete sampling grid. If we choose only one location within each grid square (usually the center) and determine the color to be used by sampling the desired image at that point, we see some apparent artifacts. This is called POINT SAMPLING and is illustrated in Figure 17.1 (B). The result is ugly aliasing artifacts for edges that don't line up naturally with the sampling grid (see Figure 17.1 (C)). (The drawing is idealized because pixels on a standard CRT do not produce light in the shape of a square, but the artifacts are obvious even when the sampled points are reconstructed as overlapping circles on the computer display.)

Aliasing takes on other forms as well. If you are developing a sequence of images for an animation and you don't properly sample objects that are in

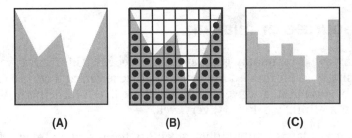

(A)   (B)   (C)

Figure 17.1   Aliasing artifacts caused by point sampling. The gray region represents the shape of the object to be rendered (A). The computer graphics display presents us with a limited sampling grid (B). The result of choosing to draw or not draw gray at each pixel results in jaggies, or aliasing artifacts (C).

motion, you might notice TEMPORAL ALIASING. This is caused by objects that are moving too rapidly for the sampling frequency being used. Objects may appear to stutter as they move or blink on and off. The classic example of temporal aliasing comes from the movies: A vehicle (car, truck, or covered wagon) in motion is going forward, but the spokes of its wheels appear to be rotating backwards. This effect is caused when the sampling rate (movie frames per second) is too low relative to the motion of the wheel spokes. In reality, the wheel may be rotating two- and three-quarter revolutions per frame, but on film it looks like it's rotating one-quarter revolution *backwards* each frame.

To render images that look truly realistic rather than computer generated, we need to develop techniques for overcoming the inherent limitations of the graphics display.

17.2 Avoiding Aliasing

One way to achieve good results without aliasing is to avoid situations in which aliasing occurs.

For instance, if you know that a particular object will always be a certain size in the final rendered image, you can design a shader that looks good while rendering that object at that size. This is the assumption behind some of the shaders presented previously in this book. The **smoothstep**, **mix**, and **clamp** functions are handy functions to use to avoid sharp transitions and to make a procedural texture look good at a particular scale.

Aliasing is often a problem when you are rendering an object at different sizes. Mipmap textures address this very issue, and you can do something similar with shaders. If you know that a particular object must appear at different sizes in the final rendering, you can design a shader for each different size. Each of these shaders would provide an appropriate level of detail and avoid aliasing for an object of that size. For this to work, the application must determine the approximate size of the final rendered object before it is drawn and then install the appropriate shader. In addition, if a continuous zoom (in or out) is applied to a single object, some "popping" will occur when the level of detail changes.

You can avoid aliasing in some situations by using a texture instead of computing something procedurally. This lets you take advantage of the FILTERING (i.e., antialiasing) support that is built into the texture-mapping hardware. However, there are issues with using stored textures as opposed to doing things procedurally, as discussed in Chapter 11.

17.3 Increasing Resolution

The effects of aliasing can be reduced through a brute force method called SUPERSAMPLING that performs sampling at several locations within a pixel and averages the result of those samples. This is exactly the approach supported in today's graphics hardware with the multisample buffer. This method of antialiasing replaces a single point sampling operation with several, so it doesn't actually eliminate aliasing, but it can reduce aliasing to the point that it is no longer objectionable. You may be able to ignore the issue of aliasing if your shaders will always be used in conjunction with a multisample buffer.

But this approach does use up hardware resources (graphics board memory for storing the multisample buffer), and even with hardware acceleration, it still may be slower than performing the antialiasing as part of the procedural texture-generation algorithm. And, because this approach doesn't eliminate aliasing, your texture is still apt to exhibit signs of aliasing, albeit at a higher frequency than before.

Supersampling is illustrated in Figure 17.2. Each of the pixels is rendered by sampling at four locations rather than at one. The average of the four samples is used as the value for the pixel. This averaging provides a better result, but it is not sufficient to eliminate aliasing because high-frequency components can still be misrepresented.

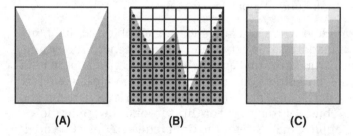

(A)   (B)   (C)

Figure 17.2   Supersampling with four samples per pixel yields a better result, but aliasing artifacts are still present. The shape of the object to be rendered is shown in (A). Sampling occurs at four locations within each pixel as shown in (B). The results are averaged to produce the final pixel value as shown in (C). Some samples that are almost half covered were sampled with just one supersample point instead of two, and one pixel contains image data that was missed entirely, even with supersampling.

Supersampling can also be implemented within a fragment shader. The code that is used to produce the fragment color can be constructed as a function, and this function can be called several times from within the main function of the fragment shader to sample the function at several discrete locations. The returned values can be averaged to create the final value for the fragment. Results are improved if the sample positions are varied stochastically rather than spaced on a regular grid. Supersampling within a fragment shader has the obvious downside of requiring N times as much processing per fragment, where N is the number of samples computed at each fragment.

There will be times when aliasing is unavoidable and supersampling is infeasible. If you want to perform procedural texturing and you want a single shader that is useful at a variety of scales, there's little choice but to address the aliasing issue and take steps to counteract aliasing in your shaders.

17.4   Antialiased Stripe Example

Aliasing does not occur until we attempt to represent a continuous image in screen space. This conversion occurs during rasterization; therefore, our attempts to mitigate its effects always occur in the fragment shader. The OpenGL Shading Language has several functions for this purpose that are available only to fragment shaders. To help explain the motivation for some of the language facilities for filter estimation, we develop a "worst case" scenario—alternating black and white stripes drawn on a sphere. Developing a fragment shader that performs antialiasing enables us to further illustrate the aliasing problem and the methods for reducing aliasing artifacts. Bert Freudenberg developed the first version of the GLSL shaders discussed in this section during the process of creating the antialiased hatching shader described in Section 18.1.

17.4.1   Generating Stripes

The antialiasing fragment shader determines whether each fragment is to be drawn as white or black to create lines on the surface of an object. The first step is to determine the method to be used for drawing lines. We use a single parameter as the basis for our stripe pattern. For illustration, let's assume that the parameter is the s coordinate of the object's texture coordinate. We have the vertex shader pass this value to us as a floating-point out variable named *V,* eventually giving us a method for creating vertical stripes on a sphere. Figure 17.3 (A) shows the result of using the *s* texture coordinate directly as the intensity (grayscale) value on the surface of the sphere. The viewing position is slightly above the sphere, so we are looking down at the "north pole." The *s* texture coordinate starts off at 0 (black) and increases to 1 (white) as it goes around the sphere. The edge where black meets white can be seen at the pole, and it runs down the back side of the sphere. The front side of the sphere looks mostly gray but increases from left to right.

We create a sawtooth wave by multiplying the *s* texture coordinate by 16 and taking the fractional part (see Figure 17.3 (B)). This causes the intensity value to start at 0, rise quickly to 1, and then drop back down to 0. (To get a feel for what a sawtooth wave looks like, see the illustrations for the built-in functions **fract** (refer to Figure 5.6) and **mod** (refer to Figure 5.7).) This sequence is repeated 16 times. The OpenGL shader code to implement this is

```
float sawtooth = fract(V * 16.0);
```

This isn't quite the stripe pattern we're after. To get closer, we employ the absolute value function (see Figure 17.3 (C)). By multiplying the value of *sawtooth* by 2 and subtracting 1, we get a function that varies in the range [–1,1]. Taking the absolute value of this function results in a function that

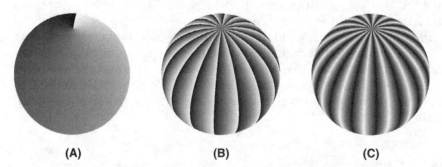

(A)   (B)   (C)

Figure 17.3   Using the *s* texture coordinate to create stripes on a sphere. In (A), the *s* texture coordinate is used directly as the intensity (gray) value. In (B), a modulus function creates a sawtooth function. In (C), the absolute value function turns the sawtooth function into a triangle function. (Courtesy of Bert Freudenberg, University of Magdeburg, 2002.)

goes from 1 down to 0 and then back to 1 (i.e., a *triangle* wave). The line of code to do this is

```
float triangle = abs(2.0 * sawtooth - 1.0);
```

A stripe pattern is starting to appear, but it's either too blurry or our glasses need adjustment. We make the stripes pure black and white by using the **step** function. When we compare our triangle variable to 0.5, this function returns 0 whenever *triangle* is less than or equal to 0.5, and 1 whenever *triangle* is greater than 0.5. This could be written as

```
float square = step(0.5, triangle);
```

This effectively produces a square wave, and the result is illustrated in Figure 17.4 (A). We can modify the relative size of the alternating stripes by adjusting the threshold value provided in the **step** function.

17.4.2 Analytic Prefiltering

In Figure 17.4 (A), we see that the stripes are now distinct, but aliasing has reared its ugly head. The **step** function returns values that are either 0 or 1, with nothing in between, so the jagged edges in the transitions between white and black are easy to spot. They will not go away if we increase the resolution of the image; they'll just be smaller. The problem is caused by the fact that the **step** function introduced an immediate transition from white to black or an edge with infinite frequency (see Figure 5.11). There is no way to sample this transition at a high enough frequency to eliminate the aliasing artifacts. To get good results, we need to take steps within our shader to remove such high frequencies.

A variety of antialiasing techniques rely on eliminating extremely high frequencies before sampling. This is called LOW-PASS FILTERING because low frequencies are passed through unmodified, whereas high frequencies are eliminated. The visual effect of low-pass filtering is that the resulting image is blurred.

To eliminate the high frequencies from the stripe pattern, we use the **smoothstep** function. We know that this function produces a smooth transition between white and black. It requires that we specify two edges, and a smooth transition occurs between those two edges. Figure 17.4 (B) illustrates the result from the following line of code:

```
float square = smoothstep(0.4, 0.6, triangle);
```

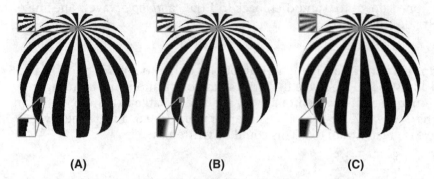

(A)   (B)   (C)

Figure 17.4   Antialiasing the stripe pattern. We can see that the square wave produced by the **step** function produces aliasing artifacts (A). The **smoothstep** function with a fixed-width filter produces too much blurring near the equator but not enough at the pole (B). An adaptive approach provides reasonable antialiasing in both regions (C). (Courtesy of Bert Freudenberg, University of Magdeburg, 2002.)

17.4.3 Adaptive Analytic Prefiltering

Analytic prefiltering produces acceptable results in some regions of the sphere but not in others. The size of the smoothing filter (0.2) is defined in parameter space. But the parameter does not vary at a constant rate in screen space. In this case, the *s* texture coordinate varies quite rapidly in screen space near the poles and less rapidly at the equator. Our fixed-width filter produces blurring across several pixels at the equator and very little effect at the poles. What we need is a way to determine the size of the smoothing filter adaptively so that transition can be appropriate at all scales in screen space. This requires a measurement of how rapidly the function we're interested in is changing at a particular position in screen space.

Fortunately, the OpenGL Shading Language provides a built-in function that can give us the rate of change (derivative) of any parameter in screen space. The function **dFdx** gives the rate of change in screen coordinates in the *x* direction, and **dFdy** gives the rate of change in the *y* direction. Because these functions deal with screen space, they are available only in a fragment shader. These two functions can provide the information needed to compute a GRADIENT VECTOR for the position of interest.

Given a function $f(x,y)$, the gradient of f at the position (x, y) is defined as the vector

$$G[f(x, y)] = \begin{bmatrix} \dfrac{\partial f}{\partial x} \\ \dfrac{\partial f}{\partial y} \end{bmatrix}$$

In English, the gradient vector comprises the partial derivative of function f with respect to x (i.e., the measure of how rapidly f is changing in the x direction) and the partial derivative of the function f with respect to y (i.e., the measure of how rapidly f is changing in the y direction). The important properties of the gradient vector are that it points in the direction of the maximum rate of increase of the function $f(x,y)$ (the gradient direction) and that the magnitude of this vector equals the maximum rate of increase of $f(x,y)$ in the gradient direction. (These properties are useful for image processing too, as we see later.) The built-in functions **dFdx** and **dFdy** give us exactly what we need to define the gradient vector for functions used in fragment shaders.

The magnitude of the gradient vector for the function $f(x,y)$ is commonly called the GRADIENT of the function $f(x,y)$. It is defined as

$$\textbf{mag}[G[f(x, y)]] = \textbf{sqrt}((\partial f/\partial x)^2 + (\partial f/\partial y)^2)$$

In practice, it is not always necessary to perform the (possibly costly) square root operation. The gradient can be approximated with absolute values:

$$\textbf{mag}[G[f(x, y)]] \cong \textbf{abs}(f(x, y) - f(x + 1, y)) + \textbf{abs}(f(x, y) - f(x, y + 1))$$

This is exactly what is returned by the built-in function **fwidth**. The sum of the absolute values is an upper bound on the width of the sampling filter needed to eliminate aliasing. If it is too large, the resulting image looks somewhat blurrier than it should, but this is usually acceptable.

The two methods of computing the gradient are compared in Figure 17.5. As you can see, there is little visible difference. Because the value of the gradient was quite small for the function being evaluated on this object, the values were scaled so that they would be visible.

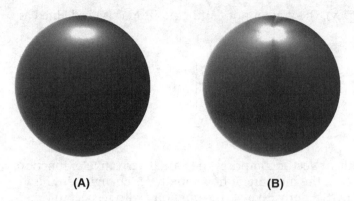

(A)   **(B)**

Figure 17.5 Visualizing the gradient. In (A), the magnitude of the gradient vector is used as the intensity (gray) value. In (B), the gradient is approximated with absolute values. (Actual gradient values are scaled for visualization.) (Courtesy of Bert Freudenberg, University of Magdeburg, 2002.)

To compute the actual gradient for the in variable *V* within a fragment shader, we use

```
float width = length(vec2(dFdx(V), dFdy(V)));
```

To approximate it, we use the potentially higher-performance calculation.

```
float width = fwidth(V);
```

We then use the filter width within our call to **smoothstep** as follows:

```
float edge = dp * Frequency * 2.0;
float square = smoothstep(0.5 - edge, 0.5 + edge, triangle);
```

If we put this all together in a fragment shader, we get Listing 17.1.

Listing 17.1 Fragment shader for adaptive analytic antialiasing

```
#version 140

uniform float Frequency;        // Stripe frequency = 6
uniform vec3  Color0;
uniform vec3  Color1;

in  float V;                    // generic varying
in  float LightIntensity;

out vec4 FragColor;
```

```
void main()
{
    float sawtooth = fract(V * Frequency);
    float triangle = abs(2.0 * sawtooth - 1.0);
    float dp = length(vec2(dFdx(V), dFdy(V)));
    float edge = dp * Frequency * 2.0;
    float square = smoothstep(0.5 - edge, 0.5 + edge, triangle);
    vec3  color = mix(Color0, Color1, square);
    FragColor = vec4(color, 1.0);
    FragColor.rgb *= LightIntensity;
}
```

If we scale the frequency of our texture, we must also increase the filter width accordingly. After the value of the function is computed, it is replicated across the red, green, and blue components of a **vec3** and used as the color of the fragment. The results of this adaptive antialiasing approach are shown in Figure 17.4 (C). The results are much more consistent across the surface of the sphere. A simple lighting computation is added, and the resulting shader is applied to the teapot in Figure 17.6.

This approach to antialiasing works well until the filter width gets larger than the frequency. This is the situation that occurs at the north pole of the sphere. The stripes very close to the pole are much thinner than one pixel, so no step function will produce the correct gray value here. In such regions, you need to switch to integration or frequency clamping, both of which are discussed in subsequent sections.

Figure 17.6 Effect of adaptive analytical antialiasing on striped teapots. On the left, the teapot is drawn with no antialiasing. On the right, the adaptive antialiasing shader is used. A small portion of the striped surface is magnified 200 percent to make it easier to see the difference.

17.4.4 Analytic Integration

The weighted average of a function over a specified interval is called a CONVOLUTION. The values that do the weighting are called the CONVOLUTION KERNEL or the CONVOLUTION FILTER. In some cases, we can reduce or eliminate aliasing by determining the convolution of a function ahead of time and then sampling the convolved function rather than the original function. The convolution can be performed over a fixed interval in a computation that is equivalent to convolving the input function with a box filter. A box filter is far from ideal, but it is simple and easy to compute and often good enough.

This method corresponds to the notion of antialiasing by AREA SAMPLING. It is different from point sampling or supersampling in that we attempt to calculate the area of the object being rendered relative to the sampling region. Referring to Figure 17.2, if we used an area sampling technique, we would get more accurate values for each of the pixels, and we wouldn't miss that pixel that just had a sliver of coverage.

In *Advanced RenderMan: Creating CGI for Motion Pictures*, Apodaca and Gritz (1999) explain how to perform analytic antialiasing of a periodic step function, sometimes called a PULSE TRAIN. Darwyn Peachey described how to apply this method to his procedural brick RenderMan shader in *Texturing and Modeling: A Procedural Approach*, and Dave Baldwin published a GLSL version of this shader in the original paper on the OpenGL Shading Language. We use this technique to analytically antialias the procedural brick GLSL shader we described back in Chapter 6. Recall that the simple brick example used the **step** function to produce the periodic brick pattern. The function that creates the brick pattern in the horizontal direction is illustrated in Figure 17.7. From 0 to *BrickPct.x* (the brick width fraction), the function is 1.0. At the value of *BrickPct.x*, there is an edge with infinite slope as the function drops to 0. At the value 1, the function jumps back up to 1.0, and the process is repeated for the next brick.

The key to antialiasing this function is to compute its integral, or accumulated, value. We have to consider the possibility that, in areas of high complexity, the filter width that is computed by **fwidth** will cover several of these pulses. By sampling the integral rather than the function itself, we get a properly weighted average and avoid the high frequencies caused by point sampling that would produce aliasing artifacts.

So what is the integral of this function? It is illustrated in Figure 17.8. From 0 to *BrickPct.x*, the function value is 1, so the integral increases with a slope of 1. From *BrickPct.x* to 1.0, the function has a value of 0, so the integral stays constant in this region. At 1, the function jumps back to 1.0, so the integral increases until the function reaches *BrickPct.x* + 1. At this point, the integral changes to a slope of 0 again, and this pattern of ramps and plateaus continues.

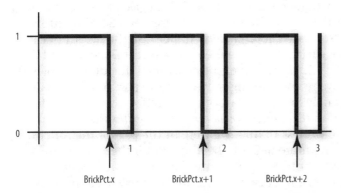

Figure 17.7   The periodic step function, or pulse train, that defines the horizontal component of the procedural brick texture

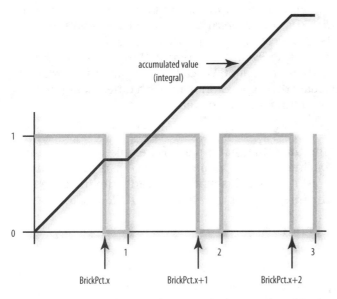

Figure 17.8   Periodic step function (pulse train) and its integral

We perform antialiasing by determining the value of the integral over the area of the filter, and we do that by evaluating the integral at the edges of the filter and subtracting the two values. The integral for this function consists of two parts: the sum of the area for all the pulses that have been fully completed before the edge we are considering and the area of the possibly partially completed pulse for the edge we are considering.

For our procedural brick shader, we use the variable *position.x* as the basis for generating the pulse function in the horizontal direction. So, the number of fully completed pulses is just **floor**(*position.x*). Because the height of each pulse is 1.0, the area of each fully completed pulse is just *BrickPct.x*. Multiplying **floor**(*position.x*) by *BrickPct.x* gives the area for all the fully completed pulses. The edge that we're considering may be in the part of the function that is equal to 0, or it may be in the part of the function that is equal to 1. We can find out by computing **fract**(*position.x*) – (1.0 – *BrickPct.x*). If the result of this subtraction is less than 0, we were in the part of the function that returns 0, so nothing more needs to be done. But if the value is greater than zero, we are partway into a region of the function that is equal to 1. Because the height of the pulse is 1, the area of this partial pulse is **fract**(*position.x*) – (1.0 – *BrickPct.x*). Therefore, the second part of our integral is the expression **max**(**fract**(*position.x*) – (1.0 – *BrickPct.x*), 0.0).

We use this integral for both the horizontal and vertical components of our procedural brick pattern. Because the application knows the brick width and height fractions (*BrickPct.x* and *BrickPct.y*), it can easily compute 1.0 – *BrickPct.x* and 1.0 – *BrickPct.y* and provide them to our fragment shader as well. This keeps us from unnecessarily computing these values several times for every fragment that is rendered. We call these values the mortar percentage. Because we evaluate this expression twice with different arguments, we define it as a macro or a function for convenience.

```
#define Integral(x, p, notp) ((floor(x)*(p)) + max(fract(x)-(notp), 0.0))
```

The parameter *p* indicates the value that is part of the pulse (i.e., when the function is 1.0), and *notp* indicates the value that is not part of the pulse (i.e., when the function is 0). Using this macro, we can write the code to compute the value of the integral over the width of the filter as follows:

```
vec2 fw, useBrick;

fw = fwidth(position);

useBrick = (Integral(position + fw, BrickPct, MortarPct) -
            Integral(position, BrickPct, MortarPct)) / fw;
```

The result is divided by the area of the filter (a box filter is assumed in this case) to obtain the average value for the function in the selected interval.

17.4.5 Antialiased Brick Fragment Shader

Now we can put all this to work to build better bricks. We replace the simple point sampling technique used in the example in Chapter 6 with analytic integration. The resulting shader is shown in Listing 17.2. The difference between the aliased and antialiased brick shaders is shown in Color Plate 34.

Listing 17.2 Source code for an antialiased brick fragment shader

```
#version 140

uniform vec3  BrickColor, MortarColor;
uniform vec2  BrickSize;
uniform vec2  BrickPct;
uniform vec2  MortarPct;

in  vec2  MCPosition;
in  float LightIntensity;

out vec4  FragColor;

#define Integral(x, p, notp) ((floor(x)*(p)) + max(fract(x)-(notp), 0.0))

void main()
{
    vec2 position, fw, useBrick;
    vec3 color;

    // Determine position within the brick pattern
    position = MCPosition / BrickSize;

    // Adjust every other row by an offset of half a brick
    if (fract(position.y * 0.5) > 0.5)
        position.x += 0.5;

    // Calculate filter size
    fw = fwidth(position);

    // Perform filtering by integrating the 2D pulse made by the
    // brick pattern over the filter width and height
    useBrick = (Integral(position + fw, BrickPct, MortarPct) -
               Integral(position, BrickPct, MortarPct)) / fw;

    // Determine final color
    color  = mix(MortarColor, BrickColor, useBrick.x * useBrick.y);
    color *= LightIntensity;
    FragColor = vec4(color, 1.0);
}
```

17.5 Frequency Clamping

Certain functions do not have an analytic solution, or they are just too diffi-cult to solve. If this is the case, you might try a technique called FREQUENCY CLAMPING. In this technique, the average value of the function replaces the actual value of the function when the filter width is too large. This is conve-nient for functions such as sine and noise whose average is known.

17.5.1 Antialiased Checkerboard Fragment Shader

The checkerboard pattern is the standard measure of the quality of an antialiasing technique (see Figure 17.9). Larry Gritz wrote a checkerboard

Figure 17.9   Checkerboard pattern rendered with the antialiased checkerboard shader. On the left, the filter width is set to 0, so aliasing occurs. On the right, the filter width is computed using the **fwidth** function.

RenderMan shader that performs antialiasing by frequency sampling, and Dave Baldwin translated this shader to GLSL. Listing 17.3 shows a fragment shader that produces a procedurally generated, antialiased checkerboard pattern. The vertex shader transforms the vertex position and passes along the texture coordinate, nothing more. The application provides values for the two colors of the checkerboard pattern, the average of these two colors (the application can compute this and provide it through a uniform variable, rather than having the fragment shader compute it for every fragment), and the frequency of the checkerboard pattern.

The fragment shader computes the appropriate size of the filter and uses it to perform smooth interpolation between adjoining checkerboard squares. If the filter is too wide (i.e., the in variable is changing too quickly for proper filtering), the average color is substituted. Even though this fragment shader uses a conditional statement, care is taken to avoid aliasing. In the transition zone between the **if** clause and the **else** clause, a smooth interpolation is performed between the computed color and the average color.

Listing 17.3 Source code for an antialiased checkerboard fragment shader

```
#version 140

uniform vec3  Color0;
uniform vec3  Color1;
uniform vec3  AvgColor;
uniform float Frequency;

in  vec2 TexCoord;
out vec4 FragColor;

void main()
{
    vec3 color;

    // Determine the width of the projection of one pixel into s-t space
    vec2 fw = fwidth(TexCoord);

    // Determine the amount of fuzziness
    vec2 fuzz = fw * Frequency * 2.0;

    float fuzzMax = max(fuzz.s, fuzz.t);

    // Determine the position in the checkerboard pattern
    vec2 checkPos = fract(TexCoord * Frequency);

    if (fuzzMax < 0.5)
    {
        // If the filter width is small enough,
        // compute the pattern color
```

```
        vec2 p = smoothstep(vec2(0.5), fuzz + vec2(0.5), checkPos) +
                 (1.0 - smoothstep(vec2(0.0), fuzz, checkPos));

        color = mix(Color0, Color1,
                    p.x * p.y + (1.0 - p.x) * (1.0 - p.y));

        // Fade in the average color when we get close to the limit
        color = mix(color, AvgColor, smoothstep(0.125, 0.5, fuzzMax));
    }
    else
    {
        // Otherwise, use only the average color
        color = AvgColor;
    }

    FragColor = vec4(color, 1.0);
}
```

17.6 Summary

With increased freedom comes increased responsibility. The OpenGL Shading Language permits the computation of procedural textures without restriction. It is quite easy to write a shader that exhibits unsightly aliasing artifacts (using a conditional or a step function is all it takes), and it can be difficult to eliminate these artifacts. After describing the aliasing problem in general terms, this chapter explored several options for antialiasing procedural textures. Facilities in the language, such as the built-in functions for smooth interpolation (**smoothstep**), for determining derivatives in screen space (**dFdx**, **dFdy**), and for estimating filter width (**fwidth**) can assist in the fight against jaggies. These functions were fundamental components of shaders that were presented to perform antialiasing by prefiltering, adaptive prefiltering, integration, and frequency clamping.

17.7 Further Information

Most signal processing and image processing books contain a discussion of the concepts of sampling, reconstruction, and aliasing. Books by Glassner, Wolberg, and Gonzalez and Woods can be consulted for additional information on these topics. Technical memos by Alvy Ray Smith address the issues of aliasing in computer graphics directly.

The book *Advanced RenderMan: Creating CGI for Motion Pictures* by Anthony A. Apodaca and Larry Gritz (1999) contains a chapter that describes shader antialiasing in terms of the RenderMan shading language, and much of the discussion is germane to the OpenGL Shading Language as well. Darwyn Peachey has a similar discussion in *Texturing & Modeling: A Procedural Approach, Third Edition*, by David Ebert et al. (2002).

Bert Freudenberg developed an OpenGL shader to do adaptive antialiasing and presented this work at the SIGGRAPH 2002 in San Antonio, Texas. In this chapter, I've re-created the images Bert used in his talk, but he deserves the credit for originally developing the images and the shaders to illustrate some of the topics I've covered. This subject is also covered in his Ph.D. thesis, *Real-Time Stroke-based Halftoning*.

[1] *Former 3Dlabs developer Web site.* Now at http://3dshaders.com/.

[2] Apodaca, Anthony A., and Larry Gritz, *Advanced RenderMan: Creating CGI for Motion Pictures*, Morgan Kaufmann Publishers, San Francisco, 1999. www.renderman.org/RMR/Books/arman/materials.html

[3] Baldwin, Dave, *OpenGL 2.0 Shading Language White Paper, Version 1.0*, 3Dlabs, October, 2001.

[4] Cook, Robert L., *Stochastic Sampling in Computer Graphics*, ACM Transactions on Graphics, vol. 5, no. 1, pp. 51–72, January 1986.

[5] Crow, Franklin C., *The Aliasing Problem in Computer-Generated Shaded Images*, Communications of the ACM, 20(11), pp. 799–805, November 1977.

[6] Crow, Franklin C., *Summed-Area Tables for Texture Mapping*, Computer Graphics (SIGGRAPH '84 Proceedings), pp. 207–212, July 1984.

[7] Dippé, Mark A. Z., and Erling Henry Wold, *Antialiasing Through Stochastic Sampling*, Computer Graphics (SIGGRAPH '85 Proceedings), pp. 69–78, July 1985.

[8] Ebert, David S., John Hart, Bill Mark, F. Kenton Musgrave, Darwyn Peachey, Ken Perlin, and Steven Worley, *Texturing and Modeling: A Procedural Approach, Third Edition*, Morgan Kaufmann Publishers, San Francisco, 2002. www.texturingandmodeling.com

[9] Freudenberg, Bert, *A Non-Photorealistic Fragment Shader in OpenGL 2.0*, Presented at the SIGGRAPH 2002 Exhibition in San Antonio, July 2002. http://isgwww.cs.uni-magdeburg.de/~bert/publications

[10] Freudenberg, Bert, *Real-Time Stroke-based Halftoning*, Ph.D. thesis, University of Magdeburg, submitted in 2003.

[11] Glassner, Andrew S., *Principles of Digital Image Synthesis*, Vol. 1, Morgan Kaufmann Publishers, San Francisco, 1995.

[12] Glassner, Andrew S., *Principles of Digital Image Synthesis*, Vol. 2, Morgan Kaufmann Publishers, San Francisco, 1995.

[13] Gonzalez, Rafael C., and Richard E. Woods, *Digital Image Processing, Second Edition*, Prentice Hall, Upper Saddle River, New Jersey, 2002.

[14] Gritz, Larry, *LGAntialiasedChecks.sl*, RenderMan Repository Web site. www.renderman.org/RMR/Shaders/LGShaders/index.html

[15] Smith, Alvy Ray, *Digital Filtering Tutorial for Computer Graphics*, Lucasfilm Technical Memo 27, revised March 1983. www.alvyray.com/memos/default.htm

[16] Smith, Alvy Ray, *Digital Filtering Tutorial, Part II*, Lucasfilm Technical Memo 27, revised March 1983. www.alvyray.com/memos/default.htm

[17] Smith, Alvy Ray, *A Pixel Is Not a Little Square, a Pixel Is Not a Little Square, a Pixel Is Not a Little Square! (And a Voxel Is Not a Little Cube)*, Technical Memo 6, Microsoft Research, July 1995. www.alvyray.com/memos/default.htm

[18] Wolberg, George, *Digital Image Warping*, Wiley-IEEE Press, 2002.

Chapter 18

Non-photorealistic Shaders

A significant amount of computer graphics research has been aimed at achieving more and more realistic renditions of synthetic scenes. A long-time goal has been to render a scene so perfectly that it is indistinguishable from a photograph of the real scene, a goal called PHOTOREALISM. With the latest graphics hardware, some photorealistic effects are becoming possible in real-time rendering.

This quest for realism is also reflected in graphics APIs such as OpenGL. The OpenGL specification defines specific formulas for calculating effects such as illumination from light sources, material properties, and fog. These formulas attempt to define effects as realistically as possible while remaining relatively easy to implement in hardware, and they have duly been cast into silicon by intrepid graphics hardware designers.

But the collection of human art and literature shows us that photorealism is not the only important style for creating images. The availability of low-cost programmable graphics hardware has sparked the growth of an area called NON-PHOTOREALISTIC RENDERING, or NPR. Researchers and practitioners in this field are attempting to use computer graphics to produce a wide range of artistic effects other than photorealism. In this chapter, we look at a few examples of shaders whose main focus is something other than generating results that are as realistic as possible.

18.1 Hatching Example

Bert Freudenberg of the University of Magdeburg in Germany was one of the first people outside 3Dlabs to come up with a unique OpenGL shader. His area of research has been to use programmable hardware to produce real-time NPR effects such as hatching and half-toning. He experimented with a prototype implementation of the OpenGL Shading Language in the summer of 2002 and produced a hatching shader that he agreed to share with us for this book.

This shader has a few unique features, and the steps involved in designing this shader are described in Bert's Ph.D. thesis, *Real-Time Stroke-based Half-toning* (2003). Bert's hatching shader is based on a woodblock printing shader by Scott Johnston that is discussed in *Advanced RenderMan: Creating CGI for Motion Pictures* by Anthony A. Apodaca and Larry Gritz (1999).

The goal in a hatching shader is to render an object in a way that makes it look hand-drawn, for instance with strokes that look like they may have been drawn with pen and ink. Each stroke contributes to the viewer's ability to comprehend the tone, texture, and shape of the object being viewed. The effect being sought in this shader is that of a woodcut print. In a woodcut, a wooden block carved with small grooves is covered with ink and pressed onto a surface. The image left on the surface is the mirror image of the image carved into the wood block. No ink is left where the grooves are cut, only where the wood is left uncut. Lighting is simulated by varying the width of the grooves according to light intensity.

We face a number of challenges in developing a shader that simulates the look of a woodcut print. The first thing we need is a way of generating stripes that defines the tone and texture of the object. Alternating white and black lines provides the highest-contrast edges and thus represents a worst-case scenario for aliasing artifacts; thus, antialiasing is a prime consideration. We also want our lines to "stay put" on the object so that we can use the object in an animation sequence. Finally, the lines in a woodcut print are not always perfectly straight and uniform as though they were drawn by a computer. They are cut into the wood by a human artist, so they have some character. We'd like the lines that our shader generates to have some character as well.

18.1.1 Application Setup

The application needs to send vertex positions, normals, and a single set of texture coordinates to the hatching shader. The normals are used in a simple lighting formula, and the texture coordinates are used as the base for

procedurally defining the hatching pattern. The light position is passed in
as a uniform variable, and the application also updates the value of the *Time*
uniform variable at each frame so that the behavior of the shader can be
modified slightly each frame. What do you suppose we use to give our lines
some character? You guessed it—the noise function. In this case, we have
the application generate the noise values that are needed and store the
results in a 3D texture. For this reason, the value for a uniform variable of
type **sampler3D** is provided by the application to inform the fragment
shader which texture unit should be accessed to obtain the noise values.

18.1.2 Vertex Shader

The hatch vertex shader is shown in Listing 18.1. The first line is the only
line that looks different from shaders we've discussed previously. The out
variable *ObjPos* is the basis for our hatching stroke computation in the fragment shader. To animate the wiggle of the lines, the vertex shader adds the
uniform variable *Time* to the *z* coordinate of the incoming vertex position.
This makes it appear as though the wiggles are "flowing" along the
z axis. A scaling value is also used to make the hatching strokes match the
scale of the object being rendered. (To accommodate a variety of objects, we
should probably replace this value with a uniform variable.) The remainder
of the vertex shader performs a simple diffuse lighting equation, copies the
t coordinate of the incoming texture coordinate into the out variable *V*, and
computes the value of the built-in variable *gl_Position*.

Listing 18.1   Vertex shader for hatching

```
#version 140

uniform mat4 MVMatrix;
uniform mat4 MVPMatrix;
uniform mat3 NormalMatrix;

uniform vec3  LightPosition;
uniform float Time;

in   vec4  MCVertex;
in   vec3  MCNormal;
in   vec2  TexCoord0;

out vec3  ObjPos;
out float V;
out float LightIntensity;

void main()
{
    ObjPos          = (vec3(MCVertex) + vec3(0.0, 0.0, Time)) * 0.2;
```

```
vec3 pos        = vec3(MVMatrix * MCVertex);
vec3 tnorm      = normalize(NormalMatrix * MCNormal);
vec3 lightVec   = normalize(LightPosition - pos);

LightIntensity  = max(dot(lightVec, tnorm), 0.0);

V = TexCoord0.t;  // try .s for vertical stripes

gl_Position = MVPMatrix * MCVertex;
}
```

18.1.3 Generating Hatching Strokes

The purpose of our fragment shader is to determine whether each fragment
is to be drawn as white or black in order to create lines on the surface of the
object. As we mentioned, there are some challenges along the way. To prepare for the full-blown hatching shader, we develop some of the techniques
we need and illustrate them on a simple object: a sphere.

We start with the same code that was presented in Section 17.4.1 for generating vertical stripes, namely,

```
float sawtooth = fract(V * 16.0);
float triangle = abs(2.0 * sawtooth - 1.0);
float square = step(0.5, triangle);
```

Recall that V was an out variable passed from the vertex shader. It was equal
to the s texture coordinate if we wanted to generate vertical stripes and
equal to the t texture coordinate if we wanted to generate horizontal stripes.
We chose the number 16 to give us 16 white stripes and 16 black stripes. The
result of this code is illustrated in Figure 18.1. We can modify the relative

Figure 18.1   A sphere with a stripe pattern generated procedurally based on the s
texture coordinate (courtesy of Bert Freudenberg, University of Magdeburg, 2002)

size of the white and black stripes by adjusting the threshold value provided in the **step** function.

18.1.4 Obtaining Uniform Line Density

We now have reasonable-looking stripes, but they aren't of uniform width. They appear fatter along the equator and pinched in at the pole. We'd like to end up with lines that are of roughly equal width in screen space. This requires the use of the **dFdx** and **dFdy** functions:

```
float dp = length(vec2(dFdx(V), dFdy(V)));
```

As we learned in Section 17.4.3, this computation provides us with the gradient (i.e., how rapidly *V* is changing at this point on the surface). We can use this value to adjust the density of lines in screen space.

Computing the actual gradient with the **length** function involves a potentially costly square root operation. Why not use the approximation to the gradient discussed in Section 17.4.3? In this case we must compute the actual gradient because the approximation to the gradient isn't quite good enough for our purposes. We're not using this value to estimate the filter width for antialiasing; instead, we're using it to compute the stripe frequency. This computation needs to be rotationally invariant so that our stripes don't jump around just because we rotate the object. For this reason, we need to compute the actual length of the gradient vector, not just the sum of the absolute values of the two components of the gradient vector.

So, we use the base 2 logarithm of this value (shown applied to the sphere in Figure 18.2 (A)) to adjust the density in discrete steps—each time *dp* doubles, the number of lines doubles unless we do something about it. The stripes get too thin and too dense if doubling occurs. To counteract this effect (because we are interested in getting a constant line density in screen space), we decrease the number of stripes when the density gets too high. We do this by negating the logarithm.

```
float logdp      = -log2(dp);
float ilogdp     = floor(logdp);
float frequency  = exp2(ilogdp);
float sawtooth   = fract(V * frequency * stripes);
```

A sphere with a higher stripe frequency is shown in Figure 18.2 (B). As you can see, the lines look reasonable in the lower part of the sphere, but there are too many at the pole. By applying the stripe frequency adjustment, we

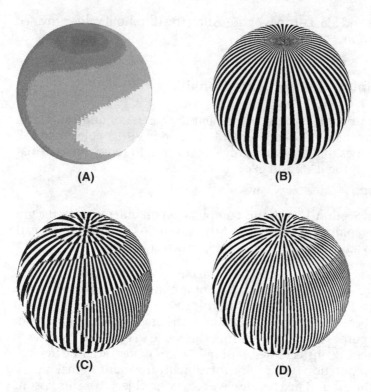

Figure 18.2 Adjusting the stripe frequency. The integer part of the logarithm of the gradient (A) is the basis for determining stripe frequency. First, the sphere is shown with a higher frequency of stripes (B). The integer part of the logarithm then adjusts the stripe frequency in (C), and the effect of tapering the ends is shown in (D). (Courtesy of Bert Freudenberg, University of Magdeburg, 2002.)

end up with stripes of roughly equal width across the sphere (see Figure 18.2 (C)). Notice the correlation between Figure 18.2 (A) and Figure 18.2 (C).

The next issue to address is the abrupt changes that occur as we jump from one stroke frequency to the next. Our eyes detect a distinct edge along these transitions, and we need to take steps to soften this edge so that it is less distracting. We can accomplish this by using the fractional part of *logdp* to do a smooth blend between two frequencies of the triangle wave. This value is 0 at the start of one frequency, and it increases to 1.0 at the point where the jump to the next frequency occurs.

```
float transition = logdp - ilogdp;
```

As we saw earlier, we can generate a triangle wave with frequency double that of a triangle wave with frequency t by taking **abs**$(2.0 * t - 1.0)$. We can use the value of *transition* to linearly interpolate between t and **abs**$(2.0 * t - 1.0)$ by computing $(1.0 - transition) * t + transition * $ **abs**$(2.0 * t - 1.0)$. This is exactly the same as if we did **mix**(**abs**$(2.0 * t - 1.0)$, t, *transition*). But instead of using **mix**, we note that this is equivalent to **abs**$((1.0 - transition) * t - transition)$. Using the previously computed value for our base frequency (*triangle*), we end up with the following code:

```
triangle = abs((1.0 - transition) * triangle - transition);
```

The result of drawing the sphere with uniform stripe density and tapered ends is shown in Figure 18.2 (D).

18.1.5 Simulating Lighting

To simulate the effect of lighting, we'd like to make the dark stripes more prominent in regions that are in shadow and the white stripes more prominent in regions that are lit. We can do this by using the computed light intensity to modify the threshold value used in the **step** function. In regions that are lit, the threshold value is decreased so that black stripes get thinner. In regions that are in shadow, the threshold value is increased so that the black stripes get wider.

```
const float edgew = 0.2;            // width of smooth step

float edge0  = clamp(LightIntensity - edgew, 0.0, 1.0);
float edge1  = clamp(LightIntensity, 0.0, 1.0);
float square = 1.0 - smoothstep(edge0, edge1, triangle);
```

Once again, we use the **smoothstep** function to antialias the transition. Because our stripe pattern is a (roughly) constant width in screen space, we can use a constant filter width rather than an adaptive one. The results of the lighting effect can be seen in Figure 18.3.

18.1.6 Adding Character

If a woodcut block is made by a human artist and not by a machine, the cuts in the wood aren't perfect in thickness and spacing. How do we add some imperfections into our mathematically perfect description of hatching lines? With noise (see Chapter 15). For this shader, we don't need anything fancy; we just want to add some "wiggle" to our otherwise perfect lines or

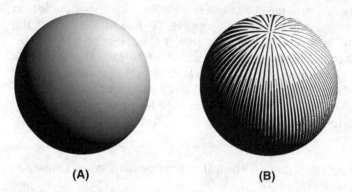

(A)   **(B)**

Figure 18.3 Applying lighting to the sphere. In (A), the sphere is lit with a simple lighting model and no stripes. In (B), the light intensity modulates the width of the stripes to simulate the effect of lighting. (Courtesy of Bert Freudenberg, University of Magdeburg, 2002.)

perhaps some "patchiness" to our simple lighting equation. We can use a tileable 3D texture containing Perlin noise in the same way for this shader as for the shaders in Chapter 15.

To add wiggle to our lines, we modify the sawtooth generation function.

```
float sawtooth = fract((V + noise * 0.1) * frequency * stripes);
```

The result of noise added to our stripe pattern is illustrated in Figure 18.4.

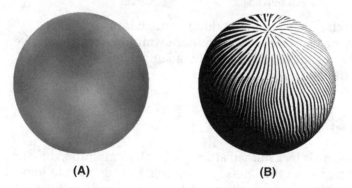

(A)   **(B)**

Figure 18.4 Adding noise to the hatching algorithm. In (A), the Perlin noise function is applied directly to the sphere's surface. In (B), it modulates the parameter that defines the frequency of the hatching strokes. (Courtesy of Bert Freudenberg, University of Magdeburg, 2002.)

Figure 18.5   Woodcut-style teapot rendered with the hatching shader (courtesy of Bert Freudenberg, University of Magdeburg, 2002)

18.1.7 Hatching Fragment Shader

The pieces described in the preceding sections are put together in the general-purpose hatching shader shown in Listing 18.2. It bases its hatching stroke computation on the *t* texture coordinate, so the result is horizontal stripes rather than vertical ones. The results of applying this shader to the teapot model are shown in Figure 18.5.

Listing 18.2   Fragment shader for woodcut-style rendering

```
#version 140

uniform sampler3D Noise;            // value of Noise = 3;

const float frequency = 1.0;

in  vec3  ObjPos;            // object space coord (noisy)
in  float V;                 // generic varying
in  float LightIntensity;

out vec4  FragColor;


void main()
{
    float dp        = length(vec2(dFdx(V), dFdy(V)));
    float logdp     = -log2(dp * 8.0);
```

```
float ilogdp   = floor(logdp);
float stripes  = exp2(ilogdp);

float noise    = texture(Noise, ObjPos).x;

float sawtooth = fract((V + noise * 0.1) * frequency * stripes);
float triangle = abs(2.0 * sawtooth - 1.0);

// adjust line width
float transition = logdp - ilogdp;

// taper ends
triangle = abs((1.0 + transition) * triangle - transition);

const float edgew = 0.3;                // width of smooth step

float edge0  = clamp(LightIntensity - edgew, 0.0, 1.0);
float edge1  = clamp(LightIntensity, 0.0, 1.0);
float square = 1.0 - smoothstep(edge0, edge1, triangle);

FragColor = vec4(vec3(square), 1.0);
}
```

18.2 Technical Illustration Example

Pick up just about any instruction manual, technical book, or encyclopedia
and you will see a variety of illustrations other than photographs or photorealistic graphics. Technical illustrators have learned various techniques
over the years to convey relevant information as simply and as clearly as
possible. Details that do not contribute to understanding are omitted, and
details that are crucial to understanding are clear and straightforward. This
style of illustration differs from mainstream computer graphics for which
an enormous amount of detail may be presented in an image to make it look
more realistic. The effort to convey information as succinctly as possible in
a technical illustration is summed up by a strategy referred to by Edward
Tufte (1997) as "the smallest effective difference." In his book *Visual Explanations*, Tufte says, "Make all visual distinctions as subtle as possible, but
still clear and effective."

Various NPR practitioners are attempting to develop algorithms to create
technical illustrations. The goal is to simplify or even automate the task of
creating high-quality technical illustrations according to time-honored
illustration techniques. Much of our comprehension about an object's
shape comes from lighting. Yet the traditional lighting equation is defi-
cient at conveying shape information in areas that are not lit directly,

because these areas appear flat. The only lighting in these areas comes from the ambient term, which is constant. Technical illustrations also highlight important edges in black so that they are distinct and clearly convey the shape of the object. If a small ambient term is used in the traditional lighting model, black edge highlights typically are indistinguishable from unlit regions of the object, which are also very near black.

In 1998, Bruce and Amy Gooch, Peter Shirley, and Elaine Cohen surveyed illustrations and came up with a list of common characteristics for color illustrations done with airbrush and pen.

- Surface boundaries, silhouette edges, and discontinuities in the surface of an object are usually drawn with black curves.

- A single light source is used, and it produces a white highlight on objects.

- The light source is usually positioned above the object so that the diffuse reflection term varies in the range [0,1] across the visible portion of the object.

- Effects that add complexity (realism) such as shadows, reflections, and multiple light sources are not shown.

- Matte objects are shaded with intensities far from white and black so as to be clearly distinct from (black) edges and (white) highlights.

- The warmth or coolness of the color indicates the surface normal (and hence the curvature of the surface).

These characteristics were incorporated into a "low dynamic range artistic tone algorithm" that we now refer to as GOOCH SHADING.

One of the important aspects of Gooch shading is the generation of black curves that represent important edges. There are a number of techniques for rendering such edges. Perhaps the best method is to have them identified during the modeling process by the person designing the model. In this case, the edges can be rendered as antialiased black lines that are drawn on top of the object itself, that is, in a second rendering pass that draws the edges after the objects in the scene have been completely rendered.

If important edges have not been identified during the modeling process, several methods can generate them automatically. Quality of results varies according to the method used and the characteristics of the objects in the scene. Interior boundary or crease edges should also be identified, and these are sometimes critical to comprehension. A technique that identifies boundary or crease edges as well as silhouette edges involves using vertex and fragment shaders to write world-space normals and depth values into the framebuffer. The result is stored as a texture, and a subsequent rendering pass with different vertex and fragment shaders can use an edge detection algorithm on this "image" to detect discontinuities (i.e., edges) in the scene (Jason Mitchell (2002)).

A technique for drawing silhouette edges for simple objects, described by Jeff Lander (2000) in *Under the Shade of the Rendering Tree*, requires drawing the geometry twice. First, we draw just the front-facing polygons using filled polygons and the depth comparison mode set to GL_LESS. The Gooch shaders are active when we do this. Then, we draw the back-facing polygons as lines with the depth comparison mode set to GL_LEQUAL. This has the effect of drawing lines such that a front-facing polygon shares an edge with a back-facing polygon. We draw these lines with a trivial fragment shader that outputs black FragColor with polygon mode set so that back-facing polygons are drawn as lines. The OpenGL calls to do this are shown in Listing 18.3.

Listing 18.3   C code for drawing silhouette edges on simple objects

```
// Enable culling
glEnable(GL_CULL_FACE);

// Draw front-facing polygons as filled using the Gooch shader
glPolygonMode(GL_FRONT_AND_BACK, GL_FILL);
glDepthFunc(GL_LESS);
glCullFace(GL_BACK);
glUseProgram(ProgramGooch);
drawSphere(0.6f, 64);

// Draw back-facing polygons as black lines using standard OpenGL
glLineWidth(5.0);
glPolygonMode(GL_BACK_AND_BACK, GL_LINE);
glDepthFunc(GL_LEQUAL);
glCullFace(GL_FRONT);
glUseProgram(ProgramBlackFragment);
drawSphere(0.6f, 64);
```

A second aspect of Gooch shading is that specular highlights are computed with the exponential specular term of the Phong lighting model and are rendered in white. Highlights convey information about the curvature of the surface, and choosing white as the highlight color ensures that highlights are distinct from edges (which are black) and from the colors shading the object (which are chosen to be visually distinct from white or black).

A third aspect of the algorithm is that a limited range of luminance values is used to convey information about the curvature of the surfaces that are being rendered. This part of the shading uses the color of the object, which is typically chosen to be an intermediate value that doesn't interfere visually with white or black.

Because the range of luminance values is limited, a warm-to-cool color gradient is also added to convey more information about the object's surface. Artists use "warm" colors (yellow, red, and orange) and "cool" colors (blue, violet, and green) to communicate a sense of depth. Warm colors, which appear to advance, indicate objects that are closer. Cool colors, which appear to recede, indicate objects that are farther away.

The actual shading of the object depends on two factors. The diffuse reflection factor generates luminance values in a limited range to provide one part of the shading. A color ramp that blends between two colors provides the other part of the shading. One of the two colors is chosen to be a cool (recessive) color, such as blue, to indicate surfaces that are angled away from the light source. The other color is chosen to be a warm (advancing) color, such as yellow, to indicate surfaces facing toward the light source. The blue-to-yellow ramp provides an undertone that ensures a cool-to-warm transition regardless of the diffuse object color that is chosen.

The formulas used to compute the colors used for Gooch shading are as follows:

$$k_{cool} = k_{blue} + \alpha k_{diffuse}$$

$$k_{warm} = k_{yellow} + \beta k_{diffuse}$$

$$k_{final} = \left(\frac{1 + N \cdot L}{2}\right) k_{cool} + \left(1 - \frac{1 + N \cdot L}{2}\right) k_{warm}$$

k_{cool} is the color for the areas that are not illuminated by the light source. We compute this value by adding the blue undertone color and the diffuse color of the object, $k_{diffuse}$. The value α is a variable that defines how much of the object's diffuse color will be added to the blue undertone color. k_{warm} is the color for the areas that are fully illuminated by the light source. This value is computed as the sum of the yellow undertone color and the object's diffuse color multiplied by a scale factor, β.

The final color is just a linear blend between the colors k_{cool} and k_{warm} based on the diffuse reflection term $N \cdot L$, where N is the normalized surface normal and L is the unit vector in the direction of the light source. Since $N \cdot L$ can vary from [–1,1], we add 1 and divide the result by 2 to get a value in the range [0,1]. This value determines the ratio of k_{cool} and k_{warm} to produce the final color value.

18.2.1 Application Setup

We implement this shading algorithm in two passes (i.e., we draw the geometry twice). We use the Lander technique to render silhouette edges in black. In the first pass, we cull back-facing polygons and render the front-facing polygons with the Gooch shader. In the second pass, we cull all the front-facing polygons and use a trivial fragment shader to render the edges of the back-facing polygons in black. We draw the edges with a line width greater than one pixel so that they can be seen outside the object. For this shader to work properly, only vertex positions and normals need to be passed to the vertex shader.

18.2.2 Vertex Shader

The goals of the Gooch vertex shader are to produce a value for the $(1 + N \cdot L) / 2$ term in the previous equations and to pass on the reflection vector and the view vector so that the specular reflection can be computed in the fragment shader (see Listing 18.4). Other elements of the shader are identical to shaders discussed earlier.

Listing 18.4   Vertex shader for Gooch matte shading

```
#version 140

uniform mat4 MVMatrix;
uniform mat4 MVPMatrix;
uniform mat3 NormalMatrix;

uniform vec3  LightPosition;  // (0.0, 10.0, 4.0)

in  vec4  MCVertex;
in  vec3  MCNormal;
in  vec2  TexCoord0;

out float NdotL;
out vec3  ReflectVec;
out vec3  ViewVec;

void main()
{
    vec3 ecPos      = vec3(MVMatrix * MCVertex);
    vec3 tnorm      = normalize(NormalMatrix * MCNormal);
    vec3 lightVec   = normalize(LightPosition - ecPos);
    ReflectVec      = normalize(reflect(-lightVec, tnorm));
    ViewVec         = normalize(-ecPos);
    NdotL           = dot(lightVec, tnorm) * 0.5 + 0.5;
    gl_Position     = MVPMatrix * MCVertex;
}
```

18.2.3 Fragment Shader

The fragment shader implements the tone-based shading portion of the Gooch shading algorithm and adds the specular reflection component (see Listing 18.5). The colors and ratios are defined as uniform variables so that they can be easily modified by the application. The reflection and view vectors are normalized in the fragment shader because interpolation may have caused them to have a length other than 1.0. The result of rendering with the Gooch shader and the silhouette edge algorithm described by Lander is shown in Color Plate 27.

Listing 18.5   Fragment shader for Gooch matte shading

```
#version 140

uniform vec3  SurfaceColor; // (0.75, 0.75, 0.75)
uniform vec3  WarmColor;    // (0.6, 0.6, 0.0)
uniform vec3  CoolColor;    // (0.0, 0.0, 0.6)
uniform float DiffuseWarm;  // 0.45
uniform float DiffuseCool;  // 0.45

in  float NdotL;
in  vec3  ReflectVec;
in  vec3  ViewVec;

out vec4 FragColor;

void main()
{
    vec3 kcool    = min(CoolColor + DiffuseCool * SurfaceColor, 1.0);
    vec3 kwarm    = min(WarmColor + DiffuseWarm * SurfaceColor, 1.0);
    vec3 kfinal   = mix(kcool, kwarm, NdotL);

    vec3 nreflect = normalize(ReflectVec);
    vec3 nview    = normalize(ViewVec);

    float spec    = max(dot(nreflect, nview), 0.0);
    spec          = pow(spec, 32.0);

    FragColor = vec4(min(kfinal + spec, 1.0), 1.0);
}
```

18.3 Mandelbrot Example

C'mon, now, what kind of a book on graphics programming would this be without an example of drawing the Mandelbrot set?

Our last shader of the chapter doesn't fall into the category of attempting to achieve an artistic or painterly effect, but it's an example of performing a type of general-purpose computation on the graphics hardware for scientific visualization. In this case, the graphics hardware enables us to do real-time exploration of a famous mathematical function that computes the Mandelbrot set. In 1998, Michael Rivero created a RenderMan shader that creates the Mandelbrot set as a texture. Subsequently, Dave Baldwin adapted this shader for GLSL, Steve Koren then made some modifications to it to get it working on programmable hardware for the first time, and I've adapted this shader further for inclusion in this book.

The point of including this shader is to emphasize the fact that with the OpenGL Shading Language, computations that were previously possible only in the realm of the CPU can now be executed on the graphics hardware. Performing the computations completely on the graphics hardware is a big performance win because the computations can be carried out on many pixels in parallel. Visualization of a complex mathematical function such as the Mandelbrot set barely begins to tap the potential for using programmable shader technology for scientific visualization.

18.3.1 About the Mandelbrot Set

To understand the Mandelbrot set, we must first recall a few things from our high school mathematics days. No real number, when multiplied by itself, yields a negative value. But the imaginary number called i is defined to be equal to the square root of -1. With i, the square root of any negative number can easily be described. For instance, $3i$ squared is -9, and conversely the square root of -9 is $3i$.

Numbers that consist of a real number and an imaginary number, such as $6 + 4i$, are called COMPLEX NUMBERS. Arithmetic operations can be performed on complex numbers just as on real numbers. The result of multiplying two complex numbers is as follows:

$$x = a + bi$$

$$y = c + di$$

$$xy = ac + adi + cbi - bd$$

$$= (ac - bd) + (ad + bc)i$$

Because complex numbers contain two parts, the set of complex numbers is two-dimensional. Complex numbers can be plotted on the complex number plane, which uses the horizontal axis to represent the real part and the vertical axis to represent the imaginary part (see Figure 18.6).

In Figure 18.6, we see three symbols plotted on the complex number plane. A small square is plotted at the complex number $2 + i$, a small circle is plotted at $-1 + 2i$, and a triangle is plotted at $-1.5 - 0.5i$.

With the assistance of 1970s computer technology (quite inferior by today's consumer PC standards), a mathematician named Benoit Mandelbrot began studying a recursive function involving complex numbers.

$$Z_0 = c$$

$$Z_{n+1} = Z_n^2 + c$$

In this function, the value of Z is initialized to c, the value of the complex number being tested. For each iteration, the value of Z is squared and added to c to determine a new value for Z. This amazingly simple iterative formula produces what has been called the most complex object in mathematics, and perhaps the most complex structure ever seen!

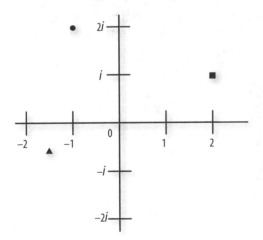

Figure 18.6   A portion of the complex number plane

It turns out that for some values of c, the function eventually approaches infinity, and for other values it does not. Quite simply, values of c that go off to infinity are not part of the Mandelbrot set, and the rest are. If we use a computer (or an OpenGL Shading Language–capable graphics accelerator!) to test thousands of points on the complex number plane and assign a gray level to those that go off to infinity and black to those that don't, we see the following familiar cardioid/prickly pear shape start to appear (see Figure 18.7).

How exactly do we test whether these values go off to infinity? Well, Mandelbrot helped us out a bit here. He showed that if the magnitude of Z (its distance from the origin) was greater than 2, the value of the function would go to infinity. To encode this function in a programming language, all we need to do is stop iterating when the magnitude of Z surpasses 2. Even easier, because we're always dealing with Z^2, we can simply check to see if Z^2 is greater than 4.

The values inside the black region of Figure 18.7 do not go off to infinity in any reasonable number of iterations. How do we deal with these? To prevent our computer or graphics hardware from locking up in an infinite loop, we need to decide on the maximum number of iterations to allow before we give up and assume the point is inside the Mandelbrot set. With these two exit criteria, we can write a simple loop that computes the Mandelbrot set.

The beauty of the Mandelbrot set can be enhanced if we color code the number of iterations needed to determine whether a particular point is inside the set. Values determined to be outside the set on the first iteration

Figure 18.7   Simple plot of the Mandelbrot set

are given one color value, values determined to be outside the set on the second iteration are given another color value, and so on. In Figure 18.7, I've used gray levels to indicate the number of iterations. The medium gray on the outside represents values that are identified as outside the Mandelbrot set on the very first iteration. Values in white along the edge took 20 iterations to be identified as being outside the Mandelbrot set.

The edges of the Mandelbrot set hold an infinite amount of self-similar variety. By continuing to zoom in on the edge detail, you can find complex numbers whose magnitude stayed below 2 for hundreds or even thousands of iterations of the function before finally exceeding the threshold and zooming off to infinity.

Here are a few other deep thoughts that you can use to amaze and amuse your friends:

* The length of the border for the Mandelbrot set is infinite.

* All the regions inside the Mandelbrot set (i.e., the black regions) are connected.

* There is exactly one band surrounding the Mandelbrot set for each iteration value (e.g., a band that exceeded the threshold on the first iteration, a band that exceeded on the second iteration, and so on). The iteration bands go completely around the Mandelbrot set, do not break, and do not cross each other. When you've zoomed in to explore an edge region with amazing complexity, this is pretty astonishing.

* There are an infinite number of "mini-Mandelbrots" (regions that look like warped or transformed versions of the full Mandelbrot set) within the original.

18.3.2 Vertex Shader

The vertex shader for the Mandelbrot set (see Listing 18.6) is almost exactly the same as the vertex shader for the simple brick example that was described in Section 6.2. The only difference is that we assume that texture coordinates will be provided in the range of [0,1] for both s and t, and we map these values into the range [−2.5, 2.5] and store the result into an out variable named *Position*. This enables the fragment shader to plot values directly onto a coordinate system that is just the right size for plotting the Mandelbrot set, and it has the point (0,0) in the middle. If the application draws a single polygon that is a screen-aligned square and has texture coordinate (0,0) in the lower-left corner and (1,1) in the upper right, the result is a standard representation of the Mandelbrot set. Of course, with our OpenGL Mandelbrot shader, the Mandelbrot set can be "textured" onto any geometry, and we even apply a simple lighting model as an added bonus.

Listing 18.6   Vertex shader for drawing the Mandelbrot set

```
#version 140

uniform mat4 MVMatrix;
uniform mat4 MVPMatrix;
uniform mat3 NormalMatrix;

uniform vec3  LightPosition;
uniform float SpecularContribution;
uniform float DiffuseContribution;
uniform float Shininess;

in  vec4  MCVertex;
in  vec3  MCNormal;
in  vec3  TexCoord0;

out float LightIntensity;
out vec3  Position;

void main()
{
    vec3 ecPosition = vec3(MVMatrix * MCVertex);
    vec3 tnorm      = normalize(NormalMatrix * MCNormal);
    vec3 lightVec   = normalize(LightPosition - ecPosition);
    vec3 reflectVec = reflect(-lightVec, tnorm);
    vec3 viewVec    = normalize(-ecPosition);
    float spec      = max(dot(reflectVec, viewVec), 0.0);
    spec            = pow(spec, Shininess);
    LightIntensity  = DiffuseContribution *
                      max(dot(lightVec, tnorm), 0.0) +
                      SpecularContribution * spec;
    Position        = TexCoord0 * 5.0 - 2.5;
    gl_Position     = MVPMatrix * MCVertex;
}
```

18.3.3 Fragment Shader

The fragment shader implements the algorithm described in the previous section. Uniform variables establish the maximum number of iterations and the starting point for viewing the Mandelbrot set (center value and zoom factor). The application is given artistic license to use uniform variables to set one color for points inside the set and two colors to use for points outside the set. For values outside the set, the color gradient from *OuterColor1* to *OuterColor2* is broken into 20 separate bands, and the cycle is repeated if the number of iterations goes past 20. It is repeated again if the number of iterations goes past 40, and so on.

This shader maps the *x* coordinate of the computed position in the complex number plane (i.e., the value in *Position.x*) to the real number in the iterative function, and the *y* coordinate to the imaginary number. After the initial conditions have been established, the shader enters a loop with two exit criteria—if we reach the maximum number of iterations allowed or if the point proves to be outside the set. Within the loop, the function $Z^2 + c$ is computed for use in the next iteration. After the loop is exited, we compute the color of the fragment. If we're inside the set, we use the inside color. If we're on the edge or outside, we blend the edge color and the outer color, depending on the number of iterations that have occurred.

The complete fragment shader is shown in Listing 18.7.

Listing 18.7 Fragment shader for computing the Mandelbrot set

```
#version 140

uniform float MaxIterations;
uniform float Zoom;
uniform float Xcenter;
uniform float Ycenter;
uniform vec3  InnerColor;
uniform vec3  OuterColor1;
uniform vec3  OuterColor2;

in  vec3  Position;
in  float LightIntensity;
out vec4  FragColor;

void main()
{
    float   real  = Position.x * Zoom + Xcenter;
    float   imag  = Position.y * Zoom + Ycenter;
    float   Creal = real;    // Change this line...
    float   Cimag = imag;    // ...and this one to get a Julia set

    float r2 = 0.0;
    float iter;

    for (iter = 0.0; iter < MaxIterations && r2 < 4.0; ++iter)
    {
        float tempreal = real;
```

```
        real = (tempreal * tempreal) - (imag * imag) + Creal;
        imag = 2.0 * tempreal * imag + Cimag;
        r2   = (real * real) + (imag * imag);
    }

    // Base the color on the number of iterations

    vec3 color;

    if (r2 < 4.0)
        color = InnerColor;
    else
        color = mix(OuterColor1, OuterColor2, fract(iter * 0.05));

    color *= LightIntensity;

    FragColor = vec4(color, 1.0);
}
```

There is obviously room for improvement in this shader. One thing you might do is improve the color selection algorithm. One possibility is to use a 1D texture to store a color lookup table. The number of iterations could be used to index into this table to obtain the color for drawing the fragment.

After you've invented a pleasing coloring scheme, you can explore some of the popular Mandelbrot "tourist locations." Various books and Web sites have published the coordinates of interesting locations in the Mandelbrot set, and these shaders are set up so that you can plug those coordinates in directly and zoom in and see for yourself. Figure 18.8 shows a few that I explored.

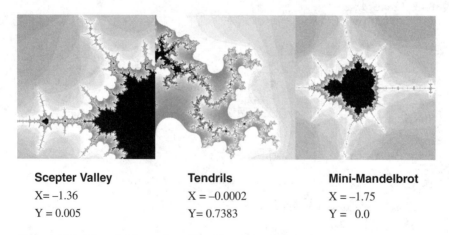

Scepter Valley	**Tendrils**	**Mini-Mandelbrot**
X= −1.36	X = −0.0002	X = −1.75
Y = 0.005	Y= 0.7383	Y = 0.0

Figure 18.8   Results from the Mandelbrot shader

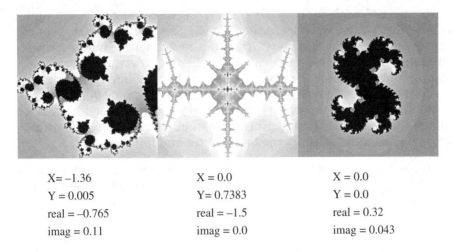

X= −1.36	X = 0.0	X = 0.0
Y = 0.005	Y = 0.7383	Y = 0.0
real = −0.765	real = −1.5	real = 0.32
imag = 0.11	imag = 0.0	imag = 0.043

Figure 18.9 Some Julia sets rendered with the Mandelbrot shader

18.3.4 Julia Sets

Julia sets are related to the Mandelbrot set. Each point in the Mandelbrot set can be used to generate a Julia set, and these are just as much fun to explore as the Mandelbrot set. The only difference is that the constant *c* in the equation term $Z^2 + c$ is initialized to the value of a point in the Mandelbrot set other than the one currently being plotted. To change the Mandelbrot shader into a fragment shader for doing Julia sets, change the two lines of code that initialize the value of *c*.

```
float    Creal = -1.36;    // Now we'll see an interesting Julia set
float    Cimag = 0.11;
```

Figure 18.9 shows a few examples of the Julia sets that can be rendered with this shader. You might want to change this shader so that the values for *Creal* and *Cimag* can be passed in as uniform variables when you want to draw a Julia set. The numbers are no longer imaginary. Now we can do real-time exploration of the mathematical universe through the OpenGL Shading Language!

18.4 Summary

Realism is no longer the goal for all applications of interactive computer graphics. Because of the flexibility of programmable graphics hardware, we no longer have to settle for the classic "look" of computer graphics. A high-level procedural language such as the OpenGL Shading Language enables artists and practitioners to express algorithms for rendering in more artistic styles such as pen-and-ink, woodcut, and paints. A procedural hatching shader was presented and described to illustrate how such rendering can be accomplished. Various styles of technical illustration can be done interactively, as shown by the Gooch shader described in this chapter. It is also possible to write shaders that assist in the visualization of mathematical functions, as demonstrated by the Mandelbrot and Julia set shaders.

The history of human art shows that there is an endless variety of artistic styles. The OpenGL Shading Language can be used to create shaders that emulate some of these styles and perhaps to invent new ones.

18.5 Further Information

Books devoted to the topic of non-photorealistic rendering include *Non-Photorealistic Rendering* by Amy Gooch and Bruce Gooch (2001) and *Non-Photorealistic Computer Graphics* by Thomas Strothotte and Stefan Schlechtweg (2002).

The Gooch shading algorithm is defined and described in the SIGGRAPH 1998 paper, *A Non-Photorealistic Lighting Model for Automatic Technical Illustration*, by Amy Gooch, Bruce Gooch, Peter Shirley, and Elaine Cohen. This paper draws on concepts presented by Edward Tufte in *Visual Explanations* (1997). A short discussion of NPR can be found in *Real-Time Rendering, Second Edition*, by Tomas Akenine-Möller and Eric Haines (2002). I've also included a lot of references to NPR resources in the main bibliography at the end of this book.

The classic text on fractals and the Mandelbrot set is, of course, *The Fractal Geometry of Nature, Updated and Augmented,* by Benoit Mandelbrot (1983). In 1986, Heinz-Otto Peitgen and Peter Richter wrote *The Beauty of Fractals,* another book you can enjoy looking at as well as reading. Peitgen and Dietmer Saupe (1988) edited a book called *The Science of Fractal Images,* which contains numerous examples and algorithms and additional material by Mandelbrot, Richard Voss, and others. A couple of the Mandelbrot "tourist destinations" that I've listed were described by Paul Derbyshire on the now defunct Web site, *PGD's Quick Guide to the Mandelbrot Set.*

[1] Akenine-Möller, Tomas, E. Haines, *Real-Time Rendering, Second Edition,* AK Peters, Ltd., Natick, Massachusetts, 2002. www.realtimerendering.com

[2] Baldwin, Dave, *OpenGL 2.0 Shading Language White Paper, Version 1.0*, 3Dlabs, October, 2001.

[3] Derbyshire, Paul, *PGD's Quick Guide to the Mandelbrot Set*, personal Web site. www.globalserve.net/~derbyshire/manguide.html (defunct)

[4] Freudenberg, Bert, Maic Masuch, and Thomas Strothotte, *Walk-Through Illustrations: Frame-Coherent Pen-and-Ink Style in a Game Engine*, Computer Graphics Forum, Volume 20 (2001), Number 3, Manchester, U.K. http://isgwww.cs.uni-magdeburg.de/~bert/publications

[5] Freudenberg, Bert, Maic Masuch, and Thomas Strothotte, *Real-Time Halftoning: A Primitive For Non-Photorealistic Shading*, Rendering Techniques 2002, Proceedings 13th Eurographics Workshop, pp. 227–231, 2002. http://isgwww.cs.uni-magdeburg.de/~bert/publications

[6] Freudenberg, Bert, and Maic Masuch, *Non-Photorealistic Shading in an Educational Game Engine*, SIGGRAPH and Eurographics Campfire, Snowbird, Utah, June 1–June 4, 2002. http://isgwww.cs.uni-magdeburg.de/~bert/publications

[7] Freudenberg, Bert, *Real-Time Stroke-based Halftoning*, Ph.D. thesis, University of Magdeburg, submitted in 2003.

[8] Gooch, Amy, *Interactive Non-Photorealistic Technical Illustration*, Master's thesis, University of Utah, December 1998. www.cs.utah.edu/~gooch/publication.html

[9] Gooch, Amy, Bruce Gooch, Peter Shirley, and Elaine Cohen, *A Non-Photorealistic Lighting Model for Automatic Technical Illustration*, Computer Graphics (SIGGRAPH '98 Proceedings), pp. 447–452, July 1998. www.cs.utah.edu/~gooch/publication.html

[10] Gooch, Bruce, Peter-Pike J. Sloan, Amy Gooch, Peter Shirley, and Richard Riesenfeld, *Interactive Technical Illustration*, Proceedings 1999 Symposium on Interactive 3D Graphics, pp. 31–38, April 1999. www.cs.utah.edu/~gooch/publication.html

[11] Gooch, Bruce, and Amy Gooch, *Non-Photorealistic Rendering*, AK Peters Ltd., Natick, Massachusetts, 2001. www.cs.utah.edu/~gooch/book.html

[12] Lander, Jeff, *Under the Shade of the Rendering Tree*, Game Developer Magazine, vol. 7, no. 2, pp. 17–21, Feb. 2000. www.darwin3d.com/gdm2000.htm

[13] Mandelbrot, Benoit B., *The Fractal Geometry of Nature, Updated and Augmented*, W. H. Freeman and Company, New York, 1983.

[14] Mitchell, Jason L., *Image Processing with Pixel Shaders in Direct3D*, in Engel, Wolfgang, ed., ShaderX, Wordware, May 2002. www.pixelmaven.com/jason

[15] Peitgen, Heinz-Otto, and P. H. Richter, *The Beauty of Fractals, Images of Complex Dynamical Systems,* Springer Verlag, Berlin Heidelberg, 1986.

[16] Peitgen, Heinz-Otto, D. Saupe, M. F. Barnsley, R. L. Devaney, B. B. Mandelbrot, R. F. Voss, *The Science of Fractal Images,* Springer Verlag, New York, 1988.

[17] Strothotte, Thomas, and S. Schlectweg, *Non-Photorealistic Computer Graphics, Modeling, Rendering, and Animation,* Morgan Kaufmann Publishers, San Francisco, 2002.

[18] Tufte, Edward, *Visual Explanations,* Graphics Press, Cheshire, Connecticut, 1997.

Chapter 19

Shaders for Imaging

In this chapter, we describe shaders whose primary function is to operate on two-dimensional images rather than on three-dimensional geometric primitives.

A fragment shader can be used to process texture values read from a texture map. We can divide imaging operations into two broad categories: those that require access to a single pixel at a time and those that require access to multiple pixels at a time. With the OpenGL Shading Language, you can easily implement in a fragment shader the imaging operations that require access to only a single pixel at a time. Operations that require access to multiple pixels at a time require that the image first be stored in texture memory. You can then access the image multiple times from within a fragment shader to achieve the desired result.

An OpenGL shader typically can perform imaging operations much faster on the graphics hardware than on the CPU because of the highly parallel nature of the graphics hardware. So, we let the fragment shader handle the task. This approach also frees the CPU to perform other useful tasks. If the image to be modified is stored as a texture on the graphics accelerator, the user can interact with it in real time to correct color, remove noise, sharpen an image, and do other such operations, and all the work can be done on the graphics board, with very little traffic on the I/O bus.

19.1 Geometric Image Transforms

If you want to rotate an image, the traditional response has always been "Load the image into texture memory, use it to draw a textured rectangle, and transform the rectangle." Although this approach does require an extra read and write of the image within the graphics system—the image must be written into texture memory and then read as the rectangle is drawn—the speed and bandwidth of today's graphics accelerators make this an acceptable approach for all but the most demanding applications. With the OpenGL Shading Language, you can even provide the same rectangle coordinates every time you draw the image and let the vertex shader do the scaling, translation, or rotation of the rectangle. You can perform image warping by texturing a polygon mesh instead of a single rectangle. Hardware support for texture filtering can produce high-quality results for any of these operations.

19.2 Mathematical Mappings

A common imaging operation supported by OpenGL fixed functionality is scale-and-bias. In this operation, each incoming color component is multiplied by a scale factor, and a bias value is added. You can use the result to map color values from one linear range to another. This is straightforward in the OpenGL Shading Language with the use of the standard math operators. You can do more complex mathematical mappings on pixel values with built-in functions such as **pow**, **exp2**, and **log2**.

The built-in dot product function (**dot**) can produce a single intensity value from a color value. The following code computes a CIE luminance value from linear RGB values defined according to *ITU-R Recommendation BT.709* (the HDTV color standard):

```
float luminance = dot(vec3(0.2125, 0.7154, 0.0721), rgbColor);
```

This luminance mapping function is the standard used in manufacturing contemporary monitors, and it defines a linear RGB color space. The coefficients 0.299, 0.587, and 0.114 are often used to convert an RGB value to a luminance value. However, these values were established with the inception of the NTSC standard in 1953 to compute luminance for the monitors of that time, and they are used to convert nonlinear RGB values to luminance values. They do not accurately calculate luminance for today's CRT monitors, but they are still appropriate for computing nonlinear video luma from nonlinear RGB input values as follows:

```
float luma = dot(vec3(0.299, 0.587, 0.114), rgbColor);
```

19.3 Lookup Table Operations

OpenGL defines a number of lookup tables as part of its fixed functionality. Several are defined as part of the imaging subset. Lookup tables are simply a way of mapping an input value to one or more output values. This operation provides a level of indirection that is often useful for processing color information. The fact that OpenGL has programmable processors means that you can compute the input values as part of a shader and use the output value as part of further computation within the shader. This creates a lot of new possibilities for lookup tables.

A flexible and efficient way to perform lookup table operations with an OpenGL shader is to use a 1D texture map. The lookup table can be an arbitrary size (thus overcoming a common gripe about OpenGL lookup tables often being limited by implementations to 256 entries). You can use the lookup table to map a single input value to a single output value or to a two-, three-, or four-component value. If you want the values returned to be discrete values, set the 1D texture's filtering modes to GL_NEAREST. If you want interpolation to occur between neighboring lookup table values, use GL_LINEAR.

You can use an intensity value in the range [0,1] as the texture coordinate for a 1D texture access. The built-in texture functions always return an RGBA value. If a texture with a single channel has been bound to the texture unit specified by the sampler, the value of that texture is contained in each of the red, green, and blue channels, so you can pick any of them.

```
float color = texture(lut, intensity).r; // GL_PIXEL_MAP_I_TO_I
```

You can perform an intensity-to-RGBA lookup with a single texture access.

```
vec4  color = texture(lut, intensity);   // GL_PIXEL_MAP_I_TO_R,G,B,A
```

An RGBA-to-RGBA lookup operation requires four texture accesses.

```
vec4 colorOut;
colorOut.r = texture(lut, colorIn.r).r;  // GL_PIXEL_MAP_R_TO_R
colorOut.g = texture(lut, colorIn.g).g;  // GL_PIXEL_MAP_G_TO_G
colorOut.b = texture(lut, colorIn.b).b;  // GL_PIXEL_MAP_B_TO_B
colorOut.a = texture(lut, colorIn.a).a;  // GL_PIXEL_MAP_A_TO_A
```

However, if you don't need alpha and you are willing to use a 3D texture to store the color table, you can do an RGB-to-RGB lookup with a single texture access.

```
colorOut.rgb = texture(lut, colorIn.rgb).rgb;
```

In this case, the variable *lut* must be defined as a **sampler3d**, whereas in the previous cases it needed to be defined as a **sampler1d**.

19.4 Color Space Conversions

A variety of color space conversions can be implemented in OpenGL shaders. In this section, we look at converting CIE colors to RGB, and vice versa. Conversions between other color spaces can be done similarly.

The CIE system was defined in 1931 by the Committee Internationale de L'Èclairage (CIE). It defines a device-independent color space based on the characteristics of human color perception. The CIE set up a hypothetical set of primaries, XYZ, that correspond to the way the eye's retina behaves. After experiments based on color matching by human observers, the CIE defined the primaries so that all visible light maps into a positive mixture of X, Y, and Z and so that Y correlates approximately to the apparent lightness of a color. The CIE system precisely defines any color. With this as a standard reference, colors can be transformed from the native (device-dependent) color space of one device to the native color space of another device.

A matrix formulation is convenient for performing such conversions. The HDTV standard as defined in *ITU-R Recommendation BT.709* (1990) has the following CIE XYZ primaries and uses the D_{65} (natural sunlight) white point:

	R	G	B	white
x	0.640	0.300	0.150	0.3127
y	0.330	0.600	0.060	0.3290
z	0.030	0.100	0.790	0.3582

Listing 19.1 shows the OpenGL shader code that transforms CIE color values to HDTV standard RGB values by using the D_{65} white point, and Listing 19.2 shows the reverse transformation. The matrices look like they are transposed compared to the colorimetry literature because in the OpenGL Shading Language matrix values are provided in column major order.

Listing 19.1   OpenGL shader code to transform CIE values to RGB

```
const mat3 CIEtoRGBmat = mat3(3.240479, -0.969256,  0.055648,
                             -1.537150,  1.875992, -0.204043,
                             -0.498535,  0.041556,  1.057311);

vec3 rgbColor = cieColor * CIEtoRGBmat;
```

Listing 19.2   OpenGL shader code to transform RGB values to CIE

```
const mat3 RGBtoCIEmat = mat3(0.412453, 0.212671, 0.019334,
                              0.357580, 0.715160, 0.119193,
                              0.180423, 0.072169, 0.950227);

vec3 cieColor = rgbColor * RGBtoCIEmat;
```

19.5 Image Interpolation and Extrapolation

In 1994, Paul Haeberli and Douglas Voorhies published an interesting paper that described imaging operations that could be performed with interpolation and extrapolation operations. These operations could actually be programmed on the high-end graphics systems of that time; today, thanks to the OpenGL Shading Language, they can be done quite easily on consumer graphics hardware.

The technique is quite simple. The idea is to determine a target image that can be used together with the source image to perform interpolation and extrapolation. The equation is set up as a simple linear interpolation that blends two images:

$$Image_{out} = (1 - \alpha) \cdot Image_{target} + \alpha \cdot Image_{source}$$

The target image is actually an image that you want to interpolate or extrapolate away from. Values of *alpha* between 0 and 1 interpolate between the two images, and values greater than 1 extrapolate between the two images. For instance, to adjust brightness, the target image is one in which every pixel is black. When *alpha* is 1, the result is the source image. When *alpha* is 0, the result is that all pixels are black. When *alpha* is between 0 and 1, the result is a linear blend of the source image and the black image, effectively darkening the image. When *alpha* is greater than 1, the image is brightened.

Such operations can be applied to images (pixel rectangles in OpenGL jargon) with a fragment shader as they are being sent to the display. In cases in which a target image is really needed (in many cases, it is not needed, as we shall see), it can be stored in a texture and accessed by the fragment shader. If the source and target images are downloaded into memory on the graphics card (i.e., stored as textures), these operations can be blazingly fast, limited only by the memory speed and the fill rate of the graphics hardware. This should be much faster than performing the same operations on the CPU and downloading the image across the I/O bus every time it's modified.

19.5.1 Brightness

Brightness is the easiest example. The target image is composed entirely of black pixels (e.g., pixel values (0,0,0)). Therefore, the first half of the interpolation equation goes to zero, and the equation reduces to a simple scaling of the source pixel values. This is implemented with the fragment shader in

Listing 19.3, and the results for several values of *alpha* are shown in Color
Plate 29.

Listing 19.3   Fragment shader for adjusting brightness uniform float Alpha;

```
#version 140

uniform float Alpha;

in  vec4 Color;
out vec4 FragColor;

void main(void)
{
    FragColor = Color * Alpha;
}
```

19.5.2 Contrast

A somewhat more interesting example is contrast (see Listing 19.4). Here
the target image is chosen to be a constant gray image with each pixel containing a value equal to the average luminance of the image. This value and
the *alpha* value are assumed to be computed by the application and sent
to the shader as uniform variables. The results of the contrast shader are
shown in Color Plate 30.

Listing 19.4   Fragment shader for adjusting contrast

```
#version 140

uniform vec3  AvgLuminance;
uniform float Alpha;

in  vec3  Color;
out vec4  FragColor;

void main()
{
    vec3 color  = mix(AvgLuminance, Color, Alpha);
    FragColor   = vec4(color, 1.0);
}
```

19.5.3 Saturation

The target image for a saturation adjustment is an image containing only
luminance information (i.e., a grayscale version of the source image). This
image can be computed pixel-by-pixel by extraction of the luminance value

from each RGB value. The proper computation depends on knowing the color space in which the RGB values are specified. For RGB values specified according to the HDTV color standard, you could use the coefficients shown in the shader in Listing 19.5. Results of this shader are shown in Color Plate 31. As you can see, extrapolation can provide useful results for values that are much greater than 1.0.

Listing 19.5 Fragment shader for adjusting saturation

```
#version 140

const    vec3  lumCoeff = vec3(0.2125, 0.7154, 0.0721);
uniform float Alpha;

in  vec4 Color;
out vec4 FragColor;

void main()
{
    vec3 intensity = vec3(dot(Color.rgb, lumCoeff));
    vec3 color     = mix(intensity, Color.rgb, Alpha);
    FragColor      = vec4(color, 1.0);
}
```

19.5.4 Sharpness

Remarkably, this technique also lends itself to adjusting any image convolution operation (see Listing 19.6). For instance, you can construct a target image by blurring the original image. Interpolation from the source image to the blurred image reduces high frequencies, and extrapolation (*alpha* greater than 1) increases them. The result is image sharpening through UNSHARP MASKING. The results of the sharpness fragment shader are shown in Color Plate 32.

Listing 19.6 Fragment shader for adjusting sharpness

```
#version 140

uniform sampler2D Blurry;
uniform float Alpha;

in  vec2  TexCoord;
in  vec4  Color;
out vec4  FragColor;

void main()
{
    vec3 blurred  = vec3(texture(Blurry, TexCoord.st));
    vec3 color    = Color.rgb * Alpha + blurred * (1.0 - Alpha);
    FragColor     = vec4(color, 1.0);
}
```

These examples showed the simple case in which the entire image is modified with a single *alpha* value. More complex processing is possible. The *alpha* value could be a function of other variables. A control texture could define a complex shape that indicates the portion of the image to be modified. A brush pattern could apply the operation selectively to small regions of the image. The operation could be applied selectively to pixels with a certain luminance range (e.g., shadows, highlights, or midtones).

Fragment shaders can also interpolate between more than two images, and the interpolation need not be linear. Interpolation can be done along several axes simultaneously with a single target image. A blurry, desaturated version of the source image can be used with the source image to produce a sharpened, saturated version in a single operation.

19.6 Blend Modes

With the expressiveness of a high-level language, it is easy to combine, or blend, two images in a variety of ways. Both images can be stored in texture memory, or one can be in texture memory and one can be downloaded by the application with **glDrawPixels**. For example, here's a fragment shader that adds together two images:

```
#version 140

uniform sampler2D BaseImage;
uniform sampler2D BlendImage;
uniform float Opacity;

in  vec2 TexCoord;
out vec4 FragColor;

void main (void)
{
    vec4 base  = texture(BaseImage, TexCoord.xy);
    vec4 blend = texture(BlendImage, TexCoord.xy);

    vec4 result = blend + base;
        result = clamp(result, 0.0, 1.0);

    FragColor = mix(base, result, Opacity);
}
```

The following sections contain snippets of OpenGL shader code that perform pixel-by-pixel blending for some of the common blend modes. In each case,

- *base* is a **vec4** containing the RGBA color value from the base (original) image.

- *blend* is a **vec4** containing the RGBA color value from the image that is being blended into the base image.

- *result* is a **vec4** containing the RGBA color that results from the blending operation.

- If it's needed in the computation, *white* is a **vec4** containing (1.0, 1.0, 1.0, 1.0).

- If it's needed in the computation, *lumCoeff* is a **vec4** containing (0.2125, 0.7154, 0.0721, 1.0).

- As a final step, *base* and *result* are combined by use of a floating-point value called *Opacity*, which determines the contribution of each.

There is no guarantee that the results of the code snippets provided here will produce results identical to those of your favorite image editing program, but the effects should be similar. The OpenGL shader code for the various blend modes is based on information published by Jens Gruschel in his article *Blend Modes*, available at www.pegtop.net/delphi/blendmodes. Unless otherwise noted, the blend operations are not commutative (you will get different results if you swap the base and blend images).

Results of the blend mode shaders are shown in Color Plate 33.

19.6.1 Normal

NORMAL is often used as the default blending mode. The blend image is placed over the base image. The resulting image equals the blend image when the opacity is 1.0 (i.e., the base image is completely covered). For opacities other than 1.0, the result is a linear blend of the two images based on *Opacity*.

```
result = blend;
```

19.6.2 Average

The AVERAGE blend mode adds the two images and divides by two. The result is the same as NORMAL when the opacity is set to 0.5. This operation is commutative.

```
result = (base + blend) * 0.5;
```

19.6.3 Dissolve

In the DISSOLVE mode, either *blend* or *base* is chosen randomly at every pixel. The value of *Opacity* is used as a probability factor for choosing the *blend* value. Thus, as the opacity gets closer to 1.0, the *blend* value is more likely to be chosen than the *base* value. If we draw the image as a texture on a rectangular polygon, we can use the texture coordinate values as the argument to **noise1D** to provide a value with which we can select in a pseudo-random, but repeatable, way. We can apply a scale factor to the texture coordinates to obtain noise of a higher frequency and give the appearance of randomness. The value returned by the noise function is in the range $[-1,1]$ so we add 1 and multiply by 0.5 to get it in the range $[0,1]$.

```
float noise = (noise1(vec2(TexCoord * noiseScale)) + 1.0) * 0.5;
result = (noise < Opacity) ? blend : base;
```

19.6.4 Behind

BEHIND chooses the *blend* value only where the base image is completely transparent (i.e., *base.a* = 0.0). You can think of the base image as a piece of clear acetate, and the effect of this mode is as if you were painting the blend image on the back of the acetate—only the areas painted behind transparent pixels are visible.

```
result = (base.a == 0.0) ? blend : base;
```

19.6.5 Clear

CLEAR always uses the *blend* value, and the alpha value of *result* is set to 0 (transparent). This blend mode is more apt to be used with drawing tools than on complete images.

```
result.rgb = blend.rgb;
result.a   = 0.0;
```

19.6.6 Darken

In DARKEN mode, the two values are compared, and the minimum value is chosen for each component. This operation makes images darker because the blend image can do nothing except make the base image darker. A blend image that is completely white (RGB = 1.0, 1.0, 1.0) does not alter the base image. Regions of black (0, 0, 0) in either image cause the result to be black.

It is commutative—the result is the same if the blend image and the base image are swapped.

```
result = min(blend, base);
```

19.6.7 Lighten

LIGHTEN can be considered the opposite of DARKEN. Instead of taking the minimum of each component, we take the maximum. The blend image can therefore never do anything but make the result lighter. A blend image that is completely black (RGB = 0, 0, 0) does not alter the base image. Regions of white (1.0, 1.0, 1.0) in either image cause the result to be white. The operation is commutative because swapping the two images does not change the result.

```
result = max(blend, base);
```

19.6.8 Multiply

In MULTIPLY mode, the two values are multiplied together. This produces a darker result in all areas in which neither image is completely white. White is effectively an identity (or transparency) operator because any color multiplied by white will be the original color. Regions of black (0, 0, 0) in either image cause the result to be black. The result is similar to the effect of stacking two color transparencies on an overhead projector. This operation is commutative.

```
result = blend * base;
```

19.6.9 Screen

SCREEN can be thought of as the opposite of MULTIPLY because it multiplies the inverse of the two input values. The result of this multiplication is then inverted to produce the final result. Black is effectively an identity (or transparency) operator because any color multiplied by the inverse of black (i.e., white) will be the original color. This blend mode is commutative.

```
result = white - ((white - blend) * (white - base));
```

19.6.10 Color Burn

COLOR BURN darkens the base color as indicated by the blend color by decreasing luminance. There is no effect if the *blend* value is white. This computation can result in some values less than 0, so truncation may occur when the resulting color is clamped.

```
result = white - (white - base) / blend;
```

19.6.11 Color Dodge

COLOR DODGE brightens the base color as indicated by the blend color by increasing luminance. There is no effect if the *blend* value is black. This computation can result in some values greater than 1, so truncation may occur when the result is clamped.

```
result = base / (white - blend);
```

19.6.12 Overlay

OVERLAY first computes the luminance of the base value. If the luminance value is less than 0.5, the *blend* and *base* values are multiplied together. If the luminance value is greater than 0.5, a screen operation is performed. The effect is that the *base* value is mixed with the *blend* value, rather than being replaced. This allows patterns and colors to overlay the base image, but shadows and highlights in the base image are preserved. A discontinuity occurs where luminance = 0.5. To provide a smooth transition, we actually do a linear blend of the two equations for luminance in the range [0.45,0.55].

```
float luminance = dot(base, lumCoeff);
if (luminance < 0.45)
    result = 2.0 * blend * base;
else if (luminance > 0.55)
    result = white - 2.0 * (white - blend) * (white - base);
else
{
    vec4 result1 = 2.0 * blend * base;
    vec4 result2 = white - 2.0 * (white - blend) * (white - base);
    result = mix(result1, result2, (luminance - 0.45) * 10.0);
}
```

19.6.13 Soft Light

SOFT LIGHT produces an effect similar to a soft (diffuse) light shining through the blend image and onto the base image. The resulting image is essentially a muted combination of the two images.

```
result = 2.0 * base * blend + base * base - 2.0 * base * base * blend;
```

19.6.14 Hard Light

HARD LIGHT mode is identical to OVERLAY mode, except that the luminance value is computed with the *blend* value rather than the *base* value. The effect is similar to shining a harsh light through the blend image and onto the base image. Pixels in the blend image with a luminance of 0.5 have no effect on the base image. This mode is often used to produce embossing effects. The **mix** function provides a linear blend between the two functions for luminance in the range [0.45,0.55].

```
float luminance = dot(blend, lumCoeff);
if (luminance < 0.45)
    result = 2.0 * blend * base;
else if (luminance > 0.55)
    result = white - 2.0 * (white - blend) * (white - base);
else
{
    vec4 result1 = 2.0 * blend * base;
    vec4 result2 = white - 2.0 * (white - blend) * (white - base);
    result = mix(result1, result2, (luminance - 0.45) * 10.0);
}
```

19.6.15 Add

In the ADD mode, the result is the sum of the blend image and the base image. Truncation may occur because resulting values can exceed 1.0. The blend and base images can be swapped, and the result will be the same.

```
result = blend + base;
```

19.6.16 Subtract

SUBTRACT subtracts the blend image from the base image. Truncation may occur because resulting values may be less than 0.

```
result = base - blend;
```

19.6.17 Difference

In the DIFFERENCE mode, the result is the absolute value of the difference between the *blend* value and the *base* value. A result of black means the two initial values were equal. A result of white means they were opposite. This mode can be useful for comparing images because identical images produce a completely black result. An all-white blend image can be used to invert the base image. Blending with black produces no change. Because of the absolute value operation, this blend mode is commutative.

```
result = abs(blend - base);
```

19.6.18 Inverse Difference

The INVERSE DIFFERENCE blend mode performs the "opposite" of DIFFERENCE. Blend values of white and black produce the same results as for DIFFERENCE (white inverts and black has no effect), but colors in between white and black become lighter instead of darker. This operation is commutative.

```
result = white - abs(white - base - blend);
```

19.6.19 Exclusion

EXCLUSION is similar to DIFFERENCE, but it produces an effect that is lower in contrast (softer). The effect for this mode is in between the effects of the DIFFERENCE and INVERSE DIFFERENCE modes. Blending with white inverts the base image, blending with black has no effect, and colors in between become gray. This is also a commutative blend mode.

```
result = base + blend - (2.0 * base * blend);
```

19.6.20 Opacity

In OPACITY mode, an opacity value in the range [0,1] can also specify the relative contribution of the base image and the computed result. The *result* value from any of the preceding formulas can be further modified to compute the effect of the *opacity* value as follows:

```
finalColor = mix(base, result, Opacity);
```

19.7 Convolution

CONVOLUTION is a common image processing operation that filters an image by computing the sum of products between the source image and a smaller image called the CONVOLUTION KERNEL or the CONVOLUTION FILTER. Depending on the choice of values in the convolution kernel, a convolution operation can perform blurring, sharpening, noise reduction, edge detection, and other useful imaging operations.

Mathematically, the discrete 2D convolution operation is defined as

$$H(x, y) = \sum_{j=0}^{height-1} \sum_{i=0}^{width-1} F(x+i, y+j) \cdot G(i,j)$$

In this equation, the function *F* represents the base image, and *G* represents the convolution kernel. The double summation is based on the width and height of the convolution kernel. We compute the value for a particular pixel in the output image by aligning the center of the convolution kernel with the pixel at the same position in the base image, multiplying the values of the base image pixels covered by the convolution kernel by the values in the corresponding locations in the convolution kernel, and then summing the results.

The flexibility of the OpenGL Shading Language enables convolution operations with arbitrary-sized kernels and full floating-point precision. Furthermore, the convolution operation can be written in an OpenGL shader such that the minimum number of multiplication operations is actually performed (i.e., kernel values equal to 0 do not need to be stored or used in the convolution computation).

But there are a couple of hurdles to overcome. First, this operation seems naturally suited to implementation as a fragment shader, but the fragment shader is not allowed to access the values of any neighboring fragments. How can we perform a neighborhood operation such as convolution without access to the "neighborhood"?

The answer to this dilemma is that we store the base image in texture memory and access it as a texture. We can draw a screen-aligned rectangle that's the same size on the screen as the base image and enable texturing to render the image perfectly. We can introduce a fragment shader into this process, and instead of sampling the image just once during the texturing process, we can access each of the values under the convolution kernel and compute the convolution result at every pixel.

A second hurdle is that, although the OpenGL Shading Language supports loops, even nested loops, it does not currently support two-dimensional arrays. We can easily overcome this by "unrolling" the convolution kernel and storing it as a one-dimensional array. Each location in this array stores an x- and y-offset from the center of the convolution kernel and the value of the convolution kernel at that position. In the fragment shader, we process this array in a single loop, adding the specified offsets to the current texture location, accessing the base image, and multiplying the retrieved pixel value by the convolution kernel value. Storing the convolution kernel this way means that we can store the values in row major order, column major order, backwards, or all mixed up. We don't even need to include convolution kernel values that are zero, because they do not contribute to the convolved image.

The interesting work for performing convolution is done with fragment shaders. The vertex shader is required to perform an identity mapping of the input geometry (a screen-aligned rectangle that is the size of the base image), and it is required to pass on texture coordinates. The texture coordinate (0,0) should be assigned to the lower-left corner of the rectangle, and the texture coordinate (1,1) should be assigned to the upper-right corner of the rectangle.

One additional issue with convolution operations is deciding what to do when the convolution kernel extends beyond the edges of the base image. A convenient side effect of using OpenGL texture operations to perform the convolution is that the texture-wrapping modes defined by OpenGL map nicely to the common methods of treating convolution borders. Thus,

- To achieve the same effect as the GL_CONSTANT_BORDER, set the GL_TEXTURE_WRAP_S and GL_TEXTURE_WRAP_T parameters of the texture containing the base image to GL_CLAMP_TO_BORDER. This method uses the border color when the convolution kernel extends past the image boundary.

- If the desired behavior is the same as GL_REPLICATE_BORDER, set the GL_TEXTURE_WRAP_S and GL_TEXTURE_WRAP_T parameters of the texture containing the base image to GL_CLAMP_TO_EDGE. This method uses the pixel value at the edge of the image when the convolution kernel extends past the image boundary.

- If you want to mimic the GL_REDUCE convolution border mode, draw a rectangle that is smaller than the image to be convolved. For a 3 × 3 convolution kernel, the rectangle should be smaller by two pixels in *width* and two pixels in *height*. In this case, the texture coordinate of the lower-left corner is (1/*width*, 1/*height*), and the texture coordinate of the upper-right corner is (1 − 1/*width*, 1 − 1/*height*).

The texture filtering modes should be set to GL_NEAREST to avoid unintended interpolation.

19.7.1 Smoothing

Image smoothing operations can attenuate high frequencies in an image. A common image smoothing operation is known as NEIGHBORHOOD AVERAGING. This method uses a convolution kernel that contains a weighting of 1.0 in each location. The final sum is divided by a value equal to the number of locations in the convolution kernel. For instance, a 3×3 neighborhood averaging convolution filter would look like this:

1	1	1
1	1	1
1	1	1

The resulting sum would be divided by 9 (or multiplied by 1/9). Neighborhood averaging, as the name implies, has the effect of averaging all the pixels in a region with equal weighting. It effectively smears the value of each pixel to its neighbors, resulting in a blurry version of the original image.

Because all the elements of the convolution kernel are equal to 1, we can write a simplified fragment shader to implement neighborhood averaging (see Listing 19.7). This shader can be used for neighborhood averaging for any kernel size where *width * height* is less than or equal to 25 (i.e., up to 5×5). The results of this operation are shown in Figure 19.1 (B).

Listing 19.7 Fragment shader for the neighborhood averaging convolution operation

```
#version 140

// maximum size supported by this shader
const int MaxKernelSize = 25;

// array of offsets for accessing the base image
uniform vec2 Offset[MaxKernelSize];

// size of kernel (width * height) for this execution
uniform int KernelSize;

// final scaling value
uniform vec4 ScaleFactor;
```

```
// image to be convolved
uniform sampler2D BaseImage;

// texture coordinate output from vertex shader
in vec2 TexCoord;

// fragment shader output
out vec4 FragColor;

void main()
{
    int i;
    vec4 sum = vec4(0.0);

    for (i = 0; i < KernelSize; i++)
        sum += texture(BaseImage, TexCoord.st + Offset[i]);

    FragColor = sum * ScaleFactor;
}
```

Image smoothing by means of convolution is often used to reduce noise. This works well in regions of solid color or intensity, but it has the side effect of blurring high frequencies (edges). A convolution filter that applies higher weights to values nearer the center can do a better job of eliminating noise while preserving edge detail. Such a filter is the Gaussian filter, which can be encoded in a convolution kernel as follows:

1/273	4/273	7/273	4/273	1/273
4/273	16/273	26/273	16/273	4/273
7/273	26/273	41/273	26/273	7/273
4/273	16/273	26/273	16/273	4/273
1/273	4/273	7/273	4/273	1/273

Listing 19.8 contains the code for a more general convolution shader. This shader can handle convolution kernels containing up to 25 entries. In this shader, each convolution kernel entry is expected to have been multiplied by the final scale factor, so there is no need to scale the final sum.

Listing 19.8   Fragment shader general convolution computation

```
#version 140

// maximum size supported by this shader
const int MaxKernelSize = 25;
```

```
// array of offsets for accessing the base image
uniform vec2 Offset[MaxKernelSize];

// size of kernel (width * height) for this execution
uniform int KernelSize;

// value for each location in the convolution kernel
uniform vec4 KernelValue[MaxKernelSize];

// image to be convolved
uniform sampler2D BaseImage;

// texture coordinate output from vertex shader
in vec2 TexCoord;

// fragment shader output
out vec4 FragColor;

void main()
{
    int i;
    vec4 sum = vec4(0.0);

    for (i = 0; i < KernelSize; i++)
    {
        vec4 tmp = texture(BaseImage, TexCoord.st + Offset[i]);
        sum += tmp * KernelValue[i];
    }

    FragColor = sum;
}
```

The original image in Figure 19.1 (A) has had uniform noise added to it to create the image in Figure 19.1 (C). The Gaussian smoothing filter is then applied to this image to remove noise, and the result is shown in Figure 19.1 (D). Notice in particular that the noise has been significantly reduced in areas of nearly constant intensity.

As the size of the convolution kernel goes up, the number of texture reads that is required increases as the square of the kernel size. For larger kernels, this can become the limiting factor for performance. Some kernels, including the Gaussian kernel just described, are said to be separable because the convolution operation with a *width* × *height* kernel can be performed as two passes, with one-dimensional convolutions of size *width* × 1 and 1 × *height*. With this approach, there is an extra write for each pixel (the result of the first pass), but the number of texture reads is reduced from *width* × *height* to *width* + *height*.

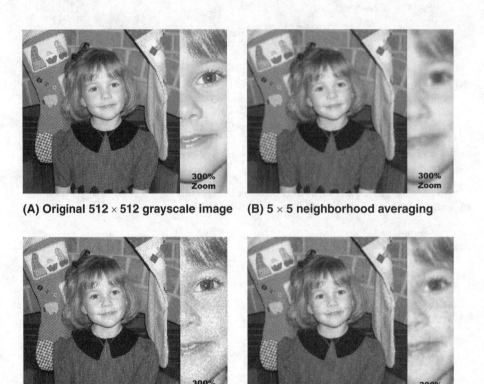

(A) Original 512 × 512 grayscale image   **(B) 5 × 5 neighborhood averaging**

(C) Original with noise added   **(D) Noise reduction with Gaussian filter**

Figure 19.1   Results of various convolution operations

19.7.2 Edge Detection

Another common use for the convolution operation is edge detection. This operation is useful for detecting meaningful discontinuities in intensity level. The resulting image can aid in image comprehension or can enhance the image in other ways.

One method for detecting edges involves the Laplacian operator.

0	1	0
1	−4	1
0	1	0

We can plug the Laplacian convolution kernel into the fragment shader shown in Listing 19.8. This results in the image shown in Figure 19.2.

Figure 19.2 Edge detection with the Laplacian convolution kernel (image scaled for display)

19.7.3 Sharpening

A common method of image sharpening is to add the results of an edge detection filter back onto the original image. To control the degree of sharpening, a scaling factor scales the edge image as it is added.

One way to sharpen an image is with the negative Laplacian operator. This convolution filter is defined as

0	−1	0
−1	4	−1
0	−1	0

The fragment shader that implements image sharpening in this fashion is almost identical to the general convolution shader shown in the previous section (see Listing 19.9). The only difference is that the result of the convolution operation is added to the original image. Before it is added, the convolution result is scaled by a scale factor provided by the application through a uniform variable. The results of unsharp masking are shown in Figure 19.3 and Figure 19.4.

Listing 19.9 Fragment shader for unsharp masking

```
#version 140

// maximum size supported by this shader
const int MaxKernelSize = 25;

// array of offsets for accessing the base image
uniform vec2 Offset[MaxKernelSize];
```

```
// size of kernel (width * height) for this execution
uniform int KernelSize;

// value for each location in the convolution kernel
uniform vec4 KernelValue[MaxKernelSize];

// scaling factor for edge image
uniform vec4 ScaleFactor;

// image to be convolved
uniform sampler2D BaseImage;

// texture coordinate output from vertex shader
in vec2 TexCoord;

// fragment shader output
out vec4 FragColor;


void main()
{
    int i;
    vec4 sum = vec4(0.0);

    for (i = 0; i < KernelSize; i++)
    {
        vec4 tmp = texture(BaseImage, TexCoord.st + Offset[i]);
        sum += tmp * KernelValue[i];
    }

    vec4 baseColor = texture(BaseImage, vec2(TexCoord));
    FragColor = ScaleFactor * sum + baseColor;
}
```

Figure 19.3 Results of the unsharp masking shader. (Laplacian image in center is scaled for display.) Zoomed views of the original and resulting images are shown in Figure 19.4.

Figure 19.4   Results of the unsharp masking shader. Original image is on the left, sharpened image on the right.

19.8 Summary

In addition to support for rendering 3D geometry, OpenGL also contains a great deal of support for rendering images. The OpenGL Shading Language allows fully programmable processing of images. With this programmability and the parallel processing nature of the underlying graphics hardware, image processing operations can be performed orders-of-magnitude faster on the graphics accelerator than on the CPU. This programmability can be used to implement traditional image processing operations such as image blurring, sharpening, and noise removal; high-quality color correction; brightness, saturation, and contrast adjustment; geometric transformations such as rotation and warping; blending; and many other image processing operations. Furthermore, applications no longer need to be constrained to manipulating monochrome or color images. Multispectral processing and analysis are also possible.

The world of digital imagery is exploding as a result of the rapid development and acceptance of consumer products for digital photography and digital video. The OpenGL Shading Language will undoubtedly be at the heart of many tools that support this revolution in the future.

19.9 Further Information

The OpenGL literature doesn't always do justice to the imaging capabilities of OpenGL. In 1996, I wrote a paper called *Using OpenGL for Imaging* that attempted to describe and highlight clearly the fixed functionality imaging capabilities of OpenGL, including the capabilities of several pertinent imaging extensions. This paper was published as part of the SPIE Medical Imaging '96 Image Display Conference in Newport Beach, CA, and is available on this book's companion Web site at http://3dshaders.com/pubs. Another good resource for understanding how to use OpenGL for imaging is the course notes for the SIGGRAPH '99 course *Advanced Graphics Programming Techniques Using OpenGL* by Tom McReynolds and David Blythe. These can be found online at www.opengl.org/resources/tutorials/sig99/advanced99/notes/notes.html. This material has also been published in a recent book by Morgan Kaufmann.

Charles Poynton (1997) is one of the luminaries (pun intended) of the color technology field, and his *Frequently Asked Questions about Color* and *Frequently Asked Questions about Gamma* are informative and approachable treatments of a variety of topics relating to color and imaging. I found these on the Web on Charles's home page at www.poynton.com/Poynton-color.html.

The CIE color system is defined in Publication CIE 17.4–1987, *International Lighting Vocabulary*, Vienna, Austria, Central Bureau of the Committee Internationale de L'Èclairage, currently in its fourth edition. The HDTV color standard is defined in *ITU-R BT.709-2–Parameter Values for the HDTV Standards for Production and International Programme Exchange*, Geneva: ITU, 1990.

The paper *Image Processing by Interpolation and Extrapolation* by Paul Haeberli and Douglas Voorhies appeared in IRIS Universe Magazine in1994. A slightly shorter version of this paper is available online at www.graficaobscura.com/interp/.

A classic textbook on image processing is *Digital Image Processing, Second Edition*, by Rafael C. Gonzalez and Richard E. Woods, Addison-Wesley, 2002. An amazing little book (literally amazing, and literally little) is the *Pocket Handbook of Image Processing Algorithms in C* by Harley Myler and Arthur Weeks (1993).

[1] Gonzalez, Rafael C., and Richard E. Woods, *Digital Image Processing, Second Edition*, Prentice Hall, Upper Saddle River, New Jersey, 2002.

[2] Gruschel, Jens, *Blend Modes,* Pegtop Software Web site. www.pegtop.net/delphi/blendmodes

[3] Haeberli, Paul, and Douglas Voorhies, *Image Processing by Interpolation and Extrapolation*, IRIS Universe Magazine No. 28, Silicon Graphics, August, 1994. www.graficaobscura.com/interp/

[4] Hall, Roy, *Illumination and Color in Computer Generated Imagery*, Springer-Verlag, New York, 1989.

[5] *International Lighting Vocabulary*, Publication CIE No. 17.4, Joint publication IEC (International Electrotechnical Commission) and CIE (Committee Internationale de L'Èclairage), Geneva, 1987. www.cie.co.at/framepublications.html

[6] ITU-R Recommendation BT.709, *Basic Parameter Values for the HDTV Standard for the Studio and for International Programme Exchange*, [formerly CCIR Rec. 709], Geneva, ITU, 1990.

[7] Lindbloom, Bruce J., *Accurate Color Reproduction for Computer Graphics Applications*, Computer Graphics (SIGGRAPH '89 Proceedings), pp. 117–126, July 1989.

[8] Lindbloom, Bruce J., personal Web site, 2003. www.brucelindbloom.com/

[9] McReynolds, Tom, David Blythe, Brad Grantham, and Scott Nelson, *Advanced Graphics Programming Techniques Using OpenGL*, SIGGRAPH '99 course notes, 1999. www.opengl.org/resources/tutorials/sig99/advanced99/notes/notes.html

[10] McReynolds, Tom, and David Blythe, *Advanced Graphics Programming Techniques Using OpenGL*, Morgan Kaufmann, 2005.

[11] Myler, Harley R., and Arthur R. Weeks, *The Pocket Handbook of Image Processing Algorithms in C*, Prentice Hall, Upper Saddle River, NJ, 1993.

[12] Poynton, Charles A., *A Technical Introduction to Digital Video*, John Wiley & Sons, New York, 1996.

[13] Poynton, Charles A., *Frequently Asked Questions about Color*, 1997. www.poynton.com/Poynton-color.html

[14] Rost, Randi, *Using OpenGL for Imaging*, SPIE Medical Imaging '96 Image Display Conference, February 1996. http://3dshaders.com/pubs

[15] Wolberg, George, *Digital Image Warping*, Wiley-IEEE Press, 2002.

Chapter 20

Language Comparison

The OpenGL Shading Language is by no means the first graphics shading language ever defined. Here are a few other notable shading languages and a little about how each one compares to the OpenGL Shading Language. Compare the diagrams in this chapter with the OpenGL Shading Language execution model in Figure 2.4 for a visual summary.

20.1 Chronology of Shading Languages

Rob Cook and Ken Perlin are usually credited with being the first to develop languages to describe shading calculations. Both of these efforts targeted offline (noninteractive) rendering systems. Perlin's work included the definition of the noise function and the introduction of control constructs. Cook's work on shade trees at Lucasfilm (later Pixar) introduced the classification of shaders as surface shaders, light shaders, atmosphere shaders, and so on, and the ability to describe the operation of each through an expression. This work evolved into the effort to develop a full-featured language for describing shading calculations, which was taken up by Pat Hanrahan and culminated in the 1988 release of the first version of the *RenderMan Interface Specification* by Pixar. Subsequently, RenderMan became the de facto industry-standard shading language for offline rendering systems for the entertainment industry. It remains in widespread use today.

The first interactive shading language was demonstrated at the University of North Carolina on a massively parallel graphics architecture called PixelFlow that was developed over the decade of the 1990s. The shading language used on PixelFlow could render scenes with procedural shading at 30 frames per second or more. The shading language component of this system was described by Marc Olano in 1998.

After leaving UNC, Olano joined a team at SGI that was defining and implementing an interactive shading language that would run on top of OpenGL and use multipass rendering methods to execute the shaders. This work culminated in the release in 2000 of a product from SGI called OpenGL Shader, the first commercially available real-time, high-level shading language.

In June 1999, the Computer Graphics Laboratory at Stanford embarked on an effort to define a real-time shading language that could be accelerated by existing consumer graphics hardware. This language was called the Stanford Real-Time Shading Language. Results of this system were demonstrated in 2001.

The OpenGL Shading Language, Microsoft's HLSL, and NVIDIA's Cg are all efforts to define a commercially viable, real-time, high-level shading language. The white paper that first described the shading language that would become the OpenGL Shading Language was published in October 2001 by Dave Baldwin of 3Dlabs. NVIDIA's Cg specification was published in June of 2002, and Microsoft's HLSL specification was published in November 2002 as part of the beta release of the DirectX 9.0 Software Development Kit. Some cross-pollination of ideas occurred among these three efforts because of the interrelationships of the companies involved.

In subsequent sections, we compare the OpenGL Shading Language with other commercially available high-level shading languages.

20.2 RenderMan

In 1988, after several years of development, Pixar published the *RenderMan Interface Specification*. This was an interface intended to define the communications protocol between modeling programs and rendering programs aimed at producing images of photorealistic quality, as shown in Figure 20.1. The original target audience for this interface was animation production, and the interface has proved to be very successful for this market. It has been used as the interface for producing computer graphics special effects for films such as *Jurassic Park*, *Star Wars Episode 1: The Phantom Menace*, *The Lord of the Rings: The Two Towers*, and others. It has also been used for films that have been done entirely with computer graphics such as *Finding Nemo*, *Toy Story*, *A Bug's Life*, and *Monsters, Inc.*

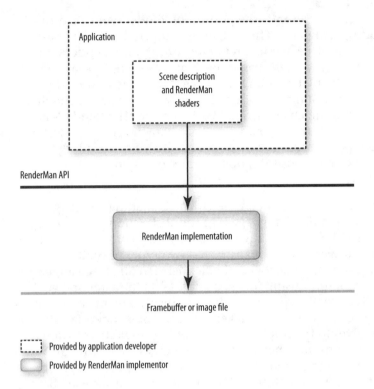

Application

Scene description
and RenderMan
shaders

RenderMan API

RenderMan implementation

Framebuffer or image file

Provided by application developer

Provided by RenderMan implementor

Figure 20.1   RenderMan execution environment

One of the main differences between the OpenGL Shading Language
and RenderMan is that RenderMan attempts to define the entire interface
between modeling programs and rendering programs. It provides an entire
graphics processing pipeline of its own that has no relationship to OpenGL.
Although a hardware implementation was envisioned at the time Render-
Man was first defined, it was primarily designed as a high-quality, realistic
rendering interface; therefore, it provides no compromises for interactivity
or direct hardware implementation on today's graphics hardware. Render-
Man includes support for describing geometric primitives, hierarchical
modeling, stacking geometric transformations, camera attributes, shading
attributes, and constructive solid geometry. OpenGL already provides many
of these capabilities; therefore, they need not be addressed in the OpenGL
Shading Language.

Of particular interest, however, is the portion of RenderMan called the RenderMan Shading Language. This language completely describes arbitrary shaders that can be passed to a renderer through the RenderMan interface. This language was also based on C, and as such, it bears some resemblance to the OpenGL Shading Language. In a general way, the RenderMan interface is similar to OpenGL, and the RenderMan Shading Language is similar to the OpenGL Shading Language. The RenderMan interface and OpenGL both let you define the characteristics of a scene (viewing parameters, primitives to be rendered, etc.). Both shading languages compute the color, position, opacity, and other characteristics of a point in the scene.

One of the main differences between the OpenGL Shading Language and the RenderMan Shading Language is in the abstraction of the shading problem. The OpenGL Shading Language closely maps onto today's commercial graphics hardware and has abstracted two types of shaders so far: vertex shaders and fragment shaders. The RenderMan Shading Language has always had uncompromising image quality as its fundamental goal, and it abstracts five shader types: light shaders, displacement shaders, surface shaders, volume shaders, and imager shaders. The RenderMan shader types lend themselves to the implementation of high-quality software rendering implementations, but they do not match up as well with hardware that has been designed to support interactive rendering with OpenGL. As a result, RenderMan implementations have typically been software based, but attempts to accelerate RenderMan shaders in hardware have been made (read *Interactive Multi-Pass Programmable Shading* by Peercy, Olano, Airey, and Ungar, 2000). The OpenGL Shading Language was designed from the beginning for acceleration by commodity graphics hardware.

There are some differences in the data types supported by the two languages. RenderMan supports native types that represent colors, points, and normals, whereas the OpenGL Shading Language includes the more generic vectors of 1, 2, 3, or 4 floating-point values that can support any of those. RenderMan goes a bit further in making the language graphics-specific by including built-in support for coordinate spaces named *object, world, camera, NDC, raster,* and *screen.*

RenderMan supports a number of predefined surface shader variables, light source variables, volume shader variables, displacement shader variables, and imager shader variables. The OpenGL Shading Language contains built-in variables that are specific to OpenGL state values, some of which are similar to the RenderMan predefined variables. Because it is aimed at producing animation, RenderMan also has built-in variables to represent time. The

OpenGL Shading Language does not, but such values can be passed to shaders through uniform variables to accomplish the same thing.

On the other hand, the two languages have much in common. In a very real sense, the OpenGL Shading Language can be thought of as a descendant of the RenderMan Shading Language. The data type qualifiers **uniform** and **varying** were invented in RenderMan and have been carried forward to mean the same things in the OpenGL Shading Language. Expressions and precedence of operators in both languages are very much like C. Keywords such as **if, else, while, for, break**, and **return** are the same in both languages. The list of built-in math functions for the OpenGL Shading Language is largely similar to the list of built-in math functions for the RenderMan Shading Language.

20.3 OpenGL Shader (ISL)

OpenGL Shader was a software package developed by SGI and released in 2000. It was available as a commercial product for several years, but is no longer available. OpenGL Shader defined both a shading language (Interactive Shading Language, or ISL) and a set of API calls that defined shaders and used them in the rendering process.

The fundamental premise of OpenGL Shader was that the OpenGL API could be used as an assembly language for executing programmable shaders (see Figure 20.2). Hardware with more features (e.g., multitexture and fragment programmability) could be viewed as having a more powerful assembly language. A sequence of statements in an ISL shader could end up being translated into one or more rendering passes. Each pass could be a geometry pass (geometry is drawn to use vertex, rasterization, and fragment operations), a copy pass (a region of the framebuffer is copied back into the same place in the framebuffer to use pixel, rasterization, and fragment operations), or a copy texture pass (a region of the framebuffer is copied to a texture to use pixel operations). Compiler optimization technology determined the type of pass required to execute a sequence of source code instructions and, if possible, to reduce the number of passes needed overall. The final version of OpenGL Shader was optimized for multiple hardware back ends and could exploit the features exposed on a particular platform to reduce the number of passes required.

Like every other shading language worth its salt, ISL is based on C. However, because of its fundamental premise, ISL shaders end up looking quite

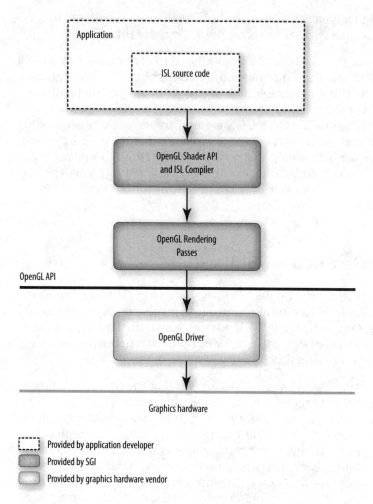

Figure 20.2   OpenGL Shader (ISL) execution environment

different from OpenGL shaders. Many of the instructions in an ISL shader end up look like directives to perform a rendering pass. For example, consider the following ISL source code:

```
varying color b;
FB  = diffuse();
FB *= color(.5, .2, 0, 1);
b   = FB;
FB  = specular(30.0);
FB += b;
```

The identifier *FB* specifies a result to be stored in the framebuffer. This sequence of operations first calls a subshader that executes a light shader to compute a diffuse color for the geometry being rendered. This value is multiplied by the color value (.5, .2, 0, 1), and the result is then stored in a region of texture memory called *b*. A specular reflection calculation is performed next, and finally the diffuse component and specular components are added together. Although it has the appearance of requiring multiple passes, this sequence of instructions can actually be executed in a single pass on a number of different graphics accelerators.

ISL supports surface and light shaders, which are merged and compiled. In this regard, it is more similar to the RenderMan way of doing things than it is to the OpenGL distinction of vertex and fragment shaders.

Another difference between the OpenGL Shading Language and ISL is that ISL was designed to provide portability for interactive shading by means of the OpenGL capabilities of both past and current hardware, whereas the OpenGL Shading Language was designed to expose the programmability of current and future hardware. The OpenGL Shading Language is not intended for hardware without a significant degree of programmability, but ISL executes shaders with the identical visual effect on a variety of hardware, including hardware with little or no explicit support for programmability.

Yet another difference between ISL and the OpenGL Shading Language is that ISL was designed with the constraints of using the OpenGL API as an assembly language, without requiring any changes in the underlying hardware. The OpenGL Shading Language was designed to define new capabilities for the underlying hardware, and so it supports a more natural syntax for expressing graphics algorithms. The high-level language defined by the OpenGL Shading Language can be translated into the machine code native to the graphics hardware with an optimizing compiler written by the graphics hardware vendor.

20.4 HLSL

HLSL stands for High-Level Shader Language, and it was defined by Microsoft and introduced with DirectX 9 in 2002. In terms of its syntax and functionality, HLSL is much closer to the OpenGL Shading Language than either RenderMan or ISL. HLSL supports the paradigm of programmability at the vertex level and at the fragment level just as in the OpenGL Shading Language. An HLSL vertex shader corresponds to an OpenGL vertex shader, and an HLSL pixel shader corresponds to an OpenGL fragment shader.

One of the main differences between the OpenGL Shading Language and HLSL is in the execution environment (see Figure 20.3). The HLSL compiler is really a translator that lives outside DirectX in the sense that HLSL programs are never sent directly to the DirectX 9 or DirectX 10 API for execution. Instead, the HLSL compiler translates HLSL source into assembly-level source or binary programs called VERTEX SHADERS and PIXEL SHADERS (in Microsoft DirectX parlance). Various levels of functionality have been defined for these assembly level shaders, and they are differentiated by

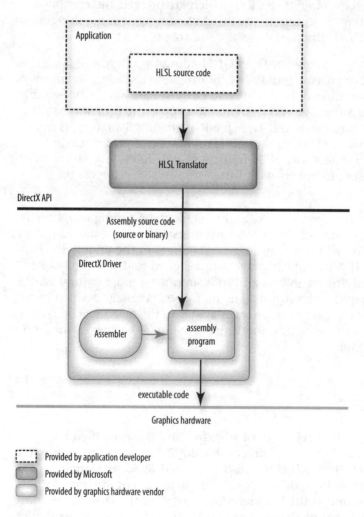

Figure 20.3 Execution environment for Microsoft's HLSL

a version number (e.g., Vertex Shader 1.0, 2.0, 3.0, 4.0; Pixel Shader 1.1, 1.4, 2.0, 3.0, 4.0).

One advantage of this approach is that HLSL programs can be translated offline, or long before the application is actually executed. However, the translation is done to a binary representation of assembly code. This binary representation may still need to be translated to native machine code at execution time. This is in contrast to the OpenGL Shading Language model, in which the compiler is part of the driver, and the graphics hardware vendor writes the compiler. Giving the graphics hardware vendor the responsibility of translating from high-level shading language source to machine code grants these vendors a lot of room for shader optimization and architectural innovation.

HLSL is designed to make it easier for application developers to deal with the various levels of functionality found in these assembly-level shaders. Using HLSL and the support environment that has been built around it, application developers can write shaders in a high-level shading language and be reasonably confident that their shaders will run on hardware with widely varying capabilities.

However, because HLSL is more expressive than the capabilities of graphics hardware that exists today and much more expressive than hardware shipped in the past, HLSL shaders are not guaranteed to run on every platform. Shader writers have two choices: They can write their shader for the lowest common denominator (i.e., hardware with very little programmability), or they can target their shader at a certain class of hardware by using a language feature called PROFILES. Microsoft provides supporting software called the DirectX Effects Framework to help developers organize and deploy a set of shaders that do the same thing for hardware with differing capabilities.

The fundamental data types in HLSL are the same as those in the OpenGL Shading Language except for slight naming differences. HLSL also supports half- and double-precision floats. Like the OpenGL Shading Language, HLSL accommodates vectors, matrices, structures, and arrays. Expressions in HLSL are as in C/C++. User-defined functions and conditionals are supported in the same manner as in the OpenGL Shading Language. Looping constructs (**for, do,** and **while**) are defined in HLSL, but the current documentation states that they are not yet implemented. HLSL has a longer list of built-in functions than does the OpenGL Shading Language, but those that are in both languages are very similar or identical.

One area of difference is the way in which values are passed between vertex shaders and pixel (HLSL) or fragment (OpenGL Shading Language) shaders. HLSL defines both input semantics and output semantics (annotations that identify data usage) for both vertex shaders and pixel shaders. This provides the same functionality as the OpenGL Shading Language varying and built-in variables. You are allowed to pass arbitrary data into and out of vertex and pixel shaders, but you must do so in named locations such as *POSITION*, *COLOR[i]*, *TEXCOORD[i]*, and so on. This requirement means that you may have to pass your light direction variable *lightdir* in a semantic slot named *TEXCOORD[i]*, for instance—a curious feature for a high-level language. The OpenGL Shading Language lets you use arbitrary names for passing values between vertex shaders and fragment shaders.

Another obvious difference between HLSL and the OpenGL Shading Language is that HLSL was designed for DirectX, Microsoft's proprietary graphics API, and the OpenGL Shading Language was designed for OpenGL. Microsoft can add to and change DirectX, whereas OpenGL is an open, cross-platform standard that changes more slowly but retains compatibility with previous versions.

20.5 Cg

Cg is a high-level shading language that is similar to HLSL. Cg has been defined, implemented, and supported by NVIDIA. Comparing Cg to the OpenGL Shading Language is virtually the same as comparing HLSL to the OpenGL Shading Language. There are a few minor differences between Cg and HLSL (for instance, HLSL has a double data type but Cg does not), but Cg and HLSL were developed by Microsoft and NVIDIA working together, so their resulting products are very similar.

One advantage that Cg has over both HLSL and the OpenGL Shading Language is that the Cg translator can generate either DirectX vertex shader/pixel shader assembly code or OpenGL vertex/fragment program (assembly-level) code. This provides the potential for using Cg shaders in either the DirectX environment or the OpenGL environment (see Figure 20.4). However, it also requires the application to make calls to a library provided by NVIDIA that sits between the application and the underlying graphics API (either OpenGL or DirectX). This library is called the Cg Runtime library. For simple applications, it can help cover up the limitations of the underlying driver (for instance, it can cover up the fact that a DirectX driver supports multiple versions of vertex and pixel shaders and automatically selects the most appropriate version to use). But this intervening layer can also complicate things for more complicated applications because it covers up details of shader management.

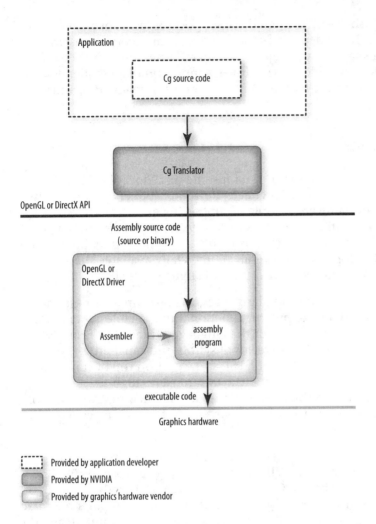

Figure 20.4 The Cg execution environment

NVIDIA has its own version of the framework that surrounds the shading language. CgFX is a shader specification and interchange format whose file format is the same as that supported by the .fx Effect format for DirectX 9. The CgFX runtime library, like the Cg runtime library, supports both OpenGL and DirectX, so in this way the Microsoft and NVIDIA products differ.

Because it is so similar to HLSL, the advantages and disadvantages of Cg with respect to the OpenGL Shading Language are also similar: proprietary versus standard (thus earlier to market), support for less capable hardware at the cost of hardware dependencies in shader source code, translation from high-level shading language to "standard" assembly interface offline versus a compiler embedded in the driver, a more complete shader development system but with the requirement of extra runtime libraries, and so on.

20.6   Summary

Shading languages have been around for some time now. The first shading languages were non-real-time languages aimed at producing photorealistic imagery. Graphics hardware capable of supporting an interactive shading language showed up in research labs in the 1990s, and today, this type of programmable graphics hardware is available at consumer price points. This has led to the development of several commercially available shading languages, notably, ISL, the OpenGL Shading Language, HLSL, and Cg.

In the spectrum of programming languages, the last three are extremely similar. Each was designed to provide functionality available in RenderMan by the use of C/C++ as the basis for the language syntax. The result is that all three languages are similar in terms of syntax and capability. The single biggest technical difference is that HLSL and Cg sit on top of standard interfaces such as DirectX and OpenGL and translate high-level source code to assembly outside those APIs. The OpenGL Shading Language, on the other hand, translates high-level source code to machine code within the OpenGL driver.

As far as nontechnical differences, the HLSL and CG specifications are controlled by Microsoft and NVIDIA, respectively. The OpenGL Shading Language is controlled by the OpenGL ARB, a standards body made up of representatives from a variety of graphics hardware and computer manufacturers. HLSL is designed for use in Microsoft's DirectX environment, and the OpenGL Shading Language is designed for use with OpenGL in a variety of operating environments. Cg is designed to be used in either DirectX or OpenGL environments.

20.7   Further Information

The RenderMan Shading Language is specified in Pixar's *The RenderMan Interface Specification* (2000), and its use is described in the books *The RenderMan Companion: A Programmer's Guide to Realistic Computer Graphics*

(Upstill 1990) and *Advanced RenderMan: Creating CGI for Motion Pictures* (Apodaca and Gritz 1999).

OpenGL Shader and ISL are described in the SIGGRAPH 2000 paper *Interactive Multi-Pass Programmable Shading*. The book *Real-Time Shading* by Olano, Hart, Heidrich, and McCool (2002) contains chapters describing various shading languages, including RenderMan, ISL, and shading languages defined and implemented by researchers at the University of North Carolina, Stanford, and the University of Waterloo.

The Stanford Real-Time Shading Language is described in the SIGGRAPH 2001 paper, *A Real-Time Procedural Shading System for Programmable Graphics Hardware*, and in the course notes for *Real-Time Shading*, Course 24, SIGGRAPH 2001.

There are sure to be books out that describe Microsoft's HLSL, but at the time of this writing, the only documentation I could find is available from Microsoft on the DirectX 9 page of its Web site, www.microsoft.com/directx. A good starting point is *Introduction to the DirectX 9 High-Level Shader Language* by Craig Peeper and Jason Mitchell. This paper also appears as a chapter in the book *ShaderX2: Shader Programming Tips and Tricks with DirectX 9.0* by Wolfgang Engel.

Cg is described in documentation from NVIDIA in the book *The Cg Tutorial: The Definitive Guide to Programmable Real-Time Graphics* by Fernando and Kilgard (2003) and in the SIGGRAPH 2003 paper *Cg: A System for Programming Graphics Hardware in a C-like Language*.

The bibliography at the end of this book contains references to other notable noncommercial shading languages.

[1] Apodaca, Anthony A., and Larry Gritz, *Advanced RenderMan: Creating CGI for Motion Pictures*, Morgan Kaufmann Publishers, San Francisco, 1999. www.renderman.org/RMR/Books/arman/materials.html

[2] Baldwin, Dave, *OpenGL 2.0 Shading Language White Paper, Version 1.0*, 3Dlabs, October, 2001.

[3] Cook, Robert L., *Shade Trees*, Computer Graphics (SIGGRAPH '84 Proceedings), pp. 223–231, July 1984.

[4] Fernando, Randima, and Mark Kilgard, *The Cg Tutorial, the Definitive Guide to Programmable Real-Time Graphics*, Addison-Wesley, Boston, Massachusetts, 2003.

[5] Kessenich, John, Dave Baldwin, and Randi Rost, *The OpenGL Shading Language, Version 1.10*, 3Dlabs, April 2004. www.opengl.org/documentation/spec.html

[6] Mark, William R., *Real-Time Shading: Stanford Real-Time Procedural Shading System*, SIGGRAPH 2001, Course 24, course notes, 2001. http://graphics.stanford.edu/projects/shading/pubs/sigcourse2001.pdf

[7] Mark, William R., R. Steven Glanville, Kurt Akeley, and Mark Kilgard, *Cg: A System for Programming Graphics Hardware in a C-like Language*, Computer Graphics (SIGGRAPH 2003 Proceedings), pp. 896–907, July 2003. www.cs.utexas.edu/users/billmark/papers/Cg

[8] Microsoft, *DirectX 10.0 SDK*, 2007. http://msdn.microsoft.com/directx

[9] NVIDIA Corporation, Cg Toolkit, Release 1.4, software and documentation. http://developer.nvidia.com/object/cg_toolkit.html

[10] Olano, Marc, and Anselmo Lastra, *A Shading Language on Graphics Hardware: The PixelFlow Shading System*, Computer Graphics (SIGGRAPH '98 Proceedings), pp. 159–168, July 1998. www.csee.umbc.edu/~olano/papers

[11] Olano, Marc, John Hart, Wolfgang Heidrich, and Michael McCool, *Real-Time Shading*, AK Peters, Ltd., Natick, Massachusetts, 2002.

[12] Peeper, Craig, and Jason Mitchell, *Introduction to the DirectX 9 High-Level Shader Language*, in *ShaderX2 : Shader Programming Tips and Tricks with DirectX 9.0*, Editor: Wolfgang Engel, Wordware Publishing, 2003. www.ati.com/developer/ShaderX2_IntroductionToHLSL.pdf

[13] Peercy, Mark S., Marc Olano, John Airey, and P. Jeffrey Ungar, *Interactive Multi-Pass Programmable Shading*, Computer Graphics (SIGGRAPH 2000 Proceedings), pp. 425–432, July 2000. www.csee.umbc.edu/~olano/papers

[14] Perlin, Ken, *An Image Synthesizer*, Computer Graphics (SIGGRAPH '85 Proceedings), pp. 287–296, July 1985.

[15] Pixar, *The RenderMan Interface Specification*, Version 3.2, Pixar, July 2000. https://renderman.pixar.com/products/rispec/index.htm

[16] Proudfoot, Kekoa, William R. Mark, Svetoslav Tzvetkov, and Pat Hanrahan, *A Real-Time Procedural Shading System for Programmable Graphics Hardware*, Computer Graphics (SIGGRAPH 2001 Proceedings), pp. 159–170, August 2001. http://graphics.stanford.edu/projects/shading/pubs/sig2001

[17] *SGI OpenGL Shader Web site*. www.sgi.com/software/shader (defunct)

[18] *ShaderX2 : Shader Programming Tips and Tricks with DirectX 9.0*, Editor: Wolfgang Engel, Wordware Publishing, 2003. www.shaderx2.com

[19] Upstill, Steve, *The RenderMan Companion: A Programmer's Guide to Realistic Computer Graphics*, Addison-Wesley, Reading, Massachusetts, 1990.

Language Grammar

The grammar is fed from the output of lexical analysis. The tokens returned from lexical analysis are

```
ATTRIBUTE CONST BOOL FLOAT INT UINT
BREAK CONTINUE DO ELSE FOR IF DISCARD RETURN SWITCH CASE DEFAULT
BVEC2 BVEC3 BVEC4 IVEC2 IVEC3 IVEC4 UVEC2 UVEC3 UVEC4 VEC2 VEC3 VEC4
MAT2 MAT3 MAT4 CENTROID IN OUT INOUT UNIFORM VARYING

NOPERSPECTIVE FLAT SMOOTH LAYOUT
MAT2X2 MAT2X3 MAT2X4
MAT3X2 MAT3X3 MAT3X4
MAT4X2 MAT4X3 MAT4X4
SAMPLER1D SAMPLER2D SAMPLER3D SAMPLERCUBE SAMPLER1DSHADOW
SAMPLER2DSHADOW
SAMPLERCUBESHADOW SAMPLER1DARRAY SAMPLER2DARRAY SAMPLER1DARRAYSHADOW
SAMPLER2DARRAYSHADOW ISAMPLER1D ISAMPLER2D ISAMPLER3D ISAMPLERCUBE
ISAMPLER1DARRAY ISAMPLER2DARRAY USAMPLER1D USAMPLER2D USAMPLER3D
USAMPLERCUBE USAMPLER1DARRAY USAMPLER2DARRAY
STRUCT VOID WHILE

IDENTIFIER TYPE_NAME FLOATCONSTANT INTCONSTANT UINTCONSTANT BOOLCONSTANT
FIELD_SELECTION
LEFT_OP RIGHT_OP
INC_OP DEC_OP LE_OP GE_OP EQ_OP NE_OP
AND_OP OR_OP XOR_OP MUL_ASSIGN DIV_ASSIGN ADD_ASSIGN
MOD_ASSIGN LEFT_ASSIGN RIGHT_ASSIGN AND_ASSIGN XOR_ASSIGN OR_ASSIGN
SUB_ASSIGN

LEFT_PAREN RIGHT_PAREN LEFT_BRACKET RIGHT_BRACKET LEFT_BRACE RIGHT_BRACE
DOT COMMA COLON EQUAL SEMICOLON BANG DASH TILDE PLUS STAR SLASH PERCENT
LEFT_ANGLE RIGHT_ANGLE VERTICAL_BAR CARET AMPERSAND QUESTION

INVARIANT
HIGH_PRECISION MEDIUM_PRECISION LOW_PRECISION PRECISION
```

The following describes the grammar for the OpenGL Shading Language in terms of the preceding tokens:

variable_identifier:
    IDENTIFIER

primary_expression:
    variable_identifier
    INTCONSTANT
    UINTCONSTANT
    FLOATCONSTANT
    BOOLCONSTANT
    LEFT_PAREN expression RIGHT_PAREN

postfix_expression:
    primary_expression
    postfix_expression LEFT_BRACKET integer_expression
      RIGHT_BRACKET
    function_call
    postfix_expression DOT FIELD_SELECTION
    postfix_expression INC_OP
    postfix_expression DEC_OP

integer_expression:
    expression

function_call:
    function_call_or_method

function_call_or_method:
    function_call_generic
    postfix_expression DOT function_call_generic

function_call_generic:

> *function_call_header_with_parameters RIGHT_PAREN*

> *function_call_header_no_parameters RIGHT_PAREN*

function_call_header_no_parameters:

> *function_call_header VOID*

> *function_call_header*

function_call_header_with_parameters:

> *function_call_header assignment_expression*

> *function_call_header_with_parameters COMMA*
> *assignment_expression*

function_call_header:

> *function_identifier LEFT_PAREN*

// Grammar Note: Constructors look like functions,
// but lexical analysis recognized most of them as keywords.
// They are now recognized through "type_specifier".

function_identifier:

> *type_specifier*
> *IDENTIFIER*
> *FIELD_SELECTION*

unary_expression:

> *postfix_expression*
> *INC_OP unary_expression*
> *DEC_OP unary_expression*
> *unary_operator unary_expression*

// Grammar Note: No traditional style type casts.

unary_operator:
    PLUS
    DASH
    BANG
    TILDE

// Grammar Note: No '' or '&' unary ops. Pointers are not
    supported.*

multiplicative_expression:
    unary_expression
    multiplicative_expression STAR unary_expression
    multiplicative_expression SLASH unary_expression
    multiplicative_expression PERCENT unary_expression

additive_expression:
    multiplicative_expression
    additive_expression PLUS multiplicative_expression
    additive_expression DASH multiplicative_expression

shift_expression:
    additive_expression
    shift_expression LEFT_OP additive_expression
    shift_expression RIGHT_OP additive_expression

relational_expression:
    shift_expression
    relational_expression LEFT_ANGLE shift_expression
    relational_expression RIGHT_ANGLE shift_expression
    relational_expression LE_OP shift_expression
    relational_expression GE_OP shift_expression

equality_expression:

    relational_expression

    equality_expression EQ_OP relational_expression

    equality_expression NE_OP relational_expression

and_expression:

    equality_expression

    and_expression AMPERSAND equality_expression

exclusive_or_expression:

    and_expression

    exclusive_or_expression CARET and_expression

inclusive_or_expression:

    exclusive_or_expression

    inclusive_or_expression VERTICAL_BAR
      exclusive_or_expression

logical_and_expression:

    inclusive_or_expression

    logical_and_expression AND_OP inclusive_or_expression

logical_xor_expression:

    logical_and_expression

    logical_xor_expression XOR_OP logical_and_expression

logical_or_expression:

    logical_xor_expression

    logical_or_expression OR_OP logical_xor_expression

conditional_expression:

    logical_or_expression

    logical_or_expression QUESTION expression COLON
      assignment_expression

assignment_expression:
    conditional_expression
    unary_expression assignment_operator assignment_expression

assignment_operator:
    EQUAL
    MUL_ASSIGN
    DIV_ASSIGN
    MOD_ASSIGN
    ADD_ASSIGN
    SUB_ASSIGN
    LEFT_ASSIGN
    RIGHT_ASSIGN
    AND_ASSIGN
    XOR_ASSIGN
    OR_ASSIGN

expression:
    assignment_expression
    expression COMMA assignment_expression

constant_expression:
    conditional_expression

declaration:
    function_prototype SEMICOLON
    init_declarator_list SEMICOLON
    PRECISION precision_qualifier type_specifier_no_prec
        SEMICOLON
    type_qualifier IDENTIFIER LEFT_BRACE
        struct_declaration_list RIGHT_BRACE SEMICOLON
    type_qualifier SEMICOLON

function_prototype:

    function_declarator RIGHT_PAREN

function_declarator:

    function_header

    function_header_with_parameters

function_header_with_parameters:

    function_header parameter_declaration

    function_header_with_parameters COMMA
       parameter_declaration

function_header:

    fully_specified_type IDENTIFIER LEFT_PAREN

parameter_declarator:

    type_specifier IDENTIFIER

    type_specifier IDENTIFIER LEFT_BRACKET
       constant_expression RIGHT_BRACKET

parameter_declaration:

    parameter_type_qualifier parameter_qualifier
       parameter_declarator

    parameter_qualifier parameter_declarator

    parameter_type_qualifier parameter_qualifier
       parameter_type_specifier

    parameter_qualifier parameter_type_specifier

parameter_qualifier:

    / empty */*

    IN

    OUT

    INOUT

parameter_type_specifier:
> *type_specifier*

init_declarator_list:
> *single_declaration*
>
> *init_declarator_list COMMA IDENTIFIER*
>
> *init_declarator_list COMMA IDENTIFIER LEFT_BRACKET*
> *RIGHT_BRACKET*
>
> *init_declarator_list COMMA IDENTIFIER LEFT_BRACKET*
> *constant_expression*
> *RIGHT_BRACKET*
>
> *init_declarator_list COMMA IDENTIFIER LEFT_BRACKET*
> *RIGHT_BRACKET EQUAL initializer*
>
> *init_declarator_list COMMA IDENTIFIER LEFT_BRACKET*
> *constant_expression RIGHT_BRACKET EQUAL initializer*
>
> *init_declarator_list COMMA IDENTIFIER EQUAL initializer*

single_declaration:
> *fully_specified_type*
>
> *fully_specified_type IDENTIFIER*
>
> *fully_specified_type IDENTIFIER LEFT_BRACKET*
> *RIGHT_BRACKET*
>
> *fully_specified_type IDENTIFIER LEFT_BRACKET*
> *constant_expression RIGHT_BRACKET*
>
> *fully_specified_type IDENTIFIER LEFT_BRACKET*
> *RIGHT_BRACKET EQUAL initializer*
>
> *fully_specified_type IDENTIFIER LEFT_BRACKET*
> *constant_expression RIGHT_BRACKET EQUAL initializer*
>
> *fully_specified_type IDENTIFIER EQUAL initializer*
>
> *INVARIANT IDENTIFIER   // Vertex only.*

// Grammar Note: No 'enum' or 'typedef'.

fully_specified_type:
> *type_specifier*
>
> *type_qualifier type_specifier*

invariant_qualifier:
>   *INVARIANT*

interpolation_qualifier:
>   *SMOOTH*
>   *FLAT*
>   *NOPERSPECTIVE*

layout_qualifier:
>   *LAYOUT LEFT_PAREN layout_list RIGHT_PAREN*

layout_list:
>   *IDENTIFIER*
>   *layout_list COMMA IDENTIFIER*

parameter_type_qualifier:
>   *CONST*

type_qualifier:
>   *storage_qualifier*
>   *layout_qualifier*
>   *layout_qualifier storage_qualifier*
>   *interpolation_qualifier type_qualifier*
>   *invariant_qualifier type_qualifier*
>   *invariant_qualifier interpolation_qualifier type_qualifier*

storage_qualifier:
>   *CONST*
>   *ATTRIBUTE   // Vertex only.*
>   *VARYING*
>   *CENTROID VARYING*
>   *IN*
>   *OUT*
>   *CENTROID IN*
>   *CENTROID OUT*
>   *UNIFORM*

type_specifier:

    type_specifier_no_prec

    precision_qualifier type_specifier_no_prec

type_specifier_no_prec:

    type_specifier_nonarray

    type_specifier_nonarray LEFT_BRACKET RIGHT_BRACKET

    type_specifier_nonarray LEFT_BRACKET constant_expression RIGHT_BRACKET

type_specifier_nonarray:

    VOID

    FLOAT

    INT

    UINT

    BOOL

    VEC2

    VEC3

    VEC4

    BVEC2

    BVEC3

    BVEC4

    IVEC2

    IVEC3

    IVEC4

    UVEC2

    UVEC3

    UVEC4

    MAT2

    MAT3

    MAT4

    MAT2X2

MAT2X3

MAT2X4

MAT3X2

MAT3X3

MAT3X4

MAT4X2

MAT4X3

MAT4X4

SAMPLER1D

SAMPLER2D

SAMPLER3D

SAMPLERCUBE

SAMPLER1DSHADOW

SAMPLER2DSHADOW

SAMPLERCUBESHADOW

SAMPLER1DARRAY

SAMPLER2DARRAY

SAMPLER1DARRAYSHADOW

SAMPLER2DARRAYSHADOW

ISAMPLER1D

ISAMPLER2D

ISAMPLER3D

ISAMPLERCUBE

ISAMPLER1DARRAY

ISAMPLER2DARRAY

USAMPLER1D

USAMPLER2D

USAMPLER3D

USAMPLERCUBE

USAMPLER1DARRAY

USAMPLER2DARRAY

struct_specifier:
   TYPE_NAME

precision_qualifier:
   HIGH_PRECISION
   MEDIUM_PRECISION
   LOW_PRECISION

struct_specifier:
   STRUCT IDENTIFIER LEFT_BRACE struct_declaration_list
      RIGHT_BRACE
   *STRUCT LEFT_BRACE struct_declaration_list RIGHT_*
      BRACE

struct_declaration_list:
   struct_declaration
   struct_declaration_list struct_declaration

struct_declaration:
   type_specifier struct_declarator_list SEMICOLON
   type_qualifier type_specifier struct_declarator_list
      SEMICOLON

struct_declarator_list:
   struct_declarator
   struct_declarator_list COMMA struct_declarator

struct_declarator:
   IDENTIFIER
   IDENTIFIER LEFT_BRACKET constant_expression
      RIGHT_BRACKET

initializer:
   assignment_expression

declaration_statement:
>   *declaration*

statement:
>   *compound_statement*
>   *simple_statement*

// Grammar Note: labeled statements for SWITCH only;
// 'goto' is not supported.

simple_statement:
>   *declaration_statement*
>   *expression_statement*
>   *selection_statement*
>   *switch_statement*
>   *case_label*
>   *iteration_statement*
>   *jump_statement*

compound_statement:
>   *LEFT_BRACE RIGHT_BRACE*
>   *LEFT_BRACE statement_list RIGHT_BRACE*

statement_no_new_scope:
>   *compound_statement_no_new_scope*
>   *simple_statement*

compound_statement_no_new_scope:
>   *LEFT_BRACE RIGHT_BRACE*
>   *LEFT_BRACE statement_list RIGHT_BRACE*

statement_list:
>   *statement*
>   *statement_list statement*

expression_statement:
    SEMICOLON
    expression SEMICOLON

selection_statement:
    IF LEFT_PAREN expression RIGHT_PAREN
      selection_rest_statement

selection_rest_statement:
    statement ELSE statement
    statement

condition:
    expression
    fully_specified_type IDENTIFIER EQUAL initializer

switch_statement:
    SWITCH LEFT_PAREN expression RIGHT_PAREN
      LEFT_BRACE switch_statement_list RIGHT_BRACE

switch_statement_list:
    / nothing */*
    statement_list

case_label:
    CASE expression COLON
    DEFAULT COLON

iteration_statement:
    WHILE LEFT_PAREN condition RIGHT_PAREN
      statement_no_new_scope
    DO statement WHILE LEFT_PAREN expression
      RIGHT_PAREN SEMICOLON
    FOR LEFT_PAREN for_init_statement for_rest_statement
      RIGHT_PAREN statement_no_new_scope

for_init_statement:
  expression_statement
  declaration_statement

conditionopt:
  condition
  / empty */*

for_rest_statement:
  conditionopt SEMICOLON
  conditionopt SEMICOLON expression

jump_statement:
  CONTINUE SEMICOLON
  BREAK SEMICOLON
  RETURN SEMICOLON
  RETURN expression SEMICOLON
  DISCARD SEMICOLON   // Fragment shader only.

// Grammar Note: No 'goto'. Gotos are not supported.

translation_unit:
  external_declaration
  translation_unit external_declaration

external_declaration:
  function_definition
  declaration

function_definition:
  function_prototype compound_statement_no_new_scope

API Function Reference

This section contains detailed information on the OpenGL commands that support the creation, compilation, linking, and usage of shaders written in the OpenGL Shading Language, as well as the OpenGL commands added to provide generic vertex attributes and user-defined uniform variables to such shaders.

The reference pages in this section are copyrighted by 3Dlabs, Inc., Ltd. © 2003–2005 and are reprinted with permission.

Implementation-Dependent API Values for GLSL

A number of new implementation-dependent values have been defined in OpenGL 3.1 to support the requirements of the OpenGL Shading Language. Each value can be queried with one of the variants of **glGet**.

GL_MAX_COMBINED_TEXTURE_IMAGE_UNITS
> Defines the total number of hardware units that can access texture maps from the vertex processor and the fragment processor combined. The minimum legal value is 32.

GL_MAX_DRAW_BUFFERS
> Defines the maximum number of buffers that can be simultaneously written into from within a fragment shader using the special output variable array *gl_FragData.* This constant effectively defines the size of the *gl_FragData* array.

GL_MAX_FRAGMENT_UNIFORM_COMPONENTS
> Defines the number of components (i.e., floating-point values) that are available for fragment shader uniform variables. The minimum legal value is 1024.

GL_MAX_TEXTURE_IMAGE_UNITS
> Defines the total number of hardware units that can access texture maps from the fragment processor. The minimum legal value is 16.

GL_MAX_VARYING_COMPONENTS
> Defines the number of floating-point variables available for varying variables. The minimum legal value is 64.

GL_MAX_VERTEX_ATTRIBS
> Defines the number of active vertex attributes that are available. The minimum legal value is 16.

GL_MAX_VERTEX_TEXTURE_IMAGE_UNITS
> Defines the number of hardware units that can access texture maps from the vertex processor. The minimum legal value is 16.

GL_MAX_VERTEX_UNIFORM_COMPONENTS
> Defines the number of components (i.e., floating-point values) that are available for vertex shader uniform variables. The minimum legal value is 1024.

Other Queriable Values for GLSL

GL_CURRENT_PROGRAM

>   Contains the name of the program object that is currently installed
>   as part of current state. If no program object is active, this value is
>   0. This value can be obtained with one of the variants of **glGet**.

GL_SHADING_LANGUAGE_VERSION

>   Contains the OpenGL Shading Language version that is supported
>   by the implementation. It is organized as a dot-delimited sequence
>   of multidigit integers. This value can be obtained with **glGetString**.

glAttachShader

NAME

glAttachShader—Attaches a shader object to a program object

C SPECIFICATION

```
void glAttachShader(GLuint program,
                    GLuint shader)
```

PARAMETERS

program   Specifies the program object to which a shader object will be attached

shader   Specifies the shader object that is to be attached

DESCRIPTION

For an executable to be created, there must be a way to specify the list of things that will be linked. Program objects provide this mechanism. Shaders that are to be linked in a program object must first be attached to that program object. **glAttachShader** attaches the shader object specified by *shader* to the program object specified by *program*. This signifies that *shader* will be included in link operations that will be performed on *program*.

All operations that can be performed on a shader object are valid whether or not the shader object is attached to a program object. It is permissible to attach a shader object to a program object before source code has been loaded into the shader object or before the shader object has been compiled. It is permissible to attach multiple shader objects of the same type because each may contain a portion of the complete shader. It is also permissible to attach a shader object to more than one program object. If a shader object is deleted while it is attached to a program object, it is flagged for deletion, and deletion does not occur until **glDetachShader** is called to detach it from all program objects to which it is attached.

NOTES

glAttachShader is available only if the GL version is 2.0 or greater.

ERRORS

GL_INVALID_VALUE is generated if either *program* or *shader* is not a value generated by OpenGL.

GL_INVALID_OPERATION is generated if *program* is not of type GL_PROGRAM_OBJECT.

GL_INVALID_OPERATION is generated if *shader* is not of type GL_SHADER_OBJECT.

GL_INVALID_OPERATION is generated if *shader* is already attached to *program*.

GL_INVALID_OPERATION is generated if **glAttachShader** is executed between the execution of **glBegin** and the corresponding execution of **glEnd**.

ASSOCIATED GETS

glGetAttachedShaders with the handle of a valid program object

glIsProgram

glIsShader

SEE ALSO

glCompileShader, **glDetachShader**, **glLinkProgram**, **glShaderSource**

glBindAttribLocation

NAME

glBindAttribLocation—Associates a generic vertex attribute index with a named attribute variable

C SPECIFICATION

```
void glBindAttribLocation(GLuint program,
                          GLuint index,
                          const GLchar *name)
```

PARAMETERS

program   Specifies the handle of the program object in which the association is to be made

index   Specifies the index of the generic vertex attribute to be bound

name   Specifies a null-terminated string containing the name of the vertex shader attribute variable to which *index* is to be bound

DESCRIPTION

glBindAttribLocation associates a user-defined attribute variable in the program object specified by *program* with a generic vertex attribute index. The name of the user-defined attribute variable is passed as a null-terminated string in *name.* The generic vertex attribute index to be bound to this variable is specified by *index.* When *program* is made part of current state, values provided through the generic vertex attribute *index* modify the value of the user-defined attribute variable specified by *name.*

If *name* refers to a matrix attribute variable, *index* refers to the first column of the matrix. Other matrix columns are then automatically bound to locations *index+1* for a matrix of type mat2; *index+1* and *index+2* for a matrix of type mat3; and *index+1, index+2,* and *index+3* for a matrix of type mat4.

This command makes it possible for vertex shaders to use descriptive names for attribute variables rather than generic variables that are numbered from 0 to GL_MAX_VERTEX_ATTRIBS–1. The values sent to each generic attribute index are part of current state, just like standard vertex attributes such as color, normal, and vertex position. If a different program object is made current by calling **glUseProgram**, the generic vertex attributes are tracked in such a way that the same values will be observed by attributes in the new program object that are also bound to *index*.

Attribute variable name-to-generic attribute index bindings for a program object can be explicitly assigned at any time with **glBindAttribLocation**. Attribute bindings do not go into effect until **glLinkProgram** is called. After a program object has been linked successfully, the index values for generic attributes remain fixed (and their values can be queried) until the next link command occurs.

Applications are not allowed to bind any of the standard OpenGL vertex attributes with this command, because they are bound automatically when needed. Any attribute binding that occurs after the program object has been linked does not take effect until the next time the program object is linked.

NOTES

glBindAttribLocation is available only if the GL version is 2.0 or greater.

glBindAttribLocation can be called before any vertex shader objects are bound to the specified program object. It is also permissible to bind a generic attribute index to an attribute variable name that is never used in a vertex shader.

If *name* was bound previously, that information is lost. Thus, you cannot bind one user-defined attribute variable to multiple indices, but you can bind multiple user-defined attribute variables to the same index.

Applications are allowed to bind more than one user-defined attribute variable to the same generic vertex attribute index. This is called *aliasing*, and it is allowed only if just one of the aliased attributes is active in the executable program or if no path through the shader consumes more than one attribute of a set of attributes aliased to the same location. The compiler and linker are allowed to assume that no aliasing is done and are free to employ optimizations that work only in the absence of aliasing. OpenGL implementations are not required to do error checking to detect aliasing. Because there is no way to bind standard attributes, it is not possible to alias generic attributes with conventional ones (except for generic attribute 0).

Active attributes that are not explicitly bound are bound by the linker when **glLinkProgram** is called. The locations assigned can be queried with **glGetAttribLocation**.

OpenGL copies the *name* string when **glBindAttribLocation** is called, so an application can free its copy of the *name* string immediately after the function returns.

ERRORS

GL_INVALID_VALUE is generated if *index* is greater than or equal to GL_MAX_ VERTEX_ATTRIBS.

GL_INVALID_OPERATION is generated if *name* starts with the reserved prefix "gl_".

GL_INVALID_VALUE is generated if *program* is not a value generated by OpenGL.

GL_INVALID_OPERATION is generated if *program* is not of type GL_PROGRAM_ OBJECT.

GL_INVALID_OPERATION is generated if **glBindAttribLocation** is executed between the execution of **glBegin** and the corresponding execution of **glEnd**.

ASSOCIATED GETS

glGet with argument GL_MAX_VERTEX_ATTRIBS

glGetActiveAttrib with argument *program*

glGetAttribLocation with arguments *program* and *name*

glIsProgram

SEE ALSO

glDisableVertexAttribArray, glEnableVertexAttribArray, glUseProgram, glVertexAttrib, glVertexAttribPointer

glCompileShader

NAME

glCompileShader—Compiles a shader object

C SPECIFICATION

```
void glCompileShader(GLuint shader)
```

PARAMETERS

shader   Specifies the shader object to be compiled

DESCRIPTION

glCompileShader compiles the source code strings that have been stored in the shader object specified by *shader.*

The compilation status is stored as part of the shader object's state. This value is set to GL_TRUE if the shader was compiled without errors and is ready for use, and GL_FALSE otherwise. It can be queried by calling **glGetShader** with arguments *shader* and GL_COMPILE_STATUS.

Compilation of a shader can fail for a number of reasons, as specified by the *OpenGL Shading Language Specification.* Whether or not the compilation was successful, information about the compilation can be obtained from the shader object's information log by calling **glGetShaderInfoLog**.

NOTES

glCompileShader is available only if the GL version is 2.0 or greater.

ERRORS

GL_INVALID_VALUE is generated if *shader* is not a value generated by OpenGL.

GL_INVALID_OPERATION is generated if *shader* is not of type GL_SHADER_OBJECT.

GL_INVALID_OPERATION is generated if **glCompileShader** is executed between the execution of **glBegin** and the corresponding execution of **glEnd**.

ASSOCIATED GETS

glGetShaderInfoLog with argument *shader*

glGetShader with arguments *shader* and GL_COMPILE_STATUS

glIsShader

SEE ALSO

glCreateShader, **glLinkProgram**, **glShaderSource**

glCreateProgram

NAME

glCreateProgram—Creates a program object

C SPECIFICATION

```
GLuint glCreateProgram(void)
```

DESCRIPTION

glCreateProgram creates an empty program object and returns a nonzero value by which it can be referenced. A program object is an object to which shader objects can be attached. This provides a mechanism to specify the shader objects that will be linked to create a program. It also provides a means for checking the compatibility of the shaders that will be used to create a program (for instance, checking the compatibility between a vertex shader and a fragment shader). When no longer needed as part of a program object, shader objects can be detached.

One or more executables are created in a program object by these actions: successfully attaching shader objects to the program object with **glAttachShader**, successfully compiling the shader objects with **glCompileShader**, and successfully linking the program object with **glLinkProgram**. These executables are made part of current state when **glUseProgram** is called. Program objects can be deleted with **glDeleteProgram**. The memory associated with the program object is deleted when it is no longer part of current rendering state for any context.

NOTES

glCreateProgram is available only if the GL version is 2.0 or greater.

Like display lists and texture objects, the namespace for program objects may be shared across a set of contexts, as long as the server sides of the contexts share the same address space. If the namespace is shared across contexts, any attached objects and the data associated with those attached objects are shared as well.

Applications are responsible for synchronizing across API calls when objects are accessed from different execution threads.

ERRORS

This function returns 0 if an error occurs creating the program object.

GL_INVALID_OPERATION is generated if **glCreateProgram** is executed between the execution of **glBegin** and the corresponding execution of **glEnd**.

ASSOCIATED GETS

glGet with the argument GL_CURRENT_PROGRAM

glGetActiveAttrib with a valid program object and the index of an active attribute variable

glGetActiveUniform with a valid program object and the index of an active uniform variable

glGetAttachedShaders with a valid program object

glGetAttribLocation with a valid program object and the name of an attribute variable

glGetProgram with a valid program object and the parameter to be queried

glGetProgramInfoLog with a valid program object

glGetUniform with a valid program object and the location of a uniform variable

glGetUniformLocation with a valid program object and the name of a uniform variable

glIsProgram

SEE ALSO

glAttachShader, glBindAttribLocation, glCreateShader, glDeleteProgram, glDetachShader, glLinkProgram, glUniform, glUseProgram, glValidateProgram

glCreateShader

NAME

glCreateShader—Creates a shader object

C SPECIFICATION

`GLuint glCreateShader(GLenum shaderType)`

PARAMETERS

shaderType   Specifies the type of shader to be created. Must
                        be either GL_VERTEX_SHADER or GL_FRAGMENT_
                        SHADER.

DESCRIPTION

glCreateShader creates an empty shader object and returns a nonzero value
by which it can be referenced. A shader object maintains the source code
strings that define a shader. *shaderType* specifies the type of shader to be
created. Two types of shaders are supported. A shader of type GL_VERTEX_
SHADER is a shader that is intended to run on the programmable vertex
processor and replace the fixed functionality vertex processing in OpenGL.
A shader of type GL_FRAGMENT_SHADER is a shader that is intended to run
on the programmable fragment processor and replace the fixed functionality fragment processing in OpenGL.

When created, a shader object's GL_SHADER_TYPE parameter is set to either
GL_VERTEX_SHADER or GL_FRAGMENT_SHADER, depending on the value of
shaderType.

NOTES

glCreateShader is available only if the GL version is 2.0 or greater.

Like display lists and texture objects, the namespace for shader objects may
be shared across a set of contexts, as long as the server sides of the contexts
share the same address space. If the namespace is shared across contexts,
any attached objects and the data associated with those attached objects are
shared as well.

Applications are responsible for providing the synchronization across API
calls when objects are accessed from different execution threads.

ERRORS

This function returns 0 if an error occurs creating the shader object.

GL_INVALID_ENUM is generated if *shaderType* is not an accepted value.

GL_INVALID_OPERATION is generated if **glCreateShader** is executed between the execution of **glBegin** and the corresponding execution of **glEnd**.

ASSOCIATED GETS

glGetShader with a valid shader object and the parameter to be queried

glGetShaderInfoLog with a valid shader object

glGetShaderSource with a valid shader object

glIsShader

SEE ALSO

glAttachShader, glCompileShader, glCreateProgram, glDeleteShader, glDetachShader, glShaderSource

glDeleteProgram

NAME

glDeleteProgram—Deletes a program object

C SPECIFICATION

```
void glDeleteProgram(GLuint program)
```

PARAMETERS

program   Specifies the program object to be deleted

DESCRIPTION

glDeleteProgram frees the memory and invalidates the name associated with the program object specified by *program*. This command effectively undoes the effects of a call to **glCreateProgram**.

If a program object is in use as part of current rendering state, it is flagged for deletion but is not deleted until it is no longer part of the current state for any rendering context. If a program object to be deleted has shader objects attached to it, those shader objects are automatically detached but not deleted unless they have already been flagged for deletion by a previous call to **glDeleteShader**. A value of 0 for *program* is silently ignored.

To determine whether a program object has been flagged for deletion, call **glGetProgram** with arguments *program* and GL_DELETE_STATUS.

NOTES

glDeleteProgram is available only if the GL version is 2.0 or greater.

ERRORS

GL_INVALID_VALUE is generated if *program* is not a value generated by OpenGL.

GL_INVALID_OPERATION is generated if **glDeleteProgram** is executed between the execution of **glBegin** and the corresponding execution of **glEnd**.

ASSOCIATED GETS

glGet with argument GL_CURRENT_PROGRAM

glGetProgram with arguments *program* and GL_DELETE_STATUS

glIsProgram

SEE ALSO

glCreateProgram, **glCreateShader**, **glDetachShader**, **glUseProgram**

glDeleteShader

NAME

glDeleteShader—Deletes a shader object

C SPECIFICATION

```
void glDeleteShader(GLuint shader)
```

PARAMETERS

shader   Specifies the shader object to be deleted

DESCRIPTION

glDeleteShader frees the memory and invalidates the name associated with the shader object specified by *shader*. This command effectively undoes the effects of a call to **glCreateShader**.

If a shader object to be deleted is attached to a program object, it is flagged for deletion but is not deleted until it is no longer attached to any program object, for any rendering context (i.e., it must be detached from wherever it was attached before it can be deleted). A value of 0 for *shader* is silently ignored.

To determine whether an object has been flagged for deletion, call **glGetShader** with arguments *shader* and GL_DELETE_STATUS.

NOTES

glDeleteShader is available only if the GL version is 2.0 or greater.

ERRORS

GL_INVALID_VALUE is generated if *shader* is not a value generated by OpenGL.

GL_INVALID_OPERATION is generated if **glDeleteShader** is executed between the execution of **glBegin** and the corresponding execution of **glEnd**.

ASSOCIATED GETS

glGetAttachedShaders with the program object to be queried

glGetShader with arguments *shader* and GL_DELETE_STATUS

glIsShader

SEE ALSO

glCreateProgram, glCreateShader, glDetachShader, glUseProgram

glDetachShader

NAME

glDetachShader—Detaches a shader object from a program object to which it is attached

C SPECIFICATION

```
void glDetachShader(GLuint program,
                    GLuint shader)
```

PARAMETERS

program   Specifies the program object from which to detach the shader object

shader   Specifies the shader object to be detached

DESCRIPTION

glDetachShader detaches the shader object specified by *shader* from the program object specified by *program*. This command undoes the effect of the command **glAttachShader**.

If *shader* has already been flagged for deletion by a call to **glDeleteShader** and it is not attached to any other program object, it is deleted after it has been detached.

NOTES

glDetachShader is available only if the GL version is 2.0 or greater.

ERRORS

GL_INVALID_VALUE is generated if either *program* or *shader* is a value that was not generated by OpenGL.

GL_INVALID_OPERATION is generated if *program* is not a program object.

GL_INVALID_OPERATION is generated if *shader* is not a shader object.

GL_INVALID_OPERATION is generated if *shader* is not attached to *program*.

GL_INVALID_OPERATION is generated if **glDetachShader** is executed between the execution of **glBegin** and the corresponding execution of **glEnd**.

ASSOCIATED GETS

glGetAttachedShaders with the handle of a valid program object

glGetShader with arguments *shader* and GL_DELETE_STATUS

glIsProgram

glIsShader

SEE ALSO

glAttachShader

glDrawBuffers

NAME

glDrawBuffers—Specifies a list of color buffers to be drawn into

C SPECIFICATION

```
void glDrawBuffers(GLsizei n,
                   const GLenum *bufs)
```

PARAMETERS

n   Specifies the number of buffers in *bufs*

bufs   Points to an array of symbolic constants specifying the
            buffers into which fragment colors or data values will
            be written

DESCRIPTION

glDrawBuffers defines an array of buffers into which fragment color values or fragment data will be written. If no fragment shader is active, rendering operations generate only one fragment color per fragment, and that fragment is written into each of the buffers specified by *bufs*. If a fragment shader is active and it writes a value to the output variable *gl_FragColor*, then that value is written into each of the buffers specified by *bufs*. If a fragment shader is active and it writes a value to one or more elements of the output array variable *gl_FragData[]*, then the value of *gl_FragData[0]* is written into the first buffer specified by *bufs*, the value of *gl_FragData[1]* is written into the second buffer specified by *bufs*, and so on, up to *gl_FragData[n-1]*. The draw buffer used for *gl_FragData[n]* and beyond is implicitly set to be GL_NONE.

The symbolic constants contained in *bufs* may be any of the following:

GL_NONE
    The fragment color/data value is not written into any color buffer.

GL_FRONT_LEFT
    The fragment color/data value is written into the front-left color buffer.

GL_FRONT_RIGHT
> The fragment color/data value is written into the front-right color buffer.

GL_BACK_LEFT
> The fragment color/data value is written into the back-left color buffer.

GL_BACK_RIGHT
> The fragment color/data value is written into the back-right color buffer.

GL_AUXi
> The fragment color/data value is written into auxiliary buffer i.

Except for GL_NONE, the preceding symbolic constants may not appear more than once in *bufs*. The maximum number of draw buffers supported is implementation dependent and can be queried by calling **glGet** with the argument GL_MAX_DRAW_BUFFERS. The number of auxiliary buffers can be queried by calling **glGet** with the argument GL_AUX_BUFFERS.

NOTES

glDrawBuffers is available only if the GL version is 2.0 or greater.

It is always the case that GL_AUXi = GL_AUX0 + i.

The symbolic constants GL_FRONT, GL_BACK, GL_LEFT, GL_RIGHT, and GL_FRONT_AND_BACK are not allowed in the *bufs* array since they may refer to multiple buffers.

If a fragment shader writes to neither *gl_FragColor* nor *gl_FragData*, the values of the fragment colors following shader execution are undefined. For each fragment generated in this situation, a different value may be written into each of the buffers specified by *bufs*.

ERRORS

GL_INVALID_ENUM is generated if one of the values in *bufs* is not an accepted value.

GL_INVALID_ENUM is generated if n is less than 0.

GL_INVALID_OPERATION is generated if a symbolic constant other than GL_NONE appears more than once in *bufs*.

GL_INVALID_OPERATION is generated if any entry in *bufs* (other than GL_NONE) indicates a color buffer that does not exist in the current GL context.

GL_INVALID_VALUE is generated if *n* is greater than GL_MAX_DRAW_BUFFERS.

GL_INVALID_OPERATION is generated if **glDrawBuffers** is executed between the execution of **glBegin** and the corresponding execution of **glEnd**.

ASSOCIATED GETS

glGet with argument GL_MAX_DRAW_BUFFERS

glGet with argument GL_DRAW_BUFFERSi where *i* indicates the number of the draw buffer whose value is to be queried

SEE ALSO

glBlendFunc, glColorMask, glDrawBuffer, glIndexMask, glLogicOp, glReadBuffer

glEnableVertexAttribArray

NAME

glEnableVertexAttribArray, **glDisableVertexAttribArray**—Enable or disable a generic vertex attribute array

C SPECIFICATION

```
void glEnableVertexAttribArray(GLuint index)
void glDisableVertexAttribArray(GLuint index)
```

PARAMETERS

index   Specifies the index of the generic vertex attribute to be enabled or disabled

DESCRIPTION

glEnableVertexAttribArray enables the generic vertex attribute array specified by *index*. **glDisableVertexAttribArray** disables the generic vertex attribute array specified by *index*. By default, all client-side capabilities are disabled, including all generic vertex attribute arrays. If enabled, the values in the generic vertex attribute array are accessed and used for rendering when calls are made to vertex array commands such as **glDrawArrays**, **glDrawElements**, **glDrawRangeElements**, **glArrayElement**, **glMultiDrawElements**, or **glMultiDraw-Arrays**.

NOTES

glEnableVertexAttribArray and **glDisableVertexAttribArray** are available only if the GL version is 2.0 or greater.

ERRORS

GL_INVALID_VALUE is generated if *index* is greater than or equal to GL_MAX_VERTEX_ATTRIBS.

GL_INVALID_OPERATION is generated if either **glEnableVertexAttribArray** or **glDisableVertexAttribArray** is executed between the execution of **glBegin** and the corresponding execution of **glEnd**.

ASSOCIATED GETS

glGet with argument GL_MAX_VERTEX_ATTRIBS

glGetVertexAttrib with arguments *index* and GL_VERTEX_ATTRIB_ARRAY_ENABLED

glGetVertexAttribPointer with arguments *index* and GL_VERTEX_ATTRIB_ARRAY_POINTER

SEE ALSO

glArrayElement, glBindAttribLocation, glDrawArrays, glDrawElements, glDrawRangeElements, glMultiDrawArrays, glMultiDrawElements, glPopClientAttrib, glPushClientAttrib, glVertexAttrib, glVertexAttribPointer

glGetActiveAttrib

NAME

glGetActiveAttrib—Returns information about an active attribute variable for the specified program object

C SPECIFICATION

```
void glGetActiveAttrib(GLuint program,
                       GLuint index,
                       GLsizei bufSize,
                       GLsizei *length,
                       GLint *size,
                       GLenum *type,
                       GLchar *name)
```

PARAMETERS

program	Specifies the program object to be queried
index	Specifies the index of the attribute variable to be queried
bufSize	Specifies the maximum number of characters OpenGL is allowed to write in the character buffer indicated by *name*
length	Returns the number of characters actually written by OpenGL in the string indicated by *name* (excluding the null terminator) if a value other than NULL is passed
size	Returns the size of the attribute variable
type	Returns the data type of the attribute variable
name	Returns a null-terminated string containing the name of the attribute variable

DESCRIPTION

glGetActiveAttrib returns information about an active attribute variable in the program object specified by *program*. The number of active attributes can be obtained by calling **glGetProgram** with the value GL_ACTIVE_ATTRIBUTES. A value of 0 for *index* selects the first active attribute variable. Permissible values for *index* range from 0 to the number of active attribute variables minus 1.

A vertex shader may use built-in attribute variables, user-defined attribute variables, or both. Built-in attribute variables have a prefix of "gl_" and reference conventional OpenGL vertex attributes (e.g., *gl_Vertex*, *gl_Normal*; see the OpenGL Shading Language specification for a complete list). User-defined attribute variables have arbitrary names and obtain their values through numbered generic vertex attributes. An attribute variable (either built-in or user-defined) is considered active if during the link operation, the determination is made that the attribute variable can be accessed during program execution. Therefore, *program* should have previously been the target of a call to **glLinkProgram**, but it is not necessary for it to have been linked successfully.

The size of the character buffer required to store the longest attribute variable name in *program* can be obtained by calling **glGetProgram** with the value GL_ACTIVE_ATTRIBUTE_MAX_LENGTH. This value should be used to allocate a buffer of sufficient size to store the returned attribute name. The size of this character buffer is passed in *bufSize*, and a pointer to this character buffer is passed in *name*.

glGetActiveAttrib returns the name of the attribute variable indicated by *index*, storing it in the character buffer specified by *name*. The string returned is null terminated. The actual number of characters written into this buffer is returned in *length*, and this count does not include the null termination character. If the length of the returned string is not required, a value of NULL can be passed in the *length* argument.

The *type* argument returns a pointer to the attribute variable's data type. The symbolic constants GL_FLOAT, GL_FLOAT_VEC2, GL_FLOAT_VEC3, GL_FLOAT_VEC4, GL_FLOAT_MAT2, GL_FLOAT_MAT3, and GL_FLOAT_MAT4 may be returned. The *size* argument returns the size of the attribute, in units of the type returned in *type*.

The list of active attribute variables may include both built-in attribute variables (which begin with the prefix "gl_") as well as user-defined attribute variable names.

This function returns as much information as it can about the specified active attribute variable. If no information is available, *length* is 0, and *name* is an empty string. This situation could occur if this function is called after a link operation that failed. If an error occurs, the return values *length*, *size*, *type*, and *name* are unmodified.

NOTES

glGetActiveAttrib is available only if the GL version is 2.0 or greater.

ERRORS

GL_INVALID_VALUE is generated if *program* is not a value generated by OpenGL.

GL_INVALID_OPERATION is generated if *program* is not a program object.

GL_INVALID_VALUE is generated if *index* is greater than or equal to the number of active attribute variables in *program*.

GL_INVALID_OPERATION is generated if **glGetActiveAttrib** is executed between the execution of **glBegin** and the corresponding execution of **glEnd**.

GL_INVALID_VALUE is generated if *bufSize* is less than 0.

ASSOCIATED GETS

glGet with argument GL_MAX_VERTEX_ATTRIBS

glGetProgram with argument GL_ACTIVE_ATTRIBUTES or GL_ACTIVE_ATTRIBUTE_MAX_LENGTH

glIsProgram

SEE ALSO

glBindAttribLocation, **glLinkProgram**, **glVertexAttrib**, **glVertexAttribPointer**

glGetActiveUniform

NAME

glGetActiveUniform—Returns information about an active uniform variable for the specified program object

C SPECIFICATION

```
void glGetActiveUniform(GLuint program,
                        GLuint index,
                        GLsizei bufSize,
                        GLsizei *length,
                        GLint *size,
                        GLenum *type,
                        GLchar *name)
```

PARAMETERS

program	Specifies the program object to be queried
index	Specifies the index of the uniform variable to be queried
bufSize	Specifies the maximum number of characters OpenGL is allowed to write in the character buffer indicated by *name*
length	Returns the number of characters actually written by OpenGL in the string indicated by *name* (excluding the null terminator) if a value other than NULL is passed
size	Returns the size of the uniform variable
type	Returns the data type of the uniform variable
name	Returns a null-terminated string containing the name of the uniform variable

DESCRIPTION

glGetActiveUniform returns information about an active uniform variable in the program object specified by *program*. The number of active uniform variables can be obtained by calling **glGetProgram** with the value GL_ACTIVE_UNIFORMS. A value of 0 for *index* selects the first active uniform variable. Permissible values for *index* range from 0 to the number of active uniform variables minus 1.

Shaders may use built-in uniform variables, user-defined uniform variables, or both. Built-in uniform variables have a prefix of "gl_" and reference existing OpenGL state or values derived from such state (e.g., *gl_Fog*, *gl_ModelViewMatrix*; see the OpenGL Shading Language specification for a complete list). User-defined uniform variables have arbitrary names and obtain their values from the application through calls to **glUniform.** A uniform variable (either built-in or user-defined) is considered active if during the link operation, a determination is made that the uniform variable can be accessed during program execution. Therefore, *program* should have previously been the target of a call to **glLinkProgram,** but it is not necessary for it to have been linked successfully.

The size of the character buffer required to store the longest uniform variable name in *program* can be obtained by calling **glGetProgram** with the value GL_ACTIVE_UNIFORM_MAX_LENGTH. This value should be used to allocate a buffer of sufficient size to store the returned uniform variable name. The size of this character buffer is passed in *bufSize*, and a pointer to this character buffer is passed in *name*.

glGetActiveUniform returns the name of the uniform variable indicated by *index*, storing it in the character buffer specified by *name.* The string returned is null terminated. The actual number of characters written into this buffer is returned in *length*, and this count does not include the null termination character. If the length of the returned string is not required, a value of NULL can be passed in the *length* argument.

The *type* argument returns a pointer to the uniform variable's data type. The symbolic constants GL_FLOAT, GL_FLOAT_VEC2, GL_FLOAT_VEC3, GL_FLOAT_VEC4, GL_INT, GL_INT_VEC2, GL_INT_VEC3, GL_INT_VEC4, GL_BOOL, GL_BOOL_VEC2, GL_BOOL_VEC3, GL_BOOL_VEC4, GL_FLOAT_MAT2, GL_FLOAT_MAT3, GL_FLOAT_MAT4, GL_SAMPLER_1D, GL_SAMPLER_2D, GL_SAMPLER_3D, GL_SAMPLER_CUBE, GL_SAMPLER_1D_SHADOW, or GL_SAMPLER_2D_SHADOW may be returned.

If one or more elements of an array are active, the name of the array is returned in *name*, the type is returned in *type*, and the *size* parameter returns the highest array element index used, plus one, as determined by the compiler and/or linker. Only one active uniform variable is reported for a uniform array.

Uniform variables that are declared as structures or arrays of structures are not returned directly by this function. Instead, each of these uniform variables is reduced to its fundamental components containing the "." and "[]" operators such that each of the names is valid as an argument to **glGetUniformLocation**. Each of these reduced uniform variables is counted as one active uniform variable and is assigned an index. A valid name cannot be a structure, an array of structures, or a subcomponent of a vector or matrix.

The size of the uniform variable is returned in *size*. Uniform variables other than arrays have a size of 1. Structures and arrays of structures are reduced as described earlier, such that each of the names returned is a data type in the earlier list. If this reduction results in an array, the size returned is as described for uniform arrays; otherwise, the size returned is 1.

The list of active uniform variables may include both built-in uniform variables (which begin with the prefix "gl_") as well as user-defined uniform variable names.

This function returns as much information as it can about the specified active uniform variable. If no information is available, *length* is 0, and *name* is an empty string. This situation could occur if this function is called after a link operation that failed. If an error occurs, the return values *length*, *size*, *type*, and *name* are unmodified.

NOTES

glGetActiveUniform is available only if the GL version is 2.0 or greater.

ERRORS

GL_INVALID_VALUE is generated if *program* is not a value generated by OpenGL.

GL_INVALID_OPERATION is generated if *program* is not a program object.

GL_INVALID_VALUE is generated if *index* is greater than or equal to the number of active uniform variables in *program*.

GL_INVALID_OPERATION is generated if **glGetActiveUniform** is executed between the execution of **glBegin** and the corresponding execution of **glEnd**.

GL_INVALID_VALUE is generated if *bufSize* is less than 0.

ASSOCIATED GETS

glGet with argument GL_MAX_VERTEX_UNIFORM_COMPONENTS or GL_MAX_FRAGMENT_UNIFORM_COMPONENTS

glGetProgram with argument GL_ACTIVE_UNIFORMS or GL_ACTIVE_UNIFORM_MAX_LENGTH

glIsProgram

SEE ALSO

glGetUniform, **glGetUniformLocation**, **glLinkProgram**, **glUniform**, **glUseProgram**

glGetAttachedShaders

NAME

glGetAttachedShaders—Returns the handles of the shader objects attached to a program object

C SPECIFICATION

```
void glGetAttachedShaders(GLuint program,
                          GLsizei maxCount,
                          GLsizei *count,
                          GLuint *shaders)
```

PARAMETERS

program	Specifies the program object to be queried
maxCount	Specifies the size of the array for storing the returned object names
count	Returns the number of names actually returned in *objects*
shaders	Specifies an array that is used to return the names of attached shader objects

DESCRIPTION

glGetAttachedShaders returns the names of the shader objects attached to *program*. The names of shader objects that are attached to *program* are returned in *shaders*. The actual number of shader names written into *shaders* is returned in *count*. If no shader objects are attached to *program*, *count* is set to 0. The maximum number of shader names that may be returned in *shaders* is specified by *maxCount*.

If the number of names actually returned is not required (for instance, if it has just been obtained with **glGetProgram**), a value of NULL may be passed for count. If no shader objects are attached to *program*, a value of 0 is returned in *count*. The actual number of attached shaders can be obtained by calling **glGetProgram** with the value GL_ATTACHED_SHADERS.

NOTES

glGetAttachedShaders is available only if the GL version is 2.0 or greater.

ERRORS

GL_INVALID_VALUE is generated if *program* is not a value generated by OpenGL.

GL_INVALID_OPERATION is generated if *program* is not a program object.

GL_INVALID_VALUE is generated if *maxCount* is less than 0.

GL_INVALID_OPERATION is generated if **glGetAttachedShaders** is executed between the execution of **glBegin** and the corresponding execution of **glEnd**.

ASSOCIATED GETS

glGetProgram with argument GL_ATTACHED_SHADERS

glIsProgram

SEE ALSO

glAttachShader, glDetachShader

glGetAttribLocation

NAME

glGetAttribLocation—Returns the location of an attribute variable

C SPECIFICATION

```
GLint glGetAttribLocation(GLuint program,
                          const GLchar *name)
```

PARAMETERS

program   Specifies the program object to be queried

name   Points to a null-terminated string containing the
                 name of the attribute variable whose location is to be
                 queried

DESCRIPTION

glGetAttribLocation queries the previously linked program object specified
by *program* for the attribute variable specified by *name* and returns the
index of the generic vertex attribute that is bound to that attribute variable.
If *name* is a matrix attribute variable, the index of the first column of the
matrix is returned. If the named attribute variable is not an active attribute
in the specified program object or if *name* starts with the reserved prefix
"gl_", a value of –1 is returned.

The association between an attribute variable name and a generic attribute
index can be specified at any time with **glBindAttribLocation**. Attribute bindings do not take effect until **glLinkProgram** is called. After a program object
has been linked successfully, the index values for attribute variables remain
fixed until the next link command occurs. The attribute bindings can be
queried only after a link if the link was successful. **glGetAttribLocation** returns
the binding that actually went into effect the last time **glLinkProgram** was
called for the specified program object. Attribute bindings that have been
specified since the last link operation are not returned by **glGetAttribLocation**.

NOTES

glGetAttribLocation is available only if the GL version is 2.0 or greater.

ERRORS

GL_INVALID_OPERATION is generated if *program* is not a value generated by OpenGL.

GL_INVALID_OPERATION is generated if *program* is not a program object.

GL_INVALID_OPERATION is generated if *program* has not been successfully linked.

GL_INVALID_OPERATION is generated if **glGetAttribLocation** is executed between the execution of **glBegin** and the corresponding execution of **glEnd**.

ASSOCIATED GETS

glGetActiveAttrib with argument *program* and the index of an active attribute

glIsProgram

SEE ALSO

glBindAttribLocation, glLinkProgram, glVertexAttrib, glVertexAttribPointer

glGetProgram

NAME

glGetProgramiv—Returns a parameter from a program object

C SPECIFICATION

```
void glGetProgramiv(GLuint program,
                    GLenum pname,
                    GLint *params)
```

PARAMETERS

program   Specifies the program object to be queried.

pname   Specifies the object parameter. Accepted symbolic
                names are GL_DELETE_STATUS, GL_LINK_STATUS,
                GL_VALIDATE_STATUS, GL_INFO_LOG_LENGTH,
                GL_ATTACHED_SHADERS, GL_ACTIVE_ATTRIBUTES,
                GL_ACTIVE_ATTRIBUTE_MAX_LENGTH, GL_ACTIVE_
                UNIFORMS, and GL_ACTIVE_UNIFORM_MAX_LENGTH.

params   Returns the requested object parameter.

DESCRIPTION

glGetProgram returns in *params* the value of a parameter for a specific
program object. The following parameters are defined:

GL_DELETE_STATUS
          params returns GL_TRUE if *program* is currently flagged for deletion,
          and GL_FALSE otherwise.

GL_LINK_STATUS
          params returns GL_TRUE if the last link operation on *program* was
          successful, and GL_FALSE otherwise.

GL_VALIDATE_STATUS
          params returns GL_TRUE or if the last validation operation on
          program was successful, and GL_FALSE otherwise.

GL_INFO_LOG_LENGTH
>   *params* returns the number of characters in the information log for *program* including the null termination character (i.e., the size of the character buffer required to store the information log). If *program* has no information log, a value of 0 is returned.

GL_ATTACHED_SHADERS
>   *params* returns the number of shader objects attached to *program*.

GL_ACTIVE_ATTRIBUTES
>   *params* returns the number of active attribute variables for *program*.

GL_ACTIVE_ATTRIBUTE_MAX_LENGTH
>   *params* returns the length of the longest active attribute name for *program*, including the null termination character (i.e., the size of the character buffer required to store the longest attribute name). If no active attributes exist, 0 is returned.

GL_ACTIVE_UNIFORMS
>   *params* returns the number of active uniform variables for *program*.

GL_ACTIVE_UNIFORM_MAX_LENGTH
>   *params* returns the length of the longest active uniform variable name for *program*, including the null termination character (i.e., the size of the character buffer required to store the longest uniform variable name). If no active uniform variables exist, 0 is returned.

NOTES

glGetProgram is available only if the GL version is 2.0 or greater.

If an error is generated, no change is made to the contents of *params*.

ERRORS

GL_INVALID_VALUE is generated if *program* is not a value generated by OpenGL.

GL_INVALID_OPERATION is generated if *program* does not refer to a program object.

GL_INVALID_ENUM is generated if *pname* is not an accepted value.

GL_INVALID_OPERATION is generated if **glGetProgram** is executed between the execution of **glBegin** and the corresponding execution of **glEnd**.

ASSOCIATED GETS

glGetActiveAttrib with argument *program*

glGetActiveUniform with argument *program*

glGetAttachedShaders with argument *program*

glGetProgramInfoLog with argument *program*

glIsProgram

SEE ALSO

glAttachShader, **glCreateProgram**, **glDeleteProgram**, **glGetShader**, **glLinkProgram**, **glValidateProgram**

glGetProgramInfoLog

NAME

glGetProgramInfoLog—Returns the information log for a program object

C SPECIFICATION

```
void glGetProgramInfoLog(GLuint program,
                         GLsizei maxLength,
                         GLsizei *length,
                         GLchar *infoLog)
```

PARAMETERS

program	Specifies the program object whose information log is to be queried
maxLength	Specifies the size of the character buffer for storing the returned information log
length	Returns the length of the string returned in *infoLog* (excluding the null terminator)
infoLog	Specifies an array of characters that is used to return the information log

DESCRIPTION

glGetProgramInfoLog returns the information log for the specified program object. The information log for a program object is modified when the program object is linked or validated. The string that is returned is null terminated.

glGetProgramInfoLog returns in *infoLog* as much of the information log as it can, up to a maximum of *maxLength* characters. The number of characters actually returned, excluding the null termination character, is specified by *length.* If the length of the returned string is not required, a value of NULL can be passed in the *length* argument. The size of the buffer required to store the returned information log can be obtained by calling **glGetProgram** with the value GL_INFO_LOG_LENGTH.

The information log for a program object is either an empty string, a string containing information about the last link operation, or a string containing information about the last validation operation. It may contain diagnostic messages, warning messages, and other information. When a program object is created, its information log is a string of length 0.

NOTES

glGetProgramInfoLog is available only if the GL version is 2.0 or greater.

The information log for a program object is the OpenGL implementor's primary mechanism for conveying information about linking and validating. Therefore, the information log can be helpful to application developers during the development process, even when these operations are successful. Application developers should not expect different OpenGL implementations to produce identical information logs.

ERRORS

GL_INVALID_VALUE is generated if *program* is not a value generated by OpenGL.

GL_INVALID_OPERATION is generated if *program* is not a program object.

GL_INVALID_VALUE is generated if *maxLength* is less than 0.

GL_INVALID_OPERATION is generated if **glGetProgramInfoLog** is executed between the execution of **glBegin** and the corresponding execution of **glEnd**.

ASSOCIATED GETS

glGetProgram with argument GL_INFO_LOG_LENGTH

glsProgram

SEE ALSO

glCompileShader, glGetShaderInfoLog, glLinkProgram, glValidateProgram

glGetShader

NAME

glGetShaderiv—Returns a parameter from a shader object

C SPECIFICATION

```
void glGetShaderiv(GLuint shader,
                   GLenum pname,
                   GLint *params)
```

PARAMETERS

shader   Specifies the shader object to be queried.

pname   Specifies the object parameter. Accepted symbolic
                names are GL_SHADER_TYPE, GL_DELETE_STATUS,
                GL_COMPILE_STATUS, GL_INFO_LOG_LENGTH,
                GL_SHADER_SOURCE_LENGTH.

params   Returns the requested object parameter.

DESCRIPTION

glGetShader returns in *params* the value of a parameter for a specific shader
object. The following parameters are defined:

GL_SHADER_TYPE
        params returns GL_VERTEX_SHADER if *shader* is a vertex shader
        object, and GL_FRAGMENT_SHADER if *shader* is a fragment shader
        object.

GL_DELETE_STATUS
        params returns GL_TRUE if *shader* is currently flagged for deletion,
        and GL_FALSE otherwise.

GL_COMPILE_STATUS
        params returns GL_TRUE if the last compile operation on *shader*
        was successful, and GL_FALSE otherwise.

GL_INFO_LOG_LENGTH
        params returns the number of characters in the information log for
        shader including the null termination character (i.e., the size of the
        character buffer required to store the information log). If *shader*
        has no information log, a value of 0 is returned.

GL_SHADER_SOURCE_LENGTH

> *params* returns the length of the concatenation of the source strings that make up the shader source for the *shader*, including the null termination character (i.e., the size of the character buffer required to store the shader source). If no source code exists, 0 is returned.

NOTES

glGetShader is available only if the GL version is 2.0 or greater.

If an error is generated, no change is made to the contents of *params*.

ERRORS

GL_INVALID_VALUE is generated if *shader* is not a value generated by OpenGL.

GL_INVALID_OPERATION is generated if *shader* does not refer to a shader object.

GL_INVALID_ENUM is generated if *pname* is not an accepted value.

GL_INVALID_OPERATION is generated if **glGetShader** is executed between the execution of **glBegin** and the corresponding execution of **glEnd**.

ASSOCIATED GETS

glGetShaderInfoLog with argument *shader*

glGetShaderSource with argument *shader*

glIsShader

SEE ALSO

glCompileShader, glCreateShader, glDeleteShader, glGetProgram, glShaderSource

glGetShaderInfoLog

NAME

glGetShaderInfoLog—Returns the information log for a shader object

C SPECIFICATION

```
void glGetShaderInfoLog(GLuint shader,
                        GLsizei maxLength,
                        GLsizei *length,
                        GLchar *infoLog)
```

PARAMETERS

shader   Specifies the shader object whose information log is to
              be queried

maxLength   Specifies the size of the character buffer for storing the
              returned information log

length   Returns the length of the string returned in *infoLog*
              (excluding the null terminator)

infoLog   Specifies an array of characters that returns the infor-
              mation log

DESCRIPTION

glGetShaderInfoLog returns the information log for the specified shader
object. The information log for a shader object is modified when the shader
is compiled. The string that is returned is null terminated.

glGetShaderInfoLog returns in *infoLog* as much of the information log as it
can, up to a maximum of *maxLength* characters. The number of characters
actually returned, excluding the null termination character, is specified by
length. If the length of the returned string is not required, a value of NULL
can be passed in the *length* argument. The size of the buffer required to store
the returned information log can be obtained by calling **glGetShader** with
the value GL_INFO_LOG_LENGTH.

The information log for a shader object is a string that may contain diagnostic messages, warning messages, and other information about the last

compile operation. When a shader object is created, its information log is a string of length 0.

NOTES

glGetShaderInfoLog is available only if the GL version is 2.0 or greater.

The information log for a shader object is the OpenGL implementor's primary mechanism for conveying information about the compilation process. Therefore, the information log can be helpful to application developers during the development process, even when compilation is successful. Application developers should not expect different OpenGL implementations to produce identical information logs.

ERRORS

GL_INVALID_VALUE is generated if *shader* is not a value generated by OpenGL.

GL_INVALID_OPERATION is generated if *shader* is not a shader object.

GL_INVALID_VALUE is generated if *maxLength* is less than 0.

GL_INVALID_OPERATION is generated if **glGetShaderInfoLog** is executed between the execution of **glBegin** and the corresponding execution of **glEnd**.

ASSOCIATED GETS

glGetShader with argument GL_INFO_LOG_LENGTH

glIsShader

SEE ALSO

glCompileShader, **glGetProgramInfoLog**, **glLinkProgram**, **glValidateProgram**

glGetShaderSource

NAME

glGetShaderSource—Returns the source code string from a shader object

C SPECIFICATION

```
void glGetShaderSource(GLuint shader,
                       GLsizei bufSize,
                       GLsizei *length,
                       GLchar *source)
```

PARAMETERS

shader	Specifies the shader object to be queried
bufSize	Specifies the size of the character buffer for storing the returned source code string
length	Returns the length of the string returned in *source* (excluding the null terminator)
source	Specifies an array of characters that is used to return the source code string

DESCRIPTION

glGetShaderSource returns the concatenation of the source code strings from the shader object specified by *shader*. The source code strings for a shader object are the result of a previous call to **glShaderSource**. The string returned by the function is null terminated.

glGetShaderSource returns in *source* as much of the source code string as it can, up to a maximum of *bufSize* characters. The number of characters actually returned, excluding the null termination character, is specified by *length*. If the length of the returned string is not required, a value of NULL can be passed in the *length* argument. The size of the buffer required to store the returned source code string can be obtained by calling **glGetShader** with the value GL_SHADER_SOURCE_LENGTH.

NOTES

glGetShaderSource is available only if the GL version is 2.0 or greater.

ERRORS

GL_INVALID_VALUE is generated if *shader* is not a value generated by OpenGL.

GL_INVALID_OPERATION is generated if *shader* is not a shader object.

GL_INVALID_VALUE is generated if *bufSize* is less than 0.

GL_INVALID_OPERATION is generated if **glGetShaderSource** is executed between the execution of **glBegin** and the corresponding execution of **glEnd**.

ASSOCIATED GETS

glGetShader with argument GL_SHADER_SOURCE_LENGTH

glIsShader

SEE ALSO

glCreateShader, **glShaderSource**

glGetUniform

NAME

glGetUniformfv, **glGetUniformiv**—Return the value of a uniform variable

C SPECIFICATION

```
void glGetUniformfv(GLuint program,
                    GLint location,
                    GLfloat *params)

void glGetUniformiv(GLuint program,
                    GLint location,
                    GLint *params)
```

PARAMETERS

program   Specifies the program object to be queried

location   Specifies the location of the uniform variable to be
                   queried

params   Returns the value of the specified uniform variable

DESCRIPTION

glGetUniform returns in *params* the value or values of the specified uniform variable. The type of the uniform variable specified by *location* determines the number of values returned. If the uniform variable is defined in the shader as a Boolean, int, or float, a single value is returned. If it is defined as a vec2, ivec2, or bvec2, two values are returned. If it is defined as a vec3, ivec3, or bvec3, three values are returned, and so on. To query values stored in uniform variables declared as arrays, call **glGetUniform** for each element of the array. To query values stored in uniform variables declared as structures, call **glGetUniform** for each field in the structure. The values for uniform variables declared as a matrix are returned in column major order.

The locations assigned to uniform variables are not known until the program object is linked. After linking has occurred, the command **glGetUniformLocation** obtains the location of a uniform variable. This location value can then be passed to **glGetUniform** to query the current value of the uniform variable. After a program object has been linked successfully, the index values for uniform variables remain fixed until the next link command occurs. The uniform variable values can be queried only after a link if the link was successful.

NOTES

glGetUniform is available only if the GL version is 2.0 or greater.

If an error is generated, no change is made to the contents of *params*.

ERRORS

GL_INVALID_VALUE is generated if *program* is not a value generated by OpenGL.

GL_INVALID_OPERATION is generated if *program* is not a program object.

GL_INVALID_OPERATION is generated if *program* has not been successfully linked.

GL_INVALID_OPERATION is generated if *location* does not correspond to a valid uniform variable location for the specified program object.

GL_INVALID_OPERATION is generated if **glGetUniform** is executed between the execution of **glBegin** and the corresponding execution of **glEnd**.

ASSOCIATED GETS

glGetActiveUniform with arguments *program* and the index of an active uniform variable

glGetProgram with arguments *program* and GL_ACTIVE_UNIFORMS or GL_ACTIVE_UNIFORM_MAX_LENGTH

glGetUniformLocation with arguments *program* and the name of a uniform variable

glIsProgram

SEE ALSO

glCreateProgram, **glLinkProgram**, **glUniform**

glGetUniformLocation

NAME

glGetUniformLocation—Returns the location of a uniform variable

C SPECIFICATION

```
GLint glGetUniformLocation(GLuint program,
                           const GLchar *name)
```

PARAMETERS

program   Specifies the program object to be queried

name   Points to a null-terminated string containing the
                name of the uniform variable whose location is to
                be queried

DESCRIPTION

glGetUniformLocation returns an integer that represents the location of a specific uniform variable within a program object. *name* must be a null-terminated string that contains no white space. *name* must be an active uniform variable name in *program* that is not a structure, an array of structures, or a subcomponent of a vector or a matrix. This function returns –1 if *name* does not correspond to an active uniform variable in *program* or if *name* starts with the reserved prefix "gl_".

Uniform variables that are structures or arrays of structures may be queried with **glGetUniformLocation** for each field within the structure. The array element operator "[]" and the structure field operator "." may be used in *name* to select elements within an array or fields within a structure. The result of using these operators is not allowed to be another structure, an array of structures, or a subcomponent of a vector or a matrix. Except if the last part of *name* indicates a uniform variable array, the location of the first element of an array can be retrieved with the name of the array or with the name appended by "[0]".

The actual locations assigned to uniform variables are not known until the program object is linked successfully. After linking has occurred, the command **glGetUniformLocation** obtains the location of a uniform variable. This location value can then be passed to **glUniform** to set the value of the uniform variable or to **glGetUniform** to query the current value of the uniform variable. After a program object has been linked successfully, the index values for uniform variables remain fixed until the next link command occurs. Uniform variable locations and values can be queried after a link only if the link was successful.

NOTES

glGetUniformLocation is available only if the GL version is 2.0 or greater.

ERRORS

GL_INVALID_VALUE is generated if *program* is not a value generated by OpenGL.

GL_INVALID_OPERATION is generated if *program* is not a program object.

GL_INVALID_OPERATION is generated if *program* has not been successfully linked.

GL_INVALID_OPERATION is generated if **glGetUniformLocation** is executed between the execution of **glBegin** and the corresponding execution of **glEnd**.

ASSOCIATED GETS

glGetActiveUniform with arguments *program* and the index of an active uniform variable

glGetProgram with arguments *program* and GL_ACTIVE_UNIFORMS or GL_ACTIVE_UNIFORM_MAX_LENGTH

glGetUniform with arguments *program* and the name of a uniform variable

glIsProgram

SEE ALSO

glLinkProgram, glUniform

glGetVertexAttrib

NAME

glGetVertexAttribdv, **glGetVertexAttribfv**, **glGetVertexAttribiv**—Return a generic vertex attribute parameter

C SPECIFICATION

```
void glGetVertexAttribdv(GLuint index,
                         GLenum pname,
                         GLdouble *params)

void glGetVertexAttribfv(GLuint index,
                         GLenum pname,
                         GLfloat *params)

void glGetVertexAttribiv(GLuint index,
                         GLenum pname,
                         GLint *params)
```

PARAMETERS

index   Specifies the generic vertex attribute to be queried.

pname   Specifies the symbolic name of the vertex attribute parameter to be queried. GL_VERTEX_ATTRIB_ARRAY_ ENABLED, GL_VERTEX_ATTRIB_ARRAY_SIZE, GL_ VERTEX_ATTRIB_ARRAY_STRIDE, GL_VERTEX_ATTRIB_ ARRAY_TYPE, GL_VERTEX_ATTRIB_ARRAY_NORMALIZED, and GL_CURRENT_VERTEX_ATTRIB are accepted.

params   Returns the requested data.

DESCRIPTION

glGetVertexAttrib returns in params the value of a generic vertex attribute parameter. The generic vertex attribute to be queried is specified by *index*, and the parameter to be queried is specified by *pname.*

The accepted parameter names are as follows:

GL_VERTEX_ATTRIB_ARRAY_ENABLED
> *params* returns a single value that is nonzero (true) if the vertex attribute array for *index* is enabled and 0 (false) if it is disabled. The initial value is GL_FALSE.

GL_VERTEX_ATTRIB_ARRAY_SIZE
> *params* returns a single value, the size of the vertex attribute array for *index*. The size is the number of values for each element of the vertex attribute array, and it is 1, 2, 3, or 4. The initial value is 4.

GL_VERTEX_ATTRIB_ARRAY_STRIDE
> *params* returns a single value, the array stride for (number of bytes between successive elements in) the vertex attribute array for *index*. A value of 0 signifies that the array elements are stored sequentially in memory. The initial value is 0.

GL_VERTEX_ATTRIB_ARRAY_TYPE
> *params* returns a single value, a symbolic constant indicating the array type for the vertex attribute array for *index*. Possible values are GL_BYTE, GL_UNSIGNED_BYTE, GL_SHORT, GL_UNSIGNED_SHORT, GL_INT, GL_UNSIGNED_INT, GL_FLOAT, and GL_DOUBLE. The initial value is GL_FLOAT.

GL_VERTEX_ATTRIB_ARRAY_NORMALIZED
> *params* returns a single value that is non-zero (true) if fixed-point data types for the vertex attribute array indicated by *index* are normalized when they are converted to floating point, and 0 (false) otherwise. The initial value is GL_FALSE.

GL_CURRENT_VERTEX_ATTRIB
> *params* returns four values that represent the current value for the generic vertex attribute specified by *index*. Generic vertex attribute 0 is unique in that it has no current state, so an error is generated if *index* is 0. The initial value for all other generic vertex attributes is (0,0,0,1).

All the parameters except GL_CURRENT_VERTEX_ATTRIB represent client-side state.

NOTES

glGetVertexAttrib is available only if the GL version is 2.0 or greater.

If an error is generated, no change is made to the contents of *params*.

ERRORS

GL_INVALID_VALUE is generated if *index* is greater than or equal to GL_MAX_VERTEX_ATTRIBS.

GL_INVALID_ENUM is generated if *pname* is not an accepted value.

GL_INVALID_OPERATION is generated if *index* is 0 and *pname* is GL_CURRENT_VERTEX_ATTRIB.

ASSOCIATED GETS

glGet with argument GL_MAX_VERTEX_ATTRIBS

glGetVertexAttribPointer with arguments *index* and GL_VERTEX_ATTRIB_ARRAY_POINTER

SEE ALSO

glBindAttribLocation, glDisableVertexAttribArray, glEnableVertexAttribArray, glVertexAttrib, glVertexAttribPointer

glGetVertexAttribPointer

NAME

glGetVertexAttributePointerv—Returns the address of the specified pointer

C SPECIFICATION

```
void glGetVertexAttribPointerv(GLuint index,
                               GLenum pname,
                               GLvoid **pointer)
```

PARAMETERS

index   Specifies the generic vertex attribute to be queried.

pname   Specifies the symbolic name of the generic vertex attri-
                bute parameter to be queried. Must be GL_VERTEX_
                ATTRIB_ARRAY_POINTER.

params   Returns the requested data.

DESCRIPTION

glGetVertexAttribPointer returns pointer information. *index* is the generic
vertex attribute to be queried, *pname* is a symbolic constant indicating the
pointer to be returned, and *params* is a pointer to a location in which to
place the returned data. The accepted parameter names are as follows:

GL_VERTEX_ATTRIB_ARRAY_POINTER
        params returns a single value that is a pointer to the vertex
        attribute array for the generic vertex attribute specified by *index*.

NOTES

glGetVertexAttribPointer is available only if the GL version is 2.0 or greater.

The pointer returned is client-side state.

The initial value for each pointer is NULL.

ERRORS

GL_INVALID_VALUE is generated if *index* is greater than or equal to GL_MAX_
VERTEX_ATTRIBS.

GL_INVALID_ENUM is generated if *pname* is not an accepted value.

ASSOCIATED GETS

glGet with argument GL_MAX_VERTEX_ATTRIBS

glGetVertexAttrib with arguments *index* and the name of a generic vertex
attribute parameter

SEE ALSO

glVertexAttribPointer

glIsProgram

NAME

glIsProgram—Determines whether a name corresponds to a program object

C SPECIFICATION

```
GLboolean glIsProgram(GLuint program)
```

PARAMETERS

program   Specifies a potential program object

DESCRIPTION

glIsProgram returns GL_TRUE if *program* is the name of a program object. If *program* is zero or a nonzero value that is not the name of a program object, **glIsProgram** returns GL_FALSE.

NOTES

glIsProgram is available only if the GL version is 2.0 or greater.

No error is generated if *program* is not a valid program object name.

ERRORS

GL_INVALID_OPERATION is generated if **glIsProgram** is executed between the execution of **glBegin** and the corresponding execution of **glEnd**.

ASSOCIATED GETS

glGet with the argument GL_CURRENT_PROGRAM

glGetActiveAttrib with arguments *program* and the index of an active attribute variable

glGetActiveUniform with arguments *program* and the index of an active uniform variable

glGetAttachedShaders with argument *program*

glGetAttribLocation with arguments *program* and the name of an attribute variable

glGetProgram with arguments *program* and the parameter to be queried

glGetProgramInfoLog with argument *program*

glGetUniform with arguments *program* and the location of a uniform variable

glGetUniformLocation with arguments *program* and the name of a uniform variable

SEE ALSO

glAttachShader, glBindAttribLocation, glCreateProgram, glDeleteProgram, glDetachShader, glLinkProgram, glUniform, glUseProgram, glValidateProgram

glIsShader

NAME

glIsShader—Determines whether a name corresponds to a shader object

C SPECIFICATION

```
GLboolean glIsShader(GLuint shader)
```

PARAMETERS

shader   Specifies a potential shader object

DESCRIPTION

glIsShader returns GL_TRUE if *shader* is the name of a shader object. If *shader* is zero or a nonzero value that is not the name of a shader object, **glIsShader** returns GL_FALSE.

NOTES

glIsShader is available only if the GL version is 2.0 or greater.

No error is generated if *shader* is not a valid shader object name.

ERRORS

GL_INVALID_OPERATION is generated if **glIsShader** is executed between the execution of **glBegin** and the corresponding execution of **glEnd**.

ASSOCIATED GETS

glGetAttachedShaders with a valid program object

glGetShader with arguments *shader* and a parameter to be queried

glGetShaderInfoLog with argument *object*

glGetShaderSource with argument *object*

SEE ALSO

glAttachShader, glCompileShader, glCreateShader, glDeleteShader, glDetachShader, glLinkProgram, glShaderSource

glLinkProgram

NAME

glLinkProgram—Links a program object

C SPECIFICATION

```
void glLinkProgram(GLuint program)
```

PARAMETERS

program   Specifies the handle of the program object to be linked

DESCRIPTION

glLinkProgram links the program object specified by *program.* If any shader objects of type GL_VERTEX_SHADER are attached to *program*, they are used to create an executable that will run on the programmable vertex processor. If any shader objects of type GL_FRAGMENT_SHADER are attached to *program*, they are used to create an executable that will run on the programmable fragment processor.

The status of the link operation is stored as part of the program object's state. This value is set to GL_TRUE if the program object was linked without errors and is ready for use, and GL_FALSE otherwise. It can be queried by calling **glGetProgram** with arguments *program* and GL_LINK_STATUS.

As a result of a successful link operation, all active user-defined uniform variables belonging to *program* are initialized to 0, and each of the program object's active uniform variables is assigned a location that can be queried with **glGetUniformLocation**. Also, any active user-defined attribute variables that have not been bound to a generic vertex attribute index are bound to one at this time.

Linking of a program object can fail for a number of reasons as specified in the OpenGL Shading Language Specification. The following lists some of the conditions that cause a link error:

*   The number of active attribute variables supported by the implementation has been exceeded.

*   The storage limit for uniform variables has been exceeded.

- The number of active uniform variables supported by the implementation has been exceeded.

- The **main** function is missing for the vertex shader or the fragment shader.

- A varying variable actually used in the fragment shader is not declared in the same way (or is not declared at all) in the vertex shader.

- A reference to a function or variable name is unresolved.

- A shared global is declared with two different types or two different initial values.

- One or more of the attached shader objects has not been successfully compiled.

- Binding a generic attribute matrix caused some rows of the matrix to fall outside the allowed maximum of GL_MAX_VERTEX_ATTRIBS.

- Not enough contiguous vertex attribute slots could be found to bind attribute matrices.

When a program object has been successfully linked, the program object can be made part of current state with **glUseProgram**. Whether or not the link operation was successful, the program object's information log is overwritten. The information log can be retrieved with **glGetProgramInfoLog**.

glLinkProgram also installs the generated executables as part of the current rendering state if the link operation was successful and the specified program object is already currently in use as a result of a previous call to **glUseProgram**. If the program object currently in use is relinked unsuccessfully, its link status is set to GL_FALSE, but the executables and associated state remain part of the current state until a subsequent call to **glUseProgram** removes it from use. After it is removed from use, it cannot be made part of current state until it has been successfully relinked.

If *program* contains shader objects of type GL_VERTEX_SHADER but does not contain shader objects of type GL_FRAGMENT_SHADER, the vertex shader is linked against the implicit interface for fixed functionality fragment processing. Similarly, if *program* contains shader objects of type GL_FRAGMENT_SHADER but does not contain shader objects of type GL_VERTEX_SHADER, the fragment shader is linked against the implicit interface for fixed functionality vertex processing.

The program object's information log is updated, and the program is generated at the time of the link operation. After the link operation, applications are free to modify attached shader objects, compile attached shader objects, detach shader objects, delete shader objects, and attach additional shader objects. None of these operations affect the information log or the program that is part of the program object.

NOTES

glLinkProgram is available only if the GL version is 2.0 or greater.

If the link operation is unsuccessful, any information about a previous link operation on *program* is lost (i.e., a failed link does not restore the old state of *program*). Certain information can still be retrieved from *program* even after an unsuccessful link operation. See, for instance, **glGetActiveAttrib** and **glGetActiveUniform**.

ERRORS

GL_INVALID_VALUE is generated if *program* is not a value generated by OpenGL.

GL_INVALID_OPERATION is generated if *program* is not a program object.

GL_INVALID_OPERATION is generated if **glLinkProgram** is executed between the execution of **glBegin** and the corresponding execution of **glEnd**.

ASSOCIATED GETS

glGet with the argument GL_CURRENT_PROGRAM

glGetActiveAttrib with argument *program* and the index of an active attribute variable

glGetActiveUniform with argument *program* and the index of an active uniform variable

glGetAttachedShaders with argument *program*

glGetAttribLocation with argument *program* and an attribute variable name

glGetProgram with arguments *program* and GL_LINK_STATUS

glGetProgramInfoLog with argument *program*

glGetUniform with argument *program* and a uniform variable location

glGetUniformLocation with argument *program* and a uniform variable name

glIsProgram

SEE ALSO

glAttachShader, glBindAttribLocation, glCompileShader, glCreateProgram, glDeleteProgram, glDetachShader, glUniform, glUseProgram, glValidateProgram

glShaderSource

NAME

glShaderSource—Replaces the source code in a shader object

C SPECIFICATION

```
void glShaderSource(GLuint shader,
                    GLsizei count,
                    const GLchar **string,
                    const GLint *length)
```

PARAMETERS

shader   Specifies the handle of the shader object whose source
              code is to be replaced

count   Specifies the number of elements in the *string* and
              length arrays

string   Specifies an array of pointers to strings containing the
              source code to be loaded into the shader

length   Specifies an array of string lengths

DESCRIPTION

glShaderSource sets the source code in *shader* to the source code in the array
of strings specified by *string*. Any source code previously stored in the shader
object is completely replaced. The number of strings in the array is specified
by *count*. If *length* is NULL, each string is assumed to be null terminated. If
length is a value other than NULL, it points to an array containing a string
length for each of the corresponding elements of *string*. Each element in the
length array may contain the length of the corresponding string (the null
character is not counted as part of the string length) or a value less than 0
to indicate that the string is null terminated. The source code strings are not
scanned or parsed at this time; they are simply copied into the specified
shader object.

NOTES

glShaderSource is available only if the GL version is 2.0 or greater.

OpenGL copies the shader source code strings when **glShaderSource** is called, so an application can free its copy of the source code strings immediately after the function returns.

ERRORS

GL_INVALID_VALUE is generated if *shader* is not a value generated by OpenGL.

GL_INVALID_OPERATION is generated if *shader* is not a shader object.

GL_INVALID_VALUE is generated if *count* is less than 0.

GL_INVALID_OPERATION is generated if **glShaderSource** is executed between the execution of **glBegin** and the corresponding execution of **glEnd**.

ASSOCIATED GETS

glGetShader with arguments *shader* and GL_SHADER_SOURCE_LENGTH

glGetShaderSource with argument *shader*

glIsShader

SEE ALSO

glCompileShader, **glCreateShader**, **glDeleteShader**

glUniform

NAME

glUniform1f, glUniform2f, glUniform3f, glUniform4f, glUniform1i, glUniform2i, glUniform3i, glUniform4i, glUniform1fv, glUniform2fv, glUniform3fv, glUniform4fv, glUniform1iv, glUniform2iv, glUniform3iv, glUniform4iv, glUniformMatrix2fv, glUniformMatrix3fv, glUniformMatrix4fv—Specify the value of a uniform variable for the current program object

C SPECIFICATION

```
void glUniform1f(GLint location,
                 GLfloat v0)
void glUniform2f(GLint location,
                 GLfloat v0,
                 GLfloat v1)
void glUniform3f(GLint location,
                 GLfloat v0,
                 GLfloat v1,
                 GLfloat v2)
void glUniform4f(GLint location,
                 GLfloat v0,
                 GLfloat v1,
                 GLfloat v2,
                 GLfloat v3)

void glUniform1i(GLint location,
                 GLint v0)
void glUniform2i(GLint location,
                 GLint v0,
                 GLint v1)
void glUniform3i(GLint location,
                 GLint v0,
                 GLint v1,
                 GLint v2)
void glUniform4i(GLint location,
                 GLint v0,
                 GLint v1,
                 GLint v2,
                 GLint v3)
```

PARAMETERS

location   Specifies the location of the uniform variable to be modified

v0, v1, v2, v3   Specify the new values to be used for the specified uniform variable

C SPECIFICATION

```
void glUniform1fv(GLint location,
                  GLsizei count,
                  const GLfloat *value)
void glUniform2fv(GLint location,
                  GLsizei count,
                  const GLfloat *value)
void glUniform3fv(GLint location,
                  GLsizei count,
                  const GLfloat *value)
void glUniform4fv(GLint location,
                  GLsizei count,
                  const GLfloat *value)

void glUniform1iv(GLint location,
                  GLsizei count,
                  const GLint *value)
void glUniform2iv(GLint location,
                  GLsizei count,
                  const GLint *value)
void glUniform3iv(GLint location,
                  GLsizei count,
                  const GLint *value)
void glUniform4iv(GLint location,
                  GLsizei count,
                  const GLint *value)
```

PARAMETERS

location   Specifies the location of the uniform value to be modified

count   Specifies the number of elements that are to be modified (this should be 1 if the targeted uniform variable is not an array, 1 or more if it is an array)

value   Specifies a pointer to an array of *count* values that are used to update the specified uniform variable

C SPECIFICATION

```
void glUniformMatrix2fv(GLint location,
                        GLsizei count,
                        GLboolean transpose,
                        const GLfloat *value)
void glUniformMatrix3fv(GLint location,
                        GLsizei count,
                        GLboolean transpose,
                        const GLfloat *value)
void glUniformMatrix4fv(GLint location,
                        GLsizei count,
                        GLboolean transpose,
                        const GLfloat *value)
```

PARAMETERS

location Specifies the location of the uniform value to be modified

count Specifies the number of elements that are to be modified (this should be 1 if the targeted uniform variable is not an array, 1 or more if it is an array)

transpose Specifies whether to transpose the matrix as the values are loaded into the uniform variable

value Specifies a pointer to an array of *count* values that are used to update the specified uniform variable

DESCRIPTION

glUniform modifies the value of a uniform variable or a uniform variable array. The location of the uniform variable to be modified is specified by *location*, which should be a value returned by **glGetUniformLocation**. **glUniform** operates on the program object that was made part of current state with **glUseProgram**.

The commands **glUniform{1|2|3|4}{f|i}** change the value of the uniform variable specified by *location*, using the values passed as arguments. The number specified in the command should match the number of components in the data type of the specified uniform variable (e.g., **1** for float, int, bool; **2** for vec2, ivec2, bvec2). The suffix **f** means that floating-point values are being passed; the suffix **i** means that integer values are being passed, and this type should also match the data type of the specified uniform variable. The **i** variants of this function provide values for uniform variables defined as int, ivec2, ivec3, ivec4, or arrays of these. The **f** variants provide values for uniform variables of type float, vec2, vec3, vec4, or arrays of these. Either the **i** or the **f** variants can provide values for uniform variables of type bool, bvec2, bvec3, bvec4, or arrays of these. The uniform variable is set to false if the input value is 0 or 0.0f, and it is set to true otherwise.

All active uniform variables defined in a program object are initialized to 0 when the program object is linked successfully. They retain the values assigned to them with **glUniform** until the next successful link operation occurs on the program object, when they are once again initialized to 0.

The commands **glUniform{1|2|3|4}{f|i}v** modify a single uniform variable or a uniform variable array. These commands pass a count and a pointer to the values to be loaded into a uniform variable or a uniform variable array. Use a count of 1 if modifying the value of a single uniform variable, and a count of 1 or greater if modifying an entire array or part of an array. When n elements starting at an arbitrary position m in a uniform variable array are loaded, elements $m + n - 1$ in the array are replaced with the new values. If $m + n - 1$ is larger than the size of the uniform variable array, values for all array elements beyond the end of the array are ignored. The number specified in the name of the command indicates the number of components for each element in *value*, and it should match the number of components in the data type of the specified uniform variable (e.g., **1** for float, int, bool; **2** for vec2, ivec2, bvec2). The data type specified in the name of the command must match the data type for the specified uniform variable as described previously for **glUniform{1|2|3|4}{f|i}**.

For uniform variable arrays, each element of the array is considered to be of the type indicated in the name of the command (e.g., **glUniform3f** or **glUniform3fv** can be used to load a uniform variable array of type vec3). The number of elements of the uniform variable array to be modified is specified by *count*.

The commands **glUniformFloatMatrix{2|3|4}fv** modify a matrix or an array of matrices. The number in the command name is interpreted as the dimensionality of the matrix. The number **2** indicates a 2×2 matrix (i.e., 4 values), the number **3** indicates a 3×3 matrix (i.e., 9 values), and the number **4** indicates a 4×4 matrix (i.e., 16 values). If *transpose* is GL_FALSE, each matrix is assumed to be supplied in column major order. If *transpose* is GL_TRUE, each matrix is assumed to be supplied in row major order. The *count* argument specifies the number of matrices to be passed. Use a count of 1 if modifying the value of a single matrix, and use a count greater than 1 if modifying an array of matrices.

NOTES

glUniform is available only if the GL version is 2.0 or greater.

glUniform1i and **glUniform1iv** are the only two functions that may load uniform variables defined as sampler types. Loading samplers with any other function results in a GL_INVALID_OPERATION error.

If *count* is greater than 1 and the indicated uniform variable is not an array, a GL_INVALID_OPERATION error is generated, and the specified uniform variable remains unchanged.

Other than the preceding exceptions, if the type and size of the uniform variable as defined in the shader do not match the type and size specified in the name of the command used to load a value for the uniform variable, a GL_INVALID_OPERATION error is generated, and the specified uniform variable remains unchanged.

If *location* is a value other than –1 and it does not represent a valid uniform variable location in the current program object, an error is generated, and no changes are made to the uniform variable storage of the current program object. If *location* is equal to –1, the data passed in is silently ignored, and the specified uniform variable is unchanged.

ERRORS

GL_INVALID_OPERATION is generated if there is no current program object.

GL_INVALID_OPERATION is generated if the size of the uniform variable declared in the shader does not match the size indicated by the **glUniform** command.

GL_INVALID_OPERATION is generated if one of the integer variants of this function loads a uniform variable of type float, vec2, vec3, vec4, or an array of these, or if one of the floating-point variants of this function loads a uniform variable of type int, ivec2, ivec3, or ivec4, or an array of these.

GL_INVALID_OPERATION is generated if *location* is an invalid uniform location for the current program object and *location* is not equal to –1.

GL_INVALID_VALUE is generated if *count* is less than 0.

GL_INVALID_OPERATION is generated if *count* is greater than 1 and the indicated uniform variable is not an array variable.

GL_INVALID_OPERATION is generated if a sampler is loaded with a command other than **glUniform1i** and **glUniform1iv**.

GL_INVALID_OPERATION is generated if **glUniform** is executed between the execution of **glBegin** and the corresponding execution of **glEnd**.

ASSOCIATED GETS

glGet with the argument GL_CURRENT_PROGRAM

glGetActiveUniform with the handle of a program object and the index of an active uniform variable

glGetUniform with the handle of a program object and the location of a uniform variable

glGetUniformLocation with the handle of a program object and the name of a uniform variable

SEE ALSO

glLinkProgram, **glUseProgram**

glUseProgram

NAME

glUseProgram—Installs a program object as part of current rendering state

C SPECIFICATION

```
void glUseProgram(GLuint program)
```

PARAMETERS

program   Specifies the handle of the program object whose executables are to be used as part of current rendering state

DESCRIPTION

glUseProgram installs the program object specified by *program* as part of current rendering state. Creating one or more executables in a program object involves successfully attaching shader objects to it with **glAttachShader**, successfully compiling the shader objects with **glCompileShader**, and successfully linking the program object with **glLinkProgram**.

A program object contains an executable that will run on the vertex processor if it contains one or more shader objects of type GL_VERTEX_SHADER that have been successfully compiled and linked. Similarly, a program object contains an executable that will run on the fragment processor if it contains one or more shader objects of type GL_FRAGMENT_SHADER that have been successfully compiled and linked.

Successfully installing an executable on a programmable processor disables the corresponding fixed functionality of OpenGL. Specifically, if an executable is installed on the vertex processor, the OpenGL fixed functionality is disabled as follows:

- The modelview matrix is not applied to vertex coordinates.
- The projection matrix is not applied to vertex coordinates.
- The texture matrices are not applied to texture coordinates.
- Normals are not transformed to eye coordinates.
- Normals are not rescaled or normalized.

- Normalization of GL_AUTO_NORMAL evaluated normals is not performed.

- Texture coordinates are not generated automatically.

- Per-vertex lighting is not performed.

- Color material computations are not performed.

- Color index lighting is not performed.

This list also applies to setting the current raster position.

The executable that is installed on the vertex processor is expected to implement any or all of the desired functionality from the preceding list. Similarly, if an executable is installed on the fragment processor, the OpenGL fixed functionality is disabled as follows:

- Texture environment and texture functions are not applied.

- Texture application is not applied.

- Color sum is not applied.

- Fog is not applied.

Again, the fragment shader that is installed is expected to implement any or all of the desired functionality from the preceding list.

While a program object is in use, applications are free to modify attached shader objects, compile attached shader objects, attach additional shader objects, and detach or delete shader objects. None of these operations affect the executables that are part of the current state. However, relinking the program object that is currently in use installs the program object as part of the current rendering state if the link operation was successful (see **glLinkProgram**). If the program object currently in use is relinked unsuccessfully, its link status is set to GL_FALSE, but the executables and associated state remain part of the current state until a subsequent call to **glUseProgram** removes the program object from use. After it is removed from use, it cannot be made part of current state until it has been successfully relinked.

If *program* contains shader objects of type GL_VERTEX_SHADER but does not contain shader objects of type GL_FRAGMENT_SHADER, an executable is installed on the vertex processor, but fixed functionality is used for fragment processing. Similarly, if *program* contains shader objects of type GL_FRAGMENT_SHADER but does not contain shader objects of type

GL_VERTEX_SHADER, an executable is installed on the fragment processor, but fixed functionality is used for vertex processing. If *program* is 0, the programmable processors are disabled, and fixed functionality is used for both vertex and fragment processing.

NOTES

glUseProgram is available only if the GL version is 2.0 or greater.

While a program object is in use, the state that controls the disabled fixed functionality may also be updated with the normal OpenGL calls.

Like display lists and texture objects, the namespace for program objects may be shared across a set of contexts, as long as the server sides of the contexts share the same address space. If the namespace is shared across contexts, any attached objects and the data associated with those attached objects are shared as well.

Applications are responsible for synchronizing across API calls when objects are accessed from different execution threads.

ERRORS

GL_INVALID_VALUE is generated if *program* is neither 0 nor a value generated by OpenGL.

GL_INVALID_OPERATION is generated if *program* is not a program object.

GL_INVALID_OPERATION is generated if *program* could not be made part of current state.

GL_INVALID_OPERATION is generated if **glUseProgram** is executed between the execution of **glBegin** and the corresponding execution of **glEnd**.

ASSOCIATED GETS

glGet with the argument GL_CURRENT_PROGRAM

glGetActiveAttrib with a valid program object and the index of an active attribute variable

glGetActiveUniform with a valid program object and the index of an active uniform variable

glGetAttachedShaders with a valid program object

glGetAttribLocation with a valid program object and the name of an attribute variable

glGetProgram with a valid program object and the parameter to be queried

glGetProgramInfoLog with a valid program object

glGetUniform with a valid program object and the location of a uniform variable

glGetUniformLocation with a valid program object and the name of a uniform variable

glIsProgram

SEE ALSO

glIAttachShader, **glBindAttribLocation**, **glCompileShader**, **glCreateProgram**, **glDeleteProgram**, **glDetachShader**, **glLinkProgram**, **glUniform**, **glValidateProgram**, **glVertexAttrib**

glValidateProgram

NAME

glValidateProgram—Validates a program object

C SPECIFICATION

```
void glValidateProgram(GLuint program)
```

PARAMETERS

program   Specifies the handle of the program object to be validated

DESCRIPTION

glValidateProgram checks to see whether the executables contained in *program* can execute given the current OpenGL state. The information generated by the validation process is stored in *program*'s information log. The validation information may consist of an empty string, or it may be a string containing information about how the current program object interacts with the rest of current OpenGL state. This function provides a way for OpenGL implementors to convey more information about why the current program is inefficient, suboptimal, failing to execute, and so on.

The status of the validation operation is stored as part of the program object's state. This value is set to GL_TRUE if the validation succeeded, and GL_FALSE otherwise. It can be queried by calling **glGetProgram** with arguments *program* and GL_VALIDATE_STATUS. If validation is successful, *program* is guaranteed to execute given the current state. Otherwise, *program* is guaranteed to not execute.

This function is typically useful only during application development. The informational string stored in the information log is completely implementation dependent; therefore, different OpenGL implementations cannot be expected to produce identical information strings.

NOTES

glValidateProgram is available only if the GL version is 2.0 or greater.

This function mimics the validation operation that OpenGL implementations must perform when rendering commands are issued while programmable shaders are part of current state. The error GL_INVALID_OPERATION is generated by **glBegin**, **glRasterPos**, or any command that performs an implicit call to **glBegin** if

- any two active samplers in the current program object are of different types but refer to the same texture image unit;

- any active sampler in the current program object refers to a texture image unit in which fixed function fragment processing accesses a texture target that does not match the sampler type; or

- the sum of the number of active samplers in the program and the number of texture image units enabled for fixed function fragment processing exceeds the combined limit on the total number of texture image units allowed.

Difficulties or performance degradation may occur if applications try to catch these errors when issuing rendering commands. Therefore, applications are advised to make calls to **glValidateProgram** to detect these issues during application development.

ERRORS

GL_INVALID_VALUE is generated if *program* is not a value generated by OpenGL.

GL_INVALID_OPERATION is generated if *program* is not a program object.

GL_INVALID_OPERATION is generated if **glValidateProgram** is executed between the execution of **glBegin** and the corresponding execution of **glEnd**.

ASSOCIATED GETS

glGetProgram with arguments *program* and GL_VALIDATE_STATUS

glGetProgramInfoLog with argument *program*

glIsProgram

SEE ALSO

glLinkProgram, **glUseProgram**

glVertexAttrib

NAME

glVertexAttrib1f, glVertexAttrib1s, glVertexAttrib1d, glVertexAttrib2f, glVertexAttrib2s, glVertexAttrib2d, glVertexAttrib3f, glVertexAttrib3s, glVertexAttrib3d, glVertexAttrib4f, glVertexAttrib4s, glVertexAttrib4d, glVertexAttrib4Nub, glVertexAttrib1fv, glVertexAttrib1sv, glVertexAttrib1dv, glVertexAttrib2fv, glVertexAttrib2sv, glVertexAttrib2dv, glVertexAttrib3fv, glVertexAttrib3sv, glVertexAttrib3dv, glVertexAttrib4fv, glVertexAttrib4sv, glVertexAttrib4dv, glVertexAttrib4iv, glVertexAttrib4bv, glVertexAttrib4ubv, glVertexAttrib4usv, glVertexAttrib4uiv, glVertexAttrib4Nbv, glVertexAttrib4Nsv, glVertexAttrib4Niv, glVertexAttrib4Nubv, glVertexAttrib4Nusv, glVertexAttrib4Nuiv—Specify the value of a generic vertex attribute

C SPECIFICATION

```
void glVertexAttrib1f(GLuint index,
                      GLfloat v0)
void glVertexAttrib1s(GLuint index,
                      GLshort v0)
void glVertexAttrib1d(GLuint index,
                      GLdouble v0)


void glVertexAttrib2f(GLuint index,
                      GLfloat v0,
                      GLfloat v1)
void glVertexAttrib2s(GLuint index,
                      GLshort v0,
                      GLshort v1)
void glVertexAttrib2d(GLuint index,
                      GLdouble v0,
                      GLdouble v1)


void glVertexAttrib3f(GLuint index,
                      GLfloat v0,
                      GLfloat v1,
                      GLfloat v2)
void glVertexAttrib3s(GLuint index,
                      GLshort v0,
                      GLshort v1,
                      GLshort v2)
```

```
void glVertexAttrib3d(GLuint index,
                      GLdouble v0,
                      GLdouble v1,
                      GLdouble v2)

void glVertexAttrib4f(GLuint index,
                      GLfloat v0,
                      GLfloat v1,
                      GLfloat v2,
                      GLfloat v3)
void glVertexAttrib4s(GLuint index,
                      GLshort v0,
                      GLshort v1,
                      GLshort v2,
                      GLshort v3)
void glVertexAttrib4d(GLuint index,
                      GLdouble v0,
                      GLdouble v1,
                      GLdouble v2,
                      GLdouble v3)

void glVertexAttrib4Nub(GLuint index,
                        GLubyte v0,
                        GLubyte v1,
                        GLubyte v2,
                        GLubyte v3)
```

PARAMETERS

index   Specifies the index of the generic vertex attribute to be
                   modified

v0, v1, v2, v3   Specify the new values to be used for the specified
                   vertex attribute

C SPECIFICATION

```
void glVertexAttrib1fv(GLuint index, const GLfloat *v)
void glVertexAttrib1sv(GLuint index, const GLshort *v)
void glVertexAttrib1dv(GLuint index, const GLdouble *v)

void glVertexAttrib2fv(GLuint index, const GLfloat *v)
void glVertexAttrib2sv(GLuint index, const GLshort *v)
void glVertexAttrib2dv(GLuint index, const GLdouble *v)

void glVertexAttrib3fv(GLuint index, const GLfloat *v)
void glVertexAttrib3sv(GLuint index, const GLshort *v)
void glVertexAttrib3dv(GLuint index, const GLdouble *v)

void glVertexAttrib4fv(GLuint index, const GLfloat *v)
void glVertexAttrib4sv(GLuint index, const GLshort *v)
void glVertexAttrib4dv(GLuint index, const GLdouble *v)
void glVertexAttrib4iv(GLuint index, const GLint *v)
void glVertexAttrib4bv(GLuint index, const GLbyte *v)

void glVertexAttrib4ubv(GLuint index, const GLubyte *v)
void glVertexAttrib4usv(GLuint index, const GLushort *v)
void glVertexAttrib4uiv(GLuint index, const GLuint *v)

void glVertexAttrib4Nbv(GLuint index, const GLbyte *v)
void glVertexAttrib4Nsv(GLuint index, const GLshort *v)
void glVertexAttrib4Niv(GLuint index, const GLint *v)
void glVertexAttrib4Nubv(GLuint index, const GLubyte *v)
void glVertexAttrib4Nusv(GLuint index, const GLushort *v)
void glVertexAttrib4Nuiv(GLuint index, const GLuint *v)
```

PARAMETERS

index   Specifies the index of the generic vertex attribute to be
              modified

v   Specifies a pointer to an array of values to be used for
              the generic vertex attribute

DESCRIPTION

OpenGL defines a number of standard vertex attributes that applications can modify with standard API entry points (color, normal, texture coordinates, etc.). The **glVertexAttrib** family of entry points allows an application to pass generic vertex attributes into numbered locations.

Generic attributes are defined as four-component values that are organized into an array. The first entry of this array is numbered 0, and the size of the array is specified by the implementation-dependent constant GL_MAX_VERTEX_ATTRIBS. Individual elements of this array can be modified with a **glVertexAttrib** call that specifies the index of the element to be modified and a value for that element.

These commands can specify one, two, three, or all four components of the generic vertex attribute specified by *index*. A **1** in the command name means that only one value is passed and that it modifies the first component of the generic vertex attribute. The second and third components are set to 0, and the fourth component is set to 1. Similarly, a **2** in the command name means that values are provided for the first two components, the third component is set to 0, and the fourth component is set to 1. A **3** in the command name means that values are provided for the first three components and that the fourth component is set to 1, and a **4** in the command name means that values are provided for all four components.

The letters **s**, **f**, **i**, **d**, **ub**, **us**, and **ui** specify whether the arguments are of type short, float, int, double, unsigned byte, unsigned short, or unsigned int. When **v** is appended to the name, the commands can take a pointer to an array of such values. The letter **N** in a command name means that the arguments are passed as fixed-point values that are scaled to a normalized range according to the component conversion rules defined by the OpenGL specification. Signed values are understood to represent fixed-point values in the range [−1,1], and unsigned values are understood to represent fixed-point values in the range [0,1].

OpenGL Shading Language attribute variables are allowed to be of type mat2, mat3, or mat4. Attributes of these types can be loaded by the **glVertexAttrib** entry points. Matrices must be loaded into successive generic attribute slots in column major order, with one column of the matrix in each generic attribute slot.

A user-defined attribute variable declared in a vertex shader can be bound to a generic attribute index with **glBindAttribLocation**. Such binding allows an application to use more descriptive variable names in a vertex shader. A subsequent change to the specified generic vertex attribute is immediately reflected as a change to the corresponding attribute variable in the vertex shader.

The binding between a generic vertex attribute index and a user-defined attribute variable in a vertex shader is part of the state of a program object, but the current value of the generic vertex attribute is not. The value of each generic vertex attribute is part of current state, just like standard vertex attributes, and it is maintained even if a different program object is used.

An application may freely modify generic vertex attributes that are not bound to a named vertex shader attribute variable. These values are simply maintained as part of current state and are not accessed by the vertex shader. If a generic vertex attribute bound to an attribute variable in a vertex shader is not updated while the vertex shader is executing, the vertex shader repeatedly uses the current value for the generic vertex attribute.

The generic vertex attribute with index 0 is the same as the vertex position attribute previously defined by OpenGL. A **glVertex2**, **glVertex3**, or **glVertex4** command is completely equivalent to the corresponding **glVertexAttrib** command with an index argument of 0. A vertex shader can access generic vertex attribute 0 by using the built-in attribute variable *gl_Vertex*. There are no current values for generic vertex attribute 0. This is the only generic vertex attribute with this property; calls to set other standard vertex attributes can be freely mixed with calls to set any of the other generic vertex attributes.

NOTES

glVertexAttrib is available only if the GL version is 2.0 or greater.

Generic vertex attributes can be updated at any time. In particular, **glVertexAttrib** can be called between a call to **glBegin** and the corresponding call to **glEnd**.

An application can bind more than one attribute name to the same generic vertex attribute index. This is referred to as aliasing, and it is allowed only if just one of the aliased attribute variables is active in the vertex shader or if no path through the vertex shader consumes more than one of the attributes aliased to the same location. OpenGL implementations are not required to do error checking to detect aliasing; they are allowed to assume that aliasing does not occur, and they are allowed to employ optimizations that work only in the absence of aliasing.

There is no provision for binding standard vertex attributes; therefore, it is not possible to alias generic attributes with standard attributes.

ERRORS

GL_INVALID_VALUE is generated if *index* is greater than or equal to GL_MAX_
VERTEX_ATTRIBS.

ASSOCIATED GETS

glGet with the argument GL_CURRENT_PROGRAM

glGetActiveAttrib with argument *program* and the index of an active attribute
variable

glGetAttribLocation with argument *program* and an attribute variable name

glGetVertexAttrib with arguments GL_CURRENT_VERTEX_ATTRIB and *index*

SEE ALSO

glBindAttribLocation, glVertex, glVertexAttribPointer

glVertexAttribPointer

NAME

glVertexAttribPointer—Defines a generic vertex attribute array

C SPECIFICATION

```
void glVertexAttribPointer(GLuint index,
                           GLint size,
                           GLenum type,
                           GLboolean normalized,
                           GLsizei stride,
                           const GLvoid *pointer)
```

PARAMETERS

index	Specifies the index of the generic vertex attribute to be modified.
size	Specifies the number of values for each element of the generic vertex attribute array. Must be 1, 2, 3, or 4.
type	Specifies the data type of each component in the array. Symbolic constants GL_BYTE, GL_UNSIGNED_BYTE, GL_SHORT, GL_UNSIGNED_SHORT, GL_INT, GL_UNSIGNED_INT, GL_FLOAT, and GL_DOUBLE are accepted.
normalized	Specifies whether fixed-point data values should be normalized (GL_TRUE) or converted directly as fixed-point values (GL_FALSE) when they are accessed.
stride	Specifies the byte offset between consecutive attribute values. If *stride* is 0 (the initial value), the attribute values are understood to be tightly packed in the array.
pointer	Specifies a pointer to the first component of the first attribute value in the array.

DESCRIPTION

glVertexAttribPointer specifies the location and data format of an array of generic vertex attribute values to use when rendering. *size* specifies the number of components per attribute and must be 1, 2, 3, or 4. *type* specifies the data type of each component, and *stride* specifies the byte stride from one attribute to the next, allowing attribute values to be intermixed with other attribute values or stored in a separate array. A value of 0 for *stride* means that the values are stored sequentially in memory with no gaps between successive elements. If set to GL_TRUE, *normalized* means that values stored in an integer format are to be mapped to the range [–1,1] (for signed values) or [0,1] (for unsigned values) when they are accessed and converted to floating point. Otherwise, values are converted to floats directly without normalization.

When a generic vertex attribute array is specified, *size*, *type*, *normalized*, *stride*, and *pointer* are saved as client-side state.

To enable and disable the generic vertex attribute array, call **glEnableVertexAttribArray** and **glDisableVertexAttribArray** with *index*. If enabled, the generic vertex attribute array is used when **glDrawArrays**, **glDrawElements**, **glDrawRangeElements**, **glArrayElement**, **glMultiDrawElements**, or **glMultiDrawArrays** is called.

NOTES

glVertexAttribPointer is available only if the GL version is 2.0 or greater.

Each generic vertex attribute array is initially disabled and is not accessed when **glDrawArrays**, **glDrawElements**, **glDrawRangeElements**, **glArrayElement**, **glMultiDrawElements**, or **glMultiDrawArrays** is called.

Execution of **glVertexAttribPointer** is not allowed between the execution of **glBegin** and **glEnd**, but an error may or may not be generated. If no error is generated, the operation is undefined.

glVertexAttribPointer is typically implemented on the client side.

Generic vertex attribute array parameters are client-side state and are therefore not saved or restored by **glPushAttrib** and **glPopAttrib**. Use **glPushClientAttrib** and **glPopClientAttrib** instead.

ERRORS

GL_INVALID_VALUE is generated if *index* is greater than or equal to GL_MAX_VERTEX_ATTRIBS.

GL_INVALID_VALUE is generated if *size* is not 1, 2, 3, or 4.

GL_INVALID_ENUM is generated if *type* is not an accepted value.

GL_INVALID_VALUE is generated if *stride* is negative.

ASSOCIATED GETS

glGet with argument GL_MAX_VERTEX_ATTRIBS

glGetVertexAttrib with arguments *index* and the name of a vertex attribute parameter

glGetVertexAttribPointer with arguments *index* and GL_VERTEX_ATTRIB_ARRAY_POINTER

SEE ALSO

glArrayElement, glBindAttribLocation, glDisableVertexAttribArray, glDraw-Arrays, glDrawElements, glDrawRangeElements, glEnableVertexAttribArray, glMultiDrawArrays, glMultiDrawElements, glPopClientAttrib, glPushClientAttrib, glVertexAttrib

OpenGL 1.5 to OpenGL 2.0 GLSL Migration Guide

The OpenGL Shading Language was initially supported through ARB extensions to OpenGL 1.5. The following table (originally compiled by Teri Morrison) documents the mapping of OpenGL 1.5 ARB extension API entry points to the OpenGL 2.0 API entry points.

glAttachObjectARB	Renamed to **glAttachShader**. Input arguments *program* and *shader* were changed from GLhandleARB to GLuint.
glBindAttribLocationARB	Renamed to **glBindAttribLocation**. Input argument *program* was changed from GLhandleARB to GLuint. Input argument *name* was changed from const GLcharARB* to const GLchar*.
glCompileShaderARB	Renamed to **glCompileShader**. Input argument *shader* was changed from GLhandleARB to GLuint.
glCreateProgramObjectARB	Renamed to **glCreateProgram**. Function return value was changed from GLhandleARB to GLuint.
glCreateShaderObjectARB	Renamed to **glCreateShader**. Function return value was changed from GLhandleARB to GLuint.
glDeleteObjectARB	Split into two functions, **glDeleteProgram** and **glDeleteShader**. Input argument *object* was changed from GLhandleARB to GLuint. Additional error checking was added to ensure that the input argument in the new function (*program* or *shader*) is the proper object type.
glDetachObjectARB	Renamed to **glDetachShader**. Input arguments *program* and *shader* were changed from GLhandleARB to GLuint.

glDisableVertexAttribArrayARB	Renamed to **glDisableVertexAttribArray**.
glEnableVertexAttribArrayARB	Renamed to **glEnableVertexAttribArray**.
glGetActiveAttribARB	Renamed to **glGetActiveAttrib**. Input argument *program* was changed from GLhandleARB to GLuint. Input argument *name* was changed from GLcharARB* to GLchar*.
glGetActiveUniformARB	Renamed to **glGetActiveUniform**. Input argument *program* was changed from GLhandleARB to GLuint. Input argument *name* was changed from GLcharARB* to GLchar*.
glGetAttachedObjectsARB	Renamed to **glGetAttachedShaders**. Input argument *program* was changed from GLhandleARB to GLuint. Input argument *objects* was changed from GLhandleARB* to GLuint*.
glGetAttribLocationARB	Renamed to **glGetAttribLocation**. Input argument *program* was changed from GLhandleARB to GLuint. Input argument *name* was changed from const GLcharARB* to const GLchar*.
glGetHandleARB	Replaced by calling **glGet** with the symbolic constant GL_CURRENT_PROGRAM.
glGetInfoLogARB	Split into two functions, **glGetProgramInfoLog** and **glGetShaderInfoLog**. Input argument *object* was changed from GLhandleARB to GLuint. Output argument *infoLog* was changed from const GLcharARB* to const GLchar*. New error checking was added to ensure that the input argument in the new function *(program* or *shader)* is the proper object type.

glGetObjectParameterARB	Split into two functions, **glGetProgram** and **glGetShader**. Input argument *object* was changed from GLhandleARB to GLuint. Additional error checking was added to ensure that the input argument in the new function *(program* or *shader)* is the proper object type. In OpenGL 2.0 there is no equivalent for the floating-point version of the ARB function **glGetObjectParameterfvARB**.
glGetShaderSourceARB	Renamed to **glGetShaderSource**. Input argument *shader* was changed from GLhandleARB to GLuint. Output argument *source* was changed from const GLcharARB* to const GLchar*.
glGetUniformARB	Renamed to **glGetUniform**. Input argument *program* was changed from GLhandleARB to GLuint.
glGetUniformLocationARB	Renamed to **glGetUniformLocation**. Input argument *program* was changed from GLhandleARB to GLuint. Input argument *name* was changed from const GLcharARB* to const GLchar*.
glGetVertexAttribARB	Renamed to **glGetVertexAttrib**.
glGetVertexAttribPointerARB	Renamed to **glGetVertexAttribPointer**.
glLinkProgramARB	Renamed to **glLinkProgram**. Input argument *program* was changed from GLhandleARB to GLuint.
glShaderSourceARB	Renamed to **glShaderSource**. Input argument *shader* was changed from GLhandleARB to GLuint. Input argument *strings* was changed from const GLcharARB** to const GLchar**.
glUniformARB	Renamed to **glUniform**.

glUseProgramObjectARB	Renamed to **glUseProgram**. Input argument *program* was changed from GLhandleARB to GLuint.
glValidateProgramARB	Renamed to **glValidateProgram**. Input argument *program* was changed from GLhandleARB to GLuint.
glVertexAttribARB	Renamed to **glVertexAttrib**.
glVertexAttribPointerARB	Renamed to **glVertexAttribPointer**.
New functions	The functions **glIsProgram** and **glIsShader** were added in OpenGL 2.0 and have no equivalent in the ARB extensions that support GLSL.
	The function **glDrawBuffers** was promoted to OpenGL 2.0 from the ARB_draw_buffers extension specification, where it was called **glDrawBuffersARB**.

Afterword

Writing a book requires a lot of time and effort. Sometimes authors refer to the finished product as "a labor of love." I have to say that, for me, writing this book has been "a labor of fun."

I have been fortunate to participate in a major architectural revolution in computer graphics hardware. In the last few years, consumer graphics hardware has undergone a sea change—from pure fixed functionality to almost complete user programmability. In many ways, this time feels like the late 1970s and early 1980s, when significant advances were being made in computer graphics at places like the University of Utah, NYU, Lucasfilm, JPL, UNC, and Cornell. The difference this time is that graphics hardware is now cheap enough and fast enough that you don't have to work at a research institute or attend an elite graduate school to play with it. You can explore the brave new world on your own personal computer.

It is relatively rare to participate in establishing even one industry standard, but I have had the good fortune to play a role in the definition of three important graphics standards. First was PEX in the late 1980s. Next was OpenGL in the early 1990s and, now, the OpenGL Shading Language in the first years of the new millennium. These efforts have been gratifying to me because they provide graphics hardware capabilities to people in an industry-standard way. Applications written to a standard are portable, and therefore the technology they are built on is accessible to a wider audience.

It's been a labor of fun because it is a lot of fun and truly remarkable to be one of the first people to implement classic rendering algorithms by using a high-level language on low-cost but high-performance graphics hardware. When our team first got the brick shader running on 3Dlabs Wildcat VP graphics hardware, it was a jaw-dropping "Wow!" moment. A similar feeling occurred when I got a shader I was developing to run successfully for the first time or saw, working for the first time, a shader written by someone else in the group. It seems to me that this feeling must be similar to that felt by the graphics pioneers twenty to twenty-five years ago when they got the first successful results from their new algorithms. And it is great fun to hear from end users who experience those same sorts of jaw-dropping "Wow!" moments.

Because of the architectural revolution in consumer graphics hardware, today people like you and me can quickly and easily write shaders that implement the rendering algorithms devised twenty years ago by the pioneers of computer graphics. To implement bump mapping, we looked up Blinn's 1978 paper, and to implement particle systems, we looked at Reeves's 1983 paper. I chuckled to myself when I saw the hand-drawn diagrams in Alvy Ray Smith's 1983 memo on digital filtering. Images that took hours to generate take milliseconds to render today. And shader code that took weeks to develop can now be written in minutes with a high-level shading language developed specifically for this task. It is mind-boggling to think how painstaking it must have been for Mandelbrot to generate images of his famous set in the late 1970s, compared to how easy it is to do today with the OpenGL Shading Language.

And part of the reason that I've so enjoyed writing this book is that I know there are significant new discoveries to be made in the area of computer graphics. If someone like me can simply and easily implement rendering algorithms that previously could run only on software on CPUs, imagine how much more is possible with the programmable graphics hardware that is available today. The availability of low-cost programmable graphics hardware makes it possible for many more people to experiment with new rendering techniques. Algorithms of much higher complexity can be developed. And I know that some of you out there will invent some exciting new rendering techniques when using the OpenGL Shading Language. This technology is moving rapidly to handheld devices such as PDAs and cell phones. A version of the OpenGL Shading Language for embedded devices was approved as part of OpenGL ES in the summer of 2005. That means that millions of devices will soon be running applications that use GLSL to unlock the power of the underlying programmable graphics hardware.

My mission in writing this book has been to educate you and, perhaps more important, to try to open your eyes to the rendering possibilities that exist beyond the fixed functionality with which we've been shackled for so many years. In my view, there's no longer any reason to continue to use the fixed functionality of OpenGL. Everyone should be writing shaders to render things the way they want instead of the way the fixed functionality graphics hardware has allowed. I encourage you to think outside the box, explore new ways of getting pixels on the screen, and share your discoveries with others. If you want, you can send your discoveries to me at randi@3dshaders.com and I'll make them available to others on my Web site.

Keep on pushing the pixels, and best of luck in all your rendering endeavors!

—Randi Rost,
Fort Collins, CO
June 2003, 1st edition
August 2005, 2nd edition

The path to the OpenGL Shading Language began in the hot, crowded ballroom of the Wilshire Grand at the OpenGL Birds of a Feather at SIGGRAPH 2001 in Los Angeles. By June of 2002, the "arb-gl2" workgroup formed, and I was privileged to be elected the chair of the group. The first draft of the OpenGL Shading Language specification was published February 27, 2003, followed in an astonishingly short time by the first edition of this book.

It is the collaboration of the people who work together on the OpenGL Architecture Review Board (ARB) who create and continue to evolve the OpenGL Shading Language. These people share their gifts of intelligence, passion, and endurance. It is a joy to work with these colleagues, no matter who signs their paychecks.

What a journey we are on together!

—Bill Licea-Kane,
Boston, MA
April 2009, 3rd edition

Glossary

1D TEXTURE—A one-dimensional (width only) array of values stored in texture memory.

2D TEXTURE—A two-dimensional (width and height) array of values stored in texture memory.

3D TEXTURE—A three-dimensional (width, height, and depth) array of values stored in texture memory.

ACCUMULATION BUFFER—An OpenGL offscreen memory buffer that can accumulate the results of multiple rendering operations. This buffer often has more bits per pixel than the other offscreen memory buffers in order to support such accumulation operations.

ACTIVE ATTRIBUTES—In variables that can be accessed when a vertex shader is executed. (It is allowed to have in variables that are defined but never used within a vertex shader.)

ACTIVE SAMPLERS—Samplers that can be accessed when a program is executed.

ACTIVE TEXTURE UNIT—The texture unit currently defined as the target of commands that modify texture access state such as the current 1D/2D/3D/cube map texture, texture unit enable/disable, texture environment state, and so on.

ACTIVE UNIFORMS—Uniform variables that can be accessed when a shader is executed, including built-in uniform variables and user-defined uniform variables. (It is allowed to have uniform variables that are defined but never used within a shader.)

ALIASING—Artifacts caused by insufficient sampling or inadequate representation of high-frequency components in a computer graphics image. These artifacts are also commonly referred to as "jaggies."

ALPHA—The fourth component of a color value (after red, green, and blue). Alpha indicates the opacity of a pixel (1.0 means the pixel is fully opaque; 0.0 means the pixel is fully transparent). Alpha is used in color blending operations.

ALPHA TEST—An OpenGL pipeline stage that discards fragments depending on the outcome of a comparison between the current fragment's alpha value and a constant reference alpha value.

AMBIENT OCCLUSION—A technique for producing more realistic lighting and shadowing effects that uses a precomputed occlusion (or accessibility) factor to scale the diffuse illumination at each point on the surface of an object.

AMPLITUDE—The distance of a function's maximum or minimum from the mean of the function.

ANISOTROPIC—Something with properties that differ when measured in different directions, such as the property of a material (anisotropic reflection) or a characteristic of an algorithm (anisotropic texture filtering). Contrast with ISOTROPIC.

ANTIALIASING—The effort to reduce or eliminate artifacts caused by insufficient sampling or inadequate representation of high-frequency components in a computer graphics image.

APPLICATION PROGRAMMING INTERFACE (API)—A source-level interface provided for use by applications.

AREA SAMPLING—An antialiasing technique that considers the area of the primitive being sampled. This method usually produces better results than either point sampling or supersampling, but it can be more expensive to compute.

ATTENUATION—In the lighting computation, the effect of light intensity diminishing as a function of distance from the light source.

ATTRIBUTE ALIASING—Binding more than one user-defined in variable to the same generic vertex attribute index. This binding is allowed only if just one of the aliased attributes is active in the executable program or if no path through the shader consumes more than one in variable of a set of in variables aliased to the same location.

ATTRIBUTE VARIABLE—An OpenGL Shading Language variable that is qualified with the **in** keyword. Attribute variables contain the values that an application passes through the OpenGL API by using generic, numbered vertex attributes. With attribute variables, a vertex shader can obtain unique data at every vertex. These variables are read-only and can be defined only in vertex shaders. Attribute variables are used to pass frequently changing data to a shader.

AUXILIARY BUFFER—A region of offscreen memory that stores arbitrary or generic data, for example, intermediate results from a multipass rendering algorithm. A framebuffer may have more than one associated auxiliary buffer.

BENT NORMAL—A surface attribute that represents the average direction of the available light that is received at that point on the surface. This value is computed as follows: Cast rays from the point on the surface in the hemisphere indicated by the surface normal and then average all rays that are unoccluded by other parts of the model.

BIDIRECTIONAL REFLECTANCE DISTRIBUTION FUNCTION (BRDF)—A model for computing the reflection from a surface. The elevation and azimuth angles of the incoming and outgoing energy directions are used to compute the relative amount of energy reflected in the outgoing direction. Measurements of real-world materials can be used in this computation to create a more realistic looking surface. BRDFs can more accurately render materials with anisotropic reflection properties.

BRDF—See BIDIRECTIONAL REFLECTANCE DISTRIBUTION FUNCTION.

BUFFERS—Regions of memory on the graphics accelerator devoted to storing a particular type of data. A color buffer stores color values, a depth buffer stores depth values, etc.

BUMP MAP—A two-dimensional array of normal perturbation values that can be stored in texture memory.

BUMP MAPPING—A rendering technique that simulates the appearance of bumps, wrinkles, or other surface irregularities by perturbing surface normals before lighting calculations are performed.

CALL BY VALUE-RETURN—A subroutine calling convention whereby input parameters are copied into the function at call time and output parameters are copied back to the caller before the function exits.

CHROMATIC ABERRATION—The tendency of a lens to bend light of different colors by unequal amounts because of differences in the indices of refraction of the constituent wavelengths of the light.

CHROMATIC DISPERSION—The effect of distributing a light source into its constituent wavelengths, for example, by passing it through a prism.

CLIP SPACE—See CLIPPING COORDINATE SYSTEM.

CLIPPING—The process of comparing incoming graphics primitives to one or more reference planes and discarding any portion of primitives that are deemed to be outside those reference planes.

CLIPPING COORDINATE SYSTEM—The coordinate system in which view-volume clipping occurs. Graphics primitives are transformed from the eye coordinate system into the clipping coordinate system by the projection matrix.

COLOR SUM—The OpenGL pipeline stage that adds together the primary color and the secondary color. This stage occurs after texturing to allow a specular highlight that is the color of the light source to be applied on top of the textured surface.

COMPILER FRONT END—The part of the compiler that performs lexical, syntactical, and semantic analysis of source code and produces a binary representation of the code that is suitable for consumption by subsequent phases of compilation.

CONSTRUCTOR—A programming language feature for initializing aggregate data types or converting between data types.

CONTROL TEXTURE—A texture map whose primary function is to provide values that determine the behavior of a rendering algorithm rather than provide data for the rendering process.

CONVOLUTION—The weighted average of a function over a specified interval.

CONVOLUTION FILTER—See CONVOLUTION KERNEL.

CONVOLUTION KERNEL—The values that are used for weighting in a convolution operation.

CUBE MAP—A texture map comprising six 2D textures that correspond to faces on a cube. The faces are identified by their axial direction ($\pm x$, $\pm y$, $\pm z$), and the proper face is automatically selected when a texture access is performed.

CUBE MAPPING—The process of accessing the proper face of a cube map texture to retrieve the value that will be used in texture application. Cube mapping is one method for performing environment mapping.

CULLING—The act of discarding graphics primitives according to a particular criterion, such as whether the primitives are back facing with respect to the current viewing position.

DEFERRED SHADING—A shading algorithm that first identifies the visible surfaces in a scene and then applies a shading effect only to those visible surfaces.

DEPENDENT TEXTURE READ—A texture access operation that depends on values obtained from a previous texture-access operation.

DEPTH BUFFER—An OpenGL offscreen memory buffer that maintains depth values. This buffer stores the depth of the topmost visible graphics primitive at each pixel. In conjunction with the depth test operation, this buffer can perform hidden surface elimination.

DEPTH-CUING—A graphics rendering technique that alters the appearance of a graphics primitive according to its distance from the viewer. Depth-cuing is often used to fade the color of distant primitives to the background color to make them appear more distant.

DEPTH MAP—See SHADOW MAP.

DEPTH TEST—An OpenGL pipeline stage that compares the depth associated with the incoming fragment with the depth value retrieved from the framebuffer. If the test fails, the fragment is discarded.

DIFFRACTION—The change in the directions and intensities of a group of waves (e.g., light waves) as they pass by an obstacle or pass through an aperture.

DIFFRACTION GRATING—A glass or metal surface with large numbers of small, parallel, equally spaced grooves or slits that produces a diffraction effect.

DISPLAY MEMORY—Framebuffer memory that is allocated to maintaining the image displayed on the computer monitor or LCD. Display memory is read many times per second (the refresh rate) and updates the visible display surface.

DOUBLE BUFFERING—A graphics rendering technique that involves rendering to a back buffer while displaying a front buffer. When rendering is completed, the two buffers are swapped. In this way, the end user never sees partially complete images, and animation can be smoother and more realistic.

DRIVER—A piece of software that interacts with the native operating system and controls a specific piece of hardware in the system.

ENVIRONMENT MAPPING—A rendering technique that involves saving the scene surrounding an object as one or more specialized texture maps and then, when rendering the object, accessing these texture maps to compute accurate reflections of that environment.

EQUIRECTANGULAR TEXTURE MAP—A rectangular 2D texture that can be used as an environment map. The texture spans 360° horizontally and 180° vertically. Significant distortion occurs toward the top and bottom of the texture. Also known as a LATITUDE-LONGITUDE (or LAT-LONG) TEXTURE MAP.

EXECUTABLE—The machine code intended for execution on the vertex processor or the fragment processor.

EYE COORDINATE SYSTEM—The coordinate system that is defined to have the eye (viewing) position at the origin. Graphics primitives are transformed by the modelview matrix from the modeling (or object) coordinate system into the eye coordinate system.

EYE SPACE—see EYE COORDINATE SYSTEM.

FILTERING—The process of calculating a single value according to the values of multiple samples in the neighborhood of that value.

FIXED FUNCTIONALITY—The term used to describe portions of the OpenGL pipeline that are not programmable. These portions of OpenGL operate in a fixed fashion, and the behavior can be altered only when a predefined set of state variables is changed through the OpenGL API.

FLAT SHADING—The term used to describe the application of a single value of one vertex to the extent of a primitive (contrast with SMOOTH SHADING).

FOG—A rendering technique that simulates atmospheric effects due to particulates such as those contained in clouds and smog. Fog is computed by attenuation of the object color as a function of distance from the viewer.

FRACTAL—A geometrically complex object, the complexity of which arises through the repetition of a given form over a range of scales. (*Ken Musgrave*)

FRAGMENT—The set of data that is generated by rasterization and that represents the information necessary to update a single framebuffer location. A fragment consists of a window coordinate position and associated data such as color, depth, texture coordinates, and the like.

FRAGMENT PROCESSING—An OpenGL pipeline stage that defines the operations that occur to a fragment produced by rasterization before the back-end processing stages. For OpenGL fixed functionality, fragment processing operations included texture access, texture application, fog, and color sum. For the OpenGL programmable fragment processor, any type of per-fragment processing may be performed.

FRAGMENT PROCESSOR—A programmable unit that replaces the traditional fixed functionality fragment processing stage of OpenGL. Fragment shaders are executed on the fragment processor.

FRAGMENT SHADER—A program written in the OpenGL Shading Language for execution on the fragment processor. The fragment shader's **main** function is executed once for each fragment generated by rasterization and can be programmed to perform both traditional operations (texture access, texture application, fog) and nontraditional operations.

FRAMEBUFFER—The region of graphics memory that stores the results of OpenGL rendering operations. Part of the framebuffer (the front buffer) is visible on the display device, and part of it is not.

FRAMEBUFFER OPERATIONS—An OpenGL pipeline stage containing operations that control or affect the whole framebuffer (e.g., buffer masking operations, buffer clear operations).

FREQUENCY—The measure of periodicity in a function (i.e., how often the pattern of a function repeats).

FRESNEL EFFECT—The result of transparent materials causing light to be both reflected and refracted, with the amount of light reflected and refracted depending on the viewing angle.

FRUSTUM—See VIEW FRUSTUM.

FRUSTUM CLIPPING—An OpenGL pipeline stage that clips primitives to the view frustum.

GEOMETRIC PRIMITIVE—A point, line, or polygon.

GLOSS MAP—A texture map that controls the reflective characteristics of a surface rather than supply image data for the texturing operation.

GLYPH BOMBING—TEXTURE BOMBING using character glyphs from a texture map.

GOOCH SHADING—A non-photorealistic rendering technique that attempts to duplicate the look of a technical illustration. This technique is also called a low dynamic range artistic tone algorithm.

GOURAUD SHADING—See SMOOTH SHADING.

GRADIENT—The measure of how rapidly a function is changing in a particular direction. Properly, this is a vector (see GRADIENT VECTOR). More commonly, the magnitude of the gradient vector for the function $f(x,y)$ in a particular direction is referred to as the gradient of the function $f(x,y)$ in that direction.

GRADIENT NOISE—See PERLIN NOISE.

GRADIENT VECTOR—A vector that defines the rate of change of a function in all directions. The gradient vector for the function $f(x,y)$ contains two components: the partial derivative of f with respect to x and the partial derivative of f with respect to y.

GRAPHICS ACCELERATOR—Hardware dedicated to the process of rendering and displaying graphics.

GRAPHICS CONTEXT—The OpenGL data structure that contains the state needed to control the operation of the rendering pipeline.

GRAPHICS PROCESSING PIPELINE—The sequence of operations that occurs when geometry or image data defined by an application is transformed into something that is stored in the framebuffer. This processing is divided into stages that occur in a specific order. Each stage has defined inputs and outputs and can be precisely described.

HEMISPHERE LIGHTING—The process of illuminating scenes and objects by modeling global illumination as two hemispheres, one representing the color of the sky and the other representing the color of the ground (or shadows). Computing the illumination at any surface point is done by integrating the light from the visible hemisphere at that point.

IMAGE-BASED LIGHTING—The process of illuminating scenes and objects with images of light captured from the real world.

IMAGING SUBSET—A collection of imaging-related functionality that was added to OpenGL as an optional subset in OpenGL 1.2. The imaging subset supports color matrix, convolution, histogram, and various blending operations. Graphics hardware vendors are not required to support this functionality as part of their OpenGL implementation.

IMMEDIATE MODE—A mode of rendering in which graphics commands are executed when they are specified.

INDEX OF REFRACTION—The property of a material that defines the ratio of the speed of light in a vacuum to the speed of light in that material.

ISOTROPIC—Something with properties that are the same along a pair of orthogonal axes from which they are measured (i.e., rotationally invariant). Contrast with ANISOTROPIC.

KEY-FRAME INTERPOLATION—An animation technique that produces "in-between" results based on interpolation between two key frames. This technique can save time and effort because the objects in the scene do not need to be painstakingly animated for every frame, only for those frames that provide the key to the overall animation sequence.

L-VALUE—An expression identifying an object in memory that can be written to. For example, variables that are writable are l-values. Array indexing and structure member selection are expressions that can result in l-values.

LACUNARITY—The frequency multiplier (or gap) between successive iterations of a summed noise (fractal) function.

LATITUDE-LONGITUDE TEXTURE MAP—see EQUIRECTANGULAR TEXTURE MAP.

LEVEL-OF-DETAIL—The value that selects a mipmap level from a mipmap texture. Incrementing the level-of-detail by 1 results in the selection of a mipmap level that is half the resolution of the previous one. Thus, increasing the value used for level-of-detail results in the selection of mipmap levels that contain smaller and smaller textures (suitable for use on smaller and smaller objects on the screen).

LEXICAL ANALYSIS—The process of scanning the input text to produce a sequence of tokens (or terminal symbols) for the syntactical analysis phase that follows. Characters or tokens that are not part of the language can be identified as errors during this process. Sometimes this process is referred to as scanning.

LIGHT PROBE—A device or a system that captures an omnidirectional, high dynamic range image of light from a real-world scene.

LIGHT PROBE IMAGE—An omnidirectional, high dynamic range image of light captured from the real world.

LOOKAT POINT—The lookat point is a reference point indicating the center of the scene.

LOW-PASS FILTERING—A method of filtering that eliminates high frequencies but leaves low frequencies unmodified. Low-pass filters are sometimes called SMOOTHING FILTERS because high frequencies are blurred (smoothed).

MIPMAP LEVEL—A specific texel array within a mipmap texture.

MIPMAP TEXTURE—An ordered set of texel arrays representing the same image. Typically, each array has a resolution that is half the previous one in each dimension.

MODEL SPACE—See MODELING COORDINATE SYSTEM.

MODEL TRANSFORMATION MATRIX—The matrix that transforms coordinates from the modeling coordinate system into the world coordinate system. In OpenGL, this matrix is not available separately; it is always part of the modelview matrix.

MODELING—The process of defining a numerical representation of an object that is to be rendered, for instance, defining the Bezier curves that specify a teapot, or the vertex positions, colors, surface normals, and texture coordinates that define a bowling pin.

MODELING COORDINATE SYSTEM—A coordinate system that is defined in a way that makes it convenient to specify and orient a single object. Also known as the OBJECT COORDINATE SYSTEM or OBJECT SPACE.

MODELING TRANSFORMATION—The transformation that takes coordinates from the modeling coordinate system into the world coordinate system.

MODELVIEW MATRIX—The matrix that transforms coordinates from the modeling coordinate system into the eye coordinate system.

MODELVIEW-PROJECTION MATRIX—The matrix that transforms coordinates from the modeling coordinate system into the clipping coordinate system.

MULTIFRACTAL—A function whose fractal dimension varies according to location.

MULTISAMPLE BUFFER—A region of offscreen memory that can perform supersampling by maintaining more than one sample per pixel and automatically averaging the samples to produce the final, antialiased image.

NEIGHBORHOOD AVERAGING—An image processing technique that low-pass filters (smooths) an image by computing the weighted average of pixels in close proximity to one another.

NOISE—A continuous, irregular function with a defined range that creates complex and interesting patterns.

NON-PHOTOREALISTIC RENDERING (NPR)—A class of rendering techniques whose purpose is to achieve something other than the most realistic result possible. Such techniques may strive to achieve a painterly or hand-drawn appearance, the look of a technical illustration, or a cartoonlike appearance. Hatching and Gooch shading are examples of NPR techniques.

NORMAL MAP—A texture map that contains normals rather than image data.

NORMALIZED DEVICE COORDINATE SPACE—The coordinate space that contains the view volume in an axis-aligned cube with a minimum corner at $(-1,-1,-1)$ and a maximum corner at $(1,1,1)$.

NPR—See NON-PHOTOREALISTIC RENDERING.

OBJECT COORDINATE SYSTEM—See MODELING COORDINATE SYSTEM.

OBJECT SPACE—See MODELING COORDINATE SYSTEM.

OCTAVE—Two frequencies that are related by a ratio of 2:1.

OFFSCREEN MEMORY—Framebuffer memory that stores things, such as depth buffers and textures, that are never directly visible on the display screen (contrast with DISPLAY MEMORY).

OPENGL SHADER—A term applied to a shader written in the OpenGL Shading Language to differentiate from a shader written in another shading language.

OPENGL SHADING LANGUAGE—The high-level programming language defined to allow application writers to write programs that execute on the programmable processors defined within OpenGL.

OPENGL SHADING LANGUAGE API—The set of function calls added to OpenGL to allow OpenGL shaders to be created, deleted, queried, compiled, linked, and used.

PARSING—See SYNTACTIC ANALYSIS.

PARTICLE SYSTEM—A rendering primitive that consists of a large number of points or short lines that are suitable for rendering a class of objects with ill-defined boundaries (e.g., fire, sparks, liquid sprays).

PER-FRAGMENT OPERATIONS—An OpenGL pipeline stage that occurs after fragment processing and before framebuffer operations. It includes a variety of tests, such as the stencil, alpha, and depth tests, aimed at determining whether the fragment should be used to update the framebuffer.

PERLIN NOISE—A noise function that is defined to have a value of 0 for integer input values and whose variability is introduced by defining pseudorandom gradient values at each of those points. Also called GRADIENT NOISE.

PHOTOREALISM—The effort to use computer graphics to model, render, and animate a scene in such a way that it is indistinguishable from a photograph or film sequence of the same scene in real life.

PIXEL GROUP—A value that will ultimately be used to update the framebuffer (i.e., a color, depth, or stencil value).

PIXEL OWNERSHIP TEST—An OpenGL pipeline stage that decides whether a fragment can be used to update the framebuffer or whether the targeted framebuffer location belongs to another window or to another OpenGL graphics context.

PIXEL PACKING—An OpenGL pipeline stage that writes pixels retrieved from OpenGL into application-controlled memory.

PIXEL RECTANGLE—A rectangular array of pixels (i.e., an image).

PIXEL TRANSFER—An OpenGL pipeline stage that processes pixel data while it is being transferred within OpenGL. At this stage, operations can occur for the following: scaling and biasing, lookup table, convolution, histogram, color matrix, and the like.

PIXEL UNPACKING—An OpenGL pipeline stage that reads pixels (i.e., image data) from application-controlled memory and sends them on for further processing by OpenGL.

POINT SAMPLING—The process of determining the value at each pixel by sampling the function at just one point. This is the typical behavior of graphics hardware and many graphics algorithms, and it can lead to aliasing artifacts. Contrast with SUPERSAMPLING and AREA SAMPLING.

POINT SPRITE—A screen-aligned quadrilateral that has texture coordinates and that is drawn by rasterizing a single point primitive. Normally, points are drawn as a single pixel or as a round circle. A point sprite can be used to draw an image stored in a texture map at each point position.

POLYNOMIAL TEXTURE MAP (PTM)—A light-dependent texture map that can reconstruct the color of a surface under varying lighting conditions.

PRIMITIVE ASSEMBLY—An OpenGL pipeline stage that occurs after vertex processing and that assembles individual vertex values into a primitive. The primary function of this stage is to buffer vertex values until enough accumulate to define the desired primitive. Points require one vertex, lines require two, triangles require three, and so on.

PRIMITIVES—In OpenGL parlance, things that can be rendered: points, lines, polygons, bitmaps, and images.

PROCEDURAL TEXTURE SHADER—A shader that produces its results primarily by synthesizing rather than by relying heavily on precomputed values.

PROCEDURAL TEXTURING—The process of computing a texture primarily by synthesizing rather than by relying heavily on precomputed values.

PROGRAM—The set of executables that result from successful linking of a program object. This program can be installed as part of OpenGL's current state to provide programmable vertex and fragment processing.

PROGRAM OBJECT—An OpenGL-managed data structure that serves as a container object for one or more shader objects. Program objects are used when shaders are linked. Linking a program object results in one or more executables that are part of the program object and that can be installed as part of current state.

PROJECTION MATRIX—The matrix that transforms coordinates from the eye coordinate system to the clipping coordinate system.

PROJECTION TRANSFORMATION—The transformation that takes coordinates from the eye coordinate system into the clipping coordinate system.

PTM—See POLYNOMIAL TEXTURE MAP.

PULSE TRAIN—A periodic function that varies abruptly between two values (i.e., a square wave).

R-VALUE—An expression identifying a declared or temporary object in memory that can be read—for example, a variable name is an r-value, but function names are not. Expressions result in r-values.

RASTER POSITION—A piece of OpenGL state that positions bitmap and image write operations.

RASTERIZATION—The process of converting graphics primitives such as points, lines, polygons, bitmaps, and images into fragments.

READ CONTROL—An OpenGL pipeline stage that contains state to define the region of framebuffer memory that is read during pixel read operations.

RENDERING—The process of converting geometry or image data defined by an application into something that is stored in the framebuffer.

RENDERING PIPELINE—See GRAPHICS PROCESSING PIPELINE.

SAMPLER—An opaque data type in the OpenGL Shading Language that stores the information needed to access a particular texture from within a shader.

SCANNING—See LEXICAL ANALYSIS.

SCENE GRAPH—Either a hierarchical data structure containing a description of a scene to be rendered or a rendering engine for traversing and rendering such data structures.

SCISSOR TEST—An OpenGL pipeline stage that, when enabled, allows drawing operations to occur only within a specific rectangular region that has been defined in window coordinates.

SEMANTIC ANALYSIS—The process of determining whether the input text conforms to the semantic rules defined or implied by a programming language. Semantic errors in the input text can be identified during this phase of compilation.

SHADER—Source code written in the OpenGL Shading Language that is intended for execution on one of OpenGL's programmable processors.

SHADER OBJECT—An OpenGL-managed data structure that stores the source code and the compiled code for a shader written in the OpenGL Shading Language. Shader objects can be compiled, and compiled shader objects can be linked to produce executable code (see PROGRAM OBJECT).

SHADOW MAP—A texture created by rendering a scene from the point of view of a light source. This texture is then used during a final rendering pass to determine the parts of the scene that are in shadow. Also known as a DEPTH MAP.

SHADOW MAPPING—An algorithm that computes shadows by rendering the scene once for each shadow-causing light source in the scene and once for the final rendering of the scene, including shadows. The per-light rendering passes are rendered from the light source's point of view and create shadow maps. These textures are then accessed on the final pass to determine the parts of the scene that are in shadow.

SMOOTH SHADING—The term used to describe the application of linearly interpolated vertex values across the extent of a primitive (contrast with FLAT SHADING). Also called GOURAUD SHADING.

SMOOTHING FILTERS—See LOW-PASS FILTERING.

SPHERE MAPPING—A method for performing environment mapping that simulates the projection of the environment onto a sphere surrounding the object to be rendered. The mapped environment is treated as a 2D texture map and accessed with the polar coordinates of the reflection vector.

STENCIL BUFFER—An offscreen region of framebuffer memory that can be used with the stencil test to mask regions. A complex shape can be stored in the stencil buffer, and subsequent drawing operations can use the contents of the stencil buffer to determine whether to update each pixel.

STENCIL TEST—An OpenGL pipeline stage that conditionally eliminates a pixel according to the results of a comparison between the value stored in the stencil buffer and a reference value. Applications can specify the action taken when the stencil test fails, the action taken when the stencil test passes and the depth test fails, and the action to be taken when both the stencil test and the depth test pass.

SUPERSAMPLING—A rendering technique that involves taking two or more point samples per pixel and then filtering these values to determine the value to be used for the pixel. Supersampling does not eliminate aliasing but can reduce it to the point at which it is no longer objectionable.

SURFACE-LOCAL COORDINATE SPACE—A coordinate system that assumes that each point on a surface is at (0,0,0) and that the unperturbed surface normal at each point is (0,0,1).

SWIZZLE—To duplicate or switch around the order of the components of a vector (e.g., to create a value that contains alpha, green, blue, red from one that contains red, green, blue, alpha).

SYNTACTIC ANALYSIS—The process of determining whether the structure of an input text is valid according to the grammar that defines the language. Syntax errors in the input text can be identified during this phase of compilation. Sometimes referred to as parsing.

TANGENT SPACE—A particular surface-local coordinate system that is defined with a tangent vector as one of the basis vectors.

T&L—See TRANSFORMATION AND LIGHTING.

TEMPORAL ALIASING—Aliasing artifacts that are caused by insufficient sampling in the time domain or inadequate representation of objects that are in motion.

TEXEL—A single pixel in a texture map.

TEXTURE ACCESS—The process of reading from a texture map in texture memory, including the filtering that occurs, the level-of-detail calculation for mipmap textures, and so on.

TEXTURE APPLICATION—The process of using the value read from texture memory to compute the color of a fragment. OpenGL's fixed functionality has fixed formulas for this process, but with programmability, this operation has become much more general.

TEXTURE BOMBING—The process of applying irregularly spaced decorative elements (stars, polka dots, character glyphs, etc.) to an object's surface. Decorative elements can be computed procedurally or obtained from a texture map. They can also be randomly scaled and rotated to add further interest.

TEXTURE MAPPING—The combination of texture access and texture application. Traditionally, this mapping involves reading image data from a texture map stored in texture memory and using it as the color for the primitive being rendered. With programmability, this operation has become much more general.

TEXTURE MEMORY—A region of memory on the graphics accelerator that is used for storing textures.

TEXTURE OBJECT—The OpenGL-managed data structure that contains information that describes a texture map, including the texels that define the texture, the wrapping behavior, the filtering method, and so on.

TEXTURE UNIT—An OpenGL abstraction for the graphics hardware that performs texture access and texture application. Since version 1.2, OpenGL has allowed the possibility of more than one texture unit, thus allowing access to more than one texture at a time.

TRANSFORMATION AND LIGHTING (T&L)—The process of converting vertex positions from object coordinates into window coordinates, and for converting vertex colors into colors that are displayable on the screen, taking into account the effects of simulated light sources.

TURBULENCE—A variation of Perlin noise that sums noise functions of different frequencies. These frequencies include an absolute value function to introduce discontinuities to the function in order to give the appearance of turbulent flow.

UNIFORM VARIABLE—An OpenGL Shading Language variable that is qualified with the **uniform** keyword. The values for these variables are provided by the application or through OpenGL state. They are read-only from within a shader and may be accessed from either vertex shaders or fragment shaders. They pass data that changes relatively infrequently.

UNSHARP MASKING—A method of sharpening an image by subtracting a blurred version of the image from itself.

USER CLIPPING—An OpenGL operation that compares graphics primitives to user-specified clip distances and discards everything that is deemed to be outside the intersection of those clip distances.

VALUE NOISE—A noise function that is defined as follows: Assign pseudorandom values in a defined range (e.g., [0,1] or [–1,1]) to each integer input value and then smoothly interpolate between those values.

VARYING VARIABLE—An OpenGL Shading Language variable that is qualified with the **varying** keyword. These variables are defined at each vertex and interpolated across a graphics primitive to produce a perspective-correct value at each fragment. They must be declared in both the vertex shader and the fragment shader with the same type. They are the output values from vertex shaders and the input values for fragment shaders.

VERTEX—A point in three-dimensional space.

VERTEX ATTRIBUTES—Values that are associated with a vertex. OpenGL defines both standard and generic vertex attributes. Standard attributes include vertex position, color, normal, and texture coordinates. Generic vertex attributes can be defined to be arbitrary data values that are passed to OpenGL for each vertex.

VERTEX PROCESSING—An OpenGL pipeline stage that defines the operations that occur to each vertex from the time the vertex is provided to OpenGL until the primitive assembly stage. For OpenGL fixed functionality, this processing included transformation, lighting, texture coordinate generation, and other operations. For the OpenGL programmable vertex processor, any type of per-vertex processing may be performed.

VERTEX PROCESSOR—A programmable unit that replaces the traditional fixed functionality vertex processing stage of OpenGL. Vertex shaders are executed on the vertex processor.

VERTEX SHADER—A program written in the OpenGL Shading Language that executes on the vertex processor. The vertex shader's **main** function is executed once for each vertex provided to OpenGL and can be programmed to perform both traditional operations (transformation, lighting) and nontraditional operations.

VIEW FRUSTUM—The view volume after it has been warped by the perspective division calculation.

VIEW VOLUME—The volume in the clipping coordinate system whose coordinates x, y, z, and w all satisfy the conditions that $-w \leq x \leq w$, $-w \leq y \leq w$, and $-w \leq z \leq w$. Any portion of a geometric primitive that extends beyond this volume will be clipped.

VIEWING MATRIX—The matrix that transforms coordinates from the world coordinate system into the eye coordinate system. In OpenGL, this matrix is not available separately; it is always part of the modelview matrix.

VIEWING TRANSFORMATION—The transformation that takes coordinates from the world coordinate system into the eye coordinate system.

VIEWPORT TRANSFORMATION—The transformation that takes coordinates from the normalized device coordinate system into the window coordinate system.

WINDOW COORDINATE SYSTEM—The coordinate system used to identify pixels within a window on the display device. In this coordinate system, x values range from 0 to the width of the window minus 1, and y values range from 0 to the height of the window minus 1. OpenGL defines the pixel with window coordinates (0,0) to be the pixel at the lower-left corner of the window.

WORLD COORDINATE SYSTEM—A coordinate system that is defined in a way that is convenient for the placement and orientation of all of the objects in a scene.

WORLD SPACE—See WORLD COORDINATE SYSTEM.

Further Reading

This section contains references to other useful papers, articles, books, and Web sites. Over the course of time, some Web addresses may change. Please see this book's companion Web site at http://3dshaders.com for current links.

Former 3Dlabs developer Web site: now at http://3dshaders.com

Abram, G. D., and T. Whitted, *Building Block Shaders*, Computer Graphics (SIGGRAPH '90 Proceedings), pp. 283–288, August 1990.

Akenine-Möller, Tomas, and E. Haines, *Real-Time Rendering, Second Edition*, AK Peters, Ltd., Natick, Massachusetts, 2002. www.realtimerendering.com

Apodaca, Anthony A., and Larry Gritz, *Advanced RenderMan: Creating CGI for Motion Pictures*, Morgan Kaufmann Publishers, San Francisco, 1999. www.renderman.org/RMR/Books/arman/materials.html

Arvo, James, ed., *Graphics Gems II*, Academic Press, San Diego, 1991. www.acm.org/pubs/tog/GraphicsGems

ATI developer Web site. www.ati.com/developer

Baker, Dan, and C. Boyd, *Advanced Shading and Lighting*, Microsoft Corp. Meltdown 2001 Presentation. www.microsoft.com/mscorp/corpevents/meltdown2001/ppt/DXGLighting.ppt

Baldwin, Dave, *OpenGL 2.0 Shading Language White Paper, Version 1.0*, 3Dlabs, October, 2001.

Barzel, Ronen, *Lighting Controls for Computer Cinematography,* Journal of Graphics Tools, 2(1), 1997, pp. 1–20.

Blinn, James, *Models of Light Reflection for Computer Synthesized Pictures*, Computer Graphics (SIGGRAPH '77 Proceedings), pp. 192–198, July 1977.

————, *Simulation of Wrinkled Surfaces*, Computer Graphics (SIGGRAPH '78 Proceedings), pp. 286–292, August 1978.

————, *Light Reflection Functions for Simulation of Clouds and Dusty Surfaces*, Computer Graphics (SIGGRAPH '82 Proceedings), pp. 21–29, July 1982.

Blinn, James, and M. E. Newell, *Texture and Reflection in Computer Generated Images*, Communications of the ACM, vol. 19, no. 10, pp. 542–547, October 1976.

Bunnell, Michael, *Dynamic Ambient Occlusion and Indirect Lighting*, in *GPU Gems 2: Programming Techniques for High-Performance Graphics and General-Purpose Computation*, Editor: Matt Pharr, Addison-Wesley, Reading, Massachusetts, 2005. http://download.nvidia.com/developer/GPU_Gems_2/GPU_Gems2_ch14.pdf

Bunnell, Michael, and Fabio Pellacini, *Shadow Map Antialiasing*, in *GPU Gems: Programming Techniques, Tips, and Tricks for Real-Time Graphics*, Editor: Randima Fernando, Addison-Wesley, Reading, Massachusetts, 2004. http://developer.nvidia.com/object/gpu_gems_home.html

Cabral, B., N. Max, and R. Springmeyer, *Bidirectional Reflection Functions from Surface Bump Maps*, Computer Graphics (SIGGRAPH '87 Proceedings), pp. 273–281, July 1987.

Card, Drew, and Jason L. Mitchell, *Non-Photorealistic Rendering with Pixel and Vertex Shaders*, in Engel, Wolfgang, ed., ShaderX, Wordware, May 2002. www.shaderx.com

Cook, Robert L., *Shade Trees*, Computer Graphics (SIGGRAPH '84 Proceedings), pp. 223–231, July 1984.

————, *Stochastic Sampling in Computer Graphics*, ACM Transactions on Graphics, vol. 5, no. 1, pp. 51–72, January 1986.

Cook, Robert L., and Kenneth E. Torrance, *A Reflectance Model for Computer Graphics*, Computer Graphics (SIGGRAPH '81 Proceedings), pp. 307–316, July 1981.

————, *A Reflectance Model for Computer Graphics*, ACM Transactions on Graphics, vol. 1, no. 1, pp. 7–24, January 1982.

Cornell University Program of Computer Graphics Measurement Data. www.graphics.cornell.edu/online/measurements

Crow, Franklin C., *The Aliasing Problem in Computer-Generated Shaded Images*, Communications of the ACM, vol. 20, no. 11, pp. 799–805, November 1977.

————, *Shadow Algorithms for Computer Graphics*, Computer Graphics (SIGGRAPH '77 Proceedings), vol. 11, no. 2, pp. 242–248, July 1977.

————, *Summed-Area Tables for Texture Mapping*, Computer Graphics (SIGGRAPH '84 Proceedings), pp. 207–212, July 1984.

Curtis, Cassidy J., *Loose and Sketchy Animation*, SIGGRAPH '98 Technical Sketch, p. 317, 1998. www.otherthings.com/uw/loose/sketch.html

Curtis, Cassidy J., Sean E. Anderson, Kurt W. Fleischer, and David H. Salesin, *Computer-Generated Watercolor*, Computer Graphics (SIGGRAPH '97 Proceedings), pp. 421–430, August 1997. http://grail.cs.washington.edu/projects/watercolor

Dawson, Bruce, *What Happened to My Colours!?!* Game Developers Conference, pp. 251–268, March 2001. www.gdconf.com/archives/2001/ dawson.doc

Debevec, Paul, *Image-Based Lighting*, IEEE Computer Graphics and Applications, vol. 22, no. 2, pp. 26–34. www.debevec.org/CGAIBL2/ibl-tutorial-cga2002.pdf

Debevec, Paul, personal Web site. www.debevec.org

Debevec, Paul, *Rendering Synthetic Objects into Real Scenes: Bridging Traditional and Image-Based Graphics with Global Illumination and High Dynamic Range Photography*, Computer Graphics (SIGGRAPH '98 Proceedings), pp. 189–198. http://athens.ict.usc.edu/Research/IBL

Debevec, Paul, and J. Malik, *Recovering High Dynamic Range Radiance Maps from Photographs*, Computer Graphics (SIGGRAPH '97 Proceedings), pp. 369–378. www.debevec.org/Research/HDR

Delphi3D Web site. http://delphi3d.net

DeLoura, Mark, ed., *Game Programming Gems*, Charles River Media, Hingham, Massachusetts, 2000.

———, *Game Programming Gems II*, Charles River Media, Hingham, Massachusetts, 2001.

———, *Game Programming Gems III*, Charles River Media, Hingham, Massachusetts, 2002.

Derbyshire, Paul, *PGD's Quick Guide to the Mandelbrot Set*, personal Web site. www.globalserve.net/~derbyshire/manguide.html (defunct)

Dippé, Mark A. Z., and Erling Henry Wold, *Antialiasing Through Stochastic Sampling*, Computer Graphics (SIGGRAPH '85 Proceedings), pp. 69–78, July 1985.

Duff, Tom, *Compositing 3-D Rendered Images*, Computer Graphics (SIGGRAPH '85 Proceedings), pp. 41–44, July 1985.

Ebert, David S., John Hart, Bill Mark, F. Kenton Musgrave, Darwyn Peachey, Ken Perlin, and Steven Worley, *Texturing and Modeling: A Procedural Approach, Third Edition*, Morgan Kaufmann Publishers, San Francisco, 2002. www.texturingandmodeling.com

Fernando, Randima, and Mark J. Kilgard, *The Cg Tutorial: The Definitive Guide to Programmable Real-Time Graphics*, Addison-Wesley, Boston, Massachusetts, 2003.

Foley, J. D., A. van Dam, S.K. Feiner, and J. F. Hughes, *Computer Graphics: Principles and Practice in C, Second Edition*, Addison-Wesley, Reading, Massachusetts, 1996.

Foley, J. D., A. van Dam, S.K. Feiner, J. F. Hughes, and R.L. Philips, *Introduction to Computer Graphics*, Addison-Wesley, Reading, Massachusetts, 1994.

Fosner, Ron, *Real-Time Shader Programming, Covering DirectX 9.0*, Morgan Kaufmann Publishers, San Francisco, 2003.

Freudenberg, Bert, *A Non-Photorealistic Fragment Shader in OpenGL 2.0*, SIGGRAPH 2002 Exhibition, San Antonio, Texas, July 2002. http://isgwww.cs.uni-magdeburg.de/~bert/publications

———, *Stroke-based Real-Time Halftoning Rendering*, Ph.D. thesis, University of Magdeburg, submitted in 2003.

Freudenberg, Bert, and Maic Masuch, *Non-Photorealistic Shading in an Educational Game Engine*, SIGGRAPH and Eurographics Campfire, Snowbird, Utah, June 1–June 4, 2002. http://isgwww.cs.uni-magdeburg.de/~bert/publications

Freudenberg, Bert, Maic Masuch, and Thomas Strothotte, *Walk-Through Illustrations: Frame-Coherent Pen-and-Ink Style in a Game Engine*, Computer Graphics Forum, vol. 20 (2001), no. 3, Manchester, U.K. http://isgwww.cs.uni-magdeburg.de/~bert/publications

———, *Real-Time Halftoning: A Primitive For Non-Photorealistic Shading*, Rendering Techniques 2002, Proceedings 13th Eurographics Workshop, pp. 227–231, 2002. http://isgwww.cs.uni-magdeburg.de/~bert/publications

Glaeser, Georg, *Reflections on Spheres and Cylinders of Revolution*, Journal for Geometry and Graphics, Volume 3 (1999), No. 2, pp. 121–139. www.heldermann-verlag.de/jgg/jgg01_05/jgg0312.pdf

Glanville, Steve, *Texture Bombing*, in *GPU Gems: Programming Techniques, Tips, and Tricks for Real-Time Graphics*, Editor: Randima Fernando, Addison-Wesley, Reading, Massachusetts, 2004. http://developer.nvidia.com/object/gpu_gems_home.html

Glassner, Andrew S., ed., *Graphics Gems*, Academic Press, San Diego, 1990. www.acm.org/pubs/tog/GraphicsGems

Glassner, Andrew S., *Principles of Digital Image Synthesis*, vol. 1, Morgan Kaufmann Publishers, San Francisco, 1995.

———, *Principles of Digital Image Synthesis*, vol. 2, Morgan Kaufmann Publishers, San Francisco, 1995.

Gonzalez, Rafael C., and Richard E. Woods, *Digital Image Processing, Second Edition*, Prentice Hall, Upper Saddle River, New Jersey, 2002.

Gooch, Amy, *Interactive Non-Photorealistic Technical Illustration*, Master's thesis, University of Utah, December 1998. www.cs.utah.edu/~gooch/publication.html

Gooch, Amy, Bruce Gooch, Peter Shirley, and Elaine Cohen, *A Non-Photorealistic Lighting Model for Automatic Technical Illustration*, Computer Graphics (SIGGRAPH '98 Proceedings), pp. 447–452, July 1998. www.cs.utah.edu/~gooch/publication.html

Gooch, Bruce, and Amy Gooch, *Non-Photorealistic Rendering*, AK Peters Ltd., Natick, Massachusetts, 2001. www.cs.utah.edu/~gooch/book.html

Gooch, Bruce, Peter-Pike J. Sloan, Amy Gooch, Peter Shirley, and Richard Riesenfeld, *Interactive Technical Illustration*, Proceedings 1999 Symposium on Interactive 3D Graphics, pp. 31–38, April 1999. www.cs.utah.edu/~gooch/publication.html

Goral, Cindy M., K. Torrance, D. Greenberg, and B. Battaile, *Modeling the Interaction of Light Between Diffuse Surfaces*, Computer Graphics (SIGGRAPH '84 Proceedings), pp. 213–222, July 1984.

Gouraud, H., *Continuous Shading of Curved Surfaces*, IEEE Transactions on Computers, vol. C-20, pp. 623–629, June 1971.

GPU Gems: Programming Techniques, Tips, and Tricks for Real-Time Graphics, Editor: Randima Fernando, Addison-Wesley, Reading, Massachusetts, 2004. http://developer.nvidia.com/object/gpu_gems_home.html

GPU Gems 2: Programming Techniques for High-Performance Graphics and General-Purpose Computation, Editor: Matt Pharr, Addison-Wesley, Reading, Massachusetts, 2005. http://developer.nvidia.com/object/gpu_gems_2_home.html

Green, Robin, *Spherical Harmonic Lighting: The Gritty Details*, GDC 2003 Presentation. www.research.scea.com/gdc2003/spherical-harmonic-lighting.html

Greene, Ned, *Environment Mapping and Other Applications of World Projections*, IEEE Computer Graphics and Applications, vol. 6, no. 11, pp. 21–29, November 1986.

Gritz, Larry, *LGAntialiasedChecks.sl*, RenderMan Repository Web site. www.renderman.org/RMR/Shaders/LGShaders/index.html

Gruschel, Jens, *Blend Modes*, Pegtop Software Web site. www.pegtop.net/delphi/blendmodes

Haeberli, Paul, *Paint by Numbers: Abstract Image Representation*, Computer Graphics (SIGGRAPH '90 Proceedings), pp. 207–214, August 1990.

———, *Matrix Operations for Image Processing*, Silicon Graphics Inc., 1993. www.sgi.com/grafica/matrix

Haeberli, Paul, and Douglas Voorhies, *Image Processing by Interpolation and Extrapolation*, IRIS Universe Magazine, no. 28, Silicon Graphics, August 1994. http://www.sgi.com/grafica/interp

Haeberli, Paul, and Kurt Akeley, *The Accumulation Buffer: Hardware Support for High-Quality Rendering*, Computer Graphics (SIGGRAPH '90 Proceedings), pp. 289–298, August 1990.

Haeberli, Paul, and Mark Segal, *Texture Mapping as a Fundamental Drawing Primitive*, 4th Eurographics Workshop on Rendering, pp. 259–266, 1993. www.sgi.com/grafica/texmap

Haines, Eric, *Real-Time Shadows*, GDC 2001 Presentation. www.gdconf.com/archives/2001/haines.pdf

Hall, Roy, *Illumination and Color in Computer Generated Imagery*, Springer-Verlag, New York, 1989.

Hanrahan, Pat, and Wolfgang Krueger, *Reflection From Layered Surfaces Due to Subsurface Scattering*, Computer Graphics (SIGGRAPH '93 Proceedings), pages 165–174, August 1993. www.graphics.stanford.edu/papers/subsurface

Hanrahan, Pat, and J. Lawson, *A Language for Shading and Lighting Calculations*, Computer Graphics (SIGGRAPH '90 Proceedings), pp. 289–298, August 1990.

Hart, Evan, Dave Gosselin, and John Isidoro, *Vertex Shading with Direct3D and OpenGL*, Game Developers Conference, San Jose, March 2001. www.ati.com/developer/ATIGDC2001Vertex.PDF

Hart, John C., *Perlin Noise Pixel Shaders*, ACM SIGGRAPH/Eurographics Workshop on Graphics Hardware, pp. 87–94, August 2001. http://graphics.cs.uiuc.edu/~jch/papers/pixelnoise.pdf

Heckbert, Paul S., *Survey of Texture Mapping*, IEEE Computer Graphics and Applications, vol. 6, no. 11, pp. 56–67, November 1986. www.cs.cmu.edu/~ph

——, *Fundamentals of Texture Mapping and Image Warping*, Report No. 516, Computer Science Division, University of California, Berkeley, June 1989. www.cs.cmu.edu/~ph

——, ed., *Graphics Gems IV*, Academic Press, San Diego, 1994. www.acm.org/pubs/tog/GraphicsGems

Heidrich, Wolfgang, and Hans-Peter Seidel, *View-Independent Environment Maps*, ACM SIGGRAPH/Eurographics Workshop on Graphics Hardware, pp. 39–45, August 1998.

——, *Realistic, Hardware-Accelerated Shading and Lighting*, Computer Graphics (SIGGRAPH '99 Proceedings), pp. 171–178, August 1999. www.cs.ubc.ca/~heidrich/Papers

Heidrich, Wolfgang, *Environment Maps and Their Applications*, SIGGRAPH 2000, Course 27, course notes. www.csee.umbc.edu/~olano/s2000c27/envmap.pdf

Hertzmann, Aaron, *Painterly Rendering with Curved Brush Strokes of Multiple Sizes*, Computer Graphics (SIGGRAPH '98 Proceedings), pp. 453–460, 1998. http://mrl.nyu.edu/publications/painterly98

——, *Introduction to 3D Non-Photorealistic Rendering: Silhouettes and Outlines*, SIGGRAPH '99 Non-Photorealistic Rendering course notes, 1999. www.mrl.nyu.edu/~hertzman/hertzmann-intro3d.pdf

Hewlett-Packard, *Polynomial Texture Mapping*, Web site. www.hpl.hp.com/ptm

Hoffman, Nathaniel, and A. Preetham, *Rendering Outdoor Light Scattering in Real Time*, Game Developers Conference 2002. www.ati.com/developer/dx9/ATI-LightScattering.pdf

Hook, Brian, *Multipass Rendering and the Magic of Alpha Blending*, Game Developer, vol. 4, no. 5, pp. 12–19, August 1997.

Hughes, John F., and Tomas Möller, *Building an Orthonormal Basis from a Unit Vector*, Journal of Graphics Tools, vol. 4, no. 4, pp. 33–35, 1999. www.acm.org/jgt/papers/HughesMoller99

International Lighting Vocabulary, Publication CIE No. 17.4, Joint publication IEC (International Electrotechnical Commission) and CIE (Committee Internationale de L'Èclairage), Geneva, 1987. www.cie.co.at/framepublications.html

ITU-R Recommendation BT.709, *Basic Parameter Values for the HDTV Standard for the Studio and for International Programme Exchange*, [formerly CCIR Rec. 709], Geneva, ITU, 1990.

Kajiya, James T., *Anisotropic Reflection Models*, Computer Graphics (SIGGRAPH '85 Proceedings), pp. 15–21, July 1985.

———, *The Rendering Equation*, Computer Graphics (SIGGRAPH '86 Proceedings), pp. 143–150, August 1986.

Kaplan, Matthew, Bruce Gooch, and Elaine Cohen, *Interactive Artistic Rendering*, Proceedings of the First International Symposium on Non-Photorealistic Animation and Rendering (NPAR), pp. 67–74, June 2000. www.cs.utah.edu/npr/utah_papers.html

Kautz, Jan, and Michael D. McCool, *Interactive Rendering with Arbitrary BRDFs Using Separable Approximations*, 10th Eurographics Workshop on Rendering, pp. 281–292, June 1999. www.mpi-sb.mpg.de/~jnkautz/publications

———, *Approximation of Glossy Reflection with Prefiltered Environment Maps*, Graphics Interface 2000, pp. 119–126, May 2000. www.mpi-sb.mpg.de/~jnkautz/publications

Kautz, Jan, P.-P. Vázquez, W. Heidrich, and H.-P. Seidel, *A Unified Approach to Prefiltered Environment Maps*, 11th Eurographics Workshop on Rendering, pp. 185–196, June 2000. www.mpi-sb.mpg.de/~jnkautz/publications

Kautz, Jan, and Hans-Peter Seidel, *Hardware Accelerated Displacement Mapping for Image Based Rendering*, Graphics Interface 2001, pp. 61–70, May 2001.

———, *Towards Interactive Bump Mapping with Anisotropic Shift-Variant BRDFs*, ACM SIGGRAPH/Eurographics Workshop on Graphics Hardware, pp. 51–58, 2000. www.mpi-sb.mpg.de/~jnkautz/projects/anisobumpmaps

Kautz, Jan, Chris Wynn, Jonathan Blow, Chris Blasband, Anis Ahmad, and Michael McCool, *Achieving Real-Time Realistic Reflectance, Part 1*, Game Developer, vol. 8, no. 1, pp. 32–37, January 2001.

————, *Achieving Real-Time Realistic Reflectance, Part 2*, Game Developer, vol. 8, no. 2, pp. 38–44, February 2001. www.gdmag.com/code.htm

Kerlow, Isaac V., *The Art of 3-D: Computer Animation and Imaging, Second Edition*, John Wiley & Sons, New York, 2000.

Kernighan, Brian, and Dennis Ritchie, *The C Programming Language, Second Edition*, Prentice Hall, Englewood Cliffs, New Jersey, 1988.

Kessenich, John, Dave Baldwin, and Randi Rost, *The OpenGL Shading Language, Version 1.10*, 3Dlabs, April 2004. www.opengl.org/documentation/spec.html

Kilgard, Mark J., *A Practical and Robust Bump-mapping Technique for Today's GPUs*, Game Developers Conference, NVIDIA White Paper, 2000. http://developer.nvidia.com/object/Practical_Bumpmapping_Tech.html

Kirk, David, ed., *Graphics Gems III*, Academic Press, San Diego, 1992. www.acm.org/pubs/tog/GraphicsGems

Lander, Jeff, *Collision Response: Bouncy, Trouncy, Fun*, Game Developer, vol. 6, no. 3, pp. 15–19, March 1999. www.darwin3d.com/gdm1999.htm

————, *The Era of Post-Photorealism*, Game Developer, vol. 8, no. 6, pp. 18–22, June 2001.

————, *Graphics Programming and the Tower of Babel*, Game Developer, vol. 8, no. 3, pp. 13–16, March 2001. www.gdmag.com/code.htm

————, *Haunted Trees for Halloween*, Game Developer Magazine, vol. 7, no. 11, pp. 17–21, November 2000. www.gdmag.com/code.htm

————, *A Heaping Pile of Pirate Booty*, Game Developer, vol. 8, no. 4, pp. 22–30, April 2001.

————, *Images from Deep in the Programmer's Cave*, Game Developer, vol. 8, no. 5, pp. 23–28, May 2001. www.gdmag.com/code.htm

————, *The Ocean Spray in Your Face*, Game Developer, vol. 5, no. 7, pp. 13–19, July 1998. www.darwin3d.com/gdm1998.htm

————, *Physics on the Back of a Cocktail Napkin*, Game Developer, vol. 6, no. 9, pp. 17–21, September 1999. www.darwin3d.com/gdm1999.htm

————, *Return to Cartoon Central*, Game Developer Magazine, vol. 7, no. 8, pp. 9–14, August 2000. www.gdmag.com/code.htm

————, *Shades of Disney: Opaquing a 3D World*, Game Developer Magazine, vol. 7, no. 3, pp. 15–20, March 2000. www.darwin3d.com/gdm2000.htm

————, *Skin Them Bones: Game Programming for the Web Generation*, Game Developer, vol. 5, no. 5, pp. 11–16, May 1998. www.darwin3d.com/gdm1998.htm

————, *Slashing Through Real-Time Character Animation*, Game Developer, vol. 5, no. 4, pp. 13–15, April 1998. www.darwin3d.com/gdm1998.htm

————, *That's a Wrap: Texture Mapping Methods*, Game Developer Magazine, vol. 7, no. 10, pp. 21–26, October 2000. www.gdmag.com/code.htm

———, *Under the Shade of the Rendering Tree*, Game Developer Magazine, vol. 7, no. 2, pp. 17–21, February 2000. www.darwin3d.com/gdm2000.htm

Landis, Hayden, *Production-Ready Global Illumination*, SIGGRAPH 2002 Course Notes, course 16, RenderMan In Production. www.debevec.org/HDRI2004/landis-S2002-course16-prodreadyGI.pdf

Lasseter, John, *Principles of Traditional Animation Applied to 3D Computer Animation*, Computer Graphics, (SIGGRAPH '87 Proceedings) pp. 35–44, July 1987.

———, *Tricks to Animating Characters with a Computer*, SIGGRAPH '94, Course 1, course notes. www.siggraph.org/education/materials/HyperGraph/animation/character_animation/principles/lasseter_s94.htm

Lichtenbelt, Barthold, *Integrating the OpenGL Shading Language*, 3Dlabs internal white paper, July 2003.

Lindbloom, Bruce J., *Accurate Color Reproduction for Computer Graphics Applications*, Computer Graphics (SIGGRAPH '89 Proceedings), pp. 117–126, July 1989.

———, personal Web site, 2003. www.brucelindbloom.com

Litwinowicz, Peter, *Processing Images and Video for an Impressionist Effect*, Computer Graphics (SIGGRAPH '97 Proceedings), pp. 407–414, August 1997.

Lorensen, William E., and Harvey E. Cline, *Marching Cubes: A High Resolution 3D Surface Construction Algorithm*, Computer Graphics (SIGGRAPH '87 Proceedings), pp. 163–169, July 1987.

Lowell, Ross, *Matters of Light & Depth*, Lowel-Light Manufacturing, 1992.

Malzbender, Tom, Dan Gelb, and Hans Wolters, *Polynomial Texture Maps*, Computer Graphics (SIGGRAPH 2001 Proceedings), pp. 519–528, August 2001. www.hpl.hp.com/research/ptm/papers/ptm.pdf

Mandelbrot, Benoit B., *The Fractal Geometry of Nature, Updated and Augmented*, W. H. Freeman and Company, New York, 1983.

Mark, William R., *Real-Time Shading: Stanford Real-Time Procedural Shading System*, SIGGRAPH 2001, Course 24, course notes, 2001. http://graphics.stanford.edu/projects/shading/pubs/sigcourse2001.pdf

Mark, William R., R. Steven Glanville, Kurt Akeley, and Mark Kilgard, *Cg: A System for Programming Graphics Hardware in a C-like Language*, Computer Graphics (SIGGRAPH 2003 Proceedings), pp. 896–907, July 2003. www.cs.utexas.edu/users/billmark/papers/Cg

Markosian, Lee, Michael A. Kowalski, Daniel Goldstein, Samuel J. Trychin, John F. Hughes, and Lubomir D. Bourdev, *Real-time Nonphotorealistic Rendering*, Computer Graphics (SIGGRAPH '97 Proceedings), pp. 415–420, August 1997. www.eecs.umich.edu/~sapo/pubs

McCool, Michael D., *SMASH: A Next-Generation API for Programmable Graphics Accelerators*, Technical Report CS-2000-14, University of Waterloo, August 2000. www.cgl.uwaterloo.ca/Projects/rendering/Papers/smash.pdf

McCool, Michael D., Jason Ang, and Anis Ahmad, *Homomorphic Factorization of BRDFs for High-performance Rendering*, Computer Graphics (SIGGRAPH 2001 Proceedings), pp. 171–178, August 2001. www.cgl.uwaterloo.ca/Projects/rendering/Papers

McReynolds, Tom, David Blythe, Brad Grantham, and Scott Nelson, *Advanced Graphics Programming Techniques Using OpenGL*, SIGGRAPH '99 course notes, 1999. www.opengl.org/resources/tutorials/sig99/advanced99/notes/notes.html

McReynolds, Tom, and David Blythe, *Advanced Graphics Programming Techniques Using OpenGL*, Morgan Kaufmann Publishers, San Francisco, 2005.

Meier, Barbara J, *Painterly Rendering for Animation*, Computer Graphics (SIGGRAPH '96 Proceedings), pp. 477–484, August 1996. www.cs.virginia.edu/~dbrogan/CS551.851.animation.sp.2000/Papers/p477-meier.pdf

Microsoft, *Advanced Shading and Lighting*, Meltdown 2001, July 2001. www.microsoft.com/mscorp/corpevents/meltdown2001/presentations.asp

———, *DirectX 9.0 SDK*, 2003. http://msdn.microsoft.com/directx

Mitchell, Jason L., *Advanced Vertex and Pixel Shader Techniques*, European Game Developers Conference, London, September 2001. www.pixelmaven.com/jason

———, *Image Processing with Pixel Shaders in Direct3D*, in Engel, Wolfgang, ed., ShaderX, Wordware, May 2002. www.pixelmaven.com/jason

Muchnick, Steven, *Advanced Compiler Design and Implementation*, Morgan Kaufmann Publishers, San Francisco, 1997.

Myler, Harley R., and Arthur R. Weeks, *The Pocket Handbook of Image Processing Algorithms in C*, Prentice Hall, Upper Saddle River, NJ, 1993.

NASA, *Earth Observatory*, Web site. http://earthobservatory.nasa.gov/Newsroom/BlueMarble

Nishita, Tomoyuki, Takao Sirai, Katsumi Tadamura, and Eihachiro Nakamae, *Display of the Earth Taking into Account Atmospheric Scattering*, Computer Graphics (SIGGRAPH '93 Proceedings), pp. 175–182, August 1993. http://nis-lab.is.s.u-tokyo.ac.jp/~nis/abs_sig.html#sig93

NVIDIA developer Web site. http://developer.nvidia.com

NVIDIA Corporation, Cg Toolkit, Release 1.4, software and documentation. http://developer.nvidia.com/object/cg_toolkit.html

Olano, Marc, and Anselmo Lastra, *A Shading Language on Graphics Hardware: The PixelFlow Shading System*, Computer Graphics (SIGGRAPH '98 Proceedings), pp. 159–168, July 1998. www.csee.umbc.edu/~olano/papers

Olano, Marc, John Hart, Wolfgang Heidrich, and Michael McCool, *Real-Time Shading*, AK Peters, Ltd., Natick, Massachusetts, 2002.

OpenGL Architecture Review Board, *ARB_fragment_program Extension Specification*, OpenGL Extension Registry. http://oss.sgi.com/projects/ogl-sample/registry

———, *ARB_fragment_shader Extension Specification*, OpenGL Extension Registry. http://oss.sgi.com/projects/ogl-sample/registry

———, *ARB_shader_objects Extension Specification*, OpenGL Extension Registry. http://oss.sgi.com/projects/ogl-sample/registry

———, *ARB_vertex_program Extension Specification*, OpenGL Extension Registry. http://oss.sgi.com/projects/ogl-sample/registry

———, *ARB_vertex_shader Extension Specification*, OpenGL Extension Registry. http://oss.sgi.com/projects/ogl-sample/registry

———, *OpenGL Reference Manual, Fourth Edition: The Official Reference to OpenGL, Version 1.4*, Editor: Dave Shreiner, Addison-Wesley, Reading, Massachusetts, 2004.

OpenGL, official Web site. http://opengl.org

OpenGL Performer Web site. www.sgi.com/products/software/performer/

OpenSceneGraph Web site. www.openscenegraph.org/

OpenSG Web site. www.opensg.org

Owen, G. Scott, *Computer Animation*, Web site. www.siggraph.org/education/materials/HyperGraph/animation/anim0.htm

Pandromeda Web site. www.pandromeda.com

Parent, Rick, *Computer Animation: Algorithms and Techniques*, Morgan Kaufmann Publishers, San Francisco, 2001.

Peachey, Darwyn, *Solid Texturing of Complex Surfaces*, Computer Graphics (SIGGRAPH '85 Proceedings), pp. 279–286, July 1985.

Peeper, Craig, and Jason Mitchell, *Introduction to the DirectX 9 High-Level Shader Language*, in *ShaderX2 : Shader Programming Tips and Tricks with DirectX 9.0*, Editor: Wolfgang Engel, Wordware Publishing, 2003. www.ati.com/developer/ShaderX2_IntroductionToHLSL.pdf

Peercy, Mark S., Marc Olano, John Airey, and P. Jeffrey Ungar, *Interactive Multi-Pass Programmable Shading*, Computer Graphics (SIGGRAPH 2000 Proceedings), pp. 425–432, July 2000. www.csee.umbc.edu/~olano/papers

Peitgen, Heinz-Otto, and P. H. Richter, *The Beauty of Fractals, Images of Complex Dynamical Systems*, Springer Verlag, Berlin Heidelberg, 1986.

Peitgen, Heinz-Otto, D. Saupe, M. F. Barnsley, R. L. Devaney, B. B. Mandelbrot, and R. F. Voss, *The Science of Fractal Images,* Springer Verlag, New York, 1988.

Perlin, Ken, *An Image Synthesizer*, Computer Graphics (SIGGRAPH '85 Proceedings), pp. 287–296, July 1985.

——, *Implementing Improved Perlin Noise* in *GPU Gems: Programming Techniques, Tips, and Tricks for Real-Time Graphics*, Editor: Randima Fernando, Addison-Wesley, Reading, Massachusetts, 2004. http://developer.nvidia.com/object/gpu_gems_home.html

——, *Improving Noise*, Computer Graphics (SIGGRAPH 2002 Proceedings), pp. 681–682, July 2002. http://mrl.nyu.edu/perlin/paper445.pdf

——, personal Web site. www.noisemachine.com

——, personal Web site. http://mrl.nyu.edu/~perlin

Pharr, Matt, and Simon Green, *Ambient Occlusion,* in *GPU Gems: Programming Techniques, Tips, and Tricks for Real-Time Graphics*, Editor: Randima Fernando, Addison-Wesley, Reading, Massachusetts, 2004. http://developer.nvidia.com/object/gpu_gems_home.html

Pharr, Matt, and Greg Humphreys, *Physically Based Rendering: From Theory to Implementation*, Morgan Kaufmann, San Francisco, 2004. http://pbrt.org/

Phong, Bui Tuong, *Illumination for Computer Generated Pictures*, Communications of the ACM, vol. 18, no. 6, pp. 311–317, June 1975.

Pixar, *The RenderMan Interface Specification*, Version 3.2, Pixar, July 2000. https://renderman.pixar.com/products/rispec/index.htm

Porter, Thomas, and Tom Duff, *Compositing Digital Images*, Computer Graphics (SIGGRAPH '84 Proceedings), pp. 253–259, July 1984.

Poulin, P., and A. Fournier, *A Model for Anisotropic Reflection*, Computer Graphics (SIGGRAPH '90 Proceedings), pp. 273–282, August 1990.

Poynton, Charles A., *Frequently Asked Questions about Color*, 1997. www.poynton.com/Poynton-color.html

——, *Frequently Asked Questions about Gamma*, 1997. www.poynton.com/Poynton-color.html

——, *A Technical Introduction to Digital Video*, John Wiley & Sons, New York, 1996.

Praun, Emil, Adam Finkelstein, and Hugues Hoppe, *Lapped Textures*, Computer Graphics (SIGGRAPH 2000 Proceedings), pp. 465–470, July 2000. www.cs.princeton.edu/gfx/proj/lapped_tex

Praun, Emil, Hugues Hoppe, Matthew Webb, and Adam Finkelstein, *Real-time Hatching*, Computer Graphics (SIGGRAPH 2000 Proceedings), pp. 581–586, August 2001. www.cs.princeton.edu/gfx/proj/hatching

Proakis, John G., and Dimitris G. Manolakis, *Digital Signal Processing: Principles, Algorithms, and Applications, Third Edition*, Prentice Hall, Upper Saddle River, New Jersey, 1995.

Proudfoot, Kekoa, William R. Mark, Svetoslav Tzvetkov, and Pat Hanrahan, *A Real-Time Procedural Shading System for Programmable Graphics Hardware*, Computer Graphics (SIGGRAPH 2001 Proceedings), pp. 159–170, August 2001. http://graphics.stanford.edu/projects/shading/pubs/sig2001

Purcell, Timothy J., Ian Buck, William R. Mark, and Pat Hanrahan, *Ray Tracing on Programmable Graphics Hardware*, Computer Graphics (SIGGRAPH 2002 Proceedings), July 2002. www-graphics.stanford.edu/papers/rtongfx

Ramamoorthi, Ravi, and P. Hanrahan, *An Efficient Representation for Irradiance Environment Maps*, Computer Graphics (SIGGRAPH 2001 Proceedings), pp. 497–500, August 2001. www1.cs.columbia.edu/~ravir/papers/envmap/index.html

Raskar, Ramesh, and Michael Cohen, *Image Precision Silhouette Edges*, Proceedings 1999 Symposium on Interactive 3D Graphics, pp. 135–140, April 1999. www.cs.unc.edu/~raskar/NPR

Raskar, Ramesh, *Hardware Support for Non-photorealistic Rendering*, ACM SIGGRAPH/Eurographics Workshop on Graphics Hardware, pp. 41–46, 2001. www.cs.unc.edu/~raskar/HWWS

Reeves, William T., *Particle Systems—A Technique for Modeling a Class of Fuzzy Objects*, ACM Transactions on Graphics, vol. 2, no. 2, pp. 91–108, April 1983.

Reeves, William T., and Ricki Blau, *Approximate and Probabilistic Algorithms for Shading and Rendering Structured Particle Systems*, Computer Graphics (SIGGRAPH '85 Proceedings), pp. 313–322, July 1985.

Reeves, William T., David H. Salesin, and Robert L. Cook, *Rendering Antialiased Shadows with Depth Maps*, Computer Graphics (SIGGRAPH '87 Proceedings), pp. 283–291, July 1987.

Reynolds, Craig, *Stylized Depiction in Computer Graphics*, Web site. www.red3d.com/cwr/npr

Rost, Randi J., *The OpenGL Shading Language*, SIGGRAPH 2002, Course 17, course notes. http://3dshaders.com/pubs

———, *Using OpenGL for Imaging*, SPIE Medical Imaging '96 Image Display Conference, February 1996. http://3dshaders.com/pubs

Salisbury, Michael, Sean E. Anderson, Ronen Barzel, and David H. Salesin, *Interactive Pen-and-Ink Illustration*, Computer Graphics (SIGGRAPH '94 Proceedings), pp. 101–108, July 1994. http://grail.cs.washington.edu/pub

Salisbury, Michael, *Image-Based Pen-and-Ink Illustration*, Ph.D. thesis, University of Washington, 1997. http://grail.cs.washington.edu/theses

Saito, Takafumi, and Tokiichiro Takahashi, *Comprehensible Rendering of 3-D Shapes*, Computer Graphics (SIGGRAPH '90 Proceedings), pp. 197–206, August 1990.

Schlick, Christophe, *An Inexpensive BRDF Model for Physically Based Rendering*, Eurographics '94, published in Computer Graphics Forum, vol. 13., no. 3, pp. 149–162, September 1994.

Schneider, Philip, and David Eberly, *Geometric Tools for Computer Graphics*, Morgan Kaufmann Publishers, San Francisco, 2002.

Segal, Mark, C. Korobkin, R. van Widenfelt, J. Foran, and P. Haeberli, *Fast Shadows and Lighting Effects Using Texture Mapping*, Computer Graphics (SIGGRAPH '92 Proceedings), pp. 249–252, July 1992.

Segal, Mark, and Kurt Akeley, *The Design of the OpenGL Graphics Interface*, Silicon Graphics Inc., 1994. wwws.sun.com/software/graphics/opengl/OpenGLdesign.pdf

———, *The OpenGL Graphics System: A Specification (Version 2.0)*, Editor (v1.1): Chris Frazier, (v1.2–1.5): Jon Leech, (v2.0): Jon Leech and Pat Brown, September 2004. www.opengl.org/documentation/spec.html

SGI OpenGL Web site. www.sgi.com/software/opengl

SGI OpenGL Shader Web site. www.sgi.com/software/shader (defunct)

ShaderX2 : Shader Programming Tips and Tricks with DirectX 9.0, Editor: Wolfgang Engel, Wordware Publishing, 2003. www.shaderx2.com

Shishkovtsov, Oles, *Deferred Shading in S.T.A.L.K.E.R.*, in *GPU Gems 2: Programming Techniques for High-Performance Graphics and General-Purpose Computation*, Editor: Matt Pharr, Addison-Wesley, Reading, Massachusetts, 2005. http://developer.nvidia.com/object/gpu_gems_2_home.html

Shreiner, Dave, and The Khronos OpenGL ARB Working Group, *OpenGL Programming Guide, Seventh Edition: The Official Guide to Learning OpenGL, Versions 3.0 and 3.1*, Addison-Wesley, Boston, Massachusetts, 2010.

SIGGRAPH Proceedings, Web site of online materials. http://portal.acm.org.

Sillion, François, and Claude Puech, *Radiosity and Global Illumination*, Morgan Kaufmann Publishers, San Francisco, 1994.

Sloup, Jaroslav, *Physically-based Simulation: A Survey of the Modelling and Rendering of the Earth's Atmosphere*, Proceedings of the 18th Spring Conference on Computer Graphics, pp. 141–150, April 2002. http://sgi.felk.cvut.cz/~sloup/html/research/project

Smith, Alvy Ray, *Color Gamut Transform Pairs*, Computer Graphics (SIGGRAPH '78 Proceedings), pp. 12–19, August 1978. www.alvyray.com

———, *Digital Filtering Tutorial for Computer Graphics*, Lucasfilm Technical Memo 27, revised March 1983. www.alvyray.com/memos/default.htm

———, *Digital Filtering Tutorial, Part II*, Lucasfilm Technical Memo 27, revised March 1983. www.alvyray.com/memos/default.htm

———, *A Pixel Is Not a Little Square, A Pixel Is Not a Little Square, A Pixel Is Not a Little Square! (And a Voxel is Not a Little Cube)*, Technical Memo 6, Microsoft Research, July 1995. www.alvyray.com/memos/default.htm

SMPTE RP 177–1993, *Derivation of Basic Television Color Equations*.

Stam, Jos, *Diffraction Shaders*, Computer Graphics (SIGGRAPH '99 Proceedings), pp. 101–110, August 1999. www.dgp.toronto.edu/people/stam/ reality/Research/pdf/diff.pdf

——, *Simulating Diffraction*, in *GPU Gems: Programming Techniques, Tips, and Tricks for Real-Time Graphics*, Editor: Randima Fernando, Addison-Wesley, Reading, Massachusetts, 2004. http://developer.nvidia.com/object/ gpu_gems_home.html

Stokes, Michael, Matthew Anderson, Srinivasan Chandrasekar, and Ricardo Motta, *A Standard Default Color Space for the Internet—sRGB*, Version 1.10, November 1996. www.color.org/sRGB.html

Stone, Maureen, *A Survey of Color for Computer Graphics*, Course 4 at SIGGRAPH 2001, August 2001. www.stonesc.com

Strothotte, Thomas, and S. Schlectweg, *Non-Photorealistic Computer Graphics, Modeling, Rendering, and Animation*, Morgan Kaufmann Publishers, San Francisco, 2002.

Stroustrup, Bjarne, *The C++ Programming Language (Special 3rd Edition)*, Addison-Wesley, Reading, Massachusetts, 2000.

Taylor, Philip, *Per-Pixel Lighting*, Microsoft Corp., November 2001.

Thomas, Frank, and Ollie Johnston, *Disney Animation—The Illusion of Life*, Abbeville Press, New York, 1981.

——, *The Illusion of Life—Disney Animation, Revised Edition*, Hyperion, 1995.

Torrance, K., and E. Sparrow, *Theory for Off-Specular Reflection from Roughened Surfaces*, J. Optical Society of America, vol. 57, September 1967.

Tufte, Edward, *Visual Explanations*, Graphics Press, Cheshire, Connecticut, 1997.

Upstill, Steve, *The RenderMan Companion: A Programmer's Guide to Realistic Computer Graphics*, Addison-Wesley, Reading, Massachusetts, 1990.

Verbeck, Channing P., and D. Greenberg, *A Comprehensive Light Source Description for Computer Graphics*, IEEE Computer Graphics and Applications, vol. 4, no. 7, July 1984, pp. 66–75.

Ward, Gregory, *Measuring and Modeling Anisotropic Reflection*, Computer Graphics (SIGGRAPH '92 Proceedings), pp. 265–272, July 1992. http://radsite.lbl.gov/radiance/papers/sg92/paper.html

Watt, Alan H., and Mark Watt, *Advanced Animation and Rendering Techniques: Theory and Practice*, Addison-Wesley, Reading, Massachusetts, 1992.

Whitted, Turner, *An Improved Illumination Model for Shaded Display*, Communications of the ACM vol. 23, no. 6, pp. 343–349, 1980.

Williams, Lance, *Pyramidal Parametrics*, Computer Graphics (SIGGRAPH '83 Proceedings), pp. 1–11, July 1983.

Winkenbach, Georges, and David Salesin, *Computer-Generated Pen-and-Ink Illustration*, Computer Graphics (SIGGRAPH '94 Proceedings), pp. 91–100, July 1994. http://grail.cs.washington.edu/pub

Winkenbach, Georges, *Computer-Generated Pen-and-Ink Illustration*, Ph.D. Dissertation, University of Washington, 1996. http://grail.cs.washington.edu/theses

Wolberg, George, *Digital Image Warping*, Wiley-IEEE Press, 2002.

Woo, Andrew, P. Poulin, and A. Fournier, *A Survey of Shadow Algorithms*, IEEE Computer Graphics and Applications, vol. 10, no. 6, pp.13–32, November 1990.

Worley, Steven, *A Cellular Texture Basis Function*, Computer Graphics (SIGGRAPH '96 Proceedings), pp. 291–294, August 1996.

Wright, Richard, *Understanding and Using OpenGL Texture Objects*, Gamasutra, July 23, 1999. www.gamasutra.com/features/19990723/opengl_texture_objects_01.htm

Wright, Richard, and Benjamin Lipchak, *OpenGL SuperBible, Third Edition*, Sams Publishing, 2005. www.starstonesoftware.com/OpenGL/opengl_superbbile.htm

Zhukov, Sergei, A. Iones, G. Kronin, *An Ambient Light Illumination Model*, Proceedings of Eurographics Rendering Workshop '98.

Zwillinger, Dan, *CRC Standard Mathematical Tables and Formulas*, 30th Edition, CRC Press, 1995. http://geom.math.uiuc.edu/docs/reference/CRC-formulas/

Index

noise shader example, 448
point size mode, 111
refraction, 406
shadow maps, 388
simple texture shader example, 302
for soft volume shadows, 395, 397
sphere morph vertex shader, 466
spheres, 338
spherical harmonic lighting, 367
for spherical harmonic lighting, 383
for stripes, 333
technical illustration example, 520
texture access functions, 140
Überlight model, 372
user-defined variables, 200
for using noise to modify and animate
  objects' shape, 468
variables, 61
for Ward's BRDF model, 420
View frustum, defined, 702
Viewing direction
  directional lights and point lights, 278
  eye coordinate system, 277
Viewing matrix, defined, 702
Viewing parameters, specifying, 24

Viewing transformation, defined, 24, 702
Viewport transformation, defined, 27, 702
View volume, defined, 702
Void, data type, 75
Volume shadows, deferred shading, 392–400

W

Ward, Greg, BRDF models, 417
warn behavior, 96
Water surfaces, example of specular
  reflections, 304
Wavelength, diffraction, 411
WGL, 7
Window coordinate system
  about, 27
  defined, 703
Window system, memory allocation, 7
Wobble, animation, 476–480
Wood shader example, 454
World coordinate system, defined, 23, 703
World space. *See* World coordinate system

X

X Window System, GLX, 7

OpenGL® Titles from Addison-Wesley

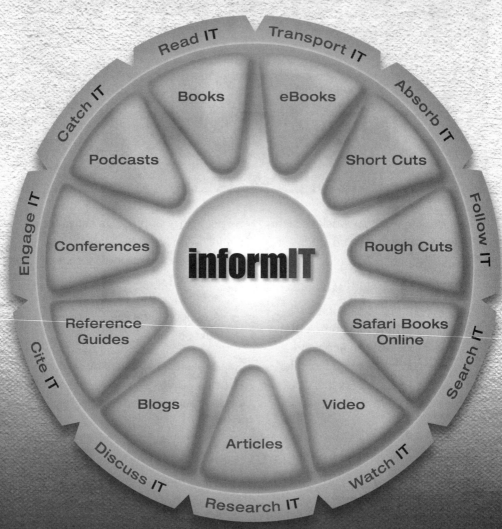

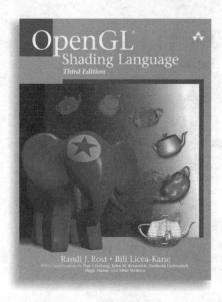

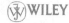

OpenGL®
Programming Guide
Seventh Edition

OpenGL®
Programming Guide
Seventh Edition

The Official Guide to
Learning OpenGL®, Versions 3.0 and 3.1

Dave Shreiner
The Khronos OpenGL ARB Working Group

♦♦Addison-Wesley

Upper Saddle River, NJ • Boston • Indianapolis • San Francisco
New York • Toronto • Montreal • London • Munich • Paris • Madrid
Capetown • Sydney • Tokyo • Singapore • Mexico City

Many of the designations used by manufacturers and sellers to distinguish their products are claimed as trademarks. Where those designations appear in this book, and the publisher was aware of a trademark claim, the designations have been printed with initial capital letters or in all capitals.

The authors and publisher have taken care in the preparation of this book, but make no expressed or implied warranty of any kind and assume no responsibility for errors or omissions. No liability is assumed for incidental or consequential damages in connection with or arising out of the use of the information or programs contained herein.

The publisher offers excellent discounts on this book when ordered in quantity for bulk purchases or special sales, which may include electronic versions and/or custom covers and content particular to your business, training goals, marketing focus, and branding interests. For more information, please contact:

U.S. Corporate and Government Sales
(800) 382-3419
corpsales@pearsontechgroup.com

For sales outside of the U.S., please contact:

International Sales
international@pearsoned.com

Visit us on the Web: informit.com/aw

Library of Congress Cataloging-in-Publication Data

Shreiner, Dave.
  OpenGL programming guide : the official guide to learning OpenGL, versions 3.0 and 3.1 / Dave Shreiner; the Khronos OpenGL ARB Working Group — 7th ed.
    p. cm.
  Includes index.
  ISBN 978-0-321-55262-4 (pbk. : alk. paper)
  1. Computer graphics. 2. OpenGL. I. Title.
  T385.O635 2009
  006.6'6—dc22

                                                                    2009018793

Pearson Education, Inc.
Rights and Contracts Department
501 Boylston Street, Suite 900
Boston, MA 02116
Fax (617) 671-3447

ISBN 13: 978-0-321-55262-4
ISBN 10:   0-321-55262-8
Text printed in the United States on recycled paper at Edwards Brothers in Ann Arbor, Michigan.
Second printing, February 2010

For my family—Felicity, Max, Sarah, and Scout.
—JLN

For my family—Ellyn, Ricky, and Lucy.
—TRD

To Tom Doeppner and Andy van Dam, who started me along this path.
—MW

For my family—Vicki, Bonnie, Bob, Phantom, Squiggles, Tuxedo, and Toby.
—DRS

In memory of Phil Karlton, Celeste Fowler, and Ben Cheatham.

Contents

The following appendices are available online at
`http://www.opengl-redbook.com/appendices/`.

E. Order of Operations

F. Programming Tips

G. OpenGL Invariance

H. Calculating Normal Vectors

I. Built-In OpenGL Shading Language Variables and Functions

J. Floating-Point Formats for Textures, Framebuffers, and Renderbuffers

K. RGTC Compressed Texture Format

L. std140 Uniform Buffer Layout

Figures

Tables

Examples

About This Guide

The OpenGL graphics system is a software interface to graphics hardware. "GL" stands for "Graphics Library." It allows you to create interactive programs that produce color images of moving, three-dimensional objects. With OpenGL, you can control computer-graphics technology to produce realistic pictures, or ones that depart from reality in imaginative ways. This guide explains how to program with the OpenGL graphics system to deliver the visual effect you want.

What This Guide Contains

This guide has 15 chapters. The first five chapters present basic information that you need to understand to be able to draw a properly colored and lit three-dimensional object on the screen.

- Chapter 1, **"Introduction to OpenGL,"** provides a glimpse into the kinds of things OpenGL can do. It also presents a simple OpenGL program and explains essential programming details you need to know for subsequent chapters.

- Chapter 2, **"State Management and Drawing Geometric Objects,"** explains how to create a three-dimensional geometric description of an object that is eventually drawn on the screen.

- Chapter 3, **"Viewing,"** describes how such three-dimensional models are transformed before being drawn on a two-dimensional screen. You can control these transformations to show a particular view of a model.

- Chapter 4, **"Color,"** describes how to specify the color and shading method used to draw an object.

- Chapter 5, **"Lighting,"** explains how to control the lighting conditions surrounding an object and how that object responds to light (that is, how it reflects or absorbs light). Lighting is an important topic, since objects usually don't look three-dimensional until they're lit.

The remaining chapters explain how to optimize or add sophisticated features to your three-dimensional scene. You might choose not to take advantage of many of these features until you're more comfortable with OpenGL. Particularly advanced topics are noted in the text where they occur.

- Chapter 6, **"Blending, Antialiasing, Fog, and Polygon Offset,"** describes techniques essential to creating a realistic scene—alpha blending (to create transparent objects), antialiasing (to eliminate jagged edges), atmospheric effects (to simulate fog or smog), and polygon offset (to remove visual artifacts when highlighting the edges of filled polygons).

- Chapter 7, **"Display Lists,"** discusses how to store a series of OpenGL commands for execution at a later time. You'll want to use this feature to increase the performance of your OpenGL program.

- Chapter 8, **"Drawing Pixels, Bitmaps, Fonts, and Images,"** discusses how to work with sets of two-dimensional data as bitmaps or images. One typical use for bitmaps is describing characters in fonts.

- Chapter 9, **"Texture Mapping,"** explains how to map one-, two-, and three-dimensional images called *textures* onto three-dimensional objects. Many marvelous effects can be achieved through texture mapping.

- Chapter 10, **"The Framebuffer,"** describes all the possible buffers that can exist in an OpenGL implementation and how you can control them. You can use the buffers for such effects as hidden-surface elimination, stenciling, masking, motion blur, and depth-of-field focusing.

- Chapter 11, **"Tessellators and Quadrics,"** shows how to use the tessellation and quadrics routines in the GLU (OpenGL Utility Library).

- Chapter 12, **"Evaluators and NURBS,"** gives an introduction to advanced techniques for efficient generation of curves or surfaces.

- Chapter 13, **"Selection and Feedback,"** explains how you can use OpenGL's selection mechanism to select an object on the screen. Additionally, the chapter explains the feedback mechanism, which allows you to collect the drawing information OpenGL produces, rather than having it be used to draw on the screen.

- Chapter 14, **"Now That You Know,"** describes how to use OpenGL in several clever and unexpected ways to produce interesting results. These techniques are drawn from years of experience with both OpenGL and the technological precursor to OpenGL, the Silicon Graphics IRIS Graphics Library.

- Chapter 15, **"The OpenGL Shading Language,"** discusses the changes that occurred starting with OpenGL Version 2.0. This includes an introduction to the OpenGL Shading Language, also commonly called the "GLSL," which allows you to take control of portions of OpenGL's processing for *vertices* and *fragments*. This functionality can greatly enhance the image quality and computational power of OpenGL.

There are also several appendices that you will likely find useful:

- Appendix A, **"Basics of GLUT: The OpenGL Utility Toolkit,"** discusses the library that handles window system operations. GLUT is portable and it makes code examples shorter and more comprehensible.

- Appendix B, **"State Variables,"** lists the state variables that OpenGL maintains and describes how to obtain their values.

- Appendix C, **"Homogeneous Coordinates and Transformation Matrices,"** explains some of the mathematics behind matrix transformations.

- Appendix D, **"OpenGL and Window Systems,"** briefly describes the routines available in window-system-specific libraries, which are extended to support OpenGL rendering. Window system interfaces to the X Window System, Apple's Mac OS, and Microsoft Windows are discussed here.

Finally, an extensive Glossary defines the key terms used in this guide.

In addition, the appendices listed below are available at the following Web site:

`http://www.opengl-redbook.com/appendices/`

- Appendix E, **"Order of Operations,"** gives a technical overview of the operations OpenGL performs, briefly describing them in the order in which they occur as an application executes.

- Appendix F, **"Programming Tips,"** lists some programming tips based on the intentions of the designers of OpenGL that you might find useful.

- Appendix G, **"OpenGL Invariance,"** describes when and where an OpenGL implementation must generate the exact pixel values described in the OpenGL specification.

- Appendix H, **"Calculating Normal Vectors,"** tells you how to calculate normal vectors for different types of geometric objects.

- Appendix I, **"Built-In OpenGL Shading Language Variables and Functions,"** describes the built-in variables and functions available in the OpenGL Shading Language.

- Appendix J, **"Floating-Point Formats for Textures, Framebuffers, and Renderbuffers,"** documents the various floating-point and shared-exponent pixel and texel formats.

- Appendix K, **"RGTC Compressed Texture Format,"** describes the texture format for storing one- and two-component compressed textures.

- Appendix L, **"std140 Uniform Buffer Layout,"** documents the standard memory layout of uniform-variable buffers for GLSL 1.40.

What's New in This Edition

This seventh edition of the *OpenGL Programming Guide* includes new and updated material covering OpenGL Versions 3.0 and 3.1. With those versions, OpenGL—which is celebrating its eighteenth birthday the year of this writing—has undergone a drastic departure from its previous revisions. Version 3.0 added a number of new features as well as a *depreciation model,* which sets the way for antiquated features to be removed from the library. Note that only new features were added to Version 3.0, making it completely source and binary backward compatible with previous versions. However, a number of features were marked as *deprecated,* indicating that they may potentially be removed from future versions of the API.

Updates related to OpenGL Version 3.0 that are discussed in this edition include the following items:

- New features in OpenGL:

    - An update to the OpenGL Shading Language, creating version 1.30 of GLSL

    - Conditional rendering

    - Finer-grained access to mapping buffer objects' memory for update and reading

    - Floating-point pixel formats for framebuffers in addition to texture map formats (which were added in OpenGL Version 2.1)

- Framebuffer and *renderbuffer* objects

- Compact floating-point representations for reducing the memory storage usage for small dynamic-range data

- Improved support for multisample buffer interactions when copying data

- Non-normalized integer values in texture maps and renderbuffers whose values retain their original representation, as compared to OpenGL's normal operation of mapping those values into the range [0,1]

- One- and two-dimensional texture array support

- Additional packed-pixel formats allowing access to the new renderbuffer support

- Separate blending and writemask control for multiple rendering targets

- Texture compression format

- Single- and double-component internal formats for textures

- Transform feedback

- Vertex-array objects

- sRGB framebuffer format

• An in-depth discussion of the deprecation model

• Bug fixes and updated token names

And for OpenGL Version 3.1:

• Identification of features removed due to deprecation in Version 3.0

• New features:

- An update to the OpenGL Shading Language, creating version 1.40 of GLSL

- Instanced rendering

- Efficient server-side copies of data between buffers

- Rendering of multiple similar primitives within a single draw call using a special (user-specified) token to indicate when to restart a primitive

- Texture buffer objects

- Texture rectangles
- Uniform buffer objects
- Signed normalized texel formats

What You Should Know Before Reading This Guide

This guide assumes only that you know how to program in the C language and that you have some background in mathematics (geometry, trigonometry, linear algebra, calculus, and differential geometry). Even if you have little or no experience with computer graphics technology, you should be able to follow most of the discussions in this book. Of course, computer graphics is an ever-expanding subject, so you may want to enrich your learning experience with supplemental reading:

- *Computer Graphics: Principles and Practice* by James D. Foley, Andries van Dam, Steven K. Feiner, and John F. Hughes (Addison-Wesley, 1990)—This book is an encyclopedic treatment of the subject of computer graphics. It includes a wealth of information but is probably best read after you have some experience with the subject.

- *3D Computer Graphics* by Andrew S. Glassner (The Lyons Press, 1994)—This book is a nontechnical, gentle introduction to computer graphics. It focuses on the visual effects that can be achieved, rather than on the techniques needed to achieve them.

Another great place for all sorts of general information is the official OpenGL Web site. This Web site contains software, sample programs, documentation, FAQs, discussion boards, and news. It is always a good place to start any search for answers to your OpenGL questions:

`http://www.opengl.org/`

Additionally, full documentation of all the procedures that compose OpenGL Versions 3.0 and 3.1 will be documented at the official OpenGL Web site. These Web pages replace the *OpenGL Reference Manual* that was published by the OpenGL Architecture Review Board and Addison-Wesley.

OpenGL is really a hardware-independent specification of a programming interface, and you use a particular implementation of it on a particular kind of hardware. This guide explains how to program with any OpenGL implementation. However, since implementations may vary slightly—in performance and in providing additional, optional features, for example—you might want to investigate whether supplementary documentation is available for the particular implementation you're using. In addition, the provider of your particular implementation might have OpenGL-related utilities, toolkits, programming and debugging support, widgets, sample programs, and demos available at its Web site.

How to Obtain the Sample Code

This guide contains many sample programs to illustrate the use of particular OpenGL programming techniques. As the audience for this guide has a wide range of experience—from novice to seasoned veteran—with both computer graphics and OpenGL, the examples published in these pages usually present the simplest approach to a particular rendering situation, demonstrated using the OpenGL Version 3.0 interface. This is done mainly to make the presentation straightforward and obtainable to those readers just starting with OpenGL. For those of you with extensive experience looking for implementations using the latest features of the API, we first thank you for your patience with those following in your footsteps, and ask that you please visit our Web site:

`http://www.opengl-redbook.com/`

There, you will find the source code for all examples in this text, implementations using the latest features, and additional discussion describing the modifications required in moving from one version of OpenGL to another.

All of the programs contained within this book use the OpenGL Utility Toolkit (GLUT), originally authored by Mark Kilgard. For this edition, we use the open-source version of the GLUT interface from the folks developing the freeglut project. They have enhanced Mark's original work (which is thoroughly documented in his book, *OpenGL Programming for the X Window System* (Addison-Wesley, 1996)). You can find their open-source project page at the following address:

`http://freeglut.sourceforge.net/`

You can obtain code and binaries of their implementation at this site.

The section "OpenGL-Related Libraries" in Chapter 1 and Appendix A give more information about using GLUT. Additional resources to help accelerate your learning and programming of OpenGL and GLUT can be found at the OpenGL Web site's resource pages:

`http://www.opengl.org/resources/`

Many implementations of OpenGL might also include the code samples as part of the system. This source code is probably the best source for your implementation, because it might have been optimized for your system. Read your machine-specific OpenGL documentation to see where those code samples can be found.

Errata

Unfortunately, it is likely this book will have errors. Additionally, OpenGL is updated during the publication of this guide: Errors are corrected and clarifications are made to the specification, and new specifications are released. We keep a list of bugs and updates at our Web site, `http://www.opengl-redbook.com/`, where we also offer facilities for reporting any new bugs you might find. If you find an error, please accept our apologies, and our thanks in advance for reporting it. We'll get it corrected as soon as possible.

Style Conventions

These style conventions are used in this guide:

- **Bold**—Command and routine names and matrices

- *Italics*—Variables, arguments, parameter names, spatial dimensions, matrix components, and first occurrences of key terms

- Regular—Enumerated types and defined constants

Code examples are set off from the text in a monospace font, and command summaries are shaded with gray boxes.

In a command summary, braces are used to identify options among data types. In the following example, **glCommand** has four possible suffixes: s, i, f, and d, which stand for the data types GLshort, GLint, GLfloat, and GLdouble. In the function prototype for **glCommand**, *TYPE* is a wildcard that represents the data type indicated by the suffix.

> void **glCommand**{sifd}(*TYPE x1, TYPE y1, TYPE x2, TYPE y2*);

Distinguishing Deprecated Features

As mentioned, this edition of the *OpenGL Programming Guide* details
Versions 3.0 and 3.1. OpenGL Version 3.0 is entirely backward compatible
with all of the versions made available to this point. However, Version 3.1
employed the deprecation model to remove a number of older features that
were less compatible with modern graphics systems. While numerous
features were removed from the "core" of OpenGL, to ease the transition
between versions, the OpenGL ARB released the GL_ARB_compatibility
extension. If your implementation supports this extension, it will be able to
use all of the removed functionality. To easily identify features that were
removed from OpenGL in Version 3.1, but are still supported by the
compatibility extension, an informational table listing the affected
functions or tokens will be shown in the margin of this book next to where
the command or feature is introduced in its gray box.

Compatibility Extension
glBegin   **GL_POLYGON**

While only features from OpenGL were deprecated and removed, some of
those features affect libraries, such as the OpenGL Utility Library, commonly
called GLU. Those functions that are affected by the changes in OpenGL
Version 3.1 are also listed in a table in the margin.

Acknowledgments

The Seventh Edition

OpenGL Versions 3.0 and 3.1, which this guide covers, mark a new era in the evolution of OpenGL. Once again, the members of the OpenGL ARB Working Group, as part of the Khronos Group, have worked tirelessly to provide new versions that leverage the latest developments in graphics technology. Barthold Lichtenbelt, Bill Licea-Kane, Jeremy Sandmel, and Jon Leech, all of whom lead the technical sub-groups of the OpenGL ARB Working group deserve our thanks. Additionally, without the tireless efforts of Neil Trevett, President of the Khronos Group, who has carried the torch on open-standard media APIs.

The staff at Addison-Wesley once again worked miracles in producing this edition. Debra Williams Cauley, Anna Popick, John Fuller, Molly Sharp, and Jill Hobbs helped with advice and recommendations in making this manuscript better. A thorough technical review was provided by Sean Carmody and Bob Kuehne. Their help is greatly appreciated.

The Sixth Edition

As with the seven preceding versions of OpenGL, the guidance of the OpenGL Architecture Review Board was paramount in its evolution and development. Without the ARB's guidance and devotion, OpenGL would surely languish, and once again we express our gratitude for their efforts.

Once again, the staff of Addison-Wesley provided the support and encouragement to have this edition come to fruition. Debra Williams Cauley, Tyrrell Albaugh, and John Fuller once again worked miracles in producing this manuscript. Thanks once again for an effort second to none.

The Fifth Edition

OpenGL continued its evolutionary track under the careful guidance of the OpenGL Architecture Review Board and its working groups. The small committees that help unify the various business and technical differences among the ARB's membership deserve our thanks and gratitude. They continue to push OpenGL's success to new levels.

As always, the ever-patient and helpful staff at Addison-Wesley were indispensable. Once again, Mary O'Brien, perhaps OpenGL's most devoted non-programming (at least to our knowledge) proponent, continues to encourage us to update the programming guide for the community. Tyrrell Albaugh and John Fuller worked tirelessly in preparing the manuscript for production. Thanks to you all.

The Fourth Edition

OpenGL continued its evolution and success with the aid of many individuals. The OpenGL Architecture Review Board, along with its many participants, help to mold OpenGL. Their contributions were much appreciated.

Numerous example programs were written by Stace Peterson. Helpful discussions and clarifications were provided by Maryann Simmons, Patrick Brown, Alan Commike, Brad Grantham, Bob Kuehne, Jon Leech, Benjamin Lipchak, Marc Olano, and Vicki Shreiner.

Once again, the editorial and production staff at Addison-Wesley were extremely helpful. Thanks to Mary O'Brien, John Fuller, and Brenda Mulligan.

The Third Edition

The third edition of this book required the support of many individuals.

Special thanks are due to the reviewers who volunteered and trudged through the now seven hundred pages of technical material that constitute the third edition: Bill Armstrong, Bob Beretta, David Blythe, Dan Brokenshire, Norman Chin, Steve Cunningham, Angus Dorbie, Laurence Feldman, Celeste Fowler, Jeffery Galinovsky, Brad Grantham, Eric Haines, David Ishimoto, Mark Kilgard, Dale Kirkland, Jon Leech, Seth Livingston, Chikai Ohazama, Bimal Poddar, Mike Schmit, John Stauffer, R. Scott Thompson, David Yu, and Hansong Zhang. Their careful diligence has greatly improved the quality of this book.

An immeasurable debt of gratitude goes to Laura Cooper, Dany Galgani, and Dan Young for their production support, and to Mary O'Brien, Elizabeth Spainhour, Chanda Leary, and John Fuller of Addison-Wesley. Additionally, Miriam Geller, Shawn Hopwood, Stacy Maller, and David Story were instrumental in the coordination and marketing of this effort.

The First and Second Editions

Thanks to the long list of pioneers and past contributors to the success of OpenGL and of this book.

Thanks to the chief architects of OpenGL: Mark Segal and Kurt Akeley. Special recognition goes to the pioneers who heavily contributed to the initial design and functionality of OpenGL: Allen Akin, David Blythe, Jim Bushnell, Dick Coulter, John Dennis, Raymond Drewry, Fred Fisher, Celeste Fowler, Chris Frazier, Momi Furuya, Bill Glazier, Kipp Hickman, Paul Ho, Rick Hodgson, Simon Hui, Lesley Kalmin, Phil Karlton, On Lee, Randi Rost, Kevin P. Smith, Murali Sundaresan, Pierre Tardif, Linas Vepstas, Chuck Whitmer, Jim Winget, and Wei Yen.

The impetus for the second edition began with Paula Womack and Tom McReynolds of Silicon Graphics, who recognized the need for a revision and also contributed some of the new material. John Schimpf, OpenGL Product Manager at Silicon Graphics, was instrumental in getting the revision off and running.

Many thanks go to the people who contributed to the success of the first and second editions of this book: Cindy Ahuna, Kurt Akeley, Bill Armstrong, Otto Berkes, Andy Bigos, Drew Bliss, Patrick Brown, Brian Cabral, Norman Chin, Bill Clifford, Jim Cobb, Dick Coulter, Kathleen Danielson, Suzy Deffeyes, Craig Dunwoody, Fred Fisher, Chris Frazier, Ken Garnett, Kathy Gochenour, Michael Gold, Mike Heck, Paul Ho, Deanna Hohn, Brian Hook, Kevin Hunter, Phil Huxley, Renate Kempf, Mark Kilgard, Dale Kirkland, David Koller, Kevin LeFebvre, Hock San Lee, Zicheng Liu, Rob Mace, Kay Maitz, Tim Misner, Jeremy Morris, Dave Orton, Bimal Poddar, Susan Riley, Randi Rost, Mark Segal, Igor Sinyak, Bill Sweeney, Pierre Tardif, Andy Vesper, Henri Warren, Paula Womack, Gilman Wong, Steve Wright, and David Yu.

The color plates received a major overhaul for this edition. The sequence of plates based on the cover image (Plates 1 through 9) was created by Thad Beier, Seth Katz, and Mason Woo. Plates 10 through 20, 22, and 23 are snapshots of programs created by Mason Woo. Plate 21 was created by Paul Haeberli. Plate 24 was created by Cyril Kardassevitch of the Institue de

Recherche en Informatique de Toulouse. Plate 25 was created by Yukari Ito and Keisuke Kirii of Nihon SGI. Plate 26 was created by John Coggi and David Stodden of The Aerospace Company. Plate 27 was created by Rainer Goebel, Max Planck Institute for Brain Research. Plate 28 was created by Stefan Brabec and Wolfgang Heidrich of the Max Planck Institute for Computer Science. Plate 29 was created by Mikko Blomqvist, Mediaclick OY. Plate 30 was created by Bernd Lutz of Fraunhofer IGD. Finally, Plates 31 and 32, screenshots from the Quake series of games, were created by id Software.

For the color plates that appeared in the previous editions, we would like to thank Gavin Bell, Barry Brouillette, Rikk Carey, Sharon Clay, Mark Daly, Alain Dumesny, Ben Garlick, Kevin Goldsmith, Jim Helman, Dave Immel, Paul Isaacs, Michael Jones, Carl Korobkin, Howard Look, David Mott, Craig Phillips, John Rohlf, Linda Roy, Paul Strauss, and Doug Voorhies.

And now, each of the authors would like to take the 15 minutes that have been allotted to them by Andy Warhol to say thank you.

From the first and second editions:

I'd like to thank my managers at Silicon Graphics—Dave Larson and Way Ting—and the members of my group—Patricia Creek, Arthur Evans, Beth Fryer, Jed Hartman, Ken Jones, Robert Reimann, Eve Stratton (aka Margaret-Anne Halse), John Stearns, and Josie Wernecke—for their support during this lengthy process. Last, but surely not least, I want to thank those whose contributions toward this project are too deep and mysterious to elucidate: Yvonne Leach, Kathleen Lancaster, Caroline Rose, Cindy Kleinfeld, and my parents, Florence and Ferdinand Neider.

—JLN

In addition to my parents, Edward and Irene Davis, I'd like to thank the people who taught me most of what I know about computers and computer graphics—Doug Engelbart and Jim Clark.

—TRD

I'd like to thank the many past and current members of Silicon Graphics whose accommodation and enlightenment were essential to my contribution to this book: Gerald Anderson, Wendy Chin, Bert Fornaciari, Bill Glazier, Jill Huchital, Howard Look, Bill Mannel, David Marsland, Dave Orton, Linda Roy, Keith Seto, and Dave Shreiner. Very special thanks to Karrin Nicol, Leilani Gayles, Kevin Dankwardt, Kiyoshi Hasegawa, and Raj Singh for their guidance throughout my career. I also bestow much gratitude to my teammates on the Stanford B ice hockey team for periods of glorious distraction throughout the initial writing of this book. Finally, I'd like to thank my family, especially my mother, Bo, and my late father, Henry.

—MW

And for the third edition:

I'd first like to acknowledge Mason, who aside from helping me with this undertaking, has been a great friend and mentor over the years. My knowledge of OpenGL would be nothing without the masters who have patiently answered my questions: Kurt Akeley, Allen Akin, David Blythe, Chris Frazier, Mark Kilgard, Mark Segal, Paula Womack, and David Yu and my current teammates working on OpenGL: Paul Ho, George Kyriazis, Jon Leech, Ken Nicholson, and David Yu. Additionally, I'd like to recognize Doug Doren, Kerwin Dobbs, and Karl Sohlberg, who started me on this odyssey so long ago, and Andrew Walton, John Harechmak, and Alan Dare, who have provided illuminating conversations about graphics over the years. Finally and most important, I'd like to thank Vicki, my loving wife, my parents, Bonnie and Bob, and Squiggles and Phantom, who endlessly encourage me in all that I do and have taught me to enjoy life to the fullest.

—DRS

And for the fourth edition:

Once again, I owe Mason a debt of thanks for helping to jump start this project. Without him, we all might be waiting for an update. I'd also like to extend my appreciation to Alan Chalmers, James Gain, Geoff Leach, and their students for their enthusiasm and encouragement. I'd also like to thank ACM/SIGGRAPH, Afrigraph, Seagraph, and SGI for the ample opportunities to talk about OpenGL to wonderful audiences worldwide. Brad Grantham, who's been willing to help out with all my OpenGL escapades, deserves special thanks. A couple of friends who deserve special mention are Eric England and Garth Honhart. The biggest thanks goes to those I love most: Vicki, my folks, and Squiggles, Phantom, and Toby. They continue to make me more successful than I ever imagined.

—DRS

And for the fifth edition:

First and foremost, a tremendous thanks goes to Vicki, my wife, who patiently waited the countless hours needed to finish this project, and to the rest of my family: Phantom, Toby, Bonnie, and Bob. I also wish to thank the OpenGL and SIGGRAPH communities, which continue to encourage me in these endeavors. And thanks to Alan Commike, Bob Kuehne, Brad Grantham, and Tom True for their help and support in the various OpenGL activities I coerce them into helping me with.

—DRS

And for the sixth edition:

As always, my deepest appreciation goes to Vicki and Phantom who waited patiently while I toiled on this edition, and to my parents: Bonnie and Bob, who still encourage and compliment my efforts (and dig the fact that I actually wound up doing something useful in life). I'd also like to thank the members of the OpenGL ARB Working Group (now part of the Khronos Group) and its Ecosystem Technical Subgroup for their efforts in making documentation and information about OpenGL all the more accessible.

A great thanks goes to the Graphics group at the University of Cape Town's Visual Computing Laboratory: James Gain, Patrick Marais, Gary Marsden, Bruce Merry, Carl Hultquist, Christopher de Kadt, Ilan Angel, and Shaun Nirenstein; and Jason Moore. Last, but certainly not least, thanks once again to the OpenGL and SIGGRAPH communities for encouraging me to continue this project and providing ever needed feedback. Thanks to you all.

—DRS

And for the seventh edition:

As with every edition, I am entirely endebted to Vicki and Phantom, for their support and patience. Likewise, my parents, Bonnie and Bob, who wax lyrical over my efforts; no son could be luckier or prouder.

A very large thanks goes to my employer, ARM, Inc., and in particular to Jem Davies, my manager, for his patience and support when this project interrupted my responsibilties at work. Likewise, Bruce Merry of ARM whose attention to detail helped clarify a number of points. Additionally, I'd like to thank my colleagues at ARM who provide endless entertainment and discussions on graphics and media. And as with every edition, my sincerest appreciation to the readers of this guide, and the practitioners of OpenGL worldwide. Thanks for giving me a reason to keep writing.

—DRS

Chapter 1

Introduction to OpenGL

Chapter Objectives

After reading this chapter, you'll be able to do the following:

- Appreciate in general terms what OpenGL does

- Identify different levels of rendering complexity

- Understand the basic structure of an OpenGL program

- Recognize OpenGL command syntax

- Identify the sequence of operations of the OpenGL rendering pipeline

- Understand in general terms how to animate graphics in an OpenGL program

This chapter introduces OpenGL. It has the following major sections:

- "What Is OpenGL?" explains what OpenGL is, what it does and doesn't do, and how it works.

- "A Smidgen of OpenGL Code" presents a small OpenGL program and briefly discusses it. This section also defines a few basic computer-graphics terms.

- "OpenGL Command Syntax" explains some of the conventions and notations used by OpenGL commands.

- "OpenGL as a State Machine" describes the use of state variables in OpenGL and the commands for querying, enabling, and disabling states.

- "OpenGL Rendering Pipeline" shows a typical sequence of operations for processing geometric and image data.

- "OpenGL-Related Libraries" describes sets of OpenGL-related routines, including a detailed introduction to GLUT (Graphics Library Utility Toolkit), a portable toolkit.

- "Animation" explains in general terms how to create pictures on the screen that move.

- "OpenGL and Its Deprecation Mechanism" describes which changes deprecation brought into the latest version(s) of OpenGL, how those changes will affect your applications, and how OpenGL will evolve in the future in light of those changes.

What Is OpenGL?

OpenGL is a software interface to graphics hardware. This interface consists of more than 700 distinct commands (about 670 commands as specified for OpenGL Version 3.0 and another 50 in the OpenGL Utility Library) that you use to specify the objects and operations needed to produce interactive three-dimensional applications.

OpenGL is designed as a streamlined, hardware-independent interface to be implemented on many different hardware platforms. To achieve these qualities, no commands for performing windowing tasks or obtaining user input are included in OpenGL; instead, you must work through whatever windowing system controls the particular hardware you're using. Similarly, OpenGL doesn't provide high-level commands for describing models of three-dimensional objects. Such commands might allow you to specify relatively complicated shapes such as automobiles, parts of the body, airplanes, or molecules. With OpenGL, you must build your desired model from a small set of *geometric primitives*—points, lines, and polygons.

A sophisticated library that provides these features could certainly be built on top of OpenGL. The OpenGL Utility Library (GLU) provides many of the modeling features, such as quadric surfaces and NURBS curves and surfaces. GLU is a standard part of every OpenGL implementation.

Now that you know what OpenGL *doesn't* do, here's what it *does* do. Take a look at the color plates—they illustrate typical uses of OpenGL. They show the scene on the cover of this book, *rendered* (which is to say, drawn) by a computer using OpenGL in successively more complicated ways. The following list describes in general terms how these pictures were made.

- Plate 1 shows the entire scene displayed as a *wireframe* model—that is, as if all the objects in the scene were made of wire. Each *line* of wire corresponds to an edge of a primitive (typically a polygon). For example, the surface of the table is constructed from triangular polygons that are positioned like slices of pie.

  Note that you can see portions of objects that would be obscured if the objects were solid rather than wireframe. For example, you can see the entire model of the hills outside the window even though most of this model is normally hidden by the wall of the room. The globe appears to be nearly solid because it's composed of hundreds of colored blocks, and you see the wireframe lines for all the edges of all the blocks, even those forming the back side of the globe. The way the globe is constructed gives you an idea of how complex objects can be created by assembling lower-level objects.

- Plate 2 shows a *depth-cued* version of the same wireframe scene. Note that the lines farther from the eye are dimmer, just as they would be in real life, thereby giving a visual cue of *depth*. OpenGL uses atmospheric effects (collectively referred to as *fog*) to achieve depth cueing.

- Plate 3 shows an *antialiased* version of the wireframe scene. Antialiasing is a technique for reducing the jagged edges (also known as *jaggies*) created when approximating smooth edges using *pixels*—short for *picture elements*—which are confined to a rectangular grid. Such jaggies are usually the most visible, with near-horizontal or near-vertical lines.

- Plate 4 shows a *flat-shaded*, *unlit* version of the scene. The objects in the scene are now shown as solid. They appear "flat" in the sense that only one color is used to render each polygon, so they don't appear smoothly rounded. There are no effects from any light sources.

- Plate 5 shows a *lit, smooth-shaded* version of the scene. Note how the scene looks much more realistic and three-dimensional when the objects are shaded to respond to the light sources in the room, as if the objects were smoothly rounded.

- Plate 6 adds *shadows* and *textures* to the previous version of the scene. Shadows aren't an explicitly defined feature of OpenGL (there is no "shadow command"), but you can create them yourself using the techniques described in Chapter 9 and Chapter 14. *Texture mapping* allows you to apply a two-dimensional image onto a three-dimensional object. In this scene, the top on the table surface is the most vibrant example of texture mapping. The wood grain on the floor and table surface are all texture mapped, as well as the wallpaper and the toy top (on the table).

- Plate 7 shows a *motion-blurred* object in the scene. The sphinx (or dog, depending on your Rorschach tendencies) appears to be captured moving forward, leaving a blurred trace of its path of motion.

- Plate 8 shows the scene as it was drawn for the cover of the book from a different viewpoint. This plate illustrates that the image really is a snapshot of models of three-dimensional objects.

- Plate 9 brings back the use of fog, which was shown in Plate 2 to simulate the presence of smoke particles in the air. Note how the same effect in Plate 2 now has a more dramatic impact in Plate 9.

- Plate 10 shows the *depth-of-field effect*, which simulates the inability of a camera lens to maintain all objects in a photographed scene in focus. The camera focuses on a particular spot in the scene. Objects that are significantly closer or farther than that spot are somewhat blurred.

The color plates give you an idea of the kinds of things you can do with the OpenGL graphics system. The following list briefly describes the major graphics operations that OpenGL performs to render an image on the screen. (See "OpenGL Rendering Pipeline" on page 10 for detailed information on this order of operations.)

1. Construct shapes from geometric primitives, thereby creating mathematical descriptions of objects. (OpenGL considers points, lines, polygons, images, and bitmaps to be primitives.)

2. Arrange the objects in three-dimensional space and select the desired vantage point for viewing the composed scene.

3. Calculate the colors of all the objects. The colors might be explicitly assigned by the application, determined from specified lighting

conditions, obtained by pasting textures onto the objects, or some combination of these operations. These actions may be carried out using *shaders*, where you explicitly control all the color computations, or they may be performed internally in OpenGL using its preprogrammed algorithms (by what is commonly termed the *fixed-function pipeline*).

4. Convert the mathematical description of objects and their associated color information to pixels on the screen. This process is called *rasterization*.

During these stages, OpenGL might perform other operations, such as eliminating parts of objects that are hidden by other objects. In addition, after the scene is rasterized but before it's drawn on the screen, you can perform some operations on the pixel data if you want.

In some implementations (such as with the X Window System), OpenGL is designed to work even if the computer that displays the graphics you create isn't the computer that runs your graphics program. This might be the case if you work in a networked computer environment where many computers are connected to one another by a network. In this situation, the computer on which your program runs and issues OpenGL drawing commands is called the *client*, and the computer that receives those commands and performs the drawing is called the *server*. The format for transmitting OpenGL commands (called the *protocol*) from the client to the server is always the same, so OpenGL programs can work across a *network* even if the client and server are different kinds of computers. If an OpenGL program isn't running across a network, then there's only one computer, and it is both the client and the server.

A Smidgen of OpenGL Code

Because you can do so many things with the OpenGL graphics system, an OpenGL program can be complicated. However, the basic structure of a useful program can be simple: its tasks are to initialize certain states that control how OpenGL renders and to specify objects to be rendered.

Before you look at some OpenGL code, let's go over a few terms. *Rendering*, which you've already seen used, is the process by which a computer creates images from models. These *models*, or objects, are constructed from geometric primitives—points, lines, and polygons—that are specified by their *vertices*.

The final rendered image consists of pixels drawn on the screen; a pixel is the smallest visible element the display hardware can put on the screen.

Information about the pixels (for instance, what color they're supposed to be) is organized in memory into bitplanes. A *bitplane* is an area of memory that holds one *bit* of information for every pixel on the screen; the bit might indicate how red a particular pixel is supposed to be, for example. The bitplanes are themselves organized into a *framebuffer*, which holds all the information that the graphics display needs to control the color and intensity of all the pixels on the screen.

Now look at what an OpenGL program might look like. Example 1-1 renders a white rectangle on a black background, as shown in Figure 1-1.

Figure 1-1   White Rectangle on a Black Background

Example 1-1   Chunk of OpenGL Code

```
#include <whateverYouNeed.h>

main() {
    InitializeAWindowPlease();

    glClearColor(0.0, 0.0, 0.0, 0.0);
    glClear(GL_COLOR_BUFFER_BIT);
    glColor3f(1.0, 1.0, 1.0);
    glOrtho(0.0, 1.0, 0.0, 1.0, -1.0, 1.0);
    glBegin(GL_POLYGON);
        glVertex3f(0.25, 0.25, 0.0);
        glVertex3f(0.75, 0.25, 0.0);
        glVertex3f(0.75, 0.75, 0.0);
        glVertex3f(0.25, 0.75, 0.0);
    glEnd();
    glFlush();
    UpdateTheWindowAndCheckForEvents();
}
```

The first line of the **main()** routine initializes a *window* on the screen: The **InitializeAWindowPlease()** routine is meant as a placeholder for window-system-specific routines, which are generally not OpenGL calls. The next two lines are OpenGL commands that clear the window to black: **glClearColor()** establishes what color the window will be cleared to, and **glClear()** actually clears the window. Once the clearing color is set, the window is cleared to that color whenever **glClear()** is called. This clearing color can be changed with another call to **glClearColor()**. Similarly, the **glColor3f()** command establishes what color to use for drawing objects—in this case, the color is white. All objects drawn after this point use this color, until it's changed with another call to set the color.

The next OpenGL command used in the program, **glOrtho()**, specifies the *coordinate system* OpenGL assumes as it draws the final image and how the image is mapped to the screen. The next calls, which are bracketed by **glBegin()** and **glEnd()**, define the object to be drawn—in this example, a polygon with four vertices. The polygon's "corners" are defined by the **glVertex3f()** commands. As you might be able to guess from the arguments, which are (x, y, z) coordinates, the polygon is a rectangle on the $z = 0$ plane.

Finally, **glFlush()** ensures that the drawing commands are actually executed, rather than stored in a *buffer* awaiting additional OpenGL commands. The **UpdateTheWindowAndCheckForEvents()** placeholder routine manages the contents of the window and begins event processing.

Actually, this piece of OpenGL code isn't well structured. You may be asking, "What happens if I try to move or resize the window?" or "Do I need to reset the coordinate system each time I draw the rectangle?". Later in this chapter, you will see replacements for both **InitializeAWindowPlease()** and **UpdateTheWindowAndCheckForEvents()** that actually work but require restructuring of the code to make it efficient.

OpenGL Command Syntax

As you might have observed from the simple program in the preceding section, OpenGL commands use the prefix **gl** and initial capital letters for each word making up the command name (recall **glClearColor()**, for example). Similarly, OpenGL defined constants begin with GL_, use all capital letters, and use underscores to separate words (for example, GL_COLOR_BUFFER_BIT).

You might also have noticed some seemingly extraneous letters appended to some command names (for example, the **3f** in **glColor3f()** and **glVertex3f()**).

It's true that the **Color** part of the command name **glColor3f()** is enough to define the command as one that sets the current color. However, more than one such command has been defined so that you can use different types of arguments. In particular, the **3** part of the suffix indicates that three arguments are given; another version of the **Color** command takes four arguments. The **f** part of the suffix indicates that the arguments are floating-point numbers. Having different formats allows OpenGL to accept the user's data in his or her own data format.

Some OpenGL commands accept as many as eight different data types for their arguments. The letters used as suffixes to specify these data types for ISO C implementations of OpenGL are shown in Table 1-1, along with the corresponding OpenGL type definitions. The particular implementation of OpenGL that you're using might not follow this scheme exactly; an implementation in C++ or Ada that supports function overloading, for example, wouldn't necessarily need to.

Suffix	Data Type	Typical Corresponding C-Language Type	OpenGL Type Definition
b	8-bit integer	signed char	GLbyte
s	16-bit integer	short	GLshort
i	32-bit integer	int or long	GLint, GLsizei
f	32-bit floating-point	float	GLfloat, GLclampf
d	64-bit floating-point	double	GLdouble, GLclampd
ub	8-bit unsigned integer	unsigned char	GLubyte, GLboolean
us	16-bit unsigned integer	unsigned short	GLushort
ui	32-bit unsigned integer	unsigned int or unsigned long	GLuint, GLenum, GLbitfield

Table 1-1   Command Suffixes and Argument Data Types

Thus, the two commands

```
glVertex2i(1, 3);
glVertex2f(1.0, 3.0);
```

are equivalent, except that the first specifies the vertex's coordinates as 32-bit integers, and the second specifies them as single-precision floating-point numbers.

Note: Implementations of OpenGL have leeway in selecting which C data type to use to represent OpenGL data types. If you resolutely use the OpenGL defined data types throughout your application, you will avoid mismatched types when porting your code between different implementations.

Some OpenGL commands can take a final letter **v**, which indicates that the command takes a pointer to a vector (or array) of values, rather than a series of individual arguments. Many commands have both vector and nonvector versions, but some commands accept only individual arguments and others require that at least some of the arguments be specified as a vector. The following lines show how you might use a vector and a nonvector version of the command that sets the current color:

```
glColor3f(1.0, 0.0, 0.0);

GLfloat color_array[] = {1.0, 0.0, 0.0};
glColor3fv(color_array);
```

Finally, OpenGL defines the type of GLvoid. This is most often used for OpenGL commands that accept pointers to arrays of values.

In the rest of this guide (except in actual code examples), OpenGL commands are referred to by their base names only, and an asterisk is included to indicate that there may be more to the command name. For example, **glColor*()** stands for all variations of the command you use to set the current color. If we want to make a specific point about one version of a particular command, we include the suffix necessary to define that version. For example, **glVertex*v()** refers to all the vector versions of the command you use to specify vertices.

OpenGL as a State Machine

OpenGL is a state machine, particularly if you're using the fixed-function pipeline. You put it into various states (or modes) that then remain in effect until you change them. As you've already seen, the current color is a state variable. You can set the current color to white, red, or any other color, and thereafter every object is drawn with that color until you set the current color to something else. The current color is only one of many state variables that OpenGL maintains. Others control such things as the current viewing and projection transformations, line and polygon stipple patterns, polygon drawing modes, pixel-packing conventions, positions and characteristics of lights, and material properties of the objects being drawn. Many state variables refer to modes that are enabled or disabled with the command **glEnable()** or **glDisable()**.

If you're using programmable shaders, depending on which version of OpenGL you're using, the amount of state that is exposed to your shaders will vary.

Each state variable or mode has a default value, and at any point you can query the system for each variable's current value. Typically, you use one of the six following commands to do this: **glGetBooleanv()**, **glGetDoublev()**, **glGetFloatv()**, **glGetIntegerv()**, **glGetPointerv()**, or **glIsEnabled()**. Which of these commands you select depends on what data type you want the answer to be given in. Some state variables have a more specific query command (such as **glGetLight*()**, **glGetError()**, or **glGetPolygonStipple()**). In addition, you can save a collection of state variables on an attribute stack with **glPushAttrib()** or **glPushClientAttrib()**, temporarily modify them, and later restore the values with **glPopAttrib()** or **glPopClientAttrib()**. For temporary state changes, you should use these commands rather than any of the query commands, as they're likely to be more efficient.

See Appendix B for the complete list of state variables you can query. For each variable, the appendix also lists a suggested **glGet*()** command that returns the variable's value, the attribute class to which it belongs, and the variable's default value.

OpenGL Rendering Pipeline

Most implementations of OpenGL have a similar order of operations, a series of processing stages called the OpenGL rendering pipeline. This ordering, as shown in Figure 1-2, is not a strict rule about how OpenGL is implemented, but it provides a reliable guide for predicting what OpenGL will do.

If you are new to three-dimensional graphics, the upcoming description may seem like drinking water out of a fire hose. You can skim this now, but come back to Figure 1-2 as you go through each chapter in this book.

The following diagram shows the Henry Ford assembly line approach, which OpenGL takes to processing data. Geometric data (vertices, lines, and polygons) follow the path through the row of boxes that includes evaluators and per-vertex operations, while pixel data (pixels, images, and bitmaps) are treated differently for part of the process. Both types of data undergo the same final steps (rasterization and per-fragment operations) before the final pixel data is written into the framebuffer.

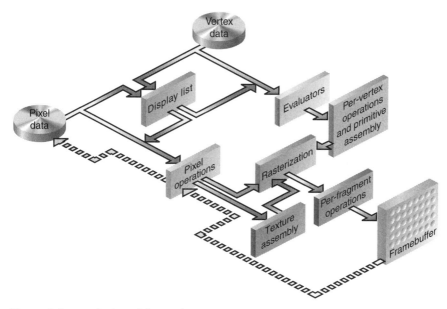

Figure 1-2   Order of Operations

Now you'll see more detail about the key stages in the OpenGL rendering pipeline.

Display Lists

All data, whether it describes geometry or pixels, can be saved in a *display list* for current or later use. (The alternative to retaining data in a display list is processing the data immediately—also known as *immediate mode*.) When a display list is executed, the retained data is sent from the display list just as if it were sent by the application in immediate mode. (See Chapter 7 for more information about display lists.)

Evaluators

All geometric primitives are eventually described by vertices. Parametric curves and surfaces may be initially described by control points and polynomial functions called *basis functions*. Evaluators provide a method for deriving the vertices used to represent the surface from the control points.

The method is a polynomial mapping, which can produce surface normal, texture coordinates, colors, and spatial coordinate values from the control points. (See Chapter 12 to learn more about evaluators.)

Per-Vertex Operations

For vertex data, next is the "per-vertex operations" stage, which converts the vertices into primitives. Some types of vertex data (for example, spatial coordinates) are transformed by 4 × 4 floating-point matrices. Spatial coordinates are projected from a position in the 3D world to a position on your screen. (See Chapter 3 for details about the transformation matrices.)

If advanced features are enabled, this stage is even busier. If texturing is used, texture coordinates may be generated and transformed here. If lighting is enabled, the lighting calculations are performed using the transformed vertex, surface normal, light source position, material properties, and other lighting information to produce a color value.

Since OpenGL Version 2.0, you've had the option of using fixed-function vertex processing, as just previously described, or completely controlling the operation of the per-vertex operations by using vertex shaders. If you employ shaders, all of the operations in the per-vertex operations stage are replaced by your shader. In Version 3.1, all of the fixed-function vertex operations are removed (unless your implementation supports the GL_ARB_compatibility extension), and using a vertex shader is mandatory.

Primitive Assembly

Clipping, a major part of primitive assembly, is the elimination of portions of geometry that fall outside a half-space, defined by a plane. Point clipping simply passes or rejects vertices; line or polygon clipping can add additional vertices depending on how the line or polygon is clipped.

In some cases, this is followed by perspective division, which makes distant geometric objects appear smaller than closer objects. Then viewport and depth (z-coordinate) operations are applied. If culling is enabled and the primitive is a polygon, it then may be rejected by a culling test. Depending on the polygon mode, a polygon may be drawn as points or lines. (See "Polygon Details" in Chapter 2.)

The results of this stage are complete geometric primitives, which are the transformed and clipped vertices with related color, depth, and sometimes texture-coordinate values and guidelines for the rasterization step.

Pixel Operations

While geometric data takes one path through the OpenGL rendering pipeline, pixel data takes a different route. Pixels from an array in system memory are first unpacked from one of a variety of formats into the proper number of components. Next the data is scaled, biased, and processed by a pixel map. The results are clamped and then either written into texture memory or sent to the rasterization step. (See "Imaging Pipeline" in Chapter 8.)

If pixel data is read from the framebuffer, pixel-transfer operations (scale, bias, mapping, and clamping) are performed. Then these results are packed into an appropriate format and returned to an array in system memory.

There are special pixel copy operations for copying data in the framebuffer to other parts of the framebuffer or to the texture memory. A single pass is made through the pixel-transfer operations before the data is written to the texture memory or back to the framebuffer.

Many of the pixel operations described are part of the fixed-function pixel pipeline and often move large amounts of data around the system. Modern graphics implementations tend to optimize performance by trying to localize graphics operations to the memory local to the graphics hardware (this description is a generalization, of course, but it is how most systems are currently implemented). OpenGL Version 3.0, which supports all of these operations, also introduces *framebuffer objects* that help optimize these data movements, in particular, these objects can eliminate some of these transfers entirely. Framebuffer objects, combined with programmable fragment shaders replace many of these operations (most notably, those classified as pixel transfers) and provide significantly more flexibility.

Texture Assembly

OpenGL applications can apply texture images to geometric objects to make the objects look more realistic, which is one of the numerous techniques enabled by texture mapping. If several texture images are used, it's wise to put them into texture objects so that you can easily switch among them.

Almost all OpenGL implementations have special resources for accelerating texture performance (which may be allocated from a shared pool of resources in the graphics implementation). To help your OpenGL implementation manage these memory resources efficiently, texture objects may be prioritized to help control potential caching and locality issues of texture maps. (See Chapter 9.)

Rasterization

Rasterization is the conversion of both geometric and pixel data into *fragments*. Each fragment square corresponds to a pixel in the framebuffer. Line and polygon stipples, line width, point size, shading model, and coverage calculations to support antialiasing are taken into consideration as vertices are connected into lines or the interior pixels are calculated for a filled polygon. Color and depth values are generated for each fragment square.

Fragment Operations

Before values are actually stored in the framebuffer, a series of operations are performed that may alter or even throw out fragments. All these operations can be enabled or disabled.

The first operation that a fragment might encounter is texturing, where a *texel* (texture element) is generated from texture memory for each fragment and applied to the fragment. Next, primary and secondary colors are combined, and a fog calculation may be applied. If your application is employing fragment shaders, the preceding three operations may be done in a shader.

After the final color and depth generation of the previous operations, the scissor test, the alpha test, the stencil test, and the depth-buffer test (the depth buffer is does hidden-surface removal) are evaluated, if enabled. Failing an enabled test may end the continued processing of a fragment's square. Then, blending, dithering, logical operation, and masking by a bitmask may be performed. (See Chapter 6 and Chapter 10.) Finally, the thoroughly processed fragment is drawn into the appropriate buffer, where it has finally become a pixel and achieved its final resting place.

OpenGL-Related Libraries

OpenGL provides a powerful but primitive set of rendering commands, and all higher-level drawing must be done in terms of these commands. Also, OpenGL programs have to use the underlying mechanisms of the windowing system. Several libraries enable you to simplify your programming tasks, including the following:

- The OpenGL Utility Library (GLU) contains several routines that use lower-level OpenGL commands to perform such tasks as setting up matrices for specific viewing orientations and projections, performing polygon tessellation, and rendering surfaces. This library is provided as part of every OpenGL implementation. The more useful GLU routines are described in this guide, where they're relevant to the topic being discussed, such as in all of Chapter 11 and in the section "The GLU NURBS Interface" in Chapter 12. GLU routines use the prefix **glu**.

- For every window system, there is a library that extends the functionality of that window system to support OpenGL rendering. For machines that use the X Window System, the OpenGL Extension to the X Window System (GLX) is provided as an adjunct to OpenGL. GLX routines use the prefix **glX**. For Microsoft Windows, the WGL routines provide the Windows to OpenGL interface. All WGL routines use the prefix **wgl**. For Mac OS, three interfaces are available: AGL (with prefix **agl**), CGL (**cgl**), and Cocoa (**NSOpenGL** classes).

  All of these window system extension libraries are described in more detail in Appendix D.

- The OpenGL Utility Toolkit (GLUT) is a window-system-independent toolkit, originally written by Mark Kilgard, that hides the complexities of differing window system APIs. In this edition, we use an open-source implementation of GLUT named **freeglut**, which extends the original functionality of GLUT. The next section describes the fundamental routines necessary to author programs using GLUT, all of which are prefixed with **glut**. In most parts of the text, we continue to use the term GLUT, with the understanding that we are using the Freeglut implementation.

Include Files

For all OpenGL applications, you want to include the OpenGL header files in every file. Many OpenGL applications may use GLU, the aforementioned OpenGL Utility Library, which requires inclusion of the glu.h header file. So almost every OpenGL source file begins with

```
#include <GL/gl.h>
#include <GL/glu.h>
```

Note: Microsoft Windows requires that windows.h be included before either gl.h or glu.h, because some macros used internally in the Microsoft Windows version of gl.h and glu.h are defined in windows.h.

The OpenGL library changes all the time. The various vendors that make graphics hardware add new features that may be too new to have been incorporated in gl.h. In order for you to take advantage of these new *extensions* to OpenGL, an additional header file is available, named glext.h. This header contains all of the latest version and extension functions and tokens and is available in the OpenGL Registry at the OpenGL Web site (`http://www.opengl.org/registry`). The Registry also contains the specifications for every OpenGL extension published. As with any header, you could include it with the following statement:

```
#include "glext.h"
```

You probably noticed the quotes around the filename, as compared to the normal angle brackets. Because glext.h is how graphics card vendors enable access to new extensions, you will probably need to download versions frequently from the Internet, so having a local copy to compile your program is not a bad idea. Additionally, you may not have permission to place the glext.h header file in a system header-file include directory (such as `/usr/include` on Unix-type systems).

If you are directly accessing a window interface library to support OpenGL, such as GLX, WGL, or CGL, you must include additional header files. For example, if you are calling GLX, you may need to add these lines to your code:

```
#include <X11/Xlib.h>
#include <GL/glx.h>
```

In Microsoft Windows, the WGL routines are made accessible with

```
#include <windows.h>
```

If you are using GLUT for managing your window manager tasks, you should include

```
#include <freeglut.h>
```

Note: The original GLUT header file was named glut.h. Both glut.h and freeglut.h guarantee that gl.h and glu.h are properly included for you, so including all three files is redundant. Additionally, these headers make sure that any internal operating system dependent macros are properly defined before including gl.h and glu.h. To make your GLUT programs portable, include glut.h or freeglut.h and do not explicitly include either gl.h or glu.h.

Most OpenGL applications also use standard C library system calls, so it is common to include header files that are not related to graphics, such as

```
#include <stdlib.h>
#include <stdio.h>
```

We don't include the header file declarations for our examples in this text, so our examples are less cluttered.

Header Files for OpenGL Version 3.1

As compared to OpenGL Version 3.0, which only added new functions and features to the sum of OpenGL's functionality, OpenGL Version 3.1 removed functions marked as deprecated. To make that transition easier for software authors, OpenGL Version 3.1 provides an entire new set of header files, and recommends a location for vendor to integrate them into the respective operating systems. You can still use the gl.h and glext.h files, which will continue to document all OpenGL entry points, regardless of version.

However, if you're porting code to be used only with Version 3.1, you might consider using the new OpenGL Version 3.1 headers:

```
#include <GL3/gl3.h>
#include <GL3/gl3ext.h>
```

They include functions and tokens for Version 3.1 (for future versions, the features set will be restricted to that particular version). You should find that these headers simplify the process of moving existing OpenGL code to newer versions. Like any OpenGL headers, these files are available for download from the OpenGL Registry (http://www.opengl.org/registry).

GLUT, the OpenGL Utility Toolkit

As you know, OpenGL contains rendering commands but is designed to be independent of any window system or operating system. Consequently, it contains no commands for opening windows or reading events from the keyboard or mouse. Unfortunately, it's impossible to write a complete graphics program without at least opening a window, and most interesting programs require a bit of user input or other services from the operating system or window system. In many cases, complete programs make the most interesting examples, so this book uses GLUT to simplify opening windows, detecting input, and so on. If you have implementations of OpenGL and GLUT on your system, the examples in this book should run without change when linked with your OpenGL and GLUT libraries.

In addition, since OpenGL drawing commands are limited to those that generate simple geometric primitives (points, lines, and polygons), GLUT includes several routines that create more complicated three-dimensional objects, such as a sphere, a torus, and a teapot. This way, snapshots of program output can be interesting to look at. (Note that the OpenGL Utility Library, GLU, also has quadrics routines that create some of the same three-dimensional objects as GLUT, such as a sphere, cylinder, or cone.)

GLUT may not be satisfactory for full-featured OpenGL applications, but you may find it a useful starting point for learning OpenGL. The rest of this section briefly describes a small subset of GLUT routines so that you can follow the programming examples in the rest of this book. (See Appendix A for more details GLUT).

Window Management

Several routines perform tasks necessary for initializing a window:

- **glutInit**(int *argc*, char **argv*) initializes GLUT and processes any command line arguments (for X, this would be options such as -display and -geometry). **glutInit()** should be called before any other GLUT routine.

- **glutInitDisplayMode**(unsigned int *mode*) specifies whether to use an *RGBA* or color-index color model. You can also specify whether you want a single- or double-buffered window. (If you're working in color-index mode, you'll want to load certain colors into the color map; use **glutSetColor()** to do this.) Finally, you can use this routine to indicate that you want the window to have an associated depth, stencil, multisampling, and/or accumulation buffer. For example, if you want a window with double buffering, the RGBA color model, and a depth buffer, you might call **glutInitDisplayMode(GLUT_DOUBLE | GLUT_RGBA | GLUT_DEPTH).**

- **glutInitWindowPosition**(int *x*, int *y*) specifies the screen location for the upper-left corner of your window.

- **glutInitWindowSize**(int *width*, int *height*) specifies the size, in pixels, of your window.

- **glutInitContextVersion**(int *majorVersion*, int *minorVersion*) specifies which version of OpenGL you want to use. (This is a new addition available only when using Freeglut, and was introduced with OpenGL

Version 3.0. See "OpenGL Contexts" on page 27 for more details on OpenGL contexts and versions.)

- **glutInitContextFlags**(int *flags*) specifes the type of OpenGL context you want to use. For normal OpenGL operation, you can omit this call from your program. However, if you want to use a forward-compatible OpenGL context, you will need to call this routine. (This is also a new addition available only in Freeglut, and was introduced with OpenGL Version 3.0. See "OpenGL Contexts" on page 27 for more details on the types of OpenGL contexts.)

- int **glutCreateWindow**(char **string*) creates a window with an OpenGL context. It returns a unique identifier for the new window. Be warned: until **glutMainLoop()** is called, the window is not yet displayed.

The Display Callback

glutDisplayFunc(void (**func*)(void)) is the first and most important event callback function you will see. Whenever GLUT determines that the contents of the window need to be redisplayed, the callback function registered by **glutDisplayFunc()** is executed. Therefore, you should put all the routines you need to redraw the scene in the display callback function.

If your program changes the contents of the window, sometimes you will have to call **glutPostRedisplay()**, which gives **glutMainLoop()** a nudge to call the registered display callback at its next opportunity.

Running the Program

The very last thing you must do is call **glutMainLoop()**. All windows that have been created are now shown, and rendering to those windows is now effective. Event processing begins, and the registered display callback is triggered. Once this loop is entered, it is never exited!

Example 1-2 shows how you might use GLUT to create the simple program shown in Example 1-1. Note the restructuring of the code. To maximize efficiency, operations that need to be called only once (setting the background color and coordinate system) are now in a procedure called **init()**. Operations to render (and possibly re-render) the scene are in the **display()** procedure, which is the registered GLUT display callback.

Example 1-2   Simple OpenGL Program Using GLUT: hello.c

```
void display(void)
{
/*   clear all pixels   */
    glClear(GL_COLOR_BUFFER_BIT);
```

```
/*  draw white polygon (rectangle) with corners at
 *  (0.25, 0.25, 0.0) and (0.75, 0.75, 0.0)
 */
    glColor3f(1.0, 1.0, 1.0);
    glBegin(GL_POLYGON);
        glVertex3f(0.25, 0.25, 0.0);
        glVertex3f(0.75, 0.25, 0.0);
        glVertex3f(0.75, 0.75, 0.0);
        glVertex3f(0.25, 0.75, 0.0);
    glEnd();

/*  don't wait!
 *  start processing buffered OpenGL routines
 */
    glFlush();
}

void init(void)
{
/*  select clearing (background) color        */
    glClearColor(0.0, 0.0, 0.0, 0.0);

/*  initialize viewing values  */
    glMatrixMode(GL_PROJECTION);
    glLoadIdentity();
    glOrtho(0.0, 1.0, 0.0, 1.0, -1.0, 1.0);
}

/*
 *  Declare initial window size, position, and display mode
 *  (single buffer and RGBA).  Open window with "hello"
 *  in its title bar.  Call initialization routines.
 *  Register callback function to display graphics.
 *  Enter main loop and process events.
 */
int main(int argc, char** argv)
{
    glutInit(&argc, argv);
    glutInitDisplayMode(GLUT_SINGLE | GLUT_RGB);
    glutInitWindowSize(250, 250);
    glutInitWindowPosition(100, 100);
    glutCreateWindow("hello");
    init();
    glutDisplayFunc(display);
    glutMainLoop();
    return 0;   /* ISO C requires main to return int. */
}
```

Handling Input Events

You can use the following routines to register callback commands that are invoked when specified events occur:

- **glutReshapeFunc**(void (*func)(int w, int h)) indicates what action should be taken when the window is resized.

- **glutKeyboardFunc**(void (*func)(unsigned char key, int x, int y)) and **glutMouseFunc**(void (*func)(int button, int state, int x, int y)) allow you to link a keyboard key or a mouse button with a routine that's invoked when the key or mouse button is pressed or released.

- **glutMotionFunc**(void (*func)(int x, int y)) registers a routine to call back when the mouse is moved while a mouse button is also pressed.

Managing a Background Process

You can specify a function that's to be executed if no other events are pending—for example, when the event loop would otherwise be idle—with **glutIdleFunc**(void (*func)(void)). This routine takes a pointer to the function as its only argument. Pass in NULL (zero) to disable the execution of the function.

Drawing Three-Dimensional Objects

GLUT includes several routines for drawing these three-dimensional objects:

cone	icosahedron	teapot
cube	octahedron	tetrahedron
dodecahedron	sphere	torus

You can draw these objects as wireframes or as solid shaded objects with surface normals defined. For example, the routines for a cube and a sphere are as follows:

void **glutWireCube**(GLdouble *size*);

void **glutSolidCube**(GLdouble *size*);

void **glutWireSphere**(GLdouble *radius*, GLint *slices*, GLint *stacks*);

void **glutSolidSphere**(GLdouble *radius*, GLint *slices*, GLint *stacks*);

All these models are drawn centered at the origin of the world coordinate system. (See Appendix A for information on the prototypes of all these drawing routines.)

Animation

One of the most exciting things you can do on a graphics computer is draw pictures that move. Whether you're an engineer trying to see all sides of a mechanical part you're designing, a pilot learning to fly an airplane using a simulation, or merely a computer-game aficionado, it's clear that *animation* is an important part of computer graphics.

In a movie theater, motion is achieved by taking a sequence of pictures and projecting them at 24 frames per second on the screen. Each frame is moved into position behind the lens, the shutter is opened, and the frame is displayed. The shutter is momentarily closed while the film is advanced to the next frame, then that frame is displayed, and so on. Although you're watching 24 different frames each second, your brain blends them all into a smooth animation. (The old Charlie Chaplin movies were shot at 16 frames per second and are noticeably jerky.) Computer-graphics screens typically refresh (redraw the picture) approximately 60 to 76 times per second, and some even run at about 120 refreshes per second. Clearly, 60 per second is smoother than 30, and 120 is perceptively better than 60. Refresh rates faster than 120, however, may approach a point of diminishing returns, depending on the limits of perception.

The key reason that motion picture projection works is that each frame is complete when it is displayed. Suppose you try to do computer animation of your million-frame movie with a program such as this:

```
open_window();
for (i = 0; i < 1000000; i++) {
   clear_the_window();
   draw_frame(i);
   wait_until_a_24th_of_a_second_is_over();
}
```

If you add the time it takes for your system to clear the screen and to draw a typical frame, this program gives increasingly poor results, depending on how close to 1/24 second it takes to clear and draw. Suppose the drawing takes nearly a full 1/24 second. Items drawn first are visible for the full 1/24 second and present a solid image on the screen; items drawn toward the end are instantly cleared as the program starts on the next frame. This presents at best a ghostlike image, as for most of the 1/24 second your eye is viewing the cleared background instead of the items that were unlucky enough to be drawn last. The problem is that this program doesn't display completely drawn frames; instead, you watch the drawing as it happens.

Most OpenGL implementations provide *double-buffering*—hardware or software that supplies two complete color buffers. One is displayed while the other is being drawn. When the drawing of a frame is complete, the two buffers are swapped, so the one that was being viewed is now used for drawing, and vice versa. This is like a movie projector with only two frames in a loop; while one is being projected on the screen, an artist is desperately erasing and redrawing the frame that's not visible. As long as the artist is quick enough, the viewer notices no difference between this setup and one in which all the frames are already drawn, and the projector is simply displaying them one after the other. With double-buffering, every frame is shown only when the drawing is complete; the viewer never sees a partially drawn frame.

A modified version that displays smoothly animated graphics using double-buffering might look like the following:

```
open_window_in_double_buffer_mode();
for (i = 0; i < 1000000; i++) {
   clear_the_window();
   draw_frame(i);
   swap_the_buffers();
}
```

The Refresh That Pauses

For some OpenGL implementations, in addition to simply swapping the viewable and drawable buffers, the **swap_the_buffers()** routine waits until the current screen refresh period is over so that the previous buffer is completely displayed. This routine also allows the new buffer to be completely displayed, starting from the beginning. Assuming that your system refreshes the display 60 times per second, this means that the fastest frame rate you can achieve is 60 frames per second (*fps*), and if all your frames can be cleared and drawn in under 1/60 second, your animation will run smoothly at that rate.

What often happens on such a system is that the frame is too complicated to draw in 1/60 second, so each frame is displayed more than once. If, for example, it takes 1/45 second to draw a frame, you get 30 fps, and the graphics are idle for 1/30 − 1/45 = 1/90 second per frame, or one-third of the time.

In addition, the video refresh rate is constant, which can have some unexpected performance consequences. For example, with the 1/60 second per refresh monitor and a constant frame rate, you can run at 60 fps, 30 fps, 20 fps, 15 fps, 12 fps, and so on (60/1, 60/2, 60/3, 60/4, 60/5,...). This means that if you're writing an application and gradually adding features (say it's a flight simulator, and you're adding ground scenery), at first each feature you add has no effect on the overall performance—you still get 60 fps. Then, all of a sudden, you add one new feature, and the system can't quite draw the whole thing in 1/60 of a second, so the animation slows from 60 fps to 30 fps because it misses the first possible buffer-swapping time. A similar thing happens when the drawing time per frame is more than 1/30 second—the animation drops from 30 to 20 fps.

If the scene's complexity is close to any of the magic times (1/60 second, 2/60 second, 3/60 second, and so on in this example), then, because of random variation, some frames go slightly over the time and some slightly under. Then the frame rate is irregular, which can be visually disturbing. In this case, if you can't simplify the scene so that all the frames are fast enough, it might be better to add an intentional, tiny delay to make sure they all miss, giving a constant, slower frame rate. If your frames have drastically different complexities, a more sophisticated approach might be necessary.

Motion = Redraw + Swap

The structure of real animation programs does not differ very much from this description. Usually, it is easier to redraw the entire buffer from scratch for each frame than to figure out which parts require redrawing. This is especially true with applications such as three-dimensional flight simulators, where a tiny change in the plane's orientation changes the position of everything outside the window.

In most animations, the objects in a scene are simply redrawn with different transformations—the *viewpoint* of the viewer moves, or a car moves down the road a bit, or an object is rotated slightly. If significant recomputation is required for nondrawing operations, the attainable frame rate often slows down. Keep in mind, however, that the idle time after the **swap_the_buffers()** routine can often be used for such calculations.

OpenGL doesn't have a **swap_the_buffers()** command because the feature might not be available on all hardware and, in any case, it's highly dependent on the window system. For example, if you are using the

X Window System and accessing it directly, you might use the following GLX routine:

```
void glXSwapBuffers(Display *dpy, Window window);
```

(See Appendix D for equivalent routines for other window systems.)

If you are using the GLUT library, you'll want to call this routine:

```
void glutSwapBuffers(void);
```

Example 1-3 illustrates the use of **glutSwapBuffers()** in drawing a spinning square, as shown in Figure 1-3. This example also shows how to use GLUT to control an input device and turn on and off an idle function. In this example, the mouse buttons toggle the spinning on and off.

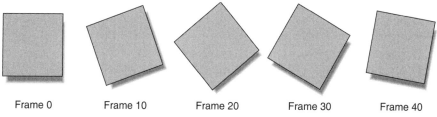

| Frame 0 | Frame 10 | Frame 20 | Frame 30 | Frame 40 |

Figure 1-3   Double-Buffered Rotating Square

Example 1-3   Double-Buffered Program: double.c

```
static GLfloat spin = 0.0;

void init(void)
{
    glClearColor(0.0, 0.0, 0.0, 0.0);
    glShadeModel(GL_FLAT);
}

void display(void)
{
    glClear(GL_COLOR_BUFFER_BIT);
    glPushMatrix();
    glRotatef(spin, 0.0, 0.0, 1.0);
    glColor3f(1.0, 1.0, 1.0);
    glRectf(-25.0, -25.0, 25.0, 25.0);
    glPopMatrix();
    glutSwapBuffers();
}
```

```
void spinDisplay(void)
{
   spin = spin + 2.0;
   if (spin > 360.0)
      spin = spin - 360.0;
   glutPostRedisplay();
}

void reshape(int w, int h)
{
   glViewport(0, 0, (GLsizei) w, (GLsizei) h);
   glMatrixMode(GL_PROJECTION);
   glLoadIdentity();
   glOrtho(-50.0, 50.0, -50.0, 50.0, -1.0, 1.0);
   glMatrixMode(GL_MODELVIEW);
   glLoadIdentity();
}

void mouse(int button, int state, int x, int y)
{
   switch (button) {
      case GLUT_LEFT_BUTTON:
         if (state == GLUT_DOWN)
            glutIdleFunc(spinDisplay);
         break;

      case GLUT_MIDDLE_BUTTON:
         if (state == GLUT_DOWN)
            glutIdleFunc(NULL);
         break;

      default:
         break;
   }
}

/*
 *  Request double buffer display mode.
 *  Register mouse input callback functions
 */
int main(int argc, char** argv)
{
   glutInit(&argc, argv);
   glutInitDisplayMode(GLUT_DOUBLE | GLUT_RGB);
   glutInitWindowSize(250, 250);
   glutInitWindowPosition(100, 100);
   glutCreateWindow(argv[0]);
   init();
```

```
    glutDisplayFunc(display);
    glutReshapeFunc(reshape);
    glutMouseFunc(mouse);
    glutMainLoop();
    return 0;
}
```

OpenGL and Its Deprecation Mechanism

Advanced

Advanced

As mentioned earlier, OpenGL is continuously undergoing improvement and refinement. New ways of doing graphics operations are developed, and entire new fields, such as *GPGPU* (short for "general-purpose computing on graphics processing units"), arise that lead to evolution in graphics hardware capabilities. New extensions to OpenGL are suggested by vendors, and eventually some of those extensions are incorporated as part of a new core revision of OpenGL. Over the years, this development process has allowed numerous redundant methods for accomplishing the same activity to appear in the API. In many cases, while the functionality was similar, the methods' application performance generally was not, giving the impression that aspects of the OpenGL API were slow and didn't work well on modern hardware. With OpenGL Version 3.0, the Khronos OpenGL ARB Working Group specified a *depreciation model* that indicated how features could be removed from the API. However, this change required more than just changes to the core OpenGL API—it also affected how OpenGL contexts were created, and the types of contexts available.

OpenGL Contexts

An OpenGL *context* is the data structure where OpenGL stores state information to be used when you're rendering images. It includes things like textures, server-side buffer objects, function entry points, blending states, and compiled shader objects—in short, all the things discussed in the chapters that follow. In versions of OpenGL prior to Version 3.0, there was a single type of OpenGL context—the *full context*; it contained everything available in that implementation of OpenGL, and there was only one way to create a context (which is window-system dependent).

With Version 3.0, a new type of context was created—the *forward-compatible context*—which hides the features marked for future removal from the

OpenGL API to help application developers modify their applications to accommodate future versions of OpenGL.

Profiles

In addition to the various types of contexts added to Version 3.0, the concept of *profiles* was introduced. A profile is subset of OpenGL functionality specific to an application domain, such as gaming, computer-aided design (CAD), or programs written for embedded platforms.

Currently, only a single profile is defined, which exposes the entire set of functionality supported in the created OpenGL context. New types of profiles may be introduced in future versions of OpenGL.

Each window system has its own set of functions for incorporating OpenGL into its operation (e.g., WGL for Microsoft Windows), which is what really creates the type of OpenGL context you request (also based on the profile). As such, while the procedure is basically the same, the function calls used are window-system specific. Fortunately, GLUT hides the details of this operation. At some point, you may need to know the details. We defer that conversation to Appendix D where you can find information about the routines specific to your windowing system.

Specifying OpenGL Context Versions with GLUT

The GLUT library automatically takes care of creating an OpenGL context when **glutCreateWindow()** is called. Be default, the requested OpenGL context will be compatible with OpenGL Version 2.1. To allocate a context for OpenGL Version 3.0 and later, you'll need to call **glutInitContextVersion()**. Likewise, if you want to use a forward-compatible context for porting, you will also need to specify that context attribute by calling **glutInitContextFlags()**. Both of these concepts are demonstrated in Example 1-4. These functions are described in more detail in Appendix A, "Basics of GLUT: The OpenGL Utility Toolkit."

Example 1-4   Creating an OpenGL Version 3.0 Context Using GLUT

```
glutInit(&argc, argv);
glutInitDisplayMode(GLUT_RGBA | GLUT_DEPTH | GLUT_DOUBLE);
glutInitWindowSize(width, height);
glutInitWindowPosition(xPos, yPos);
glutInitContextVersion(3, 0);
glutInitContextFlags(GLUT_FORWARD_COMPATIBLE);
glutCreateWindow(argv[0]);
```

Accessing OpenGL Functions

Depending on the operating system on which you're developing your applications, you may need to do some additional work to access certain OpenGL functions. You'll know when this need arises because your compiler will report that various functions are undefined (of course, every compiler will report this error differently, but that's crux of the matter). In these situations, you'll need to retrieve the function's address (into a function pointer). There are various ways to accomplish this:

- If your application uses the native windowing system for opening windows and event processing, then use the appropriate ***GetProcAddress**() function for the operating system your application will be using. Examples of these functions include **wglGetProcAddress**() and **glXGetProcAddress**().

- If you are using GLUT, then use GLUT's function pointer retrieval routine, **glutGetProcAddress**().

- Use the open-source project GLEW (short for "OpenGL Extension Wrangler"). GLEW defines every OpenGL function, retrieving function pointers and verifying extensions automatically for you. Go to `http://glew.sourceforge.net/` to find more details and to obtain the code or binaries.

While we don't explicitly show any of these options in the programs included in the text, we use GLEW to simplify the process for us.

Chapter 2

State Management and Drawing Geometric Objects

Chapter Objectives

After reading this chapter, you'll be able to do the following:

- Clear the window to an arbitrary color

- Force any pending drawing to complete

- Draw with any geometric primitive—point, line, or polygon—in two or three dimensions

- Turn states on and off and query state variables

- Control the display of geometric primitives—for example, draw dashed lines or outlined polygons

- Specify *normal vectors* at appropriate points on the surfaces of solid objects

- Use *vertex arrays* and *buffer objects* to store and access geometric data with fewer function calls

- Save and restore several state variables at once

Although you can draw complex and interesting pictures using OpenGL, they're all constructed from a small number of primitive graphical items. This shouldn't be too surprising—look at what Leonardo da Vinci accomplished with just pencils and paintbrushes.

At the highest level of abstraction, there are three basic drawing operations: clearing the window, drawing a geometric object, and drawing a raster object. Raster objects, which include such things as two-dimensional images, bitmaps, and character fonts, are covered in Chapter 8. In this chapter, you learn how to clear the screen and draw geometric objects, including points, straight lines, and flat polygons.

You might think to yourself, "Wait a minute. I've seen lots of computer graphics in movies and on television, and there are plenty of beautifully shaded curved lines and surfaces. How are those drawn if OpenGL can draw only straight lines and flat polygons?" Even the image on the cover of this book includes a round table and objects on the table that have curved surfaces. It turns out that all the curved lines and surfaces you've seen are approximated by large numbers of little flat polygons or straight lines, in much the same way that the globe on the cover is constructed from a large set of rectangular blocks. The globe doesn't appear to have a smooth surface because the blocks are relatively large compared with the globe. Later in this chapter, we show you how to construct curved lines and surfaces from lots of small geometric primitives.

This chapter has the following major sections:

- "A Drawing Survival Kit" explains how to clear the window and force drawing to be completed. It also gives you basic information about controlling the colors of geometric objects and describing a coordinate system.

- "Describing Points, Lines, and Polygons" shows you the set of primitive geometric objects and how to draw them.

- "Basic State Management" describes how to turn on and off some states (modes) and query state variables.

- "Displaying Points, Lines, and Polygons" explains what control you have over the details of how primitives are drawn—for example, what diameters points have, whether lines are solid or dashed, and whether polygons are outlined or filled.

- "Normal Vectors" discusses how to specify normal vectors for geometric objects and (briefly) what these vectors are for.

- "Vertex Arrays" shows you how to put large amounts of geometric data into just a few arrays and how, with only a few function calls, to render the geometry it describes. Reducing function calls may increase the efficiency and performance of rendering.

- "Buffer Objects" details how to use server-side memory buffers to store vertex array data for more efficient geometric rendering.

- "Vertex-Array Objects" expands the discussions of vertex arrays and buffer objects by describing how to efficiently change among sets of vertex arrays.

- "Attribute Groups" reveals how to query the current value of state variables and how to save and restore several related state values all at once.

- "Some Hints for Building Polygonal Models of Surfaces" explores the issues and techniques involved in constructing polygonal approximations to surfaces.

One thing to keep in mind as you read the rest of this chapter is that with OpenGL, unless you specify otherwise, every time you issue a drawing command, the specified object is drawn. This might seem obvious, but in some systems, you first make a list of things to draw. When your list is complete, you tell the graphics hardware to draw the items in the list. The first style is called *immediate-mode* graphics and is the default OpenGL style. In addition to using immediate mode, you can choose to save some commands in a list (called a *display list*) for later drawing. Immediate-mode graphics are typically easier to program, but display lists are often more efficient. Chapter 7 tells you how to use display lists and why you might want to use them.

Version 1.1 of OpenGL introduced vertex arrays.

In Version 1.2, scaling of surface normals (GL_RESCALE_NORMAL) was added to OpenGL. Also, **glDrawRangeElements()** supplemented vertex arrays.

Version 1.3 marked the initial support for texture coordinates for multiple texture units in the OpenGL core feature set. Previously, multitexturing had been an optional OpenGL extension.

In Version 1.4, fog coordinates and secondary colors may be stored in vertex arrays, and the commands **glMultiDrawArrays()** and **glMultiDrawElements()** may be used to render primitives from vertex arrays.

In Version 1.5, vertex arrays may be stored in buffer objects that may be able to use server memory for storing arrays and potentially accelerating their rendering.

Version 3.0 added support for vertex array objects, allowing all of the state related to vertex arrays to be bundled and activated with a single call. This, in turn, makes switching between sets of vertex arrays simpler and faster.

Version 3.1 removed most of the immediate-mode routines and added the primitive restart index, which allows you to render multiple primitives (of the same type) with a single drawing call.

A Drawing Survival Kit

This section explains how to clear the window in preparation for drawing, set the colors of objects that are to be drawn, and force drawing to be completed. None of these subjects has anything to do with geometric objects in a direct way, but any program that draws geometric objects has to deal with these issues.

Clearing the Window

Drawing on a computer screen is different from drawing on paper in that the paper starts out white, and all you have to do is draw the picture. On a computer, the memory holding the picture is usually filled with the last picture you drew, so you typically need to clear it to some background color before you start to draw the new scene. The color you use for the background depends on the application. For a word processor, you might clear to white (the color of the paper) before you begin to draw the text. If you're drawing a view from a spaceship, you clear to the black of space before beginning to draw the stars, planets, and alien spaceships. Sometimes you might not need to clear the screen at all; for example, if the image is the inside of a room, the entire graphics window is covered as you draw all the walls.

At this point, you might be wondering why we keep talking about *clearing* the window—why not just draw a rectangle of the appropriate color that's large enough to cover the entire window? First, a special command to clear a window can be much more efficient than a general-purpose drawing command. In addition, as you'll see in Chapter 3, OpenGL allows you to set the coordinate system, viewing position, and viewing direction arbitrarily, so it might be difficult to figure out an appropriate size and location for a window-clearing rectangle. Finally, on many machines, the graphics hardware consists of multiple buffers in addition to the buffer containing colors of the pixels that are displayed. These other buffers must be cleared from time to time, and it's convenient to have a single command that can clear any combination of them. (See Chapter 10 for a discussion of all the possible buffers.)

You must also know how the colors of pixels are stored in the graphics hardware known as *bitplanes*. There are two methods of storage. Either the red, green, blue, and alpha (RGBA) values of a pixel can be directly stored in the bitplanes, or a single index value that references a color lookup table is stored. RGBA color-display mode is more commonly used, so most of the examples in this book use it. (See Chapter 4 for more information about both display modes.) You can safely ignore all references to alpha values until Chapter 6.

As an example, these lines of code clear an RGBA mode window to black:

```
glClearColor(0.0, 0.0, 0.0, 0.0);
glClear(GL_COLOR_BUFFER_BIT);
```

The first line sets the clearing color to black, and the next command clears the entire window to the current clearing color. The single parameter to **glClear()** indicates which buffers are to be cleared. In this case, the program clears only the color buffer, where the image displayed on the screen is kept. Typically, you set the clearing color once, early in your application, and then you clear the buffers as often as necessary. OpenGL keeps track of the current clearing color as a state variable, rather than requiring you to specify it each time a buffer is cleared.

Chapter 4 and Chapter 10 discuss how other buffers are used. For now, all you need to know is that clearing them is simple. For example, to clear both the color buffer and the depth buffer, you would use the following sequence of commands:

```
glClearColor(0.0, 0.0, 0.0, 0.0);
glClearDepth(1.0);
glClear(GL_COLOR_BUFFER_BIT | GL_DEPTH_BUFFER_BIT);
```

In this case, the call to **glClearColor()** is the same as before, the **glClearDepth()** command specifies the value to which every pixel of the depth buffer is to be set, and the parameter to the **glClear()** command now consists of the bitwise logical OR of all the buffers to be cleared. The following summary of **glClear()** includes a table that lists the buffers that can be cleared, their names, and the chapter in which each type of buffer is discussed.

void **glClearColor**(GLclampf *red*, GLclampf *green*, GLclampf *blue*, GLclampf *alpha*);		

Sets the current clearing color for use in clearing color buffers in RGBA mode. (See Chapter 4 for more information on RGBA mode.) The *red*, *green*, *blue*, and *alpha* values are clamped if necessary to the range [0, 1]. The default clearing color is (0, 0, 0, 0), which is black.

void **glClear**(GLbitfield *mask*);	

Clears the specified buffers to their current clearing values. The *mask* argument is a bitwise logical OR combination of the values listed in Table 2-1.

Buffer	Name	Reference
Color buffer	GL_COLOR_BUFFER_BIT	Chapter 4
Depth buffer	GL_DEPTH_BUFFER_BIT	Chapter 10
Accumulation buffer	GL_ACCUM_BUFFER_BIT	Chapter 10
Stencil buffer	GL_STENCIL_BUFFER_BIT	Chapter 10

Compatibility
Extension

**GL_ACCUM_
BUFFER_BIT**

Table 2-1   Clearing Buffers

Before issuing a command to clear multiple buffers, you have to set the values to which each buffer is to be cleared if you want something other than the default RGBA color, depth value, accumulation color, and stencil index. In addition to the **glClearColor()** and **glClearDepth()** commands that set the current values for clearing the color and depth buffers, **glClearIndex()**, **glClearAccum()**, and **glClearStencil()** specify the *color index*, accumulation color, and stencil index used to clear the corresponding buffers. (See Chapter 4 and Chapter 10 for descriptions of these buffers and their uses.)

OpenGL allows you to specify multiple buffers because clearing is generally a slow operation, as every pixel in the window (possibly millions) is touched, and some graphics hardware allows sets of buffers to be cleared simultaneously. Hardware that doesn't support simultaneous clears performs them sequentially. The difference between

```
glClear(GL_COLOR_BUFFER_BIT | GL_DEPTH_BUFFER_BIT);
```

and

```
glClear(GL_COLOR_BUFFER_BIT);
glClear(GL_DEPTH_BUFFER_BIT);
```

is that although both have the same final effect, the first example might run faster on many machines. It certainly won't run more slowly.

Specifying a Color

With OpenGL, the description of the shape of an object being drawn is independent of the description of its color. Whenever a particular geometric object is drawn, it's drawn using the currently specified coloring scheme. The coloring scheme might be as simple as "draw everything in fire-engine red" or as complicated as "assume the object is made out of blue plastic, that there's a yellow spotlight pointed in such and such a direction, and that there's a general low-level reddish-brown light everywhere else." In general, an OpenGL programmer first sets the color or coloring scheme and then draws the objects. Until the color or coloring scheme is changed, all objects are drawn in that color or using that coloring scheme. This method helps OpenGL achieve higher drawing performance than would result if it didn't keep track of the current color.

For example, the pseudocode

```
set_current_color(red);
draw_object(A);
draw_object(B);
set_current_color(green);
set_current_color(blue);
draw_object(C);
```

draws objects A and B in red, and object C in blue. The command on the fourth line that sets the current color to green is wasted.

Coloring, lighting, and shading are all large topics with entire chapters or large sections devoted to them. To draw geometric primitives that can be seen, however, you need some basic knowledge of how to set the current color; this information is provided in the next few paragraphs. (See Chapter 4 and Chapter 5 for details on these topics.)

To set a color, use the command **glColor3f()**. It takes three parameters, all of which are floating-point numbers between 0.0 and 1.0. The parameters are, in order, the red, green, and blue *components* of the color. You can think of these three values as specifying a "mix" of colors: 0.0 means don't use any of that component, and 1.0 means use all you can of that component. Thus, the code

```
glColor3f(1.0, 0.0, 0.0);
```

makes the brightest red the system can draw, with no green or blue components. All zeros makes black; in contrast, all ones makes white. Setting all three components to 0.5 yields gray (halfway between black and white). Here are eight commands and the colors they would set:

```
glColor3f(0.0, 0.0, 0.0);       /* black */
glColor3f(1.0, 0.0, 0.0);       /* red */
glColor3f(0.0, 1.0, 0.0);       /* green */
glColor3f(1.0, 1.0, 0.0);       /* yellow */
glColor3f(0.0, 0.0, 1.0);       /* blue */
glColor3f(1.0, 0.0, 1.0);       /* magenta */
glColor3f(0.0, 1.0, 1.0);       /* cyan */
glColor3f(1.0, 1.0, 1.0);       /* white */
```

You might have noticed earlier that the routine for setting the clearing color, **glClearColor()**, takes four parameters, the first three of which match the parameters for **glColor3f()**. The fourth parameter is the alpha value; it's covered in detail in "Blending" in Chapter 6. For now, set the fourth parameter of **glClearColor()** to 0.0, which is its default value.

Forcing Completion of Drawing

As you saw in "OpenGL Rendering Pipeline" in Chapter 1, most modern graphics systems can be thought of as an assembly line. The main central processing unit (CPU) issues a drawing command. Perhaps other hardware does geometric transformations. Clipping is performed, followed by shading and/or texturing. Finally, the values are written into the bitplanes for display. In high-end architectures, each of these operations is performed by a different piece of hardware that's been designed to perform its particular task quickly. In such an architecture, there's no need for the CPU to wait for each drawing command to complete before issuing the next one. While the CPU is sending a vertex down the pipeline, the transformation hardware is working on transforming the last one sent, the one before that is being clipped, and so on. In such a system, if the CPU waited for each command to complete before issuing the next, there could be a huge performance penalty.

In addition, the application might be running on more than one machine. For example, suppose that the main program is running elsewhere (on a machine called the client) and that you're viewing the results of the drawing on your workstation or terminal (the server), which is connected by a network to the client. In that case, it might be horribly inefficient to send each command over the network one at a time, as considerable overhead is often associated with each network transmission. Usually, the client gathers a collection of commands into a single network packet before sending it. Unfortunately, the network code on the client typically has no way of knowing that the graphics program is finished drawing a frame or scene. In the worst case, it waits forever for enough additional drawing commands to fill a packet, and you never see the completed drawing.

For this reason, OpenGL provides the command **glFlush()**, which forces the client to send the network packet even though it might not be full. Where there is no network and all commands are truly executed immediately on the server, **glFlush()** might have no effect. However, if you're writing a program that you want to work properly both with and without a network, include a call to **glFlush()** at the end of each frame or scene. Note that **glFlush()** doesn't wait for the drawing to complete—it just forces the drawing to begin execution, thereby guaranteeing that all previous commands *execute* in finite time even if no further rendering commands are executed.

There are other situations in which **glFlush()** is useful:

- Software renderers that build images in system memory and don't want to constantly update the screen.

- Implementations that gather sets of rendering commands to amortize start-up costs. The aforementioned network transmission example is one instance of this.

---

void **glFlush**(void);

Forces previously issued OpenGL commands to begin execution, thus guaranteeing that they complete in finite time.

A few commands—for example, commands that swap buffers in double-buffer mode—automatically flush pending commands onto the network before they can occur.

If **glFlush()** isn't sufficient for you, try **glFinish()**. This command flushes the network as **glFlush()** does and then waits for notification from the graphics hardware or network indicating that the drawing is complete in the framebuffer. You might need to use **glFinish()** if you want to synchronize tasks—for example, to make sure that your three-dimensional rendering is on the screen before you use Display PostScript to draw labels on top of the rendering. Another example would be to ensure that the drawing is complete before it begins to accept user input. After you issue a **glFinish()** command, your graphics process is blocked until it receives notification from the graphics hardware that the drawing is complete. Keep in mind that excessive use of **glFinish()** can reduce the performance of your application, especially if you're running over a network, because it requires round-trip communication. If **glFlush()** is sufficient for your needs, use it instead of **glFinish()**.

---

void **glFinish**(void);

Forces all previously issued OpenGL commands to complete. This command doesn't return until all effects from previous commands are fully realized.

Coordinate System Survival Kit

Whenever you initially open a window or later move or resize that window, the window system will send an event to notify you. If you are using GLUT, the notification is automated; whatever routine has been registered to **glutReshapeFunc()** will be called. You must register a callback function that will

- Reestablish the rectangular region that will be the new rendering canvas

- Define the coordinate system to which objects will be drawn

In Chapter 3, you'll see how to define three-dimensional coordinate systems, but right now just create a simple, basic two-dimensional coordinate system into which you can draw a few objects. Call **glutReshapeFunc(reshape)**, where **reshape()** is the following function shown in Example 2-1.

Example 2-1   Reshape Callback Function

```
void reshape(int w, int h)
{
   glViewport(0, 0, (GLsizei) w, (GLsizei) h);
   glMatrixMode(GL_PROJECTION);
   glLoadIdentity();
   gluOrtho2D(0.0, (GLdouble) w, 0.0, (GLdouble) h);
}
```

The kernel of GLUT will pass this function two arguments: the width and height, in pixels, of the new, moved, or resized window. **glViewport()** adjusts the pixel rectangle for drawing to be the entire new window. The next three routines adjust the coordinate system for drawing so that the lower left corner is (0, 0) and the upper right corner is (w, h) (see Figure 2-1).

To explain it another way, think about a piece of graphing paper. The w and h values in **reshape()** represent how many columns and rows of squares are on your graph paper. Then you have to put axes on the graph paper. The **gluOrtho2D()** routine puts the origin, (0, 0), in the lowest, leftmost square, and makes each square represent one unit. Now, when you render the points, lines, and polygons in the rest of this chapter, they will appear on this paper in easily predictable squares. (For now, keep all your objects two-dimensional.)

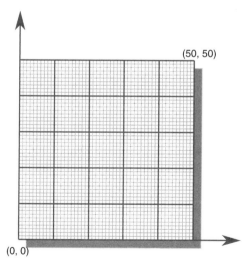

(50, 50)

(0, 0)

Figure 2-1   Coordinate System Defined by w = 50, h = 50

Describing Points, Lines, and Polygons

This section explains how to describe OpenGL geometric primitives. All geometric primitives are eventually described in terms of their *vertices*—coordinates that define the points themselves, the endpoints of line segments, or the corners of polygons. The next section discusses how these primitives are displayed and what control you have over their display.

What Are Points, Lines, and Polygons?

You probably have a fairly good idea of what a mathematician means by the terms *point*, *line*, and *polygon*. The OpenGL meanings are similar, but not quite the same.

One difference comes from the limitations of computer-based calculations. In any OpenGL implementation, floating-point calculations are of finite precision, and they have round-off errors. Consequently, the coordinates of OpenGL points, lines, and polygons suffer from the same problems.

A more important difference arises from the limitations of a raster graphics display. On such a display, the smallest displayable unit is a pixel, and although pixels might be less than 1/100 of an inch wide, they are still much larger than the mathematician's concepts of infinitely small (for points) and infinitely thin (for lines). When OpenGL performs calculations, it assumes that points are represented as vectors of floating-point numbers. However, a point is typically (but not always) drawn as a single pixel, and many different points with slightly different coordinates could be drawn by OpenGL on the same pixel.

Points

A point is represented by a set of floating-point numbers called a *vertex*. All internal calculations are done as if vertices are three-dimensional. Vertices specified by the user as two-dimensional (that is, with only *x*- and *y*-coordinates) are assigned a *z*-coordinate equal to zero by OpenGL.

Advanced

OpenGL works in the *homogeneous coordinates* of three-dimensional projective geometry, so for internal calculations, all vertices are represented with four floating-point coordinates (x, y, z, w). If w is different from zero, these coordinates correspond to the Euclidean, three-dimensional point (x/w, y/w, z/w). You can specify the w-coordinate in OpenGL commands, but this is rarely done. If the *w*-coordinate isn't specified, it is understood to be 1.0. (See Appendix C for more information about homogeneous coordinate systems.)

Lines

In OpenGL, the term *line* refers to a *line segment*, not the mathematician's version that extends to infinity in both directions. There are easy ways to specify a connected series of line segments, or even a closed, connected series of segments (see Figure 2-2). In all cases, though, the lines constituting the connected series are specified in terms of the vertices at their endpoints.

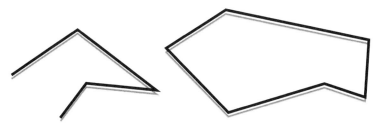

Figure 2-2   Two Connected Series of Line Segments

Polygons

Polygons are the areas enclosed by single closed loops of line segments, where the line segments are specified by the vertices at their endpoints. Polygons are typically drawn with the pixels in the interior filled in, but you can also draw them as outlines or a set of points. (See "Polygon Details" on page 60.)

In general, polygons can be complicated, so OpenGL imposes some strong restrictions on what constitutes a primitive polygon. First, the edges of OpenGL polygons can't intersect (a mathematician would call a polygon satisfying this condition a *simple polygon*). Second, OpenGL polygons must be *convex*, meaning that they cannot have indentations. Stated precisely, a region is convex if, given any two points in the interior, the line segment joining them is also in the interior. See Figure 2-3 for some examples of valid and invalid polygons. OpenGL, however, doesn't restrict the number of line segments making up the boundary of a convex polygon. Note that polygons with holes can't be described. They are *nonconvex*, and they can't be drawn with a boundary made up of a single closed loop. Be aware that if you present OpenGL with a nonconvex filled polygon, it might not draw it as you expect. For instance, on most systems, no more than the *convex hull* of the polygon would be filled. On some systems, less than the convex hull might be filled.

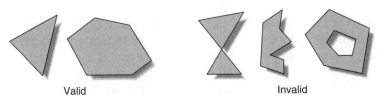

Valid   Invalid

Figure 2-3   Valid and Invalid Polygons

The reason for the OpenGL restrictions on valid polygon types is that it's simpler to provide fast polygon-rendering hardware for that restricted class of polygons. Simple polygons can be rendered quickly. The difficult cases are hard to detect quickly, so for maximum performance, OpenGL crosses its fingers and assumes the polygons are simple.

Many real-world surfaces consist of nonsimple polygons, nonconvex polygons, or polygons with holes. Since all such polygons can be formed from unions of simple convex polygons, some routines to build more complex objects are provided in the GLU library. These routines take complex descriptions and tessellate them, or break them down into groups of the simpler OpenGL polygons that can then be rendered. (See "Polygon Tessellation" in Chapter 11 for more information about the *tessellation* routines.)

Since OpenGL vertices are always three-dimensional, the points forming the boundary of a particular polygon don't necessarily lie on the same plane in space. (Of course, they do in many cases—if all the z-coordinates are zero, for example, or if the polygon is a *triangle*.) If a polygon's vertices don't lie in the same plane, then after various rotations in space, changes in the viewpoint, and projection onto the display screen, the points might no longer form a simple convex polygon. For example, imagine a four-point *quadrilateral* where the points are slightly out of plane, and look at it almost edge-on. You can get a nonsimple polygon that resembles a bow tie, as shown in Figure 2-4, which isn't guaranteed to be rendered correctly. This situation isn't all that unusual if you approximate curved surfaces by quadrilaterals made of points lying on the true surface. You can always avoid the problem by using triangles, as any three points always lie on a plane.

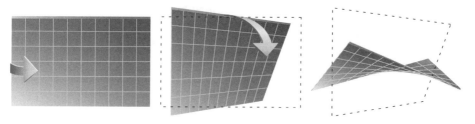

Figure 2-4   Nonplanar Polygon Transformed to Nonsimple Polygon

Rectangles

Since rectangles are so common in graphics applications, OpenGL provides a filled-rectangle drawing primitive, **glRect*()**. You can draw a rectangle as a polygon, as described in "OpenGL Geometric Drawing Primitives" on page 47, but your particular implementation of OpenGL might have optimized **glRect*()** for rectangles.

void **glRect**{sifd}(*TYPE x1, TYPE y1, TYPE x2, TYPE y2*);
void **glRect**{sifd}**v**(const *TYPE *v1*, const *TYPE *v2*);

Draws the rectangle defined by the corner points (*x1, y1*) and (*x2, y2*). The rectangle lies in the plane $z = 0$ and has sides parallel to the *x*- and *y*-axes. If the vector form of the function is used, the corners are given by two pointers to arrays, each of which contains an (*x, y*) pair.

Note that although the rectangle begins with a particular orientation in three-dimensional space (in the *xy*-plane and parallel to the axes), you can change this by applying rotations or other transformations. (See Chapter 3 for information about how to do this.)

Curves and Curved Surfaces

Any smoothly curved line or surface can be approximated—to any arbitrary degree of accuracy—by short line segments or small polygonal regions. Thus, subdividing curved lines and surfaces sufficiently and then approximating them with straight line segments or flat polygons makes them appear curved (see Figure 2-5). If you're skeptical that this really works, imagine subdividing until each line segment or polygon is so tiny that it's smaller than a pixel on the screen.

Figure 2-5   Approximating Curves

Even though curves aren't geometric primitives, OpenGL provides some direct support for subdividing and drawing them. (See Chapter 12 for information about how to draw curves and curved surfaces.)

Specifying Vertices

With OpenGL, every geometric object is ultimately described as an ordered set of vertices. You use the **glVertex*()** command to specify a vertex.

void **glVertex**[234]{sifd}(*TYPE coords*);
void **glVertex**[234]{sifd}v(const *TYPE* coords*);

Specifies a vertex for use in describing a geometric object. You can supply up to four coordinates (*x, y, z, w*) for a particular vertex or as few as two (*x, y*) by selecting the appropriate version of the command. If you use a version that doesn't explicitly specify *z* or *w*, *z* is understood to be 0, and *w* is understood to be 1. Calls to **glVertex*()** are effective only between a **glBegin()** and **glEnd()** pair.

Example 2-2 provides some examples of using **glVertex*()**.

Example 2-2   Legal Uses of glVertex*()

```
glVertex2s(2, 3);
glVertex3d(0.0, 0.0, 3.1415926535898);
glVertex4f(2.3, 1.0, -2.2, 2.0);

GLdouble dvect[3] = {5.0, 9.0, 1992.0};
glVertex3dv(dvect);
```

The first example represents a vertex with three-dimensional coordinates (2, 3, 0). (Remember that if it isn't specified, the *z*-coordinate is understood to be 0.) The coordinates in the second example are (0.0, 0.0,

3.1415926535898) (double-precision floating-point numbers). The third example represents the vertex with three-dimensional coordinates (1.15, 0.5, −1.1) as a homogenous coordinate. (Remember that the *x*-, *y*-, and *z*-coordinates are eventually divided by the *w*-coordinate.) In the final example, *dvect* is a pointer to an array of three double-precision floating-point numbers.

On some machines, the vector form of **glVertex*()** is more efficient, since only a single parameter needs to be passed to the graphics subsystem. Special hardware might be able to send a whole series of coordinates in a single batch. If your machine is like this, it's to your advantage to arrange your data so that the vertex coordinates are packed sequentially in memory. In this case, there may be some gain in performance by using the vertex array operations of OpenGL. (See "Vertex Arrays" on page 70.)

OpenGL Geometric Drawing Primitives

Now that you've seen how to specify vertices, you still need to know how to tell OpenGL to create a set of points, a line, or a polygon from those vertices. To do this, you bracket each set of vertices between a call to **glBegin()** and a call to **glEnd()**. The argument passed to **glBegin()** determines what sort of geometric primitive is constructed from the vertices. For instance, Example 2-3 specifies the vertices for the polygon shown in Figure 2-6.

Example 2-3 Filled Polygon

```
glBegin(GL_POLYGON);
    glVertex2f(0.0, 0.0);
    glVertex2f(0.0, 3.0);
    glVertex2f(4.0, 3.0);
    glVertex2f(6.0, 1.5);
    glVertex2f(4.0, 0.0);
glEnd();
```

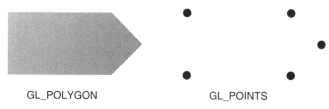

GL_POLYGON   GL_POINTS

Figure 2-6   Drawing a Polygon or a Set of Points

If you had used GL_POINTS instead of GL_POLYGON, the primitive would have been simply the five points shown in Figure 2-6. Table 2-2 in the following function summary for **glBegin()** lists the 10 possible arguments and the corresponding types of primitives.

void **glBegin**(GLenum *mode*);

Marks the beginning of a vertex-data list that describes a geometric primitive. The type of primitive is indicated by *mode*, which can be any of the values shown in Table 2-2.

Value	Meaning
GL_POINTS	Individual points
GL_LINES	Pairs of vertices interpreted as individual line segments
GL_LINE_STRIP	Series of connected line segments
GL_LINE_LOOP	Same as above, with a segment added between last and first vertices
GL_TRIANGLES	Triples of vertices interpreted as triangles
GL_TRIANGLE_STRIP	Linked strip of triangles
GL_TRIANGLE_FAN	Linked fan of triangles
GL_QUADS	Quadruples of vertices interpreted as four-sided polygons
GL_QUAD_STRIP	Linked strip of quadrilaterals
GL_POLYGON	Boundary of a simple, convex polygon

Table 2-2   Geometric Primitive Names and Meanings

void **glEnd**(void);

Marks the end of a vertex-data list.

Figure 2-7 shows examples of all the geometric primitives listed in Table 2-2, with descriptions of the pixels that are drawn for each of the objects. Note that in addition to points, several types of lines and polygons are defined. Obviously, you can find many ways to draw the same primitive. The method you choose depends on your vertex data.

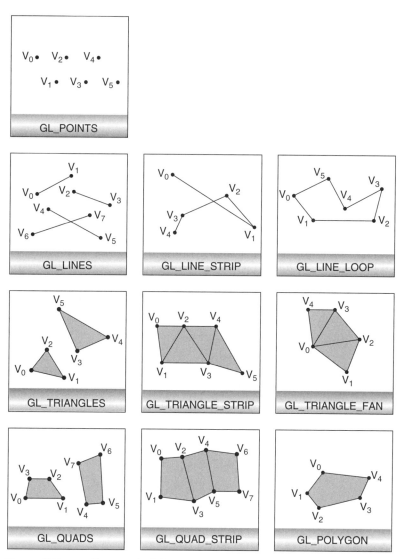

Figure 2-7   Geometric Primitive Types

As you read the following descriptions, assume that n vertices (v_0, v_1, v_2, ... , v_{n-1}) are described between a **glBegin()** and **glEnd()** pair.

GL_POINTS	Draws a point at each of the n vertices.
GL_LINES	Draws a series of unconnected line segments. Segments are drawn between v_0 and v_1, between v_2 and v_3, and so on. If n is odd, the last segment is drawn between v_{n-3} and v_{n-2}, and v_{n-1} is ignored.
GL_LINE_STRIP	Draws a line segment from v_0 to v_1, then from v_1 to v_2, and so on, finally drawing the segment from v_{n-2} to v_{n-1}. Thus, a total of $n-1$ line segments are drawn. Nothing is drawn unless n is larger than 1. There are no restrictions on the vertices describing a line strip (or a line loop); the lines can intersect arbitrarily.
GL_LINE_LOOP	Same as GL_LINE_STRIP, except that a final line segment is drawn from v_{n-1} to v_0, completing a loop.
GL_TRIANGLES	Draws a series of triangles (three-sided polygons) using vertices v_0, v_1, v_2, then v_3, v_4, v_5, and so on. If n isn't a multiple of 3, the final one or two vertices are ignored.
GL_TRIANGLE_STRIP	Draws a series of triangles (three-sided polygons) using vertices v_0, v_1, v_2, then v_2, v_1, v_3 (note the order), then v_2, v_3, v_4, and so on. The ordering is to ensure that the triangles are all drawn with the same orientation so that the strip can correctly form part of a surface. Preserving the orientation is important for some operations, such as culling (see "Reversing and Culling Polygon Faces" on page 61). n must be at least 3 for anything to be drawn.
GL_TRIANGLE_FAN	Same as GL_TRIANGLE_STRIP, except that the vertices are v_0, v_1, v_2, then v_0, v_2, v_3, then v_0, v_3, v_4, and so on (see Figure 2-7).

GL_QUADS	Draws a series of quadrilaterals (four-sided polygons) using vertices v_0, v_1, v_2, v_3, then v_4, v_5, v_6, v_7, and so on. If n isn't a multiple of 4, the final one, two, or three vertices are ignored.
GL_QUAD_STRIP	Draws a series of quadrilaterals (four-sided polygons) beginning with v_0, v_1, v_3, v_2, then v_2, v_3, v_5, v_4, then v_4, v_5, v_7, v_6, and so on (see Figure 2-7). n must be at least 4 before anything is drawn. If n is odd, the final vertex is ignored.
GL_POLYGON	Draws a polygon using the points v_0, ... , v_{n-1} as vertices. n must be at least 3, or nothing is drawn. In addition, the polygon specified must not intersect itself and must be convex. If the vertices don't satisfy these conditions, the results are unpredictable.

Restrictions on Using glBegin() and glEnd()

The most important information about vertices is their coordinates, which are specified by the **glVertex*()** command. You can also supply additional vertex-specific data for each vertex—a color, a normal vector, texture coordinates, or any combination of these—using special commands. In addition, a few other commands are valid between a **glBegin()** and **glEnd()** pair. Table 2-3 contains a complete list of such valid commands.

Command	Purpose of Command	Reference
glVertex*()	set vertex coordinates	Chapter 2
glColor*()	set RGBA color	Chapter 4
glIndex*()	set color index	Chapter 4
glSecondaryColor*()	set secondary color for post-texturing application	Chapter 9
glNormal*()	set normal vector coordinates	Chapter 2
glMaterial*()	set material properties	Chapter 5
glFogCoord*()	set fog coordinates	Chapter 6

Table 2-3   Valid Commands between glBegin() and glEnd()

Command	Purpose of Command	Reference
glTexCoord*()	set texture coordinates	Chapter 9
glMultiTexCoord*()	set texture coordinates for multitexturing	Chapter 9
glVertexAttrib*()	set generic vertex attribute	Chapter 15
glEdgeFlag*()	control drawing of edges	Chapter 2
glArrayElement()	extract vertex array data	Chapter 2
glEvalCoord*(), glEvalPoint*()	generate coordinates	Chapter 12
glCallList(), glCallLists()	execute display list(s)	Chapter 7

Table 2-3   (continued)   Valid Commands between glBegin() and glEnd()

No other OpenGL commands are valid between a **glBegin()** and **glEnd()** pair, and making most other OpenGL calls generates an error. Some vertex array commands, such as **glEnableClientState()** and **glVertexPointer()**, when called between **glBegin()** and **glEnd()**, have undefined behavior but do not necessarily generate an error. (Also, routines related to OpenGL, such as **glX*()** routines, have undefined behavior between **glBegin()** and **glEnd()**.) These cases should be avoided, and debugging them may be more difficult.

Note, however, that only OpenGL commands are restricted; you can certainly include other programming-language constructs (except for calls, such as the aforementioned **glX*()** routines). For instance, Example 2-4 draws an outlined circle.

Example 2-4   Other Constructs between glBegin() and glEnd()

```
#define PI 3.1415926535898
GLint circle_points = 100;
glBegin(GL_LINE_LOOP);
for (i = 0; i < circle_points; i++) {
   angle = 2*PI*i/circle_points;
   glVertex2f(cos(angle), sin(angle));
}
glEnd();
```

Note: This example isn't the most efficient way to draw a circle, especially if you intend to do it repeatedly. The graphics commands used are typically very fast, but this code calculates an angle and calls the **sin()** and **cos()** routines for each vertex; in addition, there's the loop overhead. (Another way to calculate the vertices of a circle is to use a GLU routine; see "Quadrics: Rendering Spheres, Cylinders, and Disks" in Chapter 11.) If you need to draw numerous circles, calculate the coordinates of the vertices once and save them in an array and create a display list (see Chapter 7), or use vertex arrays to render them.

Unless they are being compiled into a display list, all **glVertex*()** commands should appear between a **glBegin()** and **glEnd()** combination. (If they appear elsewhere, they don't accomplish anything.) If they appear in a display list, they are executed only if they appear between a **glBegin()** and a **glEnd()**. (See Chapter 7 for more information about display lists.)

Although many commands are allowed between **glBegin()** and **glEnd()**, vertices are generated only when a **glVertex*()** command is issued. At the moment **glVertex*()** is called, OpenGL assigns the resulting vertex the current color, texture coordinates, normal vector information, and so on. To see this, look at the following code sequence. The first point is drawn in red, and the second and third ones in blue, despite the extra color commands:

```
glBegin(GL_POINTS);
    glColor3f(0.0, 1.0, 0.0);                /* green */
    glColor3f(1.0, 0.0, 0.0);                /* red */
    glVertex(...);
    glColor3f(1.0, 1.0, 0.0);                /* yellow */
    glColor3f(0.0, 0.0, 1.0);                /* blue */
    glVertex(...);
    glVertex(...);
glEnd();
```

You can use any combination of the 24 versions of the **glVertex*()** command between **glBegin()** and **glEnd()**, although in real applications all the calls in any particular instance tend to be of the same form. If your vertex-data specification is consistent and repetitive (for example, **glColor***, **glVertex***, **glColor***, **glVertex***,...), you may enhance your program's performance by using vertex arrays. (See "Vertex Arrays" on page 70.)

Basic State Management

In the preceding section, you saw an example of a state variable, the current RGBA color, and how it can be associated with a primitive. OpenGL maintains many states and state variables. An object may be rendered with lighting, texturing, hidden surface removal, fog, and other states affecting its appearance.

By default, most of these states are initially inactive. These states may be costly to activate; for example, turning on texture mapping will almost certainly slow down the process of rendering a primitive. However, the image will improve in quality and will look more realistic, owing to the enhanced graphics capabilities.

To turn many of these states on and off, use these two simple commands:

void **glEnable**(GLenum *capability*);
void **glDisable**(GLenum *capability*);

glEnable() turns on a capability, and **glDisable()** turns it off. More than 60 enumerated values can be passed as parameters to **glEnable()** or **glDisable()**. Some examples are GL_BLEND (which controls blending of RGBA values), GL_DEPTH_TEST (which controls depth comparisons and updates to the depth buffer), GL_FOG (which controls fog), GL_LINE_STIPPLE (patterned lines), and GL_LIGHTING (you get the idea).

You can also check whether a state is currently enabled or disabled.

GLboolean **glIsEnabled**(GLenum *capability*)

Returns GL_TRUE or GL_FALSE, depending on whether or not the queried capability is currently activated.

The states you have just seen have two settings: on and off. However, most OpenGL routines set values for more complicated state variables. For example, the routine **glColor3f()** sets three values, which are part of the GL_CURRENT_COLOR state. There are five querying routines used to find out what values are set for many states:

void **glGetBooleanv**(GLenum *pname*, GLboolean **params*);
void **glGetIntegerv**(GLenum *pname*, GLint **params*);
void **glGetFloatv**(GLenum *pname*, GLfloat **params*);
void **glGetDoublev**(GLenum *pname*, GLdouble **params*);
void **glGetPointerv**(GLenum *pname*, GLvoid ***params*);

Obtains Boolean, integer, floating-point, double-precision, or pointer state variables. The *pname* argument is a symbolic constant indicating the state variable to return, and *params* is a pointer to an array of the indicated type in which to place the returned data. See the tables in Appendix B for the possible values for *pname*. For example, to get the current RGBA color, a table in Appendix B suggests you use **glGetIntegerv**(GL_CURRENT_ COLOR, *params*) or **glGetFloatv**(GL_CURRENT_COLOR, *params*). A type conversion is performed, if necessary, to return the desired variable as the requested data type.

These querying routines handle most, but not all, requests for obtaining state information. (See "The Query Commands" in Appendix B for a list of all of the available OpenGL state querying routines.)

Displaying Points, Lines, and Polygons

By default, a point is drawn as a single pixel on the screen, a line is drawn solid and 1 pixel wide, and polygons are drawn solidly filled in. The following paragraphs discuss the details of how to change these default display modes.

Point Details

To control the size of a rendered point, use **glPointSize**() and supply the desired size in pixels as the argument.

void **glPointSize**(GLfloat *size*);

Sets the width in pixels for rendered points; *size* must be greater than 0.0 and by default is 1.0.

The actual collection of pixels on the screen that are drawn for various point widths depends on whether antialiasing is enabled. (Antialiasing is a technique for smoothing points and lines as they're rendered; see "Antialiasing" and "Point Parameters" in Chapter 6 for more detail.) If antialiasing is disabled (the default), fractional widths are rounded to integer widths, and a screen-aligned square region of pixels is drawn. Thus, if the width is 1.0, the square is 1 pixel by 1 pixel; if the width is 2.0, the square is 2 pixels by 2 pixels; and so on.

With antialiasing or multisampling enabled, a circular group of pixels is drawn, and the pixels on the boundaries are typically drawn at less than full intensity to give the edge a smoother appearance. In this mode, noninteger widths aren't rounded.

Most OpenGL implementations support very large point sizes. You can query the minimum and maximum sized for aliased points by using GL_ALIASED_POINT_SIZE_RANGE with **glGetFloatv**(). Likewise, you can obtain the range of supported sizes for antialiased points by passing GL_SMOOTH_POINT_SIZE_RANGE to **glGetFloatv**(). The sizes of supported antialiased points are evenly spaced between the minimum and maximum sizes for the range. Calling **glGetFloatv**() with the parameter GL_SMOOTH_POINT_SIZE_GRANULARITY will return how accurately a given antialiased point size is supported. For example, if you request **glPointSize(2.37)** and the granularity returned is 0.1, then the point size is rounded to 2.4.

Line Details

With OpenGL, you can specify lines with different widths and lines that are *stippled* in various ways—dotted, dashed, drawn with alternating dots and dashes, and so on.

Wide Lines

void **glLineWidth**(GLfloat *width*);

Sets the width, in pixels, for rendered lines; *width* must be greater than 0.0 and by default is 1.0.

Version 3.1 does not support values greater than 1.0, and will generate a GL_INVALID_VALUE error if a value greater than 1.0 is specified.

The actual rendering of lines is affected if either antialiasing or multisampling is enabled. (See "Antialiasing Points or Lines" on page 269 and "Antialiasing Geometric Primitives with Multisampling" on page 275.) Without antialiasing, widths of 1, 2, and 3 draw lines 1, 2, and 3 pixels wide. With antialiasing enabled, noninteger line widths are possible, and pixels on the boundaries are typically drawn at less than full intensity. As with point sizes, a particular OpenGL implementation might limit the width of non-antialiased lines to its maximum antialiased line width, rounded to the nearest integer value. You can obtain the range of supported aliased line

widths by using GL_ALIASED_LINE_WIDTH_RANGE with **glGetFloatv**().
To determine the supported minimum and maximum sizes of antialiased
line widths, and what granularity your implementation supports, call
glGetFloatv(), with GL_SMOOTH_LINE_WIDTH_RANGE and GL_
SMOOTH_LINE_WIDTH_GRANULARITY.

Note: Keep in mind that, by default, lines are 1 pixel wide, so they appear
wider on lower-resolution screens. For computer displays, this isn't
typically an issue, but if you're using OpenGL to render to a high-
resolution plotter, 1-pixel lines might be nearly invisible. To obtain
resolution-independent line widths, you need to take into account
the physical dimensions of pixels.

Advanced

Advanced

With non-antialiased wide lines, the line width isn't measured perpendicular to the line. Instead, it's measured in the *y*-direction if the absolute value
of the slope is less than 1.0; otherwise, it's measured in the *x*-direction. The
rendering of an antialiased line is exactly equivalent to the rendering of a
filled rectangle of the given width, centered on the exact line.

Stippled Lines

To make stippled (dotted or dashed) lines, you use the command
glLineStipple() to define the *stipple* pattern, and then you enable line
stippling with **glEnable**().

```
glLineStipple(1, 0x3F07);
glEnable(GL_LINE_STIPPLE);
```

---

void **glLineStipple**(GLint *factor*, GLushort *pattern*);

Sets the current stippling pattern for lines. The *pattern* argument is a 16-bit
series of 0s and 1s, and it's repeated as necessary to stipple a given line. A
1 indicates that drawing occurs, and a 0 that it does not, on a pixel-by-
pixel basis, beginning with the low-order bit of the pattern. The pattern
can be stretched out by using *factor*, which multiplies each subseries of
consecutive 1s and 0s. Thus, if three consecutive 1s appear in the pattern,
they're stretched to six if *factor* is 2. *factor* is clamped to lie between 1 and
256. Line stippling must be enabled by passing GL_LINE_STIPPLE to
glEnable(); it's disabled by passing the same argument to **glDisable**().

Compatibility Extension
glLineStipple
GL_LINE_
STIPPLE

With the preceding example and the pattern 0x3F07 (which translates
to 0011111100000111 in binary), a line would be drawn with 3 pixels on,
then 5 off, 6 on, and 2 off. (If this seems backward, remember that the

low-order bit is used first.) If *factor* had been 2, the pattern would have been elongated: 6 pixels on, 10 off, 12 on, and 4 off. Figure 2-8 shows lines drawn with different patterns and repeat factors. If you don't enable line stippling, drawing proceeds as if *pattern* were 0xFFFF and *factor* were 1. (Use **glDisable()** with GL_LINE_STIPPLE to disable stippling.) Note that stippling can be used in combination with wide lines to produce wide stippled lines.

PATTERN	FACTOR	
0x00FF	1	——— ——— ———
0x00FF	2	————— —————
0x0C0F	1	—— — —— — —— —
0x0C0F	3	——————— ———
0xAAAA	1	- - - - - - - - - - - - - - - - - - -
0xAAAA	2	— — — — — — — — — —
0xAAAA	3	— — — — — — —
0xAAAA	4	—— —— —— —— ——

Figure 2-8   Stippled Lines

One way to think of the stippling is that as the line is being drawn, the pattern is shifted by 1 bit each time a pixel is drawn (or *factor* pixels are drawn, if *factor* isn't 1). When a series of connected line segments is drawn between a single **glBegin()** and **glEnd()**, the pattern continues to shift as one segment turns into the next. This way, a stippling pattern continues across a series of connected line segments. When **glEnd()** is executed, the pattern is reset, and if more lines are drawn before stippling is disabled the stippling restarts at the beginning of the pattern. If you're drawing lines with GL_LINES, the pattern resets for each independent line.

Example 2-5 illustrates the results of drawing with a couple of different stipple patterns and line widths. It also illustrates what happens if the lines are drawn as a series of individual segments instead of a single connected line strip. The results of running the program appear in Figure 2-9.

Figure 2-9   Wide Stippled Lines

Example 2-5   Line Stipple Patterns: lines.c

```c
#define drawOneLine(x1,y1,x2,y2)  glBegin(GL_LINES);  \
   glVertex2f((x1),(y1)); glVertex2f((x2),(y2)); glEnd();

void init(void)
{
   glClearColor(0.0, 0.0, 0.0, 0.0);
   glShadeModel(GL_FLAT);
}

void display(void)
{
   int i;

   glClear(GL_COLOR_BUFFER_BIT);
/* select white for all lines  */
   glColor3f(1.0, 1.0, 1.0);

/* in 1st row, 3 lines, each with a different stipple  */
   glEnable(GL_LINE_STIPPLE);

   glLineStipple(1, 0x0101);  /*  dotted  */
   drawOneLine(50.0, 125.0, 150.0, 125.0);
   glLineStipple(1, 0x00FF);  /*  dashed  */
   drawOneLine(150.0, 125.0, 250.0, 125.0);
   glLineStipple(1, 0x1C47);  /*  dash/dot/dash  */
   drawOneLine(250.0, 125.0, 350.0, 125.0);

/* in 2nd row, 3 wide lines, each with different stipple */
   glLineWidth(5.0);
   glLineStipple(1, 0x0101);  /*  dotted  */
   drawOneLine(50.0, 100.0, 150.0, 100.0);
   glLineStipple(1, 0x00FF);  /*  dashed  */
   drawOneLine(150.0, 100.0, 250.0, 100.0);
   glLineStipple(1, 0x1C47);  /*  dash/dot/dash  */
   drawOneLine(250.0, 100.0, 350.0, 100.0);
   glLineWidth(1.0);

/* in 3rd row, 6 lines, with dash/dot/dash stipple  */
/* as part of a single connected line strip          */
   glLineStipple(1, 0x1C47);  /*  dash/dot/dash  */
   glBegin(GL_LINE_STRIP);
   for (i = 0; i < 7; i++)
      glVertex2f(50.0 + ((GLfloat) i * 50.0), 75.0);
   glEnd();
```

```
/* in 4th row, 6 independent lines with same stipple  */
   for (i = 0; i < 6; i++) {
      drawOneLine(50.0 + ((GLfloat) i * 50.0), 50.0,
                  50.0 + ((GLfloat)(i+1) * 50.0), 50.0);
   }

/* in 5th row, 1 line, with dash/dot/dash stipple    */
/* and a stipple repeat factor of 5                  */
   glLineStipple(5, 0x1C47);   /*  dash/dot/dash  */
   drawOneLine(50.0, 25.0, 350.0, 25.0);

   glDisable(GL_LINE_STIPPLE);
   glFlush();
}

void reshape(int w, int h)
{
   glViewport(0, 0, (GLsizei) w, (GLsizei) h);
   glMatrixMode(GL_PROJECTION);
   glLoadIdentity();
   gluOrtho2D(0.0, (GLdouble) w, 0.0, (GLdouble) h);
}

int main(int argc, char** argv)
{
   glutInit(&argc, argv);
   glutInitDisplayMode(GLUT_SINGLE | GLUT_RGB);
   glutInitWindowSize(400, 150);
   glutInitWindowPosition(100, 100);
   glutCreateWindow(argv[0]);
   init();
   glutDisplayFunc(display);
   glutReshapeFunc(reshape);
   glutMainLoop();
   return 0;
}
```

Polygon Details

Polygons are typically drawn by filling in all the pixels enclosed within the
boundary, but you can also draw them as outlined polygons or simply as
points at the vertices. A filled polygon might be solidly filled or stippled with
a certain pattern. Although the exact details are omitted here, filled polygons
are drawn in such a way that if adjacent polygons share an edge or vertex,
the pixels making up the edge or vertex are drawn exactly once—they're

included in only one of the polygons. This is done so that partially transparent polygons don't have their edges drawn twice, which would make those edges appear darker (or brighter, depending on what color you're drawing with). Note that it might result in narrow polygons having no filled pixels in one or more rows or columns of pixels.

To antialias filled polygons, multisampling is highly recommended. For details, see "Antialiasing Geometric Primitives with Multisampling" in Chapter 6.

Polygons as Points, Outlines, or Solids

A polygon has two sides—front and back—and might be rendered differently depending on which side is facing the viewer. This allows you to have cutaway views of solid objects in which there is an obvious distinction between the parts that are inside and those that are outside. By default, both front and back faces are drawn in the same way. To change this, or to draw only outlines or vertices, use **glPolygonMode()**.

---

void **glPolygonMode**(GLenum *face*, GLenum *mode*);

Controls the drawing mode for a polygon's front and back faces. The parameter *face* can be GL_FRONT_AND_BACK, GL_FRONT, or GL_BACK; *mode* can be GL_POINT, GL_LINE, or GL_FILL to indicate whether the polygon should be drawn as points, outlined, or filled. By default, both the front and back faces are drawn filled.

Version 3.1 only accepts GL_FRONT_AND_BACK as a value for *face*, and renders polygons the same way regardless of whether they're front- or back-facing.

> Compatibility
> Extension
>
> **GL_FRONT**
> **GL_BACK**

For example, you can have the *front faces* filled and the *back faces* outlined with two calls to this routine:

```
glPolygonMode(GL_FRONT, GL_FILL);
glPolygonMode(GL_BACK, GL_LINE);
```

Reversing and Culling Polygon Faces

By convention, polygons whose vertices appear in counterclockwise order on the screen are called *front-facing*. You can construct the surface of any "reasonable" solid—a mathematician would call such a surface an orientable manifold (spheres, donuts, and teapots are orientable; Klein bottles and Möbius strips aren't)—from polygons of consistent orientation. In other words, you can use all clockwise polygons or all counterclockwise polygons. (This is essentially the mathematical definition of *orientable*.)

Suppose you've consistently described a model of an orientable surface but happen to have the clockwise orientation on the outside. You can swap what OpenGL considers the back face by using the function **glFrontFace()**, supplying the desired orientation for front-facing polygons.

> void **glFrontFace**(GLenum *mode*);
>
> Controls how front-facing polygons are determined. By default, *mode* is GL_CCW, which corresponds to a counterclockwise orientation of the ordered vertices of a projected polygon in window coordinates. If *mode* is GL_CW, faces with a clockwise orientation are considered front-facing.

Note: The orientation (clockwise or counterclockwise) of the vertices is also known as its *winding*.

In a completely enclosed surface constructed from opaque polygons with a consistent orientation, none of the back-facing polygons are ever visible— they're always obscured by the front-facing polygons. If you are outside this surface, you might enable *culling* to discard polygons that OpenGL determines are back-facing. Similarly, if you are inside the object, only back-facing polygons are visible. To instruct OpenGL to discard front- or back-facing polygons, use the command **glCullFace()** and enable culling with **glEnable()**.

> void **glCullFace**(GLenum *mode*);
>
> Indicates which polygons should be discarded (culled) before they're converted to screen coordinates. The mode is either GL_FRONT, GL_BACK, or GL_FRONT_AND_BACK to indicate front-facing, back-facing, or all polygons. To take effect, culling must be enabled using **glEnable()** with GL_CULL_FACE; it can be disabled with **glDisable()** and the same argument.

Advanced

Advanced

In more technical terms, deciding whether a face of a polygon is front- or back-facing depends on the sign of the polygon's area computed in window coordinates. One way to compute this area is

$$a = \frac{1}{2} \sum_{i=0}^{n-1} x_i \, y_{i \oplus 1} - x_{i \oplus 1} \, y_i$$

where x_i and y_i are the x and y window coordinates of the ith vertex of the n-vertex polygon and

$i \oplus 1$ is $(i+1)$ mod n.

Assuming that GL_CCW has been specified, if $a > 0$, the polygon corresponding to that vertex is considered to be front-facing; otherwise, it's back-facing. If GL_CW is specified and if $a < 0$, then the corresponding polygon is front-facing; otherwise, it's back-facing.

Try This

Modify Example 2-5 by adding some filled polygons. Experiment with different colors. Try different polygon modes. Also, enable culling to see its effect.

Try This

Stippling Polygons

By default, filled polygons are drawn with a solid pattern. They can also be filled with a 32-bit by 32-bit *window-aligned* stipple pattern, which you specify with **glPolygonStipple()**.

Compatibility Extension

glPolygonStipple
GL_POLYGON_
STIPPLE

void **glPolygonStipple**(const GLubyte *mask*);

Defines the current stipple pattern for filled polygons. The argument *mask* is a pointer to a 32 × 32 bitmap that's interpreted as a mask of 0s and 1s. Where a 1 appears, the corresponding pixel in the polygon is drawn, and where a 0 appears, nothing is drawn. Figure 2-10 shows how a stipple pattern is constructed from the characters in *mask*. Polygon stippling is enabled and disabled by using **glEnable()** and **glDisable()** with GL_POLYGON_STIPPLE as the argument. The interpretation of the *mask* data is affected by the **glPixelStore*()** GL_UNPACK* modes. (See "Controlling Pixel-Storage Modes" in Chapter 8.)

In addition to defining the current polygon stippling pattern, you must enable stippling:

```
glEnable(GL_POLYGON_STIPPLE);
```

Use **glDisable()** with the same argument to disable polygon stippling.

Figure 2-11 shows the results of polygons drawn unstippled and then with two different stippling patterns. The program is shown in Example 2-6. The reversal of white to black (from Figure 2-10 to Figure 2-11) occurs because the program draws in white over a black background, using the pattern in Figure 2-10 as a stencil.

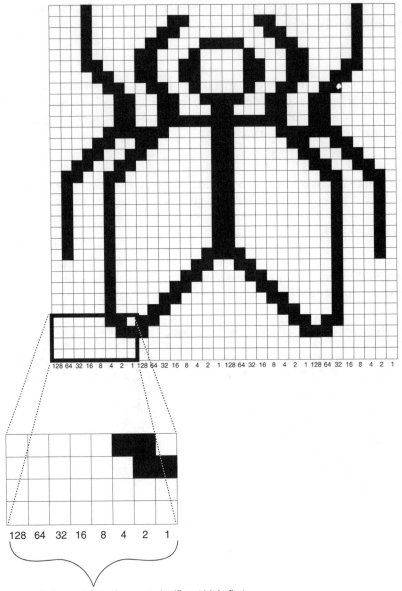

128 64 32 16 8 4 2 1   128 64 32 16 8 4 2 1   128 64 32 16 8 4 2 1   128 64 32 16 8 4 2 1

128 64 32 16 8 4 2 1

By default, for each byte the most significant bit is first.
Bit ordering can be changed by calling **glPixelStore*()**.

Figure 2-10   Constructing a Polygon Stipple Pattern

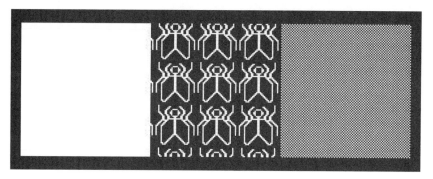

Figure 2-11   Stippled Polygons

Example 2-6   Polygon Stipple Patterns: polys.c

```
void display(void)
{
    GLubyte fly[] = {
        0x00, 0x00, 0x00, 0x00, 0x00, 0x00, 0x00, 0x00,
        0x03, 0x80, 0x01, 0xC0, 0x06, 0xC0, 0x03, 0x60,
        0x04, 0x60, 0x06, 0x20, 0x04, 0x30, 0x0C, 0x20,
        0x04, 0x18, 0x18, 0x20, 0x04, 0x0C, 0x30, 0x20,
        0x04, 0x06, 0x60, 0x20, 0x44, 0x03, 0xC0, 0x22,
        0x44, 0x01, 0x80, 0x22, 0x44, 0x01, 0x80, 0x22,
        0x44, 0x01, 0x80, 0x22, 0x44, 0x01, 0x80, 0x22,
        0x44, 0x01, 0x80, 0x22, 0x44, 0x01, 0x80, 0x22,
        0x66, 0x01, 0x80, 0x66, 0x33, 0x01, 0x80, 0xCC,
        0x19, 0x81, 0x81, 0x98, 0x0C, 0xC1, 0x83, 0x30,
        0x07, 0xe1, 0x87, 0xe0, 0x03, 0x3f, 0xfc, 0xc0,
        0x03, 0x31, 0x8c, 0xc0, 0x03, 0x33, 0xcc, 0xc0,
        0x06, 0x64, 0x26, 0x60, 0x0c, 0xcc, 0x33, 0x30,
        0x18, 0xcc, 0x33, 0x18, 0x10, 0xc4, 0x23, 0x08,
        0x10, 0x63, 0xC6, 0x08, 0x10, 0x30, 0x0c, 0x08,
        0x10, 0x18, 0x18, 0x08, 0x10, 0x00, 0x00, 0x08};

    GLubyte halftone[] = {
        0xAA, 0xAA, 0xAA, 0xAA, 0x55, 0x55, 0x55, 0x55,
        0xAA, 0xAA, 0xAA, 0xAA, 0x55, 0x55, 0x55, 0x55,
        0xAA, 0xAA, 0xAA, 0xAA, 0x55, 0x55, 0x55, 0x55,
        0xAA, 0xAA, 0xAA, 0xAA, 0x55, 0x55, 0x55, 0x55,
        0xAA, 0xAA, 0xAA, 0xAA, 0x55, 0x55, 0x55, 0x55,
        0xAA, 0xAA, 0xAA, 0xAA, 0x55, 0x55, 0x55, 0x55,
        0xAA, 0xAA, 0xAA, 0xAA, 0x55, 0x55, 0x55, 0x55,
        0xAA, 0xAA, 0xAA, 0xAA, 0x55, 0x55, 0x55, 0x55,
```

```
            0xAA, 0xAA, 0xAA, 0xAA, 0x55, 0x55, 0x55, 0x55,
            0xAA, 0xAA, 0xAA, 0xAA, 0x55, 0x55, 0x55, 0x55,
            0xAA, 0xAA, 0xAA, 0xAA, 0x55, 0x55, 0x55, 0x55,
            0xAA, 0xAA, 0xAA, 0xAA, 0x55, 0x55, 0x55, 0x55,
            0xAA, 0xAA, 0xAA, 0xAA, 0x55, 0x55, 0x55, 0x55,
            0xAA, 0xAA, 0xAA, 0xAA, 0x55, 0x55, 0x55, 0x55,
            0xAA, 0xAA, 0xAA, 0xAA, 0x55, 0x55, 0x55, 0x55,
            0xAA, 0xAA, 0xAA, 0xAA, 0x55, 0x55, 0x55, 0x55};

      glClear(GL_COLOR_BUFFER_BIT);
      glColor3f(1.0, 1.0, 1.0);
/*  draw one solid, unstippled rectangle,        */
/*  then two stippled rectangles                 */
      glRectf(25.0, 25.0, 125.0, 125.0);
      glEnable(GL_POLYGON_STIPPLE);
      glPolygonStipple(fly);
      glRectf(125.0, 25.0, 225.0, 125.0);
      glPolygonStipple(halftone);
      glRectf(225.0, 25.0, 325.0, 125.0);
      glDisable(GL_POLYGON_STIPPLE);
      glFlush();
}

void init(void)
{
      glClearColor(0.0, 0.0, 0.0, 0.0);
      glShadeModel(GL_FLAT);
}

void reshape(int w, int h)
{
      glViewport(0, 0, (GLsizei) w, (GLsizei) h);
      glMatrixMode(GL_PROJECTION);
      glLoadIdentity();
      gluOrtho2D(0.0, (GLdouble) w, 0.0, (GLdouble) h);
}

int main(int argc, char** argv)
{
      glutInit(&argc, argv);
      glutInitDisplayMode(GLUT_SINGLE | GLUT_RGB);
      glutInitWindowSize(350, 150);
      glutCreateWindow(argv[0]);
      init();
      glutDisplayFunc(display);
```

```
    glutReshapeFunc(reshape);
    glutMainLoop();
    return 0;
}
```

You might want to use display lists to store polygon stipple patterns to maximize efficiency. (See "Display List Design Philosophy" in Chapter 7.)

Marking Polygon Boundary Edges

Advanced

Advanced

OpenGL can render only convex polygons, but many nonconvex polygons arise in practice. To draw these nonconvex polygons, you typically subdivide them into convex polygons—usually triangles, as shown in Figure 2-12—and then draw the triangles. Unfortunately, if you decompose a general polygon into triangles and draw the triangles, you can't really use **glPolygonMode()** to draw the polygon's outline, as you get all the triangle outlines inside it. To solve this problem, you can tell OpenGL whether a particular vertex precedes a boundary edge; OpenGL keeps track of this information by passing along with each vertex a bit indicating whether that vertex is followed by a boundary edge. Then, when a polygon is drawn in GL_LINE mode, the nonboundary edges aren't drawn. In Figure 2-12, the dashed lines represent added edges.

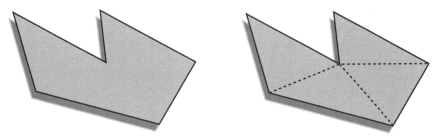

Figure 2-12   Subdividing a Nonconvex Polygon

By default, all vertices are marked as preceding a boundary edge, but you can manually control the setting of the *edge flag* with the command **glEdgeFlag*()**. This command is used between **glBegin()** and **glEnd()** pairs, and it affects all the vertices specified after it until the next **glEdgeFlag()** call is made. It applies only to vertices specified for polygons, triangles, and quads, not to those specified for strips of triangles or quads.

void **glEdgeFlag**(GLboolean *flag*);
void **glEdgeFlagv**(const GLboolean **flag*);

Indicates whether a vertex should be considered as initializing a boundary edge of a polygon. If *flag* is GL_TRUE, the edge flag is set to TRUE (the default), and any vertices created are considered to precede boundary edges until this function is called again with *flag* being GL_FALSE.

For instance, Example 2-7 draws the outline shown in Figure 2-13.

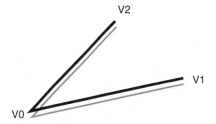

Figure 2-13   Outlined Polygon Drawn Using Edge Flags

Example 2-7   Marking Polygon Boundary Edges

```
glPolygonMode(GL_FRONT_AND_BACK, GL_LINE);
glBegin(GL_POLYGON);
    glEdgeFlag(GL_TRUE);
    glVertex3fv(V0);
    glEdgeFlag(GL_FALSE);
    glVertex3fv(V1);
    glEdgeFlag(GL_TRUE);
    glVertex3fv(V2);
glEnd();
```

Normal Vectors

A *normal vector* (or *normal*, for short) is a vector that points in a direction that's perpendicular to a surface. For a flat surface, one perpendicular direction is the same for every point on the surface, but for a general curved surface, the normal direction might be different at each point on the surface. With OpenGL, you can specify a normal for each polygon or for each vertex. Vertices of the same polygon might share the same normal (for a flat surface) or have different normals (for a curved surface). You can't assign normals anywhere other than at the vertices.

An object's normal vectors define the orientation of its surface in space—in particular, its orientation relative to light sources. These vectors are used by OpenGL to determine how much light the object receives at its vertices. Lighting—a large topic by itself—is the subject of Chapter 5, and you might want to review the following information after you've read that chapter. Normal vectors are discussed briefly here because you define normal vectors for an object at the same time you define the object's geometry.

You use **glNormal*()** to set the current normal to the value of the argument passed in. Subsequent calls to **glVertex*()** cause the specified vertices to be assigned the current normal. Often, each vertex has a different normal, which necessitates a series of alternating calls, as in Example 2-8.

Example 2-8   Surface Normals at Vertices

```
glBegin (GL_POLYGON);
    glNormal3fv(n0);
    glVertex3fv(v0);
    glNormal3fv(n1);
    glVertex3fv(v1);
    glNormal3fv(n2);
    glVertex3fv(v2);
    glNormal3fv(n3);
    glVertex3fv(v3);
glEnd();
```

---

void **glNormal3**{bsidf}(*TYPE nx, TYPE ny, TYPE nz*);
void **glNormal3**{bsidf}**v**(const *TYPE* *v*);

Compatibility
Extension

glNormal

Sets the current normal vector as specified by the arguments. The nonvector version (without the **v**) takes three arguments, which specify an (*nx, ny, nz*) vector that's taken to be the normal. Alternatively, you can use the vector version of this function (with the **v**) and supply a single array of three elements to specify the desired normal. The **b**, **s**, and **i** versions scale their parameter values linearly to the range [–1.0, 1.0].

There's no magic to finding the normals for an object—most likely, you have to perform some calculations that might include taking derivatives—but there are several techniques and tricks you can use to achieve certain effects. Appendix H, "Calculating Normal Vectors,"[1] explains how to find normal vectors for surfaces. If you already know how to do this, if you can count on always being supplied with normal vectors, or if you don't want to use the OpenGL lighting facilities, you don't need to read this appendix.

---

[1] This appendix is available online at http://www.opengl-redbook.com/appendices/.

Note that at a given point on a surface, two vectors are perpendicular to the surface, and they point in opposite directions. By convention, the normal is the one that points to the outside of the surface being modeled. (If you get inside and outside reversed in your model, just change every normal vector from (x, y, z) to $(-x, -y, -z)$).

Also, keep in mind that since normal vectors indicate direction only, their lengths are mostly irrelevant. You can specify normals of any length, but eventually they have to be converted to a length of 1 before lighting calculations are performed. (A vector that has a length of 1 is said to be of unit length, or *normalized*.) In general, you should supply normalized normal vectors. To make a normal vector of unit length, divide each of its x-, y-, z-components by the length of the normal:

$$\sqrt{x^2 + y^2 + z^2}$$

Normal vectors remain normalized as long as your model transformations include only rotations and translations. (See Chapter 3 for a discussion of transformations.) If you perform irregular transformations (such as scaling or multiplying by a shear matrix), or if you specify nonunit-length normals, then you should have OpenGL automatically normalize your normal vectors after the transformations. To do this, call **glEnable(GL_NORMALIZE)**.

Compatibility Extension

GL_NORMALIZE
GL_RESCALE_NORMAL

If you supply unit-length normals, and you perform only uniform scaling (that is, the same scaling value for x, y, and z), you can use **glEnable(GL_RESCALE_NORMAL)** to scale the normals by a constant factor, derived from the modelview transformation matrix, to return them to unit length after transformation.

Note that automatic normalization or rescaling typically requires additional calculations that might reduce the performance of your application. Rescaling normals uniformly with GL_RESCALE_NORMAL is usually less expensive than performing full-fledged normalization with GL_NORMALIZE. By default, both automatic normalizing and rescaling operations are disabled.

Vertex Arrays

You may have noticed that OpenGL requires many function calls to render geometric primitives. Drawing a 20-sided polygon requires at least 22 function calls: one call to **glBegin()**, one call for each of the vertices, and a final call to **glEnd()**. In the two previous code examples, additional information (polygon boundary edge flags or surface normals) added function calls for each vertex. This can quickly double or triple the number of function calls required for one geometric object. For some systems, function calls have a great deal of overhead and can hinder performance.

An additional problem is the redundant processing of vertices that are shared between adjacent polygons. For example, the cube in Figure 2-14 has six faces and eight shared vertices. Unfortunately, if the standard method of describing this object is used, each vertex has to be specified three times: once for every face that uses it. Therefore, 24 vertices are processed, even though eight would be enough.

Figure 2-14   Six Sides, Eight Shared Vertices

OpenGL has vertex array routines that allow you to specify a lot of vertex-related data with just a few arrays and to access that data with equally few function calls. Using vertex array routines, all 20 vertices in a 20-sided polygon can be put into one array and called with one function. If each vertex also has a surface normal, all 20 surface normals can be put into another array and also called with one function.

Arranging data in vertex arrays may increase the performance of your application. Using vertex arrays reduces the number of function calls, which improves performance. Also, using vertex arrays may allow reuse of already processed shared vertices.

Note: Vertex arrays became standard in Version 1.1 of OpenGL. Version 1.4 added support for storing fog coordinates and secondary colors in vertex arrays.

There are three steps to using vertex arrays to render geometry:

1. Activate (enable) the appropriate arrays, with each storing a different type of data: vertex coordinates, surface normals, RGBA colors, secondary colors, color indices, fog coordinates, texture coordinates, polygon edge flags, or vertex attributes for use in a vertex shader.

2. Put data into the array or arrays. The arrays are accessed by the addresses of (that is, pointers to) their memory locations. In the client-server model, this data is stored in the client's address space, unless you choose to use buffer objects (see "Buffer Objects" on page 91), for which the arrays are stored in server memory.

3. Draw geometry with the data. OpenGL obtains the data from all activated arrays by dereferencing the pointers. In the client-server model, the data is transferred to the server's address space. There are three ways to do this:

   • Accessing individual array elements (randomly hopping around)

   • Creating a list of individual array elements (methodically hopping around)

   • Processing sequential array elements

   The dereferencing method you choose may depend on the type of problem you encounter. Version 1.4 added support for multiple array access from a single function call.

Interleaved vertex array data is another common method of organization. Instead of several different arrays, each maintaining a different type of data (color, surface normal, coordinate, and so on), you may have the different types of data mixed into a single array. (See "Interleaved Arrays" on page 88.)

Step 1: Enabling Arrays

The first step is to call **glEnableClientState()** with an enumerated parameter, which activates the chosen array. In theory, you may need to call this up to eight times to activate the eight available arrays. In practice, you'll probably activate up to six arrays. For example, it is unlikely that you would activate both GL_COLOR_ARRAY and GL_INDEX_ARRAY, as your program's display mode supports either RGBA mode or color-index mode, but probably not both simultaneously.

Compatibility
Extension

glEnableClientState

void **glEnableClientState**(GLenum *array*)

Specifies the array to enable. The symbolic constants GL_VERTEX_ARRAY, GL_COLOR_ARRAY, GL_SECONDARY_COLOR_ARRAY, GL_INDEX_ARRAY, GL_NORMAL_ARRAY, GL_FOG_COORD_ARRAY, GL_TEXTURE_COORD_ARRAY, and GL_EDGE_FLAG_ARRAY are acceptable parameters.

Note: Version 3.1 supports only vertex array data stored in buffer objects (see "Buffer Objects" on page 91 for details).

If you use lighting, you may want to define a surface normal for every vertex. (See "Normal Vectors" on page 68.) To use vertex arrays for that case, you activate both the surface normal and vertex coordinate arrays:

```
glEnableClientState(GL_NORMAL_ARRAY);
glEnableClientState(GL_VERTEX_ARRAY);
```

Suppose that you want to turn off lighting at some point and just draw the geometry using a single color. You want to call **glDisable()** to turn off lighting states (see Chapter 5). Now that lighting has been deactivated, you also want to stop changing the values of the surface normal state, which is wasted effort. To do this, you call

```
glDisableClientState(GL_NORMAL_ARRAY);
```

---

void **glDisableClientState**(GLenum *array*);

Specifies the array to disable. It accepts the same symbolic constants as **glEnableClientState()**.

Compatibility
Extension

glDisableClientState

You might be asking yourself why the architects of OpenGL created these new (and long) command names, like **gl*ClientState()**, for example. Why can't you just call **glEnable()** and **glDisable()**? One reason is that **glEnable()** and **glDisable()** can be stored in a display list, but the specification of vertex arrays cannot, because the data remains on the client's side.

If multitexturing is enabled, enabling and disabling client arrays affects only the active texturing unit. See "Multitexturing" on page 467 for more details.

Step 2: Specifying Data for the Arrays

There is a straightforward way by which a single command specifies a single array in the client space. There are eight different routines for specifying arrays—one routine for each kind of array. There is also a command that can specify several client-space arrays at once, all originating from a single interleaved array.

Compatibility Extension
glVertexPointer

void **glVertexPointer**(GLint *size*, GLenum *type*, GLsizei *stride*, const GLvoid **pointer*);

Specifies where spatial coordinate data can be accessed. *pointer* is the memory address of the first coordinate of the first vertex in the array. *type* specifies the data type (GL_SHORT, GL_INT, GL_FLOAT, or GL_DOUBLE) of each coordinate in the array. *size* is the number of coordinates per vertex, which must be 2, 3, or 4. *stride* is the byte offset between consecutive vertices. If *stride* is 0, the vertices are understood to be tightly packed in the array.

To access the other seven arrays, there are seven similar routines:

Compatibility Extension
glColorPointer
glSecondaryColor Pointer
glIndexPointer
glNormalPointer
glFogCoordPointer
glTexCoordPointer
glEdgeFlagPointer

void **glColorPointer**(GLint *size*, GLenum *type*, GLsizei *stride*, const GLvoid **pointer*);
void **glSecondaryColorPointer**(GLint *size*, GLenum *type*, GLsizei *stride*, const GLvoid **pointer*);
void **glIndexPointer**(GLenum *type*, GLsizei *stride*, const GLvoid **pointer*);
void **glNormalPointer**(GLenum *type*, GLsizei *stride*, const GLvoid **pointer*);
void **glFogCoordPointer**(GLenum *type*, GLsizei *stride*, const GLvoid **pointer*);
void **glTexCoordPointer**(GLint *size*, GLenum *type*, GLsizei *stride*, const GLvoid **pointer*);
void **glEdgeFlagPointer**(GLsizei *stride*, const GLvoid **pointer*);

Note: Additional vertex attributes, used by programmable shaders, can be stored in vertex arrays. Because of their association with shaders, they are discussed in Chapter 15, "The OpenGL Shading Language," on page 720. For Version 3.1, only generic vertex arrays are supported for storing vertex data.

The main difference among the routines is whether size and type are unique or must be specified. For example, a surface normal always has three components, so it is redundant to specify its size. An edge flag is always a single Boolean, so neither size nor type needs to be mentioned. Table 2-4 displays legal values for size and data types.

For OpenGL implementations that support multitexturing, specifying a texture coordinate array with **glTexCoordPointer**() only affects the currently active texture unit. See "Multitexturing" on page 467 for more information.

Command	Sizes	Values for *type* Argument
glVertexPointer	2, 3, 4	GL_SHORT, GL_INT, GL_FLOAT, GL_DOUBLE
glColorPointer	3, 4	GL_BYTE, GL_UNSIGNED_BYTE, GL_SHORT, GL_UNSIGNED_SHORT, GL_INT, GL_UNSIGNED_INT, GL_FLOAT, GL_DOUBLE
glSecondaryColorPointer	3	GL_BYTE, GL_UNSIGNED_BYTE, GL_SHORT, GL_UNSIGNED_SHORT, GL_INT, GL_UNSIGNED_INT, GL_FLOAT, GL_DOUBLE
glIndexPointer	1	GL_UNSIGNED_BYTE, GL_SHORT, GL_INT, GL_FLOAT, GL_DOUBLE
glNormalPointer	3	GL_BYTE, GL_SHORT, GL_INT, GL_FLOAT, GL_DOUBLE
glFogCoordPointer	1	GL_FLOAT, GL_DOUBLE
glTexCoordPointer	1, 2, 3, 4	GL_SHORT, GL_INT, GL_FLOAT, GL_DOUBLE
glEdgeFlagPointer	1	no type argument (type of data must be GLboolean)

Table 2-4   Vertex Array Sizes (Values per Vertex) and Data Types

Example 2-9 uses vertex arrays for both RGBA colors and vertex coordinates. RGB floating-point values and their corresponding (*x*, *y*) integer coordinates are loaded into the GL_COLOR_ARRAY and GL_VERTEX_ARRAY.

Example 2-9   Enabling and Loading Vertex Arrays: varray.c

```
static GLint vertices[] = {25, 25,
                           100, 325,
                           175, 25,
                           175, 325,
                           250, 25,
                           325, 325};
static GLfloat colors[] = {1.0, 0.2, 0.2,
                           0.2, 0.2, 1.0,
                           0.8, 1.0, 0.2,
                           0.75, 0.75, 0.75,
                           0.35, 0.35, 0.35,
                           0.5, 0.5, 0.5};
```

```
glEnableClientState(GL_COLOR_ARRAY);
glEnableClientState(GL_VERTEX_ARRAY);

glColorPointer(3, GL_FLOAT, 0, colors);
glVertexPointer(2, GL_INT, 0, vertices);
```

Stride

The *stride* parameter for the **gl*Pointer()** routines tells OpenGL how to access the data you provide in your pointer arrays. Its value should be the number of bytes between the starts of two successive pointer elements, or zero, which is a special case. For example, suppose you stored both your vertex's RGB and (*x, y, z*) coordinates in a single array, such as the following:

```
static GLfloat intertwined[] =
    {1.0, 0.2, 1.0, 100.0, 100.0, 0.0,
     1.0, 0.2, 0.2,   0.0, 200.0, 0.0,
     1.0, 1.0, 0.2, 100.0, 300.0, 0.0,
     0.2, 1.0, 0.2, 200.0, 300.0, 0.0,
     0.2, 1.0, 1.0, 300.0, 200.0, 0.0,
     0.2, 0.2, 1.0, 200.0, 100.0, 0.0};
```

To reference only the color values in the *intertwined* array, the following call starts from the beginning of the array (which could also be passed as *&intertwined[0]*) and jumps ahead 6 * sizeof(GLfloat) bytes, which is the size of both the color and vertex coordinate values. This jump is enough to get to the beginning of the data for the next vertex:

```
glColorPointer(3, GL_FLOAT, 6*sizeof(GLfloat), &intertwined[0]);
```

For the vertex coordinate pointer, you need to start from further in the array, at the fourth element of *intertwined* (remember that C programmers start counting at zero):

```
glVertexPointer(3, GL_FLOAT, 6*sizeof(GLfloat), &intertwined[3]);
```

If your data is stored similar to the *intertwined* array above, you may find the approach described in "Interleaved Arrays" on page 88 more convenient for storing your data.

With a stride of zero, each type of vertex array (RGB color, color index, vertex coordinate, and so on) must be tightly packed. The data in the array must be homogeneous; that is, the data must be all RGB color values, all vertex coordinates, or all some other data similar in some fashion.

Step 3: Dereferencing and Rendering

Until the contents of the vertex arrays are dereferenced, the arrays remain on the client side, and their contents are easily changed. In Step 3, contents of the arrays are obtained, sent to the server, and then sent down the graphics processing pipeline for rendering.

You can obtain data from a single array element (indexed location), from an ordered list of array elements (which may be limited to a subset of the entire vertex array data), or from a sequence of array elements.

Dereferencing a Single Array Element

---
void **glArrayElement**(GLint *ith*)

Obtains the data of one (the *ith*) vertex for all currently enabled arrays. For the vertex coordinate array, the corresponding command would be **glVertex**[*size*][*type*]**v**(), where *size* is one of [2, 3, 4], and *type* is one of [s,i,f,d] for GLshort, GLint, GLfloat, and GLdouble, respectively. Both size and type were defined by **glVertexPointer**(). For other enabled arrays, **glArrayElement**() calls **glEdgeFlagv**(), **glTexCoord**[*size*][*type*]**v**(), **glColor**[*size*][*type*]**v**(), **glSecondaryColor3**[*type*]**v**(), **glIndex**[*type*]**v**(), **glNormal3**[*type*]**v**(), and **glFogCoord**[*type*]**v**(). If the vertex coordinate array is enabled, the **glVertex*v**() routine is executed last, after the execution (if enabled) of up to seven corresponding array values.

Compatibility
Extension

glArrayElement

glArrayElement() is usually called between **glBegin**() and **glEnd**(). (If called outside, **glArrayElement**() sets the current state for all enabled arrays, except for vertex, which has no current state.) In Example 2-10, a triangle is drawn using the third, fourth, and sixth vertices from enabled vertex arrays. (Again, remember that C programmers begin counting array locations with zero.)

Example 2-10   Using glArrayElement() to Define Colors and Vertices

```
glEnableClientState(GL_COLOR_ARRAY);
glEnableClientState(GL_VERTEX_ARRAY);
glColorPointer(3, GL_FLOAT, 0, colors);
glVertexPointer(2, GL_INT, 0, vertices);

glBegin(GL_TRIANGLES);
glArrayElement(2);
glArrayElement(3);
glArrayElement(5);
glEnd();
```

When executed, the latter five lines of code have the same effect as

```
glBegin(GL_TRIANGLES);
glColor3fv(colors + (2 * 3));
glVertex2iv(vertices + (2 * 2));
glColor3fv(colors + (3 * 3));
glVertex2iv(vertices + (3 * 2));
glColor3fv(colors + (5 * 3));
glVertex2iv(vertices + (5 * 2));
glEnd();
```

Since **glArrayElement()** is only a single function call per vertex, it may reduce the number of function calls, which increases overall performance.

Be warned that if the contents of the array are changed between **glBegin()** and **glEnd()**, there is no guarantee that you will receive original data or changed data for your requested element. To be safe, don't change the contents of any array element that might be accessed until the primitive is completed.

Dereferencing a List of Array Elements

glArrayElement() is good for randomly "hopping around" your data arrays. Similar routines, **glDrawElements()**, **glMultiDrawElements()**, and **glDrawRangeElements()**, are good for hopping around your data arrays in a more orderly manner.

---

void **glDrawElements**(GLenum *mode*, GLsizei *count*, GLenum *type*, const GLvoid *indices);

Defines a sequence of geometric primitives using *count* number of elements, whose indices are stored in the array *indices*. *type* must be one of GL_UNSIGNED_BYTE, GL_UNSIGNED_SHORT, or GL_UNSIGNED_INT, indicating the data type of the *indices* array. *mode* specifies what kind of primitives are constructed and is one of the same values that is accepted by **glBegin()**; for example, GL_POLYGON, GL_LINE_LOOP, GL_LINES, GL_POINTS, and so on.

The effect of **glDrawElements()** is almost the same as this command sequence:

```
glBegin(mode);
for (i = 0; i < count; i++)
   glArrayElement(indices[i]);
glEnd();
```

glDrawElements() additionally checks to make sure *mode, count,* and *type* are valid. Also, unlike the preceding sequence, executing **glDrawElements()** leaves several states indeterminate. After execution of **glDrawElements()**, current RGB color, secondary color, color index, normal coordinates, fog coordinates, texture coordinates, and edge flag are indeterminate if the corresponding array has been enabled.

With **glDrawElements()**, the vertices for each face of the cube can be placed in an array of indices. Example 2-11 shows two ways to use **glDrawElements()** to render the cube. Figure 2-15 shows the numbering of the vertices used in Example 2-11.

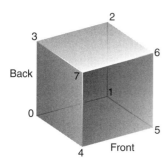

Figure 2-15   Cube with Numbered Vertices

Example 2-11   Using glDrawElements() to Dereference Several Array Elements

```
static GLubyte frontIndices[] = {4, 5, 6, 7};
static GLubyte rightIndices[] = {1, 2, 6, 5};
static GLubyte bottomIndices[] = {0, 1, 5, 4};
static GLubyte backIndices[] = {0, 3, 2, 1};
static GLubyte leftIndices[] = {0, 4, 7, 3};
static GLubyte topIndices[] = {2, 3, 7, 6};

glDrawElements(GL_QUADS, 4, GL_UNSIGNED_BYTE, frontIndices);
glDrawElements(GL_QUADS, 4, GL_UNSIGNED_BYTE, rightIndices);
glDrawElements(GL_QUADS, 4, GL_UNSIGNED_BYTE, bottomIndices);
glDrawElements(GL_QUADS, 4, GL_UNSIGNED_BYTE, backIndices);
glDrawElements(GL_QUADS, 4, GL_UNSIGNED_BYTE, leftIndices);
glDrawElements(GL_QUADS, 4, GL_UNSIGNED_BYTE, topIndices);
```

Note: It is an error to encapsulate **glDrawElements()** between a **glBegin()/glEnd()** pair.

With several primitive types (such as GL_QUADS, GL_TRIANGLES, and GL_LINES), you may be able to compact several lists of indices together into a single array. Since the GL_QUADS primitive interprets each group of four vertices as a single polygon, you may compact all the indices used in Example 2-11 into a single array, as shown in Example 2-12:

Example 2-12 Compacting Several glDrawElements() Calls into One

```
static GLubyte allIndices[] = {4, 5, 6, 7, 1, 2, 6, 5,
                               0, 1, 5, 4, 0, 3, 2, 1,
                               0, 4, 7, 3, 2, 3, 7, 6};

glDrawElements(GL_QUADS, 24, GL_UNSIGNED_BYTE, allIndices);
```

For other primitive types, compacting indices from several arrays into a single array renders a different result. In Example 2-13, two calls to **glDrawElements()** with the primitive GL_LINE_STRIP render two line strips. You cannot simply combine these two arrays and use a single call to **glDrawElements()** without concatenating the lines into a single strip that would connect vertices #6 and #7. (Note that vertex #1 is being used in both line strips just to show that this is legal.)

Example 2-13 Two glDrawElements() Calls That Render Two Line Strips

```
static GLubyte oneIndices[] = {0, 1, 2, 3, 4, 5, 6};
static GLubyte twoIndices[] = {7, 1, 8, 9, 10, 11};

glDrawElements(GL_LINE_STRIP, 7, GL_UNSIGNED_BYTE, oneIndices);
glDrawElements(GL_LINE_STRIP, 6, GL_UNSIGNED_BYTE, twoIndices);
```

The routine **glMultiDrawElements()** was introduced in OpenGL Version 1.4 to enable combining the effects of several **glDrawElements()** calls into a single call.

> void **glMultiDrawElements**(GLenum *mode*, GLsizei *count*,
> GLenum *type*, const GLvoid **indices*,
> GLsizei *primcount*);
>
> Calls a sequence of *primcount* (a number of) **glDrawElements()** commands. *indices* is an array of pointers to lists of array elements. *count* is an array of how many vertices are found in each respective array element list. *mode* (primitive type) and *type* (data type) are the same as they are in **glDrawElements()**.

The effect of **glMultiDrawElements()** is the same as

```
for (i = 0; i < primcount; i++) {
   if (count[i] > 0)
      glDrawElements(mode, count[i], type, indices[i]);
}
```

The calls to **glDrawElements()** in Example 2-13 can be combined into a single call of **glMultiDrawElements()**, as shown in Example 2-14:

Example 2-14   Use of glMultiDrawElements(): mvarray.c

```
static GLubyte oneIndices[] = {0, 1, 2, 3, 4, 5, 6};
static GLubyte twoIndices[] = {7, 1, 8, 9, 10, 11};
static GLsizei count[] = {7, 6};
static GLvoid * indices[2] = {oneIndices, twoIndices};

glMultiDrawElements(GL_LINE_STRIP, count, GL_UNSIGNED_BYTE,
                    indices, 2);
```

Like **glDrawElements()** or **glMultiDrawElements()**, **glDrawRangeElements()** is also good for hopping around data arrays and rendering their contents. **glDrawRangeElements()** also introduces the added restriction of a range of legal values for its indices, which may increase program performance. For optimal performance, some OpenGL implementations may be able to prefetch (obtain prior to rendering) a limited amount of vertex array data. **glDrawRangeElements()** allows you to specify the range of vertices to be prefetched.

---

void **glDrawRangeElements**(GLenum *mode*, GLuint *start*,
                    GLuint *end*, GLsizei *count*,
                    GLenum *type*, const GLvoid **indices*);

Creates a sequence of geometric primitives that is similar to, but more restricted than, the sequence created by **glDrawElements()**. Several parameters of **glDrawRangeElements()** are the same as counterparts in **glDrawElements()**, including *mode* (kind of primitives), *count* (number of elements), *type* (data type), and *indices* (array locations of vertex data). **glDrawRangeElements()** introduces two new parameters: *start* and *end*, which specify a range of acceptable values for *indices*. To be valid, values in the array *indices* must lie between *start* and *end*, inclusive.

It is a mistake for vertices in the array *indices* to reference outside the range [*start, end*]. However, OpenGL implementations are not required to find or report this mistake. Therefore, illegal index values may or may not generate an OpenGL error condition, and it is entirely up to the implementation to decide what to do.

You can use **glGetIntegerv()** with GL_MAX_ELEMENTS_VERTICES and GL_MAX_ELEMENTS_INDICES to find out, respectively, the recommended maximum number of vertices to be prefetched and the maximum number of indices (indicating the number of vertices to be rendered) to be referenced. If *end – start + 1* is greater than the recommended maximum of prefetched vertices, or if *count* is greater than the recommended maximum of indices, **glDrawRangeElements()** should still render correctly, but performance may be reduced.

Not all vertices in the range [*start, end*] have to be referenced. However, on some implementations, if you specify a sparsely used range, you may unnecessarily process many vertices that go unused.

With **glArrayElement()**, **glDrawElements()**, **glMultiDrawElements()**, and **glDrawRangeElements()**, it is possible that your OpenGL implementation caches recently processed (meaning transformed, lit) vertices, allowing your application to "reuse" them by not sending them down the transformation pipeline additional times. Take the aforementioned cube, for example, which has six faces (polygons) but only eight vertices. Each vertex is used by exactly three faces. Without **gl*Elements()**, rendering all six faces would require processing 24 vertices, even though 16 vertices are redundant. Your implementation of OpenGL may be able to minimize redundancy and process as few as eight vertices. (Reuse of vertices may be limited to all vertices within a single **glDrawElements()** or **glDrawRangeElements()** call, a single index array for **glMultiDrawElements()**, or, for **glArrayElement()**, within one **glBegin()**/**glEnd()** pair.)

Dereferencing a Sequence of Array Elements

While **glArrayElement()**, **glDrawElements()**, and **glDrawRangeElements()** "hop around" your data arrays, **glDrawArrays()** plows straight through them.

void **glDrawArrays**(GLenum *mode*, GLint *first*, GLsizei *count*);

Constructs a sequence of geometric primitives using array elements starting at *first* and ending at *first + count – 1* of each enabled array. *mode* specifies what kinds of primitives are constructed and is one of the same values accepted by **glBegin()**; for example, GL_POLYGON, GL_LINE_LOOP, GL_LINES, GL_POINTS, and so on.

The effect of **glDrawArrays()** is almost the same as this command sequence:

```
glBegin (mode);
for (i = 0; i < count; i++)
   glArrayElement(first + i);
glEnd();
```

As is the case with **glDrawElements()**, **glDrawArrays()** also performs error checking on its parameter values and leaves the current RGB color, secondary color, color index, normal coordinates, fog coordinates, texture coordinates, and edge flag with indeterminate values if the corresponding array has been enabled.

Try This

Change the icosahedron drawing routine in Example 2-19 on page 115 to use vertex arrays.

Try This

Similar to **glMultiDrawElements()**, the routine **glMultiDrawArrays()** was introduced in OpenGL Version 1.4 to combine several **glDrawArrays()** calls into a single call.

---

void **glMultiDrawArrays**(GLenum *mode*, GLint **first*, GLsizei **count*
GLsizei *primcount*);

Calls a sequence of *primcount* (a number of) **glDrawArrays()** commands. *mode* specifies the primitive type with the same values as accepted by **glBegin()**. *first* and *count* contain lists of array locations indicating where to process each list of array elements. Therefore, for the *i*th list of array elements, a geometric primitive is constructed starting at *first[i]* and ending at *first[i] + count[i] – 1*.

The effect of **glMultiDrawArrays()** is the same as

```
for (i = 0; i < primcount; i++) {
    if (count[i] > 0)
        glDrawArrays(mode, first[i], count[i]);
}
```

Restarting Primitives

As you start working with larger sets of vertex data, you are likely to find that you need to make numerous calls to the OpenGL drawing routines, usually rendering the same type of primitive (such as GL_TRIANGLE_STRIP, for example) that you used in the previous drawing call. Of course, you can use the **glMultiDraw*()** routines, but they require the overhead of maintaining the arrays for the starting index and length of each primitive.

OpenGL Version 3.1 added the ability to restart primitives within the same drawing call by specifying a special value, the *primitive restart index*, which is specially processed by OpenGL. When the primitive restart index is encountered in a draw call, a new rendering primitive of the same type is started with the vertex following the index. The primitive restart index is specified by the **glPrimitiveRestartIndex()** routine.

---

void **glPrimitiveRestartIndex**(GLuint *index*);

Specifies the vertex array element index used to indicate that a new primitive should be started during rendering. When processing of vertex array element indices encounters a value that matches *index*, no vertex data is processed, the current graphics primitive is terminated, and a new one of the identical type is started.

Primitive restarting is controlled by calling **glEnable()** or **glDisable()** and specifying GL_PRIMITIVE_RESTART, as demonstrated in Example 2-15.

Example 2-15   Using glPrimitiveRestartIndex() to Render Multiple Triangle Strips: primrestart.c.

```
#define BUFFER_OFFSET(offset) ((GLvoid *) NULL + offset)

#define XStart          -0.8
#define XEnd             0.8
#define YStart          -0.8
#define YEnd             0.8

#define NumXPoints              11
#define NumYPoints              11
#define NumPoints               (NumXPoints * NumYPoints)
#define NumPointsPerStrip       (2*NumXPoints)
#define NumStrips               (NumYPoints-1)
#define RestartIndex            0xffff

void
init()
{
    GLuint      vbo, ebo;
    GLfloat     *vertices;
    GLushort    *indices;

    /* Set up vertex data */
    glGenBuffers(1, &vbo);
    glBindBuffer(GL_ARRAY_BUFFER, vbo);
    glBufferData(GL_ARRAY_BUFFER, 2*NumPoints*sizeof(GLfloat),
        NULL, GL_STATIC_DRAW);
```

```
vertices = glMapBuffer(GL_ARRAY_BUFFER, GL_WRITE_ONLY);

if (vertices == NULL) {
    fprintf(stderr, "Unable to map vertex buffer\n");
    exit(EXIT_FAILURE);
}
else {
    int      i, j;
    GLfloat  dx = (XEnd - XStart) / (NumXPoints - 1);
    GLfloat  dy = (YEnd - YStart) / (NumYPoints - 1);
    GLfloat  *tmp = vertices;
    int n = 0;

    for (j = 0; j < NumYPoints; ++j) {
        GLfloat y = YStart + j*dy;

        for (i = 0; i < NumXPoints; ++i) {
            GLfloat x = XStart + i*dx;
            *tmp++ = x;
            *tmp++ = y;
        }
    }

    glUnmapBuffer(GL_ARRAY_BUFFER);
    glVertexPointer(2, GL_FLOAT, 0, BUFFER_OFFSET(0));
    glEnableClientState(GL_VERTEX_ARRAY);
}

/* Set up index data */
glGenBuffers(1, &ebo);
glBindBuffer(GL_ELEMENT_ARRAY_BUFFER, ebo);

/* We allocate an extra restart index because it simplifies
**   the element-array loop logic */
glBufferData( GL_ELEMENT_ARRAY_BUFFER,
    NumStrips*(NumPointsPerStrip+1)*sizeof(GLushort),
    NULL, GL_STATIC_DRAW );
indices = glMapBuffer(GL_ELEMENT_ARRAY_BUFFER,
    GL_WRITE_ONLY);

if (indices == NULL) {
    fprintf(stderr, "Unable to map index buffer\n");
    exit(EXIT_FAILURE);
}
else {
    int      i, j;
    GLushort *index = indices;
```

```
        for (j = 0; j < NumStrips; ++j) {
            GLushort  bottomRow = j*NumYPoints;
            GLushort  topRow = bottomRow + NumYPoints;

            for (i = 0; i < NumXPoints; ++i) {
                *index++ = topRow + i;
                *index++ = bottomRow + i;
            }
            *index++ = RestartIndex;
        }

        glUnmapBuffer(GL_ELEMENT_ARRAY_BUFFER);
    }

    glPrimitiveRestartIndex(RestartIndex);
    glEnable(GL_PRIMITIVE_RESTART);
}

void
display()
{
    int  i, start;

    glClear(GL_COLOR_BUFFER_BIT | GL_DEPTH_BUFFER_BIT);

    glColor3f(1, 1, 1);
    glDrawElements(GL_TRIANGLE_STRIP,
        NumStrips*(NumPointsPerStrip + 1),
        GL_UNSIGNED_SHORT, BUFFER_OFFSET(0));

    glutSwapBuffers();
}
```

Instanced Drawing

Advanced

Advanced

OpenGL Version 3.1 (specifically, GLSL version 1.40) added support for *instanced drawing*, which provides an additional value—gl_InstanceID, called the *instance ID*, and accessible only in a vertex shader—that is monotonically incremented for each group of primitives specified.

glDrawArraysInstanced() operates similarly to **glMultiDrawArrays()**, except that the starting index and vertex count (as specified by *first* and *count*, respectively) are the same for each call to **glDrawArrays()**.

---

void **glDrawArraysInstanced**(GLenum *mode*, GLint *first*, GLsizei *count*, GLsizei *primcount*);

Effectively calls **glDrawArrays()** *primcount* times, setting the GLSL vertex shader value gl_InstanceID before each call. *mode* specifies the primitive type. *first* and *count* specify the range of array elements that are passed to **glDrawArrays()**.

---

glDrawArraysInstanced() has the same effect as this call sequence (except that your application cannot manually update gl_InstanceID):

```
for (i = 0; i < primcount; i++) {
    gl_InstanceID = i;
    glDrawArrays(mode, first, count);
}
gl_InstanceID = 0;
```

Likewise, **glDrawElementsInstanced()** performs the same operation, but allows random-access to the data in the vertex array:

---

void **glDrawElementsInstanced**(GLenum *mode*, GLsizei *count*, GLenum *type*, const void **indicies*, GLsizei *primcount*);

Effectively calls **glDrawElements()** *primcount* times, setting the GLSL vertex shader value gl_InstanceID before each call. *mode* specifies the primitive type. *type* indicates the data type of the array *indices* and must be one of the following: GL_UNSIGNED_BYTE, GL_UNSIGNED_SHORT, or GL_UNSIGNED_INT. *indicies* and *count* specify the range of array elements that are passed to **glDrawElements()**.

The implementation of **glDrawElementsInstanced()** is shown here:

```
for (i = 0; i < primcount; i++) {
    gl_InstanceID = i;
    glDrawElements(mode, count, type, indicies);
}
gl_InstanceID = 0;
```

Interleaved Arrays

Advanced

Earlier in this chapter (see "Stride" on page 76), the special case of inter-leaved arrays was examined. In that section, the array *intertwined*, which interleaves RGB color and 3D vertex coordinates, was accessed by calls to **glColorPointer()** and **glVertexPointer()**. Careful use of *stride* helped prop-erly specify the arrays:

```
static GLfloat intertwined[] =
    {1.0, 0.2, 1.0, 100.0, 100.0, 0.0,
     1.0, 0.2, 0.2, 0.0, 200.0, 0.0,
     1.0, 1.0, 0.2, 100.0, 300.0, 0.0,
     0.2, 1.0, 0.2, 200.0, 300.0, 0.0,
     0.2, 1.0, 1.0, 300.0, 200.0, 0.0,
     0.2, 0.2, 1.0, 200.0, 100.0, 0.0};
```

There is also a behemoth routine, **glInterleavedArrays()**, that can specify several vertex arrays at once. **glInterleavedArrays()** also enables and dis-ables the appropriate arrays (so it combines "Step 1: Enabling Arrays" on page 72 and "Step 2: Specifying Data for the Arrays" on page 73). The array *intertwined* exactly fits one of the 14 data-interleaving configurations sup-ported by **glInterleavedArrays()**. Therefore, to specify the contents of the array *intertwined* into the RGB color and vertex arrays and enable both arrays, call

```
glInterleavedArrays(GL_C3F_V3F, 0, intertwined);
```

This call to **glInterleavedArrays()** enables GL_COLOR_ARRAY and GL_VERTEX_ARRAY. It disables GL_SECONDARY_COLOR_ARRAY, GL_INDEX_ARRAY, GL_NORMAL_ARRAY, GL_FOG_COORD_ARRAY, GL_TEXTURE_COORD_ARRAY, and GL_EDGE_FLAG_ARRAY.

This call also has the same effect as calling **glColorPointer()** and **glVertexPointer()** to specify the values for six vertices in each array. Now you are ready for Step 3: calling **glArrayElement()**, **glDrawElements()**, **glDrawRangeElements()**, or **glDrawArrays()** to dereference array elements.

Note that **glInterleavedArrays()** does not support edge flags.

The mechanics of **glInterleavedArrays()** are intricate and require reference to Example 2-16 and Table 2-5. In that example and table, you'll see e_t, e_c, and e_n, which are the Boolean values for the enabled or disabled texture coordinate, color, and normal arrays; and you'll see s_t, s_c, and s_v, which are the sizes (numbers of components) for the texture coordinate, color, and

void **glInterleavedArrays**(GLenum *format*,
GLsizei *stride*, const GLvoid *pointer)

Initializes all eight arrays, disabling arrays that are not specified in *format*, and enabling the arrays that are specified. *format* is one of 14 symbolic constants, which represent 14 data configurations; Table 2-5 displays *format* values. *stride* specifies the byte offset between consecutive vertices. If *stride* is 0, the vertices are understood to be tightly packed in the array. *pointer* is the memory address of the first coordinate of the first vertex in the array.

If multitexturing is enabled, **glInterleavedArrays()** affects only the active texture unit. See "Multitexturing" on page 467 for details.

vertex arrays. t_c is the data type for RGBA color, which is the only array that can have nonfloating-point interleaved values. p_c, p_n, and p_v are the calculated strides for jumping into individual color, normal, and vertex values; and s is the stride (if one is not specified by the user) to jump from one array element to the next.

The effect of **glInterleavedArrays()** is the same as calling the command sequence in Example 2-16 with many values defined in Table 2-5. All pointer arithmetic is performed in units of **sizeof**(GLubyte).

Example 2-16   Effect of glInterleavedArrays(format, stride, pointer)

```
int str;
/* set e_t, e_c, e_n, s_t, s_c, s_v, t_c, p_c, p_n, p_v, and s
 * as a function of Table 2-5 and the value of format
 */

str = stride;
if (str == 0)
   str = s;

glDisableClientState(GL_EDGE_FLAG_ARRAY);
glDisableClientState(GL_INDEX_ARRAY);
glDisableClientState(GL_SECONDARY_COLOR_ARRAY);
glDisableClientState(GL_FOG_COORD_ARRAY);

if (e_t) {
   glEnableClientState(GL_TEXTURE_COORD_ARRAY);
   glTexCoordPointer(s_t, GL_FLOAT, str, pointer);
}
else
```

```
   glDisableClientState(GL_TEXTURE_COORD_ARRAY);
if (e_c) {
   glEnableClientState(GL_COLOR_ARRAY);
   glColorPointer(s_c, t_c, str, pointer+p_c);
}
else
   glDisableClientState(GL_COLOR_ARRAY);

if (e_n) {
   glEnableClientState(GL_NORMAL_ARRAY);
   glNormalPointer(GL_FLOAT, str, pointer+p_n);
}
else
   glDisableClientState(GL_NORMAL_ARRAY);

glEnableClientState(GL_VERTEX_ARRAY);
glVertexPointer(s_v, GL_FLOAT, str, pointer+p_v);
```

In Table 2-5, T and F are True and False. f is **sizeof**(GLfloat). c is 4 times **sizeof**(GLubyte), rounded up to the nearest multiple of f.

Format	e_t	e_c	e_n	s_t	s_c	s_v	t_c	p_c	p_n	p_v	s
GL_V2F	F	F	F			2				0	2f
GL_V3F	F	F	F			3				0	3f
GL_C4UB_V2F	F	T	F		4	2	GL_UNSIGNED_BYTE	0		c	c+2f
GL_C4UB_V3F	F	T	F		4	3	GL_UNSIGNED_BYTE	0		c	c+3f
GL_C3F_V3F	F	T	F		3	3	GL_FLOAT	0		3f	6f
GL_N3F_V3F	F	F	T			3			0	3f	6f
GL_C4F_N3F_V3F	F	T	T		4	3	GL_FLOAT	0	4f	7f	10f
GL_T2F_V3F	T	F	F	2		3				2f	5f
GL_T4F_V4F	T	F	F	4		4				4f	8f
GL_T2F_C4UB_V3F	T	T	F	2	4	3	GL_UNSIGNED_BYTE	2f		c+2f	c+5f
GL_T2F_C3F_V3F	T	T	F	2	3	3	GL_FLOAT	2f		5f	8f
GL_T2F_N3F_V3F	T	F	T	2		3			2f	5f	8f
GL_T2F_C4F_N3F_V3F	T	T	T	2	4	3	GL_FLOAT	2f	6f	9f	12f
GL_T4F_C4F_N3F_V4F	T	T	T	4	4	4	GL_FLOAT	4f	8f	11f	15f

Table 2-5   Variables That Direct glInterleavedArrays()

Start by learning the simpler formats, GL_V2F, GL_V3F, and GL_C3F_V3F. If you use any of the formats with C4UB, you may have to use a struct data type or do some delicate type casting and pointer math to pack four unsigned bytes into a single 32-bit word.

For some OpenGL implementations, use of interleaved arrays may increase application performance. With an interleaved array, the exact layout of your data is known. You know your data is tightly packed and may be accessed in one chunk. If interleaved arrays are not used, the *stride* and size information has to be examined to detect whether data is tightly packed.

Note: **glInterleavedArrays()** only enables and disables vertex arrays and specifies values for the vertex-array data. It does not render anything. You must still complete "Step 3: Dereferencing and Rendering" on page 77 and call **glArrayElement()**, **glDrawElements()**, **glDrawRangeElements()**, or **glDrawArrays()** to dereference the pointers and render graphics.

Buffer Objects

Advanced

Advanced

There are many operations in OpenGL where you send a large block of data to OpenGL, such as passing vertex array data for processing. Transferring that data may be as simple as copying from your system's memory down to your graphics card. However, because OpenGL was designed as a client-server model, any time that OpenGL needs data, it will have to be transferred from the client's memory. If that data doesn't change, or if the client and server reside on different computers (distributed rendering), that data transfer may be slow, or redundant.

Buffer objects were added to OpenGL Version 1.5 to allow an application to explicitly specify which data it would like to be stored in the graphics server.

Many different types of buffer objects are used in the current versions of OpenGL:

- Vertex data in arrays can be stored in server-side buffer objects starting with OpenGL Version 1.5. They are described in "Using Buffer Objects with Vertex-Array Data" on page 102 of this chapter.

- Support for storing pixel data, such as texture maps or blocks of pixels, in buffer objects was added into OpenGL Version 2.1 It is described in "Using Buffer Objects with Pixel Rectangle Data" in Chapter 8.

- Version 3.1 added *uniform buffer objects* for storing blocks of uniform-variable data for use with shaders.

You will find many other features in OpenGL that use the term "objects," but not all apply to storing blocks of data. For example, texture objects (introduced in OpenGL Version 1.1) merely encapsulate various state settings associated with texture maps (See "Texture Objects" on page 437). Likewise, vertex-array objects, added in Version 3.0, encapsulate the state parameters associated with using vertex arrays. These types of objects allow you to alter numerous state settings with many fewer function calls. For maximum performance, you should try to use them whenever possible, once you're comfortable with their operation.

Note: An object is referred to by its name, which is an unsigned integer identifier. Starting with Version 3.1, all names must be generated by OpenGL using one of the **glGen*()** routines; user-defined names are no longer accepted.

Creating Buffer Objects

In OpenGL Version 3.0, any nonzero unsigned integer may used as a buffer object identifier. You may either arbitrarily select representative values or let OpenGL allocate and manage those identifiers for you. Why the difference? By having OpenGL allocate identifiers, you are guaranteed to avoid an already used buffer object identifier. This helps to eliminate the risk of modifying data unintentionally. In fact, OpenGL Version 3.1 requires that all object identifiers be generated, disallowing user-defined names.

To have OpenGL allocate buffer objects identifiers, call **glGenBuffers()**.

---

void **glGenBuffers**(GLsizei *n*, GLuint **buffers*);

Returns *n* currently unused names for buffer objects in the array *buffers*. The names returned in *buffers* do not have to be a contiguous set of integers.

The names returned are marked as used for the purposes of allocating additional buffer objects, but only acquire a valid state once they have been bound.

Zero is a reserved buffer object name and is never returned as a buffer object by **glGenBuffers()**.

You can also determine whether an identifier is a currently used buffer object identifier by calling **glIsBuffer()**.

GLboolean **glIsBuffer**(GLuint *buffer*);

Returns GL_TRUE if *buffer* is the name of a buffer object that has been bound, but has not been subsequently deleted. Returns GL_FALSE if *buffer* is zero or if *buffer* is a nonzero value that is not the name of a buffer object.

Making a Buffer Object Active

To make a buffer object active, it needs to be bound. Binding selects which buffer object future operations will affect, either for initializing data or using that buffer for rendering. That is, if you have more than one buffer object in your application, you'll likely call **glBindBuffer()** multiple times: once to initialize the object and its data, and then subsequent times either to select that object for use in rendering or to update its data.

To disable use of buffer objects, call **glBindBuffer()** with zero as the buffer identifier. This switches OpenGL to the default mode of not using buffer objects.

---

void **glBindBuffer**(GLenum *target*, GLuint *buffer*);

Specifies the current active buffer object. *target* must be set to one of GL_ARRAY_BUFFER, GL_ELEMENT_ARRAY_BUFFER, GL_PIXEL_PACK_ BUFFER, GL_PIXEL_UNPACK_BUFFER, GL_COPY_READ_BUFFER, GL_COPY_WRITE_BUFFER, GL_TRANSFORM_FEEDBACK_BUFFER, or GL_UNIFORM_BUFFER. *buffer* specifies the buffer object to be bound to.

glBindBuffer() does three things: 1. When using *buffer* of an unsigned integer other than zero for the first time, a new buffer object is created and assigned that name. 2. When binding to a previously created buffer object, that buffer object becomes the active buffer object. 3. When binding to a *buffer* value of zero, OpenGL stops using buffer objects.

Allocating and Initializing Buffer Objects with Data

Once you've bound a buffer object, you need to reserve space for storing your data. This is done by calling **glBufferData()**.

> void **glBufferData**(GLenum *target*, GLsizeiptr *size*, const GLvoid **data*,
> GLenum *usage*);
>
> Allocates *size* storage units (usually bytes) of OpenGL server memory for
> storing vertex array data or indices. Any previous data associated with the
> currently bound object will be deleted.
>
> *target* may be either GL_ARRAY_BUFFER for vertex data; GL_ELEMENT_
> ARRAY_BUFFER for index data; GL_PIXEL_UNPACK_BUFFER for pixel
> data being passed into OpenGL; GL_PIXEL_PACK_BUFFER for pixel data
> being retrieved from OpenGL; GL_COPY_READ_BUFFER and GL_COPY_
> WRITE_BUFFER for data copied between buffers; GL_TEXTURE_BUFFER
> for texture data stored as a texture buffer; GL_TRANSFORM_FEEDBACK_
> BUFFER for results from executing a transform feedback shader; or
> GL_UNIFORM_BUFFER for uniform variable values.
>
> *size* is the amount of storage required for storing the respective data. This
> value is generally number of elements in the data multiplied by their
> respective storage size.
>
> *data* is either a pointer to a client memory that is used to initialize the
> buffer object or NULL. If a valid pointer is passed, *size* units of storage are
> copied from the client to the server. If NULL is passed, *size* units of storage
> are reserved for use, but are left uninitialized.
>
> *usage* provides a hint as to how the data will be read and written after
> allocation. Valid values are GL_STREAM_DRAW, GL_STREAM_READ, GL_
> STREAM_COPY, GL_STATIC_DRAW, GL_STATIC_READ, GL_STATIC_COPY,
> GL_DYNAMIC_DRAW, GL_DYNAMIC_READ, GL_DYNAMIC_COPY.
>
> **glBufferData()** will generate a GL_OUT_OF_MEMORY error if the
> requested *size* exceeds what the server is able to allocate. It will generate a
> GL_INVALID_VALUE error if usage is not one of the permitted values.

glBufferData() first allocates memory in the OpenGL server for storing your
data. If you request too much memory, a GL_OUT_OF_MEMORY error will
be set. Once the storage has been reserved, and if the *data* parameter is not
NULL, *size* units of storage (usually bytes) are copied from the client's
memory into the buffer object. However, if you need to dynamically load
the data at some point after the buffer is created, pass NULL in for the *data*
pointer. This will reserve the appropriate storage for your data, but leave it
uninitialized.

The final parameter to **glBufferData()**, *usage*, is a performance hint to OpenGL. Based upon the value you specify for *usage*, OpenGL may be able to optimize the data for better performance, or it can choose to ignore the hint. There are three operations that can be done to buffer object data:

1. Drawing—the client specifies data that is used for rendering.

2. Reading—data values are read from an OpenGL buffer (such as the framebuffer) and used in the application in various computations not immediately related to rendering.

3. Copying—data values are read from an OpenGL buffer and then used as data for rendering.

Additionally, depending upon how often you intend to update the data, there are various operational hints for describing how often the data will be read or used in rendering:

• Stream mode—you specify the data once, and use it only a few times in drawing or other operations.

• Static mode—you specify the data once, but use the values often.

• Dynamic mode—you may update the data often and use the data values in the buffer object many times as well.

Possible values for *usage* are described in Table 2-6.

Parameter	Meaning
GL_STREAM_DRAW	Data is specified once and used at most a few times as the source of drawing and image specification commands.
GL_STREAM_READ	Data is copied once from an OpenGL buffer and is used at most a few times by the application as data values.
GL_STREAM_COPY	Data is copied once from an OpenGL buffer and is used at most a few times as the source for drawing or image specification commands.
GL_STATIC_DRAW	Data is specified once and used many times as the source of drawing or image specification commands.
GL_STATIC_READ	Data is copied once from an OpenGL buffer and is used many times by the application as data values.

Table 2-6   Values for *usage* Parameter of glBufferData()

Parameter	Meaning
GL_STATIC_COPY	Data is copied once from an OpenGL buffer and is used many times as the source for drawing or image specification commands.
GL_DYNAMIC_DRAW	Data is specified many times and used many times as the source of drawing and image specification commands.
GL_DYNAMIC_READ	Data is copied many times from an OpenGL buffer and is used many times by the application as data values.
GL_DYNAMIC_COPY	Data is copied many times from an OpenGL buffer and is used many times as the source for drawing or image specification commands.

Table 2-6   (continued)   Values for *usage* Parameter of glBufferData()

Updating Data Values in Buffer Objects

There are two methods for updating data stored in a buffer object. The first method assumes that you have data of the same type prepared in a buffer in your application. **glBufferSubData()** will replace some subset of the data in the bound buffer object with the data you provide.

---

void **glBufferSubData**(GLenum *target*, GLintptr *offset*, GLsizeiptr *size*,
                                 const GLvoid **data*);

Update *size* bytes starting at *offset* (also measured in bytes) in the currently bound buffer object associated with *target* using the data pointed to by *data*. *target* must be one of GL_ARRAY_BUFFER, GL_ELEMENT_ARRAY_ BUFFER, GL_PIXEL_UNPACK_BUFFER, GL_PIXEL_PACK_BUFFER, GL_COPY_READ_BUFFER, GL_COPY_WRITE_BUFFER, GL_TRANSFORM_ FEEDBACK_BUFFER, or GL_UNIFORM_BUFFER.

glBufferSubData() will generate a GL_INVALID_VALUE error if *size* is less than zero or if *size* + *offset* is greater than the original size specified when the buffer object was created.

The second method allows you more control over which data values are updated in the buffer. **glMapBuffer()** and **glMapBufferRange()** return a pointer to the buffer object memory, into which you can write new values (or simply read the data, depending on your choice of memory access permissions), just as if you were assigning values to an array. When you've completed updating the values in the buffer, you call **glUnmapBuffer()** to signify that you've completed updating the data.

glMapBuffer() provides access to the entire set of data contained in the buffer object. This approach is useful if you need to modify much of the data in buffer, but may be inefficient if you have a large buffer and need to update only a small portion of the values.

GLvoid ***glMapBuffer**(GLenum *target*, GLenum *access*);

Returns a pointer to the data storage for the currently bound buffer object associated with *target*, which must be one of GL_ARRAY_BUFFER, GL_ELEMENT_ARRAY_BUFFER, GL_PIXEL_PACK_BUFFER, GL_PIXEL_ UNPACK_BUFFER, GL_COPY_READ_BUFFER, GL_COPY_WRITE_ BUFFER, GL_TRANSFORM_FEEDBACK_BUFFER, or GL_UNIFORM_ BUFFER. *access* must be either GL_READ_ONLY, GL_WRITE_ONLY, or GL_READ_WRITE, indicating the operations that a client may do on the data.

glMapBuffer() will return NULL either if the buffer cannot be mapped (setting the OpenGL error state to GL_OUT_OF_MEMORY) or if the buffer was already mapped previously (where the OpenGL error state will be set to GL_INVALID_OPERATION).

When you've completed accessing the storage, you can unmap the buffer by calling **glUnmapBuffer()**.

GLboolean **glUnmapBuffer**(GLenum *target*);

Indicates that updates to the currently bound buffer object are complete, and the buffer may be released. *target* must be one of GL_ARRAY_BUFFER, GL_ELEMENT_ARRAY_BUFFER, GL_PIXEL_PACK_BUFFER, GL_PIXEL_ UNPACK_BUFFER, GL_COPY_READ_BUFFER, GL_COPY_WRITE_ BUFFER, GL_TRANSFORM_FEEDBACK_BUFFER, or GL_UNIFORM_ BUFFER.

As a simple example of how you might selectively update elements of your data, we'll use **glMapBuffer()** to obtain a pointer to the data in a buffer object containing three-dimensional positional coordinates, and then update only the *z*-coordinates.

```
GLfloat* data;

data = (GLfloat*) glMapBuffer(GL_ARRAY_BUFFER, GL_READ_WRITE);

if (data != (GLfloat*) NULL) {
    for( i = 0; i < 8; ++i )
        data[3*i+2] *= 2.0;   /* Modify Z values */
    glUnmapBuffer(GL_ARRAY_BUFFER);
} else {
    /* Handle not being able to update data */
}
```

If you need to update only a relatively small number of values in the buffer (as compared to its total size), or small contiguous ranges of values in a very large buffer object, it may be more efficient to use **glMapBufferRange()**. It allows you to map only the range of data values you need.

GLvoid ***glMapBufferRange**(GLenum *target*, GLintptr *offset*,
GLsizeiptr *length*, GLbitfield *access*);

Returns a pointer into the data storage for the currently bound buffer object associated with *target*, which must be one of GL_ARRAY_BUFFER, GL_ELEMENT_ARRAY_BUFFER, GL_PIXEL_PACK_BUFFER, GL_PIXEL_UNPACK_BUFFER, GL_COPY_READ_BUFFER, GL_COPY_WRITE_BUFFER, GL_TRANSFORM_FEEDBACK_BUFFER, or GL_UNIFORM_BUFFER. *offset* and *length* specify the range to be mapped. *access* is a bitmask composed of GL_MAP_READ_BIT, GL_MAP_WRITE_BIT, which indicate the operations that a client may do on the data, and optionally GL_MAP_INVALIDATE_RANGE_BIT, GL_MAP_INVALIDATE_BUFFER_BIT, GL_MAP_FLUSH_EXPLICIT_BIT, or GL_MAP_UNSYNCHRONIZED_BIT, which provide hints on how OpenGL should manage the data in the buffer.

glMapBufferRange() will return NULL if an error occurs. GL_INVALID_VALUE is generated if *offset* or *length* are negative, or *offset+length* is greater than the buffer size. GL_OUT_OF_MEMORY error is generated if adequate memory cannot be obtained to map the buffer. GL_INVALID_OPERATION is generated if any of the following occur: The buffer is already mapped; *access* does not have either GL_MAP_READ_BIT or GL_MAP_WRITE_BIT set; *access* has GL_MAP_READ_BIT set and any of GL_MAP_INVALIDATE_RANGE_BIT, GL_MAP_INVALIDATE_BUFFER_BIT, or GL_MAP_UNSYNCHRONIZED_BIT is also set; or both GL_MAP_WRITE_BIT and GL_MAP_FLUSH_EXPLICIT_BIT are set in *access*.

Using **glMapBufferRange()**, you can specify optional hints by setting additional bits within *access*. These flags describe how the OpenGL server needs to preserve data that was originally in the buffer before you mapped it. The hints are meant to aid the OpenGL implementation in determining which data values it needs to retain, or for how long, to keep any internal copies of the data correct and consistent.

Parameter	Meaning
GL_MAP_INVALIDATE_RANGE_BIT	Specify that the previous values in the mapped range may be discarded, but preserve the other values within the buffer. Data within this range are undefined unless explicitly written. No OpenGL error is generated if later OpenGL calls access undefined data, and the results of such calls are undefined (but may cause application or system errors). This flag may not be used in conjunction with the GL_READ_BIT.
GL_MAP_INVALIDATE_BUFFER_BIT	Specify that the previous values of the entire buffer may be discarded, and all values with the buffer are undefined unless explicitly written. No OpenGL error is generated if later OpenGL calls access undefined data, and the results of such calls are undefined (but may cause application or system errors). This flag may not be used in conjunction with the GL_READ_BIT.
GL_MAP_FLUSH_EXPLICIT_BIT	Indicate that discrete ranges of the mapped region may be updated, that the application will signal when modifications to a range should be considered completed by calling **glFlushMappedBufferRange()**. No OpenGL error is generated if a range of the mapped buffer is updated but not flushed, however, the values are undefined until flushed. Using this option will require any modified ranges to be explicitly flushed to the OpenGL server—**glUnmapBuffer()** will not automatically flush the buffer's data.

Table 2-7   Values for the *access* Parameter of glMapBufferRange()

Parameter	Meaning
GL_MAP_UNSYNCHRONIZED_BIT	Specify that OpenGL should not attempt to synchronize pending operations on a buffer (e.g., updating data with a call to **glBufferData()**, or the application is trying to use the data in the buffer for rendering) until the call to **glMapBufferRange()** has completed. No OpenGL errors are generated for the pending operations that access or modify the mapped region, but the results of those operations is undefined.

Table 2-7 (continued)   Values for the *access* Parameter of glMapBufferRange()

As described in Table 2-7, specifying GL_MAP_FLUSH_EXPLICIT_BIT in the access flags when mapping a buffer region with **glMapBufferRange()** requires ranges modified within the mapped buffer to be indicated to the OpenGL by a call to **glFlushMappedBufferRange()**.

GLvoid **glFlushMappedBufferRange**(GLenum *target*, GLintptr *offset*, GLsizeiptr *length*);

Signal that values within a mapped buffer range have been modified, which may cause the OpenGL server to update cached copies of the buffer object. *target* must be one of the following: GL_ARRAY_BUFFER, GL_ELEMENT_ARRAY_BUFFER, GL_PIXEL_PACK_BUFFER, GL_PIXEL_UNPACK_BUFFER, GL_COPY_READ_BUFFER, GL_COPY_WRITE_BUFFER, GL_TRANSFORM_FEEDBACK_BUFFER, or GL_UNIFORM_BUFFER. *offset* and *length* specify the range of the mapped buffer region, relative to the beginning of the mapped range of the buffer.

A GL_INVALID_VALUE error is generated if *offset* or *length* is negative or if *offset+length* is greater than the size of the mapped region. A GL_INVALID_OPERATION error is generated if there is no buffer bound to *target* (i.e., zero was specified as the buffer to be bound in a call to **glBindBuffer()** for *target*), or if the buffer bound to *target* is not mapped, or if it is mapped without having set the GL_MAP_FLUSH_EXPLICIT_BIT.

Copying Data Between Buffer Objects

On some occasions, you may need to copy data from one buffer object to another. In versions of OpenGL prior to Version 3.1, this would be a two-step process:

1. Copy the data from the buffer object into memory in your application. You would do this either by mapping the buffer and copying it into a local memory buffer, or by calling **glGetBufferSubData()** to copy the data from the server.

2. Update the data in another buffer object by binding to the new object and then sending the new data using **glBufferData()** (or **glBufferSubData()** if you're replacing only a subset). Alternatively, you could map the buffer, and then copy the data from a local memory buffer into the mapped buffer.

In OpenGL Version 3.1, the **glCopyBufferSubData()** command copies data without forcing it to make a temporary stop in your application's memory.

---

void **glCopyBufferSubData**(GLenum *readbuffer*, GLenum *writebuffer*,
    GLintptr *readoffset*, GLintptr *writeoffset*,
    GLsizeiptr *size*);

Copy data from the buffer object associated with *readbuffer* to the buffer object bound to *writebuffer*. *readbuffer* and *writebuffer* must be one of GL_ARRAY_BUFFER, GL_COPY_READ_BUFFER, GL_COPY_WRITE_BUFFER, GL_ELEMENT_ARRAY_BUFFER, GL_PIXEL_PACK_BUFFER, GL_PIXEL_UNPACK_BUFFER, GL_TEXTURE_BUFFER, GL_TRANSFORM_FEEDBACK_BUFFER, or GL_UNIFORM_BUFFER.

readoffset and *size* specify the amount of data copied into the destination buffer object, replacing the same size of data starting at *writeoffset*.

Numerous situations will cause a GL_INVALID_VALUE error to be generated: *readoffset*, *writeoffset*, or *size* being negative; *readoffset* + *size* exceeding the extent of the buffer object bound to *readbuffer*; *writeoffset* + *size* exceeding the extent of the buffer object bound to *writebuffer*; or if *readbuffer* and *writebuffer* are bound to the same object, and the regions specified by *readoffset* and *size* overlap the region defined by *writeoffset* and *size*.

A GL_INVALID_OPERATION error is generated if either *readbuffer* or *writebuffer* is bound to zero, or either buffer is currently mapped.

Cleaning Up Buffer Objects

When you're finished with a buffer object, you can release its resources and make its identifier available by calling **glDeleteBuffers**(). Any bindings to currently bound objects that are deleted are reset to zero.

---

void **glDeleteBuffers**(GLsizei *n*, const GLuint **buffers*);

Deletes *n* buffer objects, named by elements in the array *buffers*. The freed buffer objects may now be reused (for example, by **glGenBuffers**()).

If a buffer object is deleted while bound, all bindings to that object are reset to the default buffer object, as if **glBindBuffer**() had been called with zero as the specified buffer object. Attempts to delete nonexistent buffer objects or the buffer object named zero are ignored without generating an error.

Using Buffer Objects with Vertex-Array Data

To store your vertex-array data in buffer objects, you will need to add a few steps to your application.

1. (Optional) Generate buffer object identifiers.

2. Bind a buffer object, specifying that it will be used for either storing vertex data or indices.

3. Request storage for your data, and optionally initialize those data elements.

4. Specify offsets relative to the start of the buffer object to initialize the vertex-array functions, such as **glVertexPointer**().

5. Bind the appropriate buffer object to be utilized in rendering.

6. Render using an appropriate vertex-array rendering function, such as **glDrawArrays**() or **glDrawElements**().

If you need to initialize multiple buffer objects, you will repeat steps 2 through 4 for each buffer object.

Both "formats" of vertex-array data are available for use in buffer objects. As described in "Step 2: Specifying Data for the Arrays," vertex, color, lighting normal, or any other type of associated vertex data can be stored in a buffer object. Additionally, interleaved vertex array data, as described in "Interleaved Arrays," can also be stored in a buffer object. In either case, you would create a single buffer object to hold all of the data to be used as vertex arrays.

As compared to specifying a memory address in the client's memory where OpenGL should access the vertex-array data, you specify the offset in machine units (usually bytes) to the data in the buffer. To help illustrate computing the offset, and to frustrate the purists in the audience, we'll use the following macro to simplify expressing the offset:

```
#define BUFFER_OFFSET(bytes)   ((GLubyte*) NULL + (bytes))
```

For example, if you had floating-point color and position data for each vertex, perhaps represented as the following array

```
GLfloat vertexData[][6] = {
    { R₀, G₀, B₀, X₀, Y₀, Z₀ },
    { R₁, G₁, B₁, X₁, Y₁, Z₁ },
    ...
    { Rₙ, Gₙ, Bₙ, Xₙ, Yₙ, Zₙ }
};
```

that were used to initialize the buffer object, you could specify the data as two separate vertex array calls, one for colors and one for vertices:

```
glColorPointer(3, GL_FLOAT, 6*sizeof(GLfloat),BUFFER_OFFSET(0));
glVertexPointer(3, GL_FLOAT, 6*sizeof(GLfloat),
                BUFFER_OFFSET(3*sizeof(GLfloat)));
glEnableClientState(GL_COLOR_ARRAY);
glEnableClientState(GL_VERTEX_ARRAY);
```

Conversely, since the data in *vertexData* matches a format for an interleaved vertex array, you could use **glInterleavedArrays()** for specifying the vertex-array data:

```
glInterleavedArrays(GL_C3F_V3F, 0, BUFFER_OFFSET(0));
```

Putting this all together, Example 2-17 demonstrates how buffer objects of vertex data might be used. The example creates two buffer objects, one containing vertex data and the other containing index data.

Example 2-17   Using Buffer Objects with Vertex Data

```
#define VERTICES     0
#define INDICES      1
#define NUM_BUFFERS  2
```

```
GLuint  buffers[NUM_BUFFERS];

GLfloat vertices[][3] = {
    { -1.0, -1.0, -1.0 },
    {  1.0, -1.0, -1.0 },
    {  1.0,  1.0, -1.0 },
    { -1.0,  1.0, -1.0 },
    { -1.0, -1.0,  1.0 },
    {  1.0, -1.0,  1.0 },
    {  1.0,  1.0,  1.0 },
    { -1.0,  1.0,  1.0 }
};

GLubyte indices[][4] = {
    { 0, 1, 2, 3 },
    { 4, 7, 6, 5 },
    { 0, 4, 5, 1 },
    { 3, 2, 6, 7 },
    { 0, 3, 7, 4 },
    { 1, 5, 6, 2 }
};

glGenBuffers(NUM_BUFFERS, buffers);

glBindBuffer(GL_ARRAY_BUFFER, buffers[VERTICES]);
glBufferData(GL_ARRAY_BUFFER, sizeof(vertices), vertices,
            GL_STATIC_DRAW);
glVertexPointer(3, GL_FLOAT, 0, BUFFER_OFFSET(0));
glEnableClientState(GL_VERTEX_ARRAY);

glBindBuffer(GL_ELEMENT_ARRAY_BUFFER, buffers[INDICES]);
glBufferData(GL_ELEMENT_ARRAY_BUFFER, sizeof(indices), indices
            GL_STATIC_DRAW);

glDrawElements(GL_QUADS, 24, GL_UNSIGNED_BYTE,
            BUFFER_OFFSET(0));
```

Vertex-Array Objects

As your programs grow larger and use more models, you will probably find that you switch between multiple sets of vertex arrays each frame. Depending on how many vertex attributes you're using for each vertex, the number of calls—such as to **glVertexPointer()**—may start to become large.

Vertex-array objects bundle collections of calls for setting the vertex array's state. After being initialized, you can quickly change between different sets of vertex arrays with a single call.

To create a vertex-array object, first call **glGenVertexArrays()**, which will create the requested number of uninitialized objects:

---

void **glGenVertexArrays**(GLsizei *n*, GLuint **arrays*);

Returns *n* currently unused names for use as vertex-array objects in the array *arrays*. The names returned are marked as used for the purposes of allocating additional buffer objects, and initialized with values representing the default state of the collection of uninitialized vertex arrays.

After creating your vertex-array objects, you'll need to initialize the new objects, and associate the set of vertex-array data that you want to enable with the individual allocated objects. You do this with the **glBindVertexArray()** routine. Once you initialize all of your vertex-array objects, you can use **glBindVertexArray()** to switch between the different sets of vertex arrays that you've set up.

GLvoid **gBindVertexArray**(GLuint *array*);

---

glBindVertexArray() does three things. When using the value *array* that is other than zero and was returned from **glGenVertexArrays()**, a new vertex-array object is created and assigned that name. When binding to a previously created vertex-array object, that vertex array object becomes active, which additionally affects the vertex array state stored in the object. When binding to an *array* value of zero, OpenGL stops using vertex-array objects and returns to the default state for vertex arrays.

A GL_INVALID_OPERATION error is generated if *array* is not a value previously returned from **glGenVertexArrays()**, or if it is a value that has been released by **glDeleteVertexArrays()**, or if any of the **gl*Pointer()** routines are called to specify a vertex array that is not associated with a buffer object while a non-zero vertex-array object is bound (i.e., using a client-side vertex array storage).

Example 2-18 demonstrates switching between two sets of vertex arrays using vertex-arrays objects.

Example 2-18   Using Vertex-Array Objects: vao.c

```
#define BUFFER_OFFSET(offset)   ((GLvoid*) NULL + offset)
#define NumberOf(array)         (sizeof(array)/sizeof(array[0]))

typedef struct {
    GLfloat x, y, z;
} vec3;


typedef struct {
    vec3      xlate;    /* Translation */
    GLfloat   angle;
    vec3      axis;
} XForm;

enum { Cube, Cone, NumVAOs };
GLuint    VAO[NumVAOs];
GLenum    PrimType[NumVAOs];
GLsizei   NumElements[NumVAOs];
XForm     Xform[NumVAOs] = {
    { { -2.0, 0.0, 0.0 }, 0.0, { 0.0, 1.0, 0.0 } },
    { {  0.0, 0.0, 2.0 }, 0.0, { 1.0, 0.0, 0.0 } }
};
GLfloat   Angle = 0.0;

void
init()
{
    enum { Vertices, Colors, Elements, NumVBOs };
    GLuint  buffers[NumVBOs];

    glGenVertexArrays(NumVAOs, VAO);

    {
        GLfloat  cubeVerts[][3] = {
            { -1.0, -1.0, -1.0 },
            { -1.0, -1.0,  1.0 },
            { -1.0,  1.0, -1.0 },
            { -1.0,  1.0,  1.0 },
            {  1.0, -1.0, -1.0 },
            {  1.0, -1.0,  1.0 },
            {  1.0,  1.0, -1.0 },
            {  1.0,  1.0,  1.0 },
        };
```

```
GLfloat  cubeColors[][3] = {
    {  0.0,   0.0,   0.0 },
    {  0.0,   0.0,   1.0 },
    {  0.0,   1.0,   0.0 },
    {  0.0,   1.0,   1.0 },
    {  1.0,   0.0,   0.0 },
    {  1.0,   0.0,   1.0 },
    {  1.0,   1.0,   0.0 },
    {  1.0,   1.0,   1.0 },
};

GLubyte  cubeIndices[] = {
    0, 1, 3, 2,
    4, 6, 7, 5,
    2, 3, 7, 6,
    0, 4, 5, 1,
    0, 2, 6, 4,
    1, 5, 7, 3
};

glBindVertexArray(VAO[Cube]);
glGenBuffers(NumVBOs, buffers);
glBindBuffer(GL_ARRAY_BUFFER, buffers[Vertices]);
glBufferData(GL_ARRAY_BUFFER, sizeof(cubeVerts),
    cubeVerts, GL_STATIC_DRAW);
glVertexPointer(3, GL_FLOAT, 0, BUFFER_OFFSET(0));
glEnableClientState(GL_VERTEX_ARRAY);

glBindBuffer(GL_ARRAY_BUFFER, buffers[Colors]);
glBufferData(GL_ARRAY_BUFFER, sizeof(cubeColors),
    cubeColors, GL_STATIC_DRAW);
glColorPointer(3, GL_FLOAT, 0, BUFFER_OFFSET(0));
glEnableClientState(GL_COLOR_ARRAY);

glBindBuffer(GL_ELEMENT_ARRAY_BUFFER,
    buffers[Elements]);
glBufferData(GL_ELEMENT_ARRAY_BUFFER,
    sizeof(cubeIndices), cubeIndices, GL_STATIC_DRAW);

PrimType[Cube] = GL_QUADS;
NumElements[Cube] = NumberOf(cubeIndices);
}

{
    int i, idx;
    float  dTheta;
```

```
#define NumConePoints  36
        /* We add one more vertex for the cone's apex */
        GLfloat  coneVerts[NumConePoints+1][3] = {
            {0.0, 0.0, 1.0}
        };
        GLfloat  coneColors[NumConePoints+1][3] = {
            {1.0, 1.0, 1.0}
        };
        GLubyte  coneIndices[NumConePoints+1];

        dTheta = 2*M_PI / (NumConePoints - 1);
        idx = 1;
        for (i = 0; i < NumConePoints; ++i, ++idx) {
            float theta = i*dTheta;
            coneVerts[idx][0] = cos(theta);
            coneVerts[idx][1] = sin(theta);
            coneVerts[idx][2] = 0.0;

            coneColors[idx][0] = cos(theta);
            coneColors[idx][1] = sin(theta);
            coneColors[idx][2] = 0.0;

            coneIndices[idx] = idx;
        }

        glBindVertexArray(VAO[Cone]);
        glGenBuffers(NumVBOs, buffers);
        glBindBuffer(GL_ARRAY_BUFFER, buffers[Vertices]);
        glBufferData(GL_ARRAY_BUFFER, sizeof(coneVerts),
            coneVerts, GL_STATIC_DRAW);
        glVertexPointer(3, GL_FLOAT, 0, BUFFER_OFFSET(0));
        glEnableClientState(GL_VERTEX_ARRAY);

        glBindBuffer(GL_ARRAY_BUFFER, buffers[Colors]);
        glBufferData(GL_ARRAY_BUFFER, sizeof(coneColors),
            coneColors, GL_STATIC_DRAW);
        glColorPointer(3, GL_FLOAT, 0, BUFFER_OFFSET(0));
        glEnableClientState(GL_COLOR_ARRAY);

        glBindBuffer(GL_ELEMENT_ARRAY_BUFFER,
            buffers[Elements]);
        glBufferData(GL_ELEMENT_ARRAY_BUFFER,
            sizeof(coneIndices), coneIndices, GL_STATIC_DRAW);

        PrimType[Cone] = GL_TRIANGLE_FAN;
        NumElements[Cone] = NumberOf(coneIndices);
    }

    glEnable(GL_DEPTH_TEST);
}
```

```
void
display()
{
    int  i;

    glClear(GL_COLOR_BUFFER_BIT | GL_DEPTH_BUFFER_BIT);

    glPushMatrix();
    glRotatef(Angle, 0.0, 1.0, 0.0);

    for (i = 0; i < NumVAOs; ++i) {
        glPushMatrix();
        glTranslatef(Xform[i].xlate.x, Xform[i].xlate.y,
            Xform[i].xlate.z);
        glRotatef(Xform[i].angle, Xform[i].axis.x,
            Xform[i].axis.y, Xform[i].axis.z);
        glBindVertexArray(VAO[i]);
        glDrawElements(PrimType[i], NumElements[i],
            GL_UNSIGNED_BYTE, BUFFER_OFFSET(0));
        glPopMatrix();
    }

    glPopMatrix();
    glutSwapBuffers();
}
```

To delete vertex-array objects and release their names for reuse, call
glDeleteVertexArrays(). If you're using buffer objects for storing data, they
are not deleted when the vertex-array object referencing them is deleted.
They continue to exist (until you delete them). The only change that occurs
is if the buffer objects were currently bound when you deleted the vertex-
array object, they become unbound.

---

void **glDeleteVertexArrays**(GLsizei *n*, GLuint **arrays*);

Deletes the *n* vertex-arrays objects specified in *arrays*, enabling the names
for reuse as vertex arrays later. If a bound vertex array is deleted, the
bindings for that vertex array become zero (as if you had called
glBindBuffer() with a value of zero), and the default vertex array becomes
the current one. Unused names in arrays are released, but no changes to
the current vertex array state are made.

Finally, if you need to determine whether a particular value might represent an allocated (but not necessarily initialized) vertex-array object, you can check by calling **glIsVertexArray()**.

GLboolean **glIsVertexArray**(GLuint *array*);

Returns GL_TRUE if *array* is the name of a vertex-array object that was previously generated with **glGenVertexArrays()**, but has not been subsequently deleted. Returns GL_FALSE if *array* is zero or a nonzero value that is not the name of a vertex-array object.

Attribute Groups

In "Basic State Management" you saw how to set or query an individual state or state variable. You can also save and restore the values of a collection of related state variables with a single command.

OpenGL groups related state variables into an *attribute group*. For example, the GL_LINE_BIT attribute consists of five state variables: the line width, the GL_LINE_STIPPLE enable status, the line stipple pattern, the line stipple repeat counter, and the GL_LINE_SMOOTH enable status. (See "Antialiasing" in Chapter 6.) With the commands **glPushAttrib()** and **glPopAttrib()**, you can save and restore all five state variables at once.

Some state variables are in more than one attribute group. For example, the state variable GL_CULL_FACE is part of both the polygon and the enable attribute groups.

In OpenGL Version 1.1, there are now two different attribute stacks. In addition to the original attribute stack (which saves the values of server state variables), there is also a client attribute stack, accessible by the commands **glPushClientAttrib()** and **glPopClientAttrib()**.

In general, it's faster to use these commands than to get, save, and restore the values yourself. Some values might be maintained in the hardware, and getting them might be expensive. Also, if you're operating on a remote client, all the attribute data has to be transferred across the network connection and back as it is obtained, saved, and restored. However, your OpenGL implementation keeps the attribute stack on the server, avoiding unnecessary network delays.

There are about 20 different attribute groups, which can be saved and restored by **glPushAttrib()** and **glPopAttrib()**. There are two client attribute groups, which can be saved and restored by **glPushClientAttrib()** and **glPopClientAttrib()**. For both server and client, the attributes are stored on a stack, which has a depth of at least 16 saved attribute groups. (The actual stack depths for your implementation can be obtained using GL_MAX_ATTRIB_STACK_DEPTH and GL_MAX_CLIENT_ATTRIB_STACK_DEPTH with **glGetIntegerv()**.) Pushing a full stack or popping an empty one generates an error.

(See the tables in Appendix B to find out exactly which attributes are saved for particular mask values—that is, which attributes are in a particular attribute group.)

Compatibility Extension
glPushAttrib
glPopAttrib
GL_ACCUM_ BUFFER_BIT
GL_ALL_ATTRIB_ BITS
GL_COLOR_ BUFFER_BIT
GL_CURRENT_BIT
GL_DEPTH_ BUFFER_BIT
GL_ENABLE_BIT
GL_EVAL_BIT
GL_FOG_BIT
GL_HINT_BIT
GL_LIGHTING_BIT
GL_LINE_BIT
GL_LIST_BIT
GL_ MULTISAMPLE_BIT
GL_PIXEL_MODE_ BIT
GL_POINT_BIT
GL_POLYGON_BIT
GL_POLYGON_ STIPPLE_BIT
GL_SCISSOR_BIT
GL_STENCIL_ BUFFER_BIT
GL_TEXTURE_BIT
GL_TRANSFORM_ BIT
GL_VIEWPORT_BIT

> void **glPushAttrib**(GLbitfield *mask*);
> void **glPopAttrib**(void);
>
> **glPushAttrib()** saves all the attributes indicated by bits in *mask* by pushing them onto the attribute stack. **glPopAttrib()** restores the values of those state variables that were saved with the last **glPushAttrib()**. Table 2-8 lists the possible mask bits that can be logically ORed together to save any combination of attributes. Each bit corresponds to a collection of individual state variables. For example, GL_LIGHTING_BIT refers to all the state variables related to lighting, which include the current material color; the ambient, diffuse, specular, and emitted light; a list of the lights that are enabled; and the directions of the spotlights. When **glPopAttrib()** is called, all these variables are restored.

The special mask GL_ALL_ATTRIB_BITS is used to save and restore all the state variables in all the attribute groups.

Mask Bit	Attribute Group
GL_ACCUM_BUFFER_BIT	accum-buffer
GL_ALL_ATTRIB_BITS	—
GL_COLOR_BUFFER_BIT	color-buffer
GL_CURRENT_BIT	current
GL_DEPTH_BUFFER_BIT	depth-buffer

Table 2-8   Attribute Groups

Mask Bit	Attribute Group
GL_ENABLE_BIT	enable
GL_EVAL_BIT	eval
GL_FOG_BIT	fog
GL_HINT_BIT	hint
GL_LIGHTING_BIT	lighting
GL_LINE_BIT	line
GL_LIST_BIT	list
GL_MULTISAMPLE_BIT	multisample
GL_PIXEL_MODE_BIT	pixel
GL_POINT_BIT	point
GL_POLYGON_BIT	polygon
GL_POLYGON_STIPPLE_BIT	polygon-stipple
GL_SCISSOR_BIT	scissor
GL_STENCIL_BUFFER_BIT	stencil-buffer
GL_TEXTURE_BIT	texture
GL_TRANSFORM_BIT	transform
GL_VIEWPORT_BIT	viewport

Table 2-8 **(continued)**   Attribute Groups

Compatibility Extension
glPushClientAttrib
glPopClientAttrib
GL_CLIENT_ PIXEL_STORE_ BIT
GL_CLIENT_ VERTEX_ARRAY_ BIT
GL_CLIENT_ALL_ ATTRIB_BITS

void **glPushClientAttrib**(GLbitfield *mask*);
void **glPopClientAttrib**(void);

glPushClientAttrib() saves all the attributes indicated by bits in *mask* by pushing them onto the client attribute stack. **glPopClientAttrib**() restores the values of those state variables that were saved with the last **glPushClientAttrib**(). Table 2-9 lists the possible mask bits that can be logically ORed together to save any combination of client attributes.

Two client attribute groups, feedback and select, cannot be saved or restored with the stack mechanism.

Mask Bit	Attribute Group
GL_CLIENT_PIXEL_STORE_BIT	pixel-store
GL_CLIENT_VERTEX_ARRAY_BIT	vertex-array
GL_CLIENT_ALL_ATTRIB_BITS	--
can't be pushed or popped	feedback
can't be pushed or popped	select

Table 2-9   Client Attribute Groups

Some Hints for Building Polygonal Models of Surfaces

Following are some techniques that you can use as you build polygonal approximations of surfaces. You might want to review this section after you've read Chapter 5 on lighting and Chapter 7 on display lists. The lighting conditions affect how models look once they're drawn, and some of the following techniques are much more efficient when used in conjunction with display lists. As you read these techniques, keep in mind that when lighting calculations are enabled, normal vectors must be specified to get proper results.

Constructing polygonal approximations to surfaces is an art, and there is no substitute for experience. This section, however, lists a few pointers that might make it a bit easier to get started.

- Keep polygon orientations (windings) consistent. Make sure that when viewed from the outside, all the polygons on the surface are oriented in the same direction (all clockwise or all counterclockwise). Consistent orientation is important for polygon culling and two-sided lighting. Try to get this right the first time, as it's excruciatingly painful to fix the problem later. (If you use **glScale*()** to reflect geometry around some axis of symmetry, you might change the orientation with **glFrontFace()** to keep the orientations consistent.)

- When you subdivide a surface, watch out for any nontriangular polygons. The three vertices of a triangle are guaranteed to lie on a plane; any polygon with four or more vertices might not. Nonplanar polygons can be viewed from some orientation such that the edges cross each other, and OpenGL might not render such polygons correctly.

- There's always a trade-off between the display speed and the quality of the image. If you subdivide a surface into a small number of polygons, it renders quickly but might have a jagged appearance; if you subdivide it into millions of tiny polygons, it probably looks good but might take a long time to render. Ideally, you can provide a parameter to the subdivision routines that indicates how fine a subdivision you want, and if the object is farther from the eye, you can use a coarser subdivision. Also, when you subdivide, use large polygons where the surface is relatively flat, and small polygons in regions of high curvature.

- For high-quality images, it's a good idea to subdivide more on the silhouette edges than in the interior. If the surface is to be rotated relative to the eye, this is tougher to do, as the silhouette edges keep moving. Silhouette edges occur where the normal vectors are perpendicular to the vector from the surface to the viewpoint—that is, when their vector dot product is zero. Your subdivision algorithm might choose to subdivide more if this dot product is near zero.

- Try to avoid T-intersections in your models (see Figure 2-16). As shown, there's no guarantee that the line segments AB and BC lie on exactly the same pixels as the segment AC. Sometimes they do, and sometimes they don't, depending on the transformations and orientation. This can cause cracks to appear intermittently in the surface.

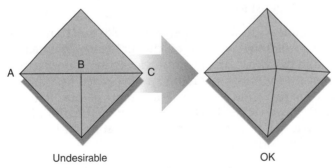

Undesirable   OK

Figure 2-16   Modifying an Undesirable T-Intersection

- If you're constructing a closed surface, be sure to use exactly the same numbers for coordinates at the beginning and end of a closed loop, or you can get gaps and cracks due to numerical round-off. Here's an example of bad code for a two-dimensional circle:

```
/* don't use this code */
#define PI 3.14159265
#define EDGES 30

/* draw a circle */
glBegin(GL_LINE_STRIP);
for (i = 0; i <= EDGES; i++)
    glVertex2f(cos((2*PI*i)/EDGES), sin((2*PI*i)/EDGES));
glEnd();
```

The edges meet exactly only if your machine manages to calculate exactly the same values for the sine and cosine of 0 and of (2*PI*EDGES/EDGES). If you trust the floating-point unit on your machine to do this right, the authors have a bridge they'd like to sell you... To correct the code, make sure that when i == EDGES, you use 0 for the sine and cosine, not 2*PI*EDGES/EDGES. (Or simpler still, use GL_LINE_LOOP instead of GL_LINE_STRIP, and change the loop termination condition to i < EDGES.)

An Example: Building an Icosahedron

To illustrate some of the considerations that arise in approximating a surface, let's look at some example code sequences. This code concerns the vertices of a regular icosahedron (which is a Platonic solid composed of 20 faces that span 12 vertices, the face of each being an equilateral triangle). An icosahedron can be considered a rough approximation of a sphere. Example 2-19 defines the vertices and triangles making up an icosahedron and then draws the icosahedron.

Example 2-19   Drawing an Icosahedron

```
#define X .525731112119133606
#define Z .850650808352039932

static GLfloat vdata[12][3] = {
    {-X, 0.0, Z}, {X, 0.0, Z}, {-X, 0.0, -Z}, {X, 0.0, -Z},
    {0.0, Z, X}, {0.0, Z, -X}, {0.0, -Z, X}, {0.0, -Z, -X},
    {Z, X, 0.0}, {-Z, X, 0.0}, {Z, -X, 0.0}, {-Z, -X, 0.0}
};
```

```
static GLuint tindices[20][3] = {
   {1,4,0}, {4,9,0}, {4,5,9}, {8,5,4}, {1,8,4},
   {1,10,8}, {10,3,8}, {8,3,5}, {3,2,5}, {3,7,2},
   {3,10,7}, {10,6,7}, {6,11,7}, {6,0,11}, {6,1,0},
   {10,1,6}, {11,0,9}, {2,11,9}, {5,2,9}, {11,2,7}
};

int i;

glBegin(GL_TRIANGLES);
for (i = 0; i < 20; i++) {
   /* color information here */
   glVertex3fv(&vdata[tindices[i][0]][0]);
   glVertex3fv(&vdata[tindices[i][1]][0]);
   glVertex3fv(&vdata[tindices[i][2]][0]);
}
glEnd();
```

The strange numbers *X* and *Z* are chosen so that the distance from the origin to any of the vertices of the icosahedron is 1.0. The coordinates of the 12 vertices are given in the array *vdata[][]*, where the zeroth vertex is {*–X, 0.0, Z*}, the first is {*X, 0.0, Z*}, and so on. The array *tindices[][]* tells how to link the vertices to make triangles. For example, the first triangle is made from the zeroth, fourth, and first vertices. If you take the vertices for triangles in the order given, all the triangles have the same orientation.

The line that mentions color information should be replaced by a command that sets the color of the *i*th face. If no code appears here, all faces are drawn in the same color, and it will be impossible to discern the three-dimensional quality of the object. An alternative to explicitly specifying colors is to define surface normals and use lighting, as described in the next subsection.

Note: In all the examples described in this section, unless the surface is to be drawn only once, you should probably save the calculated vertex and normal coordinates so that the calculations don't need to be repeated each time the surface is drawn. This can be done using your own data structures or by constructing display lists (see Chapter 7).

Calculating Normal Vectors for a Surface

If a surface is to be lit, you need to supply the vector normal to the surface. Calculating the normalized cross product of two vectors on that surface provides their normal vector. With the flat surfaces of an icosahedron, all three vertices defining a surface have the same normal vector. In this case, the normal needs to be specified only once for each set of three vertices. The code in Example 2-20 can replace the "color information here" line in Example 2-19 for drawing the icosahedron.

Example 2-20   Generating Normal Vectors for a Surface

```
GLfloat d1[3], d2[3], norm[3];
for (j = 0; j < 3; j++) {
   d1[j] = vdata[tindices[i][0]][j] - vdata[tindices[i][1]][j];
   d2[j] = vdata[tindices[i][1]][j] - vdata[tindices[i][2]][j];
}
normcrossprod(d1, d2, norm);
glNormal3fv(norm);
```

The function **normcrossprod()** produces the normalized cross product of two vectors, as shown in Example 2-21.

Example 2-21   Calculating the Normalized Cross Product of Two Vectors

```
void normalize(float v[3])
{
    GLfloat d = sqrt(v[0]*v[0]+v[1]*v[1]+v[2]*v[2]);
    if (d == 0.0) {
       error("zero length vector");
       return;
    }
    v[0] /= d;
    v[1] /= d;
    v[2] /= d;
}

void normcrossprod(float v1[3], float v2[3], float out[3])
{
    out[0] = v1[1]*v2[2] - v1[2]*v2[1];
    out[1] = v1[2]*v2[0] - v1[0]*v2[2];
    out[2] = v1[0]*v2[1] - v1[1]*v2[0];
    normalize(out);
}
```

If you're using an icosahedron as an approximation for a shaded sphere, you'll want to use normal vectors that are perpendicular to the true surface of the sphere, rather than perpendicular to the faces. For a sphere, the normal vectors are simple; each points in the same direction as the vector from the origin to the corresponding vertex. Since the icosahedron vertex data is for an icosahedron of radius 1, the normal data and vertex data are identical. Here is the code that would draw an icosahedral approximation of a smoothly shaded sphere (assuming that lighting is enabled, as described in Chapter 5):

```
glBegin(GL_TRIANGLES);
for (i = 0; i < 20; i++) {
    glNormal3fv(&vdata[tindices[i][0]][0]);
    glVertex3fv(&vdata[tindices[i][0]][0]);
    glNormal3fv(&vdata[tindices[i][1]][0]);
    glVertex3fv(&vdata[tindices[i][1]][0]);
    glNormal3fv(&vdata[tindices[i][2]][0]);
    glVertex3fv(&vdata[tindices[i][2]][0]);
}
glEnd();
```

Improving the Model

A 20-sided approximation to a sphere doesn't look good unless the image of the sphere on the screen is quite small, but there's an easy way to increase the accuracy of the approximation. Imagine the icosahedron inscribed in a sphere, and subdivide the triangles as shown in Figure 2-17. The newly introduced vertices lie slightly inside the sphere, so push them to the surface by normalizing them (dividing them by a factor to make them have length 1). This subdivision process can be repeated for arbitrary accuracy. The three objects shown in Figure 2-17 use 20, 80, and 320 approximating triangles, respectively.

Figure 2-17   Subdividing to Improve a Polygonal Approximation to a Surface

Example 2-22 performs a single subdivision, creating an 80-sided spherical approximation.

Example 2-22 Single Subdivision

```
void drawtriangle(float *v1, float *v2, float *v3)
{
    glBegin(GL_TRIANGLES);
        glNormal3fv(v1);
        glVertex3fv(v1);
        glNormal3fv(v2);
        glVertex3fv(v2);
        glNormal3fv(v3);
        glVertex3fv(v3);
    glEnd();
}



void subdivide(float *v1, float *v2, float *v3)
{
    GLfloat v12[3], v23[3], v31[3];
    GLint i;

    for (i = 0; i < 3; i++) {
        v12[i] = (v1[i]+v2[i])/2.0;
        v23[i] = (v2[i]+v3[i])/2.0;
        v31[i] = (v3[i]+v1[i])/2.0;
    }
    normalize(v12);
    normalize(v23);
    normalize(v31);
    drawtriangle(v1, v12, v31);
    drawtriangle(v2, v23, v12);
    drawtriangle(v3, v31, v23);
    drawtriangle(v12, v23, v31);
}

for (i = 0; i < 20; i++) {
    subdivide(&vdata[tindices[i][0]][0],
              &vdata[tindices[i][1]][0],
              &vdata[tindices[i][2]][0]);
}
```

Example 2-23 is a slight modification of Example 2-22 that recursively subdivides the triangles to the proper depth. If the depth value is 0, no subdivisions are performed, and the triangle is drawn as is. If the depth is 1, a single subdivision is performed, and so on.

Example 2-23   Recursive Subdivision

```
void subdivide(float *v1, float *v2, float *v3, long depth)
{
   GLfloat v12[3], v23[3], v31[3];
   GLint i;

   if (depth == 0) {
      drawtriangle(v1, v2, v3);
      return;
   }
   for (i = 0; i < 3; i++) {
      v12[i] = (v1[i]+v2[i])/2.0;
      v23[i] = (v2[i]+v3[i])/2.0;
      v31[i] = (v3[i]+v1[i])/2.0;
   }
   normalize(v12);
   normalize(v23);
   normalize(v31);
   subdivide(v1, v12, v31, depth-1);
   subdivide(v2, v23, v12, depth-1);
   subdivide(v3, v31, v23, depth-1);
   subdivide(v12, v23, v31, depth-1);
}
```

Generalized Subdivision

A recursive subdivision technique such as the one described in Example 2-23 can be used for other types of surfaces. Typically, the recursion ends if either a certain depth is reached or some condition on the curvature is satisfied (highly curved parts of surfaces look better with more subdivision).

To look at a more general solution to the problem of subdivision, consider an arbitrary surface parameterized by two variables, $u[0]$ and $u[1]$. Suppose that two routines are provided:

```
void surf(GLfloat u[2], GLfloat vertex[3], GLfloat normal[3]);
float curv(GLfloat u[2]);
```

If $u[]$ is passed to **surf**(), the corresponding three-dimensional vertex and normal vectors (of length 1) are returned. If $u[]$ is passed to **curv**(), the curvature of the surface at that point is calculated and returned. (See an introductory textbook on differential geometry for more information about measuring surface curvature.)

Example 2-24 shows the recursive routine that subdivides a triangle until either the maximum depth is reached or the maximum curvature at the three vertices is less than some cutoff.

Example 2-24 Generalized Subdivision

```
void subdivide(float u1[2], float u2[2], float u3[2],
               float cutoff, long depth)
{
   GLfloat v1[3], v2[3], v3[3], n1[3], n2[3], n3[3];
   GLfloat u12[2], u23[2], u32[2];
   GLint i;

   if (depth == maxdepth || (curv(u1) < cutoff &&
       curv(u2) < cutoff && curv(u3) < cutoff)) {
      surf(u1, v1, n1);
      surf(u2, v2, n2);
      surf(u3, v3, n3);
      glBegin(GL_POLYGON);
         glNormal3fv(n1); glVertex3fv(v1);
         glNormal3fv(n2); glVertex3fv(v2);
         glNormal3fv(n3); glVertex3fv(v3);
      glEnd();
      return;
   }

   for (i = 0; i < 2; i++) {
      u12[i] = (u1[i] + u2[i])/2.0;
      u23[i] = (u2[i] + u3[i])/2.0;
      u31[i] = (u3[i] + u1[i])/2.0;
   }
   subdivide(u1, u12, u31, cutoff, depth+1);
   subdivide(u2, u23, u12, cutoff, depth+1);
   subdivide(u3, u31, u23, cutoff, depth+1);
   subdivide(u12, u23, u31, cutoff, depth+1);
}
```

Chapter 3

Viewing

Chapter Objectives

After reading this chapter, you'll be able to do the following:

- View a *geometric model* in any orientation by transforming it in three-dimensional space

- Control the location in three-dimensional space from which the model is viewed

- Clip undesired portions of the model out of the scene that's to be viewed

- Manipulate the appropriate matrix stacks that control model transformation for viewing, and project the model onto the screen

- Combine multiple transformations to mimic sophisticated systems in motion, such as a solar system or an articulated robot arm

- Reverse or mimic the operations of the geometric processing pipeline

Note: For OpenGL Version 3.1, many of the techniques and functions described in this chapter were removed through deprecation. The concepts are still relevant, but the transformations described need to be implemented in a vertex shader, as described in "Vertex Processing" in Chapter 15.

Chapter 2 explained how to instruct OpenGL to draw the geometric models you want displayed in your scene. Now you must decide how you want to position the models in the scene, and you must choose a vantage point from which to view the scene. You can use the default positioning and vantage point, but most likely you want to specify them.

Look at the image on the cover of this book. The program that produced that image contained a single geometric description of a building block. Each block was carefully positioned in the scene: Some blocks were scattered on the floor, some were stacked on top of each other on the table, and some were assembled to make the globe. Also, a particular viewpoint had to be chosen. Obviously, we wanted to look at the corner of the room containing the globe. But how far away from the scene—and where exactly—should the viewer be? We wanted to make sure that the final image of the scene contained a good view out the window, that a portion of the floor was visible, and that all the objects in the scene were not only visible but presented in an interesting arrangement. This chapter explains how to use OpenGL to accomplish these tasks: how to position and orient models in three-dimensional space and how to establish the location—also in three-dimensional space—of the viewpoint. All of these factors help determine exactly what image appears on the screen.

You want to remember that the point of computer graphics is to create a two-dimensional image of three-dimensional objects (it has to be two-dimensional because it's drawn on a flat screen), but you need to think in three-dimensional coordinates while making many of the decisions that determine what is drawn on the screen. A common mistake people make when creating three-dimensional graphics is to start thinking too soon that the final image appears on a flat, two-dimensional screen. Avoid thinking about which pixels need to be drawn, and instead try to visualize three-dimensional space. Create your models in some three-dimensional universe that lies deep inside your computer, and let the computer do its job of calculating which pixels to color.

A series of three computer operations converts an object's three-dimensional coordinates to pixel positions on the screen:

- Transformations, which are represented by matrix multiplication, include modeling, viewing, and projection operations. Such operations include rotation, translation, scaling, reflecting, orthographic projection, and perspective projection. Generally, you use a combination of several transformations to draw a scene.

- Since the scene is rendered on a rectangular window, objects (or parts of objects) that lie outside the window must be clipped. In three-dimensional computer graphics, clipping occurs by throwing out objects on one side of a clipping plane.

- Finally, a correspondence must be established between the transformed coordinates and screen pixels. This is known as a *viewport* transformation.

This chapter describes all of these operations, and how to control them, in the following major sections:

- "Overview: The Camera Analogy" gives an overview of the transformation process by describing the analogy of taking a photograph with a camera, presents a simple example program that transforms an object, and briefly describes the basic OpenGL transformation commands.

- "Viewing and Modeling Transformations" explains in detail how to specify and imagine the effect of viewing and modeling transformations. These transformations orient the model and the camera relative to each other to obtain the desired final image.

- "Projection Transformations" describes how to specify the shape and orientation of the *viewing volume*. The viewing volume determines how a scene is projected onto the screen (with a perspective or orthographic projection) and which objects or parts of objects are clipped out of the scene.

- "Viewport Transformation" explains how to control the conversion of three-dimensional model coordinates to screen coordinates.

- "Troubleshooting Transformations" presents some tips for discovering why you might not be getting the desired effect from your modeling, viewing, projection, and viewport transformations.

- "Manipulating the Matrix Stacks" discusses how to save and restore certain transformations. This is particularly useful when you're drawing complicated objects that are built from simpler ones.

- "Additional Clipping Planes" describes how to specify additional clipping planes beyond those defined by the viewing volume.

- "Examples of Composing Several Transformations" walks you through a couple of more complicated uses for transformations.

- "Reversing or Mimicking Transformations" shows you how to take a transformed point in window coordinates and reverse the transformation to obtain its original object coordinates. The transformation itself (without reversal) can also be emulated.

In Version 1.3, new OpenGL functions were added to directly support row-major (in OpenGL terms, transposed) matrices.

Overview: The Camera Analogy

The transformation process used to produce the desired scene for viewing is analogous to taking a photograph with a camera. As shown in Figure 3-1, the steps with a camera (or a computer) might be the following:

1. Set up your tripod and point the camera at the scene (viewing transformation).

2. Arrange the scene to be photographed into the desired composition (modeling transformation).

3. Choose a camera lens or adjust the zoom (projection transformation).

4. Determine how large you want the final photograph to be—for example, you might want it enlarged (viewport transformation).

After these steps have been performed, the picture can be snapped or the scene can be drawn.

Note that these steps correspond to the order in which you specify the desired transformations in your program, not necessarily the order in which the relevant mathematical operations are performed on an object's vertices. The viewing transformations must precede the modeling transformations in your code, but you can specify the projection and viewport transformations at any point before drawing occurs. Figure 3-2 shows the order in which these operations occur on your computer.

With a camera

With a computer

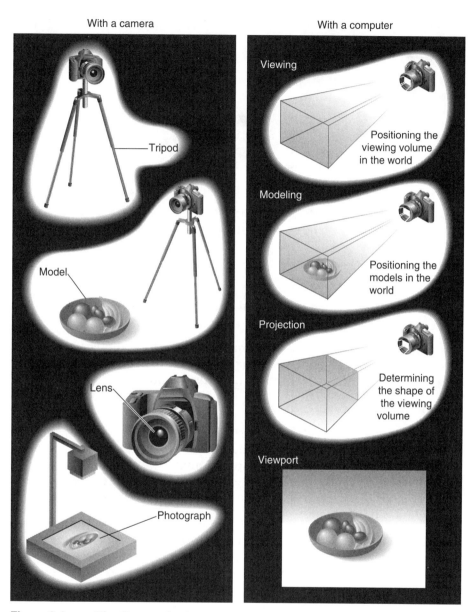

Tripod

Model

Lens

Photograph

Viewing

Positioning the
viewing volume
in the world

Modeling

Positioning the
models in the
world

Projection

Determining
the shape of
the viewing
volume

Viewport

Figure 3-1   The Camera Analogy

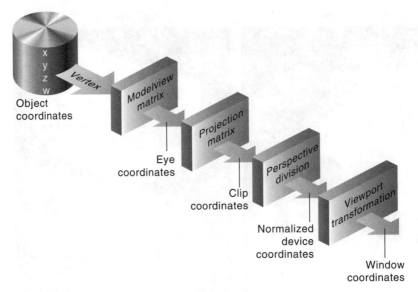

Object
coordinates

Eye
coordinates

Clip
coordinates

Normalized
device
coordinates

Window
coordinates

Figure 3-2   Stages of Vertex Transformation

To specify viewing, modeling, and projection transformations, you construct a 4 × 4 matrix **M**, which is then multiplied by the coordinates of each vertex v in the scene to accomplish the transformation:

$v' = \mathbf{M}v$

(Remember that vertices always have four coordinates (x, y, z, w), although in most cases w is 1, and for two-dimensional data, z is 0.) Note that viewing and modeling transformations are automatically applied to surface normal vectors, in addition to vertices. (Normal vectors are used only in *eye coordinates*.) This ensures that the normal vector's relationship to the vertex data is properly preserved.

The viewing and modeling transformations you specify are combined to form the modelview matrix, which is applied to the incoming *object coordinates* to yield eye coordinates. Next, if you've specified additional clipping planes to remove certain objects from the scene or to provide cutaway views of objects, these clipping planes are applied.

After that, OpenGL applies the projection matrix to yield *clip coordinates*. This transformation defines a viewing volume; objects outside this volume are clipped so that they're not drawn in the final scene. After this point, the *perspective division* is performed by dividing coordinate values by w, to produce *normalized device coordinates*. (See for more information about the meaning of the *w*-coordinate and how it affects matrix transformations.) Finally, the transformed coordinates are converted to *window coordinates* by applying the viewport transformation. You can manipulate the dimensions of the viewport to cause the final image to be enlarged, shrunk, or stretched.

You might correctly suppose that the *x*- and *y*-coordinates are sufficient to determine which pixels need to be drawn on the screen. However, all the transformations are performed on the *z*-coordinates as well. This way, at the end of this transformation process, the *z*-values correctly reflect the depth of a given vertex (measured in distance away from the screen). One use for this depth value is to eliminate unnecessary drawing. For example, suppose two vertices have the same *x*- and *y*-values but different *z*-values. OpenGL can use this information to determine which surfaces are obscured by other surfaces and can then avoid drawing the hidden surfaces. (See Chapter 5 and Chapter 10 for more information about this technique, which is called *hidden-surface removal*.)

As you've probably guessed by now, you need to know a few things about matrix mathematics to get the most out of this chapter. If you want to brush up on your knowledge in this area, you might consult a textbook on linear algebra.

A Simple Example: Drawing a Cube

Example 3-1 draws a cube that's scaled by a modeling transformation (see Figure 3-3). The viewing transformation, **gluLookAt()**, positions and aims the camera toward where the cube is drawn. A projection transformation and a viewport transformation are also specified. The rest of this section walks you through Example 3-1 and briefly explains the transformation commands it uses. The succeeding sections contain a complete, detailed discussion of all OpenGL transformation commands.

Figure 3-3   Transformed Cube

Example 3-1   Transformed Cube: cube.c

```c
void init(void)
{
   glClearColor(0.0, 0.0, 0.0, 0.0);
   glShadeModel(GL_FLAT);
}

void display(void)
{
   glClear(GL_COLOR_BUFFER_BIT);
   glColor3f(1.0, 1.0, 1.0);
   glLoadIdentity();             /* clear the matrix */
        /* viewing transformation  */
   gluLookAt(0.0, 0.0, 5.0, 0.0, 0.0, 0.0, 0.0, 1.0, 0.0);
   glScalef(1.0, 2.0, 1.0);      /* modeling transformation */
   glutWireCube(1.0);
   glFlush();
}

void reshape(int w, int h)
{
   glViewport(0, 0, (GLsizei) w, (GLsizei) h);
   glMatrixMode(GL_PROJECTION);
   glLoadIdentity();
   glFrustum(-1.0, 1.0, -1.0, 1.0, 1.5, 20.0);
   glMatrixMode(GL_MODELVIEW);
}

int main(int argc, char** argv)
{
   glutInit(&argc, argv);
   glutInitDisplayMode(GLUT_SINGLE | GLUT_RGB);
   glutInitWindowSize(500, 500);
   glutInitWindowPosition(100, 100);
   glutCreateWindow(argv[0]);
   init();
   glutDisplayFunc(display);
   glutReshapeFunc(reshape);
   glutMainLoop();
   return 0;
}
```

The Viewing Transformation

Recall that the viewing transformation is analogous to positioning and aiming a camera. In this code example, before the viewing transformation can be specified, the *current matrix* is set to the identity matrix with **glLoadIdentity()**. This step is necessary since most of the transformation commands multiply the current matrix by the specified matrix and then set the result to be the current matrix. If you don't clear the current matrix by loading it with the identity matrix, you continue to combine previous transformation matrices with the new one you supply. In some cases, you do want to perform such combinations, but you also need to clear the matrix sometimes.

In Example 3-1, after the matrix is initialized, the viewing transformation is specified with **gluLookAt()**. The arguments for this command indicate where the camera (or eye position) is placed, where it is aimed, and which way is up. The arguments used here place the camera at (0, 0, 5), aim the camera lens toward (0, 0, 0), and specify the *up-vector* as (0, 1, 0). The up-vector defines a unique orientation for the camera.

If **gluLookAt()** was not called, the camera has a default position and orientation. By default, the camera is situated at the origin, points down the negative z-axis, and has an up-vector of (0, 1, 0). Therefore, in Example 3-1, the overall effect is that **gluLookAt()** moves the camera five units along the z-axis. (See "Viewing and Modeling Transformations" on page 137 for more information about viewing transformations.)

The Modeling Transformation

You use the modeling transformation to position and orient the model. For example, you can rotate, translate, or scale the model—or perform some combination of these operations. In Example 3-1, **glScalef()** is the modeling transformation that is used. The arguments for this command specify how scaling should occur along the three axes. If all the arguments are 1.0, this command has no effect. In Example 3-1, the cube is drawn twice as large in the y-direction. Thus, if one corner of the cube had originally been at (3.0, 3.0, 3.0), that corner would wind up being drawn at (3.0, 6.0, 3.0). The effect of this modeling transformation is to transform the cube so that it isn't a cube but a rectangular box.

Try This

Change the **gluLookAt()** call in Example 3-1 to the modeling transformation **glTranslatef()** with parameters (0.0, 0.0, –5.0). The result should look exactly the same as when you used **gluLookAt()**. Why are the effects of these two commands similar?

Try This

Note that instead of moving the camera (with a viewing transformation) so that the cube could be viewed, you could have moved the cube away from the camera (with a modeling transformation). This duality in the nature of viewing and modeling transformations is why you need to think about the effects of both types of transformations simultaneously. It doesn't make sense to try to separate the effects, but sometimes it's easier to think about them in one way more than in the other. This is also why modeling and viewing transformations are combined into the *modelview matrix* before the transformations are applied. (See "Viewing and Modeling Transformations" on page 137 for more information about on how to think about modeling and viewing transformations and how to specify them to get the results you want.)

Also note that the modeling and viewing transformations are included in the **display()** routine, along with the call that's used to draw the cube, **glutWireCube()**. In this way, **display()** can be used repeatedly to draw the contents of the window if, for example, the window is moved or uncovered, and you've ensured that the cube is drawn in the desired way each time, with the appropriate transformations. The potential repeated use of **display()** underscores the need to load the identity matrix before performing the viewing and modeling transformations, especially when other transformations might be performed between calls to **display()**.

The Projection Transformation

Specifying the projection transformation is like choosing a lens for a camera. You can think of this transformation as determining what the field of view or viewing volume is and therefore what objects are inside it and to some extent how they look. This is equivalent to choosing among wide-angle, normal, and telephoto lenses, for example. With a wide-angle lens, you can include a wider scene in the final photograph than you can with a telephoto lens, but a telephoto lens allows you to photograph objects as though they're closer to you than they actually are. In computer graphics, you don't have to pay $10,000 for a 2,000-millimeter telephoto lens; once you've bought your graphics workstation, all you need to do is use a smaller number for your field of view.

In addition to the field-of-view considerations, the projection transformation determines how objects are *projected* onto the screen, as the term suggests. Two basic types of projections are provided for you by OpenGL, along with several corresponding commands for describing the relevant parameters in different ways. One type is the *perspective* projection, which matches how you see things in daily life. Perspective makes objects that are farther away appear smaller; for example, it makes railroad tracks appear to converge in the distance. If you're trying to make realistic pictures, you'll want to choose perspective projection, which is specified with the **glFrustum()** command in , "Viewing,"Example 3-1.

The other type of projection is *orthographic*, which maps objects directly onto the screen without affecting their relative sizes. Orthographic projection is used in architectural and computer-aided design applications where the final image needs to reflect the measurements of objects, rather than how they might look. Architects create perspective drawings to show how particular buildings or interior spaces look when viewed from various vantage points; the need for orthographic projection arises when blueprint plans or elevations, which are used in the construction of buildings, are generated. (See "Projection Transformations" on page 152 for a discussion of ways to specify both kinds of projection transformations.)

Before **glFrustum()** can be called to set the projection transformation, some preparation is needed. As shown in the **reshape()** routine in Example 3-1, the command called **glMatrixMode()** is used first, with the argument GL_PROJECTION. This indicates that the current matrix specifies the projection transformation and that subsequent transformation calls affect the *projection matrix*. As you can see, a few lines later, **glMatrixMode()** is called again, this time with GL_MODELVIEW as the argument. This indicates that succeeding transformations now affect the modelview matrix instead of the projection matrix. (See "Manipulating the Matrix Stacks" on page 164 for more information about how to control the projection and modelview matrices.)

Note that **glLoadIdentity()** is used to initialize the current projection matrix so that only the specified projection transformation has an effect. Now **glFrustum()** can be called, with arguments that define the parameters of the projection transformation. In this example, both the projection transformation and the viewport transformation are contained in the **reshape()** routine, which is called when the window is first created and whenever the window is moved or reshaped. This makes sense, because both projecting (the width-to-height aspect ratio of the projection viewing volume) and applying the viewport relate directly to the screen, and specifically to the size or aspect ratio of the window on the screen.

Try This

Change the **glFrustum()** call in Example 3-1 to the more commonly used Utility Library routine **gluPerspective()**, with parameters (60.0, 1.0, 1.5, 20.0). Then experiment with different values, especially for *fovy* and *aspect*.

Try This

The Viewport Transformation

Together, the projection transformation and the viewport transformation determine how a scene is mapped onto the computer screen. The projection transformation specifies the mechanics of how the mapping should occur, and the viewport indicates the shape of the available screen area into which the scene is mapped. Since the viewport specifies the region the image occupies on the computer screen, you can think of the viewport transformation as defining the size and location of the final processed photograph—for example, whether the photograph should be enlarged or shrunk.

The arguments for **glViewport()** describe the origin of the available screen space within the window—(0, 0) in this example—and the width and height of the available screen area, all measured in pixels on the screen. This is why this command needs to be called within **reshape()**: If the window changes size, the viewport needs to change accordingly. Note that the width and height are specified using the actual width and height of the window; often, you want to specify the viewport in this way, rather than give an absolute size. (See "Viewport Transformation" on page 158 for more information about how to define the viewport.)

Drawing the Scene

Once all the necessary transformations have been specified, you can draw the scene (that is, take the photograph). As the scene is drawn, OpenGL transforms each vertex of every object in the scene by the modeling and viewing transformations. Each vertex is then transformed as specified by the projection transformation and clipped if it lies outside the viewing volume described by the projection transformation. Finally, the remaining transformed vertices are divided by *w* and mapped onto the viewport.

General-Purpose Transformation Commands

This section discusses some OpenGL commands that you might find useful as you specify desired transformations. You've already seen two of these commands: **glMatrixMode()** and **glLoadIdentity()**. Four commands described here—**glLoadMatrix*()**, **glLoadTransposeMatrix*()**, **glMultMatrix*()**, and **glMultTransposeMatrix*()**—allow you to specify any transformation matrix directly or to multiply the current matrix by that specified matrix. More specific transformation commands—such as **gluLookAt()** and **glScale*()**—are described in later sections.

As described in the preceding section, you need to state whether you want to modify the modelview or projection matrix before supplying a transformation command. You choose the matrix with **glMatrixMode()**. When you use nested sets of OpenGL commands that might be called repeatedly, remember to reset the matrix mode correctly. (The **glMatrixMode()** command can also be used to indicate the *texture matrix*; texturing is discussed in detail in "The Texture Matrix Stack" in Chapter 9.)

---

void **glMatrixMode**(GLenum *mode*);

Specifies whether the modelview, projection, or texture matrix will be modified, using the argument GL_MODELVIEW, GL_PROJECTION, or GL_TEXTURE for *mode*. Subsequent transformation commands affect the specified matrix. Note that only one matrix can be modified at a time. By default, the modelview matrix is the one that's modifiable, and all three matrices contain the identity matrix.

Compatibility
Extension

glMatrixMode
GL_MODELVIEW
GL_PROJECTION
GL_TEXTURE

You use the **glLoadIdentity()** command to clear the currently modifiable matrix for future transformation commands, as these commands modify the current matrix. Typically, you always call this command before specifying projection or viewing transformations, but you might also call it before specifying a modeling transformation.

---

void **glLoadIdentity**(void);

Sets the currently modifiable matrix to the 4 × 4 identity matrix.

Compatibility
Extension

glLoadIdentity

If you want to specify explicitly a particular matrix to be loaded as the current matrix, use **glLoadMatrix*()** or **glLoadTransposeMatrix*()**. Similarly, use **glMultMatrix*()** or **glMultTransposeMatrix*()** to multiply the current matrix by the matrix passed in as an argument.

---

void **glLoadMatrix**{fd}(const *TYPE* *m*);

Sets the 16 values of the current matrix to those specified by *m*.

Compatibility
Extension

glLoadMatrix
glMultMatrix

---

void **glMultMatrix**{fd}(const *TYPE* *m*);

Multiplies the matrix specified by the 16 values pointed to by *m* by the current matrix and stores the result as the current matrix.

All matrix multiplication with OpenGL occurs as follows. Suppose the current matrix is C, and the matrix specified with **glMultMatrix*()** or any of the transformation commands is **M**. After multiplication, the final matrix is always **CM**. Since matrix multiplication isn't generally commutative, the order makes a difference.

The argument for **glLoadMatrix*()** and **glMultMatrix*()** is a vector of 16 values $(m_1, m_2, ... , m_{16})$ that specifies a matrix **M** stored in column-major order as follows:

$$M = \begin{bmatrix} m_1 & m_5 & m_9 & m_{13} \\ m_2 & m_6 & m_{10} & m_{14} \\ m_3 & m_7 & m_{11} & m_{15} \\ m_4 & m_8 & m_{12} & m_{16} \end{bmatrix}$$

If you're programming in C and you declare a matrix as *m[4][4]*, then the element *m[i][j]* is in the *i*th column and *j*th row of the common OpenGL transformation matrix. This is the reverse of the standard C convention in which *m[i][j]* is in row *i* and column *j*. One way to avoid confusion between the column and the row is to declare your matrices as *m[16]*.

Another way to avoid possible confusion is to call the OpenGL routines **glLoadTransposeMatrix*()** and **glMultTransposeMatrix*()**, which use row-major (the standard C convention) matrices as arguments.

<table>
<tr><td>
Compatibility
Extension

glLoadTranspose
Matrix

glMultTranspose
Matrix
</td><td>

void **glLoadTransposeMatrix**{fd}(const *TYPE* *m);

Sets the 16 values of the current matrix to those specified by *m*, whose values are stored in row-major order. **glLoadTransposeMatrix*(***m***)** has the same effect as **glLoadMatrix*(***m^T***)**.
</td></tr>
</table>

void **glMultTransposeMatrix**{fd}(const *TYPE* *m);

Multiplies the matrix specified by the 16 values pointed to by *m* by the current matrix and stores the result as the current matrix. **glMultTransposeMatrix*(***m***)** has the same effect as **glMultMatrix*(***m^T***)**.

You might be able to maximize efficiency by using display lists to store frequently used matrices (and their inverses), rather than recomputing them.

(See "Display List Design Philosophy" in Chapter 7.) OpenGL implementations often must compute the inverse of the modelview matrix so that normals and clipping planes can be correctly transformed to eye coordinates.

Viewing and Modeling Transformations

Viewing and modeling transformations are inextricably related in OpenGL and are, in fact, combined into a single modelview matrix. (See "A Simple Example: Drawing a Cube" on page 129.) One of the toughest problems newcomers to computer graphics face is understanding the effects of combined three-dimensional transformations. As you've already seen, there are alternative ways to think about transformations—do you want to move the camera in one direction or move the object in the opposite direction? Each way of thinking about transformations has advantages and disadvantages, but in some cases one way more naturally matches the effect of the intended transformation. If you can find a natural approach for your particular application, it's easier to visualize the necessary transformations and then write the corresponding code to specify the matrix manipulations. The first part of this section discusses how to think about transformations; later, specific commands are presented. For now, we use only the matrix-manipulation commands you've already seen. Finally, keep in mind that you must call **glMatrixMode()** with GL_MODELVIEW as its argument prior to performing modeling or viewing transformations.

Thinking about Transformations

Let's start with a simple case of two transformations: a 45-degree counterclockwise rotation about the origin around the z-axis and a translation down the x-axis. Suppose that the object you're drawing is small compared with the translation (so that you can see the effect of the translation) and that it's originally located at the origin. If you rotate the object first and then translate it, the rotated object appears on the x-axis. If you translate it down the x-axis first, however, and then rotate about the origin, the object is on the line $y = x$, as shown in Figure 3-4. In general, the order of transformations is critical. If you do transformation A and then transformation B, you almost always get something different than if you do them in the opposite order.

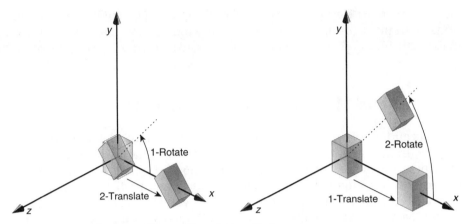

Figure 3-4   Rotating First or Translating First

Now let's talk about the order in which you specify a series of transformations. All viewing and modeling transformations are represented as 4 × 4 matrices. Each successive **glMultMatrix*()** or transformation command multiplies a new 4 × 4 matrix **M** by the current modelview matrix **C** to yield **CM**. Finally, vertices *v* are multiplied by the current modelview matrix. This process means that the last transformation command called in your program is actually the first one applied to the vertices: **CMv**. Thus, one way of looking at it is to say that you have to specify the matrices in the reverse order. Like many other things, however, once you've gotten used to thinking about this correctly, backward will seem like forward.

Consider the following code sequence, which draws a single point using three transformations:

```
glMatrixMode(GL_MODELVIEW);
glLoadIdentity();
glMultMatrixf(N);                 /* apply transformation N */
glMultMatrixf(M);                 /* apply transformation M */
glMultMatrixf(L);                 /* apply transformation L */
glBegin(GL_POINTS);
glVertex3f(v);                    /* draw transformed vertex v */
glEnd();
```

With this code, the modelview matrix successively contains **I**, **N**, **NM**, and finally **NML**, where **I** represents the identity matrix. The transformed vertex is **NMLv**. Thus, the vertex transformation is **N(M(Lv))**—that is, **v** is multiplied first by **L**, the resulting **Lv** is multiplied by **M**, and the resulting **MLv** is multiplied by **N**. Notice that the transformations to vertex **v** effectively occur in the opposite order than they were specified. (Actually, only a single multiplication of a vertex by the modelview matrix occurs; in this example, the **N**, **M**, and **L** matrices are already multiplied into a single matrix before it's applied to **v**.)

Grand, Fixed Coordinate System

Thus, if you like to think in terms of a grand, fixed coordinate system—in which matrix multiplications affect the position, orientation, and scaling of your model—you have to think of the multiplications as occurring in the opposite order from how they appear in the code. Using the simple example shown on the left side of Figure 3-4 (a rotation about the origin and a translation along the *x*-axis), if you want the object to appear on the axis after the operations, the rotation must occur first, followed by the translation. To do this, you'll need to reverse the order of operations, so the code looks something like this (where **R** is the rotation matrix and **T** is the translation matrix):

```
glMatrixMode(GL_MODELVIEW);
glLoadIdentity();
glMultMatrixf(T);                   /* translation */
glMultMatrixf(R);                   /* rotation */
draw_the_object();
```

Moving a Local Coordinate System

Another way to view matrix multiplications is to forget about a grand, fixed coordinate system in which your model is transformed and instead imagine that a local coordinate system is tied to the object you're drawing. All operations occur relative to this changing coordinate system. With this approach, the matrix multiplications now appear in the natural order in the code. (Regardless of which analogy you're using, the code is the same, but how you think about it differs.) To see this in the translation-rotation example, begin by visualizing the object with a coordinate system tied to it. The translation operation moves the object and its coordinate system down the *x*-axis. Then, the rotation occurs about the (now-translated) origin, so the object rotates in place in its position on the axis.

This approach is what you should use for applications such as articulated robot arms, where there are joints at the shoulder, elbow, and wrist, and on each of the fingers. To figure out where the tips of the fingers go relative to the body, you'd like to start at the shoulder, go down to the wrist, and so on, applying the appropriate rotations and translations at each joint. Thinking about it in reverse would be far more confusing.

This second approach can be problematic, however, in cases where scaling occurs, and especially so when the scaling is nonuniform (scaling different amounts along the different axes). After uniform scaling, translations move a vertex by a multiple of what they did before, as the coordinate system is stretched. Nonuniform scaling mixed with rotations may make the axes of the local coordinate system nonperpendicular.

As mentioned earlier, you normally issue viewing transformation commands in your program before any modeling transformations. In this way, a vertex in a model is first transformed into the desired orientation and then transformed by the viewing operation. Since the matrix multiplications must be specified in reverse order, the viewing commands need to come first. Note, however, that you don't need to specify either viewing or modeling transformations if you're satisfied with the default conditions. If there's no viewing transformation, the "camera" is left in the default position at the origin, pointing toward the negative z-axis; if there's no modeling transformation, the model isn't moved, and it retains its specified position, orientation, and size.

Since the commands for performing modeling transformations can be used to perform viewing transformations, modeling transformations are *discussed* first, even if viewing transformations are actually *issued* first. This order for discussion also matches the way many programmers think when planning their code. Often, they write all the code necessary to compose the scene, which involves transformations to position and orient objects correctly relative to each other. Next, they decide where they want the viewpoint to be relative to the scene they've composed, and then they write the viewing transformations accordingly.

Modeling Transformations

The three OpenGL routines for modeling transformations are **glTranslate*()**, **glRotate*()**, and **glScale*()**. As you might suspect, these routines transform an object (or coordinate system, if you're thinking of it in that way) by moving, rotating, stretching, shrinking, or reflecting it. All three commands are equivalent to producing an appropriate translation, rotation, or scaling matrix, and then calling **glMultMatrix*()** with that matrix as the argument. However, using these three routines might be faster than using **glMultMatrix*()**. OpenGL automatically computes the matrices for you. (See if you're interested in the details.)

In the command summaries that follow, each matrix multiplication is described in terms of what it does to the vertices of a geometric object using the fixed coordinate system approach, and in terms of what it does to the local coordinate system that's attached to an object.

Translate

void **glTranslate**{fd}(*TYPE x, TYPE y, TYPE z*);

Multiplies the current matrix by a matrix that moves (translates) an object by the given *x*-, *y*-, and *z*-values (or moves the local coordinate system by the same amounts).

Compatibility Extension

glTranslate

Figure 3-5 shows the effect of **glTranslate*()**.

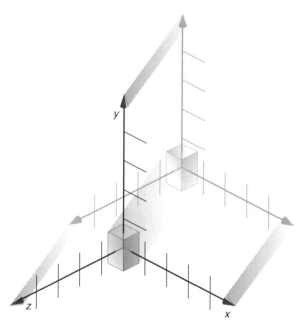

Figure 3-5   Translating an Object

Note that using (0.0, 0.0, 0.0) as the argument for **glTranslate*()** is the identity operation—that is, it has no effect on an object or its local coordinate system.

Rotate

Compatibility
Extension

glRotate

void **glRotate**{fd}(*TYPE angle, TYPE x, TYPE y, TYPE z*);

Multiplies the current matrix by a matrix that rotates an object (or the local coordinate system) in a counterclockwise direction about the ray from the origin through the point (*x, y, z*). The *angle* parameter specifies the angle of rotation in degrees.

The effect of **glRotatef**(45.0, 0.0, 0.0, 1.0), which is a rotation of 45 degrees about the *z*-axis, is shown in Figure 3-6.

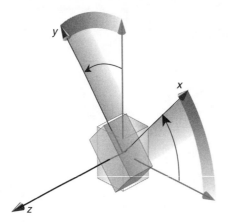

Figure 3-6   Rotating an Object

Note that an object that lies farther from the axis of rotation is more dramatically rotated (has a larger orbit) than an object drawn near the axis. Also, if the *angle* argument is zero, the **glRotate*()** command has no effect.

Scale

Compatibility
Extension

glScale

void **glScale**{fd}(*TYPE x, TYPE y, TYPE z*);

Multiplies the current matrix by a matrix that stretches, shrinks, or reflects an object along the axes. Each *x*-, *y*-, and *z*-coordinate of every point in the object is multiplied by the corresponding argument *x, y,* or *z*. With the local coordinate system approach, the local coordinate axes are stretched, shrunk, or reflected by the *x*-, *y*-, and *z*-factors, and the associated object is transformed with them.

Figure 3-7 shows the effect of **glScalef**(2.0, –0.5, 1.0).

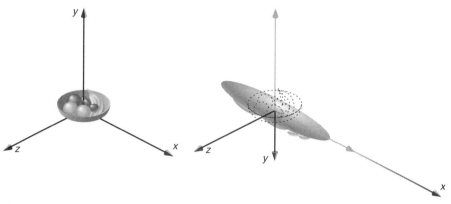

Figure 3-7   Scaling and Reflecting an Object

glScale*() is the only one of the three modeling transformations that changes the apparent size of an object: Scaling with values greater than 1.0 stretches an object, and using values less than 1.0 shrinks it. Scaling with a –1.0 value reflects an object across an axis. The identity values for scaling are (1.0, 1.0, 1.0). In general, you should limit your use of **glScale*()** to those cases where it is necessary. Using **glScale*()** decreases the performance of lighting calculations, because the normal vectors have to be renormalized after transformation.

Note: A scale value of zero collapses all object coordinates along that axis to zero. It's usually not a good idea to do this, because such an operation cannot be undone. Mathematically speaking, the matrix cannot be inverted, and inverse matrices are required for certain lighting operations (see Chapter 5). Sometimes collapsing coordinates does make sense; the calculation of shadows on a planar surface is one such application (see "Shadows" in Chapter 14). In general, if a coordinate system is to be collapsed, the projection matrix should be used, rather than the modelview matrix.

A Modeling Transformation Code Example

Example 3-2 is a portion of a program that renders a triangle four times, as shown in Figure 3-8. These are the four transformed triangles:

- A solid wireframe triangle is drawn with no modeling transformation.

- The same triangle is drawn again, but with a dashed line stipple, and translated (to the left—along the negative *x*-axis).

- A triangle is drawn with a long dashed line stipple, with its height (*y*-axis) halved and its width (*x*-axis) increased by 50 percent.

- A rotated triangle, made of dotted lines, is drawn.

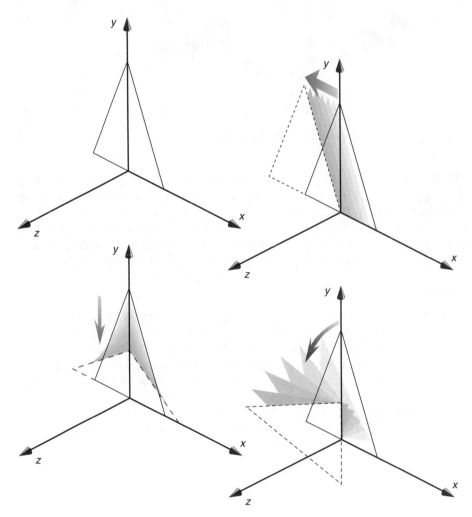

Figure 3-8   Modeling Transformation Example

Example 3-2   Using Modeling Transformations: model.c

```
glLoadIdentity();
glColor3f(1.0, 1.0, 1.0);
draw_triangle();                     /* solid lines */

glEnable(GL_LINE_STIPPLE);           /* dashed lines */
glLineStipple(1, 0xF0F0);
glLoadIdentity();
glTranslatef(-20.0, 0.0, 0.0);
draw_triangle();

glLineStipple(1, 0xF00F);            /*long dashed lines */
glLoadIdentity();
glScalef(1.5, 0.5, 1.0);
draw_triangle();

glLineStipple(1, 0x8888);            /* dotted lines */
glLoadIdentity();
glRotatef(90.0, 0.0, 0.0, 1.0);
draw_triangle();
glDisable(GL_LINE_STIPPLE);
```

Note the use of **glLoadIdentity()** to isolate the effects of modeling transformations; initializing the matrix values prevents successive transformations from having a cumulative effect. Even though using **glLoadIdentity()** repeatedly has the desired effect, it may be inefficient, because you may have to respecify viewing or modeling transformations. (See "Manipulating the Matrix Stacks" on page 164 for a better way to isolate transformations.)

Note: Sometimes, programmers who want a continuously rotating object attempt to achieve this by repeatedly applying a rotation matrix that has small values. The problem with this technique is that because of round-off errors, the product of thousands of tiny rotations gradually drifts away from the value you really want (it might even become something that isn't a rotation). Instead of using this technique, increment the angle and issue a new rotation command with the new angle at each update step.

Nate Robins' Transformation Tutorial

If you have downloaded Nate Robins' suite of tutorial programs, this is an opportune time to run the **transformation** tutorial. (For information on how and where to download these programs, see "Errata" on page xlii.) With this tutorial, you can experiment with the effects of rotation, translation, and scaling.

Viewing Transformations

A viewing transformation changes the position and orientation of the viewpoint. If you recall the camera analogy, the viewing transformation positions the camera tripod, pointing the camera toward the model. Just as you move the camera to some position and rotate it until it points in the desired direction, viewing transformations are generally composed of translations and rotations. Also remember that to achieve a certain scene composition in the final image or photograph, you can either move the camera or move all the objects in the opposite direction. Thus, a modeling transformation that rotates an object counterclockwise is equivalent to a viewing transformation that rotates the camera clockwise, for example. Finally, keep in mind that the viewing transformation commands must be called before any modeling transformations are performed, so that the modeling transformations take effect on the objects first.

You can manufacture a viewing transformation in any of several ways, as described next. You can also choose to use the default location and orientation of the viewpoint, which is at the origin, looking down the negative z-axis.

- Use one or more modeling transformation commands (that is, **glTranslate*()** and **glRotate*()**). You can think of the effect of these transformations as moving the camera position or as moving all the objects in the world, relative to a stationary camera.

- Use the Utility Library routine **gluLookAt()** to define a line of sight. This routine encapsulates a series of rotation and translation commands.

- Create your own utility routine to encapsulate rotations and translations. Some applications might require custom routines that allow you to specify the viewing transformation in a convenient way. For example, you might want to specify the roll, pitch, and heading rotation angles of a plane in flight, or you might want to specify a transformation in terms of polar coordinates for a camera that's orbiting around an object.

Using glTranslate*() and glRotate*()

When you use modeling transformation commands to emulate viewing transformations, you're trying to move the viewpoint in a desired way while keeping the objects in the world stationary. Since the viewpoint is initially located at the origin and since objects are often most easily constructed there as well (see Figure 3-9), you generally have to perform

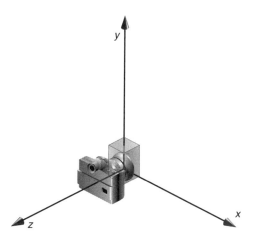

Figure 3-9   Object and Viewpoint at the Origin

some transformation so that the objects can be viewed. Note that, as shown in the figure, the camera initially points down the negative z-axis. (You're seeing the back of the camera.)

In the simplest case, you can move the viewpoint backward, away from the objects; this has the same effect as moving the objects forward, or away from the viewpoint. Remember that, by default, forward is down the negative z-axis; if you rotate the viewpoint, forward has a different meaning. Therefore, to put five units of distance between the viewpoint and the objects by moving the viewpoint, as shown in Figure 3-10, use

```
glTranslatef(0.0, 0.0, -5.0);
```

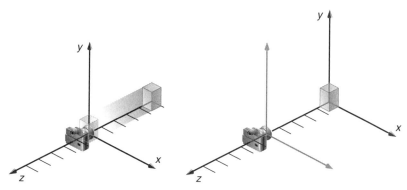

Figure 3-10   Separating the Viewpoint and the Object

This routine moves the objects in the scene –5 units along the z-axis. This is also equivalent to moving the camera +5 units along the z-axis.

Now suppose you want to view the objects from the side. Should you issue a rotate command before or after the translate command? If you're thinking in terms of a grand, fixed coordinate system, first imagine both the object and the camera at the origin. You could rotate the object first and then move it away from the camera so that the desired side is visible. You know that with the fixed coordinate system approach, commands have to be issued in the opposite order in which they should take effect, so you know that you need to write the translate command in your code first and follow it with the rotate command.

Now let's use the local coordinate system approach. In this case, think about moving the object and its local coordinate system away from the origin; then, the rotate command is carried out using the now-translated coordinate system. With this approach, commands are issued in the order in which they're applied, so once again the translate command comes first. Thus, the sequence of transformation commands to produce the desired result is

```
glTranslatef(0.0, 0.0, -5.0);
glRotatef(90.0, 0.0, 1.0, 0.0);
```

If you're having trouble keeping track of the effect of successive matrix multiplications, try using both the fixed and local coordinate system approaches and see whether one makes more sense to you. Note that with the fixed coordinate system, rotations always occur about the grand origin, whereas with the local coordinate system, rotations occur about the origin of the local system. You might also try using the **gluLookAt()** utility routine described next.

Using the gluLookAt() Utility Routine

Often, programmers construct a scene around the origin or some other convenient location and then want to look at it from an arbitrary point to get a good view of it. As its name suggests, the **gluLookAt()** utility routine is designed for just this purpose. It takes three sets of arguments, which specify the location of the viewpoint, define a reference point toward which the camera is aimed, and indicate which direction is up. Choose the viewpoint to yield the desired view of the scene. The reference point is typically somewhere in the middle of the scene. (If you've built your scene at the origin, the reference point is probably the origin.) It might be a little trickier to specify the correct up-vector. Again, if you've built some real-world scene at or around the origin and if you've been taking the positive y-axis to point upward, then that's your up-vector for **gluLookAt()**. However, if you're designing a flight simulator, up is the direction perpendicular to the plane's wings, from the plane toward the sky when the plane is right-side-up on the ground.

The **gluLookAt()** routine is particularly useful when you want to pan across a landscape, for instance. With a viewing volume that's symmetric in both *x* and *y*, the (*eyex, eyey, eyez*) point specified is always in the center of the image on the screen, so you can use a series of commands to move this point slightly, thereby panning across the scene.

---

void **gluLookAt**(GLdouble *eyex*, GLdouble *eyey*, GLdouble *eyez*,
                GLdouble *centerx*, GLdouble *centery*, GLdouble *centerz*,
                GLdouble *upx*, GLdouble *upy*, GLdouble *upz*);

Defines a viewing matrix and multiplies it to the right of the current matrix. The desired viewpoint is specified by *eyex, eyey,* and *eyez*. The *centerx, centery,* and *centerz* arguments specify any point along the desired line of sight, but typically they specify some point in the center of the scene being looked at. The *upx, upy,* and *upz* arguments indicate which direction is up (that is, the direction from the bottom to the top of the viewing volume).

In the default position, the camera is at the origin, is looking down the negative *z*-axis, and has the positive *y*-axis as straight up. This is the same as calling

```
gluLookAt(0.0, 0.0, 0.0, 0.0, 0.0, -100.0, 0.0, 1.0, 0.0);
```

The *z*-value of the reference point is −100.0, but could be any negative *z*, because the line of sight will remain the same. In this case, you don't actually want to call **gluLookAt()**, because this is the default (see Figure 3-11),

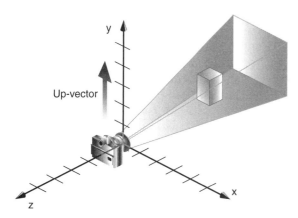

Figure 3-11   Default Camera Position

and you are already there. (The lines extending from the camera represent the viewing volume, which indicates its field of view.)

Figure 3-12 shows the effect of a typical **gluLookAt()** routine. The camera position (*eyex, eyey, eyez*) is at (4, 2, 1). In this case, the camera is looking right at the model, so the reference point is at (2, 4, –3). An orientation vector of (2, 2, –1) is chosen to rotate the viewpoint to this 45-degree angle.

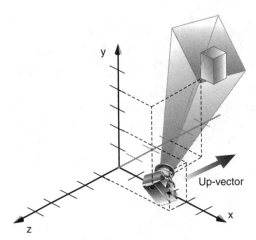

Figure 3-12   Using gluLookAt()

Therefore, to achieve this effect, call

```
gluLookAt(4.0, 2.0, 1.0, 2.0, 4.0, -3.0, 2.0, 2.0, -1.0);
```

Note that **gluLookAt()** is part of the Utility Library, rather than the basic OpenGL library. This isn't because it's not useful, but because it encapsulates several basic OpenGL commands—specifically, **glTranslate*()** and **glRotate*()**. To see this, imagine a camera located at an arbitrary viewpoint and oriented according to a line of sight, both as specified with **gluLookAt()** and a scene located at the origin. To "undo" what **gluLookAt()** does, you need to transform the camera so that it sits at the origin and points down the negative *z*-axis, the default position. A simple translate moves the camera to the origin. You can easily imagine a series of rotations about each of the three axes of a fixed coordinate system that would orient the camera so that it pointed toward negative *z*-values. Since OpenGL allows rotation about an arbitrary axis, you can accomplish any desired rotation of the camera with a single **glRotate*()** command.

Note: You can have only one active viewing transformation. You cannot try to combine the effects of two viewing transformations, any more than a camera can have two tripods. If you want to change the position of the camera, make sure you call **glLoadIdentity()** to erase the effects of any current viewing transformation.

Nate Robins' Projection Tutorial

If you have Nate Robins' suite of tutorial programs, run the **projection** tutorial. With this tutorial, you can see the effects of changes to the parameters of **gluLookAt()**.

Advanced

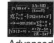

Advanced

To transform any arbitrary vector so that it's coincident with another arbitrary vector (for instance, the negative z-axis), you need to do a little mathematics. The axis about which you want to rotate is given by the cross product of the two normalized vectors. To find the angle of rotation, normalize the initial two vectors. The cosine of the desired angle between the vectors is equal to the dot product of the normalized vectors. The angle of rotation around the axis given by the cross product is always between 0 and 180 degrees. (See Appendix I, "Built-In OpenGL Shading Language Variables and Functions,"[1] for definitions of cross and dot products.)

Note that computing the angle between two normalized vectors by taking the inverse cosine of their dot product is not very accurate, especially for small angles, but it should work well enough to get you started.

Creating a Custom Utility Routine

Advanced

Advanced

For some specialized applications, you might want to define your own transformation routine. Since this is rarely done and is a fairly advanced topic, it's left mostly as an exercise for the reader. The following exercises suggest two custom viewing transformations that might be useful.

Try This

Try This

- Suppose you're writing a flight simulator and you'd like to display the world from the point of view of the pilot of a plane. The world is described in a coordinate system with the origin on the runway and the plane at coordinates (x, y, z). Suppose further that the plane has some *roll*, *pitch*, and *heading* (these are rotation angles of the plane relative to its center of gravity).

---

[1] This appendix is available online at http://www.opengl-redbook.com/appendices/.

Show that the following routine could serve as the viewing transformation:

```
void pilotView{GLdouble planex, GLdouble planey,
               GLdouble planez, GLdouble roll,
               GLdouble pitch, GLdouble heading)
{
     glRotated(roll, 0.0, 0.0, 1.0);
     glRotated(pitch, 0.0, 1.0, 0.0);
     glRotated(heading, 1.0, 0.0, 0.0);
     glTranslated(-planex, -planey, -planez);
}
```

- Suppose your application involves orbiting the camera around an object that's centered at the origin. In this case, you'd like to specify the viewing transformation by using polar coordinates. Let the *distance* variable define the radius of the orbit or how far the camera is from the origin. (Initially, the camera is moved *distance* units along the positive z-axis.) The *azimuth* describes the angle of rotation of the camera about the object in the xy-plane, measured from the positive y-axis. Similarly, *elevation* is the angle of rotation of the camera in the yz-plane measured from the positive z-axis. Finally, *twist* represents the rotation of the viewing volume around its line of sight.

Show that the following routine could serve as the viewing transformation:

```
void polarView{GLdouble distance, GLdouble twist,
               GLdouble elevation, GLdouble azimuth)
{
     glTranslated(0.0, 0.0, -distance);
     glRotated(-twist, 0.0, 0.0, 1.0);
     glRotated(-elevation, 1.0, 0.0, 0.0);
     glRotated(azimuth, 0.0, 0.0, 1.0);
}
```

Projection Transformations

The preceding section described how to compose the desired modelview matrix so that the correct modeling and viewing transformations are applied. This section explains how to define the desired projection matrix, which is also used to transform the vertices in your scene. Before you issue any of the transformation commands described in this section, remember to call

```
glMatrixMode(GL_PROJECTION);
glLoadIdentity();
```

so that the commands affect the projection matrix, rather than the model-view matrix, and so that you avoid compound projection transformations. Since each projection transformation command completely describes a particular transformation, typically you don't want to combine a projection transformation with another transformation.

The purpose of the projection transformation is to define a *viewing volume*, which is used in two ways. The viewing volume determines how an object is projected onto the screen (that is, by using a perspective or an orthographic projection), and it defines which objects or portions of objects are clipped out of the final image. You can think of the viewpoint we've been talking about as existing at one end of the viewing volume. At this point, you might want to reread "A Simple Example: Drawing a Cube" on page 129 for its overview of all the transformations, including projection transformations.

Perspective Projection

The most unmistakable characteristic of perspective projection is *fore-shortening*: The farther an object is from the camera, the smaller it appears in the final image. This occurs because the viewing volume for a perspective projection is a *frustum* of a pyramid (a truncated pyramid whose top has been cut off by a plane parallel to its base). Objects that fall within the viewing volume are projected toward the apex of the pyramid, where the camera or viewpoint is. Objects that are closer to the viewpoint appear larger because they occupy a proportionally larger amount of the viewing volume than those that are farther away, in the larger part of the frustum. This method of projection is commonly used for animation, visual simulation, and any other applications that strive for some degree of realism, because it's similar to how our eye (or a camera) works.

The command to define a frustum, **glFrustum()**, calculates a matrix that accomplishes perspective projection and multiplies the current projection matrix (typically the identity matrix) by it. Recall that the viewing volume is used to clip objects that lie outside of it; the four sides of the frustum, its top, and its base correspond to the six clipping planes of the viewing volume, as shown in Figure 3-13. Objects or parts of objects outside these planes are clipped from the final image. Note that **glFrustum()** doesn't require you to define a symmetric viewing volume.

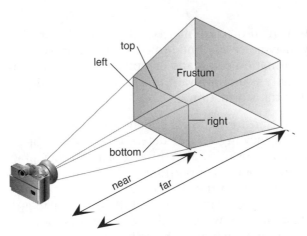

Figure 3-13   Perspective Viewing Volume Specified by glFrustum()

Compatibility
Extension

glFrustum

void **glFrustum**(GLdouble *left*, GLdouble *right*,
　　　　　　　　GLdouble *bottom*, GLdouble *top*,
　　　　　　　　GLdouble *near*, GLdouble *far*);

Creates a matrix for a perspective-view frustum and multiplies the current
matrix by it. The frustum's viewing volume is defined by the parameters:
(*left*, *bottom*, *−near*) and (*right*, *top*, *−near*) specify the (*x*, *y*, *z*) coordinates of
the lower left and upper right corners, respectively, of the near clipping
plane; *near* and *far* give the distances from the viewpoint to the near and
far clipping planes. They should always be positive.

The frustum has a default orientation in three-dimensional space. You can
perform rotations or translations on the projection matrix to alter this
orientation, but this is tricky and nearly always avoidable.

Advanced

Advanced

The frustum doesn't have to be symmetrical, and its axis isn't necessarily
aligned with the *z*-axis. For example, you can use **glFrustum()** to draw
a picture as if you were looking through a rectangular window of a house,
where the window was above and to the right of you. Photographers use
such a viewing volume to create false perspectives. You might use it to have
the hardware calculate images at resolutions much higher than normal, perhaps for use on a printer. For example, if you want an image that has twice

the resolution of your screen, draw the same picture four times, each time using the frustum to cover the entire screen with one-quarter of the image. After each quarter of the image is rendered, you can read the pixels back to collect the data for the higher-resolution image. (See Chapter 8 for more information about reading pixel data.)

Although it's easy to understand conceptually, **glFrustum()** isn't intuitive to use. Instead, you might try the Utility Library routine **gluPerspective()**. This routine creates a viewing volume of the same shape as **glFrustum()** does, but you specify it in a different way. Rather than specifying corners of the near clipping plane, you specify the angle of the field of view (Θ, or theta, in Figure 3-14) in the *y*-direction and the aspect ratio of the width to the height (*x/y*). (For a square portion of the screen, the aspect ratio is 1.0.) These two parameters are enough to determine an untruncated pyramid along the line of sight, as shown in Figure 3-14. You also specify the distance between the viewpoint and the near and far clipping planes, thereby truncating the pyramid. Note that **gluPerspective()** is limited to creating frustums that are symmetric in both the *x*- and *y*-axes along the line of sight, but this is usually what you want.

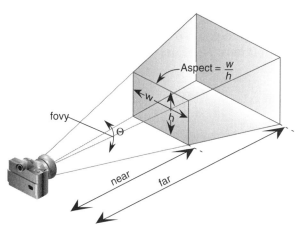

Figure 3-14   Perspective Viewing Volume Specified by gluPerspective()

Just as with **glFrustum()**, you can apply rotations or translations to change the default orientation of the viewing volume created by **gluPerspective()**. With no such transformations, the viewpoint remains at the origin, and the line of sight points down the negative *z*-axis.

With **gluPerspective()**, you need to pick appropriate values for the field of view, otherwise the image may look distorted. To get a perfect field of view, figure out how far your eye normally is from the screen and how big

void **gluPerspective**(GLdouble *fovy*, GLdouble *aspect*,
                        GLdouble *near*, GLdouble *far*);

Creates a matrix for a symmetric perspective-view frustum and multiplies the current matrix by it. *fovy* is the angle of the field of view in the *yz*-plane; its value must be in the range [0.0, 180.0]. *aspect* is the aspect ratio of the frustum, its width divided by its height. *near* and *far* values are the distances between the viewpoint and the clipping planes, along the negative *z*-axis. They should always be positive.

the window is, and calculate the angle the window subtends at that size and distance. It's probably smaller than you would guess. Another way to think about it is that a 94-degree field of view with a 35-millimeter camera requires a 20-millimeter lens, which is a very wide-angle lens. (See "Troubleshooting Transformations" on page 162 for more details on how to calculate the desired field of view.)

The preceding paragraph suggests inches and millimeters—do these really have anything to do with OpenGL? The answer is, in a word, no. The projection and other transformations are inherently unitless. If you want to think of the near and far clipping planes as located at 1.0 and 20.0 meters, inches, kilometers, or leagues, it's up to you. The only rule is that you have to use a consistent unit of measurement. Then the resulting image is drawn to scale.

Orthographic Projection

With an orthographic projection, the viewing volume is a rectangular parallelepiped, or, more informally, a box (see Figure 3-15). Unlike perspective projection, the size of the viewing volume doesn't change from one end to the other, so distance from the camera doesn't affect how large an object appears. This type of projection is used for applications for architectural blueprints and computer-aided design, where it's crucial to maintain the actual sizes of objects and the angles between them as they're projected.

The command **glOrtho()** creates an orthographic parallel viewing volume. As with **glFrustum()**, you specify the corners of the near clipping plane and the distance to the far clipping plane.

With no other transformations, the direction of projection is parallel to the *z*-axis, and the viewpoint faces toward the negative *z*-axis.

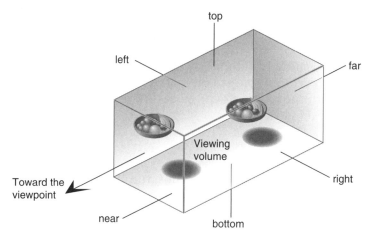

Figure 3-15   Orthographic Viewing Volume

---

void **glOrtho**(GLdouble *left*, GLdouble *right*,
              GLdouble *bottom*, GLdouble *top*,
              GLdouble *near*, GLdouble *far*);

Compatibility Extension
glOrtho

Creates a matrix for an orthographic parallel viewing volume and multiplies the current matrix by it. (*left, bottom, −near*) and (*right, top, −near*) are
points on the near clipping plane that are mapped to the lower left and
upper right corners of the viewport window, respectively. (*left, bottom,
−far*) and (*right, top, −far*) are points on the far clipping plane that are
mapped to the same respective corners of the viewport. Both *near* and
far may be positive, negative, or even set to zero. However, *near* and *far*
should not be the same value.

For the special case of projecting a two-dimensional image onto a two-
dimensional screen, use the Utility Library routine **gluOrtho2D()**. This
routine is identical to the three-dimensional version, **glOrtho()**, except that
all the *z* coordinates for objects in the scene are assumed to lie between −1.0
and 1.0. If you're drawing two-dimensional objects using the two-dimensional
vertex commands, all the *z* coordinates are zero; thus, no object is clipped
because of its *z*-value.

> void **gluOrtho2D**(GLdouble *left*, GLdouble *right*,
>   GLdouble *bottom*, GLdouble *top*);
>
> Creates a matrix for projecting two-dimensional coordinates onto the
> screen and multiplies the current projection matrix by it. The clipping
> region is a rectangle with the lower left corner at (*left*, *bottom*) and the
> upper right corner at (*right*, *top*).

Nate Robins' Projection Tutorial

If you have Nate Robins' suite of tutorial programs, run the **projection**
tutorial once again. This time, experiment with the parameters of the
gluPerspective(), **glOrtho()**, and **glFrustum()** routines.

Viewing Volume Clipping

After the vertices of the objects in the scene have been transformed by
the modelview and projection matrices, any primitives that lie outside
the viewing volume are clipped. The six clipping planes used are those
that define the sides and ends of the viewing volume. You can specify
additional clipping planes and locate them wherever you choose. (See
"Additional Clipping Planes" on page 168 for information about this
relatively advanced topic.) Keep in mind that OpenGL reconstructs the
edges of polygons that are clipped.

Viewport Transformation

Recalling the camera analogy, you know that the viewport transformation
corresponds to the stage where the size of the developed photograph is
chosen. Do you want a wallet-size or a poster-size photograph? Since this is
computer graphics, the viewport is the rectangular region of the window
where the image is drawn. Figure 3-16 shows a viewport that occupies most
of the screen. The viewport is measured in window coordinates, which
reflect the positions of pixels on the screen relative to the lower left corner
of the window. Keep in mind that all vertices have been transformed by the
modelview and projection matrices by this point, and vertices outside the
viewing volume have been clipped.

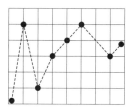 

Figure 3-16   Viewport Rectangle

Defining the Viewport

The window system, not OpenGL, is responsible for opening a window on the screen. However, by default, the viewport is set to the entire pixel rectangle of the window that's opened. You use the **glViewport()** command to choose a smaller drawing region; for example, you can subdivide the window to create a split-screen effect for multiple views in the same window.

---

void **glViewport**(GLint *x*, GLint *y*, GLsizei *width*, GLsizei *height*);

Defines a pixel rectangle in the window into which the final image is mapped. The *(x, y)* parameter specifies the lower left corner of the viewport, and *width* and *height* are the size of the viewport rectangle. By default, the initial viewport values are *(0, 0, winWidth, winHeight)*, where *winWidth* and *winHeight* specify the size of the window.

The aspect ratio of a viewport should generally equal the aspect ratio of the viewing volume. If the two ratios are different, the projected image will be distorted when mapped to the viewport, as shown in Figure 3-17. Note that subsequent changes in the size of the window don't explicitly affect the viewport. Your application should detect window resize events and modify the viewport appropriately.

In Figure 3-17, the left figure shows a projection that maps a square image onto a square viewport using these routines:

```
gluPerspective(fovy, 1.0, near, far);
glViewport(0, 0, 400, 400);
```

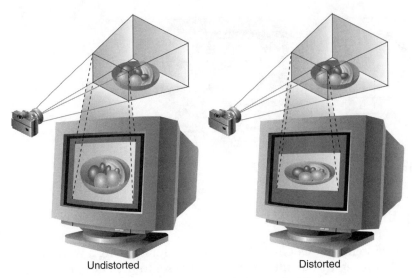

Undistorted	Distorted

Figure 3-17   Mapping the Viewing Volume to the Viewport

However, in the right figure, the window has been resized to a nonequilateral rectangular viewport, but the projection is unchanged. The image appears compressed along the *x*-axis:

```
gluPerspective(fovy, 1.0, near, far);
glViewport(0, 0, 400, 200);
```

To avoid the distortion, modify the aspect ratio of the projection to match the viewport:

```
gluPerspective(fovy, 2.0, near, far);
glViewport(0, 0, 400, 200);
```

Try This

Try This

Modify an existing program so that an object is drawn twice, in different viewports. You might draw the object with different projection and/or viewing transformations for each viewport. To create two side-by-side viewports, you might issue these commands, along with the appropriate modeling, viewing, and projection transformations:

```
glViewport(0, 0, sizex/2, sizey);
                .
                .
                .
glViewport(sizex/2, 0, sizex/2, sizey);
```

The Transformed Depth Coordinate

The depth (z) coordinate is encoded during the viewport transformation (and later stored in the depth buffer). You can scale z-values to lie within a desired range with the **glDepthRange()** command. (Chapter 10 discusses the depth buffer and the corresponding uses of the depth coordinate.) Unlike x and y window coordinates, z window coordinates are treated by OpenGL as though they always range from 0.0 to 1.0.

void **glDepthRange**(GLclampd *near*, GLclampd *far*);

Defines an encoding for z-coordinates that's performed during the viewport transformation. The *near* and *far* values represent adjustments to the minimum and maximum values that can be stored in the depth buffer. By default, they're 0.0 and 1.0, respectively, which work for most applications. These parameters are clamped to lie within [0, 1].

In perspective projection, the transformed depth coordinate (like the x- and y-coordinates) is subject to perspective division by the w-coordinate. As the transformed depth coordinate moves farther away from the near clipping plane, its location becomes increasingly less precise. (See Figure 3-18.)

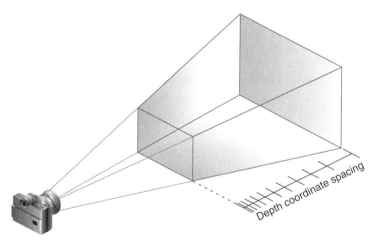

Figure 3-18   Perspective Projection and Transformed Depth Coordinates

Therefore, perspective division affects the accuracy of operations that rely on the transformed depth coordinate, especially depth-buffering, which is used for hidden-surface removal.

Troubleshooting Transformations

It's pretty easy to get a camera pointed in the right direction, but in computer graphics, you have to specify position and direction with coordinates and angles. As we can attest, it's all too easy to achieve the well-known black-screen effect. Although any number of things can go wrong, often you get this effect—which results in absolutely nothing being drawn in the window you open on the screen—from incorrectly aiming the "camera" and taking a picture with the model behind you. A similar problem arises if you don't choose a field of view that's wide enough to view your objects but narrow enough so they appear reasonably large.

If you find yourself exerting great programming effort only to create a black window, try these diagnostic steps:

1. Check the obvious possibilities. Make sure your system is plugged in. Make sure you're drawing your objects with a color that's different from the color with which you're clearing the screen. Make sure that whatever states you're using (such as lighting, texturing, alpha blending, logical operations, or antialiasing) are correctly turned on or off, as desired.

2. Remember that with the projection commands, the near and far coordinates measure distance from the viewpoint and that (by default) you're looking down the negative z-axis. Thus, if the near value is 1.0 and the far value is 3.0, objects must have z-coordinates between −1.0 and −3.0 in order to be visible. To ensure that you haven't clipped everything out of your scene, temporarily set the near and far clipping planes to some absurdly inclusive values, such as 0.001 and 1000000.0. This alters appearance for operations such as depth-buffering and fog, but it might uncover inadvertently clipped objects.

3. Determine where the viewpoint is, in which direction you're looking, and where your objects are. It might help to create a real three-dimensional space—using your hands, for instance—to figure these things out.

4. Make sure you know where you're rotating about. You might be rotating about some arbitrary location unless you translated back to the origin first. It's OK to rotate about any point unless you're expecting to rotate about the origin.

5. Check your aim. Use **gluLookAt()** to aim the viewing volume at your objects, or draw your objects at or near the origin, and use **glTranslate*()** as a viewing transformation to move the camera just far enough in the z-direction so that the objects fall within the viewing volume. Once you've managed to make your objects visible, try to change the viewing volume incrementally to achieve the exact result you want, as described next.

6. For perspective transformations, be certain the near clipping plane is not too close to the viewer (camera), otherwise depth-buffering accuracy may be adversely affected.

Even after you've aimed the camera in the correct direction and you can see your objects, they might appear too small or too large. If you're using **gluPerspective()**, you might need to alter the angle defining the field of view by changing the value of the first parameter for this command. You can use trigonometry to calculate the desired field of view given the size of the object and its distance from the viewpoint: The tangent of half the desired angle is half the size of the object divided by the distance to the object (see Figure 3-19). Thus, you can use an arctangent routine to compute half the desired angle. Example 3-3 assumes such a routine, **atan2()**, which calculates the arctangent given the length of the opposite and adjacent sides of a right triangle. This result then needs to be converted from radians to degrees.

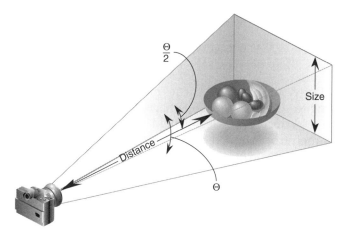

Figure 3-19   Using Trigonometry to Calculate the Field of View

Example 3-3   Calculating Field of View

```
#define PI 3.1415926535

double calculateAngle(double size, double distance)
{
    double radtheta, degtheta;

    radtheta = 2.0 * atan2 (size/2.0, distance);
    degtheta = (180.0 * radtheta) / PI;
    return degtheta;
}
```

Typically, of course, you don't know the exact size of an object, and only the distance between the viewpoint and a single point in your scene can be determined. To obtain a fairly good approximate value, find the bounding box for your scene by determining the maximum and minimum x-, y-, and z-coordinates of all the objects in your scene. Then calculate the radius of a bounding sphere for that box, and use the center of the sphere to determine the distance and the radius to determine the size.

For example, suppose all the coordinates in your object satisfy the equations $-1 \leq x \leq 3$, $5 \leq y \leq 7$, and $-5 \leq z \leq 5$. The center of the bounding box is (1, 6, 0), and the radius of a bounding sphere is the distance from the center of the box to any corner—say (3, 7, 5)—or

$$\sqrt{(3-1)^2 + (7-6)^2 + (5-0)^2} = \sqrt{30} = 5.477$$

If the viewpoint is at (8, 9, 10), the distance between it and the center is

$$\sqrt{(8-1)^2 + (9-6)^2 + (10-0)^2} = \sqrt{158} = 12.570$$

The tangent of the half-angle is 5.477 divided by 12.570, which equals 0.4357, so the half-angle is 23.54 degrees.

Remember that the field-of-view angle affects the optimal position for the viewpoint, if you're trying to achieve a realistic image. For example, if your calculations indicate that you need a 179-degree field of view, the viewpoint must be a fraction of an inch from the screen to achieve realism. If your calculated field of view is too large, you might need to move the viewpoint farther away from the object.

Manipulating the Matrix Stacks

The modelview and projection matrices you've been creating, loading, and multiplying have been only the visible tips of their respective icebergs. Each of these matrices is actually the topmost member of a stack of matrices (see Figure 3-20).

A stack of matrices is useful for constructing hierarchical models, in which complicated objects are constructed from simpler ones. For example, suppose you're drawing an automobile that has four wheels, each of which is attached to the car with five bolts. You have a single routine to draw a wheel and another to draw a bolt, since all the wheels and all the bolts look the

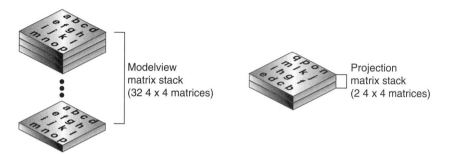

Figure 3-20   Modelview and Projection Matrix Stacks

same. These routines draw a wheel or a bolt in some convenient position and orientation; for example, centered at the origin with its axis coincident with the z-axis. When you draw the car, including the wheels and bolts, you want to call the wheel-drawing routine four times, with different transformations in effect each time to position the wheels correctly. As you draw each wheel, you want to draw the bolts five times, each time translated appropriately relative to the wheel.

Suppose for a minute that all you have to do is draw the car body and the wheels. The English description of what you want to do might be something like this:

> Draw the car body. Remember where you are, and translate to the right front wheel. Draw the wheel and throw away the last translation so your current position is back at the origin of the car body. Remember where you are, and translate to the left front wheel...

Similarly, for each wheel, you want to draw the wheel, remember where you are, and successively translate to each of the positions where bolts are drawn, throwing away the transformations after each bolt is drawn.

Since the transformations are stored as matrices, a matrix stack provides an ideal mechanism for doing this sort of successive remembering, translating, and throwing away. All the matrix operations that have been described so far (**glLoadMatrix()**, **glLoadTransposeMatrix()**, **glMultMatrix()**, **glMultTransposeMatrix()**, **glLoadIdentity()**, and the commands that create specific transformation matrices) deal with the current matrix or the top matrix on the stack. You can control which matrix is on top with the commands that perform stack operations: **glPushMatrix()**, which copies the current matrix and adds the copy to the top of the stack, and **glPopMatrix()**, which discards the top matrix on the stack, as shown in Figure 3-21. (Remember that the current matrix is always the matrix on the top.) In effect, **glPushMatrix**() means "remember where you are" and **glPopMatrix**() means "go back to where you were."

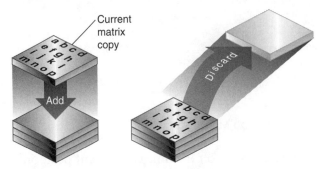

Figure 3-21   Pushing and Popping the Matrix Stack

void **glPushMatrix**(void);

Pushes all matrices in the current stack down one level. The current stack is determined by **glMatrixMode**(). The topmost matrix is copied, so its contents are duplicated in both the top and second-from-the-top matrix. If too many matrices are pushed, an error is generated.

void **glPopMatrix**(void);

Pops the top matrix off the stack, destroying the contents of the popped matrix. What was the second-from-the-top matrix becomes the top matrix. The current stack is determined by **glMatrixMode**(). If the stack contains a single matrix, calling **glPopMatrix**() generates an error.

Example 3-4 draws an automobile, assuming the existence of routines that draw the car body, a wheel, and a bolt.

Example 3-4   Pushing and Popping the Matrix

```
draw_wheel_and_bolts()
{
   int i;

   draw_wheel();
   for(i=0;i<5;i++){
      glPushMatrix();
         glRotatef(72.0*i, 0.0, 0.0, 1.0);
         glTranslatef(3.0, 0.0, 0.0);
```

```
        draw_bolt();
      glPopMatrix();
   }
}

draw_body_and_wheel_and_bolts()
{
   draw_car_body();
   glPushMatrix();
      glTranslatef(40, 0, 30);   /*move to first wheel position*/
      draw_wheel_and_bolts();
   glPopMatrix();
   glPushMatrix();
      glTranslatef(40, 0, -30);   /*move to 2nd wheel position*/
      draw_wheel_and_bolts();
   glPopMatrix();
   ...                      /*draw last two wheels similarly*/
}
```

This code assumes that the wheel and bolt axes are coincident with the z-axis; that the bolts are evenly spaced every 72 degrees, 3 units (maybe inches) from the center of the wheel; and that the front wheels are 40 units in front of and 30 units to the right and left of the car's origin.

A stack is more efficient than an individual matrix, especially if the stack is implemented in hardware. When you push a matrix, you don't need to copy the current data back to the main process, and the hardware may be able to copy more than one element of the matrix at a time. Sometimes you might want to keep an identity matrix at the bottom of the stack so that you don't need to call **glLoadIdentity()** repeatedly.

The Modelview Matrix Stack

As you've seen earlier in "Viewing and Modeling Transformations," the modelview matrix contains the cumulative product of multiplying viewing and modeling transformation matrices. Each viewing or modeling transformation creates a new matrix that multiplies the current modelview matrix; the result, which becomes the new current matrix, represents the composite transformation. The modelview matrix stack contains at least 32 4×4 matrices; initially, the topmost matrix is the identity matrix. Some implementations of OpenGL may support more than 32 matrices on the stack. To find the maximum allowable number of matrices, you can use the query command **glGetIntegerv(GL_MAX_MODELVIEW_STACK_DEPTH, GLint *params)**.

The Projection Matrix Stack

The projection matrix contains a matrix for the projection transformation, which describes the viewing volume. Generally, you don't want to compose projection matrices, so you issue **glLoadIdentity()** before performing a projection transformation. Also for this reason, the projection matrix stack need be only two levels deep; some OpenGL implementations may allow more than two 4 × 4 matrices. To find the stack depth, call **glGetIntegerv(GL_MAX_PROJECTION_STACK_DEPTH, GLint *params)**.

One use for a second matrix in the stack would be an application that needs to display a help window with text in it, in addition to its normal window showing a three-dimensional scene. Since text is most easily positioned with an orthographic projection, you could change temporarily to an orthographic projection, display the help, and then return to your previous projection:

```
glMatrixMode(GL_PROJECTION);
glPushMatrix();                        /*save the current projection*/
    glLoadIdentity();
    glOrtho(...);                      /*set up for displaying help*/
    display_the_help();
glPopMatrix();
```

Note that you'd probably also have to change the modelview matrix appropriately.

Advanced

If you know enough mathematics, you can create custom projection matrices that perform arbitrary projective transformations. For example, OpenGL and its Utility Library have no built-in mechanism for two-point perspective. If you were trying to emulate the drawings in drafting texts, you might need such a projection matrix.

Additional Clipping Planes

In addition to the six clipping planes of the viewing volume (left, right, bottom, top, near, and far), you can define up to six additional clipping planes for further restriction of the viewing volume, as shown in Figure 3-22. This is useful for removing extraneous objects in a scene—for example, if you want to display a cutaway view of an object.

Each plane is specified by the coefficients of its equation: $Ax + By + Cz + D = 0$. The clipping planes are automatically transformed appropriately by modeling and viewing transformations. The clipping volume becomes the intersection of the viewing volume and all *half-spaces* defined by the additional clipping planes. Remember that polygons that get clipped automatically have their edges reconstructed appropriately by OpenGL.

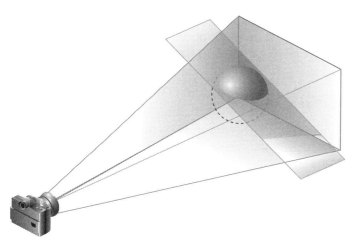

Figure 3-22   Additional Clipping Planes and the Viewing Volume

---

void **glClipPlane**(GLenum *plane*, const GLdouble **equation*);

Defines a clipping plane. The *equation* argument points to the four coefficients of the plane equation, $Ax + By + Cz + D = 0$. All points with eye coordinates (x_e, y_e, z_e, w_e) that satisfy $(A\ B\ C\ D)\mathbf{M}^{-1}(x_e\ y_e\ z_e\ w_e)^{\mathrm{T}} \geq 0$ lie in the half-space defined by the plane, where $\mathbf{M}$ is the current modelview matrix at the time **glClipPlane**() is called. All points not in this half-space are clipped away. The *plane* argument is GL_CLIP_DISTANCE*i* (named GL_CLIP_PLANE*i* prior to OpenGL version 3.0), where *i* is an integer specifying which of the available clipping planes to define. *i* is a number between 0 and one less than the maximum number of additional clipping planes.

Compatibility Extension
glClipPlane
GL_CLIP_ DISTANCE*i*
GL_CLIP_PLANE*i*
GL_MAX_CLIP_ PLANES

You need to enable each additional clipping plane you define:

`glEnable(GL_CLIP_PLANEi);`

You can disable a plane with

`glDisable(GL_CLIP_PLANEi);`

All implementations of OpenGL must support at least six additional clipping planes, although some implementations may allow more. You can use **glGetIntegerv()** with GL_MAX_CLIP_PLANES to determine how many clipping planes are supported.

Note: Clipping performed as a result of **glClipPlane()** is done in eye coordinates, not in clip coordinates. This difference is noticeable if the projection matrix is singular (that is, a real projection matrix that flattens three-dimensional coordinates to two-dimensional ones). Clipping performed in eye coordinates continues to take place in three dimensions even when the projection matrix is singular.

A Clipping Plane Code Example

Example 3-5 renders a wireframe sphere with two clipping planes that slice away three-quarters of the original sphere, as shown in Figure 3-23.

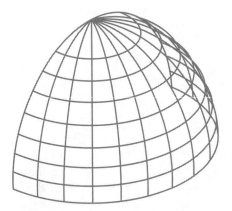

Figure 3-23   Clipped Wireframe Sphere

Example 3-5   Wireframe Sphere with Two Clipping Planes: clip.c

```
void init(void)
{
    glClearColor(0.0, 0.0, 0.0, 0.0);
    glShadeModel(GL_FLAT);
}
void display(void)
{
```

```
    GLdouble eqn[4] = {0.0, 1.0, 0.0, 0.0};
    GLdouble eqn2[4] = {1.0, 0.0, 0.0, 0.0};

    glClear(GL_COLOR_BUFFER_BIT);
    glColor3f(1.0, 1.0, 1.0);
    glPushMatrix();
    glTranslatef(0.0, 0.0, -5.0);

/*    clip lower half -- y < 0          */
    glClipPlane(GL_CLIP_PLANE0, eqn);
    glEnable(GL_CLIP_PLANE0);
/*    clip left half -- x < 0           */
    glClipPlane(GL_CLIP_PLANE1, eqn2);
    glEnable(GL_CLIP_PLANE1);

    glRotatef(90.0, 1.0, 0.0, 0.0);
    glutWireSphere(1.0, 20, 16);
    glPopMatrix();
    glFlush();
}

void reshape(int w, int h)
{
    glViewport(0, 0, (GLsizei) w, (GLsizei) h);
    glMatrixMode(GL_PROJECTION);
    glLoadIdentity();
    gluPerspective(60.0, (GLfloat) w/(GLfloat) h, 1.0, 20.0);
    glMatrixMode(GL_MODELVIEW);
}

int main(int argc, char** argv)
{
    glutInit(&argc, argv);
    glutInitDisplayMode(GLUT_SINGLE | GLUT_RGB);
    glutInitWindowSize(500, 500);
    glutInitWindowPosition(100, 100);
    glutCreateWindow(argv[0]);
    init();
    glutDisplayFunc(display);
    glutReshapeFunc(reshape);
    glutMainLoop();
    return 0;
}
```

Try This

- Try changing the coefficients that describe the clipping planes in Example 3-5.

- Try calling a modeling transformation, such as **glRotate*()**, to affect **glClipPlane()**. Make the clipping plane move independently of the objects in the scene.

Examples of Composing Several Transformations

This section demonstrates how to combine several transformations to achieve a particular result. The two examples discussed are a solar system, in which objects need to rotate on their axes as well as in orbit around each other, and a robot arm, which has several joints that effectively transform coordinate systems as they move relative to each other.

Building a Solar System

The program described in this section draws a simple solar system with a planet and a sun, both using the same sphere-drawing routine. To write this program, you need to use **glRotate*()** for the revolution of the planet around the sun and for the rotation of the planet around its own axis. You also need **glTranslate*()** to move the planet out to its orbit, away from the origin of the solar system. Remember that you can specify the desired sizes of the two spheres by supplying the appropriate arguments for the **glutWireSphere()** routine.

To draw the solar system, you first want to set up a projection and a viewing transformation. For this example, **gluPerspective()** and **gluLookAt()** are used.

Drawing the sun is straightforward, since it should be located at the origin of the grand, fixed coordinate system, which is where the sphere routine places it. Thus, drawing the sun doesn't require translation; you can use **glRotate*()** to make the sun rotate about an arbitrary axis. Drawing a planet rotating around the sun, as shown in Figure 3-24, requires several modeling transformations. The planet needs to rotate about its own axis once a day; and once a year, the planet completes one revolution around the sun.

To determine the order of modeling transformations, visualize what happens to the local coordinate system. An initial **glRotate*()** rotates the local coordinate system that initially coincides with the grand coordinate system.

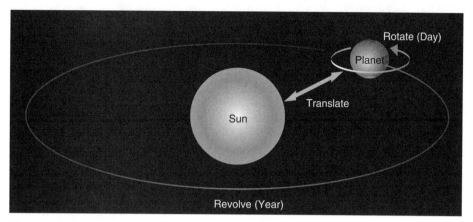

Figure 3-24 Planet and Sun

Next, **glTranslate*()** moves the local coordinate system to a position on the planet's orbit; the distance moved should equal the radius of the orbit. Thus, the initial **glRotate*()** actually determines where along the orbit the planet is (or what time of year it is).

A second **glRotate*()** rotates the local coordinate system around the local axes, thus determining the time of day for the planet. Once you've issued all these transformation commands, the planet can be drawn.

In summary, the following OpenGL commands draw the sun and planet; the full program is shown in Example 3-6:

```
glPushMatrix();
glutWireSphere(1.0, 20, 16);       /* draw sun */
glRotatef((GLfloat) year, 0.0, 1.0, 0.0);
glTranslatef(2.0, 0.0, 0.0);
glRotatef((GLfloat) day, 0.0, 1.0, 0.0);
glutWireSphere(0.2, 10, 8);        /* draw smaller planet */
glPopMatrix();
```

Example 3-6 Planetary System: planet.c

```
static int year = 0, day = 0;

void init(void)
{
    glClearColor(0.0, 0.0, 0.0, 0.0);
    glShadeModel(GL_FLAT);
}
```

```
void display(void)
{
    glClear(GL_COLOR_BUFFER_BIT);
    glColor3f(1.0, 1.0, 1.0);

    glPushMatrix();
    glutWireSphere(1.0, 20, 16);    /* draw sun */
    glRotatef((GLfloat) year, 0.0, 1.0, 0.0);
    glTranslatef(2.0, 0.0, 0.0);
    glRotatef((GLfloat) day, 0.0, 1.0, 0.0);
    glutWireSphere(0.2, 10, 8);     /* draw smaller planet */
    glPopMatrix();
    glutSwapBuffers();
}

void reshape(int w, int h)
{
    glViewport(0, 0, (GLsizei) w, (GLsizei) h);
    glMatrixMode(GL_PROJECTION);
    glLoadIdentity();
    gluPerspective(60.0, (GLfloat) w/(GLfloat) h, 1.0, 20.0);
    glMatrixMode(GL_MODELVIEW);
    glLoadIdentity();
    gluLookAt(0.0, 0.0, 5.0, 0.0, 0.0, 0.0, 0.0, 1.0, 0.0);
}

void keyboard(unsigned char key, int x, int y)
{
    switch (key) {
        case 'd':
            day = (day + 10) % 360;
            glutPostRedisplay();
            break;
        case 'D':
            day = (day - 10) % 360;
            glutPostRedisplay();
            break;
        case 'y':
            year = (year + 5) % 360;
            glutPostRedisplay();
            break;
        case 'Y':
            year = (year - 5) % 360;
            glutPostRedisplay();
            break;
        default:
```

```
        break;
    }
}

int main(int argc, char** argv)
{
    glutInit(&argc, argv);
    glutInitDisplayMode(GLUT_DOUBLE | GLUT_RGB);
    glutInitWindowSize(500, 500);
    glutInitWindowPosition(100, 100);
    glutCreateWindow(argv[0]);
    init();
    glutDisplayFunc(display);
    glutReshapeFunc(reshape);
    glutKeyboardFunc(keyboard);
    glutMainLoop();
    return 0;
}
```

Try This

Try This

- Try adding a moon to the planet, or try several moons and additional planets. Hint: Use **glPushMatrix()** and **glPopMatrix()** to save and restore the position and orientation of the coordinate system at appropriate moments. If you're going to draw several moons around a planet, you need to save the coordinate system prior to positioning each moon and restore the coordinate system after each moon is drawn.

- Try tilting the planet's axis.

Building an Articulated Robot Arm

This section discusses a program that creates an articulated robot arm with two or more segments. The arm should be connected with pivot points at the shoulder, elbow, or other joints. Figure 3-25 shows a single joint of such an arm.

You can use a scaled cube as a segment of the robot arm, but first you must call the appropriate modeling transformations to orient each segment. Since the origin of the local coordinate system is initially at the center of the cube, you need to move the local coordinate system to one edge of the cube. Otherwise, the cube rotates about its center, rather than the pivot point.

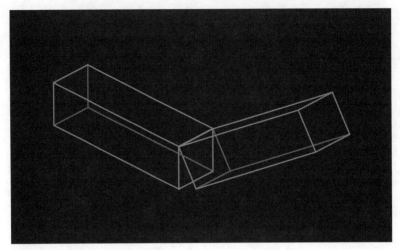

Figure 3-25   Robot Arm

After you call **glTranslate*()** to establish the pivot point and **glRotate*()** to pivot the cube, translate back to the center of the cube. Then the cube is scaled (flattened and widened) before it is drawn. The **glPushMatrix()** and **glPopMatrix()** commands restrict the effect of **glScale*()**. Here's what your code might look like for this first segment of the arm (the entire program is shown in Example 3-7):

```
glTranslatef(-1.0, 0.0, 0.0);
glRotatef((GLfloat) shoulder, 0.0, 0.0, 1.0);
glTranslatef(1.0, 0.0, 0.0);
glPushMatrix();
glScalef(2.0, 0.4, 1.0);
glutWireCube(1.0);
glPopMatrix();
```

To build a second segment, you need to move the local coordinate system to the next pivot point. Since the coordinate system has previously been rotated, the *x*-axis is already oriented along the length of the rotated arm. Therefore, translating along the *x*-axis moves the local coordinate system to the next pivot point. Once it's at that pivot point, you can use the same code to draw the second segment as you used for the first one. This can be continued for an indefinite number of segments (shoulder, elbow, wrist, fingers):

```
glTranslatef(1.0, 0.0, 0.0);
glRotatef((GLfloat) elbow, 0.0, 0.0, 1.0);
glTranslatef(1.0, 0.0, 0.0);
glPushMatrix();
glScalef(2.0, 0.4, 1.0);
glutWireCube(1.0);
glPopMatrix();
```

Example 3-7   Robot Arm: robot.c

```
static int shoulder = 0, elbow = 0;

void init(void)
{
  glClearColor(0.0, 0.0, 0.0, 0.0);
  glShadeModel(GL_FLAT);
}

void display(void)
{
   glClear(GL_COLOR_BUFFER_BIT);
   glPushMatrix();
   glTranslatef(-1.0, 0.0, 0.0);
   glRotatef((GLfloat) shoulder, 0.0, 0.0, 1.0);
   glTranslatef(1.0, 0.0, 0.0);
   glPushMatrix();
   glScalef(2.0, 0.4, 1.0);
   glutWireCube(1.0);
   glPopMatrix();

   glTranslatef(1.0, 0.0, 0.0);
   glRotatef((GLfloat) elbow, 0.0, 0.0, 1.0);
   glTranslatef(1.0, 0.0, 0.0);
   glPushMatrix();
   glScalef(2.0, 0.4, 1.0);
   glutWireCube(1.0);
   glPopMatrix();

   glPopMatrix();
   glutSwapBuffers();
}

void reshape(int w, int h)
{
   glViewport(0, 0, (GLsizei) w, (GLsizei) h);
   glMatrixMode(GL_PROJECTION);
```

```
        glLoadIdentity();
        gluPerspective(65.0, (GLfloat) w/(GLfloat) h, 1.0, 20.0);
        glMatrixMode(GL_MODELVIEW);
        glLoadIdentity();
        glTranslatef(0.0, 0.0, -5.0);
}

void keyboard(unsigned char key, int x, int y)
{
    switch (key) {
        case 's':    /*  s key rotates at shoulder  */
            shoulder = (shoulder + 5) % 360;
            glutPostRedisplay();
            break;
        case 'S':
            shoulder = (shoulder - 5) % 360;
            glutPostRedisplay();
            break;
        case 'e':  /*  e key rotates at elbow  */
            elbow = (elbow + 5) % 360;
            glutPostRedisplay();
            break;
        case 'E':
            elbow = (elbow - 5) % 360;
            glutPostRedisplay();
            break;
        default:
            break;
    }
}

int main(int argc, char** argv)
{
    glutInit(&argc, argv);
    glutInitDisplayMode(GLUT_DOUBLE | GLUT_RGB);
    glutInitWindowSize(500, 500);
    glutInitWindowPosition(100, 100);
    glutCreateWindow(argv[0]);
    init();
    glutDisplayFunc(display);
    glutReshapeFunc(reshape);
    glutKeyboardFunc(keyboard);
    glutMainLoop();
    return 0;
}
```

Try This

- Modify Example 3-7 to add additional segments to the robot arm.

- Modify Example 3-7 to add additional segments at the same position. For example, give the robot arm several "fingers" at the wrist, as shown in Figure 3-26. Hint: Use **glPushMatrix()** and **glPopMatrix()** to save and restore the position and orientation of the coordinate system at the wrist. If you're going to draw fingers at the wrist, you need to save the current matrix prior to positioning each finger, and restore the current matrix after each finger is drawn.

Try This

Figure 3-26   Robot Arm with Fingers

Nate Robins' Transformation Tutorial

If you have Nate Robins' suite of tutorial programs, go back to the **transformation** tutorial and run it again. Use the popup menu interface to change the order of **glRotate*()** and **glTranslate()**, and note the effect of swapping the order of these routines.

Reversing or Mimicking Transformations

The geometric processing pipeline is very good at using viewing and projection matrices and a viewport for clipping to transform the world (or object) coordinates of a vertex into window (or screen) coordinates. However, there are situations in which you want to reverse that process. A common situation is when an application user utilizes the mouse to choose a location in three dimensions. The mouse returns only a two-dimensional value, which is the screen location of the cursor. Therefore, the application will have to reverse the transformation process to determine where in three-dimensional space this screen location originated.

The Utility Library routines **gluUnProject()** and **gluUnProject4()** perform this reversal of the transformations. Given the three-dimensional window coordinates for a transformed vertex and all the transformations that affected it, **gluUnProject()** returns the original world coordinates of that vertex. (Use **gluUnProject4()** if the depth range is other than the default [0, 1].)

int **gluUnProject**(GLdouble *winx*, GLdouble *winy*, GLdouble *winz*,
 const GLdouble *modelMatrix[16]*,
 const GLdouble *projMatrix[16]*,
 const GLint *viewport[4]*,
 GLdouble **objx*, GLdouble **objy*, GLdouble **objz*);

Maps the specified window coordinates (*winx, winy, winz*) into object coordinates, using transformations defined by a modelview matrix (*modelMatrix*), projection matrix (*projMatrix*), and viewport (*viewport*). The resulting object coordinates are returned in *objx, objy,* and *objz*. The function returns GL_TRUE, indicating success, or GL_FALSE, indicating failure (such as a noninvertible matrix). This operation does not attempt to clip the coordinates to the viewport or eliminate depth values that fall outside of **glDepthRange()**.

There are inherent difficulties in trying to reverse the transformation process. A two-dimensional screen location could have originated from anywhere on an entire line in three-dimensional space. To disambiguate the result, **gluUnProject()** requires that a window depth coordinate (*winz*) be provided, specified in terms of **glDepthRange()**. (For more about depth range, see "The Transformed Depth Coordinate" on page 161.) For the default values of **glDepthRange()**, *winz* at 0.0 will request the world coordinates of the transformed point at the near clipping plane, while *winz* at 1.0 will request the point at the far clipping plane.

Example 3-8 demonstrates **gluUnProject()** by reading the mouse position and determining the three-dimensional points at the near and far clipping planes from which the mouse position was transformed. The computed world coordinates are printed to standard output, but the rendered window itself is just black.

Example 3-8   Reversing the Geometric Processing Pipeline: unproject.c

```
void display(void)
{
    glClear(GL_COLOR_BUFFER_BIT);
```

```
    glFlush();
}

void reshape(int w, int h)
{
    glViewport(0, 0, (GLsizei) w, (GLsizei) h);
    glMatrixMode(GL_PROJECTION);
    glLoadIdentity();
    gluPerspective(45.0, (GLfloat) w/(GLfloat) h, 1.0, 100.0);
    glMatrixMode(GL_MODELVIEW);
    glLoadIdentity();
}

void mouse(int button, int state, int x, int y)
{
    GLint viewport[4];
    GLdouble mvmatrix[16], projmatrix[16];
    GLint realy;  /*  OpenGL y coordinate position  */
    GLdouble wx, wy, wz;  /*  returned world x, y, z coords  */

    switch (button) {
        case GLUT_LEFT_BUTTON:
            if (state == GLUT_DOWN) {
                glGetIntegerv(GL_VIEWPORT, viewport);
                glGetDoublev(GL_MODELVIEW_MATRIX, mvmatrix);
                glGetDoublev(GL_PROJECTION_MATRIX, projmatrix);
/*  note viewport[3] is height of window in pixels  */
                realy = viewport[3] - (GLint) y - 1;
                printf("Coordinates at cursor are (%4d, %4d)\n",
                    x, realy);
                gluUnProject((GLdouble) x, (GLdouble) realy, 0.0,
                    mvmatrix, projmatrix, viewport, &wx, &wy, &wz);
                printf("World coords at z=0.0 are (%f, %f, %f)\n",
                    wx, wy, wz);
                gluUnProject((GLdouble) x, (GLdouble) realy, 1.0,
                    mvmatrix, projmatrix, viewport, &wx, &wy, &wz);
                printf("World coords at z=1.0 are (%f, %f, %f)\n",
                    wx, wy, wz);
            }
            break;
        case GLUT_RIGHT_BUTTON:
            if (state == GLUT_DOWN)
                exit(0);
            break;
        default:
            break;
```

```
        }
}

int main(int argc, char** argv)
{
    glutInit(&argc, argv);
    glutInitDisplayMode(GLUT_SINGLE | GLUT_RGB);
    glutInitWindowSize(500, 500);
    glutInitWindowPosition(100, 100);
    glutCreateWindow(argv[0]);
    glutDisplayFunc(display);
    glutReshapeFunc(reshape);
    glutMouseFunc(mouse);
    glutMainLoop();
    return 0;
}
```

GLU 1.3 introduces a modified version of **gluUnProject()**. **gluUnProject4()** can handle nonstandard **glDepthRange()** values and also *w*-coordinate values other than 1.

int **gluUnProject4**(GLdouble *winx*, GLdouble *winy*, GLdouble *winz*,
            GLdouble *clipw*, const GLdouble *modelMatrix[16]*,
            const GLdouble *projMatrix[16]*,
            const GLint *viewport[4]*,
            GLclampd *zNear*, GLclampd *zFar*,
            GLdouble **objx*, GLdouble **objy*,
            GLdouble **objz*, GLdouble **objw*);

Overall, the operation is similar to **gluUnProject()**. Maps the specified window coordinates (*winx, winy, winz, clipw*) into object coordinates, using transformations defined by a modelview matrix (*modelMatrix*), projection matrix (*projMatrix*), viewport (*viewport*), and the depth range values *zNear* and *zFar*. The resulting object coordinates are returned in *objx, objy, objz,* and *objw*.

gluProject() is another Utility Library routine, which is related to **gluUnProject()**. **gluProject()** mimics the actions of the transformation pipeline. Given three-dimensional world coordinates and all the transformations that affect them, **gluProject()** returns the transformed window coordinates.

int **gluProject**(GLdouble *objx*, GLdouble *objy*, GLdouble *objz*,
            const GLdouble *modelMatrix[16]*,
            const GLdouble *projMatrix[16]*,
            const GLint *viewport[4]*,
            GLdouble **winx*, GLdouble **winy*, GLdouble **winz*);

Maps the specified object coordinates (*objx, objy, objz*) into window coordinates, using transformations defined by a modelview matrix (*modelMatrix*), projection matrix (*projMatrix*), and viewport (*viewport*). The resulting window coordinates are returned in *winx, winy,* and *winz.* The function returns GL_TRUE, indicating success, or GL_FALSE, indicating failure.

Note: The matrices passed to **gluUnProject()**, **gluUnProject4()**, and **gluProject()** are in the OpenGL-standard column-major order. You might use **glGetDoublev()** and **glGetIntegerv()** to obtain the current GL_MODELVIEW_MATRIX, GL_PROJECTION_MATRIX, and GL_VIEWPORT values for use with **gluUnProject()**, **gluUnProject4()**, or **gluProject()**.

Chapter 4

Color

Chapter Objectives

After reading this chapter, you'll be able to do the following:

- Decide between using RGBA or color-index mode for your application

- Specify desired colors for drawing objects

- Use smooth shading to draw a single polygon with more than one color

Note: In OpenGL Version 3.1, many of the techniques and functions described in this chapter were removed through deprecation. In particular, color-index rendering is not supported. The concepts relating to RGBA color modes are still relevant, but need to be implemented in vertex or fragment shaders, as described in Chapter 15.

The goal of almost all OpenGL applications is to draw color pictures in a window on the screen. The window is a rectangular array of pixels, each of which contains and displays its own color. Thus, in a sense, the point of all the calculations performed by an OpenGL implementation—calculations that take into account OpenGL commands, state information, and values of parameters—is to determine the final color of every pixel that's to be drawn in the window. This chapter explains the commands for specifying colors and how OpenGL interprets them in the following major sections:

- "Color Perception" discusses how the eye perceives color.

- "Computer Color" describes the relationship between pixels on a computer *monitor* and their colors; it also defines the two display modes: RGBA and color index.

- "RGBA versus Color-Index Mode" explains how the two display modes use graphics hardware and how to decide which mode to use.

- "Specifying a Color and a Shading Model" describes the OpenGL commands you use to specify the desired color or shading model.

Color Perception

Physically, light is composed of photons—tiny particles of light, each traveling along its own path, and each vibrating at its own frequency (or wavelength or energy—any one of frequency, wavelength, or energy determines the others). A photon is completely characterized by its position, direction, and frequency/wavelength/energy. Photons with wavelengths ranging from about 390 nanometers (nm) (violet) and 720 nm (red) cover the colors of the visible spectrum, forming the colors of a rainbow (violet, indigo, blue, green, yellow, orange, red). However, your eyes perceive lots of colors that aren't in the rainbow—white, black, brown, and pink, for example. How does this happen?

What your eye actually sees is a mixture of photons of different frequencies. Real light sources are characterized by the distribution of photon frequencies they emit. Ideal white light consists of an equal amount of light of all frequencies. Laser light is usually very pure, and all photons are almost identical in frequency (and in direction and phase as well). Light from a sodium-vapor lamp has more light in the yellow frequency. Light from most stars in space has a distribution that depends heavily on their temperatures (black-body radiation). The frequency distribution of light from most sources in your immediate environment is more complicated.

The human eye perceives color when certain cells in the retina (called *cone cells*, or just *cones*) become excited after being struck by photons. The three different kinds of cone cells respond best to three different wavelengths of light: One type of cone cell responds best to red light, one to green light, and the other to blue light. (A person who is color-blind is usually missing one or more types of cone cells.) When a given mixture of photons enters the eye, the cone cells in the retina register different degrees of excitation depending on their types, and if a different mixture of photons happens to excite the three types of cone cells to the same degree, its color is indistinguishable from that of the first mixture.

Since each color is recorded by the eye as the levels of excitation of the cone cells produced by the incoming photons, the eye can perceive colors that aren't in the spectrum produced by a prism or rainbow. For example, if you send a mixture of red and blue photons so that both the red and blue cones in the retina are excited, your eye sees it as magenta, which isn't in the spectrum. Other combinations give browns, turquoises, and mauves, none of which appears in the color spectrum.

A computer-graphics monitor emulates visible colors by lighting pixels with a combination of red, green, and blue light in proportions that excite the red-, green-, and blue-sensitive cones in the retina in such a way that it matches the excitation levels generated by the photon mix it's trying to emulate. If humans had more types of cone cells, some that were yellow-sensitive for example, color monitors would probably have a yellow gun as well, and we'd use RGBY (red, green, blue, yellow) quadruples to specify colors. And if everyone were color-blind in the same way, this chapter would be simpler.

To display a particular color, the monitor sends the right amounts of red, green, and blue (RGB) light to stimulate appropriately the different types of cone cells in your eye. A color monitor can send different proportions of red, green, and blue to each of the pixels, and the eye sees a million or so pinpoints of light, each with its own color.

Note: There are many other representations of color, or color models, with acronyms such as HLS, HSV, and CMYK. If your data needs to be in one of these color models, you need to convert to and from RGB. For the formulas to perform these conversions, see Foley, van Dam, et al., *Computer Graphics: Principles and Practice* (Addison-Wesley, 1990).

This section considers only how the eye perceives combinations of photons that enter it. The situation for light bouncing off materials and entering the eye is even more complex—white light bouncing off a red ball will appear red, and yellow light shining through blue glass appears almost black, for example. (See "Real-World and OpenGL Lighting" in Chapter 5 for a discussion of these effects.)

Computer Color

On a color computer screen, the hardware causes each pixel on the screen to emit different amounts of red, green, and blue light. These are called the R, G, and B values. They're often packed together (sometimes with a fourth value, called alpha, or A), and the packed value is called the RGB (or RGBA) value. (See "Blending" in Chapter 6 for an explanation of the alpha values.) The color information at each pixel can be stored either in *RGBA mode*, in which the R, G, B, and possibly A values are kept for each pixel, or in *color-index mode*, in which a single number (called the *color index*) is stored for each pixel. Each color index indicates an entry in a table that defines a particular set of R, G, and B values. Such a table is called a *color map*.

In color-index mode, you might want to alter the values in the color map. Since color maps are controlled by the window system, there are no OpenGL commands to do this. All the examples in this book initialize the color-display mode at the time the window is opened by using routines from the GLUT library. (See Appendix A for details.)

There is a great deal of variation among the different graphics hardware platforms in both the size of the pixel array and the number of colors that can be displayed at each pixel. On any graphics system, each pixel has the same amount of memory for storing its color, and all the memory for all the pixels is called the *color buffer*. The size of a buffer is usually measured in bits, so an 8-bit buffer could store 8 bits of data (256 possible different colors) for each pixel. The size of the possible buffers varies from machine to machine. (See Chapter 10 for more information.)

The R, G, and B values can range from 0.0 (none) to 1.0 (full intensity). For example, R = 0.0, G = 0.0, and B = 1.0 represents the brightest possible blue. If R, G, and B are all 0.0, the pixel is black; if all are 1.0, the pixel is drawn in the brightest white that can be displayed on the screen. *Blending* green and blue creates shades of cyan. Blue and red combine for magenta. Red and green create yellow. To help you create the colors you want from the R, G, and B components, look at the color cube shown in Plate 12. The axes of this cube represent intensities of red, blue, and green. A black-and-white version of the cube is shown in Figure 4-1.

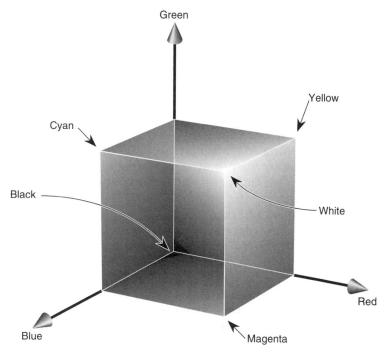

Green

Yellow

Cyan

Black

White

Red

Blue

Magenta

Figure 4-1   The Color Cube in Black and White

The commands used to specify a color for an object (in this case, a point) can be as simple as this:

```
glColor3f(1.0, 0.0, 0.0);   /* the current RGB color is red: */
                            /* full red, no green, no blue. */
glBegin(GL_POINTS);
    glVertex3fv(point_array);
glEnd();
```

In certain modes (for example, if lighting or texturing calculations are performed), the assigned color might go through other operations before arriving in the framebuffer as a value representing a color for a pixel. In fact, the color of a pixel is determined by a lengthy sequence of operations.

Early in a program's execution, the color-display mode is set to either RGBA mode or color-index mode. Once the color-display mode is initialized, it can't be changed. As the program executes, a color (either a color index or an RGBA value) is determined on a per-vertex basis for each geometric primitive. This color either is a color you've explicitly specified for a vertex or, if lighting is enabled, is determined from the interaction of the transformation matrices with the surface normals and other material properties. In other words, a red ball with a blue light shining on it looks different from the same ball with no light on it. (See Chapter 5 for details.) After the relevant lighting calculations have been performed, the chosen shading model is applied. As explained in "Specifying a Color and a Shading Model," you can choose flat or smooth shading, each of which has different effects on the eventual color of a pixel.

Next, the primitives are *rasterized*, or converted to a two-dimensional image. Rasterizing involves determining which squares of an integer grid in window coordinates are occupied by the primitive, and then assigning color and other values to each such square. A grid square along with its associated values of color, z (depth), and texture coordinates is called a *fragment*. Pixels are elements of the framebuffer; a fragment comes from a primitive and is combined with its corresponding pixel to yield a new pixel. Once a fragment has been constructed, texturing, fog, and antialiasing are applied—if they're enabled—to the fragments. After that, any specified alpha blending, *dithering*, and bitwise logical operations are carried out using the fragment and the pixel already stored in the framebuffer. Finally, the fragment's color value (either color index or RGBA) is written into the pixel and displayed in the window using the window's color-display mode.

RGBA versus Color-Index Mode

In either color-index or RGBA mode, a certain amount of color data is stored at each pixel. This amount is determined by the number of bitplanes in the framebuffer. A *bitplane* contains 1 bit of data for each pixel. If there are 8 color bitplanes, there are 8 color bits per pixel, and hence $2^8 = 256$ different values or colors that can be stored at the pixel.

Bitplanes are often divided evenly into storage for R, G, and B components (that is, a 24-bitplane system devotes 8 bits each to red, green, and blue), but this isn't always true. To find out the number of bitplanes available on your system for red, green, blue, alpha, or color-index values, use **glGetIntegerv()** with GL_RED_BITS, GL_GREEN_BITS, GL_BLUE_BITS, GL_ALPHA_BITS, and GL_INDEX_BITS.

Note: Color intensities on most computer screens aren't perceived as linear by the human eye. Consider colors consisting of just a red component, with green and blue set at zero. As the intensity varies from 0.0 (off) to 1.0 (full on), the number of electrons striking the pixels increases, but the question is, does 0.5 appear to be halfway between 0.0 and 1.0? To test this, write a program that draws alternate pixels in a checkerboard pattern to intensities 0.0 and 1.0, and compare it with a region drawn solidly in color 0.5. At a reasonable distance from the screen, the two regions should appear to have the same intensity. If they look noticeably different, you need to use whatever correction mechanism is provided on your particular system. For example, many systems have a table to adjust intensities so that 0.5 appears to be halfway between 0.0 and 1.0. The mapping generally used is an exponential one, with the exponent referred to as gamma (hence the term *gamma correction*). Using the same gamma for the red, green, and blue components gives pretty good results, but three different gamma values might give slightly better results. (For more details on this topic, see Foley, van Dam, et al., *Computer Graphics: Principles and Practice*. Addison-Wesley, 1990.)

RGBA Display Mode

In RGBA mode, the hardware sets aside a certain number of bitplanes for each of the R, G, B, and A components (not necessarily the same number for each component), as shown in Figure 4-2. The R, G, and B values are typically stored as integers, rather than floating-point numbers, and they're scaled to the number of available bits for storage and retrieval. For example, if a system has 8 bits available for the R component, integers between 0 and 255 can be stored; thus, 0, 1, 2, ..., 255 in the bitplanes would correspond to R values of 0/255 = 0.0, 1/255, 2/255, ..., 255/255 = 1.0. Regardless of the number of bitplanes, 0.0 specifies the minimum intensity, and 1.0 specifies the maximum intensity.

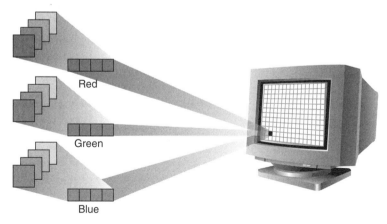

Figure 4-2   RGB Values from the Bitplanes

Note: The alpha value (the A in RGBA) has no direct effect on the color displayed on the screen. It can be used for many things, including blending and transparency, and it can have an effect on the values of R, G, and B that are written. (See "Blending" in Chapter 6 for more information about alpha values.)

The number of distinct colors that can be displayed at a single pixel depends on the number of bitplanes and the capacity of the hardware to interpret those bitplanes. The number of distinct colors can't exceed 2^n, where n is the number of bitplanes. Thus, a machine with 24 bitplanes for RGB can display up to 16.77 million distinct colors.

Dithering

Advanced

Advanced

Some graphics hardware uses dithering to increase the number of apparent colors. Dithering is the technique of using combinations of some colors to create the effects of other colors. To illustrate how dithering works, suppose your system has only 1 bit each for R, G, and B and thus can display only eight colors: black, white, red, blue, green, yellow, cyan, and magenta. To display a pink region, the hardware can fill the region in a checkerboard manner, alternating red and white pixels. If your eye is far enough away from the screen that it can't distinguish individual pixels, the region appears pink—the average of red and white. Redder pinks can be achieved by filling a higher proportion of the pixels with red, whiter pinks would use more white pixels, and so on.

With this technique, there are no pink pixels. The only way to achieve the effect of "pinkness" is to cover a region consisting of multiple pixels—you can't dither a single pixel. If you specify an RGB value for an unavailable color and fill a polygon, the hardware fills the pixels in the interior of the polygon with a mixture of nearby colors whose average appears to your eye to be the color you want. (Remember, though, that if you're reading pixel information out of the framebuffer, you get the actual red and white pixel values, since there aren't any pink ones. See Chapter 8 for more information about reading pixel values.)

Figure 4-3 illustrates some simple dithering of black and white pixels to make shades of gray. From left to right, the 4×4 patterns at the top represent dithering patterns for 50 percent, 19 percent, and 69 percent gray. Under each pattern, you can see repeated reduced copies of each pattern, but these black and white squares are still bigger than most pixels. If you look at them from across the room, you can see that they blur together and appear as three levels of gray.

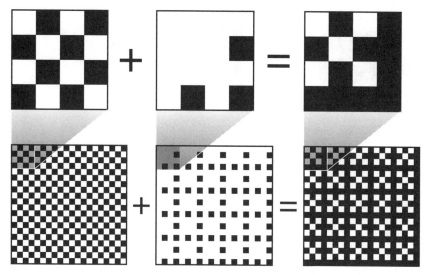

Figure 4-3   Dithering Black and White to Create Gray

With about 8 bits each of R, G, and B, you can get a fairly high-quality image without dithering. Just because your machine has 24 color bitplanes, however, doesn't mean that dithering won't be desirable. For example, if you are running in double-buffer mode, the bitplanes might be divided into two sets of 12, so there are really only 4 bits each per R, G, and B component. Without dithering, 4-bit-per-component color can give less than satisfactory results in many situations.

You enable or disable dithering by passing GL_DITHER to **glEnable()** or **glDisable()**. Note that dithering, unlike many other features, is enabled by default.

Color-Index Display Mode

With color-index mode, OpenGL uses a color map (or *lookup table*), which is similar to using a palette to mix paints to prepare for a paint-by-number scene. A painter's palette provides spaces to mix paints together; similarly, a computer's color map provides indices where the primary red, green, and blue values can be mixed, as shown in Figure 4-4.

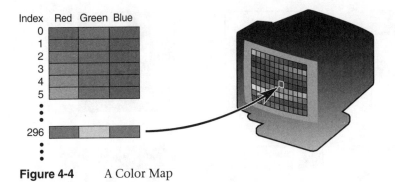

Figure 4-4   A Color Map

A painter filling in a paint-by-number scene chooses a color from the color palette and fills the corresponding numbered regions with that color. A computer stores the color index in the bitplanes for each pixel. Then those bitplane values reference the color map, and the screen is painted with the corresponding red, green, and blue values from the color map, as shown in Figure 4-5.

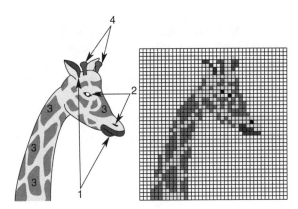

Figure 4-5   Using a Color Map to Paint a Picture

In color-index mode, the number of simultaneously available colors is limited by the size of the color map and the number of bitplanes available. The size of the color map is determined by the amount of hardware dedicated to it. The size of the color map is always a power of 2, and typical sizes range from 256 (2^8) to 4096 (2^{12}), where the exponent is the number of bitplanes being used. If there are 2^n indices in the color map and m available bit-planes, the number of usable entries is the smaller of 2^n and 2^m.

With RGBA mode, each pixel's color is independent of other pixels. However, in color-index mode, each pixel with the same index stored in its bit-planes shares the same color-map location. If the contents of an entry in the color map change, then all pixels of that color index change their color.

Choosing between RGBA and Color-Index Mode

You should base your decision to use RGBA or color-index mode on what hardware is available and on what your application requires. For most systems, more colors can be simultaneously represented with RGBA mode than with color-index mode. Also, for several effects, such as shading, lighting, texture mapping, and fog, RGBA provides more flexibility than color-index mode.

You might prefer to use color-index mode in the following cases:

*   If you're porting an existing application that makes significant use of color-index mode, it might be easier not to change to RGBA mode.

*   If you have a small number of bitplanes available, RGBA mode may produce noticeably coarse shades of colors. For example, if you have only 8 bitplanes, in RGBA mode you may have only 3 bits for red, 3 bits for green, and 2 bits for blue. You'd have only 8 (2^3) shades of red and green, and only 4 shades of blue. The gradients between color shades are likely to be very obvious.

    In this situation, if you have limited shading requirements, you can use the color-lookup table to load more shades of colors. For example, if you need only shades of blue, you can use color-index mode and store up to 256 (2^8) shades of blue in the color-lookup table, which is much better than the 4 shades you would have in RGBA mode. Of course, this example would use up your entire color-lookup table, so you would have no shades of red, green, or other combined colors.

*   Color-index mode can be useful for various tricks, such as color-map animation and drawing in layers. (See Chapter 14 for more information.)

In general, use RGBA mode wherever possible. It works with texture mapping and works better with lighting, shading, fog, antialiasing, and blending.

Changing between Display Modes

In the best of all possible worlds, you might want to avoid making a choice between RGBA and color-index display mode. For example, you may want to use color-index mode for a color-map animation effect and then, when needed, immediately change the scene to RGBA mode for texture mapping.

Similarly, you may desire to switch between single and double buffering. For example, you may have very few bitplanes; let's say 8 bitplanes. In single-buffer mode, you'll have 256 (2^8) colors, but if you are using double-buffer mode to eliminate flickering from your animated program, you may have only 16 (2^4) colors. Perhaps you want to draw a moving object without flicker and are willing to sacrifice colors for using double-buffer mode (maybe the object is moving so fast that the viewer won't notice the details). But when the object comes to rest, you will want to draw it in single-buffer mode so that you can use more colors.

Unfortunately, most window systems won't allow an easy switch. For example, with the X Window System, the color-display mode is an attribute of the X Visual. An X Visual must be specified before the window is created. Once it is specified, it cannot be changed for the life of the window. After you create a window with a double-buffered, RGBA display mode, you're stuck with it.

A tricky solution to this problem is to create more than one window, each with a different display mode. You must control the visibility of each window (for example, mapping or unmapping an X Window, or managing or unmanaging a Motif or Athena widget) and draw the object in the appropriate, visible window.

Specifying a Color and a Shading Model

OpenGL maintains a current color (in RGBA mode) and a current color index (in color-index mode). Unless you're using a more complicated coloring model such as lighting or texture mapping, each object is drawn using the current color (or color index). Look at the following pseudocode sequence:

```
set_color(RED);
draw_item(A);
draw_item(B);
set_color(GREEN);
set_color(BLUE);
draw_item(C);
```

Items A and B are drawn in red, and item C is drawn in blue. The fourth line, which sets the current color to green, has no effect (except to waste a bit of time). With no lighting or texturing, when the current color is set, all items drawn afterward are drawn in that color until the current color is changed.

Specifying a Color in RGBA Mode

In RGBA mode, use the **glColor*()** command to select a current color.

void **glColor3**{b s i f d ub us ui}(*TYPE r, TYPE g, TYPE b*);
void **glColor4**{b s i f d ub us ui}(*TYPE r, TYPE g, TYPE b, TYPE a*);
void **glColor3**{b s i f d ub us ui}**v**(const *TYPE *v*);
void **glColor4**{b s i f d ub us ui}**v**(const *TYPE *v*);

Sets the current red, green, blue, and alpha values. This command can have up to three suffixes, which differentiate variations of the parameters accepted. The first suffix is either 3 or 4, to indicate whether you supply an alpha value in addition to the red, green, and blue values. If you don't supply an alpha value, it's automatically set to 1.0. The second suffix indicates the data type for parameters: byte, short, integer, float, double, unsigned byte, unsigned short, or unsigned integer. The third suffix is an optional **v**, which indicates that the argument is a pointer to an array of values of the given data type.

Compatibility
Extension

glColor

For the versions of **glColor*()** that accept floating-point data types, the values should typically range between 0.0 and 1.0, the minimum and maximum values that can be stored in the framebuffer. Unsigned-integer color components, when specified, are linearly mapped to floating-point values such that the largest representable value maps to 1.0 (full intensity), and zero maps to 0.0 (zero intensity). Signed-integer color components, when specified, are linearly mapped to floating-point values such that the most positive representable value maps to 1.0, and the most negative representable value maps to −1.0 (see Table 4-1).

Neither floating-point nor signed-integer values are clamped to the range [0, 1] before updating the current color or current lighting material parameters. After lighting calculations, resulting color values outside the range [0, 1] are clamped to the range [0, 1] before they are interpolated or written into a color buffer. Even if lighting is disabled, the color components are clamped before rasterization.

Suffix	Data Type	Minimum Value	Min Value Maps to	Maximum Value	Max Value Maps to
b	1-byte integer	−128	−1.0	127	1.0
s	2-byte integer	−32,768	−1.0	32,767	1.0
i	4-byte integer	−2,147,483,648	−1.0	2,147,483,647	1.0
ub	unsigned 1-byte integer	0	0.0	255	1.0
us	unsigned 2-byte integer	0	0.0	65,535	1.0
ui	unsigned 4-byte integer	0	0.0	4,294,967,295	1.0

Table 4-1   Converting Color Values to Floating-Point Numbers

The similar routine **glSecondaryColor*()** is used to specify a color to be applied after texture mapping (if lighting is disabled). For more detail, see "Applying Secondary Color after Texturing" on page 478.

Color Clamping

OpenGL Version 3.0 introduced floating-point framebuffers, where RGBA color components are stored as true floating-point values. Given the greater dynamic range of floating-point values, you may want to allow color values that fall outside the range of clamped color values originally specified by OpenGL: 0.0 to 1.0.

Compatibility Extension
GL_CLAMP_VERTEX_COLOR
GL_CLAMP_FRAGMENT_COLOR

void **glClampColor**(GLenum *target*, GLenum *clamp*);

Specify whether the primary and secondary color values are clamped. *target* must be set to GL_CLAMP_VERTEX_COLOR, GL_CLAMP_FRAGMENT_COLOR, or GL_CLAMP_READ_COLOR, and *clamp* must be one of GL_TRUE, GL_FALSE, or GL_FIXED_ONLY.

The color-clamping options available in OpenGL Version 3.0 are described in Table 4-2.

Parameter	Specifies
GL_TRUE	Colors should be clamped to the range [0, 1]
GL_FALSE	Colors are not to be clamped
GL_FIXED_ONLY	Colors are only clamped if the destination framebuffer format is fixed-point

Table 4-2   Values for use with **glClampColor()**

Specifying a Color in Color-Index Mode

In color-index mode, use the **glIndex*()** command to select a single-valued color index as the current color index.

---

void **glIndex**{sifd ub}(TYPE *c*);
void **glIndex**{sifd ub}**v**(const TYPE **c*);

Compatibility Extension

glIndex

Sets the current color index to *c*. The first suffix for this command indicates the data type for parameters: short, integer, float, double, or unsigned byte. The second, optional suffix is **v**, which indicates that the argument is an array of values of the given data type (the array contains only one value).

In "Clearing the Window" in Chapter 2, you saw the specification of **glClearColor()**. For color-index mode, there is a corresponding **glClearIndex()**.

---

void **glClearIndex**(GLfloat *cindex*);

Compatibility Extension

glClearIndex

Sets the current clearing color in color-index mode. In a color-index mode window, a call to **glClear**(GL_COLOR_BUFFER_BIT) will use *cindex* to clear the buffer. The default clearing index is 0.0.

Note: OpenGL does not have any routines to load values into the color-lookup table. Window systems typically already have such operations. GLUT has the routine **glutSetColor()** to call the window-system-specific commands.

Advanced

The current index is stored as a floating-point value. Integer values are converted directly to floating-point values, with no special mapping. Index values outside the representable range of the color-index buffer aren't clamped. However, before an index is dithered (if enabled) and written to the framebuffer, it's converted to fixed-point format. Any bits in the integer portion of the resulting fixed-point value that don't correspond to bits in the framebuffer are masked out.

Specifying a Shading Model

A line or a filled polygon primitive can be drawn with a single color (flat shading) or with many different colors (smooth shading, also called *Gouraud shading*). You specify the desired shading technique with **glShadeModel**().

Compatibility Extension

glShadeModel

---

void **glShadeModel**(GLenum *mode*);

Sets the shading model. The mode parameter can be either GL_SMOOTH (the default) or GL_FLAT.

With flat shading, the color of one particular vertex of an independent primitive is duplicated across all the primitive's vertices to render that primitive. With smooth shading, the color at each vertex is treated individually. For a line primitive, the colors along the line segment are interpolated between the vertex colors. For a polygon primitive, the colors for the interior of the polygon are interpolated between the vertex colors. Example 4-1 draws a smooth-shaded triangle, as shown in Plate 11.

Example 4-1   Drawing a Smooth-Shaded Triangle: smooth.c

```
void init(void)
{
   glClearColor(0.0, 0.0, 0.0, 0.0);
   glShadeModel(GL_SMOOTH);
}

void triangle(void)
{
   glBegin(GL_TRIANGLES);
   glColor3f(1.0, 0.0, 0.0);
   glVertex2f(5.0, 5.0);
   glColor3f(0.0, 1.0, 0.0);
```

```
   glVertex2f(25.0, 5.0);
   glColor3f(0.0, 0.0, 1.0);
   glVertex2f(5.0, 25.0);
   glEnd();
}

void display(void)
{
   glClear(GL_COLOR_BUFFER_BIT);
   triangle();
   glFlush();
}

void reshape(int w, int h)
{
   glViewport(0, 0, (GLsizei) w, (GLsizei) h);
   glMatrixMode(GL_PROJECTION);
   glLoadIdentity();
   if (w <= h)
      gluOrtho2D(0.0, 30.0, 0.0, 30.0*(GLfloat) h/(GLfloat) w);
   else
      gluOrtho2D(0.0, 30.0*(GLfloat) w/(GLfloat) h, 0.0, 30.0);
   glMatrixMode(GL_MODELVIEW);
}

int main(int argc, char** argv)
{
   glutInit(&argc, argv);
   glutInitDisplayMode(GLUT_SINGLE | GLUT_RGB);
   glutInitWindowSize(500, 500);
   glutInitWindowPosition(100, 100);
   glutCreateWindow(argv[0]);
   init();
   glutDisplayFunc(display);
   glutReshapeFunc(reshape);
   glutMainLoop();
   return 0;
}
```

With smooth shading, neighboring pixels have slightly different color values. In RGBA mode, adjacent pixels with slightly different values look similar, so the color changes across a polygon appear gradual. In color-index mode, adjacent pixels may reference different locations in the color-index table, which may not have similar colors at all. Adjacent color-index entries may contain wildly different colors, so a smooth-shaded polygon in color-index mode can look psychedelic.

To avoid this problem, you have to create a color ramp of smoothly changing colors among a contiguous set of indices in the color map. Remember that loading colors into a color map is performed through your window system, rather than through OpenGL. If you use GLUT, you can use **glutSetColor()** to load a single index in the color map with specified red, green, and blue values. The first argument for **glutSetColor()** is the index, and the others are the red, green, and blue values. To load 32 contiguous color indices (color indices 16 to 47) with slightly differing shades of yellow, you might call

```
for (i = 0; i < 32; i++) {
    glutSetColor(16+i, 1.0*(i/32.0), 1.0*(i/32.0), 0.0);
}
```

Now, if you render smooth-shaded polygons that use only the colors from indices 16 to 47, those polygons will have gradually differing shades of yellow.

With flat shading, the color of a single vertex defines the color of an entire primitive. For a line segment, the color of the line is the current color when the second (ending) vertex is specified. For a polygon, the color used is the one that's in effect when a particular vertex is specified, as shown in Table 4-3. The table counts vertices and polygons starting from 1. OpenGL follows these rules consistently, but the best way to avoid uncertainty about how a flat-shaded primitive will be drawn is to specify only one color for the primitive.

Type of Polygon	Vertex Used to Select the Color for the ith Polygon
single polygon	1
triangle strip	$i + 2$
triangle fan	$i + 2$
independent triangle	$3i$
quad strip	$2i + 2$
independent quad	$4i$

Table 4-3   How OpenGL Selects a Color for the ith Flat-Shaded Polygon

Chapter 5

Lighting

Chapter Objectives

After reading this chapter, you'll be able to do the following:

- Understand how real-world lighting conditions are approximated by OpenGL

- Render illuminated objects by defining light source, material, and lighting model properties

- Define the material properties of the objects being illuminated

- Manipulate the matrix stack to control the positions of light sources

Note: In OpenGL Version 3.1, many of the techniques and functions described in this chapter were removed through deprecation. The concepts are still relevant, but computing colors through lighting must be done in either a vertex or fragment shader. These topics are briefly described in Chapter 15, and fully explained in the companion text, *The OpenGL Shading Language Guide*.

As you saw in Chapter 4, OpenGL computes the color of each pixel in a final, displayed scene that's held in the framebuffer. Part of this computation depends on what lighting is used in the scene and on how objects in the scene reflect or absorb that light. As an example of this, recall that the ocean has a different color on a bright, sunny day than it does on a gray, cloudy day. The presence of sunlight or clouds determines whether you see the ocean as bright turquoise or murky gray-green. In fact, most objects don't even look three-dimensional until they're lit. Figure 5-1 shows two versions of the exact same scene (a single sphere), one with lighting and one without.

Figure 5-1   A Lit and an Unlit Sphere

As you can see, an unlit sphere looks no different from a two-dimensional disk. This demonstrates how critical the interaction between objects and light is in creating a three-dimensional scene.

With OpenGL, you can manipulate the lighting and objects in a scene to create many different kinds of effects. This chapter begins with a primer on hidden-surface removal. Then it explains how to control the lighting in a scene, discusses the OpenGL conceptual model of lighting, and describes in detail how to set the numerous illumination parameters to achieve certain effects. Toward the end of the chapter, the mathematical computations that determine how lighting affects color are presented.

This chapter contains the following major sections:

- "A Hidden-Surface Removal Survival Kit" describes the basics of removing hidden surfaces from view.

- "Real-World and OpenGL Lighting" explains in general terms how light behaves in the world and how OpenGL models this behavior.

- "A Simple Example: Rendering a Lit Sphere" introduces the OpenGL lighting facility by presenting a short program that renders a lit sphere.

- "Creating Light Sources" explains how to define and position light sources.

- "Selecting a Lighting Model" discusses the elements of a lighting model and how to specify them.

- "Defining Material Properties" explains how to describe the properties of objects so that they interact with light in a desired way.

- "The Mathematics of Lighting" presents the mathematical calculations used by OpenGL to determine the effect of lights in a scene.

- "Lighting in Color-Index Mode" discusses the differences between using RGBA mode and color-index mode for lighting.

Lighting calculations typically take place prior to texturing. Version 1.2 introduced a lighting mode (GL_SEPARATE_SPECULAR_COLOR) whereby the calculation of the specular color is done separately from the emissive, ambient, and diffuse components, and then the application of the specular color takes place after texturing. Using a separate specular color often enhances a highlight, making it less influenced by the color of the texture image.

A Hidden-Surface Removal Survival Kit

With this section, you begin to draw shaded, three-dimensional objects in earnest. With shaded polygons, it becomes very important to draw the objects that are closer to the viewing position and to eliminate objects obscured by others nearer to the eye.

When you draw a scene composed of three-dimensional objects, some of them might obscure all or parts of others. Changing your viewpoint can change the obscuring relationship. For example, if you view the scene from the opposite direction, any object that was previously in front of another is now behind it. To draw a realistic scene, these obscuring relationships must be maintained. Suppose your code works like this:

```
while (1) {
    get_viewing_point_from_mouse_position();
    glClear(GL_COLOR_BUFFER_BIT);
    draw_3d_object_A();
    draw_3d_object_B();
}
```

For some mouse positions, object A might obscure object B. For others, the reverse may hold. If nothing special is done, the preceding code always draws object B second (and thus on top of object A) no matter what viewing position is selected. In a worst-case scenario, if objects A and B intersect one another so that part of object A obscures object B, and part of B obscures A, changing the drawing order does not provide a solution.

The elimination of parts of solid objects that are obscured by others is called *hidden-surface removal*. (Hidden-line removal, which does the same job for objects represented as wireframe skeletons, is a bit trickier and isn't discussed here. See "Hidden-Line Removal" in Chapter 14 for details.) The easiest way to achieve hidden-surface removal is to use the depth buffer (sometimes called a z-buffer). (Also see Chapter 10.)

A depth buffer works by associating a depth, or a distance, from the view plane (usually the near clipping plane), with each pixel on the window. Initially, the depth values for all pixels are set to the largest possible distance (usually the far clipping plane) using the **glClear()** command with GL_DEPTH_BUFFER_BIT. Then the objects in the scene are drawn in any order.

Graphical calculations in hardware or software convert each surface that's drawn to a set of pixels on the window where the surface will appear if it isn't obscured by something else. In addition, the distance from the view plane is computed. With depth-buffering enabled, before each pixel is drawn a comparison is done with the depth value already stored at the pixel. If the new pixel is closer than (in front of) what's there, the new pixel's color and depth values replace those that are currently written into the pixel. If the new pixel's depth is greater than what's currently there, the new pixel is obscured, and the color and depth information for the incoming pixel is discarded.

To use depth-buffering, you need to enable it. This has to be done only once. Before drawing, each time you draw the scene, you need to clear the depth buffer and then draw the objects in the scene in any order.

To convert the preceding code example so that it performs hidden-surface removal, modify it to the following:

```
glutInitDisplayMode(GLUT_DEPTH | .... );
glEnable(GL_DEPTH_TEST);
...
while (1) {
    glClear(GL_COLOR_BUFFER_BIT | GL_DEPTH_BUFFER_BIT);
    get_viewing_point_from_mouse_position();
    draw_3d_object_A();
    draw_3d_object_B();
}
```

The argument for **glClear()** clears both the depth and color buffers.

Depth-buffer testing can affect the performance of your application. Since information is discarded, rather than used for drawing, hidden-surface removal can increase your performance slightly. However, the implementation of your depth buffer probably has the greatest effect on performance. A "software" depth buffer (implemented with processor memory) may be much slower than one implemented with a specialized hardware depth buffer.

Real-World and OpenGL Lighting

When you look at a physical surface, your eye's perception of the color depends on the distribution of photon energies that arrive and trigger your cone cells. (See "Color Perception" in Chapter 4.) Those photons come from a light source or combination of sources, some of which are absorbed and some of which are reflected by the surface. In addition, different surfaces may have very different properties—some are shiny and preferentially reflect light in certain directions, while others scatter incoming light equally in all directions. Most surfaces are somewhere in between.

OpenGL approximates light and lighting as if light can be broken into red, green, and blue components. Thus, the color of a light source is characterized by the amounts of red, green, and blue light it emits, and the material of a surface is characterized by the percentages of the incoming red, green, and blue components that are reflected in various directions. The OpenGL lighting equations are just approximations, but ones that work fairly well and can be computed relatively quickly. If you want a more accurate (or just different) lighting model, you have to do your own calculations in software. Such software can be enormously complex, as a few hours of reading any optics textbook should convince you.

In the OpenGL lighting model, the light in a scene comes from several light sources that can be individually turned on and off. Some light comes from a particular direction or position, and some light is generally scattered about the scene. For example, when you turn on a lightbulb in a room, most of the light comes from the bulb, but some light results from bouncing off one, two, three, or more walls. This bounced light (called *ambient* light) is assumed to be so scattered that there is no way to tell its original direction, but it disappears if a particular light source is turned off.

Finally, there might be a general ambient light in the scene that comes from no particular source, as if it had been scattered so many times that its original source is impossible to determine.

In the OpenGL model, the light sources have effects only when there are surfaces that absorb and reflect light. Each surface is assumed to be composed of a material with various properties. A material might emit its own light (such as headlights on an automobile), it might scatter some incoming light in all directions, and it might reflect some portion of the incoming light in a preferential direction (such as a mirror or other shiny surface).

The OpenGL lighting model considers the lighting to be divided into four independent components: ambient, diffuse, specular, and emissive. All four components are computed independently and then added together.

Ambient, Diffuse, Specular, and Emissive Light

Ambient illumination is light that's been scattered so much by the environment that its direction is impossible to determine—it seems to come from all directions. Backlighting in a room has a large ambient component, since most of the light that reaches your eye has first bounced off many surfaces. A spotlight outdoors has a tiny ambient component; most of the light travels in the same direction, and since you're outdoors, very little of the light reaches your eye after bouncing off other objects. When ambient light strikes a surface, it's scattered equally in all directions.

The *diffuse* component is the light that comes from one direction, so it's brighter if it comes squarely down on a surface than if it barely glances off the surface. Once it hits a surface, however, it's scattered equally in all directions, so it appears equally bright, no matter where the eye is located. Any light coming from a particular position or direction probably has a diffuse component.

Specular light comes from a particular direction, and it tends to bounce off the surface in a preferred direction. A well-collimated laser beam bouncing off a high-quality mirror produces almost 100 percent specular reflection. Shiny metal or plastic has a high specular component, and chalk or carpet has almost none. You can think of specularity as shininess.

In addition to ambient, diffuse, and specular colors, materials may have an *emissive* color, which simulates light originating from an object. In the OpenGL lighting model, the emissive color of a surface adds intensity to the object, but is unaffected by any light sources. Also, the emissive color does not introduce any additional light into the overall scene.

Although a light source delivers a single distribution of frequencies, the ambient, diffuse, and specular components might be different. For example, if you have a white light in a room with red walls, the scattered light tends to be red, although the light directly striking objects is white. OpenGL allows you to set the red, green, and blue values for each component of light independently.

Material Colors

The OpenGL lighting model approximates a material's color from the percentages of the incoming red, green, and blue light it reflects. For example, a perfectly red ball reflects all the incoming red light and absorbs all the green and blue light that strikes it. If you view such a ball in white light (composed of equal amounts of red, green, and blue light), all the red is reflected, and you see a red ball. If the ball is viewed in pure red light, it also appears to be red. If, however, the red ball is viewed in pure green light, it appears black (all the green is absorbed and there's no incoming red, so no light is reflected).

Like lights, materials have different ambient, diffuse, and specular colors, which determine the ambient, diffuse, and specular reflectances of the material. A material's ambient reflectance is combined with the ambient component of each incoming light source, the diffuse reflectance with the light's diffuse component, and similarly for the specular reflectance and specular component. Ambient and diffuse reflectances define the color of the material and are typically similar if not identical. Specular reflectance is usually white or gray, so that specular highlights end up being the color of the light source's specular intensity. If you think of a white light shining on a shiny red plastic sphere, most of the sphere appears red, but the shiny highlight is white.

RGB Values for Lights and Materials

The color components specified for lights mean something different than for materials. For a light, the numbers correspond to a percentage of full intensity for each color. If the R, G, and B values for a light's color are all 1.0, the light is the brightest possible white. If the values are 0.5, the color is still white, but only at half intensity, so it appears gray. If R = G = 1 and B = 0 (full red and green with no blue), the light appears yellow.

For materials, the numbers correspond to the reflected proportions of those colors. So if R = 1, G = 0.5, and B = 0 for a material, that material reflects all the incoming red light, half the incoming green light, and none of the incoming blue light. In other words, if an OpenGL light has components (LR, LG, LB), and a material has corresponding components (MR, MG, MB), then, ignoring all other reflectivity effects, the light that arrives at the eye is given by (LR·MR, LG·MG, LB·MB).

Similarly, if you have two lights that send (R1, G1, B1) and (R2, G2, B2) to the eye, OpenGL adds the components, giving (R1 + R2, G1 + G2, B1 + B2). If any of the sums is greater than 1 (corresponding to a color brighter than the equipment can display), the component is clamped to 1.

A Simple Example: Rendering a Lit Sphere

These are the steps required to add lighting to your scene:

1. Define normal vectors for each vertex of every object. These normals determine the orientation of the object relative to the light sources.

2. Create, select, and position one or more light sources.

3. Create and select a *lighting model*, which defines the level of global ambient light and the effective location of the viewpoint (for the purposes of lighting calculations).

4. Define material properties for the objects in the scene.

Example 5-1 accomplishes these tasks. It displays a sphere illuminated by a single light source, as shown earlier in Figure 5-1.

Example 5-1   Drawing a Lit Sphere: light.c

```
void init(void)
{
   GLfloat mat_specular[] = { 1.0, 1.0, 1.0, 1.0 };
   GLfloat mat_shininess[] = { 50.0 };
   GLfloat light_position[] = { 1.0, 1.0, 1.0, 0.0 };
   GLfloat white_light[] = { 1.0, 1.0, 1.0, 1.0 };
   GLfloat lmodel_ambient[] = { 0.1, 0.1, 0.1, 1.0 };
   glClearColor(0.0, 0.0, 0.0, 0.0);
   glShadeModel(GL_SMOOTH);
   glMaterialfv(GL_FRONT, GL_SPECULAR, mat_specular);
   glMaterialfv(GL_FRONT, GL_SHININESS, mat_shininess);
```

```
   glLightfv(GL_LIGHT0, GL_POSITION, light_position);
   glLightfv(GL_LIGHT0, GL_DIFFUSE, white_light);
   glLightfv(GL_LIGHT0, GL_SPECULAR, white_light);
   glLightModelfv(GL_LIGHT_MODEL_AMBIENT, lmodel_ambient);

   glEnable(GL_LIGHTING);
   glEnable(GL_LIGHT0);
   glEnable(GL_DEPTH_TEST);
}

void display(void)
{
   glClear(GL_COLOR_BUFFER_BIT | GL_DEPTH_BUFFER_BIT);
   glutSolidSphere(1.0, 20, 16);
   glFlush();
}

void reshape(int w, int h)
{
   glViewport(0, 0, (GLsizei) w, (GLsizei) h);
   glMatrixMode(GL_PROJECTION);
   glLoadIdentity();
   if (w <= h)
      glOrtho(-1.5, 1.5, -1.5*(GLfloat)h/(GLfloat)w,
         1.5*(GLfloat)h/(GLfloat)w, -10.0, 10.0);
   else
      glOrtho(-1.5*(GLfloat)w/(GLfloat)h,
         1.5*(GLfloat)w/(GLfloat)h, -1.5, 1.5, -10.0, 10.0);
   glMatrixMode(GL_MODELVIEW);
   glLoadIdentity();
}

int main(int argc, char** argv)
{
   glutInit(&argc, argv);
   glutInitDisplayMode(GLUT_SINGLE | GLUT_RGB | GLUT_DEPTH);
   glutInitWindowSize(500, 500);
   glutInitWindowPosition(100, 100);
   glutCreateWindow(argv[0]);
   init();
   glutDisplayFunc(display);
   glutReshapeFunc(reshape);
   glutMainLoop();
   return 0;
}
```

The lighting-related calls are in the **init()** command; they're discussed briefly in the following paragraphs and in more detail later in this chapter. One thing to note about Example 5-1 is that it uses RGBA color mode, not color-index mode. The OpenGL lighting calculation is different for the two modes, and in fact the lighting capabilities are more limited in color-index mode. Thus, RGBA is the preferred mode when doing lighting, and all the examples in this chapter use it. (See "Lighting in Color-Index Mode" on page 246 for more information.)

Define Normal Vectors for Each Vertex of Every Object

An object's normals determine its orientation relative to the light sources. For each vertex, OpenGL uses the assigned normal to determine how much light that particular vertex receives from each light source. In this example, the normals for the sphere are defined as part of the **glutSolidSphere()** routine.

For proper lighting, surface normals must be of unit length. You must also be careful that the modelview transformation matrix does not scale the surface normal, so that the resulting normal is no longer of unit length. To ensure that normals are of unit length, you may need to call **glEnable()** with GL_NORMALIZE or GL_RESCALE_NORMAL as a parameter.

GL_RESCALE_NORMAL causes each component in a surface normal to be multiplied by the same value, which is determined from the modelview transformation matrix. Therefore, it works correctly only if the normal was scaled uniformly and was a unit-length vector to begin with. GL_NORMALIZE is a more thorough operation than GL_RESCALE_NORMAL. When GL_NORMALIZE is enabled, the length of the normal vector is calculated, and then each component of the normal is divided by the calculated length. This operation guarantees that the resulting normal is of unit length, but may be more expensive than simply rescaling normals. (See "Normal Vectors" in Chapter 2 and Appendix I, "Built-In OpenGL Shading Language Variables and Functions,"[1] for more details on how to define normals.)

Note: Some OpenGL implementations may implement GL_RESCALE_NORMAL by actually normalizing the normal vectors, not just scaling them. However, you cannot determine whether your implementation does this, nor should you usually rely on this.

---

[1] This appendix is available online at http://www.opengl-redbook.com/appendices/.

Create, Position, and Enable One or More Light Sources

Example 5-1 uses only one, white light source; its location is specified by the **glLightfv()** call. This example specifies white as the color for light zero (GL_LIGHT0) for calculations of diffuse and specular reflection. If you want a differently colored light, modify **glLight*()**.

You can also include at least eight different light sources of various colors in your scene. (The particular implementation of OpenGL you're using might allow more than eight.) The default color of lights other than GL_LIGHT0 is black. You can also locate the lights wherever you desire: You can position them near the scene, as a desk lamp would be, or infinitely far away to simulate sunlight, for example. In addition, you can control whether a light produces a narrow, focused beam or a wider beam. Remember that each light source adds significantly to the calculations needed to render the scene, so performance is affected by the number of lights in the scene. (See "Creating Light Sources" on page 214 for more information about how to create lights with the desired characteristics.)

After you've defined the characteristics of the lights you want, you have to turn them on with the **glEnable()** command. You also need to call **glEnable()** with GL_LIGHTING as a parameter to prepare OpenGL to perform lighting calculations. (See "Enabling Lighting" on page 231 for more information.)

Select a Lighting Model

As you might expect, the **glLightModel*()** command describes the parameters of a lighting model. In Example 5-1, the only element of the lighting model that's defined explicitly is the global ambient light. The lighting model also defines whether the viewer of the scene should be considered to be infinitely far away or local to the scene, and whether lighting calculations should be performed differently for the front and back surfaces of objects in the scene. Example 5-1 uses the default settings for these two aspects of the model—a viewer infinitely far away ("infinite viewer" mode) and one-sided lighting. Using a local viewer adds significantly to the complexity of the calculations that must be performed, because OpenGL must calculate the angle between the viewpoint and each object. With an infinite viewer, however, the angle is ignored, and the results are slightly less realistic. Further, since in this example the back surface of the sphere is never seen (it's the inside of the sphere), one-sided lighting is sufficient. (See "Selecting a Lighting Model" on page 227 for a more detailed description of the elements of an OpenGL lighting model.)

Define Material Properties for the Objects in the Scene

An object's material properties determine how it reflects light and therefore of what material it seems to be made. Because the interaction between an object's material surface and incident light is complex, specifying material properties so that an object has a certain desired appearance is an art. You can specify a material's ambient, diffuse, and specular colors and how shiny it is. In this example, only the last two material properties—the specular material color and shininess—are explicitly specified (with the **glMaterialfv**() calls). (See "Defining Material Properties" on page 231 for descriptions and examples of all material-property parameters.)

Some Important Notes

As you write your own lighting program, remember that you can use the default values for some lighting parameters, whereas others need to be changed. Also, don't forget to enable whatever lights you define and to enable lighting calculations. Finally, remember that you might be able to use display lists to maximize efficiency as you change lighting conditions. (See "Display List Design Philosophy" in Chapter 7.)

Creating Light Sources

Compatibility
Extension

glLight
GL_LIGHT*i*
GL_AMBIENT
GL_DIFFUSE
GL_SPECULAR
GL_POSITION
GL_SPOT_
DIRECTION
GL_SPOT_
EXPONENT
GL_SPOT_
CUTOFF
GL_CONSTANT_
ATTENUATION
GL_LINEAR_
ATTENUATION
GL_QUADRATIC_
ATTENUATION

Light sources have several properties, such as color, position, and direction. The following sections explain how to control these properties and what the resulting light looks like. The command used to specify all properties of lights is **glLight*()**. Its three arguments identify the light whose property is being specified, the property, and the desired value for that property.

void **glLight**{if}(GLenum *light*, GLenum *pname*, TYPE *param*);
void **glLight**{if}**v**(GLenum *light*, GLenum *pname*, const TYPE **param*);

Creates the light specified by *light*, which can be GL_LIGHT0, GL_LIGHT1, ... , or GL_LIGHT7. The characteristic of the light being set is defined by *pname*, which specifies a named parameter (see Table 5-1). *param* indicates the values to which the *pname* characteristic is set; it's a pointer to a group of values if the vector version is used or the value itself if the nonvector version is used. The nonvector version can be used to set only single-valued light characteristics.

Parameter Name	Default Values	Meaning
GL_AMBIENT	(0.0, 0.0, 0.0, 1.0)	ambient intensity of light
GL_DIFFUSE	(1.0, 1.0, 1.0, 1.0) or (0.0, 0.0, 0.0, 1.0)	diffuse intensity of light (default for light 0 is white; for other lights, black)
GL_SPECULAR	(1.0, 1.0, 1.0, 1.0) or (0.0, 0.0, 0.0, 1.0)	specular intensity of light (default for light 0 is white; for other lights, black)
GL_POSITION	(0.0, 0.0, 1.0, 0.0)	(x, y, z, w) position of light
GL_SPOT_DIRECTION	(0.0, 0.0, −1.0)	(x, y, z) direction of spotlight
GL_SPOT_EXPONENT	0.0	spotlight exponent
GL_SPOT_CUTOFF	180.0	spotlight cutoff angle
GL_CONSTANT_ATTENUATION	1.0	constant attenuation factor
GL_LINEAR_ATTENUATION	0.0	linear attenuation factor
GL_QUADRATIC_ATTENUATION	0.0	quadratic attenuation factor

Table 5-1   Default Values for *pname* Parameter of glLight*()

Note: The default values listed for GL_DIFFUSE and GL_SPECULAR in Table 5-1 differ from GL_LIGHT0 to other lights (GL_LIGHT1, GL_LIGHT2, etc.). For GL_LIGHT0, the default value is (1.0, 1.0, 1.0, 1.0) for both GL_DIFFUSE and GL_SPECULAR. For other lights, the default value is (0.0, 0.0, 0.0, 1.0) for the same light source properties.

Example 5-2 shows how to use **glLight*()**:

Example 5-2   Defining Colors and Position for a Light Source

```
GLfloat light_ambient[] = { 0.0, 0.0, 0.0, 1.0 };
GLfloat light_diffuse[] = { 1.0, 1.0, 1.0, 1.0 };
GLfloat light_specular[] = { 1.0, 1.0, 1.0, 1.0 };
GLfloat light_position[] = { 1.0, 1.0, 1.0, 0.0 };

glLightfv(GL_LIGHT0, GL_AMBIENT, light_ambient);
glLightfv(GL_LIGHT0, GL_DIFFUSE, light_diffuse);
glLightfv(GL_LIGHT0, GL_SPECULAR, light_specular);
glLightfv(GL_LIGHT0, GL_POSITION, light_position);
```

As you can see, arrays are defined for the parameter values, and **glLightfv()** is called repeatedly to set the various parameters. In this example, the first three calls to **glLightfv()** are superfluous, since they're being used to specify the default values for the GL_AMBIENT, GL_DIFFUSE, and GL_SPECULAR parameters.

Note: Remember to turn on each light with **glEnable()**. (See "Enabling Lighting" for more information about how to do this.)

All the parameters for **glLight*()** and their possible values are explained in the following sections. These parameters interact with those that define the overall lighting model for a particular scene and an object's material properties. (See "Selecting a Lighting Model" and "Defining Material Properties" for more information about these two topics. "The Mathematics of Lighting" explains how all these parameters interact mathematically.)

Color

OpenGL allows you to associate three different color-related parameters—GL_AMBIENT, GL_DIFFUSE, and GL_SPECULAR—with any particular light. The GL_AMBIENT parameter refers to the RGBA intensity of the ambient light that a particular light source adds to the scene. As you can see in Table 5-1, by default there is no ambient light since GL_AMBIENT is (0.0, 0.0, 0.0, 1.0). This value was used in Example 5-1. If this program had specified blue ambient light as

```
GLfloat light_ambient[] = { 0.0, 0.0, 1.0, 1.0};
glLightfv(GL_LIGHT0, GL_AMBIENT, light_ambient);
```

the result would have been as shown on the left side of Plate 13.

The GL_DIFFUSE parameter probably most closely correlates with what you naturally think of as "the color of a light." It defines the RGBA color of the diffuse light that a particular light source adds to a scene. By default, GL_DIFFUSE is (1.0, 1.0, 1.0, 1.0) for GL_LIGHT0, which produces a bright, white light, as shown on the left side of Plate 13. The default value for any other light (GL_LIGHT1, ... , GL_LIGHT7) is (0.0, 0.0, 0.0, 0.0).

The GL_SPECULAR parameter affects the color of the specular highlight on an object. Typically, a real-world object such as a glass bottle has a specular highlight that's the color of the light shining on it (which is often white). Therefore, if you want to create a realistic effect, set the GL_SPECULAR parameter to the same value as the GL_DIFFUSE parameter. By default,

GL_SPECULAR is (1.0, 1.0, 1.0, 1.0) for GL_LIGHT0, and (0.0, 0.0, 0.0, 0.0) for any other light.

Note: The alpha component of these colors is not used until blending is enabled (see Chapter 6). Until then, the alpha value can be safely ignored.

Position and Attenuation

As previously mentioned, you can choose between a light source that's treated as though it's located infinitely far away from the scene and one that's nearer to the scene. The first type is referred to as a *directional* light source; the effect of an infinite location is that the rays of light can be considered parallel by the time they reach an object. An example of a real-world directional light source is the sun. The second type is called a *positional* light source, since its exact position within the scene determines the effect it has on a scene and, specifically, the direction from which the light rays come. A desk lamp is an example of a positional light source. You can see the difference between directional and positional lights in Plate 13. The light used in Example 5-1 is a directional one:

```
GLfloat light_position[] = { 1.0, 1.0, 1.0, 0.0 };
glLightfv(GL_LIGHT0, GL_POSITION, light_position);
```

As shown, you supply a vector of four values (x, y, z, w) for the GL_POSITION parameter. If the last value, w, is zero, the corresponding light source is a directional one, and the (x, y, z) values describe its direction. This direction is transformed by the modelview matrix. By default, GL_POSITION is (0, 0, 1, 0), which defines a directional light that points along the negative z-axis. (Note that nothing prevents you from creating a directional light with the direction of (0, 0, 0), but such a light won't help you much.)

If the w-value is nonzero, the light is positional, and the (x, y, z) values specify the location of the light in homogeneous object coordinates (see Appendix C). This location is transformed by the modelview matrix and stored in eye coordinates. (See "Controlling a Light's Position and Direction" on page 221 for more information about how to control the transformation of the light's location.) Also, by default, a positional light radiates in all directions, but you can restrict it to producing a cone of illumination by defining the light as a spotlight. (See "Spotlights" on page 219 for an explanation of how to define a light as a spotlight.)

Note: Remember that the colors across the face of a smooth-shaded polygon are determined by the colors calculated for the vertices. Because of this, you probably want to avoid using large polygons with local lights. If you locate the light near the middle of the polygon, the vertices might be too far away to receive much light, and the whole polygon will look darker than you intended. To avoid this problem, break up the large polygon into smaller ones.

For real-world lights, the intensity of light decreases as distance from the light increases. Since a directional light is infinitely far away, it doesn't make sense to attenuate its intensity over distance, so attenuation is disabled for a directional light. However, you might want to attenuate the light from a positional light. OpenGL attenuates a light source by multiplying the contribution of that source by an attenuation factor:

$$\text{attenuation factor} = \frac{1}{k_c + k_l d + k_q d^2}$$

where

d = distance between the light's position and the vertex

k_c = GL_CONSTANT_ATTENUATION

k_l = GL_LINEAR_ATTENUATION

k_q = GL_QUADRATIC_ATTENUATION

By default, k_c is 1.0 and both k_l and k_q are zero, but you can give these parameters different values:

```
glLightf(GL_LIGHT0, GL_CONSTANT_ATTENUATION, 2.0);
glLightf(GL_LIGHT0, GL_LINEAR_ATTENUATION, 1.0);
glLightf(GL_LIGHT0, GL_QUADRATIC_ATTENUATION, 0.5);
```

Note that the ambient, diffuse, and specular contributions are all attenuated. Only the emission and global ambient values aren't attenuated. Also note that since attenuation requires an additional division (and possibly more math) for each calculated color, using attenuated lights may slow down application performance.

Spotlights

As previously mentioned, you can have a positional light source act as a spotlight by restricting the shape of the light it emits to a cone. To create a spotlight, you need to determine the spread of the cone of light you desire. (Remember that since spotlights are positional lights, you also have to locate them where you want them. Again, note that nothing prevents you from creating a directional spotlight, but it won't give you the result you want.) To specify the angle between the axis of the cone and a ray along the edge of the cone, use the GL_SPOT_CUTOFF parameter. The angle of the cone at the apex is then twice this value, as shown in Figure 5-2.

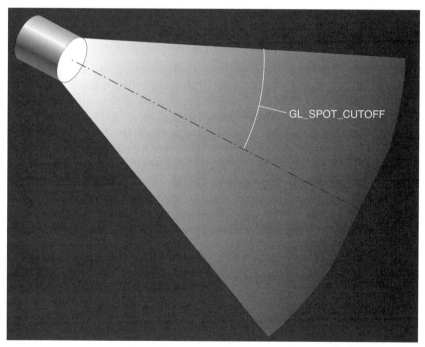

Figure 5-2   GL_SPOT_CUTOFF Parameter

Note that no light is emitted beyond the edges of the cone. By default, the spotlight feature is disabled because the GL_SPOT_CUTOFF parameter is 180.0. This value means that light is emitted in all directions (the angle at the cone's apex is 360 degrees, so it isn't a cone at all). The value for

GL_SPOT_CUTOFF is restricted to the range [0.0, 90.0] (unless it has the special value 180.0). The following line sets the cutoff parameter to 45 degrees:

```
glLightf(GL_LIGHT0, GL_SPOT_CUTOFF, 45.0);
```

You also need to specify a spotlight's direction, which determines the axis of the cone of light:

```
GLfloat spot_direction[] = { -1.0, -1.0, 0.0 };
glLightfv(GL_LIGHT0, GL_SPOT_DIRECTION, spot_direction);
```

The direction is specified in object coordinates. By default, the direction is (0.0, 0.0, −1.0), so if you don't explicitly set the value of GL_SPOT_DIRECTION, the light points down the negative z-axis. Also, keep in mind that a spotlight's direction is transformed by the modelview matrix just as though it were a normal vector, and the result is stored in eye coordinates. (See "Controlling a Light's Position and Direction" for more information about such transformations.)

In addition to the spotlight's cutoff angle and direction, there are two ways you can control the intensity distribution of the light within the cone. First, you can set the attenuation factor described earlier, which is multiplied by the light's intensity. You can also set the GL_SPOT_EXPONENT parameter, which by default is zero, to control how concentrated the light is. The light's intensity is highest in the center of the cone. It's attenuated toward the edges of the cone by the cosine of the angle between the direction of the light and the direction from the light to the vertex being lit, raised to the power of the spot exponent. Thus, higher spot exponents result in a more focused light source. (See "The Mathematics of Lighting" for more details on the equations used to calculate light intensity.)

Multiple Lights

As mentioned, you can have at least eight lights in your scene (possibly more, depending on your OpenGL implementation). Since OpenGL needs to perform calculations to determine how much light each vertex receives from each light source, increasing the number of lights adversely affects performance. The constants used to refer to the eight lights are GL_LIGHT0, GL_LIGHT1, GL_LIGHT2, GL_LIGHT3, and so on. In the preceding discussions, parameters related to GL_LIGHT0 were set. If you want an additional light, you need to specify its parameters; also, remember that the default values are different for these other lights than they are for GL_LIGHT0, as explained in Table 5-1. Example 5-3 defines a white attenuated spotlight.

Example 5-3   Second Light Source

```
GLfloat light1_ambient[] = { 0.2, 0.2, 0.2, 1.0 };
GLfloat light1_diffuse[] = { 1.0, 1.0, 1.0, 1.0 };
GLfloat light1_specular[] = { 1.0, 1.0, 1.0, 1.0 };
GLfloat light1_position[] = { -2.0, 2.0, 1.0, 1.0 };
GLfloat spot_direction[] = { -1.0, -1.0, 0.0 };

glLightfv(GL_LIGHT1, GL_AMBIENT, light1_ambient);
glLightfv(GL_LIGHT1, GL_DIFFUSE, light1_diffuse);
glLightfv(GL_LIGHT1, GL_SPECULAR, light1_specular);
glLightfv(GL_LIGHT1, GL_POSITION, light1_position);
glLightf(GL_LIGHT1, GL_CONSTANT_ATTENUATION, 1.5);
glLightf(GL_LIGHT1, GL_LINEAR_ATTENUATION, 0.5);
glLightf(GL_LIGHT1, GL_QUADRATIC_ATTENUATION, 0.2);

glLightf(GL_LIGHT1, GL_SPOT_CUTOFF, 45.0);
glLightfv(GL_LIGHT1, GL_SPOT_DIRECTION, spot_direction);
glLightf(GL_LIGHT1, GL_SPOT_EXPONENT, 2.0);

glEnable(GL_LIGHT1);
```

If these lines were added to Example 5-1, the sphere would be lit with two lights, one directional and one spotlight.

Try This

Modify Example 5-1 in the following manner:

Try This

- Change the first light to be a positional colored light, rather than a directional white one.

- Add an additional colored spotlight. Hint: Use some of the code shown in the preceding section.

- Measure how these two changes affect performance.

Controlling a Light's Position and Direction

OpenGL treats the position and direction of a light source just as it treats the position of a geometric primitive. In other words, a light source is subject to the same matrix transformations as a primitive. More specifically, when **glLight*()** is called to specify the position or the direction of a light source, the position or direction is transformed by the current modelview matrix and stored in eye coordinates. This means you can manipulate a light source's position or direction by changing the contents of the modelview matbix. (The projection matrix has no effect on a light's position or direction.) This section explains how to achieve the following three different effects by changing the point in the program at which the light position is set, relative to modeling or viewing transformations:

- A light position that remains fixed
- A light that moves around a stationary object
- A light that moves along with the viewpoint

Keeping the Light Stationary

In the simplest example, as in Example 5-1, the light position remains fixed. To achieve this effect, you need to set the light position after whatever viewing and/or modeling transformation you use. Example 5-4 shows how the relevant code from the **init()** and **reshape()** routines might look.

Example 5-4   Stationary Light Source

```
glViewport(0, 0, (GLsizei) w, (GLsizei) h);
glMatrixMode(GL_PROJECTION);
glLoadIdentity();
if (w <= h)
    glOrtho(-1.5, 1.5, -1.5*h/w, 1.5*h/w, -10.0, 10.0);
else
    glOrtho(-1.5*w/h, 1.5*w/h, -1.5, 1.5, -10.0, 10.0);
glMatrixMode(GL_MODELVIEW);
glLoadIdentity();

/* later in init() */
GLfloat light_position[] = { 1.0, 1.0, 1.0, 1.0 };
glLightfv(GL_LIGHT0, GL_POSITION, position);
```

As you can see, the viewport and projection matrices are established first. Then, the identity matrix is loaded as the modelview matrix, after which the light position is set. Since the identity matrix is used, the originally specified light position (1.0, 1.0, 1.0) isn't changed by being multiplied by the modelview matrix. Then, since neither the light position nor the modelview matrix is modified after this point, the direction of the light remains (1.0, 1.0, 1.0).

Independently Moving the Light

Now suppose you want to rotate or translate the light position so that the light moves relative to a stationary object. One way to do this is to set the light position after the modeling transformation, which is itself changed specifically to modify the light position. You can begin with the same series of calls in **init**() early in the program. Then you need to perform the desired modeling transformation (on the modelview stack) and reset the light position, probably in **display**(). Example 5-5 shows what **display**() might be.

Example 5-5   Independently Moving Light Source

```
static GLdouble spin;

void display(void)
{
    GLfloat light_position[] = { 0.0, 0.0, 1.5, 1.0 };
    glClear(GL_COLOR_BUFFER_BIT | GL_DEPTH_BUFFER_BIT);

    glPushMatrix();
        gluLookAt(0.0, 0.0, 5.0, 0.0, 0.0, 0.0, 0.0, 1.0, 0.0);
        glPushMatrix();
            glRotated(spin, 1.0, 0.0, 0.0);
            glLightfv(GL_LIGHT0, GL_POSITION, light_position);
        glPopMatrix();
        glutSolidTorus(0.275, 0.85, 8, 15);
    glPopMatrix();
    glFlush();
}
```

spin is a global variable and is probably controlled by an input device. **display**() causes the scene to be redrawn with the light rotated *spin* degrees around a stationary torus. Note the two pairs of **glPushMatrix**() and **glPopMatrix**() calls, which are used to isolate the viewing and modeling transformations, all of which occur on the modelview stack. Since in Example 5-5 the viewpoint remains constant, the current matrix is pushed down the stack, and then the desired viewing transformation is loaded with **gluLookAt**(). The matrix stack is pushed again before the modeling transformation **glRotated**() is specified. Then the light position is set in the new, rotated coordinate system so that the light itself appears to be rotated from its previous position. (Remember that the light position is stored in eye coordinates, which are obtained after transformation by the modelview matrix.) After the rotated matrix is popped off the stack, the torus is drawn.

Example 5-6 is a program that rotates a light source around an object. When the left mouse button is pressed, the light position rotates an additional 30 degrees. A small, unlit, wireframe cube is drawn to represent the position of the light in the scene.

Example 5-6   Moving a Light with Modeling Transformations: movelight.c

```
static int spin = 0;

void init(void)
{
   glClearColor(0.0, 0.0, 0.0, 0.0);
   glShadeModel(GL_SMOOTH);
   glEnable(GL_LIGHTING);
   glEnable(GL_LIGHT0);
   glEnable(GL_DEPTH_TEST);
}

/*  Here is where the light position is reset after the modeling
 *  transformation (glRotated) is called.  This places the
 *  light at a new position in world coordinates.  The cube
 *  represents the position of the light.
 */
void display(void)
{
   GLfloat position[] = { 0.0, 0.0, 1.5, 1.0 };

   glClear(GL_COLOR_BUFFER_BIT | GL_DEPTH_BUFFER_BIT);
   glPushMatrix();
   glTranslatef(0.0, 0.0, -5.0);

   glPushMatrix();
   glRotated((GLdouble) spin, 1.0, 0.0, 0.0);
   glLightfv(GL_LIGHT0, GL_POSITION, position);

   glTranslated(0.0, 0.0, 1.5);
   glDisable(GL_LIGHTING);
   glColor3f(0.0, 1.0, 1.0);
   glutWireCube(0.1);
   glEnable(GL_LIGHTING);
   glPopMatrix();

   glutSolidTorus(0.275, 0.85, 8, 15);
   glPopMatrix();
   glFlush();
}

void reshape(int w, int h)
{
   glViewport(0, 0, (GLsizei) w, (GLsizei) h);
   glMatrixMode(GL_PROJECTION);
   glLoadIdentity();
```

```
    gluPerspective(40.0, (GLfloat) w/(GLfloat) h, 1.0, 20.0);
    glMatrixMode(GL_MODELVIEW);
    glLoadIdentity();
}

void mouse(int button, int state, int x, int y)
{
    switch (button) {
        case GLUT_LEFT_BUTTON:
            if (state == GLUT_DOWN) {
                spin = (spin + 30) % 360;
                glutPostRedisplay();
            }
            break;
        default:
            break;
    }
}
int main(int argc, char** argv)
{
    glutInit(&argc, argv);
    glutInitDisplayMode(GLUT_SINGLE | GLUT_RGB | GLUT_DEPTH);
    glutInitWindowSize(500, 500);
    glutInitWindowPosition(100, 100);
    glutCreateWindow(argv[0]);
    init();
    glutDisplayFunc(display);
    glutReshapeFunc(reshape);
    glutMouseFunc(mouse);
    glutMainLoop();
    return 0;
}
```

Moving the Light Source Together with the Viewpoint

To create a light that moves along with the viewpoint, you need to set the light position before the viewing transformation. Then the viewing transformation affects both the light and the viewpoint in the same way. Remember that the light position is stored in eye coordinates, and this is one of the few times when eye coordinates are critical. In Example 5-7, the light position is defined in **init()**, which stores the light position at (0, 0, 0) in eye coordinates. In other words, the light is shining from the lens of the camera.

Example 5-7   Light Source That Moves with the Viewpoint

```
GLfloat light_position[] = { 0.0, 0.0, 0.0, 1.0 };

glViewport(0, 0, (GLint) w, (GLint) h);
glMatrixMode(GL_PROJECTION);
glLoadIdentity();
gluPerspective(40.0, (GLfloat) w/(GLfloat) h, 1.0, 100.0);
glMatrixMode(GL_MODELVIEW);
glLoadIdentity();
glLightfv(GL_LIGHT0, GL_POSITION, light_position);
```

If the viewpoint is now moved, the light will move along with it, maintaining (0, 0, 0) distance, relative to the eye. In the continuation of Example 5-7, which follows next, the global variables (*ex, ey, ez*) control the position of the viewpoint, and (*upx, upy, upz*) control the value of the up-vector. The **display()** routine that's called from the event loop to redraw the scene might be as follows:

```
static GLdouble ex, ey, ez, upx, upy, upz;

void display(void)
{
    glClear(GL_COLOR_BUFFER_BIT | GL_DEPTH_BUFFER_BIT);
    glPushMatrix();
        gluLookAt(ex, ey, ez, 0.0, 0.0, 0.0, upx, upy, upz);
        glutSolidTorus(0.275, 0.85, 8, 15);
    glPopMatrix();
    glFlush();
}
```

When the lit torus is redrawn, both the light position and the viewpoint are moved to the same location. As the values passed to **gluLookAt()** change and the eye moves, the object will never appear dark, because it is always being illuminated from the eye position. Even though you haven't respecified the light position, the light moves because the eye coordinate system has changed.

This method of moving the light can be represented by simulating the illumination from a miner's hat. Another example would be carrying a candle or lantern. The light position specified by the call to **glLightfv(GL_LIGHTi, GL_POSITION, position)** would be the *x*-, *y*-, and *z*-distances from the eye position to the illumination source. Then, as the eye position moves, the light will remain the same relative distance away.

Try This

Modify Example 5-6 in the following manner:

- Make the light translate past the object instead of rotating around it. Hint: Use **glTranslated()** rather than the first **glRotated()** in **display()**, and choose an appropriate value to use instead of *spin*.

Try This

- Change the attenuation so that the light decreases in intensity as it is moved away from the object. Hint: Add calls to **glLight*()** to set the desired attenuation parameters.

Nate Robins' Lightposition Tutorial

If you have downloaded Nate Robins' suite of tutorial programs, now run the **lightposition** tutorial. (For information on how and where to download these programs, see "Errata" on page xlii.) With this tutorial, you can experiment with the light source position and the effect of the modelview matrix.

Selecting a Lighting Model

The OpenGL notion of a lighting model has four components:

- The global ambient light intensity
- Whether the viewpoint position is local to the scene or should be considered to be an infinite distance away
- Whether lighting calculations should be performed differently for both the front and back faces of objects
- Whether the specular color should be separated from ambient and diffuse colors and applied after the texturing operation

This section explains how to specify a lighting model. It also discusses how to enable lighting—that is, how to tell OpenGL that you want lighting calculations to be performed.

The command used to specify all properties of the lighting model is **glLightModel*()**. **glLightModel*()** has two arguments: the lighting model property and the desired value for that property.

void **glLightModel**{if}(GLenum *pname, TYPE param*);
void **glLightModel**{if}v(GLenum *pname*, const *TYPE *param*);

Sets properties of the lighting model. The characteristic of the lighting model being set is defined by *pname*, which specifies a named parameter (see Table 5-2). *param* indicates the values to which the *pname* characteristic is set; it's a pointer to a group of values if the vector version is used or the value itself if the nonvector version is used. The nonvector version can be used to set only single-valued lighting model characteristics, not for GL_LIGHT_MODEL_AMBIENT.

Parameter Name	Default Value	Meaning
GL_LIGHT_MODEL_AMBIENT	(0.2, 0.2, 0.2, 1.0)	ambient RGBA intensity of the entire scene
GL_LIGHT_MODEL_LOCAL_VIEWER	0.0 or GL_FALSE	how specular reflection angles are computed
GL_LIGHT_MODEL_TWO_SIDE	0.0 or GL_FALSE	specifies one-sided or two-sided lighting
GL_LIGHT_MODEL_COLOR_CONTROL	GL_SINGLE_COLOR	whether specular color is calculated separately from ambient and diffuse

Table 5-2   Default Values for *pname* Parameter of glLightModel*()

Global Ambient Light

As discussed earlier, each light source can contribute ambient light to a scene. In addition, there can be other ambient light that's not from any particular source. To specify the RGBA intensity of such global ambient light, use the GL_LIGHT_MODEL_AMBIENT parameter as follows:

```
GLfloat lmodel_ambient[] = { 0.2, 0.2, 0.2, 1.0 };
glLightModelfv(GL_LIGHT_MODEL_AMBIENT, lmodel_ambient);
```

In this example, the values used for *lmodel_ambient* are the default values for GL_LIGHT_MODEL_AMBIENT. Since these numbers yield a small amount of white ambient light, even if you don't add a specific light source to your scene, you can still see the objects in the scene. Plate 14 shows the effects of different amounts of global ambient light.

Local or Infinite Viewpoint

The location of the viewpoint affects the calculations for highlights produced by specular reflectance. More specifically, the intensity of the highlight at a particular vertex depends on the normal at that vertex, the direction from the vertex to the light source, and the direction from the vertex to the viewpoint. Keep in mind that the viewpoint isn't actually being moved by calls to lighting commands (you need to change the projection transformation, as described in "Projection Transformations" in Chapter 3); instead, different assumptions are made for the lighting calculations, as if the viewpoint were moved.

With an infinite viewpoint, the direction between it and any vertex in the scene remains constant. A local viewpoint tends to yield more realistic results, but since the direction has to be calculated for each vertex, overall performance is decreased with a local viewpoint. By default, an infinite viewpoint is assumed. Here's how to change to a local viewpoint:

```
glLightModeli(GL_LIGHT_MODEL_LOCAL_VIEWER, GL_TRUE);
```

This call places the viewpoint at (0, 0, 0) in eye coordinates. To switch back to an infinite viewpoint, pass in GL_FALSE as the argument.

Two-Sided Lighting

Lighting calculations are performed for all polygons, whether they're front-facing or back-facing. Since you usually set up lighting conditions with the front-facing polygons in mind, however, the back-facing ones typically aren't correctly illuminated. In Example 5-1, where the object is a sphere, only the front faces are ever seen, since they're the ones on the outside of the sphere. Therefore, in this case, it doesn't matter what the back-facing polygons look like. If the sphere is going to be cut away so that its inside surface will be visible, however, you might want to have the inside surface fully lit according to the lighting conditions you've defined; you might also want to supply a different material description for the back faces. When you turn on two-sided lighting with

```
glLightModeli(GL_LIGHT_MODEL_TWO_SIDE, GL_TRUE);
```

OpenGL reverses the surface normals for back-facing polygons; typically, this means that the surface normals of visible back- and front-facing polygons face, rather than point away from, the viewer. As a result, all polygons are illuminated correctly. However, these additional operations usually make two-sided lighting perform more slowly than the default one-sided lighting.

To turn two-sided lighting off, pass in GL_FALSE as the argument in the preceding call. (See "Defining Material Properties" on page 231 for information about how to supply material properties for both faces.) You can also control which faces OpenGL considers to be front-facing with the command **glFrontFace()**. (See "Reversing and Culling Polygon Faces" on page 61 for more information.)

Secondary Specular Color

For typical lighting calculations, the ambient, diffuse, specular, and emissive contributions are calculated and simply added together. By default, texture mapping is applied after lighting, so specular highlights may appear muted, or texturing may look undesirable in other ways. To delay application of the specular color until after texturing, call

```
glLightModeli(GL_LIGHT_MODEL_COLOR_CONTROL,
              GL_SEPARATE_SPECULAR_COLOR);
```

In this mode, lighting produces two colors per vertex: a primary color, which consists of all nonspecular lighting contributions, and a secondary color, which is a sum of all specular lighting contributions. During texture mapping, only the primary color is combined with the texture colors. After texturing, the secondary color is added to the resulting combination of primary and texture colors (see "Applying Secondary Color after Texturing" on page 478). Objects that are lit and textured using a separate specular color usually have more visible and prominent specular highlights.

To restore the default, call

```
glLightModeli(GL_LIGHT_MODEL_COLOR_CONTROL, GL_SINGLE_COLOR);
```

Once again, the primary color includes all contributing colors: ambient, diffuse, specular, and emissive. Lighting contributions are not added after texturing. (If you are not performing texture mapping, there isn't any reason to separate the specular color from the other lighting components.)

Enabling Lighting

With OpenGL, you need to enable (or disable) lighting explicitly. If lighting isn't enabled, the current color is simply mapped onto the current vertex, and no calculations concerning normals, light sources, the lighting model, or material properties are performed. Here's how to enable lighting:

```
glEnable(GL_LIGHTING);
```

To disable lighting, call **glDisable()** with GL_LIGHTING as the argument.

You also need explicitly to enable each light source that you define, after you've specified the parameters for that source. Example 5-1 uses only one light, GL_LIGHT0:

```
glEnable(GL_LIGHT0);
```

Compatibility Extension
GL_LIGHTING
GL_LIGHT*i*

Defining Material Properties

You've seen how to create light sources with certain characteristics and how to define the desired lighting model. This section describes how to define the material properties of the objects in the scene: the ambient, diffuse, and specular color, the shininess, and the color of any emitted light. (See "The Mathematics of Lighting" for the equations used in the lighting and material-property calculations.) Most of the material properties are conceptually similar to ones you've already used to create light sources. The mechanism for setting them is similar, except that the command used is called **glMaterial*()**.

void **glMaterial**{if}(GLenum *face*, GLenum *pname*, *TYPE param*);
void **glMaterial**{if}**v**(GLenum *face*, GLenum *pname*, const *TYPE *param*);

Specifies a current material property for use in lighting calculations. *face* can be GL_FRONT, GL_BACK, or GL_FRONT_AND_BACK to indicate to which faces of the object the material should be applied. The particular material property being set is identified by *pname*, and the desired values for that property are given by *param*, which is either a pointer to a group of values (if the vector version is used) or the actual value (if the nonvector version is used). The nonvector version works only for setting GL_SHININESS. The possible values for *pname* are shown in Table 5-3. Note that GL_AMBIENT_AND_DIFFUSE allows you to set both the ambient and diffuse material colors simultaneously to the same RGBA value.

Parameter Name	Default Value	Meaning
GL_AMBIENT	(0.2, 0.2, 0.2, 1.0)	ambient color of material
GL_DIFFUSE	(0.8, 0.8, 0.8, 1.0)	diffuse color of material
GL_AMBIENT_AND_DIFFUSE		ambient and diffuse color of material
GL_SPECULAR	(0.0, 0.0, 0.0, 1.0)	specular color of material
GL_SHININESS	0.0	specular exponent
GL_EMISSION	(0.0, 0.0, 0.0, 1.0)	emissive color of material
GL_COLOR_INDEXES	(0, 1, 1)	ambient, diffuse, and specular color indices

Table 5-3   Default Values for *pname* Parameter of glMaterial*()

As discussed in "Selecting a Lighting Model," you can choose to have lighting calculations performed differently for the front- and back-facing polygons of objects. If the back faces might indeed be seen, you can supply different material properties for the front and back surfaces by using the *face* parameter of **glMaterial*()**. See Plate 14 for an example of an object drawn with different inside and outside material properties.

To give you an idea of the possible effects you can achieve by manipulating material properties, see Plate 16. This figure shows the same object drawn with several different sets of material properties. The same light source and lighting model are used for the entire figure. The sections that follow discuss the specific properties used to draw each of these spheres.

Note that most of the material properties set with **glMaterial*()** are (R, G, B, A) colors. Regardless of what alpha values are supplied for other parameters, the alpha value at any particular vertex is the diffuse-material alpha value (that is, the alpha value given to GL_DIFFUSE with the **glMaterial*()** command, as described in the next section). (See "Blending" in Chapter 6 for a complete discussion of alpha values.) Also, none of the RGBA material properties apply in color-index mode. (See "Lighting in Color-Index Mode" on page 246 for more information about what parameters are relevant in color-index mode.)

Diffuse and Ambient Reflection

The GL_DIFFUSE and GL_AMBIENT parameters set with **glMaterial*()** affect the colors of the diffuse and ambient light reflected by an object. Diffuse reflectance plays the most important role in determining what you perceive the color of an object to be. Your perception is affected by the color of the incident diffuse light and the angle of the incident light relative to the normal direction. (It's most intense where the incident light falls perpendicular to the surface.) The position of the viewpoint doesn't affect diffuse reflectance at all.

Ambient reflectance affects the overall color of the object. Because diffuse reflectance is brightest where an object is directly illuminated, ambient reflectance is most noticeable where an object receives no direct illumination. An object's total ambient reflectance is affected by the global ambient light and ambient light from individual light sources. Like diffuse reflectance, ambient reflectance isn't affected by the position of the viewpoint.

For real-world objects, diffuse and ambient reflectance are normally the same color. For this reason, OpenGL provides you with a convenient way of assigning the same value to both simultaneously with **glMaterial*()**:

```
GLfloat mat_amb_diff[] = { 0.1, 0.5, 0.8, 1.0 };
glMaterialfv(GL_FRONT_AND_BACK, GL_AMBIENT_AND_DIFFUSE,
          mat_amb_diff);
```

In this example, the RGBA color (0.1, 0.5, 0.8, 1.0)—a deep blue color—represents the current ambient and diffuse reflectance for both the front- and back-facing polygons.

In Plate 16, the first row of spheres has no ambient reflectance (0.0, 0.0, 0.0, 0.0), and the second row has a significant amount of it (0.7, 0.7, 0.7, 1.0).

Specular Reflection

Specular reflection from an object produces highlights. Unlike ambient and diffuse reflection, the amount of specular reflection seen by a viewer does depend on the location of the viewpoint—it is brightest along the direct angle of reflection. To see this, imagine looking at a metallic ball outdoors in the sunlight. As you move your head, the highlight created by the sunlight moves with you to some extent. However, if you move your head too much, you lose the highlight entirely.

OpenGL allows you to set the effect that the material has on reflected light (with GL_SPECULAR) and control the size and brightness of the highlight (with GL_SHININESS). You can assign a number in the range [0.0, 128.0] to GL_SHININESS: the higher the value, the smaller and brighter (more focused) the highlight. (See "The Mathematics of Lighting" on page 240 for details about how specular highlights are calculated.)

In Plate 16, the spheres in the first column have no specular reflection. In the second column, GL_SPECULAR and GL_SHININESS are assigned values as follows:

```
GLfloat mat_specular[] = { 1.0, 1.0, 1.0, 1.0 };
GLfloat low_shininess[] = { 5.0 };
glMaterialfv(GL_FRONT, GL_SPECULAR, mat_specular);
glMaterialfv(GL_FRONT, GL_SHININESS, low_shininess);
```

In the third column, the GL_SHININESS parameter is increased to 100.0.

Emission

By specifying an RGBA color for GL_EMISSION, you can make an object appear to be giving off light of that color. Since most real-world objects (except lights) don't emit light, you'll probably use this feature mostly to simulate lamps and other light sources in a scene. In Plate 16, the spheres in the fourth column have a reddish-gray value for GL_EMISSION:

```
GLfloat mat_emission[] = {0.3, 0.2, 0.2, 0.0};
glMaterialfv(GL_FRONT, GL_EMISSION, mat_emission);
```

Notice that the spheres appear to be slightly glowing; however, they're not actually acting as light sources. You would need to create a light source and position it at the same location as the sphere to create such an effect.

Changing Material Properties

Example 5-1 uses the same material properties for all vertices of the only object in the scene (the sphere). In other situations, you might want to assign different material properties for different vertices on the same object. More likely, you have more than one object in the scene, and each object has different material properties. For example, the code that produced Plate 16 has to draw 12 different objects (all spheres), each with different material properties. Example 5-8 shows a portion of the code in **display()**.

Example 5-8   Different Material Properties: material.c

```
GLfloat no_mat[] = { 0.0, 0.0, 0.0, 1.0 };
GLfloat mat_ambient[] = { 0.7, 0.7, 0.7, 1.0 };
GLfloat mat_ambient_color[] = { 0.8, 0.8, 0.2, 1.0 };
GLfloat mat_diffuse[] = { 0.1, 0.5, 0.8, 1.0 };
GLfloat mat_specular[] = { 1.0, 1.0, 1.0, 1.0 };
GLfloat no_shininess[] = { 0.0 };
GLfloat low_shininess[] = { 5.0 };
GLfloat high_shininess[] = { 100.0 };
GLfloat mat_emission[] = {0.3, 0.2, 0.2, 0.0};

glClear(GL_COLOR_BUFFER_BIT | GL_DEPTH_BUFFER_BIT);

/*  draw sphere in first row, first column
 *  diffuse reflection only; no ambient or specular
 */
glPushMatrix();
glTranslatef(-3.75, 3.0, 0.0);
glMaterialfv(GL_FRONT, GL_AMBIENT, no_mat);
glMaterialfv(GL_FRONT, GL_DIFFUSE, mat_diffuse);
glMaterialfv(GL_FRONT, GL_SPECULAR, no_mat);
glMaterialfv(GL_FRONT, GL_SHININESS, no_shininess);
glMaterialfv(GL_FRONT, GL_EMISSION, no_mat);
glutSolidSphere(1.0, 16, 16);
glPopMatrix();

/*  draw sphere in first row, second column
 *  diffuse and specular reflection; low shininess; no ambient
 */
glPushMatrix();
glTranslatef(-1.25, 3.0, 0.0);
glMaterialfv(GL_FRONT, GL_AMBIENT, no_mat);
glMaterialfv(GL_FRONT, GL_DIFFUSE, mat_diffuse);
```

```
    glMaterialfv(GL_FRONT, GL_SPECULAR, mat_specular);
    glMaterialfv(GL_FRONT, GL_SHININESS, low_shininess);
    glMaterialfv(GL_FRONT, GL_EMISSION, no_mat);
    glutSolidSphere(1.0, 16, 16);
    glPopMatrix();

/*  draw sphere in first row, third column
 *  diffuse and specular reflection; high shininess; no ambient
 */
    glPushMatrix();
    glTranslatef(1.25, 3.0, 0.0);
    glMaterialfv(GL_FRONT, GL_AMBIENT, no_mat);
    glMaterialfv(GL_FRONT, GL_DIFFUSE, mat_diffuse);
    glMaterialfv(GL_FRONT, GL_SPECULAR, mat_specular);
    glMaterialfv(GL_FRONT, GL_SHININESS, high_shininess);
    glMaterialfv(GL_FRONT, GL_EMISSION, no_mat);
    glutSolidSphere(1.0, 16, 16);
    glPopMatrix();

/*  draw sphere in first row, fourth column
 *  diffuse reflection; emission; no ambient or specular refl.
 */
    glPushMatrix();
    glTranslatef(3.75, 3.0, 0.0);
    glMaterialfv(GL_FRONT, GL_AMBIENT, no_mat);
    glMaterialfv(GL_FRONT, GL_DIFFUSE, mat_diffuse);
    glMaterialfv(GL_FRONT, GL_SPECULAR, no_mat);
    glMaterialfv(GL_FRONT, GL_SHININESS, no_shininess);
    glMaterialfv(GL_FRONT, GL_EMISSION, mat_emission);
    glutSolidSphere(1.0, 16, 16);
    glPopMatrix();
```

As you can see, **glMaterialfv()** is called repeatedly to set the desired material property for each sphere. Note that it needs to be called only to change a property that has to be respecified. The second, third, and fourth spheres use the same ambient and diffuse properties as the first sphere, so these properties do not need to be respecified. Since **glMaterial*()** has a performance cost associated with its use, Example 5-8 could be rewritten to minimize material-property changes.

Nate Robins' Lightmaterial Tutorial

If you have downloaded Nate Robins' suite of tutorial programs, now run the **lightmaterial** tutorial. With this tutorial, you can experiment with the colors of material properties, including ambient, diffuse, and specular colors, as well as the shininess exponent.

Color Material Mode

Another technique for minimizing performance costs associated with changing material properties is to use **glColorMaterial()**.

---

void **glColorMaterial**(GLenum *face*, GLenum *mode*);

Causes the material property (or properties) specified by *mode* of the specified material face (or faces) specified by *face* to track the value of the current color at all times. A change to the current color (using **glColor*()**) immediately updates the specified material properties. The *face* parameter can be GL_FRONT, GL_BACK, or GL_FRONT_AND_BACK (the default). The *mode* parameter can be GL_AMBIENT, GL_DIFFUSE, GL_SPECULAR, GL_AMBIENT_AND_DIFFUSE (the default), or GL_EMISSION. At any given time, only one mode is active. **glColorMaterial()** has no effect on color-index lighting.

Compatibility
Extension

glColorMaterial

Note that **glColorMaterial()** specifies two independent values: The first determines which face or faces are updated, and the second determines which material property or properties of those faces are updated. OpenGL does *not* maintain separate *mode* variables for each face.

After calling **glColorMaterial()**, you need to call **glEnable()** with GL_COLOR_MATERIAL as the parameter. Then, you can change the current color using **glColor*()** (or other material properties, using **glMaterial*()**) as needed as you draw:

```
glEnable(GL_COLOR_MATERIAL);
glColorMaterial(GL_FRONT, GL_DIFFUSE);
/* now glColor* changes diffuse reflection  */
glColor3f(0.2, 0.5, 0.8);
/* draw some objects here */
glColorMaterial(GL_FRONT, GL_SPECULAR);
/* glColor* no longer changes diffuse reflection
 * now glColor* changes specular reflection  */
glColor3f(0.9, 0.0, 0.2);
/* draw other objects here */
glDisable(GL_COLOR_MATERIAL);
```

You should use **glColorMaterial()** whenever you need to change a single material parameter for most vertices in your scene. If you need to change more than one material parameter, as was the case for Plate 16, use **glMaterial*()**. When you don't need the capabilities of **glColorMaterial()** anymore, be sure to disable it so that you don't get undesired material properties and don't incur the performance cost associated with it. The performance value in using **glColorMaterial()** varies, depending on your OpenGL implementation. Some implementations may be able to optimize the vertex routines so that they can quickly update material properties based on the current color.

Example 5-9 shows an interactive program that uses **glColorMaterial()** to change material parameters. Pressing each of the three mouse buttons changes the color of the diffuse reflection.

Example 5-9   Using glColorMaterial(): colormat.c

```
GLfloat diffuseMaterial[4] = { 0.5, 0.5, 0.5, 1.0 };

void init(void)
{
    GLfloat mat_specular[] = { 1.0, 1.0, 1.0, 1.0 };
    GLfloat light_position[] = { 1.0, 1.0, 1.0, 0.0 };

    glClearColor(0.0, 0.0, 0.0, 0.0);
    glShadeModel(GL_SMOOTH);
    glEnable(GL_DEPTH_TEST);
    glMaterialfv(GL_FRONT, GL_DIFFUSE, diffuseMaterial);
    glMaterialfv(GL_FRONT, GL_SPECULAR, mat_specular);
    glMaterialf(GL_FRONT, GL_SHININESS, 25.0);
    glLightfv(GL_LIGHT0, GL_POSITION, light_position);
    glEnable(GL_LIGHTING);
    glEnable(GL_LIGHT0);

    glColorMaterial(GL_FRONT, GL_DIFFUSE);
    glEnable(GL_COLOR_MATERIAL);
}

void display(void)
{
    glClear(GL_COLOR_BUFFER_BIT | GL_DEPTH_BUFFER_BIT);
    glutSolidSphere(1.0, 20, 16);
    glFlush();
}

void reshape(int w, int h)
{
    glViewport(0, 0, (GLsizei) w, (GLsizei) h);
    glMatrixMode(GL_PROJECTION);
```

```
        glLoadIdentity();
        if (w <= h)
            glOrtho(-1.5, 1.5, -1.5*(GLfloat)h/(GLfloat)w,
                1.5*(GLfloat)h/(GLfloat)w, -10.0, 10.0);
        else
            glOrtho(-1.5*(GLfloat)w/(GLfloat)h,
                1.5*(GLfloat)w/(GLfloat)h, -1.5, 1.5, -10.0, 10.0);
        glMatrixMode(GL_MODELVIEW);
        glLoadIdentity();
}

void mouse(int button, int state, int x, int y)
{
        switch (button) {
            case GLUT_LEFT_BUTTON:
                if (state == GLUT_DOWN) {        /*  change red  */
                    diffuseMaterial[0] += 0.1;
                    if (diffuseMaterial[0] > 1.0)
                        diffuseMaterial[0] = 0.0;
                    glColor4fv(diffuseMaterial);
                    glutPostRedisplay();
                }
                break;
            case GLUT_MIDDLE_BUTTON:
                if (state == GLUT_DOWN) {        /*  change green  */
                    diffuseMaterial[1] += 0.1;
                    if (diffuseMaterial[1] > 1.0)
                        diffuseMaterial[1] = 0.0;
                    glColor4fv(diffuseMaterial);
                    glutPostRedisplay();
                }
                break;
            case GLUT_RIGHT_BUTTON:
                if (state == GLUT_DOWN) {        /*  change blue  */
                    diffuseMaterial[2] += 0.1;
                    if (diffuseMaterial[2] > 1.0)
                        diffuseMaterial[2] = 0.0;
                    glColor4fv(diffuseMaterial);
                    glutPostRedisplay();
                }
                break;
            default:
                break;
        }
}
```

```
int main(int argc, char** argv)
{
    glutInit(&argc, argv);
    glutInitDisplayMode(GLUT_SINGLE | GLUT_RGB | GLUT_DEPTH);
    glutInitWindowSize(500, 500);
    glutInitWindowPosition(100, 100);
    glutCreateWindow(argv[0]);
    init();
    glutDisplayFunc(display);
    glutReshapeFunc(reshape);
    glutMouseFunc(mouse);
    glutMainLoop();
    return 0;
}
```

Try This

Modify Example 5-8 in the following manner:

Try This

- Change the global ambient light in the scene. Hint: Alter the value of the GL_LIGHT_MODEL_AMBIENT parameter.

- Change the diffuse, ambient, and specular reflection parameters, the shininess exponent, and the emission color. Hint: Use the **glMaterial*()** command, but avoid making excessive calls.

- Use two-sided materials and add a user-defined clipping plane so that you can see the inside and outside of a row or column of spheres. (See "Additional Clipping Planes" in Chapter 3, if you need to recall user-defined clipping planes.) Hint: Turn on two-sided lighting with GL_LIGHT_MODEL_TWO_SIDE, set the desired material properties, and add a clipping plane.

- Remove the **glMaterialfv()** call for setting the GL_DIFFUSE value, and use the more efficient **glColorMaterial()** calls to achieve the same lighting.

The Mathematics of Lighting

Advanced

This section presents the equations used by OpenGL to perform lighting calculations to determine colors when in RGBA mode. (See "The Mathematics

Advanced

of Color-Index Mode Lighting" for corresponding calculations for color-index mode.) You don't need to read this section if you're willing to experiment to obtain the lighting conditions you want. Even after reading this section, you'll probably have to experiment, but you'll have a better idea of how the values of parameters affect a vertex's color. Remember that if lighting is not enabled, the color of a vertex is simply the current color; if it is enabled, the lighting computations described here are carried out in eye coordinates.

In the following equations, mathematical operations are performed separately on the R, G, and B components. Thus, for example, when three terms are shown as added together, the R values, the G values, and the B values for each term are separately added to form the final RGB color $(R_1 + R_2 + R_3, G_1 + G_2 + G_3, B_1 + B_2 + B_3)$. When three terms are multiplied, the calculation is $(R_1 R_2 R_3, G_1 G_2 G_3, B_1 B_2 B_3)$. (Remember that the final A or alpha component at a vertex is equal to the material's diffuse alpha value at that vertex.)

The color produced by lighting a vertex is computed as follows:

vertex color =   the material emission at that vertex +

the global ambient light scaled by the material's ambient property at that vertex   +

the ambient, diffuse, and specular contributions from all the light sources, properly attenuated

After lighting calculations are performed, the color values are clamped (in RGBA mode) to the range [0, 1].

Note that OpenGL lighting calculations don't take into account the possibility of one object blocking light from another; as a result, shadows aren't automatically created. (See "Shadows" in Chapter 14 for a technique used to create shadows.) Also keep in mind that with OpenGL, illuminated objects don't radiate light onto other objects.

Material Emission

The material emission term is the simplest. It's the RGB value assigned to the GL_EMISSION parameter.

Scaled Global Ambient Light

The second term is computed by multiplying the global ambient light (as defined by the GL_LIGHT_MODEL_AMBIENT parameter) by the material's ambient property (GL_AMBIENT value as assigned with **glMaterial*()**):

ambient$_{\text{light model}}$ * ambient$_{\text{material}}$

Each of the R, G, and B values for these two parameters are multiplied separately to compute the final RGB value for this term: (R_1R_2, G_1G_2, B_1B_2).

Contributions from Light Sources

Each light source may contribute to a vertex's color, and these contributions are added together. The equation for computing each light source's contribution is as follows:

contribution = attenuation factor * spotlight effect *

(ambient term + diffuse term + specular term)

Attenuation Factor

The *attenuation factor* was described in "Position and Attenuation":

$$\text{attenuation factor} = \frac{1}{k_c + k_l d + k_q d^2}$$

where

d = distance between the light's position and the vertex

k_c = GL_CONSTANT_ATTENUATION

k_l = GL_LINEAR_ATTENUATION

k_q = GL_QUADRATIC_ATTENUATION

If the light is a directional one, the attenuation factor is 1.

Spotlight Effect

The *spotlight effect* evaluates to one of three possible values, depending on whether or not the light is actually a spotlight and whether the vertex lies inside or outside the cone of illumination produced by the spotlight:

- 1 if the light isn't a spotlight (GL_SPOT_CUTOFF is 180.0).

- 0 if the light is a spotlight, but the vertex lies outside the cone of illumination produced by the spotlight.

- $(\max \{\mathbf{v} \cdot \mathbf{d}, 0\})^{GL\_SPOT\_EXPONENT}$ where:

    $\mathbf{v} = (v_x, v_y, v_z)$ is the unit vector that points from the spotlight (GL_POSITION) to the vertex.

    $\mathbf{d} = (d_x, d_y, d_z)$ is the spotlight's direction (GL_SPOT_DIRECTION), assuming the light is a spotlight and the vertex lies inside the cone of illumination produced by the spotlight.

    The dot product of the two vectors $\mathbf{v}$ and $\mathbf{d}$ varies as the cosine of the angle between them; hence, objects directly in line get maximum illumination, and objects off the axis have their illumination drop as the cosine of the angle.

To determine whether a particular vertex lies within the cone of illumination, OpenGL evaluates $(\max \{\mathbf{v} \cdot \mathbf{d}, 0\})$, where $\mathbf{v}$ and $\mathbf{d}$ are as defined in the preceding discussion. If this value is less than the cosine of the spotlight's cutoff angle (GL_SPOT_CUTOFF), then the vertex lies outside the cone; otherwise, it's inside the cone.

Ambient Term

The ambient term is simply the ambient color of the light scaled by the ambient material property:

$$ambient_{light} * ambient_{material}$$

Diffuse Term

The diffuse term needs to take into account whether or not light falls directly on the vertex, the diffuse color of the light, and the diffuse material property:

$$(\max \{\mathbf{L} \cdot \mathbf{n}, 0\}) * diffuse_{light} * diffuse_{material}$$

where

   $\mathbf{L} = (\mathbf{L}_x, \mathbf{L}_y, \mathbf{L}_z)$ is the unit vector that points from the vertex to the light position (GL_POSITION).

   $\mathbf{n} = (\mathbf{n}_x, \mathbf{n}_y, \mathbf{n}_z)$ is the unit normal vector at the vertex.

Specular Term

The specular term also depends on whether or not light falls directly on the vertex. If $L \cdot n$ is less than or equal to zero, there is no specular component at the vertex. (If it's less than zero, the light is on the wrong side of the surface.) If there's a specular component, it depends on the following:

- The unit normal vector at the vertex (n_x, n_y, n_z)

- The sum of the two unit vectors that point between (1) the vertex and the light position (or light direction) and (2) the vertex and the viewpoint (assuming that GL_LIGHT_MODEL_LOCAL_VIEWER is true; if it's not true, the vector (0, 0, 1) is used as the second vector in the sum). This vector sum is normalized (by dividing each component by the magnitude of the vector) to yield $s = (s_x, s_y, s_z)$.

- The specular exponent (GL_SHININESS)

- The specular color of the light (GL_SPECULAR$_{light}$)

- The specular property of the material (GL_SPECULAR$_{material}$)

Using these definitions, here's how OpenGL calculates the specular term:

$$(\max \{s \cdot n, 0\})^{shininess} * specular_{light} * specular_{material}$$

However, if $L \cdot n = 0$, the specular term is 0.

Putting It All Together

Using the definitions of terms described in the preceding paragraphs, the following represents the entire lighting calculation in RGBA mode:

vertex color = emission$_{material}$ +

ambient$_{light\ model}$ * ambient$_{material}$ +

$$\sum_{i=0}^{n-1} \left(\frac{1}{k_c + k_l d + k_q d^2} \right)_i * (\text{spotlight effect})_i *$$

[ambient$_{light}$ * ambient$_{material}$ +

$(\max \{L \cdot n, 0\}) * diffuse_{light} * diffuse_{material}$ +

$(\max \{s \cdot n, 0\})^{shininess} * specular_{light} * specular_{material}]_i$

Secondary Specular Color

If GL_SEPARATE_SPECULAR_COLOR is the current lighting model color control, then a primary and secondary color are produced for each vertex, which are computed as follows:

primary color =   the material emission at that vertex +

the global ambient light scaled by the material's ambient property at that vertex   +

the ambient and diffuse contributions from all the light sources, properly attenuated

secondary color =   the specular contributions from all the light sources, properly attenuated

The following two equations represent the lighting calculations for the primary and secondary colors:

primary color = $\text{emission}_{\text{material}}$ +

$\text{ambient}_{\text{light model}}$ * $\text{ambient}_{\text{material}}$ +

$$\sum_{i=0}^{n-1} \left(\frac{1}{k_c + k_l d + k_q d^2} \right)_i \text{ * (spotlight effect)}_i \text{ *}$$

$[\text{ambient}_{\text{light}}$ * $\text{ambient}_{\text{material}}$ +

$(\max \{ \mathbf{L} \cdot \mathbf{n} , 0 \})$ * $\text{diffuse}_{\text{light}}$ * $\text{diffuse}_{\text{material}}]_i$

secondary color =

$$\sum_{i=0}^{n-1} \left(\frac{1}{k_c + k_l d + k_q d^2} \right)_i \text{ * (spotlight effect)}_i \text{ *}$$

$[(\max \{ \mathbf{s} \cdot \mathbf{n} , 0 \})^{\text{shininess}}$ * $\text{specular}_{\text{light}}$ * $\text{specular}_{\text{material}}]_i$

During texture mapping, only the primary color is combined with the texture colors. After the texturing operation, the secondary color is added to the resulting combination of the primary and texture colors.

Lighting in Color-Index Mode

In color-index mode, the parameters comprising RGBA values either have no effect or have a special interpretation. Since it's much harder to achieve certain effects in color-index mode, you should use RGBA whenever possible. In fact, the only light-source, lighting-model, or material parameters in an RGBA form that are used in color-index mode are the light-source parameters GL_DIFFUSE and GL_SPECULAR, and the material parameter GL_SHININESS. GL_DIFFUSE and GL_SPECULAR (d_l and s_l, respectively) are used to compute color-index diffuse and specular light intensities (d_{ci} and s_{ci}), as follows:

$$d_{ci} = 0.30R(d_l) + 0.59G(d_l) + 0.11B(d_l)$$

$$s_{ci} = 0.30R(s_l) + 0.59G(s_l) + 0.11B(s_l)$$

where $R(x)$, $G(x)$, and $B(x)$ refer to the red, green, and blue components, respectively, of color x. The weighting values 0.30, 0.59, and 0.11 reflect the "perceptual" weights that red, green, and blue have for your eye—your eye is most sensitive to green and least sensitive to blue.

To specify material colors in color-index mode, use **glMaterial*()** with the special parameter GL_COLOR_INDEXES, as follows:

```
GLfloat mat_colormap[] = { 16.0, 47.0, 79.0 };
glMaterialfv(GL_FRONT, GL_COLOR_INDEXES, mat_colormap);
```

The three numbers supplied for GL_COLOR_INDEXES specify the color indices for the ambient, diffuse, and specular material colors, respectively. In other words, OpenGL regards the color associated with the first index (16.0 in this example) as the pure ambient color, with the second index (47.0) as the pure diffuse color, and with the third index (79.0) as the pure specular color. (By default, the ambient color index is 0.0, and the diffuse and specular color indices are both 1.0. Note that **glColorMaterial()** has no effect on color-index lighting.)

As it draws a scene, OpenGL uses colors associated with indices between these numbers to shade objects in the scene. Therefore, you must build a color ramp between the indicated indices (in this example, between indices 16 and 47, and then between indices 47 and 79). Often, the color ramp is built smoothly, but you might want to use other formulations to achieve different effects. Here's an example of a smooth color ramp that starts with a black ambient color and goes through a magenta diffuse color to a white specular color:

```
for (i = 0; i < 32; i++) {
   glutSetColor(16 + i, 1.0 * (i/32.0), 0.0, 1.0 * (i/32.0));
   glutSetColor(48 + i, 1.0, 1.0 * (i/32.0), 1.0);
}
```

The GLUT library command **glutSetColor()** takes four arguments. It associates the color index indicated by the first argument with the RGB triplet specified by the last three arguments. When $i = 0$, the color index 16 is assigned the RGB value (0.0, 0.0, 0.0), or black. The color ramp builds smoothly up to the diffuse material color at index 47 (when $i = 31$), which is assigned the pure magenta RGB value (1.0, 0.0, 1.0). The second loop builds the ramp between the magenta diffuse color and the white (1.0, 1.0, 1.0) specular color (index 79). Plate 15 shows the result of using this color ramp with a single lit sphere.

The Mathematics of Color-Index Mode Lighting

Advanced

Advanced

As you might expect, since the allowable parameters are different for color-index mode than for RGBA mode, the calculations are different as well. Since there's no material emission and no ambient light, the only terms of interest from the RGBA equations are the diffuse and specular contributions from the light sources and the shininess. Even these terms need to be modified, however, as explained next.

Begin with the diffuse and specular terms from the RGBA equations. In the diffuse term, instead of diffuse$_{light}$ * diffuse$_{material}$, substitute d_{ci} as defined in the preceding section for color-index mode. Similarly, in the specular term, instead of specular$_{light}$ * specular$_{material}$, use s_{ci} as defined in the preceding section. (Calculate the attenuation, the spotlight effect, and all other components of these terms as before.) Call these modified diffuse and specular terms d and s, respectively. Now, let $s' = \min\{ s, 1 \}$, and then compute

$$c = a_m + d(1 - s')(d_m - a_m) + s'(s_m - a_m)$$

where a_m, d_m, and s_m are the ambient, diffuse, and specular material indices specified using GL_COLOR_INDEXES. The final color index is

$$c' = \min \{ c, s_m \}$$

After lighting calculations are performed, the color-index values are converted to fixed-point (with an unspecified number of bits to the right of the binary point). Then the integer portion is masked (bitwise ANDed) with $2^n - 1$, where n is the number of bits in a color in the color-index buffer.

Chapter 6

Blending, Antialiasing, Fog, and Polygon Offset

Chapter Objectives

After reading this chapter, you'll be able to do the following:

- Blend colors to achieve such effects as making objects appear translucent

- Smooth jagged edges of lines and polygons with antialiasing

- Create scenes with realistic atmospheric effects

- Render rounded (antialiased) points with varying sizes, based upon distance from the viewpoint

- Draw geometry at or near the same depth, but avoid unaesthetic artifacts from intersecting geometry

The preceding chapters have given you the basic information you need to create a computer-graphics scene; you've learned how to do the following:

- Draw geometric shapes

- Transform those geometric shapes so that they can be viewed from whatever perspective you wish

- Specify how the geometric shapes in your scene should be colored and shaded

- Add lights and indicate how they should affect the shapes in your scene

Now you're ready to get a little fancier. This chapter discusses five techniques that can add extra detail and polish to your scene. None of these techniques is hard to use—in fact, it's probably harder to explain them than to use them. Each of these techniques is described in its own major section:

- "Blending" tells you how to specify a blending function that combines color values from a source and a destination. The final effect is that parts of your scene appear translucent.

- "Antialiasing" explains this relatively subtle effect that alters colors so that the edges of points, lines, and polygons appear smooth rather than angular and jagged. Multisampling is a powerful technique to antialias all of the primitives in your entire scene.

- "Fog" describes how to create the illusion of depth by computing the color values of an object based on its distance from the viewpoint. Thus, objects that are far away appear to fade into the background, just as they do in real life.

- "Point Parameters" discusses an efficient technique for rendering point primitives with different sizes and color, depending upon distance from the viewpoint. Point parameters can be useful for modeling particle systems.

- If you've tried to draw a wireframe outline atop a shaded object and used the same vertices, you've probably noticed some ugly visual artifacts. "Polygon Offset" shows you how to tweak (offset) depth values to make an outlined, shaded object look beautiful.

OpenGL Version 1.1 added the polygon offset capability.

Version 1.2 of OpenGL introduced a selectable blending equation (**glBlendEquation()**), a constant blending color (**glBlendColor()**), and the blending factors: GL_CONSTANT_COLOR, GL_ONE_MINUS_CONSTANT_COLOR, GL_CONSTANT_ALPHA, and GL_ONE_MINUS_CONSTANT_ALPHA.

In Version 1.2 and 1.3, these features were supported only if the OpenGL implementation supported the imaging subset. In Version 1.4, the blending equation, constant blending color, and constant blending factors became mandatory.

In Version 1.3, multisampling became a core feature of OpenGL.

Version 1.4 also added the following new features, which are covered in this chapter:

- Use of GL_SRC_COLOR and GL_ONE_MINUS_SRC_COLOR as source blending factors. (Prior to Version 1.4, GL_SRC_COLOR and GL_ONE_MINUS_SRC_COLOR had to be destination factors.)

- Use of GL_DST_COLOR and GL_ONE_MINUS_DST_COLOR as destination blending factors. (Prior to Version 1.4, GL_DST_COLOR and GL_ONE_MINUS_DST_COLOR had to be source factors.)

- Explicit specification of fog coordinates

- Point parameters to control characteristics of point primitives

- Capability to blend RGB and alpha color components with separate blending functions

Blending

What's it all about, alpha? You've already seen alpha values (alpha is the A in RGBA), but they've been ignored until now. Alpha values are specified with **glColor*()** when using **glClearColor()** to specify a clearing color and when specifying certain lighting parameters such as a material property or light source intensity. As you learned in Chapter 4, the pixels on a monitor screen emit red, green, and blue light, which is controlled by the red, green, and blue color values. So how does an alpha value affect what is drawn in a window on the screen?

When blending is enabled, the alpha value is often used to combine the color value of the fragment being processed with that of the pixel already stored in the framebuffer. Blending occurs after your scene has been rasterized and converted to fragments, but just before the final pixels are drawn in the framebuffer. Alpha values can also be used in the alpha test to accept or reject a fragment based on its alpha value. (See Chapter 10 for more information about this process.)

Without blending, each new fragment overwrites any existing color values in the framebuffer, as though the fragment were opaque. With blending, you can control how (and how much of) the existing color value should be combined with the new fragment's value. Thus, you can use alpha blending to create a translucent fragment that lets some of the previously stored color value "show through." Color blending lies at the heart of techniques such as transparency, digital compositing, and painting.

Note: Alpha values aren't specified in color-index mode, so blending operations aren't performed in color-index mode.

The most natural way to think of blending operations is to think of the RGB components of a fragment as representing its color, and the alpha component as representing opacity. Transparent or translucent surfaces have lower opacity than opaque ones and, therefore, lower alpha values. For example, if you're viewing an object through green glass, the color you see is partly green from the glass and partly the color of the object. The percentage varies depending on the transmission properties of the glass: If the glass transmits 80 percent of the light that strikes it (that is, has an opacity of 20 percent), the color you see is a combination of 20 percent glass color and 80 percent the color of the object behind it. You can easily imagine situations with multiple translucent surfaces. If you look at an automobile, for instance, its interior has one piece of glass between it and your viewpoint; some objects behind the automobile are visible through two pieces of glass.

The Source and Destination Factors

During blending, color values of the incoming fragment (the *source*) are combined with the color values of the corresponding currently stored pixel (the *destination*) in a two-stage process. First you specify how to compute source and destination factors. These factors are RGBA quadruplets that are multiplied by each component of the R, G, B, and A values in the source and destination, respectively. Then the corresponding components in the two sets of RGBA quadruplets are combined. To show this mathematically, let the source and destination blending factors be (S_r, S_g, S_b, S_a) and (D_r, D_g, D_b, D_a), respectively, and let the RGBA values of the source and destination be indicated with a subscript of s or d. Then the final, blended RGBA values are given by

$$(R_s S_r + R_d D_r,\ G_s S_g + G_d D_g,\ B_s S_b + B_d D_b,\ A_s S_a + A_d D_a)$$

Each component of this quadruplet is eventually clamped to [0, 1] (unless color clamping is disabled. See "Color Clamping" on page 198).

The default way to combine the source and destination fragments is to add their values together (C_sS+C_dD). See "Combining Pixels Using Blending Equations" on page 255 for information on how to select other mathematical operations to combine fragments.

You have two different ways to choose the source and destination blending factors. You may call **glBlendFunc()** and choose two blending factors: the first factor for the source RGBA and the second for the destination RGBA. Or, you may use **glBlendFuncSeparate()** and choose four blending factors, which allows you to use one blending operation for RGB and a different one for its corresponding alpha.

---

void **glBlendFunc**(GLenum *srcfactor*, GLenum *destfactor*);

Controls how color values in the fragment being processed (the source) are combined with those already stored in the framebuffer (the destination). The possible values for these arguments are explained in Table 6-1. The argument *srcfactor* indicates how to compute a source blending factor; *destfactor* indicates how to compute a destination blending factor.

The blend factors are assumed to lie in the range [0, 1]. After the color values in the source and destination are combined, they're clamped to the range [0, 1].

---

void **glBlendFuncSeparate**(GLenum *srcRGB*, GLenum *destRGB*,
GLenum *srcAlpha*, GLenum *destAlpha*);

Similar to **glBlendFunc()**, **glBlendFuncSeparate()** also controls how source color values (fragment) are combined with destination values (framebuffer). **glBlendFuncSeparate()** also accepts the same arguments (shown in Table 6-1) as **glBlendFunc()**. The argument *srcRGB* indicates the source blending factor for color values; *destRGB* is the destination blending factor for color values. The argument *srcAlpha* indicates the source blending factor for alpha values; *destAlpha* is the destination blending factor for alpha values.

The blend factors are assumed to lie in the range [0, 1]. After the color values in the source and destination are combined, they're clamped to the range [0, 1].

Note: In Table 6-1, the RGBA values of the source, destination, and constant colors are indicated with the subscripts s, d, and c, respectively. Subtraction of quadruplets means subtracting them componentwise. GL_SRC_ALPHA_SATURATE may be used only as a source blend factor.

Constant	RGB Blend Factor	Alpha Blend Factor
GL_ZERO	$(0, 0, 0)$	0
GL_ONE	$(1, 1, 1)$	1
GL_SRC_COLOR	(R_s, G_s, B_s)	A_s
GL_ONE_MINUS_SRC_COLOR	$(1, 1, 1) - (R_s, G_s, B_s)$	$1 - A_s$
GL_DST_COLOR	(R_d, G_d, B_d)	A_d
GL_ONE_MINUS_DST_COLOR	$(1, 1, 1) - (R_d, G_d, B_d)$	$1 - A_d$
GL_SRC_ALPHA	(A_s, A_s, A_s)	A_s
GL_ONE_MINUS_SRC_ALPHA	$(1, 1, 1) - (A_s, A_s, A_s)$	$1 - A_s$
GL_DST_ALPHA	(A_d, A_d, A_d)	A_d
GL_ONE_MINUS_DST_ALPHA	$(1, 1, 1) - (A_d, A_d, A_d)$	$1 - A_d$
GL_CONSTANT_COLOR	(R_c, G_c, B_c)	A_c
GL_ONE_MINUS_CONSTANT_COLOR	$(1, 1, 1) - (R_c, G_c, B_c)$	$1 - A_c$
GL_CONSTANT_ALPHA	(A_c, A_c, A_c)	A_c
GL_ONE_MINUS_CONSTANT_ALPHA	$(1, 1, 1) - (A_c, A_c, A_c)$	$1 - A_c$
GL_SRC_ALPHA_SATURATE	$(f, f, f); f = \min(A_s, 1 - A_d)$	1

Table 6-1   Source and Destination Blending Factors

If you use one of the GL*CONSTANT* blending functions, you need to use **glBlendColor()** to specify a constant color.

> void **glBlendColor**(GLclampf *red*, GLclampf *green*, GLclampf *blue*, GLclampf *alpha*);
>
> Sets the current *red*, *green*, *blue*, and *alpha* values for use as the constant color (R_c, G_c, B_c, A_c) in blending operations.

Enabling Blending

No matter how you specify the blending function, you also need to enable blending to have it take effect:

```
glEnable(GL_BLEND);
```

Use **glDisable()** with GL_BLEND to disable blending. Note that using the constants GL_ONE (source) and GL_ZERO (destination) gives the same results as when blending is disabled; these values are the default.

Advanced

Advanced

OpenGL Version 2.0 introduced the ability to render into multiple buffers simultaneously (see "Selecting Color Buffers for Writing and Reading" on page 497 for details). In versions prior to OpenGL Version 3.0, all buffers enabled and disabled blending simultaneously (using **glEnable()** and **glDisable()**). As of Version 3.0, however, blending settings can be managed on a per-buffer basis, using **glEnablei()** and **glDisablei()** (described on page 516).

Combining Pixels Using Blending Equations

With standard blending, colors in the framebuffer are combined (using addition) with incoming fragment colors to produce the new framebuffer color. Either **glBlendEquation()** or **glBlendEquationSeparate()** may be used to select other mathematical operations to compute the difference, minimum, or maximum between color fragments and framebuffer pixels.

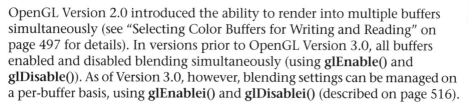

void **glBlendEquation**(GLenum *mode*);

Specifies how framebuffer and source colors are blended together. The allowable values for *mode* are GL_FUNC_ADD (the default), GL_FUNC_SUBTRACT, GL_FUNC_REVERSE_SUBTRACT, GL_MIN, and GL_MAX, of GL_LOGIC_OP. The possible modes are described in Table 6-2.

void **glBlendEquationSeparate**(GLenum *modeRGB*,
                                  GLenum *modeAlpha*);

Specifies how framebuffer and source colors are blended together, but allows for different blending modes for the rgb and alpha color components. The allowable values for *modeRGB* and *modeAlpha* are identical for the modes accepted by **glBlendEquation()**.

In Table 6-2, C_s and C_d represent the source and destination colors. The S and D parameters in the table represent the source and destination blending factors as specified with **glBlendFunc()** or **glBlendFuncSeparate()**. For GL_LOGIC_OP, the logical operator is specified by calling **glLogicOp()**. (See Table 10-4, "Sixteen Logical Operations," on page 518 for the list of supported logical operations.)

Blending Mode Parameter	Mathematical Operation
GL_FUNC_ADD	$C_sS + C_dD$
GL_FUNC_SUBTRACT	$C_sS - C_dD$
GL_FUNC_REVERSE_SUBTRACT	$C_dD - C_sS$
GL_MIN	$\min(C_sS, C_dD)$
GL_MAX	$\max(C_sS, C_dD)$
GL_LOGIC_OP	$C_S \ op \ C_D$

Table 6-2   Blending Equation Mathematical Operations

In Example 6-1, the different blending equation modes are demonstrated. The 'a', 's', 'r', 'm', and 'x' keys are used to select which blending mode to use. A blue square is used for the source color, and the yellow background is used as the destination color. The blending factor for each color is set to GL_ONE using **glBlendFunc()**.

Example 6-1   Demonstrating the Blend Equation Modes: blendeqn.c

```
/*  The following keys change the selected blend equation mode
 *
 *       'a'  ->  GL_FUNC_ADD
 *       's'  ->  GL_FUNC_SUBTRACT
 *       'r'  ->  GL_FUNC_REVERSE_SUBTRACT
 *       'm'  ->  GL_MIN
 *       'x'  ->  GL_MAX
 */

void init(void)
{
   glClearColor(1.0, 1.0, 0.0, 0.0);

   glBlendFunc(GL_ONE, GL_ONE);
   glEnable(GL_BLEND);
}
```

```
void display(void)
{
   glClear(GL_COLOR_BUFFER_BIT);
   glColor3f(0.0, 0.0, 1.0);
   glRectf(-0.5, -0.5, 0.5, 0.5);
   glFlush();
}

void keyboard(unsigned char key, int x, int y)
{
   switch (key) {
      case 'a': case 'A':
       /* Colors are added as: (1,1,0) + (0,0,1) = (1,1,1) which
        * will produce a white square on a yellow background. */
         glBlendEquation(GL_FUNC_ADD);
         break;

      case 's': case 'S':
      /* Colors are subtracted as: (0,0,1) - (1,1,0) = (-1,-1,1)
       * which is clamped to (0, 0, 1), producing a blue square
       * on a yellow background. */
         glBlendEquation(GL_FUNC_SUBTRACT);
         break;

      case 'r': case 'R':
      /* Colors are subtracted as: (1,1,0) - (0,0,1) = (1,1,-1)
       * which is clamped to (1, 1, 0). This produces yellow for
       * both the square and the background. */
         glBlendEquation(GL_FUNC_REVERSE_SUBTRACT);
         break;

      case 'm': case 'M':
      /* The minimum of each component is computed, as
       * [min(1,0),min(1,0),min(0,1)] which equates to (0,0,0).
       * This will produce a black square on the yellow
       * background. */
         glBlendEquation(GL_MIN);
         break;

      case 'x': case 'X':
      /* The minimum of each component is computed, as
       * [max(1, 0), max(1, 0), max(0, 1)] which equates to
       * (1, 1, 1).  This will produce a white square on the
       * yellow background. */
         glBlendEquation(GL_MAX);
         break;
```

```
        case 27:
            exit(0);
    }       break;

    glutPostRedisplay();
}
```

Sample Uses of Blending

Not all combinations of source and destination factors make sense. Most applications use a small number of combinations. The following paragraphs describe typical uses for particular combinations of source and destination factors. Some of these examples use only the incoming alpha value, so they work even when alpha values aren't stored in the framebuffer. Note that often there's more than one way to achieve some of these effects.

•   One way to draw a picture composed half of one image and half of another, equally blended, is to set the source factor to GL_ONE and the destination factor to GL_ZERO, and draw the first image. Then set the source factor to GL_SRC_ALPHA and the destination factor to GL_ONE_MINUS_SRC_ALPHA, and draw the second image with alpha equal to 0.5. This pair of factors probably represents the most commonly used blending operation. If the picture is supposed to be blended with 0.75 of the first image and 0.25 of the second, draw the first image as before, and draw the second with an alpha of 0.25.

•   To blend three different images equally, set the destination factor to GL_ONE and the source factor to GL_SRC_ALPHA. Draw each of the images with alpha equal to 0.3333333. With this technique, each image is only one-third of its original brightness, which is noticeable where the images don't overlap.

•   Suppose you're writing a paint program, and you want to have a brush that gradually adds color so that each brush stroke blends in a little more color with whatever is currently in the image (say, 10 percent color with 90 percent image on each pass). To do this, draw the image of the brush with alpha of 10 percent and use GL_SRC_ALPHA (source) and GL_ONE_MINUS_SRC_ALPHA (destination). Note that you can vary the alphas across the brush to make the brush add more of its color in the middle and less on the edges, for an antialiased brush shape (see "Antialiasing"). Similarly, erasers can be implemented by setting the eraser color to the background color.

- The blending functions that use the source or destination colors—GL_DST_COLOR or GL_ONE_MINUS_DST_COLOR for the source factor and GL_SRC_COLOR or GL_ONE_MINUS_SRC_COLOR for the destination factor—effectively allow you to modulate each color component individually. This operation is equivalent to applying a simple filter—for example, multiplying the red component by 80 percent, the green component by 40 percent, and the blue component by 72 percent would simulate viewing the scene through a photographic filter that blocks 20 percent of red light, 60 percent of green, and 28 percent of blue.

- Suppose you want to draw a picture composed of three translucent surfaces, some obscuring others, and all over a solid background. Assume the farthest surface transmits 80 percent of the color behind it, the next transmits 40 percent, and the closest transmits 90 percent. To compose this picture, draw the background first with the default source and destination factors, and then change the blending factors to GL_SRC_ALPHA (source) and GL_ONE_MINUS_SRC_ALPHA (destination). Next, draw the farthest surface with an alpha of 0.2, then the middle surface with an alpha of 0.6, and finally the closest surface with an alpha of 0.1.

- If your system has alpha planes, you can render objects one at a time (including their alpha values), read them back, and then perform interesting matting or compositing operations with the fully rendered objects. (See "Compositing 3D Rendered Images" by Tom Duff, *SIGGRAPH 1985 Proceedings*, pp. 41–44, for examples of this technique.) Note that objects used for picture composition can come from any source—they can be rendered using OpenGL commands, rendered using techniques such as ray-tracing or radiosity that are implemented in another graphics library, or obtained by scanning in existing images.

- You can create the effect of a nonrectangular raster image by assigning different alpha values to individual fragments in the image. In most cases, you would assign an alpha of 0 to each "invisible" fragment and an alpha of 1.0 to each opaque fragment. For example, you can draw a polygon in the shape of a tree and apply a texture map of foliage; the viewer can see through parts of the rectangular texture that aren't part of the tree if you've assigned them alpha values of 0. This method, sometimes called *billboarding*, is much faster than creating the tree out of three-dimensional polygons. An example of this technique is shown in Figure 6-1, in which the tree is a single rectangular polygon that can be rotated about the center of the trunk, as shown by the outlines, so that it's always facing the viewer. (See "Texture Functions" in Chapter 9 for more information about blending textures.)

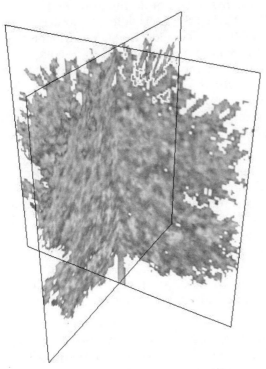

Figure 6-1   Creating a Nonrectangular Raster Image

- Blending is also used for *antialiasing*, which is a rendering technique to reduce the jagged appearance of primitives drawn on a raster screen. (See "Antialiasing" for more information.)

A Blending Example

Example 6-2 draws two overlapping colored triangles, each with an alpha of 0.75. Blending is enabled and the source and destination blending factors are set to GL_SRC_ALPHA and GL_ONE_MINUS_SRC_ALPHA, respectively.

When the program starts up, a yellow triangle is drawn on the left and then a cyan triangle is drawn on the right so that in the center of the window, where the triangles overlap, cyan is blended with the original yellow. You can change which triangle is drawn first by typing 't' in the window.

Example 6-2   Blending Example: alpha.c

```
static int leftFirst = GL_TRUE;

/*  Initialize alpha blending function.  */
static void init(void)
{
   glEnable(GL_BLEND);
   glBlendFunc(GL_SRC_ALPHA, GL_ONE_MINUS_SRC_ALPHA);
   glShadeModel(GL_FLAT);
   glClearColor(0.0, 0.0, 0.0, 0.0);
}

static void drawLeftTriangle(void)
{
/* draw yellow triangle on LHS of screen */
   glBegin(GL_TRIANGLES);
      glColor4f(1.0, 1.0, 0.0, 0.75);
      glVertex3f(0.1, 0.9, 0.0);
      glVertex3f(0.1, 0.1, 0.0);
      glVertex3f(0.7, 0.5, 0.0);
   glEnd();
}

static void drawRightTriangle(void)
{
/* draw cyan triangle on RHS of screen */
   glBegin(GL_TRIANGLES);
      glColor4f(0.0, 1.0, 1.0, 0.75);
      glVertex3f(0.9, 0.9, 0.0);
      glVertex3f(0.3, 0.5, 0.0);
      glVertex3f(0.9, 0.1, 0.0);
   glEnd();
}

void display(void)
{
   glClear(GL_COLOR_BUFFER_BIT);

   if (leftFirst) {
      drawLeftTriangle();
      drawRightTriangle();
   }
```

```
      else {
         drawRightTriangle();
         drawLeftTriangle();
      }
      glFlush();
}

void reshape(int w, int h)
{
   glViewport(0, 0, (GLsizei) w, (GLsizei) h);
   glMatrixMode(GL_PROJECTION);
   glLoadIdentity();
   if (w <= h)
      gluOrtho2D(0.0, 1.0, 0.0, 1.0*(GLfloat)h/(GLfloat)w);
   else
      gluOrtho2D(0.0, 1.0*(GLfloat)w/(GLfloat)h, 0.0, 1.0);
}

void keyboard(unsigned char key, int x, int y)
{
   switch (key) {
      case 't':
      case 'T':
         leftFirst = !leftFirst;
         glutPostRedisplay();
         break;
      case 27:  /*  Escape key  */
         exit(0);
         break;
      default:
         break;
   }
}

int main(int argc, char** argv)
{
   glutInit(&argc, argv);
   glutInitDisplayMode(GLUT_SINGLE | GLUT_RGB);
   glutInitWindowSize(200, 200);
   glutCreateWindow(argv[0]);
   init();
   glutReshapeFunc(reshape);
   glutKeyboardFunc(keyboard);
   glutDisplayFunc(display);
   glutMainLoop();
   return 0;
}
```

The order in which the triangles are drawn affects the color of the overlapping region. When the left triangle is drawn first, cyan fragments (the source) are blended with yellow fragments, which are already in the framebuffer (the destination). When the right triangle is drawn first, yellow is blended with cyan. Because the alpha values are all 0.75, the actual blending factors become 0.75 for the source and $1.0 - 0.75 = 0.25$ for the destination. In other words, the source fragments are somewhat translucent, but they have more effect on the final color than do the destination fragments.

Three-Dimensional Blending with the Depth Buffer

As you saw in the previous example, the order in which polygons are drawn greatly affects the blended result. When drawing three-dimensional translucent objects, you can get different appearances depending on whether you draw the polygons from back to front or from front to back. You also need to consider the effect of the depth buffer when determining the correct order. (See "A Hidden-Surface Removal Survival Kit" in Chapter 5 for an introduction to the depth buffer. Also see "Depth Test" in Chapter 10 for more information.) The depth buffer keeps track of the distance between the viewpoint and the portion of the object occupying a given pixel in a window on the screen; when another candidate color arrives for that pixel, it's drawn only if its object is closer to the viewpoint, in which case its depth value is stored in the depth buffer. With this method, obscured (or hidden) portions of surfaces aren't necessarily drawn and therefore aren't used for blending.

If you want to render both opaque and translucent objects in the same scene, then you want to use the depth buffer to perform hidden-surface removal for any objects that lie behind the opaque objects. If an opaque object hides either a translucent object or another opaque object, you want the depth buffer to eliminate the more distant object. If the translucent object is closer, however, you want to blend it with the opaque object. You can generally figure out the correct order in which to draw the polygons if everything in the scene is stationary, but the problem can quickly become too hard if either the viewpoint or the object is moving.

The solution is to enable depth buffering but make the depth buffer read-only while drawing the translucent objects. First you draw all the opaque objects, with the depth buffer in normal operation. Then you preserve these depth values by making the depth buffer read-only. When the translucent objects are drawn, their depth values are still compared with the values established by the opaque objects, so they aren't drawn if they're behind the opaque ones. If they're closer to the viewpoint, however, they don't eliminate the opaque objects, since the depth-buffer values can't change. Instead, they're blended with the opaque objects. To control whether the depth buffer is writable, use **glDepthMask()**; if you pass GL_FALSE as the argument, the buffer becomes read-only, whereas GL_TRUE restores the normal, writable operation.

Example 6-3 demonstrates how to use this method to draw opaque and translucent three-dimensional objects. In the program, typing 'a' triggers an animation sequence in which a translucent cube moves through an opaque sphere. Pressing the 'r' key resets the objects in the scene to their initial positions. To get the best results when transparent objects overlap, draw the objects from back to front.

Example 6-3   Three-Dimensional Blending: alpha3D.c

```
#define MAXZ 8.0
#define MINZ -8.0
#define ZINC 0.4
static float solidZ = MAXZ;
static float transparentZ = MINZ;
static GLuint sphereList, cubeList;

static void init(void)
{
   GLfloat mat_specular[] = { 1.0, 1.0, 1.0, 0.15 };
   GLfloat mat_shininess[] = { 100.0 };
   GLfloat position[] = { 0.5, 0.5, 1.0, 0.0 };

   glMaterialfv(GL_FRONT, GL_SPECULAR, mat_specular);
   glMaterialfv(GL_FRONT, GL_SHININESS, mat_shininess);
   glLightfv(GL_LIGHT0, GL_POSITION, position);

   glEnable(GL_LIGHTING);
   glEnable(GL_LIGHT0);
   glEnable(GL_DEPTH_TEST);

   sphereList = glGenLists(1);
   glNewList(sphereList, GL_COMPILE);
      glutSolidSphere(0.4, 16, 16);
   glEndList();
   cubeList = glGenLists(1);
   glNewList(cubeList, GL_COMPILE);
      glutSolidCube(0.6);
   glEndList();
}
```

```c
void display(void)
{
   GLfloat mat_solid[] = { 0.75, 0.75, 0.0, 1.0 };
   GLfloat mat_zero[] = { 0.0, 0.0, 0.0, 1.0 };
   GLfloat mat_transparent[] = { 0.0, 0.8, 0.8, 0.6 };
   GLfloat mat_emission[] = { 0.0, 0.3, 0.3, 0.6 };

   glClear(GL_COLOR_BUFFER_BIT | GL_DEPTH_BUFFER_BIT);

   glPushMatrix();
      glTranslatef(-0.15, -0.15, solidZ);
      glMaterialfv(GL_FRONT, GL_EMISSION, mat_zero);
      glMaterialfv(GL_FRONT, GL_DIFFUSE, mat_solid);
      glCallList(sphereList);
   glPopMatrix();

   glPushMatrix();
      glTranslatef(0.15, 0.15, transparentZ);
      glRotatef(15.0, 1.0, 1.0, 0.0);
      glRotatef(30.0, 0.0, 1.0, 0.0);
      glMaterialfv(GL_FRONT, GL_EMISSION, mat_emission);
      glMaterialfv(GL_FRONT, GL_DIFFUSE, mat_transparent);
      glEnable(GL_BLEND);
      glDepthMask(GL_FALSE);
      glBlendFunc(GL_SRC_ALPHA, GL_ONE);
      glCallList(cubeList);
      glDepthMask(GL_TRUE);
      glDisable(GL_BLEND);
   glPopMatrix();

   glutSwapBuffers();
}

void reshape(int w, int h)
{
   glViewport(0, 0, (GLint) w, (GLint) h);
   glMatrixMode(GL_PROJECTION);
   glLoadIdentity();
   if (w <= h)
      glOrtho(-1.5, 1.5, -1.5*(GLfloat)h/(GLfloat)w,
            1.5*(GLfloat)h/(GLfloat)w, -10.0, 10.0);
   else
      glOrtho(-1.5*(GLfloat)w/(GLfloat)h,
            1.5*(GLfloat)w/(GLfloat)h, -1.5, 1.5, -10.0, 10.0);
   glMatrixMode(GL_MODELVIEW);
   glLoadIdentity();
}
```

```
void animate(void)
{
   if (solidZ <= MINZ || transparentZ >= MAXZ)
      glutIdleFunc(NULL);
   else {
      solidZ -= ZINC;
      transparentZ += ZINC;
      glutPostRedisplay();
   }
}

void keyboard(unsigned char key, int x, int y)
{
   switch (key) {
      case 'a':
      case 'A':
         solidZ = MAXZ;
         transparentZ = MINZ;
         glutIdleFunc(animate);
         break;
      case 'r':
      case 'R':
         solidZ = MAXZ;
         transparentZ = MINZ;
         glutPostRedisplay();
         break;
      case 27:
        exit(0);
   }    break;
}

int main(int argc, char** argv)
{
   glutInit(&argc, argv);
   glutInitDisplayMode(GLUT_DOUBLE | GLUT_RGB | GLUT_DEPTH);
   glutInitWindowSize(500, 500);
   glutCreateWindow(argv[0]);
   init();
   glutReshapeFunc(reshape);
   glutKeyboardFunc(keyboard);
   glutDisplayFunc(display);
   glutMainLoop();
   return 0;
}
```

Antialiasing

You might have noticed in some of your OpenGL pictures that lines, especially nearly horizontal and nearly vertical ones, appear jagged. These "jaggies" appear because the ideal line is approximated by a series of pixels that must lie on the pixel grid. The jaggedness is called *aliasing*, and this section describes antialiasing techniques for reducing it. Figure 6-2 shows two intersecting lines, both aliased and antialiased. The pictures have been magnified to show the effect.

Figure 6-2   Aliased and Antialiased Lines

Figure 6-3 shows how a diagonal line 1 pixel wide covers more of some pixel squares than others. In fact, when performing antialiasing, OpenGL calculates a *coverage* value for each fragment based on the fraction of the pixel square on the screen that it would cover. Figure 6-3 shows these coverage values for the line. In RGBA mode, OpenGL multiplies the fragment's alpha value by its coverage. You can then use the resulting alpha value to blend the fragment with the corresponding pixel already in the framebuffer. In color-index mode, OpenGL sets the least significant 4 bits of the color index based on the fragment's coverage (0000 for no coverage and 1111 for complete coverage). It's up to you to load your color map and apply it appropriately to take advantage of this coverage information.

The details of calculating coverage values are complex, are difficult to specify in general, and in fact may vary slightly depending on your particular implementation of OpenGL. You can use the **glHint()** command to exercise some control over the trade-off between image quality and speed, but not all implementations will take the hint.

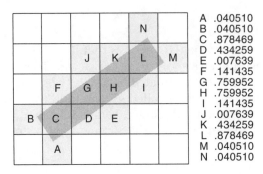

	.040510
A	.040510
B	.040510
C	.878469
D	.434259
E	.007639
F	.141435
G	.759952
H	.759952
I	.141435
J	.007639
K	.434259
L	.878469
M	.040510
N	.040510

Figure 6-3   Determining Coverage Values

<table>
<tr><td rowspan="8">

Compatibility
Extension

**GL_
PERSPECTIVE_
CORRECTION_
HINT**

GL_FOG_HINT

**GL_POINT_
SMOOTH_HINT**

**GL_GENERATE_
MIPMAP_HINT**
</td><td>

void **glHint**(GLenum *target*, GLenum *hint*);

Controls certain aspects of OpenGL behavior. The *target* parameter indicates which behavior is to be controlled; its possible values are shown in Table 6-3. The *hint* parameter can be GL_FASTEST to indicate that the most efficient option should be chosen, GL_NICEST to indicate the highest-quality option, or GL_DONT_CARE to indicate no preference. The interpretation of hints is implementation-dependent; an OpenGL implementation can ignore them entirely. (For more information about the relevant topics, see this section for details about sampling and "Fog" for details about fog.)

The GL_PERSPECTIVE_CORRECTION_HINT target parameter refers to how color values and texture coordinates are interpolated across a primitive: either linearly in screen space (a relatively simple calculation) or in a perspective-correct manner (which requires more computation). Often, systems perform linear color interpolation because the results, while not technically correct, are visually acceptable; however, in most cases, textures require perspective-correct interpolation to be visually acceptable. Thus, an OpenGL implementation can choose to use this parameter to control the method used for interpolation. (See Chapter 3 for a discussion of perspective projection, Chapter 4 for a discussion of color, and Chapter 9 for a discussion of texture mapping.)
</td></tr>
</table>

Parameter	Specifies
GL_POINT_SMOOTH_HINT, GL_LINE_SMOOTH_HINT, GL_POLYGON_SMOOTH_HINT	sampling quality of points, lines, or polygons during antialiasing operations
GL_FOG_HINT	whether fog calculations are done per pixel (GL_NICEST) or per vertex (GL_FASTEST)
GL_PERSPECTIVE_CORRECTION_HINT	quality of color and texture-coordinate interpolation
GL_GENERATE_MIPMAP_HINT	quality and performance of automatic mipmap level generation
GL_TEXTURE_COMPRESSION_HINT	quality and performance of compressing texture images
GL_FRAGMENT_SHADER_DERIVATIVE_HINT	derivative accuracy for fragment processing for built-in GLSL shader functions dFdx, dFdy, and fwidth

Table 6-3   Values for Use with glHint()

Antialiasing Points or Lines

One way to antialias points or lines is to turn on antialiasing with **glEnable()**, passing in GL_POINT_SMOOTH or GL_LINE_SMOOTH, as appropriate. You might also want to provide a quality hint with **glHint()**. (Remember that you can set the size of a point or the width of a line. You can also stipple a line. See "Line Details" in Chapter 2.) Then follow the procedures described in one of the following sections, depending on whether you're in RGBA or color-index mode.

Another way to antialias points or lines is to use multisampling, as described in "Antialiasing Geometric Primitives with Multisampling."

Antialiasing in RGBA Mode

In RGBA mode, you need to enable blending. The blending factors you most likely want to use are GL_SRC_ALPHA (source) and GL_ONE_MINUS_SRC_ALPHA (destination). Alternatively, you can use GL_ONE for the destination factor to make lines a little brighter where they intersect. Now you're ready to draw whatever points or lines you want antialiased. The antialiased effect is most noticeable if you use a fairly high alpha value. Remember that since you're performing blending, you might need to consider the rendering order as described in "Three-Dimensional Blending with the Depth Buffer." However, in most cases, the ordering can be ignored without significant adverse effects. Example 6-4 initializes the necessary modes for antialiasing and then draws two intersecting diagonal lines. When you run this program, press the 'r' key to rotate the lines so that you can see the effect of antialiasing on lines of different slopes. Note that the depth buffer isn't enabled in this example.

Example 6-4   Antialiased Lines: aargb.c

```
static float rotAngle = 0.;

/*  Initialize antialiasing for RGBA mode, including alpha
 *  blending, hint, and line width.  Print out implementation-
 *  specific info on line width granularity and width.
 */
void init(void)
{
   GLfloat values[2];
   glGetFloatv(GL_LINE_WIDTH_GRANULARITY, values);
   printf("GL_LINE_WIDTH_GRANULARITY value is %3.1f\n",
      values[0]);
   glGetFloatv(GL_LINE_WIDTH_RANGE, values);
   printf("GL_LINE_WIDTH_RANGE values are %3.1f %3.1f\n",
      values[0], values[1]);

   glEnable(GL_LINE_SMOOTH);
   glEnable(GL_BLEND);
   glBlendFunc(GL_SRC_ALPHA, GL_ONE_MINUS_SRC_ALPHA);
   glHint(GL_LINE_SMOOTH_HINT, GL_DONT_CARE);
   glLineWidth(1.5);

   glClearColor(0.0, 0.0, 0.0, 0.0);
}

/* Draw 2 diagonal lines to form an X */
void display(void)
{
   glClear(GL_COLOR_BUFFER_BIT);

   glColor3f(0.0, 1.0, 0.0);
   glPushMatrix();
   glRotatef(-rotAngle, 0.0, 0.0, 0.1);
```

```
   glBegin(GL_LINES);
      glVertex2f(-0.5, 0.5);
      glVertex2f(0.5, -0.5);
   glEnd();
   glPopMatrix();

   glColor3f(0.0, 0.0, 1.0);
   glPushMatrix();
   glRotatef(rotAngle, 0.0, 0.0, 0.1);
   glBegin(GL_LINES);
      glVertex2f(0.5, 0.5);
      glVertex2f(-0.5, -0.5);
   glEnd();
   glPopMatrix();

   glFlush();
}

void reshape(int w, int h)
{
   glViewport(0, 0, (GLint) w, (GLint) h);
   glMatrixMode(GL_PROJECTION);
   glLoadIdentity();
   if (w <= h)
      gluOrtho2D(-1.0, 1.0,
         -1.0*(GLfloat)h/(GLfloat)w, 1.0*(GLfloat)h/(GLfloat)w);
   else
      gluOrtho2D(-1.0*(GLfloat)w/(GLfloat)h,
         1.0*(GLfloat)w/(GLfloat)h, -1.0, 1.0);
   glMatrixMode(GL_MODELVIEW);
   glLoadIdentity();
}

void keyboard(unsigned char key, int x, int y)
{
   switch (key) {
      case 'r':
      case 'R':
         rotAngle += 20.;
         if (rotAngle >= 360.) rotAngle = 0.;
         glutPostRedisplay();
         break;
      case 27:  /*  Escape Key  */
         exit(0);
         break;
      default:
         break;
```

```
    }
}

int main(int argc, char** argv)
{
    glutInit(&argc, argv);
    glutInitDisplayMode(GLUT_SINGLE | GLUT_RGB);
    glutInitWindowSize(200, 200);
    glutCreateWindow(argv[0]);
    init();
    glutReshapeFunc(reshape);
    glutKeyboardFunc(keyboard);
    glutDisplayFunc(display);
    glutMainLoop();
    return 0;
}
```

Antialiasing in Color-Index Mode

The tricky part about antialiasing in color-index mode is loading and using
the color map. Since the last 4 bits of the color index indicate the coverage
value, you need to load 16 contiguous indices with a color ramp from the
background color to the object's color. (The ramp has to start with an index
value that's a multiple of 16.) Then you clear the color buffer to the first of
the 16 colors in the ramp and draw your points or lines using colors in the
ramp. Example 6-5 demonstrates how to construct the color ramp to draw
antialiased lines in color-index mode. In this example, two color ramps
are created: One contains shades of green and the other shades of blue.

Example 6-5   Antialiasing in Color-Index Mode: aaindex.c

```
#define RAMPSIZE 16
#define RAMP1START 32
#define RAMP2START 48

static float rotAngle = 0.;

/*  Initialize antialiasing for color-index mode,
 *  including loading a green color ramp starting
 *  at RAMP1START and a blue color ramp starting
 *  at RAMP2START. The ramps must be a multiple of 16.
 */
```

```
void init(void)
{
    int i;

    for (i = 0; i < RAMPSIZE; i++) {
        GLfloat shade;
        shade = (GLfloat) i/(GLfloat) RAMPSIZE;
        glutSetColor(RAMP1START+(GLint)i, 0., shade, 0.);
        glutSetColor(RAMP2START+(GLint)i, 0., 0., shade);
    }
    glEnable(GL_LINE_SMOOTH);
    glHint(GL_LINE_SMOOTH_HINT, GL_DONT_CARE);
    glLineWidth(1.5);

    glClearIndex((GLfloat) RAMP1START);
}
/*  Draw 2 diagonal lines to form an X */
void display(void)
{
    glClear(GL_COLOR_BUFFER_BIT);

    glIndexi(RAMP1START);
    glPushMatrix();
    glRotatef(-rotAngle, 0.0, 0.0, 0.1);
    glBegin(GL_LINES);
        glVertex2f(-0.5, 0.5);
        glVertex2f(0.5, -0.5);
    glEnd();
    glPopMatrix();

    glIndexi(RAMP2START);
    glPushMatrix();
    glRotatef(rotAngle, 0.0, 0.0, 0.1);
    glBegin(GL_LINES);
        glVertex2f(0.5, 0.5);
        glVertex2f(-0.5, -0.5);
    glEnd();
    glPopMatrix();

    glFlush();
}

void reshape(int w, int h)
{
    glViewport(0, 0, (GLsizei) w, (GLsizei) h);
    glMatrixMode(GL_PROJECTION);
    glLoadIdentity();
```

```
    if (w <= h)
        gluOrtho2D(-1.0, 1.0,
            -1.0*(GLfloat)h/(GLfloat)w, 1.0*(GLfloat)h/(GLfloat)w);
    else
        gluOrtho2D(-1.0*(GLfloat)w/(GLfloat)h,
            1.0*(GLfloat)w/(GLfloat)h, -1.0, 1.0);
    glMatrixMode(GL_MODELVIEW);
    glLoadIdentity();
}

void keyboard(unsigned char key, int x, int y)
{
    switch (key) {
        case 'r':
        case 'R':
            rotAngle += 20.;
            if (rotAngle >= 360.) rotAngle = 0.;
            glutPostRedisplay();
            break;
        case 27:  /*  Escape Key */
            exit(0);
            break;
        default:
            break;
    }
}

int main(int argc, char** argv)
{
    glutInit(&argc, argv);
    glutInitDisplayMode(GLUT_SINGLE | GLUT_INDEX);
    glutInitWindowSize(200, 200);
    glutCreateWindow(argv[0]);
    init();
    glutReshapeFunc(reshape);
    glutKeyboardFunc(keyboard);
    glutDisplayFunc(display);
    glutMainLoop();
    return 0;
}
```

Since the color ramp goes from the background color to the object's color, the antialiased lines look correct only in the areas where they are drawn on top of the background. When the blue line is drawn, it erases part of the green line at the point where the lines intersect. To fix this, you would need to redraw the area where the lines intersect using a ramp that goes from green (the color of the line in the framebuffer) to blue (the color of the line being drawn). However, this requires additional calculations, and it is usually not worth the effort since the intersection area is small. Note that this is not a problem in RGBA mode, since the colors of objects being drawn are blended with the color already in the framebuffer.

You may also want to enable the depth test when drawing antialiased points and lines in color-index mode. In this example, the depth test is disabled since both of the lines lie in the same z-plane. However, if you want to draw a three-dimensional scene, you should enable the depth buffer so that the resulting pixel colors correspond to the "nearest" objects.

The trick described in "Three-Dimensional Blending with the Depth Buffer" can also be used to mix antialiased points and lines with aliased, depth-buffered polygons. To do this, draw the polygons first, then make the depth buffer read-only and draw the points and lines. The points and lines intersect nicely with each other but will be obscured by nearer polygons.

Try This

Take a previous program, such as the robot arm or solar system examples described in "Examples of Composing Several Transformations" in Chapter 3, and draw wireframe objects with antialiasing. Try it in either RGBA or color-index mode. Also try different line widths and point sizes to see their effects.

Try This

Antialiasing Geometric Primitives with Multisampling

Multisampling is a technique that uses additional color, depth, and stencil information (samples) to antialias OpenGL primitives: points, lines, polygons, bitmaps, and images. Each fragment, instead of having a single color, single depth, and single set of texture coordinates, has multiple colors, depths, and texture coordinate sets, based upon the number of subpixel samples. Calculations aren't at the dead center of each pixel (as they typically are when you have one sample), but are dispersed at several sample locations. Instead of using alpha values to represent how much a primitive covers a pixel, antialiasing coverage values are calculated from the samples saved in a multisample buffer.

Multisampling is especially good for antialiasing the edges of polygons, because sorting isn't needed. (If you are using alpha values to antialias polygons, the order in which translucent objects are drawn affects the color of the results.) Multisampling takes care of traditionally difficult cases, such as intersecting or adjacent polygons.

Multisampling is trivial to add to an application. Just follow these three steps:

1. Obtain a window that supports multisampling. With GLUT, you can ask for one by calling

```
glutInitDisplayMode(GLUT_DOUBLE | GLUT_RGB |
    GLUT_MULTISAMPLE);
```

2. After you've opened a window, you will need to verify that multisampling is available. For instance, GLUT may give you a window with "almost" what you have asked for. If querying the state variable GL_SAMPLE_BUFFERS returns a value of one and GL_SAMPLES returns a value greater than one, then you'll be able to use multisampling. (GL_SAMPLES returns the number of subpixel samples. If there is only one sample, multisampling is effectively disabled.)

```
GLint bufs, samples;
glGetIntegerv(GL_SAMPLE_BUFFERS, &bufs);
glGetIntegerv(GL_SAMPLES, &samples);
```

3. To turn on multisampling, call

```
glEnable(GL_MULTISAMPLE);
```

Example 6-6 displays two sets of primitives side-by-side so that you can see the difference that multisampling makes. **init()** checks the multisampling state variables and then two display lists are compiled: one list with a "pinwheel" of lines of different widths and triangles (filled polygons) and the other with a checkerboard background. In **display()**, the pinwheel is drawn both with multisampling (on the left) and without (right). You should compare the aliasing of the two objects. A contrasting background sometimes accentuates aliasing, and other times it may obscure it. You can press the 'b' key to redraw the scene with or without the checkerboard background.

Example 6-6   Enabling Multisampling: multisamp.c

```
static int bgtoggle = 1;

/*
 *  Print out state values related to multisampling.
 *  Create display list with "pinwheel" of lines and
 *  triangles.
 */
void init(void)
{
```

```
    GLint buf, sbuf;
    int i, j;

    glClearColor(0.0, 0.0, 0.0, 0.0);
    glGetIntegerv(GL_SAMPLE_BUFFERS, &buf);
    printf("number of sample buffers is %d\n", buf);
    glGetIntegerv(GL_SAMPLES, &sbuf);
    printf("number of samples is %d\n", sbuf);

    glNewList(1, GL_COMPILE);
    for (i = 0; i < 19; i++) {
        glPushMatrix();
        glRotatef(360.0*(float)i/19.0, 0.0, 0.0, 1.0);
        glColor3f (1.0, 1.0, 1.0);
        glLineWidth((i%3)+1.0);
        glBegin(GL_LINES);
            glVertex2f(0.25, 0.05);
            glVertex2f(0.9, 0.2);
        glEnd();
        glColor3f(0.0, 1.0, 1.0);
        glBegin(GL_TRIANGLES);
            glVertex2f(0.25, 0.0);
            glVertex2f(0.9, 0.0);
            glVertex2f(0.875, 0.10);
        glEnd();
        glPopMatrix();
    }
    glEndList();

    glNewList(2, GL_COMPILE);
    glColor3f(1.0, 0.5, 0.0);
    glBegin(GL_QUADS);
    for (i = 0; i < 16; i++) {
        for (j = 0; j < 16; j++) {
            if (((i + j) % 2) == 0) {
                glVertex2f(-2.0 + (i * 0.25), -2.0 + (j * 0.25));
                glVertex2f(-2.0 + (i * 0.25), -1.75 + (j * 0.25));
                glVertex2f(-1.75 + (i * 0.25), -1.75 + (j * 0.25));
                glVertex2f(-1.75 + (i * 0.25), -2.0 + (j * 0.25));
            }
        }
    }
    glEnd();
    glEndList();
}
```

```
/*  Draw two sets of primitives so that you can
 *  compare the user of multisampling against its absence.
 *
 *  This code enables antialiasing and draws one display list,
 *  and then it disables and draws the other display list.
 */
void display(void)
{
   glClear(GL_COLOR_BUFFER_BIT);

   if (bgtoggle)
      glCallList(2);

   glEnable(GL_MULTISAMPLE);
   glPushMatrix();
   glTranslatef(-1.0, 0.0, 0.0);
   glCallList(1);
   glPopMatrix();

   glDisable(GL_MULTISAMPLE);
   glPushMatrix();
   glTranslatef(1.0, 0.0, 0.0);
   glCallList(1);
   glPopMatrix();
   glutSwapBuffers();
}


void keyboard(unsigned char key, int x, int y)
{
   switch (key) {
      case 'b':
      case 'B':
         bgtoggle = !bgtoggle;
         glutPostRedisplay();
         break;
      case 27:  /*  Escape Key  */
         exit(0);
         break;
      default:
         break;
   }

}
```

With a standard implementation, you can't fine-tune multisampling. You can't change the number of samples or specify (or even query) the subpixel sample locations.

If multisampling is enabled and there's also a multisample buffer, then points, lines, and polygons generate fragments that are intended for antialiasing. For example, a large-sized point primitive is rounded, not square, whether GL_POINT_SMOOTH has been enabled or disabled. The states of GL_LINE_SMOOTH and GL_POLYGON_SMOOTH are similarly ignored. Other primitive attributes, such as point size and line width, are supported during multisampling.

Alpha and Multisampling Coverage

By default, multisampling calculates fragment coverage values that are independent of alpha. However, if you enable one of the following special modes, then a fragment's alpha value is taken into consideration when calculating the coverage. The special modes are as follows:

- GL_SAMPLE_ALPHA_TO_COVERAGE uses the alpha value of the fragment to compute the final coverage value.

- GL_SAMPLE_ALPHA_TO_ONE sets the fragment's alpha value to one, the maximum alpha value, and then uses that value in the coverage calculation.

- GL_SAMPLE_COVERAGE uses the value set with the **glSampleCoverage()** routine, which is combined (ANDed) with the calculated coverage value. Additionally, this mode can be inverted by setting the *invert* flag with the **glSampleCoverage()** routine.

---

void **glSampleCoverage**(GLclampf *value*, GLboolean *invert*);

Sets parameters to be used to interpret alpha values while computing multisampling coverage. *value* is a temporary coverage value that is used if GL_SAMPLE_COVERAGE or GL_SAMPLE_ALPHA_TO_COVERAGE has been enabled. *invert* is a Boolean that indicates whether the temporary coverage value ought to be bitwise inverted before it is used (ANDed) with the fragment coverage.

Antialiasing Polygons

Antialiasing the edges of filled polygons is similar to antialiasing points and lines. When different polygons have overlapping edges, you need to blend the color values appropriately. You can use the method described in this section, or you can use the accumulation buffer to perform antialiasing for your entire scene. Using the accumulation buffer, which is described in

Chapter 10, is easier from your point of view, but it's much more computation-intensive and therefore slower. However, as you'll see, the method described here is rather cumbersome.

Note: If you draw your polygons as points at the vertices or as outlines— that is, by passing GL_POINT or GL_LINE to **glPolygonMode()**— point or line antialiasing is applied, if enabled as described earlier. The rest of this section addresses polygon antialiasing when you're using GL_FILL as the polygon mode.

In theory, you can antialias polygons in either RGBA or color-index mode. However, object intersections affect polygon antialiasing more than they affect point or line antialiasing, so rendering order and blending accuracy become more critical. In fact, they're so critical that if you're antialiasing more than one polygon, you need to order the polygons from front to back, and then use **glBlendFunc()** with GL_SRC_ALPHA_SATURATE for the source factor and GL_ONE for the destination factor. Thus, antialiasing polygons in color-index mode normally isn't practical.

To antialias polygons in RGBA mode, you use the alpha value to represent coverage values of polygon edges. You need to enable polygon antialiasing by passing GL_POLYGON_SMOOTH to **glEnable()**. This causes pixels on the edges of the polygon to be assigned fractional alpha values based on their coverage, as though they were lines being antialiased. Also, if you desire, you can supply a value for GL_POLYGON_SMOOTH_HINT.

Now you need to blend overlapping edges appropriately. First, turn off the depth buffer so that you have control over how overlapping pixels are drawn. Then set the blending factors to GL_SRC_ALPHA_SATURATE (source) and GL_ONE (destination). With this specialized blending function, the final color is the sum of the destination color and the scaled source color; the scale factor is the smaller of either the incoming source alpha value or 1 minus the destination alpha value. This means that for a pixel with a large alpha value, successive incoming pixels have little effect on the final color because 1 minus the destination alpha is almost zero. With this method, a pixel on the edge of a polygon might be blended eventually with the colors from another polygon that's drawn later. Finally, you need to sort all the polygons in your scene so that they're ordered from front to back before drawing them.

Fog

Computer images sometimes seem unrealistically sharp and well defined. Antialiasing makes an object appear more realistic by smoothing its edges.

Additionally, you can make an entire image appear more natural by adding *fog*, which makes objects fade into the distance. "Fog" is a general term that describes similar forms of atmospheric effects; it can be used to simulate haze, mist, smoke, or pollution (see Plate 9). Fog is essential in visual-simulation applications, where limited visibility needs to be approximated. It's often incorporated into flight-simulator displays.

When fog is enabled, objects that are farther from the viewpoint begin to fade into the fog color. You can control the density of the fog, which determines the rate at which objects fade as the distance increases, as well as the fog's color. You can also explicitly specify a fog coordinate per-vertex for fog distance calculations, rather than use an automatically calculated depth value.

Fog is available in both RGBA and color-index modes, although the calculations are slightly different in the two modes. Since fog is applied after matrix transformations, lighting, and texturing are performed, it affects transformed, lit, and textured objects. Note that with large simulation programs, fog can improve performance, since you can choose not to draw objects that would be too fogged to be visible.

All types of geometric primitives can be fogged, including points and lines. Using the fog effect on points and lines is also called *depth-cuing* (as shown in Plate 2) and is popular in molecular modeling and other applications.

Using Fog

Using fog is easy. You enable it by passing GL_FOG to **glEnable()**, and you choose the color and the equation that controls the density with **glFog*()**. If you want, you can supply a value for GL_FOG_HINT with **glHint()**, as described in Table 6-3. Example 6-7 draws five red spheres, each at a different distance from the viewpoint. Pressing the 'f' key selects among the three different fog equations, which are described in the next section.

Example 6-7   Five Fogged Spheres in RGBA Mode: fog.c

```
static GLint fogMode;

static void init(void)
{
   GLfloat position[] = { 0.5, 0.5, 3.0, 0.0 };

   glEnable(GL_DEPTH_TEST);

   glLightfv(GL_LIGHT0, GL_POSITION, position);
```

```
glEnable(GL_LIGHTING);
glEnable(GL_LIGHT0);
{
    GLfloat mat[3] = {0.1745, 0.01175, 0.01175};
    glMaterialfv(GL_FRONT, GL_AMBIENT, mat);
    mat[0] = 0.61424; mat[1] = 0.04136; mat[2] = 0.04136;
    glMaterialfv(GL_FRONT, GL_DIFFUSE, mat);
    mat[0] = 0.727811; mat[1] = 0.626959; mat[2] = 0.626959;
    glMaterialfv(GL_FRONT, GL_SPECULAR, mat);
    glMaterialf(GL_FRONT, GL_SHININESS, 0.6*128.0);
}

glEnable(GL_FOG);
{
    GLfloat fogColor[4] = {0.5, 0.5, 0.5, 1.0};

    fogMode = GL_EXP;
    glFogi(GL_FOG_MODE, fogMode);
    glFogfv(GL_FOG_COLOR, fogColor);
    glFogf(GL_FOG_DENSITY, 0.35);
    glHint(GL_FOG_HINT, GL_DONT_CARE);
    glFogf(GL_FOG_START, 1.0);
    glFogf(GL_FOG_END, 5.0);
}
glClearColor(0.5, 0.5, 0.5, 1.0);  /* fog color */
}

static void renderSphere(GLfloat x, GLfloat y, GLfloat z)
{
    glPushMatrix();
    glTranslatef(x, y, z);
    glutSolidSphere(0.4, 16, 16);
    glPopMatrix();
}

/* display() draws 5 spheres at different z positions.
 */
void display(void)
{
    glClear(GL_COLOR_BUFFER_BIT | GL_DEPTH_BUFFER_BIT);
    renderSphere(-2., -0.5, -1.0);
    renderSphere(-1., -0.5, -2.0);
    renderSphere(0., -0.5, -3.0);
    renderSphere(1., -0.5, -4.0);
    renderSphere(2., -0.5, -5.0);
    glFlush();
}
```

```
void reshape(int w, int h)
{
    glViewport(0, 0, (GLsizei) w, (GLsizei) h);
    glMatrixMode(GL_PROJECTION);
    glLoadIdentity();
    if (w <= h)
        glOrtho(-2.5, 2.5, -2.5*(GLfloat)h/(GLfloat)w,
            2.5*(GLfloat)h/(GLfloat)w, -10.0, 10.0);
    else
        glOrtho(-2.5*(GLfloat)w/(GLfloat)h,
            2.5*(GLfloat)w/(GLfloat)h, -2.5, 2.5, -10.0, 10.0);
    glMatrixMode(GL_MODELVIEW);
    glLoadIdentity();
}

void keyboard(unsigned char key, int x, int y)
{
    switch (key) {
        case 'f':
        case 'F':
            if (fogMode == GL_EXP) {
                fogMode = GL_EXP2;
                printf("Fog mode is GL_EXP2\n");
            }
            else if (fogMode == GL_EXP2) {
                fogMode = GL_LINEAR;
                printf("Fog mode is GL_LINEAR\n");
            }
            else if (fogMode == GL_LINEAR) {
                fogMode = GL_EXP;
                printf("Fog mode is GL_EXP\n");
            }
            glFogi(GL_FOG_MODE, fogMode);
            glutPostRedisplay();
            break;
        case 27:
            exit(0);
            break;
        default:
            break;
    }
}

int main(int argc, char** argv)
{
    glutInit(&argc, argv);
    glutInitDisplayMode(GLUT_SINGLE | GLUT_RGB | GLUT_DEPTH);
```

```
glutInitWindowSize(500, 500);
glutCreateWindow(argv[0]);
init();
glutReshapeFunc(reshape);
glutKeyboardFunc(keyboard);
glutDisplayFunc(display);
glutMainLoop();
return 0;
}
```

Fog Equations

Fog blends a fog color with an incoming fragment's color using a fog blending factor. This factor, f, is computed with one of these three equations and then clamped to the range [0, 1]:

$$f = e^{-(density \cdot z)} \quad (GL\_EXP)$$

$$f = e^{-(density \cdot z)^2} \quad (GL\_EXP2)$$

$$f = \frac{end - z}{end - start} \quad (GL\_LINEAR)$$

In these three equations, z is the eye-coordinate distance between the viewpoint and the fragment center. You may have added control over the z eye-coordinate distance with per-vertex fog coordinates, which is described in "Fog Coordinates." The values for *density, start*, and *end* are all specified with **glFog*()**. The f factor is used differently, depending on whether you're in RGBA mode or color-index mode, as explained in the following subsections.

Compatibility
Extension

glFog and all
tokens accepted
by it, and **GL_FOG**

void **glFog**{if}(GLenum *pname, TYPE param*);
void **glFog**{if}**v**(GLenum *pname*, const *TYPE *params*);

Sets the parameters and function for calculating fog. If *pname* is GL_FOG_MODE, then *param* is GL_EXP (the default), GL_EXP2, or GL_LINEAR to select one of the three fog factors. If *pname* is GL_FOG_DENSITY, GL_FOG_START, or GL_FOG_END, then *param* is (or points to, with the vector version of the command) a value for *density, start*, or *end* in the equations. (The default values are 1, 0, and 1, respectively.) In RGBA mode, *pname* can be GL_FOG_COLOR, in which case *params* points to four values that specify the fog's RGBA color values. The corresponding value for *pname* in color-index mode is GL_FOG_INDEX, for which *param* is a single value specifying the fog's color index.

Figure 6-4 plots the fog-density equations for various values of the parameters.

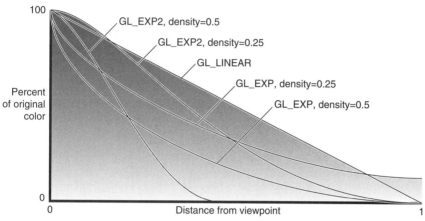

Figure 6-4   Fog-Density Equations

Fog in RGBA Mode

In RGBA mode, the fog factor f is used as follows to calculate the final fogged color:

$$C = f\,C_i + (1 - f)\,C_f$$

where C_i represents the incoming fragment's RGBA values and C_f the fog-color values assigned with GL_FOG_COLOR.

Fog in Color-Index Mode

In color-index mode, the final fogged color index is computed as follows:

$$I = I_i + (1 - f)\,I_f$$

where I_i is the incoming fragment's color index and I_f is the fog's color index as specified with GL_FOG_INDEX.

To use fog in color-index mode, you have to load appropriate values in a color ramp. The first color in the ramp is the color of the object without fog, and the last color in the ramp is the color of the completely fogged object. You probably want to use **glClearIndex()** to initialize the background color index so that it corresponds to the last color in the ramp; this way, totally fogged objects blend into the background. Similarly, before objects are drawn, you should call **glIndex*()** and pass in the index of the first color in the ramp (the unfogged color). Finally, to apply fog to different colored objects in the scene, you need to create several color ramps and call **glIndex*()** before each object is drawn to set the current color index to the start of each color ramp. Example 6-8 illustrates how to initialize appropriate conditions and then apply fog in color-index mode.

Example 6-8   Fog in Color-Index Mode: fogindex.c

```
/*  Initialize color map and fog.  Set screen clear color
 *  to end of color ramp.
 */
#define NUMCOLORS 32
#define RAMPSTART 16

static void init(void)
{
   int i;

   glEnable(GL_DEPTH_TEST);

   for (i = 0; i < NUMCOLORS; i++) {
      GLfloat shade;
      shade = (GLfloat) (NUMCOLORS-i)/(GLfloat) NUMCOLORS;
      glutSetColor(RAMPSTART + i, shade, shade, shade);
   }
   glEnable(GL_FOG);

   glFogi(GL_FOG_MODE, GL_LINEAR);
   glFogi(GL_FOG_INDEX, NUMCOLORS);
   glFogf(GL_FOG_START, 1.0);
   glFogf(GL_FOG_END, 6.0);
   glHint(GL_FOG_HINT, GL_NICEST);
   glClearIndex((GLfloat) (NUMCOLORS+RAMPSTART-1));
}

static void renderSphere(GLfloat x, GLfloat y, GLfloat z)
{
   glPushMatrix();
   glTranslatef(x, y, z);
   glutWireSphere(0.4, 16, 16);
   glPopMatrix();
}
```

```
/*  display() draws 5 spheres at different z positions.
 */
void display(void)
{
   glClear(GL_COLOR_BUFFER_BIT | GL_DEPTH_BUFFER_BIT);
   glIndexi(RAMPSTART);

   renderSphere(-2., -0.5, -1.0);
   renderSphere(-1., -0.5, -2.0);
   renderSphere(0., -0.5, -3.0);
   renderSphere(1., -0.5, -4.0);
   renderSphere(2., -0.5, -5.0);

   glFlush();
}

void reshape(int w, int h)
{
   glViewport(0, 0, w, h);
   glMatrixMode(GL_PROJECTION);
   glLoadIdentity();
   if (w <= h)
      glOrtho(-2.5, 2.5, -2.5*(GLfloat)h/(GLfloat)w,
         2.5*(GLfloat)h/(GLfloat)w, -10.0, 10.0);
   else
      glOrtho(-2.5*(GLfloat)w/(GLfloat)h,
         2.5*(GLfloat)w/(GLfloat)h, -2.5, 2.5, -10.0, 10.0);
   glMatrixMode(GL_MODELVIEW);
   glLoadIdentity();
}

void keyboard(unsigned char key, int x, int y)
{

   switch (key) {
      case 27:
         exit(0);
   }
}

int main(int argc, char** argv)
{
   glutInit(&argc, argv);
   glutInitDisplayMode(GLUT_SINGLE | GLUT_INDEX | GLUT_DEPTH);
   glutInitWindowSize(500, 500);
   glutCreateWindow(argv[0]);
```

```
    init();
    glutReshapeFunc(reshape);
    glutKeyboardFunc(keyboard);
    glutDisplayFunc(display);
    glutMainLoop();
    return 0;
}
```

Fog Coordinates

As discussed earlier, the fog equations use a fog coordinate, *z*, to calculate a color value:

$$f = e^{-(density \cdot z)} \quad (GL\_EXP)$$
$$f = e^{-(density \cdot z)^2} \quad (GL\_EXP2)$$
$$f = \frac{end - z}{end - start} \quad (GL\_LINEAR)$$

By default, *z* is automatically calculated as the distance from the eye to a fragment, but you may want greater control over how fog is calculated. You may want to simulate a fog equation other than those offered by OpenGL. For example, you might want a flight simulation with "ground-based" fog, so you'll use denser fog closer to sea level.

In OpenGL Version 1.4, you can explicitly specify values for *z* on a per-vertex basis by calling **glFog(GL_FOG_COORD_SRC, GL_FOG_COORD)**. In explicit fog coordinate mode, you may specify the fog coordinate at each vertex with **glFogCoord*()**.

Compatibility Extension
glFogCoord

void **glFogCoord**{fd}(*TYPE z*);
void **glFogCoord**{fd}**v**(const *TYPE *z*);

Sets the current fog coordinate to *z*. If GL_FOG_COORD is the current fog coordinate source, the current fog coordinate is used by the current fog equation (GL_LINEAR, GL_EXP, or GL_EXP2) to calculate fog.

Values of *z* should be positive, representing eye-coordinate distance. You should avoid using negative values for fog coordinates, because the calculations may result in strange colors.

Within a geometric primitive, the fog coordinates may be interpolated for each fragment.

The sample program in Example 6-9 renders a triangle and allows you to change the fog coordinate at each vertex by pressing several numerical keys. While in explicit fog coordinate mode, moving the viewpoint forward and backward (pressing the 'f' and 'b' keys) does not transform the fog coordinates and therefore does not affect the colors of the vertices. If you stop using explicit fog coordinates (pressing the 'c' key), moving the viewpoint once again dramatically affects colors calculated for fog.

Example 6-9   Fog Coordinates: fogcoord.c

```
static GLfloat f1, f2, f3;

/*  Initialize fog
 */
static void init(void)
{
   GLfloat fogColor[4] = {0.0, 0.25, 0.25, 1.0};
   f1 = 1.0f;
   f2 = 5.0f;
   f3 = 10.0f;

   glEnable(GL_FOG);
   glFogi (GL_FOG_MODE, GL_EXP);
   glFogfv (GL_FOG_COLOR, fogColor);
   glFogf (GL_FOG_DENSITY, 0.25);
   glHint (GL_FOG_HINT, GL_DONT_CARE);
   glFogi(GL_FOG_COORD_SRC, GL_FOG_COORD);
   glClearColor(0.0, 0.25, 0.25, 1.0);  /* fog color */
}
   /* display() draws a triangle at an angle.
 */
void display(void)
{
   glClear(GL_COLOR_BUFFER_BIT);

   glColor3f(1.0f, 0.75f, 0.0f);
   glBegin(GL_TRIANGLES);
   glFogCoordf(f1);
   glVertex3f(2.0f, -2.0f, 0.0f);
   glFogCoordf(f2);
   glVertex3f(-2.0f, 0.0f, -5.0f);
   glFogCoordf(f3);
   glVertex3f(0.0f, 2.0f, -10.0f);
   glEnd();
```

```
            glutSwapBuffers();
}

void keyboard(unsigned char key, int x, int y)
{
    switch (key) {
        case 'c':
            glFogi(GL_FOG_COORD_SRC, GL_FRAGMENT_DEPTH);
            glutPostRedisplay();
            break;
        case 'C':
            glFogi(GL_FOG_COORD_SRC, GL_FOG_COORD);
            glutPostRedisplay();
            break;
        case '1':
            f1 = f1 + 0.25;
            glutPostRedisplay();
            break;
        case '2':
            f2 = f2 + 0.25;
            glutPostRedisplay();
            break;
        case '3':
            f3 = f3 + 0.25;
            glutPostRedisplay();
            break;
        case '8':
            if (f1 > 0.25) {
                f1 = f1 - 0.25;
                glutPostRedisplay();
            }
            break;
        case '9':
            if (f2 > 0.25) {
                f2 = f2 - 0.25;
                glutPostRedisplay();
            }
            break;
        case '0':
            if (f3 > 0.25) {
                f3 = f3 - 0.25;
                glutPostRedisplay();
            }
            break;
        case 'b':
```

```
        glMatrixMode(GL_MODELVIEW);
        glTranslatef(0.0, 0.0, -0.25);
        glutPostRedisplay();
        break;
    case 'f':
        glMatrixMode(GL_MODELVIEW);
        glTranslatef(0.0, 0.0, 0.25);
        glutPostRedisplay();
        break;
    case 27:
        exit(0);
        break;
    default:
        break;
    }
}
```

Point Parameters

In some situations, you may want to render objects that resemble small circles or spheres, but you don't want to use inefficient, multisided polygonal models. For example, in a flight-simulation application, you may want to model runway landing lights—so as an aircraft approaches a runway, the landing lights appear larger and possibly also brighter. Or, when rendering liquid droplets (such as rain or, for you videogamers, splattered blood), you want to simulate the phenomena using a particle system.

The landing lights or drops of liquid may be rendered as point primitives, but the points may need to be able to change apparent size and brightness. Using **glPointSize()** and **glEnable**(GL_POINT_SMOOTH) to make larger, rounded points is a step toward a solution, possibly using fog to suggest distance. However, **glPointSize()** can't be called within **glBegin()** and **glEnd()**, so it's hard to vary the size of different points. You would have to recalculate the point sizes on the fly and then, for best performance, regroup them by size.

Point parameters are an automated, elegant solution, attenuating the size of point primitives and optionally their brightness, based upon distance to the view point. You use **glPointParameterf*()** to specify the coefficients of the attenuation equation and the alpha component of points (which controls brightness).

void **glPointParameter{if}**(GLenum *pname*, GLfloat *param*);
void **glPointParameter{if}v**(GLenum *pname*, const *TYPE *param*);

Sets values related to rendering point primitives.

If *pname* is GL_POINT_DISTANCE_ATTENUATION, then *param* is an array of three floating-point values (*a*, *b*, *c*), containing the constant, linear, and quadratic coefficients for deriving the size and brightness of a point, based upon eye-coordinate distance, *d*:

$$derivedSize \; = \; clamp\left(size \times \sqrt{\left(\frac{1}{a + b \times d + c \times d^2} \right)} \right)$$

If *pname* is set to GL_POINT_SIZE_MIN or GL_POINT_SIZE_MAX, *param* is an absolute limit (either lower or upper bound, respectively) used in the previous equation to clamp the derived point size.

If multisampling is enabled and *pname* is GL_POINT_FADE_THRESHOLD_SIZE, then *param* specifies a different lower limit (*threshold*) for the size of a point. If *derivedSize < threshold*, then the factor *fade* is computed to modulate the point's alpha, thus diminishing its brightness:

$$fade \; = \; \left(\frac{derivedSize}{threshold} \right)^2$$

If *pname* is GL_POINT_SPRITE_COORD_ORIGIN, and *param* is GL_LOWER_LEFT, then the origin for iterated texture coordinates on point sprites is the lower-left fragment, with the *t* texture coordinate increasing vertically from bottom to top across the fragments. Alternatively, if *param* is set to GL_UPPER_LEFT, the *t* texture coordinate decreases from top to bottom vertically.

The GL_POINT_DISTANCE_ATTENUATION distance calculation is similar to the math used with the coefficients for attenuated local light sources. In Example 6-10, pressing the 'c', 'l', or 'q' key switches the attenuation equation among constant, linear, and quadratic attenuation. Pressing the 'f' or 'b' key moves the viewer forward or backward, which makes the points appear larger or smaller for the linear and quadratic attenuation modes.

Example 6-10   Point Parameters: pointp.c

```
static GLfloat constant[3] = {1.0, 0.0, 0.0};
static GLfloat linear[3] = {0.0, 0.12, 0.0};
static GLfloat quadratic[3] = {0.0, 0.0, 0.01};
...
```

```
void keyboard(unsigned char key, int x, int y) {
 switch (key) {
 case 'c':
  glPointParameterfv (GL_POINT_DISTANCE_ATTENUATION, constant);
  glutPostRedisplay();
 break;
 case 'l':
  glPointParameterfv (GL_POINT_DISTANCE_ATTENUATION, linear);
  glutPostRedisplay();
 break;
 case 'q':
  glPointParameterfv (GL_POINT_DISTANCE_ATTENUATION, quadratic);
  glutPostRedisplay();
 break;
 case 'b':
  glMatrixMode (GL_MODELVIEW);
  glTranslatef (0.0, 0.0, -0.5);
  glutPostRedisplay();
 break;
 case 'f':
  glMatrixMode (GL_MODELVIEW);
  glTranslatef (0.0, 0.0, 0.5);
  glutPostRedisplay();
break;
 ...
```

With the chosen linear and quadratic attenuation coefficients in
Example 6-10, moving the eye very close to a point may actually increase
the derived point size, by dividing the original point size by a proper fraction. To lessen or prevent this, you can increase the constant attenuation
coefficient or add a size limiting value with GL_POINT_SIZE_MAX.

With point parameters, you almost certainly want round, rather than
square, points, so you'll have to enable point antialiasing, as described in
"Antialiasing Points or Lines" on page 269. These lines of code will do
the trick:

```
glEnable(GL_POINT_SMOOTH);
glEnable(GL_BLEND);
glBlendFunc(GL_SRC_ALPHA, GL_ONE_MINUS_SRC_ALPHA);
```

Polygon Offset

If you want to highlight the edges of a solid object, you might draw the
object with polygon mode set to GL_FILL, and then draw it again, but in

a different color and with the polygon mode set to GL_LINE. However, because lines and filled polygons are not rasterized in exactly the same way, the depth values generated for the line and polygon edge are usually not the same, even between the same two vertices. The highlighting lines may fade in and out of the coincident polygons, which is sometimes called "stitching" and is visually unpleasant.

This undesirable effect can be eliminated by using polygon offset, which adds an appropriate offset to force coincident z-values apart, separating a polygon edge from its highlighting line. (The stencil buffer, described in "Stencil Test" in Chapter 10, can also be used to eliminate stitching. However, polygon offset is almost always faster than stenciling.) Polygon offset is also useful for applying decals to surfaces by rendering images with hidden-line removal. In addition to lines and filled polygons, this technique can also be used with points.

There are three different ways to turn on polygon offset, one for each type of polygon rasterization mode: GL_FILL, GL_LINE, and GL_POINT. You enable the polygon offset by passing the appropriate parameter to **glEnable()**—either GL_POLYGON_OFFSET_FILL, GL_POLYGON_OFFSET_LINE, or GL_POLYGON_OFFSET_POINT. You must also call **glPolygonMode()** to set the current polygon rasterization method.

---

void **glPolygonOffset**(GLfloat *factor*, GLfloat *units*);

When enabled, the depth value of each fragment is modified by adding a calculated offset value before the depth test is performed. The offset value *offset* is calculated by

$$offset = m \cdot factor + r \cdot units$$

where *m* is the maximum depth slope of the polygon (computed during rasterization), and *r* is the smallest value guaranteed to produce a resolvable difference in depth values and is an implementation-specific constant. Both *factor* and *units* may be negative.

To achieve a nice rendering of the highlighted solid object without visual artifacts, you can add either a positive offset to the solid object (push it away from you) or a negative offset to the wireframe (pull it toward you). The big question is: How much offset is enough? Unfortunately, the offset required depends on various factors, including the depth slope of each polygon and the width of the lines in the wireframe.

OpenGL calculates the depth slope (see Figure 6-5), which is the z- (depth) value divided by the change in either x- or y-coordinates as you traverse the polygon. The depth values are clamped to the range [0, 1], and the x- and y-coordinates are in window coordinates. To estimate the maximum depth slope of a polygon (m in the offset equation), use the formula

$$m = \sqrt{\left(\frac{\partial z}{\partial x}\right)^2 + \left(\frac{\partial z}{\partial y}\right)^2}$$ (or an implementation may use the approximation $m = max\left(\frac{\partial z}{\partial x}, \frac{\partial z}{\partial y}\right)$).

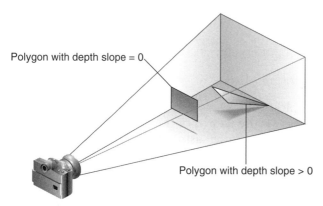

Polygon with depth slope = 0

Polygon with depth slope > 0

Figure 6-5   Polygons and Their Depth Slopes

For polygons that are parallel to the near and far clipping planes, the depth slope is zero. Those polygons can use a small constant offset, which you can specify by setting *factor* = 0.0 and *units* = 1.0 in your call to **glPolygonOffset()**.

For polygons that are at a great angle to the clipping planes, the depth slope can be significantly greater than zero, and a larger offset may be needed. A small, nonzero value for *factor*, such as 0.75 or 1.0, is probably enough to generate distinct depth values and eliminate the unpleasant visual artifacts.

Example 6-11 shows a portion of code where a display list (which presumably draws a solid object) is first rendered with lighting, the default polygon mode of GL_FILL, and polygon offset with a *factor* value of 1.0 and a *units* value of 1.0. These values ensure that the offset is enough for all polygons in your scene, regardless of depth slope. (These values may actually be a little more offset than the minimum needed, but too much offset is less noticeable than too little.) Then, to highlight the edges of the first object, the object is rendered as an unlit wireframe with the offset disabled.

Example 6-11   Polygon Offset to Eliminate Visual Artifacts: polyoff.c

```
glEnable(GL_LIGHT0);
glEnable(GL_LIGHTING);
glPolygonOffset(1.0, 1.0);

glEnable(GL_POLYGON_OFFSET_FILL);
glCallList(list);
glDisable(GL_POLYGON_OFFSET_FILL);

glDisable(GL_LIGHTING);
glDisable(GL_LIGHT0);
glColor3f(1.0, 1.0, 1.0);
glPolygonMode(GL_FRONT_AND_BACK, GL_LINE);
glCallList(list);
glPolygonMode(GL_FRONT_AND_BACK, GL_FILL);
```

In some situations, the simplest values for *factor* and *units* (1.0 and 1.0) aren't the answer. For instance, if the widths of the lines that are highlighting the edges are greater than 1, then increasing the value of *factor* may be necessary. Also, since depth values while using a perspective projection are unevenly transformed into window coordinates (see "The Transformed Depth Coordinate" in Chapter 3), less offset is needed for polygons that are closer to the near clipping plane, and more offset is needed for polygons that are farther away. You may need to experiment with the values you pass to **glPolygonOffset()** to get the result you're looking for.

Chapter 7

Display Lists

Chapter Objectives

After reading this chapter, you'll be able to do the following:

- Understand how display lists can be used along with commands in immediate mode to organize your data and improve performance

- Maximize performance by knowing how and when to use display lists

Note: In OpenGL Version 3.1, all of the techniques and functions described in this chapter were removed through deprecation.

A *display list* is a group of OpenGL commands that have been stored for later execution. When a display list is invoked, the commands in it are executed in the order in which they were issued. Most OpenGL commands can be either stored in a display list or issued in *immediate mode*, which causes them to be executed immediately. You can freely mix immediate-mode programming and display lists within a single program. The programming examples you've seen so far have used immediate mode. This chapter discusses what display lists are and how best to use them. It has the following major sections:

- "Why Use Display Lists?" explains when to use display lists.

- "An Example of Using a Display List" gives a brief example, showing the basic commands for using display lists.

- "Display List Design Philosophy" explains why certain design choices were made (such as making display lists uneditable) and what performance optimizations you might expect to see when using display lists.

- "Creating and Executing a Display List" discusses in detail the commands for creating, executing, and deleting display lists.

- "Executing Multiple Display Lists" shows how to execute several display lists in succession, using a small character set as an example.

- "Managing State Variables with Display Lists" illustrates how to use display lists to save and restore OpenGL commands that set state variables.

Why Use Display Lists?

Display lists may improve performance since you can use them to store OpenGL commands for later execution. It is often a good idea to cache commands in a display list if you plan to redraw the same geometry multiple times, or if you have a set of state changes that need to be applied multiple times. Using display lists, you can define the geometry and/or state changes once and execute them multiple times.

To see how you can use display lists to store geometry just once, consider drawing a tricycle. The two wheels on the back are the same size but are offset from each other. The front wheel is larger than the back wheels and also in a different location. An efficient way to render the wheels on the tricycle would be to store the geometry for one wheel in a display list and then execute the list three times. You would need to set the modelview matrix appropriately each time before executing the list to calculate the correct size and location of each wheel.

When running OpenGL programs remotely to another machine on the network, it is especially important to cache commands in a display list. In this case, the server is a machine other than the host. (See "What Is OpenGL?" in Chapter 1 for a discussion of the OpenGL client-server model.) Since display lists are part of the server state and therefore reside on the server machine, you can reduce the cost of repeatedly transmitting that data over a network if you store repeatedly used commands in a display list.

When running locally, you can often improve performance by storing frequently used commands in a display list. Some graphics hardware may store display lists in dedicated memory or may store the data in an optimized form that is more compatible with the graphics hardware or software. (See "Display List Design Philosophy" for a detailed discussion of these optimizations.)

An Example of Using a Display List

A display list is a convenient and efficient way to name and organize a set of OpenGL commands. For example, suppose you want to draw a torus and view it from different angles. The most efficient way to do this would be to store the torus in a display list. Then, whenever you want to change the view, you would change the modelview matrix and execute the display list to draw the torus. Example 7-1 illustrates this.

Example 7-1   Creating a Display List: torus.c

```
GLuint theTorus;

/* Draw a torus */
static void torus(int numc, int numt)
{
   int i, j, k;
   double s, t, x, y, z, twopi;

   twopi = 2 * (double)M_PI;
   for (i = 0; i < numc; i++) {
      glBegin(GL_QUAD_STRIP);
```

```
        for (j = 0; j <= numt; j++) {
            for (k = 1; k >= 0; k--) {
                s = (i + k) % numc + 0.5;
                t = j % numt;

                x = (1+.1*cos(s*twopi/numc))*cos(t*twopi/numt);
                y = (1+.1*cos(s*twopi/numc))*sin(t*twopi/numt);
                z = .1 * sin(s * twopi / numc);
                glVertex3f(x, y, z);
            }
        }
        glEnd();
    }
}

/* Create display list with Torus and initialize state */
static void init(void)
{
    theTorus = glGenLists(1);
    glNewList(theTorus, GL_COMPILE);
    torus(8, 25);
    glEndList();

    glShadeModel(GL_FLAT);
    glClearColor(0.0, 0.0, 0.0, 0.0);
}

void display(void)
{
    glClear(GL_COLOR_BUFFER_BIT);
    glColor3f(1.0, 1.0, 1.0);
    glCallList(theTorus);
    glFlush();
}

void reshape(int w, int h)
{
    glViewport(0, 0, (GLsizei) w, (GLsizei) h);
    glMatrixMode(GL_PROJECTION);
    glLoadIdentity();
    gluPerspective(30, (GLfloat) w/(GLfloat) h, 1.0, 100.0);
    glMatrixMode(GL_MODELVIEW);
    glLoadIdentity();
    gluLookAt(0, 0, 10, 0, 0, 0, 0, 1, 0);
}
```

```
/* Rotate about x-axis when "x" typed; rotate about y-axis
   when "y" typed; "i" returns torus to original view */
void keyboard(unsigned char key, int x, int y)
{
    switch (key) {
    case 'x':
    case 'X':
        glRotatef(30., 1.0, 0.0, 0.0);
        glutPostRedisplay();
        break;
    case 'y':
    case 'Y':
        glRotatef(30., 0.0, 1.0, 0.0);
        glutPostRedisplay();
        break;
    case 'i':
    case 'I':
        glLoadIdentity();
        gluLookAt(0, 0, 10, 0, 0, 0, 0, 1, 0);
        glutPostRedisplay();
        break;
    case 27:
        exit(0);
        break;
    }
}

int main(int argc, char **argv)
{
    glutInitWindowSize(200, 200);
    glutInit(&argc, argv);
    glutInitDisplayMode(GLUT_SINGLE | GLUT_RGB);
    glutCreateWindow(argv[0]);
    init();
    glutReshapeFunc(reshape);
    glutKeyboardFunc(keyboard);
    glutDisplayFunc(display);
    glutMainLoop();
    return 0;
}
```

Let's start by looking at **init()**. It creates a display list for the torus and initializes the OpenGL rendering state. Note that the routine for drawing a torus (**torus()**) is bracketed by **glNewList()** and **glEndList()**, which defines a display list. The argument *listName* for **glNewList()** is an integer index, generated by **glGenLists()**, that uniquely identifies this display list.

The user can rotate the torus about the *x*- or *y*-axis by pressing the 'x' or 'y' key when the window has focus. Whenever this happens, the callback function **keyboard()** is called, which concatenates a 30-degree rotation matrix (about the *x*- or *y*-axis) with the current modelview matrix. Then **glutPostRedisplay()** is called, which will cause **glutMainLoop()** to call **display()** and render the torus after other events have been processed. When the 'i' key is pressed, **keyboard()** restores the initial modelview matrix and returns the torus to its original location.

The **display()** function is very simple. It clears the window and then calls **glCallList()** to execute the commands in the display list. If we hadn't used display lists, **display()** would have to reissue the commands to draw the torus each time it was called.

A display list contains only OpenGL commands. In Example 7-1, only the **glBegin()**, **glVertex()**, and **glEnd()** calls are stored in the display list. Their parameters are *evaluated*, and the resulting values are copied into the display list when it is created. All the trigonometry to create the torus is done only once, which should increase rendering performance. However, the values in the display list can't be changed later, and once a command has been stored in a list it is not possible to remove it. Neither can you add any new commands to the list after it has been defined. You can delete the entire display list and create a new one, but you can't edit it.

Note: Display lists also work well with GLU commands, since those operations are ultimately broken down into low-level OpenGL commands, which can easily be stored in display lists. Use of display lists with GLU is particularly important for optimizing performance of GLU tessellators (see Chapter 11) and NURBS (see Chapter 12).

Display List Design Philosophy

To optimize performance, an OpenGL display list is a cache of commands, rather than a dynamic database. In other words, once a display list is created, it can't be modified. If a display list were modifiable, performance could be reduced by the overhead required to search through the display list and perform memory management. As portions of a modifiable display list were changed, memory allocation and deallocation might lead to memory fragmentation. Any modifications that the OpenGL implementation made to the display list commands in order to make them more efficient to render would need to be redone. Also, the display list might be difficult to access, cached somewhere over a network or a system bus.

The way in which the commands in a display list are optimized may vary from implementation to implementation. For example, a command as simple as **glRotate*()** might show a significant improvement if it's in a display list, since the calculations to produce the rotation matrix aren't trivial (they can involve square roots and trigonometric functions). In the display list, however, only the final rotation matrix needs to be stored, so a display list rotation command can be executed as fast as the hardware can execute **glMultMatrix*()**. A sophisticated OpenGL implementation might even concatenate adjacent transformation commands into a single matrix multiplication.

Although you're not guaranteed that your OpenGL implementation optimizes display lists for any particular uses, executing display lists is no slower than executing the commands contained within them individually. There is some overhead, however, involved in jumping to a display list. If a particular list is small, this overhead could exceed any execution advantage. The most likely possibilities for optimization are listed next, with references to the chapters in which the topics are discussed:

- Matrix operations (Chapter 3). Most matrix operations require OpenGL to compute inverses. Both the computed matrix and its inverse might be stored by a particular OpenGL implementation in a display list.

- Raster bitmaps and images (Chapter 8). The format in which you specify raster data isn't likely to be one that's ideal for the hardware. When a display list is compiled, OpenGL might transform the data into the representation preferred by the hardware. This can have a significant effect on the speed of raster character drawing, since character strings usually consist of a series of small bitmaps.

- Lights, material properties, and lighting models (Chapter 5). When you draw a scene with complex lighting conditions, you might change the materials for each item in the scene. Setting the materials can be slow, since it might involve significant calculations. If you put the material definitions in display lists, these calculations don't have to be done each time you switch materials, since only the results of the calculations need to be stored; as a result, rendering lit scenes might be faster. (See "Encapsulating Mode Changes" for more details on using display lists to change such values as lighting conditions.)

- Polygon stipple patterns (Chapter 2).

Note: To optimize texture images, you should store texture data in *texture objects* instead of display lists.

Some of the commands used for specifying the properties listed here are context-sensitive, so you need to take this into account to ensure optimum performance. For example, when GL_COLOR_MATERIAL is enabled, some of the material properties will track the current color (see Chapter 5). Any **glMaterial*()** calls that set the same material properties are ignored.

It may improve performance to store state settings with geometry. For example, suppose you want to apply a transformation to some geometric objects and then draw the results. Your code may look like this:

```
glNewList(1, GL_COMPILE);
draw_some_geometric_objects();
glEndList();

glLoadMatrix(M);
glCallList(1);
```

However, if the geometric objects are to be transformed in the same way each time, it is better to store the matrix in the display list. For example, if you write your code as follows, some implementations may be able to improve performance by transforming the objects when they are defined instead of each time they are drawn:

```
glNewList(1, GL_COMPILE);
glLoadMatrix(M);
draw_some_geometric_objects();
glEndList();
glCallList(1);
```

A more likely situation occurs during rendering of images. As you will see in Chapter 8, you can modify pixel-transfer state variables and control the way images and bitmaps are rasterized. If the commands that set these state variables precede the definition of the image or bitmap in the display list, the implementation may be able to perform some of the operations ahead of time and cache the results.

Remember that display lists have some disadvantages. Very small lists may not perform well since there is some overhead when executing a list. Another disadvantage is the immutability of the contents of a display list. To optimize performance, an OpenGL display list can't be changed, and its contents can't be read. If the application needs to maintain data separately from the display list (for example, for continued data processing), then a lot of additional memory may be required.

Creating and Executing a Display List

As you've already seen, **glNewList()** and **glEndList()** are used to begin and end the definition of a display list, which is then invoked by supplying its identifying index with **glCallList()**. In Example 7-2, a display list is created in the **init()** routine. This display list contains OpenGL commands to draw a red triangle. Then, in the **display()** routine, the display list is executed 10 times. In addition, a line is drawn in immediate mode. Note that the display list allocates memory to store the commands and the values of any necessary variables.

Example 7-2   Using a Display List: list.c

```
GLuint listName;

static void init(void)
{
   listName = glGenLists(1);
   glNewList(listName, GL_COMPILE);
      glColor3f(1.0, 0.0, 0.0);  /*  current color red  */
      glBegin(GL_TRIANGLES);
      glVertex2f(0.0, 0.0);
      glVertex2f(1.0, 0.0);
      glVertex2f(0.0, 1.0);
      glEnd();
      glTranslatef(1.5, 0.0, 0.0); /*  move position  */
   glEndList();
   glShadeModel(GL_FLAT);
}

static void drawLine(void)
{
   glBegin(GL_LINES);
   glVertex2f(0.0, 0.5);
   glVertex2f(15.0, 0.5);
   glEnd();
}

void display(void)
{
   GLuint i;
```

```
glClear(GL_COLOR_BUFFER_BIT);
glColor3f(0.0, 1.0, 0.0);    /*  current color green  */
for (i = 0; i < 10; i++)     /*  draw 10 triangles     */
    glCallList(listName);
drawLine();   /* Is this line green?  NO!  */
              /* Where is the line drawn?  */
glFlush();
}
```

The **glTranslatef()** routine in the display list alters the position of the next object to be drawn. Without it, calling the display list twice would just draw the triangle on top of itself. The **drawLine()** routine, which is called in immediate mode, is also affected by the 10 **glTranslatef()** calls that precede it. Therefore, if you call transformation commands within a display list, don't forget to take into account the effect those commands will have later in your program.

Only one display list can be created at a time. In other words, you must eventually follow **glNewList()** with **glEndList()** to end the creation of a display list before starting another one. As you might expect, calling **glEndList()** without having started a display list generates the error GL_INVALID_OPERATION. (See "Error Handling" in Chapter 14 for more information about processing errors.)

Naming and Creating a Display List

Each display list is identified by an integer index. When creating a display list, you want to be careful that you don't accidentally choose an index that's already in use, thereby overwriting an existing display list. To avoid accidental deletions, use **glGenLists()** to generate one or more unused indices.

Compatibility
Extension

glGenLists

GLuint **glGenLists**(GLsizei *range*);

Allocates *range* number of contiguous, previously unallocated display list indices. The integer returned is the index that marks the beginning of a contiguous block of empty display list indices. The returned indices are all marked as empty and used, so subsequent calls to **glGenLists()** don't return these indices until they're deleted. Zero is returned if the requested number of indices isn't available, or if *range* is zero.

In the following example, a single index is requested, and if it proves to be available it's used to create a new display list:

```
listIndex = glGenLists(1);
if (listIndex != 0) {
    glNewList(listIndex,GL_COMPILE);
        ...
    glEndList();
}
```

Note: Zero is not a valid display list index.

---

void **glNewList**(GLuint *list*, GLenum *mode*);

Specifies the start of a display list. OpenGL routines that are called subsequently (until **glEndList()** is called to end the display list) are stored in a display list, except for a few restricted OpenGL routines that can't be stored. (Those restricted routines are executed immediately, during the creation of the display list.) *list* is a nonzero positive integer that uniquely identifies the display list. The possible values for *mode* are GL_COMPILE and GL_COMPILE_AND_EXECUTE. Use GL_COMPILE if you don't want the OpenGL commands executed as they're placed in the display list; to cause the commands to be both executed immediately and placed in the display list for later use, specify GL_COMPILE_AND_EXECUTE.

Compatibility Extension
glNewList
glEndList
GL_COMPILE
GL_COMPILE_ AND_EXECUTE

---

void **glEndList**(void);

Marks the end of a display list.

When a display list is created, it is stored with the current OpenGL context. Thus, when the context is destroyed, the display list is also destroyed. Some windowing systems allow multiple contexts to share display lists. In this case, the display list is destroyed when the last context in the *share group* is destroyed.

What's Stored in a Display List?

When you're building a display list, only the values for expressions are stored in the list. If values in an array are subsequently changed, the display list values don't change. In the following code fragment, the display list contains a command to set the current RGBA color to black (0.0, 0.0, 0.0). The subsequent change of the value of the *color_vector* array to red (1.0, 0.0, 0.0) has no effect on the display list because the display list contains the values that were in effect when it was created:

```
GLfloat color_vector[3] = {0.0, 0.0, 0.0};
glNewList(1, GL_COMPILE);
    glColor3fv(color_vector);
glEndList();
color_vector[0] = 1.0;
```

Not all OpenGL commands can be stored and executed from within a display list. For example, commands that set client state and commands that retrieve state values aren't stored in a display list. (Many of these commands are easily identifiable because they return values in parameters passed by reference or return a value directly.) If these commands are called when making a display list, they're executed immediately.

Table 7-1 enumerates OpenGL commands that cannot be stored in a display list. (Note also that **glNewList()** itself generates an error if it's called while already creating a display list.) Some of these commands haven't been described yet; you can look in the index to see where they're discussed.

glAreTexturesResident	glEdgeFlagPointer	glIsShader
glAttachShader	glEnableClientState	glIsTexture
glBindAttribLocation	glEnableVertexAttribArray	glLinkProgram
glBindBuffer	glFeedbackBuffer	glMapBuffer
glBufferData	glFinish	glNormalPointer
glBufferSubData	glFlush	glPixelStore
glClientActiveTexture	glFogCoordPointer	glPopClientAttrib
glColorPointer	glFogCoordPointer	glPushClientAttrib
glCompileShader	glGenBuffers	glReadPixels
glCreateProgram	glGenLists	glRenderMode
glCreateShader	glGenQueries	glSecondaryColorPointer
glDeleteBuffers	glGenTextures	glSecondaryColorPointer
glDeleteLists	glGet*	glSelectBuffer
glDeleteProgram	glIndexPointer	glShaderSource
glDeleteQueries	glInterleavedArrays	glTexCoordPointer
glDeleteShader	glIsBuffer	glUnmapBuffer
glDeleteTextures	glIsEnabled	glValidateProgram

Table 7-1   OpenGL Functions That Cannot Be Stored in Display Lists

glDetachShader	glIsList	glVertexAttribPointer
glDisableClientState	glIsProgram	glVertexPointer
glDisableVertexAttribArray	glIsQuery	

Table 7-1 (continued)   OpenGL Functions That Cannot Be Stored in Display Lists

To understand more clearly why these commands can't be stored in a display list, remember that when you're using OpenGL across a network, the client may be on one machine and the server on another. After a display list is created, it resides with the server, so the server can't rely on the client for any information related to the display list. If querying commands, such as **glGet*()** or **glIs*()**, were allowed in a display list, the calling program would be surprised at random times by data returned over the network. Without parsing the display list as it was sent, the calling program wouldn't know where to put the data. Therefore, any command that returns a value can't be stored in a display list.

Commands that change client state, such as **glPixelStore()**, **glSelectBuffer()**, and the commands to define vertex arrays, can't be stored in a display list. For example, the vertex-array specification routines (such as **glVertexPointer()**, **glColorPointer()**, and **glInterleavedArrays()**) set client state pointers and cannot be stored in a display list. **glArrayElement()**, **glDrawArrays()**, and **glDrawElements()** send data to the server state to construct primitives from elements in the enabled arrays, so these operations can be stored in a display list. (See "Vertex Arrays" in Chapter 2.) The vertex-array data stored in this display list is obtained by dereferencing data from the pointers, not by storing the pointers themselves. Therefore, subsequent changes to the data in the vertex arrays will not affect the definition of the primitive in the display list.

In addition, any commands that use the pixel-storage modes use the modes that are in effect when they are placed in the display list. (See "Controlling Pixel-Storage Modes" in Chapter 8.) Other routines that rely upon client state—such as **glFlush()** and **glFinish()**—can't be stored in a display list because they depend on the client state that is in effect when they are executed.

Executing a Display List

After you've created a display list, you can execute it by calling **glCallList()**. Naturally, you can execute the same display list many times, and you can mix calls to execute display lists with calls to perform immediate-mode graphics, as you've already seen.

void **glCallList**(GLuint *list*);

This routine executes the display list specified by *list*. The commands in the display list are executed in the order they were saved, just as if they were issued without using a display list. If *list* hasn't been defined, nothing happens.

You can call **glCallList()** from anywhere within a program, as long as an OpenGL context that can access the display list is active (that is, the context that was active when the display list was created or a context in the same share group). A display list can be created in one routine and executed in a different one, since its index uniquely identifies it. Also, there is no facility for saving the contents of a display list into a data file, nor a facility for creating a display list from a file. In this sense, a display list is designed for temporary use.

Hierarchical Display Lists

You can create a *hierarchical display list*, which is a display list that executes another display list by calling **glCallList()** between a **glNewList()** and **glEndList()** pair. A hierarchical display list is useful for an object made of components, especially if some of those components are used more than once. For example, this is a display list that renders a bicycle by calling other display lists to render parts of the bicycle:

```
glNewList(listIndex,GL_COMPILE);
    glCallList(handlebars);
    glCallList(frame);
    glTranslatef(1.0, 0.0, 0.0);
    glCallList(wheel);
    glTranslatef(3.0, 0.0, 0.0);
    glCallList(wheel);
glEndList();
```

To avoid infinite recursion, there's a limit on the nesting level of display lists; the limit is at least 64, but it might be higher, depending on the implementation. To determine the nesting limit for your implementation of OpenGL, call

```
glGetIntegerv(GL_MAX_LIST_NESTING, GLint *data);
```

OpenGL allows you to create a display list that calls another list that hasn't been created yet. Nothing happens when the first list calls the second, undefined one.

You can use a hierarchical display list to approximate an editable display list by wrapping a list around several lower-level lists. For example, to put a polygon in a display list while allowing yourself to be able to edit its vertices easily, you could use the code in Example 7-3.

Example 7-3   Hierarchical Display List

```
glNewList(1,GL_COMPILE);
    glVertex3fv(v1);
glEndList();
glNewList(2,GL_COMPILE);
    glVertex3fv(v2);
glEndList();
glNewList(3,GL_COMPILE);
    glVertex3fv(v3);
glEndList();

glNewList(4,GL_COMPILE);
    glBegin(GL_POLYGON);
        glCallList(1);
        glCallList(2);
        glCallList(3);
    glEnd();
glEndList();
```

To render the polygon, call display list number 4. To edit a vertex, you need only re-create the single display list corresponding to that vertex. Since an index number uniquely identifies a display list, creating one with the same index as an existing one automatically deletes the old one. Keep in mind that this technique doesn't necessarily provide optimal memory usage or peak performance, but it's acceptable and useful in some cases.

Managing Display List Indices

So far, we've recommended the use of **glGenLists()** to obtain unused display list indices. If you insist on avoiding **glGenLists()**, then be sure to use **glIsList()** to determine whether a specific index is in use.

You can explicitly delete a specific display list or a contiguous range of lists with **glDeleteLists()**. Using **glDeleteLists()** makes those indices available again.

GLboolean **glIsList**(GLuint *list*);

Returns GL_TRUE if *list* is already used for a display list, and GL_FALSE otherwise.

void **glDeleteLists**(GLuint *list*, GLsizei *range*);

Deletes *range* display lists, starting at the index specified by *list*. An attempt to delete a list that has never been created is ignored.

Executing Multiple Display Lists

OpenGL provides an efficient mechanism for executing several display lists in succession. This mechanism requires that you put the display list indices in an array and call **glCallLists**(). An obvious use for such a mechanism occurs when display list indices correspond to meaningful values. For example, if you're creating a font, each display list index might correspond to the ASCII value of a character in that font. To have several such fonts, you would need to establish a different initial display list index for each font. You can specify this initial index by using **glListBase**() before calling **glCallLists**().

void **glListBase**(GLuint *base*);

Specifies the offset that's added to the display list indices in **glCallLists**() to obtain the final display list indices. The default display list base is 0. The list base has no effect on **glCallList**(), which executes only one display list, or on **glNewList**().

void **glCallLists**(GLsizei *n*, GLenum *type*, const GLvoid **lists*);

Executes *n* display lists. The indices of the lists to be executed are computed by adding the offset indicated by the current display list base (specified with **glListBase**()) to the signed integer values in the array pointed to by *lists*.

The *type* parameter indicates the data type of the values in *lists*. It can be set to GL_BYTE, GL_UNSIGNED_BYTE, GL_SHORT, GL_UNSIGNED_SHORT, GL_INT, GL_UNSIGNED_INT, or GL_FLOAT, indicating that *lists* should be treated as an array of bytes, unsigned bytes, shorts, unsigned shorts, integers, unsigned integers, or floats, respectively. *Type* can also be GL_2_BYTES, GL_3_BYTES, or GL_4_BYTES, in which case sequences of 2, 3, or 4 bytes are read from *lists* and then shifted and added together, byte by byte, to calculate the display list offset. The following algorithm is used (where *byte[0]* is the start of a byte sequence):

```
/* b = 2, 3, or 4; bytes are numbered 0, 1, 2, 3 in array */
offset = 0;
for (i = 0; i < b; i++) {
   offset = offset << 8;
   offset += byte[i];
}
index = offset + listbase;
```

For multiple-byte data, the highest-order data comes first, as bytes are taken from the array in order.

As an example of the use of multiple display lists, look at the program fragments in Example 7-4 taken from the full program in Example 7-5. This program draws characters with a stroked font (a set of letters made from line segments). The routine **initStrokedFont()** sets up the display list indices for each letter so that they correspond with their ASCII values.

Example 7-4   Defining Multiple Display Lists

```
void initStrokedFont(void)
{
   GLuint base;

   base = glGenLists(128);
   glListBase(base);
   glNewList(base+'A', GL_COMPILE);
      drawLetter(Adata); glEndList();
   glNewList(base+'E', GL_COMPILE);
      drawLetter(Edata); glEndList();
   glNewList(base+'P', GL_COMPILE);
      drawLetter(Pdata); glEndList();
   glNewList(base+'R', GL_COMPILE);
      drawLetter(Rdata); glEndList();
   glNewList(base+'S', GL_COMPILE);
      drawLetter(Sdata); glEndList();
   glNewList(base+' ', GL_COMPILE);    /* space character */
      glTranslatef(8.0, 0.0, 0.0);
   glEndList();
}
```

The **glGenLists()** command allocates 128 contiguous display list indices. The first of the contiguous indices becomes the display list base. A display list is made for each letter; each display list index is the sum of the base and the ASCII value of that letter. In this example, only a few letters and the space character are created.

After the display lists have been created, **glCallLists()** can be called to execute the display lists. For example, you can pass a character string to the subroutine **printStrokedString()**:

```
void printStrokedString(GLbyte *s)
{
   GLint len = strlen(s);
   glCallLists(len, GL_BYTE, s);
}
```

The ASCII value for each letter in the string is used as the offset into the display list indices. The current list base is added to the ASCII value of each letter to determine the final display list index to be executed. The output produced by Example 7-5 is shown in Figure 7-1.

Figure 7-1   Stroked Font That Defines the Characters A, E, P, R, S

Example 7-5   Multiple Display Lists to Define a Stroked Font: stroke.c

```
#define PT 1
#define STROKE 2
#define END 3

typedef struct charpoint {
   GLfloat   x, y;
   int       type;
} CP;

CP Adata[] = {
   { 0, 0, PT}, {0, 9, PT}, {1, 10, PT}, {4, 10, PT},
   {5, 9, PT}, {5, 0, STROKE}, {0, 5, PT}, {5, 5, END}
};
```

```
CP Edata[] = {
    {5, 0, PT}, {0, 0, PT}, {0, 10, PT}, {5, 10, STROKE},
    {0, 5, PT}, {4, 5, END}
};

CP Pdata[] = {
    {0, 0, PT}, {0, 10, PT}, {4, 10, PT}, {5, 9, PT}, {5, 6, PT},
    {4, 5, PT}, {0, 5, END}
};

CP Rdata[] = {
    {0, 0, PT}, {0, 10, PT}, {4, 10, PT}, {5, 9, PT}, {5, 6, PT},
    {4, 5, PT}, {0, 5, STROKE}, {3, 5, PT}, {5, 0, END}
};

CP Sdata[] = {
    {0, 1, PT}, {1, 0, PT}, {4, 0, PT}, {5, 1, PT}, {5, 4, PT},
    {4, 5, PT}, {1, 5, PT}, {0, 6, PT}, {0, 9, PT}, {1, 10, PT},
    {4, 10, PT}, {5, 9, END}
};

/*  drawLetter() interprets the instructions from the array
 *  for that letter and renders the letter with line segments.
 */
static void drawLetter(CP *l)
{
    glBegin(GL_LINE_STRIP);
    while (1) {
        switch (l->type) {
            case PT:
                glVertex2fv(&l->x);
                break;
            case STROKE:
                glVertex2fv(&l->x);
                glEnd();
                glBegin(GL_LINE_STRIP);
                break;
            case END:
                glVertex2fv(&l->x);
                glEnd();
                glTranslatef(8.0, 0.0, 0.0);
                return;
        }
        l++;
    }
}
```

```
/*  Create a display list for each of 6 characters. */
static void init(void)
{
   GLuint base;

   glShadeModel(GL_FLAT);

   base = glGenLists(128);
   glListBase(base);
   glNewList(base+'A', GL_COMPILE);
   drawLetter(Adata);
   glEndList();
   glNewList(base+'E', GL_COMPILE);
   drawLetter(Edata);
   glEndList();
   glNewList(base+'P', GL_COMPILE);
   drawLetter(Pdata);
   glEndList();
   glNewList(base+'R', GL_COMPILE);
   drawLetter(Rdata);
   glEndList();
   glNewList(base+'S', GL_COMPILE);
   drawLetter(Sdata);
   glEndList();
   glNewList(base+' ', GL_COMPILE);
   glTranslatef(8.0, 0.0, 0.0);
   glEndList();
}

char *test1 = "A SPARE SERAPE APPEARS AS";
char *test2 = "APES PREPARE RARE PEPPERS";

static void printStrokedString(char *s)
{
   GLsizei len = strlen(s);
   glCallLists(len, GL_BYTE, (GLbyte *)s);
}

void display(void)
{
   glClear(GL_COLOR_BUFFER_BIT);
   glColor3f(1.0, 1.0, 1.0);
   glPushMatrix();
   glScalef(2.0, 2.0, 2.0);
```

```
      glTranslatef(10.0, 30.0, 0.0);
      printStrokedString(test1);
      glPopMatrix();
      glPushMatrix();
      glScalef(2.0, 2.0, 2.0);
      glTranslatef(10.0, 13.0, 0.0);
      printStrokedString(test2);
      glPopMatrix();
      glFlush();
}

void reshape(int w, int h)
{
   glViewport(0, 0, (GLsizei) w, (GLsizei) h);
   glMatrixMode(GL_PROJECTION);
   glLoadIdentity();
   gluOrtho2D(0.0, (GLdouble) w, 0.0, (GLdouble) h);
}

void keyboard(unsigned char key, int x, int y)
{
   switch (key) {
      case ' ':
         glutPostRedisplay();
         break;
      case 27:
         exit(0);
         break;
   }
}

int main(int argc, char** argv)
{
   glutInit(&argc, argv);
   glutInitDisplayMode(GLUT_SINGLE | GLUT_RGB);
   glutInitWindowSize(440, 120);
   glutCreateWindow(argv[0]);
   init();
   glutReshapeFunc(reshape);
   glutKeyboardFunc(keyboard);
   glutDisplayFunc(display);
   glutMainLoop();
   return 0;
}
```

Managing State Variables with Display Lists

A display list can contain calls that change the values of OpenGL state variables. These values change as the display list is executed, just as if the commands were called in immediate mode, and the changes persist after execution of the display list is completed. As previously seen in Example 7-2, and as shown in Example 7-6, which follows, the changes in the current color and current matrix made during the execution of the display list remain in effect after it has been called.

Example 7-6   Persistence of State Changes after Execution of a Display List

```
glNewList(listIndex,GL_COMPILE);
    glColor3f(1.0, 0.0, 0.0);
    glBegin(GL_POLYGON);
        glVertex2f(0.0, 0.0);
        glVertex2f(1.0, 0.0);
        glVertex2f(0.0, 1.0);
    glEnd();
    glTranslatef(1.5, 0.0, 0.0);
glEndList();
```

If you now call the following sequence, the line drawn after the display list is drawn with red as the current color and translated by an additional (1.5, 0.0, 0.0):

```
glCallList(listIndex);
glBegin(GL_LINES);
    glVertex2f(2.0,-1.0);
    glVertex2f(1.0, 0.0);
glEnd();
```

Sometimes you want state changes to persist, but other times you want to save the values of state variables before executing a display list and then restore these values after the list has been executed. Remember that you cannot use **glGet*()** in a display list, so you must use another way to query and store the values of state variables.

You can use **glPushAttrib()** to save a group of state variables and **glPopAttrib()** to restore the values when you're ready for them. To save and restore the current matrix, use **glPushMatrix()** and **glPopMatrix()** as described in "Manipulating the Matrix Stacks" in Chapter 3. These push and pop routines can be legally cached in a display list. To restore the state variables in Example 7-6, you might use the code shown in Example 7-7.

Example 7-7   Restoring State Variables within a Display List

```
glNewList(listIndex,GL_COMPILE);
   glPushMatrix();
   glPushAttrib(GL_CURRENT_BIT);
   glColor3f(1.0, 0.0, 0.0);
   glBegin(GL_POLYGON);
      glVertex2f(0.0, 0.0);
      glVertex2f(1.0, 0.0);
      glVertex2f(0.0, 1.0);
   glEnd();
   glTranslatef(1.5, 0.0, 0.0);
   glPopAttrib();
   glPopMatrix();
glEndList();
```

If you use the display list from Example 7-7, which restores values, the code in Example 7-8 draws a green, untranslated line. With the display list in Example 7-6, which doesn't save and restore values, the line is drawn red, and its position is translated 10 times (1.5, 0.0, 0.0).

Example 7-8   The Display List May or May Not Affect drawLine()

```
void display(void)
{
   GLint i;

   glClear(GL_COLOR_BUFFER_BIT);
   glColor3f(0.0, 1.0, 0.0);   /* set current color to green   */
   for (i = 0; i < 10; i++)
      glCallList(listIndex);   /* display list called 10 times */
   drawLine();                 /* how and where does this line appear? */
   glFlush();
}
```

Encapsulating Mode Changes

You can use display lists to organize and store groups of commands to change various modes or set various parameters. When you want to switch from one group of settings to another, using display lists might be more efficient than making the calls directly, since the settings might be cached in a format that matches the requirements of your graphics system.

Display lists may be more efficient than immediate mode for switching among various lighting, lighting-model, and material-parameter settings. You might also use display lists for stipple patterns, fog parameters, and clipping-plane equations. In general, you'll find that executing display lists is at least as fast as making the relevant calls directly, but remember that some overhead is involved in jumping to a display list.

Example 7-9 shows how to use display lists to switch among three different line stipples. First, you call **glGenLists()** to allocate a display list for each stipple pattern and create a display list for each pattern. Then, you use **glCallList()** to switch from one stipple pattern to another.

Example 7-9   Display Lists for Mode Changes

```
GLuint offset;
offset = glGenLists(3);

glNewList(offset, GL_COMPILE);
    glDisable(GL_LINE_STIPPLE);
glEndList();

glNewList(offset+1, GL_COMPILE);
    glEnable(GL_LINE_STIPPLE);
    glLineStipple(1, 0x0F0F);
glEndList();

glNewList(offset+2, GL_COMPILE);
    glEnable(GL_LINE_STIPPLE);
    glLineStipple(1, 0x1111);
glEndList();


#define drawOneLine(x1,y1,x2,y2) glBegin(GL_LINES); \
    glVertex2f((x1),(y1)); glVertex2f((x2),(y2)); glEnd();

glCallList(offset);
drawOneLine(50.0, 125.0, 350.0, 125.0);

glCallList(offset+1);
drawOneLine(50.0, 100.0, 350.0, 100.0);

glCallList(offset+2);
drawOneLine(50.0, 75.0, 350.0, 75.0);
```

Chapter 8

Drawing Pixels, Bitmaps, Fonts, and Images

Chapter Objectives

After reading this chapter, you'll be able to do the following:

- Position and draw bitmapped data

- Read pixel data (bitmaps and images) from the framebuffer into processor memory and from memory into the framebuffer

- Copy pixel data from one color buffer to another, or to another location in the same buffer

- Magnify or reduce an image as it's written to the framebuffer

- Control pixel data formatting and perform other transformations as the data is moved to and from the framebuffer

- Perform pixel processing using the Imaging Subset

- Use buffer objects for storing pixel data

Note: Much of the functionality discussed in this chapter was deprecated in OpenGL Version 3.0, and was removed from Version 3.1. It was replaced with more capable functionality using framebuffer objects, which are described in Chapter 10.

So far, most of the discussion in this guide has concerned the rendering of geometric data—points, lines, and polygons. Two other important classes of data can be rendered by OpenGL:

- Bitmaps, typically used for characters in fonts

- Image data, which might have been scanned in or calculated

Both bitmaps and image data take the form of rectangular arrays of pixels. One difference between them is that a *bitmap* consists of a single bit of information about each pixel, and image data typically includes several pieces of data per pixel (the complete red, green, blue, and alpha color components, for example). Also, bitmaps are like masks in that they're used to overlay another image, but image data simply overwrites or is blended with whatever data is in the framebuffer.

This chapter describes first how to draw pixel data (bitmaps and images) from processor memory to the framebuffer and how to read pixel data from the framebuffer into processor memory. It also describes how to copy pixel data from one position to another, either from one buffer to another or within a single buffer.

Note: OpenGL does not support reading or saving pixels and images to files.

This chapter contains the following major sections:

- "Bitmaps and Fonts" describes the commands for positioning and drawing bitmapped data. Such data may describe a font.

- "Images" presents basic information about drawing, reading, and copying pixel data.

- "Imaging Pipeline" describes the operations that are performed on images and bitmaps when they are read from the framebuffer and when they are written to the framebuffer.

- "Reading and Drawing Pixel Rectangles" covers all the details about how pixel data is stored in memory and how to transform it as it's moved into or out of memory.

- "Using Buffer Objects with Pixel Rectangle Data" discusses using server-side buffer objects to store and retrieve pixel data more efficiently.

- "Tips for Improving Pixel Drawing Rates" lists tips for getting better performance when drawing pixel rectangles.

- "Imaging Subset" presents additional pixel processing operations found in this OpenGL extension.

In most cases, the necessary pixel operations are simple, so the first three sections might be all you need to read for your application. However, pixel manipulation can be complex—there are many ways to store pixel data in memory, and you can apply any of several operations to pixels as they're moved to and from the framebuffer. These details are the subject of the fourth section of this chapter. Most likely, you'll want to read this section only when you actually need to make use of the information. "Tips for Improving Pixel Drawing Rates" provides useful tips to get the best performance when rendering bitmaps and images.

OpenGL Version 1.2 added packed data types (such as GL_UNSIGNED_BYTE_3_3_2 and GL_UNSIGNED_INT_10_10_10_2) and swizzled pixel formats (such as BGR and BGRA), which match some windowing-system formats better.

Also in Version 1.2, a set of imaging operations, including color matrix transformations, color lookup tables, histograms, and new blending operations (**glBlendEquation()**, **glBlendColor()**, and several constant blending modes), became an ARB-approved extension named the *Imaging Subset*. In Version 1.4, the blending operations of the Imaging Subset were promoted to the core OpenGL feature set, and are no longer optional functionality.

Version 1.4 introduced use of GL_SRC_COLOR and GL_ONE_MINUS_SRC_COLOR as source blending functions as well as use of GL_DST_COLOR and GL_ONE_MINUS_DST_COLOR as destination blending functions. Also introduced in Version 1.4 was **glWindowPos*()** for specifying the raster position in window coordinates.

Version 3.0 introduced numerous additional data types and pixel formats described in this chapter. Many of these formats are more useful as texture formats (see Chapter 9, "Texture Mapping," for details) and as renderbuffer formats, which are part of the new functionality of framebuffer objects (details are discussed in "Framebuffer Objects" in Chapter 10).

Bitmaps and Fonts

A bitmap is a rectangular array of 0s and 1s that serves as a drawing mask for a rectangular portion of the window. Suppose you're drawing a bitmap and the current raster color is red. Wherever there's a 1 in the bitmap, the corresponding pixel in the framebuffer is replaced by a red pixel (or combined with a red pixel, depending on which per-fragment operations are in effect). (See "Testing and Operating on Fragments" in Chapter 10.) If there's a 0 in the bitmap, no fragments are generated, and the contents of the pixel are unaffected. The most common use of bitmaps is for drawing characters on the screen.

OpenGL provides only the lowest level of support for drawing strings of characters and manipulating fonts. The commands **glRasterPos*()** (or alternatively **glWindowPos*()**) and **glBitmap()** position and draw a single bitmap on the screen. In addition, through the display-list mechanism, you can use a sequence of character codes to index into a corresponding series of bitmaps representing those characters. (See Chapter 7 for more information about display lists.) You'll have to write your own routines to provide any other support you need for manipulating bitmaps, fonts, and strings of characters.

Consider Example 8-1, which draws the character F three times on the screen. Figure 8-1 shows the F as a bitmap and its corresponding bitmap data.

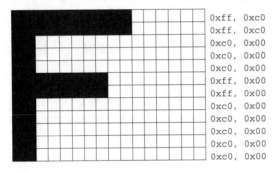

Figure 8-1   Bitmapped F and Its Data

Example 8-1   Drawing a Bitmapped Character: drawf.c

```
GLubyte rasters[24] = {
    0xc0, 0x00, 0xc0, 0x00, 0xc0, 0x00, 0xc0, 0x00, 0xc0, 0x00,
    0xff, 0x00, 0xff, 0x00, 0xc0, 0x00, 0xc0, 0x00, 0xc0, 0x00,
    0xff, 0xc0, 0xff, 0xc0};

void init(void)
{
    glPixelStorei(GL_UNPACK_ALIGNMENT, 1);
    glClearColor(0.0, 0.0, 0.0, 0.0);
}

void display(void)
```

```
{
    glClear(GL_COLOR_BUFFER_BIT);
    glColor3f(1.0, 1.0, 1.0);
    glRasterPos2i(20, 20);
    glBitmap(10, 12, 0.0, 0.0, 11.0, 0.0, rasters);
    glBitmap(10, 12, 0.0, 0.0, 11.0, 0.0, rasters);
    glBitmap(10, 12, 0.0, 0.0, 11.0, 0.0, rasters);
    glFlush();
}
```

In Figure 8-1, note that the visible part of the F character is at most 10 bits wide. Bitmap data is always stored in chunks that are multiples of 8 bits, but the width of the actual bitmap doesn't have to be a multiple of 8. The bits making up a bitmap are drawn starting from the lower left corner: First, the bottom row is drawn, then the next row above it, and so on. As you can tell from the code, the bitmap is stored in memory in this order—the array of rasters begins with 0xc0, 0x00, 0xc0, 0x00 for the bottom two rows of the F and continues to 0xff, 0xc0, 0xff, 0xc0 for the top two rows.

The commands of interest in this example are **glRasterPos2i()** and **glBitmap()**; they're discussed in detail in the next section. For now, ignore the call to **glPixelStorei()**; it describes how the bitmap data is stored in computer memory. (See "Controlling Pixel-Storage Modes" for more information.)

The Current Raster Position

The *current raster position* is the screen position where the next bitmap (or image) is to be drawn. In the F example, the raster position was set by calling **glRasterPos*()** with coordinates (20, 20), which is where the lower left corner of the F was drawn:

```
glRasterPos2i(20, 20);
```

---

void **glRasterPos{234}{sifd}**(*TYPE x, TYPE y, TYPE z, TYPE w*);
void **glRasterPos{234}{sifd}v**(const *TYPE *coords*);

Compatibility
Extension

glRasterPos

Sets the current raster position. The *x*, *y*, *z*, and *w* arguments specify the coordinates of the raster position. If the vector form of the function is used, the *coords* array contains the coordinates of the raster position. If **glRasterPos2*()** is used, *z* is implicitly set to zero and *w* is implicitly set to 1; similarly, with **glRasterPos3*()**, *w* is set to 1.

The coordinates of the raster position are transformed to screen coordinates in exactly the same way as coordinates supplied with a **glVertex*()** command (that is, with the modelview and perspective matrices). After transformation, either they define a valid spot in the viewport, or they're clipped because the coordinates were outside the viewing volume. If the transformed point is clipped out, the current raster position is invalid.

Prior to Version 1.4, if you wanted to specify the raster position in window (screen) coordinates, you had to set up the modelview and projection matrices for simple 2D rendering, with something like the following sequence of commands, where *width* and *height* are also the size (in pixels) of the viewport:

```
glMatrixMode(GL_PROJECTION);
glLoadIdentity();
gluOrtho2D(0.0, (GLfloat) width, 0.0, (GLfloat) height);
glMatrixMode(GL_MODELVIEW);
glLoadIdentity();
```

In Version 1.4, **glWindowPos*()** was introduced as an alternative to **glRasterPos*()**. **glWindowPos*()** specifies the current raster position in window coordinates, without the transformation of its *x* and *y* coordinates by the modelview or projection matrices, nor clipping to the viewport. **glWindowPos*()** makes it much easier to intermix 2D text and 3D graphics at the same time without the repetitive switching of transformation state.

Compatibility
Extension

glWindowPos

void **glWindowPos{23}{sifd}**(*TYPE x, TYPE y, TYPE z*);
void **glWindowPos{23}{sifd}v**(const *TYPE *coords*);

Sets the current raster position using the *x* and *y* arguments as window coordinates without matrix transformation, clipping, lighting, or texture coordinate generation. The *z* value is transformed by (and clamped to) the current near and far values set by **glDepthRange()**. If the vector form of the function is used, the *coords* array contains the coordinates of the raster position. If **glWindowPos2*()** is used, *z* is implicitly set to zero.

To obtain the current raster position (whether set by **glRasterPos*()** or **glWindowPos*()**), you can use the query command **glGetFloatv()** with GL_CURRENT_RASTER_POSITION as the first argument. The second argument should be a pointer to an array that can hold the (*x, y, z, w*) values as floating-point numbers. Call **glGetBooleanv()** with GL_CURRENT_RASTER_POSITION_VALID as the first argument to determine whether the current raster position is valid.

Drawing the Bitmap

Once you've set the desired raster position, you can use the **glBitmap()** command to draw the data.

void **glBitmap**(GLsizei *width*, GLsizei *height*,
    GLfloat x_{bo}, GLfloat y_{bo},
    GLfloat x_{bi}, GLfloat y_{bi},
    const GLubyte **bitmap*);

Compatibility
Extension

glBitmap

Draws the bitmap specified by *bitmap*, which is a pointer to the bitmap image. The origin of the bitmap is placed at the current raster position. If the current raster position is invalid, nothing is drawn, and the raster position remains invalid. The *width* and *height* arguments indicate the width and height, in pixels, of the bitmap. The width need not be a multiple of 8, although the data is stored in unsigned characters of 8 bits each. (In the F example, it wouldn't matter if there were garbage bits in the data beyond the tenth bit; since **glBitmap()** was called with a width of 10, only 10 bits of the row are rendered.) Use x_{bo} and y_{bo} to define the origin of the bitmap, which is positioned at the current raster position (positive values move the origin up and to the right of the raster position; negative values move it down and to the left); x_{bi} and y_{bi} indicate the *x* and *y* increments that are added to the raster position after the bitmap is rasterized (see Figure 8-2).

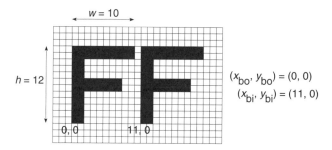

Figure 8-2   Bitmap and Its Associated Parameters

Allowing the origin of the bitmap to be placed arbitrarily makes it easy for characters to extend below the origin (typically used for characters with descenders, such as g, j, and y), or to extend beyond the left of the origin (used for various swash characters, which have extended flourishes, or for characters in fonts that lean to the left).

After the bitmap is drawn, the current raster position is advanced by x_{bi} and y_{bi} in the x- and y-directions, respectively. (If you just want to advance the current raster position without drawing anything, call **glBitmap()** with the *bitmap* parameter set to NULL and the *width* and *height* parameters set to zero.) For standard Latin fonts, y_{bi} is typically 0.0 and x_{bi} is positive (since successive characters are drawn from left to right). For Hebrew, where characters go from right to left, the x_{bi} values would typically be negative. Fonts that draw successive characters vertically in columns would use zero for x_{bi} and nonzero values for y_{bi}. In Figure 8-2, each time the F is drawn, the current raster position advances by 11 pixels, allowing a 1-pixel space between successive characters.

Since x_{bo}, y_{bo}, x_{bi}, and y_{bi} are floating-point values, characters need not be an integral number of pixels apart. Actual characters are drawn on exact pixel boundaries, but the current raster position is kept in floating point so that each character is drawn as close as possible to where it belongs. For example, if the code in the F example were modified such that x_{bi} was 11.5 instead of 12, and if more characters were drawn, the space between letters would alternate between 1 and 2 pixels, giving the best approximation to the requested 1.5-pixel space.

Note: You can't rotate bitmap fonts because the bitmap is always drawn aligned to the x and y framebuffer axes. Additionally, bitmaps can't be zoomed.

Choosing a Color for the Bitmap

You are familiar with using **glColor*()** and **glIndex*()** to set the current color or index for drawing geometric primitives. The same commands are used to set different state variables, GL_CURRENT_RASTER_COLOR and GL_CURRENT_RASTER_INDEX, for rendering bitmaps. The raster color state variables are set from the current color when **glRasterPos*()** is called, which can lead to a trap. In the following sequence of code, what is the color of the bitmap?

```
glColor3f(1.0, 1.0, 1.0);   /* white */
glRasterPos3fv(position);
glColor3f(1.0, 0.0, 0.0);   /* red   */
glBitmap(....);
```

Are you surprised to learn that the bitmap is white? The GL_CURRENT_RASTER_COLOR is set to white when **glRasterPos3fv()** is called. The second call to **glColor3f()** changes the value of GL_CURRENT_COLOR for future geometric rendering, but the color used to render the bitmap is unchanged.

To obtain the current raster color or index, you can use the query commands **glGetFloatv()** or **glGetIntegerv()** with GL_CURRENT_RASTER_COLOR or GL_CURRENT_RASTER_INDEX as the first argument.

Fonts and Display Lists

Display lists are discussed in general terms in Chapter 7. However, a few of the display-list management commands have special relevance for drawing strings of characters. As you read this section, keep in mind that the ideas presented here apply equally well to characters that are drawn using bitmap data and those drawn using geometric primitives (points, lines, and polygons). (See "Executing Multiple Display Lists" in Chapter 7 for an example of a geometric font.)

A font typically consists of a set of characters, where each character has an identifying number (usually the ASCII code) and a drawing method. For a standard ASCII character set, the capital letter A is number 65, B is 66, and so on. The string "DAB" would be represented by the three indices 68, 65, 66. In the simplest approach, display-list number 65 draws an A, number 66 draws a B, and so on. To draw the string 68, 65, 66, just execute the corresponding display lists.

You can use the command **glCallLists()** in just this way:

```
void glCallLists(GLsizei n, GLenum type, const GLvoid *lists);
```

The first argument, *n*, indicates the number of characters to be drawn, *type* is usually GL_BYTE, and *lists* is an array of character codes.

Since many applications need to draw character strings in multiple fonts and sizes, this simplest approach isn't convenient. Instead, you'd like to use 65 as A no matter what font is currently active. You could force font 1 to encode A, B, and C as 1065, 1066, 1067, and font 2 as 2065, 2066, 2067, but then any numbers larger than 256 would no longer fit in an 8-bit byte. A better solution is to add an offset to every entry in the string before choosing the display list. In this case, font 1 has A, B, and C represented by 1065,

1066, and 1067, and in font 2, they might be 2065, 2066, and 2067. To draw characters in font 1, set the offset to 1000 and draw display lists 65, 66, and 67. To draw that same string in font 2, set the offset to 2000 and draw the same lists.

To set the offset, use the command **glListBase()**. For the preceding examples, it should be called with 1000 or 2000 as the (only) argument. Now what you need is a contiguous list of unused display-list numbers, which you can obtain from **glGenLists()**:

```
GLuint glGenLists(GLsizei range);
```

This function returns a block of *range* display-list identifiers. The returned lists are all marked as "used" even though they're empty, so that subsequent calls to **glGenLists()** never return the same lists (unless you've explicitly deleted them previously). Therefore, if you use 4 as the argument and if **glGenLists()** returns 81, you can use display-list identifiers 81, 82, 83, and 84 for your characters. If **glGenLists()** can't find a block of unused identifiers of the requested length, it returns 0. (Note that the command **glDeleteLists()** makes it easy to delete all the lists associated with a font in a single operation.)

Most American and European fonts have a small number of characters (fewer than 256), so it's easy to represent each character with a different code that can be stored in a single byte. Asian fonts, among others, may require much larger character sets, so a byte-per-character encoding is impossible. OpenGL allows strings to be composed of 1-, 2-, 3-, or 4-byte characters through the *type* parameter in **glCallLists()**. This parameter can have any of the following values:

GL_BYTE	GL_UNSIGNED_BYTE
GL_SHORT	GL_UNSIGNED_SHORT
GL_INT	GL_UNSIGNED_INT
GL_FLOAT	GL_2_BYTES
GL_3_BYTES	GL_4_BYTES

(See "Executing Multiple Display Lists" in Chapter 7 for more information about these values.)

Defining and Using a Complete Font

The **glBitmap()** command and the display-list mechanism described in the preceding section make it easy to define a raster font. In Example 8-2, the upper-case characters of an ASCII font are defined. In this example, each character has the same width, but this is not always the case. Once the characters are defined, the program prints the message "THE QUICK BROWN FOX JUMPS OVER A LAZY DOG."

The code in Example 8-2 is similar to the F example, except that each character's bitmap is stored in its own display list. When combined with the offset returned by **glGenLists()**, the display list identifier is equal to the ASCII code for the character.

Example 8-2   Drawing a Complete Font: font.c

```
GLubyte space[] =
    {0x00, 0x00, 0x00, 0x00, 0x00, 0x00, 0x00, 0x00, 0x00, 0x00, 0x00, 0x00, 0x00};
GLubyte letters[][13] = {
    {0x00, 0x00, 0xc3, 0xc3, 0xc3, 0xc3, 0xff, 0xc3, 0xc3, 0xc3, 0x66, 0x3c, 0x18},
    {0x00, 0x00, 0xfe, 0xc7, 0xc3, 0xc3, 0xc7, 0xfe, 0xc7, 0xc3, 0xc3, 0xc7, 0xfe},
    {0x00, 0x00, 0x7e, 0xe7, 0xc0, 0xc0, 0xc0, 0xc0, 0xc0, 0xc0, 0xc0, 0xe7, 0x7e},
    {0x00, 0x00, 0xfc, 0xce, 0xc7, 0xc3, 0xc3, 0xc3, 0xc3, 0xc3, 0xc7, 0xce, 0xfc},
    {0x00, 0x00, 0xff, 0xc0, 0xc0, 0xc0, 0xc0, 0xfc, 0xc0, 0xc0, 0xc0, 0xc0, 0xff},
    {0x00, 0x00, 0xc0, 0xc0, 0xc0, 0xc0, 0xc0, 0xc0, 0xfc, 0xc0, 0xc0, 0xc0, 0xff},
    {0x00, 0x00, 0x7e, 0xe7, 0xc3, 0xc3, 0xcf, 0xc0, 0xc0, 0xc0, 0xc0, 0xe7, 0x7e},
    {0x00, 0x00, 0xc3, 0xc3, 0xc3, 0xc3, 0xc3, 0xff, 0xc3, 0xc3, 0xc3, 0xc3, 0xc3},
    {0x00, 0x00, 0x7e, 0x18, 0x18, 0x18, 0x18, 0x18, 0x18, 0x18, 0x18, 0x18, 0x7e},
    {0x00, 0x00, 0x7c, 0xee, 0xc6, 0x06, 0x06, 0x06, 0x06, 0x06, 0x06, 0x06, 0x06},
    {0x00, 0x00, 0xc3, 0xc6, 0xcc, 0xd8, 0xf0, 0xe0, 0xf0, 0xd8, 0xcc, 0xc6, 0xc3},
    {0x00, 0x00, 0xff, 0xc0, 0xc0, 0xc0, 0xc0, 0xc0, 0xc0, 0xc0, 0xc0, 0xc0, 0xc0},
    {0x00, 0x00, 0xc3, 0xc3, 0xc3, 0xc3, 0xc3, 0xc3, 0xdb, 0xff, 0xff, 0xe7, 0xc3},
    {0x00, 0x00, 0xc7, 0xc7, 0xcf, 0xcf, 0xdf, 0xdb, 0xfb, 0xf3, 0xf3, 0xe3, 0xe3},
    {0x00, 0x00, 0x7e, 0xe7, 0xc3, 0xc3, 0xc3, 0xc3, 0xc3, 0xc3, 0xc3, 0xe7, 0x7e},
    {0x00, 0x00, 0xc0, 0xc0, 0xc0, 0xc0, 0xc0, 0xfe, 0xc7, 0xc3, 0xc3, 0xc7, 0xfe},
    {0x00, 0x00, 0x3f, 0x6e, 0xdf, 0xdb, 0xc3, 0xc3, 0xc3, 0xc3, 0xc3, 0x66, 0x3c},
    {0x00, 0x00, 0xc3, 0xc6, 0xcc, 0xd8, 0xf0, 0xfe, 0xc7, 0xc3, 0xc3, 0xc7, 0xfe},
    {0x00, 0x00, 0x7e, 0xe7, 0x03, 0x03, 0x07, 0x7e, 0xe0, 0xc0, 0xc0, 0xe7, 0x7e},
    {0x00, 0x00, 0x18, 0x18, 0x18, 0x18, 0x18, 0x18, 0x18, 0x18, 0x18, 0x18, 0xff},
    {0x00, 0x00, 0x7e, 0xe7, 0xc3, 0xc3, 0xc3, 0xc3, 0xc3, 0xc3, 0xc3, 0xc3, 0xc3},
    {0x00, 0x00, 0x18, 0x3c, 0x3c, 0x66, 0x66, 0xc3, 0xc3, 0xc3, 0xc3, 0xc3, 0xc3},
    {0x00, 0x00, 0xc3, 0xe7, 0xff, 0xff, 0xdb, 0xdb, 0xc3, 0xc3, 0xc3, 0xc3, 0xc3},
    {0x00, 0x00, 0xc3, 0x66, 0x66, 0x3c, 0x3c, 0x18, 0x3c, 0x3c, 0x66, 0x66, 0xc3},
    {0x00, 0x00, 0x18, 0x18, 0x18, 0x18, 0x18, 0x18, 0x3c, 0x3c, 0x66, 0x66, 0xc3},
    {0x00, 0x00, 0xff, 0xc0, 0xc0, 0x60, 0x30, 0x7e, 0x0c, 0x06, 0x03, 0x03, 0xff}
};
GLuint fontOffset;
void makeRasterFont(void)
{
```

```
      GLuint i, j;
      glPixelStorei(GL_UNPACK_ALIGNMENT, 1);
      fontOffset = glGenLists(128);
      for (i = 0,j = 'A'; i < 26; i++,j++) {
         glNewList(fontOffset + j, GL_COMPILE);
         glBitmap(8, 13, 0.0, 2.0, 10.0, 0.0, letters[i]);
         glEndList();
      }
      glNewList(fontOffset + ' ', GL_COMPILE);
      glBitmap(8, 13, 0.0, 2.0, 10.0, 0.0, space);
      glEndList();
}
void init(void)
{
      glShadeModel(GL_FLAT);
      makeRasterFont();
}

void printString(char *s)
{
      glPushAttrib(GL_LIST_BIT);
      glListBase(fontOffset);
      glCallLists(strlen(s), GL_UNSIGNED_BYTE, (GLubyte *) s);
      glPopAttrib();
}

/* Everything above this line could be in a library
 * that defines a font.  To make it work, you've got
 * to call makeRasterFont() before you start making
 * calls to printString().
 */
void display(void)
{
      GLfloat white[3] = { 1.0, 1.0, 1.0 };

      glClear(GL_COLOR_BUFFER_BIT);
      glColor3fv(white);

      glRasterPos2i(20, 60);
      printString("THE QUICK BROWN FOX JUMPS");
      glRasterPos2i(20, 40);
      printString("OVER A LAZY DOG");
      glFlush();
}
```

Images

An image—or more precisely, a pixel rectangle—is similar to a bitmap. Instead of containing only a single bit for each pixel in a rectangular region of the screen, however, an image can contain much more information. For example, an image can contain a complete (R, G, B, A) color stored at each pixel. Images can come from several sources, such as

- A photograph that's digitized with a scanner

- An image that was first generated on the screen by a graphics program using the graphics hardware and then read back pixel by pixel

- A software program that generated the image in memory pixel by pixel

The images you normally think of as pictures come from the color buffers. However, you can read or write rectangular regions of pixel data from or to the depth buffer or the stencil buffer. (See Chapter 10 for an explanation of these other buffers.)

In addition to simply being displayed on the screen, images can be used for texture maps, in which case they're essentially pasted onto polygons that are rendered on the screen in the normal way. (See Chapter 9 for more information about this technique.)

Reading, Writing, and Copying Pixel Data

OpenGL provides three basic commands that manipulate image data:

- **glReadPixels()**—Reads a rectangular array of pixels from the framebuffer and stores the data in processor memory.

- **glDrawPixels()**—Writes a rectangular array of pixels from data kept in processor memory into the framebuffer at the current raster position specified by **glRasterPos*()**.

- **glCopyPixels()**—Copies a rectangular array of pixels from one part of the framebuffer to another. This command behaves similarly to a call to **glReadPixels()** followed by a call to **glDrawPixels()**, but the data is never written into processor memory.

For the aforementioned commands, the order of pixel data processing operations is shown in Figure 8-3.

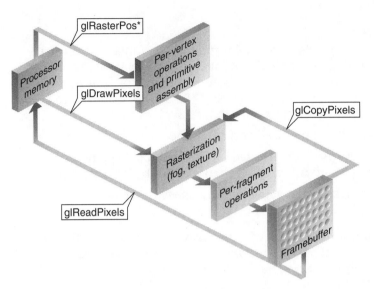

Figure 8-3   Simplistic Diagram of Pixel Data Flow

Figure 8-3 presents the basic flow of pixels as they are processed. The coordinates of **glRasterPos*()**, which specify the current raster position used by **glDrawPixels()** and **glCopyPixels()**, are transformed by the geometric processing pipeline. Both **glDrawPixels()** and **glCopyPixels()** are affected by rasterization and per-fragment operations. (But when drawing or copying a pixel rectangle, there's almost never a reason to have fog or texture enabled.)

However, complications arise because there are many kinds of framebuffer data, many ways to store pixel information in computer memory, and various data conversions that can be performed during the reading, writing, and copying operations. These possibilities translate to many different modes of operation. If all your program does is copy images on the screen or read them into memory temporarily so that they can be copied out later, you can ignore most of these modes. However, if you want your program to modify the data while it's in memory—for example, if you have an image stored in one format but the window requires a different format, or if you want to save image data to a file for future restoration in another session or on another kind of machine with significantly different graphical capabilities—you have to understand the various modes.

The rest of this section describes the basic commands in detail. The following sections discuss the details of the series of imaging operations that comprise the Imaging Pipeline: pixel-storage modes, pixel-transfer operations, and pixel-mapping operations.

Reading Pixel Data from Framebuffer to Processor Memory

void **glReadPixels**(GLint *x*, GLint *y*, GLsizei *width*, GLsizei *height*, GLenum *format*, GLenum *type*, GLvoid **pixels*);

Reads pixel data from the framebuffer rectangle whose lower-left corner is at (*x, y*) in window coordinates and whose dimensions are *width* and *height,* and then stores the data in the array pointed to by *pixels. format* indicates the kind of pixel data elements that are read (a color-index, depth, or stencil value or an R, G, B, or A component value, as listed in Table 8-1), and *type* indicates the data type of each element (see Table 8-2).

glReadPixels() can generate a few OpenGL errors: A GL_INVALID_OPERATION error will be generated if *format* is set to GL_DEPTH, and there is no depth buffer; or if *format* is GL_STENCIL, and there is no stencil buffer; or if *format* is set to GL_DEPTH_STENCIL, and there are not both a depth and a stencil buffer associated with the framebuffer, or if *type* is neither GL_UNSIGNED_INT_24_8, nor GL_FLOAT_32_UNSIGNED_INT_24_8_REV, then GL_INVALID_ENUM is set.

If you are using **glReadPixels**() to obtain RGBA or color-index information, you may need to clarify which buffer you are trying to access. For example, if you have a double-buffered window, you need to specify whether you are reading data from the front buffer or back buffer. To control the current read source buffer, call **glReadBuffer**(). (See "Selecting Color Buffers for Writing and Reading" in Chapter 10.)

format Constant	Pixel Format
GL_COLOR_INDEX	a single color index
GL_RG or GL_RG_INTEGER	a red color component, followed by a green color component
GL_RGB or GL_RGB_INTEGER	a red color component, followed by green and blue color components
GL_RGBA or GL_RGBA_INTEGER	a red color component, followed by green, blue, and alpha color components

Table 8-1   Pixel Formats for glReadPixels() or glDrawPixels()

format Constant	Pixel Format
GL_BGR or GL_BGR_INTEGER	a blue color component, followed by green and red color components
GL_BGRA or GL_BGRA_INTEGER	a blue color component, followed by green, red, and alpha color components
GL_RED or GL_RED_INTEGER	a single red color component
GL_GREEN or GL_GREEN_INTEGER	a single green color component
GL_BLUE or GL_BLUE_INTEGER	a single blue color component
GL_ALPHA or GL_ALPHA_INTEGER	a single alpha color component
GL_LUMINANCE	a single luminance component
GL_LUMINANCE_ALPHA	a luminance component followed by an alpha color component
GL_STENCIL_INDEX	a single stencil index
GL_DEPTH_COMPONENT	a single depth component
GL_DEPTH_STENCIL	combined depth and stencil components

Table 8-1   (continued)   Pixel Formats for glReadPixels() or glDrawPixels()

type Constant	Data Type
GL_UNSIGNED_BYTE	unsigned 8-bit integer
GL_BYTE	signed 8-bit integer
GL_BITMAP	single bits in unsigned 8-bit integers using the same format as **glBitmap()**
GL_UNSIGNED_SHORT	unsigned 16-bit integer
GL_SHORT	signed 16-bit integer
GL_UNSIGNED_INT	unsigned 32-bit integer
GL_INT	signed 32-bit integer

Table 8-2   Data Types for glReadPixels() or glDrawPixels()

type Constant	Data Type
GL_FLOAT	single-precision floating point
GL_HALF_FLOAT	a 16-bit floating-point value
GL_UNSIGNED_BYTE_3_3_2	packed into unsigned 8-bit integer
GL_UNSIGNED_BYTE_2_3_3_REV	packed into unsigned 8-bit integer
GL_UNSIGNED_SHORT_5_6_5	packed into unsigned 16-bit integer
GL_UNSIGNED_SHORT_5_6_5_REV	packed into unsigned 16-bit integer
GL_UNSIGNED_SHORT_4_4_4_4	packed into unsigned 16-bit integer
GL_UNSIGNED_SHORT_4_4_4_4_REV	packed into unsigned 16-bit integer
GL_UNSIGNED_SHORT_5_5_5_1	packed into unsigned 16-bit integer
GL_UNSIGNED_SHORT_1_5_5_5_REV	packed into unsigned 16-bit integer
GL_UNSIGNED_INT_8_8_8_8	packed into unsigned 32-bit integer
GL_UNSIGNED_INT_8_8_8_8_REV	packed into unsigned 32-bit integer
GL_UNSIGNED_INT_10_10_10_2	packed into unsigned 32-bit integer
GL_UNSIGNED_INT_2_10_10_10_REV	packed into unsigned 32-bit integer
GL_UNSIGNED_INT_24_8	packed into unsigned 32-bit integer. (For use exclusively with a format of GL_DEPTH_STENCIL)
GL_UNSIGNED_INT_10F_11F_10F_11F_REV	10- and 11-bit floating-point values packed into unsigned 32-bit integer
GL_UNSIGNED_INT_5_9_9_9_REV	three 9-bit floating-poing values sharing their exponent 5-bit value packed into an unsigned 32-bit integer
GL_FLOAT_32_ UNSIGNED_INT_24_8_REV	depth and stencil values packed into two 32-bit quantities: 32-bit floating-point depth value, and an 8-bit unsigned stencil value. (The "middle" 24 bits are unused.)

Table 8-2   (continued)   Data Types for glReadPixels() or glDrawPixels()

Note: The GL_*_REV pixel formats are particularly useful on Microsoft's Windows operating systems.

Remember that, depending on the format, anywhere from one to four elements are read (or written). For example, if the format is GL_RGBA and you're reading into 32-bit integers (that is, if *type* is equal to GL_UNSIGNED_INT or GL_INT), then every pixel read requires 16 bytes of storage (four components × four bytes/component).

Each element of the image is stored in memory, as indicated in Table 8-2. If the element represents a continuous value, such as a red, green, blue, or *luminance* component, each value is scaled to fit into the available number of bits. For example, assume the red component is initially specified as a floating-point value between 0.0 and 1.0. If it needs to be packed into an unsigned byte, only 8 bits of precision are kept, even if more bits are allocated to the red component in the framebuffer. GL_UNSIGNED_SHORT and GL_UNSIGNED_INT give 16 and 32 bits of precision, respectively. The signed versions of GL_BYTE, GL_SHORT, and GL_INT have 7, 15, and 31 bits of precision, since the negative values are typically not used.

If the element is an index (a color index or a stencil index, for example), and the type is not GL_FLOAT, the value is simply masked against the available bits in the type. The signed versions—GL_BYTE, GL_SHORT, and GL_INT—have masks with one fewer bit. For example, if a color index is to be stored in a signed 8-bit integer, it's first masked against 0x7f. If the type is GL_FLOAT, the index is simply converted into a single-precision floating-point number (for example, the index 17 is converted to the float 17.0).

For integer-based packed data types (denoted by constants that begin with GL_UNSIGNED_BYTE_*, GL_UNSIGNED_SHORT_*, or GL_UNSIGNED_INT_*), color components of each pixel are squeezed into a single unsigned data type: one of byte, short integer, or standard integer. Valid formats are limited for each type, as indicated in Table 8-3. If an invalid pixel format is used for a packed pixel data type, a GL_INVALID_OPERATION error is generated.

Packed type Constants	Valid Pixel Formats
GL_UNSIGNED_BYTE_3_3_2	GL_RGB
GL_UNSIGNED_BYTE_2_3_3_REV	GL_RGB
GL_UNSIGNED_SHORT_5_6_5	GL_RGB
GL_UNSIGNED_SHORT_5_6_5_REV	GL_RGB

Table 8-3   Valid Pixel Formats for Packed Data Types

Packed type Constants	Valid Pixel Formats
GL_UNSIGNED_SHORT_4_4_4_4	GL_RGBA, GL_BGRA
GL_UNSIGNED_SHORT_4_4_4_4_REV	GL_RGBA, GL_BGRA
GL_UNSIGNED_SHORT_5_5_5_1	GL_RGBA, GL_BGRA
GL_UNSIGNED_SHORT_1_5_5_5_REV	GL_RGBA, GL_BGRA
GL_UNSIGNED_INT_8_8_8_8	GL_RGBA, GL_BGRA
GL_UNSIGNED_INT_8_8_8_8_REV	GL_RGBA, GL_BGRA
GL_UNSIGNED_INT_10_10_10_2	GL_RGBA, GL_BGRA
GL_UNSIGNED_INT_2_10_10_10_REV	GL_RGBA, GL_BGRA
GL_UNSIGNED_INT_24_8	GL_DEPTH_STENCIL
GL_UNSIGNED_INT_10F_11F_11F	GL_RGB
GL_UNSIGNED_INT_5_9_9_9_REV	GL_RGB
GL_FLOAT_32_UNSIGNED_INT_24_8_REV	GL_DEPTH_STENCIL

Table 8-3 (continued)   Valid Pixel Formats for Packed Data Types

The order of color values in bitfield locations of packed pixel data is determined by both the pixel format and whether the type constant contains _REV. Without the _REV suffix, the color components are normally assigned with the first color component occupying the most significant locations. With the _REV suffix, the component packing order is reversed, with the first color component starting with the least significant locations.

To illustrate this, Figure 8-4 shows the bitfield ordering of GL_UNSIGNED_ BYTE_3_3_2, GL_UNSIGNED_BYTE_2_3_3_REV, and four valid combinations of GL_UNSIGNED_SHORT_4_4_4_4 (and _REV) data types and the RGBA/BGRA pixel formats. The bitfield organizations for the other 14 valid combinations of packed pixel data types and pixel formats follow similar patterns.

The most significant bit of each color component is always packed in the most significant bit location. Storage of a single component is not affected by any pixel storage modes, although storage of an entire pixel may be affected by the byte swapping mode. (For details on byte swapping, see "Controlling Pixel-Storage Modes" on page 347.)

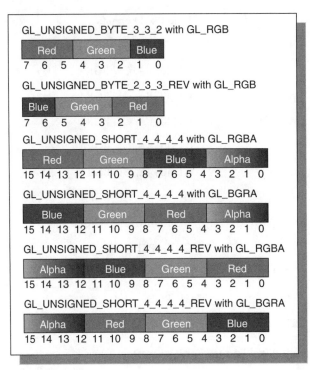

Figure 8-4   Component Ordering for Some Data Types and Pixel Formats

Writing Pixel Data from Processor Memory to Framebuffer

Compatibility
Extension

glDrawPixels

void **glDrawPixels**(GLsizei *width*, GLsizei *height*, GLenum *format*,
    GLenum *type*, const GLvoid **pixels*);

Draws a rectangle of pixel data with dimensions *width* and *height*. The pixel rectangle is drawn with its lower-left corner at the current raster position. *format* and *type* have the same meaning as with **glReadPixels**(). (For legal values for *format* and *type*, see Tables 8-1 and 8-2.) The array pointed to by *pixels* contains the pixel data to be drawn. If the current raster position is invalid, nothing is drawn, and the raster position remains invalid.

A GL_INVALID_OPERATION is generated if *format* is GL_STENCIL and there isn't a stencil buffer associated with the framebuffer, or likewise, if *format* is GL_DEPTH_STENCIL, and there is not both a depth and stencil buffer.

Example 8-3 is a portion of a program that uses **glDrawPixels()** to draw a pixel rectangle in the lower left corner of a window. **makeCheckImage()** creates a 64 × 64 RGB array of a black-and-white checkerboard image. **glRasterPos2i**(0, 0) positions the lower left corner of the image. For now, ignore **glPixelStorei()**.

Example 8-3   Use of glDrawPixels(): image.c

```
#define checkImageWidth 64
#define checkImageHeight 64
GLubyte checkImage[checkImageHeight][checkImageWidth][3];

void makeCheckImage(void)
{
   int i, j, c;

   for (i = 0; i < checkImageHeight; i++) {
      for (j = 0; j < checkImageWidth; j++) {
         c = (((i&0x8)==0)^((j&0x8)==0))*255;
         checkImage[i][j][0] = (GLubyte) c;
         checkImage[i][j][1] = (GLubyte) c;
         checkImage[i][j][2] = (GLubyte) c;
      }
   }
}

void init(void)
{
   glClearColor(0.0, 0.0, 0.0, 0.0);
   glShadeModel(GL_FLAT);
   makeCheckImage();
   glPixelStorei(GL_UNPACK_ALIGNMENT, 1);
}
void display(void)
{
   glClear(GL_COLOR_BUFFER_BIT);
   glRasterPos2i(0, 0);
   glDrawPixels(checkImageWidth, checkImageHeight, GL_RGB,
            GL_UNSIGNED_BYTE, checkImage);
   glFlush();
}
```

When using **glDrawPixels()** to write RGBA or color-index information, you may need to control the current drawing buffers with **glDrawBuffer()**, which, along with **glReadBuffer()**, is also described in "Selecting Color Buffers for Writing and Reading" in Chapter 10.

glDrawPixels() operates slightly differently when the *format* parameter is set to GL_STENCIL or GL_DEPTH_STENCIL. In the cases where the stencil buffer is affected, the window positions that would be written have their stencil values updated (subject to the current front stencil mask), but no values in the color buffer are generated or affected (i.e., no fragments are generated; if a fragment shader is bound, it is not executed for those positions during that drawing operation). Likewise, if a depth is also provided, and you can write to the depth buffer (i.e., the depth mask is GL_TRUE), then the depth values are written directly to the depth buffer, which remains unaffected by the settings of the depth test.

Copying Pixel Data within the Framebuffer

Compatibility
Extension

glCopyPixels

void **glCopyPixels**(GLint *x*, GLint *y*, GLsizei *width*, GLsizei *height*, GLenum *buffer*);

Copies pixel data from the read framebuffer rectangle whose lower left corner is at (*x*, *y*) and whose dimensions are *width* and *height*. The data is copied to a new position in the write framebuffer whose lower left corner is given by the current raster position. *buffer* is either GL_COLOR, GL_STENCIL, GL_DEPTH, or GL_DEPTH_STENCIL specifying the framebuffer that is used. **glCopyPixels()** behaves similarly to a **glReadPixels()** followed by a **glDrawPixels()**, with the following translation for the *buffer* to *format* parameter:

- If *buffer* is GL_DEPTH or GL_STENCIL, then GL_DEPTH_COMPONENT or GL_STENCIL_INDEX is used, respectively. If GL_DEPTH_STENCIL is specified for *buffer* and any of those buffers are not present (e.g., there's no stencil buffer associated with the framebuffer), then it's as if there were zeroes in the channel for the data for the missing buffer.

- If GL_COLOR is specified, GL_RGBA or GL_COLOR_INDEX is used, depending on whether the system is in RGBA or color-index mode.

Note that there's no need for a *format* or *data* parameter for **glCopyPixels()**, since the data is never copied into processor memory. The read source buffer and the destination buffer of **glCopyPixels()** are specified by **glReadBuffer()**

and **glDrawBuffer()**, respectively. Both **glDrawPixels()** and **glCopyPixels()** are used in Example 8-4.

For all three functions, the exact conversions of the data going to or coming from the framebuffer depend on the modes in effect at the time. See the next section for details.

OpenGL Version 3.0 introduced a new pixel copy command called **glBlitFramebuffer()**, which subsumes the functionality of **glCopyPixels()** and **glPixelZoom()**. It is described in full detail at "Copying Pixel Rectangles" on page 539, as it leverages some of the functionality of framebuffer objects.

Imaging Pipeline

This section discusses the complete Imaging Pipeline: the pixel-storage modes and pixel-transfer operations, which include how to set up an arbitrary mapping to convert pixel data. You can also magnify or reduce a pixel rectangle before it's drawn by calling **glPixelZoom()**. The order of these operations is shown in Figure 8-5.

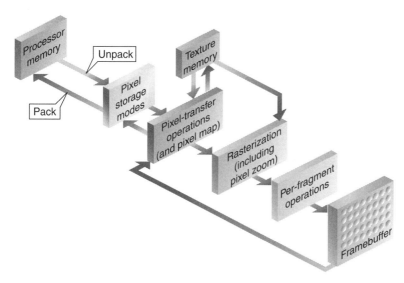

Figure 8-5   Imaging Pipeline

When **glDrawPixels()** is called, the data is first unpacked from processor memory according to the pixel-storage modes that are in effect, and then the pixel-transfer operations are applied. The resulting pixels are then rasterized. During rasterization, the pixel rectangle may be zoomed up or down, depending on the current state. Finally, the fragment operations are applied, and the pixels are written into the framebuffer. (See "Testing and Operating on Fragments" in Chapter 10 for a discussion of the fragment operations.)

When **glReadPixels()** is called, data is read from the framebuffer, the pixel-transfer operations are performed, and then the resulting data is packed into processor memory.

glCopyPixels() applies all the pixel-transfer operations during what would be the **glReadPixels()** activity. The resulting data is written as it would be by **glDrawPixels()**, but the transformations aren't applied a second time. Figure 8-6 shows how **glCopyPixels()** moves pixel data, starting from the framebuffer.

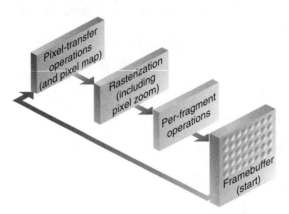

Figure 8-6   glCopyPixels() Pixel Path

From "Drawing the Bitmap" and Figure 8-7, you can see that rendering bitmaps is simpler than rendering images. Neither the pixel-transfer operations nor the pixel-zoom operation are applied.

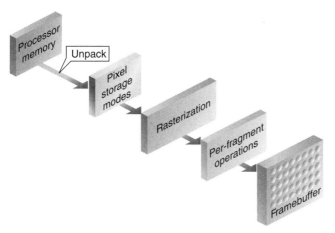

Figure 8-7   glBitmap() Pixel Path

Note that the pixel-storage modes and pixel-transfer operations are applied to textures as they are read from or written to texture memory. Figure 8-8 shows the effect on **glTexImage*()**, **glTexSubImage*()**, and **glGetTexImage()**.

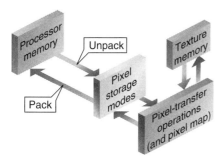

Figure 8-8   glTexImage*(), glTexSubImage*(), and glGetTexImage() Pixel Paths

As shown in Figure 8-9, when pixel data is copied from the framebuffer into texture memory (**glCopyTexImage*()** or **glCopyTexSubImage*()**), only pixel-transfer operations are applied. (See Chapter 9 for more information on textures.)

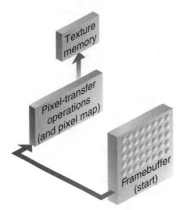

Figure 8-9   glCopyTexImage*() and glCopyTexSubImage*() Pixel Paths

Pixel Packing and Unpacking

Packing and unpacking refer to the way in which pixel data is written to and read from processor memory.

An image stored in memory has between one and four chunks of data, called *elements*. The data might consist of just the color index or the luminance (luminance is the weighted sum of the red, green, and blue values), or it might consist of the red, green, blue, and alpha components for each pixel. The possible arrangements of pixel data, or *formats*, determine the number of elements stored for each pixel and their order.

Some elements (such as a color index or a stencil index) are integers, and others (such as the red, green, blue, and alpha components, or the depth component) are floating-point values, typically ranging between 0.0 and 1.0. Floating-point components are usually stored in the framebuffer with lower resolution than a full floating-point number would require (for example, color components may be stored in 8 bits). The exact number of bits used to represent the components depends on the particular hardware being used. Thus, it's often wasteful to store each component as a full 32-bit floating-point number, especially since images can easily contain a million pixels.

Elements can be stored in memory as various data types, ranging from 8-bit bytes to 32-bit integers or floating-point numbers. OpenGL explicitly defines the conversion of each component in each format to each of the possible data types. Keep in mind that you may lose data if you try to store a high-resolution component in a type represented by a small number of bits.

Controlling Pixel-Storage Modes

Image data is typically stored in processor memory in rectangular two- or three-dimensional arrays. Often, you want to display or store a subimage that corresponds to a subrectangle of the array. In addition, you might need to take into account that different machines have different byte-ordering conventions. Finally, some machines have hardware that is far more efficient at moving data to and from the framebuffer if the data is aligned on 2-byte, 4-byte, or 8-byte boundaries in processor memory. For such machines, you probably want to control the byte alignment. All the issues raised in this paragraph are controlled as pixel-storage modes, which are discussed in the next subsection. You specify these modes by using **glPixelStore*()**, which you've already seen used in a couple of example programs.

All pixel-storage modes that OpenGL supports are controlled with the **glPixelStore*()** command. Typically, several successive calls are made with this command to set several parameter values.

---

void **glPixelStore{if}**(GLenum *pname*, *TYPE param*);

Sets the pixel-storage modes, which affect the operation of **glDrawPixels()**, **glReadPixels()**, **glBitmap()**, **glPolygonStipple()**, **glTexImage1D()**, **glTexImage2D()**, **glTexImage3D()**, **glTexSubImage1D()**, **glTexSubImage2D()**, **glTexSubImage3D()**, **glGetTexImage()**, and, if the Imaging Subset is available (see "Imaging Subset" on page 367), also **glGetColorTable()**, **glGetConvolutionFilter()**, **glGetSeparableFilter()**, **glGetHistogram()**, and **glGetMinmax()**.

The possible parameter names for *pname* are shown in Table 8-4, along with their data types, initial values, and valid ranges of values. The GL_UNPACK* parameters control how data is unpacked from memory by **glDrawPixels()**, **glBitmap()**, **glPolygonStipple()**, **glTexImage1D()**, **glTexImage2D()**, **glTexImage3D()**, **glTexSubImage1D()**, **glTexSubImage2D()**, and **glTexSubImage3D()**. The GL_PACK* parameters control how data is packed into memory by **glReadPixels()** and **glGetTexImage()**, and, if the Imaging Subset is available, also **glGetColorTable()**, **glGetConvolutionFilter()**, **glGetSeparableFilter()**, **glGetHistogram()**, and **glGetMinmax()**.

GL_UNPACK_IMAGE_HEIGHT, GL_PACK_IMAGE_HEIGHT, GL_UNPACK_SKIP_IMAGES, and GL_PACK_SKIP_IMAGES affect only 3D texturing (**glTexImage3D()**, **glTexSubImage3D()**, and **glGetTexImage(GL_TEXTURE_3D,...)**).

Parameter Name	Type	Initial Value	Valid Range
GL_UNPACK_SWAP_BYTES, GL_PACK_SWAP_BYTES	GLboolean	FALSE	TRUE/FALSE
GL_UNPACK_LSB_FIRST, GL_PACK_LSB_FIRST	GLboolean	FALSE	TRUE/FALSE
GL_UNPACK_ROW_LENGTH, GL_PACK_ROW_LENGTH	GLint	0	any non-negative integer
GL_UNPACK_SKIP_ROWS, GL_PACK_SKIP_ROWS	GLint	0	any non-negative integer
GL_UNPACK_SKIP_PIXELS, GL_PACK_SKIP_PIXELS	GLint	0	any non-negative integer
GL_UNPACK_ALIGNMENT, GL_PACK_ALIGNMENT	GLint	4	1, 2, 4, 8
GL_UNPACK_IMAGE_HEIGHT, GL_PACK_IMAGE_HEIGHT	GLint	0	any non-negative integer
GL_UNPACK_SKIP_IMAGES, GL_PACK_SKIP_IMAGES	GLint	0	any non-negative integer

Table 8-4   glPixelStore() Parameters

Since the corresponding parameters for packing and unpacking have the same meanings, they're discussed together in the rest of this section and referred to without the GL_PACK or GL_UNPACK prefix. For example, *SWAP_BYTES refers to GL_PACK_SWAP_BYTES and GL_UNPACK_SWAP_BYTES.

If the *SWAP_BYTES parameter is FALSE (the default), the ordering of the bytes in memory is whatever is native for the OpenGL client; otherwise, the bytes are reversed. The byte reversal applies to any size element, but has a meaningful effect only for multibyte elements.

The effect of swapping bytes may differ among OpenGL implementations. If on an implementation, GLubyte has 8 bits, GLushort has 16 bits, and GLuint has 32 bits, then Figure 8-10 illustrates how bytes are swapped for different data types. Note that byte swapping has no effect on single-byte data.

Note: As long as your OpenGL application doesn't share images with other machines, you can ignore the issue of byte ordering. If your application must render an OpenGL image that was created on a different machine and the two machines have different byte orders, byte ordering can be swapped using *SWAP_BYTES. However, *SWAP_BYTES does not allow you to reorder elements (for example, to swap red and green).

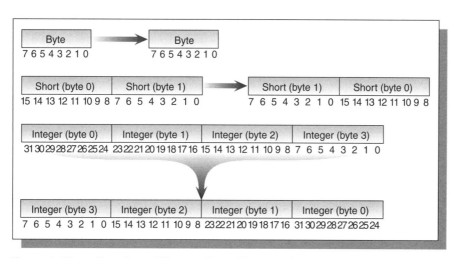

Figure 8-10 Byte Swap Effect on Byte, Short, and Integer Data

The *LSB_FIRST parameter applies only when drawing or reading 1-bit images or bitmaps for which a single bit of data is saved or restored for each pixel. If *LSB_FIRST is FALSE (the default), the bits are taken from the bytes starting with the most significant bit; otherwise, they're taken in the opposite order. For example, if *LSB_FIRST is FALSE, and the byte in question is 0x31, the bits, in order, are {0, 0, 1, 1, 0, 0, 0, 1}. If *LSB_FIRST is TRUE, the order is {1, 0, 0, 0, 1, 1, 0, 0}.

Sometimes you want to draw or read only a subrectangle of the entire rectangle of image data stored in memory. If the rectangle in memory is larger than the subrectangle that's being drawn or read, you need to specify the actual length (measured in pixels) of the larger rectangle with *ROW_LENGTH. If *ROW_LENGTH is zero (which it is by default), the row length is understood to be the same as the width that's specified with **glReadPixels()**, **glDrawPixels()**, or **glCopyPixels()**. You also need to specify the number of rows and pixels to skip before starting to copy the data for the subrectangle. These numbers are set using the parameters *SKIP_ROWS and *SKIP_PIXELS, as shown in Figure 8-11. By default, both parameters are 0, so you start at the lower left corner.

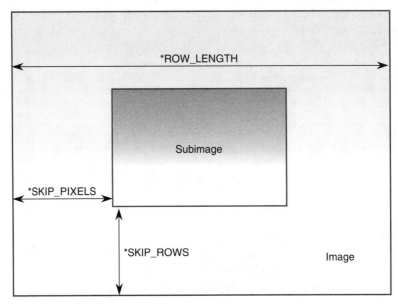

Figure 8-11   *SKIP_ROWS, *SKIP_PIXELS, and *ROW_LENGTH Parameters

Often a particular machine's hardware is optimized for moving pixel data to and from memory, if the data is saved in memory with a particular byte alignment. For example, in a machine with 32-bit words, hardware can often retrieve data much faster if it's initially aligned on a 32-bit boundary, which typically has an address that is a multiple of 4. Likewise, 64-bit architectures might work better when the data is aligned to 8-byte boundaries. On some machines, however, byte alignment makes no difference.

As an example, suppose your machine works better with pixel data aligned to a 4-byte boundary. Images are most efficiently saved by forcing the data for each row of the image to begin on a 4-byte boundary. If the image is 5 pixels wide and each pixel consists of 1 byte each of red, green, and blue information, a row requires 5 × 3 = 15 bytes of data. Maximum display efficiency can be achieved if the first row, and each successive row, begins on a 4-byte boundary, so there is 1 byte of waste in the memory storage for each row. If your data is stored in this way, set the *ALIGNMENT parameter appropriately (to 4, in this case).

If *ALIGNMENT is set to 1, the next available byte is used. If it's 2, a byte is skipped if necessary at the end of each row so that the first byte of the next row has an address that's a multiple of 2. In the case of bitmaps (or 1-bit images), where a single bit is saved for each pixel, the same byte alignment works, although you have to count individual bits. For example, if you're saving a single bit per pixel, if the row length is 75, and if the alignment is 4, then each row requires 75/8, or 9 3/8 bytes. Since 12 is the smallest multiple of 4 that is bigger than 9 3/8, 12 bytes of memory are used for each row. If the alignment is 1, then 10 bytes are used for each row, as 9 3/8 is rounded up to the next byte. (There is a simple use of **glPixelStorei**() shown in Example 8-4.)

Note: The default value for *ALIGNMENT is 4. A common programming mistake is assuming that image data is tightly packed and byte aligned (which assumes that *ALIGNMENT is set to 1).

The parameters *IMAGE_HEIGHT and *SKIP_IMAGES affect only the defining and querying of three-dimensional textures. For details on these pixel-storage modes, see "Pixel-Storage Modes for Three-Dimensional Textures" on page 417.

Pixel-Transfer Operations

As image data is transferred from memory into the framebuffer, or from the framebuffer into memory, OpenGL can perform several operations on it. For example, the ranges of components can be altered—normally, the red component is between 0.0 and 1.0, but you might prefer to keep it in some other range; or perhaps the data you're using from a different graphics system stores the red component in a different range. You can even create maps to perform arbitrary conversions of color indices or color components during pixel transfer. Such conversions performed during the transfer of pixels to and from the framebuffer are called *pixel-transfer operations*. They're controlled with the **glPixelTransfer***() and **glPixelMap***() commands.

Be aware that although color, depth, and stencil buffers have many similarities, they don't behave identically, and a few of the modes have special cases. All the mode details are covered in this section and the sections that follow, including all the special cases.

Some of the pixel-transfer function characteristics are set with **glPixelTransfer*()**. The other characteristics are specified with **glPixelMap*()**, which is described in the next section.

void **glPixelTransfer**{if}(GLenum *pname*, *TYPE param*);

Sets pixel-transfer modes that affect the operation of **glDrawPixels()**, **glReadPixels()**, **glCopyPixels()**, **glTexImage1D()**, **glTexImage2D()**, **glTexImage3D()**, **glCopyTexImage1D()**, **glCopyTexImage2D()**, **glTexSubImage1D()**, **glTexSubImage2D()**, **glTexSubImage3D()**, **glCopyTexSubImage1D()**, **glCopyTexSubImage2D()**, **glCopyTexSubImage3D()**, and **glGetTexImage()**. The parameter *pname* must be one of those listed in the first column of Table 8-5, and its value, *param*, must be in the valid range shown.

Parameter Name	Type	Initial Value	Valid Range
GL_MAP_COLOR	GLboolean	FALSE	TRUE/FALSE
GL_MAP_STENCIL	GLboolean	FALSE	TRUE/FALSE
GL_INDEX_SHIFT	GLint	0	$(-\infty, \infty)$
GL_INDEX_OFFSET	GLint	0	$(-\infty, \infty)$
GL_RED_SCALE	GLfloat	1.0	$(-\infty, \infty)$
GL_GREEN_SCALE	GLfloat	1.0	$(-\infty, \infty)$
GL_BLUE_SCALE	GLfloat	1.0	$(-\infty, \infty)$
GL_ALPHA_SCALE	GLfloat	1.0	$(-\infty, \infty)$
GL_DEPTH_SCALE	GLfloat	1.0	$(-\infty, \infty)$
GL_RED_BIAS	GLfloat	0.0	$(-\infty, \infty)$
GL_GREEN_BIAS	GLfloat	0.0	$(-\infty, \infty)$
GL_BLUE_BIAS	GLfloat	0.0	$(-\infty, \infty)$
GL_ALPHA_BIAS	GLfloat	0.0	$(-\infty, \infty)$
GL_DEPTH_BIAS	GLfloat	0.0	$(-\infty, \infty)$

Table 8-5   glPixelTransfer*() Parameters

Parameter Name	Type	Initial Value	Valid Range
GL_POST_CONVOLUTION_RED_SCALE	GLfloat	1.0	$(-\infty, \infty)$
GL_POST_CONVOLUTION_GREEN_SCALE	GLfloat	1.0	$(-\infty, \infty)$
GL_POST_CONVOLUTION_BLUE_SCALE	GLfloat	1.0	$(-\infty, \infty)$
GL_POST_CONVOLUTION_ALPHA_SCALE	GLfloat	1.0	$(-\infty, \infty)$
GL_POST_CONVOLUTION_RED_BIAS	GLfloat	0.0	$(-\infty, \infty)$
GL_POST_CONVOLUTION_GREEN_BIAS	GLfloat	0.0	$(-\infty, \infty)$
GL_POST_CONVOLUTION_BLUE_BIAS	GLfloat	0.0	$(-\infty, \infty)$
GL_POST_CONVOLUTION_ALPHA_BIAS	GLfloat	0.0	$(-\infty, \infty)$
GL_POST_COLOR_MATRIX_RED_SCALE	GLfloat	1.0	$(-\infty, \infty)$
GL_POST_COLOR_MATRIX_GREEN_SCALE	GLfloat	1.0	$(-\infty, \infty)$
GL_POST_COLOR_MATRIX_BLUE_SCALE	GLfloat	1.0	$(-\infty, \infty)$
GL_POST_COLOR_MATRIX_ALPHA_SCALE	GLfloat	1.0	$(-\infty, \infty)$
GL_POST_COLOR_MATRIX_RED_BIAS	GLfloat	0.0	$(-\infty, \infty)$
GL_POST_COLOR_MATRIX_GREEN_BIAS	GLfloat	0.0	$(-\infty, \infty)$
GL_POST_COLOR_MATRIX_BLUE_BIAS	GLfloat	0.0	$(-\infty, \infty)$
GL_POST_COLOR_MATRIX_ALPHA_BIAS	GLfloat	0.0	$(-\infty, \infty)$

Table 8-5   (continued)   glPixelTransfer*() Parameters

Caution: GL_POST_CONVOLUTION_* and GL_POST_COLOR_MATRIX_*
parameters are present only if the Imaging Subset is supported by
your OpenGL implementation. See "Imaging Subset" on
page 367 for more details.

If the GL_MAP_COLOR or GL_MAP_STENCIL parameter is TRUE, then
mapping is enabled. See the next subsection to learn how the mapping is
done and how to change the contents of the maps. All the other parameters
directly affect the pixel component values.

A scale and bias can be applied to the red, green, blue, alpha, and depth
components. For example, you may wish to scale red, green, and blue

components that were read from the framebuffer before converting them to a luminance format in processor memory. Luminance is computed as the sum of the red, green, and blue components, so if you use the default value for GL_RED_SCALE, GL_GREEN_SCALE, and GL_BLUE_SCALE, the components all contribute equally to the final intensity or luminance value. If you want to convert RGB to luminance, according to the NTSC standard, you set GL_RED_SCALE to .30, GL_GREEN_SCALE to .59, and GL_BLUE_SCALE to .11.

Indices (color and stencil) can also be transformed. In the case of indices, a shift and an offset are applied. This is useful if you need to control which portion of the color table is used during rendering.

Pixel Mapping

All the color components, color indices, and stencil indices can be modified by means of a table lookup before they are placed in screen memory. The command for controlling this mapping is **glPixelMap*()**.

<table>
<tr>
<td>

Compatibility Extension

glPixelMap and any accepted tokens

</td>
<td>

void **glPixelMap**{ui us f}**v**(GLenum *map*, GLint *mapsize*, const *TYPE *values*);

Loads the pixel map indicated by *map* with *mapsize* entries, whose values are pointed to by *values*. Table 8-6 lists the map names and values; the default sizes are all 1, and the default values are all 0. Each map's size must be a power of 2.

</td>
</tr>
</table>

Map Name	Address	Value
GL_PIXEL_MAP_I_TO_I	color index	color index
GL_PIXEL_MAP_S_TO_S	stencil index	stencil index
GL_PIXEL_MAP_I_TO_R	color index	R
GL_PIXEL_MAP_I_TO_G	color index	G
GL_PIXEL_MAP_I_TO_B	color index	B

Table 8-6   glPixelMap*() Parameter Names and Values

Map Name	Address	Value
GL_PIXEL_MAP_I_TO_A	color index	A
GL_PIXEL_MAP_R_TO_R	R	R
GL_PIXEL_MAP_G_TO_G	G	G
GL_PIXEL_MAP_B_TO_B	B	B
GL_PIXEL_MAP_A_TO_A	A	A

Table 8-6 (continued)   glPixelMap*() Parameter Names and Values

The maximum size of the maps is machine-dependent. You can find the sizes of the pixel maps supported on your machine with **glGetIntegerv()**. Use the query argument GL_MAX_PIXEL_MAP_TABLE to obtain the maximum size for all the pixel map tables, and use GL_PIXEL_MAP_*_TO_*_SIZE to obtain the current size of the specified map. The six maps whose address is a color index or stencil index must always be sized to an integral power of 2. The four RGBA maps can be any size from 1 through GL_MAX_PIXEL_MAP_TABLE.

To understand how a table works, consider a simple example. Suppose that you want to create a 256-entry table that maps color indices to color indices using GL_PIXEL_MAP_I_TO_I. You create a table with an entry for each of the values between 0 and 255 and initialize the table with **glPixelMap*()**. Assume you're using the table for thresholding and want to map indices below 101 (indices 0 to 100) to 0, and all indices 101 and above to 255. In this case, your table consists of 101 0s and 155 255s. The pixel map is enabled using the routine **glPixelTransfer*()** to set the parameter GL_MAP_COLOR to TRUE. Once the pixel map is loaded and enabled, incoming color indices below 101 come out as 0, and incoming pixels from 101 to 255 are mapped to 255. If the incoming pixel is larger than 255, it's first masked by 255, throwing out all the bits above the eighth, and the resulting masked value is looked up in the table. If the incoming index is a floating-point value (say 88.14585), it's rounded to the nearest integer value (giving 88), and that number is looked up in the table (giving 0).

Using pixel maps, you can also map stencil indices or convert color indices to RGB. (See "Reading and Drawing Pixel Rectangles" for information about the conversion of indices.)

Magnifying, Reducing, or Flipping an Image

After the pixel-storage modes and pixel-transfer operations are applied, images and bitmaps are rasterized. Normally, each pixel in an image is written to a single pixel on the screen. However, you can arbitrarily magnify, reduce, or even flip (reflect) an image by using **glPixelZoom()**.

---

void **glPixelZoom**(GLfloat *zoom_x*, GLfloat *zoom_y*);

Sets the magnification or reduction factors for pixel-write operations (**glDrawPixels()** and **glCopyPixels()**) in the *x*- and *y*-dimensions. By default, $zoom_x$ and $zoom_y$ are 1.0. If they're both 2.0, each image pixel is drawn to 4 screen pixels. Note that fractional magnification or reduction factors are allowed, as are negative factors. Negative zoom factors reflect the resulting image about the current raster position.

During rasterization, each image pixel is treated as a $zoom_x \times zoom_y$ rectangle, and fragments are generated for all the pixels whose centers lie within the rectangle. More specifically, let (x_{rp}, y_{rp}) be the current raster position. If a particular group of elements (indices or components) is the *n*th in a row and belongs to the *m*th column, consider the region in window coordinates bounded by the rectangle with corners at

$(x_{rp} + zoom_x \cdot n, y_{rp} + zoom_y \cdot m)$ and $(x_{rp} + zoom_x(n+1), y_{rp} + zoom_y(m+1))$

Any fragments whose centers lie inside this rectangle (or on its bottom or left boundaries) are produced in correspondence with this particular group of elements.

A negative zoom can be useful for flipping an image. OpenGL describes images from the bottom row of pixels to the top (and from left to right). If you have a "top to bottom" image, such as a frame of video, you may want to use **glPixelZoom**(1.0, –1.0) to make the image right side up for OpenGL. Be sure that you reset the current raster position appropriately, if needed.

Example 8-4 shows the use of **glPixelZoom()**. A checkerboard image is initially drawn in the lower left corner of the window. By pressing a mouse button and moving the mouse, you can use **glCopyPixels()** to copy the lower left corner of the window to the current cursor location. (If you copy the image onto itself, it looks wacky!) The copied image is zoomed, but initially it is zoomed by the default value of 1.0, so you won't notice. The 'z' and 'Z' keys increase and decrease the zoom factors by 0.5. Any window damage causes the contents of the window to be redrawn. Pressing the 'r' key resets the image and zoom factors.

Example 8-4   Drawing, Copying, and Zooming Pixel Data: image.c

```c
#define checkImageWidth 64
#define checkImageHeight 64
GLubyte checkImage[checkImageHeight][checkImageWidth][3];

static GLdouble zoomFactor = 1.0;
static GLint height;

void makeCheckImage(void)
{
   int i, j, c;

   for (i = 0; i < checkImageHeight; i++) {
      for (j = 0; j < checkImageWidth; j++) {
         c = (((i&0x8)==0)^((j&0x8)==0))*255;
         checkImage[i][j][0] = (GLubyte) c;
         checkImage[i][j][1] = (GLubyte) c;
         checkImage[i][j][2] = (GLubyte) c;
      }
   }
}

void init(void)
{
   glClearColor(0.0, 0.0, 0.0, 0.0);
   glShadeModel(GL_FLAT);
   makeCheckImage();
   glPixelStorei(GL_UNPACK_ALIGNMENT, 1);
}

void display(void)
{
   glClear(GL_COLOR_BUFFER_BIT);
   glRasterPos2i(0, 0);
   glDrawPixels(checkImageWidth, checkImageHeight, GL_RGB,
                GL_UNSIGNED_BYTE, checkImage);
   glFlush();
}

void reshape(int w, int h)
{
   glViewport(0, 0, (GLsizei) w, (GLsizei) h);
   height = (GLint) h;
   glMatrixMode(GL_PROJECTION);
   glLoadIdentity();
   gluOrtho2D(0.0, (GLdouble) w, 0.0, (GLdouble) h);
```

```
        glMatrixMode(GL_MODELVIEW);
        glLoadIdentity();
}

void motion(int x, int y)
{
        static GLint screeny;

        screeny = height - (GLint) y;
        glRasterPos2i(x, screeny);
        glPixelZoom(zoomFactor, zoomFactor);
        glCopyPixels(0, 0, checkImageWidth, checkImageHeight,
                     GL_COLOR);
        glPixelZoom(1.0, 1.0);
        glFlush();
}

void keyboard(unsigned char key, int x, int y)
{
        switch (key) {
            case 'r':
            case 'R':
                zoomFactor = 1.0;
                glutPostRedisplay();
                printf("zoomFactor reset to 1.0\n");
                break;
            case 'z':
                zoomFactor += 0.5;
                if (zoomFactor >= 3.0)
                    zoomFactor = 3.0;
                printf("zoomFactor is now %4.1f\n", zoomFactor);
                break;
            case 'Z':
                zoomFactor -= 0.5;
                if (zoomFactor <= 0.5)
                    zoomFactor = 0.5;
                printf("zoomFactor is now %4.1f\n", zoomFactor);
                break;
            case 27:
                exit(0);
                break;
            default:
                break;
        }
}
```

Reading and Drawing Pixel Rectangles

This section describes the reading and drawing processes in detail. The pixel conversions performed when going from framebuffer to memory (reading) are similar but not identical to the conversions performed when going in the opposite direction (drawing), as explained in the following sections. You may wish to skip this section the first time through, especially if you do not plan to use the pixel-transfer operations right away.

The Pixel Rectangle Drawing Process

Figure 8-12 and the following list describe the operation of drawing pixels into the framebuffer.

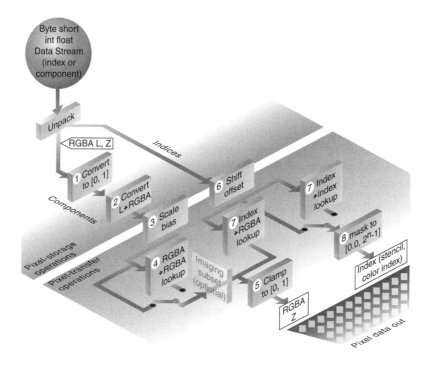

Figure 8-12   Drawing Pixels with glDrawPixels()

1. If the pixels are not indices (that is, if the format isn't GL_COLOR_INDEX or GL_STENCIL_INDEX), the first step is to convert the components to floating-point format if necessary. (See Table 4-1 for the details of the conversion.)

2. If the format is GL_LUMINANCE or GL_LUMINANCE_ALPHA, the luminance element is converted into R, G, and B by using the luminance value for each of the R, G, and B components. In GL_LUMINANCE_ALPHA format, the alpha value becomes the A value. If GL_LUMINANCE is specified, the A value is set to 1.0.

3. Each component (R, G, B, A, or depth) is multiplied by the appropriate scale, and the appropriate bias is added. For example, the R component is multiplied by the value corresponding to GL_RED_SCALE and added to the value corresponding to GL_RED_BIAS.

4. If GL_MAP_COLOR is TRUE, each of the R, G, B, and A components is clamped to the range [0.0, 1.0], multiplied by an integer 1 less than the table size, truncated, and looked up in the table. (See "Tips for Improving Pixel Drawing Rates" for more details.)

5. Next, the R, G, B, and A components are clamped to [0.0, 1.0], if they weren't already, and are converted to fixed-point with as many bits to the left of the binary point as there are in the corresponding framebuffer component.

6. If you're working with index values (stencil or color indices), then the values are first converted to fixed-point (if they were initially floating-point numbers), with some unspecified bits to the right of the binary point. Indices that were initially fixed-point remain so, and any bits to the right of the binary point are set to zero.

   The resulting index value is then shifted right or left by the absolute value of GL_INDEX_SHIFT bits; the value is shifted left if GL_INDEX_SHIFT > 0, and right otherwise. Finally, GL_INDEX_OFFSET is added to the index.

7. The next step with indices depends on whether you're using RGBA mode or color-index mode. In RGBA mode, a color index is converted to RGBA using the color components specified by GL_PIXEL_MAP_I_TO_R, GL_PIXEL_MAP_I_TO_G, GL_PIXEL_MAP_I_TO_B, and GL_PIXEL_MAP_I_TO_A (see "Pixel Mapping" for details). Otherwise, if GL_MAP_COLOR is GL_TRUE, a color index is looked up through the table GL_PIXEL_MAP_I_TO_I. (If GL_MAP_COLOR is GL_FALSE, the index is unchanged). If the image is made up of stencil indices rather

than color indices, and if GL_MAP_STENCIL is GL_TRUE, the index is looked up in the table corresponding to GL_PIXEL_MAP_S_TO_S. If GL_MAP_STENCIL is FALSE, the stencil index is unchanged.

8. Finally, if the indices haven't been converted to RGBA, the indices are then masked to the number of bits of either the color-index or stencil buffer, whichever is appropriate.

The Pixel Rectangle Reading Process

Many of the conversions done during the pixel rectangle drawing process are also done during the pixel rectangle reading process. The pixel reading process is shown in Figure 8-13 and described in the following list.

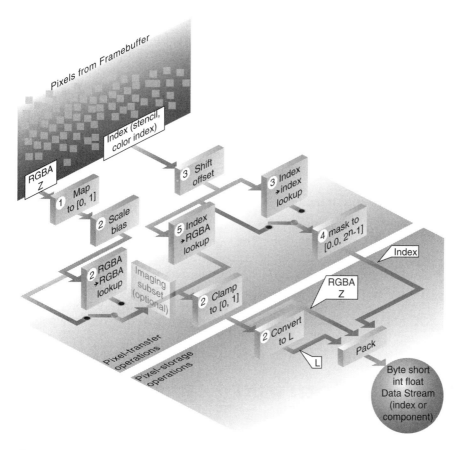

Figure 8-13   Reading Pixels with glReadPixels()

1. If the pixels to be read aren't indices (that is, if the format isn't GL_COLOR_INDEX or GL_STENCIL_INDEX), the components are mapped to [0.0, 1.0]—that is, in exactly the opposite way that they are when written.

2. Next, the scales and biases are applied to each component. If GL_MAP_COLOR is GL_TRUE, they're mapped and again clamped to [0.0, 1.0]. If luminance is desired instead of RGB, the R, G, and B components are added (L = R + G + B).

3. If the pixels are indices (color or stencil), they're shifted, offset, and, if GL_MAP_COLOR is GL_TRUE, also mapped.

4. If the storage format is either GL_COLOR_INDEX or GL_STENCIL_INDEX, the pixel indices are masked to the number of bits of the storage type (1, 8, 16, or 32) and packed into memory as previously described.

5. If the storage format is one of the component types (such as luminance or RGB), the pixels are always mapped by the index-to-RGBA maps. Then, they're treated as though they had been RGBA pixels in the first place (including potential conversion to luminance).

6. Finally, for both index and component data, the results are packed into memory according to the GL_PACK* modes set with **glPixelStore*()**.

The scaling, bias, shift, and offset values are the same as those used in drawing pixels, so if you're both reading and drawing pixels, be sure to reset these components to the appropriate values before doing a read or a draw. Similarly, the various maps must be properly reset if you intend to use maps for both reading and drawing.

Note: It might seem that luminance is handled incorrectly in both the reading and drawing operations. For example, luminance is not usually equally dependent on the R, G, and B components as it may be assumed from both Figure 8-12 and Figure 8-13. For example, if you want your luminance to be calculated such that the R, G, and B components contribute 30, 59, and 11 percent, respectively, you can set GL_RED_SCALE to 0.30, GL_RED_BIAS to 0.0, and so on. The computed L is then .30R + .59G + .11B.

Using Buffer Objects with Pixel Rectangle Data

Advanced

In the same way that storing vertex-array data in buffer objects, as described in "Using Buffer Objects with Vertex-Array Data" in Chapter 2, can increase application performance, storing pixel data in buffer objects can yield similar performance benefits.

By storing pixel rectangles in server-side buffer objects, you can eliminate the need to transfer data from the client's memory to the OpenGL server each frame. You might do this if you render an image as the background, instead of calling **glClear()**, for example.

Compared to vertex-array data in buffer objects, pixel buffer objects can be both read from (just like their vertex counterparts) and written to. Writing to a buffer object occurs when you retrieve pixel data from OpenGL, like when you call **glReadPixels()** or when you retrieve a texture's texels with **glGetTexImage()**.

Using Buffer Objects to Transfer Pixel Data

OpenGL functions that transfer data from the client application's memory to the OpenGL server, such as **glDrawPixels()**, **glTexImage*D()**, **glCompressedTexImage*D()**, **glPixelMap*()**, and similar functions in the Imaging Subset that take an array of pixels, can use buffer objects for storing pixel data on the server.

To store your pixel rectangle data in buffer objects, you will need to add a few steps to your application.

1. (Optional) Generate buffer object identifiers by calling **glGenBuffers()**.

2. Bind a buffer object for pixel unpacking by calling **glBindBuffer()** with a GL_PIXEL_UNPACK_BUFFER.

3. Request storage for your data and optionally initialize those data elements using **glBufferData()**, once again specifying GL_PIXEL_UNPACK_BUFFER as the *target* parameter.

4. Bind the appropriate buffer object to be used during rendering by once again calling **glBindBuffer()**.

5. Use the data by calling the appropriate function, such as **glDrawPixels()** or **glTexImage2D()**.

If you need to initialize multiple buffer objects, you will repeat steps 2 and 3 for each buffer object.

Example 8-5 modifies the image.c program (shown in Example 8-4) to use pixel buffer objects.

Example 8-5   Drawing, Copying, and Zooming Pixel Data Stored in a Buffer
Object: pboimage.c

```
#define BUFFER_OFFSET(bytes)   ((GLubyte*) NULL + (bytes))

/*Create checkerboard image*/
#definecheckImageWidth 64
#definecheckImageHeight 64
GLubyte checkImage[checkImageHeight][checkImageWidth][3];

static GLdouble zoomFactor = 1.0;
static GLint height;
static GLuint pixelBuffer;

void makeCheckImage(void)
{
   int i, j, c;

   for (i = 0; i < checkImageHeight; i++) {
      for (j = 0; j < checkImageWidth; j++) {
         c = (((i&0x8)==0)^((j&0x8)==0))*255;
         checkImage[i][j][0] = (GLubyte) c;
         checkImage[i][j][1] = (GLubyte) c;
         checkImage[i][j][2] = (GLubyte) c;
      }
   }
}

void init(void)
{
   glewInit();
   glClearColor (0.0, 0.0, 0.0, 0.0);
   glShadeModel(GL_FLAT);
   makeCheckImage();
   glPixelStorei(GL_UNPACK_ALIGNMENT, 1);

   glGenBuffers(1, &pixelBuffer);
   glBindBuffer(GL_PIXEL_UNPACK_BUFFER, pixelBuffer);
   glBufferData(GL_PIXEL_UNPACK_BUFFER,
               3*checkImageWidth*checkImageHeight,
               checkImage, GL_STATIC_DRAW);
}

void display(void)
{
   glClear(GL_COLOR_BUFFER_BIT);
```

```
    glRasterPos2i(0, 0);
    glBindBuffer(GL_PIXEL_UNPACK_BUFFER, pixelBuffer);
    glDrawPixels(checkImageWidth, checkImageHeight, GL_RGB,
                 GL_UNSIGNED_BYTE, BUFFER_OFFSET(0));
    glFlush();
}
```

Using Buffer Objects to Retrieve Pixel Data

Pixel buffer objects can also be used as destinations for operations that read pixels from OpenGL buffers and pass those pixels back to the application. Functions like **glReadPixels()** and **glGetTexImage()** can be provided an offset into a currently bound pixel buffer and update the data values in the buffer objects with the retrieved pixels.

Initializing and using a buffer object as the destination for pixel retrieval operations is almost identical to those steps described in "Using Buffer Objects to Transfer Pixel Data," except that the buffer *target* parameter for all buffer object-related calls needs to be GL_PIXEL_PACK_BUFFER.

After the completion of the OpenGL function retrieving the pixels, you can access the data values in the buffer object either by using the **glMapBuffer()** function (described in "Buffer Objects" in Chapter 2) or by **glGetBufferSubData()**. In some cases, **glGetBufferSubData()** may result in a more efficient transfer of data than **glMapBuffer()**.

Example 8-6 demonstrates using a pixel buffer object to store and access the pixels rendered after retrieving the image by calling **glReadPixels()**.

Example 8-6   Retrieving Pixel Data Using Buffer Objects

```
#define BUFFER_OFFSET(bytes) ((GLubyte*) NULL + (bytes))

GLuint pixelBuffer;
GLsizei imageWidth;
GLsizei imageHeight;
GLsizei numComponents = 4; /* four components for GL_RGBA */
GLsizei bufferSize;

void
init(void)
{
    bufferSize = imageWidth * imageHeight * numComponents
                 * sizeof(GLfloat); /* machine storage size */

    glGenBuffers(1, &pixelBuffer);
```

```
    glBindBuffer(GL_PIXEL_PACK_BUFFER, pixelBuffer);
    glBufferData(GL_PIXEL_PACK_BUFFER, bufferSize,
                 NULL, /* allocate but don't initialize data */
                 GL_STREAM_READ);
}

void
display(void)
{
    int i;
    GLsizei numPixels = imageWidth * imageHeight;

    /* Draw frame */

    glReadPixels(0, 0, imageWidth, imageHeight, GL_RGBA,
                 GL_FLOAT, BUFFER_OFFSET(0));

    GLfloat *pixels = glMapBuffer(GL_PIXEL_PACK_BUFFER,
                                  GL_READ_ONLY);

    for ( i = 0; i < numPixels; ++i ) {
        /* insert your pixel processing here
            process( &pixels[i*numComponents] );
        */
    }
    glUnmapBuffer(GL_PIXEL_PACK_BUFFER);
}
```

Tips for Improving Pixel Drawing Rates

As you can see, OpenGL has a rich set of features for reading, drawing, and manipulating pixel data. Although these features are often very useful, they can also decrease performance. Here are some tips for improving pixel draw rates:

- For best performance, set all pixel-transfer parameters to their default values, and set pixel zoom to (1.0, 1.0).

- A series of fragment operations is applied to pixels as they are drawn into the framebuffer. (See "Testing and Operating on Fragments" in Chapter 10.) For optimum performance, disable all necessary fragment operations.

- While performing pixel operations, disable other costly states, such as texture mapping or blending.

- If you use a pixel format and type that match those of the framebuffer, your OpenGL implementation doesn't need to convert the pixels into the format that matches the framebuffer. For example, if you are writing images to an RGB framebuffer with 8 bits per component, call **glDrawPixels()** with *format* set to RGB and *type* set to GL_ UNSIGNED_BYTE.

- For many implementations, unsigned image formats are faster to use than signed image formats.

- It is usually faster to draw a large pixel rectangle than to draw several small ones, since the cost of transferring the pixel data can be amortized over many pixels.

- If possible, reduce the amount of data that needs to be copied by using small data types (for example, use GL_UNSIGNED_BYTE) and fewer components (for example, use format GL_LUMINANCE_ALPHA).

- Pixel-transfer operations, including pixel mapping and values for scale, bias, offset, and shift other than the defaults, may decrease performance.

- If you need to render the same image each frame (as a background, for example), render it as a textured quadrilateral, as compared to calling **glDrawPixels()**. Having it stored as a texture requires that the data be downloaded into OpenGL once. See Chapter 9 for a discussion of texture mapping.

Imaging Subset

The Imaging Subset is a collection of routines that provide additional pixel processing capabilities. With it, you can:

- Use color lookup tables to replace pixel values.

- Use convolutions to filter images.

- Use color matrix transformations to do color space conversions and other linear transformations.

- Collect histogram statistics and minimum and maximum color component information about images.

You should use the Imaging Subset if you need more pixel processing capabilities than those provided by **glPixelTransfer*()** and **glPixelMap*()**.

The Imaging Subset is an extension to OpenGL. If the token *GL_ARB_imaging* is defined in the strings returned when querying extensions, then the subset is present, and all the functionality that is described in the following sections is available for you to use. If the token is not defined, none of the functionality is present in your implementation. To see if your implementation supports the Imaging Subset, see "Extensions to the Standard" on page 641.

Note: Although the Imaging Subset has always been an OpenGL extension, its functionality was deprecated in OpenGL Version 3.0, and was removed from Version 3.1 of the OpenGL specification.

Whenever pixels are passed to or read from OpenGL, they are processed by any of the enabled features of the subset. Routines that are affected by the Imaging Subset include functions that

- Draw and read pixel rectangles: **glReadPixels()**, **glDrawPixels()**, **glCopyPixels()**.

- Define textures: **glTexImage1D()**, **glTexImage2D()**, **glCopyTexImage*D()**, **glTexSubImage1D()**, **glTexSubImage2d()** and **glCopyTexSubImage*D()**.

Figure 8-14 illustrates the operations that the Imaging Subset performs on pixels that are passed into or read from OpenGL. Most of the features of the Imaging Subset may be enabled and disabled, with the exception of the color matrix transformation, which is always enabled.

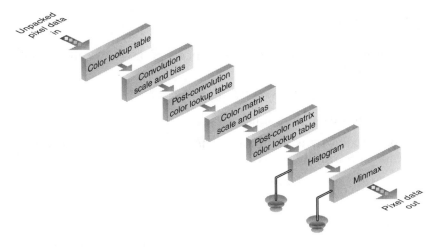

Figure 8-14   Imaging Subset Operations

Color Tables

Color tables are lookup tables used to replace a pixel's color. In applications, color tables may be used for contrast enhancement, filtering, and image equalization.

There are three different color lookup tables available, which operate at different stages of the pixel pipeline. Table 8-7 shows where in the pipeline pixels may be replaced by the respective color table.

Color Table Parameter	Operates on Pixels
GL_COLOR_TABLE	when they enter the imaging pipeline
GL_POST_CONVOLUTION_COLOR_TABLE	after convolution
GL_POST_COLOR_MATRIX_COLOR_TABLE	after the color matrix transformation

Table 8-7   When Color Table Operations Occur in the Imaging Pipeline

Each color table can be enabled separately using **glEnable()** with the respective parameter from Table 8-7.

Specifying Color Tables

Color tables are specified similarly to one-dimensional images. As shown in Figure 8-14, there are three color tables available for updating pixel values. **glColorTable()** is used to define each color table.

---

void **glColorTable**(GLenum *target*, GLenum *internalFormat*,
           GLsizei *width*, GLenum *format*, GLenum *type*,
           const GLvoid **data*);

Defines the specified color table when *target* is set to GL_COLOR_TABLE, GL_POST_CONVOLUTION_COLOR_TABLE, or GL_POST_COLOR_MATRIX_COLOR_TABLE. If *target* is set to GL_PROXY_COLOR_TABLE, GL_PROXY_POST_CONVOLUTION_COLOR_TABLE, or GL_PROXY_POST_COLOR_MATRIX_COLOR_TABLE, then **glColorTable()** verifies that the specified color table fits into the available resources.

The *internalFormat* variable is used to determine the internal OpenGL representation of *data*. It can be one of the following symbolic constants: GL_ALPHA, GL_ALPHA4, GL_ALPHA8, GL_ALPHA12, GL_ALPHA16, GL_LUMINANCE, GL_LUMINANCE4, GL_LUMINANCE8, GL_LUMINANCE12, GL_LUMINANCE16, GL_LUMINANCE_ALPHA, GL_LUMINANCE4_ALPHA4, GL_LUMINANCE6_ALPHA2, GL_LUMINANCE8_ALPHA8, GL_LUMINANCE12_ALPHA4, GL_LUMINANCE12_ALPHA12, GL_LUMINANCE16_ALPHA16, GL_INTENSITY, GL_INTENSITY4, GL_INTENSITY8, GL_INTENSITY12, GL_INTENSITY16, GL_RGB, GL_R3_G3_B2, GL_RGB4, GL_RGB5, GL_RGB8, GL_RGB10, GL_RGB12, GL_RGB16, GL_RGBA, GL_RGBA2, GL_RGBA4, GL_RGB5_A1, GL_RGBA8, GL_RGB10_A2, GL_RGBA12, and GL_RGBA16.

The *width* parameter, which must be a power of 2, indicates the number of pixels in the color table. The *format* and *type* describe the format and data type of the color table data. They have the same meaning as equivalent parameters of **glDrawPixels()**.

The internal format of the table determines which components of the image's pixels are replaced. For example, if you specify the format to be GL_RGB, then the red, green, and blue components of each incoming pixel are looked up in the appropriate color table and replaced. Table 8-8 describes which pixel components are replaced for a given base internal format.

Base Internal Format	Red Component	Green Component	Blue Component	Alpha Component
GL_ALPHA	Unchanged	Unchanged	Unchanged	A_t
GL_LUMINANCE	L_t	L_t	L_t	Unchanged
GL_LUMINANCE_ALPHA	L_t	L_t	L_t	A_t
GL_INTENSITY	I_t	I_t	I_t	I_t
GL_RGB	R_t	G_t	B_t	Unchanged
GL_RGBA	R_t	G_t	B_t	A_t

Table 8-8 Color Table Pixel Replacement

In Table 8-8, L_t represents luminance entries in the defined color table, which affect only red, green, and blue components. I_t represents intensity entries, which affect red, green, blue, and alpha identically.

After the appropriate color table has been applied to the image, the pixels can be scaled and biased, after which their values are clamped to the range [0, 1]. The GL_COLOR_TABLE_SCALE and GL_COLOR_TABLE_BIAS factors are set for each color table with the **glColorTableParameter*()** routine.

---

void **glColorTableParameter{if}v**(GLenum *target*, GLenum *pname*,
                               *TYPE *param)*;

Sets the GL_COLOR_TABLE_SCALE and GL_COLOR_TABLE_BIAS parameters for each color table. The *target* parameter is one of GL_COLOR_TABLE, GL_POST_CONVOLUTION_COLOR_TABLE, or GL_POST_COLOR_MATRIX_COLOR_TABLE, and it specifies which color table's scale and bias values to set.

The possible values for *pname* are GL_COLOR_TABLE_SCALE and GL_COLOR_TABLE_BIAS.

The value for *param* points to an array of four values, representing the red, green, blue, and alpha modifiers, respectively.

Example 8-7 shows how an image can be inverted using color tables. The color table is set up to replace each color component with its inverse color.

Example 8-7   Pixel Replacement Using Color Tables: colortable.c

```
extern GLubyte*  readImage(const char*, GLsizei*, GLsizei* );

GLubyte  *pixels;
GLsizei   width, height;

void init(void)
{
   int    i;
   GLubyte  colorTable[256][3];

   pixels = readImage("Data/leeds.bin", &width, &height);
   glPixelStorei(GL_UNPACK_ALIGNMENT, 1);
   glClearColor(0, 0, 0, 0);
```

```
        /* Set up an inverting color table */
        for (i = 0; i < 256; ++i) {
            colorTable[i][0] = 255 - i;
            colorTable[i][1] = 255 - i;
            colorTable[i][2] = 255 - i;
        }

        glColorTable(GL_COLOR_TABLE, GL_RGB, 256, GL_RGB,
            GL_UNSIGNED_BYTE, colorTable);
        glEnable(GL_COLOR_TABLE);
    }

void display(void)
{
    glClear(GL_COLOR_BUFFER_BIT);
    glRasterPos2i(1, 1);
    glDrawPixels(width, height, GL_RGB, GL_UNSIGNED_BYTE,
        pixels);
    glFlush();
}
```

Note: Example 8-7 introduces a new function, **readImage()**, which is presented to simplify the example programs. In general, you need to use a routine that can read the image file format that you require. The file format that **readImage()** understands is listed below. The data is listed sequentially in the file.

- Width of the image, stored as a *GLsizei*

- Height of the image, stored as a *GLsizei*

- *width · height* RGB triples, stored with a *GLubyte* per color component

In addition to specifying a color table explicitly from your application, you may want to use an image created in the framebuffer as the definition for a color table. The **glCopyColorTable()** routine lets you specify a single row of pixels that are read from the framebuffer and used to define a color table.

---

void **glCopyColorTable**(GLenum *target*, GLenum *internalFormat*,
                         GLint *x*, GLint *y*, GLsizei *width*);

Creates a color table using framebuffer data to define the elements of the color table. The pixels are read from the current GL_READ_BUFFER and are processed exactly as if **glCopyPixels()** had been called but stopped before final conversion. The **glPixelTransfer*()** settings are applied.

The *target* parameter must be set to one of the targets of **glColorTable()**. The *internalFormat* parameter uses the same symbolic constants as the *internalFormat* parameter of **glColorTable()**. The color array is defined by the *width* pixels in the row starting at (*x, y*) in the framebuffer.

Replacing All or Part of a Color Table

If you would like to replace a part of a color table, then color subtable commands let you reload an arbitrary section of a color table with new values.

---

void **glColorSubTable**(GLenum *target*, GLsizei *start*, GLsizei *count*,
  GLenum *format*, GLenum *type*,
  const GLvoid **data*);

Replaces color table entries *start* to *start + count − 1* with values stored in *data*.

The *target* parameter is GL_COLOR_TABLE, GL_POST_CONVOLUTION_ COLOR_TABLE, or GL_POST_COLOR_MATRIX_COLOR_TABLE. The *format* and *type* parameters are identical to those of **glColorTable()** and describe the pixel values stored in *data*.

---

void **glCopyColorSubTable**(GLenum *target*, GLsizei *start*, GLint *x*,
  GLint *y*, GLsizei *count*);

Replaces color table entries *start* to *start + count − 1* with *count* color pixel values from the row in the framebuffer starting at position (*x, y*). The pixels are converted into the *internalFormat* of the original color table.

Querying a Color Table's Values

The pixel values stored in the color tables can be retrieved using the **glGetColorTable()** function. Refer to "The Query Commands" on page 740 for more details.

Color Table Proxies

Color table proxies provide a way to query OpenGL to see if there are enough resources available to store your color table. If **glColorTable()** is called with one of the following proxy targets:

- GL_PROXY_COLOR_TABLE

- GL_PROXY_POST_CONVOLUTION_COLOR_TABLE

- GL_PROXY_POST_COLOR_MATRIX_COLOR_TABLE

then OpenGL determines if the required color table resources are available. If the color table does not fit, the width, format, and component resolution values are all set to zero. To check if your color table fits, query one of the state values mentioned above. For example:

```
glColorTable(GL_PROXY_COLOR_TABLE, GL_RGB, 1024, GL_RGB,
    GL_UNSIGNED_BYTE, null);
glGetColorTableParameteriv(GL_PROXY_COLOR_TABLE,
    GL_COLOR_TABLE_WIDTH, &width);
if (width == 0)
    /* color table didn't fit as requested */
```

For more details on **glGetColorTableParameter*()**, see "The Query Commands" on page 740.

Convolutions

Convolutions are pixel filters that replace each pixel with a weighted average of its neighboring pixels and itself. Blurring and sharpening images, finding edges, and adjusting image contrast are examples of how convolutions are used.

Figure 8-15 shows how pixel P_{00} and related pixels are processed by the 3×3 convolution filter to produce pixel P'_{11}.

Convolutions are arrays of pixel weights and operate only on RGBA pixels. A filter, which is also known as a *kernel*, is simply a two-dimensional array of pixel weights. Each pixel in the output image of the convolution process is created by multiplying a set of the input image's pixels by the pixel weights in the convolution kernel and summing the results. For example, in Figure 8-15, pixel P'_{11} is computed by summing the products of the nine pixels from the input image and the nine pixel weights in the convolution filter.

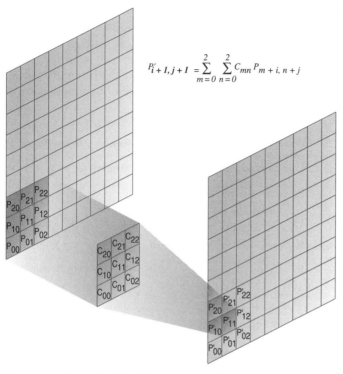

$$P'_{i+1,j+1} = \sum_{m=0}^{2} \sum_{n=0}^{2} C_{mn} P_{m+i,n+j}$$

Figure 8-15   The Pixel Convolution Operation

void **glConvolutionFilter2D**(GLenum *target*, GLenum *internalFormat*,
                    GLsizei *width*, GLsizei *height*,
                    GLenum *format*, GLenum *type*,
                    const GLvoid **image*);

Defines a two-dimensional convolution filter where the *target* parameter
must be GL_CONVOLUTION_2D.

The *internalFormat* parameter defines which pixel components the
convolution operation is performed on, and can be one of the 38 symbolic
constants that are used for the *internalFormat* parameter for **glColorTable**().

The *width* and *height* parameters specify the size of the filter in pixels. The
maximum width and height for convolution filters may be queried with
glGetConvolutionParameter*(). Refer to "The Query Commands" on
page 740 for more details.

As with **glDrawPixels**(), the *format* and *type* parameters specify the format
of the pixels stored in *image*.

Similar to color tables, the internal format of the convolution filter determines which components of the image are operated on. Table 8-9 describes how the different base filter formats affect pixels. R_s, G_s, B_s, and A_s represent the color components of the source pixels. L_f represents the luminance value of a GL_LUMINANCE filter, and I_f corresponds to the intensity value of a GL_INTENSITY filter. Finally, R_f, G_f, B_f, and A_f represent the red, green, blue, and alpha components of the convolution filter.

Base Filter Format	Red Result	Green Result	Blue Result	Alpha Result
GL_ALPHA	Unchanged	Unchanged	Unchanged	$A_s * A_f$
GL_LUMINANCE	$R_s * L_f$	$G_s * L_f$	$B_s * L_f$	Unchanged
GL_LUMINANCE_ALPHA	$R_s * L_f$	$G_s * L_f$	$B_s * L_f$	$A_s * A_f$
GL_INTENSITY	$R_s * I_f$	$Gs * I_f$	$B_s * I_f$	$A_s * I_f$
GL_RGB	$R_s * R_f$	$G_s * G_f$	$B_s * B_f$	Unchanged
GL_RGBA	$R_s * R_f$	$G_s * G_f$	$Bs * B_f$	$A_s * A_f$

Table 8-9   How Convolution Filters Affect RGBA Pixel Components

Use **glEnable(GL_CONVOLUTION_2D)** to enable 2D convolution processing.

Example 8-8 demonstrates the use of several 3 × 3 GL_LUMINANCE convolution filters to find edges in an RGB image. The 'h', 'l', and 'v' keys change among the various filters.

Example 8-8   Using Two-Dimensional Convolution Filters: convolution.c

```
extern GLubyte*  readImage(const char*, GLsizei*, GLsizei*);

GLubyte  *pixels;
GLsizei   width, height;

/* Define convolution filters */
GLfloat  horizontal[3][3] = {
   { 0, -1, 0 },
   { 0,  1, 0 },
   { 0,  0, 0 }
};
```

```
GLfloat  vertical[3][3] = {
    {  0, 0, 0 },
    { -1, 1, 0 },
    {  0, 0, 0 }
};

GLfloat  laplacian[3][3] = {
    { -0.125, -0.125, -0.125 },
    { -0.125,  1.0,   -0.125 },
    { -0.125, -0.125, -0.125 }
};

void display(void)
{
    glClear(GL_COLOR_BUFFER_BIT);
    glRasterPos2i(1, 1);
    glDrawPixels(width, height, GL_RGB, GL_UNSIGNED_BYTE,
        pixels);
    glFlush();
}

void init(void)
{
    pixels = readImage("Data/leeds.bin", &width, &height);
    glPixelStorei(GL_UNPACK_ALIGNMENT, 1);
    glClearColor(0.0, 0.0, 0.0, 0.0);

    printf("Using horizontal filter\n");
    glConvolutionFilter2D(GL_CONVOLUTION_2D, GL_LUMINANCE, 3, 3,
        GL_LUMINANCE, GL_FLOAT, horizontal);
    glEnable(GL_CONVOLUTION_2D);
}

void keyboard(unsigned char key, int x, int y)
{
    switch (key) {
        case 'h' :
            printf("Using horizontal filter\n");
            glConvolutionFilter2D(GL_CONVOLUTION_2D, GL_LUMINANCE,
                3, 3, GL_LUMINANCE, GL_FLOAT, horizontal );
            break;

        case 'v' :
            printf("Using vertical filter\n" );
```

```
        glConvolutionFilter2D( GL_CONVOLUTION_2D, GL_LUMINANCE,
            3, 3, GL_LUMINANCE, GL_FLOAT, vertical );
        break;

    case 'l' :
        printf("Using laplacian filter\n");
        glConvolutionFilter2D(GL_CONVOLUTION_2D, GL_LUMINANCE,
            3, 3, GL_LUMINANCE, GL_FLOAT, laplacian );
        break;

    case 27: /* Escape Key */
        exit(0)
        break;
}
    glutPostRedisplay();
}
```

As with color tables, you may want to specify a convolution filter with pixel values from the framebuffer. **glCopyConvolutionFilter2D()** copies a rectangle of pixels from the current GL_READ_BUFFER to use as the definition of the convolution filter. If GL_LUMINANCE or GL_INTENSITY is specified for the *internalFormat,* the red component of the pixel is used to define the convolution filter's value.

---

void **glCopyConvolutionFilter2D**(GLenum *target,*
                                   GLenum *internalFormat,*
                                   GLint *x,* GLint *y,*
                                   GLsizei *width,* GLsizei *height*);

Defines a two-dimensional convolution filter initialized with pixels from the color framebuffer. *target* must be GL_CONVOLUTION_2D, and *internalFormat* must be set to one of the internal formats defined for **glConvolutionFilter2D()**.

The pixel rectangle with lower left pixel (*x, y*) and size *width* by *height* is read from the framebuffer and converted into the specified *internalFormat.*

Specifying Separable Two-Dimensional Convolution Filters

Convolution filters are separable if they can be represented by the *outer product* of two one-dimensional filters.

glSeparableFilter2D() is used to specify the two one-dimensional filters that represent the separable two-dimensional convolution filter. As with

glConvolutionFilter2D(), the internal format of the convolution filter determines how an image's pixels are processed.

---

void **glSeparableFilter2D**(GLenum *target*, GLenum *internalFormat*,
GLsizei *width*, GLsizei *height*, GLenum *format*,
GLenum *type*, const GLvoid **row*,
const GLvoid **column*);

Defines a two-dimensional separable convolution filter. *target* must be set to GL_SEPARABLE_2D. The *internalFormat* parameter uses the same values that are used for **glConvolutionFilter2D()**.

width specifies the number of pixels in the *row* array. Likewise, *height* specifies the number of pixels in the *column* array. *type* and *format* define the storage format for *row* and *column* in the same manner as **glConvolutionFilter2D()**.

Use **glEnable(GL_SEPARABLE_2D)** to enable convolutions using a two-dimensional separable convolution filter. GL_CONVOLUTION_2D takes precedence if both GL_CONVOLUTION_2D and GL_SEPARABLE_2D are specified.

A GL_INVALID_OPERATION error is set if an unpack pixel buffer object is bound and the combination of *width, height, format,* and *type*, plus the specified offsets into the bound buffer object would cause a memory access outside of the memory allocated when the buffer object was created.

For example, you might construct a 3 × 3 convolution filter by specifying the one-dimensional filter [−1/2, 1, −1/2] for both *row* and *column* for a GL_LUMINANCE separable convolution filter. OpenGL would compute the convolution of the source image using the two one-dimensional filters in the same manner as if it computed a complete two-dimensional filter by computing the following outer product:

$$
\begin{bmatrix} -1/2 \\ 1 \\ -1/2 \end{bmatrix} \begin{bmatrix} -1/2 & 1 & -1/2 \end{bmatrix} = \begin{bmatrix} 1/4 & -1/2 & 1/4 \\ -1/2 & 1 & -1/2 \\ 1/4 & -1/2 & 1/4 \end{bmatrix}
$$

Using separable convolution filters is computationally more efficient than using a nonseparable two-dimensional convolution filter.

One-Dimensional Convolution Filters

One-dimensional convolutions are identical to the two-dimensional version except that the filter's *height* parameter is assumed to be 1. However, they affect only the specification of one-dimensional textures (see "Texture Rectangles" on page 412 for details).

---

void **glConvolutionFilter1D**(GLenum *target*, GLenum *internalFormat*,
 GLsizei *width*, GLenum *format*,
 GLenum *type*, const GLvoid **image*);

Specifies a one-dimensional convolution filter. *target* must be set to GL_CONVOLUTION_1D. *width* specifies the number of pixels in the filter. The *internalFormat*, *format*, and *type* have the same meanings as they do for the respective parameters to **glConvolutionFilter2D**(). *image* points to the one-dimensional image to be used as the convolution filter.

Use **glEnable(GL_CONVOLUTION_1D)** to enable one-dimensional convolutions.

You may want to specify the convolution filter with values generated from the framebuffer. **glCopyConvolutionFilter1D**() copies a row of pixels from the current GL_READ_BUFFER, converts them into the specified *internalFormat*, and uses them to define the convolution filter.

A GL_INVALID_OPERATION error is set if an unpack pixel buffer object is bound and the combination of *width, format,* and *type*, plus the specified offset into the bound buffer object would cause a memory access outside of the memory allocated when the buffer object was created.

---

void **glCopyConvolutionFilter1D**(GLenum *target*,
 GLenum *internalFormat*, GLint *x*,
 GLint *y*, GLsizei *width*);

Defines a one-dimensional convolution filter with pixel values from the framebuffer. **glCopyConvolutionFilter1D**() copies *width* pixels starting at (*x, y*) and converts the pixels into the specified *internalFormat*.

When a convolution filter is specified, it can be scaled and biased. The scale and bias values are specified with the **glConvolutionParameter***(). No clamping of the convolution filter occurs after scaling or biasing.

void **glConvolutionParameter**{if}(GLenum *target*, GLenum *pname*,
TYPE param);
void **glConvolutionParameter**{if}v(GLenum *target*, GLenum *pname*,
const *TYPE *params*);

Sets parameters that control how a convolution is performed. *target* must be GL_CONVOLUTION_1D, GL_CONVOLUTION_2D, or GL_SEPARABLE_2D.

pname must be GL_CONVOLUTION_BORDER_MODE, GL_CONVOLUTION_FILTER_SCALE, or GL_CONVOLUTION_FILTER_BIAS. Specifying *pname* as GL_CONVOLUTION_BORDER_MODE defines the convolution border mode. In this case, *params* must be GL_REDUCE, GL_CONSTANT_BORDER, or GL_REPLICATE_BORDER. If *pname* is set to either GL_CONVOLUTION_FILTER_SCALE or GL_CONVOLUTION_FILTER_BIAS, then *params* points to an array of four color values for red, green, blue, and alpha, respectively.

Convolution Border Modes

The convolutions of pixels at the edges of an image are handled differently from the interior pixels. Their convolutions are modified by the convolution border mode. There are three options for computing border convolutions:

- GL_REDUCE mode causes the resulting image to shrink in each dimension by the size of the convolution filter. The width of the resulting image is *(width − W_f)*, and the height of the resulting image is *(height − H_f)*, where W_f and H_f are the width and height of the convolution filter, respectively. If this produces an image with zero or negative width or height, no output is generated, nor are any errors.

- GL_CONSTANT_BORDER computes the convolutions of border pixels by using a constant pixel value for pixels outside of the source image. The constant pixel value is set using the **glConvolutionParameter*()** function. The resulting image's size matches that of the source image.

- GL_REPLICATE_BORDER computes the convolution in the same manner as in GL_CONSTANT_BORDER mode, except the outermost row or column of pixels is used for the pixels that lie outside of the source image. The resulting image's size matches that of the source image.

Post-Convolution Operations

After the convolution operation is completed, the pixels of the resulting image may be scaled and biased, and are clamped to the range [0, 1]. The scale and bias values are specified by calling **glPixelTransfer*()**, with either GL_POST_CONVOLUTION_*_SCALE or GL_POST_CONVOLUTION_*_BIAS, respectively. Specifying a GL_POST_CONVOLUTION_COLOR_TABLE with **glColorTable()** allows pixel components to be replaced using a color lookup table.

Color Matrix

For color space conversions and linear transformations on pixel values, the Imaging Subset supports a 4 × 4 matrix stack, selected by setting **glMatrixMode(GL_COLOR)**. For example, to convert from RGB color space to CMY (cyan, magenta, yellow) color space, you might call

```
GLfloat rgb2cmy[16] = {
    -1,  0,  0, 0,
     0, -1,  0, 0,
     0,  0, -1, 0,
     1,  1,  1, 1
};

glMatrixMode(GL_COLOR);  /* enter color matrix mode */
glLoadMatrixf(rgb2cmy);
glMatrixMode(GL_MODELVIEW);  /* back to modelview mode */
```

Note: Recall that OpenGL matrices are stored in a column-major format. See "General-Purpose Transformation Commands" on page 134 for more detail about using matrices with OpenGL.

The color matrix stack has at least two matrix entries. (See "The Query Commands" on page 740 for details on determining the depth of the color matrix stack.) Unlike the other parts of the Imaging Subset, the color matrix transformation is always performed and cannot be disabled.

Example 8-9 illustrates using the color matrix to exchange the red and green color components of an image.

Example 8-9   Exchanging Color Components Using the Color Matrix: colormatrix.c

```
extern GLubyte*  readImage(const char*, GLsizei*, GLsizei*);

GLubyte  *pixels;
GLsizei  width, height;
```

```
void init(void)
{
    /* Specify a color matrix to reorder a pixel's components
     * from RGB to GBR */
    GLfloat  m[16] = {
        0.0, 1.0, 0.0, 0.0,
        0.0, 0.0, 1.0, 0.0,
        1.0, 0.0, 0.0, 0.0,
        0.0, 0.0, 0.0, 1.0
    };

    pixels = readImage("Data/leeds.bin", &width, &height);
    glPixelStorei(GL_UNPACK_ALIGNMENT, 1);
    glClearColor(0.0, 0.0, 0.0, 0.0);

    glMatrixMode(GL_COLOR);
    glLoadMatrixf(m);
    glMatrixMode(GL_MODELVIEW);
}

void display(void)
{
    glClear(GL_COLOR_BUFFER_BIT);
    glRasterPos2i(1, 1);
    glDrawPixels(width, height, GL_RGB, GL_UNSIGNED_BYTE,
        pixels);
    glFlush();
}
```

Post-Color Matrix Transformation Operations

Similar to the post-convolution operations, pixels can be scaled and biased after the color matrix step. Calling **glPixelTransfer*()** with either GL_POST_COLOR_MATRIX_*_SCALE or GL_POST_COLOR_MATRIX_*_BIAS defines the scale and bias values for the post color matrix operation. Pixel values after scaling and biasing are clamped to the range [0, 1].

Histogram

Using the Imaging Subset, you can collect statistics about images. Histogramming determines the distribution of color values in an image, which can be used to determine how to balance an image's contrast, for example.

glHistogram() specifies what components of the image you want to histogram, and whether you want only to collect statistics or to continue processing the image. To collect histogram statistics, you must call **glEnable(GL_HISTOGRAM)**.

Similar to the color tables described in "Color Tables" on page 369, a proxy mechanism is available with **glHistogram**() to determine if there are enough resources to store the requested histogram. If resources are not available, the histogram's width, format, and component resolutions are set to zero. You can query the results of a histogram proxy using **glGetHistogramParameter**(), described in "The Query Commands" on page 740.

---

void **glHistogram**(GLenum *target*, GLsizei *width*,
                     GLenum *internalFormat*, GLboolean *sink*);

Defines how an image's histogram data should be stored. The *target* parameter must be set to either GL_HISTOGRAM or GL_PROXY_HISTOGRAM. The *width* parameter specifies the number of entries in the histogram table. Its value must be a power of 2.

The *internalFormat* parameter defines how the histogram data should be stored. The allowable values are GL_ALPHA, GL_ALPHA4, GL_ALPHA8, GL_ALPHA12, GL_ALPHA16, GL_LUMINANCE, GL_LUMINANCE4, GL_LUMINANCE8, GL_LUMINANCE12, GL_LUMINANCE16, GL_LUMINANCE_ALPHA, GL_LUMINANCE4_ALPHA4, GL_LUMINANCE6_ALPHA2, GL_LUMINANCE8_ALPHA8, GL_LUMINANCE12_ALPHA4, GL_LUMINANCE12_ALPHA12, GL_LUMINANCE16_ALPHA16, GL_RGB, GL_RGB2, GL_RGB4, GL_RGB5, GL_RGB8, GL_RGB10, GL_RGB12, GL_RGB16, GL_RGBA, GL_RGBA2, GL_RGBA4, GL_RGB5_A1, GL_RGBA8, GL_RGB10_A2, GL_RGBA12, and GL_RGBA16. This list does not include GL_INTENSITY* values. This differs from the list of values accepted by **glColorTable**().

The *sink* parameter indicates whether the pixels should continue to the minmax stage of the pipeline or be discarded.

After you've passed the pixels to the imaging pipeline using **glDrawPixels**(), you can retrieve the results of the histogram using **glGetHistogram**(). In addition to returning the histogram's values, **glGetHistogram**() can be used to reset the histogram's internal storage. The internal storage can also be reset using **glResetHistogram**(), which is described on page 386.

void **glGetHistogram**(GLenum *target*, GLboolean *reset*, GLenum *format*, GLenum *type*, GLvoid **values*);

Returns the collected histogram statistics. *target* must be GL_HISTOGRAM. *reset* specifies if the internal histogram tables should be cleared.

The *format* and *type* parameters specify the storage type of *values*, and how the histogram data should be returned to the application. They accept the same values at their respective parameters in **glDrawPixels**().

In Example 8-10, the program computes the histogram of an image and plots resulting distributions in the window. The 's' key in the example shows the effect of the *sink* parameter, which controls whether the pixels are passed to the subsequent imaging pipeline operations.

Example 8-10   Computing and Diagramming an Image's Histogram: histogram.c

```
#define HISTOGRAM_SIZE  256    /* Must be a power of 2 */

extern GLubyte*  readImage(const char*, GLsizei*, GLsizei*);

GLubyte   *pixels;
GLsizei   width, height;


void init(void)
{
   pixels = readImage("Data/leeds.bin", &width, &height);
   glPixelStorei(GL_UNPACK_ALIGNMENT, 1);
   glClearColor(0.0, 0.0, 0.0, 0.0);

   glHistogram(GL_HISTOGRAM, HISTOGRAM_SIZE, GL_RGB, GL_FALSE);
   glEnable(GL_HISTOGRAM);
}

void display(void)
{
   int i;
   GLushort values[HISTOGRAM_SIZE][3];

   glClear(GL_COLOR_BUFFER_BIT);
   glRasterPos2i(1, 1);
   glDrawPixels(width, height, GL_RGB, GL_UNSIGNED_BYTE,
      pixels);
   glGetHistogram(GL_HISTOGRAM, GL_TRUE, GL_RGB,
      GL_UNSIGNED_SHORT, values);
```

```
    /* Plot histogram */

    glBegin(GL_LINE_STRIP);
    glColor3f(1.0, 0.0, 0.0);
    for (i = 0; i < HISTOGRAM_SIZE; i++)
        glVertex2s(i, values[i][0]);
    glEnd();

    glBegin(GL_LINE_STRIP);
    glColor3f(0.0, 1.0, 0.0);
    for (i = 0; i < HISTOGRAM_SIZE; i++)
        glVertex2s(i, values[i][1]);
    glEnd();

    glBegin(GL_LINE_STRIP);
    glColor3f(0.0, 0.0, 1.0);
    for (i = 0; i < HISTOGRAM_SIZE; i++)
        glVertex2s(i, values[i][2]);
    glEnd();
    glFlush();
}

void keyboard(unsigned char key, int x, int y)
{
    static GLboolean sink = GL_FALSE;

    switch (key) {
       case 's' :
          sink = !sink;
          glHistogram(GL_HISTOGRAM, HISTOGRAM_SIZE, GL_RGB,
             sink);
          break;

       case 27: /* Escape Key */
          exit(0);
          break;
}
    glutPostRedisplay();
}
```

glResetHistogram() will discard the histogram without retrieving the values.

void **glResetHistogram**(GLenum *target*);

Resets the histogram counters to zero. The *target* parameter must be GL_HISTOGRAM.

Minmax

glMinmax() computes the minimum and maximum pixel component values for a pixel rectangle. As with **glHistogram()**, you can compute the minimum and maximum values and either render the image or discard the pixels.

---
void **glMinmax**(GLenum *target*, GLenum *internalFormat*,
        GLboolean *sink*);

Computes the minimum and maximum pixel values for an image. *target* must be GL_MINMAX.

internalFormat specifies for which color components the minimum and maximum values should be computed. **glMinmax()** accepts the same values for *internalFormat* as **glHistogram()** accepts.

If GL_TRUE is specified for *sink*, then the pixels are discarded and not written to the framebuffer. GL_FALSE renders the image.

glGetMinmax() is used to retrieve the computed minimum and maximum values. Similar to **glHistogram()**, the internal values for the minimum and maximum can be reset when they are accessed.

---
void **glGetMinmax**(GLenum *target*, GLboolean *reset*, GLenum *format*,
        GLenum *type*, GLvoid **values*);

Returns the results of the minmax operation. *target* must be GL_MINMAX. If the *reset* parameter is set to GL_TRUE, the minimum and maximum values are reset to their initial values. The *format* and *type* parameters describe the format of the minmax data returned in *values*, and use the same values as **glDrawPixels()**.

Example 8-11 demonstrates the use of **glMinmax()** to compute the minimum and maximum pixel values in GL_RGB format. The minmax operation must be enabled with **glEnable(GL_MINMAX)**.

The minimum and maximum values returned in the array *values* from **glMinmax()** command are grouped by component. For example, if you request GL_RGB values as the *format*, the first three values in the *values* array represent the minimum red, green, and blue values, followed by the maximum red, green, and blue values for the processed pixels.

Example 8-11   Computing Minimum and Maximum Pixel Values: minmax.c

```
extern GLubyte*  readImage(const char*, GLsizei*, GLsizei*);

GLubyte  *pixels;
GLsizei   width, height;


void init(void)
{
    pixels = readImage("Data/leeds.bin", &width, &height);
    glPixelStorei(GL_UNPACK_ALIGNMENT, 1);
    glClearColor(0.0, 0.0, 0.0, 0.0);

    glMinmax(GL_MINMAX, GL_RGB, GL_FALSE);
    glEnable(GL_MINMAX);
}

void display(void)
{
    GLubyte  values[6];

    glClear(GL_COLOR_BUFFER_BIT);
    glRasterPos2i(1, 1);
    glDrawPixels(width, height, GL_RGB, GL_UNSIGNED_BYTE,
        pixels);
    glGetMinmax(GL_MINMAX, GL_TRUE, GL_RGB, GL_UNSIGNED_BYTE,
        values);
    glFlush();
    printf("Red  : min = %d  max = %d\n", values[0], values[3]);
    printf("Green: min = %d  max = %d\n", values[1], values[4]);
    printf("Blue : min = %d  max = %d\n", values[2], values[5]);
}
```

Even though **glGetMinmax()** can reset the minmax values when they are retrieved, you can explicitly reset the internal tables at any time by calling **glResetMinmax()**.

---

void **glResetMinmax**(GLenum *target*);

Resets the minimum and maximum values to their initial values. The *target* parameter must be GL_MINMAX.

Chapter 9

Texture Mapping

Chapter Objectives

After reading this chapter, you'll be able to do the following:

- Understand what texture mapping can add to your scene

- Specify texture images in compressed and uncompressed formats

- Control how a texture image is filtered as it is applied to a fragment

- Create and manage texture images in texture objects, and control a high-performance working set of those texture objects

- Specify how the texture and fragment colors are combined

- Supply texture coordinates describing how the texture image should be mapped onto objects in your scene

- Generate texture coordinates automatically to produce effects such as contour maps and environment maps

- Perform complex texture operations in a single pass with multitexturing (sequential texture units)

- Use texture combiner functions to mathematically operate on texture, fragment, and constant color values

- After texturing, process fragments with secondary colors

- Specify textures to be used for processing point sprites

- Transform texture coordinates using the texture matrix

- Render shadowed objects, using depth textures

So far, every geometric primitive has been drawn as either a solid color or smoothly shaded between the colors at its vertices—that is, they've been drawn without texture mapping. If you want to draw a large brick wall without texture mapping, for example, each brick must be drawn as a separate polygon. Without texturing, a large flat wall—which is really a single rectangle—might require thousands of individual bricks, and even then the bricks may appear too smooth and regular to be realistic.

Texture mapping allows you to glue an image of a brick wall (obtained, perhaps, by taking a photograph of a real wall) to a polygon and to draw the entire wall as a single polygon. Texture mapping ensures that all the right things happen as the polygon is transformed and rendered. For example, when the wall is viewed in perspective, the bricks may appear smaller as the wall gets farther from the viewpoint. Other uses for texture mapping include depicting vegetation on large polygons representing the ground in flight simulation; wallpaper patterns; and textures that make polygons look like natural substances such as marble, wood, and cloth. The possibilities are endless. Although it's most natural to think of applying textures to polygons, textures can be applied to all primitives—points, lines, polygons, bitmaps, and images. Plates 6, 8, 18–21, and 24–32 all demonstrate the use of textures.

Because there are so many possibilities, texture mapping is a fairly large, complex subject, and you must make several programming choices when using it. For starters, most people intuitively understand a two-dimensional texture, but a texture may be one-dimensional or even three-dimensional. You can map textures to surfaces made of a set of polygons or to curved surfaces, and you can repeat a texture in one, two, or three directions (depending on how many dimensions the texture is described in) to cover the surface. In addition, you can automatically map a texture onto an object in such a way that the texture indicates contours or other properties of the item being viewed. Shiny objects can be textured so that they appear to be in the center of a room or other environment, reflecting the surroundings from their surfaces. Finally, a texture can be applied to a surface in different ways. It can be painted on directly (like a decal placed on a surface), used to modulate the color the surface would have been painted otherwise, or used to blend a texture color with the surface color. If this is your first exposure to texture mapping, you might find that the discussion in this chapter moves fairly quickly. As an additional reference, you might look at the chapter on texture mapping in *3D Computer Graphics* by Alan Watt (Addison-Wesley, 1999).

Textures are simply rectangular arrays of data—for example, color data, luminance data, or color and alpha data. The individual values in a texture array are often called *texels*. What makes texture mapping tricky is that a rectangular texture can be mapped to nonrectangular regions, and this must be done in a reasonable way.

Figure 9-1 illustrates the texture-mapping process. The left side of the figure represents the entire texture, and the black outline represents a quadrilateral shape whose corners are mapped to those spots on the texture. When the quadrilateral is displayed on the screen, it might be distorted by applying various transformations—rotations, translations, scaling, and projections. The right side of the figure shows how the texture-mapped quadrilateral might appear on your screen after these transformations. (Note that this quadrilateral is concave and might not be rendered correctly by OpenGL without prior tessellation. See Chapter 11 for more information about tessellating polygons.)

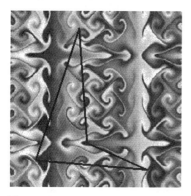 

Figure 9-1   Texture-Mapping Process

Notice how the texture is distorted to match the distortion of the quadrilateral. In this case, it's stretched in the *x*-direction and compressed in the *y*-direction; there's a bit of rotation and shearing going on as well. Depending on the texture size, the quadrilateral's distortion, and the size of the screen image, some of the texels might be mapped to more than one fragment, and some fragments might be covered by multiple texels. Since the texture is made up of discrete texels (in this case, 256×256 of them), filtering operations must be performed to map texels to fragments. For example, if many texels correspond to a fragment, they're averaged down to fit; if texel boundaries fall across fragment boundaries, a weighted average of the applicable texels is performed. Because of these calculations, texturing is computationally expensive, which is why many specialized graphics systems include hardware support for texture mapping.

An application may establish texture objects, with each texture object representing a single texture (and possible associated mipmaps). Some implementations of OpenGL can support a special *working set* of texture objects that have better performance than texture objects outside the working set. These high-performance texture objects are said to be *resident* and may have special hardware and/or software acceleration available. You may use OpenGL to create and delete texture objects and to determine which textures constitute your working set.

This chapter covers the OpenGL's texture-mapping facility in the following major sections.

- "An Overview and an Example" gives a brief, broad look at the steps required to perform texture mapping. It also presents a relatively simple example of texture mapping.

- "Specifying the Texture" explains how to specify one-, two-, or three-dimensional textures. It also discusses how to use a texture's borders, how to supply a series of related textures of different sizes, and how to control the filtering methods used to determine how an applied texture is mapped to screen coordinates.

- "Filtering" details how textures are either magnified or minified as they are applied to the pixels of polygons. Minification using special mipmap textures is also explained.

- "Texture Objects" describes how to put texture images into objects so that you can control several textures at one time. With texture objects, you may be able to create a working set of high-performance textures, which are said to be resident. You may also prioritize texture objects to increase or decrease the likelihood that a texture object is resident.

- "Texture Functions" discusses the methods used for painting a texture onto a surface. You can choose to have the texture color values replace those that would be used if texturing were not in effect, or you can have the final color be a combination of the two.

- "Assigning Texture Coordinates" describes how to compute and assign appropriate texture coordinates to the vertices of an object. It also explains how to control the behavior of coordinates that lie outside the default range—that is, how to repeat or clamp textures across a surface.

- "Automatic Texture-Coordinate Generation" shows how to have OpenGL automatically generate texture coordinates so that you can achieve such effects as contour and environment maps.

- "Multitexturing" details how textures may be applied in a serial pipeline of successive texturing operations.

- "Texture Combiner Functions" explains how you can control mathematical operations (multiplication, addition, subtraction, interpolation, and even dot products) on the RGB and alpha values of textures, constant colors, and incoming fragments. Combiner functions expose flexible, programmable fragment processing.

- "Applying Secondary Color after Texturing" shows how secondary colors are applied to fragments after texturing.

- "Point Sprites" discusses how textures can be applied to large points to improve their visual quality.

- "The Texture Matrix Stack" explains how to manipulate the texture matrix stack and use the q texture coordinate.

- "Depth Textures" describes the process for using the values stored in the depth buffer as a texture for use in determining shadowing for a scene.

Version 1.1 of OpenGL introduced several texture-mapping operations:

- Additional internal texture image formats

- Texture proxy, to query whether there are enough resources to accommodate a given texture image

- Texture subimage, to replace all or part of an existing texture image, rather than completely delete and create a texture to achieve the same effect

- Specifying texture data from framebuffer memory (as well as from system memory)

- Texture objects, including resident textures and prioritizing

Version 1.2 added:

- 3D texture images

- A new texture-coordinate wrapping mode, GL_CLAMP_TO_EDGE, which derives texels from the edge of a texture image, not its border

- Greater control over mipmapped textures to represent different levels of detail (LOD)

- Calculating specular highlights (from lighting) after texturing operations

Version 1.3 granted more texture-mapping operations:

- Compressed textures
- Cube map textures
- Multitexturing, which is applying several textures to render a single primitive
- Texture-wrapping mode, GL_CLAMP_TO_BORDER
- Texture environment modes: GL_ADD and GL_COMBINE (including the dot product combination function)

Version 1.4 supplied these texture capabilities:

- Texture-wrapping mode, GL_MIRRORED_REPEAT
- Automatic mipmap generation with GL_GENERATE_MIPMAP
- Texture parameter GL_TEXTURE_LOD_BIAS, which alters selection of the mipmap level of detail
- Application of a secondary color (specified by **glSecondaryColor*()**) after texturing
- During the texture combine environment mode, the ability to use texture color from different texture units as sources for the texture combine function
- Use of depth (*r* coordinate) as an internal texture format and texturing modes that compare depth texels to decide upon texture application

Version 1.5 added support for:

- Additional texture-comparison modes for use of textures for shadow mapping

Version 2.0 modified texture capabilities by:

- Removing the power-of-two restriction on texture maps
- Iterated texture coordinates across point sprites

Version 2.1 added the following enhancements:

- Specifying textures in sRGB format, which accepts gamma-corrected red, green, and blue texture components
- Specifying and retrieving pixel rectangle data in server-side buffer objects. See "Using Buffer Objects with Pixel Rectangle Data" in Chapter 8 for details on using pixel buffer objects.

Version 3.0 contributed even more texturing features:

- Storing texels in floating-point, signed integer, and unsigned integer formats without being normalized (mapped into the range [-1,1] or [0,1] respectively)

- One- and two-dimensional texture arrays, which allow indexing into an array of one- or two-dimensional texture maps using the next-higher-dimension texture coordinate

- A standardized texture format, RGTC, for one- and two-component textures

If you try to use one of these texture-mapping operations and can't find it, check the version number of your implementation of OpenGL to see if it actually supports it. (See "Which Version Am I Using?" in Chapter 14.) In some implementations, a particular feature may be available only as an extension.

For example, in OpenGL Version 1.2, multitexturing was approved by the Khronos OpenGL ARB Working Group, the governing body for OpenGL, as an optional extension. An implementation of OpenGL 1.2 supporting multitexturing would have function and constant names suffixed with **ARB**, such as **glActiveTextureARB(GL_TEXTURE1_ARB)**. In OpenGL 1.3, multitexturing became mandatory, and the ARB suffix was removed.

An Overview and an Example

This section gives an overview of the steps necessary to perform texture mapping. It also presents a relatively simple texture-mapping program. Of course, you know that texture mapping can be a very involved process.

Steps in Texture Mapping

To use texture mapping, you perform the following steps:

1. Create a texture object and specify a texture for that object.

2. Indicate how the texture is to be applied to each pixel.

3. Enable texture mapping.

4. Draw the scene, supplying both texture and geometric coordinates.

Keep in mind that texture mapping works only in RGBA mode. Texture mapping results in color-index mode are undefined.

Create a Texture Object and Specify a Texture for That Object

A texture is usually thought of as being two-dimensional, like most images, but it can also be one-dimensional or three-dimensional. The data describing a texture may consist of one, two, three, or four elements per texel and may represent an (R, G, B, A) quadruple, a modulation constant, or a depth component.

In Example 9-1, which is very simple, a single texture object is created to maintain a single uncompressed, two-dimensional texture. This example does not find out how much memory is available. Since only one texture is created, there is no attempt to prioritize or otherwise manage a working set of texture objects. Other advanced techniques, such as texture borders, mipmaps, or cube maps, are not used in this simple example.

Indicate How the Texture Is to Be Applied to Each Pixel

You can choose any of four possible functions for computing the final RGBA value from the fragment color and the texture image data. One possibility is simply to use the texture color as the final color; this is the *replace* mode, in which the texture is painted on top of the fragment, just as a decal would be applied. (Example 9-1 uses *replace* mode.) Another method is to use the texture to *modulate*, or scale, the fragment's color; this technique is useful for combining the effects of lighting with texturing. Finally, a constant color can be blended with that of the fragment, based on the texture value.

Enable Texture Mapping

You need to enable texturing before drawing your scene. Texturing is enabled or disabled using **glEnable()** or **glDisable()**, with the symbolic constant GL_TEXTURE_1D, GL_TEXTURE_2D, GL_TEXTURE_3D, or GL_TEXTURE_CUBE_MAP for one-, two-, three-dimensional, or cube map texturing, respectively. (If two or all three of the dimensional texturing modes are enabled, the largest dimension enabled is used. If cube map textures are enabled, it trumps all the others. For the sake of clean programs, you should enable only the one you want to use.)

Draw the Scene, Supplying Both Texture and Geometric Coordinates

You need to indicate how the texture should be aligned relative to the fragments to which it's to be applied before it's "glued on." That is, you need to specify both texture coordinates and geometric coordinates as you specify the objects in your scene. For a two-dimensional texture map, for example, the texture coordinates range from 0.0 to 1.0 in both directions, but the coordinates of the items being textured can be anything. To apply the brick texture to a wall, for example, assuming the wall is square and meant to represent one copy of the texture, the code would probably assign texture coordinates (0, 0), (1, 0), (1, 1), and (0, 1) to the four corners of the wall. If the wall is large, you might want to paint several copies of the texture map on it. If you do so, the texture map must be designed so that the bricks at the left edge match up nicely with the bricks at the right edge, and similarly for the bricks at the top and bottom.

You must also indicate how texture coordinates outside the range [0.0, 1.0] should be treated. Do the textures repeat to cover the object, or are they clamped to a boundary value?

A Sample Program

One of the problems with showing sample programs to illustrate texture mapping is that interesting textures are large. Typically, textures are read from an image file, since specifying a texture programmatically could take hundreds of lines of code. In Example 9-1, the texture—which consists of alternating white and black squares, like a checkerboard—is generated by the program. The program applies this texture to two squares, which are then rendered in perspective, one of them facing the viewer squarely and the other tilting back at 45 degrees, as shown in Figure 9-2. In object coordinates, both squares are the same size.

Figure 9-2   Texture-Mapped Squares

Example 9-1   Texture-Mapped Checkerboard: checker.c

```c
/*  Create checkerboard texture  */
#define checkImageWidth 64
#define checkImageHeight 64
static GLubyte checkImage[checkImageHeight][checkImageWidth][4];

static GLuint texName;

void makeCheckImage(void)
{
   int i, j, c;

   for (i = 0; i < checkImageHeight; i++) {
      for (j = 0; j < checkImageWidth; j++) {
         c = (((i&0x8)==0)^((j&0x8))==0)*255;
         checkImage[i][j][0] = (GLubyte) c;
         checkImage[i][j][1] = (GLubyte) c;
         checkImage[i][j][2] = (GLubyte) c;
         checkImage[i][j][3] = (GLubyte) 255;
      }
   }
}

void init(void)
{
   glClearColor(0.0, 0.0, 0.0, 0.0);
   glShadeModel(GL_FLAT);
   glEnable(GL_DEPTH_TEST);
   makeCheckImage();
   glPixelStorei(GL_UNPACK_ALIGNMENT, 1);

   glGenTextures(1, &texName);
   glBindTexture(GL_TEXTURE_2D, texName);

   glTexParameteri(GL_TEXTURE_2D, GL_TEXTURE_WRAP_S, GL_REPEAT);
   glTexParameteri(GL_TEXTURE_2D, GL_TEXTURE_WRAP_T, GL_REPEAT);
   glTexParameteri(GL_TEXTURE_2D, GL_TEXTURE_MAG_FILTER,
                   GL_NEAREST);
   glTexParameteri(GL_TEXTURE_2D, GL_TEXTURE_MIN_FILTER,
                   GL_NEAREST);
   glTexImage2D(GL_TEXTURE_2D, 0, GL_RGBA, checkImageWidth,
                checkImageHeight, 0, GL_RGBA, GL_UNSIGNED_BYTE,
                checkImage);
}

void display(void)
{
```

```
    glClear(GL_COLOR_BUFFER_BIT | GL_DEPTH_BUFFER_BIT);
    glEnable(GL_TEXTURE_2D);
    glTexEnvf(GL_TEXTURE_ENV, GL_TEXTURE_ENV_MODE, GL_REPLACE);
    glBindTexture(GL_TEXTURE_2D, texName);
    glBegin(GL_QUADS);
    glTexCoord2f(0.0, 0.0); glVertex3f(-2.0, -1.0, 0.0);
    glTexCoord2f(0.0, 1.0); glVertex3f(-2.0, 1.0, 0.0);
    glTexCoord2f(1.0, 1.0); glVertex3f(0.0, 1.0, 0.0);
    glTexCoord2f(1.0, 0.0); glVertex3f(0.0, -1.0, 0.0);

    glTexCoord2f(0.0, 0.0); glVertex3f(1.0, -1.0, 0.0);
    glTexCoord2f(0.0, 1.0); glVertex3f(1.0, 1.0, 0.0);
    glTexCoord2f(1.0, 1.0); glVertex3f(2.41421, 1.0, -1.41421);
    glTexCoord2f(1.0, 0.0); glVertex3f(2.41421, -1.0, -1.41421);
    glEnd();
    glFlush();
    glDisable(GL_TEXTURE_2D);
}

void reshape(int w, int h)
{
    glViewport(0, 0, (GLsizei) w, (GLsizei) h);
    glMatrixMode(GL_PROJECTION);
    glLoadIdentity();
    gluPerspective(60.0, (GLfloat) w/(GLfloat) h, 1.0, 30.0);
    glMatrixMode(GL_MODELVIEW);
    glLoadIdentity();
    glTranslatef(0.0, 0.0, -3.6);
}
/*  keyboard() and main() deleted to reduce printing  */
```

The checkerboard texture is generated in the routine **makeCheckImage()**, and all the texture-mapping initialization occurs in the routine **init()**. **glGenTextures()** and **glBindTexture()** name and create a texture object for a texture image. (See "Texture Objects" on page 437.) The single, full-resolution texture map is specified by **glTexImage2D()**, whose parameters indicate the size, type, location, and other properties of the texture image. (See "Specifying the Texture" below for more information about **glTexImage2D()**.)

The four calls to **glTexParameter*()** specify how the texture is to be wrapped and how the colors are to be filtered if there isn't an exact match between texels in the texture and pixels on the screen. (See "Filtering" on page 434 and "Repeating and Clamping Textures" on page 452.)

In **display()**, **glEnable()** turns on texturing. **glTexEnv*()** sets the drawing mode to GL_REPLACE so that the textured polygons are drawn using the colors from the texture map (rather than taking into account the color in which the polygons would have been drawn without the texture).

Then, two polygons are drawn. Note that texture coordinates are specified along with vertex coordinates. The **glTexCoord*()** command behaves similarly to the **glNormal()** command. **glTexCoord*()** sets the current texture coordinates; any subsequent vertex command has those texture coordinates associated with it until **glTexCoord*()** is called again.

Note: The checkerboard image on the tilted polygon might look wrong when you compile and run it on your machine—for example, it might look like two triangles with different projections of the checkerboard image on them. If so, try setting the parameter GL_PERSPECTIVE_CORRECTION_HINT to GL_NICEST and running the example again. To do this, use **glHint()**.

Specifying the Texture

The command **glTexImage2D()** defines a two-dimensional texture. It takes several arguments, which are described briefly here and in more detail in the subsections that follow. The related commands for one- and three-dimensional textures, **glTexImage1D()** and **glTexImage3D()**, are described in "Texture Rectangles" and "Three-Dimensional Textures," respectively.

---

void **glTexImage2D**(GLenum *target*, GLint *level*, GLint *internalFormat*,
GLsizei *width*, GLsizei *height*, GLint *border*,
GLenum *format*, GLenum *type*, const GLvoid **texels*);

Defines a two-dimensional texture, or a one-dimensional texture array. The *target* parameter is set to one of the constants: GL_TEXTURE_2D, GL_PROXY_TEXTURE_2D, GL_TEXTURE_CUBE_MAP_POSITIVE_X, GL_TEXTURE_CUBE_MAP_NEGATIVE_X, GL_TEXTURE_CUBE_MAP_POSITIVE_Y, GL_TEXTURE_CUBE_MAP_NEGATIVE_Y, GL_TEXTURE_CUBE_MAP_POSITIVE_Z, GL_TEXTURE_CUBE_MAP_NEGATIVE_Z, or GL_PROXY_TEXTURE_CUBE_MAP for defining two-dimensional textures, (See "Cube Map Textures" for information about use of the GL_*CUBE_MAP* constants with **glTexImage2D** and related functions), and GL_TEXTURE_1D_ARRAY and GL_PROXY_TEXTURE_1D_ARRAY for defining a one-dimensional texture array (which are only available if the OpenGL version is 3.0 or greater. See "Texture Arrays" on page 419.), or GL_TEXTURE_RECTANGLE and GL_PROXY_TEXTURE_RECTANGLE.

You use the *level* parameter if you're supplying multiple resolutions of the texture map; with only one resolution, *level* should be 0. (See "Mipmaps: Multiple Levels of Detail" for more information about using multiple resolutions.)

The next parameter, *internalFormat*, indicates which components (RGBA, depth, luminance, or intensity) are selected for the texels of an image. There are three groups of internal formats. First, the following symbolic constants for *internalFormat* specify that texel values should be normalized (mapped into the range [0,1]) and stored in a fixed-point representation (of the number of bits specified if there's a numeric value included in the token name): GL_ALPHA, GL_ALPHA4, GL_ALPHA8, GL_ALPHA12, GL_ALPHA16, GL_COMPRESSED_ALPHA, GL_COMPRESSED_LUMINANCE, GL_COMPRESSED_LUMINANCE_ ALPHA, GL_COMPRESSED_INTENSITY, GL_COMPRESSED_RGB, GL_COMPRESSED_RGBA, GL_DEPTH_COMPONENT, GL_DEPTH_ COMPONENT16, GL_DEPTH_COMPONENT24, GL_DEPTH_ COMPONENT32, GL_DEPTH_STENCIL, GL_INTENSITY, GL_INTENSITY4, GL_INTENSITY8, GL_INTENSITY12, GL_INTENSITY16, GL_LUMINANCE, GL_LUMINANCE4, GL_LUMINANCE8, GL_LUMINANCE12, GL_LUMINANCE16, GL_LUMINANCE_ALPHA, GL_LUMINANCE4_ALPHA4, GL_LUMINANCE6_ALPHA2, GL_LUMINANCE8_ALPHA8, GL_LUMINANCE12_ALPHA4, GL_LUMINANCE12_ALPHA12, GL_LUMINANCE16_ALPHA16, GL_RED, GL_R8, GL_R16, GL_RG, GL_RG8, GL_RG16, GL_RGB, GL_R3_G3_B2, GL_RGB4, GL_RGB5, GL_RGB8, GL_RGB10, GL_RGB12, GL_RGB16, GL_RGBA, GL_RGBA2, GL_RGBA4, GL_RGB5_A1, GL_RGBA8, GL_RGB10_A2, GL_RGBA12, GL_RGBA16, GL_SRGB, GL_SRGB8, GL_SRGB_ALPHA, GL_SRGB8_ALPHA8, GL_SLUMINANCE_ALPHA, GL_SLUMINANCE8_ ALPHA8, GL_SLUMINANCE, GL_SLUMINANCE8, GL_COMPRESSED_ SRGB, GL_COMPRESSED_SRGB_ALPHA, GL_COMPRESSED_ SLUMINANCE, or GL_COMPRESSED_SLUMINANCE_ALPHA. (See "Texture Functions" for a discussion of how these selected components are applied, and see "Compressed Texture Images" for a discussion of how compressed textures are handled.)

The next sets of symbolic constants for *internalFormat* were added in OpenGL version 3.0, and specify floating-point pixel formats, which are not normalized (and stored in floating-point values of the specified number of bits): GL_R16F, GL_R32F, GL_RG16F, GL_RG32F, GL_RGB16F, GL_RGB32F, GL_RGBA16F, GL_RGBA32F, GL_R11F_G11F_B10F, and GL_RGB9_E5. Another set of symbolic constants accepted represent signed- and unsigned-integer (denoted with the additional "U" in the token) formats (stored in the respective integer types of the specified bitwidth): GL_R8I, GL_R8UI, GL_R16I, GL_R16UI, GL_R32I, GL_R32UI, GL_RG8I, GL_RG8UI, GL_RG16I, GL_RG16UI, GL_RG32I, GL_RG32UI, GL_RGB8I, GL_RGB8UI, GL_RGB16I, GL_RGB16UI, GL_RGB32I, GL_RGB32UI, GL_RGBA8I, GL_RGBA8UI, GL_RGBA16I, GL_RGBA16UI, GL_RGBA32I, and GL_RGBA32UI. Additionally, textures can be stored in a compressed form if *internalFormat* is one of: GL_COMPRESSED_RED, GL_COMPRESSED_ RG, and in the specific compressed texture formats: GL_COMPRESSED_ RED_RGTC1, GL_COMPRESSED_SIGNED_RED_RGTC1, GL_ COMPRESSED_RG_RGTC2, and GL_COMPRESSED_SIGNED_RG_RGTC2, and for sized depth and stencil formats, OpenGL version 3.0 added: GL_DEPTH_COMPONENT16, GL_DEPTH_COMPONENT24, GL_DEPTH_ COMPONENT32F, and GL_DEPTH24_STENCIL8, and GL_DEPTH32F_ STENCIL8 for packed stencil-depth dual-channel texels.

OpenGL version 3.1 added support for signed normalized values (which are mapped the range [-1,1]), and are specified for *internalFormat* with the tokens: GL_R8_SNORM, GL_R16_SNORM, GL_RG8_SNORM, GL_RG16_ SNORM, GL_RGB8_SNORM, GL_RGB16_SNORM, GL_RGBA8_SNORM, GL_RGBA16_SNORM.

The *internalFormat* may request a specific resolution of components. For example, if *internalFormat* is GL_R3_G3_B2, you are asking that texels be 3 bits of red, 3 bits of green, and 2 bits of blue. By definition, GL_INTENSITY, GL_LUMINANCE, GL_LUMINANCE_ALPHA, GL_DEPTH_COMPONENT, GL_RGB, GL_RGBA, GL_SRGB, GL_SRGB_ALPHA, GL_SLUMINANCE, GL_SLUMINANCE_ALPHA, and the compressed forms of the above tokens are lenient, because they do not ask for a specific resolution. (For compatibility with the OpenGL release 1.0, the numeric values 1, 2, 3, and 4 for *internalFormat* are equivalent to the symbolic constants GL_LUMINANCE, GL_LUMINANCE_ALPHA, GL_RGB, and GL_RGBA, respectively.)

The *width* and *height* parameters give the dimensions of the texture image; *border* indicates the width of the border, which is either 0 (no border) or 1 (and must be 0 for version 3.1 implementations). For OpenGL implementations that do not support version 2.0 or greater, both *width* and *height* must have the form $2^m + 2b$, where m is a non-negative integer (which can have a different value for *width* than for *height*) and b is the value of *border*. The maximum size of a texture map depends on the implementation of OpenGL, but it must be at least 64×64 (or 66×66 with borders). For OpenGL implementations supporting version 2.0 and greater, textures may be of any size. The *format* and *type* parameters describe the format and data type of the texture image data. They have the same meaning as they do for **glDrawPixels**(). (See "Imaging Pipeline" in Chapter 8.) In fact, texture data is in the same format as the data used by **glDrawPixels**(), so the settings of **glPixelStore*** () and **glPixelTransfer*** () are applied. (In Example 9-1, the call

```
glPixelStorei(GL_UNPACK_ALIGNMENT, 1);
```

is made because the data in the example isn't padded at the end of each texel row.) The *format* parameter can be GL_COLOR_INDEX, GL_DEPTH_COMPONENT, GL_RGB, GL_RGBA, GL_RED, GL_GREEN, GL_BLUE, GL_ALPHA, GL_LUMINANCE, or GL_LUMINANCE_ALPHA—that is, the same formats available for **glDrawPixels**() with the exception of GL_STENCIL_INDEX. OpenGL version 3.0 additionally permits the following formats: GL_DEPTH_STENCIL, GL_RG, GL_RED_INTEGER, GL_GREEN_INTEGER, GL_BLUE_INTEGER, GL_ALPHA_INTEGER, GL_RG_INTEGER, GL_RGB_INTEGER, GL_RGBA_INTEGER, GL_BGR_INTEGER, and GL_BGRA_INTEGER.

Similarly, the *type* parameter can be GL_BYTE, GL_UNSIGNED_BYTE, GL_SHORT, GL_UNSIGNED_SHORT, GL_INT, GL_UNSIGNED_INT, GL_FLOAT, GL_BITMAP, or one of the packed pixel data types.

Finally, *texels* contains the texture image data. This data describes the texture image itself as well as its border.

As you can see by the myriad of accepted values, the internal format of a texture image may affect the performance of texture operations. For example, some implementations perform texturing faster with GL_RGBA than with GL_RGB, because the color components align to processor memory better. Since this varies, you should check specific information about your implementation of OpenGL.

The internal format of a texture image also may control how much memory a texture image consumes. For example, a texture of internal format GL_RGBA8 uses 32 bits per texel, while a texture of internal format GL_R3_G3_B2 uses only 8 bits per texel. Of course, there is a corresponding trade-off between memory consumption and color resolution.

A GL_DEPTH_COMPONENT texture stores depth values, as compared to colors, and is most often used for rendering shadows (as described in "Depth Textures" on page 483). Similarly a GL_DEPTH_STENCIL texture stores depth and stencil values in the same texture.

Textures specified with an internal format of GL_SRGB, GL_SRGB8, GL_SRGB_ALPHA, GL_SRGB8_ALPHA8, GL_SLUMINANCE_ALPHA,

GL_SLUMINANCE8_ALPHA8, GL_SLUMINANCE, GL_SLUMINANCE8, GL_COMPRESSED_SRGB, GL_COMPRESSED_SRGB_ALPHA, GL_COMPRESSED_SLUMINANCE, or GL_COMPRESSED_SLUMINANCE_ALPHA) are expected to have their red, green, and blue color components specified in the sRGB color space (officially known as the International Electrotechnical Commission IEC standard 61966-2-1). The sRGB color space is approximately the same as the 2.2 gamma-corrected linear RGB color space. For sRGB textures, the alpha values in the texture should not be gamma corrected.

For internal formats with the suffixes of "F", "I", or "UI", the format of a texel is stored in a floating-point value, signed integer, or unsigned integer, respectively, of the specified number of bits (e.g., GL_R16F would store a single channel texture with each texel being a 16-bit floating-point value). All of these formats were added in OpenGL Version 3.0. For these formats, the values are not mapped into the range [0,1], but rather are allowed their full numeric precision. One other special format that involves floating-point values is the *packed shared-exponent* format, which specifies the red, green, and blue values as floating-point values, all of which have the same exponent value. All of these formats are described in the online appendix Appendix J, "Floating-Point Formats for Textures, Framebuffers, and Renderbuffers."[1]

Integer internal texture formats (those with an "I" or "UI" suffix) require their input data to match the specified integer size.

Signed-normalized values specified with internal formats including GL_*_SNORM are converted into the range [-1,1].

Although texture mapping results in color-index mode are undefined, you can still specify a texture with a GL_COLOR_INDEX image. In that case, pixel-transfer operations are applied to convert the indices to RGBA values by table lookup before they're used to form the texture image.

If your OpenGL implementation supports the *Imaging Subset* and any of its features are enabled, the texture image will be affected by those features. For example, if the two-dimensional convolution filter is enabled, then the convolution will be performed on the texture image. (The convolution may change the image's width and/or height.)

For OpenGL versions prior to Version 2.0, the number of texels for both the width and the height of a texture image, not including the optional border, must be a power of 2. If your original image does not have dimensions that fit that limitation, you can use the OpenGL Utility Library routine **gluScaleImage()** to alter the sizes of your textures.

---

[1] This appendix is available online at http://www.opengl-redbook.com/appendices/.

int **gluScaleImage**(GLenum *format*, GLint *widthin*, GLint *heightin*,
GLenum *typein*, const void **datain*, GLint *widthout*,
GLint *heightout*, GLenum *typeout*, void **dataout*);

Scales an image using the appropriate pixel-storage modes to unpack the data from *datain*. The *format*, *typein*, and *typeout* parameters can refer to any of the formats or data types supported by **glDrawPixels()**. The image is scaled using linear interpolation and box filtering (from the size indicated by *widthin* and *heightin* to *widthout* and *heightout*), and the resulting image is written to *dataout*, using the pixel GL_PACK* storage modes. The caller of **gluScaleImage()** must allocate sufficient space for the output buffer. A value of 0 is returned on success, and a GLU error code is returned on failure.

Note: In GLU 1.3, **gluScaleImage()** supports packed pixel formats (and their related data types), but likely does not support those of OpenGL Version 3.0 and later.

The framebuffer itself can also be used as a source for texture data. **glCopyTexImage2D()** reads a rectangle of pixels from the framebuffer and uses that rectangle as texels for a new texture.

void **glCopyTexImage2D**(GLenum *target*, GLint *level*,
GLint *internalFormat*, GLint *x*, GLint *y*,
GLsizei *width*, GLsizei *height*, GLint *border*);

Creates a two-dimensional texture, using framebuffer data to define the texels. The pixels are read from the current GL_READ_BUFFER and are processed exactly as if **glCopyPixels()** had been called, but instead of going to the framebuffer, the pixels are placed into texture memory. The settings of **glPixelTransfer*()** and other pixel-transfer operations are applied.

The *target* parameter must be one of the constants GL_TEXTURE_2D, GL_TEXTURE_CUBE_MAP_POSITIVE_X, GL_TEXTURE_CUBE_MAP_ NEGATIVE_X, GL_TEXTURE_CUBE_MAP_POSITIVE_Y, GL_TEXTURE_ CUBE_MAP_NEGATIVE_Y, GL_TEXTURE_CUBE_MAP_POSITIVE_Z, or GL_TEXTURE_CUBE_MAP_NEGATIVE_Z (see "Cube Map Textures" on page 465 for information about use of the *CUBE_MAP* constants), or GL_TEXTURE_1D_ARRAY (see "Texture Arrays" on page 419). The *level*, *internalFormat*, and *border* parameters have the same effects that they have for **glTexImage2D()**. The texture array is taken from a screen-aligned pixel rectangle with the lower left corner at coordinates specified by the (x, y) parameters. The *width* and *height* parameters specify the size of this pixel rectangle. For OpenGL implementations that do not support Version 2.0, both *width* and *height* must have the form $2^m + 2b$, where m is a non-negative integer (which can have a different value for *width* than for *height*) and b is the value of *border*. For implementations supporting OpenGL Version 2.0 and greater, textures may be of any size.

If your OpenGL implementation is Version 3.0 or later, you can use framebuffer objects to effectively perform the same operation as **glCopyPixels2D()** by rendering directly into texture memory. This process is described in detail in "Framebuffer Objects" in Chapter 10.

The next sections give more detail about texturing, including the use of the *target*, *border*, and *level* parameters. The *target* parameter can be used to query accurately the size of a texture (by creating a texture proxy with **glTexImage*D()**) and whether a texture possibly can be used within the texture resources of an OpenGL implementation. Redefining a portion of a texture is described in "Replacing All or Part of a Texture Image" on page 408. One- and three-dimensional textures are discussed in "Texture Rectangles" on page 412 and "Three-Dimensional Textures" on page 414, respectively. The texture border, which has its size controlled by the *border* parameter, is detailed in "Compressed Texture Images" on page 420. The *level* parameter is used to specify textures of different resolutions and is incorporated into the special technique of *mipmapping*, which is explained in "Mipmaps: Multiple Levels of Detail" on page 423. Mipmapping requires understanding how to filter textures as they are applied; filtering is covered on page 434.

Texture Proxy

To an OpenGL programmer who uses textures, size is important. Texture resources are typically limited, and texture format restrictions vary among OpenGL implementations. There is a special texture proxy target to evaluate whether your OpenGL implementation is capable of supporting a particular texture format at a particular texture size.

glGetIntegerv(GL_MAX_TEXTURE_SIZE,...) tells you a lower bound on the largest width or height (without borders) of a texture image; typically, the size of the largest square texture supported. For 3D textures, GL_MAX_3D_TEXTURE_SIZE may be used to query the largest allowable dimension (width, height, or depth, without borders) of a 3D texture image. For cube map textures, GL_MAX_CUBE_MAP_TEXTURE_SIZE is similarly used.

However, use of any of the GL_MAX*TEXTURE_SIZE queries does not consider the effect of the internal format or other factors. A texture image that stores texels using the GL_RGBA16 internal format may be using 64 bits per texel, so its image may have to be 16 times smaller than an image with the GL_LUMINANCE4 internal format. Textures requiring borders or mipmaps further reduce the amount of available memory.

A special placeholder, or *proxy*, for a texture image allows the program to query more accurately whether OpenGL can accommodate a texture of a desired internal format.

For instance, to find out whether there are enough resources available for a standard 2D texture, call **glTexImage2D()** with a *target* parameter of GL_PROXY_TEXTURE_2D and the given *level, internalFormat, width, height, border, format,* and *type.* For a proxy, you should pass NULL as the pointer for the *texels* array. (For a cube map, use **glTexImage2D()** with the target GL_PROXY_TEXTURE_CUBE_MAP. For one- or three-dimensional textures, texture rectangles, and texture arrays, use the corresponding routines and symbolic constants.)

After the texture proxy has been created, query the texture state variables with **glGetTexLevelParameter*()**. If there aren't enough resources to accommodate the texture proxy, the texture state variables for width, height, border width, and component resolutions are set to 0.

---

void **glGetTexLevelParameter**{if}**v**(GLenum *target*, GLint *level*,
                              GLenum *pname*, TYPE **params*);

Returns in *params* texture parameter values for a specific level of detail, specified as *level*. *target* defines the target texture and is GL_TEXTURE_1D, GL_TEXTURE_2D, GL_TEXTURE_3D, GL_TEXTURE_CUBE_MAP_POSITIVE_X, GL_TEXTURE_CUBE_MAP_NEGATIVE_X, GL_TEXTURE_CUBE_MAP_POSITIVE_Y, GL_TEXTURE_CUBE_MAP_NEGATIVE_Y, GL_TEXTURE_CUBE_MAP_POSITIVE_Z, GL_TEXTURE_CUBE_MAP_NEGATIVE_Z, GL_TEXTURE_1D_ARRAY, GL_TEXTURE_2D_ARRAY, GL_TEXTURE_RECTANGLE, GL_PROXY_TEXTURE_1D, GL_PROXY_TEXTURE_1D_ARRAY, GL_PROXY_TEXTURE_2D, GL_PROXY_TEXTURE_2D_ARRAY, GL_PROXY_TEXTURE_3D, GL_PROXY_TEXTURE_CUBE_MAP, or GL_PROXY_TEXTURE_RECTANGLE. (GL_TEXTURE_CUBE_MAP is not valid, because it does not specify a particular face of a cube map.) Accepted values for *pname* are GL_TEXTURE_WIDTH, GL_TEXTURE_HEIGHT, GL_TEXTURE_DEPTH, GL_TEXTURE_BORDER, GL_TEXTURE_INTERNAL_FORMAT, GL_TEXTURE_RED_SIZE, GL_TEXTURE_GREEN_SIZE, GL_TEXTURE_BLUE_SIZE, GL_TEXTURE_ALPHA_SIZE, GL_TEXTURE_LUMINANCE_SIZE, and GL_TEXTURE_INTENSITY_SIZE.

Example 9-2 demonstrates how to use the texture proxy to find out if there are enough resources to create a 64 × 64 texel texture with RGBA components with 8 bits of resolution. If this succeeds, then **glGetTexLevelParameteriv()** stores the internal format (in this case, GL_RGBA8) into the variable *format*.

Example 9-2   Querying Texture Resources with a Texture Proxy

```
GLint width;

glTexImage2D(GL_PROXY_TEXTURE_2D, 0, GL_RGBA8,
             64, 64, 0, GL_RGBA, GL_UNSIGNED_BYTE, NULL);
glGetTexLevelParameteriv(GL_PROXY_TEXTURE_2D, 0,
             GL_TEXTURE_WIDTH, &width);
```

Note: There is one major limitation with texture proxies: The texture proxy answers the question of whether a texture is capable of being loaded into texture memory. The texture proxy provides the same answer, regardless of how texture resources are currently being used. If other textures are using resources, then the texture proxy query may respond affirmatively, but there may not be enough resources to make your texture resident (that is, part of a possibly high-performance working set of textures). The texture proxy does not answer the question of whether there is sufficient capacity to handle the requested texture. (See "Texture Objects" for more information about managing resident textures.)

Replacing All or Part of a Texture Image

Creating a texture may be more computationally expensive than modifying an existing one. Often it is better to replace all or part of a texture image with new information, rather than create a new one. This can be helpful for certain applications, such as using real-time, captured video images as texture images. For that application, it makes sense to create a single texture and use **glTexSubImage2D()** to replace repeatedly the texture data with new video images. Also, there are no size restrictions for **glTexSubImage2D()** that force the height or width to be a power of 2. (This is helpful for processing video images, which generally do not have sizes that are powers of 2. However, you must load the video images into an initial, larger image that must have 2^n texels for each dimension, and adjust texture coordinates for the subimages.)

void **glTexSubImage2D**(GLenum *target,* GLint *level,* GLint *xoffset,*
                        GLint *yoffset,* GLsizei *width,* GLsizei *height,*
                        GLenum *format,* GLenum *type,*
                        const GLvoid **texels*);

Defines a two-dimensional texture image that replaces all or part of a contiguous subregion (in 2D, it's simply a rectangle) of the current, existing two-dimensional texture image. The *target* parameter must be set to one of the same options that are available for **glCopyTexImage2D**.

The *level, format,* and *type* parameters are similar to the ones used for **glTexImage2D()**. *level* is the mipmap level-of-detail number. It is not an error to specify a width or height of 0, but the subimage will have no effect. *format* and *type* describe the format and data type of the texture image data. The subimage is also affected by modes set by **glPixelStore*()** and **glPixelTransfer*()** and other pixel-transfer operations.

texels contains the texture data for the subimage. *width* and *height* are the dimensions of the subregion that is replacing all or part of the current texture image. *xoffset* and *yoffset* specify the texel offset in the *x*- and *y*-directions—with (0, 0) at the lower left corner of the texture—and specify where in the existing texture array the subimage should be placed. This region may not include any texels outside the range of the originally defined texture array.

In Example 9-3, some of the code from Example 9-1 has been modified so that pressing the 's' key drops a smaller checkered subimage into the existing image. (The resulting texture is shown in Figure 9-3.) Pressing the 'r' key restores the original image. Example 9-3 shows the two routines, **makeCheckImages()** and **keyboard()**, that have been substantially changed. (See "Texture Objects" for more information about **glBindTexture()**.)

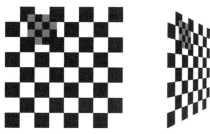

Figure 9-3   Texture with Subimage Added

Example 9-3 Replacing a Texture Subimage: texsub.c

```
/*  Create checkerboard textures  */
#define checkImageWidth 64
#define checkImageHeight 64
#define subImageWidth 16
#define subImageHeight 16
static GLubyte checkImage[checkImageHeight][checkImageWidth][4];
static GLubyte subImage[subImageHeight][subImageWidth][4];

void makeCheckImages(void)
{
   int i, j, c;

   for (i = 0; i < checkImageHeight; i++) {
      for (j = 0; j < checkImageWidth; j++) {
         c = (((i&0x8)==0) ^ ((j&0x8)==0))*255;
         checkImage[i][j][0] = (GLubyte) c;
         checkImage[i][j][1] = (GLubyte) c;
         checkImage[i][j][2] = (GLubyte) c;
         checkImage[i][j][3] = (GLubyte) 255;
      }
   }
   for (i = 0; i < subImageHeight; i++) {
      for (j = 0; j < subImageWidth; j++) {
         c = (((i&0x4)==0) ^ ((j&0x4)==0))*255;
         subImage[i][j][0] = (GLubyte) c;
         subImage[i][j][1] = (GLubyte) 0;
         subImage[i][j][2] = (GLubyte) 0;
         subImage[i][j][3] = (GLubyte) 255;
      }
   }
}

void keyboard(unsigned char key, int x, int y)
{
   switch (key) {
      case 's':
      case 'S':
         glBindTexture(GL_TEXTURE_2D, texName);
         glTexSubImage2D(GL_TEXTURE_2D, 0, 12, 44,
                     subImageWidth, subImageHeight, GL_RGBA,
                     GL_UNSIGNED_BYTE, subImage);
         glutPostRedisplay();
         break;
      case 'r':
```

```
   case 'R':
      glBindTexture(GL_TEXTURE_2D, texName);
      glTexImage2D(GL_TEXTURE_2D, 0, GL_RGBA,
                   checkImageWidth, checkImageHeight, 0,
                   GL_RGBA, GL_UNSIGNED_BYTE, checkImage);
      glutPostRedisplay();
      break;
   case 27:
      exit(0);
      break;
   default:
      break;
   }
}
```

Once again, the framebuffer itself can be used as a source for texture data—this time, a texture subimage. **glCopyTexSubImage2D()** reads a rectangle of pixels from the framebuffer and replaces a portion of an existing texture array. (**glCopyTexSubImage2D()** is something of a cross between **glCopyTexImage2D()** and **glTexSubImage2D()**.)

---

void **glCopyTexSubImage2D**(GLenum *target*, GLint *level*, GLint *xoffset*,
                            GLint *yoffset*, GLint *x*, GLint *y*,
                            GLsizei *width*, GLsizei *height*);

Uses image data from the framebuffer to replace all or part of a contiguous subregion of the current, existing two-dimensional texture image. The pixels are read from the current GL_READ_BUFFER and are processed exactly as if **glCopyPixels()** had been called, but instead of going to the framebuffer, the pixels are placed into texture memory. The settings of **glPixelTransfer*()** and other pixel-transfer operations are applied.

The *target* parameter must be set to one of the same options that are available for **glCopyTexImage2D**. *level* is the mipmap level-of-detail number. *xoffset* and *yoffset* specify the texel offset in the *x*- and *y*-directions—with (0, 0) at the lower left corner of the texture—and specify where in the existing texture array the subimage should be placed. The subimage texture array is taken from a screen-aligned pixel rectangle with the lower left corner at coordinates specified by the (*x*, *y*) parameters. The *width* and *height* parameters specify the size of this subimage rectangle.

For OpenGL Version 3.1, a GL_INVALID_VALUE error is generated if *target* is GL_TEXTURE_RECTANGLE, and *level* is not zero.

Texture Rectangles

OpenGL Version 3.1 added textures that are addressed by their texel locations, and not normalized texture coordinates. These textures, specified by a target of GL_TEXTURE_RECTANGLE, are very useful when you want a direct mapping of texels to pixels during rendering. A few restrictions apply when using texture rectangles, as they are called: No mipmap-based filtering is done (e.g,. texture rectangles may not have mipmaps), nor can they be compressed.

One-Dimensional Textures

Sometimes a one-dimensional texture is sufficient—for example, if you're drawing textured bands where all the variation is in one direction. A one-dimensional texture behaves as a two-dimensional one with *height* = 1, and without borders along the top and bottom. All the two-dimensional texture and subtexture definition routines have corresponding one-dimensional routines. To create a simple one-dimensional texture, use **glTexImage1D()**.

---

void **glTexImage1D**(GLenum *target*, GLint *level*, GLint *internalFormat*,
                GLsizei *width*, GLint *border*, GLenum *format*,
                GLenum *type*, const GLvoid **texels*);

Defines a one-dimensional texture. All the parameters have the same meanings as for **glTexImage2D()**, except that *texels* is now a one-dimensional array. As before, for OpenGL implementations that do not support OpenGL Version 2.0 or greater, the value of *width* is 2^m (or $2^m + 2$, if there's a border), where *m* is a non-negative integer. You can supply mipmaps and proxies (set *target* to GL_PROXY_TEXTURE_1D), and the same filtering options are available as well.

For a sample program that uses a one-dimensional texture map, see Example 9-8.

If your OpenGL implementation supports the *Imaging Subset* and if the one-dimensional convolution filter is enabled (GL_CONVOLUTION_1D), then the convolution is performed on the texture image. (The convolution may change the width of the texture image.) Other pixel operations may also be applied.

To replace all or some of the texels of a one-dimensional texture, use **glTexSubImage1D()**.

> void **glTexSubImage1D**(GLenum *target*, GLint *level*, GLint *xoffset*,
> GLsizei *width*, GLenum *format*,
> GLenum *type*, const GLvoid **texels*);
>
> Defines a one-dimensional texture array that replaces all or part of
> a contiguous subregion (in 1D, a row) of the current, existing one-
> dimensional texture image. The *target* parameter must be set to
> GL_TEXTURE_1D.
>
> The *level*, *format*, and *type* parameters are similar to the ones used for
> **glTexImage1D**(). *level* is the mipmap level-of-detail number. *format*
> and *type* describe the format and data type of the texture image data.
> The subimage is also affected by modes set by **glPixelStore***(),
> **glPixelTransfer***(), or other pixel-transfer operations.
>
> *texels* contains the texture data for the subimage. *width* is the number of
> texels that replace part or all of the current texture image. *xoffset* specifies
> the texel offset in the existing texture array where the subimage should be
> placed.

To use the framebuffer as the source of a new one-dimensional texture
or a replacement for an old one-dimensional texture, use either
glCopyTexImage1D() or glCopyTexSubImage1D().

> void **glCopyTexImage1D**(GLenum *target*, GLint *level*,
> GLint *internalFormat*, GLivnt *x*, GLint *y*,
> GLsizei *width*, GLint *border*);
>
> Creates a one-dimensional texture using framebuffer data to define the
> texels. The pixels are read from the current GL_READ_BUFFER and are
> processed exactly as if **glCopyPixels**() had been called, but instead of
> going to the framebuffer, the pixels are placed into texture memory.
> The settings of **glPixelStore***() and **glPixelTransfer***() are applied.
>
> The *target* parameter must be set to the constant GL_TEXTURE_1D. The
> *level*, *internalFormat*, and *border* parameters have the same effects that they
> have for **glCopyTexImage2D**(). The texture array is taken from a row of
> pixels with the lower left corner at coordinates specified by the (x, y)
> parameters. The *width* parameter specifies the number of pixels in this
> row. For OpenGL implementations that do not support Version 2.0, the
> value of *width* is 2^m (or $2^m + 2$ if there's a border), where m is a non-
> negative integer.

> void **glCopyTexSubImage1D**(GLenum *target*, GLint *level*, GLint *xoffset*,
> GLint *x*, GLint *y*, GLsizei *width*);
>
> Uses image data from the framebuffer to replace all or part of a contiguous subregion of the current, existing one-dimensional texture image. The pixels are read from the current GL_READ_BUFFER and are processed exactly as if **glCopyPixels()** had been called, but instead of going to the framebuffer, the pixels are placed into texture memory. The settings of **glPixelTransfer*()** and other pixel-transfer operations are applied.
>
> The *target* parameter must be set to GL_TEXTURE_1D. *level* is the mipmap level-of-detail number. *xoffset* specifies the texel offset and where to put the subimage within the existing texture array. The subimage texture array is taken from a row of pixels with the lower left corner at coordinates specified by the (*x*, *y*) parameters. The *width* parameter specifies the number of pixels in this row.

Three-Dimensional Textures

Advanced

Three-dimensional textures are most often used for rendering in medical and geoscience applications. In a medical application, a three-dimensional texture may represent a series of layered computed tomography (CT) or magnetic resonance imaging (MRI) images. To an oil and gas researcher, a three-dimensional texture may model rock strata. (Three-dimensional texturing is part of an overall category of applications, called *volume rendering*. Some advanced volume rendering applications deal with *voxels*, which represent data as volume-based entities.)

Due to their size, three-dimensional textures may consume a lot of texture resources. Even a relatively coarse three-dimensional texture may use 16 or 32 times the amount of texture memory that a single two-dimensional texture uses. (Most of the two-dimensional texture and subtexture definition routines have corresponding three-dimensional routines.)

A three-dimensional texture image can be thought of as layers of two-dimensional subimage rectangles. In memory, the rectangles are arranged in a sequence. To create a simple three-dimensional texture, use **glTexImage3D()**.

Note: There are no three-dimensional convolutions in the *Imaging Subset*. However, 2D convolution filters may be used to affect three-dimensional texture images.

void **glTexImage3D**(GLenum *target*, GLint *level*, GLint *internalFormat*,
    GLsizei *width*, GLsizei *height*, GLsizei *depth*,
    GLint *border*, GLenum *format*, GLenum *type*,
    const GLvoid *texels);

Defines either a three-dimensional texture or an array of two-dimensional
textures. All the parameters have the same meanings as for **glTexImage2D()**,
except that *texels* is now a three-dimensional array, and the parameter *depth*
has been added for 3D textures. For GL_TEXTURE_2D_ARRAY, *depth*
represents the length of the texture array. If the OpenGL implementation does
not support Version 2.0, the value of *depth* is 2^m (or $2^m + 2$, if there's a border),
where *m* is a non-negative integer. For OpenGL 2.0 implementations, the
power-of-two dimension requirement has been eliminated. You can supply
mipmaps and proxies (set *target* to GL_PROXY_TEXTURE_3D), and the same
filtering options are available as well.

For a portion of a program that uses a three-dimensional texture map, see
Example 9-4.

Example 9-4   Three-Dimensional Texturing: texture3d.c

```
#define iWidth 16
#define iHeight 16
#define iDepth 16

static GLubyte image [iDepth][iHeight][iWidth][3];
static GLuint texName;

/*  Create a 16x16x16x3 array with different color values in
 *  each array element [r, g, b]. Values range from 0 to 255.
 */
void makeImage(void)
{
   int s, t, r;

   for (s = 0 ; s < 16 ; s++)
      for (t = 0 ; t < 16 ; t++)
         for (r = 0 ; r < 16 ; r++) {
            image[r][t][s][0] = s * 17;
            image[r][t][s][1] = t * 17;
            image[r][t][s][2] = r * 17;
         }
}
```

```
/*  Initialize state: the 3D texture object and its image
 */
void init(void)
{
    glClearColor(0.0, 0.0, 0.0, 0.0);
    glShadeModel(GL_FLAT);
    glEnable(GL_DEPTH_TEST);

    makeImage();
    glPixelStorei(GL_UNPACK_ALIGNMENT, 1);

    glGenTextures(1, &texName);
    glBindTexture(GL_TEXTURE_3D, texName);

    glTexParameteri(GL_TEXTURE_3D, GL_TEXTURE_WRAP_S, GL_CLAMP);
    glTexParameteri(GL_TEXTURE_3D, GL_TEXTURE_WRAP_T, GL_CLAMP);
    glTexParameteri(GL_TEXTURE_3D, GL_TEXTURE_WRAP_R, GL_CLAMP);

    glTexParameteri(GL_TEXTURE_3D, GL_TEXTURE_MAG_FILTER,
                    GL_NEAREST);
    glTexParameteri(GL_TEXTURE_3D, GL_TEXTURE_MIN_FILTER,
                    GL_NEAREST);
    glTexImage3D(GL_TEXTURE_3D, 0, GL_RGB, iWidth, iHeight,
                 iDepth, 0, GL_RGB, GL_UNSIGNED_BYTE, image);
}
```

To replace all or some of the texels of a three-dimensional texture, use **glTexSubImage3D()**.

---

void **glTexSubImage3D**(GLenum *target*, GLint *level*, GLint *xoffset*,
        GLint *yoffset*, GLint *zoffset*, GLsizei *width*,
        GLsizei *height*, GLsizei *depth*, GLenum *format*,
        GLenum *type*, const GLvoid **texels*);

Defines a three-dimensional texture array that replaces all or part of a contiguous subregion of the current, existing three-dimensional texture image. The *target* parameter must be set to GL_TEXTURE_3D.

The *level*, *format*, and *type* parameters are similar to the ones used for **glTexImage3D()**. *level* is the mipmap level-of-detail number. *format* and *type* describe the format and data type of the texture image data. The subimage is also affected by modes set by **glPixelStore*()**, **glPixelTransfer*()**, and other pixel-transfer operations.

texels contains the texture data for the subimage. *width*, *height*, and *depth* specify the size of the subimage in texels. *xoffset*, *yoffset*, and *zoffset* specify the texel offset indicating where to put the subimage within the existing texture array.

To use the framebuffer as the source of replacement for a portion of an existing three-dimensional texture, use **glCopyTexSubImage3D()**.

---

void **glCopyTexSubImage3D**(GLenum *target*, GLint *level*, GLint *xoffset*,
GLint *yoffset*, GLint *zoffset*, GLint *x*,
GLint *y*, GLsizei *width*, GLsizei *height*);

Uses image data from the framebuffer to replace part of a contiguous subregion of the current, existing three-dimensional texture image. The pixels are read from the current GL_READ_BUFFER and are processed exactly as if **glCopyPixels()** had been called, but instead of going to the framebuffer, the pixels are placed into texture memory. The settings of **glPixelTransfer*()** and other pixel-transfer operations are applied.

The *target* parameter must be set to GL_TEXTURE_3D. *level* is the mipmap level-of-detail number. The subimage texture array is taken from a screen-aligned pixel rectangle with the lower left corner at coordinates specified by the (*x, y*) parameters. The *width* and *height* parameters specify the size of this subimage rectangle. *xoffset, yoffset,* and *zoffset* specify the texel offset indicating where to put the subimage within the existing texture array. Since the subimage is a two-dimensional rectangle, only a single slice of the three-dimensional texture (the slice at *zoffset*) is replaced.

Pixel-Storage Modes for Three-Dimensional Textures

Pixel-storage values control the row-to-row spacing of each layer (in other words, of one 2D rectangle). **glPixelStore*()** sets pixel-storage modes, with parameters such as *ROW_LENGTH, *ALIGNMENT, *SKIP_PIXELS, and *SKIP_ROWS (where * is either GL_UNPACK_ or GL_PACK_), which control referencing of a subrectangle of an entire rectangle of pixel or texel data. (These modes were previously described in "Controlling Pixel-Storage Modes" on page 347.)

The aforementioned pixel-storage modes remain useful for describing two of the three dimensions, but additional pixel-storage modes are needed to support referencing of subvolumes of three-dimensional texture image data. New parameters, *IMAGE_HEIGHT and *SKIP_IMAGES, allow the routines **glTexImage3D()**, **glTexSubImage3D()**, and **glGetTexImage()** to delimit and access any desired subvolume.

If the three-dimensional texture in memory is larger than the subvolume that is defined, you need to specify the height of a single subimage with the *IMAGE_HEIGHT parameter. Also, if the subvolume does not start with the very first layer, the *SKIP_IMAGES parameter needs to be set.

*IMAGE_HEIGHT is a pixel-storage parameter that defines the height (number of rows) of a single layer of a three-dimensional texture image. If the *IMAGE_HEIGHT value is zero (a negative number is invalid), then the number of rows in each two-dimensional rectangle is the value of *height*, which is the parameter passed to **glTexImage3D()** or **glTexSubImage3D()**. (This is commonplace because *IMAGE_HEIGHT is zero, by default.) Otherwise, the height of a single layer is the *IMAGE_HEIGHT value.

Figure 9-4 shows how *IMAGE_HEIGHT determines the height of an image (when the parameter *height* determines only the height of the subimage.) This figure shows a three-dimensional texture with only two layers.

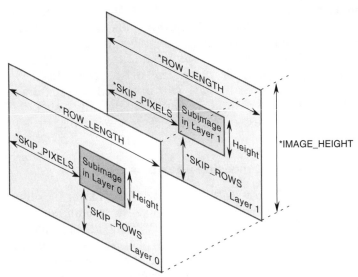

Figure 9-4   *IMAGE_HEIGHT Pixel-Storage Mode

*SKIP_IMAGES defines how many layers to bypass before accessing the first data of the subvolume. If the *SKIP_IMAGES value is a positive integer (call the value *n*), then the pointer in the texture image data is advanced that many layers (*n* * the size of one layer of texels). The resulting subvolume starts at layer *n* and is several layers deep—how many layers deep is determined by the *depth* parameter passed to **glTexImage3D()** or **glTexSubImage3D()**. If the

*SKIP_IMAGES value is zero (the default), then accessing the texel data begins with the very first layer described in the texel array.

Figure 9-5 shows how the *SKIP_IMAGES parameter can bypass several layers to get to where the subvolume is actually located. In this example, *SKIP_IMAGES == 3, and the subvolume begins at layer 3.

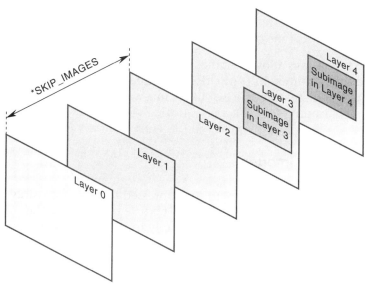

Figure 9-5   *SKIP_IMAGES Pixel-Storage Mode

Texture Arrays

Advanced

Advanced

For certain applications, you may have a number of one- or two-dimensional textures that you might like to access simultaneously within the confines of a draw call. For instance, suppose you're authoring a game that features multiple characters of basically the same geometry, but each of which has its own costume. Without the OpenGL Version 3.0 feature of texture arrays, you would probably use a set of calls similar to the technique used in Example 9-5.

The call to **glBindTexture()** for each draw call could have performance implications for the application if the texture objects needed to be updated in the OpenGL server (due to perhaps a shortage of texture storage resources).

Texture arrays allow you to combine a collection of one- or two-dimensional textures, all of the same size, in a texture of the next higher dimension (e.g., an array of two-dimensional textures becomes something of a three-dimensional texture). If you were to try using a three-dimensional texture to store a collection of two-dimensional textures, you would encounter a few inconveniences: The indexing texture coordinate—*r* in this case—is normalized to the range [0,1]. To access the third texture in a stack of seven, you would need to pass .35714 (or thereabouts) to access what you would probably like to access as "2" (textures are indexed from zero, just like "C"). Texture arrays permit this type of texture selection.

Additionally, texture arrays allow suitable mipmap filtering within the texture accessed by the index. In comparison, a three-dimensional texture would filter between the texture "slices," likely in a way that doesn't return the results you were hoping for.

Compressed Texture Images

Texture maps can be stored internally in a compressed format to possibly reduce the amount of texture memory used. A texture image can either be compressed as it is being loaded or loaded directly in its compressed form.

Compressing a Texture Image While Loading

To have OpenGL compress a texture image while it's being downloaded, specify one of the GL_COMPRESSED_* enumerants for the *internalformat* parameter. The image will automatically be compressed after the texels have been processed by any active pixel-store (See "Controlling Pixel-Storage Modes") or pixel-transfer modes (See "Pixel-Transfer Operations").

Once the image has been loaded, you can determine if it was compressed, and into which format, using the following:

```
GLboolean compressed;
GLenum    textureFormat;
GLsizei   imageSize;

glGetTexLevelParameteriv(GL_TEXTURE_2D, GL_TEXTURE_COMPRESSED,
    &compressed);
if (compressed == GL_TRUE) {
```

```
    glGetTexLevelParameteriv(GL_TEXTURE_2D,
        GL_TEXTURE_INTERNAL_FORMAT, &textureFormat);
    glGetTexLevelParameteriv(GL_TEXTURE_2D,
        GL_TEXTURE_COMPRESSED_IMAGE_SIZE, &imageSize);
}
```

Loading a Compressed Texture Images

OpenGL doesn't specify the internal format that should be used for compressed textures; each OpenGL implementation is allowed to specify a set of OpenGL extensions that implement a particular texture compression format. For compressed textures that are to be loaded directly, it's important to know their storage format and to verify that the texture's format is available in your OpenGL implementation.

To load a texture stored in a compressed format, use the **glCompressedTexImage*D()** calls.

---

void **glCompressedTexImage1D**(GLenum *target*, GLint *level*,
                               GLenum *internalformat*, GLsizei *width*,
                               GLint *border*, GLsizei *imageSize*,
                               const GLvoid **texels*);
void **glCompressedTexImage2D**(GLenum *target*, GLint *level*,
                               GLenum *internalformat*, GLsizei *width*,
                               GLsizei *height*, GLint *border*,
                               GLsizei *imageSize*, const GLvoid **texels*);
void **glCompressedTexImage3D**(GLenum *target*, GLint *level*,
                               GLenum *internalformat*, GLsizei *width*,
                               GLsizei *height*, GLsizei *depth*,
                               GLint *border*, GLsizei *imageSize*,
                               const GLvoid **texels*);

Defines a one-, two-, or three-dimensional texture from a previously compressed texture image.

Use the *level* parameter if you're supplying multiple resolutions of the texture map; with only one resolution, *level* should be 0. (See "Mipmaps: Multiple Levels of Detail" for more information about using multiple resolutions.)

internalformat specifies the format of the compressed texture image. It must be a supported compression format of the implementation loading the texture, otherwise a GL_INVALID_ENUM error is specified. To determine supported compressed texture formats, see Appendix B for details.

width, *height*, and *depth* represent the dimensions of the texture image for one-, two-, and three-dimensional texture images, respectively. As with uncompressed textures, *border* indicates the width of the border, which is either 0 (no border) or 1. Each value must have the form $2^m + 2b$, where m is a non-negative integer and b is the value of *border*. For OpenGL 2.0 implementations, the power-of-two dimension requirement has been eliminated.

For OpenGL Version 3.1, a GL_INVALID_ENUM error is generated if *target* is GL_TEXTURE_RECTANGLE, or GL_PROXY_TEXTURE_RECTANGLE for **glCompressedTexImage2D()**.

Additionally, compressed textures can be used, just like uncompressed texture images, to replace all or part of an already loaded texture. Use the **glCompressedTexSubImage*D()** calls.

---

void **glCompressedTexSubImage1D**(GLenum *target*, GLint *level*,
                                   GLint *xoffset*, GLsizei *width*,
                                   GLenum *format*, GLsizei *imageSize*,
                                   const GLvoid **texels*);
void **glCompressedTexSubImage2D**(GLenum *target*, GLint *level*,
                                   GLint *xoffset*, GLint *yoffet*,
                                   GLsizei *width*, GLsizei *height*,
                                   GLsizei *imageSize*,
                                   const GLvoid **texels*);
void **glCompressedTexSubImage3D**(GLenum *target*, GLint *level*,
                                   GLint *xoffset* GLint *yoffset*,
                                   GLint *zoffset*, GLsizei *width*,
                                   GLsizei *height*, GLsizei *depth*,
                                   GLsizei *imageSize*,
                                   const GLvoid **texels*);

Defines a one-, two-, or three-dimensional texture from a previously compressed texture image.

The *xoffset*, *yoffset*, and *zoffset* parameters specify the pixel offsets for the respective texture dimension where to place the new image inside of the texture array.

width, *height*, and *depth* specify the size of the one-, two-, or three-dimensional texture image to be used to update the texture image.

imageSize specifies the number of bytes stored in the *texels* array.

Using a Texture's Borders

Advanced

If you need to apply a larger texture map than your implementation of OpenGL allows, you can, with a little care, effectively make larger textures by tiling with several different textures. For example, if you need a texture twice as large as the maximum allowed size mapped to a square, draw the square as four subsquares, and load a different texture before drawing each piece.

Since only a single texture map is available at one time, this approach might lead to problems at the edges of the textures, especially if some form of linear filtering is enabled. The texture value to be used for pixels at the edges must be averaged with something beyond the edge, which, ideally, should come from the adjacent texture map. If you define a border for each texture whose texel values are equal to the values of the texels at the edge of the adjacent texture map, then the correct behavior results when linear filtering takes place.

To do this correctly, notice that each map can have eight neighbors—one adjacent to each edge and one touching each corner. The values of the texels in the corner of the border need to correspond with the texels in the texture maps that touch the corners. If your texture is an edge or corner of the whole tiling, you need to decide what values would be reasonable to put in the borders. The easiest reasonable thing to do is to copy the value of the adjacent texel in the texture map with **glTexSubImage2D()**.

A texture's border color is also used if the texture is applied in such a way that it only partially covers a primitive. (See "Repeating and Clamping Textures" on page 452 for more information about this situation.)

Note: Texture borders are not supported in OpenGL Version 3.1 and later. When specifying a texture in those implementations, the value of the border must be 0.

Mipmaps: Multiple Levels of Detail

Advanced

Textured objects can be viewed, like any other objects in a scene, at different distances from the viewpoint. In a dynamic scene, as a textured object moves farther from the viewpoint, the texture map must decrease in size along with the size of the projected image. To accomplish this, OpenGL has to filter the texture map down to an appropriate size for mapping onto the object, without introducing visually disturbing artifacts, such as shimmering, flashing, and scintillation. For example, to render a brick wall, you may use a large texture image (say 128×128 texels) when the wall is close to the viewer. But if the wall is moved farther away from the viewer until it appears on the screen as a single pixel, then the filtered textures may appear to change abruptly at certain transition points.

To avoid such artifacts, you can specify a series of prefiltered texture maps of decreasing resolutions, called *mipmaps*, as shown in Figure 9-6. The term *mipmap* was coined by Lance Williams, when he introduced the idea in his paper "Pyramidal Parametrics" (*SIGGRAPH 1983 Proceedings*). *Mip* stands for the Latin *multum in parvo*, meaning "many things in a small place." Mipmapping uses some clever methods to pack image data into memory.

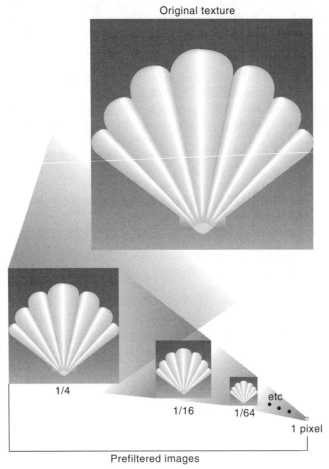

Figure 9-6   Mipmaps

Note: To acquire a full understanding of mipmaps, you need to understand minification filters, which are described in "Filtering" on page 434.

When using mipmapping, OpenGL automatically determines which texture map to use based on the size (in pixels) of the object being mapped. With this approach, the level of detail in the texture map is appropriate for the image that's drawn on the screen—as the image of the object gets smaller, the size of the texture map decreases. Mipmapping requires some extra computation and texture storage area; however, when it's not used, textures that are mapped onto smaller objects might shimmer and flash as the objects move.

To use mipmapping, you must provide all sizes of your texture in powers of 2 between the largest size and a 1 × 1 map. For example, if your highest-resolution map is 64 × 16, you must also provide maps of size 32 × 8, 16 × 4, 8 × 2, 4 × 1, 2 × 1, and 1 × 1. The smaller maps are typically filtered and averaged-down versions of the largest map in which each texel in a smaller texture is an average of the corresponding 4 texels in the higher-resolution texture. (Since OpenGL doesn't require any particular method for calculating the lower-resolution maps, the differently sized textures could be totally unrelated. In practice, unrelated textures would make the transitions between mipmaps extremely noticeable, as in Plate 20.)

To specify these textures, call **glTexImage2D()** once for each resolution of the texture map, with different values for the *level*, *width*, *height*, and *image* parameters. Starting with zero, *level* identifies which texture in the series is specified; with the previous example, the highest-resolution texture of size 64 × 16 would be declared with *level* = 0, the 32 × 8 texture with *level* = 1, and so on. In addition, for the mipmapped textures to take effect, you need to choose the appropriate filtering method as described in "Filtering" on page 434.

Note: This description of OpenGL mipmapping avoids detailed discussion of the scale factor (known as λ) between texel size and polygon size. This description also assumes default values for parameters related to mipmapping. To see an explanation of λ and the effects of mipmapping parameters, see "Calculating the Mipmap Level" on page 430 and "Mipmap Level of Detail Control" on page 431.

Example 9-5 illustrates the use of a series of six texture maps decreasing in size from 32 × 32 to 1 × 1. This program draws a rectangle that extends from the foreground far back in the distance, eventually disappearing at a point, as shown in Plate 20. Note that the texture coordinates range from 0.0 to 8.0, so 64 copies of the texture map are required to tile the rectangle—eight in each direction. To illustrate how one texture map succeeds another, each map has a different color.

Example 9-5   Mipmap Textures: mipmap.c

```
GLubyte mipmapImage32[32][32][4];
GLubyte mipmapImage16[16][16][4];
GLubyte mipmapImage8[8][8][4];
GLubyte mipmapImage4[4][4][4];
GLubyte mipmapImage2[2][2][4];
GLubyte mipmapImage1[1][1][4];

static GLuint texName;

void makeImages(void)
{
   int i, j;

   for (i = 0; i < 32; i++) {
      for (j = 0; j < 32; j++) {
         mipmapImage32[i][j][0] = 255;
         mipmapImage32[i][j][1] = 255;
         mipmapImage32[i][j][2] = 0;
         mipmapImage32[i][j][3] = 255;
      }
   }
   for (i = 0; i < 16; i++) {
      for (j = 0; j < 16; j++) {
         mipmapImage16[i][j][0] = 255;
         mipmapImage16[i][j][1] = 0;
         mipmapImage16[i][j][2] = 255;
         mipmapImage16[i][j][3] = 255;
      }
   }
   for (i = 0; i < 8; i++) {
      for (j = 0; j < 8; j++) {
         mipmapImage8[i][j][0] = 255;
         mipmapImage8[i][j][1] = 0;
         mipmapImage8[i][j][2] = 0;
         mipmapImage8[i][j][3] = 255;
      }
   }
   for (i = 0; i < 4; i++) {
      for (j = 0; j < 4; j++) {
         mipmapImage4[i][j][0] = 0;
         mipmapImage4[i][j][1] = 255;
         mipmapImage4[i][j][2] = 0;
         mipmapImage4[i][j][3] = 255;
      }
   }
   for (i = 0; i < 2; i++) {
      for (j = 0; j < 2; j++) {
```

```
            mipmapImage2[i][j][0] = 0;
            mipmapImage2[i][j][1] = 0;
            mipmapImage2[i][j][2] = 255;
            mipmapImage2[i][j][3] = 255;
        }
    }
    mipmapImage1[0][0][0] = 255;
    mipmapImage1[0][0][1] = 255;
    mipmapImage1[0][0][2] = 255;
    mipmapImage1[0][0][3] = 255;
}

void init(void)
{
    glEnable(GL_DEPTH_TEST);
    glShadeModel(GL_FLAT);

    glTranslatef(0.0, 0.0, -3.6);
    makeImages();
    glPixelStorei(GL_UNPACK_ALIGNMENT, 1);

    glGenTextures(1, &texName);
    glBindTexture(GL_TEXTURE_2D, texName);
    glTexParameteri(GL_TEXTURE_2D, GL_TEXTURE_WRAP_S, GL_REPEAT);
    glTexParameteri(GL_TEXTURE_2D, GL_TEXTURE_WRAP_T, GL_REPEAT);
    glTexParameteri(GL_TEXTURE_2D, GL_TEXTURE_MAG_FILTER,
                    GL_NEAREST);
    glTexParameteri(GL_TEXTURE_2D, GL_TEXTURE_MIN_FILTER,
                    GL_NEAREST_MIPMAP_NEAREST);
    glTexImage2D(GL_TEXTURE_2D, 0, GL_RGBA, 32, 32, 0,
                 GL_RGBA, GL_UNSIGNED_BYTE, mipmapImage32);
    glTexImage2D(GL_TEXTURE_2D, 1, GL_RGBA, 16, 16, 0,
                 GL_RGBA, GL_UNSIGNED_BYTE, mipmapImage16);
    glTexImage2D(GL_TEXTURE_2D, 2, GL_RGBA, 8, 8, 0,
                 GL_RGBA, GL_UNSIGNED_BYTE, mipmapImage8);
    glTexImage2D(GL_TEXTURE_2D, 3, GL_RGBA, 4, 4, 0,
                 GL_RGBA, GL_UNSIGNED_BYTE, mipmapImage4);
    glTexImage2D(GL_TEXTURE_2D, 4, GL_RGBA, 2, 2, 0,
                 GL_RGBA, GL_UNSIGNED_BYTE, mipmapImage2);
    glTexImage2D(GL_TEXTURE_2D, 5, GL_RGBA, 1, 1, 0,
                 GL_RGBA, GL_UNSIGNED_BYTE, mipmapImage1);

    glTexEnvf(GL_TEXTURE_ENV, GL_TEXTURE_ENV_MODE, GL_REPLACE);
    glEnable(GL_TEXTURE_2D);
}

void display(void)
{
```

```
    glClear(GL_COLOR_BUFFER_BIT | GL_DEPTH_BUFFER_BIT);
    glBindTexture(GL_TEXTURE_2D, texName);
    glBegin(GL_QUADS);
    glTexCoord2f(0.0, 0.0); glVertex3f(-2.0, -1.0, 0.0);
    glTexCoord2f(0.0, 8.0); glVertex3f(-2.0, 1.0, 0.0);
    glTexCoord2f(8.0, 8.0); glVertex3f(2000.0, 1.0, -6000.0);
    glTexCoord2f(8.0, 0.0); glVertex3f(2000.0, -1.0, -6000.0);
    glEnd();
    glFlush();
}
```

Building Mipmaps in Real Applications

Example 9-5 illustrates mipmapping by making each mipmap a different color so that it's obvious when one map is replaced by another. In a real situation, you define mipmaps such that the transition is as smooth as possible. Thus, the maps of lower resolution are usually filtered versions of an original, high-resolution texture map.

There are several ways to create mipmaps using OpenGL features. In the most modern versions of OpenGL (i.e., Version 3.0 and later), you can use **glGenerateMipmap()**, which will build the *mipmap stack* for the current texture image (see "Texture Objects" and its discussion of **glBindTexture()**) bound to a specific texture target.

---

int **glGenerateMipmap**(GLenum *target*);

Generates a complete set of mipmaps for the texture image associated with *target*, which must be one of: GL_TEXTURE_1D, GL_TEXTURE_2D, GL_TEXTURE_3D, GL_TEXTURE_1D_ARRAY, GL_TEXTURE_2D_ARRAY, or GL_TEXTURE_CUBE_MAP.

The mipmap levels constructed are controlled by the GL_TEXTURE_BASE_LEVEL, and GL_TEXTURE_MAX_LEVEL (see "Mipmap Level of Detail Control" on page 431 for details describing these values). If those values are left to their defaults, an entire mipmap stack down to a single-texel texture map is created. The filtering method used in creating each successive level is implementation dependent.

A GL_INVALID_OPERATION error will be generated if *target* is GL_TEXTURE_CUBE_MAP, and not all cube map faces are initialized and consistent.

The use of **glGenerateMipmap()** makes explicit which mipmaps you would like, and puts them under the control of the OpenGL implementation. If you don't have access to a Version 3.0 or later implementation, you can still have OpenGL generate mipmaps for you. Use **glTexParameter*()** to set GL_ GENERATE_MIPMAP to GL_TRUE; then any change to the texels (interior or border) of a BASE_LEVEL mipmap will automatically cause all textures at all mipmap levels from BASE_LEVEL+1 to MAX_LEVEL to be recomputed and replaced. Textures at all other mipmap levels, including at BASE_LEVEL, remain unchanged.

Note: In OpenGL Version 3.1 and later, use of GL_GENERATE_MIPMAP has been replaced with the more explicit **glGenerateMipmap()** routine. Trying to set GL_GENERATE_MIPMAP on a texture object in Version 3.1 will generate a GL_INVALID_OPERATION error.

Finally, if you are using an older OpenGL implementation (any version prior to 1.4), you would need to construct the mipmap stack manually, without OpenGL's aid. However, because mipmap construction is such an important operation, the OpenGL Utility Library contains routines that can help you manipulate of images to be used as mipmapped textures.

Assuming you have constructed the level 0, or highest-resolution, map, the routines **gluBuild1DMipmaps()**, **gluBuild2DMipmaps()**, and **gluBuild3DMipmaps()** construct and define the pyramid of mipmaps down to a resolution of 1×1 (or 1, for one-dimensional, or $1 \times 1 \times 1$, for three-dimensional). If your original image has dimensions that are not exact powers of 2, **gluBuild*DMipmaps()** helpfully scales the image to the nearest power of 2. Also, if your texture is too large, **gluBuild*DMipmaps()** reduces the size of the image until it fits (as measured by the GL_PROXY_ TEXTURE mechanism).

int **gluBuild1DMipmaps**(GLenum *target*, GLint *internalFormat*, GLint *width*, GLenum *format*, GLenum *type*, const void **texels*);
int **gluBuild2DMipmaps**(GLenum *target*, GLint *internalFormat*, GLint *width*, GLint *height*, GLenum *format*, GLenum *type*, const void **texels*);
int **gluBuild3DMipmaps**(GLenum *target*, GLint *internalFormat*, GLint *width*, GLint *height*, GLint *depth*, GLenum *format*, GLenum *type*, const void **texels*);

Constructs a series of mipmaps and calls **glTexImage*D()** to load the images. The parameters for *target, internalFormat, width, height, depth, format, type*, and *texels* are exactly the same as those for **glTexImage1D()**, **glTexImage2D()**, and **glTexImage3D()**. A value of 0 is returned if all the mipmaps are constructed successfully; otherwise, a GLU error code is returned.

With increased control over level of detail (using BASE_LEVEL, MAX_
LEVEL, MIN_LOD, and MAX_LOD), you may need to create only a subset
of the mipmaps defined by **gluBuild*DMipmaps()**. For example, you may
want to stop at a 4 × 4 texel image, rather than go all the way to the smallest
1 × 1 texel image. To calculate and load a subset of mipmap levels, call
gluBuild*DMipmapLevels().

---

int **gluBuild1DMipmapLevels**(GLenum *target*, GLint *internalFormat*,
                      GLint *width*, GLenum *format*,
                      GLenum *type*, GLint *level*, GLint *base*,
                      GLint *max*, const void *texels);
int **gluBuild2DMipmapLevels**(GLenum *target*, GLint *internalFormat*,
                      GLint *width*, GLint *height*, GLenum *format*,
                      GLenum *type*, GLint *level*, GLint *base*,
                      GLint *max*, const void *texels);
int **gluBuild3DMipmapLevels**(GLenum *target*, GLint *internalFormat*,
                      GLint *width*, GLint *height*, GLint *depth*,
                      GLenum *format*, GLenum *type*,
                      GLint *level*, GLint *base*, GLint *max*,
                      const void *texels);

Constructs a series of mipmaps and calls **glTexImage*D()** to load the
images. *level* indicates the mipmap level of the *texels* image. *base* and *max*
determine which mipmap levels will be derived from *texels*. Otherwise,
the parameters for *target, internalFormat, width, height, depth, format, type*, and
texels are exactly the same as those for **glTexImage1D()**, **glTexImage2D()**,
and **glTexImage3D()**. A value of 0 is returned if all the mipmaps are
constructed successfully; otherwise, a GLU error code is returned.

Calculating the Mipmap Level

Computing which level of mipmap to texture a particular polygon depends
on the scale factor between the texture image and the size of the polygon
to be textured (in pixels). Let's call this scale factor ρ and also define a sec-
ond value, λ, where $\lambda = \log_2 \rho + \text{lod}_{\text{bias}}$. (Since texture images can be multi-
dimensional, it is important to clarify that ρ is the maximum scale factor of
all dimensions.)

lod_{bias} is the level-of-detail bias, a constant value set by **glTexEnv*()** to
adjust λ. (For information about how to use **glTexEnv*()** to set level-of-
detail bias, see "Texture Functions" on page 444.) By default, $\text{lod}_{\text{bias}} = 0.0$,
which has no effect. It's best to start with this default value and adjust in
small amounts, if needed.

If $\lambda \leq 0.0$, then the texture is smaller than the polygon, so a magnification filter is used. If $\lambda > 0.0$, then a minification filter is used. If the minification filter selected uses mipmapping, then λ indicates the mipmap level. (The minification-to-magnification switchover point is usually at $\lambda = 0.0$, but not always. The choice of mipmapping filter may shift the switchover point.)

For example, if the texture image is 64×64 texels and the polygon size is 32×32 pixels, then $\rho = 2.0$ (not 4.0), and therefore $\lambda = 1.0$. If the texture image is 64×32 texels and the polygon size is 8×16 pixels, then $\rho = 8.0$ (x scales by 8.0, y by 2.0; use the maximum value) and therefore $\lambda = 3.0$.

Mipmap Level of Detail Control

By default, you must provide a mipmap for every level of resolution, down to 1 texel in every dimension. For some techniques, you want to avoid representing your data with very small mipmaps. For instance, you might use a technique called *mosaicing*, where several smaller images are combined on a single texture. One example of mosaicing is shown in Figure 9-7, where many characters are on a single texture, which may be more efficient than creating a texture image for each character. To map only a single letter from the texture, you make smart use of texture coordinates to isolate the letter you want.

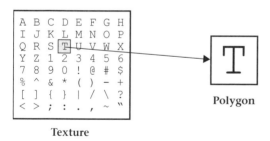

Texture

Figure 9-7   Using a Mosaic Texture

If you have to supply very small mipmaps, the lower-resolution mipmaps of the mosaic crush together detail from many different letters. Therefore, you may want to set restrictions on how low your resolution can go. Generally, you want the capability to add or remove levels of mipmaps as needed.

Another visible mipmapping problem is *popping*—the sudden transition from using one mipmap to using a radically higher- or lower-resolution mipmap, as a mipmapped polygon becomes larger or smaller.

Note: Many mipmapping features were introduced in later versions of OpenGL. Check the version of your implementation to see if a particular feature is supported. In some versions, a particular feature may be available as an extension.

To control mipmapping levels, the constants GL_TEXTURE_BASE_LEVEL, GL_TEXTURE_MAX_LEVEL, GL_TEXTURE_MIN_LOD, and GL_TEXTURE_ MAX_LOD are passed to **glTexParameter*()**. The first two constants (for brevity, shortened to BASE_LEVEL and MAX_LEVEL in the remainder of this section) control which mipmap levels are used and therefore which levels need to be specified. The other two constants (shortened to MIN_LOD and MAX_LOD) control the active range of the aforementioned scale factor λ.

These texture parameters address several of the previously described problems. Effective use of BASE_LEVEL and MAX_LEVEL may reduce the number of mipmaps that need to be specified and thereby streamline texture resource usage. Selective use of MAX_LOD may preserve the legibility of a mosaic texture, and MIN_LOD may reduce the popping effect with higher-resolution textures.

BASE_LEVEL and MAX_LEVEL are used to set the boundaries for which mipmap levels are used. BASE_LEVEL is the level of the highest-resolution (largest texture) mipmap level that is used. The default value for BASE_ LEVEL is 0. However, you may later change the value for BASE_LEVEL, so that you add additional higher-resolution textures "on the fly." Similarly, MAX_LEVEL limits the lowest-resolution mipmap to be used. The default value for MAX_LEVEL is 1000, which almost always means that the smallest-resolution texture is 1 texel.

To set the base and maximum mipmap levels, use **glTexParameter*()** with the first argument set to GL_TEXTURE_1D, GL_TEXTURE_2D, GL_ TEXTURE_3D, or GL_TEXTURE_CUBE_MAP, depending on your textures. The second argument is one of the parameters described in Table 9-1. The third argument denotes the value for the parameter.

Parameter	Description	Values
GL_TEXTURE_BASE_ LEVEL	level for highest-resolution texture (lowest numbered mipmap level) in use	any non-negative integer
GL_TEXTURE_MAX_ LEVEL	level for smallest-resolution texture (highest numbered mipmap level) in use	any non-negative integer

Table 9-1   Mipmapping Level Parameter Controls

The code in Example 9-6 sets the base and maximum mipmap levels to 2 and 5, respectively. Since the image at the base level (level 2) has a 64 × 32 texel resolution, the mipmaps at levels 3, 4, and 5 must have the appropriate lower resolution.

Example 9-6   Setting Base and Maximum Mipmap Levels

```
glTexParameteri(GL_TEXTURE_2D, GL_TEXTURE_BASE_LEVEL, 2);
glTexParameteri(GL_TEXTURE_2D, GL_TEXTURE_MAX_LEVEL, 5);
glTexImage2D(GL_TEXTURE_2D, 2, GL_RGBA, 64, 32, 0, GL_RGBA,
            GL_UNSIGNED_BYTE, image1);
glTexImage2D(GL_TEXTURE_2D, 3, GL_RGBA, 32, 16, 0, GL_RGBA,
            GL_UNSIGNED_BYTE, image2);
glTexImage2D(GL_TEXTURE_2D, 4, GL_RGBA, 16, 8, 0, GL_RGBA,
            GL_UNSIGNED_BYTE, image3);
glTexImage2D(GL_TEXTURE_2D, 5, GL_RGBA, 8, 4, 0, GL_RGBA,
            GL_UNSIGNED_BYTE, image4);
```

Later on, you may decide to add additional higher-or lower-resolution mipmaps. For example, you may add a 128 × 64 texel texture to this set of mipmaps at level 1, but you must remember to reset BASE_LEVEL.

Note: For mipmapping to work, all mipmaps between BASE_LEVEL and the *largest possible level*, inclusive, must be loaded. The largest possible level is the smaller of either the value for MAX_LEVEL or the level at which the size of the mipmap is only 1 texel (either 1, 1 × 1, or 1 × 1 × 1). If you fail to load a necessary mipmap level, then texturing may be mysteriously disabled. If you are mipmapping and texturing does not appear, ensure that each required mipmap level has been loaded with a legal texture.

As with BASE_LEVEL and MAX_LEVEL, **glTexParameter*()** sets MIN_LOD and MAX_LOD. Table 9-2 lists possible values.

Parameter	Description	Values
GL_TEXTURE_MIN_LOD	minimum value for λ (scale factor of texture image versus polygon size)	any value
GL_TEXTURE_MAX_LOD	maximum value for λ	any value

Table 9-2   Mipmapping Level-of-Detail Parameter Controls

The following code is an example of using **glTexParameter*()** to specify the level-of-detail parameters:

```
glTexParameterf(GL_TEXTURE_2D, GL_TEXTURE_MIN_LOD, 2.5);
glTexParameterf(GL_TEXTURE_2D, GL_TEXTURE_MAX_LOD, 4.5);
```

MIN_LOD and MAX_LOD provide minimum and maximum values for λ (the scale factor from texture image to polygon) for mipmapped minification, which indirectly specifies which mipmap levels are used.

If you have a 64 × 64 pixel polygon and MIN_LOD is the default value of 0.0, then a level 0 64 × 64 texel texture map may be used for minification (provided BASE_LEVEL = 0; as a rule, BASE_LEVEL ≤ MIN_LOD). However, if MIN_LOD is set to 2.0, then the largest texture map that may be used for minification is 16 × 16 texels, which corresponds to $\lambda = 2.0$.

MAX_LOD has influence only if it is less than the maximum λ (which is either MAX_LEVEL or where the mipmap is reduced to 1 texel). In the case of a 64 × 64 texel texture map, $\lambda = 6.0$ corresponds to a 1 × 1 texel mipmap. In the same case, if MAX_LOD is 4.0, then no mipmap smaller than 4 × 4 texels will be used for minification.

You may find that a MIN_LOD that is fractionally greater than BASE_LEVEL or a MAX_LOD that is fractionally less than MAX_LEVEL is best for reducing visual effects (such as popping) related to transitions between mipmaps.

Filtering

Texture maps are square or rectangular, but after being mapped to a polygon or surface and transformed into screen coordinates, the individual texels of a texture rarely correspond to individual pixels of the final screen image. Depending on the transformations used and the texture mapping applied, a single pixel on the screen can correspond to anything from a tiny portion of a texel (magnification) to a large collection of texels (minification), as shown in Figure 9-8. In either case, it's unclear exactly which texel values should be used and how they should be averaged or interpolated. Consequently, OpenGL allows you to specify any of several filtering options to determine these calculations. The options provide different trade-offs between speed and image quality. Also, you can specify independently the filtering methods for magnification and minification.

In some cases, it isn't obvious whether magnification or minification is called for. If the texture map needs to be stretched (or shrunk) in both the *x*- and *y*- directions, then magnification (or minification) is needed. If the

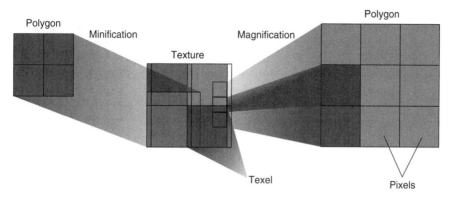

Figure 9-8   Texture Magnification and Minification

texture map needs to be stretched in one direction and shrunk in the other, OpenGL makes a choice between magnification and minification that in most cases gives the best result possible. It's best to try to avoid these situations by using texture coordinates that map without such distortion. (See "Computing Appropriate Texture Coordinates" on page 450.)

The following lines are examples of how to use **glTexParameter*()** to specify the magnification and minification filtering methods:

```
glTexParameteri(GL_TEXTURE_2D, GL_TEXTURE_MAG_FILTER,
                GL_NEAREST);
glTexParameteri(GL_TEXTURE_2D, GL_TEXTURE_MIN_FILTER,
                GL_NEAREST);
```

The first argument to **glTexParameter*()** is GL_TEXTURE_1D, GL_TEXTURE_2D, GL_TEXTURE_3D, or GL_TEXTURE_CUBE_MAP, whichever is appropriate. For the purposes of this discussion, the second argument is either GL_TEXTURE_MAG_FILTER, or GL_TEXTURE_MIN_FILTER, to indicate whether you're specifying the filtering method for magnification or minification. The third argument specifies the filtering method; Table 9-3 lists the possible values.

Parameter	Values
GL_TEXTURE_MAG_FILTER	GL_NEAREST or GL_LINEAR
GL_TEXTURE_MIN_FILTER	GL_NEAREST, GL_LINEAR, GL_NEAREST_MIPMAP_NEAREST, GL_NEAREST_MIPMAP_LINEAR, GL_LINEAR_MIPMAP_NEAREST, or GL_LINEAR_MIPMAP_LINEAR

Table 9-3   Filtering Methods for Magnification and Minification

If you choose GL_NEAREST, the texel with coordinates nearest the center of the pixel is used for both magnification and minification. This can result in aliasing artifacts (sometimes severe). If you choose GL_LINEAR, a weighted linear average of the 2 × 2 array of texels that lie nearest to the center of the pixel is used, again for both magnification and minification. (For three-dimensional textures, it's a 2 × 2 × 2 array; for one-dimensional, it's an average of 2 texels.) When the texture coordinates are near the edge of the texture map, the nearest 2 × 2 array of texels might include some that are outside the texture map. In these cases, the texel values used depend on which wrapping mode is in effect and whether you've assigned a border for the texture. (See "Repeating and Clamping Textures" on page 452.) GL_NEAREST requires less computation than GL_LINEAR and therefore might execute more quickly, but GL_LINEAR provides smoother results.

With magnification, even if you've supplied mipmaps, only the base level texture map is used. With minification, you can choose a filtering method that uses the most appropriate one or two mipmaps, as described in the next paragraph. (If GL_NEAREST or GL_LINEAR is specified with minification, only the base level texture map is used.)

As shown in Table 9-3, four additional filtering options are available when minifying with mipmaps. Within an individual mipmap, you can choose the nearest texel value with GL_NEAREST_MIPMAP_NEAREST, or you can interpolate linearly by specifying GL_LINEAR_MIPMAP_NEAREST. Using the nearest texels is faster but yields less desirable results. The particular mipmap chosen is a function of the amount of minification required, and there's a cutoff point from the use of one particular mipmap to the next. To avoid a sudden transition, use GL_NEAREST_MIPMAP_LINEAR or GL_LINEAR_MIPMAP_LINEAR for linear interpolation of texel values from the two nearest best choices of mipmaps. GL_NEAREST_MIPMAP_LINEAR selects the nearest texel in each of the two maps and then interpolates linearly between these two values. GL_LINEAR_MIPMAP_LINEAR uses linear interpolation to compute the value in each of two maps and then interpolates linearly between these two values. As you might expect, GL_LINEAR_MIPMAP_LINEAR generally produces the highest-quality results, but it requires the most computation and therefore might be the slowest.

Caution: If you request a mipmapped texture filter, but you have not supplied a full and consistent set of mipmaps (all correct-sized texture images between GL_TEXTURE_BASE_LEVEL and GL_TEXTURE_MAX_LEVEL), OpenGL will, without any error, implicitly disable texturing. If you are trying to use mipmaps and no texturing appears at all, check the texture images at all your mipmap levels.

Some of these texture filters are known by more popular names. GL_NEAREST is often called *point sampling*. GL_LINEAR is known as *bilinear sampling*, because for two-dimensional textures, a 2×2 array of texels is sampled. GL_LINEAR_MIPMAP_LINEAR is sometimes known as *trilinear sampling*, because it is a linear average between two bilinearly sampled mipmaps.

Note: The minification-to-magnification switchover point is usually at $\lambda = 0.0$, but is affected by the type of minification filter you choose. If the current magnification filter is GL_LINEAR and the minification filter is GL_NEAREST_MIPMAP_NEAREST or GL_NEAREST_MIPMAP_LINEAR, then the switch between filters occurs at $\lambda = 0.5$. This prevents the minified texture from looking sharper than its magnified counterpart.

Nate Robins' Texture Tutorial

If you have downloaded Nate Robins' suite of tutorial programs, now run the **texture** tutorial. (For information on how and where to download these programs, see "Errata" on page xlii.) With this tutorial, you can experiment with the texture-mapping filtering method, switching between GL_NEAREST and GL_LINEAR.

Texture Objects

A texture object stores texture data and makes it readily available. You may control many textures and go back to textures that have been previously loaded into your texture resources. Using texture objects is usually the fastest way to apply textures, resulting in big performance gains, because it is almost always much faster to bind (reuse) an existing texture object than it is to reload a texture image using **glTexImage*D()**.

Also, some implementations support a limited *working set* of high-performance textures. You can use texture objects to load your most often used textures into this limited area.

To use texture objects for your texture data, take these steps:

1. Generate texture names.
2. Initially bind (create) texture objects to texture data, including the image arrays and texture properties.
3. If your implementation supports a working set of high-performance textures, see if you have enough space for all your texture objects. If there isn't enough space, you may wish to establish priorities for each texture object so that more often used textures stay in the working set.

4. Bind and rebind texture objects, making their data currently available for rendering textured models.

Naming a Texture Object

Any nonzero unsigned integer may be used as a texture name. To avoid accidentally reusing names, consistently use **glGenTextures()** to provide unused texture names.

---

void **glGenTextures**(GLsizei *n*, GLuint **textureNames*);

Returns *n* currently unused names for texture objects in the array *textureNames*. The names returned in *textureNames* do not have to be a contiguous set of integers.

The names in *textureNames* are marked as used, but they acquire texture state and dimensionality (1D, 2D, or 3D) only when they are first bound.

Zero is a reserved texture name and is never returned as a texture name by **glGenTextures()**.

glIsTexture() determines if a texture name is actually in use. If a texture name was returned by **glGenTextures()** but has not yet been bound (calling **glBindTexture()** with the name at least once), then **glIsTexture()** returns GL_FALSE.

GLboolean **glIsTexture**(GLuint *textureName*);

Returns GL_TRUE if *textureName* is the name of a texture that has been bound and has not been subsequently deleted, and returns GL_FALSE if *textureName* is zero or *textureName* is a nonzero value that is not the name of an existing texture.

Creating and Using Texture Objects

The same routine, **glBindTexture()**, both creates and uses texture objects. When a texture name is initially bound (used with **glBindTexture()**), a new texture object is created with default values for the texture image and texture properties. Subsequent calls to **glTexImage*()**, **glTexSubImage*()**, **glCopyTexImage*()**, **glCopyTexSubImage*()**, **glTexParameter*()**, and

glPrioritizeTextures() store data in the texture object. The texture object may contain a texture image and associated mipmap images (if any), including associated data such as width, height, border width, internal format, resolution of components, and texture properties. Saved texture properties include minification and magnification filters, wrapping modes, border color, and texture priority.

When a texture object is subsequently bound once again, its data becomes the current texture state. (The state of the previously bound texture is replaced.)

---

void **glBindTexture**(GLenum *target*, GLuint *textureName*);

---

glBindTexture() does three things. When using the *textureName* of an unsigned integer other than zero for the first time, a new texture object is created and assigned that name. When binding to a previously created texture object, that texture object becomes active. When binding to a *textureName* value of zero, OpenGL stops using texture objects and returns to the unnamed default texture.

When a texture object is initially bound (that is, created), it assumes the dimensionality of *target*, which is GL_TEXTURE_1D, GL_TEXTURE_2D, GL_TEXTURE_3D, GL_TEXTURE_CUBE_MAP, GL_TEXTURE_1D_ARRAY, GL_TEXTURE_2D_ARRAY, GL_TEXTURE_RECTANGLE, or GL_TEXTURE_BUFFER. Immediately on its initial binding, the state of the texture object is equivalent to the state of the default *target* dimensionality at the initialization of OpenGL. In this initial state, texture properties such as minification and magnification filters, wrapping modes, border color, and texture priority are set to their default values.

In Example 9-7, two texture objects are created in **init()**. In **display()**, each texture object is used to render a different four-sided polygon.

Example 9-7   Binding Texture Objects: texbind.c

```
#define checkImageWidth 64
#define checkImageHeight 64
static GLubyte checkImage[checkImageHeight][checkImageWidth][4];
static GLubyte otherImage[checkImageHeight][checkImageWidth][4];

static GLuint texName[2];

void makeCheckImages(void)
{
```

```
    int i, j, c;

    for (i = 0; i < checkImageHeight; i++) {
        for (j = 0; j < checkImageWidth; j++) {
            c = (((i&0x8)==0)^((j&0x8)==0))*255;
            checkImage[i][j][0] = (GLubyte) c;
            checkImage[i][j][1] = (GLubyte) c;
            checkImage[i][j][2] = (GLubyte) c;
            checkImage[i][j][3] = (GLubyte) 255;
            c = (((i&0x10)==0)^((j&0x10)==0))*255;
            otherImage[i][j][0] = (GLubyte) c;
            otherImage[i][j][1] = (GLubyte) 0;
            otherImage[i][j][2] = (GLubyte) 0;
            otherImage[i][j][3] = (GLubyte) 255;
        }
    }
}

void init(void)
{
    glClearColor(0.0, 0.0, 0.0, 0.0);
    glShadeModel(GL_FLAT);
    glEnable(GL_DEPTH_TEST);

    makeCheckImages();
    glPixelStorei(GL_UNPACK_ALIGNMENT, 1);

    glGenTextures(2, texName);
    glBindTexture(GL_TEXTURE_2D, texName[0]);
    glTexParameteri(GL_TEXTURE_2D, GL_TEXTURE_WRAP_S, GL_CLAMP);
    glTexParameteri(GL_TEXTURE_2D, GL_TEXTURE_WRAP_T, GL_CLAMP);
    glTexParameteri(GL_TEXTURE_2D, GL_TEXTURE_MAG_FILTER,
                    GL_NEAREST);
    glTexParameteri(GL_TEXTURE_2D, GL_TEXTURE_MIN_FILTER,
                    GL_NEAREST);
    glTexImage2D(GL_TEXTURE_2D, 0, GL_RGBA, checkImageWidth,
                 checkImageHeight, 0, GL_RGBA, GL_UNSIGNED_BYTE,
                 checkImage);

    glBindTexture(GL_TEXTURE_2D, texName[1]);
    glTexParameteri(GL_TEXTURE_2D, GL_TEXTURE_WRAP_S, GL_CLAMP);
    glTexParameteri(GL_TEXTURE_2D, GL_TEXTURE_WRAP_T, GL_CLAMP);
    glTexParameteri(GL_TEXTURE_2D, GL_TEXTURE_MAG_FILTER,
                    GL_NEAREST);
    glTexParameteri(GL_TEXTURE_2D, GL_TEXTURE_MIN_FILTER,
                    GL_NEAREST);
    glTexEnvf(GL_TEXTURE_ENV, GL_TEXTURE_ENV_MODE, GL_REPLACE);
```

```
      glTexImage2D(GL_TEXTURE_2D, 0, GL_RGBA, checkImageWidth,
                   checkImageHeight, 0, GL_RGBA, GL_UNSIGNED_BYTE,
                   otherImage);
   glEnable(GL_TEXTURE_2D);
}

void display(void)
{
   glClear(GL_COLOR_BUFFER_BIT | GL_DEPTH_BUFFER_BIT);
   glBindTexture(GL_TEXTURE_2D, texName[0]);
   glBegin(GL_QUADS);
   glTexCoord2f(0.0, 0.0); glVertex3f(-2.0, -1.0, 0.0);
   glTexCoord2f(0.0, 1.0); glVertex3f(-2.0, 1.0, 0.0);
   glTexCoord2f(1.0, 1.0); glVertex3f(0.0, 1.0, 0.0);
   glTexCoord2f(1.0, 0.0); glVertex3f(0.0, -1.0, 0.0);
   glEnd();
   glBindTexture(GL_TEXTURE_2D, texName[1]);
   glBegin(GL_QUADS);
   glTexCoord2f(0.0, 0.0); glVertex3f(1.0, -1.0, 0.0);
   glTexCoord2f(0.0, 1.0); glVertex3f(1.0, 1.0, 0.0);
   glTexCoord2f(1.0, 1.0); glVertex3f(2.41421, 1.0, -1.41421);
   glTexCoord2f(1.0, 0.0); glVertex3f(2.41421, -1.0, -1.41421);
   glEnd();
   glFlush();
}
```

Whenever a texture object is bound once again, you may edit the contents of the bound texture object. Any commands you call that change the texture image or other properties change the contents of the currently bound texture object as well as the current texture state.

In Example 9-7, after completion of **display**(), you are still bound to the texture named by the contents of *texName[1]*. Be careful that you don't call a spurious texture routine that changes the data in that texture object.

When mipmaps are used, all related mipmaps of a single texture image must be put into a single texture object. In Example 9-5, levels 0–5 of a mip-mapped texture image are put into a single texture object named *texName*.

Cleaning Up Texture Objects

As you bind and unbind texture objects, their data still sits around some-where among your texture resources. If texture resources are limited, deleting textures may be one way to free up resources.

void **glDeleteTextures**(GLsizei *n*, const GLuint **textureNames*);

Deletes *n* texture objects, named by elements in the array *textureNames*. The freed texture names may now be reused (for example, by **glGenTextures**()).

If a texture that is currently bound is deleted, the binding reverts to the default texture, as if **glBindTexture**() were called with zero for the value of *textureName*. Attempts to delete nonexistent texture names or the texture name of zero are ignored without generating an error.

A Working Set of Resident Textures

Some OpenGL implementations support a working set of high-performance textures, which are said to be resident. Typically, these implementations have specialized hardware to perform texture operations and a limited hardware cache to store texture images. In this case, using texture objects is recommended, because you are able to load many textures into the working set and then control them.

If all the textures required by the application exceed the size of the cache, some textures cannot be resident. If you want to find out if a single texture is currently resident, bind its object, and then call **glGetTexParameter*v**() to determine the value associated with the GL_TEXTURE_RESIDENT state. If you want to know about the texture residence status of many textures, use **glAreTexturesResident**().

GLboolean **glAreTexturesResident**(GLsizei *n*,
                              const GLuint **textureNames*,
                              GLboolean **residences*);

Queries the texture residence status of the *n* texture objects, named in the array *textureNames*. *residences* is an array in which texture residence status is returned for the corresponding texture objects in the array *textureNames*. If all the named textures in *textureNames* are resident, the **glAreTexturesResident**() function returns GL_TRUE, and the contents of the array *residences* are undisturbed. If any texture in *textureNames* is not resident, then **glAreTexturesResident**() returns GL_FALSE, and the elements in *residences*, which correspond to nonresident texture objects in *textureNames*, are also set to GL_FALSE.

Note that **glAreTexturesResident**() returns the current residence status. Texture resources are very dynamic, and texture residence status may change at any time. Some implementations cache textures when they are first used. It may be necessary to draw with the texture before checking residency.

If your OpenGL implementation does not establish a working set of high-performance textures, then the texture objects are always considered resident. In that case, **glAreTexturesResident()** always returns GL_TRUE and basically provides no information.

Texture Residence Strategies

If you can create a working set of textures and want to get the best texture performance possible, you really have to know the specifics of your implementation and application. For example, with a visual simulation or video game, you have to maintain performance in all situations. In that case, you should never access a nonresident texture. For these applications, you want to load up all your textures on initialization and make them all resident. If you don't have enough texture memory available, you may need to reduce the size, resolution, and levels of mipmaps for your texture images, or you may use **glTexSubImage*()** to repeatedly reuse the same texture memory.

Note: If you have several short-lived textures of the same size, you can use **glTexSubImage*()** to reload existing texture objects with different images. This technique may be more efficient than deleting textures and reestablishing new textures from scratch.

For applications that create textures "on the fly," nonresident textures may be unavoidable. If some textures are used more frequently than others, you may assign a higher priority to those texture objects to increase their likelihood of being resident. Deleting texture objects also frees up space. Short of that, assigning a lower priority to a texture object may make it first in line for being moved out of the working set, as resources dwindle. **glPrioritizeTextures()** is used to assign priorities to texture objects.

---

void **glPrioritizeTextures**(GLsizei *n*, const GLuint **textureNames*,
const GLclampf **priorities*);

Assigns the *n* texture objects, named in the array *textureNames*, the texture residence priorities in the corresponding elements of the array *priorities*. The priority values in the array *priorities* are clamped to the range [0.0, 1.0] before being assigned. Zero indicates the lowest priority (textures least likely to be resident), and 1 indicates the highest priority.

glPrioritizeTextures() does not require that any of the textures in *textureNames* be bound. However, the priority might not have any effect on a texture object until it is initially bound.

---

glTexParameter*() also may be used to set a single texture's priority, but only if the texture is currently bound. In fact, use of **glTexParameter*()** is the only way to set the priority of a default texture.

If texture objects have equal priority, typical implementations of OpenGL apply a least recently used (LRU) strategy to decide which texture objects to move out of the working set. If you know that your OpenGL implementation uses this algorithm, then having equal priorities for all texture objects creates a reasonable LRU system for reallocating texture resources.

If your implementation of OpenGL doesn't use an LRU strategy for texture objects of equal priority (or if you don't know how it decides), you can implement your own LRU strategy by carefully maintaining the texture object priorities. When a texture is used (bound), you can maximize its priority, which reflects its recent use. Then, at regular (time) intervals, you can degrade the priorities of all texture objects.

Note: Fragmentation of texture memory can be a problem, especially if you're deleting and creating numerous new textures. Although it may be possible to load all the texture objects into a working set by binding them in one sequence, binding them in a different sequence may leave some textures nonresident.

Texture Functions

In each of the examples presented so far in this chapter, the values in the texture map have been used directly as colors to be painted on the surface being rendered. You can also use the values in the texture map to modulate the color in which the surface would be rendered without texturing or to combine the color in the texture map with the original color of the surface. You choose texturing functions by supplying the appropriate arguments to **glTexEnv*()**.

Compatibility Extension
glTexEnv and all associated tokens

void **glTexEnv**{if}(GLenum *target*, GLenum *pname*, *TYPE param*);
void **glTexEnv**{if}**v**(GLenum *target*, GLenum *pname*, const *TYPE *param*);

Sets the current texturing function. *target* must be either GL_TEXTURE_FILTER_CONTROL or GL_TEXTURE_ENV.

If *target* is GL_TEXTURE_FILTER_CONTROL, then *pname* must be GL_TEXTURE_LOD_BIAS, and *param* is a single, floating-point value used to bias the mipmapping level-of-detail parameter.

If *target* is GL_TEXTURE_ENV and if *pname* is GL_TEXTURE_ENV_MODE, then *param* is one of GL_DECAL, GL_REPLACE, GL_MODULATE, GL_BLEND, GL_ADD, or GL_COMBINE, which specifies how texture values are combined with the color values of the fragment being processed. If *pname* is GL_TEXTURE_ENV_COLOR, then *param* is an array of 4 floating-point numbers (R, G, B, A) which denotes a color to be used for GL_BLEND operations.

If *target* is GL_POINT_SPRITE and if *pname* is GL_COORD_REPLACE, then setting *param* to GL_TRUE will enable the iteration of texture coordinates across a point sprite. Texture coordinates will remain constant across the primitive if *param* is set to GL_FALSE.

Note: This is only a partial list of acceptable values for **glTexEnv*()**, excluding texture combiner functions. For complete details about GL_COMBINE and a complete list of options for *pname* and *param* for **glTexEnv*()**, see "Texture Combiner Functions" on page 472 and Table 9-8.

The combination of the texturing function and the base internal format determines how the textures are applied for each component of the texture. The texturing function operates on selected components of the texture and the color values that would be used with no texturing. (Note that the selection is performed after the pixel-transfer function has been applied.) Recall that when you specify your texture map with **glTexImage*D()**, the third argument is the internal format to be selected for each texel.

There are six base internal formats: GL_ALPHA, GL_LUMINANCE, GL_LUMINANCE_ALPHA, GL_INTENSITY, GL_RGB, and GL_RGBA. Other internal formats (such as GL_LUMINANCE6_ALPHA2 or GL_R3_G3_B2) specify desired resolutions of the texture components and can be matched to one of these six base internal formats.

Texturing calculations are ultimately in RGBA, but some internal formats are not in RGB. Table 9-4 shows how the RGBA color values are derived from different texture formats, including the less obvious derivations.

Base Internal Format	Derived Source Color (R, G, B, A)
GL_ALPHA	(0, 0, 0, A)
GL_LUMINANCE	(L, L, L, 1)

Table 9-4 Deriving Color Values from Different Texture Formats

Base Internal Format	Derived Source Color (R, G, B, A)
GL_LUMINANCE_ALPHA	(L, L, L, A)
GL_INTENSITY	(I, I, I, I)
GL_RGB	(R, G, B, 1)
GL_RGBA	(R, G, B, A)

Table 9-4   (continued)   Deriving Color Values from Different Texture Formats

Table 9-5 and Table 9-6 show how a texturing function (except for GL_COMBINE) and base internal format determine the texturing application formula used for each component of the texture.

In Table 9-5 and Table 9-6, note the following use of subscripts:

- s indicates a texture source color, as determined in Table 9-4.
- f indicates an incoming fragment value.
- c indicates values assigned with GL_TEXTURE_ENV_COLOR.
- No subscript indicates a final, computed value.

In these tables, multiplication of a color triple by a scalar means multiplying each of the R, G, and B components by the scalar; multiplying (or adding) two color triples means multiplying (or adding) each component of the second by (or to) the corresponding component of the first.

Base Internal Format	GL_REPLACE Function	GL_MODULATE Function	GL_DECAL Function
GL_ALPHA	$C = C_f$ $A = A_s$	$C = C_f$ $A = A_f A_s$	undefined
GL_LUMINANCE	$C = C_s$ $A = A_f$	$C = C_f C_s$ $A = A_f$	undefined
GL_LUMINANCE_ALPHA	$C = C_s$ $A = A_s$	$C = C_f C_s$ $A = A_f A_s$	undefined
GL_INTENSITY	$C = C_s$ $A = C_s$	$C = C_f C_s$ $A = A_f C_s$	undefined

Table 9-5   Replace, Modulate, and Decal Texture Functions

Base Internal Format	GL_REPLACE Function	GL_MODULATE Function	GL_DECAL Function
GL_RGB	$C = C_s$ $A = A_f$	$C = C_f C_s$ $A = A_f$	$C = C_s$ $A = A_f$
GL_RGBA	$C = C_s$ $A = A_s$	$C = C_f C_s$ $A = A_f A_s$	$C = C_f(1 - A_s) + C_s A_s$ $A = A_f$

Table 9-5 (continued) Replace, Modulate, and Decal Texture Functions

Base Internal Format	GL_BLEND Function	GL_ADD Function
GL_ALPHA	$C = C_f$ $A = A_f A_s$	$C = C_f$ $A = A_f A_s$
GL_LUMINANCE	$C = C_f(1 - C_s) + C_c C_s$ $A = A_f$	$C = C_f + C_s$ $A = A_f$
GL_LUMINANCE_ALPHA	$C = C_f(1 - C_s) + C_c C_s$ $A = A_f A_s$	$C = C_f + C_s$ $A = A_f A_s$
GL_INTENSITY	$C = C_f(1 - C_s) + C_c C_s$ $A = A_f(1 - A_s) + A_c A_s$	$C = C_f + C_s$ $A = A_f + A_s$
GL_RGB	$C = C_f(1 - C_s) + C_c C_s$ $A = A_f$	$C = C_f + C_s$ $A = A_f$
GL_RGBA	$C = C_f(1 - C_s) + C_c C_s$ $A = A_f A_s$	$C = C_f + C_s$ $A = A_f A_s$

Table 9-6 Blend and Add Texture Functions

The replacement texture function simply takes the color that would have been painted in the absence of any texture mapping (the fragment's color), tosses it away, and replaces it with the texture color. You use the replacement texture function in situations where you want to apply an opaque texture to an object—such as, for example, if you were drawing a soup can with an opaque label.

The decal texture function is similar to replacement, except that it works for only the RGB and RGBA internal formats, and it processes alpha differently. With the RGBA internal format, the fragment's color is blended with the texture color in a ratio determined by the texture alpha, and the fragment's alpha is unchanged. The decal texture function may be used to apply an alpha blended texture, such as an insignia on an airplane wing.

For modulation, the fragment's color is modulated by the contents of the texture map. If the base internal format is GL_LUMINANCE, GL_LUMINANCE_ALPHA, or GL_INTENSITY, the color values are multiplied by the same value, so the texture map modulates between the fragment's color (if the luminance or intensity is 1) to black (if it's 0). For the GL_RGB and GL_RGBA internal formats, each of the incoming color components is multiplied by a corresponding (possibly different) value in the texture. If there's an alpha value, it's multiplied by the fragment's alpha. Modulation is a good texture function for use with lighting, since the lit polygon color can be used to attenuate the texture color. Most of the texture-mapping examples in the color plates use modulation for this reason. White, specular polygons are often used to render lit, textured objects, and the texture image provides the diffuse color.

The additive texture function simply adds the texture color to the fragment color. If there's an alpha value, it's multiplied by the fragment alpha, except for the GL_INTENSITY format, where the texture's intensity is added to the fragment alpha. Unless the texture and fragment colors are carefully chosen, the additive texture function easily results in oversaturated or clamped colors.

The blending texture function is the only function that uses the color specified by GL_TEXTURE_ENV_COLOR. The luminance, intensity, or color value is used somewhat like an alpha value to blend the fragment's color with the GL_TEXTURE_ENV_COLOR. (See "Sample Uses of Blending" in Chapter 6 for the billboarding example, which uses a blended texture.)

Nate Robins' Texture Tutorial

If you have downloaded Nate Robins' suite of tutorial programs, run the **texture** tutorial. Change the texture-mapping environment attribute and see the effects of several texture functions. If you use GL_MODULATE, note the effect of the color specified by **glColor4f()**. If you choose GL_BLEND, see what happens if you change the color specified by the *env_color* array.

Assigning Texture Coordinates

As you draw your texture-mapped scene, you must provide both object coordinates and texture coordinates for each vertex. After transformation, the object's coordinates determine where on the screen that particular vertex is rendered. The texture coordinates determine which texel in the texture map is assigned to that vertex. In exactly the same way that colors are interpolated between two vertices of shaded polygons and lines, texture coordinates are interpolated between vertices. (Remember that textures are rectangular arrays of data.)

Texture coordinates can comprise one, two, three, or four coordinates. They're usually referred to as the *s-*, *t-*, *r-*, and *q*-coordinates to distinguish them from object coordinates (*x, y, z,* and *w*) and from evaluator coordinates (*u* and *v*; see Chapter 12). For one-dimensional textures, you use the *s*-coordinate; for two-dimensional textures, you use *s* and *t*; and for three-dimensional textures, you use *s, t,* and *r*. The *q*-coordinate, like *w*, is typically given the value 1 and can be used to create homogeneous coordinates; it's described as an advanced feature in "The *q*-Coordinate." The command to specify texture coordinates, **glTexCoord*()**, is similar to **glVertex*()**, **glColor*()**, and **glNormal*()**—it comes in similar variations and is used the same way between **glBegin()** and **glEnd()** pairs. Usually, texture-coordinate values range from 0 to 1; values can be assigned outside this range, however, with the results described in "Repeating and Clamping Textures."

---

void **glTexCoord**{1234}{sifd}(*TYPE coords*);
void **glTexCoord**{1234}{sifd}**v**(const *TYPE *coords*);

Compatibility
Extension

glTexCoord

Sets the current texture coordinates (*s, t, r, q*). Subsequent calls to **glVertex*()** result in those vertices being assigned the current texture coordinates. With **glTexCoord1*()**, the *s*-coordinate is set to the specified value, *t* and *r* are set to 0, and *q* is set to 1. Using **glTexCoord2*()** allows you to specify *s* and *t*; *r* and *q* are set to 0 and 1, respectively. With **glTexCoord3*()**, *q* is set to 1 and the other coordinates are set as specified. You can specify all coordinates with **glTexCoord4*()**. Use the appropriate suffix (s, i, f, or d) and the corresponding value for *TYPE* (GLshort, GLint, GLfloat, or GLdouble) to specify the coordinates' data type. You can supply the coordinates individually, or you can use the vector version of the command to supply them in a single array. Texture coordinates are multiplied by the 4×4 texture matrix before any texture mapping occurs. (See "The Texture Matrix Stack" on page 481.) Note that integer texture coordinates are interpreted directly, rather than being mapped to the range [–1, 1] as normal coordinates are.

The next subsection discusses how to calculate appropriate texture coordinates. Instead of explicitly assigning them yourself, you can choose to have texture coordinates calculated automatically by OpenGL as a function of the vertex coordinates. (See "Automatic Texture-Coordinate Generation" on page 457.)

Nate Robins' Texture Tutorial

If you have Nate Robins' **texture** tutorial, run it, and experiment with the parameters of **glTexCoord2f()** for the four different vertices. See how you can map from a portion of the entire texture. (What happens if you make a texture coordinate less than 0 or greater than 1?)

Computing Appropriate Texture Coordinates

Two-dimensional textures are square or rectangular images that are typically mapped to the polygons that make up a polygonal model. In the simplest case, you're mapping a rectangular texture onto a model that's also rectangular—for example, your texture is a scanned image of a brick wall, and your rectangle represents a brick wall of a building. Suppose the brick wall is square and the texture is square, and you want to map the whole texture to the whole wall. The texture coordinates of the texture square are (0, 0), (1, 0), (1, 1), and (0, 1) in counterclockwise order. When you're drawing the wall, just give those four coordinate sets as the texture coordinates as you specify the wall's vertices in counterclockwise order.

Now suppose that the wall is two-thirds as high as it is wide, and that the texture is again square. To avoid distorting the texture, you need to map the wall to a portion of the texture map so that the aspect ratio of the texture is preserved. Suppose that you decide to use the lower two-thirds of the texture map to texture the wall. In this case, use texture coordinates of (0, 0), (1, 0), (1, 2/3), and (0, 2/3) for the texture coordinates, as the wall vertices are traversed in a counterclockwise order.

As a slightly more complicated example, suppose you'd like to display a tin can with a label wrapped around it on the screen. To obtain the texture, you purchase a can, remove the label, and scan it in. Suppose the label is 4 units tall and 12 units around, which yields an aspect ratio of 3 to 1. Since textures must have aspect ratios of 2^n to 1, you can either simply not use the top third of the texture, or you can cut and paste the texture until it has the necessary aspect ratio. Suppose you decide not to use the top third. Now suppose the tin can is a cylinder approximated by 30 polygons of length 4 units (the height of the can) and width 12/30 (1/30 of the circumference of the can). You can use the following texture coordinates for each of the 30 approximating rectangles:

1: (0, 0), (1/30, 0), (1/30, 2/3), (0, 2/3)

2: (1/30, 0), (2/30, 0), (2/30, 2/3), (1/30, 2/3)

3: (2/30, 0), (3/30, 0), (3/30, 2/3), (2/30, 2/3)

. . .

30: (29/30, 0), (1, 0), (1, 2/3), (29/30, 2/3)

Only a few curved surfaces such as cones and cylinders can be mapped to a flat surface without geodesic distortion. Any other shape requires some distortion. In general, the higher the curvature of the surface, the more distortion of the texture is required.

If you don't care about texture distortion, it's often quite easy to find a reasonable mapping. For example, consider a sphere whose surface coordinates are given by $(\cos \theta \cos \phi, \cos \theta \sin \phi, \sin \theta)$, where $0 \leq \theta \leq 2\pi$ and $0 \leq \phi \leq \pi$. The θ-ϕ rectangle can be mapped directly to a rectangular texture map, but the closer you get to the poles, the more distorted the texture is. The entire top edge of the texture map is mapped to the north pole, and the entire bottom edge to the south pole. For other surfaces, such as that of a torus (doughnut) with a large hole, the natural surface coordinates map to the texture coordinates in a way that produces only a little distortion, so it might be suitable for many applications. Figure 9-9 shows two toruses, one with a small hole (and therefore a lot of distortion near the center) and one with a large hole (and only a little distortion).

Figure 9-9   Texture-Map Distortion

If you're texturing spline surfaces generated with evaluators (see Chapter 12), the u and v parameters for the surface can sometimes be used as texture coordinates. In general, however, there's a large artistic component to successful mapping of textures to polygonal approximations of curved surfaces.

Repeating and Clamping Textures

You can assign texture coordinates outside the range [0, 1] and have them either clamp or repeat in the texture map. With repeating textures, if you have a large plane with texture coordinates running from 0.0 to 10.0 in both directions, for example, you'll get 100 copies of the texture tiled together on the screen. During repeating, the integer parts of texture coordinates are ignored, and copies of the texture map tile the surface. For most applications in which the texture is to be repeated, the texels at the top of the texture should match those at the bottom, and similarly for the left and right edges.

A "mirrored" repeat is available, where the surface tiles "flip-flop." For instance, within texture coordinate range [0, 1], a texture may appear oriented from left-to-right (or top-to-bottom or near-to-far), but the "mirrored" repeat wrapping reorients the texture from right-to-left for texture coordinate range [1, 2], then back again to left-to-right for coordinates [2, 3], and so on.

Another possibility is to clamp the texture coordinates: Any values greater than 1.0 are set to 1.0, and any values less than 0.0 are set to 0.0. Clamping is useful for applications in which you want a single copy of the texture to appear on a large surface. If the texture coordinates of the surface range from 0.0 to 10.0 in both directions, one copy of the texture appears in the lower left corner of the surface.

If you are using textures with borders or have specified a texture border color, both the wrapping mode and the filtering method (see "Filtering" on page 434) influence whether and how the border information is used.

If you're using the filtering method GL_NEAREST, the closest texel in the texture is used. For most wrapping modes, the border (or border color) is ignored. However, if the texture coordinate is outside the range [0, 1] and the wrapping mode is GL_CLAMP_TO_BORDER, then the nearest border texel is chosen. (If no border is present, the constant border color is used.)

If you've chosen GL_LINEAR as the filtering method, a weighted combination in a 2 × 2 array (for two-dimensional textures) of color data is used for texture application. If there is a border or border color, the texture and border colors are used together, as follows:

- For the wrapping mode GL_REPEAT, the border is always ignored. The 2 × 2 array of weighted texels wraps to the opposite edge of the texture. Thus, texels at the right edge are averaged with those at the left edge, and top and bottom texels are also averaged.

- For the wrapping mode GL_CLAMP, the texel from the border (or GL_TEXTURE_BORDER_COLOR) is used in the 2 × 2 array of weighted texels.

- For the wrapping mode GL_CLAMP_TO_EDGE, the border is always ignored. Texels at or near the edge of the texture are used for texturing calculations, but not the border.

- For the wrapping mode GL_CLAMP_TO_BORDER, if the texture coordinate is outside the range [0, 1], then only border texels (or if no border is present, the constant border color) are used for texture application. Near the edge of texture coordinates, texels from both the border and the interior texture may be sampled in a 2 × 2 array.

If you are using clamping, you can avoid having the rest of the surface affected by the texture. To do this, use alpha values of 0 for the edges (or borders, if they are specified) of the texture. The decal texture function directly uses the texture's alpha value in its calculations. If you are using one of the other texture functions, you may also need to enable blending with good source and destination factors. (See "Blending" in Chapter 6.)

To see the effects of wrapping, you must have texture coordinates that venture beyond [0.0, 1.0]. Start with Example 9-1, and modify the texture coordinates for the squares by mapping the texture coordinates from 0.0 to 4.0, as follows:

```
glBegin(GL_QUADS);
  glTexCoord2f(0.0, 0.0); glVertex3f(-2.0, -1.0, 0.0);
  glTexCoord2f(0.0, 4.0); glVertex3f(-2.0, 1.0, 0.0);
  glTexCoord2f(4.0, 4.0); glVertex3f(0.0, 1.0, 0.0);
  glTexCoord2f(4.0, 0.0); glVertex3f(0.0, -1.0, 0.0);

  glTexCoord2f(0.0, 0.0); glVertex3f(1.0, -1.0, 0.0);
  glTexCoord2f(0.0, 4.0); glVertex3f(1.0, 1.0, 0.0);
  glTexCoord2f(4.0, 4.0); glVertex3f(2.41421, 1.0, -1.41421);
  glTexCoord2f(4.0, 0.0); glVertex3f(2.41421, -1.0, -1.41421);
glEnd();
```

With GL_REPEAT wrapping, the result is as shown in Figure 9-10.

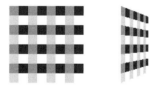

Figure 9-10   Repeating a Texture

In this case, the texture is repeated in both the *s*- and *t*- directions, since the following calls are made to **glTexParameter*()**:

```
glTexParameteri(GL_TEXTURE_2D, GL_TEXTURE_WRAP_S, GL_REPEAT);
glTexParameteri(GL_TEXTURE_2D, GL_TEXTURE_WRAP_T, GL_REPEAT);
```

Some OpenGL implementations support GL_MIRRORED_REPEAT wrapping, which reverses orientation at every integer texture coordinate boundary. Figure 9-11 shows the contrast between ordinary repeat wrapping (left) and the mirrored repeat (right).

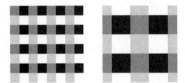

Figure 9-11   Comparing GL_REPEAT to GL_MIRRORED_REPEAT

In Figure 9-12, GL_CLAMP is used for each direction. Where the texture coordinate s or t is greater than one, the texel used is from where each texture coordinate is exactly one.

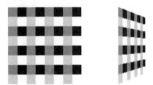

Figure 9-12   Clamping a Texture

Wrapping modes are independent for each direction. You can also clamp in one direction and repeat in the other, as shown in Figure 9-13.

Figure 9-13   Repeating and Clamping a Texture

Plate 1. The scene from the cover of this book, with the objects rendered as wireframe models. See Chapter 2.

Plate 2. The same scene using fog for depth-cueing (lines further from the eye are dimmer). See Chapter 6.

Plate 3. The same scene
with antialiased lines that
smooth the jagged edges.
See Chapter 6.

Plate 4. The scene
drawn with flat-shaded
polygons (a single color
for each filled polygon).
See Chapter 4.

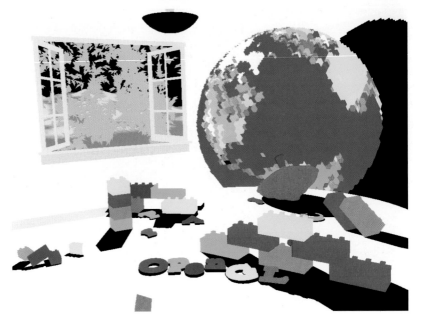

Plate 3. The same scene with antialiased lines that smooth the jagged edges. See Chapter 6.

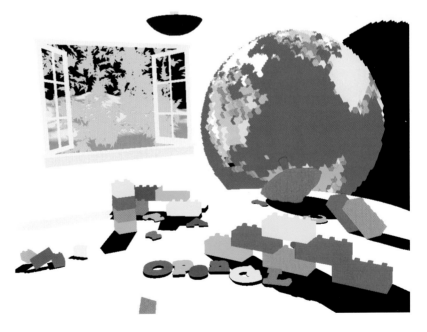

Plate 4. The scene drawn with flat-shaded polygons (a single color for each filled polygon). See Chapter 4.

Plate 1. The scene from the cover of this book, with the objects rendered as wireframe models. See Chapter 2.

Plate 2. The same scene using fog for depth-cueing (lines further from the eye are dimmer). See Chapter 6.

Plate 5. The scene rendered with lighting and smooth-shaded polygons. See Chapters 4 and 5.

Plate 6. The scene with texture maps and shadows added. See Chapters 9 and 14.

Plate 7. The scene drawn with one of the objects motion-blurred. The accumulation buffer is used to compose the sequence of images needed to blur the moving object. See Chapter 10.

Plate 8. A close-up shot—the scene is rendered from a new viewpoint. See Chapter 3.

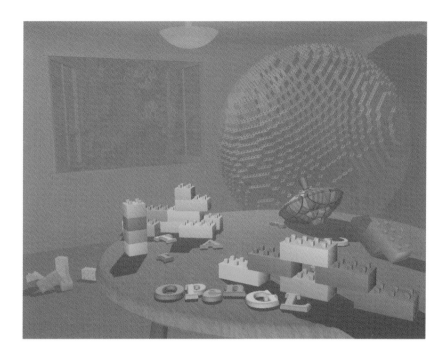

Plate 9. The scene drawn using atmospheric effects (fog) to simulate a smoke-filled room. See Chapter 6.

Plate 10. Teapots drawn with jittered viewing volumes into the accumulation buffer for a depth-of-field effect. The gold teapot is in sharpest focus. See Chapter 10.

Plate 11. A smooth-shaded triangle. The three vertices at the corners are drawn in red, green, and blue; the rest of the triangle is smoothly shaded between these three colors. See Chapter 4.

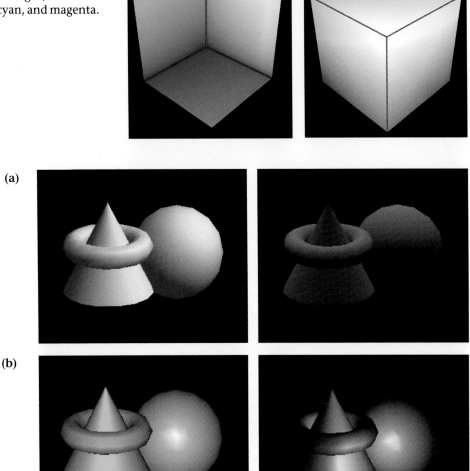

Plate 12. The color cube. On the left, the red, green, and blue axes are shown; on the right, the axes denote yellow, cyan, and magenta. See Chapter 4.

(a)

(b)

Plate 13. Objects drawn with gray material parameters and colored light sources. **(a)** The scene on the left has pale blue ambient light and a white diffuse light source. The scene on the right has a pale blue diffuse light source and almost no ambient light. **(b)** On the left, an infinite light source is used; on the right, a local light source is used. With the infinite light source, the highlight (specular reflection) is centered on both the cone and the sphere because the angle between the object and the line of sight is ignored. With a local light source, the angle is taken into account, so the highlights are located appropriately on both objects. See Chapter 5.

(a)

(b)

Plate 15. A lighted sphere drawn using color index mode. See Chapter 5.

Plate 14. Gray teapots drawn with different lighting conditions. **(a)** Each of the three teapots is drawn with increasing ambient light. **(b)** The teapots are clipped to expose their interiors. The top teapot uses one-sided lighting, the middle one uses two-sided lighting with the same material for both front and back faces, and the bottom teapot uses two-sided lighting and different materials for the front and back faces. See Chapter 5.

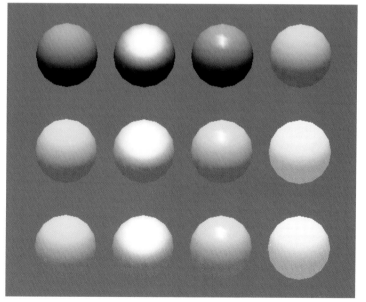

— No ambient reflection.

— Grey ambient reflection.

— Blue ambient reflection.

Plate 16. Twelve spheres, each with different material parameters. The row properties are as labeled above. The first column uses a blue diffuse material color with no specular properties. The second column adds white specular reflection with a low shininess exponent. The third column uses a high shininess exponent and thus has a more concentrated highlight. The fourth column uses the blue diffuse color and, instead of specular reflection, adds an emissive component. See Chapter 5.

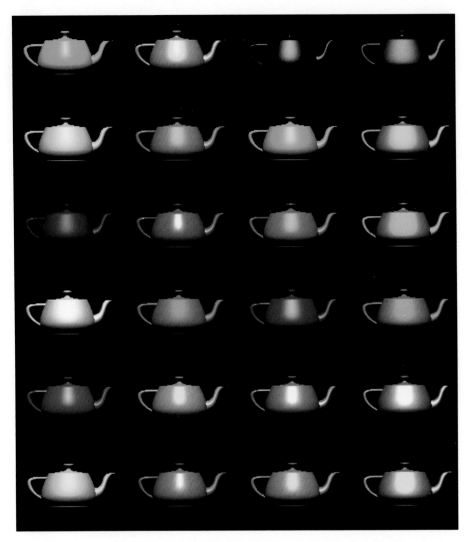

Plate 17. Lighted, smooth-shaded teapots drawn with different material properties that approximate real materials. The first column has materials that resemble (from top to bottom) emerald, jade, obsidian, pearl, ruby, and turquoise. The second column resembles brass, bronze, chrome, copper, gold, and silver. The third column represents various colors of plastic: black, cyan, green, red, white, and yellow. The fourth column is drawn with similar colors of rubber. See Chapter 5.

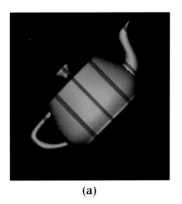 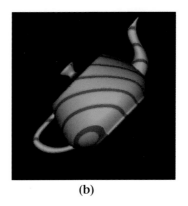 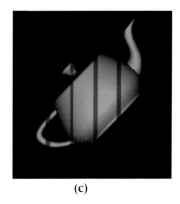

| (a) | (b) | (c) |

Plate 18. Lighted, green teapots drawn using automatic texture-coordinate generation and a red contour texture map. **(a)** The texture contour stripes are parallel to the plane x = 0, relative to the transformed object (that is, using GL_OBJECT_LINEAR). As the object moves, the texture appears to be attached to it. **(b)** A different planar equation (x + y + z = 0) is used, so the stripes have a different orientation. **(c)** The texture coordinates are calculated relative to eye coordinates and hence aren't fixed to the object (GL_EYE_LINEAR). As the object moves, it appears to "swim" through the texture. See Chapter 9.

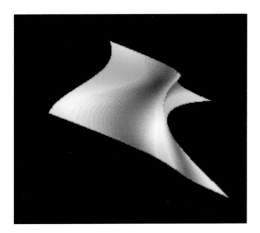

Plate 19. A texture-mapped Bezier surface mesh created using evaluators. See Chapters 9 and 12.

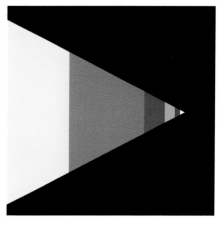

Plate 20. A single polygon drawn using a set of mipmapped textures. In this case, each texture is simply a different color. The polygon is actually a rectangle oriented so that it recedes into the distance, appearing to become progressively smaller. As the visible area of the polygon becomes smaller, correspondingly smaller mipmaps are used. See Chapter 9.

Plate 21. An environment-mapped object. On the left is the original texture, a processed photograph of a coffee shop in Palo Alto, taken with a very wide-angle lens. Below is a goblet with the environment map applied; because of the mapping, the goblet appears to reflect the coffee shop off its surface. See Chapter 9.

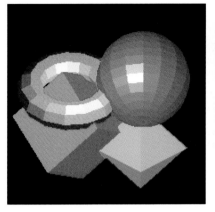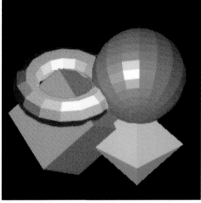

Plate 22. A scene with several flat-shaded objects. On the left, the scene is aliased. On the right, the accumulation buffer is used for scene antialiasing: the scene is rendered several times, each time jittered less than one pixel, and the images are accumulated and then averaged. See Chapter 10.

Plate 23. A magnification of the previous scenes. The left image shows the aliased, jagged edges. In the right image, the edges are blurred, or antialiased, and hence less jagged. See Chapter 10.

Plate 24. An architectural rendering using OpenGL. This is a rendering of a VRML scene using texture mapping (see Chapter 9) for illumination control and stencil buffering (see Chapter 10). (Image courtesy of Cyril Kardassevitch, Institut de Recherche en Informatique de Toulouse, Toulouse, France)

Plate 25. An image representing a manufacturing prototype. Environment mapping is used to enhance the illumination in the scene. See Chapter 9. (Image courtesy of Yukari Ito and Keisuke Kirii, Visual Systems Technology Center, Nihon SGI, Tokyo, Japan)

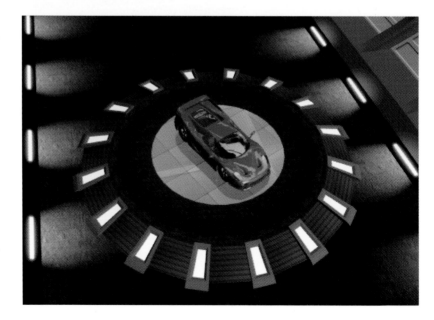

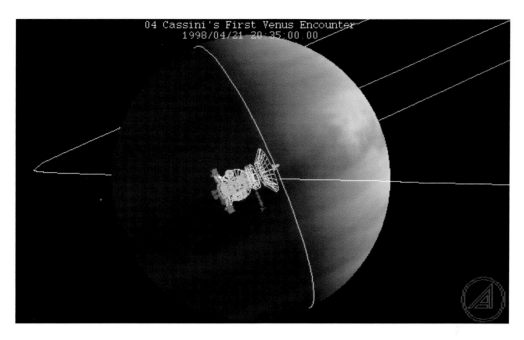

Plate 26. Scientific visualization of the interplanetary probe, Cassini, after its initial rendezvous with Venus. (Image courtesy of John Coggi and David Stodden, The Aerospace Company, Los Angeles, California, USA)

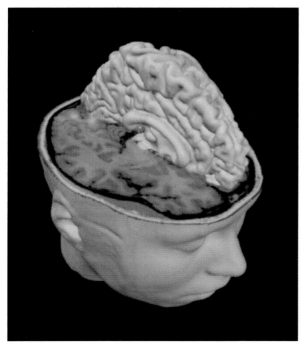

Plate 27. Medical visualization based on slices from a magnetic resonance imaging scan. The image is composed of surfaces generated from the slices. (Image courtesy of Rainer Goebel, Max Planck Institute for Brain Research, Frankfurt, Germany)

Plate 28. Projected texture mapping. See Chapter 9. (Image courtesy of Stefan Brabec and Wolfgang Heidrich, Max Planck Institute for Computer Science, Saarbrücken, Germany)

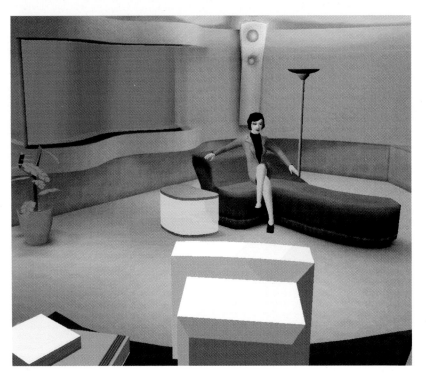

Plate 29. A synthetic being. The illumination in the scene is augmented using texture mapping. (Image courtesy of Mikko Blomqvist, Mediaclick OY, Tampere, Finland)

Plate 30. An image of a virutal oceanarium. Texture mapping and fog are used to generate the underwater effects. See Chapter 6. (Image courtesy of Bernd Lutz, Fraunhofer IGD, Darmstadt, Germany)

Plates 31 and 32. Screen images from Quake II and Quake III Arena, both of which use OpenGL for image generation. Multiple texture mapping passes are used to provide the image quality. Also note the use of fog and alpha blending to increase realism in the scene. (Images courtesy of id Software, Mesquite, Texas, USA)

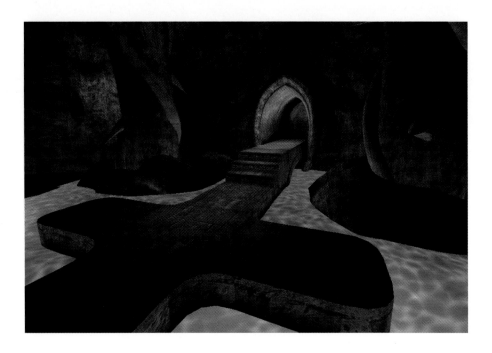

You've now seen several arguments for **glTexParameter*()**, which are summarized as follows.

void **glTexParameter**{if}(GLenum *target*, GLenum *pname*, TYPE *param*);
void **glTexParameter**{if}**v**(GLenum *target*, GLenum *pname*,
                          const TYPE **param*);
void **glTexParameterI**{i ui}**v**(GLenum *target*, GLenum *pname*,
                          const TYPE **param);*

Sets various parameters that control how a texture is treated as it's applied to a fragment or stored in a texture object. The *target* parameter is GL_TEXTURE_1D, GL_TEXTURE_2D, GL_TEXTURE_3D, GL_TEXTURE_1D_ARRAY, GL_TEXTURE_2D_ARRAY, GL_TEXTURE_CUBE_MAP, and GL_TEXTURE_RECTANGLE to match the intended texture. The possible values for *pname* and *param* are shown in Table 9-7. You can use the vector version of the command to supply an array of values for GL_TEXTURE_BORDER_COLOR, or you can supply individual values for other parameters using the nonvector version. If values are supplied as integers using **glTexParameterf*()**, they're converted to floating-point numbers according to Table 4-1; they're also clamped to the range [0, 1]. Integer values passed into **glTexParameterI*()** are not converted. Likewise, if integer values are supplied using **glTexParameterI*()** to set floating-point parameters, they are converted as described in Table 4-1.

Parameter	Values
GL_TEXTURE_WRAP_S	GL_CLAMP, GL_CLAMP_TO_EDGE, GL_CLAMP_TO_BORDER, GL_REPEAT, GL_MIRRORED_REPEAT
GL_TEXTURE_WRAP_T	GL_CLAMP, GL_CLAMP_TO_EDGE, GL_CLAMP_TO_BORDER, GL_REPEAT, GL_MIRRORED_REPEAT
GL_TEXTURE_WRAP_R	GL_CLAMP, GL_CLAMP_TO_EDGE, GL_CLAMP_TO_BORDER, GL_REPEAT, GL_MIRRORED_REPEAT
GL_TEXTURE_MAG_FILTER	GL_NEAREST, GL_LINEAR

Table 9-7   glTexParameter*() Parameters

Parameter	Values
GL_TEXTURE_MIN_FILTER	GL_NEAREST, GL_LINEAR, GL_NEAREST_MIPMAP_NEAREST, GL_NEAREST_MIPMAP_LINEAR, GL_LINEAR_MIPMAP_NEAREST, GL_LINEAR_MIPMAP_LINEAR
GL_TEXTURE_BORDER_COLOR	any four values in [0.0, 1.0] (for non-integer texture formats), or signed or unsigned integer values (for integer texture formats)
GL_TEXTURE_PRIORITY	[0.0, 1.0] for the current texture object
GL_TEXTURE_MIN_LOD	any floating-point value
GL_TEXTURE_MAX_LOD	any floating-point value
GL_TEXTURE_BASE_LEVEL	any non-negative integer
GL_TEXTURE_MAX_LEVEL	any non-negative integer
GL_TEXTURE_LOD_BIAS	any floating-point value
GL_DEPTH_TEXTURE_MODE	GL_RED, GL_LUMINANCE, GL_INTENSITY, GL_ALPHA
GL_TEXTURE_COMPARE_MODE	GL_NONE, GL_COMPARE_REF_TO_TEXTURE (for Version 3.0 and later), or GL_COMPARE_R_TO_TEXTURE (for versions up to and including Version 2.1)
GL_TEXTURE_COMPARE_FUNC	GL_LEQUAL, GL_GEQUAL, GL_LESS, GL_GREATER, GL_EQUAL, GL_NOTEQUAL, GL_ALWAYS, GL_NEVER
GL_GENERATE_MIPMAP	GL_TRUE, GL_FALSE

Table 9-7 (continued)   glTexParameter*() Parameters

Try This

Figures 9-12 and 9-13 are drawn using GL_NEAREST for the minification and magnification filters. What happens if you change the filter values to GL_LINEAR? The resulting image should look more blurred.

Border information may be used while calculating texturing. For the simplest demonstration of this, set GL_TEXTURE_BORDER_COLOR to

Try This

a noticeable color. With the filters set to GL_NEAREST and the wrapping mode set to GL_CLAMP_TO_BORDER, the border color affects the textured object (for texture coordinates beyond the range [0, 1]). The border also affects the texturing with the filters set to GL_LINEAR and the wrapping mode set to GL_CLAMP.

What happens if you switch the wrapping mode to GL_CLAMP_TO_EDGE or GL_REPEAT? In both cases, the border color is ignored.

Nate Robins' Texture Tutorial

Run the Nate Robins' **texture** tutorial and see the effects of the wrapping parameters GL_REPEAT and GL_CLAMP. You will need to make the texture coordinates at the vertices (parameters to **glTexCoord2f()**) less than 0 and/or greater than 1 to see any repeating or clamping effect.

Automatic Texture-Coordinate Generation

You can use texture mapping to make contours on your models or to simulate the reflections from an arbitrary environment on a shiny model. To achieve these effects, let OpenGL automatically generate the texture coordinates for you, rather than explicitly assign them with **glTexCoord*()**. To generate texture coordinates automatically, use the command **glTexGen()**.

---

void **glTexGen**{ifd}(GLenum *coord*, GLenum *pname*, *TYPE param*);
void **glTexGen**{ifd}v(GLenum *coord*, GLenum *pname*, const *TYPE *param*);

Specifies the functions for automatically generating texture coordinates. The first parameter, *coord*, must be GL_S, GL_T, GL_R, or GL_Q to indicate whether texture coordinate *s, t, r,* or *q* is to be generated. The *pname* parameter is GL_TEXTURE_GEN_MODE, GL_OBJECT_PLANE, or GL_EYE_PLANE. If it's GL_TEXTURE_GEN_MODE, *param* is an integer (or, in the vector version of the command, points to an integer) that is one of GL_OBJECT_LINEAR, GL_EYE_LINEAR, GL_SPHERE_MAP, GL_REFLECTION_MAP, or GL_NORMAL_MAP. These symbolic constants determine which function is used to generate the texture coordinate. With either of the other possible values for *pname, param* is a pointer to an array of values (for the vector version) specifying parameters for the texture-generation function.

Compatibility
Extension

glTexGen and all accpted tokens.

The different methods of texture-coordinate generation have different uses. Specifying the reference plane in object coordinates is best when a texture image remains fixed to a moving object. Thus, GL_OBJECT_LINEAR would be used for putting a wood grain on a tabletop. Specifying the reference plane in eye coordinates (GL_EYE_LINEAR) is best for producing dynamic contour lines on moving objects. GL_EYE_LINEAR may be used by specialists in the geosciences who are drilling for oil or gas. As the drill goes deeper into the ground, the drill may be rendered with different colors to represent the layers of rock at increasing depths. GL_SPHERE_MAP and GL_REFLECTION_MAP are used mainly for spherical environment mapping, and GL_NORMAL_MAP is used for cube maps. (See "Sphere Map" on page 463 and "Cube Map Textures" on page 465.)

Creating Contours

When GL_TEXTURE_GEN_MODE and GL_OBJECT_LINEAR are specified, the generation function is a linear combination of the object coordinates of the vertex (x_0, y_0, z_0, w_0):

generated coordinate = $p_1 x_0 + p_2 y_0 + p_3 z_0 + p_4 w_0$

The $p_1, ..., p_4$ values are supplied as the *param* argument to **glTexGen*v**(), with *pname* set to GL_OBJECT_PLANE. With $p_1, ..., p_4$ correctly normalized, this function gives the distance from the vertex to a plane. For example, if $p_2 = p_3 = p_4 = 0$ and $p_1 = 1$, the function gives the distance between the vertex and the plane $x = 0$. The distance is positive on one side of the plane, negative on the other, and zero if the vertex lies on the plane.

Initially, in Example 9-8, equally spaced contour lines are drawn on a teapot; the lines indicate the distance from the plane $x = 0$. The coefficients for the plane $x = 0$ are in this array:

```
static GLfloat xequalzero[] = {1.0, 0.0, 0.0, 0.0};
```

Since only one property is being shown (the distance from the plane), a one-dimensional texture map suffices. The texture map is a constant green color, except that at equally spaced intervals it includes a red mark. Since the teapot is sitting on the *xy*-plane, the contours are all perpendicular to its base. Plate 18 shows the picture drawn by the program.

In the same example, pressing the 's' key changes the parameters of the reference plane to

```
static GLfloat slanted[] = {1.0, 1.0, 1.0, 0.0};
```

The contour stripes are parallel to the plane $x + y + z = 0$, slicing across the teapot at an angle, as shown in Plate 18. To restore the reference plane to its initial value, $x = 0$, press the 'x' key.

Example 9-8   Automatic Texture-Coordinate Generation: texgen.c

```
#define stripeImageWidth 32
GLubyte stripeImage[4*stripeImageWidth];

static GLuint texName;

void makeStripeImage(void)
{
   int j;

   for (j = 0; j < stripeImageWidth; j++) {
      stripeImage[4*j]   = (GLubyte) ((j<=4) ? 255 : 0);
      stripeImage[4*j+1] = (GLubyte) ((j>4) ? 255 : 0);
      stripeImage[4*j+2] = (GLubyte) 0;
      stripeImage[4*j+3] = (GLubyte) 255;
   }
}

/*  planes for texture-coordinate generation  */
static GLfloat xequalzero[] = {1.0, 0.0, 0.0, 0.0};
static GLfloat slanted[] = {1.0, 1.0, 1.0, 0.0};
static GLfloat *currentCoeff;
static GLenum currentPlane;
static GLint currentGenMode;

void init(void)
{
   glClearColor(0.0, 0.0, 0.0, 0.0);
   glEnable(GL_DEPTH_TEST);
   glShadeModel(GL_SMOOTH);

   makeStripeImage();
   glPixelStorei(GL_UNPACK_ALIGNMENT, 1);

   glGenTextures(1, &texName);
   glBindTexture(GL_TEXTURE_1D, texName);
   glTexParameteri(GL_TEXTURE_1D, GL_TEXTURE_WRAP_S, GL_REPEAT);
   glTexParameteri(GL_TEXTURE_1D, GL_TEXTURE_MAG_FILTER,
                   GL_LINEAR);
   glTexParameteri(GL_TEXTURE_1D, GL_TEXTURE_MIN_FILTER,
                   GL_LINEAR);
```

```
      glTexImage1D(GL_TEXTURE_1D, 0, GL_RGBA, stripeImageWidth, 0,
                   GL_RGBA, GL_UNSIGNED_BYTE, stripeImage);

      glTexEnvf(GL_TEXTURE_ENV, GL_TEXTURE_ENV_MODE, GL_MODULATE);
      currentCoeff = xequalzero;
      currentGenMode = GL_OBJECT_LINEAR;
      currentPlane = GL_OBJECT_PLANE;
      glTexGeni(GL_S, GL_TEXTURE_GEN_MODE, currentGenMode);
      glTexGenfv(GL_S, currentPlane, currentCoeff);

      glEnable(GL_TEXTURE_GEN_S);
      glEnable(GL_TEXTURE_1D);
      glEnable(GL_CULL_FACE);
      glEnable(GL_LIGHTING);
      glEnable(GL_LIGHT0);
      glEnable(GL_AUTO_NORMAL);
      glEnable(GL_NORMALIZE);
      glFrontFace(GL_CW);
      glCullFace(GL_BACK);
      glMaterialf(GL_FRONT, GL_SHININESS, 64.0);
   }

   void display(void)
   {
      glClear(GL_COLOR_BUFFER_BIT | GL_DEPTH_BUFFER_BIT);

      glPushMatrix();
      glRotatef(45.0, 0.0, 0.0, 1.0);
      glBindTexture(GL_TEXTURE_1D, texName);
      glutSolidTeapot(2.0);
      glPopMatrix();
      glFlush();
   }

   void reshape(int w, int h)
   {
      glViewport(0, 0, (GLsizei) w, (GLsizei) h);
      glMatrixMode(GL_PROJECTION);
      glLoadIdentity();
      if (w <= h)
         glOrtho(-3.5, 3.5, -3.5*(GLfloat)h/(GLfloat)w,
                 3.5*(GLfloat)h/(GLfloat)w, -3.5, 3.5);
      else
         glOrtho(-3.5*(GLfloat)w/(GLfloat)h,
                 3.5*(GLfloat)w/(GLfloat)h, -3.5, 3.5, -3.5, 3.5);
```

```c
    glMatrixMode(GL_MODELVIEW);
    glLoadIdentity();
}

void keyboard(unsigned char key, int x, int y)
{
    switch (key) {
        case 'e':
        case 'E':
            currentGenMode = GL_EYE_LINEAR;
            currentPlane = GL_EYE_PLANE;
            glTexGeni(GL_S, GL_TEXTURE_GEN_MODE, currentGenMode);
            glTexGenfv(GL_S, currentPlane, currentCoeff);
            glutPostRedisplay();
            break;
        case 'o':
        case 'O':
            currentGenMode = GL_OBJECT_LINEAR;
            currentPlane = GL_OBJECT_PLANE;
            glTexGeni(GL_S, GL_TEXTURE_GEN_MODE, currentGenMode);
            glTexGenfv(GL_S, currentPlane, currentCoeff);
            glutPostRedisplay();
            break;
        case 's':
        case 'S':
            currentCoeff = slanted;
            glTexGenfv(GL_S, currentPlane, currentCoeff);
            glutPostRedisplay();
            break;
        case 'x':
        case 'X':
            currentCoeff = xequalzero;
            glTexGenfv(GL_S, currentPlane, currentCoeff);
            glutPostRedisplay();
            break;
        case 27:
            exit(0);
            break;
        default:
            break;
    }
}

int main(int argc, char** argv)
{
    glutInit(&argc, argv);
    glutInitDisplayMode(GLUT_SINGLE | GLUT_RGB | GLUT_DEPTH);
```

```
    glutInitWindowSize(256, 256);
    glutInitWindowPosition(100, 100);
    glutCreateWindow(argv[0]);
    init();
    glutDisplayFunc(display);
    glutReshapeFunc(reshape);
    glutKeyboardFunc(keyboard);
    glutMainLoop();
    return 0;
}
```

You enable texture-coordinate generation for the *s*-coordinate by passing
GL_TEXTURE_GEN_S to **glEnable()**. To generate other coordinates, enable
them with GL_TEXTURE_GEN_T, GL_TEXTURE_GEN_R, or GL_TEXTURE_
GEN_Q. Use **glDisable()** with the appropriate constant to disable coordinate generation. Also note the use of GL_REPEAT to cause the contour lines
to be repeated across the teapot.

The GL_OBJECT_LINEAR function calculates the texture coordinates in
the model's coordinate system. Initially, in Example 9-8, the GL_OBJECT_
LINEAR function is used, so the contour lines remain perpendicular to the
base of the teapot, no matter how the teapot is rotated or viewed. However,
if you press the 'e' key, the texture-generation mode is changed from
GL_OBJECT_LINEAR to GL_EYE_LINEAR, and the contour lines are calculated relative to the eye coordinate system. (Pressing the 'o' key restores
GL_OBJECT_LINEAR as the texture-generation mode.) If the reference plane
is $x = 0$, the result is a teapot with red stripes parallel to the *yz*-plane from
the eye's point of view, as shown in Plate 18. Mathematically, you are multiplying the vector $(p_1\ p_2\ p_3\ p_4)$ by the inverse of the modelview matrix to
obtain the values used to calculate the distance to the plane. The texture
coordinate is generated with the following function:

generated coordinate = $p_1'x_e + p_2'y_e + p_3'z_e + p_4'w_e$

where $(p_1'\ p_2'\ p_3'\ p_4') = (p_1\ p_2\ p_3\ p_4)\mathbf{M}^{-1}$

In this case, (x_e, y_e, z_e, w_e) are the eye coordinates of the vertex, and p_1, ...,
p_4 are supplied as the *param* argument to **glTexGen*()**, with *pname* set to
GL_EYE_PLANE. The primed values are calculated only at the time they're
specified, so this operation isn't as computationally expensive as it looks.

In all these examples, a single texture coordinate is used to generate contours. *s*, *t*, and (if needed) *r* texture coordinates can be generated independently, however, to indicate the distances to two or three different planes.
With a properly constructed two- or three-dimensional texture map, the
resulting two or three sets of contours can be viewed simultaneously. For an

added level of complexity, you can mix generation functions. For example, you can calculate the *s*-coordinate using GL_OBJECT_LINEAR, and the *t*-coordinate using GL_EYE_LINEAR.

Sphere Map

Advanced

Advanced

The goal of environment mapping is to render an object as if it were perfectly reflective, so that the colors on its surface are those reflected to the eye from its surroundings. In other words, if you look at a perfectly polished, perfectly reflective silver object in a room, you see the reflections of the walls, floor, and other items in the room from the object. (A classic example of using environment mapping is the evil, morphing cyborg in the film *Terminator 2*.) The objects whose reflections you see depend on the position of your eye and on the position and surface angles of the silver object. To perform environment mapping, all you have to do is create an appropriate texture map and then have OpenGL generate the texture coordinates for you.

Environment mapping is an approximation based on the assumption that the items in the environment are far away in comparison with the surfaces of the shiny object—that is, it's a small object in a large room. With this assumption, to find the color of a point on the surface, take the ray from the eye to the surface, and reflect the ray off the surface. The direction of the reflected ray completely determines the color to be painted there. Encoding a color for each direction on a flat texture map is equivalent to putting a polished perfect sphere in the middle of the environment and taking a picture of it with a camera that has a lens with a very long focal length placed far away. Mathematically, the lens has an infinite focal length and the camera is infinitely far away. The encoding therefore covers a circular region of the texture map, tangent to the top, bottom, left, and right edges of the map. The texture values outside the circle make no difference, because they are never accessed in environment mapping.

To make a perfectly correct environment texture map, you need to obtain a large silvered sphere, take a photograph of it in some environment with a camera located an infinite distance away and with a lens that has an infinite focal length, and scan in the photograph. To approximate this result, you can use a scanned-in photograph of an environment taken with an extremely wide-angle (or fish-eye) lens. Plate 21 shows a photograph taken with such a lens and the results when that image is used as an environment map.

Once you've created a texture designed for environment mapping, you need to invoke OpenGL's environment-mapping algorithm. This algorithm finds the point on the surface of the sphere with the same tangent surface as that of the point on the object being rendered, and it paints the object's point with the color visible on the sphere at the corresponding point.

To generate automatically the texture coordinates to support environment mapping, use this code in your program:

```
glTexGeni(GL_S, GL_TEXTURE_GEN_MODE, GL_SPHERE_MAP);
glTexGeni(GL_T, GL_TEXTURE_GEN_MODE, GL_SPHERE_MAP);
glEnable(GL_TEXTURE_GEN_S);
glEnable(GL_TEXTURE_GEN_T);
```

The GL_SPHERE_MAP constant creates the proper texture coordinates for the environment mapping. As shown, you need to specify it for both the s- and t-directions. However, you don't have to specify any parameters for the texture-coordinate generation function.

The GL_SPHERE_MAP texture function generates texture coordinates using the following mathematical steps:

1. **u** is the unit vector pointing from the origin to the vertex (in eye coordinates).

2. **n'** is the current normal vector, after transformation to eye coordinates.

3. **r** is the reflection vector, $(r_x \ r_y \ r_z)^T$, which is calculated by $\mathbf{u} - 2\mathbf{n'}\mathbf{n'}^T\mathbf{u}$.

4. An interim value, m, is calculated by

$$m = 2\sqrt{r_x^2 + r_y^2 + (r_z + 1)^2}$$

5. Finally, the s and t texture coordinates are calculated by

$$s = r_x/m + \frac{1}{2}$$

and

$$t = r_y/m + \frac{1}{2}$$

Cube Map Textures

Advanced

Advanced

Cube map textures are a special technique that uses a set of six two-dimensional texture images to form a texture cube centered at the origin. For each fragment, the texture coordinates (s, t, r) are treated as a direction vector, with each texel representing what on the texture cube is "seen" from the origin. Cube maps are ideal for environment, reflection, and lighting effects. Cube maps can also wrap a spherical object with textures, distributing texels relatively evenly on all its sides.

The cube map textures are supplied by calling **glTexImage2D()** six times, with the *target* argument indicating the face of the cube (+X, −X, +Y, −Y, +Z, or −Z). As the name implies, each cube map texture must have the same dimensions so that a cube is formed with the same number of texels on each side, as shown in this code, where *imageSize* has been set to a power of 2:

```
glTexImage2D(GL_TEXTURE_CUBE_MAP_POSITIVE_X, 0, GL_RGBA,
  imageSize, imageSize, 0, GL_RGBA, GL_UNSIGNED_BYTE, image1);
glTexImage2D(GL_TEXTURE_CUBE_MAP_NEGATIVE_X, 0, GL_RGBA,
  imageSize, imageSize, 0, GL_RGBA, GL_UNSIGNED_BYTE, image4);
glTexImage2D(GL_TEXTURE_CUBE_MAP_POSITIVE_Y, 0, GL_RGBA,
  imageSize, imageSize, 0, GL_RGBA, GL_UNSIGNED_BYTE, image2);
glTexImage2D(GL_TEXTURE_CUBE_MAP_NEGATIVE_Y, 0, GL_RGBA,
  imageSize, imageSize, 0, GL_RGBA, GL_UNSIGNED_BYTE, image5);
glTexImage2D(GL_TEXTURE_CUBE_MAP_POSITIVE_Z, 0, GL_RGBA,
  imageSize, imageSize, 0, GL_RGBA, GL_UNSIGNED_BYTE, image3);
glTexImage2D(GL_TEXTURE_CUBE_MAP_NEGATIVE_Z, 0, GL_RGBA,
  imageSize, imageSize, 0, GL_RGBA, GL_UNSIGNED_BYTE, image6);
```

Useful cube map texture images may be generated by setting up a (real or synthetic) camera at the origin of a scene and taking six "snapshots" with 90-degree field-of-view, oriented along the positive and negative axes. The "snapshots" break up the entire 3D space into six frustums, which intersect at the origin.

Cube map functionality is orthogonal to many other texturing operations, so cube maps work with standard texturing features, such as texture borders, mipmaps, copying images, subimages, and multitexturing. There is a special proxy texture target for cube maps (GL_PROXY_TEXTURE_CUBE_MAP) because a cube map generally uses six times as much memory as an ordinary 2D texture. Texture parameters and texture objects should be established for the entire cube map as a whole, not for the six individual cube faces. The following code is an example of setting wrapping and filtering methods with the *target* GL_TEXTURE_CUBE_MAP:

```
glTexParameteri(GL_TEXTURE_CUBE_MAP, GL_TEXTURE_WRAP_S,
                GL_REPEAT);
glTexParameteri(GL_TEXTURE_CUBE_MAP, GL_TEXTURE_WRAP_T,
                GL_REPEAT);
glTexParameteri(GL_TEXTURE_CUBE_MAP, GL_TEXTURE_WRAP_R,
                GL_REPEAT);
glTexParameteri(GL_TEXTURE_CUBE_MAP, GL_TEXTURE_MAG_FILTER,
                GL_NEAREST);
glTexParameteri(GL_TEXTURE_CUBE_MAP, GL_TEXTURE_MIN_FILTER,
                GL_NEAREST);
```

To determine which texture (and texels) to use for a given fragment, the current texture coordinates (s, t, r) first select one of the six textures, based upon which of s, t, and r has the largest absolute value (major axis) and its sign (orientation). The remaining two coordinates are divided by the coordinate with the largest value to determine a new (s', t'), which is used to look up the corresponding texel(s) in the selected texture of the cube map.

Although you can calculate and specify the texture coordinates explicitly, this is generally laborious and unnecessary. Almost always, you'll want to use **glTexGen*()** to automatically generate cube map texture coordinates, using one of the two special texture coordinate generation modes: GL_REFLECTION_MAP or GL_NORMAL_MAP.

GL_REFLECTION_MAP uses the same calculations (until step 3 of the sphere-mapping coordinate computation described in "Sphere Map" on page 463) as the GL_SPHERE_MAP texture coordinate generation to determine $(r_x\ r_y\ r_z)$ for use as (s, t, r). The reflection map mode is well-suited for environment mapping as an alternative to sphere mapping.

GL_NORMAL_MAP is particularly useful for rendering scenes with infinite (or distant local) light sources and diffuse reflection. GL_NORMAL_MAP uses the model-view matrix to transform the vertex's normal into eye coordinates. The resulting $(n_x\ n_y\ n_z)$ becomes texture coordinates (s, t, r). In Example 9-9, the normal map mode is used for texture generation and cube map texturing is also enabled.

Example 9-9   Generating Cube Map Texture Coordinates: cubemap.c

```
glTexGeni(GL_S, GL_TEXTURE_GEN_MODE, GL_NORMAL_MAP);
glTexGeni(GL_T, GL_TEXTURE_GEN_MODE, GL_NORMAL_MAP);
glTexGeni(GL_R, GL_TEXTURE_GEN_MODE, GL_NORMAL_MAP);
```

```
glEnable(GL_TEXTURE_GEN_S);
glEnable(GL_TEXTURE_GEN_T);
glEnable(GL_TEXTURE_GEN_R);
/*  turn on cube map texturing  */
glEnable(GL_TEXTURE_CUBE_MAP);
```

Multitexturing

During standard texturing, a single texture image is applied once to a polygon. Multitexturing allows several textures to be applied, one by one in a pipeline of texture operations, to the same polygon. There is a series of *texture units*, where each texture unit performs a single texturing operation and successively passes its result onto the next texture unit, until all defined units are completed. Figure 9-14 shows how a fragment might undergo four texturing operations—one for each of four texture units.

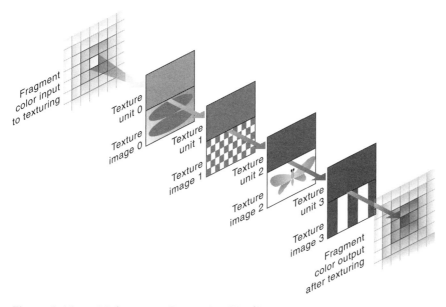

Figure 9-14   Multitexture Processing Pipeline

Multitexturing enables advanced rendering techniques, such as lighting effects, decals, compositing, and detail textures.

Steps in Multitexturing

To write code that uses multitexturing, perform the following steps:

Note: In feedback mode, multitexturing is undefined beyond the first texture unit.

1. For each texturing unit, establish the texturing state, including texture image, filter, environment, coordinate generation, and matrix. Use **glActiveTexture()** to change the current texture unit. This is discussed further in the next subsection, "Establishing Texture Units." You may also call **glGetIntegerv(GL_MAX_TEXTURE_UNITS,...)** to see how many texturing units are available on your implementation. In a worst-case scenario, there are at least two texture units.

2. During vertex specification, use **glMultiTexCoord*()** to specify more than one texture coordinate per vertex. A different texture coordinate may be used for each texturing unit. Each texture coordinate will be used during a different texturing pass. Automatic texture-coordinate generation and specification of texture coordinates in vertex arrays are special cases of this situation. The special cases are described in "Other Methods of Texture-Coordinate Specification" on page 471.

Establishing Texture Units

Multitexturing introduces multiple texture units, which are additional texture application passes. Each texture unit has identical capabilities and houses its own texturing state, including the following:

- Texture image
- Filtering parameters
- Environment application
- Texture matrix stack
- Automatic texture-coordinate generation
- Vertex-array specification (if needed)

Each texture unit combines the previous fragment color with its texture image, according to its texture state. The resulting fragment color is passed onto the next texture unit, if it is active.

To assign texture information to each texture unit, the routine **glActiveTexture()** selects the current texture unit to be modified. After that, calls to **glTexImage*()**, **glTexParameter*()**, **glTexEnv*()**, **glTexGen*()**, and **glBindTexture**() affect only the current texture unit. Queries of these texture states also apply to the current texture unit, as well as queries of the current texture coordinates and current raster texture coordinates.

---

void **glActiveTexture**(GLenum *texUnit*);

Selects the texture unit that is currently modified by texturing routines. *texUnit* is a symbolic constant of the form GL_TEXTURE*i*, where *i* is in the range from 0 to *k* – 1, and *k* is the maximum number of texture units.

If you use texture objects, you can bind a texture to the current texture unit. The current texture unit has the values of the texture state contained within the texture object (including the texture image).

The following code fragment, Example 9-10, has two distinct parts. In the first part, two ordinary texture objects are created (assume the arrays *texels0* and *texels1* define texture images). In the second part, the two texture objects are used to set up two texture units.

Example 9-10   Initializing Texture Units for Multitexturing: multitex.c

```
/*  Two ordinary texture objects are created  */
GLuint texNames[2];
glGenTextures(2, texNames);
glBindTexture(GL_TEXTURE_2D, texNames[0]);
glTexImage2D(GL_TEXTURE_2D, 0, GL_RGBA, 32, 32, 0, GL_RGBA,
             GL_UNSIGNED_BYTE, texels0);
glTexParameteri(GL_TEXTURE_2D,GL_TEXTURE_MIN_FILTER,GL_NEAREST);
glTexParameteri(GL_TEXTURE_2D,GL_TEXTURE_MAG_FILTER,GL_NEAREST);
glTexParameteri(GL_TEXTURE_2D, GL_TEXTURE_WRAP_S, GL_REPEAT);
glTexParameteri(GL_TEXTURE_2D, GL_TEXTURE_WRAP_T, GL_REPEAT);
glBindTexture(GL_TEXTURE_2D, texNames[1]);
glTexImage2D(GL_TEXTURE_2D, 0, GL_RGBA, 16, 16, 0, GL_RGBA,
             GL_UNSIGNED_BYTE, texels1);
glTexParameteri(GL_TEXTURE_2D,GL_TEXTURE_MIN_FILTER,GL_LINEAR);
glTexParameteri(GL_TEXTURE_2D,GL_TEXTURE_MAG_FILTER,GL_LINEAR);
glTexParameteri(GL_TEXTURE_2D, GL_TEXTURE_WRAP_S,
                GL_CLAMP_TO_EDGE);
glTexParameteri(GL_TEXTURE_2D, GL_TEXTURE_WRAP_T,
                GL_CLAMP_TO_EDGE);
/*  Use the two texture objects to define two texture units
 *  for use in multitexturing.  */
glActiveTexture(GL_TEXTURE0);
glEnable(GL_TEXTURE_2D);
```

```
glBindTexture(GL_TEXTURE_2D, texNames[0]);
glTexEnvi(GL_TEXTURE_ENV, GL_TEXTURE_ENV_MODE, GL_REPLACE);
glMatrixMode(GL_TEXTURE);
    glLoadIdentity();
    glTranslatef(0.5f, 0.5f, 0.0f);
    glRotatef(45.0f, 0.0f, 0.0f, 1.0f);
    glTranslatef(-0.5f, -0.5f, 0.0f);
glMatrixMode(GL_MODELVIEW);
glActiveTexture(GL_TEXTURE1);
glEnable(GL_TEXTURE_2D);
glBindTexture(GL_TEXTURE_2D, texNames[1]);
glTexEnvi(GL_TEXTURE_ENV, GL_TEXTURE_ENV_MODE, GL_MODULATE);
```

When a textured polygon is now rendered, it is rendered with two texturing units. In the first unit, the *texels0* texture image is applied with nearest texel filtering, repeat wrapping, replacement texture environment, and a texture matrix that rotates the texture image. After the first unit is completed, the newly textured polygon is sent onto the second texture unit (GL_TEXTURE1), where it is processed with the *texels1* texture image with linear filtering, edge clamping, modulation texture environment, and the default identity texture matrix.

Note: Operations to a texture attribute group (using **glPushAttrib()**, **glPushClientAttrib()**, **glPopAttrib()**, or **glPopClientAttrib()**) save or restore the texture state of *all* texture units (except for the texture matrix stack).

Specifying Vertices and Their Texture Coordinates

With multitexturing, it isn't enough to have one set of texture coordinates per vertex. You need to have one set for each texture unit for each vertex. Instead of using **glTexCoord*()**, you must use **glMultiTexCoord*()**, which specifies the texture unit, as well as the texture coordinates.

<table>
<tr>
<td>
Compatibility
Extension

glMultiTexCoord
</td>
<td>
void **glMultiTexCoord{1234}{sifd}**(GLenum *texUnit, TYPE coords*);
void **glMultiTexCoord{1234}{sifd}v**(GLenum *texUnit*, const *TYPE *coords*);

Sets the texture-coordinate data (*s, t, r, q*) in *coords* for use with the texture unit *texUnit*. The enumerated values for *texUnit* are the same as for **glActiveTexture()**.
</td>
</tr>
</table>

In Example 9-11, a triangle is given the two sets of texture coordinates necessary for multitexturing with two active texture units.

Example 9-11 Specifying Vertices for Multitexturing

```
glBegin(GL_TRIANGLES);
glMultiTexCoord2f(GL_TEXTURE0, 0.0, 0.0);
glMultiTexCoord2f(GL_TEXTURE1, 1.0, 0.0);
glVertex2f(0.0, 0.0);
glMultiTexCoord2f(GL_TEXTURE0, 0.5, 1.0);
glMultiTexCoord2f(GL_TEXTURE1, 0.5, 0.0);
glVertex2f(50.0, 100.0);
glMultiTexCoord2f(GL_TEXTURE0, 1.0, 0.0);
glMultiTexCoord2f(GL_TEXTURE1, 1.0, 1.0);
glVertex2f(100.0, 0.0);
glEnd();
```

Note: If you are multitexturing and you use **glTexCoord*()**, you are setting the texture coordinates for the first texture unit. In other words, using **glTexCoord*()** is equivalent to using **glMultiTexCoord* (GL_TEXTURE0,...)**.

In the rare case that you are multitexturing a bitmap or image rectangle, you need to associate several texture coordinates with each raster position. Therefore, you must call **glMultiTexCoord*()** several times, once for each active texture unit, for each **glRasterPos*()** or **glWindowPos*()** call. (Since there is only one current raster position for the entire bitmap or image rectangle, there is only one corresponding texture coordinate per unit, so the aesthetic possibilities are extremely limited.)

Other Methods of Texture-Coordinate Specification

Explicitly calling **glMultiTexCoord*()** is only one of three ways to specify texture coordinates when multitexturing. The other two ways are to use automatic texture-coordinate generation (with **glTexGen*()**) or vertex arrays (with **glTexCoordPointer()**).

If you are multitexturing and using automatic texture-coordinate generation, then **glActiveTexture()** directs which texture unit is affected by the following automatic texture-coordinate generation routines:

- **glTexGen*(...)**
- **glEnable(GL_TEXTURE_GEN_*)**
- **glDisable(GL_TEXTURE_GEN_*)**

If you are multitexturing and specifying texture coordinates in vertex arrays, then **glClientActiveTexture()** directs the texture unit for which **glTexCoordPointer()** specifies its texture-coordinate data.

void **glClientActiveTexture**(GLenum *texUnit*);

Selects the current texture unit for specifying texture-coordinate data with vertex arrays. *texUnit* is a symbolic constant of the form GL_TEXTURE*i*, with the same values that are used for **glActiveTexture**().

Reverting to a Single Texture Unit

If you are using multitexturing and want to return to a single texture unit, then you need to disable texturing for all units, except for texture unit 0, with code as shown in Example 9-12.

Example 9-12 Reverting to Texture Unit 0

```
/*  disable texturing for other texture units  */
glActiveTexture (GL_TEXTURE1);
glDisable (GL_TEXTURE_2D);
glActiveTexture (GL_TEXTURE2);
glDisable (GL_TEXTURE_2D);
/*  make texture unit 0 current  */
glActiveTexture (GL_TEXTURE0);
```

Texture Combiner Functions

Advanced

Advanced

OpenGL has evolved from its early focus on vertex processing (transformation, clipping) toward more concern with rasterization and fragment operations. Texturing functionality is increasingly exposed to the programmer to improve fragment processing.

In addition to multipass texture techniques, flexible texture combiner functions provide the programmer with finer control over mixing fragments with texture or other color values. Texture combiner functions support high-quality texture effects, such as bump mapping, more realistic specular lighting, and texture fade effects (such as interpolating between two textures). A combiner function takes color and alpha data from up to three sources and processes them, generating RGBA values as output for subsequent operations.

glTexEnv*() is used extensively to configure combiner functions. In "Texture Functions," you encountered an abbreviated description of **glTexEnv***(), and now here's the complete description:

void **glTexEnv**{if}(GLenum *target*, GLenum *pname*, *TYPE param*);
void **glTexEnv**{if}**v**(GLenum *target*, GLenum *pname*, const *TYPE *param*);

Compatibility
Extension

glTexEnv and all
accepted tokens

Sets the current texturing function. *target* must be either GL_TEXTURE_
FILTER_CONTROL or GL_TEXTURE_ENV.

If *target* is GL_TEXTURE_FILTER_CONTROL, then *pname* must be
GL_TEXTURE_LOD_BIAS, and *param* is a single, floating-point value
used to bias the mipmapping level-of-detail parameter.

If *target* is GL_TEXTURE_ENV, acceptable values for the second and
third arguments (*pname* and *param)* are listed in Table 9-8. If *pname* is
GL_TEXTURE_ENV_MODE, *param* specifies how texture values are combined with the color values of the fragment being processed. Several environment modes (GL_BLEND, GL_COMBINE, GL_COMBINE_RGB, and
GL_COMBINE_ALPHA) determine whether other environment modes are
useful.

If the texture environment mode is GL_BLEND, then the GL_TEXTURE_
ENV_COLOR setting is used.

If the texture environment mode is GL_COMBINE, then the GL_COMBINE_
RGB, GL_COMBINE_ALPHA, GL_RGB_SCALE, or GL_ALPHA_SCALE
parameters are also used. For the GL_COMBINE_RGB function, the
GL_SOURCE*i*_RGB and GL_OPERAND*i*_RGB parameters (where *i* is 0, 1,
or 2) also may be specified. Similarly for the GL_COMBINE_ALPHA
function, GL_SOURCE*i*_ALPHA and GL_OPERAND*i*_ALPHA may be
specified.

glTexEnv pname	glTexEnv param
GL_TEXTURE_ENV_MODE	GL_DECAL, GL_REPLACE, GL_MODULATE, GL_BLEND, GL_ADD, or GL_COMBINE
GL_TEXTURE_ENV_COLOR	array of 4 floating-point numbers: (R, G, B, A)
GL_COMBINE_RGB	GL_REPLACE, GL_MODULATE, GL_ADD, GL_ADD_SIGNED, GL_INTERPOLATE, GL_SUBTRACT, GL_DOT3_RGB, or GL_DOT3_RGBA
GL_COMBINE_ALPHA	GL_REPLACE, GL_MODULATE, GL_ADD, GL_ADD_SIGNED, GL_INTERPOLATE, or GL_SUBTRACT

Table 9-8 Texture Environment Parameters If *target* Is GL_TEXTURE_ENV

glTexEnv pname	glTexEnv param
GL_SRC*i*_RGB or GL_SRC*i*_ALPHA (where *i* is 0, 1, or 2)	GL_TEXTURE, GL_TEXTURE*n* (where *n* denotes the *n*th texture unit and multitexturing is enabled), GL_CONSTANT, GL_PRIMARY_COLOR, or GL_PREVIOUS
GL_OPERAND*i*_RGB (where *i* is 0, 1, or 2)	GL_SRC_COLOR, GL_ONE_MINUS_SRC_COLOR, GL_SRC_ALPHA, or GL_ONE_MINUS_SRC_ALPHA
GL_OPERAND*i*_ALPHA (where *i* is 0, 1, or 2)	GL_SRC_ALPHA, or GL_ONE_MINUS_SRC_ALPHA
GL_RGB_SCALE	floating-point color scaling factor
GL_ALPHA_SCALE	floating-point alpha scaling factor

Table 9-8 (continued) Texture Environment Parameters If *target* Is GL_TEXTURE_

Here are the steps for using combiner functions. If you are multitexturing, you may use a different combiner function for every texture unit and thus repeat these steps for each unit.

- To use any combiner function, you must call

```
glTexEnvf(GL_TEXTURE_ENV, GL_TEXTURE_ENV_MODE, GL_COMBINE);
```

- You should specify how you want RGB or alpha values to be combined (see Table 9-9). For instance, Example 9-13 directs the current texture unit to subtract RGB and alpha values of one source from another source.

Example 9-13 Setting the Programmable Combiner Functions

```
glTexEnvf(GL_TEXTURE_ENV, GL_COMBINE_RGB, GL_SUBTRACT);
glTexEnvf(GL_TEXTURE_ENV, GL_COMBINE_ALPHA, GL_SUBTRACT);
```

glTexEnv param	Combiner Function
GL_REPLACE	*Arg0*
GL_MODULATE (default)	*Arg0 * Arg1*
GL_ADD	*Arg0 + Arg1*
GL_ADD_SIGNED	*Arg0 + Arg1 – 0.5*
GL_INTERPOLATE	*Arg0 * Arg2 + Arg1 * (1 – Arg2)*

Table 9-9 GL_COMBINE_RGB and GL_COMBINE_ALPHA Functions

glTexEnv param	Combiner Function
GL_SUBTRACT	$Arg0 - Arg1$
GL_DOT3_RGB GL_DOT3_RGBA	$4 * ((Arg0_r - 0.5) * (Arg1_r - 0.5) +$ $(Arg0_g - 0.5) * (Arg1_g - 0.5) +$ $(Arg0_b - 0.5) * (Arg1_b - 0.5))$

Table 9-9 (continued)   GL_COMBINE_RGB and GL_COMBINE_ALPHA Functions

Note: GL_DOT3_RGB and GL_DOT3_RGBA are used only for
GL_COMBINE_RGB and not used for GL_COMBINE_ALPHA.

The GL_DOT3_RGB and GL_DOT3_RGBA modes differ subtly. With
GL_DOT3_RGB, the same dot product is placed into all three (R, G, B)
values. For GL_DOT3_RGBA, the result is placed into all four (R, G, B, A).

- Specify the source for the *i*th argument of the combiner function with
  the constant GL_SOURCE*i*_RGB. The number of arguments (up to three)
  depends upon the type of function chosen. As shown in Table 9-9,
  GL_SUBTRACT requires two arguments, which may be set with the
  following code:

Example 9-14   Setting the Combiner Function Sources

```
glTexEnvf(GL_TEXTURE_ENV, GL_SRC0_RGB, GL_TEXTURE);
glTexEnvf(GL_TEXTURE_ENV, GL_SRC1_RGB, GL_PREVIOUS);
```

When *pname* is GL_SOURCE*i*_RGB, these are your options for *param* along
with how the source is determined:

- GL_TEXTURE—the source for the *i*th argument is the texture of the
  current texture unit

- GL_TEXTURE*n*—the texture associated with texture unit *n*. (If you
  use this source, texture unit *n* must be enabled and valid, or the
  result will be undefined.)

- GL_CONSTANT—the constant color set with GL_TEXTURE_
  ENV_COLOR

- GL_PRIMARY_COLOR—the incoming fragment to texture unit 0,
  which is the fragment color, prior to texturing

- GL_PREVIOUS—the incoming fragment from the previous texture
  unit (for texture unit 0, this is the same as GL_PRIMARY_COLOR)

If you suppose that the GL_SUBTRACT combiner code in Example 9-14 is set for texture unit 2, then the output from texture unit 1 (GL_PREVIOUS, *Arg1*) is subtracted from texture unit 2 (GL_TEXTURE, *Arg0*).

- Specify which values (RGB or alpha) of the sources are used and how they are used:

  - GL_OPERAND*i*_RGB matches the corresponding GL_SOURCE*i*_RGB and determines the color values for the current GL_COMBINE_ RGB function. If GL_OPERAND*i*_RGB is *pname*, then *param* must be one of GL_SRC_COLOR, GL_ONE_MINUS_SRC_COLOR, GL_SRC_ALPHA, or GL_ONE_MINUS_SRC_ALPHA.

  - Similarly, GL_OPERAND*i*_ALPHA matches the corresponding GL_SOURCE*i*_ALPHA and determines the alpha values for the current GL_COMBINE_ALPHA function. However, *param* is limited to either GL_SRC_ALPHA or GL_ONE_MINUS_SRC_ALPHA.

When GL_SRC_ALPHA is used for the GL_COMBINE_RGB function, the alpha values for the combiner source are interpreted as R, G, B values. In Example 9-15, the three R, G, B components for *Arg2* are (0.4, 0.4, 0.4).

Example 9-15   Using an Alpha Value for RGB Combiner Operations

```
static GLfloat constColor[4] = {0.1, 0.2, 0.3, 0.4};
glTexEnvfv(GL_TEXTURE_ENV, GL_TEXTURE_ENV_COLOR, constColor);
glTexEnvf(GL_TEXTURE_ENV, GL_SRC2_RGB, GL_CONSTANT);
glTexEnvf(GL_TEXTURE_ENV, GL_OPERAND2_RGB, GL_SRC_ALPHA);
```

In Example 9-15, if the operand had instead been GL_SRC_COLOR, the RGB components would be (0.1, 0.2, 0.3). For GL_ONE_MINUS* modes, a value's complement (either 1–color or 1–alpha) is used for combiner calculations. In Example 9-15, if the operand is GL_ONE_MINUS_SRC_ COLOR, the RGB components are (0.9, 0.8, 0.7). For GL_ONE_MINUS_ SRC_ALPHA, the result is (0.6, 0.6, 0.6).

- Optionally choose RGB or alpha scaling factors. The defaults are

```
glTexEnvf(GL_TEXTURE_ENV, GL_RGB_SCALE, 1.0);
glTexEnvf(GL_TEXTURE_ENV, GL_ALPHA_SCALE, 1.0);
```

- Finally draw the geometry, ensuring vertices have associated texture coordinates.

The Interpolation Combiner Function

The interpolation function helps illustrate texture combiners, because it uses the maximum number of arguments and several source and operand modes. Example 9-16 is a portion of the sample program combiner.c.

Example 9-16 Interpolation Combiner Function: combiner.c

```
/* for use as constant texture color */
static GLfloat constColor[4] = {0.0, 0.0, 0.0, 0.0};

constColor[3] = 0.2;
glTexEnvfv(GL_TEXTURE_ENV, GL_TEXTURE_ENV_COLOR, constColor);
glBindTexture(GL_TEXTURE_2D, texName[0]);
glTexEnvf(GL_TEXTURE_ENV, GL_TEXTURE_ENV_MODE, GL_COMBINE);
glTexEnvf(GL_TEXTURE_ENV, GL_COMBINE_RGB, GL_INTERPOLATE);
glTexEnvf(GL_TEXTURE_ENV, GL_SRC0_RGB, GL_TEXTURE);
glTexEnvf(GL_TEXTURE_ENV, GL_OPERAND0_RGB, GL_SRC_COLOR);
glTexEnvf(GL_TEXTURE_ENV, GL_SRC1_RGB, GL_PREVIOUS);
glTexEnvf(GL_TEXTURE_ENV, GL_OPERAND1_RGB, GL_SRC_COLOR);
glTexEnvf(GL_TEXTURE_ENV, GL_SRC2_RGB, GL_CONSTANT);
glTexEnvf(GL_TEXTURE_ENV, GL_OPERAND2_RGB, GL_SRC_ALPHA);

/* geometry is now rendered */
```

In Example 9-16, there is only one active texture unit. Since GL_INTERPOLATE is the combiner function, there are three arguments, and they are combined with the following formula: *(Arg0 * Arg2) + (Arg1 * (1 – Arg2))*. The three arguments are as follows:

- *Arg0*, GL_TEXTURE, the texture image associated with the currently bound texture object (*texName[0]*)

- *Arg1*, GL_PREVIOUS, the result of the previous texture unit, but since this is texture unit 0, GL_PREVIOUS is the fragment prior to texturing

- *Arg2*, GL_CONSTANT, a constant color; currently (0.0, 0.0, 0.0, 0.2)

The interpolated result you get is a weighted blending of the texture image and the untextured fragment. Because GL_SRC_ALPHA is specified for GL_OPERAND2_RGB, the alpha value of the constant color (*Arg2*) serves as the weighting.

If you run the sample program combiner.c, you'll see 20 percent of the texture blended with 80 percent of a smooth-shaded polygon. combiner.c also varies the alpha value of the constant color, so you'll see the results of different weightings.

Examining the interpolation function explains why several of the OpenGL default values were chosen. The third argument for interpolation is intended as weight for the two other sources. Since interpolation is the only combiner function to use three arguments, it's safe to make GL_CONSTANT the default for *Arg2*. At first glance, it may seem odd that the default value for GL_OPERAND2_RGB is GL_SRC_ALPHA. But the interpolation weight is usually the same for all three color components, so using a single value makes sense, and taking it from the alpha value of the constant is convenient.

glTexEnv pname	Initial Value for param
GL_SRC0_RGB	GL_TEXTURE
GL_SRC1_RGB	GL_PREVIOUS
GL_SRC2_RGB	GL_CONSTANT
GL_OPERAND0_RGB	GL_SRC_COLOR
GL_OPERAND1_RGB	GL_SRC_COLOR
GL_OPERAND2_RGB	GL_SRC_ALPHA

Table 9-10   Default Values for Some Texture Environment Modes

Applying Secondary Color after Texturing

While applying a texture to a typical fragment, only a primary color is combined with the texel colors. The primary color may be the result of lighting calculations or **glColor*()**.

After texturing, but before fog calculations, sometimes a secondary color is also applied to a fragment. Application of a secondary color may result in a more realistic highlight on a textured object.

Secondary Color When Lighting Is Disabled

If lighting is not enabled and the color sum mode is enabled (by **glEnable(GL_COLOR_SUM)**), then the current secondary color (set by **glSecondaryColor*()**) is added to the post-texturing fragment color.

void **glSecondaryColor3**{b s i f d ub us ui}(*TYPE r, TYPE g, TYPE b*);
void **glSecondaryColor3**{b s i f d ub us ui}**v**(const *TYPE *values*);

Sets the red, green, and blue values for the current secondary color. The first suffix indicates the data type for parameters: byte, short, integer, float, double, unsigned byte, unsigned short, or unsigned integer. If there is a second suffix, **v**, then *values* is a pointer to an array of values of the given data type.

glSecondaryColor*() accepts the same data types and interprets values the same way that **glColor*()** does. (See Table 4-1 on page 198.) Secondary colors may also be specified in vertex arrays.

Secondary Specular Color When Lighting Is Enabled

Texturing operations are applied after lighting, but blending specular highlights with a texture's colors usually lessens the effect of lighting. As discussed earlier (in "Selecting a Lighting Model" on page 227), you can calculate two colors per vertex: a primary color, which consists of all nonspecular contributions, and a secondary color, which is a sum of all specular contributions. If specular color is separated, the secondary (specular) color is added to the fragment after the texturing calculation.

Note: If lighting is enabled, the secondary specular color is applied, regardless of the GL_COLOR_SUM mode, and any secondary color set by **glSecondaryColor*()** is ignored.

Point Sprites

While OpenGL supports antialiasing of points with a point size greater than one (as set with **glPointSize()**), the visual results may not be precisely what your application requires. Point *sprites* allow better control over the shading of large points. By default, when point sprites are enabled, every fragment in the sprite is assigned the same state as the vertex that initiated the point's rendering. Point sprites modify how fragment data is generated by iterating texture coordinates across the fragments of the expanded point.

To enable point sprites, call **glEnable()** with a parameter of GL_POINT_SPRITE. This will cause OpenGL to ignore the current settings for point antialiasing. Each fragment in the point will be assigned the associated vertex data, and those values will be used in shading.

Note: OpenGL Version 3.1 renders all points as if point sprites were enabled. **glTexEnv()** and all of the parameters associated with point sprites have been removed.

To enable the iteration of texture coordinates across the point sprite, you need to call **glTexEnv***(GL_POINT_SPRITE, GL_COORD_REPLACE, GL_TRUE). This needs to be done for each texture unit with a texture map that you want applied to the sprite. Figure 9-15 illustrates the differences between antialiased points and texture-mapped point sprites. On the left is an image of a 10-pixel antialiased point. The right image is a 10-pixel texture-mapped point sprite.

Figure 9-15   Comparison of Antialiased Points and Textured Point Sprites

The texture coordinates for point sprites are automatically assigned by OpenGL during rasterization. Figure 9-16 illustrates how texture coordinates are assigned to the point sprite. The s texture coordinate increases from zero to one from left to right across the fragments of the sprite. However, for t texture coordinates, values are controlled by where the sprite's texture-coordinate origin is specified. Control of the origin is specified by calling **glPointParameter()** with GL_POINT_SPRITE_COORD_ORIGIN and setting the value to either GL_LOWER_LEFT or GL_UPPER_LEFT.

When the sprite origin is specified to be the GL_LOWER_LEFT, the t-coordinate increases from zero to one going from bottom to top of the sprite. Conversely, when the value is specified to be GL_UPPER_LEFT, the t-coordinate increases from zero to one going from top to bottom.

Example 9-17 demonstrates a 10-pixel-wide point sprite with an applied texture map.

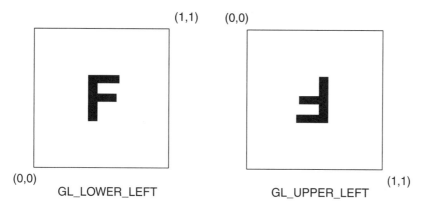

(1,1)   (0,0)

(0,0)
GL_LOWER_LEFT

(1,1)
GL_UPPER_LEFT

Figure 9-16   Assignment of Texture Coordinates Based on the Setting of
GL_POINT_SPRITE_COORD_ORIGIN

Example 9-17   Configuring a Point Sprite for Texture Mapping: sprite.c

```
glPointSize(10.0);
glTexEnvi(GL_POINT_SPRITE, GL_COORD_REPLACE, GL_TRUE);
glPointParameteri(GL_POINT_SPRITE_COORD_ORIGIN, GL_LOWER_LEFT);
glEnable(GL_POINT_SPRITE);
```

The Texture Matrix Stack

Advanced

Advanced

Just as your model coordinates are transformed by a matrix before being
rendered, texture coordinates are multiplied by a 4 × 4 matrix before any
texture mapping occurs. By default, the texture matrix is the identity, so the
texture coordinates you explicitly assign or those that are automatically
generated remain unchanged. By modifying the texture matrix while
redrawing an object, however, you can make the texture slide over the
surface, rotate around it, stretch and shrink, or any combination of the
three. In fact, since the texture matrix is a completely general 4 × 4 matrix,
effects such as perspective can be achieved.

The texture matrix is actually the top matrix on a stack, which must have a
stack depth of at least two matrices. All the standard matrix-manipulation

commands such as **glPushMatrix()**, **glPopMatrix()**, **glMultMatrix()**, and **glRotate*()** can be applied to the texture matrix. To modify the current texture matrix, you need to set the matrix mode to GL_TEXTURE, as follows:

```
glMatrixMode(GL_TEXTURE); /* enter texture matrix mode */
glRotated(...);
/* ... other matrix manipulations ... */
glMatrixMode(GL_MODELVIEW); /* back to modelview mode */
```

The q-Coordinate

The mathematics of the fourth texture coordinate, q, are similar to the w-coordinate of the (x, y, z, w) object coordinates. When the four texture coordinates (s, t, r, q) are multiplied by the texture matrix, the resulting vector (s', t', r', q') is interpreted as homogeneous texture coordinates. In other words, the texture map is indexed by s'/q', t'/q', and r'/q'.

You can make use of q in cases where more than one projection or perspective transformation is needed. For example, suppose you want to model a spotlight that has some nonuniform pattern—brighter in the center, perhaps, or noncircular, because of flaps or lenses that modify the shape of the beam. You can emulate shining such a light onto a flat surface by making a texture map that corresponds to the shape and intensity of a light, and then projecting it onto the surface in question using projection transformations. Projecting the cone of light onto surfaces in the scene requires a perspective transformation ($q \neq 1$), since the lights might shine on surfaces that aren't perpendicular to them. A second perspective transformation occurs because the viewer sees the scene from a different (but perspective) point of view. (See Plate 28 for an example; and see "Fast Shadows and Lighting Effects Using Texture Mapping" by Mark Segal, Carl Korobkin, Rolf van Widenfelt, Jim Foran, and Paul Haeberli, SIGGRAPH 1992 Proceedings [*Computer Graphics*, 26:2, July 1992, pp. 249–252] for more details.)

Another example might arise if the texture map to be applied comes from a photograph that itself was taken in perspective. As with spotlights, the final view depends on the combination of two perspective transformations.

Nate Robins' Texture Tutorial

In Nate Robins' **texture** tutorial, you can use the popup menu to view the 4×4 texture matrix, make changes in matrix values, and then see their effects.

Depth Textures

After lighting a surface (see Chapter 5), you'll soon notice that OpenGL light sources don't cast shadows. The color at each vertex is calculated without regard to any other objects in the scene. To have shadows, you need to determine and record which surfaces (or portions of the surfaces) are occluded from a direct path to a light source.

A multipass technique using depth textures provides a solution to rendering shadows. If you temporarily move the viewpoint to the light source position, you notice that everything you see is lit—there are no shadows from that perspective. A depth texture provides the mechanism to save the depth values for all "unshadowed" fragments in a *shadow map*. As you render your scene, if you compare each incoming fragment to the corresponding depth value in the shadow map, you can choose what to render, depending upon whether it is or isn't shadowed. The idea is similar to the depth test, except that it's done from the point of view of the light source.

The condensed description is as follows:

1. Render the scene from the point of view of the light source. It doesn't matter how the scene looks; you only want the depth values. Create a shadow map by capturing the depth buffer values and storing them in a texture map (shadow map).

2. Generate texture coordinates with (s, t) coordinates referencing locations within the shadow map, with the third texture coordinate (r), as the distance from the light source. Then draw the scene a second time, comparing the r value with the corresponding depth texture value to determine whether the fragment is lit or in shadow.

The following sections provide a more detailed discussion, along with sample code illustrating each of the steps.

Creating a Shadow Map

The first step is to create a texture map of depth values. You create this by rendering the scene with the viewpoint positioned at the light source's position. Example 9-18 calls **glGetLightfv()** to obtain the current light source position, calculates an up-vector, and then uses it as the viewing transformation.

Example 9-18 begins by setting the viewport size to match that of the texture map. It then sets up the appropriate projection and viewing matrices. The objects for the scene are rendered, and the resulting depth image is copied into texture memory for use as a shadow map. Finally, the viewport is reset to it's original size and position.

Note a few more points:

- The projection matrix controls the shape of the light's "lampshade." The variables *lightFovy* and *lightAspect* in the **gluPerspective()** control the size of the lampshade. A small *lightFovy* value will be more like a spotlight, and a larger value will be more like a floodlight.

- The near and far clipping planes for the light (*lightNearPlane* and *lightFarPlane*) are used to control the precision of the depth values. Try to keep the separation between the near and far planes as small as possible to maximize the precision of the values.

- After the depth values have been established in the depth buffer, you want to capture them and put them into a GL_DEPTH_COMPONENT format texture map. Example 9-18 uses **glCopyTexImage2D()** to make a texture image from the depth buffer contents. As with any texture, ensure that the image width and height are powers of two.

Example 9-18   Rendering Scene with Viewpoint at Light Source: shadowmap.c

```
GLint     viewport[4];
GLfloat   lightPos[4];

glGetLightfv(GL_LIGHT0, GL_POSITION, lightPos);
glGetIntegerv(GL_VIEWPORT, viewport);

glViewport(0, 0, SHADOW_MAP_WIDTH, SHADOW_MAP_HEIGHT);

glClear(GL_COLOR_BUFFER_BIT | GL_DEPTH_BUFFER_BIT);

glMatrixMode(GL_PROJECTION);
glPushMatrix();
glLoadIdentity();
gluPerspective(lightFovy, lightAspect, lightNearPlane,
               lightFarPlane);
glMatrixMode(GL_MODELVIEW);

glPushMatrix();
glLoadIdentity();
```

```
gluLookAt(lightPos[0], lightPos[1], lightPos[2],
    lookat[0], lookat[1], lookat[2],
    up[0], up[1], up[2]);
drawObjects();
glPopMatrix();

glMatrixMode(GL_PROJECTION);
glPopMatrix();
glMatrixMode(GL_MODELVIEW);

glCopyTexImage2D(GL_TEXTURE_2D, 0, GL_DEPTH_COMPONENT, 0, 0,
    SHADOW_MAP_WIDTH, SHADOW_MAP_HEIGHT, 0);

glViewport(viewport[0], viewport[1],
    viewport[2], viewport[3]);
```

Generating Texture Coordinates and Rendering

Now use **glTexGen*()** to automatically generate texture coordinates that
compute the eye-space distance from the light source position. The value of
the *r* coordinate should correspond to the distance from the primitives to
the light source. You can do this by using the same projection and viewing
transformations that you used to create the shadow map. Example 9-19 uses
the GL_MODELVIEW matrix stack to do all the matrix computations.

Note that the generated (*s, t, r, q*) texture coordinates and the depth values
in the shadow map are not similarly scaled. The texture coordinates are
generated in eye coordinates, so they fall in the range [–1, 1]. The depth
values in the texels are within [0, 1]. Therefore, an initial translation and
scaling maps the texture coordinates into the same range of values as the
shadow map.

Example 9-19 Calculating Texture Coordinates: shadowmap.c

```
GLfloat  tmpMatrix[16];

glMatrixMode(GL_MODELVIEW);
glPushMatrix();
glLoadIdentity();
glTranslatef(0.5, 0.5, 0.0);
glScalef(0.5, 0.5, 1.0);
gluPerspective(lightFovy, lightAspect,
    lightNearPlane, lightFarPlane);
gluLookAt(lightPos[0], lightPos[1], lightPos[2],
    lookat[0], lookat[1], lookat[2],
    up[0], up[1], up[2]);
```

```
glGetFloatv(GL_MODELVIEW_MATRIX, tmpMatrix);
glPopMatrix();

transposeMatrix(tmpMatrix);

glTexGeni(GL_S, GL_TEXTURE_GEN_MODE, GL_OBJECT_LINEAR);
glTexGeni(GL_T, GL_TEXTURE_GEN_MODE, GL_OBJECT_LINEAR);
glTexGeni(GL_R, GL_TEXTURE_GEN_MODE, GL_OBJECT_LINEAR);
glTexGeni(GL_Q, GL_TEXTURE_GEN_MODE, GL_OBJECT_LINEAR);

glTexGenfv(GL_S, GL_OBJECT_PLANE, &tmpMatrix[0]);
glTexGenfv(GL_T, GL_OBJECT_PLANE, &tmpMatrix[4]);
glTexGenfv(GL_R, GL_OBJECT_PLANE, &tmpMatrix[8]);
glTexGenfv(GL_Q, GL_OBJECT_PLANE, &tmpMatrix[12]);

glEnable(GL_TEXTURE_GEN_S);
glEnable(GL_TEXTURE_GEN_T);
glEnable(GL_TEXTURE_GEN_R);
glEnable(GL_TEXTURE_GEN_Q);
```

In Example 9-20, before the scene is rendered for the second and final time, the texture comparison mode GL_COMPARE_R_TO_TEXTURE instructs OpenGL to compare the fragment's r-coordinate with the texel value. If the r distance is less than or equal to (the comparison function GL_LEQUAL) the texel value, there is nothing between this fragment and the light source, and it is effectively treated as having a luminance value of one. If the comparison fails, then there is another primitive between this fragment and the light source, so this fragment is shadowed and has an effective luminance of zero.

Example 9-20   Rendering Scene Comparing r Coordinate: shadowmap.c

```
glTexParameteri(GL_TEXTURE_2D, GL_TEXTURE_WRAP_S,
    GL_CLAMP_TO_EDGE);
glTexParameteri(GL_TEXTURE_2D, GL_TEXTURE_WRAP_T,
    GL_CLAMP_TO_EDGE);
glTexParameteri(GL_TEXTURE_2D, GL_TEXTURE_MIN_FILTER,
    GL_LINEAR);
glTexParameteri(GL_TEXTURE_2D, GL_TEXTURE_MAG_FILTER,
    GL_LINEAR);
glTexParameteri(GL_TEXTURE_2D, GL_TEXTURE_COMPARE_FUNC,
    GL_LEQUAL);
glTexParameteri(GL_TEXTURE_2D, GL_DEPTH_TEXTURE_MODE,
    GL_LUMINANCE);
glTexParameteri( GL_TEXTURE_2D, GL_TEXTURE_COMPARE_MODE,
    GL_COMPARE_R_TO_TEXTURE);
glEnable(GL_TEXTURE_2D);
```

This technique can produce some unintended visual artifacts:

- Self-shadowing, whereby an object incorrectly casts a shadow upon itself, is a common problem.

- Aliasing of the projected texture, particularly in the regions farthest from the light sources, can occur. Using higher resolution shadow maps can help reduce the aliasing.

- GL_MODULATE mode, when used with depth texturing, may cause sharp transitions between shadowed and unshadowed regions.

Unfortunately, there are no steadfast rules for overcoming these issues. Some experimentation may be required to produce the best-looking image.

Chapter 10

The Framebuffer

Chapter Objectives

After reading this chapter, you'll be able to do the following:

- Understand the buffers that make up the framebuffer and how they're used

- Clear selected buffers and enable them for writing

- Control the parameters of the scissor, alpha, stencil, and depth tests that are applied to pixels

- Use occlusion queries to determine if objects will be visible

- Perform dithering and logical operations

- Use the accumulation buffer for such purposes as scene antialiasing

- Create and use framebuffer objects for advanced techniques, and to minimizing copying of data between buffers

Note: In OpenGL Version 3.1, some of the techniques and functions described in this chapter were removed through deprecation. The concepts are still relevant, but are available using more modern features.

An important goal of almost every graphics program is to draw pictures on the screen. The screen is composed of a rectangular array of pixels, each capable of displaying a tiny square of color at that point in the image. After the rasterization stage (including texturing and fog), the data is not yet pixels—just fragments. Each fragment has coordinate data that corresponds to a pixel, as well as color and depth values. Then each fragment undergoes a series of tests and operations, some of which have been previously described (see "Blending" in Chapter 6), and others that are discussed in this chapter.

If the tests and operations are survived, the fragment values are ready to become pixels. To draw these pixels, you need to know what color they are, which is the information that's stored in the color buffer. Whenever data is stored uniformly for each pixel, such storage for all the pixels is called a *buffer*. Different buffers might contain different amounts of data per pixel, but within a given buffer, each pixel is assigned the same amount of data. A buffer that stores a single bit of information about pixels is called a *bitplane*, and the number of bitplanes in a buffer is usually called its "depth" (not to be confused with a pixel's depth value, which is used in depth-buffer testing, as described in "Depth Test" later in this chapter).

As shown in Figure 10-1, the lower left pixel in an OpenGL window is pixel (0, 0), corresponding to the window coordinates of the lower left corner of the 1×1 region occupied by this pixel. In general, pixel (x, y) fills the region bounded by x on the left, $x + 1$ on the right, y on the bottom, and $y + 1$ on the top.

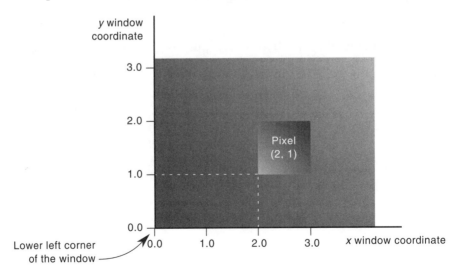

Figure 10-1   Region Occupied by a Pixel

As an example of a buffer, let's look more closely at the color buffer, which holds the color information that's to be displayed on the screen. Assume that the screen is 1280 pixels wide and 1024 pixels high and that it's a full 24-bit color screen—in other words, that there are 2^{24} (or 16,777,216) different colors that can be displayed. Since 24 bits translates to 3 bytes (8 bits per byte), the color buffer in this example has to store at least 3 bytes of data for each of the 1,310,720 (1280*1024) pixels on the screen. A particular hardware system might have more or fewer pixels on the physical screen as well as more or less color data per pixel. Any particular color buffer, however, has the same amount of data saved for each pixel on the screen.

The color buffer is only one of several buffers that hold information about a pixel. For example, in "A Hidden-Surface Removal Survival Kit" on page 205, you learned that the depth buffer holds depth information for each pixel. The color buffer itself can consist of several subbuffers. The *framebuffer* on a system comprises all of these buffers. With the exception of the color buffer(s), you don't view these other buffers directly; instead, you use them to perform such tasks as hidden-surface elimination, antialiasing of an entire scene, stenciling, drawing smooth motion, and other operations.

This chapter describes all the buffers that can exist in an OpenGL implementation and explains how they're used. It also discusses the series of tests and pixel operations that are performed before any data is written to the viewable color buffer. Finally, for completeness, the chapter concludes by explaining how to use the accumulation buffer, which holds images that are drawn into the color buffer. Originally, the accumulation buffer was marginally more capable of storing higher-precision color values. With OpenGL Version 3.0, color buffers that support native floating-point values were introduced, which effectively makes the accumulation buffer obsolete, though not necessarily the techniques that were enabled by it. These can easily be implemented on floating-point buffers.

This chapter has the following major sections.

- "Buffers and Their Uses" describes the possible buffers, what they're for, and how to clear them and enable them for writing.

- "Testing and Operating on Fragments" explains the scissor, alpha, stencil, and depth tests that occur after a pixel's position and color have been calculated but before this information is drawn on the screen. Several operations—blending, dithering, and logical operations—can also be performed before a fragment updates the screen.

- "The Accumulation Buffer" describes how to perform several advanced techniques using the accumulation buffer. These techniques include antialiasing an entire scene, using motion blur, and simulating photographic depth of field.

- "Framebuffer Objects" discusses a new type of object in OpenGL Version 3.0 that enables rendering to occur in buffers other than the color buffer displayed on the screen. They enable *off-screen rendering* and the ability to update texture maps using *render-to-texture*.

Version 1.4 of OpenGL added

- Stencil operations GL_INCR_WRAP and GL_DECR_WRAP.

Version 3.0 enhanced support by adding

- Framebuffer objects for off-screen and render-to-texture capabilities.

- sRGB-formatted framebuffers for rendering.

Version 3.1 modified the feature set by

- Removing support for the accumulation and auxiliary buffers.

Buffers and Their Uses

An OpenGL system can manipulate the following buffers:

- Color buffers: front-left, front-right, back-left, back-right, and any number of auxiliary color buffers

- Depth buffer

- Stencil buffer

- Accumulation buffer

Your particular OpenGL implementation determines which buffers are available and how many bits per pixel each buffer holds. Additionally, you can have multiple visuals, or window types, that have different buffers available. Table 10-1 lists the parameters to use with **glGetIntegerv()** to query your OpenGL system about per-pixel buffer storage for a particular visual.

Note: If you're using the X Window System, you're guaranteed, at a minimum, to have a visual with one color buffer for use in RGBA mode, with associated stencil, depth, and accumulation buffers that have color components of nonzero size. Also, if your X Window System implementation supports a Pseudo-Color visual, you are also guaranteed to have one OpenGL visual that has a color buffer for use in color-index mode, with associated depth and stencil buffers. You'll probably want to use **glXGetConfig()** to query your visuals; see Appendix C for more information about this routine.

Parameter	Meaning
GL_RED_BITS, GL_GREEN_BITS, GL_BLUE_BITS, GL_ALPHA_BITS	number of bits per R, G, B, or A component in the color buffers
GL_INDEX_BITS	number of bits per index in the color buffers
GL_DEPTH_BITS	number of bits per pixel in the depth buffer
GL_STENCIL_BITS	number of bits per pixel in the stencil buffer
GL_ACCUM_RED_BITS, GL_ACCUM_GREEN_BITS, GL_ACCUM_BLUE_BITS, GL_ACCUM_ALPHA_BITS	number of bits per R, G, B, or A component in the accumulation buffer

Table 10-1   Query Parameters for Per-Pixel Buffer Storage

Color Buffers

The color buffers are the ones to which you usually draw. They contain either color-index or RGB color data and may also contain alpha values. An OpenGL implementation that supports stereoscopic viewing has left and right color buffers for the left and right stereo images. If stereo isn't supported, only the left buffers are used. Similarly, double-buffered systems have front and back buffers, and a single-buffered system has the front buffers only. Every OpenGL implementation must provide a front-left color buffer.

Optional, nondisplayable auxiliary color buffers may also be supported. OpenGL doesn't specify any particular uses for these buffers, so you can define and use them however you please. For example, you might use them for saving an image that you use repeatedly. Then, rather than redrawing the image, you can just copy it from an auxiliary buffer into the usual color buffers. (See the description of **glCopyPixels()** in "Reading, Writing, and Copying Pixel Data" on page 333 for more information about how to do this.)

Note: In OpenGL Version 3.0, color-index mode rendering and auxiliary buffers were deprecated; these features were entirely removed from OpenGL in Version 3.1. They are available as part of the GL_ARB_ compatibility extension, if your OpenGL implementation supports this extension.

You can use GL_STEREO or GL_DOUBLEBUFFER with **glGetBooleanv()** to find out if your system supports stereo (that is, has left and right buffers) or double-buffering (front and back buffers). To find out how many, if any, auxiliary buffers are present, use **glGetIntegerv()** with GL_AUX_BUFFERS.

Depth Buffer

The depth buffer stores a depth value for each pixel. As described in "A Hidden-Surface Removal Survival Kit" on page 205, depth is usually measured in terms of distance to the eye, so pixels with larger depth-buffer values are overwritten by pixels with smaller values. This is just a useful convention, however, and the depth buffer's behavior can be modified as described in "Depth Test" on page 510. The depth buffer is sometimes called the *z buffer* (the *z* comes from the fact that *x*- and *y*-values measure horizontal and vertical displacement on the screen, and the *z*-value measures distance perpendicular to the screen).

Stencil Buffer

One use for the stencil buffer is to restrict drawing to certain portions of the screen, just as a cardboard stencil can be used with a can of spray paint to make fairly precise painted images. For example, if you want to draw an image as it would appear through an odd-shaped windshield, you can store an image of the windshield's shape in the stencil buffer, and then draw the entire scene. The stencil buffer prevents anything that wouldn't be visible through the windshield from being drawn. Thus, if your application is a driving simulation, you can draw all the instruments and other items inside the automobile once, and as the car moves, only the outside scene need be updated.

Accumulation Buffer

The accumulation buffer holds RGBA color data just as the color buffers do in RGBA mode. (The results of using the accumulation buffer in color-index mode are undefined.) It's typically used for accumulating a series of images into a final, composite image. With this method, you can perform operations such as scene antialiasing by supersampling an image and then averaging the samples to produce the values that are finally painted into the pixels of the color buffers. You don't draw directly into the accumulation buffer; accumulation operations are always performed in rectangular blocks, which are usually transfers of data to or from a color buffer.

Clearing Buffers

In graphics programs, clearing the screen (or any of the buffers) is typically one of the most expensive operations you can perform—on a 1280×1024 monitor, it requires touching well over a million pixels. For simple graphics applications, the clear operation can take more time than the rest of the drawing. If you need to clear not only the color buffer but also the depth and stencil buffers, the clear operation can be three times as expensive.

To address this problem, some machines have hardware that can clear more than one buffer at once. The OpenGL clearing commands are structured to take advantage of such architectures. First, you specify the values to be written into each buffer to be cleared. Then you issue a single command to perform the clear operation, passing in a list of all the buffers to be cleared. If the hardware is capable of simultaneous clears, they all occur at once; otherwise, the buffers are cleared sequentially.

The following commands set the clearing values for each buffer:

> void **glClearColor**(GLclampf *red*, GLclampf *green*, GLclampf *blue*,
>   GLclampf *alpha*);
> void **glClearIndex**(GLfloat *index*);
> void **glClearDepth**(GLclampd *depth*);
> void **glClearStencil**(GLint *s*);
> void **glClearAccum**(GLfloat *red*, GLfloat *green*, GLfloat *blue*,
>   GLfloat *alpha*);

Compatibility Extension
glClearIndex
glClearAccum

Specifies the current clearing values for the color buffer (in RGBA mode), the color buffer (in color-index mode), the depth buffer, the stencil buffer, and the accumulation buffer. The GLclampf and GLclampd types (clamped GLfloat and clamped GLdouble) are clamped to be between 0.0 and 1.0. The default depth-clearing value is 1.0; all the other default clearing values are 0. The values set with the clear commands remain in effect until they're changed by another call to the same command.

After you've selected your clearing values and you're ready to clear the buffers, use **glClear();**

void **glClear**(GLbitfield *mask*);

Clears the specified buffers. The value of *mask* is the bitwise logical OR of some combination of GL_COLOR_BUFFER_BIT, GL_DEPTH_BUFFER_BIT, GL_STENCIL_BUFFER_BIT, and GL_ACCUM_BUFFER_BIT to identify which buffers are to be cleared. GL_COLOR_BUFFER_BIT clears either the RGBA color buffer or the color-index buffer, depending on the mode of the system at the time. When you clear the color or color-index buffer, all the color buffers that are enabled for writing (see the next section) are cleared. The pixel ownership test, scissor test, and dithering, if enabled, are applied to the clearing operation. Masking operations, such as **glColorMask()** and **glIndexMask()**, are also effective. The alpha test, stencil test, and depth test do not affect the operation of **glClear()**.

Advanced

If you're using multiple draw buffers—particularly those that have floating-point or non-normalized integer pixel formats—you can clear each individually bound buffer using **glClearBuffer*()** functions, which were introduced in OpenGL Version 3.0. Unlike functions such as **glClearColor()** and **glClearDepth()**, which set a clear value within OpenGL that's used when **glClear()** is called, **glClearBuffer*()** uses the values passed to it to immediately clear the bound drawing buffers.

void **glClearBuffer**{fi ui}v(GLenum *buffer*, GLint *drawbuffer*,
                    const *TYPE *value*);

Clears the buffer indexed by *drawbuffer* associated with *buffer* to *value*. *buffer* must be one of GL_COLOR, GL_DEPTH, or GL_STENCIL.

If *buffer* is GL_COLOR, *drawbuffer* specifies an index to a particular draw buffer, and *value* is a four-element array containing for clear color. If the buffer indexed by *drawbuffer* has multiple draw buffers (as specified by a call to **glDrawBuffers()**), all draw buffers are cleared to *value*.

If *buffer* is GL_DEPTH or GL_STENCIL, *drawbuffer* must be zero, and *value* is a single-element array containing an appropriate clear value (subject to clamping and type conversion for depth values, and masking and type conversion for stencil values).

A GL_INVALID_ENUM is generated if *buffer* is not one of the accepted values listed above. GL_INVALID_VALUE is generated if *buffer* is GL_COLOR, and *drawbuffer* is less than zero, or greater than or equal to GL_MAX_DRAW_BUFFERS; or if *buffer* is GL_DEPTH, or GL_STENCIL, and *drawbuffer* is not zero. Finally, a GL_INVALID_OPERATION is set if *buffer* is GL_COLOR, and applied to a color-index mode buffer.

To reduce the number of functions calls associated with using multiple draw buffers, you can call **glClearBufferfi()** to simultaneously clear the depth and stencil buffers (which is effectively equivalent to calling **glClearBuffer*()** twice—once for the depth buffer and once for the stencil buffer):

void **glClearBufferfi**(GLenum *buffer*, GLint *drawbuffer*,
  GLfloat *depth*, GLint *stencil*);

Clear both the depth and stencil buffers of the currently bound framebuffer simultaneously (which may be faster on some implementations). *buffer* must be GL_DEPTH_STENCIL, and *drawbuffer* must be zero. *depth* and *stencil* will be used as the clear values for the respective buffers.

A GL_INVALID_ENUM is generated if *buffer* is not GL_DEPTH_STENCIL. and a GL_INVALID_VALUE is generated if *drawbuffer* is not zero.

Selecting Color Buffers for Writing and Reading

The results of a drawing or reading operation can go into or come from any of the color buffers: front, back, front-left, back-left, front-right, back-right, or any of the auxiliary buffers. You can choose an individual buffer to be the drawing or reading target. For drawing, you can also set the target to draw into more than one buffer at the same time. You use **glDrawBuffer()** to select the buffers to be written and **glReadBuffer()** to select the buffer as the source for **glReadPixels()**, **glCopyPixels()**, **glCopyTexImage*()**, and **glCopyTexSubImage*()**.

If you are using double-buffering, you usually want to draw only in the back buffer (and swap the buffers when you're finished drawing). In some situations, you might want to treat a double-buffered window as though it were single-buffered by calling **glDrawBuffer**(GL_FRONT_AND_BACK) to enable you to draw to both front and back buffers at the same time.

glDrawBuffer() is also used to select buffers to render stereo images (GL*LEFT and GL*RIGHT) and to render into auxiliary buffers (GL_AUX*i*).

void **glDrawBuffer**(GLenum *mode*);
void **glDrawBuffers**(GLsizei *n*, const GLenum **buffers*);

Selects the color buffers enabled for writing or clearing and disables buffers enabled by previous calls to **glDrawBuffer**(). More than one buffer may be enabled at one time. The value of *mode* can be one of the following:

GL_FRONT	GL_FRONT_LEFT	GL_AUX*i*
GL_BACK	GL_FRONT_RIGHT	GL_FRONT_AND_BACK
GL_LEFT	GL_BACK_LEFT	GL_NONE
GL_RIGHT	GL_BACK_RIGHT	GL_COLOR_ATTACHMENT*i*

Arguments that omit LEFT or RIGHT refer to both the left and right stereo buffers; similarly, arguments that omit FRONT or BACK refer to both. The *i* in GL_AUX*i* is a digit identifying a particular auxiliary buffer.

By default, *mode* is GL_FRONT for single-buffered contexts and GL_BACK for double-buffered contexts.

OpenGL Version 2.0 added the **glDrawBuffers**() routine, which specifies multiple color buffers capable of receiving color values. *buffers* is an array of buffer enumerates. Only GL_NONE, GL_FRONT_LEFT, GL_FRONT_RIGHT, GL_BACK_LEFT, GL_BACK_RIGHT, and GL_AUX*i* are accepted.

With OpenGL Version 3.0's addition of framebuffer objects, GL_COLOR_ATTACHMENT*i* was added to specify which color renderbuffers are draw targets when OpenGL is bound to a user-defined framebuffer object.

If the fixed-function OpenGL pipeline is used for generating fragment colors, each of the specified buffers receives the same color value. If a fragment shader is employed and specifies output to multiple buffers, then each buffer will be written with the color specified in the shader's output. See "Rendering to Multiple Output Buffers" in Chapter 15 for details.

Note: You can enable drawing to nonexistent buffers as long as you enable drawing to at least one buffer that does exist. If none of the specified buffers exists, an error results.

void **glReadBuffer**(GLenum *mode*);

Selects the color buffer enabled as the source for reading pixels for subsequent calls to **glReadPixels**(), **glCopyPixels**(), **glCopyTexImage***(), **glCopyTexSubImage***(), and **glCopyConvolutionFilter***(), and disables buffers enabled by previous calls to **glReadBuffer**(). The value of *mode* can be one of the following:

GL_FRONT	GL_FRONT_LEFT	GL_AUX*i*
GL_BACK	GL_FRONT_RIGHT	GL_COLOR_ATTACHMENT*i*
GL_LEFT	GL_BACK_LEFT	
GL_RIGHT	GL_BACK_RIGHT	

The buffers for **glReadBuffer**() are the same as those described for **glDrawBuffer**(). By default, *mode* is GL_FRONT for single-buffered contexts and GL_BACK for double-buffered contexts.

Use GL_COLOR_ATTACHMENT*i* with OpenGL Versions 3.0 and later when reading from a user-defined framebuffer object. The value of *i* must be between 0 and GL_MAX_COLOR_ATTACHMENTS (as returned by calling **glGetIntegerv**())

Note: You must enable reading from a buffer that exists or an error results.

Masking Buffers

Before OpenGL writes data into the enabled color, depth, or stencil buffers, a masking operation is applied to the data, as specified with one of the following commands. A bitwise logical AND is performed with each mask and the corresponding data to be written.

void **glIndexMask**(GLuint *mask*);
void **glColorMask**(GLboolean *red*, GLboolean *green*, GLboolean *blue*,
        GLboolean *alpha*);
void **glColorMaski**(GLuint *buf*, GLboolean *red*, GLboolean *green*,
        GLboolean *blue*, GLboolean *alpha*);
void **glDepthMask**(GLboolean *flag*);
void **glStencilMask**(GLuint *mask*);
void **glStencilMaskSeparate**(GLenum *face*, GLuint *mask*);

Sets the masks used to control writing into the indicated buffers. The mask set by **glIndexMask**() applies only in color-index mode. If a 1 appears in *mask*, the corresponding bit in the color-index buffer is written; if a 0 appears, the bit isn't written. Similarly, **glColorMask()** affects drawing in RGBA mode only. The *red*, *green*, *blue*, and *alpha* values control whether the corresponding component is written. (GL_TRUE means it is written.

If *flag* is GL_TRUE for **glDepthMask()**, the depth buffer is enabled for writing; otherwise, it's disabled. The mask for **glStencilMask()** is used for stencil data in the same way as the mask is used for color-index data in **glIndexMask()**. The default values of all the GLboolean masks are GL_TRUE, and the default values for the two GLuint masks are all 1's.

OpenGL Version 2.0 includes the **glStencilMaskSeparate()** function that allows separate mask values for front- and back-facing polygons.

OpenGL Version 3.0 added the **glColorMaski()** function to allow setting of the color mask for an individual buffer specified by *buf* when rendering to multiple color buffers (see "Selecting Color Buffers for Writing and Reading" on page 497 for more details on using multiple buffers).

You can do plenty of tricks with color masking in color-index mode. For example, you can use each bit in the index as a different layer and set up interactions between arbitrary layers with appropriate settings of the color map. You can create overlays and underlays, and do so-called color-map animations. (See Chapter 14 for examples of using color masking.) Masking in RGBA mode is useful less often, but you can use it for loading separate image files into the red, green, and blue bitplanes, for example.

You've seen one use for disabling the depth buffer in "Three-Dimensional Blending with the Depth Buffer" on page 263. Disabling the depth buffer for writing can also be useful if a common background is desired for a series of frames, and you want to add some features that may be obscured by parts of the background. For example, suppose your background is a forest, and you would like to draw repeated frames with the same trees, but with objects moving among them. After the trees are drawn and their depths recorded in the depth buffer, the image of the trees is saved, and the new items are drawn with the depth buffer disabled for writing. As long as the new items don't overlap each other, the picture is correct. To draw the next frame, restore the image of the trees and continue. You don't need to restore the values in the depth buffer. This trick is most useful if the background is extremely complex—so complex that it's much faster just to recopy the image into the color buffer than to recompute it from the geometry.

Masking the stencil buffer can allow you to use a multiple-bit stencil buffer to hold multiple stencils (one per bit). You might use this technique to perform capping as explained in "Stencil Test" on page 504 or to implement the Game of Life as described in "Life in the Stencil Buffer" on page 664.

Note: The mask specified by **glStencilMask()** controls which stencil bitplanes are written. This mask isn't related to the mask that's specified as the third parameter of **glStencilFunc()**, which specifies which bitplanes are considered by the stencil function.

Testing and Operating on Fragments

When you draw geometry, text, or images on the screen, OpenGL performs several calculations to rotate, translate, scale, determine the lighting, project the object(s) into perspective, execute a vertex shader, figure out which pixels in the window are affected, and determine the colors in which those pixels should be drawn. Many of the earlier chapters in this book provide some information about how to control these operations. After OpenGL determines that an individual fragment should be generated and what its color should be, several processing stages remain that control how and whether the fragment is drawn as a pixel into the framebuffer. For example, if it's outside a rectangular region or if it's farther from the viewpoint than the pixel that's already in the framebuffer, it isn't drawn. In another stage, the fragment's color is blended with the color of the pixel already in the framebuffer.

This section describes both the complete set of tests that a fragment must pass before it goes into the framebuffer and the possible final operations that can be performed on the fragment as it's written. The tests and operations occur in the following order; if a fragment is eliminated in an early test, none of the later tests or operations takes place:

1. Scissor test

2. Alpha test

3. Stencil test

4. Depth test

5. Blending

6. Dithering

7. Logical operations

All of these tests and operations are described in detail in the following subsections.

Scissor Test

You can define a rectangular portion of your window and restrict drawing to take place within it by using the **glScissor()** command. If a fragment lies inside the rectangle, it passes the scissor test.

---

void **glScissor**(GLint *x*, GLint *y*, GLsizei *width*, GLsizei *height*);

Sets the location and size of the scissor rectangle (also known as the scissor box). The parameters define the lower left corner (*x*, *y*) and the width and height of the rectangle. Pixels that lie inside the rectangle pass the scissor test. Scissoring is enabled and disabled by passing GL_SCISSOR_TEST to **glEnable()** and **glDisable()**. By default, the rectangle matches the size of the window and scissoring is disabled.

The scissor test is just a version of a stencil test using a rectangular region of the screen. It's fairly easy to create a blindingly fast hardware implementation of scissoring, while a given system might be much slower at stenciling—perhaps because the stenciling is performed in software.

Advanced

Advanced

An advanced use of scissoring is performing nonlinear projection. First divide the window into a regular grid of subregions, specifying viewport and scissor parameters that limit rendering to one region at a time. Then project the entire scene to each region using a different projection matrix.

To determine whether scissoring is enabled and to obtain the values that define the scissor rectangle, you can use GL_SCISSOR_TEST with **glIsEnabled()** and GL_SCISSOR_BOX with **glGetIntegerv()**.

Alpha Test

| Compatibility |
| Extension |
| GL_ALPHA_TEST |

In RGBA mode, the alpha test allows you to accept or reject a fragment based on its alpha value. The alpha test is enabled and disabled by passing GL_ALPHA_TEST to **glEnable()** and **glDisable()**. To determine whether the alpha test is enabled, use GL_ALPHA_TEST with **glIsEnabled()**.

Note: The alpha fragment test was deprecated in OpenGL Version 3.0, and replaced in OpenGL Version 3.1 by discarding fragments in a fragment shader using the `discard` operation. See the description of `discard` in "Flow Control Statements" on page 705.

If enabled, the test compares the incoming alpha value with a reference value. The fragment is accepted or rejected depending on the result of the comparison. Both the reference value and the comparison function are set with **glAlphaFunc()**. By default, the reference value is 0, the comparison function is GL_ALWAYS, and the alpha test is disabled. To obtain the alpha comparison function or reference value, use GL_ALPHA_TEST_FUNC or GL_ALPHA_TEST_REF with **glGetIntegerv()**.

---

void **glAlphaFunc**(GLenum *func*, GLclampf *ref*);

Sets the reference value and comparison function for the alpha test. The reference value *ref* is clamped to be between 0 and 1. The possible values for *func* and their meanings are listed in Table 10-2.

Compatibility
Extension

glAlphaFunc

Parameter	Meaning
GL_NEVER	never accept the fragment
GL_ALWAYS	always accept the fragment
GL_LESS	accept fragment if fragment alpha < reference alpha
GL_LEQUAL	accept fragment if fragment alpha ≤ reference alpha
GL_EQUAL	accept fragment if fragment alpha = reference alpha
GL_GEQUAL	accept fragment if fragment alpha ≥ reference alpha
GL_GREATER	accept fragment if fragment alpha > reference alpha
GL_NOTEQUAL	accept fragment if fragment alpha ≠ reference alpha

Table 10-2   glAlphaFunc() Parameter Values

One application for the alpha test is implementation of a transparency algorithm. Render your entire scene twice, the first time accepting only fragments with alpha values of 1, and the second time accepting fragments with alpha values that aren't equal to 1. Turn the depth buffer on during both passes, but disable depth buffer writing during the second pass.

Another use might be to make decals with texture maps whereby you can see through certain parts of the decals. Set the alphas in the decals to 0.0

where you want to see through, set them to 1.0 otherwise, set the reference value to 0.5 (or anything between 0.0 and 1.0), and set the comparison function to GL_GREATER. The decal has see-through parts, and the values in the depth buffer aren't affected. This technique, called *billboarding*, is described in "Sample Uses of Blending" on page 258.

Stencil Test

The stencil test takes place only if there is a stencil buffer. (If there is no stencil buffer, the stencil test always passes.) Stenciling applies a test that compares a reference value with the value stored at a pixel in the stencil buffer. Depending on the result of the test, the value in the stencil buffer is modified. You can choose the particular comparison function used, the reference value, and the modification performed with the **glStencilFunc()** and **glStencilOp()** commands.

---

void **glStencilFunc**(GLenum *func*, GLint *ref*, GLuint *mask*);
void **glStencilFuncSeparate**(GLenum *face*,
        GLenum *func*, GLint *ref*, GLuint *mask*);

Sets the comparison function (*func*), the reference value (*ref*), and a mask (*mask*) for use with the stencil test. The reference value is compared with the value in the stencil buffer using the comparison function, but the comparison applies only to those bits for which the corresponding bits of the mask are 1. The function can be GL_NEVER, GL_ALWAYS, GL_LESS, GL_LEQUAL, GL_EQUAL, GL_GEQUAL, GL_GREATER, or GL_NOTEQUAL. If it's GL_LESS, for example, then the fragment passes if *ref* is less than the value in the stencil buffer. If the stencil buffer contains *s* bitplanes, the low-order *s* bits of *mask* are bitwise ANDed with the value in the stencil buffer and with the reference value before the comparison is performed. The masked values are all interpreted as non-negative values. The stencil test is enabled and disabled by passing GL_STENCIL_TEST to **glEnable()** and **glDisable()**. By default, *func* is GL_ALWAYS, *ref* is 0, *mask* is all 1s, and stenciling is disabled.

OpenGL 2.0 includes the **glStencilFuncSeparate()** function that allows separate stencil function parameters to be specified for front- and back-facing polygons.

void **glStencilOp**(GLenum *fail*, GLenum *zfail*, GLenum *zpass*);
void **glStencilOpSeparate**(GLenum *face*, GLenum *fail*, GLenum *zfail*,
GLenum *zpass*);

Specifies how the data in the stencil buffer is modified when a fragment passes or fails the stencil test. The three functions *fail*, *zfail*, and *zpass* can be GL_KEEP, GL_ZERO, GL_REPLACE, GL_INCR, GL_INCR_WRAP, GL_DECR, GL_DECR_WRAP, or GL_INVERT. They correspond to keeping the current value, replacing it with zero, replacing it with the reference value, incrementing it with saturation, incrementing it without saturation, decrementing it with saturation, decrementing it without saturation, and bitwise-inverting it. The result of the increment and decrement functions is clamped to lie between zero and the maximum unsigned integer value ($2^s - 1$ if the stencil buffer holds *s* bits).

The *fail* function is applied if the fragment fails the stencil test; if it passes, then *zfail* is applied if the depth test fails and *zpass* is applied if the depth test passes, or if no depth test is performed. (See "Depth Test" on page 510.) By default, all three stencil operations are GL_KEEP.

OpenGL 2.0 includes the **glStencilOpSeparate**() function that allows separate stencil tests to be specified for front- and back-facing polygons.

"With saturation" means that the stencil value will clamp to extreme values. If you try to decrement zero with saturation, the stencil value remains zero. "Without saturation" means that going outside the indicated range wraps around. If you try to decrement zero without saturation, the stencil value becomes the maximum unsigned integer value (quite large!).

Stencil Queries

You can obtain the values for all six stencil-related parameters by using the query function **glGetIntegerv**() and one of the values shown in Table 10-3. You can also determine whether the stencil test is enabled by passing GL_STENCIL_TEST to **glIsEnabled**().

Query Value	Meaning
GL_STENCIL_FUNC	stencil function
GL_STENCIL_REF	stencil reference value
GL_STENCIL_VALUE_MASK	stencil mask
GL_STENCIL_FAIL	stencil fail action
GL_STENCIL_PASS_DEPTH_FAIL	stencil pass and depth buffer fail action
GL_STENCIL_PASS_DEPTH_PASS	stencil pass and depth buffer pass action

Table 10-3   Query Values for the Stencil Test

Stencil Examples

Probably the most typical use of the stencil test is to mask out an irregularly shaped region of the screen to prevent drawing from occurring within it (as in the windshield example in "Buffers and Their Uses"). To do this, fill the stencil mask with 0's, and then draw the desired shape in the stencil buffer with 1's. You can't draw geometry directly into the stencil buffer, but you can achieve the same result by drawing into the color buffer and choosing a suitable value for the *zpass* function (such as GL_REPLACE). (You can use **glDrawPixels**() to draw pixel data directly into the stencil buffer.) Whenever drawing occurs, a value is also written into the stencil buffer (in this case, the reference value). To prevent the stencil-buffer drawing from affecting the contents of the color buffer, set the color mask to zero (or GL_FALSE). You might also want to disable writing into the depth buffer.

After you've defined the stencil area, set the reference value to 1, and set the comparison function such that the fragment passes if the reference value is equal to the stencil-plane value. During drawing, don't modify the contents of the stencil planes.

Example 10-1 demonstrates how to use the stencil test in this way. Two toruses are drawn, with a diamond-shaped cutout in the center of the scene. Within the diamond-shaped stencil mask, a sphere is drawn. In this example, drawing into the stencil buffer takes place only when the window is redrawn, so the color buffer is cleared after the stencil mask has been created.

Example 10-1 Using the Stencil Test: stencil.c

```
#define YELLOWMAT    1
#define BLUEMAT      2

void init(void)
{
   GLfloat yellow_diffuse[] = { 0.7, 0.7, 0.0, 1.0 };
   GLfloat yellow_specular[] = { 1.0, 1.0, 1.0, 1.0 };

   GLfloat blue_diffuse[] = { 0.1, 0.1, 0.7, 1.0 };
   GLfloat blue_specular[] = { 0.1, 1.0, 1.0, 1.0 };

   GLfloat position_one[] = { 1.0, 1.0, 1.0, 0.0 };

   glNewList(YELLOWMAT, GL_COMPILE);
   glMaterialfv(GL_FRONT, GL_DIFFUSE, yellow_diffuse);
   glMaterialfv(GL_FRONT, GL_SPECULAR, yellow_specular);
   glMaterialf(GL_FRONT, GL_SHININESS, 64.0);
   glEndList();

   glNewList(BLUEMAT, GL_COMPILE);
   glMaterialfv(GL_FRONT, GL_DIFFUSE, blue_diffuse);
   glMaterialfv(GL_FRONT, GL_SPECULAR, blue_specular);
   glMaterialf(GL_FRONT, GL_SHININESS, 45.0);
   glEndList();

   glLightfv(GL_LIGHT0, GL_POSITION, position_one);

   glEnable(GL_LIGHT0);
   glEnable(GL_LIGHTING);
   glEnable(GL_DEPTH_TEST);

   glClearStencil(0x0);
   glEnable(GL_STENCIL_TEST);
}

/* Draw a sphere in a diamond-shaped section in the
 * middle of a window with 2 tori.
 */
void display(void)
{
   glClear(GL_COLOR_BUFFER_BIT | GL_DEPTH_BUFFER_BIT);

/* draw blue sphere where the stencil is 1 */
   glStencilFunc(GL_EQUAL, 0x1, 0x1);
   glStencilOp(GL_KEEP, GL_KEEP, GL_KEEP);
   glCallList(BLUEMAT);
   glutSolidSphere(0.5, 15, 15);
```

```
   /* draw the tori where the stencil is not 1 */
      glStencilFunc(GL_NOTEQUAL, 0x1, 0x1);
      glPushMatrix();
         glRotatef(45.0, 0.0, 0.0, 1.0);
         glRotatef(45.0, 0.0, 1.0, 0.0);
         glCallList(YELLOWMAT);
         glutSolidTorus(0.275, 0.85, 15, 15);
         glPushMatrix();
            glRotatef(90.0, 1.0, 0.0, 0.0);
            glutSolidTorus(0.275, 0.85, 15, 15);
         glPopMatrix();
      glPopMatrix();
}

/*  Whenever the window is reshaped, redefine the
 *  coordinate system and redraw the stencil area.
 */
void reshape(int w, int h)
{
   glViewport(0, 0, (GLsizei) w, (GLsizei) h);

/* create a diamond shaped stencil area */
   glMatrixMode(GL_PROJECTION);
   glLoadIdentity();
   if (w <= h)
      gluOrtho2D(-3.0, 3.0, -3.0*(GLfloat)h/(GLfloat)w,
                 3.0*(GLfloat)h/(GLfloat)w);
   else
      gluOrtho2D(-3.0*(GLfloat)w/(GLfloat)h,
                 3.0*(GLfloat)w/(GLfloat)h, -3.0, 3.0);
   glMatrixMode(GL_MODELVIEW);
   glLoadIdentity();

   glClear(GL_STENCIL_BUFFER_BIT);
   glStencilFunc(GL_ALWAYS, 0x1, 0x1);
   glStencilOp(GL_REPLACE, GL_REPLACE, GL_REPLACE);
   glBegin(GL_QUADS);
      glVertex2f(-1.0, 0.0);
      glVertex2f(0.0, 1.0);
      glVertex2f(1.0, 0.0);
      glVertex2f(0.0, -1.0);
   glEnd();

   glMatrixMode(GL_PROJECTION);
   glLoadIdentity();
   gluPerspective(45.0, (GLfloat) w/(GLfloat) h, 3.0, 7.0);
```

```
   glMatrixMode(GL_MODELVIEW);
   glLoadIdentity();
   glTranslatef(0.0, 0.0, -5.0);
}

/* Main Loop
 * Be certain to request stencil bits.
 */
int main(int argc, char** argv)
{
   glutInit(&argc, argv);
   glutInitDisplayMode(GLUT_SINGLE | GLUT_RGB |
                       GLUT_DEPTH | GLUT_STENCIL);
   glutInitWindowSize(400, 400);
   glutInitWindowPosition(100, 100);
   glutCreateWindow(argv[0]);
   init();
   glutReshapeFunc(reshape);
   glutDisplayFunc(display);
   glutMainLoop();
   return 0;
}
```

The following examples illustrate other uses of the stencil test. (See Chapter 14 for additional ideas.)

- Capping—Suppose you're drawing a closed convex object (or several of them, as long as they don't intersect or enclose each other) made up of several polygons, and you have a clipping plane that may or may not slice off a piece of it. Suppose that if the plane does intersect the object, you want to cap the object with some constant-colored surface, rather than see the inside of it. To do this, clear the stencil buffer to zeros, and begin drawing with stenciling enabled and the stencil comparison function set always to accept fragments. Invert the value in the stencil planes each time a fragment is accepted. After all the objects are drawn, regions of the screen where no capping is required have zeros in the stencil planes, and regions requiring capping are nonzero. Reset the stencil function so that it draws only where the stencil value is nonzero, and draw a large polygon of the capping color across the entire screen.

- Overlapping translucent polygons—Suppose you have a translucent surface that's made up of polygons that overlap slightly. If you simply use alpha blending, portions of the underlying objects are covered by more than one transparent surface, which doesn't look right. Use the stencil planes to make sure that each fragment is covered by at most one portion of the transparent surface. Do this by clearing the stencil planes to zeros, drawing only when the stencil plane is zero, and incrementing the value in the stencil plane when you draw.

- Stippling—Suppose you want to draw an image with a stipple pattern. (See "Displaying Points, Lines, and Polygons" on page 55 for more information about stippling.) You can do this by writing the stipple pattern into the stencil buffer and then drawing conditionally on the contents of the stencil buffer. After the original stipple pattern is drawn, the stencil buffer isn't altered while drawing the image, so the object is stippled by the pattern in the stencil planes.

Depth Test

For each pixel on the screen, the depth buffer keeps track of the distance between the viewpoint and the object occupying that pixel. Then, if the specified depth test passes, the incoming depth value replaces the value already in the depth buffer.

The depth buffer is generally used for hidden-surface elimination. If a new candidate color for that pixel appears, it's drawn only if the corresponding object is closer than the previous object. In this way, after the entire scene has been rendered, only objects that aren't obscured by other items remain. Initially, the clearing value for the depth buffer is a value that's as far from the viewpoint as possible, so the depth of any object is nearer than that value. If this is how you want to use the depth buffer, you simply have to enable it by passing GL_DEPTH_TEST to **glEnable()** and remember to clear the depth buffer before you redraw each frame. (See "Clearing Buffers" on page 495.) You can also choose a different comparison function for the depth test with **glDepthFunc()**.

---

void **glDepthFunc**(GLenum *func*);

Sets the comparison function for the depth test. The value for *func* must be GL_NEVER, GL_ALWAYS, GL_LESS, GL_LEQUAL, GL_EQUAL, GL_GEQUAL, GL_GREATER, or GL_NOTEQUAL. An incoming fragment passes the depth test if its z-value has the specified relation to the value already stored in the depth buffer. The default is GL_LESS, which means that an incoming fragment passes the test if its z-value is less than that already stored in the depth buffer. In this case, the z-value represents the distance from the object to the viewpoint, and smaller values mean that the corresponding objects are closer to the viewpoint.

Occlusion Query

Advanced

Advanced

The depth buffer determines visibility on a per-pixel basis. For performance reasons, it would be nice to be able to determine if a geometric object is visible before sending all of its (perhaps complex) geometry for rendering. *Occlusion queries* enable you to determine if a representative set of geometry will be visible after depth testing.

This is particularly useful for complex geometric objects with many polygons. Instead of rendering all of the geometry for a complex object, you might render its bounding box or another simplified representation that require less rendering resources. If OpenGL returns that no fragments or samples would have been modified by rendering that piece of geometry, you know that none of your complex object will be visible for that frame, and you can skip rendering that object for the frame.

The following steps are required to utilize occlusion queries:

1. (Optional) Generate a query id for each occlusion query that you need.

2. Specify the start of an occlusion query by calling **glBeginQuery()**.

3. Render the geometry for the occlusion test.

4. Specify that you've completed the occlusion query by calling **glEndQuery()**.

5. Retrieve the number of samples that passed the depth test.

In order to make the occlusion query process as efficient as possible, you'll want to disable all rendering modes that will increase the rendering time but won't change the visibility of a pixel.

Generating Query Objects

An occlusion query object identifier is just an unsigned integer. While not strictly necessary, it's a good practice to have OpenGL generate a set of ids for your use. **glGenQueries()** will generate the requested number of unused query ids for your subsequent use.

> void **glGenQueries**(GLsizei *n*, GLuint **ids*);
>
> Returns *n* currently unused names for occlusion query objects in the array *ids* The names returned in *ids* do not have to be a contiguous set of integers.
>
> The names returned are marked as used for the purposes of allocating additional query objects, but only acquire valid state once they have been specified in a call to **glBeginQuery**().
>
> Zero is a reserved occlusion query object name and is never returned as a valid value by **glGenQueries**().

You can also determine if an identifier is currently being used as an occlusion query by calling **glIsQuery**().

> GLboolean **glIsQuery**(GLuint *id*);
>
> Returns GL_TRUE if *id* is the name of an occlusion query object. Returns GL_FALSE if *id* is zero or if *id* is a nonzero value that is not the name of a buffer object.

Initiating an Occlusion Query Test

To specify geometry that's to be used in an occlusion query, merely bracket the rendering operations between calls to **glBeginQuery**() and **glEndQuery**(), as demonstrated in Example 10-2.

Example 10-2   Rendering Geometry with Occlusion Query: occquery.c

```
glBeginQuery(GL_SAMPLES_PASSED, Query);
glBegin(GL_TRIANGLES);
glVertex3f( 0.0, 0.0, 1.0);
glVertex3f(-1.0, 0.0, 0.0);
glVertex3f( 1.0, 0.0, 0.0);
glEnd();
glEndQuery(GL_SAMPLES_PASSED);
```

All OpenGL operations are available while an occlusion query is active, with the exception of **glGenQueries**() and **glDeleteQueries**(), which will raise a GL_INVALID_OPERATION error.

void **glBeginQuery**(GLenum *target*, GLuint *id*);

Specifies the start of an occlusion query operation. *target* must be GL_SAMPLES_PASSED. *id* is an unsigned integer identifier for this occlusion query operation.

void **glEndQuery**(GLenum *target*);

Ends an occlusion query. *target* must be GL_SAMPLES_PASSED.

Determining the Results of an Occlusion Query

Once you've completed rendering the geometry for the occlusion query, you need to retrieve the results. This is done with a call to **glGetQueryObject[u]iv**(), as shown in Example 10-3, which will return the number of fragments, or samples, if you're using multisampling (see "Alpha and Multisampling Coverage" on page 279 for details).

void **glGetQueryObjectiv**(GLenum *id*, GLenum *pname*,
                     GLint **params*);
void **glGetQueryObjectuiv**(GLenum *id*, GLenum *pname*,
                     GLuint **params*);

Queries the state of an occlusion query object. *id* is the name of a query object. If *pname* is GL_QUERY_RESULT, then *params* will contain the number of fragments or samples (if multisampling is enabled) that passed the depth test, with a value of zero representing the object being entirely occluded.

There may be a delay in completing the occlusion query operation. If *pname* is GL_QUERY_RESULT_AVAILABLE, *params* will contain GL_TRUE if the results for query *id* are available, or GL_FALSE otherwise.

Example 10-3   Retrieving the Results of an Occlusion Query: occquery.c

```
count = 1000; /* counter to avoid a possible infinite loop */
while (!queryReady && count--) {
    glGetQueryObjectiv(Query, GL_QUERY_RESULT_AVAILABLE,
        &queryReady);
}
```

```
if (queryReady) {
    glGetQueryObjectiv(Query, GL_QUERY_RESULT, &samples);
    fprintf(stderr, "   Samples rendered: %d\n", samples);
}
else {
    fprintf(stderr, "   Result not ready ... rendering
        anyways\n");
    samples = 1; /* make sure we render */
}

if (samples > 0)
    glDrawArrays(GL_TRIANGLE_FAN, 0, NumVertices);
```

Cleaning Up Occlusion Query Objects

After you've completed your occlusion query tests, you can release the
resources related to those queries by calling **glDeleteQueries()**.

---

void **glDeleteQueries**(GLsizei *n*, const GLuint **ids*);

Deletes *n* occlusion query objects, named by elements in the array *ids*. The
freed query objects may now be reused (for example, by **glGenQueries()**).

Conditional Rendering

Advanced

Advanced

One of the issues with occlusion queries is that they require OpenGL to
pause processing geometry and fragments, count the number of affected
samples in the depth buffer, and return the value to your application.
Stopping modern graphics hardware in this manner usually
catastrophically affects performance in performance-sensitive
applications. To eliminate the need to pause OpenGL's operation,
conditional rendering allows the graphics server (hardware) to decide if
an occlusion query yielded any fragments, and to render the intervening
commands. Conditional rendering is enabled by surrounding the
rendering operations you would have conditionally executed using the
results of **glGetQuery*()**.

> void **glBeginConditionalRender**(GLuint *id*, GLenum *mode*);
> void **glEndConditionalRender**(void);
>
> Delineates a sequence of OpenGL rendering commands that may be discarded based on the results of the occlusion query object *id*. *mode* specifies how the OpenGL implementation uses the results of the occlusion query, and must be one of: GL_QUERY_WAIT, GL_QUERY_NO_WAIT, GL_QUERY_BY_REGION_WAIT, or GL_QUERY_BY_REGION_NO_WAIT.
>
> A GL_INVALID_VALUE is set if *id* is not an existing occlusion query. A GL_INVALID_OPERATION is generated if **glBeginConditionalRender()** is called while a conditional rendering sequence is in operation; if **glEndConditionalRender()** is called when no conditional render is underway; if *id* is the name of a occlusion query object with a target different than GL_SAMPLES_PASSED; or if *id* is the name of an occlusion query in progress.

The code shown in Example 10-4 completely replaces the sequence of code in Example 10-3. Not only it the code more compact, it is far more efficient as it completely removes the results query to the OpenGL server, which is a major performance inhibitor.

Example 10-4   Rendering Using Conditional Rendering: condrender.c

```
glBeginConditionalRender(Query, GL_QUERY_WAIT);
glDrawArrays(GL_TRIANGLE_FAN, 0, NumVertices);
glEndConditionalRender();
```

Blending, Dithering, and Logical Operations

Once an incoming fragment has passed all the tests described in "Testing and Operating on Fragments," it can be combined with the current contents of the color buffer in one of several ways. The simplest way, which is also the default, is to overwrite the existing values. Alternatively, if you're using RGBA mode and you want the fragment to be translucent or anti-aliased, you might average its value with the value already in the buffer (blending). On systems with a small number of available colors, you might want to dither color values to increase the number of colors available at the cost of a loss in resolution. In the final stage, you can use arbitrary bitwise logical operations to combine the incoming fragment and the pixel that's already written.

Blending

Blending combines the incoming fragment's R, G, B, and alpha values with those of the pixel already stored at the location. Different blending operations can be applied, and the blending that occurs depends on the values of the incoming alpha value and the alpha value (if any) stored at the pixel. (See "Blending" on page 251 for an extensive discussion of this topic.)

Control of blending is available on a per-buffer basis starting with OpenGL Version 3.0, using the following commands:

> void **glEnablei**(GLenum *target*, GLuint *index*);
> void **glDisablei**(GLenum *target*, GLuint *index*);
>
> Enables or disables blending for buffer *index*. *target* must be GL_BLEND.
>
> A GL_INVALID_VALUE is generated if *index* is greater than or equal to GL_MAX_DRAW_BUFFERS.

To determine if blending is enabled for a particular buffer, use **glIsEnabledi**().

> GLboolean **glIsEnabledi**(GLenum *target*, GLuint *index*);
>
> Specifies whether *target* is enabled for buffer *index*.
>
> For OpenGL Version 3.0, target must be GL_BLEND, or a GL_INVALID_ENUM is generated.
>
> A GL_INVALID_VALUE is generated if *index* is outside of the range supported for *target*.

Dithering

On systems with a small number of color bitplanes, you can improve the color resolution at the expense of spatial resolution by dithering the color in the image. Dithering is like halftoning in newspapers. Although *The New York Times* has only two colors—black and white—it can show photographs by representing the shades of gray with combinations of black and white dots. Comparing a newspaper image of a photo (having no shades of gray) with the original photo (with grayscale) makes the loss of spatial resolution obvious. Similarly, systems with a small number of color bitplanes may dither values of red, green, and blue on neighboring pixels for the appearance of a wider range of colors.

The dithering operation that takes place is hardware-dependent; all OpenGL allows you to do is to turn it on and off. In fact, on some machines, enabling dithering might do nothing at all, which makes sense if the machine already has high color resolution. To enable and disable dithering, pass GL_DITHER to **glEnable()** and **glDisable()**. Dithering is enabled by default.

Dithering applies in both RGBA and color-index mode. The colors or color indices alternate in some hardware-dependent way between the two nearest possibilities. For example, in color-index mode, if dithering is enabled and the color index to be painted is 4.4, then 60 percent of the pixels may be painted with index 4, and 40 percent of the pixels with index 5. (Many dithering algorithms are possible, but a dithered value produced by any algorithm must depend on only the incoming value and the fragment's x- and y-coordinates.) In RGBA mode, dithering is performed separately for each component (including alpha). To use dithering in color-index mode, you generally need to arrange the colors in the color map appropriately in ramps; otherwise, bizarre images might result.

Logical Operations

The final operation on a fragment is the *logical operation*, such as an OR, XOR, or INVERT, which is applied to the incoming fragment values (source) and/or those currently in the color buffer (destination). Such fragment operations are especially useful on bit-blt-type machines, on which the primary graphics operation is copying a rectangle of data from one place in the window to another, from the window to processor memory, or from memory to the window. Typically, the copy doesn't write the data directly into memory but instead allows you to perform an arbitrary logical operation on the incoming data and the data already present; then it replaces the existing data with the results of the operation.

Since this process can be implemented fairly cheaply in hardware, many such machines are available. As an example of using a logical operation, XOR can be used to draw on an image in an undoable way; simply XOR the same drawing again, and the original image is restored. As another example, when using color-index mode, the color indices can be interpreted as bit patterns. Then you can compose an image as combinations of drawings on different layers, use writemasks to limit drawing to different sets of bitplanes, and perform logical operations to modify different layers.

You enable and disable logical operations by passing GL_INDEX_LOGIC_OP or GL_COLOR_LOGIC_OP to **glEnable()** and **glDisable()** for color-index mode or RGBA mode, respectively. You also must choose among the 16 logical operations with **glLogicOp()**, or you'll just get the effect of the default value, GL_COPY. (For backward compatibility with OpenGL Version 1.0, **glEnable**(GL_LOGIC_OP) also enables logical operation in color-index mode.)

---

void **glLogicOp**(GLenum *opcode*);

Selects the logical operation to be performed, given an incoming (source) fragment and the pixel currently stored in the color buffer (destination). Table 10-4 shows the possible values for *opcode* and their meaning (*s* represents source and *d* destination). The default value is GL_COPY.

Parameter	Operation	Parameter	Operation
GL_CLEAR	0	GL_AND	$s \wedge d$
GL_COPY	s	GL_OR	$s \vee d$
GL_NOOP	d	GL_NAND	$\neg(s \wedge d)$
GL_SET	1	GL_NOR	$\neg(s \vee d)$
GL_COPY_INVERTED	$\neg s$	GL_XOR	$s \ XOR \ d$
GL_INVERT	$\neg d$	GL_EQUIV	$\neg(s \ XOR \ d)$
GL_AND_REVERSE	$s \wedge \neg d$	GL_AND_INVERTED	$\neg s \wedge d$
GL_OR_REVERSE	$s \vee \neg d$	GL_OR_INVERTED	$\neg s \vee d$

Table 10-4   Sixteen Logical Operations

The Accumulation Buffer

Note: The accumulation buffer was removed through deprecation from OpenGL Version 3.1. Some of the techniques described in this chapter in prior editions—full-scene antialiasing, principally—have been replaced by other techniques (see "Alpha and Multisampling Coverage" on page 279). The remaining techniques are easy to implement using floating-point pixel formats in the framebuffer—a feature added in OpenGL Version 3.0. The concepts of these techniques are similar to those mentioned here.

Advanced

The accumulation buffer can be used for such things as scene antialiasing, motion blur, simulating photographic depth of field, and calculating the soft shadows that result from multiple light sources. Other techniques are possible, especially in combination with some of the other buffers. (See *The Accumulation Buffer: Hardware Support for High-Quality Rendering* by Paul Haeberli and Kurt Akeley [SIGGRAPH 1990 Proceedings, pp. 309–318] for more information about uses for the accumulation buffer.)

OpenGL graphics operations don't write directly into the accumulation buffer. Typically, a series of images is generated in one of the standard color buffers, and these images are accumulated, one at a time, into the accumulation buffer. When the accumulation is finished, the result is copied back into a color buffer for viewing. To reduce rounding errors, the accumulation buffer may have higher precision (more bits per color) than the standard color buffers. Rendering a scene several times obviously takes longer than rendering it once, but the result is higher quality. You can decide what trade-off between quality and rendering time is appropriate for your application.

You can use the accumulation buffer the same way a photographer can use film for multiple exposures. A photographer typically creates a multiple exposure by taking several pictures of the same scene without advancing the film. If anything in the scene moves, that object appears blurred. Not surprisingly, a computer can do more with an image than a photographer can do with a camera. For example, a computer has exquisite control over the viewpoint, but a photographer can't shake a camera a predictable and controlled amount. (See "Clearing Buffers" on page 495 for information about how to clear the accumulation buffer; use **glAccum()** to control it.)

---

void **glAccum**(GLenum *op*, GLfloat *value*);

Compatibility Extension

glAccum and all accepted tokens

Controls the accumulation buffer. The *op* parameter selects the operation, and *value* is a number to be used in that operation. The possible operations are GL_ACCUM, GL_LOAD, GL_RETURN, GL_ADD, and GL_MULT:

- GL_ACCUM reads each pixel from the buffer currently selected for reading with **glReadBuffer()**, multiplies the R, G, B, and alpha values by *value*, and adds the resulting values to the accumulation buffer.

- GL_LOAD is the same as GL_ACCUM, except that the values replace those in the accumulation buffer, rather than being added to them.

- GL_RETURN takes values from the accumulation buffer, multiplies them by *value*, and places the results in the color buffer(s) enabled for writing.

- GL_ADD and GL_MULT simply add and multiply, respectively, the value of each pixel in the accumulation buffer to or by *value* and then return it to the accumulation buffer. For GL_MULT, *value* is clamped to be in the range [–1.0, 1.0]. For GL_ADD, no clamping occurs.

Motion Blur

Similar methods can be used to simulate motion blur, as shown in Plate 7 and Figure 10-2. Suppose your scene has some stationary and some moving objects in it, and you want to make a motion-blurred image extending over a small interval of time. Set up the accumulation buffer in the same way, but instead of jittering the images spatially, jitter them temporally. The entire scene can be made successively dimmer by calling

```
glAccum(GL_MULT, decayFactor);
```

as the scene is drawn into the accumulation buffer, where *decayFactor* is a number from 0.0 to 1.0. Smaller numbers for *decayFactor* cause the object to appear to be moving faster. You can transfer the completed scene, with the object's current position and a "vapor trail" of previous positions, from the accumulation buffer to the standard color buffer with

```
glAccum(GL_RETURN, 1.0);
```

The image looks correct even if the items move at different speeds or if some of them are accelerated. As before, the more jitter points (temporal, in this case) you use, the better the final image, at least up to the point where you begin to lose resolution because of the finite precision in the accumulation buffer. You can combine motion blur with antialiasing by jittering in both the spatial and temporal domains, but you pay for higher quality with longer rendering times.

Depth of Field

A photograph made with a camera is in perfect focus only for items lying in a single plane a certain distance from the film. The farther an item is from

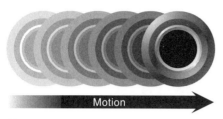

Figure 10-2   Motion-Blurred Object

this plane, the more out of focus it is. The *depth of field* for a camera is a region about the plane of perfect focus where items are out of focus by a small enough amount.

Under normal conditions, everything you draw with OpenGL is in focus (unless your monitor is bad; in which case, everything is out of focus). The accumulation buffer can be used to approximate what you would see in a photograph, where items are increasingly blurred as their distance from the plane of perfect focus increases. It isn't an exact simulation of the effects produced in a camera, but the result looks similar to what a camera would produce.

To achieve this result, draw the scene repeatedly using calls with different argument values to **glFrustum**(). Choose the arguments so that the position of the viewpoint varies slightly around its true position and so that each frustum shares a common rectangle that lies in the plane of perfect focus, as shown in Figure 10-3. The results of all the renderings should be averaged in the usual way using the accumulation buffer.

Plate 10 shows an image of five teapots drawn using the depth-of-field effect. The gold teapot (second from the left) is in focus, and the other teapots get progressively blurrier, depending on their distance from the focal plane (gold teapot). The code used to draw this image is shown in Example 10-5 (which assumes that **accPerspective**() and **accFrustum**() are defined as described in Example 10-5). The scene is drawn eight times, each with a slightly jittered viewing volume, by calling **accPerspective**(). As you recall, with scene antialiasing, the fifth and sixth parameters jitter the viewing volumes in the x- and y-directions. For the depth-of-field effect, however, you want to jitter the volume while holding it stationary at the focal plane. The focal plane is the depth value defined by the ninth (last) parameter to **accPerspective**(), which is $z = 5.0$ in this example. The amount of blur is determined by multiplying the x and y jitter values (seventh and eighth parameters of **accPerspective**()) by a constant. Determining the constant is not a science; experiment with values until the depth of field is as

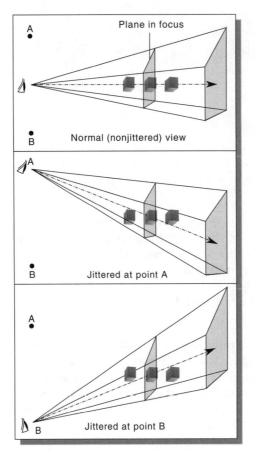

Figure 10-3 Jittered Viewing Volume for Depth-of-Field Effects

pronounced as you want. (Note that in Example 10-5, the fifth and sixth
parameters to **accPerspective**() are set to 0.0, so scene antialiasing is
turned off.)

Example 10-5 Depth-of-Field Effect: dof.c

```
void init(void)
{
    GLfloat ambient[] = { 0.0, 0.0, 0.0, 1.0 };
    GLfloat diffuse[] = { 1.0, 1.0, 1.0, 1.0 };
    GLfloat specular[] = { 1.0, 1.0, 1.0, 1.0 };
    GLfloat position[] = { 0.0, 3.0, 3.0, 0.0 };
```

```
    GLfloat lmodel_ambient[] = { 0.2, 0.2, 0.2, 1.0 };
    GLfloat local_view[] = { 0.0 };

    glLightfv(GL_LIGHT0, GL_AMBIENT, ambient);
    glLightfv(GL_LIGHT0, GL_DIFFUSE, diffuse);
    glLightfv(GL_LIGHT0, GL_POSITION, position);

    glLightModelfv(GL_LIGHT_MODEL_AMBIENT, lmodel_ambient);
    glLightModelfv(GL_LIGHT_MODEL_LOCAL_VIEWER, local_view);

    glFrontFace(GL_CW);
    glEnable(GL_LIGHTING);
    glEnable(GL_LIGHT0);
    glEnable(GL_AUTO_NORMAL);
    glEnable(GL_NORMALIZE);
    glEnable(GL_DEPTH_TEST);

    glClearColor(0.0, 0.0, 0.0, 0.0);
    glClearAccum(0.0, 0.0, 0.0, 0.0);
/*  make teapot display list */
    teapotList = glGenLists(1);
    glNewList(teapotList, GL_COMPILE);
    glutSolidTeapot(0.5);
    glEndList();
}

void renderTeapot(GLfloat x, GLfloat y, GLfloat z,
    GLfloat ambr, GLfloat ambg, GLfloat ambb,
    GLfloat difr, GLfloat difg, GLfloat difb,
    GLfloat specr, GLfloat specg, GLfloat specb, GLfloat shine)
{
    GLfloat mat[4];

    glPushMatrix();
    glTranslatef(x, y, z);
    mat[0] = ambr; mat[1] = ambg; mat[2] = ambb; mat[3] = 1.0;
    glMaterialfv(GL_FRONT, GL_AMBIENT, mat);
    mat[0] = difr; mat[1] = difg; mat[2] = difb;
    glMaterialfv(GL_FRONT, GL_DIFFUSE, mat);
    mat[0] = specr; mat[1] = specg; mat[2] = specb;
    glMaterialfv(GL_FRONT, GL_SPECULAR, mat);
    glMaterialf(GL_FRONT, GL_SHININESS, shine*128.0);
    glCallList(teapotList);
    glPopMatrix();
}
```

```
void display(void)
{
    int jitter;
    GLint viewport[4];

    glGetIntegerv(GL_VIEWPORT, viewport);
    glClear(GL_ACCUM_BUFFER_BIT);

    for (jitter = 0; jitter < 8; jitter++) {
        glClear(GL_COLOR_BUFFER_BIT | GL_DEPTH_BUFFER_BIT);
        accPerspective(45.0,
            (GLdouble) viewport[2]/(GLdouble) viewport[3],
            1.0, 15.0, 0.0, 0.0,
            0.33*j8[jitter].x, 0.33*j8[jitter].y, 5.0);

/*        ruby, gold, silver, emerald, and cyan teapots    */
        renderTeapot(-1.1, -0.5, -4.5, 0.1745, 0.01175,
                        0.01175, 0.61424, 0.04136, 0.04136,
                        0.727811, 0.626959, 0.626959, 0.6);
        renderTeapot(-0.5, -0.5, -5.0, 0.24725, 0.1995,
                        0.0745, 0.75164, 0.60648, 0.22648,
                        0.628281, 0.555802, 0.366065, 0.4);
        renderTeapot(0.2, -0.5, -5.5, 0.19225, 0.19225,
                        0.19225, 0.50754, 0.50754, 0.50754,
                        0.508273, 0.508273, 0.508273, 0.4);
        renderTeapot(1.0, -0.5, -6.0, 0.0215, 0.1745, 0.0215,
                        0.07568, 0.61424, 0.07568, 0.633,
                        0.727811, 0.633, 0.6);
        renderTeapot(1.8, -0.5, -6.5, 0.0, 0.1, 0.06, 0.0,
                        0.50980392, 0.50980392, 0.50196078,
                        0.50196078, 0.50196078, .25);
        glAccum(GL_ACCUM, 0.125);
    }
    glAccum(GL_RETURN, 1.0);
    glFlush();
}

void reshape(int w, int h)
{
    glViewport(0, 0, (GLsizei) w, (GLsizei) h);
}

/*  Main Loop
 *  Be certain you request an accumulation buffer.
 */
int main(int argc, char** argv)
{
```

```
glutInit(&argc, argv);
glutInitDisplayMode(GLUT_SINGLE | GLUT_RGB |
                    GLUT_ACCUM | GLUT_DEPTH);
glutInitWindowSize(400, 400);
glutInitWindowPosition(100, 100);
glutCreateWindow(argv[0]);
init();
glutReshapeFunc(reshape);
glutDisplayFunc(display);
glutMainLoop();
return 0;
}
```

Soft Shadows

To accumulate soft shadows resulting from multiple light sources, render the shadows with one light turned on at a time, and accumulate them together. This can be combined with spatial jittering to antialias the scene at the same time. (See "Shadows" on page 658 for more information about drawing shadows.)

Jittering

If you need to take 9 or 16 samples to antialias an image, you might think that the best choice of points is an equally spaced grid across the pixel. Surprisingly, this is not necessarily true. In fact, sometimes it's a good idea to take points that lie in adjacent pixels. You might want a uniform distribution or a normalized distribution, clustering toward the center of the pixel. In addition, Table 10-5 shows a few sets of reasonable jittering values to be used for some selected sample counts. Most of the examples in this table are uniformly distributed in the pixel, and all lie within the pixel.

Count	Values
2	{0.25, 0.75}, {0.75, 0.25}
3	{0.5033922635, 0.8317967229}, {0.7806016275, 0.2504380877}, {0.2261828938, 0.4131553612}
4	{0.375, 0.25}, {0.125, 0.75}, {0.875, 0.25}, {0.625, 0.75}

Table 10-5   Sample Jittering Values

Count	Values
5	{0.5, 0.5}, {0.3, 0.1}, {0.7, 0.9}, {0.9, 0.3}, {0.1, 0.7}
6	{0.4646464646, 0.4646464646}, {0.1313131313, 0.7979797979}, {0.5353535353, 0.8686868686}, {0.8686868686, 0.5353535353}, {0.7979797979, 0.1313131313}, {0.2020202020, 0.2020202020}
8	{0.5625, 0.4375}, {0.0625, 0.9375}, {0.3125, 0.6875}, {0.6875, 0.8125}, {0.8125, 0.1875}, {0.9375, 0.5625}, {0.4375, 0.0625}, {0.1875, 0.3125}
9	{0.5, 0.5}, {0.1666666666, 0.9444444444}, {0.5, 0.1666666666}, {0.5, 0.8333333333}, {0.1666666666, 0.2777777777}, {0.8333333333, 0.3888888888}, {0.1666666666, 0.6111111111}, {0.8333333333, 0.7222222222}, {0.8333333333, 0.0555555555}
12	{0.4166666666, 0.625}, {0.9166666666, 0.875}, {0.25, 0.375}, {0.4166666666, 0.125}, {0.75, 0.125}, {0.0833333333, 0.125}, {0.75, 0.625}, {0.25, 0.875}, {0.5833333333, 0.375}, {0.9166666666, 0.375}, {0.0833333333, 0.625}, {0.583333333, 0.875}
16	{0.375, 0.4375}, {0.625, 0.0625}, {0.875, 0.1875}, {0.125, 0.0625}, {0.375, 0.6875}, {0.875, 0.4375}, {0.625, 0.5625}, {0.375, 0.9375}, {0.625, 0.3125}, {0.125, 0.5625}, {0.125, 0.8125}, {0.375, 0.1875}, {0.875, 0.9375}, {0.875, 0.6875}, {0.125, 0.3125}, {0.625, 0.8125}

Table 10-5   **(continued)**   Sample Jittering Values

Framebuffer Objects

Advanced

Advanced

Up to this point, all of our discussion regarding buffers has focused on the buffers provided by the windowing system, as you requested when you called **glutCreateWindow()** (and configured by your call to **glutInitDisplayMode()**). Although you can quite successfully use any technique with just those buffers, quite often various operations require moving data between buffers superfluously. This is where framebuffer objects enter the picture (as part of OpenGL Version 3.0). Using framebuffer objects, you can create our own framebuffers and use their attached *renderbuffers* to minimize data copies and optimize performance.

Framebuffer objects are quite useful for performing off-screen-rendering, updating texture maps, and engaging in *buffer ping-ponging* (a data-transfer techniques used in GPGPU).

The framebuffer that is provided by the windowing system is the only framebuffer that is available to the display system of your graphics server—that is, it is the only one you can see on your screen. It also places restrictions on the use of the buffers that were created when your window opened. By comparison, the framebuffers that your application creates cannot be displayed on your monitor; they support only *off-screen rendering*.

Another difference between window-system-provided framebuffers and framebuffers you create is that those managed by the window system allocate their buffers—color, depth, stencil, and accumulation—when your window is created. When you create an application-managed framebuffer object, you need to create additional *renderbuffers* that you associate with the framebuffer objects you created. The buffers with the window-system-provided buffers can never be associated with an application-created framebuffer object, and vice versa.

To allocate an application-generated framebuffer object name, you need to call **glGenFramebuffers**() which will allocate an unused identifier for the framebuffer object. As compared to some other objects within OpenGL (e.g., texture objects and display lists), you always need to use an name returned from **glGenFramebuffers**().

---

void **glGenFramebuffers**(GLsize *n*, GLuint **ids*);

Allocate *n* unused framebuffer object names, and return those names in *ids*.

Allocating a framebuffer object name doesn't actually create the framebuffer object or allocate any storage for it. Those tasks are handled through a call to **glBindFramebuffer**(). **glBindFramebuffer**() operates in a similar manner to many of the other **glBind***() routines you've seen in OpenGL. The first time it is called for a particular framebuffer, it causes storage for the object to be allocated and initialized. Any subsequent calls will bind the provided framebuffer object name as the active one.

---

void **glBindFramebuffer**(GLenum *target*, GLuint *framebuffer*);

Specifies either a framebuffer for either reading or writing. When *target* is GL_DRAW_FRAMEBUFFER, *framebuffer* specifies the destination framebuffer for rendering. Similarly, when *target* is set to GL_READ_FRAMEBUFFER, *framebuffer* specifies the source of read operations. Passing GL_FRAMEBUFFER for *target* sets both the read and write framebuffer bindings to *framebuffer*.

framebuffer must either be zero, which binds *target* to the default; a window-system provided framebuffer; or a framebuffer object generated by a call to **glGenFramebuffers**().

A GL_INVALID_OPERATION error is generated if *framebuffer* is neither zero nor a valid framebuffer object previously generated by calling **glGenFramebuffers**(), but not deleted by calling **glDeleteFramebuffers**().

As with all of the other objects you have encountered in OpenGL, you can release an application-allocated framebuffer by calling **glDeleteFramebuffers**(). That function will mark the framebuffer object's name as unallocated and release any resources associated with the framebuffer object.

---

void **glDeleteFramebuffers**(GLsize *n*, const GLuint **ids*);

Deallocates the *n* framebuffer objects associated with the names provided in *ids*. If a framebuffer object is currently bound (i.e., its name was passed to the most recent call to **glBindFramebuffer**()), and is deleted, the framebuffer target is immediately bound to *id* zero (the window-system provided framebuffer), and the framebuffer object is released.

No errors are generated by **glDeleteFramebuffers**(). Unused names or zero are simply ignored.

For completeness, you can determine whether a particular unsigned integer is an application-allocated framebuffer object by calling **glIsFramebuffer**():.

GLboolean **glIsFramebuffer**(GLuint *framebuffer*);

Returns GL_TRUE if *framebuffer* is the name of a framebuffer returned from **glGenFramebuffers**(). Returns GL_FALSE if *framebuffer* is zero (the window-system default framebuffer) or a value that's either unallocated or been deleted by a call to **glDeleteFramebuffers**().

Once a framebuffer object is created, you still can't do much with it. You need to provide a place for drawing to go and reading to come from; those places are called *framebuffer attachments*. We'll discuss those in more detail after we examine renderbuffers, which are one type of buffer you can attach to a framebuffer object.

Renderbuffers

Renderbuffers are effectively memory managed by OpenGL that contains formatted image data. The data that a renderbuffer holds takes meaning once it is attached to a framebuffer object, assuming that the format of the image buffer matches what OpenGL is expecting to render into (e.g., you can't render colors into the depth buffer).

As with many other buffers in OpenGL, the process of allocating and deleting buffers is similar to what you've seen before. To create a new renderbuffer, you would call **glGenRenderbuffers**().

---
void **glGenRenderbuffers**(GLsizei *n*, GLuint **ids*);

Allocate *n* unused renderbuffer object names, and return those names in *ids*. Names are unused until bound with a call to **glBindRenderbuffer**().

Likewise, a call to **glDeleteRenderbuffers**() will release the storage associated with a renderbuffer.

---
void **glDeleteRenderbuffers**(GLsizei *n*, const GLuint **ids*);

Deallocates the *n* renderbuffer objects associated with the names provided in *ids*. If one of the renderbuffers is currently bound and passed to **glDeleteRenderbuffers**(), a binding of zero replaces the binding at the current framebuffer attachment point, in addition to the renderbuffer being released.

No errors are generated by **glDeleteRenderbuffers**(). Unused names or zero are simply ignored.

Likewise, you can determine whether a name represents a valid renderbuffer by calling **glIsRenderbuffer()**.

---

void **glIsRenderbuffer**(GLuint *renderbuffer*);

Returns GL_TRUE if *renderbuffer* is the name of a renderbuffer returned from **glGenRenderbuffers()**. Returns GL_FALSE if *renderbuffer* is zero (the window-system default framebuffer) or a value that's either unallocated or been deleted by a call to **glDeleteRenderbuffers()**.

Similar to the process of binding a framebuffer object so that you can modify its state, you call **glBindRenderbuffer()** to affect a renderbuffer's creation and to modify the state associated with it, which includes the format of the image data that it contains.

---

void **glBindRenderbuffer**(GLenum *target*, GLuint *renderbuffer*);

Creates a renderbuffer and associates it with the name *renderbuffer*. *target* must be GL_RENDERBUFFER. *renderbuffer* must either be zero, which removes any renderbuffer binding, or a name that was generated by a call to **glGenRenderbuffers()**; otherwise, a GL_INVALID_OPERATION error will be generated.

Creating Renderbuffer Storage

When you first call **glBindRenderbuffer()** with an unused renderbuffer name, the OpenGL server creates a renderbuffer with all its state information set to the default values. In this configuration, no storage has been allocated to store image data. Before you can attach a renderbuffer to a framebuffer and render into it, you need to allocate storage and specify its image format. This is done by calling either **glRenderbufferStorage()** or **glRenderbufferStorageMultisample()**.

---

void **glRenderbufferStorage**(GLenum *target*, GLenum *internalformat*,
        GLsizei *width*, GLsizei *height*);
void **glRenderbufferStorageMultisample**(GLenum *target*,
        GLsizei *samples*, GLenum *internalformat*, GLsizei *width*,
        GLsizei *height*);

Allocates storage for image data for the bound renderbuffer. *target* must be GL_RENDERBUFFER. For a color-renderable buffer, *internalformat* must be one of: GL_RED, GL_R8, GL_R16, GL_RG, GL_RG8, GL_RG16, GL_RGB, GL_R3_G3_B2, GL_RGB4, GL_RGB5, GL_RGB8, GL_RGB10, GL_RGB12, GL_RGB16, GL_RGBA, GL_RGBA2, GL_RGBA4, GL_RGB5_A1, GL_RGBA8, GL_RGB10_A2, GL_RGBA12, GL_RGBA16, GL_SRGB, GL_SRGB8, GL_SRGB_ALPHA, GL_SRGB8_ALPHA8,GL_R16F, GL_R32F, GL_RG16F, GL_RG32F, GL_RGB16F, GL_RGB32F, GL_RGBA16F, GL_RGBA32F, GL_R11F_G11F_B10F, GL_RGB9_E5, GL_R8I, GL_R8UI, GL_R16I, GL_R16UI, GL_R32I, GL_R32UI, GL_RG8I, GL_RG8UI, GL_RG16I, GL_RG16UI, GL_RG32I, GL_RG32UI, GL_RGB8I, GL_RGB8UI, GL_RGB16I, GL_RGB16UI, GL_RGB32I, GL_RGB32UI, GL_RGBA8I, GL_RGBA8UI, GL_RGBA16I, GL_RGBA16UI, GL_RGBA32I. OpenGL version 3.1 adds the additional following formats: GL_R8_SNORM, GL_R16_SNORM, GL_RG8_SNORM, GL_RG16_SNORM, GL_RGB8_SNORM, GL_RGB16_SNORM, GL_RGBA8_SNORM, GL_RGBA16_SNORM.

To use a renderbuffer as a depth buffer, it must be depth-renderable, which is specified by setting *internalformat* to either GL_DEPTH_COMPONENT, GL_DEPTH_COMPONENT16, GL_DEPTH_COMPONENT32, GL_DEPTH_COMPONENT32, or GL_DEPTH_COMPONENT32F.

For use exclusively as a stencil buffer, *internalformat* should be specified as either GL_STENCIL_INDEX, GL_STENCIL_INDEX1, GL_STENCIL_INDEX4, GL_STENCIL_INDEX8, or GL_STENCIL_INDEX16.

For packed depth-stencil storage, *internalformat* must be GL_DEPTH_STENCIL, which allows the renderbuffer to be attached as the depth buffer, stencil buffer, or at the combined depth-stencil attachment point.

width and *height* specify the size of the renderbuffer in pixels, and *samples* specifies the number of multisample samples per pixel. Setting *samples* to zero in a call to **glRenderbufferStorageMultisample**() is identical to calling **glRenderbufferStorage**().

A GL_INVALID_VALUE is generated if *width* or *height* is greater than the value returned when querying GL_MAX_RENDERBUFFER_SIZE, or if *samples* is greater than the value returned when querying GL_MAX_SAMPLES. A GL_INVALID_OPERATION is generated if *internalformat* is a signed- or unsigned-integer format (e.g., a format containing a "I", or "UI" in its token), and *samples* is not zero, and the implementation doesn't support multisampled integer buffers. Finally, if the renderbuffer size and format combined exceed the available memory able to be allocated, then a GL_OUT_OF_MEMORY error is generated.

Example 10-6   Creating an RGBA Color Renderbuffer: fbo.c

```
glGenRenderbuffers( 1, &color );
glBindRenderbuffer( GL_RENDERBUFFER, color );
glRenderbufferStorage( GL_RENDERBUFFER, GL_RGBA, 256, 256 );
```

Once you have created storage for your renderbuffer, you need to attach it to a framebuffer object before you can render into it.

Framebuffer Attachments

When you render, you can send the results of that rendering to a number of places:

* The color buffer to create an image, or even multiple color buffers if you're using multiple render targets (see "Special Output Values" in Chapter 15)

* The depth buffer to store occlusion information

* The stencil buffer for storing per-pixel masks to control rendering

Each of those buffers represents a framebuffer attachment, to which you can attach suitable image buffers that you later render into, or read from. The possible framebuffer attachment points are listed in Table 10-6.

Attachment Name	Description
GL_COLOR_ATTACHMENTi	The ith color buffer. i can range from zero (the default color buffer) to GL_MAX_COLOR_ATTACHMENTS–1
GL_DEPTH_ATTACHMENT	The depth buffer
GL_STENCIL_ATTACHMENT	The stencil buffer
GL_DEPTH_STENCIL_ATTACHMENT	A special attachment for packed depth-stencil buffers (which require the renderbuffer to have been allocated as a GL_DEPTH_STENCIL pixel format)

Table 10-6   Framebuffer Attachments

Currently, there are two types of rendering surfaces you can associate with one of those attachments: renderbuffers and a level of a texture image.

We'll first discuss attaching a renderbuffer to a framebuffer object, which is done by calling **glFramebufferRenderbuffer()**.

---

void **glFramebufferRenderbuffer**(GLenum *target*, GLenum *attachment*,
 GLenum *renderbuffertarget*, GLuint *renderbuffer*);

Attaches *renderbuffer* to *attachment* of the currently bound framebuffer object. *target* must either be GL_READ_FRAMEBUFFER, GL_DRAW_FRAMEBUFFER, or GL_FRAMEBUFFER (which is equivalent to GL_DRAW_FRAMEBUFFER).

attachment is one of GL_COLOR_ATTACHMENT*i*, GL_DEPTH_ATTACHMENT, GL_STENCIL_ATTACHMENT, or GL_DEPTH_STENCIL_ATTACHMENT.

renderbuffertarget must be GL_RENDERBUFFER, and *renderbuffer* must either be zero, which removes any renderbuffer attachment at *attachment*, or a renderbuffer name returned from **glGenRenderbuffers()**, or a GL_INVALID_OPERATION error is generated.

In Example 10-7, we create and attach two renderbuffers: one for color, and the other for depth. We then proceed to render, and finally copy the results back to the window-system-provided framebuffer to display the results. You might use this technique to generate frames for a movie rendering off-screen, where you don't have to worry about the visible framebuffer being corrupted by overlapping windows or someone resizing the window and interrupting rendering.

One important point to remember is that you might need to reset the viewport for each framebuffer before rendering, particularly if the size of your application-defined framebuffers differs from the window-system provided framebuffer.

Example 10-7   Attaching a Renderbuffer for Rendering: fbo.c

```
enum { Color, Depth, NumRenderbuffers };
GLuint framebuffer, renderbuffer[NumRenderbuffers]

void
init()
{
    glGenRenderbuffers( NumRenderbuffers, renderbuffer );
    glBindRenderbuffer( GL_RENDERBUFFER, renderbuffer[Color] );
    glRenderbufferStorage( GL_RENDERBUFFER, GL_RGBA, 256, 256 );
```

```
    glBindRenderbuffer( GL_RENDERBUFFER, renderbuffer[Depth] );
    glRenderbufferStorage( GL_RENDERBUFFER, GL_DEPTH_COMPONENT24,
        256, 256 );

    glGenFramebuffers( 1, &framebuffer );
    glBindFramebuffer( GL_DRAW_FRAMEBUFFER, framebuffer );
    glFramebufferRenderbuffer( GL_DRAW_FRAMEBUFFER,
        GL_COLOR_ATTACHMENT0, GL_RENDERBUFFER,
        renderbuffer[Color] );
    glFramebufferRenderbuffer( GL_DRAW_FRAMEBUFFER,
        GL_DEPTH_ATTACHMENT, GL_RENDERBUFFER,
        renderbuffer[Depth] );

    glEnable( GL_DEPTH_TEST );
}


void
display()
{
    /* Prepare to render into the renderbuffer */
    glBindFramebuffer( GL_DRAW_FRAMEBUFFER, framebuffer );
    glViewport( 0, 0, 256, 256 );

    /* Render into renderbuffer */
    glClearColor( 1.0, 0.0, 0.0, 1.0 );
    glClear( GL_COLOR_BUFFER_BIT | GL_DEPTH_BUFFER_BIT );
    /* Do other rendering */

    /* Set up to read from the renderbuffer and draw to
    ** window-system framebuffer */
    glBindFramebuffer( GL_READ_FRAMEBUFFER, framebuffer );
    glBindFramebuffer( GL_DRAW_FRAMEBUFFER, 0 );
    glViewport(0, 0, windowWidth, windowHeight);
    glClearColor( 0.0, 0.0, 1.0, 1.0 );
    glClear( GL_COLOR_BUFFER_BIT | GL_DEPTH_BUFFER_BIT );

    /* Do the copy */
    glBlitFramebuffer( 0, 0, 255, 255, 0, 0, 255, 255,
        GL_COLOR_BUFFER_BIT, GL_NEAREST );

    glutSwapBuffers();
}
```

Another very common use for framebuffer objects is to update textures dynamically. You might do this to indicate changes in a surface's appearance (such as bullet holes in a wall in a game) or to update values in a lookup table if you're doing GPGPU-like computations. In these cases, you bind a level of a texture map as the framebuffer attachment, as compared to a renderbuffer. After rendering, the texture map can be detached from the framebuffer so that it can be used in subsequent rendering.

Note: Nothing prevents you from reading from a texture that is simultaneously bound as a framebuffer attachment for writing. In this scenario, called a *framebuffer rendering loop*, the results are undefined for both operations. That is, the values returned from sampling the bound texture map, as well as the values written into the texture level while bound, will likely be incorrect.

---

void **glFramebufferTexture1D**(GLenum *target*, GLenum *attachment*,
        GLenum *texturetarget*, GLuint *texture*, GLint *level*);
void **glFramebufferTexture2D**(GLenum *target*, GLenum *attachment*,
        GLenum *texturetarget*, GLuint *texture*, GLint *level*);
void **glFramebufferTexture3D**(GLenum *target*, GLenum *attachment*,
        GLenum *texturetarget*, GLuint *texture*, GLint *level*,
        GLint *layer*);

Attaches a level of a texture objects as a rendering attachment to a framebuffer object. *target* must be either GL_READ_FRAMEBUFFER, GL_DRAW_FRAMEBUFFER, or GL_FRAMEBUFFER (which is equivalent to GL_DRAW_FRAMEBUFFER). *attachment* must be one of the framebuffer attachment points: GL_COLOR_ATTACHMENT*i*, GL_DEPTH_ATTACHMENT, GL_STENCIL_ATTACHMENT, or GL_DEPTH_STENCIL_ATTACHMENT (in which case, the internal format of the texture must be GL_DEPTH_STENCIL).

For **glFramebufferTexture1D**(), *texturetarget* must be GL_TEXTURE_1D, if *texture* is not zero. For **glFramebufferTexture2D**(), *texturetarget* must be GL_TEXTURE_2D, GL_TEXTURE_RECTANGLE, GL_TEXTURE_CUBE_MAP_POSITIVE_X, GL_TEXTURE_CUBE_MAP_POSITIVE_Y, GL_TEXTURE_CUBE_MAP_POSITIVE_Z, GL_TEXTURE_CUBE_MAP_NEGATIVE_X, GL_TEXTURE_CUBE_MAP_NEGATIVE_Y, GL_TEXTURE_CUBE_MAP_NEGATIVE_Z, and for **glFramebufferTexture3D**() *texturetarget* must be GL_TEXTURE_3D.

If *texture* is zero, indicating that any texture bound to *attachment* is released, and no subsequent bind to *attachment* is made. In this case, *texturetarget*, *level*, and *layer* are ignored.

If *texture* is not zero, it must be the name of an existing texture object (created with **glGenTextures()**), with *texturetarget* matching the texture type (e.g., GL_TEXTURE_1D, etc.) associated with the texture object, or if *texture* is a cube map, then *texturetarget* must be one of the cube map face targets: GL_TEXTURE_CUBE_MAP_POSITIVE_X, GL_TEXTURE_CUBE_MAP_POSITIVE_Y, GL_TEXTURE_CUBE_MAP_POSITIVE_Z, GL_TEXTURE_CUBE_MAP_NEGATIVE_X, GL_TEXTURE_CUBE_MAP_NEGATIVE_Y, GL_TEXTURE_CUBE_MAP_NEGATIVE_Z, otherwise, a GL_INVALID_OPERATION error is generated.

level represents the mipmap level of the associated texture image to be attached as a render target, and for three-dimensional textures, *layer* represents the layer of the texture to be used. If *texturetarget* is GL_TEXTURE_RECTANGLE (from OpenGL version 3.1), then level must be zero.

Similar to the previous example, Example 10-8 demonstrates the process of dynamically updating a texture, using the texture after its update is completed, and then rendering with it later.

Example 10-8   Attaching a Texture Level as a Framebuffer Attachment: fbotexture.c

```
GLuint framebuffer, texture;

void
init()
{
    GLuint renderbuffer;

    /* Create an empty texture */
    glGenTextures( 1, &texture );
    glBindTexture( GL_TEXTURE_2D, texture );
    glTexImage2D( GL_TEXTURE_2D, 0, GL_RGBA8, TexWidth,
        TexHeight, 0, GL_RGBA, GL_UNSIGNED_BYTE, NULL );

    /* Create a depth buffer for our framebuffer */
    glGenRenderbuffers( 1, &renderbuffer );
    glBindRenderbuffer( GL_RENDERBUFFER, renderbuffer );
```

```
    glRenderbufferStorage( GL_RENDERBUFFER, GL_DEPTH_COMPONENT24,
        TexWidth, TexHeight );

    /* Attach the texture and depth buffer to the framebuffer */
    glGenFramebuffers( 1, &framebuffer );
    glBindFramebuffer( GL_DRAW_FRAMEBUFFER, framebuffer );
    glFramebufferTexture2D( GL_DRAW_FRAMEBUFFER,
        GL_COLOR_ATTACHMENT0, GL_TEXTURE_2D, texture, 0 );
    glFramebufferRenderbuffer( GL_DRAW_FRAMEBUFFER,
        GL_DEPTH_ATTACHMENT, GL_RENDERBUFFER, renderbuffer );

    glEnable( GL_DEPTH_TEST );
}

void
display()
{
    /* Render into the renderbuffer */
    glBindFramebuffer( GL_DRAW_FRAMEBUFFER, framebuffer );
    glViewport( 0, 0, TexWidth, TexHeight );
    glClearColor( 1.0, 0.0, 1.0, 1.0 );
    glClear( GL_COLOR_BUFFER_BIT | GL_DEPTH_BUFFER_BIT );
    /* Do other rendering */

    /* Generate mipmaps of our texture */
    glGenerateMipmap( GL_TEXTURE_2D );

    /* Bind to the window-system framebuffer, unbinding from
    ** the texture, which we can use to texture other objects */
    glBindFramebuffer( GL_FRAMEBUFFER, 0 );
    glViewport( 0, 0, windowWidth, windowHeight );
    glClearColor( 0.0, 0.0, 1.0, 1.0 );
    glClear( GL_COLOR_BUFFER_BIT | GL_DEPTH_BUFFER_BIT );

    /* Render using the texture */
    glEnable( GL_TEXTURE_2D );
    ...

    glutSwapBuffers();
}
```

void **glFramebufferTextureLayer**(GLenum *target*, GLenum *attachment*, GLuint *texture*, GLint *level*, GLint *layer*);

Attaches a layer of a three-dimensional texture, or a one- or two-dimensional array texture as a framebuffer attachment, in a similar manner to **glFramebufferTexture3D**().

target must be one of GL_READ_FRAMEBUFFER, GL_DRAW_FRAMEBUFFER, or GL_FRAMEBUFFER (which is equivalent to GL_DRAW_FRAMEBUFFER). *attachment* must be one of GL_COLOR_ATTACHMENT*i*, GL_DEPTH_ATTACHMENT, GL_STENCIL_ATTACHMENT, or GL_DEPTH_STENCIL_ATTACHMENT.

texture must be either zero, indicating that the current binding for the attachment should be released, or a texture object name (as returned from **glGenTextures**()). *level* indicates the mipmap level of the texture object, and *layer* represents which layer of the texture (or array element) should be bound as an attachment.

Framebuffer Completeness

Given the myriad of combinations between texture and buffer formats, and between framebuffer attachments, various situations can arise that prevent the completion of rendering when you are using application-defined framebuffer objects. After modifying the attachments to a framebuffer object, it's best to check the framebuffer's status by calling **glCheckFramebufferStatus**().

GLenum **glCheckFramebufferStatus**(GLenum *target*);

Returns one of the framebuffer completeness status enums listed in Table 10-7. *target* must be one of GL_READ_FRAMEBUFFER, GL_DRAW_FRAMEBUFFER, or GL_FRAMEBUFFER (which is equivalent to GL_DRAW_FRAMEBUFFER).

If **glCheckFramebufferStatus**() generates an error, zero is returned.

The errors representing the various violations of framebuffer configurations are listed in Table 10-7.

Of the listed errors, GL_FRAMEBUFFER_UNSUPPORTED is very implementation dependent, and may be the most complicated to debug.

Framebuffer Completeness Status Enum	Description
GL_FRAMEBUFFER_COMPLETE	The framebuffer and its attachments match the rendering or reading state required.
GL_FRAMEBUFFER_UNDEFINED	The bound framebuffer is specified to be the default framebuffer (i.e., **glBindFramebuffer()** with zero specified as the framebuffer), and the default framebuffer doesn't exist.
GL_FRAMEBUFFER_ INCOMPLETE_ATTACHMENT	A necessary attachment to the bound framebuffer is uninitialized
GL_FRAMEBUFFER_ INCOMPLETE_MISSING_ ATTACHMENT	There are no images (e.g., texture layers or renderbuffers) attached to the framebuffer.
GL_FRAMEBUFFER_ INCOMPLETE_DRAW_BUFFER	Every drawing buffer (e.g., GL_DRAW_BUFFERi as specified by **glDrawBuffers()**) has an attachment.
GL_FRAMEBUFFER_ INCOMPLETE_READ_BUFFER	An attachment exists for the buffer specified for the buffer specified by **glReadBuffer()**.
GL_FRAMEBUFFER_ UNSUPPORTED	The combination of images attached to the framebuffer object is incompatible with the requirements of the OpenGL implementation.
GL_FRAMEBUFFER_ INCOMPLETE_MULTISAMPLE	The number of samples for all images across the framebuffer's attachments do not match.

Table 10-7   Errors returned by glCheckFramebufferStatus()

Copying Pixel Rectangles

While **glCopyPixels()** has been the default routine for replicating blocks of pixels since OpenGL Version 1.0, as OpenGL expanded its rendering facilities, a more substantial pixel-copying routine was required. **glBlitFramebuffer()**, described below, subsumes the operations of **glCopyPixels()** and **glPixelZoom()** in a single, enhanced call. **glBlitFramebuffer()** allows greater pixel filtering during the copy operation, much in the same manner as texture mapping (in fact, the same filtering operations, GL_NEAREST and GL_LINEAR are used during the copy). Additionally, this routine is aware of multisampled buffers, and supports copying between different framebuffers (as controlled by framebuffer objects).

void **glBlitFramebuffer**(GLint *srcX0*, GLint *srcY0*,
                     GLint *srcX1*, GLint *srcY1*, GLint *dstX0*, GLint *dstY0*,
                     GLint *dstX1*, GLint *dstY1*, GLbitfield *buffers*,
                     GLenum *filter*);

Copies a rectangle of pixel values from one region of the read framebuffer to another region of the draw framebuffer, potentially resizing, reversing, converting, and filtering the pixels in the process. *srcX0*, *srcY0*, *srcX1*, *srcY1* represent the source region where pixels are sourced from, and written to the rectangular region specified by *dstX0*, *dstY0*, *dstX1*, *dstY1*. *buffers* is the bitwise-or of GL_COLOR_BUFFER_BIT, GL_DEPTH_BUFFER_BIT, and GL_STENCIL_BUFFER_BIT, which represent the buffers in which the copy should occur. Finally, *filter* specifies the method of interpolation done if the two rectangular regions are different sizes, and must be one of GL_NEAREST or GL_LINEAR; no filtering is applied if the regions are the same size.

If there are multiple color draw buffers (See "Rendering to Multiple Output Buffers" on page 729), each buffer receives a copy of the source region.

If srcX1 < srcX0, or dstX1 < dstX0, the image is reversed in the horizontal direction. Likewise, if srcY1 < srcY0 or dstY1 < dstY0, the image is reverse in the vertical direction. However, If both the source and destination sizes are negative in the same direction, no reversal is done.

If the source and destination buffers are of different formats, conversion of the pixel values is done in most situations. However, if the read color buffer is a floating-point format, and any of the write color buffers are not, or vice verse; and if the read color buffer is a signed (unsigned) integer format and not all of the draw buffers are signed (unsigned) integer values, the call will generate a GL_INVALID_OPERATION, and no pixels will be copied.

Multisampled buffers also have an effect on the copying of pixels. If the source buffer is multisampled, and the destination is not, the samples are resolved to a single pixel value for the destination buffer. Conversely, if the source buffer is not multisampled, and the destination is, the source pixel's data is replicated for each sample. Finally, if both buffers are multisampled and the number of samples for each buffer is the same, the samples are copied without modification. However, if the buffers have a different number of samples, no pixels are copied, and a GL_INVALID_OPERATION error is generated.

A GL_INVALID_VALUE error is generated if *buffers* has other bits set than those permitted, or if *filter* is other than GL_LINEAR or GL_NEAREST.

Chapter 11

Tessellators and Quadrics

Chapter Objectives

After reading this chapter, you'll be able to do the following:

- Render concave filled polygons by first tessellating them into convex polygons, which can be rendered using standard OpenGL routines

- Use the OpenGL Utility Library to create quadrics objects to render and model the surfaces of spheres and cylinders, and to tessellate disks (circles) and partial disks (arcs)

Note: In OpenGL Version 3.1, some of the techniques and functions described in this chapter—particularly those relating to quadric objects—were likely affected by deprecation. While many of these features can be found in the GLU library, they rely on OpenGL functions that were removed.

The OpenGL Library (GL) is designed for low-level operations, both stream-lined and accessible to hardware acceleration. The OpenGL Utility Library (GLU) complements the OpenGL library, supporting higher-level operations. Some of the GLU operations are covered in other chapters. Mipmapping (**gluBuild*DMipmaps()**) and image scaling (**gluScaleImage()**) are discussed along with other facets of texture mapping in Chapter 9. Several matrix trans-formation GLU routines (**gluOrtho2D()**, **gluPerspective()**, **gluLookAt()**, **gluProject()**, **gluUnProject()**, and **gluUnProject4()**) are described in Chapter 3. The use of **gluPickMatrix()** is explained in Chapter 13. The GLU NURBS facilities, which are built atop OpenGL evaluators, are covered in Chapter 12. Only two GLU topics remain: polygon tessellators and quad-ric surfaces; these topics are discussed in this chapter.

To optimize performance, the basic OpenGL renders only convex polygons, but the GLU contains routines for tessellating concave polygons into con-vex ones, which the basic OpenGL can handle. Where the basic OpenGL operates on simple primitives, such as points, lines, and filled polygons, the GLU can create higher-level objects, such as the surfaces of spheres, cylin-ders, and cones.

This chapter has the following major sections.

- "Polygon Tessellation" explains how to tessellate concave polygons into easier-to-render convex polygons.

- "Quadrics: Rendering Spheres, Cylinders, and Disks" describes how to generate spheres, cylinders, circles and arcs, including data such as surface normals and texture coordinates.

Polygon Tessellation

As discussed in "Describing Points, Lines, and Polygons" in Chapter 2, OpenGL can directly display only simple convex polygons. A polygon is simple if the edges intersect only at vertices, there are no duplicate vertices, and exactly two edges meet at any vertex. If your application requires the display of concave polygons, polygons containing holes, or polygons with intersecting edges, these polygons must first be subdivided into simple convex polygons before they can be displayed. Such subdivision is called *tessellation*, and the GLU provides a collection of routines that perform tessellation. These routines take as input arbitrary contours, which describe hard-to-render polygons, and they return some combination of triangles, triangle meshes, triangle fans, and lines.

Figure 11-1 shows some contours of polygons that require tessellation: from left to right, a concave polygon, a polygon with a hole, and a self-intersecting polygon.

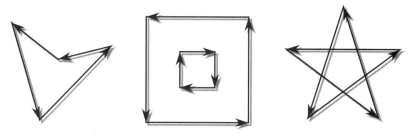

Figure 11-1   Contours That Require Tessellation

If you think a polygon may need tessellation, follow these typical steps:

1. Create a new tessellation object with **gluNewTess()**.

2. Use **gluTessCallback()** several times to register callback functions to perform operations during the tessellation. The trickiest case for a callback function is when the tessellation algorithm detects an intersection and must call the function registered for the GLU_TESS_COMBINE callback.

3. Specify tessellation properties by calling **gluTessProperty()**. The most important property is the winding rule, which determines the regions that should be filled and those that should remain unshaded.

4. Create and render tessellated polygons by specifying the contours of one or more closed polygons. If the data for the object is static, encapsulate the tessellated polygons in a display list. (If you don't have to recalculate the tessellation repeatedly, using display lists is more efficient.)

5. If you need to tessellate something else, you may reuse your tessellation object. If you are forever finished with your tessellation object, you may delete it with **gluDeleteTess()**.

Note: The tessellator described here was introduced in Version 1.2 of the GLU. If you are using an older version of the GLU, you must use routines described in "Describing GLU Errors" on page 557. To query which version of GLU you have, use **gluGetString(GLU_VERSION)**, which returns a string with your GLU version number. If you don't seem to have **gluGetString()** in your GLU, then you have GLU 1.0, which did not yet have the **gluGetString()** routine.

Creating a Tessellation Object

As a complex polygon is being described and tessellated, it has associated data, such as the vertices, edges, and callback functions. All this data is tied to a single tessellation object. To perform tessellation, your program first has to create a tessellation object using the routine **gluNewTess()**.

GLUtesselator* gluNewTess(void);

Creates a new tessellation object and returns a pointer to it. A null pointer is returned if the creation fails.

A single tessellation object can be reused for all your tessellations. This object is required only because library routines might need to do their own tessellations, and they should be able to do so without interfering with any tessellation that your program is doing. It might also be useful to have multiple tessellation objects if you want to use different sets of callbacks for different tessellations. A typical program, however, allocates a single tessellation object and uses it for all its tessellations. There's no real need to free it, because it uses a small amount of memory. On the other hand, it never hurts to be tidy.

Tessellation Callback Routines

After you create a tessellation object, you must provide a series of callback routines to be called at appropriate times during the tessellation. After specifying the callbacks, you describe the contours of one or more polygons using GLU routines. When the description of the contours is complete, the tessellation facility invokes your callback routines as necessary.

Any functions that are omitted are simply not called during the tessellation, and any information they might have returned to your program is lost. All are specified by the single routine **gluTessCallback()**.

void **gluTessCallback**(GLUtesselator *tessobj*, GLenum *type*, void (**fn*)());

Associates the callback function *fn* with the tessellation object *tessobj*. The type of the callback is determined by the parameter *type*, which can be GLU_TESS_BEGIN, GLU_TESS_BEGIN_DATA, GLU_TESS_EDGE_FLAG, GLU_TESS_EDGE_FLAG_DATA, GLU_TESS_VERTEX, GLU_TESS_VERTEX_DATA, GLU_TESS_END, GLU_TESS_END_DATA, GLU_TESS_COMBINE, GLU_TESS_COMBINE_DATA, GLU_TESS_ERROR, or GLU_TESS_ERROR_DATA. The 12 possible callback functions have the following prototypes:

GLU_TESS_BEGIN	void **begin**(GLenum *type*);
GLU_TESS_BEGIN_DATA	void **begin**(GLenum *type*, void *user_data*);
GLU_TESS_EDGE_FLAG	void **edgeFlag**(GLboolean *flag*);
GLU_TESS_EDGE_FLAG_DATA	void **edgeFlag**(GLboolean *flag*, void *user_data*);
GLU_TESS_VERTEX	void **vertex**(void *vertex_data*);
GLU_TESS_VERTEX_DATA	void **vertex**(void *vertex_data*, void *user_data*);
GLU_TESS_END	void **end**(void);
GLU_TESS_END_DATA	void **end**(void *user_data*);
GLU_TESS_COMBINE	void **combine**(GLdouble *coords*[3], void *vertex_data*[4], GLfloat *weight*[4], void **outData*);
GLU_TESS_COMBINE_DATA	void **combine**(GLdouble *coords*[3], void *vertex_data*[4], GLfloat *weight*[4], void **outData*, void *user_data*);
GLU_TESS_ERROR	void **error**(GLenum *errno*);
GLU_TESS_ERROR_DATA	void **error**(GLenum *errno*, void *user_data*);

To change a callback routine, simply call **gluTessCallback()** with the new routine. To eliminate a callback routine without replacing it with a new one, pass **gluTessCallback()** a null pointer for the appropriate function.

As tessellation proceeds, the callback routines are called in a manner similar to how you use the OpenGL commands **glBegin()**, **glEdgeFlag*()**, **glVertex*()**, and **glEnd()**. (See "Marking Polygon Boundary Edges" in Chapter 2 for more information about **glEdgeFlag*()**.) The combine callback is used to create new vertices where edges intersect. The error callback is invoked during the tessellation only if something goes wrong.

For every tessellator object created, a GLU_TESS_BEGIN callback is invoked with one of four possible parameters: GL_TRIANGLE_FAN, GL_TRIANGLE_STRIP, GL_TRIANGLES, or GL_LINE_LOOP. When the tessellator decomposes the polygons, the tessellation algorithm decides which type of triangle primitive is most efficient to use. (If the GLU_TESS_BOUNDARY_ONLY property is enabled, then GL_LINE_LOOP is used for rendering.)

Since edge flags make no sense in a triangle fan or triangle strip, if there is a callback associated with GLU_TESS_EDGE_FLAG that enables edge flags, the GLU_TESS_BEGIN callback is called only with GL_TRIANGLES. The GLU_TESS_EDGE_FLAG callback works exactly analogously to the OpenGL **glEdgeFlag*()** call.

After the GLU_TESS_BEGIN callback routine is called and before the callback associated with GLU_TESS_END is called, some combination of the GLU_TESS_EDGE_FLAG and GLU_TESS_VERTEX callbacks is invoked (usually by calls to **gluTessVertex()**, which is described on page 555). The associated edge flags and vertices are interpreted exactly as they are in OpenGL between **glBegin()** and the matching **glEnd()**.

If something goes wrong, the error callback is passed a GLU error number. A character string describing the error is obtained using the routine **gluErrorString()**. (See "Describing GLU Errors" on page 557 for more information about this routine.)

Example 11-1 shows a portion of tess.c, in which a tessellation object is created and several callbacks are registered.

Example 11-1 Registering Tessellation Callbacks: tess.c

```
#ifndef CALLBACK
#define CALLBACK
#endif
```

```
/*  a portion of init() */

tobj = gluNewTess();
gluTessCallback(tobj, GLU_TESS_VERTEX, glVertex3dv);
gluTessCallback(tobj, GLU_TESS_BEGIN, beginCallback);
gluTessCallback(tobj, GLU_TESS_END, endCallback);
gluTessCallback(tobj, GLU_TESS_ERROR, errorCallback);

/*  the callback routines registered by gluTessCallback() */
void CALLBACK beginCallback(GLenum which)
{
   glBegin(which);
}

void CALLBACK endCallback(void)
{
   glEnd();
}

void CALLBACK errorCallback(GLenum errorCode)
{
   const GLubyte *estring;

   estring = gluErrorString(errorCode);
   fprintf(stderr, "Tessellation Error: %s\n", estring);
   exit(0);
}
```

Note: Type casting of callback functions is tricky, especially if you wish to make code that runs equally well on Microsoft Windows and UNIX. To run on Microsoft Windows, programs that declare callback functions, such as tess.c, need the symbol CALLBACK in the declarations of functions. The trick of using an empty definition for CALLBACK (as demonstrated below) allows the code to run well on both Microsoft Windows and UNIX:

```
#ifndef CALLBACK
#define CALLBACK
#endif

void CALLBACK callbackFunction(...) {
   ....
}
```

In Example 11-1, the registered GLU_TESS_VERTEX callback is simply **glVertex3dv()**, and only the coordinates at each vertex are passed along. However, if you want to specify more information at every vertex, such as a color value, a surface normal vector, or a texture coordinate, you'll have to make a more complex callback routine. Example 11-2 shows the start of another tessellated object, further along in program tess.c. The registered function **vertexCallback()** expects to receive a parameter that is a pointer to six double-length floating-point values: the *x*-, *y*-, and *z*-coordinates and the red, green, and blue color values for that vertex.

Example 11-2   Vertex and Combine Callbacks: tess.c

```
/*  a different portion of init() */
   gluTessCallback(tobj, GLU_TESS_VERTEX, vertexCallback);
   gluTessCallback(tobj, GLU_TESS_BEGIN, beginCallback);
   gluTessCallback(tobj, GLU_TESS_END, endCallback);
   gluTessCallback(tobj, GLU_TESS_ERROR, errorCallback);
   gluTessCallback(tobj, GLU_TESS_COMBINE, combineCallback);

/*  new callback routines registered by these calls */
void CALLBACK vertexCallback(GLvoid *vertex)
{
   const GLdouble *pointer;

   pointer = (GLdouble *) vertex;
   glColor3dv(pointer+3);
   glVertex3dv(vertex);
}

void CALLBACK combineCallback(GLdouble coords[3],
                   GLdouble *vertex_data[4],
                   GLfloat weight[4], GLdouble **dataOut )
{
   GLdouble *vertex;
   int i;

   vertex = (GLdouble *) malloc(6 * sizeof(GLdouble));
   vertex[0] = coords[0];
   vertex[1] = coords[1];
   vertex[2] = coords[2];
   for (i = 3; i < 6; i++)
      vertex[i] = weight[0] * vertex_data[0][i]
               + weight[1] * vertex_data[1][i]
               + weight[2] * vertex_data[2][i]
               + weight[3] * vertex_data[3][i];
   *dataOut = vertex;
}
```

Example 11-2 also shows the use of the GLU_TESS_COMBINE callback. Whenever the tessellation algorithm examines the input contours, detects an intersection, and decides it must create a new vertex, the GLU_TESS_COMBINE callback is invoked. The callback is also called when the tessellator decides to merge features of two vertices that are very close to one another. The newly created vertex is a linear combination of up to four existing vertices, referenced by *vertex_data*[0..3] in Example 11-2. The coefficients of the linear combination are given by *weight*[0..3]; these weights sum to 1.0. *coords* gives the location of the new vertex.

The registered callback routine must allocate memory for another vertex, perform a weighted interpolation of data using *vertex_data* and *weight*, and return the new vertex pointer as *dataOut*. **combineCallback()** in Example 11-2 interpolates the RGB color value. The function allocates a six-element array, puts the *x*-, *y*-, and *z*-coordinates in the first three elements, and then puts the weighted average of the RGB color values in the last three elements.

User-Specified Data

Six kinds of callbacks can be registered. Since there are two versions of each kind of callback, there are 12 callbacks in all. For each kind of callback, there is one with user-specified data and one without. The user-specified data is given by the application to **gluTessBeginPolygon()** and is then passed, unaltered, to each *DATA callback routine. With GLU_TESS_BEGIN_DATA, the user-specified data may be used for "per-polygon" data. If you specify both versions of a particular callback, the callback with *user_data* is used, and the other is ignored. Therefore, although there are 12 callbacks, you can have a maximum of six callback functions active at any one time.

For instance, Example 11-2 uses smooth shading, so **vertexCallback()** specifies an RGB color for every vertex. If you want to do lighting and smooth shading, the callback would specify a surface normal for every vertex. However, if you want lighting and flat shading, you might specify only one surface normal for every polygon, not for every vertex. In that case, you might choose to use the GLU_TESS_BEGIN_DATA callback and pass the vertex coordinates and surface normal in the *user_data* pointer.

Tessellation Properties

Prior to tessellation and rendering, you may use **gluTessProperty()** to set several properties to affect the tessellation algorithm. The most important and complicated of these properties is the winding rule, which determines what is considered "interior" and "exterior."

---

void **gluTessProperty**(GLUtesselator *tessobj*, GLenum *property*,
GLdouble *value*);

For the tessellation object *tessobj*, the current value of *property* is set to *value*. *property* is GLU_TESS_BOUNDARY_ONLY, GLU_TESS_TOLERANCE, or GLU_TESS_WINDING_RULE.

If *property* is GLU_TESS_BOUNDARY_ONLY, *value* is either GL_TRUE or GL_FALSE. When it is set to GL_TRUE, polygons are no longer tessellated into filled polygons; line loops are drawn to outline the contours that separate the polygon interior and exterior. The default value is GL_FALSE. (See **gluTessNormal**() to see how to control the winding direction of the contours.)

If *property* is GLU_TESS_TOLERANCE, *value* is a distance used to calculate whether two vertices are close enough together to be merged by the GLU_TESS_COMBINE callback. The tolerance value is multiplied by the largest coordinate magnitude of an input vertex to determine the maximum distance any feature can move as a result of a single merge operation. Feature merging may not be supported by your implementation, and the tolerance value is only a hint. The default tolerance value is zero.

The GLU_TESS_WINDING_RULE property determines which parts of the polygon are on the interior and which are on the exterior and should not be filled. *value* can be GLU_TESS_WINDING_ODD (the default), GLU_TESS_WINDING_NONZERO, GLU_TESS_WINDING_POSITIVE, GLU_TESS_WINDING_NEGATIVE, or GLU_TESS_WINDING_ABS_GEQ_TWO.

Winding Numbers and Winding Rules

For a single contour, the winding number of a point is the signed number of revolutions we make around that point while traveling once around the contour (where a counterclockwise revolution is positive and a clockwise revolution is negative). When there are several contours, the individual winding numbers are summed. This procedure associates a signed integer value with each point in the plane. Note that the winding number is the same for all points in a single region.

Figure 11-2 shows three sets of contours and winding numbers for points inside those contours. In the set at the left, all three contours are counterclockwise, so each nested interior region adds 1 to the winding number. In the middle set, the two interior contours are drawn clockwise, so the winding number decreases and actually becomes negative.

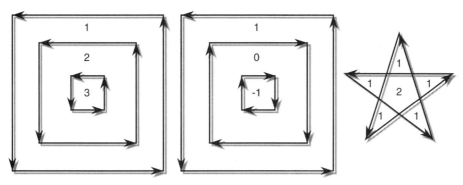

Figure 11-2   Winding Numbers for Sample Contours

The winding rule classifies a region as *inside* if its winding number belongs to the chosen category (odd, nonzero, positive, negative, or "absolute value greater than or equal to 2"). The odd and nonzero rules are common ways to define the interior. The positive, negative, and "absolute value ≥ 2" winding rules have some limited use for polygon CSG (computational solid geometry) operations.

The program tesswind.c demonstrates the effects of winding rules. The four sets of contours shown in Figure 11-3 are rendered. The user can then cycle through the different winding rule properties to see their effects. For each winding rule, the dark areas represent interiors. Note the effects of clockwise and counterclockwise winding.

CSG Uses for Winding Rules

GLU_TESS_WINDING_ODD and GLU_TESS_WINDING_NONZERO are the most commonly used winding rules. They work for the most typical cases of shading.

The winding rules are also designed for CSG operations, making it easy to find the union, difference, or intersection (Boolean operations) of several contours.

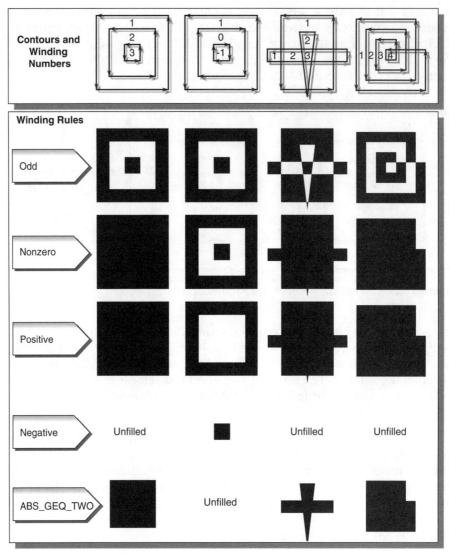

Figure 11-3   How Winding Rules Define Interiors

First, assume that each contour is defined so that the winding number is 0 for each exterior region and 1 for each interior region. (Each contour must not intersect itself.) Under this model, counterclockwise contours define the outer boundary of the polygon, and clockwise contours define holes. Contours may be nested, but a nested contour must be oriented oppositely from the contour that contains it.

If the original polygons do not satisfy this description, they can be converted to this form by first running the tessellator with the GLU_TESS_BOUNDARY_ONLY property turned on. This returns a list of contours satisfying the restriction just described. By creating two tessellator objects, the callbacks from one tessellator can be fed directly as input to the other.

Given two or more polygons of the preceding form, CSG operations can be implemented as follows:

- UNION—To calculate the union of several contours, draw all input contours as a single polygon. The winding number of each resulting region is the number of original polygons that cover it. The union can be extracted by using the GLU_TESS_WINDING_NONZERO or GLU_TESS_WINDING_POSITIVE winding rule. Note that with the nonzero winding rule, we would get the same result if all contour orientations were reversed.

- INTERSECTION—This works only for two contours at a time. Draw a single polygon using two contours. Extract the result using GLU_TESS_WINDING_ABS_GEQ_TWO.

- DIFFERENCE—Suppose you want to compute A diff (B union C union D). Draw a single polygon consisting of the unmodified contours from A, followed by the contours of B, C, and D, with their vertex order reversed. To extract the result, use the GLU_TESS_WINDING_POSITIVE winding rule. (If B, C, and D are the result of a GLU_TESS_BOUNDARY_ONLY operation, an alternative to reversing the vertex order is to use **gluTessNormal**() to reverse the sign of the supplied normal.)

Other Tessellation Property Routines

There are also complementary routines, which work alongside **gluTessProperty**(). **gluGetTessProperty**() retrieves the current values of tessellator properties. If the tessellator is being used to generate wireframe outlines instead of filled polygons, **gluTessNormal**() can be used to determine the winding direction of the tessellated polygons.

void **gluGetTessProperty**(GLUtesselator *tessobj*, GLenum *property*, GLdouble *value*);

For the tessellation object *tessobj*, the current value of *property* is returned to *value*. Values for *property* and *value* are the same as for **gluTessProperty**().

> void **gluTessNormal**(GLUtesselator *tessobj*, GLdouble *x*, GLdouble *y*,
>   GLdouble *z*);
>
> For the tessellation object *tessobj*, **gluTessNormal**() defines a normal vec-
> tor, which controls the winding direction of generated polygons. Before
> tessellation, all input data is projected into a plane perpendicular to the
> normal. Then, all output triangles are oriented counterclockwise, with
> respect to the normal. (Clockwise orientation can be obtained by revers-
> ing the sign of the supplied normal.) The default normal is (0, 0, 0).

If you have some knowledge about the location and orientation of the input
data, then using **gluTessNormal**() can increase the speed of the tessellation.
For example, if you know that all polygons lie on the *xy*-plane, call
gluTessNormal(*tessobj*, 0, 0, 1).

As stated above, the default normal is (0, 0, 0), and its effect is not immediately obvious. In this case, it is expected that the input data lies approximately
in a plane, and a plane is fitted to the vertices, no matter how they are truly
connected. The sign of the normal is chosen so that the sum of the signed
areas of all input contours is non-negative (where a counterclockwise contour has a positive area). Note that if the input data does not lie approximately in a plane, then projection perpendicular to the computed normal
may substantially change the geometry.

Polygon Definition

After all the tessellation properties have been set and the callback actions
have been registered, it is finally time to describe the vertices that comprise
input contours and tessellate the polygons.

> void **gluTessBeginPolygon**(GLUtesselator *tessobj*, void *user_data*);
> void **gluTessEndPolygon**(GLUtesselator *tessobj*);
>
> Begins and ends the specification of a polygon to be tessellated and
> associates a tessellation object, *tessobj*, with it. *user_data* points to a user-
> defined data structure, which is passed along all the GLU_TESS_*_DATA
> callback functions that have been bound.

Calls to **gluTessBeginPolygon**() and **gluTessEndPolygon**() surround the
definition of one or more contours. When **gluTessEndPolygon**() is called,
the tessellation algorithm is implemented, and the tessellated polygons are

generated and rendered. The callback functions and tessellation properties that were bound and set to the tessellation object using **gluTessCallback()** and **gluTessProperty()** are used.

---

void **gluTessBeginContour**(GLUtesselator *tessobj*);
void **gluTessEndContour**(GLUtesselator *tessobj*);

Begins and ends the specification of a closed contour, which is a portion of a polygon. A closed contour consists of zero or more calls to **gluTessVertex()**, which defines the vertices. The last vertex of each contour is automatically linked to the first.

In practice, a minimum of three vertices is needed for a meaningful contour.

---

void **gluTessVertex**(GLUtesselator *tessobj*, GLdouble *coords*[3],
                    void *vertex_data*);

Specifies a vertex in the current contour for the tessellation object. *coords* contains the three-dimensional vertex coordinates, and *vertex_data* is a pointer that's sent to the callback associated with GLU_TESS_VERTEX or GLU_TESS_VERTEX_DATA. Typically, *vertex_data* contains vertex coordinates, surface normals, texture coordinates, color information, or whatever else the application may find useful.

In the program tess.c, a portion of which is shown in Example 11-3, two polygons are defined. One polygon is a rectangular contour with a triangular hole inside, and the other is a smooth-shaded, self-intersecting, five-pointed star. For efficiency, both polygons are stored in display lists. The first polygon consists of two contours; the outer one is wound counterclockwise, and the "hole" is wound clockwise. For the second polygon, the *star* array contains both the coordinate and color data, and its tessellation callback, **vertexCallback()**, uses both.

It is important that each vertex is in a different memory location because the vertex data is not copied by **gluTessVertex()**; only the pointer (*vertex_data*) is saved. A program that reuses the same memory for several vertices may not get the desired result.

Note: In **gluTessVertex()**, it may seem redundant to specify the vertex coordinate data twice, for both the *coords* and *vertex_data* parameters; however, both are necessary. *coords* refers only to the vertex coordinates. *vertex_data* uses the coordinate data, but may also use other information for each vertex.

Example 11-3 Polygon Definition: tess.c

```c
GLdouble rect[4][3] = {50.0, 50.0, 0.0,
                       200.0, 50.0, 0.0,
                       200.0, 200.0, 0.0,
                       50.0, 200.0, 0.0};
GLdouble tri[3][3] = {75.0, 75.0, 0.0,
                      125.0, 175.0, 0.0,
                      175.0, 75.0, 0.0};
GLdouble star[5][6] = {250.0, 50.0, 0.0, 1.0, 0.0, 1.0,
                       325.0, 200.0, 0.0, 1.0, 1.0, 0.0,
                       400.0, 50.0, 0.0, 0.0, 1.0, 1.0,
                       250.0, 150.0, 0.0, 1.0, 0.0, 0.0,
                       400.0, 150.0, 0.0, 0.0, 1.0, 0.0};

startList = glGenLists(2);
tobj = gluNewTess();
gluTessCallback(tobj, GLU_TESS_VERTEX, glVertex3dv);
gluTessCallback(tobj, GLU_TESS_BEGIN, beginCallback);
gluTessCallback(tobj, GLU_TESS_END, endCallback);
gluTessCallback(tobj, GLU_TESS_ERROR, errorCallback);

glNewList(startList, GL_COMPILE);
glShadeModel(GL_FLAT);
gluTessBeginPolygon(tobj, NULL);
    gluTessBeginContour(tobj);
        gluTessVertex(tobj, rect[0], rect[0]);
        gluTessVertex(tobj, rect[1], rect[1]);
        gluTessVertex(tobj, rect[2], rect[2]);
        gluTessVertex(tobj, rect[3], rect[3]);
    gluTessEndContour(tobj);
    gluTessBeginContour(tobj);
        gluTessVertex(tobj, tri[0], tri[0]);
        gluTessVertex(tobj, tri[1], tri[1]);
        gluTessVertex(tobj, tri[2], tri[2]);
    gluTessEndContour(tobj);
gluTessEndPolygon(tobj);
glEndList();

gluTessCallback(tobj, GLU_TESS_VERTEX, vertexCallback);
gluTessCallback(tobj, GLU_TESS_BEGIN, beginCallback);
gluTessCallback(tobj, GLU_TESS_END, endCallback);
gluTessCallback(tobj, GLU_TESS_ERROR, errorCallback);
gluTessCallback(tobj, GLU_TESS_COMBINE, combineCallback);

glNewList(startList + 1, GL_COMPILE);
glShadeModel(GL_SMOOTH);
```

```
gluTessProperty(tobj, GLU_TESS_WINDING_RULE,
                GLU_TESS_WINDING_POSITIVE);
gluTessBeginPolygon(tobj, NULL);
    gluTessBeginContour(tobj);
        gluTessVertex(tobj, star[0], star[0]);
        gluTessVertex(tobj, star[1], star[1]);
        gluTessVertex(tobj, star[2], star[2]);
        gluTessVertex(tobj, star[3], star[3]);
        gluTessVertex(tobj, star[4], star[4]);
    gluTessEndContour(tobj);
gluTessEndPolygon(tobj);
glEndList();
```

Deleting a Tessellation Object

If you no longer need a tessellation object, you can delete it and free all associated memory with **gluDeleteTess**().

---

void **gluDeleteTess**(GLUtesselator *tessobj*);

Deletes the specified tessellation object, *tessobj*, and frees all associated memory.

Tessellation Performance Tips

For best performance, remember these rules:

- Cache the output of the tessellator in a display list or other user structure. To obtain the post-tessellation vertex coordinates, tessellate the polygons while in feedback mode. (See "Feedback" in Chapter 13.)

- Use **gluTessNormal**() to supply the polygon normal.

- Use the same tessellator object to render many polygons, rather than allocate a new tessellator for each one. (In a multithreaded, multi-processor environment, you may get better performance using several tessellators.)

Describing GLU Errors

The GLU provides a routine for obtaining a descriptive string for an error code. This routine is not limited to tessellation but is also used for NURBS and quadrics errors, as well as for errors in the base GL. (See "Error

Handling" in Chapter 14 for information about OpenGL's error-handling facility.)

Backward Compatibility

If you are using the 1.0 or 1.1 version of GLU, you have a much less powerful tessellator. The 1.0/1.1 tessellator handles only simple nonconvex polygons or simple polygons containing holes. It does not properly tessellate intersecting contours (no COMBINE callback) or process per-polygon data. The 1.0/1.1 tessellator still works in either GLU 1.2 or 1.3, but its use is no longer recommended.

The 1.0/1.1 tessellator has some similarities to the current tessellator. **gluNewTess()** and **gluDeleteTess()** are used for both tessellators. The main vertex specification routine remains **gluTessVertex()**. The callback mechanism is controlled by **gluTessCallback()**, although only five callback functions can be registered, a subset of the current 12.

Here are the prototypes for the 1.0/1.1 tessellator:

void **gluBeginPolygon**(GLUtriangulatorObj *tessobj*);
void **gluNextContour**(GLUtriangulatorObj *tessobj*, GLenum *type*);
void **gluEndPolygon**(GLUtriangulatorObj *tessobj*);

The outermost contour must be specified first, and it does not require an initial call to **gluNextContour()**. For polygons without holes, only one contour is defined, and **gluNextContour()** is not used. If a polygon has multiple contours (that is, holes or holes within holes), the contours are specified one after the other, each preceded by **gluNextContour()**. **gluTessVertex()** is called for each vertex of a contour.

For **gluNextContour()**, *type* can be GLU_EXTERIOR, GLU_INTERIOR, GLU_CCW, GLU_CW, or GLU_UNKNOWN. These serve only as hints to the tessellation. If you get them right, the tessellation might go faster. If you get them wrong, they're ignored, and the tessellation still works. For polygons with holes, one contour is the exterior contour and the other is the interior. The first contour is assumed to be of type GLU_EXTERIOR. Choosing clockwise or counterclockwise orientation is arbitrary in three dimensions; however, there are two different orientations in any plane, and the GLU_CCW and GLU_CW types should be used consistently. Use GLU_UNKNOWN if you don't have a clue.

It is highly recommended that you convert GLU 1.0/1.1 code to the new tessellation interface for GLU 1.2 by following these steps:

1. Change references to the major data structure type from GLUtriangulatorObj to GLUtesselator. In GLU 1.2, GLUtriangulatorObj and GLUtesselator are defined to be the same type.

2. Convert **gluBeginPolygon()** to two commands: **gluTessBeginPolygon()** and **gluTessBeginContour()**. All contours must be explicitly started, including the first one.

3. Convert **gluNextContour()** to both **gluTessEndContour()** and **gluTessBeginContour()**. You have to end the previous contour before starting the next one.

4. Convert **gluEndPolygon()** to both **gluTessEndContour()** and **gluTessEndPolygon()**. The final contour must be closed.

5. Change references to constants to **gluTessCallback()**. In GLU 1.2, GLU_BEGIN, GLU_VERTEX, GLU_END, GLU_ERROR, and GLU_EDGE_FLAG are defined as synonyms for GLU_TESS_BEGIN, GLU_TESS_VERTEX, GLU_TESS_END, GLU_TESS_ERROR, and GLU_TESS_EDGE_FLAG.

Quadrics: Rendering Spheres, Cylinders, and Disks

The base OpenGL Library provides support only for modeling and rendering simple points, lines, and convex filled polygons. Neither 3D objects nor commonly used 2D objects such as circles are directly available.

Throughout this book, you've been using GLUT to create some 3D objects. The GLU also provides routines to model and render tessellated, polygonal approximations for a variety of 2D and 3D shapes (spheres, cylinders, disks, and parts of disks), which can be calculated with quadric equations. This includes routines for drawing the quadric surfaces in a variety of styles and orientations. Quadric surfaces are defined by the following general quadratic equation:

$$a_1 x^2 + a_2 y^2 + a_3 z^2 + a_4 xy + a_5 yz + a_6 xz + a_7 x + a_8 y + a_9 z + a_{10} = 0$$

(See David Rogers' *Procedural Elements for Computer Graphics,* New York, NY: McGraw-Hill, 1985.) Creating and rendering a quadric surface is similar to using the tessellator. To use a quadrics object, follow these steps:

1. To create a quadrics object, use **gluNewQuadric()**.

2. Specify the rendering attributes for the quadrics object (unless you're satisfied with the default values).

   a. Use **gluQuadricOrientation()** to control the winding direction and differentiate the interior from the exterior.

   b. Use **gluQuadricDrawStyle()** to choose between rendering the object as points, lines, or filled polygons.

   c. For lit quadrics objects, use **gluQuadricNormals()** to specify one normal per vertex or one normal per face. The default specifies that no normals are generated at all.

   d. For textured quadrics objects, use **gluQuadricTexture()** if you want to generate texture coordinates.

3. Prepare for problems by registering an error-handling routine with **gluQuadricCallback()**. Then, if an error occurs during rendering, the routine you've specified is invoked.

4. Now invoke the rendering routine for the desired type of quadrics object: **gluSphere()**, **gluCylinder()**, **gluDisk()**, or **gluPartialDisk()**. For best performance for static data, encapsulate the quadrics object in a display list.

5. When you're completely finished with it, destroy this object with **gluDeleteQuadric()**. If you need to create another quadric, it's best to reuse your quadrics object.

Managing Quadrics Objects

A quadrics object consists of parameters, attributes, and callbacks that are stored in a data structure of type GLUquadricObj. A quadrics object may generate vertices, normals, texture coordinates, and other data, all of which may be used immediately or stored in a display list for later use. The following routines create, destroy, and report errors in a quadrics object.

GLUquadricObj* **gluNewQuadric**(void);

Creates a new quadrics object and returns a pointer to it. A null pointer is returned if the routine fails.

void **gluDeleteQuadric**(GLUquadricObj *qobj);

Destroys the quadrics object *qobj* and frees up any memory used by it.

void **gluQuadricCallback**(GLUquadricObj *qobj, GLenum *which*,
                    void (*fn)());

Defines a function *fn* to be called in special circumstances. GLU_ERROR is the only legal value for *which*, so *fn* is called when an error occurs. If *fn* is NULL, any existing callback is erased.

For GLU_ERROR, *fn* is called with one parameter, which is the error code. **gluErrorString**() can be used to convert the error code into an ASCII string.

Controlling Quadrics Attributes

The following routines affect the kinds of data generated by the quadrics routines. Use these routines before you actually specify the primitives.

Example 11-4, quadric.c, on page 565, demonstrates changing the drawing style and the kinds of normals generated as well as creation of quadrics objects, error handling, and drawing the primitives.

void **gluQuadricDrawStyle**(GLUquadricObj *qobj, GLenum *drawStyle*);

For the quadrics object *qobj*, *drawStyle* controls the rendering style. Legal values for *drawStyle* are GLU_POINT, GLU_LINE, GLU_SILHOUETTE, and GLU_FILL.

GLU_POINT and GLU_LINE specify that primitives should be rendered as a point at every vertex or a line between each pair of connected vertices.

GLU_SILHOUETTE specifies that primitives are rendered as lines, except that edges separating coplanar faces are not drawn. This is most often used for **gluDisk()** and **gluPartialDisk()**.

GLU_FILL specifies rendering by filled polygons, where the polygons are drawn in a counterclockwise fashion with respect to their normals. This may be affected by **gluQuadricOrientation()**.

---

void **gluQuadricOrientation**(GLUquadricObj *qobj*, GLenum *orientation*);

For the quadrics object *qobj*, *orientation* is either GLU_OUTSIDE (the default) or GLU_INSIDE, which controls the direction in which normals are pointing.

For **gluSphere()** and **gluCylinder()**, the definitions of outside and inside are obvious. For **gluDisk()** and **gluPartialDisk()**, the positive *z* side of the disk is considered to be outside.

---

void **gluQuadricNormals**(GLUquadricObj *qobj*, GLenum *normals*);

For the quadrics object *qobj*, *normals* is GLU_NONE (the default), GLU_FLAT, or GLU_SMOOTH.

---

gluQuadricNormals() is used to specify when to generate normal vectors. GLU_NONE means that no normals are generated, and is intended for use without lighting. GLU_FLAT generates one normal for each facet, which is often best for lighting with flat shading. GLU_SMOOTH generates one normal for every vertex of the quadric, which is usually best for lighting with smooth shading.

---

void **gluQuadricTexture**(GLUquadricObj *qobj*,
                          GLboolean *textureCoords*);

For the quadrics object *qobj*, *textureCoords* is either GL_FALSE (the default) or GL_TRUE. If the value of *textureCoords* is GL_TRUE, then texture coordinates are generated for the quadrics object. The manner in which the texture coordinates are generated varies, depending on the type of quadrics object rendered.

Quadrics Primitives

The following routines actually generate the vertices and other data that constitute a quadrics object. In each case, *qobj* refers to a quadrics object created by **gluNewQuadric**().

---

void **gluSphere**(GLUquadricObj *qobj*, GLdouble *radius*, GLint *slices*,
        GLint *stacks*);

Draws a sphere of the given *radius*, centered around the origin, (0, 0, 0). The sphere is subdivided around the *z*-axis into a number of *slices* (similar to longitude) and along the *z*-axis into a number of *stacks* (latitude).

If texture coordinates are also generated by the quadrics facility, the *t*-coordinate ranges from 0.0 at *z* = –radius to 1.0 at *z* = radius, with *t* increasing linearly along longitudinal lines. Meanwhile, *s* ranges from 0.0 at the +*y* axis, to 0.25 at the +*x* axis, to 0.5 at the –*y* axis, to 0.75 at the –*x* axis, and back to 1.0 at the +*y* axis.

---

void **gluCylinder**(GLUquadricObj *qobj*, GLdouble *baseRadius*,
        GLdouble *topRadius*, GLdouble *height*,
        GLint *slices*, GLint *stacks*);

Draws a cylinder oriented along the *z*-axis, with the base of the cylinder at *z* = 0 and the top at *z* = height. Like a sphere, the cylinder is subdivided around the *z*-axis into a number of *slices* and along the *z*-axis into a number of *stacks*. *baseRadius* is the radius of the cylinder at *z* = 0. *topRadius* is the radius of the cylinder at *z* = height. If *topRadius* is set to 0, then a cone is generated.

If texture coordinates are generated by the quadrics facility, then the *t*-coordinate ranges linearly from 0.0 at *z* = 0 to 1.0 at *z* = *height*. The *s* texture coordinates are generated the same way as they are for a sphere.

Note: The cylinder is not closed at the top or bottom. The disks at the base and at the top are not drawn.

void **gluDisk**(GLUquadricObj *qobj*, GLdouble *innerRadius*,
　　　　GLdouble *outerRadius*, GLint *slices*, GLint *rings*);

Draws a disk on the *z* = 0 plane, with a radius of *outerRadius* and a concentric circular hole with a radius of *innerRadius*. If *innerRadius* is 0, then no hole is created. The disk is subdivided around the *z*-axis into a number of *slices* (like slices of pizza) and also about the *z*-axis into a number of concentric *rings*.

With respect to orientation, the +*z* side of the disk is considered to be "outside"; that is, any normals generated point along the +*z* axis. Otherwise, the normals point along the −*z* axis.

If texture coordinates are generated by the quadrics facility, then the texture coordinates are generated linearly such that where R = *outerRadius*, the values for *s* and *t* at (R, 0, 0) are (1, 0.5), at (0, R, 0) they are (0.5, 1), at (−R, 0, 0) they are (0, 0.5), and at (0, −R, 0) they are (0.5, 0).

---

void **gluPartialDisk**(GLUquadricObj *qobj*, GLdouble *innerRadius*,
　　　　GLdouble *outerRadius*, GLint *slices*, GLint *rings*,
　　　　GLdouble *startAngle*, GLdouble *sweepAngle*);

Draws a partial disk on the *z* = 0 plane. A partial disk is similar to a complete disk, in terms of *outerRadius*, *innerRadius*, *slices*, and *rings*. The difference is that only a portion of a partial disk is drawn, starting from *startAngle* through *startAngle* + *sweepAngle* (where *startAngle* and *sweepAngle* are measured in degrees, where 0 degrees is along the +*y* axis, 90 degrees along the +*x* axis, 180 along the −*y* axis, and 270 along the −*x* axis).

A partial disk handles orientation and texture coordinates in the same way as a complete disk.

Note: For all quadrics objects, it's better to use the *Radius, height,* and similar arguments to scale them, rather than the **glScale*()** command, so that the unit-length normals that are generated don't have to be renormalized. Set the *rings* and *stacks* arguments to values other than 1 to force lighting calculations at a finer granularity, especially if the material specularity is high.

Example 11-4 shows each of the quadrics primitives being drawn, as well as the effects of different drawing styles.

Example 11-4   Quadrics Objects: quadric.c

```c
#ifndef CALLBACK
#define CALLBACK
#endif

GLuint startList;

void CALLBACK errorCallback(GLenum errorCode)
{
   const GLubyte *estring;

   estring = gluErrorString(errorCode);
   fprintf(stderr, "Quadric Error: %s\n", estring);
   exit(0);
}

void init(void)
{
   GLUquadricObj *qobj;
   GLfloat mat_ambient[] = { 0.5, 0.5, 0.5, 1.0 };
   GLfloat mat_specular[] = { 1.0, 1.0, 1.0, 1.0 };
   GLfloat mat_shininess[] = { 50.0 };
   GLfloat light_position[] = { 1.0, 1.0, 1.0, 0.0 };
   GLfloat model_ambient[] = { 0.5, 0.5, 0.5, 1.0 };

   glClearColor(0.0, 0.0, 0.0, 0.0);

   glMaterialfv(GL_FRONT, GL_AMBIENT, mat_ambient);
   glMaterialfv(GL_FRONT, GL_SPECULAR, mat_specular);
   glMaterialfv(GL_FRONT, GL_SHININESS, mat_shininess);
   glLightfv(GL_LIGHT0, GL_POSITION, light_position);
   glLightModelfv(GL_LIGHT_MODEL_AMBIENT, model_ambient);

   glEnable(GL_LIGHTING);
   glEnable(GL_LIGHT0);
   glEnable(GL_DEPTH_TEST);

/* Create 4 display lists, each with a different quadric object.
 * Different drawing styles and surface normal specifications
 * are demonstrated.
 */
   startList = glGenLists(4);
   qobj = gluNewQuadric();
   gluQuadricCallback(qobj, GLU_ERROR, errorCallback);

   gluQuadricDrawStyle(qobj, GLU_FILL); /* smooth shaded */
```

```
        gluQuadricNormals(qobj, GLU_SMOOTH);
        glNewList(startList, GL_COMPILE);
            gluSphere(qobj, 0.75, 15, 10);
        glEndList();

        gluQuadricDrawStyle(qobj, GLU_FILL); /* flat shaded */
        gluQuadricNormals(qobj, GLU_FLAT);
        glNewList(startList+1, GL_COMPILE);
            gluCylinder(qobj, 0.5, 0.3, 1.0, 15, 5);
        glEndList();

        gluQuadricDrawStyle(qobj, GLU_LINE); /* wireframe */
        gluQuadricNormals(qobj, GLU_NONE);
        glNewList(startList+2, GL_COMPILE);
            gluDisk(qobj, 0.25, 1.0, 20, 4);
        glEndList();

        gluQuadricDrawStyle(qobj, GLU_SILHOUETTE);
        gluQuadricNormals(qobj, GLU_NONE);
        glNewList(startList+3, GL_COMPILE);
            gluPartialDisk(qobj, 0.0, 1.0, 20, 4, 0.0, 225.0);
        glEndList();
    }

    void display(void)
    {
        glClear(GL_COLOR_BUFFER_BIT | GL_DEPTH_BUFFER_BIT);
        glPushMatrix();

        glEnable(GL_LIGHTING);
        glShadeModel(GL_SMOOTH);
        glTranslatef(-1.0, -1.0, 0.0);
        glCallList(startList);

        glShadeModel(GL_FLAT);
        glTranslatef(0.0, 2.0, 0.0);
        glPushMatrix();
        glRotatef(300.0, 1.0, 0.0, 0.0);
        glCallList(startList+1);
        glPopMatrix();

        glDisable(GL_LIGHTING);
        glColor3f(0.0, 1.0, 1.0);
        glTranslatef(2.0, -2.0, 0.0);
        glCallList(startList+2);
```

```
   glColor3f(1.0, 1.0, 0.0);
   glTranslatef(0.0, 2.0, 0.0);
   glCallList(startList+3);

   glPopMatrix();
   glFlush();
}

void reshape(int w, int h)
{
   glViewport(0, 0, (GLsizei) w, (GLsizei) h);
   glMatrixMode(GL_PROJECTION);
   glLoadIdentity();
   if (w <= h)
      glOrtho(-2.5, 2.5, -2.5*(GLfloat)h/(GLfloat)w,
         2.5*(GLfloat)h/(GLfloat)w, -10.0, 10.0);
   else
      glOrtho(-2.5*(GLfloat)w/(GLfloat)h,
         2.5*(GLfloat)w/(GLfloat)h, -2.5, 2.5, -10.0, 10.0);
   glMatrixMode(GL_MODELVIEW);
   glLoadIdentity();
}

void keyboard(unsigned char key, int x, int y)
{
   switch (key) {
      case 27:
         exit(0);
         break;
   }
}

int main(int argc, char** argv)
{
   glutInit(&argc, argv);
   glutInitDisplayMode(GLUT_SINGLE | GLUT_RGB | GLUT_DEPTH);
   glutInitWindowSize(500, 500);
   glutInitWindowPosition(100, 100);
   glutCreateWindow(argv[0]);
   init();
   glutDisplayFunc(display);
   glutReshapeFunc(reshape);
   glutKeyboardFunc(keyboard);
   glutMainLoop();
   return 0;
}
```

Chapter 12

Evaluators and NURBS

Chapter Objectives

Advanced

Advanced

After reading this chapter, you'll be able to do the following:

- Use OpenGL evaluator commands to draw basic curves and surfaces

- Use the GLU's higher-level NURBS facility to draw more complex curves and surfaces and to return data on the vertices of geometric objects, which result from the tessellation of the curves and surfaces

Note that this chapter presumes a number of prerequisites; they're listed in "Prerequisites" on page 571.

Note: In OpenGL Version 3.1, all of the techniques and functions described in this chapter were removed through deprecation. Even though some of this functionality is part of the GLU library, it relies on functionality that has been removed from the core OpenGL library.

At the lowest level, graphics hardware draws points, line segments, and polygons, which are usually triangles and quadrilaterals. Smooth curves and surfaces are drawn by approximating them with large numbers of small line segments or polygons. However, many useful curves and surfaces can be described mathematically by a small number of parameters such as a few *control points*. Saving the 16 control points for a surface requires much less storage than saving 1000 triangles together with the normal vector information at each vertex. In addition, the 1000 triangles only approximate the true surface, but the control points accurately describe the real surface.

Evaluators provide a way to specify points on a curve or surface (or part of one) using only the control points. The curve or surface can then be rendered at any precision. In addition, normal vectors can be calculated for surfaces automatically. You can use the points generated by an evaluator in many ways—to draw dots where the surface would be; to draw a wireframe version of the surface; or to draw a fully lighted, shaded, and even textured version.

You can use evaluators to describe any polynomial or rational polynomial splines or surfaces of any degree. These include almost all splines and spline surfaces in use today, including B-splines, NURBS (Non-Uniform Rational B-Spline) surfaces, Bézier curves and surfaces, and Hermite splines. Since evaluators provide only a low-level description of the points on a curve or surface, they're typically used underneath utility libraries that provide a higher-level interface to the programmer. The GLU's NURBS facility is such a higher-level interface—the NURBS routines encapsulate extensive complicated code. Much of the final rendering is done with evaluators, but for some conditions (trimming curves, for example) the NURBS routines use planar polygons for rendering.

This chapter contains the following major sections:

- "Prerequisites" discusses what knowledge is assumed for this chapter. It also gives several references where you can obtain this information.

- "Evaluators" explains how evaluators work and how to control them using the appropriate OpenGL commands.

- "The GLU NURBS Interface" describes the GLU routines for creating, rendering, and returning the tessellated vertices of NURBS curves and surfaces.

Prerequisites

Evaluators make splines and surfaces that are based on a Bézier (or Bernstein) basis. The defining formulas for the functions in this basis are given in this chapter, but the discussion doesn't include derivations or even lists of all their interesting mathematical properties. If you want to use evaluators to draw curves and surfaces using other bases, you must know how to convert your basis to a Bézier basis. In addition, when you render a Bézier surface or part of it using evaluators, you need to determine the granularity of your subdivision. Your decision needs to take into account the trade-off between high-quality (highly subdivided) images and high speed. Determining an appropriate subdivision strategy can be quite complicated—too complicated to be discussed here.

Similarly, a complete discussion of NURBS is beyond the scope of this book. The GLU NURBS interface is documented here, and programming examples are provided for readers who already understand the subject. In what follows, you already should know about NURBS control points, knot sequences, and trimming curves.

If you lack some of these prerequisites, the following references will help:

- Farin, Gerald E., *Curves and Surfaces for Computer-Aided Geometric Design, Fourth Edition.* San Diego, CA: Academic Press, 1996.

- Farin, Gerald E., *NURB Curves and Surfaces: From Projective Geometry to Practical Use.* Wellesley, MA: A. K. Peters Ltd., 1995.

- Farin, Gerald E., editor, *NURBS for Curve and Surface Design*, Society for Industrial and Applied Mathematics, Philadelphia, PA, 1991.

- Hoschek, Josef, and Dieter Lasser, *Fundamentals of Computer Aided Geometric Design.* Wellesley, MA: A. K. Peters Ltd., 1993.

- Piegl, Les, and Wayne Tiller, *The NURBS Book.* New York, NY: Springer-Verlag, 1995.

Note: Some terms used in this chapter might have slightly different meanings in other books on spline curves and surfaces, since there isn't total agreement among the practitioners of this art. Generally, the OpenGL meanings are a bit more restrictive. For example, OpenGL evaluators always use Bézier bases; in other contexts, evaluators might refer to the same concept, but with an arbitrary basis.

Evaluators

A Bézier curve is a vector-valued function of one variable

$$C(u) = [X(u) \ Y(u) \ Z(u)]$$

where u varies in some domain (say [0, 1]). A Bézier surface patch is a vector-valued function of two variables

$$S(u,v) = [X(u,v) \ Y(u,v) \ Z(u,v)]$$

where u and v can both vary in some domain. The range isn't necessarily three-dimensional as shown here. You might want two-dimensional output for curves on a plane or texture coordinates, or you might want four-dimensional output to specify RGBA information. Even one-dimensional output may make sense for gray levels.

For each u (or u and v, in the case of a surface), the formula for C() (or S()) calculates a point on the curve (or surface). To use an evaluator, first define the function C() or S(), enable it, and then use the **glEvalCoord1**() or **glEvalCoord2**() command instead of **glVertex***(). This way, the curve or surface vertices can be used just as any other vertices are used—to form points or lines, for example. In addition, other commands automatically generate a series of vertices that produce a regular mesh uniformly spaced in u (or in u and v). One- and two-dimensional evaluators are similar, but the description is somewhat simpler in one dimension, so that case is discussed first.

One-Dimensional Evaluators

This subsection presents an example of using one-dimensional evaluators to draw a curve. It then describes the commands and equations that control evaluators.

One-Dimensional Example: A Simple Bézier Curve

The program shown in Example 12-1 draws a cubic Bézier curve using four control points, as shown in Figure 12-1.

Figure 12-1   Bézier Curve

Example 12-1   Bézier Curve with Four Control Points: bezcurve.c

```
GLfloat ctrlpoints[4][3] = {
        { -4.0, -4.0, 0.0}, { -2.0, 4.0, 0.0},
        {2.0, -4.0, 0.0}, {4.0, 4.0, 0.0}};

void init(void)
{
   glClearColor(0.0, 0.0, 0.0, 0.0);
   glShadeModel(GL_FLAT);
   glMap1f(GL_MAP1_VERTEX_3, 0.0, 1.0, 3, 4, &ctrlpoints[0][0]);
   glEnable(GL_MAP1_VERTEX_3);
}

void display(void)
{
   int i;

   glClear(GL_COLOR_BUFFER_BIT);
   glColor3f(1.0, 1.0, 1.0);
   glBegin(GL_LINE_STRIP);
      for (i = 0; i <= 30; i++)
         glEvalCoord1f((GLfloat) i/30.0);
   glEnd();
   /* The following code displays the control points as dots. */
   glPointSize(5.0);
   glColor3f(1.0, 1.0, 0.0);
   glBegin(GL_POINTS);
      for (i = 0; i < 4; i++)
         glVertex3fv(&ctrlpoints[i][0]);
   glEnd();
   glFlush();
}
```

```
void reshape(int w, int h)
{
    glViewport(0, 0, (GLsizei) w, (GLsizei) h);
    glMatrixMode(GL_PROJECTION);
    glLoadIdentity();
    if (w <= h)
        glOrtho(-5.0, 5.0, -5.0*(GLfloat)h/(GLfloat)w,
                5.0*(GLfloat)h/(GLfloat)w, -5.0, 5.0);
    else
        glOrtho(-5.0*(GLfloat)w/(GLfloat)h,
                5.0*(GLfloat)w/(GLfloat)h, -5.0, 5.0, -5.0, 5.0);
    glMatrixMode(GL_MODELVIEW);
    glLoadIdentity();
}

int main(int argc, char** argv)
{
    glutInit(&argc, argv);
    glutInitDisplayMode(GLUT_SINGLE | GLUT_RGB);
    glutInitWindowSize(500, 500);
    glutInitWindowPosition(100, 100);
    glutCreateWindow(argv[0]);
    init();
    glutDisplayFunc(display);
    glutReshapeFunc(reshape);
    glutMainLoop();
    return 0;
}
```

A cubic Bézier curve is described by four control points, which appear in this example in the *ctrlpoints[][]* array. This array is one of the arguments for **glMap1f()**. The other arguments for this command are:

GL_MAP1_VERTEX_3	Specifies that three-dimensional control points are provided and that three-dimensional vertices should be produced
0.0	Low value of parameter u
1.0	High value of parameter u
3	The number of floating-point values to advance in the data between one control point and the next
4	The order of the spline, which is the degree plus 1: in this case, the degree is 3 (since this is a cubic curve)
&ctrlpoints[0][0]	Pointer to the first control point's data

Note that the second and third arguments control the parameterization of the curve—as the variable u ranges from 0.0 to 1.0, the curve goes from one end to the other. The call to **glEnable()** enables the one-dimensional evaluator for three-dimensional vertices.

The curve is drawn in the routine **display()** between the **glBegin()** and **glEnd()** calls. Since the evaluator is enabled, giving the command **glEvalCoord1f()** is just like issuing a **glVertex()** command with the coordinates of a vertex on the curve corresponding to the input parameter u.

Defining and Evaluating a One-Dimensional Evaluator

The Bernstein polynomial of degree n (or order $n + 1$) is given by

$$B_i^n (u) = \binom{n}{i} u^i (1-u)^{n-i}$$

If P_i represents a set of control points (one-, two-, three-, or even four-dimensional), then the equation

$$C (u) = \sum_{i=0}^{n} B_i^n (u) P_i$$

represents a Bézier curve as u varies from 0.0 to 1.0. To represent the same curve but allowing u to vary between u_1 and u_2 instead of 0.0 and 1.0, evaluate

$$C \left(\frac{u - u_1}{u_2 - u_1} \right)$$

The command **glMap1()** defines a one-dimensional evaluator that uses these equations.

void **glMap1**{fd}(GLenum *target*, *TYPE u1*, *TYPE u2*, GLint *stride*, GLint *order*, const *TYPE *points*);

Defines a one-dimensional evaluator. The *target* parameter specifies what the control points represent, as shown in Table 12-1, and therefore how many values need to be supplied in *points*. The points can represent vertices, RGBA color data, normal vectors, or texture coordinates. For example, with GL_MAP1_COLOR_4, the evaluator generates color data along a curve in four-dimensional (RGBA) color space. You also use the parameter values listed in Table 12-1 to enable each defined evaluator before you invoke it. Pass the appropriate value to **glEnable()** or **glDisable()** to enable or disable the evaluator.

The second two parameters for **glMap1*()**, *u1* and *u2*, indicate the range for the variable *u*. The variable *stride* is the number of single- or double-precision values (as appropriate) in each block of storage. Thus, it's an offset value between the beginning of one control point and the beginning of the next.

The *order* is the degree plus 1, and it should agree with the number of control points. The *points* parameter points to the first coordinate of the first control point. Using the example data structure for **glMap1*()**, use the following for *points*:

```
(GLfloat *)(&ctlpoints[0].x)
```

Parameter	Meaning
GL_MAP1_VERTEX_3	*x, y, z* vertex coordinates
GL_MAP1_VERTEX_4	*x, y, z, w* vertex coordinates
GL_MAP1_INDEX	color index
GL_MAP1_COLOR_4	R, G, B, A
GL_MAP1_NORMAL	normal coordinates
GL_MAP1_TEXTURE_COORD_1	*s* texture coordinates
GL_MAP1_TEXTURE_COORD_2	*s, t* texture coordinates
GL_MAP1_TEXTURE_COORD_3	*s, t, r* texture coordinates
GL_MAP1_TEXTURE_COORD_4	*s, t, r, q* texture coordinates

Table 12-1   Types of Control Points for glMap1*()

More than one evaluator can be evaluated at a time. If you have both a GL_MAP1_VERTEX_3 and a GL_MAP1_COLOR_4 evaluator defined and enabled, for example, then calls to **glEvalCoord1()** generate both a position and a color. Only one of the vertex evaluators can be enabled at a time, although you might have defined both of them. Similarly, only one of the texture evaluators can be active. Otherwise, however, evaluators can be used to generate any combination of vertex, normal, color, and texture-coordinate data. If you define and enable more than one evaluator of the same type, the one of highest dimension is used.

Use **glEvalCoord1*()** to evaluate a defined and enabled one-dimensional map.

---

void **glEvalCoord1**{fd}(*TYPE u*);
void **glEvalCoord1**{fd}v(const *TYPE *u*);

Compatibility
Extension

glEvalCoord1

Causes evaluation of the enabled one-dimensional maps. The argument *u* is the value (or a pointer to the value, in the vector version of the command) of the domain coordinate.

For evaluated vertices, generation of values for color, color index, normal vectors, and texture coordinates is done by evaluation. Calls to **glEvalCoord*()** do not use the current values for color, color index, normal vectors, and texture coordinates. **glEvalCoord*()** also leaves those values unchanged.

Defining Evenly Spaced Coordinate Values in One Dimension

You can use **glEvalCoord1()** with any values of *u*, but by far the most common practice is to use evenly spaced values, as shown previously in Example 12-1. To obtain evenly spaced values, define a one-dimensional grid using **glMapGrid1*()** and then apply it using **glEvalMesh1()**.

---

void **glMapGrid1**{fd}(GLint *n*, *TYPE u1*, *TYPE u2*);

Compatibility
Extension

glMapGrid1

Defines a grid that goes from *u1* to *u2* in *n* steps, which are evenly spaced.

---

void **glEvalMesh1**(GLenum *mode*, GLint *p1*, GLint *p2*);

Applies the currently defined map grid to all enabled evaluators. The *mode* can be either GL_POINT or GL_LINE, depending on whether you want to draw points or a connected line along the curve. The call has exactly the same effect as issuing a **glEvalCoord1**() for each of the steps from *p1* to *p2*, inclusive, where $0 \le p1, p2 \le n$. Programmatically, it's equivalent to

```
glBegin(GL_POINTS);      /* OR glBegin(GL_LINE_STRIP); */
  for (i = p1; i <= p2; i++)
    glEvalCoord1(u1 + i*(u2-u1)/n);
glEnd();
```

except that if $i = 0$ or $i = n$, then **glEvalCoord1**() is called with exactly *u1* or *u2* as its parameter.

Two-Dimensional Evaluators

In two dimensions, everything is similar to the one-dimensional case, except that all the commands must take two parameters, *u* and *v*, into account. Points, colors, normals, or texture coordinates must be supplied over a surface instead of a curve. Mathematically, the definition of a Bézier surface patch is given by

$$S(u, v) = \sum_{i=0}^{n} \sum_{j=0}^{m} B_i^n(u) B_j^m(v) P_{ij}$$

where the P_{ij} values are a set of $m \cdot n$ control points, and the B_i functions are the same Bernstein polynomials for one dimension. As before, the P_{ij} values can represent vertices, normals, colors, or texture coordinates.

The procedure for using two-dimensional evaluators is similar to the procedure for one dimension:

1. Define the evaluator(s) with **glMap2***().

2. Enable them by passing the appropriate value to **glEnable**().

3. Invoke them either by calling **glEvalCoord2**() between a **glBegin**() and **glEnd**() pair or by specifying and then applying a mesh with **glMapGrid2**() and **glEvalMesh2**().

Defining and Evaluating a Two-Dimensional Evaluator

Use **glMap2*()** and **glEvalCoord2*()** to define and then invoke a two-dimensional evaluator.

---

void **glMap2**{fd}(GLenum *target*, TYPE *u1*, TYPE *u2*, GLint *ustride*,
  GLint *uorder*, TYPE *v1*, TYPE *v2*, GLint *vstride*,
  GLint *vorder*, TYPE *points*);

The *target* parameter can have any of the values in Table 12-1, except that the string MAP1 is replaced with MAP2. As before, these values are also used with **glEnable()** to enable the corresponding evaluator. Minimum and maximum values for both *u* and *v* are provided as *u1*, *u2*, *v1*, and *v2*. The parameters *ustride* and *vstride* indicate the numbers of single- and double-precision values (as appropriate) between independent settings for these values, allowing users to select a subrectangle of control points out of a much larger array. For example, if the data appears in the form

```
GLfloat ctlpoints[100][100][3];
```

and you want to use the 4 × 4 subset beginning at ctlpoints[20][30], choose *ustride* to be 100*3 and *vstride* to be 3. The starting point, *points*, should be set to &ctlpoints[20][30][0]. Finally, the order parameters, *uorder* and *vorder*, can be different—allowing patches that are cubic in one direction and quadratic in the other, for example.

---

void **glEvalCoord2**{fd}(*TYPE u, TYPE v*);
void **glEvalCoord2**{fd}v(const *TYPE *values*);

Causes evaluation of the enabled two-dimensional maps. The arguments *u* and *v* are the values (or a pointer to the *values u* and *v*, in the vector version of the command) for the domain coordinates. If either of the vertex evaluators is enabled (GL_MAP2_VERTEX_3 or GL_MAP2_VERTEX_4), then the normal to the surface is computed analytically. This normal is associated with the generated vertex if automatic normal generation has been enabled by passing GL_AUTO_NORMAL to **glEnable()**. If it's disabled, the corresponding enabled normal map is used to produce a normal. If no such map exists, the current normal is used.

Two-Dimensional Example: A Bézier Surface

Example 12-2 draws a wireframe Bézier surface using evaluators, as shown in Figure 12-2. In this example, the surface is drawn with nine curved lines in each direction. Each curve is drawn as 30 segments. To get the whole program, add the **reshape()** and **main()** routines from Example 12-1.

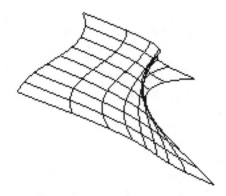

Figure 12-2   Bézier Surface

Example 12-2   Bézier Surface: bezsurf.c

```
GLfloat ctrlpoints[4][4][3] = {
   {{-1.5, -1.5, 4.0}, {-0.5, -1.5, 2.0},
    {0.5, -1.5, -1.0}, {1.5, -1.5, 2.0}},
   {{-1.5, -0.5, 1.0}, {-0.5, -0.5, 3.0},
    {0.5, -0.5, 0.0}, {1.5, -0.5, -1.0}},
   {{-1.5, 0.5, 4.0}, {-0.5, 0.5, 0.0},
    {0.5, 0.5, 3.0}, {1.5, 0.5, 4.0}},
   {{-1.5, 1.5, -2.0}, {-0.5, 1.5, -2.0},
    {0.5, 1.5, 0.0}, {1.5, 1.5, -1.0}}
};

void display(void)
{
   int i, j;

   glClear(GL_COLOR_BUFFER_BIT | GL_DEPTH_BUFFER_BIT);
   glColor3f(1.0, 1.0, 1.0);
   glPushMatrix();
   glRotatef(85.0, 1.0, 1.0, 1.0);
   for (j = 0; j <= 8; j++) {
      glBegin(GL_LINE_STRIP);
```

```
        for (i = 0; i <= 30; i++)
            glEvalCoord2f((GLfloat)i/30.0, (GLfloat)j/8.0);
        glEnd();
        glBegin(GL_LINE_STRIP);
        for (i = 0; i <= 30; i++)
            glEvalCoord2f((GLfloat)j/8.0, (GLfloat)i/30.0);
        glEnd();
    }
    glPopMatrix();
    glFlush();
}

void init(void)
{
    glClearColor(0.0, 0.0, 0.0, 0.0);
    glMap2f(GL_MAP2_VERTEX_3, 0, 1, 3, 4,
            0, 1, 12, 4, &ctrlpoints[0][0][0]);
    glEnable(GL_MAP2_VERTEX_3);
    glMapGrid2f(20, 0.0, 1.0, 20, 0.0, 1.0);
    glEnable(GL_DEPTH_TEST);
    glShadeModel(GL_FLAT);
}
```

Defining Evenly Spaced Coordinate Values in Two Dimensions

In two dimensions, the **glMapGrid2*()** and **glEvalMesh2()** commands
are similar to the one-dimensional versions, except that both *u* and *v*
information must be included.

void **glMapGrid2**{fd}(GLint *nu, TYPE u1, TYPE u2,* GLint *nv, TYPE v1, TYPE v2*); void **glEvalMesh2**(GLenum *mode*, GLint *i1,* GLint *i2*, GLint *j1*, GLint *j2*);	Compatibility Extension **glMapGrid2** **glEvalMesh2**

Defines a two-dimensional map grid that goes from *u1* to *u2* in *nu* evenly
spaced steps, goes from *v1* to *v2* in *nv* steps (**glMapGrid2*()**), and then
applies this grid to all enabled evaluators (**glEvalMesh2()**). The only significant difference from the one-dimensional versions of these two commands is that in **glEvalMesh2()**, the *mode* parameter can be GL_FILL as
well as GL_POINT or GL_LINE. GL_FILL generates filled polygons using
the quad-mesh primitive. Stated precisely, **glEvalMesh2()** is nearly equivalent to one of the following three code fragments. (It's nearly equivalent
because when *i* is equal to *nu*, or *j* to *nv*, the parameter is exactly equal to
u2 or *v2*, not to *u1* + *nu*∗(*u2* − *u1*)/*nu*, which might be slightly different
due to round-off error.)

```
glBegin(GL_POINTS);                          /* mode == GL_POINT */
for (i = nu1; i <= nu2; i++)
    for (j = nv1; j <= nv2; j++)
        glEvalCoord2(u1 + i*(u2-u1)/nu, v1+j*(v2-v1)/nv);
glEnd();
```

or

```
for (i = nu1; i <= nu2; i++) {       /* mode == GL_LINE */
    glBegin(GL_LINES);
        for (j = nv1; j <= nv2; j++)
            glEvalCoord2(u1 + i*(u2-u1)/nu, v1+j*(v2-v1)/nv);
    glEnd();
}
for (j = nv1; j <= nv2; j++) {
    glBegin(GL_LINES);
    for (i = nu1; i <= nu2; i++)
        glEvalCoord2(u1 + i*(u2-u1)/nu, v1+j*(v2-v1)/nv);
    glEnd();
}
```

or

```
for (i = nu1; i < nu2; i++) {       /* mode == GL_FILL */
    glBegin(GL_QUAD_STRIP);
    for (j = nv1; j <= nv2; j++) {
        glEvalCoord2(u1 + i*(u2-u1)/nu, v1+j*(v2-v1)/nv);
        glEvalCoord2(u1 + (i+1)*(u2-u1)/nu, v1+j*(v2-v1)/nv);
    glEnd();
}
```

Example 12-3 shows the differences necessary to draw the same Bézier surface as in Example 12-2, but using **glMapGrid2()** and **glEvalMesh2()** to subdivide the square domain into a uniform 8 × 8 grid. This program also adds lighting and shading, as shown in Figure 12-3.

Example 12-3   Lit, Shaded Bézier Surface Using a Mesh: bezmesh.c

```
void initlights(void)
{
    GLfloat ambient[] = {0.2, 0.2, 0.2, 1.0};
    GLfloat position[] = {0.0, 0.0, 2.0, 1.0};
    GLfloat mat_diffuse[] = {0.6, 0.6, 0.6, 1.0};
    GLfloat mat_specular[] = {1.0, 1.0, 1.0, 1.0};
    GLfloat mat_shininess[] = {50.0};

    glEnable(GL_LIGHTING);
    glEnable(GL_LIGHT0);
```

```
   glLightfv(GL_LIGHT0, GL_AMBIENT, ambient);
   glLightfv(GL_LIGHT0, GL_POSITION, position);

   glMaterialfv(GL_FRONT, GL_DIFFUSE, mat_diffuse);
   glMaterialfv(GL_FRONT, GL_SPECULAR, mat_specular);
   glMaterialfv(GL_FRONT, GL_SHININESS, mat_shininess);
}

void display(void)
{
   glClear(GL_COLOR_BUFFER_BIT | GL_DEPTH_BUFFER_BIT);
   glPushMatrix();
   glRotatef(85.0, 1.0, 1.0, 1.0);
   glEvalMesh2(GL_FILL, 0, 20, 0, 20);
   glPopMatrix();
   glFlush();
}

void init(void)
{
   glClearColor(0.0, 0.0, 0.0, 0.0);
   glEnable(GL_DEPTH_TEST);
   glMap2f(GL_MAP2_VERTEX_3, 0, 1, 3, 4,
           0, 1, 12, 4, &ctrlpoints[0][0][0]);
   glEnable(GL_MAP2_VERTEX_3);
   glEnable(GL_AUTO_NORMAL);
   glMapGrid2f(20, 0.0, 1.0, 20, 0.0, 1.0);
   initlights();
}
```

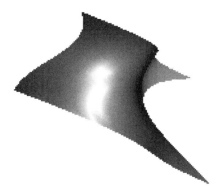

Figure 12-3   Lit, Shaded Bézier Surface Drawn with a Mesh

Using Evaluators for Textures

Example 12-4 enables two evaluators at the same time: The first generates three-dimensional points on the same Bézier surface as in Example 12-3, and the second generates texture coordinates. In this case, the texture coordinates are the same as the *u*- and *v*-coordinates of the surface, but a special flat Bézier patch must be created to do this.

The flat patch is defined over a square with corners at (0, 0), (0, 1), (1, 0), and (1, 1); it generates (0, 0) at corner (0, 0), (0, 1) at corner (0, 1), and so on. Since it's of order 2 (linear degree plus 1), evaluating this texture at the point (*u*, *v*) generates texture coordinates (*s*, *t*). It's enabled at the same time as the vertex evaluator, so both take effect when the surface is drawn (see Plate 19). If you want the texture to repeat three times in each direction, change every 1.0 in the array *texpts[][][]* to 3.0. Since the texture wraps in this example, the surface is rendered with nine copies of the texture map.

Example 12-4   Using Evaluators for Textures: texturesurf.c

```
GLfloat ctrlpoints[4][4][3] = {
    {{ -1.5, -1.5, 4.0}, { -0.5, -1.5, 2.0},
     {0.5, -1.5, -1.0}, {1.5, -1.5, 2.0}},
    {{ -1.5, -0.5, 1.0}, { -0.5, -0.5, 3.0},
     {0.5, -0.5, 0.0}, {1.5, -0.5, -1.0}},
    {{ -1.5, 0.5, 4.0}, { -0.5, 0.5, 0.0},
     {0.5, 0.5, 3.0}, {1.5, 0.5, 4.0}},
    {{ -1.5, 1.5, -2.0}, { -0.5, 1.5, -2.0},
     {0.5, 1.5, 0.0}, {1.5, 1.5, -1.0}}
};
GLfloat texpts[2][2][2] = {{{0.0, 0.0}, {0.0, 1.0}},
                           {{1.0, 0.0}, {1.0, 1.0}}};

void display(void)
{
    glClear(GL_COLOR_BUFFER_BIT | GL_DEPTH_BUFFER_BIT);
    glColor3f(1.0, 1.0, 1.0);
    glEvalMesh2(GL_FILL, 0, 20, 0, 20);
    glFlush();
}
#define imageWidth 64
#define imageHeight 64
GLubyte image[3*imageWidth*imageHeight];
```

```c
void makeImage(void)
{
   int i, j;
   float ti, tj;

   for (i = 0; i < imageWidth; i++) {
      ti = 2.0*3.14159265*i/imageWidth;
      for (j = 0; j < imageHeight; j++) {
         tj = 2.0*3.14159265*j/imageHeight;
         image[3*(imageHeight*i+j)] =
             (GLubyte) 127*(1.0+sin(ti));
         image[3*(imageHeight*i+j)+1] =
             (GLubyte) 127*(1.0+cos(2*tj));
         image[3*(imageHeight*i+j)+2] =
             (GLubyte) 127*(1.0+cos(ti+tj));
      }
   }
}

void init(void)
{
   glMap2f(GL_MAP2_VERTEX_3, 0, 1, 3, 4,
           0, 1, 12, 4, &ctrlpoints[0][0][0]);
   glMap2f(GL_MAP2_TEXTURE_COORD_2, 0, 1, 2, 2,
           0, 1, 4, 2, &texpts[0][0][0]);
   glEnable(GL_MAP2_TEXTURE_COORD_2);
   glEnable(GL_MAP2_VERTEX_3);
   glMapGrid2f(20, 0.0, 1.0, 20, 0.0, 1.0);
   makeImage();
   glTexEnvf(GL_TEXTURE_ENV, GL_TEXTURE_ENV_MODE, GL_DECAL);
   glTexParameteri(GL_TEXTURE_2D, GL_TEXTURE_WRAP_S, GL_REPEAT);
   glTexParameteri(GL_TEXTURE_2D, GL_TEXTURE_WRAP_T, GL_REPEAT);
   glTexParameteri(GL_TEXTURE_2D, GL_TEXTURE_MAG_FILTER,
                   GL_NEAREST);
   glTexParameteri(GL_TEXTURE_2D, GL_TEXTURE_MIN_FILTER,
                   GL_NEAREST);
   glTexImage2D(GL_TEXTURE_2D, 0, 3, imageWidth, imageHeight, 0,
                GL_RGB, GL_UNSIGNED_BYTE, image);
   glEnable(GL_TEXTURE_2D);
   glEnable(GL_DEPTH_TEST);
   glShadeModel(GL_FLAT);
}
```

```
void reshape(int w, int h)
{
   glViewport(0, 0, (GLsizei) w, (GLsizei) h);
   glMatrixMode(GL_PROJECTION);
   glLoadIdentity();
   if (w <= h)
      glOrtho(-4.0, 4.0, -4.0*(GLfloat)h/(GLfloat)w,
              4.0*(GLfloat)h/(GLfloat)w, -4.0, 4.0);
   else
      glOrtho(-4.0*(GLfloat)w/(GLfloat)h,
              4.0*(GLfloat)w/(GLfloat)h, -4.0, 4.0, -4.0, 4.0);
   glMatrixMode(GL_MODELVIEW);
   glLoadIdentity();
   glRotatef(85.0, 1.0, 1.0, 1.0);
}

int main(int argc, char** argv)
{
   glutInit(&argc, argv);
   glutInitDisplayMode(GLUT_SINGLE | GLUT_RGB | GLUT_DEPTH);
   glutInitWindowSize(500, 500);
   glutInitWindowPosition(100, 100);
   glutCreateWindow(argv[0]);
   init();
   glutDisplayFunc(display);
   glutReshapeFunc(reshape);
   glutMainLoop();
   return 0;
}
```

The GLU NURBS Interface

Although evaluators are the only OpenGL primitives available to draw
curves and surfaces directly, and even though they can be implemented
very efficiently in hardware, they're often accessed by applications through
higher-level libraries. The GLU provides a NURBS interface built on top of
the OpenGL evaluator commands.

A Simple NURBS Example

If you understand NURBS, writing OpenGL code to manipulate NURBS curves and surfaces is relatively easy, even with lighting and texture mapping. Perform the following steps to draw NURBS curves or untrimmed NURBS surfaces. (See "Trimming a NURBS Surface" on page 601 for information about trimmed surfaces.)

1. If you intend to use lighting with a NURBS surface, call **glEnable()** with GL_AUTO_NORMAL to generate surface normals automatically. (Or you can calculate your own.)

2. Use **gluNewNurbsRenderer()** to create a pointer to a NURBS object, which is referred to when creating your NURBS curve or surface.

3. If desired, call **gluNurbsProperty()** to choose rendering values, such as the maximum size of lines or polygons that are used to render your NURBS object. **gluNurbsProperty()** can also enable a mode, where the tessellated geometric data can be retrieved through the callback interface.

4. Call **gluNurbsCallback()** if you want to be notified when an error is encountered. (Error checking may slightly degrade performance but is still highly recommended.) **gluNurbsCallback()** may also be used to register the functions to call to retrieve the tessellated geometric data.

5. Start your curve or surface by calling **gluBeginCurve()** or **gluBeginSurface()**.

6. Generate and render your curve or surface. Call **gluNurbsCurve()** or **gluNurbsSurface()** at least once with the control points (rational or nonrational), knot sequence, and order of the polynomial basis function for your NURBS object. You might call these functions additional times to specify surface normals and/or texture coordinates.

7. Call **gluEndCurve()** or **gluEndSurface()** to complete the curve or surface.

Example 12-5 renders a NURBS surface in the shape of a symmetrical hill, with control points ranging from –3.0 to 3.0. The basis function is a cubic B-spline, but the knot sequence is nonuniform, with a multiplicity of 4 at each endpoint, causing the basis function to behave as a Bézier curve in each direction. The surface is lighted, with a dark gray diffuse reflection and white specular highlights. Figure 12-4 shows the surface as a lit wireframe.

Figure 12-4 NURBS Surface

Example 12-5 NURBS Surface: surface.c

```
#ifndef CALLBACK
#define CALLBACK
#endif

GLfloat ctlpoints[4][4][3];
int showPoints = 0;

GLUnurbsObj *theNurb;

void init_surface(void)
{
    int u, v;
    for (u = 0; u < 4; u++) {
        for (v = 0; v < 4; v++) {
            ctlpoints[u][v][0] = 2.0*((GLfloat)u - 1.5);
            ctlpoints[u][v][1] = 2.0*((GLfloat)v - 1.5);

            if ( (u == 1 || u == 2) && (v == 1 || v == 2))
                ctlpoints[u][v][2] = 3.0;
            else
                ctlpoints[u][v][2] = -3.0;
        }
    }
}

void CALLBACK nurbsError(GLenum errorCode)
{
    const GLubyte *estring;
```

```
      estring = gluErrorString(errorCode);
      fprintf(stderr, "Nurbs Error: %s\n", estring);
      exit(0);
}

void init(void)
{
   GLfloat mat_diffuse[] = { 0.7, 0.7, 0.7, 1.0 };
   GLfloat mat_specular[] = { 1.0, 1.0, 1.0, 1.0 };
   GLfloat mat_shininess[] = { 100.0 };

   glClearColor(0.0, 0.0, 0.0, 0.0);
   glMaterialfv(GL_FRONT, GL_DIFFUSE, mat_diffuse);
   glMaterialfv(GL_FRONT, GL_SPECULAR, mat_specular);
   glMaterialfv(GL_FRONT, GL_SHININESS, mat_shininess);

   glEnable(GL_LIGHTING);
   glEnable(GL_LIGHT0);
   glEnable(GL_DEPTH_TEST);
   glEnable(GL_AUTO_NORMAL);
   glEnable(GL_NORMALIZE);

   init_surface();

   theNurb = gluNewNurbsRenderer();
   gluNurbsProperty(theNurb, GLU_SAMPLING_TOLERANCE, 25.0);
   gluNurbsProperty(theNurb, GLU_DISPLAY_MODE, GLU_FILL);
   gluNurbsCallback(theNurb, GLU_ERROR, nurbsError);
}

void display(void)
{
   GLfloat knots[8] = {0.0, 0.0, 0.0, 0.0, 1.0, 1.0, 1.0, 1.0};
   int i, j;

   glClear(GL_COLOR_BUFFER_BIT | GL_DEPTH_BUFFER_BIT);

   glPushMatrix();
   glRotatef(330.0, 1., 0., 0.);
   glScalef(0.5, 0.5, 0.5);

   gluBeginSurface(theNurb);
   gluNurbsSurface(theNurb,
                   8, knots, 8, knots,
                   4 * 3, 3, &ctlpoints[0][0][0],
                   4, 4, GL_MAP2_VERTEX_3);
```

```
      gluEndSurface(theNurb);

   if (showPoints) {
      glPointSize(5.0);
      glDisable(GL_LIGHTING);
      glColor3f(1.0, 1.0, 0.0);
      glBegin(GL_POINTS);
      for (i = 0; i < 4; i++) {
         for (j = 0; j < 4; j++) {
            glVertex3f(ctlpoints[i][j][0],
                       ctlpoints[i][j][1], ctlpoints[i][j][2]);
         }
      }
      glEnd();
      glEnable(GL_LIGHTING);
   }
   glPopMatrix();
   glFlush();
}

void reshape(int w, int h)
{
   glViewport(0, 0, (GLsizei) w, (GLsizei) h);
   glMatrixMode(GL_PROJECTION);
   glLoadIdentity();
   gluPerspective(45.0, (GLdouble)w/(GLdouble)h, 3.0, 8.0);
   glMatrixMode(GL_MODELVIEW);
   glLoadIdentity();
   glTranslatef(0.0, 0.0, -5.0);
}
void keyboard(unsigned char key, int x, int y)
{
   switch (key) {
      case 'c':
      case 'C':
         showPoints = !showPoints;
         glutPostRedisplay();
         break;
      case 27:
         exit(0);
         break;
      default:
         break;
   }
}
```

```
int main(int argc, char** argv)
{
   glutInit(&argc, argv);
   glutInitDisplayMode(GLUT_SINGLE | GLUT_RGB | GLUT_DEPTH);
   glutInitWindowSize(500, 500);
   glutInitWindowPosition(100, 100);
   glutCreateWindow(argv[0]);
   init();
   glutReshapeFunc(reshape);
   glutDisplayFunc(display);
   glutKeyboardFunc(keyboard);
   glutMainLoop();
   return 0;
}
```

Managing a NURBS Object

As shown in Example 12-5, **gluNewNurbsRenderer**() returns a new NURBS object, whose type is a pointer to a GLUnurbsObj structure. You must make this object before using any other NURBS routine. When you're done with a NURBS object, you may use **gluDeleteNurbsRenderer**() to free up the memory that was used.

GLUnurbsObj* **gluNewNurbsRenderer**(void);

Creates a new NURBS object, *nobj*, and returns a pointer to the new object, or zero, if OpenGL cannot allocate memory for a new NURBS object.

void **gluDeleteNurbsRenderer**(GLUnurbsObj **nobj*);

Destroys the NURBS object *nobj*.

Controlling NURBS Rendering Properties

A set of properties associated with a NURBS object affects the way the object is rendered. These properties include how the surface is rasterized (for example, filled or wireframe), whether the tessellated vertices are displayed or returned, and the precision of tessellation.

> void **gluNurbsProperty**(GLUnurbsObj *nobj*, GLenum *property*,
> GLfloat *value*);

Controls attributes of a NURBS object, *nobj*. The *property* argument specifies the property and can be GLU_DISPLAY_MODE, GLU_NURBS_ MODE, GLU_CULLING, GLU_SAMPLING_METHOD, GLU_SAMPLING_ TOLERANCE, GLU_PARAMETRIC_TOLERANCE, GLU_U_STEP, GLU_V_ STEP, or GLU_AUTO_LOAD_MATRIX. The *value* argument indicates what the property should be.

For the *property* GLU_DISPLAY_MODE, the default *value* is GLU_FILL, which causes the surface to be rendered as polygons. If GLU_OUTLINE_ POLYGON is used for the display-mode property, only the outlines of polygons created by tessellation are rendered. GLU_OUTLINE_PATCH renders the outlines of patches and trimming curves. (See "Creating a NURBS Curve or Surface" on page 595.)

The *property* GLU_NURBS_MODE controls whether the tessellated vertices are simply rendered (the default *value*, GLU_NURBS_RENDERER) or whether the callback interface is activated to allow the tessellated data to be returned (if *value* is GLU_NURBS_TESSELLATOR). For details, see "Getting Primitives Back from the NURBS Tessellator" on page 597.

GLU_CULLING can speed up performance by not performing tessellation if the NURBS object falls completely outside the viewing volume; set this property to GL_TRUE to enable culling (the default is GL_FALSE).

Since a NURBS object is rendered as primitives, it's sampled at different values of its parameter(s) (*u* and *v*) and broken down into small line segments or polygons for rendering. If *property* is GLU_SAMPLING_ METHOD, then *value* is set to GLU_PATH_LENGTH (which is the default), GLU_PARAMETRIC_ERROR, GLU_DOMAIN_DISTANCE, GLU_OBJECT_ PATH_LENGTH, or GLU_OBJECT_PARAMETRIC_ERROR, which specifies how a NURBS curve or surface should be tessellated. When *value* is set to GLU_PATH_LENGTH, the surface is rendered so that the maximum length, in pixels, of the edges of tessellated polygons is no greater than that specified by GLU_SAMPLING_TOLERANCE. When *value* is set to GLU_PARAMETRIC_ERROR, then the quantity specified by GLU_ PARAMETRIC_TOLERANCE is the maximum distance, in pixels, between tessellated polygons and the surfaces they approximate.

A *value* of GLU_OBJECT_PATH_LENGTH is similar to GLU_PATH_LENGTH, except that the maximum length (the value of GLU_SAMPLING_TOLERANCE) of a tessellated primitive is measured in object space, not pixels. Similarly, GLU_OBJECT_PARAMETRIC_ERROR is related to GLU_PARAMETRIC_ERROR, except that GLU_PARAMETRIC_TOLERANCE measures the maximum distance between tessellated polygons and the surfaces they approximate, in object space, not in pixels.

When *value* is set to GLU_DOMAIN_DISTANCE, the application specifies, in parametric coordinates, how many sample points per unit length are taken in the *u*- and *v*-dimensions, using the values for GLU_U_STEP and GLU_V_STEP.

If *property* is GLU_SAMPLING_TOLERANCE and the sampling method is GLU_PATH_LENGTH or GLU_OBJECT_PATH_LENGTH, *value* controls the maximum length, in pixels or object space units, respectively, that should be used for tessellated polygons. For example, the default value of 50.0 makes the largest sampled line segment or polygon edge 50.0 pixels long or 50.0 units long in object space. If *property* is GLU_PARAMETRIC_TOLERANCE and the sampling method is GLU_PARAMETRIC_ERROR or GLU_OBJECT_PARAMETRIC_ERROR, *value* controls the maximum distance, in pixels or object space, respectively, between the tessellated polygons and the surfaces they approximate. For either sampling method, the default value for GLU_PARAMETRIC_TOLERANCE is 0.5. For GLU_PARAMETRIC_ERROR, this value makes the tessellated polygons within one-half pixel of the approximated surface. (For GLU_OBJECT_PARAMETRIC_ERROR, the default value of 0.5 doesn't have the same obvious meaning.)

If the sampling method is GLU_DOMAIN_DISTANCE and *property* is either GLU_U_STEP or GLU_V_STEP, then *value* is the number of sample points per unit length taken along the *u*- or *v*-dimension, respectively, in parametric coordinates. The default for both GLU_U_STEP and GLU_V_STEP is 100.

The GLU_AUTO_LOAD_MATRIX property determines whether the projection matrix, modelview matrix, and viewport are downloaded from the OpenGL server (GL_TRUE, the default), or whether the application must supply these matrices with **gluLoadSamplingMatrices()** (GL_FALSE).

Note: Several of the NURBS properties (the GLU_NURBS_MODE and its nondefault value GLU_NURBS_TESSELLATOR, and the object space sampling methods GLU_OBJECT_PATH_LENGTH and GLU_ OBJECT_PARAMETRIC_ERROR) are introduced in GLU Version 1.3. Prior to GLU 1.3, these NURBS properties existed as vendor-specific extensions, if at all. Make sure you check the GLU version before you attempt to use these properties.

---

void **gluLoadSamplingMatrices**(GLUnurbsObj *nobj,
                                  const GLfloat modelMatrix[16],
                                  const GLfloat projMatrix[16],
                                  const GLint viewport[4]);

If the GLU_AUTO_LOAD_MATRIX is turned off, the modelview and projection matrices and the viewport specified in **gluLoadSamplingMatrices**() are used to compute sampling and culling matrices for each NURBS curve or surface.

If you need to query the current value of a NURBS property, you may use **gluGetNurbsProperty**().

---

void **gluGetNurbsProperty**(GLUnurbsObj *nobj, GLenum property,
                              GLfloat *value);

Given the property to be queried for the NURBS object nobj, returns its current value.

Handling NURBS Errors

Since there are 37 different errors specific to NURBS functions, it's a good idea to register an error callback to let you know if you've stumbled into one of them. In Example 12-5, the callback function was registered with

```
gluNurbsCallback(theNurb, GLU_ERROR, (GLvoid (*)()) nurbsError);
```

void **gluNurbsCallback**(GLUnurbsObj *nobj*, GLenum *which*,
void (*fn)(GLenum *errorCode*));

which is the type of callback; for error checking, it must be GLU_ERROR. When a NURBS function detects an error condition, *fn* is invoked with the error code as its only argument. *errorCode* is one of 37 error conditions, named GLU_NURBS_ERROR1 through GLU_NURBS_ERROR37. Use **gluErrorString**() to describe the meaning of these error codes.

In Example 12-5, the **nurbsError**() routine was registered as the error callback function:

```
void CALLBACK nurbsError(GLenum errorCode)
{
    const GLubyte *estring;

    estring = gluErrorString(errorCode);
    fprintf(stderr, "Nurbs Error: %s\n", estring);
    exit(0);
}
```

In GLU 1.3, additional NURBS callback functions have been added to return post-tessellation values back to the program (instead of rendering them). For more information on these new callbacks, see "Getting Primitives Back from the NURBS Tessellator" on page 597.

Creating a NURBS Curve or Surface

To render a NURBS surface, **gluNurbsSurface**() is bracketed by **gluBeginSurface**() and **gluEndSurface**(). The bracketing routines save and restore the evaluator state.

void **gluBeginSurface**(GLUnurbsObj *nobj*);
void **gluEndSurface**(GLUnurbsObj *nobj*);

After **gluBeginSurface**(), one or more calls to **gluNurbsSurface**() defines the attributes of the surface. Exactly one of these calls must have a surface type of GL_MAP2_VERTEX_3 or GL_MAP2_VERTEX_4 to generate vertices. Use **gluEndSurface**() to end the definition of a surface. Trimming of NURBS surfaces is also supported between **gluBeginSurface**() and **gluEndSurface**(). (See "Trimming a NURBS Surface" on page 601.)

---

void **gluNurbsSurface**(GLUnurbsObj *nobj*, GLint *uknot_count*,
   GLfloat *uknot*, GLint *vknot_count*, GLfloat *vknot*,
   GLint *u_stride*, GLint *v_stride*, GLfloat *ctlarray*,
   GLint *uorder*, GLint *vorder*, GLenum *type*);

Describes the vertices (or surface normals or texture coordinates) of a
NURBS surface, *nobj*. Several of the values must be specified for both *u*
and *v* parametric directions, such as the knot sequences (*uknot* and
vknot), knot counts (*uknot_count* and *vknot_count*), and the order of
the polynomial (*uorder* and *vorder*) for the NURBS surface. Note that
the number of control points isn't specified. Instead, it's derived by
determining the number of control points along each parameter as
the number of knots minus the order. Then, the number of control
points for the surface is equal to the number of control points in each
parametric direction, multiplied by one another. The *ctlarray* argument
points to an array of control points.

The last parameter, *type*, is one of the two-dimensional evaluator types.
Commonly, you might use GL_MAP2_VERTEX_3 for nonrational or GL_
MAP2_VERTEX_4 for rational control points, respectively. You might also
use other types, such as GL_MAP2_TEXTURE_COORD_* or GL_MAP2_
NORMAL to calculate and assign texture coordinates or surface normals.
For example, to create a lighted (with surface normals) and textured
NURBS surface, you may need to call this sequence:

```
gluBeginSurface(nobj);
    gluNurbsSurface(nobj, ..., GL_MAP2_TEXTURE_COORD_2);
    gluNurbsSurface(nobj, ..., GL_MAP2_NORMAL);
    gluNurbsSurface(nobj, ..., GL_MAP2_VERTEX_3);
gluEndSurface(nobj);
```

The *u_stride* and *v_stride* arguments represent the number of floating-
point values between control points in each parametric direction. The
evaluator type, as well as its order, affects the *u_stride* and *v_stride* values.
In Example 12-5, *u_stride* is 12 (4*3) because there are three coordinates
for each vertex (set by GL_MAP2_VERTEX_3) and four control points in
the parametric *v*-direction; *v_stride* is 3 because each vertex has three
coordinates, and the *v* control points are adjacent to one another in
memory.

Drawing a NURBS curve is similar to drawing a surface, except that all calculations are done with one parameter, *u*, rather than two. Also, for curves, **gluBeginCurve()** and **gluEndCurve()** are the bracketing routines.

---

void **gluBeginCurve**(GLUnurbsObj *nobj*);
void **gluEndCurve**(GLUnurbsObj *nobj*);

After **gluBeginCurve()**, one or more calls to **gluNurbsCurve()** define the attributes of the surface. Exactly one of these calls must have a surface type of GL_MAP1_VERTEX_3 or GL_MAP1_VERTEX_4 to generate vertices. Use **gluEndCurve()** to end the definition of a surface.

---

void **gluNurbsCurve**(GLUnurbsObj *nobj*, GLint *uknot_count*,
                GLfloat *uknot*, GLint *u_stride*, GLfloat *ctlarray*,
                GLint *uorder*, GLenum *type*);

Defines a NURBS curve for the object *nobj*. The arguments have the same meaning as those for **gluNurbsSurface()**. Note that this routine requires only one knot sequence and one declaration of the order of the NURBS object. If this curve is defined within a **gluBeginCurve()**/ **gluEndCurve()** pair, then the type can be any of the valid one-dimensional evaluator types (such as GL_MAP1_VERTEX_3 or GL_MAP1_VERTEX_4).

Getting Primitives Back from the NURBS Tessellator

By default, the NURBS tessellator breaks down a NURBS object into geometric lines and polygons, and then renders them. In GLU 1.3, additional callback functions have been added, so instead of rendering the post-tessellation values, they can be returned for use by the application.

To do this, call **gluNurbsProperty()** to set the GLU_NURBS_MODE *property* to the *value* GLU_NURBS_TESSELLATOR. The other necessary step is to call **gluNurbsCallback()** several times to register callback functions, which the NURBS tessellator will now call.

---

void **gluNurbsCallback**(GLUnurbsObj *nobj*, GLenum *which*,
                    void (**fn*)());

---

nobj is the NURBS object to be tessellated. *which* is the enumerant
identifying the callback function. If the *property* GLU_NURBS_MODE is set
to GLU_NURBS_TESSELLATOR, then 12 possible callback functions (in
addition to GLU_ERROR) are available. (If GLU_NURBS_MODE is set to
the default GLU_NURBS_RENDERER value, then only GLU_ERROR is
active.) The 12 callbacks have the following enumerants and prototypes:

GLU_NURBS_BEGIN	void **begin**(GLenum *type*);
GLU_NURBS_BEGIN_DATA	void **begin**(GLenum *type*, void **userData*);
GLU_NURBS_TEXTURE_COORD	void **texCoord**(GLfloat **tCrd*);
GLU_NURBS_TEXTURE_COORD_DATA	void **texCoord**(GLfloat **tCrd*, void **userData*);
GLU_NURBS_COLOR	void **color**(GLfloat **color*);
GLU_NURBS_COLOR_DATA	void **color**(GLfloat **color*, void **userData*);
GLU_NURBS_NORMAL	void **normal**(GLfloat **nml*);
GLU_NURBS_NORMAL_DATA	void **normal**(GLfloat **nml*, void **userData*);
GLU_NURBS_VERTEX	void **vertex**(GLfloat **vertex*);
GLU_NURBS_VERTEX_DATA	void **vertex**(GLfloat **vertex*, void **userData*);
GLU_NURBS_END	void **end**(void);
GLU_NURBS_END_DATA	void **end**(void **userData*);

To change a callback routine, call **gluNurbsCallback**() with the new routine.
To eliminate a callback routine without replacing it, pass **gluNurbsCallback**()
a null pointer for the appropriate function.

Six of the callback functions allow the user to pass some data to it. To specify that user data, you must call **gluNurbsCallbackData()**.

---

void **gluNurbsCallbackData**(GLUnurbsObj *nobj,
void *userData);

---

nobj is the NURBS object to be tessellated. *userData* is the data to be passed to the callback functions.

As tessellation proceeds, the callback routines are called in a manner similar to that in which you use the OpenGL commands **glBegin()**, **glTexCoord*()**, **glColor*()**, **glNormal*()**, **glVertex*()**, and **glEnd()**. During the GLU_NURBS_TESSELLATOR mode, the curve or surface is not directly rendered, but you can capture the vertex data passed as parameters to the callback functions.

To demonstrate these new callbacks, Example 12-6 and Example 12-7 show portions of surfpoints.c, which is a modification of the earlier surface.c program. Example 12-6 shows part of the **init()** subroutine, where the NURBS object is created, GLU_NURBS_MODE is set to perform the tessellation, and the callback functions are registered.

Example 12-6   Registering NURBS Tessellation Callbacks: surfpoints.c

```
void init(void)
{
/* only a portion of init() shown here--several lines deleted */

   theNurb = gluNewNurbsRenderer();
   gluNurbsProperty(theNurb, GLU_NURBS_MODE,
                    GLU_NURBS_TESSELLATOR);
   gluNurbsProperty(theNurb, GLU_SAMPLING_TOLERANCE, 100.0);
   gluNurbsProperty(theNurb, GLU_DISPLAY_MODE, GLU_FILL);
   gluNurbsCallback(theNurb, GLU_ERROR, nurbsError);
   gluNurbsCallback(theNurb, GLU_NURBS_BEGIN, beginCallback);
   gluNurbsCallback(theNurb, GLU_NURBS_VERTEX, vertexCallback);
   gluNurbsCallback(theNurb, GLU_NURBS_NORMAL, normalCallback);
   gluNurbsCallback(theNurb, GLU_NURBS_END, endCallback);
}
```

Example 12-7 shows the callback functions of surfpoints.c. In these callbacks, **printf()** statements act as diagnostics to show what rendering directives and vertex data are returned from the tessellator. In addition, the post-tessellation data is resubmitted to the pipeline for ordinary rendering.

Example 12-7 The NURBS Tessellation Callbacks: surfpoints.c

```
void CALLBACK beginCallback(GLenum whichType)
{
   glBegin(whichType);   /*  resubmit rendering directive */
   printf("glBegin(");
   switch (whichType) {  /*  print diagnostic message  */
      case GL_LINES:
         printf("GL_LINES)\n"); break;
      case GL_LINE_LOOP:
         printf("GL_LINE_LOOP)\n"); break;
      case GL_LINE_STRIP:
         printf("GL_LINE_STRIP)\n"); break;
      case GL_TRIANGLES:
         printf("GL_TRIANGLES)\n"); break;
      case GL_TRIANGLE_STRIP:
         printf("GL_TRIANGLE_STRIP)\n"); break;
      case GL_TRIANGLE_FAN:
         printf("GL_TRIANGLE_FAN)\n"); break;
      case GL_QUADS:
         printf("GL_QUADS)\n"); break;
      case GL_QUAD_STRIP:
         printf("GL_QUAD_STRIP)\n"); break;
      case GL_POLYGON:
         printf("GL_POLYGON)\n"); break;
      default:
         break;
   }
}
void CALLBACK endCallback()
{
   glEnd();  /*  resubmit rendering directive */
   printf("glEnd()\n");
}

void CALLBACK vertexCallback(GLfloat *vertex)
{
   glVertex3fv(vertex);  /*  resubmit tessellated vertex */
   printf("glVertex3f (%5.3f, %5.3f, %5.3f)\n",
          vertex[0], vertex[1], vertex[2]);
}

void CALLBACK normalCallback(GLfloat *normal)
{
   glNormal3fv(normal);  /*  resubmit tessellated normal */
   printf("glNormal3f (%5.3f, %5.3f, %5.3f) ",
          normal[0], normal[1], normal[2]);
}
```

Trimming a NURBS Surface

To create a trimmed NURBS surface with OpenGL, start as if you were creating an untrimmed surface. After calling **gluBeginSurface()** and **gluNurbsSurface()** but before calling **gluEndSurface()**, start a trim by calling **gluBeginTrim()**.

---

void **gluBeginTrim**(GLUnurbsObj *nobj*);
void **gluEndTrim**(GLUnurbsObj *nobj*);

Marks the beginning and end of the definition of a trimming loop. A trimming loop is a set of oriented, trimming curve segments (forming a closed curve) that defines the boundaries of a NURBS surface.

You can create two kinds of trimming curves: a piecewise linear curve with **gluPwlCurve()** or a NURBS curve with **gluNurbsCurve()**. A piecewise linear curve doesn't look like what is conventionally called a curve, because it's a series of straight lines. A NURBS curve for trimming must lie within the unit square of parametric (u, v) space. The type for a NURBS trimming curve is usually GLU_MAP1_TRIM2. Less often, the type is GLU_MAP1_TRIM3, where the curve is described in a two-dimensional homogeneous space (u', v', w') by $(u, v) = (u'/w', v'/w')$.

---

void **gluPwlCurve**(GLUnurbsObj *nobj*, GLint *count*, GLfloat *array*,
                 GLint *stride*, GLenum *type*);

Describes a piecewise linear trimming curve for the NURBS object *nobj*. There are *count* points on the curve, and they're given by *array*. The *type* can be either GLU_MAP1_TRIM_2 (the most common) or GLU_MAP1_TRIM_3 ((u, v, w) homogeneous parameter space). The value of *type* determines whether *stride* is 2 or 3. *stride* represents the number of floating-point values to the next vertex in *array*.

You need to consider the orientation of trimming curves—that is, whether they're counterclockwise or clockwise—to make sure you include the desired part of the surface. If you imagine walking along a curve, everything to the left is included and everything to the right is trimmed away. For example, if your trim consists of a single counterclockwise loop, everything inside the loop is included. If the trim consists of two nonintersecting counterclockwise loops with nonintersecting interiors, everything inside either of them is included. If it consists of a counterclockwise loop with two clockwise loops inside it, the trimming region has two holes in it. The outermost trimming curve must be counterclockwise. Often, you run a trimming curve around the entire unit square to include everything within it, which is what you get by default by not specifying any trimming curves.

Trimming curves must be closed and nonintersecting. You can combine trimming curves, as long as the endpoints of the trimming curves meet to form a closed curve. You can nest curves, creating islands that float in space. Be sure to get the curve orientations right. For example, an error results if you specify a trimming region with two counterclockwise curves, one enclosed within the other: the region between the curves is to the left of one and to the right of the other, so it must be both included and excluded, which is impossible. Figure 12-5 illustrates a few valid possibilities.

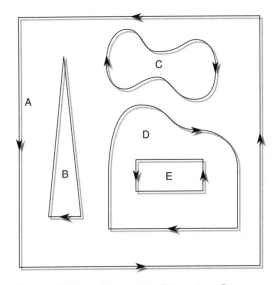

```
gluBeginSurface();
gluNurbsSurface(...);
gluBeginTrim();
gluPwlCurve(...); /* A */
gluEndTrim();
gluBeginTrim();
gluPwlCurve(...); /* B */
gluEndTrim();
gluBeginTrim();
gluNurbsCurve(...); */ C */
gluEndTrim();
gluBeginTrim();
gluNurbsCurve(...); */ D */
gluPwlCurve(...); /* D */
gluEndTrim();
gluBeginTrim();
gluPwlCurve(...); /* E */
gluEndTrim();
gluEndSurface();
```

Figure 12-5   Parametric Trimming Curves

Figure 12-6 shows the same small hill shown in Figure 12-4, but with a trimming curve that's a combination of a piecewise linear curve and a NURBS curve. The program that creates this figure is similar to the one shown in Example 12-5; the differences are in the routines shown in Example 12-8.

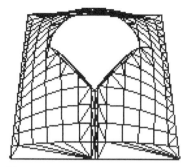 

Figure 12-6   Trimmed NURBS Surface

Example 12-8   Trimming a NURBS Surface: trim.c

```
void display(void)
{
   GLfloat knots[8] = {0.0, 0.0, 0.0, 0.0, 1.0, 1.0, 1.0, 1.0};
   GLfloat edgePt[5][2] = /* counter clockwise */
      {{0.0, 0.0}, {1.0, 0.0}, {1.0, 1.0}, {0.0, 1.0},
       {0.0, 0.0}};
   GLfloat curvePt[4][2] = /* clockwise */
      {{0.25, 0.5}, {0.25, 0.75}, {0.75, 0.75}, {0.75, 0.5}};
   GLfloat curveKnots[8] =
      {0.0, 0.0, 0.0, 0.0, 1.0, 1.0, 1.0, 1.0};
   GLfloat pwlPt[3][2] = /* clockwise */
      {{0.75, 0.5}, {0.5, 0.25}, {0.25, 0.5}};

   glClear(GL_COLOR_BUFFER_BIT | GL_DEPTH_BUFFER_BIT);
   glPushMatrix();
   glRotatef(330.0, 1., 0., 0.);
   glScalef(0.5, 0.5, 0.5);

   gluBeginSurface(theNurb);
   gluNurbsSurface(theNurb, 8, knots, 8, knots,
                   4 * 3, 3, &ctlpoints[0][0][0],
                   4, 4, GL_MAP2_VERTEX_3);
   gluBeginTrim(theNurb);
      gluPwlCurve(theNurb, 5, &edgePt[0][0], 2,
                  GLU_MAP1_TRIM_2);
   gluEndTrim(theNurb);
   gluBeginTrim(theNurb);
      gluNurbsCurve(theNurb, 8, curveKnots, 2,
                    &curvePt[0][0], 4, GLU_MAP1_TRIM_2);
```

```
        gluPwlCurve(theNurb, 3, &pwlPt[0][0], 2,
                    GLU_MAP1_TRIM_2);
    gluEndTrim(theNurb);
    gluEndSurface(theNurb);

    glPopMatrix();
    glFlush();
}
```

In Example 12-8, **gluBeginTrim()** and **gluEndTrim()** bracket each trimming curve. The first trim, with vertices defined by the array *edgePt[][]*, goes counterclockwise around the entire unit square of parametric space. This ensures that everything is drawn, provided it isn't removed by a clockwise trimming curve inside of it. The second trim is a combination of a NURBS trimming curve and a piecewise linear trimming curve. The NURBS curve ends at the points (0.9, 0.5) and (0.1, 0.5), where it is met by the piecewise linear curve, forming a closed clockwise curve.

Chapter 13

Selection and Feedback

Chapter Objectives

After reading this chapter, you'll be able to do the following:

- Create applications that allow the user to select a region of the screen or pick an object drawn on the screen

- Use the OpenGL feedback mode to obtain the results of rendering calculations

Note: In OpenGL Version 3.1, all of the techniques and functions described in this chapter were removed through deprecation. Even though some of this functionality is part of the GLU library, it relies on functionality that has been removed from the core OpenGL library

Some graphics applications simply draw static images of two- and three-dimensional objects. Other applications allow the user to identify objects on the screen and then to move, modify, delete, or otherwise manipulate those objects. OpenGL is designed to support exactly such interactive applications. Since objects drawn on the screen typically undergo multiple rotations, translations, and perspective transformations, it can be difficult for you to determine which object a user is selecting in a three-dimensional scene. To help you, OpenGL provides a selection mechanism that automatically tells you which objects are drawn inside a specified region of the window. You can use this mechanism together with a special utility routine to determine which object within the region the user is specifying, or *picking*, with the cursor.

Selection is actually a mode of operation for OpenGL; feedback is another such mode. In feedback mode, you use your graphics hardware and OpenGL to perform the usual rendering calculations. Instead of using the calculated results to draw an image on the screen, however, OpenGL returns (or feeds back) the drawing information to you. For example, if you want to draw three-dimensional objects on a plotter rather than the screen, you would draw the items in feedback mode, collect the drawing instructions, and then convert them to commands the plotter can understand.

In both selection and feedback modes, drawing information is returned to the application rather than being sent to the framebuffer, as it is in rendering mode. Thus, the screen remains frozen—no drawing occurs—while OpenGL is in selection or feedback mode. In these modes, the contents of the color, depth, stencil, and accumulation buffers are not affected. This chapter explains each of these modes in its own section:

- "Selection" discusses how to use selection mode and related routines to allow a user of your application to pick an object drawn on the screen.

- "Feedback" describes how to obtain information about what would be drawn on the screen and how that information is formatted.

Selection

Typically, when you're planning to use OpenGL's selection mechanism, you first draw your scene into the framebuffer, and then you enter selection mode and redraw the scene. However, once you're in selection mode, the contents of the framebuffer don't change until you exit selection mode. When you exit selection mode, OpenGL returns a list of the primitives that intersect the viewing volume. (Remember that the viewing volume is defined by the current modelview and projection matrices and any additional clipping planes, as explained in Chapter 3.) Each primitive that intersects the viewing volume causes a selection *hit*. The list of primitives is actually returned as an array of integer-valued *names* and related data—the *hit records*—that correspond to the current contents of the *name stack*. You construct the name stack by loading names onto it as you issue primitive drawing commands while in selection mode. Thus, when the list of names is returned, you can use it to determine which primitives might have been selected on the screen by the user.

In addition to this selection mechanism, OpenGL provides a utility routine designed to simplify selection in some cases by restricting drawing to a small region of the viewport. Typically, you use this routine to determine which objects are drawn near the cursor, so that you can identify which object the user is picking. (You can also delimit a selection region by specifying additional clipping planes. Remember that these planes act in world space, not in screen space.) Since picking is a special case of selection, selection is described first in this chapter, and then picking.

The Basic Steps

To use the selection mechanism, you need to perform the following steps:

1. Specify the array to be used for the returned hit records with **glSelectBuffer()**.

2. Enter selection mode by specifying GL_SELECT with **glRenderMode()**.

3. Initialize the name stack using **glInitNames()** and **glPushName()**.

4. Define the viewing volume you want to use for selection. Usually this is different from the viewing volume you originally used to draw the scene, so you probably want to save and then restore the current transformation state with **glPushMatrix()** and **glPopMatrix()**.

5. Alternately issue primitive drawing commands and commands to manipulate the name stack so that each primitive of interest is assigned an appropriate name.

6. Exit selection mode and process the returned selection data (the hit records).

The following two paragraphs describe **glSelectBuffer()** and **glRenderMode()**. In the next subsection, the commands for manipulating the name stack are described.

void **glSelectBuffer**(GLsizei *size*, GLuint **buffer*);

Specifies the array to be used for the returned selection data. The *buffer* argument is a pointer to an array of unsigned integers into which the data is put, and *size* indicates the maximum number of values that can be stored in the array. You need to call **glSelectBuffer**() before entering selection mode.

GLint **glRenderMode**(GLenum *mode*);

Controls whether the application is in rendering, selection, or feedback mode. The *mode* argument can be GL_RENDER (the default), GL_SELECT, or GL_FEEDBACK. The application remains in a given mode until **glRenderMode**() is called again with a different argument. Before selection mode is entered, **glSelectBuffer**() must be called to specify the selection array. Similarly, before feedback mode is entered, **glFeedbackBuffer**() must be called to specify the feedback array. The return value for **glRenderMode**() has meaning if the current render mode (that is, not the *mode* parameter) is either GL_SELECT or GL_FEEDBACK. The return value is the number of selection hits or the number of values placed in the feedback array when either mode is exited; a negative value means that the selection or feedback array has overflowed. You can use GL_RENDER_MODE with **glGetIntegerv**() to obtain the current mode.

Creating the Name Stack

As mentioned in the preceding subsection, the name stack forms the basis for the selection information that's returned to you. To create the name stack, first initialize it with **glInitNames**(), which simply clears the stack, and then add integer names to it while issuing corresponding drawing commands. As you might expect, the commands to manipulate the stack allow you to push a name onto it (**glPushName**()), pop a name off of it (**glPopName**()), and replace the name at the top of the stack with a different one (**glLoadName**()). Example 13-1 shows what your name-stack manipulation code might look like with these commands.

Example 13-1 Creating a Name Stack

```
glInitNames();
glPushName(0);

glPushMatrix();    /* save the current transformation state */

    /* create your desired viewing volume here */

    glLoadName(1);
    drawSomeObject();
    glLoadName(2);
    drawAnotherObject();
    glLoadName(3);
    drawYetAnotherObject();
    drawJustOneMoreObject();

glPopMatrix();    /* restore the previous transformation state*/
```

In this example, the first two objects to be drawn have their own names, and the third and fourth objects share a single name. With this setup, if either or both of the third and fourth objects cause a selection hit, only one hit record is returned to you. You can have multiple objects share the same name if you don't need to differentiate between them when processing the hit records.

---

void **glInitNames**(void);

Clears the name stack so that it's empty.

---

void **glPushName**(GLuint *name*);

Pushes *name* onto the name stack. Pushing a name beyond the capacity of the stack generates the error GL_STACK_OVERFLOW. The name stack's depth can vary among different OpenGL implementations, but it must be able to contain at least 64 names. You can use the parameter GL_NAME_STACK_DEPTH with **glGetIntegerv**() to obtain the depth of the name stack.

---

void **glPopName**(void);

Pops one name off the top of the name stack. Popping an empty stack generates the error GL_STACK_UNDERFLOW.

Compatibility Extension
glInitNames
glPushName
glPopName
glLoadName

---

void **glLoadName**(GLuint *name*);

Replaces the value at the top of the name stack with *name*. If the stack is empty, which it is right after **glInitNames()** is called, **glLoadName()** generates the error GL_INVALID_OPERATION. To avoid this, if the stack is initially empty, call **glPushName()** at least once to put something on the name stack before calling **glLoadName()**.

Calls to **glPushName()**, **glPopName()**, and **glLoadName()** are ignored if you're not in selection mode. You might find that it simplifies your code to use these calls throughout your drawing code, and then use the same drawing code for both selection and normal rendering modes.

The Hit Record

In selection mode, a primitive that intersects the viewing volume causes a selection hit. Whenever a name-stack manipulation command is executed or **glRenderMode()** is called, OpenGL writes a hit record into the selection array if there's been a hit since the last time the stack was manipulated or **glRenderMode()** was called. With this process, objects that share the same name—for example, an object composed of more than one primitive—don't generate multiple hit records. Also, hit records aren't guaranteed to be written into the array until **glRenderMode()** is called.

Note: In addition to geometric primitives, valid raster position coordinates produced by **glRasterPos()** or **glWindowPos()** cause a selection hit. Also, during selection mode, if culling is enabled and a polygon is processed and culled, then no hit occurs.

Each hit record consists of the following four items, in the order shown:

*   The number of names on the name stack when the hit occurred.

*   Both the minimum and maximum window-coordinate *z*-values of all vertices of the primitives that have intersected the viewing volume since the last recorded hit. These two values, which lie in the range [0, 1], are each multiplied by $2^{32} - 1$ and rounded to the nearest unsigned integer.

*   The contents of the name stack at the time of the hit, with the bottommost element first.

When you enter selection mode, OpenGL initializes a pointer to the beginning of the selection array. Each time a hit record is written into the array, the pointer is updated accordingly. If writing a hit record would cause the number of values in the array to exceed the *size* argument specified with **glSelectBuffer()**, OpenGL writes as much of the record as will fit in the array and sets an overflow flag. When you exit selection mode with **glRenderMode()**, this command returns the number of hit records that were written (including a partial record if there was one), clears the name stack, resets the overflow flag, and resets the stack pointer. If the overflow flag has been set, the return value is –1.

A Selection Example

In Example 13-2, four triangles (a green, a red, and two yellow triangles, created by calling **drawTriangle()**) and a wireframe box representing the viewing volume (**drawViewVolume()**) are drawn on the screen. Then the triangles are rendered again (**selectObjects()**), but this time in selection mode. The corresponding hit records are processed in **processHits()**, and the selection array is printed out. The first triangle generates a hit, the second one doesn't, and the third and fourth ones together generate a single hit.

Example 13-2 Selection Example: select.c

```
void drawTriangle(GLfloat x1, GLfloat y1, GLfloat x2,
    GLfloat y2, GLfloat x3, GLfloat y3, GLfloat z)
{
   glBegin(GL_TRIANGLES);
   glVertex3f(x1, y1, z);
   glVertex3f(x2, y2, z);
   glVertex3f(x3, y3, z);
   glEnd();
}

void drawViewVolume(GLfloat x1, GLfloat x2, GLfloat y1,
                    GLfloat y2, GLfloat z1, GLfloat z2)
{
   glColor3f(1.0, 1.0, 1.0);
   glBegin(GL_LINE_LOOP);
   glVertex3f(x1, y1, -z1);
   glVertex3f(x2, y1, -z1);
   glVertex3f(x2, y2, -z1);
   glVertex3f(x1, y2, -z1);
   glEnd();
```

```
        glBegin(GL_LINE_LOOP);
        glVertex3f(x1, y1, -z2);
        glVertex3f(x2, y1, -z2);
        glVertex3f(x2, y2, -z2);
        glVertex3f(x1, y2, -z2);
        glEnd();

        glBegin(GL_LINES);  /*  4 lines     */
        glVertex3f(x1, y1, -z1);
        glVertex3f(x1, y1, -z2);
        glVertex3f(x1, y2, -z1);
        glVertex3f(x1, y2, -z2);
        glVertex3f(x2, y1, -z1);
        glVertex3f(x2, y1, -z2);
        glVertex3f(x2, y2, -z1);
        glVertex3f(x2, y2, -z2);
        glEnd();
}

void drawScene(void)
{
    glMatrixMode(GL_PROJECTION);
    glLoadIdentity();
    gluPerspective(40.0, 4.0/3.0, 1.0, 100.0);

    glMatrixMode(GL_MODELVIEW);
    glLoadIdentity();
    gluLookAt(7.5, 7.5, 12.5, 2.5, 2.5, -5.0, 0.0, 1.0, 0.0);
    glColor3f(0.0, 1.0, 0.0);   /*  green triangle     */
    drawTriangle(2.0, 2.0, 3.0, 2.0, 2.5, 3.0, -5.0);
    glColor3f(1.0, 0.0, 0.0);   /*  red triangle       */
    drawTriangle(2.0, 7.0, 3.0, 7.0, 2.5, 8.0, -5.0);
    glColor3f(1.0, 1.0, 0.0);   /*  yellow triangles   */
    drawTriangle(2.0, 2.0, 3.0, 2.0, 2.5, 3.0, 0.0);
    drawTriangle(2.0, 2.0, 3.0, 2.0, 2.5, 3.0, -10.0);
    drawViewVolume(0.0, 5.0, 0.0, 5.0, 0.0, 10.0);
}

void processHits(GLint hits, GLuint buffer[])
{
    unsigned int i, j;
    GLuint names, *ptr;

    printf("hits = %d\n", hits);
    ptr = (GLuint *) buffer;
```

```
        for (i = 0; i < hits; i++) {  /*  for each hit  */
            names = *ptr;
            printf(" number of names for hit = %d\n", names); ptr++;
            printf("   z1 is %g;", (float) *ptr/0x7fffffff); ptr++;
            printf(" z2 is %g\n", (float) *ptr/0x7fffffff); ptr++;
            printf("    the name is ");
            for (j = 0; j < names; j++) {       /*  for each name */
                printf("%d ", *ptr); ptr++;
            }
            printf("\n");
        }
}

#define BUFSIZE 512

void selectObjects(void)
{
    GLuint selectBuf[BUFSIZE];
    GLint hits;

    glSelectBuffer(BUFSIZE, selectBuf);
    (void) glRenderMode(GL_SELECT);

    glInitNames();
    glPushName(0);

    glPushMatrix();
    glMatrixMode(GL_PROJECTION);
    glLoadIdentity();
    glOrtho(0.0, 5.0, 0.0, 5.0, 0.0, 10.0);
    glMatrixMode(GL_MODELVIEW);
    glLoadIdentity();
    glLoadName(1);
    drawTriangle(2.0, 2.0, 3.0, 2.0, 2.5, 3.0, -5.0);
    glLoadName(2);
    drawTriangle(2.0, 7.0, 3.0, 7.0, 2.5, 8.0, -5.0);
    glLoadName(3);
    drawTriangle(2.0, 2.0, 3.0, 2.0, 2.5, 3.0, 0.0);
    drawTriangle(2.0, 2.0, 3.0, 2.0, 2.5, 3.0, -10.0);
    glPopMatrix();
    glFlush();

    hits = glRenderMode(GL_RENDER);
    processHits(hits, selectBuf);
}
```

```
void init(void)
{
    glEnable(GL_DEPTH_TEST);
    glShadeModel(GL_FLAT);
}

void display(void)
{
    glClearColor(0.0, 0.0, 0.0, 0.0);
    glClear(GL_COLOR_BUFFER_BIT | GL_DEPTH_BUFFER_BIT);
    drawScene();
    selectObjects();
    glFlush();
}

int main(int argc, char** argv)
{
    glutInit(&argc, argv);
    glutInitDisplayMode(GLUT_SINGLE | GLUT_RGB | GLUT_DEPTH);
    glutInitWindowSize(200, 200);
    glutInitWindowPosition(100, 100);
    glutCreateWindow(argv[0]);
    init();
    glutDisplayFunc(display);
    glutMainLoop();
    return 0;
}
```

Picking

As an extension of the process described in the preceding section, you can use selection mode to determine if objects are picked. To do this, you use a special picking matrix in conjunction with the projection matrix to restrict drawing to a small region of the viewport, typically near the cursor. Then you allow some form of input, such as clicking a mouse button, to initiate selection mode. With selection mode established and with the special picking matrix used, objects that are drawn near the cursor cause selection hits. Thus, during picking, you're typically determining which objects are drawn near the cursor.

Picking is set up almost exactly the same as regular selection mode with the following major differences:

- Picking is usually triggered by an input device. In the following code examples, pressing the left mouse button invokes a function that performs picking.

- You use the utility routine **gluPickMatrix()** to multiply the current projection matrix by a special picking matrix. This routine should be called prior to multiplying a standard projection matrix (such as **gluPerspective()** or **glOrtho()**). You'll probably want to save the contents of the projection matrix first, so the sequence of operations may look like this:

```
glMatrixMode(GL_PROJECTION);
glPushMatrix();
glLoadIdentity();
gluPickMatrix(...);
gluPerspective, glOrtho, gluOrtho2D, or glFrustum
    /* ... draw scene for picking ; perform picking ... */
glPopMatrix();
```

Another completely different way to perform picking is described in "Object Selection Using the Back Buffer" in Chapter 14. This technique uses color values to identify different components of an object.

---

void **gluPickMatrix**(GLdouble *x*, GLdouble *y*, GLdouble *width*, GLdouble *height*, GLint *viewport[4]*);

Creates a projection matrix that restricts drawing to a small region of the viewport and multiplies that matrix onto the current matrix stack. The center of the picking region is (*x*, *y*) in window coordinates, typically the cursor location. *width* and *height* define the size of the picking region in screen coordinates. (You can think of the width and height as the sensitivity of the picking device.) *viewport[]* indicates the current viewport boundaries, which can be obtained by calling

```
glGetIntegerv(GL_VIEWPORT, GLint *viewport);
```

Advanced

The net result of the matrix created by **gluPickMatrix()** transforms the clipping region into the unit cube $-1 \leq (x, y, z) \leq 1$ (or $-w \leq (wx, wy, wz) \leq w$). The picking matrix effectively performs an orthogonal transformation that maps the clipping region to the unit cube. Since the transformation is arbitrary, you can make picking work for different sorts of regions—for example, for rotated rectangular portions of the window. In certain situations, you might find it easier to specify additional clipping planes to define the picking region.

Example 13-3 illustrates simple picking. It also demonstrates how to use multiple names to identify different components of a primitive; in this case, the row and column of a selected object. A 3 × 3 grid of squares is drawn, with each square a different color. The *board*[3][3] array maintains the current amount of blue for each square. When the left mouse button is pressed, the **pickSquares()** routine is called to identify which squares were picked by the mouse. Two names identify each square in the grid—one identifies the row, and the other the column. Also, when the left mouse button is pressed, the colors of all squares under the cursor position change.

Example 13-3   Picking Example: picksquare.c

```
int board[3][3];   /*  amount of color for each square  */

/*  Clear color value for every square on the board  */
void init(void)
{
    int i, j;
    for (i = 0; i < 3; i++)
        for (j = 0; j < 3; j ++)
            board[i][j] = 0;
    glClearColor(0.0, 0.0, 0.0, 0.0);
}

void drawSquares(GLenum mode)
{
    GLuint i, j;
    for (i = 0; i < 3; i++) {
        if (mode == GL_SELECT)
            glLoadName(i);
        for (j = 0; j < 3; j ++) {
            if (mode == GL_SELECT)
                glPushName(j);
            glColor3f((GLfloat) i/3.0, (GLfloat) j/3.0,
                    (GLfloat) board[i][j]/3.0);
```

```
            glRecti(i, j, i+1, j+1);
            if (mode == GL_SELECT)
                glPopName();
        }
    }
}

/*  processHits prints out the contents of the
 *  selection array.
 */
void processHits(GLint hits, GLuint buffer[])
{
    unsigned int i, j;
    GLuint ii, jj, names, *ptr;

    printf("hits = %d\n", hits);
    ptr = (GLuint *) buffer;
    for (i = 0; i < hits; i++) { /*  for each hit  */
        names = *ptr;
        printf(" number of names for this hit = %d\n", names);
            ptr++;
        printf(" z1 is %g;", (float) *ptr/0x7fffffff); ptr++;
        printf(" z2 is %g\n", (float) *ptr/0x7fffffff); ptr++;
        printf("   names are ");
        for (j = 0; j < names; j++) { /*  for each name */
            printf("%d ", *ptr);
            if (j == 0)  /*  set row and column  */
                ii = *ptr;
            else if (j == 1)
                jj = *ptr;
            ptr++;
        }
        printf("\n");
        board[ii][jj] = (board[ii][jj] + 1) % 3;
    }
}

#define BUFSIZE 512

void pickSquares(int button, int state, int x, int y)
{
    GLuint selectBuf[BUFSIZE];
    GLint hits;
    GLint viewport[4];
```

```
      if (button != GLUT_LEFT_BUTTON || state != GLUT_DOWN)
         return;

      glGetIntegerv(GL_VIEWPORT, viewport);

      glSelectBuffer(BUFSIZE, selectBuf);
      (void) glRenderMode(GL_SELECT);

      glInitNames();
      glPushName(0);

      glMatrixMode(GL_PROJECTION);
      glPushMatrix();
      glLoadIdentity();
/*  create 5x5 pixel picking region near cursor location       */
      gluPickMatrix((GLdouble) x, (GLdouble) (viewport[3] - y),
                    5.0, 5.0, viewport);
      gluOrtho2D(0.0, 3.0, 0.0, 3.0);
      drawSquares(GL_SELECT);

      glMatrixMode(GL_PROJECTION);
      glPopMatrix();
      glFlush();

      hits = glRenderMode(GL_RENDER);
      processHits(hits, selectBuf);
      glutPostRedisplay();
}

void display(void)
{
      glClear(GL_COLOR_BUFFER_BIT);
      drawSquares(GL_RENDER);
      glFlush();
}

void reshape(int w, int h)
{
      glViewport(0, 0, w, h);
      glMatrixMode(GL_PROJECTION);
      glLoadIdentity();
      gluOrtho2D(0.0, 3.0, 0.0, 3.0);
      glMatrixMode(GL_MODELVIEW);
      glLoadIdentity();
}

int main(int argc, char** argv)
{
```

```
glutInit(&argc, argv);
glutInitDisplayMode(GLUT_SINGLE | GLUT_RGB);
glutInitWindowSize(100, 100);
glutInitWindowPosition(100, 100);
glutCreateWindow(argv[0]);
init();
glutMouseFunc(pickSquares);
glutReshapeFunc(reshape);
glutDisplayFunc(display);
glutMainLoop();
return 0;
}
```

Picking with Multiple Names and a Hierarchical Model

Multiple names can also be used to choose parts of a hierarchical object in a scene. For example, if you were rendering an assembly line of automobiles, you might want the user to move the mouse to pick the third bolt on the left front wheel of the third car in line. A different name can be used to identify each level of hierarchy: which car, which wheel, and finally which bolt. As another example, one name can be used to describe a single molecule among other molecules, and additional names can differentiate individual atoms within that molecule.

Example 13-4 is a modification of Figure 3-4, which draws an automobile with four identical wheels, each of which has five identical bolts. Code has been added to manipulate the name stack with the object hierarchy.

Example 13-4   Creating Multiple Names

```
draw_wheel_and_bolts()
{
    long i;

    draw_wheel_body();
    for (i = 0; i < 5; i++) {
        glPushMatrix();
            glRotate(72.0*i, 0.0, 0.0, 1.0);
            glTranslatef(3.0, 0.0, 0.0);
            glPushName(i);
                draw_bolt_body();
            glPopName();
        glPopMatrix();
    }
}
```

```
draw_body_and_wheel_and_bolts()
{
    draw_car_body();
    glPushMatrix();
        glTranslate(40, 0, 20);   /* first wheel position*/
        glPushName(1);            /* name of wheel number 1 */
            draw_wheel_and_bolts();
        glPopName();
    glPopMatrix();
    glPushMatrix();
        glTranslate(40, 0, -20); /* second wheel position */
        glPushName(2);            /* name of wheel number 2 */
            draw_wheel_and_bolts();
        glPopName();
    glPopMatrix();

    /* draw last two wheels similarly */
}
```

Example 13-5 uses the routines in Example 13-4 to draw three different cars, numbered 1, 2, and 3.

Example 13-5   Using Multiple Names

```
draw_three_cars()
{
    glInitNames();
    glPushMatrix();
        translate_to_first_car_position();
        glPushName(1);
            draw_body_and_wheel_and_bolts();
        glPopName();
    glPopMatrix();

    glPushMatrix();
        translate_to_second_car_position();
        glPushName(2);
            draw_body_and_wheel_and_bolts();
        glPopName();
    glPopMatrix();

    glPushMatrix();
        translate_to_third_car_position();
        glPushName(3);
            draw_body_and_wheel_and_bolts();
        glPopName();
    glPopMatrix();
}
```

Assuming that picking is performed, the following are some possible name-stack return values and their interpretations. In these examples, at most one hit record is returned; also, *d1* and *d2* are depth values.

2 *d1 d2* 2 1	Car 2, wheel 1
1 *d1 d2* 3	Car 3 body
3 *d1 d2* 1 1 0	Bolt 0 on wheel 1 on car 1
empty	The pick was outside all cars

The last interpretation assumes that the bolt and wheel don't occupy the same picking region. A user might well pick both the wheel and the bolt, yielding two hits. If you receive multiple hits, you have to decide which hit to process, perhaps by using the depth values to determine which picked object is closest to the viewpoint. The use of depth values is explored further in the next subsection.

Picking and Depth Values

Example 13-6 demonstrates how to use depth values when picking to determine which object is picked. This program draws three overlapping rectangles in normal rendering mode. When the left mouse button is pressed, the **pickRects()** routine is called. This routine returns the cursor position, enters selection mode, initializes the name stack, and multiplies the picking matrix with the current orthographic projection matrix. A selection hit occurs for each rectangle the cursor is over when the left mouse button is clicked. Finally, the contents of the selection buffer are examined to identify which named objects were within the picking region near the cursor.

The rectangles in this program are drawn at different depth, or *z*-, values. Since only one name is used to identify all three rectangles, only one hit can be recorded. However, if more than one rectangle is picked, that single hit has different minimum and maximum *z*-values.

Example 13-6 Picking with Depth Values: pickdepth.c

```
void init(void)
{
   glClearColor(0.0, 0.0, 0.0, 0.0);
   glEnable(GL_DEPTH_TEST);
   glShadeModel(GL_FLAT);
   glDepthRange(0.0, 1.0);   /* The default z mapping */
}
```

```
void drawRects(GLenum mode)
{
   if (mode == GL_SELECT)
      glLoadName(1);
   glBegin(GL_QUADS);
   glColor3f(1.0, 1.0, 0.0);
   glVertex3i(2, 0, 0);
   glVertex3i(2, 6, 0);
   glVertex3i(6, 6, 0);
   glVertex3i(6, 0, 0);
   glEnd();
   if (mode == GL_SELECT)
      glLoadName(2);
   glBegin(GL_QUADS);
   glColor3f(0.0, 1.0, 1.0);
   glVertex3i(3, 2, -1);
   glVertex3i(3, 8, -1);
   glVertex3i(8, 8, -1);
   glVertex3i(8, 2, -1);
   glEnd();
   if (mode == GL_SELECT)
      glLoadName(3);
   glBegin(GL_QUADS);
   glColor3f(1.0, 0.0, 1.0);
   glVertex3i(0, 2, -2);
   glVertex3i(0, 7, -2);
   glVertex3i(5, 7, -2);
   glVertex3i(5, 2, -2);
   glEnd();
}

void processHits(GLint hits, GLuint buffer[])
{
   unsigned int i, j;
   GLuint names, *ptr;

   printf("hits = %d\n", hits);
   ptr = (GLuint *) buffer;
   for (i = 0; i < hits; i++) {   /* for each hit  */
      names = *ptr;
      printf(" number of names for hit = %d\n", names); ptr++;
      printf(" z1 is %g;", (float) *ptr/0x7fffffff); ptr++;
```

```
        printf(" z2 is %g\n", (float) *ptr/0x7fffffff); ptr++;
        printf("   the name is ");
        for (j = 0; j < names; j++) {  /* for each name */
            printf("%d ", *ptr); ptr++;
        }
        printf("\n");
    }
}

#define BUFSIZE 512

void pickRects(int button, int state, int x, int y)
{
    GLuint selectBuf[BUFSIZE];
    GLint hits;
    GLint viewport[4];

    if (button != GLUT_LEFT_BUTTON || state != GLUT_DOWN)
        return;
    glGetIntegerv(GL_VIEWPORT, viewport);

    glSelectBuffer(BUFSIZE, selectBuf);
    (void) glRenderMode(GL_SELECT);

    glInitNames();
    glPushName(0);

    glMatrixMode(GL_PROJECTION);
    glPushMatrix();
    glLoadIdentity();
/*  create 5x5 pixel picking region near cursor location */
    gluPickMatrix((GLdouble) x, (GLdouble) (viewport[3] - y),
                  5.0, 5.0, viewport);
    glOrtho(0.0, 8.0, 0.0, 8.0, -0.5, 2.5);
    drawRects(GL_SELECT);
    glPopMatrix();
    glFlush();

    hits = glRenderMode(GL_RENDER);
    processHits(hits, selectBuf);
}
```

```
void display(void)
{
   glClear(GL_COLOR_BUFFER_BIT | GL_DEPTH_BUFFER_BIT);
   drawRects(GL_RENDER);
   glFlush();
}

void reshape(int w, int h)
{
   glViewport(0, 0, (GLsizei) w, (GLsizei) h);
   glMatrixMode(GL_PROJECTION);
   glLoadIdentity();
   glOrtho(0.0, 8.0, 0.0, 8.0, -0.5, 2.5);
   glMatrixMode(GL_MODELVIEW);
   glLoadIdentity();
}

int main(int argc, char **argv)
{
   glutInit(&argc, argv);
   glutInitDisplayMode(GLUT_SINGLE | GLUT_RGB | GLUT_DEPTH);
   glutInitWindowSize(200, 200);
   glutInitWindowPosition(100, 100);
   glutCreateWindow(argv[0]);
   init();
   glutMouseFunc(pickRects);
   glutReshapeFunc(reshape);
   glutDisplayFunc(display);
   glutMainLoop();
   return 0;
}
```

Try This

Try This

- Modify Example 13-6 to add additional calls to **glPushName()** so that multiple names are on the stack when the selection hit occurs. What will the contents of the selection buffer be?

- By default, **glDepthRange()** sets the mapping of the z-values to [0.0, 1.0]. Try modifying the **glDepthRange()** values and see how these modifications affect the z-values that are returned in the selection array.

Hints for Writing a Program That Uses Selection

Most programs that allow a user to edit geometric objects interactively provide a mechanism for the user to pick items or groups of items for editing. For two-dimensional drawing programs (for example, text editors, page-layout programs, and circuit-design programs), it might be easier to do your own picking calculations instead of using the OpenGL picking mechanism. Often, it's easy to find bounding boxes for two-dimensional objects and to organize them in some hierarchical data structure to speed up searches. For example, picking that uses the OpenGL style in a VLSI layout program containing millions of rectangles can be relatively slow. However, using simple bounding-box information when rectangles are typically aligned with the screen could make picking in such a program extremely fast. The code is probably simpler to write, too.

As another example, since only geometric objects cause hits, you might want to create your own method for picking text. Setting the current raster position is a geometric operation, but it effectively creates only a single pickable point at the current raster position, which is typically at the lower left corner of the text. If your editor needs to manipulate individual characters within a text string, some other picking mechanism must be used. You could draw little rectangles around each character during picking mode, but it's almost certainly easier to handle text as a special case.

If you decide to use OpenGL picking, organize your program and its data structures so that it's easy to draw appropriate lists of objects in either selection or normal drawing mode. This way, when the user picks something, you can use the same data structures for the pick operation that you use to display the items on the screen. Also, consider whether you want to allow the user to select multiple objects. One way to do this is to store a bit for each item, indicating whether it's selected (this method, however, requires you to traverse your entire list of items to find the selected items). You might find it useful to maintain a list of pointers to selected items to speed up this search. It's probably a good idea to keep the selection bit for each item as well, because when you're drawing the entire picture, you might want to draw selected items differently (for example, in a different color or within a selection box). Finally, consider the selection user interface. You might want to allow the user to

*   Select an item

*   Sweep-select a group of items

- Add an item to the selection

- Add a sweep selection to the current selections

- Delete an item from a selection

- Choose a single item from a group of overlapping items

A typical solution for a two-dimensional drawing program might work as follows:

1. All selection is done by pointing with the mouse cursor and using the left mouse button. In the steps that follow, *cursor* means the cursor tied to the mouse, and *button* means the left mouse button.

2. Clicking on an item selects it and deselects all other currently selected items. If the cursor is on top of multiple items, the smallest is selected. (In three dimensions, there are many other strategies for disambiguating a selection.)

3. Clicking down where there is no item, holding the button down while dragging the cursor, and then releasing the button selects all the items in a screen-aligned rectangle whose corners are determined by the cursor positions when the button went down and where it came up. This is called a *sweep selection*. All items not in the swept-out region are deselected. (You must decide whether an item is selected only if it's completely within the sweep region, or if any part of it falls within the region. The "completely within" strategy usually works best.)

4. If the Shift key is held down and the user clicks on an item that isn't currently selected, that item is added to the selected list. If the clicked-on item is selected, it's deleted from the selection list.

5. If a sweep selection is performed with the Shift key pressed, the items swept out are added to the current selection.

6. In an extremely cluttered region, it's often hard to do a sweep selection. When the button goes down, the cursor might lie on top of some item, and normally that item would be selected. You can make any operation a sweep selection, but a typical user interface interprets a button down on an item plus a mouse motion as a select-plus-drag operation. To solve this problem, you can have an enforced sweep selection by holding down, say, the Alt key. With this procedure, the following set of operations constitutes a sweep selection: Alt button down, sweep, button up. Items under the cursor when the button goes down are ignored.

7. If the Shift key is held during this sweep selection, the items enclosed in the sweep region are added to the current selection.

8. Finally, if the user clicks on multiple items, select just one of them. If the cursor isn't moved (or maybe not moved more than a pixel), and the user clicks again in the same place, deselect the item originally selected, and select a different item under the cursor. Use repeated clicks at the same point to cycle through all the possibilities.

Different rules can apply in particular situations. In a text editor, you probably don't have to worry about characters on top of each other, and selections of multiple characters are always contiguous characters in the document. Thus, you need to mark only the first and last selected characters to identify the complete selection. With text, often the best way to handle selection is to identify the positions between characters, rather than the characters themselves. This allows you to have an empty selection when the beginning and end of the selection are between the same pair of characters; it also allows you to put the cursor before the first character in the document or after the final one with no special-case code.

In a three-dimensional editor, you might provide ways to rotate and zoom between selections, so sophisticated schemes for cycling through the possible selections might be unnecessary. On the other hand, selection in three dimensions is difficult because the cursor's position on the screen usually gives no indication of its depth.

Feedback

Feedback is similar to selection in that once you're in either mode, no pixels are produced and the screen is frozen. Drawing does not occur; instead, information about primitives that would have been rendered is sent back to the application. The key difference between selection and feedback modes is the information that is sent back. In selection mode, assigned names are returned to an array of integer values. In feedback mode, information about transformed primitives is sent back to an array of floating-point values. The values sent back to the feedback array consist of tokens that specify what type of primitive (point, line, polygon, image, or bitmap) has been processed and transformed, followed by vertex, color, or other data for that primitive. The values returned are fully transformed by lighting and viewing operations. Feedback mode is initiated by calling **glRenderMode()** with GL_FEEDBACK as the argument.

Here's how you enter and exit feedback mode:

1. Call **glFeedbackBuffer**() to specify the array to hold the feedback information. The arguments for this command describe what type of data and how much of it is written into the array.

2. Call **glRenderMode**() with GL_FEEDBACK as the argument to enter feedback mode. (For this step, you can ignore the value returned by **glRenderMode**().) After this point, primitives aren't rasterized to produce pixels until you exit feedback mode, and the contents of the framebuffer don't change.

3. Draw your primitives. While issuing drawing commands, you can make several calls to **glPassThrough**() to insert markers into the returned feedback data and thus facilitate parsing.

4. Exit feedback mode by calling **glRenderMode**() with GL_RENDER as the argument if you want to return to normal drawing mode. The integer value returned by **glRenderMode**() is the number of values stored in the feedback array.

5. Parse the data in the feedback array.

<table>
<tr><td>
Compatibility
Extension

glFeedbackBuffer
and all associated
tokens
</td><td>

void **glFeedbackBuffer**(GLsizei *size*, GLenum *type*, GLfloat **buffer*);

Establishes a buffer for the feedback data: *buffer* is a pointer to an array where the data is stored. The *size* argument indicates the maximum number of values that can be stored in the array. The *type* argument describes the information fed back for each vertex in the feedback array; its possible values and their meanings are shown in Table 13-1. **glFeedbackBuffer**() must be called before feedback mode is entered. In the table, *k* is 1 in color-index mode and 4 in RGBA mode.

</td></tr>
</table>

type **Argument**	Coordinates	Color	Texture	Total Values
GL_2D	*x, y*	-	-	2
GL_3D	*x, y, z*	-	-	3
GL_3D_COLOR	*x, y, z*	*k*	-	3 + *k*
GL_3D_COLOR_TEXTURE	*x, y, z*	*k*	4	7 + *k*
GL_4D_COLOR_TEXTURE	*x, y, z, w*	*k*	4	8 + *k*

Table 13-1   glFeedbackBuffer() *type* Values

Note: When multitexturing is supported, feedback returns only the texture coordinates of texture unit 0.

The Feedback Array

In feedback mode, each primitive that would be rasterized (or each call to **glBitmap()**, **glDrawPixels()**, or **glCopyPixels()**, if the raster position is valid) generates a block of values that's copied into the feedback array. The number of values is determined by the *type* argument of **glFeedbackBuffer()**, as listed in Table 13-1. Use the appropriate value for the type of primitives you're drawing: GL_2D or GL_3D for unlit two- or three-dimensional primitives; GL_3D_COLOR for lit, three-dimensional primitives; and GL_3D_COLOR_TEXTURE or GL_4D_COLOR_TEXTURE for lit, textured, three- or four-dimensional primitives.

Each block of feedback values begins with a code indicating the primitive type, followed by values that describe the primitive's vertices and associated data. Entries are also written for pixel rectangles. In addition, pass-through markers that you've explicitly created can be returned in the array; the next subsection explains these markers in more detail. Table 13-2 shows the syntax for the feedback array; remember that the data associated with each returned vertex is as described in Table 13-1. Note that a polygon can have *n* vertices returned. Also, the *x*-, *y*-, and *z*-coordinates returned by feedback are window coordinates; if *w* is returned, it's in clip coordinates. For bitmaps and pixel rectangles, the coordinates returned are those of the current raster position. In Table 13-2, note that GL_LINE_RESET_TOKEN is returned only when the line stipple is reset for that line segment.

Primitive Type	Code	Associated Data
Point	GL_POINT_TOKEN	vertex
Line	GL_LINE_TOKEN or GL_LINE_RESET_TOKEN	vertex vertex
Polygon	GL_POLYGON_TOKEN	*n* vertex vertex … vertex
Bitmap	GL_BITMAP_TOKEN	vertex
Pixel Rectangle	GL_DRAW_PIXEL_TOKEN or GL_COPY_PIXEL_TOKEN	vertex
Pass-through	GL_PASS_THROUGH_TOKEN	a floating-point number

Table 13-2   Feedback Array Syntax

Using Markers in Feedback Mode

Feedback occurs after transformations, lighting, polygon culling, and interpretation of polygons by **glPolygonMode()**. It might also occur after polygons with more than three edges are broken up into triangles (if your particular OpenGL implementation renders polygons by performing this decomposition). Thus, it might be hard for you to recognize the primitives you drew in the feedback data you receive. To help parse the feedback data, call **glPassThrough()** as needed in your sequence of drawing commands to insert a marker. You might use the markers to separate the feedback values returned from different primitives, for example. This command causes GL_PASS_THROUGH_TOKEN to be written into the feedback array, followed by the floating-point value you pass in as an argument.

void **glPassThrough**(GLfloat *token*);

Inserts a marker into the stream of values written into the feedback array, if called in feedback mode. The marker consists of the code GL_PASS_THROUGH_TOKEN followed by a single floating-point value, *token*. This command has no effect when called outside of feedback mode. Calling **glPassThrough()** between **glBegin()** and **glEnd()** generates a GL_INVALID_OPERATION error.

A Feedback Example

Example 13-7 demonstrates the use of feedback mode. This program draws a lit, three-dimensional scene in normal rendering mode. Then, feedback mode is entered, and the scene is redrawn. Since the program draws lit, untextured, three-dimensional objects, the type of feedback data is GL_3D_COLOR. Since RGBA mode is used, each unclipped vertex generates seven values for the feedback buffer: *x, y, z, r, g, b,* and *a*.

In feedback mode, the program draws two lines as part of a line strip and then inserts a pass-through marker. Next, a point is drawn at (–100.0, –100.0, –100.0), which falls outside the orthographic viewing volume and thus doesn't put any values into the feedback array. Finally, another pass-through marker is inserted, and another point is drawn.

Example 13-7   Feedback Mode: feedback.c

```c
void init(void)
{
   glEnable(GL_LIGHTING);
   glEnable(GL_LIGHT0);
}

void drawGeometry(GLenum mode)
{
   glBegin(GL_LINE_STRIP);
   glNormal3f(0.0, 0.0, 1.0);
   glVertex3f(30.0, 30.0, 0.0);
   glVertex3f(50.0, 60.0, 0.0);
   glVertex3f(70.0, 40.0, 0.0);
   glEnd();
   if (mode == GL_FEEDBACK)
      glPassThrough(1.0);
   glBegin(GL_POINTS);
   glVertex3f(-100.0, -100.0, -100.0);  /*  will be clipped  */
   glEnd();
   if (mode == GL_FEEDBACK)
      glPassThrough(2.0);
   glBegin(GL_POINTS);
   glNormal3f(0.0, 0.0, 1.0);
   glVertex3f(50.0, 50.0, 0.0);
   glEnd();
   glFlush();
}

void print3DcolorVertex(GLint size, GLint *count,
                        GLfloat *buffer)
{
   int i;

   printf("  ");
   for (i = 0; i < 7; i++) {
      printf("%4.2f ", buffer[size-(*count)]);
      *count = *count - 1;
   }
   printf("\n");
}
```

```
void printBuffer(GLint size, GLfloat *buffer)
{
    GLint count;
    GLfloat token;

    count = size;
    while (count) {
        token = buffer[size-count]; count--;
        if (token == GL_PASS_THROUGH_TOKEN) {
            printf("GL_PASS_THROUGH_TOKEN\n");
            printf("  %4.2f\n", buffer[size-count]);
            count--;
        }
        else if (token == GL_POINT_TOKEN) {
            printf("GL_POINT_TOKEN\n");
            print3DcolorVertex(size, &count, buffer);
        }
        else if (token == GL_LINE_TOKEN) {
            printf("GL_LINE_TOKEN\n");
            print3DcolorVertex(size, &count, buffer);
            print3DcolorVertex(size, &count, buffer);
        }
        else if (token == GL_LINE_RESET_TOKEN) {
            printf("GL_LINE_RESET_TOKEN\n");
            print3DcolorVertex(size, &count, buffer);
            print3DcolorVertex(size, &count, buffer);
        }
    }
}

void display(void)
{
    GLfloat feedBuffer[1024];
    GLint size;

    glMatrixMode(GL_PROJECTION);
    glLoadIdentity();
    glOrtho(0.0, 100.0, 0.0, 100.0, 0.0, 1.0);

    glClearColor(0.0, 0.0, 0.0, 0.0);
    glClear(GL_COLOR_BUFFER_BIT);
    drawGeometry(GL_RENDER);

    glFeedbackBuffer(1024, GL_3D_COLOR, feedBuffer);
    (void) glRenderMode(GL_FEEDBACK);
    drawGeometry(GL_FEEDBACK);
```

```
    size = glRenderMode(GL_RENDER);
    printBuffer(size, feedBuffer);
}

int main(int argc, char** argv)
{
    glutInit(&argc, argv);
    glutInitDisplayMode(GLUT_SINGLE | GLUT_RGB);
    glutInitWindowSize(100, 100);
    glutInitWindowPosition(100, 100);
    glutCreateWindow(argv[0]);
    init();
    glutDisplayFunc(display);
    glutMainLoop();
    return 0;
}
```

Running this program generates the following output:

```
GL_LINE_RESET_TOKEN
 30.00 30.00 0.00 0.84 0.84 0.84 1.00
 50.00 60.00 0.00 0.84 0.84 0.84 1.00
GL_LINE_TOKEN
 50.00 60.00 0.00 0.84 0.84 0.84 1.00
 70.00 40.00 0.00 0.84 0.84 0.84 1.00
GL_PASS_THROUGH_TOKEN
 1.00
GL_PASS_THROUGH_TOKEN
 2.00
GL_POINT_TOKEN
 50.00 50.00 0.00 0.84 0.84 0.84 1.00
```

Thus, the line strip drawn with these commands results in two primitives:

```
glBegin(GL_LINE_STRIP);
    glNormal3f(0.0, 0.0, 1.0);
    glVertex3f(30.0, 30.0, 0.0);
    glVertex3f(50.0, 60.0, 0.0);
    glVertex3f(70.0, 40.0, 0.0);
glEnd();
```

The first primitive begins with GL_LINE_RESET_TOKEN, which indicates
that the primitive is a line segment and that the line stipple is reset. The
second primitive begins with GL_LINE_TOKEN, so it's also a line segment,
but the line stipple isn't reset and hence continues from where the previous
line segment left off. Each of the two vertices for these lines generates seven
values for the feedback array. Note that the RGBA values for all four vertices

in these two lines are (0.84, 0.84, 0.84, 1.0), which is a very light gray color with the maximum alpha value. These color values are a result of the interaction of the surface normal and lighting parameters.

Since no feedback data is generated between the first and second pass-through markers, you can deduce that any primitives drawn between the first two calls to **glPassThrough**() were clipped out of the viewing volume. Finally, the point at (50.0, 50.0, 0.0) is drawn, and its associated data is copied into the feedback array.

Note: In both feedback and selection modes, information about objects is returned prior to any fragment tests. Thus, objects that would not be drawn due to failure of the scissor, alpha, depth, or stencil test may still have their data processed and returned in both feedback and selection modes.

Try This

Try This

Make changes in Example 13-7 to see how they affect the feedback values that are returned. For example, change the coordinate values of **glOrtho**(). Change the lighting variables, or eliminate lighting altogether and change the feedback type to GL_3D. Or, add more primitives to see what other geometric objects (such as filled polygons) contribute to the feedback array.

Chapter 14

Now That You Know

Chapter Objectives

This chapter doesn't have objectives in the same way that previous chapters do. It's simply a collection of topics that describe ideas you might find useful for your application. Some topics, such as error handling, don't fit into other categories, but are too short for an entire chapter.

OpenGL is a collection of low-level tools; now that you know about those tools, you can use them to implement higher-level functions. This chapter presents several examples of such higher-level capabilities.

This chapter discusses a variety of techniques based on OpenGL commands that illustrate some of the not-so-obvious uses to which you can put these commands. The examples presented are in no particular order and aren't related to each other. The idea is to read the section headings and skip to the examples that you find interesting. For your convenience, the headings are listed and explained briefly here.

Note: Most of the examples in the rest of this guide are complete and can be compiled and run as is. In this chapter, however, there are no complete programs, and you have to do a bit of work on your own to make them run.

- "Error Handling" tells you how to check for OpenGL error conditions.

- "Which Version Am I Using?" describes how to find out details about your implementation, including the version number. This can be useful for writing applications that can run on earlier versions of OpenGL.

- "Extensions to the Standard" presents techniques for identifying and using extensions (which are either specific to a vendor or approved by the Khronos OpenGL ARB Working Group) to the OpenGL standard.

- "Cheesy Translucency" explains how to use polygon stippling to achieve translucency; this is particularly useful when no blending hardware is available.

- "An Easy Fade Effect" shows how to use polygon stippling to create the effect of a fade into the background.

- "Object Selection Using the Back Buffer" describes how to use the back buffer in a double-buffered system to handle simple object picking.

- "Cheap Image Transformation" discusses how to draw a distorted version of a bitmapped image by drawing each pixel as a quadrilateral.

- "Displaying Layers" explains how to display multiple layers of different materials and indicate where the materials overlap.

- "Antialiased Characters" describes how to draw smoother fonts.

- "Drawing Round Points" describes how to draw near-round points.

- "Interpolating Images" shows how to blend smoothly from one image to another.

- "Making Decals" explains how to draw two images, where one is a sort of decal that should always appear on top of the other.

- "Drawing Filled, Concave Polygons Using the Stencil Buffer" tells you how to draw concave polygons, nonsimple polygons, and polygons with holes by using the stencil buffer.

- "Finding Interference Regions" describes how to determine where three-dimensional pieces overlap.

- "Shadows" describes how to draw shadows of lit objects.

- "Hidden-Line Removal" discusses how to draw a wireframe object with hidden lines removed by using the stencil buffer.

- "Texture Mapping Applications" describes several clever uses for texture mapping, such as rotating and warping images.

- "Drawing Depth-Buffered Images" tells you how to combine images in a depth-buffered environment.

- "Dirichlet Domains" explains how to find the Dirichlet domain of a set of points using the depth buffer.

- "Life in the Stencil Buffer" explains how to implement the Game of Life using the stencil buffer.

- "Alternative Uses for glDrawPixels() and glCopyPixels()" describes how to use these two commands for such effects as fake video, airbrushing, and transposed images.

Error Handling

The truth is, your program will make mistakes. Use of error-handling routines is essential during development and is highly recommended for commercially released applications (unless you can give a 100 percent guarantee your program will never generate an OpenGL error condition. Get real!). OpenGL has simple error-handling routines for the base GL and GLU libraries.

When OpenGL detects an error (in either the base GL or GLU), it records a current error code. The command that caused the error is ignored, so it has no effect on the OpenGL state or on the framebuffer contents. (If the error recorded was GL_OUT_OF_MEMORY, however, the results of the command are undefined.) Once recorded, the current error code isn't cleared—that is, additional errors aren't recorded—until you call the query command **glGetError()**, which returns the current error code. After you've queried and cleared the current error code, or if there's no error to begin with, **glGetError()** returns GL_NO_ERROR.

> GLenum **glGetError**(void);
>
> Returns the value of the error flag. When an error occurs in either the GL or the GLU, the error flag is set to the appropriate error code value. If GL_NO_ERROR is returned, there has been no detectable error since the last call to **glGetError()** or since the GL was initialized. No other errors are recorded until **glGetError()** is called, the error code is returned, and the flag is reset to GL_NO_ERROR.

It is strongly recommended that you call **glGetError()** at least once in each **display()** routine. Table 14-1 lists the basic defined OpenGL error codes.

Error Code	Description
GL_INVALID_ENUM	GLenum argument out of range
GL_INVALID_VALUE	numeric argument out of range
GL_INVALID_OPERATION	operation illegal in current state
GL_INVALID_FRAMEBUFFER_ OPERATION	framebuffer object is not complete
GL_STACK_OVERFLOW	command would cause a stack overflow
GL_STACK_UNDERFLOW	command would cause a stack underflow
GL_OUT_OF_MEMORY	not enough memory left to execute command
GL_TABLE_TOO_LARGE	specified table is too large

Table 14-1 OpenGL Error Codes

There are also 37 GLU NURBS errors (with nondescriptive constant names, GLU_NURBS_ERROR1, GLU_NURBS_ERROR2, and so on); 14 tessellator errors (GLU_TESS_MISSING_BEGIN_POLYGON, GLU_TESS_MISSING_ END_POLYGON, GLU_TESS_MISSING_BEGIN_CONTOUR, GLU_TESS_ MISSING_END_CONTOUR, GLU_TESS_COORD_TOO_LARGE, GLU_TESS_ NEED_COMBINE_CALLBACK, along with eight errors generically named GLU_TESS_ERROR*); and GLU_INCOMPATIBLE_GL_VERSION. Also, the GLU defines the error codes GLU_INVALID_ENUM, GLU_INVALID_VALUE, and GLU_OUT_OF_MEMORY, which have the same meanings as the related OpenGL codes.

To obtain a printable, descriptive string corresponding to either a GL or GLU error code, use the GLU routine **gluErrorString()**.

---

const GLubyte* **gluErrorString**(GLenum *errorCode*);

Returns a pointer to a descriptive string that corresponds to the OpenGL or GLU error number passed in *errorCode*.

In Example 14-1, a simple error-handling routine is shown.

Example 14-1   Querying and Printing an Error

```
GLenum errCode;
const GLubyte *errString;

while ((errCode = glGetError()) != GL_NO_ERROR) {
   errString = gluErrorString(errCode);
   fprintf (stderr, "OpenGL Error: %s\n", errString);
}
```

Note: The string returned by **gluErrorString()** must not be altered or freed by the application.

Which Version Am I Using?

The portability of OpenGL applications is one of OpenGL's attractive features. However, new versions of OpenGL introduce new features, and if you use new features, you may have problems running your code on older versions of OpenGL. In addition, you may want your application to perform equally well on a variety of implementations. For example, you might make texture mapping the default rendering mode on one machine, but have only flat shading on another. You can use **glGetString()** to obtain release information about your OpenGL implementation.

---

const GLubyte* **glGetString**(GLenum *name*);

Returns a pointer to a string that describes an aspect of the OpenGL implementation. *name* can be one of the following: GL_VENDOR, GL_RENDERER, GL_VERSION, GL_SHADING_LANGUAGE_VERSION, or GL_EXTENSIONS.

Compatibility
Extension

GL_EXTENSIONS

GL_VENDOR returns the name of the company responsible for the OpenGL implementation. GL_RENDERER returns an identifier of the renderer, which is usually the hardware platform. For more about GL_EXTENSIONS, see the section "Extensions to the Standard."

GL_VERSION and GL_SHADING_LANGUAGE_VERSION return a string that identifies the version number of your implementation of OpenGL. The version string is laid out as follows:

```
<version number><space><vendor-specific information>
```

The version number is of the form

```
major_number.minor_number
```

or

```
major_number.minor_number.release_number
```

where the numbers all have one or more digits. The vendor-specific information is optional. For example, if this OpenGL implementation is from the fictitious XYZ Corporation, the string returned might be

```
1.2.4 XYZ-OS 3.2
```

which means that this implementation is XYZ's fourth release of an OpenGL library that conforms to the specification for OpenGL Version 1.2. It probably also means that this is release 3.2 of XYZ's proprietary operating system.

At runtime, another way to query the OpenGL version is to call **glGetIntegerv()** with GL_MAJOR_VERSION and GL_MINOR_VERSION, which will return the major and minor nubmer, respectively, as in would be returned in string form from **glGetString()**. At compile time, you can use the preprocessor statement `#ifdef` to look for the symbolic constants named GL_VERSION_*m_n*, where *m*, and *n* corresponded to the major- and minor-version numbers. For example, the preprocessor token GL_VERSION_3_0, represent OpenGL version 3.0. If a particular token is present, that indicates that all versions up to, and including that version are available—at least for compilation. You should always check the version and extension strings at runtime to make sure the functionality you need is present in the implementation that you're using..

Note: If running from client to server, such as when performing indirect rendering with the OpenGL extension to the X Window System, the client and server may be different versions. If your client version is ahead of your server, your client might request an operation that is not supported on your server.

Utility Library Version

gluGetString() is a query function for the Utility Library (GLU) and is similar to **glGetString()**.

---

const GLubyte* **gluGetString**(GLenum *name*);

Returns a pointer to a string that describes an aspect of the OpenGL implementation. *name* can be GLU_VERSION or GLU_EXTENSIONS.

Note that **gluGetString()** was not available in GLU 1.0. Another way to query the GLU version number is to look for the symbolic constant GLU_VERSION_1_3. The absence of the constant GLU_VERSION_1_3 means that you have GLU 1.2 or an earlier version. The same principle is true for constants GLU_VERSION_1_1 and GLU_VERSION_1_2.

Also note that GLU extensions are different from OpenGL extensions.

Window System Extension Versions

For window system extensions for OpenGL, such as GLX, WGL, PGL, and AGL, there are similar routines (such as **glXQueryExtensionString()**) for querying version information. See Appendix D for more information.

(The aforementioned **glXQueryExtensionString()** and related routines were introduced with GLX 1.1 and are not supported with GLX 1.0.)

Extensions to the Standard

OpenGL has a formal written specification that describes the operations that comprise the library. An individual vendor or a group of vendors may decide to add additional functionality to their released implementation.

Function and symbolic constant names clearly indicate whether a feature is part of the OpenGL standard, a vendor-specific extension, or an OpenGL extension approved by the Khronos OpenGL ARB Working Group.

To make a vendor-specific name, the vendor appends a company identifier (in uppercase) and, if needed, additional information, such as a machine name. For example, if XYZ Corporation wants to add a new function and symbolic constant, they might be of the form **glCommandXYZ()** and GL_DEFINITION_XYZ. If XYZ Corporation wants to have an extension that is available only on its FooBar graphics board, the names might be **glCommandXYZfb()** and GL_DEFINITION_XYZ_FB.

If two or more vendors agree to implement the same extension, then the functions and constants are suffixed with the more generic EXT (**glCommandEXT()** and GL_DEFINITION_EXT).

Similarly, if the OpenGL ARB approves an extension, the functions and constants are suffixed with ARB (**glCommandARB()** and GL_DEFINITION_ARB).

Determining Supported Extensions

There are a number of ways of determining which extensions are supported on your OpenGL implementation:

- If your OpenGL version is less than 3.0, call **glGetString**(GL_EXTENSIONS), which returns a space-separated list of every extension supported by your implementation.

- To see whether a particular extension is supported, if you have GLU 1.3 or greater, you can call **gluCheckExtension()**, which returns a Boolean value indicating support for that extension.

GLboolean **gluCheckExtension**(char *extName*,
                              const GLubyte *extString*);

Returns GL_TRUE if *extName* is found in *extString*, or GL_FALSE if it isn't.

- If you are using OpenGL Version 3.0 or later, you can call **glGetStringi()**, which returns a single string corresponding to the extension string associated with the index provided.

---

const GLubyte *****glGetStringi**(GLenum *target*, GLuint *index*);

Returns the string associated with *index* for the indexed state *target*. *target* must be GL_EXTENSIONS. *index* must be a value between zero and GL_NUM_EXTENSIONS-1, as queried by **glGetIntegerv()**.

There is no specified ordering of extension strings; the order may vary across OpenGL implementations, or across different contexts within a single implementation.

A GL_INVALID_VALUE error is generated if *index* is less than zero, or greater than or equal to GL_NUM_EXTENSIONS.

Note: In OpenGL Version 3.1, **glGetString()** will no longer accept
GL_EXTENSIONS. You must use **glGetStringi()** to obtain the list
of extensions.

If you are using the GLEW library for managing extensions, it provides a
convenient mechanism for verifying extensions: It defines a Boolean
variable with a name identical to the extension string entry (e.g.,
"GL_ARB_multitexture").

If you have GLU 1.3, you can use **gluCheckExtension()** to see whether a
specified extension is supported.

gluCheckExtension() can check OpenGL and GLX extension strings, as
well as GLU extension strings.

Prior to GLU 1.3, to find out if a specific extension is supported, use the
code in Example 14-2 to search through the list and match the extension
name. **QueryExtension()** returns GL_TRUE if the string is found, or
GL_FALSE if it isn't.

Example 14-2 Determining if an Extension Is Supported (Prior to GLU 1.3)

```
static GLboolean QueryExtension(char *extName)
{
   char *p = (char *) glGetString(GL_EXTENSIONS);
   char *end;
   if (p == NULL)
     return GL_FALSE;
   end = p + strlen(p);
   while (p < end) {
     int n = strcspn(p, " ");
     if ((strlen(extName)==n) && (strncmp(extName,p,n)==0)) {
       return GL_TRUE;
     }
     p += (n + 1);
   }
   return GL_FALSE;
}
```

Extensions to the Standard for Microsoft Windows (WGL)

If you need access to an extension function on a Microsoft Windows
platform, you should

• Create conditional code based on the symbolic constant, which
identifies the extension.

- Query the previously discussed extension string at run-time.

- Use **wglGetProcAddress()** to locate the pointer to the extension function.

Example 14-3 demonstrates how to find a fictitious extension named **glSpecialEXT()**. Note that the conditional code (`#ifdef`) verifies the definition of GL_EXT_special. If the extension is available, a data type (in this case, PFNGLSPECIALEXTPROC) is specifically defined for the function pointer. Finally, **wglGetProcAddress()** obtains the function pointer.

Example 14-3   Locating an OpenGL Extension with **wglGetProcAddress()**

```
#ifdef GL_EXT_special
    PFNGLSPECIALEXTPROC glSpecialEXT;
#endif

/* somewhere later in the code */

#ifdef GL_EXT_special
    glSpecialEXT = (PFNGLSPECIALEXTPROC)
                    wglGetProcAddress("glSpecialEXT");
    assert(glSpecialEXT != NULL);
#endif
```

Cheesy Translucency

You can use polygon stippling to simulate a translucent material. This is an especially good solution for systems that don't have blending hardware. Since polygon stipple patterns are 32 × 32 bits, or 1024 bits, you can go from opaque to transparent in 1023 steps. (In practice, that's many more steps than you need.) For example, if you want a surface that lets through 29 percent of the light, simply make up a stipple pattern in which 29 percent (roughly 297) of the pixels in the mask are 0 and the rest are 1. Even if your surfaces have the same translucency, don't use the same stipple pattern for each one, because they cover exactly the same bits on the screen. Make up a different pattern for each surface by randomly selecting the appropriate number of pixels to be 0. (See "Displaying Points, Lines, and Polygons" in Chapter 2 for more information about polygon stippling.)

If you don't like the effect with random pixels turned on, you can use regular patterns, but they don't work as well when transparent surfaces are stacked. This is often not a problem, because most scenes have relatively few translucent regions that overlap. In a picture of an automobile with translucent windows, your line of sight can go through at most two windows, and usually it's only one.

An Easy Fade Effect

Suppose you have an image that you want to fade gradually to some background color. Define a series of polygon stipple patterns, each of which has more bits turned on so that they represent denser and denser patterns. Then use these patterns repeatedly with a polygon large enough to cover the region over which you want to fade. For example, suppose you want to fade to black in 16 steps. First define 16 different pattern arrays:

```
GLubyte stips[16][4*32];
```

Then load them in such a way that each has one-sixteenth of the pixels in a 32 × 32 stipple pattern turned on and that the bitwise OR of all the stipple patterns is all 1's. After that, the following code does the trick:

```
draw_the_picture();
glColor3f(0.0, 0.0, 0.0);      /* set color to black */
for (i = 0; i < 16; i++) {
    glPolygonStipple(&stips[i][0]);
    draw_a_polygon_large_enough_to_cover_the_whole_region();
}
```

In some OpenGL implementations, you might get better performance by first compiling the stipple patterns into display lists. During your initialization, do something like this:

```
#define STIP_OFFSET 100
for (i = 0; i < 16; i++) {
    glNewList(i+STIP_OFFSET, GL_COMPILE);
    glPolygonStipple(&stips[i][0]);
    glEndList();
}
```

Then, replace this line in the first code fragment

```
glPolygonStipple(&stips[i][0]);
```

with

```
glCallList(i);
```

By compiling the command to set the stipple into a display list, OpenGL might be able to rearrange the data in the *stips[ ][ ]* array into the hardware-specific form required for maximum stipple-setting speed.

Another application for this technique is if you're drawing a changing picture and want to leave some blur behind that gradually fades out to give some indication of past motion. For example, suppose you're simulating a planetary system and you want to leave trails on the planets to show recent portions of their paths. Again, assuming you want to fade in 16 steps, set up the stipple patterns as before (using the display-list version, say), and have the main simulation loop look something like this:

```
current_stipple = 0;
while (1) {                             /* loop forever */
    draw_the_next_frame();
    glCallList(current_stipple++);
    if (current_stipple == 16) current_stipple = 0;
    glColor3f(0.0, 0.0, 0.0);        /* set color to black */
    draw_a_polygon_large_enough_to_cover_the_whole_region();
}
```

Each time through the loop, you clear one-sixteenth of the pixels. Any pixel that hasn't had a planet on it for 16 frames is certain to be cleared to black. Of course, if your system supports blending in hardware, it's easier to blend in a certain amount of background color with each frame. (See "Displaying Points, Lines, and Polygons" in Chapter 2 for polygon stippling details, Chapter 7 for more information about display lists, and "Blending" in Chapter 6 for information about blending.)

Object Selection Using the Back Buffer

Although the OpenGL selection mechanism (see "Selection" in Chapter 13) is powerful and flexible, it can be cumbersome to use. Often, the situation is simple: Your application draws a scene composed of a substantial number of objects; the user points to an object with the mouse, and the application needs to find the item under the tip of the cursor.

One way to do this requires your application to be running in double-buffer mode. When the user picks an object, the application redraws the entire scene in the back buffer, but instead of using the normal colors for objects, it encodes some kind of object identifier for each object's color. The application then simply reads the pixel under the cursor, and the value of that pixel encodes the number of the picked object. If many picks are expected for a single, static picture, you can read the entire color buffer once and look in your copy for each attempted pick, rather than read each pixel individually.

Note that this scheme has an advantage over standard selection in that it picks the object that's in front if multiple objects appear at the same pixel, one behind the other. Since the image with false colors is drawn in the back buffer, the user never sees it; you can redraw the back buffer (or copy it from the front buffer) before swapping the buffers. In color-index mode, the encoding is simple: Send the object identifier as the index. In RGBA mode, encode the bits of the identifier into the R, G, and B components.

Be aware that you can run out of identifiers if there are too many objects in the scene. For example, suppose you're running in color-index mode on a system that has 4-bit buffers for color-index information (16 possible different indices) in each of the color buffers, but the scene has thousands of pickable items. To address this issue, the picking can be done in a few passes. To think about this in concrete terms, assume there are fewer than 4096 items, so all the object identifiers can be encoded in 12 bits. In the first pass, draw the scene using indices composed of the 4 high-order bits, and then use the second and third passes to draw the middle 4 bits and the 4 low-order bits. After each pass, read the pixel under the cursor, extract the bits, and pack them together at the end to get the object identifier.

With this method, the picking takes three times as long, but that's often acceptable. Note that after you have the 4 high-order bits, you eliminate 15/16 of all objects, so you really need to draw only 1/16 of them for the second pass. Similarly, after the second pass, 255 of the 256 possible items have been eliminated. The first pass thus takes about as long as drawing a single frame does, but the second and third passes can be up to 16 and 256 times as fast.

If you're trying to write portable code that works on different systems, break up your object identifiers into chunks that fit on the lowest common denominator of those systems. Also, keep in mind that your system might perform automatic dithering in RGB mode. If this is the case, turn off dithering.

Cheap Image Transformation

If you want to draw a distorted version of a bitmapped image (perhaps simply stretched or rotated, or perhaps drastically modified by some mathematical function), there are many possibilities. You can use the image as a texture map, which allows you to scale, rotate, or otherwise distort the image. If you just want to scale the image, you can use **glPixelZoom()**.

In many cases, you can achieve good results by drawing the image of each pixel as a quadrilateral. Although this scheme doesn't produce images as nice as those you would get by applying a sophisticated filtering algorithm (and it might not be sufficient for sophisticated users), it's a lot quicker.

To make the problem more concrete, assume that the original image is m pixels by n pixels, with coordinates chosen from $[0, m - 1] \times [0, n - 1]$. Let the distortion functions be $x(m, n)$ and $y(m, n)$. For example, if the distortion is simply a zooming by a factor of 3.2, then $x(m, n) = 3.2 \cdot m$ and $y(m, n) = 3.2 \triangleright \cdot n$. The following code draws the distorted image:

```
glShadeModel(GL_FLAT);
glScale(3.2, 3.2, 1.0);
for (j=0; j < n; j++) {
    glBegin(GL_QUAD_STRIP);
    for (i=0; i <= m; i++) {
        glVertex2i(i,j);
        glVertex2i(i, j+1);
        set_color(i,j);
    }
    glEnd();
}
```

This code draws each transformed pixel in a solid color equal to that pixel's color and scales the image size by 3.2. The routine **set_color()** stands for whatever the appropriate OpenGL command is to set the color of the image pixel.

The following is a slightly more complex version that distorts the image using the functions $x(i, j)$ and $y(i, j)$:

```
glShadeModel(GL_FLAT);
for (j=0; j < n; j++) {
    glBegin(GL_QUAD_STRIP);
    for (i=0; i <= m; i++) {
        glVertex2i(x(i,j), y(i,j));
        glVertex2i(x(i,j+1), y(i,j+1));
        set_color(i,j);
    }
    glEnd();
}
```

An even better distorted image can be drawn with the following code:

```
glShadeModel(GL_SMOOTH);
for (j=0; j < (n-1); j++) {
    glBegin(GL_QUAD_STRIP);
    for (i=0; i < m; i++) {
        set_color(i,j);
        glVertex2i(x(i,j), y(i,j));
        set_color(i,j+1);
        glVertex2i(x(i,j+1), y(i,j+1));
    }
    glEnd();
}
```

This code smoothly interpolates color across each quadrilateral. Note that this version produces one fewer quadrilateral in each dimension than do the flat-shaded versions, because the color image is being used to specify colors at the quadrilateral vertices. In addition, you can antialias the polygons with the appropriate blending function (GL_SRC_ALPHA, GL_ONE) to get an even nicer image.

Displaying Layers

In some applications, such as semiconductor layout programs, you want to display multiple layers of different materials and indicate where the materials overlap each other.

As a simple example, suppose you have three different substances that can be layered. At any point, eight possible combinations of layers can occur, as shown in Table 14-2.

	Layer 1	Layer 2	Layer 3	Color
0	absent	absent	absent	black
1	present	absent	absent	red
2	absent	present	absent	green
3	present	present	absent	blue
4	absent	absent	present	pink

Table 14-2 Eight Combinations of Layers

	Layer 1	Layer 2	Layer 3	Color
5	present	absent	present	yellow
6	absent	present	present	white
7	present	present	present	gray

Table 14-2 (continued)   Eight Combinations of Layers

You want your program to display eight different colors, depending on the layers present. One arbitrary possibility is shown in the last column of the table. To use this method, use color-index mode and load your color map so that entry 0 is black, entry 1 is red, entry 2 is green, and so on. Note that if the numbers from 0 through 7 are written in binary, the 4 bit is turned on whenever layer 3 appears, the 2 bit whenever layer 2 appears, and the 1 bit whenever layer 1 appears.

To clear the window, set the writemask to 7 (all three layers) and set the clearing color to 0. To draw your image, set the color to 7, and when you want to draw something in layer *n*, set the writemask to *n*. In other types of applications, it might be necessary to erase selectively in a layer, in which case you would use the writemasks just discussed, but set the color to 0 instead of 7. (See "Masking Buffers" in Chapter 10 for more information about writemasks.)

Antialiased Characters

Using the standard technique for drawing characters with **glBitmap()**, drawing each pixel of a character is an all-or-nothing affair—the pixel is either turned on or not. If you're drawing black characters on a white background, for example, the resulting pixels are either black or white, never a shade of gray. Much smoother, higher-quality images can be achieved if intermediate colors are used when rendering characters (grays, in this example).

Assuming that you're drawing black characters on a white background, imagine a highly magnified picture of the pixels on the screen, with a high-resolution character outline superimposed on it, as shown in the left-hand diagram in Figure 14-1.

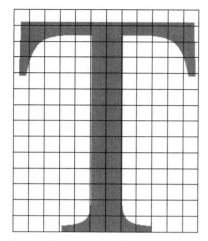

0	1	1	1	1	1	1	1	1	1	1	1
2	3	2	2	2	3	3	2	2	2	3	2
2	1	0	0	0	3	3	0	0	0	1	3
2	0	0	0	0	3	3	0	0	0	0	2
0	0	0	0	0	3	3	0	0	0	0	0
0	0	0	0	0	3	3	0	0	0	0	0
0	0	0	0	0	3	3	0	0	0	0	0
0	0	0	0	0	3	3	0	0	0	0	0
0	0	0	0	0	3	3	0	0	0	0	0
0	0	0	0	0	3	3	0	0	0	0	0
0	0	0	0	0	3	3	0	0	0	0	0
0	0	0	0	0	3	3	0	0	0	0	0
0	0	0	0	0	3	3	0	0	0	0	0
0	0	0	0	0	3	3	0	0	0	0	0
0	0	0	1	2	3	3	2	1	0	0	0

Figure 14-1   Antialiased Characters

Notice that some of the pixels are completely enclosed by the character's outline and should be painted black, some pixels are completely outside the outline and should be painted white, but many pixels should ideally be painted some shade of gray, where the darkness of the gray corresponds to the amount of black in the pixel. If this technique is used, the resulting image on the screen looks better.

If speed and memory usage are of no concern, each character can be drawn as a small image instead of as a bitmap. If you're using RGBA mode, however, this method might require up to 32 bits per pixel of the character to be stored and drawn, instead of the 1 bit per pixel for a standard character. Alternatively, you could use one 8-bit index per pixel and convert these indices to RGBA by table lookup during transfer. In many cases, a compromise is possible that allows you to draw the character with a few gray levels between black and white (say, two or three), and the resulting font description requires only 2 or 3 bits per pixel of storage.

The numbers in the right-hand diagram in Figure 14-1 indicate the approximate percentage coverage of each pixel: 0 means approximately empty, 1 means approximately one-third coverage, 2 means two-thirds, and 3 means completely covered. If pixels labeled 0 are painted white, pixels labeled 3 are painted black, and pixels labeled 1 and 2 are painted one-third and two-thirds black, respectively, the resulting character looks quite good. Only 2 bits are required to store the numbers 0, 1, 2, and 3, so for 2 bits per pixel, four levels of gray can be saved.

There are basically two methods of implementing antialiased characters, depending on whether you're in RGBA mode or color-index mode.

In RGBA mode, define three different character bitmaps, corresponding to where 1, 2, and 3 appear in Figure 14-1. Set the color to white, and clear for the background. Set the color to one-third gray (RGB = (0.666, 0.666, 0.666)), and draw all the pixels with a 1 in them. Then set RGB = (0.333, 0.333, 0.333), draw with the 2 bitmap, and use RGB = (0.0, 0.0, 0.0) for the 3 bitmap. What you're doing is defining three different fonts and redrawing the string three times, where each pass fills in the bits of the appropriate color densities.

In color-index mode, you can do exactly the same thing, but if you're willing to set up the color map correctly and use writemasks, you can get away with only two bitmaps per character and two passes per string. In the preceding example, set up one bitmap that has a 1 wherever 1 or 3 appears in the character. Set up a second bitmap that has a 1 wherever 2 or 3 appears. Load the color map so that 0 gives white, 1 gives light gray, 2 gives dark gray, and 3 gives black. Set the color to 3 (11 in binary) and the writemask to 1, and draw the first bitmap. Then change the writemask to 2, and draw the second. Where 0 appears in Figure 14-1, nothing is drawn in the framebuffer. Where 1, 2, and 3 appear, 1, 2, and 3 appear in the framebuffer.

For this example with only four gray levels, the savings are small—two passes instead of three. If eight gray levels were used instead of four, the RGBA method would require seven passes, and the color-map masking technique would require only three. With 16 gray levels, the comparison is 15 passes to four passes. (See "Masking Buffers" in Chapter 10 for more information about writemasks, and "Bitmaps and Fonts" in Chapter 8 for more information about drawing bitmaps.)

Try This

Try This

- Can you imagine how to do RGBA rendering using no more images than the optimized color-index case?

Hint: How are RGB fragments normally merged into the color buffer when antialiasing is desired?

Drawing Round Points

Draw near-round, aliased points by enabling point antialiasing, turning blending off, and using an alpha function that passes only fragments with alpha greater than 0.5. (See "Antialiasing" and "Blending" in Chapter 6 for more information about these topics.)

Interpolating Images

Suppose you have a pair of images (where *image* can mean a bitmap image or a picture generated using geometry in the usual way), and you want to blend smoothly from one to the other. This can be done easily using the alpha component and appropriate blending operations. Let's say you want to accomplish the blending in 10 steps, where image A is shown in frame 0 and image B is shown in frame 9. The obvious approach is to draw image A with an alpha of $(9 - i)/9$ and image B with an alpha of $i/9$ in frame i.

The problem with this method is that both images must be drawn in each frame. A faster approach is to draw image A in frame 0. To get frame 1, blend in 1/9 of image B and 8/9 of what's there. For frame 2, blend in 1/8 of image B with 7/8 of what's there. For frame 3, blend in 1/7 of image B with 6/7 of what's there, and so on. For the last step, you're just drawing 1/1 of image B blended with 0/1 of what's left, yielding image B exactly.

To see that this works, if for frame i you have

$$\frac{(9 - i)\,A}{9} + \frac{iB}{9}$$

and you blend in $B/(9 - i)$ with $(8 - i)/(9 - i)$ of what's there, you get

$$\frac{B}{9 - i} + \frac{8 - i}{9 - i}\left[\frac{(9 - i)\,A}{9} + \frac{iB}{9}\right] = \frac{9 - (i + 1)\,A}{9} + \frac{(i + 1)\,B}{9}$$

(See "Blending" in Chapter 6.)

Making Decals

Suppose you're drawing a complex three-dimensional picture using depth-buffering to eliminate the hidden surfaces. Suppose further that one part of your picture is composed of coplanar figures A and B, where figure B is a sort of decal that should always appear on top of figure A.

Your first approach might be to draw figure B after you've drawn figure A, setting the depth-buffering function to replace fragments when their depth is greater than or equal to the value stored in the depth buffer (GL_GEQUAL). Owing to the finite precision of the floating-point representations of the vertices, however, round-off error can cause figure B to be sometimes a bit in front of and sometimes a bit behind figure A. Here's one solution to this problem:

1. Disable the depth buffer for writing, and render A.

2. Enable the depth buffer for writing, and render B.

3. Disable the color buffer for writing, and render A again.

4. Enable the color buffer for writing.

Note that during the entire process, the depth-buffer test is enabled. In Step 1, A is rendered wherever it should be, but none of the depth-buffer values are changed; thus, in Step 2, wherever B appears over A, B is guaranteed to be drawn. Step 3 simply makes sure that all of the depth values under A are updated correctly, but since RGBA writes are disabled, the color pixels are unaffected. Finally, Step 4 returns the system to the default state (writing is enabled in both the depth buffer and the color buffer).

If a stencil buffer is available, the following, simpler technique can be used:

1. Configure the stencil buffer to write 1 if the depth test passes, and 0 otherwise. Render A.

2. Configure the stencil buffer to make no stencil value change, but to render only where stencil values are 1. Disable the depth-buffer test and its update. Render B.

With this method, it's not necessary to initialize the contents of the stencil buffer at any time, because the stencil values of all pixels of interest (that is, those rendered by A) are set when A is rendered. Be sure to reenable the depth test and disable the stencil test before additional polygons are drawn. (See "Selecting Color Buffers for Writing and Reading," "Depth Test," and "Stencil Test" in Chapter 10.)

Drawing Filled, Concave Polygons Using the Stencil Buffer

Consider the concave polygon 1234567 shown in Figure 14-2. Imagine that it's drawn as a series of triangles: 123, 134, 145, 156, and 167, all of which are shown in the figure. The heavier line represents the original polygon boundary. Drawing all these triangles divides the buffer into nine regions A, B, C, ..., I, where region I is outside all the triangles.

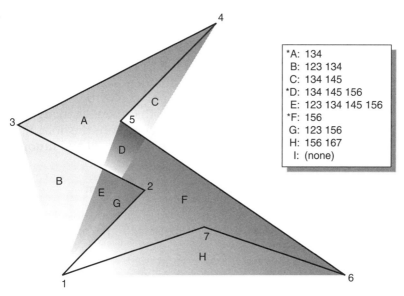

*A:	134
B:	123 134
C:	134 145
*D:	134 145 156
E:	123 134 145 156
*F:	156
G:	123 156
H:	156 167
I:	(none)

Figure 14-2   Concave Polygon

In the text of the figure, each of the region names is followed by a list of the triangles that cover it. Regions A, D, and F make up the original polygon; note that these three regions are covered by an odd number of triangles. Every other region is covered by an even number of triangles (possibly zero). Thus, to render the inside of the concave polygon, you need to render only regions that are enclosed by odd numbers of triangles. This can be done using the stencil buffer, with a two-pass algorithm.

First, clear the stencil buffer and disable writing into the color buffer. Next, draw each of the triangles in turn, using the GL_INVERT function in the stencil buffer. (For best performance, use triangle fans.) This flips the value between zero and a nonzero value every time a triangle that covers a pixel is drawn. After all the triangles are drawn, if a pixel is covered an even number of times, the value in the stencil buffers is zero; otherwise, it's nonzero. Finally, draw a large polygon over the whole region (or redraw the triangles), but allow drawing only where the stencil buffer is nonzero.

Note: There's a slight generalization of the preceding technique, where you don't need to start with a polygon vertex. In the 1234567 example, let P be any point on or off the polygon. Draw the triangles: P12, P23, P34, P45, P56, P67, and P71. Regions covered by odd numbers of triangles are inside; other regions are outside. This is a generalization in that if P happens to be one of the polygon's edges, one of the triangles is empty.

This technique can be used to fill both nonsimple polygons (polygons whose edges cross each other) and polygons with holes. The following example illustrates how to handle a complicated polygon with two regions, one four-sided and one five-sided. Assume further that there's a triangular hole and a four-sided hole (it doesn't matter in which regions the holes lie). Let the two regions be abcd and efghi, and let the holes be jkl and mnop. Let z be any point in the plane. Draw the following triangles:

zab zbc zcd zda zef zfg zgh zhi zie zjk zkl zlj zmn zno zop zpm

Mark regions covered by odd numbers of triangles as *in*, and those covered by even numbers as *out*. (See "Stencil Test" in Chapter 10 for more information about the stencil buffer.)

Finding Interference Regions

If you're designing a mechanical part made from smaller three-dimensional pieces, you often want to display regions in which the pieces overlap. In many cases, such regions indicate design errors where parts of a machine interfere with each other. In the case of moving parts, this process can be even more valuable, because a search for interfering regions can be done through a complete mechanical cycle of the design. The method for doing this is complicated, and the description here might be too brief. Complete details can be found in the paper *Interactive Inspection of Solids: Cross-sections and Interferences*, by Jarek Rossignac, Abe Megahed, and Bengt-Olaf Schneider (SIGGRAPH 1992 Proceedings).

The method is related to the capping algorithm described in "Stencil Test" in Chapter 10. The idea is to pass an arbitrary clipping plane through the objects that you want to test for interference, and then determine when a portion of the clipping plane is inside more than one object at a time. For a static image, the clipping plane can be moved manually to highlight interfering regions; for a dynamic image, it might be easier to use a grid of clipping planes to search for all possible interferences.

Draw each of the objects you want to check and clip them against the clipping plane. Note which pixels are inside the object at that clipping plane using an odd-even count in the stencil buffer, as explained in "Drawing Filled, Concave Polygons Using the Stencil Buffer." (For properly formed objects, a point is inside the object if a ray drawn from that point to the eye intersects an odd number of surfaces of the object.) To find interferences, you need to find pixels in the framebuffer where the clipping plane is in the interiors of two or more regions at once; in other words, in the intersection of the interiors of any pair of objects.

If multiple objects need to be tested for mutual intersection, store one bit every time some intersection appears, and another bit wherever the clipping buffer is inside any of the objects (the union of the objects' interiors). For each new object, determine its interior, find the intersection of that interior with the union of the interiors of the objects so far tested, and keep track of the intersection points. Then add the interior points of the new object to the union of the other objects' interiors.

You can perform the operations described in the preceding paragraph by using different bits in the stencil buffer together with various masking operations. Three bits of stencil buffer are required per pixel—one for the toggling to determine the interior of each object, one for the union of all interiors discovered so far, and one for the regions in which interference has occurred so far. To make this discussion more concrete, assume that the 1 bit of the stencil buffer is for toggling between interior and exterior, the 2 bit is the running union, and the 4 bit is for interferences so far. For each object that you're going to render, clear the 1 bit (using a stencil mask of 1 and clearing to 0), then toggle the 1 bit by keeping the stencil mask as 1 and using the GL_INVERT stencil operation.

You can find intersections and unions of the bits in the stencil buffers using the stenciling operations. For example, to make bits in buffer 2 be the union of the bits in buffers 1 and 2, mask the stencil to those 2 bits, and draw something over the entire object with the stencil function set to pass if anything nonzero occurs. This happens if the bits in buffer 1, in buffer 2, or in both are turned on. If the comparison succeeds, write a 1 in buffer 2. Also, make sure that drawing in the color buffer is disabled. An intersection calculation is similar—set the function to pass only if the value in the two buffers is equal to 3 (bits turned on in both buffers 1 and 2). Write the result into the correct buffer. (See "Stencil Test" in Chapter 10.)

Shadows

Every possible projection of three-dimensional space to three-dimensional space can be achieved with a suitable 4 × 4 invertible matrix and homogeneous coordinates. If the matrix isn't invertible but has rank 3, it projects three-dimensional space onto a two-dimensional plane. Every such possible projection can be achieved with a suitable rank-3 4 × 4 matrix. To find the shadow of an arbitrary object on an arbitrary plane from an arbitrary light source (possibly at infinity), you need to find a matrix representing that projection, multiply it on the matrix stack, and draw the object in the shadow color. Keep in mind that you need to project onto each plane that you're calling the "ground."

As a simple illustration, assume the light is at the origin, and the equation of the ground plane is $ax + by + cz + d = 0$. Given a vertex $S = (sx, sy, sz, 1)$, the line from the light through S includes all points αS, where α is an arbitrary real number. The point where this line intersects the plane occurs when

$$\alpha(a{\cdot}sx + b{\cdot}sy + c{\cdot}sz) + d = 0,$$

so

$$\alpha = -d/(a{\cdot}sx + b{\cdot}sy + c{\cdot}sz).$$

Plugging this back into the line, we get

$$-d(sx, sy, sz)/(a{\cdot}sx + b{\cdot}sy + c{\cdot}sz)$$

for the point of intersection.

The matrix that maps S to this point for every S is

$$\begin{bmatrix} -d & 0 & 0 & 0 \\ 0 & -d & 0 & 0 \\ 0 & 0 & -d & 0 \\ a & b & c & 0 \end{bmatrix}$$

This matrix can be used if you first translate the world so that the light is at the origin.

If the light is from an infinite source, all you have is a point S and a direction D = (*dx, dy, dz*). Points along the line are given by

$$S + \alpha D$$

Proceeding as before, the intersection of this line with the plane is given by

$$a(sx + \alpha{\cdot}dx) + b(sy + \alpha{\cdot}dy) + c(sz + \alpha{\cdot}dz) + d = 0$$

Solving for α, plugging that back into the equation for a line, and then determining a projection matrix gives

$$\begin{bmatrix} b \times dy + c \times dz & -b \times dx & -c \times dx & -d \times dx \\ -a \times dy & a \times dx + c \times dz & -c \times dy & -d \times dy \\ -a \times dz & -b \times dz & a \times dx + b \times dy & -d \times dz \\ 0 & 0 & 0 & a \times dx + b \times dy + c \times dz \end{bmatrix}$$

This matrix works given the plane and an arbitrary direction vector. There's no need to translate anything first. (See Chapter 3 and Appendix C.)

Hidden-Line Removal

If you want to draw a wireframe object with hidden lines removed, one approach is to draw the outlines using lines and then fill the interiors of the polygons making up the surface with polygons having the background color. With depth-buffering enabled, this interior fill covers any outlines that would be obscured by faces closer to the eye. This method would work, except that there's no guarantee that the interior of the object falls entirely inside the polygon's outline; in fact, it might overlap it in various places.

There's an easy, two-pass solution using either polygon offset or the stencil buffer. Polygon offset is usually the preferred technique, since polygon offset is almost always faster than stencil buffer. Both methods are described here, so you can see how both approaches to the problem work.

Hidden-Line Removal with Polygon Offset

To use polygon offset to accomplish hidden-line removal, the object is drawn twice. The highlighted edges are drawn in the foreground color, using filled polygons but with the polygon mode GL_LINE, to rasterize the polygons as wireframe edges. Then the filled polygons are drawn with the default polygon mode, which fills the interior of the wireframe, and with enough polygon offset to nudge the filled polygons a little farther from the eye. With the polygon offset, the interior recedes just enough that the highlighted edges are drawn without unpleasant visual artifacts.

```
glEnable(GL_DEPTH_TEST);
glPolygonMode(GL_FRONT_AND_BACK, GL_LINE);
set_color(foreground);
draw_object_with_filled_polygons();

glPolygonMode(GL_FRONT_AND_BACK, GL_FILL);
glEnable(GL_POLYGON_OFFSET_FILL);
glPolygonOffset(1.0, 1.0);
set_color(background);
draw_object_with_filled_polygons();
glDisable(GL_POLYGON_OFFSET_FILL);
```

You may have to adjust the amount of offset needed (for wider lines, for example). (See "Polygon Offset" in Chapter 6 for more information.)

Hidden-Line Removal with the Stencil Buffer

Using the stencil buffer for hidden-line removal is a more complicated procedure. For each polygon, you'll need to clear the stencil buffer and then draw the outline in both the framebuffer and the stencil buffer. Then, when you fill the interior, enable drawing only where the stencil buffer is still clear. To avoid doing an entire stencil-buffer clear for each polygon, an easy way to clear it is simply to draw 0's into the buffer using the same polygon outline. In this way, you need to clear the entire stencil buffer only once.

For example, the following code represents the inner loop you might use to perform such hidden-line removal. Each polygon is outlined in the foreground color, filled with the background color, and then outlined again in the foreground color. The stencil buffer is used to keep the fill color of each polygon from overwriting its outline. To optimize performance, the stencil and color parameters are changed only twice per loop by using the same values both times the polygon outline is drawn.

```
glEnable(GL_STENCIL_TEST);
glEnable(GL_DEPTH_TEST);
glClear(GL_STENCIL_BUFFER_BIT);
glStencilFunc(GL_ALWAYS, 0, 1);
glStencilOp(GL_INVERT, GL_INVERT, GL_INVERT);
set_color(foreground);
for (i=0; i < max; i++) {
```

```
    outline_polygon(i);
    set_color(background);
    glStencilFunc(GL_EQUAL, 0, 1);
    glStencilOp(GL_KEEP, GL_KEEP, GL_KEEP);
    fill_polygon(i);
    set_color(foreground);
    glStencilFunc(GL_ALWAYS, 0, 1);
    glStencilOp(GL_INVERT, GL_INVERT, GL_INVERT);
    outline_polygon(i);
}
```

(See "Stencil Test" in Chapter 10.)

Texture Mapping Applications

Texture mapping is quite powerful, and it can be used in some interesting ways. Here are a few advanced applications of texture mapping:

• Antialiased text—Define a texture map for each character at a relatively high resolution, and then map them onto smaller areas using the filtering provided by texturing. This also makes text appear correctly on surfaces that aren't aligned with the screen, but are tilted and have some perspective distortion.

• Antialiased lines—These can be done like antialiased text: make the line in the texture several pixels wide, and use texture filtering to antialias the lines.

• Image scaling and rotation—If you put an image into a texture map and use that texture to map onto a polygon, rotating and scaling the polygon effectively rotates and scales the image.

• Image warping—Store the image as a texture map, but map it to some spline-defined surface (using evaluators). As you warp the surface, the image follows the warping.

• Projecting images—Put the image in a texture map, and project it as a spotlight, creating a slide projector effect. (See "The q-Coordinate" in Chapter 9 for more information about how to model a spotlight using textures.)

(See Chapter 3 for information about rotating and scaling, Chapter 9 for more information about creating textures, and Chapter 12 for details on evaluators.)

Drawing Depth-Buffered Images

For complex static backgrounds, the rendering time for the geometric description of the background can be greater than the time it takes to draw a pixel image of the rendered background. If there's a fixed background and a relatively simple changing foreground, you may want to draw the background and its associated depth-buffered version as an image, rather than render it geometrically. The foreground might also consist of items that are time-consuming to render, but whose framebuffer images and depth buffers are available. You can render these items into a depth-buffered environment using a two-pass algorithm.

For example, if you're drawing a model of a molecule made of spheres, you might have an image of a beautifully rendered sphere and its associated depth-buffer values that were calculated using Phong shading or ray-tracing or some other scheme that isn't directly available through OpenGL. To draw a complex model, you might be required to draw hundreds of such spheres, which should be depth-buffered together.

To add a depth-buffered image to the scene, first draw the image's depth-buffer values into the depth buffer using **glDrawPixels()**. Then enable depth-buffering, set the writemask to 0 so that no drawing occurs, and enable stenciling such that the stencil buffers are drawn whenever a write to the depth buffer occurs.

Then draw the image into the color buffer, masked by the stencil buffer you've just written so that writing occurs only when there's a 1 in the stencil buffer. During this write, set the stenciling function to zero out the stencil buffer so that it's automatically cleared when it's time to add the next image to the scene. If the objects are to be moved nearer to or farther from the viewer, you need to use an orthographic projection; in such cases, you use GL_DEPTH_BIAS with **glPixelTransfer*()** to move the depth image. (See "Coordinate System Survival Kit" in Chapter 2, "Depth Test" and "Stencil Test" in Chapter 10, and Chapter 8 for details on **glDrawPixels()** and **glPixelTransfer*()**.)

Dirichlet Domains

Given a set S of points in a plane, the Dirichlet domain or Voronoi polygon of one of the points is the set of all points in the plane closer to that point than to any other point in the set S. These points provide the solutions to many problems in computational geometry. Figure 14-3 shows outlines of the Dirichlet domains for a set of points.

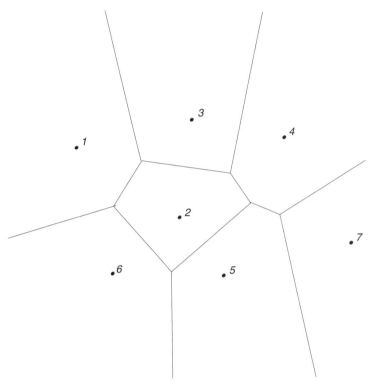

Figure 14-3   Dirichlet Domains

If for each point in S, you draw a depth-buffered cone with its apex at the point in a different color than each of the points in S, the Dirichlet domain for each point is drawn in that color. The easiest way to do this is to precompute a cone's depth in an image and use the image as the depth-buffer values as described in the preceding section, "Drawing Depth-Buffered Images." You don't need an image to draw into the framebuffer as in the case of shaded spheres, however. While you're drawing into the depth buffer, use the stencil buffer to record the pixels where drawing should occur by first clearing it and then writing nonzero values wherever the depth test succeeds. To draw the Dirichlet region, draw a polygon over the entire window, but enable drawing only where the stencil buffers are nonzero.

You can do this perhaps more easily by rendering cones of uniform color with a simple depth buffer, but a good cone might require thousands of polygons. The technique described in this section can render higher-quality cones much more quickly. (See "A Hidden-Surface Removal Survival Kit" in Chapter 5 and "Depth Test" in Chapter 10.)

Life in the Stencil Buffer

The Game of Life, invented by John Conway, is played on a rectangular grid in which each grid location is either "alive" or "dead." To calculate the next generation from the current one, count the number of live neighbors for each grid location (the eight adjacent grid locations are neighbors). A grid location is alive in generation $n + 1$ if it was alive in generation n and has exactly two or three live neighbors, or if it was dead in generation n and has exactly three live neighbors. In all other cases, it is dead in generation $n + 1$. This game generates some incredibly interesting patterns given different initial configurations. (See Martin Gardner, "Mathematical Games," *Scientific American*, vol. 223, no. 4, October 1970, pp. 120–123.) Figure 14-4 shows six generations from a game.

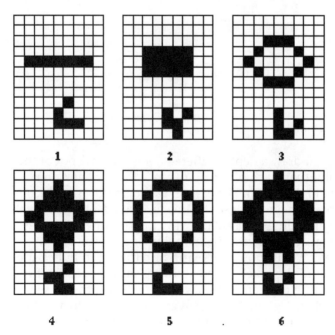

Figure 14-4   Six Generations from the Game of Life

One way to create this game using OpenGL is to use a multipass algorithm. Keep the data in the color buffer, one pixel for each grid point. Assume that black (all zeros) is the background color, and that the color of a live pixel is nonzero. Initialize by clearing the depth and stencil buffers to zero, set the depth-buffer writemask to zero, and set the depth comparison function so that it passes on not-equal. To iterate, read the image off the screen, enable drawing into the depth buffer, and set the stencil function so that it increments whenever a depth comparison succeeds but leaves the stencil buffer unchanged otherwise. Disable drawing into the color buffer.

Next, draw the image eight times, and offset one pixel in each vertical, horizontal, and diagonal direction. When you're done, the stencil buffer contains a count of the number of live neighbors for each pixel. Enable drawing to the color buffer, set the color to the color for live cells, and set the stencil function to draw only if the value in the stencil buffer is 3 (three live neighbors). In addition, if this drawing occurs, decrement the value in the stencil buffer. Then draw a rectangle covering the image; this paints each cell that has exactly three live neighbors with the "alive" color.

At this point, the stencil buffers contain 0, 1, 2, 4, 5, 6, 7, and 8, and the values under the 2's are correct. The values under 0, 1, 4, 5, 6, 7, and 8 must be cleared to the "dead" color. Set the stencil function to draw whenever the value is not 2 and to zero the stencil values in all cases. Then draw a large polygon of the "dead" color across the entire image. You're done.

For a usable demonstration program, you might want to zoom the grid up to a size larger than a single pixel; it's hard to see detailed patterns with a single pixel per grid point. (See "Coordinate System Survival Kit" in Chapter 2, and "Depth Test" and "Stencil Test" in Chapter 10.)

Alternative Uses for glDrawPixels() and glCopyPixels()

You might think of **glDrawPixels**() as a way to draw a rectangular region of pixels to the screen. Although this is often what it's used for, some other interesting uses are outlined here:

- Video—Even if your machine doesn't have special video hardware, you can display short movie clips by repeatedly drawing frames with **glDrawPixels**() in the same region of the back buffer and then swapping the buffers. The size of the frames you can display with reasonable performance using this method depends on your hardware's drawing speed, so you might be limited to 100×100 pixel movies (or smaller) if you want smooth fake video.

- Airbrush—In a paint program, your airbrush (or paintbrush) shape can be simulated using alpha values. The color of the paint is represented as the color values. To paint with a circular brush in blue, repeatedly draw a blue square with **glDrawPixels()** where the alpha values are largest in the center and taper to zero at the edges of a circle centered in the square. Draw using a blending function that uses alpha of the incoming color and (1 – alpha) of the color already at the pixel. If the alpha values in the brush are all much less than 1, you have to paint over an area repeatedly to get a solid color. If the alpha values are near 1, each brush stroke pretty much obliterates the colors underneath.

- Filtered zooms—If you zoom a pixel image by a nonintegral amount, OpenGL effectively uses a box filter, which can lead to rather severe aliasing effects. To improve the filtering, jitter the resulting image by amounts less than a pixel and redraw it multiple times, using alpha blending to average the resulting pixels. The result is a filtered zoom.

- Transposing images—You can swap same-size images in place with **glCopyPixels()** using the XOR operation. With this method, you can avoid having to read the images back into processor memory. If A and B represent the two images, the operation looks like this:

  a. A = A XOR B

  b. B = A XOR B

  c. A = A XOR B

Chapter 15

The OpenGL Shading Language

Chapter Objectives

This chapter discusses the OpenGL Shading Language. GLSL, as the OpenGL Shading Language is commonly called, is a programming language for creating programmable *shaders*. Introduced as a part of OpenGL version 2.0, the OpenGL Shading Language enables applications to explicitly specify the operations used in processing vertices and fragments. Additionally, GLSL helps unlock the computation power of modern hardware implementations of OpenGL.

After reading this chapter, you'll be able to do the following:

- Understand the structure and components of programmable shaders written in the OpenGL Shading Language

- Integrate programmable shaders into OpenGL programs

- Use exclusively shader-based techniques, including transform feedback, uniform blocks, and texture buffers

This chapter includes discussions of features in versions 1.30 and 1.40 of the OpenGL Shading Language, which are the versions associated with OpenGL versions 3.0 and 3.1, respectively. Just as OpenGL Version 3.1 removed the functionality deprecated in Version 3.0, so GLSL 1.40 removed features from GLSL 1.30. Those features are available if your implementation supports the GL_ARB_compatibility extension. This chapter discusses shaders in the context of GLSL 1.30.

The OpenGL Graphics Pipeline and Programmable Shading

You can think of the internal operation of OpenGL as two machines—one for processing vertices, the other for fragments—with dials and switches on the front of each machine. You control each machine's operation by flipping switches and twisting dials, but the internal operation of the machines is "fixed"; that is, you can't change the order of operations inside of the machine, and you're limited to the features that were built into the machine. This mode of operation for OpenGL is commonly called the *fixed-function pipeline*, and is described in detail in Appendix E, "Order of Operations."[1] Figure 15-1 illustrates the basic architecture of the OpenGL fixed-function pipeline.

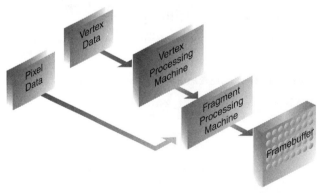

Figure 15-1   Overview of the OpenGL Fixed-Function Pipeline

OpenGL 2.0 augmented the fixed-function pipeline approach by adding a *programmable shading pipeline*, where you can control the processing of vertices and fragments with small programs, called *shaders*, written in a special language called *The OpenGL Shading Language*, or *GLSL* for short.

[1] This appendix is available online at http://www.opengl-redbook.com/appendices/.

In an application, you can use both the fixed-function and programmable pipelines for processing data, but not simultaneously. When you use a shader for processing, the corresponding portion of the fixed-function pipeline is disabled. In Version 3.1, the fixed-function pipeline was removed through deprecation. If your implementation supports the GL_ARB_ compatibility extension its functionality is made available in that extension.

While programmable shaders are not new to computer graphics, accessibility to them became available in interactive graphics libraries such as OpenGL only a few years ago. Just like the field of computer graphics itself, techniques for programmable shaders constitute a huge subject, and this chapter does not attempt to teach the theory behind programmable shaders. Rather, it covers the language available for authoring shaders available in OpenGL and how to integrate those shaders into an OpenGL application. For more information on programmable shading, you may want to broaden your knowledge of the subject with these supplemental works:

- *The RenderMan Companion: A Programmer's Guide to Realistic Computer Graphics* by Steve Upstill (Addison-Wesley, 1990)—while this text describes Pixar's RenderMan shader language (which is one of the predominant programmable shader languages used for computer-generated images in the movie industry), it describes the basics of programmable shading and presents much of the theory and practice of using shaders to generate images.

- *Real-Time Shading* by John C. Hart, Wolfgang Heidrich, Michael McCool, and Marc Olano (AK Peters, Ltd., 2002)—this modern text describes the latest advancements in programmable shading on graphics hardware and provides a survey of different techniques and implementations of programmable shaders.

- *The GPU Gems* series (Addison-Wesley)—these books describe many shader implementation tricks and techniques.

This section begins with a discussion of how shaders affect the processing of vertices and fragments. We continue describing what's required to integrate shaders to your OpenGL program, and then introduce writing shaders in GLSL. For all of the details on the OpenGL shading language, please see:

- *The OpenGL Shading Language Specification*, versions 1.30 and 1.40 by John Kessenich (available for download from `http://www.opengl.org`)

- *The OpenGL Shading Language,* 3rd editon, by Randi Rost and Bill Licea-Kane, with contributions by Dan Ginsburg, John M. Kessenich, Barthold Lichtenbelt, Hugh Malan, and Mike Weiblen (Addison-Wesley, 2009)

Vertex Processing

Figure 15-2 illustrates the processing of a vertex through the OpenGL pipeline. The shaded area indicates the functions of the vertex processing pipeline that are replaced by a vertex shader.

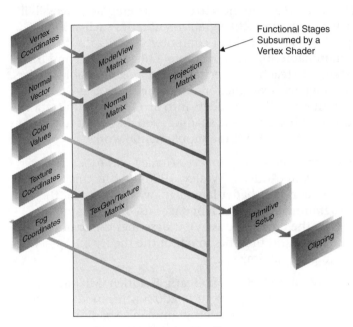

Figure 15-2   Vertex Processing Pipeline

When the fixed-function pipeline processes a vertex, it's responsible for providing the following values that are used for rasterization:

- Eye-space coordinates
- Primary and secondary colors
- Texture coordinates
- Fog coordinates
- Point size

Depending upon which features you have enabled, the vertex pipeline may not update all of those values. Those values are computed based on the input of the application through calls like **glVertex*()** and the other vertex data calls.

Not all operations in the vertex pipeline are replaced when you use a shader. After the execution of the shader, the following operations still occur, just as if the vertex were processed by the fixed-function pipeline:

- Perspective division
- Viewport mapping
- Primitive assembly
- Frustum and user clipping
- Backface culling
- Two-sided lighting selection
- Polygon-mode processing
- Polygon offset
- Depth range clamping

Fragment Processing

Similarly, Figure 15-3 illustrates the pixel processing part of the OpenGL pipeline. Once again, the shaded region indicates the functionality replaced by a fragment shader.

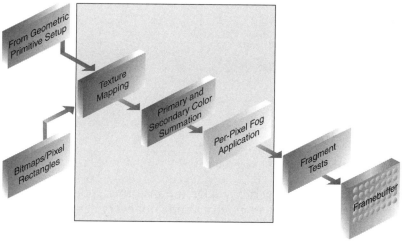

Figure 15-3   Fragment Processing Pipeline

Similar to vertex shaders, fragment shaders take over the processing of fragments. The operations subsumed in a fragment shader are:

- Texel retrieval for texture application
- Texture application
- Fogging
- Primary and secondary color summation

The operations that OpenGL does regardless of the application of a fragment shader are:

- Flat or smooth shading (which controls how values are interpolated across fragments)
- Pixel coverage computations
- Pixel ownership tests
- Scissor operations
- Stipple-pattern application (deprecated in OpenGL Version 3.0; removed in Version 3.1)
- Alpha test (in OpenGL versions up to and including 3.0. Version 3.1 removed this test, replacing it with functionality available in a fragment shader)
- Depth test
- Stencil test
- Alpha blending
- Logical operations on pixels
- Dithering of color values
- Color masking

Using GLSL Shaders

A Sample Shader

Example 15-1 shows a simple vertex shader. It transforms a point's position by simulating acceleration due to gravity. While not every detail will make sense at the moment, hopefully you'll be able to understand the basic flow of what's going on.

Example 15-1   A Sample GLSL (Version 1.30) Vertex Shader

```
#version 130

uniform float t;      // Time (passed in from the application)
attribute vec4 vel; // Particle velocity

const vec4 g = vec4( 0.0, -9.80, 0.0 );

void main()
{
    vec4 position = gl_Vertex;
    position += t*vel + t*t*g;

    gl_Position = gl_ModelViewProjectionMatrix * position;
}
```

The above preceeding is written using GLSL version 1.30 (you can tell by the
#version 130), which is compatible with OpenGL Version 3.0. Minor
changes are required to make it a version 1.40 shader, as demonstrated in
Example 15-2.

Example 15-2   The Same GLSL Vertex Shader (Version 1.40)

```
#version 140

uniform float t;      // Time (passed in from the application)
uniform mat4 MVP;     // Combined modelview and projection matrices
in vec4 pos;  // Particle position (as a homogenous coordinate)
in vec4 vel;          // Particle velocity

const vec4 g = vec4( 0.0, -9.80, 0.0 );

void main()
{
    vec4 position = pos;
    position += t*vel + t*t*g;

    gl_Position = MVP * position;
}
```

OpenGL / GLSL Interface

Writing shaders for use with OpenGL programs is similar to using a
compiler-based language like "C." You have a compiler analyze your
program, check it for errors, and then translate it into object code. Next,

a collection of object files are combined together in a linking phase generating an executable program. Using GLSL shaders in your program is a similar process, except that the compiler and linker are part of the OpenGL driver.

Figure 15-4 illustrates the steps required to create GLSL shader objects and link them together to create an executable shader program.

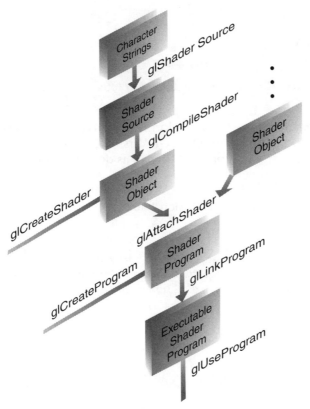

Figure 15-4   Shader Creation Flowchart

When you want to use a vertex or fragment shader in your application, you'll need to do the following sequence of steps:

For each shader object:

1. Create a shader object.

2. Compile your shader source into the object.

3. Verify that your shader successfully compiled.

Then, to link multiple shader objects into a shader program, you'll:

1. Create a shader program.

2. Attach the appropriate shader objects to the shader program.

3. Link the shader program.

4. Verify that the shader link phase completed successfully.

5. Use the shader for vertex or fragment processing.

Why create multiple shader objects? Just as you might reuse a function in different programs, the same idea applies to GLSL programs. Common routines that you create might be usable in multiple shaders. Instead of having to compile several large shaders with lots of common code, you'll merely link the appropriate shader objects together into a shader program.

To create a shader object, call **glCreateShader()**.

GLuint **glCreateShader**(GLenum *type*);

Allocates a shader object. *type* must be either GL_VERTEX_SHADER or GL_FRAGMENT_SHADER. The return value is either a non-zero integer or zero if an error occurred.

Once you have created a shader object, you need associate the source code of the shader with that object created by **glCreateShader()**. This is done by calling **glShaderSource()**.

---

void **glShaderSource**(GLuint *shader*, GLsizei *count*,
               const GLchar ***string*, const GLint **length*);

Associates the source of a shader with a shader object *shader*. *string* is an array of *count* GLchar strings that compose the shader's source. The character strings in *string* may be optionally null-terminated. *length* can be one of three values. If *length* is NULL, then it's assumed that each string provided in *string* is null-terminated. Otherwise, *length* has *count* elements, each of which specifies the length of the corresponding entry in *string*. If the value of an element in the array *length* is a positive integer, the value represents the number of characters in the corresponding *string* element. If the value is negative for particular elements, then that entry in *string* is assumed to be null-terminated.

To compile a shader object's source, use **glCompileShader()**.

---

void **glCompileShader**(GLuint *shader*);

Compiles the source code for *shader*. The results of the compilation can be queried by calling **glGetShaderiv()** with an argument of GL_COMPILE_STATUS.

Similar to when you compile a "C" program, you need to determine if the compilation finished successfully. A call to **glGetShaderiv()**, with an argument of GL_COMPILE_STATUS, will return the status of the compilation phase. If GL_TRUE is returned, the compilation succeeded, and the object can be linked into a shader program. If the compilation failed, you can determine what the error was by retrieving the compilation log. **glGetShaderInfoLog()** will return an implementation-specific set of messages describing the compilation errors. The current size of the error log can be queried by calling **glGetShaderiv()** with an argument of GL_INFO_LOG_LENGTH.

---

void **glGetShaderInfoLog**(GLuint *shader*, GLsizei *bufSize*,
                        GLsizei **length*, char **infoLog*);

Returns the log associated with the last compilation of a shader object. *shader* specifies which shader object to query. The log is returned as a null-terminated character string of *length* characters in the buffer *infoLog*. The maximum return size of the log is specified in *bufSize*.

If *length* is NULL, *infoLog*'s length is not returned.

Once you have created and compiled all of the necessary shader objects, you will need to link them together to create an executable shader program. This process is similar in nature to creating shader objects. First, you'll need to create a shader program to which you can attach the shader objects. Using **glCreateProgram()**, a shader program will be returned for further processing.

GLuint **glCreateProgram**();

Creates an empty shader program. The return value is either a non-zero integer, or zero if an error occurred.

Once you have your shader program, you'll need to populate it with the necessary shader objects to create the executable program. This is accomplished by attaching a shader object to the program by calling **glAttachShader()**.

---

void **glAttachShader**(GLuint *program*, GLuint *shader*);

Associates the shader object, *shader*, with the shader program, *program*. A shader object can be attached to a shader program at any time, although its functionality will only be available after a successful link of the shader program. A shader object can be attached to multiple shader programs simultaneously.

For parity, if you need to remove a shader object from a program to modify the shader's operation, detach the shader object by calling **glDetachShader()** with the appropriate shader object identifier.

---

void **glDetachShader**(GLuint *program*, GLuint *shader*);

Removes the association of a shader object, *shader*, from the shader program, *program*. If *shader* is detached from *program* and had been previously marked for deletion (by calling **glDeleteShader()**), it is deleted at that time.

After all the necessary shader objects have been attached to the shader program, you will need to link the objects for an executable program. This is accomplished by calling **glLinkProgram()**.

---

void **glLinkProgram**(GLuint *program*);

Processes all shader objects attached to *program* to generate a completed shader program. The result of the linking operation can be queried by calling **glGetProgramiv()** with GL_LINK_STATUS. GL_TRUE is returned for a successful link; GL_FALSE is returned otherwise.

As with shader objects, there's a chance that the linking phase may fail due to errors in the attached shader objects. You can query the result of the link operation's success by calling **glGetProgramiv()** with an argument of GL_LINK_STATUS. If GL_TRUE was returned, the link was successful, and you're able to specify the shader program for use in processing vertices or fragments. If the link failed, represented by GL_FALSE being returned, then you can determine the cause of the failure by retrieving the program link information log by calling **glGetProgramLog()**.

---

void **glGetProgramInfoLog**(GLuint *program*, GLsizei *bufSize*,
GLsizei **length*, char **infoLog*);

Returns the log associated with the last compilation of a shader program. *program* specifies which shader program to query. The log is returned as a null-terminated character string of *length* characters in the buffer *infoLog*. The maximum return size of the log is specified in *bufSize*.

If *length* is NULL, *infoLog*'s length is not returned.

After a successful program link, you can engage the vertex or fragment program by calling **glUseProgram()** with the program's object handle. To revert back to using the fixed-function pipeline, pass zero as the program object.

---

void **glUseProgram**(GLuint *program*);

Uses *program* for either vertex or fragment processing, depending upon the type of shader created with **glCreateShader()**. If *program* is zero, no shader is used for processing, and OpenGL reverts to fixed-function operation (in OpenGL Version 3.1, as there is no fixed-function pipeline, the results are undefined, but no error is generated).

While a program is in use, it can have new shader objects attached, compile attached shader objects, or detach previously attached objects. It may also be relinked. If the link phase is successful, the newly linked shader program replaces the previously active program. If the link fails, the currently bound shader program remains active and is not replaced until either a new program is specified with **glUseProgram()** or the program is successfully relinked.

Example 15-3 illustrates creating and linking a vertex shader in GLSL. The process is virtually identical for fragment shaders.

Example 15-3   Creating and Linking GLSL shaders

```
GLuint shader, program;
GLint  compiled, linked;
```

```
const GLchar* shaderSrc[] = {
    "void main()"
    "{"
    "    gl_Position = gl_ModelViewProjectionMatrix * gl_Vertex;"
    "}"
};

shader = glCreateShader(GL_VERTEX_SHADER);

glShaderSource(shader, 1, shaderSrc, NULL);
glCompileShader(shader);

glGetShaderiv(shader, GL_COMPILE_STATUS, &compiled );

if (!compiled) {
    GLint    length;
    GLchar* log;
    glGetShaderiv(shader, GL_INFO_LOG_LENGTH,
        &length );

    log = (GLchar*) malloc(length);
    glGetShaderInfoLog(shader, length, &length, log);
    fprintf(stderr, "compile log = '%s'\n", log);
    free(log);
}

program = glCreateProgram();

glAttachShader(program, shader);
glLinkProgram(program);

glGetProgramiv(program, GL_LINK_STATUS, &linked );

if (linked) {
    glUseProgram(program);
} else {
    GLint    length;
    GLchar* log;
    glGetProgramiv(progam, GL_INFO_LOG_LENGTH, &length );

    log = (GLchar*) malloc(length);
    glGetProgramInfoLog(program, length, &length, log);
    fprintf(stderr, "link log = '%s'\n", log);
    free(log);
}
```

To release the resources related to shader objects and programs, you can delete those objects by calling the respective deletion function. If either the shader program or object is currently active when it's deleted, the object is only marked for deletion. It is deleted when the program is no longer in use, or the shader object is detached from all shader program objects.

---

void **glDeleteShader**(GLuint *shader*);

Deletes *shader*. If *shader* is currently linked to one or more active shader programs, the object is tagged for deletion and deleted once the shader program is no longer being used by any shader program.

---

void **glDeleteProgram**(GLuint *program*);

Deletes *program* immediately if not currently in use in any context, or tagged for deletion when the program is no longer in use by any contexts.

To determine if an identifier is currently in use as either a shader program or object, calling **glIsProgram**() or **glIsShader**() will return a boolean value indicating if the identifier is in use.

GLboolean **glIsProgram**(GLuint *program*);

Returns GL_TRUE if *program* is the name of a shader program. If *program* is zero, or non-zero and not the name of a shader object, GL_FALSE is returned.

GLboolean **glIsShader**(GLuint *shader*);

Returns GL_TRUE if *shader* is the name of a shader object. If *shader* is zero, or non-zero and not the name of a shader object, GL_FALSE is returned.

To aid in shader development, the OpenGL call **glValidateProgram**() can help verify that a shader will execute given the current OpenGL state. Depending upon the underlying OpenGL implementation, program validation may also return hints about performance characteristics or other useful information specific to that shader's execution for that OpenGL implementation. You would validate a program in the same manner you would compile it by merely calling **glValidateProgram()** once all of the necessary shader objects were attached to the shader program. Similarly, you can query the results of the validation step by calling **glGetProgramiv()** with an argument of GL_VALIDATE_STATUS.

---

void **glValidateProgram**(GLuint *program*);

Validates *program* against the current OpenGL state settings. After validation, the value of GL_VALIDATE_STATUS will be set to either GL_TRUE, indicating that the program will execute in the current OpenGL environment, or GL_FALSE otherwise. The value of GL_VALIDATE_STATUS status can be queried by calling **glGetProgramiv()**.

The OpenGL Shading Language

This section provides an overview of the shading language used within OpenGL, commonly called GLSL. GLSL shares many traits with C++ and Java, and is used for authoring both vertex and fragment shaders, although certain features are only available for one type of shader. We will first describe GLSL's requirements, types, and other language constructs that are shared between vertex and fragment shaders, and then discuss the features unique to each type of shader.

Creating Shaders with GLSL

The Starting Point

A shader program, just like a "C" program, starts execution in **main()**. Every GLSL shader program begins life as:

```
void
main()
{
    // Your code goes here
}
```

The "//" construct is a comment and terminates at the end of the current line. "C"-type, multi-line comments—the /* and */ type—are also supported.

However, unlike ANSI "C," **main()** does not return an integer value; it is declared void.

While this is a perfectly legal GLSL vertex- or fragment-shader program that compiles and even runs, its functionality leaves something to be desired. We will continue by describing variables and their operation.

Also, as with C and its derivative languages, statements are terminated with a semicolon.

Declaring Variables

GLSL is a strongly typed language; that is, every variable must be declared and have an associated type. Variable names conform to the same rules as those for C: You can use letters, numbers, and the underscore character (_) to compose variable names. A digit cannot be the first character in a variable name.

Table 15-1 shows the basic types available in GLSL.

Type	Description
float	IEEE-like floating-point value
int	signed integer value
uint	unsigned integer value
bool	Boolean value

Table 15-1   Basic Data Types in GLSL

An additional set of types is named *samplers*, which are used as opaque handles for accessing texture maps. The various types of samplers and their uses are discussed in "Accessing Texture Maps in Shaders" on page 707.

> **Note:** An OpenGL implementation is not required to implement these types as stringently as one might like. As long as their operation is semantically and operationally correct, the underlying implementation may vary. For example, integers may be stored in floating-point registers. It is not a good idea to assume particular numeric outcomes, such as the maximum-sized integer value being 2^{15}, based upon these types.

Variable Scoping

While all variables must be declared, they may be declared any time before their use (unlike "C," where they must be the first statements in a block of code). The scoping rules of GLSL closely parallel those of C++:

- Variables declared outside of any function definition have global scope and are visible to all functions within the shader program.

- Variables declared within a set of curly braces (e.g., function definition, block following a loop or "if" statement, and so on) exist within the scope of those braces only.

- Loop iteration variables, such as *i* in the loop

```
for (int i = 0; i < 10; ++i) {
    // loop body
}
```

are only scoped for the body of the loop.

Variable Initialization

Variables may also be initialized when declared. For example:

```
int     i, numParticles = 1500;
float   force, g = -9.8;
bool    falling = true;
```

Integer constants may be expressed as octal, decimal, or hexadecimal values. An optional minus sign before a numeric value negates the constant, and a trailing 'u' or 'U' denotes an unsigned integer value.

Floating-point values must include a decimal point, unless described in scientific format (e.g., 3E-7), and may optionally include an 'f' or 'F' suffix as in "C."

Boolean values are either *true* or *false*, and can be initialized to either of those values or as the result of a operation that resolves to a boolean expression.

Constructors

As mentioned, GLSL is a strongly typed language, even more so than C++. In general, there is no implicit conversion between values, except in a few cases. For example,

```
int f = 10.0;
```

will result in a compilation error due to assigning a constant floating-point value to an integer variable. Integer values and vectors will be implicitly converted into the equivalent floating-point value or vector. Any other conversion of values requires using a conversion function (a C++-like constructor). For example,

```
float f = 10.0;
int   ten = int(f);
```

uses the **int**() function to do the conversion. Likewise, the other types also have conversion functions: **float**(), **uint**(), **bool**(). These functions also illustrate another feature of GLSL: operator overloading, whereby each function takes various input types, but all use the same base function name. We will discuss more on functions in a bit.

Aggregate Types

Three of GLSL's primitive types can be combined to better match core OpenGL's data values and to ease computational operations.

First, GLSL supports vectors of two, three, or four dimensions for each of the primitive types. Also, matrices of floats are available. Table 15-2 lists the valid vector and matrix types.

Base Type	2-D vec	3-D vec	4-D vec	Matrix Types
float	*vec2*	*vec3*	*vec4*	*mat2, mat3, mat4* *mat2x2, mat2x3, mat2x4,* *mat3x2, mat3x3, mat3x4* *mat4x2, mat4x3, mat4x4*
int	*ivec2*	*ivec3*	*ivec4*	—
uint	*uvec2*	*uvec3*	*uvec4*	—
bool	*bvec2*	*bvec3*	*bvec4*	—

Table 15-2   GLSL Vector and Matrix Types

Matrix types that list both dimensions, such as *mat4x3*, use the first value to specify the number of columns, the second the number of rows.

Variables declared with these types can be initialized similar to their scalar counterparts:

```
vec3  velocity = vec3(0.0, 2.0, 3.0);
```

and converting between types is equally accessible:

```
ivec3 steps = ivec3(velocity);
```

Vector constructors can also be used to truncate or lengthen a vector. If a longer vector is passed into the constructor of a smaller vector, the vector is truncated to the appropriate length.

```
vec4 color;
vec3 RGB = vec3(color); // now RGB only has three elements
```

Likewise, vectors are lengthened in somewhat the same manner. Scalar values can be promoted to vectors, as in

```
vec3 white = vec3(1.0);   // white = ( 1.0, 1.0, 1.0 )
vec4 translucent = vec4(white, 0.5);
```

Matrices are constructed in the same manner and can be initialized to either a diagonal matrix or a fully populated matrix.

In the case of diagonal matrices, a single value is passed into the constructor, and the diagonal elements of the matrix are set to that value, with all others being set to zero, as in

$$m = mat3(4.0) = \begin{bmatrix} 4.0 & 0.0 & 0.0 \\ 0.0 & 4.0 & 0.0 \\ 0.0 & 0.0 & 4.0 \end{bmatrix}$$

Matrices can also be created by specifying the value of every element in the matrix in the constructor. Values can be specified by combinations of scalars and vectors, as long as enough values are provided, and each column is specified in the same manner. Additionally, matrices are specified in column-major order, meaning the values are used to populate columns before rows (which is the opposite of how "C" initializes two-dimensional arrays).

For example, we could initialize a 3 × 3 matrix in any of the following ways:

```
mat3 M = mat3(1.0, 2.0, 3.0,
              4.0, 5.0, 6.0,
              7.0, 8.0, 9.0 );

vec3 column1 = vec3(1.0, 2.0, 3.0);
vec3 column2 = vec3(4.0, 5.0, 6.0);
vec3 column3 = vec3(7.0, 8.0, 9.0);

mat3 M = mat3(column1, column2, column3);
```

or even

```
vec2 column1 = vec2(1.0, 2.0);
vec2 column2 = vec2(4.0, 5.0);
vec2 column3 = vec2(7.0, 8.0);

mat3 M = mat3(column1, 3.0,
              column2, 6.0,
              column3, 9.0);
```

all yielding the same matrix

$$M = \begin{bmatrix} 1.0 & 4.0 & 7.0 \\ 2.0 & 5.0 & 8.0 \\ 3.0 & 6.0 & 9.0 \end{bmatrix}$$

Accessing Elements in Vectors and Matrices

The individual elements of vectors and matrices can be accessed and assigned. Vectors support two types of element access: a named-component method and an array-like method. Matrices use a two-dimensional array-like method.

Components of a vector can be accessed by name, as in

```
float red = color.r;
float v_y = velocity.y;
```

or using a zero-based index scheme. The following yield identical results to the above:

```
float red = color[0];
float v_y = velocity[1];
```

In fact, as shown in Table 15-3, there are three sets of component names available, all of which do the same thing. The multiple sets are useful for clarifying the operations that you're doing.

Component Accessors	Description
(x, y, z, w)	components associated with positions
(r, g, b, a)	components associated with colors
(s, t, p, q)	components associated with texture coordinates

Table 15-3   Vector Component Accessors

A common use for component-wise access to vectors is for *swizzling* components, as you might do with colors, perhaps for color space conversion. For example, you could do the following to specify a luminance value based on the red component of an input color:

```
vec3 luminance = color.rrr;
```

Likewise, if you needed to move components around in a vector, you might do:

```
color = color.abgr; // reverse the components of a color
```

The only restriction is that only one set of components can be used with a variable in one statement. That is, you can't do:

```
vec4 color = otherColor.rgz;// Error: 'z' is from a
// different group
```

Also, a compile-time error will be raised if you attempt to access an element that's outside of what the type supports. For example,

```
vec2 pos;
float zPos = pos.z; // Error: no 'z' component in 2D vectors
```

Matrix elements can be accessed using the array notation. Either a single scalar value or an array of elements can be accessed from a matrix:

```
mat4 m = mat4(2.0);
vec4 zVec = m[2];
float yScale = m[1][1]; // or m[1].y works as well
```

Structures

You can also logically group together collections of different types in a structure. Structures are convenient for passing groups of associated data into functions. When a structure is defined, it automatically creates a new type, and implicitly defines a constructor function that takes the types of the elements of the structure as parameters.

```
struct Particle {
    float lifetime;
    vec3 position;
    vec3 velocity;
};

Particle p = Particle(10.0, pos, vel); // pos, vel are vec3's
```

Likewise, to reference elements of a structure, use the familiar "dot" notation as you would in "C."

Arrays

GLSL also supports one-dimensional arrays of any type, including structures. As with "C," arrays are indexed using brackets ([ ]). The range of elements in an array of size *n* is 0 ... *n–1*. Unlike "C," however, negative array indices are not permitted, nor are two-dimensional arrays.

Arrays can be declared sized or unsized. You might use an unsized array as a forward declaration of an array variable and later redeclare it to the appropriate size. Array declarations use the bracket notation, as in:

```
float coeff[3]; // an array of 3 floats
float[3] coeff; // same thing
int   indices[]; // unsized. Redeclare later with a size
```

Arrays are first-class types in GLSL, meaning they have constructors and can be used as function parameters and return types. To statically initialize an array of values, you would use a constructor in the following manner:

```
float coeff[3] = float[3]( 2.38, 3.14, 42.0 );
```

The dimension value on the constructor is optional.

Additionally, similar to Java, GLSL arrays have an implicit method for reporting their number of elements: the **length**() method. If you would like to operate on all the values in an array, here is an example using the **length**() method:

```
for ( int i = 0; i < coeff.length(); ++i ) {
    coeff[i] *= 2.0;
}
```

Storage Qualifiers

Types can also have modifiers that affect their behavior. There are four modifiers defined in GLSL, as shown in Table 15-4.

Type Modifier	Description
const	Labels a variable as a read-only, compile-time constant.
in	Specifies that the variable is an input to the shader stage.
out	Specifies that the variable is an output from a shader stage.
uniform	Specifies that the value is passed to the shader from the application and is constant across a given primitive.

Table 15-4 GLSL Type Modifiers

Note: In GLSL versions prior to 1.30, vertex shader input variables were qualified with the keyword "attribute." Likewise, fragment shader input variables (which correspond to vertex shader outputs) were qualified with the "varying" keyword. In anticipation of potentially adding more shading stages, both of those keywords were replaced by the more generic "in" and "out" variations. In Version 1.40, both "attribute" and "varying" were removed (though they remain accessible using the GL_ARB_compatibility extension).

All storage qualifiers are valid for globally scoped variables. Additionally, *const* is applicable to local variables and function parameters.

Const **Storage Qualifier**

Just as with "C," the *const* type modifier indicates that the variable is read-only. For example, the statement

```
const float Pi = 3.141529
```

sets the variable *Pi* to an approximation of π. With the addition of the *const* modifier, it becomes an error to write to a variable after its declaration, so they must be initialized when declared.

In **Storage Qualifier**

The *in* modifier is used to qualify inputs into a shader stage. Those inputs may be vertex attributes (for vertex shaders) or interpolated variables (for fragment shaders).

Fragment shaders can further qualify their input values using some additional keywords that are valid only in combination with the *in* keyword. Those keywords are described in Table 15-5.

in **Keyword Qualifier**	**Description**
centroid	Forces the sampling of a fragment input variable to be within the area covered by the primitive for the pixel when multisampling is enabled.
smooth	Interpolates the fragment input variable in a perspective-correct manner.

Table 15-5   Additional *in* Keyword Qualifiers (for Fragment Shader Inputs)

in Keyword Qualifier	Description
flat	Doesn't interpolate the fragment input (i.e., the input will be the same for all fragments, as in flat shading).
noperspective	Linearly interpolates the fragment variable.

Table 15.5 (continued) Additional *in* Keyword Qualifiers (for Fragment Shader Inputs)

For example, if you would like a flat-shaded, centroid-sampled fragment input, you would specify

```
flat centroid in fragment;
```

in your fragment shader.

Out Storage Qualifier

The *out* modifier is used to qualify outputs from a shader stage—for example, the transformed homogenous coordinates from a vertex shader, or the final fragment color from a fragment shader.

Vertex shaders can further qualify their output values using the *centroid* keyword, which has the same meaning here as for fragment inputs. In addition, any vertex shader output qualified by *centroid* must have a matching fragment shader input variable that is also *centroid* qualified (i.e., the fragment shader has to have a variable with the identical declaration as in the vertex shader).

Uniform Storage Qualifier

The *uniform* modifier specifies that a variable's value will be specified by the application before the shader's execution and does not change across the primitive being processed. Uniform variables are shared between vertex and fragment shaders and must be declared as global variables. Any type of variable, including structures and arrays, can be specified as uniform.

Consider a shader that uses an additional color in shading a primitive. You might declare a uniform variable to pass that information into your shaders. In the shaders, you would make the declaration:

```
uniform vec4 BaseColor;
```

Within your shaders, you can reference *BaseColor* by name, but to set its value in your application, you need to do a little extra work. The GLSL compiler creates a table of all uniform variables when it links your shader program. To set *BaseColor*'s value from your application, you need to obtain the index of *BaseColor* in the table, which is done using the **glGetUniformLocation()** routine.

GLint **glGetUniformLocation**(GLuint *program*, const char **name*)

Returns the index of the uniform variable *name* associated with the shader *program*. *name* is a null-terminated character string with no spaces. A value of minus one (–1) is returned if *name* does not correspond to a uniform variable in the active shader *program*, or if a reserved shader variable name (those starting with `gl_` prefix) is specified.

name can be a single variable name, an element of an array (by including the appropriate index in brackets with the name), or a field of a structure (by specifying *name*, then "." followed by the field name, as you would in the shader program). For arrays of uniform variables, the index of the first element of the array may be queried either by specifying only the array name (for example, "arrayName"), or by specifying the index to the first element of the array (as in "arrayName[0]").

The returned value will not change unless the shader program is relinked (see **glLinkProgram()**).

Once you have the associated index for the uniform variable, you can set the value of the uniform variable using the **glUniform*()** or **glUniformMatrix*()** routines.

---

void **glUniform**{1234}{if ui}(GLint *location*, *TYPE value*);
void **glUniform**{1234}{if ui}**v**(GLint *location*, GLsizei *count*,
                const *TYPE *values*);
void **glUniformMatrix**{234}**fv**(GLint *location*, GLsizei *count*,
                GLboolean *transpose*, const GLfloat **values*);
void **glUniformMatrix**{2x3,2x4,3x2,3x4,4x2,4x3}**fv**(GLint *location*,
                GLsizei *count*, GLboolean *transpose*,
                const GLfloat **values*);

Sets the value for the uniform variable associated with the index *location* The vector form loads *count* sets of values (from one to four values, depending upon which **glUniform*()** call is used) into the uniform variables starting *location*. If location is the start of an array, *count* sequential elements of the array are loaded.

The floating-point forms can be used to load a single float, a floating-point vector, an array of floats, or an array of vectors of floats.

The integer forms can be used to update a single integer, an integer vector, an array of integers, or an array of integer vectors. Additionally, individual and arrays of texture samplers can also be loaded.

For **glUniformMatrix{234}fv()**, *count* sets of 2×2, 3×3, or 4×4 matrices are loaded from *values*.

For **glUniformMatrix{2x3,2x4,3x2,3x4,4x2,4x3}fv()**, *count* sets of like-dimensioned matrices are loaded from *values*. If *transpose* is GL_TRUE, *values* are specified in row-major order (like arrays in "C"); or if GL_FALSE is specified, *values* are taken to be in column-major order (ordered in the same manner as **glLoadMatrix()**).

Example 15-4 demonstrates obtaining a uniform variable's index and assigning values.

Example 15-4   Obtaining a Uniform Variable's Index and Assigning Values

```
GLint timeLoc; /* Uniform index for variable "time" in shader */
GLfloat timeValue; /* Application time */

timeLoc = glGetUniformLocation(program, "time");
glUniform1f(timeLoc, timeValue);
```

Uniform variables can also be declared within *named uniform blocks* that enable sharing and other features for shaders. Those uniform variables aren't accessible using the routines we just discussed, and they require usage of other routines described in the next section.

Uniform Blocks

Advanced

Advanced

As your shader programs become more complex, it's likely that the number of uniform variables they use will increase. Often the same uniform value is used within several shader programs. As uniform locations are generated when a shader is linked (i.e., when **glLinkProgram()** is called), the indices may change, even though (to you) the values of the uniform variables are identical. *Uniform buffer objects* provide a method to optimize both accessing uniform variables and enabling sharing of uniform values across shader programs.

As you might imagine, that given uniform variables can exist both in your application and in a shader, you'll need to both modify your shaders and use OpenGL routines to set up uniform buffer objects.

Note: Uniform blocks were added into OpenGL Version 3.1.

Specifying Uniform Variables Blocks in Shaders

To access a collection of uniform variables using routines such as **glMapBuffer()** (see "Buffer Objects" in Chapter 2 for more details), you need to slightly modify their declaration in your shader. Instead of declaring each uniform variable individually, you group them, just as you would do in a structure, in a *uniform block*. A uniform block is specified using the *uniform* keyword. You then enclose all the variables you want in that block within a pair of braces, as shown in Example 15-5.

Example 15-5   Declaring a Uniform Variable Block

```
uniform Matrices {
   mat4 ModelView;
   mat4 Projection;
   mat4 Color;
};
```

All types, with the exception of samplers, are permitted to be within a uniform block. Additionally, uniform blocks must be declared at global scope.

Uniform Block Layout Control

A variety of qualifiers are available to specify how to lay out the variables within a uniform block. These qualifiers can be used either for each individual uniform block or to specify how all subsequent uniform blocks are arranged (after specifying a layout declaration). The possible qualifiers are detailed in Table 15-6.

Layout Qualifier	Description
shared	Specify that the uniform block is shared among multiple programs. (This is the default sharing setting).
packed	Lay out the uniform block to minimize its memory use; however, this generally disables sharing across programs.
std140	Use the default layout as described in the OpenGL specification for uniform blocks.
row_major	Cause matrices in the uniform block to be stored in a row-major element ordering.
column_major	Specify matrices should be stored in a column-major element ordering. (This is the default ordering.)

Table 15-6   Layout Qualifiers for Uniform Blocks

For example, to specify that a single uniform block is shared and has row-major matrix storage, you would declare it in the following manner:

```
layout (shared, row_major) uniform { ... };
```

The multiple qualifying options must be separated by commas within the parentheses. To affect the layout of all subsequent uniform blocks, use the following construct:

```
layout (packed, column_major) uniform;
```

With this specification, all uniform blocks declared after that line will use that layout until the global layout is changed, or unless they include a layout override specific to their declaration.

Accessing Uniform Variables Declared in a Uniform Block

While uniform blocks are named, the uniform variables declared within them are not qualified by that name. That is, a uniform block doesn't scope a uniform variable's name, so declaring two variables of the same name within two uniform blocks of different names will cause an error. Using the block name is not necessary when accessing a uniform variable, however.

Accessing Uniform Blocks from Your Application

Because uniform variables form a bridge to share data between shaders and your application, you need to find the offsets of the various uniform variables inside the named uniform blocks in your shaders. Once you know the location of those variables, you can initialize them with data, just as you would any type of buffer object (using calls such as **glBufferData()**, for example).

To start, let's assume that you already know the names of the uniform blocks used inside the shaders in your application. The first step in initializing the uniform variables in your uniform block is to obtain the index of the block for a given program. Calling **glGetUniformBlockIndex()** returns an essential piece of information required to complete the mapping of uniform variables into your application's address space.

GLuint **glGetUniformBlockIndex**(GLuint *program*,
                                    const char **uniformBlockName*)

Returns the index of the named uniform block specified by *uniformBlockName* associated with *program*. If *uniformBlockName* is not a valid uniform block of *program*, GL_INVALID_INDEX is returned.

To initialize a buffer object to be associated with your uniform block, you'll need to bind a buffer object to a GL_UNIFORM_BUFFER target using the **glBindBuffer()** routine (see "Creating Buffer Objects" in Chapter 2 for details).

Once we have a buffer object initialized, we need to determine how large to make it to accommodate the variables in the named uniform block from our shader. To do so, we use the routine **glGetActiveUniformBlockiv()**, requesting the GL_UNIFORM_BLOCK_DATA_SIZE, which returns the size of the block as generated by the compiler (the compiler may decide to eliminate uniform variables that aren't used in the shader, depending on which uniform block layout you've selected). **glGetActiveUniformBlockiv()** can be used to obtain other parameters associated with a named uniform block. See "The Query Commands" in Appendix B for the complete list of options.

After obtaining the index of the uniform block, we need to associate a buffer object with that block. The most common method for doing so is to call either **glBindBufferRange()** or, if all the buffer storage is used for the uniform block, **glBindBufferBase()**.

---

void **glBindBufferRange**(GLenum *target*, GLuint *index*, GLuint *buffer*,
                         GLintptr *offset*, GLsizeiptr *size*);
void **glBindBufferBase**(GLenum *target*, GLuint *index*, GLuint *buffer*);

Associates the buffer object *buffer* with the named uniform block associated with *index*. *target* can either be GL_UNIFORM_BUFFER (for uniform blocks) or GL_TRANSFORM_FEEDBACK_BUFFER (for use with transform feedback; see "Transform Feedback" on page 722). *index* is the index associated with a uniform block. *offset* and *size* specify the starting index and range of the *buffer* that is to be mapped to the uniform buffer.

Calling **glBindBufferBase()** is identical to calling **glBindBufferRange()** with *offset* equal to zero and *size* equal to the size of the buffer object.

These calls can generate various OpenGL errors: A GL_INVALID_VALUE is generated if *size* is less than zero; if *offset* + *size* is greater than the size of the buffer; if either *offset* or *size* is not a multiple of 4; or if *index* is less than zero, or greater than or equal to the value returned when querying GL_MAX_UNIFORM_BUFFER_BINDINGS.

Once the association between a named uniform block and a buffer object is made, you can initialize or change values in that block by using any of the commands that affect a buffer's values, as described in "Updating Data Values in Buffer Objects" in Chapter 2.

You may also want to specify the binding for a particular named uniform block to a buffer object, as compared to the process of allowing the linker to assign a block binding and then querying the value of that assignment after the fact. You might follow this approach if you have numerous shader programs will share a uniform block. It avoids having the block be assigned a different index for each program. To explicitly control a uniform block's binding, call **glUniformBlockBinding()** before calling **glLinkProgram()**.

GLint **gUniformBlockBinding**(GLuint *program*,
                              GLuint *uniformBlockIndex*,
                              GLuint *uniformBlockBinding*)

Explicitly assigns *uniformBlockIndex* to *uniformBlockBinding* for *program*.

The layout of uniform variables in a named uniform block is controlled by the layout qualifier specified when the block was compiled and linked. If you used the default layout specification, you will need to determine the offset and date-store size of each variable in the uniform block. To do so, you will use the pair of calls: **glGetUniformIndices()**, to retrieve the index of a particular named uniform variable, and **glGetActiveUniformsiv()**, to get the offset and size for that particular index, as shown in Example 15-6.

---

void **glGetUniformIndices**(GLuint *program*, GLsizei *uniformCount*,
                    const char **uniformNames, GLuint *uniformIndices);

Returns the indices associated with the *uniformCount* uniform variables specified by name in the array *uniformNames* in the array *uniformIndices* for *program*. Each name in *uniformNames* is assumed to be NULL terminated, and both *uniformNames* and *uniformIndices* have *uniformCount* elements in each array.

If a name listed in *uniformNames* is not the name of an active uniform variables, the value GL_INVALID_INDEX is returned in the corresponding element in *uniformIndices*.

Example 15-6   Initializing Uniform Variables in a Named Uniform Block: ubo.c

```
/* Vertex and fragment shaders that share a block of uniforms
** named "Uniforms" */

const char* vShader = {
    "#version 140\n"
    "uniform Uniforms {"
    "    vec3   translation;"
    "    float scale;"
    "    vec4   rotation;"
    "    bool  enabled;"
    "};"
    "in vec2   vPos;"
    "in vec3   vColor;"
    "out vec4   fColor;"
    "void main()"
    "{"
    "    vec3    pos = vec3( vPos, 0.0 );"
    "    float   angle = radians( rotation[0] );"
    "    vec3    axis = normalize( rotation.yzw );"
    "    mat3    I = mat3( 1.0 );"

    "    mat3    S = mat3(        0, -axis.z,  axis.y,  "
```

```
"                         axis.z,         0, -axis.x, "
"                         -axis.y,   axis.x,         0 );"
"     mat3   uuT = outerProduct( axis, axis );"
"     mat3   rot = uuT + cos(angle)*(I - uuT) + sin(angle)*S;"
"     pos *= scale;"
"     pos *= rot;"
"     pos += translation;"
"     fColor = vec4( scale, scale, scale, 1 );"
"     gl_Position = vec4( pos, 1 );"
"}"
};

const char* fShader = {
    "#version 140\n"
    "uniform Uniforms {"
    "     vec3   translation;"
    "     float scale;"
    "     vec4   rotation;"
    "     bool   enabled;"
    "};"
    "in vec4   fColor;"
    "out vec4 color;"
    "void main()"
    "{"
    "     color = fColor;"
    "}"
};

/* Helper function to convert GLSL types to storage sizes */
size_t
TypeSize( GLenum type )
{
    size_t  size;

#define CASE( Enum, Count, Type ) \
    case Enum: size = Count * sizeof(Type); break

    switch( type ) {
        CASE( GL_FLOAT,            1,  GLfloat );
        CASE( GL_FLOAT_VEC2,       2,  GLfloat );
        CASE( GL_FLOAT_VEC3,       3,  GLfloat );
        CASE( GL_FLOAT_VEC4,       4,  GLfloat );
        CASE( GL_INT,              1,  GLint );
        CASE( GL_INT_VEC2,         2,  GLint );
        CASE( GL_INT_VEC3,         3,  GLint );
        CASE( GL_INT_VEC4,         4,  GLint );
        CASE( GL_UNSIGNED_INT,     1,  GLuint );
```

```
        CASE( GL_UNSIGNED_INT_VEC2,  2,   GLuint );
        CASE( GL_UNSIGNED_INT_VEC3,  3,   GLuint );
        CASE( GL_UNSIGNED_INT_VEC4,  4,   GLuint );
        CASE( GL_BOOL,               1,   GLboolean );
        CASE( GL_BOOL_VEC2,          2,   GLboolean );
        CASE( GL_BOOL_VEC3,          3,   GLboolean );
        CASE( GL_BOOL_VEC4,          4,   GLboolean );
        CASE( GL_FLOAT_MAT2,         4,   GLfloat );
        CASE( GL_FLOAT_MAT2x3,       6,   GLfloat );
        CASE( GL_FLOAT_MAT2x4,       8,   GLfloat );
        CASE( GL_FLOAT_MAT3,         9,   GLfloat );
        CASE( GL_FLOAT_MAT3x2,       6,   GLfloat );
        CASE( GL_FLOAT_MAT3x4,       12,  GLfloat );
        CASE( GL_FLOAT_MAT4,         16,  GLfloat );
        CASE( GL_FLOAT_MAT4x2,       8,   GLfloat );
        CASE( GL_FLOAT_MAT4x3,       12,  GLfloat );
        default:
            fprintf( stderr, "Unknown type: 0x%x\n", type );
            exit( EXIT_FAILURE );
            break;
    }
#undef CASE

    return size;
}


void
init()
{
    GLuint  program;

    glClearColor( 1, 0, 0, 1 );

    /* Compile and load vertex and fragment shaders (see
    ** LoadProgram.c */
    program = LoadProgram( vShader, fShader );
    glUseProgram( program );

    /* Initialize uniform values in uniform block "Uniforms" */
    {
        GLuint   uboIndex;
        GLint    uboSize;
        GLuint   ubo;
        GLvoid  *buffer;

        /* Find the uniform buffer index for "Uniforms", and
        ** determine the block's sizse*/
```

```
uboIndex = glGetUniformBlockIndex( program, "Uniforms" );

glGetActiveUniformBlockiv( program, uboIndex,
    GL_UNIFORM_BLOCK_DATA_SIZE, &uboSize );

buffer = malloc( uboSize );

if ( buffer == NULL ) {
    fprintf( stderr, "Unable to allocate buffer\n" );
    exit( EXIT_FAILURE );
}
else {
    enum { Translation, Scale, Rotation,
        Enabled, NumUniforms };

    /* Values to be stored in the buffer object */
    GLfloat    scale = 0.5;
    GLfloat    translation[] = { 0.1, 0.1, 0.0 };
    GLfloat    rotation[] = { 90, 0.0, 0.0, 1.0 };
    GLboolean  enabled = GL_TRUE;

    /* Since we know the names of the uniforms
    ** in our block, make an array of those values */
    const char* names[NumUniforms] = {
      "translation",
      "scale",
      "rotation",
      "enabled"
    };


    /* Query the necessary attributes to determine
    ** where in the buffer we should write
    ** the values */
    GLuint    indices[NumUniforms];
    GLint     size[NumUniforms];
    GLint     offset[NumUniforms];
    GLint     type[NumUniforms];

    glGetUniformIndices( program, NumUniforms,
        names, indices );
    glGetActiveUniformsiv( program, NumUniforms, indices,
        GL_UNIFORM_OFFSET, offset );
    glGetActiveUniformsiv( program, NumUniforms, indices,
        GL_UNIFORM_SIZE, size );
    glGetActiveUniformsiv( program, NumUniforms, indices,
        GL_UNIFORM_TYPE, type );
```

```
        /* Copy the uniform values into the buffer */
        memcpy( buffer + offset[Scale], &scale,
            size[Scale] * TypeSize(type[Scale]) );
        memcpy( buffer + offset[Translation], &translation,
            size[Translation] * TypeSize(type[Translation]) );
        memcpy( buffer + offset[Rotation], &rotation,
            size[Rotation] * TypeSize(type[Rotation]) );
        memcpy( buffer + offset[Enabled], &enabled,
            size[Enabled] * TypeSize(type[Enabled]) );

        /* Create the uniform buffer object, initialize
        ** its storage, and associated it with the shader
        ** program */
        glGenBuffers( 1, &ubo );
        glBindBuffer( GL_UNIFORM_BUFFER, ubo );
        glBufferData( GL_UNIFORM_BUFFER, uboSize,
            buffer, GL_STATIC_RAW );

        glBindBufferBase( GL_UNIFORM_BUFFER, uboIndex, ubo );
    }
  }
  ...
}
```

Computational Invariance

GLSL does not guarantee that two identical computations in different shaders will result in exactly the same value. The situation is no different than for computational applications executing on the CPU, where the order of compiled instructions may result in tiny differences due to the accumulation order of instructions. These tiny errors may be an issue for multipass algorithms that expect positions to be computed exactly the same for each shader pass. GLSL has a method of enforcing this type of invariance between shaders by using the *invariant* keyword.

invariant Qualifier

The *invariant* qualifier may be applied to any output varying variables of a vertex shader. The variable may be a built-in variable or a user-defined one. For example:

```
invariant gl_Position;

invariant centroid varying vec3 Color;
```

As you may recall, varying variables are used to pass data from a vertex shader into a fragment shader. Invariant variables must be declared *invariant* in both the vertex and fragment shader. The *invariant* keyword may be applied at any time before use of the variable in the shader and may be used to modify previously declared variables.

For debugging, it may be useful to impose invariance on all varying variables in shader. This can be accomplished by using the vertex shader preprocessor pragma

```
#pragma STDGL invariant(all)
```

Global invariance in this manner is useful for debugging; however, it may likely have an impact on the shader's performance. Guaranteeing invariance usually disables optimizations that may have been performed by the GLSL compiler.

Statements

The real work in a shader is done by computing values and making decisions. In the same manner as C++, GLSL has a rich set of operators for constructing arithmetic operations for computing values and a standard set of logical constructs for controlling shader execution.

Arithmetic Operations

No text describing a language is complete without the mandatory table of operator precedence (see Table 15-7). The operators are ordered in decreasing precedence. In general, the types being operated on must be the same, and for vector and matrices, the operands must be of the same dimension.

Precedence	Operators	Accepted Types	Description
1	( )	—	Grouping of operations
2	[ ] f( ) . (period) ++ --	arrays functions structures int, float, vec*, mat*	Array subscripting Function calls and constructors Structure field or method access Post-increment and -decrement
3	++ -- + - !	int, float, vec*, mat* int, float, vec*, mat*	Pre-increment and -decrement Unary operations: explicit positive or negative value, negation

Table 15-7 GLSL Operators and Their Precedence

Precedence	Operators	Accepted Types	Description
4	* /	int, float, vec*, mat*	Multiplicative operations
5	+ -	int, float, vec*, mat*	Additive operations
6	< > <= >=	int, float, vec*, mat*	Relational operations
7	== !=	int, float, vec*, mat*	Equality operations
8	&&	bool	Logical and operation
9	^^	bool	Logical exclusive-or operation
10	||	bool	Logical or operation
11	a ? b : c	bool int, float, vec*, mat*	Selection operation (inline "if" operation; if (a) then (b) else (c))
12	= += -= *= /=	int, float, vec*, mat*	Assignment Arithmetic assignment
13	, (comma)	—	Sequence of operations

Table 15-7 (continued)   GLSL Operators and Their Precedence

Note: This table lists all currently implemented operators of GLSL. Various operations that exist in C++ (%, the modulus operator, for example) are currently reserved but not implemented in GLSL.

Overload Operators

Most operators in GLSL are *overloaded*, meaning that they operate on a varied set of types. Specifically, arithmetic operations (including pre- and post-increment and -decrement) for vectors and matrices are well-defined in GLSL. For example, to multiply a vector and a matrix (recalling that the order of terms is important—matrix multiplication is non-commutative, for all you math-heads), use the following operation:

```
vec3 v;
mat3 m;
vec3 result = v * m;
```

The normal restrictions apply, that the dimensionality of the matrix and the vector must match. Additionally, scalar multiplication with a vector and matrix will produce the expected result. One notable exception is that the multiplication of two vectors will result in component-wise multiplication of components; however, multiplying two matrices will result in normal matrix multiplication.

```
vec2 a, b, c;
mat2 m, u, v;
c = a * b; //c = ( a.x*b.x, a.y*b.y )
m = u * v; //m = (u00*v00+u01*v10u00*v01+u01*v11
                   u01*v00+u11*v10u10*v01+u11*v11 )
```

Additional common vector operations (e.g., dot and cross products) are supported by function calls, as well as various per-component operations on vectors and matrices.

Logical Operations

GLSL's logical control structures are the popular if-then-else and switch statements. As with the "C" language the else clause is optional, and multiple statements require a block.

```
if ( truth ) {
    // true clause
} else {
    // false clause
}
```

Similar to the situation in C, switch statements are available (starting with GLSL 1.30) in their familiar form:

```
switch( int_value ) {
  case n:
    // statements
    break;

  case m:
    // statements
    break;

  default:
    // statements
    break;
}
```

GLSL switch statements also support "fall-through" cases—a case statement that does not end with a break statement. They do require a break for the final case in the block (before the closing brace).

Looping Constructs

GLSL supports the familiar "C" form of **for, while**, and **do ... while** loops.

The **for** loop permits the declaration of the loop iteration variable in the initialization clause of the **for** loop. The scope of iteration variables declared in this manner is only for the lifetime of the loop.

```
for (int i = 0; i < 10; ++i ) {
    ...
}

while (n < 10) {
    ...
}

do {
    ...
} while (n < 10);
```

Flow Control Statements

Additional control statements beyond conditionals and loops are available in GLSL. Table 15-8 describes available flow-control statements.

Statement	Description
break	Terminates execution of the block of a loop, and continues execution after the scope of that block.
continue	Terminates the current iteration of the enclosing block of a loop, resuming execution with the next iteration of the loop.
return [result]	Returns from the current subroutine, optionally providing a value to be returned from the function (assuming return value matches the return type of the enclosing function).
discard	Discards the current fragment and ceases shader execution. Discard statements are only valid in fragment shader programs.

Table 15-8   GLSL Flow-Control Statements

The `discard` statement is available only in fragment programs. The execution of the fragment shader may be terminated at the execution of the `discard` statement, but this is implementation dependent.

Functions

Functions permit you to replace occurrences of common code with a function call. This, of course, allows for smaller code, and less chances for errors. GLSL defines a number of built-in functions, which are listed in Appendix I, "Built-In OpenGL Shading Language Variables and Functions,"[2] as well as support for user-defined functions. User-defined functions can be defined in a single shader object, and reused in multiple shader programs.

Declarations

Function declaration syntax is very similar to "C," with the exception of the access modifiers on variables:

```
returnType functionName([accessModifier] type1 variable1,
                        [accessModifier] type2 varaible2,
                        ... )
{
    // function body
    return returnValue; // unless returnType is void
}
```

Function names can be any combination of letters, numbers, and the underscore character, with the exception that it can neither begin with a digit nor with `gl_`.

Return types can be any built-in GLSL type and user-defined structure; arrays are not available as return values. If a function doesn't return a value, its return type is `void`.

Parameters to functions can be of any type, including arrays (which must specify their size).

Functions must be either declared, or prototyped, before their use. Just as in C++, the compiler must have seen the function's definition before its use or an error will be raised. If a function is used in a shader object other than the one where it's defined, a prototype must be declared. A prototype is merely the function's signature without its accompanying body. Here's a simple example:

```
float HornerEvalPolynomial(float coeff[10], float x);
```

---

[2] This appendix is available online at http://www.opengl-redbook.com/appendices/.

Parameters Access Modifiers

While functions in GLSL are able to modify and return values after their execution, there's no concept of a pointer or reference, as in "C" or C++. Rather, parameters of functions have associated access modifiers indicating if the value should be copied into, or out of, a function after execution. Table 15-9 describes the available parameter access modifiers in GLSL.

Access Modifier	Description
in	value copied into a function (default if not specified)
const in	read-only value copied into a function
out	value copied out of a function (undefined upon entrance into the function)
inout	value copied into and out of a function

Table 15-9   GLSL Function Parameter Access Modifiers

The in keyword is optional. If a variable does not include an access modifier, then an "in" modifier is implicitly added to the parameter's declaration. However, if the variable's value needs to be copied out of a function, it must either be tagged with an "out" (for write-only variables) or an "inout" (for read-write variables). Writing to an variable not tagged with one of these modifiers will generate a compile-time error.

Additionally, to verify at compile time that a function doesn't modify an input-only variable, adding a "const in" modifier will cause the compiler to check that the variable is not written to in the function.

Using OpenGL State Values in GLSL Programs

Almost all values that you set in using the OpenGL API are accessible from within vertex and fragment shader programs. A comprehensive list of GLSL built-in variables is provided in Appendix I, "Built-In OpenGL Shading Language Variables and Functions."[3]

Accessing Texture Maps in Shaders

GLSL also supports accessing texture maps in both vertex and fragment shaders. To access a texture map, GLSL makes an association between an

---

[3] This appendix is available online at http://www.opengl-redbook.com/appendices/.

active texture unit (see "Steps in Multitexturing" in Chapter 9) configured in the OpenGL application, and a variable declared in a shader. Such variables use one of the *sampler* data types shown in Table 15-10 to allow the shader program access to the texture map's data. The dimensions of the associated texture map must match the type of the sampler.

Sampler Name	Description
sampler1D isampler1D usample1D	Accesses a 1D texture map
sampler2D isampler2D usampler2D	Accesses a 2D texture map
sampler3D isampler3D usampler3D	Accesses a 3D texture map
samplerCube isamplerCube usamplerCube	Accesses a cube map (for reflection mapping)
sampler1DArray isampler1DArray usampler1DArray	Accesses an array of 1D texture maps
sampler2DArray isampler2DArray usampler2DArray	Accesses an array of 2D texture maps
sampler2DRect isampler2DRect usampler2DRect	Accesses a 2D texture rectangle
sampler1DShadow	Accesses a 1D shadow map
sampler2DShadow	Accesses a 2D shadow map
samplerCubeShadow	Accesses a cube map of shadowmaps
sampler1DArrayShadow	Accesses an array of 1D shadow maps
sampler2DArrayShadow	Accesses an array of 2D shadow maps

Table 15-10   Fragment Shader Texture Sampler Types

Sampler Name	Description
sampler2DRectShadow	Accesses a 2D shadow texture rectangle
samplerBuffer isamplerBuffer usamplerBuffer	Accesses a texture buffer

Table 15-10   **(continued)**   Fragment Shader Texture Sampler Types

Samplers must be declared as uniform variables in the shader and must have their value assigned from within the OpenGL application. Samplers may also be used as parameters in functions, but must be used with samplers of matching type.

Samplers must have a texture unit assigned to them before their use in a shader, and can only be initialized by **glUniform1i()**, or **glUniform1iv()**, with the index of the texture unit that the sampler should use (see Example 15-7).

Example 15-7   Associating Texture Units with Sampler Variables

```
GLint texSampler; /* sampler index for shader variable "tex" */

texSampler = glGetUniformLocation(program, "tex");
glUniform1i(texSampler, 2); /* Set "tex" to use GL_TEXTURE2 */
```

Accessing Textures in GLSL

Sampling a texture map from within a GLSL shader uses the sampler variable that you've declared and associated with a texture unit. There are a number of texture access routines (described in "Texture Lookup Functions" in Appendix I, "Built-in OpenGL Shading Language Variables and Functions,"[4]) for accessing all OpenGL supported texture map types.

In Example 15-8, we sample the two-dimensional texture map associated with the sampler2D variable *tex*, and combine the results with the fragment's color, providing the same results as using GL_MODULATE mode for the texture environment mode.

Example 15-8   Sampling a Texture Within a GLSL Shader

```
uniform sampler2D tex;

void main()
{
    gl_FragColor = gl_Color * texture2D(tex, gl_TexCoord[0].st);
}
```

---

[4] This appendix is available online at http://www.opengl-redbook.com/appendices/.

Even though the example seems simple, that's truly all there is to do. However, much more interesting applications are enabled when the values in a texture map do not necessarily represent colors, but other data used for subsequent computation after retrieving the results from the texture map. Specifically, one application is using the values in one texture map as indices into another, described in "Dependent Texture Reads" below. The same results can be accomplished using the combiner texture environment (see "Texture Combiner Functions" in Chapter 9), but are much simpler to do using shaders.

The results you compute after sampling a texture are controlled by the code you write in your shader, but how the texture map is sampled is still controlled by the state settings in your application. For example, you control whether a texture map contains mipmaps, and how those mipmaps are sampled, as well as the filters used for resolving the returned texel values (basically, the parameters you set with **glTexParameter*()**). From inside the shader, you can control the biasing of mipmap selection, and using projective-texture techniques (see Appendix I, "Built-In OpenGL Shading Language Variables and Functions,"[5] for details and suitable functions).

Dependent Texture Reads

During the execution of a shader that employs texture mapping, you'll use texture coordinates to specify locations in texture maps and retrieve the resulting texel values. While texture coordinates are supplied for each active texture unit, you can use any values you might like as texture coordinates (assuming matching dimensionality) for use with a sampler, including values you may have just sampled from another texture map. Passing the results of one texture access as texture coordinates into another texture access operation is generally termed a *dependent texture read*, indicating that the results of the second operation are dependent on the first operation.

This is easy to implement in GLSL and is illustrated in Example 15-9.

Example 15-9   Dependent Texture Reads in GLSL

```
uniform sampler1D coords;
uniform sampler3D volume;

void main()
{
    vec3 texCoords = texture1D(coords, gl_TexCoord[0].s);
    vec3 volumeColor = texture3D(volume, texCoords);
    ...
}
```

---

[5] This appendix is available online at http://www.opengl-redbook.com/appendices/.

Texture Buffers

Advanced

Advanced

While GLSL makes arrays available, both as statically initialized values inside shaders, and as collections of values presented as an array in a uniform variable, you might occasionally need an array that exceeds the size limits available in those two options. Previous to OpenGL Version 3.1, you would have likely stored such a table of values in a texture map, and then manipulate the texture coordinates to obtain access to the values you wanted in the texture, usually in a less than straightforward manner. A more intuitive and direct solution to that data storage problem is the *texture buffer*. A texture buffer is a special type of buffer object, similar to a one-dimensional texture, that you can index using an integer value (like a normal array index) in your shader, but that offers the more expansive resources of texture memory, thereby allowing larger data sets.

You create a texture buffer just as you would any other buffer object. First you call **glBindBuffer()** with a target of GL_TEXTURE_BUFFER to create the object, and then you call **glBufferData()** (for example) to initialize its data. To bind that buffer to a texture buffer, you call **glTexBuffer()**.

---

void **glTexBuffer**(GLenum *target*, GLenum *internalFormat*, GLuint *buffer*);

Associates the buffer object *buffer* with *target*, causing the format of the data in *buffer* to be interpreted as having the format of *internalFormat*. *target* must be GL_TEXTURE_BUFFER, and *internalFormat* may be any of the sized texture formats: G, GL_R8, GL_R16, GL_R16F, GL_R32F, GL_R8I, GL_R16I, GL_R32I, GL_R8UI, GL_R16UI, GL_R32UI, GL_RG8, GL_RG16, GL_RG16F, GL_RG32F, GL_RG8I, GL_RG16I, GL_RG32I, GL_RG8UI, GL_RG16UI, GL_RG32UI, GL_RGBA8, GL_RGBA16, GL_RGBA16F, GL_RGBA32F, GL_RGBA8I, GL_RGBA16I, GL_RGBA32I, GL_RGBA8UI, GL_RGBA16UI, GL_RGBA32UI.

Similar to other texture maps, you specify which texture unit to associate the texture buffer with by calling **glActiveTexture()**.

Shader Preprocessor

The first step in compilation of a GLSL shader is parsing by the preprocessor. Similar to the "C" preprocessor, there are a number of directives for creating conditional compilation blocks and defining values. However, unlike the "C" preprocessor, there is no file inclusion (`#include`).

Preprocessor Directives

Table 15-11 lists the preprocessor directives accepted by the GLSL preprocessor and their functions.

Preprocessor Directive	Description
`#define` `#undef`	Control the definition of constants and macros similar to the C preprocessor

`#if`
`#ifdef`
`#ifndef`
`#else`
`#elif`
`#endif`
	Conditional code management similar to the C preprocessor, including the **defined** operator. Conditional expressions evaluate integer expressions and defined values (as specified by `#define`) only.

`#error` *text*	Cause the compiler to insert *text* (up to the first newline character) into the shader information log
`#pragma` *options*	Control compiler specific options
`#extension` *options*	Specify compiler operation with respect to specified GLSL extensions
`#version` *number*	Mandate a specific version of GLSL version support
`#line` *options*	Control diagnostic line numbering

Table 15-11   GLSL Preprocessor Directives

Macro Definition

The GLSL preprocessor allows macro definition in much the same manner as the "C" preprocessor, with the exception of the string substitution and concatenation facilities. Macros might define a single value, as in

```
#define NUM_ELEMENTS 10
```

or with parameters like

```
#define LPos(n) gl_LightSource[(n)].position
```

Additionally, there are several predefined macros for aiding in diagnostic messages (that you might issue with the `#error` directive, for example), as shown in Table 15-12.

Macro	Definition
__LINE__	Line number defined by one more than the number of newline characters processed and modified by the `#line` directive
__FILE__	Source string number currently being processed
__VERSION__	Integer representation of the OpenGL Shading Language version

Table 15-12   GLSL Preprocessor Predefined Macros

Likewise, macros (excluding those defined by GLSL) may be undefined by using the `#undef` directive. For example

```
#undef LPos
```

Preprocessor Conditionals

Identical to the processing by the "C" preprocessor, the GLSL preprocessor provides conditional code inclusion based on macro definition and integer constant evaluation.

Macro definition may be determined in two ways: Either using the `#ifdef` directive

```
#ifdef NUM_ELEMENTS
...
#endif
```

or using the **defined** operator with the `#if` or `#elif` directives

```
#if defined(NUM_ELEMENTS) && NUM_ELEMENTS > 3
...
#elif NUM_ELEMENTS < 7
...
#endif
```

Compiler Control

The `#pragma` directive provides the compiler additional information regarding how you would like your shaders compiled.

Optimization Compiler Option

The `optimize` option instructs the compiler to enable or disable optimization of the shader from the point where the directive resides forward in the shader source. You can enable or disable optimization by issuing either

```
#pragma optimize(on)
```

and

```
#pragma optimize(off)
```

respectively. These options may only be issued outside of a function definition. By default, optimization is enabled for all shaders.

Debug Compiler Option

The `debug` option enables or disables additional diagnostic output of the shader. You can enable or disable debugging by issuing either

```
#pragma debug(on)
```

and

```
#pragma debug(off)
```

respectively. Similar to the `optimize` option, these options may only be issued outside of a function definition, and by default, debugging is disabled for all shaders.

Global Shader Compilation Option

One final `#pragma` directive is available, `STDGL`. This option is currently used to enable invariance in the output of varying values. See "invariant Qualifier" on page 701 for details.

Extension Processing in Shaders

GLSL, like OpenGL itself, may be enhanced by extensions. As vendors may include extensions specific to their OpenGL implementation, it's useful to have some control over shader compilation in light of possible extensions that a shader may use.

The GLSL preprocessor uses the `#extension` directive to provide instructions to the shader compiler regarding how extension availability should be handled during compilation. For any, or all, extensions, you can specify how you would like the compiler to proceed with compilation.

```
#extension extension_name : <directive>
```

where *extensions_name* uses the same extension name returned by calling **glGetString**(GL_EXTENSIONS) or

```
#extension all : <directive>
```

to affect the behavior of all extensions.

The options available are shown in Table 15-13.

Directive	Description
require	Flag an error if the extension is not supported, or if the `all` extension specification is used.
enable	Give a warning if the particular extensions specified are not supported, or flag an error if the `all` extension specification is used.
warn	Give a warning if the particular extensions specified are not supported, or give a warning if any extension use is detected during compilation.
disable	Disable support for the particular extensions listed (that is, have the compiler act as if the extension is not supported even if it is) or all extensions if `all` is present, issuing warnings and errors as if the extension were not present.

Table 15-13   GLSL Extension Directive Modifiers

Vertex Shader Specifics

You can send data from your application into a vertex program using several mechanisms:

- By using the standard OpenGL vertex data interface (those calls that are legal between a **glBegin**() and a **glEnd**()), such as **glVertex***(), **glNormal***(), and so on. These values can vary on a per-vertex basis and are considered to be built-in attribute variables.

- By declaring uniform variables. These values remain constant across a geometric primitive.

- By declaring attribute variables, which can be updated on a per-vertex basis, in addition to the standard vertex state. (This is effectively the only method for specifying vertex attributes in OpenGL Version 3.1, unless the GL_ARB_compatibility extension is available to you.)

Likewise, a vertex program must output some data (and optionally update other variables) for continued processing by the remaining vertex processing by the OpenGL pipeline, and possibly an accompanying fragment program.

The outputs that need to be written include:

- gl_Position, which must be updated by the vertex program and contain the homogeneous coordinate of the vertex after modelview and projection transformation.

- Various other built-in variables that are declared varying for passing data into the fragment pipeline. These include colors, texture coordinates, and other per-fragment data. They are described in "Varying Output Variables" on page 721.

- User-defined varying variables.

Figure 15-5 illustrates the inputs and outputs of a vertex program.

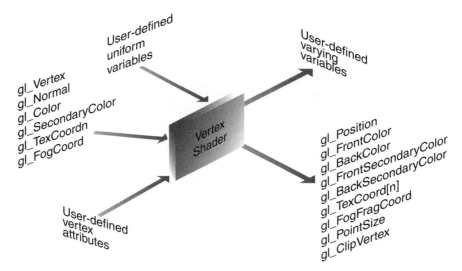

Figure 15-5   GLSL Vertex Shader Input and Output Variables

Built-In Attribute Input Variables

Table 15-14 shows variables representing those that are globally available in a vertex shader. The variables reflect the current OpenGL state, as set by the corresponding routine.

Variable	Type	Specifying function	Description
gl_Vertex	vec4	**glVertex**	Vertex's world-space coordinate
gl_Color	vec4	**glColor**	Primary color value
gl_SecondaryColor	vec4	**glSecondaryColor**	Secondary color value
gl_Normal	vec4	**glNormal**	Lighting normal
gl_MultiTexCoord$n$	vec4	**glMultiTexCoord(** $n,$ ... **);**	Texture unit n's texture coordinates, with $n = 0$ ... 7.
gl_FogCoord	float	**glFogCoord**	Fog coordinate
gl_VertexID	int	—	Index of current vertex since the start of the last rendering call
gl_InstanceID	int	**glDrawArraysInstanced** **glDrawElementsInstanced**	The instance ID for the associated primitives

Table 15-14   Vertex Shader Attribute Global Variables

User-Defined Attribute Variables

User-defined attribute variables are global variables that associate values passed from the OpenGL application to a vertex shader executing within the OpenGL implementation.

Attribute variables can be defined as float, floating-point vectors (vec*), or matrices (mat*).

Hint: In general, attribute variables are implemented as vec4's internal to OpenGL. If you have a number of single floating-point variables that you wish to use as vertex attributes, consider combining those values into one or more vec* structures. While declaring a single float is supported, it uses an entire vec4 to represent the single value.

To use user-defined attribute variables, OpenGL needs to know how to match the name of the variable you specified in your shader program with values that you pass into a shader. Similar to how OpenGL handles uniform variables, when a shader program is linked, the linker generates a table of variable names for attribute variables. To determine the maximum number of user-defined vertex attributes, call **glGetIntegerv()** with a parameter of GL_MAX_VERTEX_ATTRIBS.

To determine which index you need to update for the respective variable in the vertex program, you'll call **glGetAttribLocation()**, with the name of your variable, and the index corresponding to that name will be returned.

GLint **glGetAttribLocation**(GLuint *program*, const char **name*);

Returns the index associated with *name* for the shader *program*. *name* must be a null-terminated character string matching the declaration in *program*. If *name* is not an active variable, or it's the name of a built-in attribute variable, or an error occurs, a value of –1 is returned.

For example, in a vertex shader, you might declare

```
varying vec3 displacement;
```

Assuming that the shader compiled and linked appropriately, you would determine the index of "displacement" by calling:

```
int index = glGetAttribLocation(program, "displacement");
```

You can also explicitly set the binding of an attribute variable to an index using the **glBindAttribLocation()** call; however, this must be done before the shader program is linked.

---

void **glBindAttribLocation**(GLint *program*, GLuint *index*,
                              const char **name*);

Explicitly specifies which *index* location *name* should be assigned the next time *program* is linked. *index* must be an integer between zero and GL_MAX_VERTEX_ATTRIBS – 1, and *name* must be a null-terminated string. Built-in attribute variables (those beginning with `gl_`) will generate a GL_INVALID_OPERATION error.

To set the value associated with the returned index, you'll use a version of the **glVertexAttrib*()** function.

---

void **glVertexAttrib{1234}{sfd}**(GLuint *index*, *TYPE values*);
void **glVertexAttrib{123}{sfd}v**(GLuint *index*, const *TYPE *values*);
void **glVertexAttrib4**{bsifd ub us ui}**v**(GLuint *index*, *TYPE values*);
void **glVertexAttrib4Nub**(GLuint *index*, *TYPE values*);
void **glVertexAttrib4N**{bsi ub us ui}**v**(GLuint *index*, const *TYPE *values*);
void **glVertexAttribI{1234}{i ui}**(GLuint *index*, *TYPE values*);
void **glVertexAttribI4**{bsi ub us ui}**v**(GLint *index*, const *TYPE *values*);

Specifies the values for vertex attribute variables associated with *index* to *values*. For calls that do not explicitly set all four values, default values of 0.0 (0 for signed- and unsigned-integer values) will be set for the *y*- and *z*-coordinates, and 1.0 (1 for signed- and unsigned-integer values) for the *w*-coordinate.

Specifying values for *index* zero is identical to calling **glVertex*()**, with the same values.

The normalized version will convert integer input values into the range zero to one, using the mappings specified in Table 4-1 on page 198.

Matrices are updated by specifying consecutive values for *index*. *values* specified will be used to update the respective columns of the matrix.

While attribute variables are floating point, there's no restriction on the type of input data used to initialize their values. Specifically, integer-type input values can be normalized into the range of zero to one, using **glVertexAttrib4N*()**, before being assigned into the attribute variable.

Scalar (single-value), vector, and matrix attribute values can be set using **glVertexAttrib*()**. For the matrix case, multiple calls are required. In particular, for a matrix of dimension *n*, you would call **glVertexAttrib*()**, with indices: *index, index+1, ..., index+n−1*.

Vertex shaders also augment the vertex array facility (see "Vertex Arrays" on page 70). As with other types of vertex data, values for vertex attribute variables can be stored in vertex arrays and updated by calling **glDrawArrays()**, **glArrayElement()**, and so on. To specify the array to be used to update a variable's value, call **glVertexAttribPointer()**.

void **glVertexAttribPointer**(GLuint *index*, GLint *size*, GLenum *type*,
                          GLboolean *normalized*, GLsizei *stride*,
                          const GLvoid* *pointer*);

Specifies where the data values for *index* can be accessed. *pointer* is the memory address of the first set of values in the array. *size* represents the number of components to be updated per vertex. *type* specifies the data type (GL_SHORT, GL_INT, GL_FLOAT, or GL_DOUBLE) of each element in the array. *normalized* indicates that the vertex data should be normalized before being stored (in the same manner as **glVertexAttrib4N*()**). *stride* is the byte offset between consecutive elements in the array. If *stride* is 0, the data is assumed to be tightly packed.

As with other types of vertex arrays, specifying the array is only one part of the process. Each client-side vertex array needs to be enabled. Compared to using **glEnableClientState()**, arrays of vertex attributes are enabled by calling **glEnableVertexAttribArray()**.

void **glEnableVertexAttribArray**(GLuint *index*);
void **glDisableVertexAttribArray**(GLuint *index*);

Specifies that the vertex array associated with variable *index* be enabled or disabled. *index* must be a value between 0 and GL_MAX_VERTEX_ATTRIBS – 1.

Special Output Variables

The values shown in Table 15-15 are available for writing (and reading after being written) in a vertex shader. `gl_Position` specifies the vertex's final position upon exit of the vertex shader and is required to be written in the shader.

Variable Name	Type	Description
gl_Position	vec4	Transformed vertex position (in eye coordinates).
gl_PointSize	float	Point size of vertex.
gl_ClipVertex	vec4	Vertex position to be used with user-defined clipping planes. This value must be in the same coordinate system as the clipping planes: eye-coordinates or object-coordinates.

Table 15-15   Vertex Shader Special Global Variables

While you're able to set the output vertex position to any homogenous coordinate you might like, the final value of `gl_Position` is usually computed within a vertex program as:

```
gl_Position = gl_ModelViewProjectionMatrix * gl_Vertex;
```

Or, if you're employing a multipass algorithm (one rendering multiple images from the same geometry) that needs to have the results of the vertex shader and fixed function pipeline be consistent, set `gl_Position` using the following code:

```
gl_Position = ftransform();
```

`gl_PointSize` controls the output size of a point, similar to **glPointSize()**, but on a per-vertex basis. To control the size of points from within vertex programs, call **glEnable()** with a value of GL_VERTEX_PROGRAM_POINT_SIZE, which overrides any current point size that may have been specified.

User-defined clipping planes, as specified by **glClipPlane()**, can be used by writing a homogeneous coordinate into the `gl_ClipVertex` variable. For clipping to proceed correctly, the clipping plane specified and the coordinate written into `gl_ClipVertex` must be in the same coordinate space. The common space for clipping is eye-coordinates. You can transform the current vertex into eye-coordinates for clipping by executing:

```
gl_ClipVertex = gl_ModelViewMatrix * gl_Vertex;
```

Varying Output Variables

Table 15-16 represents those variables that can be written to in a vertex shader and have their values readable in a fragment shader. The values in the fragment shader are iterated across the fragments (or samples, if multisampling) of the primitives.

Variable Name	Type	Description
gl_FrontColor	vec4	Primary color to be used for front-facing primitives
gl_BackColor	vec4	Primary color to be used for back-facing primitives
gl_FrontSecondaryColor	vec4	Secondary color to be used for front-facing primitives

Table 15-16   Vertex Shader Varying Global Variables

Variable Name	Type	Description
gl_BackSecondaryColor	vec4	Secondary color to be used for back-facing primitives
gl_TexCoord[n]	vec4	n^{th} Texture coordinate values
gl_FogFragCoord	vec4	Fragment fog coordinate value

Table 15-16   (continued)   Vertex Shader Varying Global Variables

A vertex shader has the capability of setting both the front- and back-face color values for a vertex. Be default, regardless of the values set from within a vertex shader, the front-facing color will be chosen. This behavior can be modified by calling **glEnable()**, with a value of GL_VERTEX_PROGRAM_ TWO_SIDE, which causes OpenGL to select colors based on the orientation of the underlying primitive.

Texture Mapping in Vertex Shaders

Texture mapping is available in vertex shaders. Using textures in vertex shaders is identical to the process described in "Accessing Textures in GLSL" on page 709, with one minor exception. Automatic mipmap selection is not done in vertex shaders. However, you can manually select which mipmap level using the **texture*Lod** routines in GLSL.

To determine if your implementation is capable of using textures in vertex shaders, query GL_MAX_VERTEX_TEXTURE_IMAGE_UNITS using **glIntegerv()**. If a nonzero value is returned, texturing is supported.

Transform Feedback

Advanced

Advanced

Transform feedback allows an application to record the transformed primitives generated by rendering (and before clipping) using a vertex shader, into a buffer object, somewhat similar to the situation described in "Feedback" in Chapter 13, but with more flexible control of the data recorded.

Using transform feedback is a two-step process:

1. Specifying the mapping of outputs of a vertex shader into one or more buffer objects.

2. Rendering while in transform feedback mode.

To accomplish step 1, we'll call **glTransformFeedbackVaryings()** before linking our vertex shader. This function will set the output ordering of the varyings that we want to capture and specify how the data will be written out.

---

void **glTransformFeedbackVaryings**(GLuint *program*, GLsizei *count*,
const char **varyings*, GLenum *bufferMode*);

Assigns the ordering for *count* varying variables specified by (null-terminated) names in the array *varyings* for *program*. *bufferMode* must be either GL_SEPARATE_ATTRIBS, which specifies that the varyings should be written to *count* separate buffer objects, or GL_INTERLEAVED_ATTRIBS, which writes the *count* varying values contiguously into a single buffer object.

A program may fail to link if *count* exceeds the number of available varyings for output. A GL_INVALID_VALUE error will be generated if *program* is not a valid program object, or if *bufferMode* is set to GL_SEPARATE_ATTRIBS and *count* is greater than the value returned for a query of GL_MAX_TRANSFORM_FEEDBACK_SEPARATE_ATTRIBS.

Once the program has been successfully linked, and the ordering of varyings set, we can attach buffer objects to receive the transformed outputs. To bind a buffer, we use **glBindBufferRange()** (or **glBindBufferBase()**), associating the appropriate number of buffers if the *bufferMode* was set to GL_SEPARATE_ATTRIBS, or a single buffer if the *bufferMode* was set to GL_INTERLEAVED_ATTRIBS. The size of the buffer (as specified either by **glBindBufferRange()** or when the buffer was sized by calling **glBufferData()**, for example) dictates the number of attribute values recorded for the specified primitives. When the available buffer space is exhausted, no more primitives will be recorded.

To capture the transformed output, you enter transform feedback mode by calling **glBeginTransformFeedback()**, and specifying the type of primitives you would like recorded, as described in Table 15-17. The complete set of specified varyings is written for each vertex (up to space limitations in the buffer).

Transform Feedback Primitive Type	Permitted OpenGL Primitive Type
GL_POINTS	GL_POINTS
GL_LINES	GL_LINES GL_LINE_LOOP GL_LINE_STRIP
GL_TRIANGLES	GL_TRIANGLES GL_TRIANGLE_FAN GL_TRAINGLE_STRIP GL_QUADS GL_QUAD_STRIP GL_POLYGONS

Table 15-17   Transform Feedback Primitives and Their Permitted OpenGL Rendering Types

You then issue rendering commands. Vertices are transformed by your shader, and the varying variables you specified in step 1 are recorded.

---

void **glBeginTransformFeedback**(GLenum *primitiveMode*);
void **glEndTransformFeedback**(void);

Enters and exits transform feedback mode. *primitiveMode* must be one of GL_POINTS, GL_LINES, or GL_TRIANGLES, which represents the type of output written to the associated buffer objects.

A GL_INVALID_OPERATION error is generated if a command renders an OpenGL primitive type that is incompatible with the current transform feedback mode.

Example 15-10 illustrates the process of capturing vertex values, surface normals, and texture coordinates using transform feedback. Note that the input consists of only the vertex positions; all of the other values are generated by the vertex shader.

Example 15-10 Using Transform Feedback to Capture Geometric Primitives: xfb.c

```
GLuint
LoadTransformFeedbackShader(const char* vShader, GLsizei count,
    const GLchar** varyings)
{
    GLuint  shader, program;
    GLint   completed;
```

```
program = glCreateProgram();

/*
**   --- Load and compile the vertex shader ---
*/

if (vShader != NULL) {
    shader = glCreateShader(GL_VERTEX_SHADER);
    glShaderSource(shader, 1, &vShader, NULL);
    glCompileShader(shader);
    glGetShaderiv(shader, GL_COMPILE_STATUS, &completed);

    if (!completed) {
        GLint  len;
        char*  msg;

        glGetShaderiv(shader, GL_INFO_LOG_LENGTH, &len);
        msg = (char*) malloc(len);
        glGetShaderInfoLog(shader, len, &len, msg);
        fprintf(stderr, "Vertex shader compilation "
        "failure:\n%s\n", msg);
        free(msg);

        glDeleteProgram(program);

        exit(EXIT_FAILURE);
    }

    glAttachShader(program, shader);
}

glTransformFeedbackVaryings(program, count, varyings,
    GL_INTERLEAVED_ATTRIBS);

/*
**   --- Link program ---
*/
glLinkProgram(program);
glGetProgramiv(program, GL_LINK_STATUS, &completed);

if (!completed) {
    GLint  len;
    char*  msg;

    glGetProgramiv(program, GL_INFO_LOG_LENGTH, &len);
    msg = (char*) malloc(len);
    glGetProgramInfoLog(program, len, &len, msg);
```

```
        fprintf(stderr, "Program link failure:\n%s\n", msg);
        free(msg);

        glDeleteProgram(program);

        exit(EXIT_FAILURE);
    }

    return program;
}

void
init()
{
    /* Vertex shader generating our output values */
    const char vShader[] = {
    "#version 140\n" "in vec2  coords;"
    "out vec2 texCoords;"
    "out vec3 normal;"
    "void main() {"
    "    float angle = radians(coords[0]);"
    "    normal = vec3(cos(angle), sin(angle), 0.0);"
    "    texCoords = normal.xy;"
    "    gl_Position = vec4(normal.xy, coords[1], 1.0);"
    "}"
    };

    /* List (and ordering) of varying values written to the
    ** transform buffer */
    const char *varyings[] = {
        "texCoords",
        "normal",
        "gl_Position"
    };

    GLuint program;
    GLuint query;
    GLint  count;

    /* Load shader program and set up varyings */
    program = LoadTransformFeedbackShader(vShader, 3,
        varyings);

    glUseProgram(program);

    glGenQueries(1, &query);

    /* Bind to transform-feedback buffer */
```

```
    glBindBufferBase(GL_TRANSFORM_FEEDBACK_BUFFER, 0, xfb);

    glBeginQuery(GL_TRANSFORM_FEEDBACK_PRIMITIVES_WRITTEN,

        query);
    glBeginTransformFeedback(GL_POINTS);
    glDrawArrays(GL_POINTS, 0, 2*(NumSlices+1));
    glEndTransformFeedback();
    glEndQuery(GL_TRANSFORM_FEEDBACK_PRIMITIVES_WRITTEN);

    glGetQueryObjectiv(query, GL_QUERY_RESULT, &count);

    fprintf(stderr, "%d primitives written\n", count);
    ...
}
```

Fragment Shader Specifics

Like vertex programs, your OpenGL application can send data directly to a
fragment program, as well as having OpenGL provide values for use in your
program. All of that data, along with the inputs into a fragment shader,
result in the final color and depth value of a fragment. After execution of a
fragment shader, the computed values continue through the OpenGL
fragment pipeline to the fragment test and blending stages.

Figure 15-6 describes the inputs and outputs of a fragment programs.

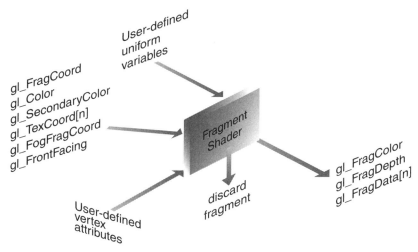

Figure 15-6   Fragment Shader Built-In Variables

Input Values

Fragment shaders receive the iterated values of the final vertex pipeline outputs. These include the fragment's position, resolved primary and secondary colors, a set of texture coordinates, and a fog coordinate distance for the fragment. All of these values are described in Table 15-18.

Variable	Type	Description
gl_FragCoord	vec4	(Read only) Position of the fragment, including the z-component, which represents the fixed-function computed depth value
gl_FrontFacing	bool	(Read only) Specifies if the fragment belongs to a front-facing primitive
gl_Color	vec4	Primary color of the fragment
gl_SecondayColor	vec4	Secondary color of the fragment
gl_TexCoord[n]	vec4	n^{th} texture coordinates for the fragment
gl_FogFragCoord	float	Fragment's fog coordinate, either specified as the z-coordinate of the primitive in eye space or the interpolated fog coordinate
gl_PointCoord	vec2	Fragment's location for a point sprite in the range [0.0, 1.0]. The value is undefined if the current primitive is not a point sprite or if point sprites are disabled

Table 15-18　Fragment Shader Varying Global Variables

Special Output Values

Input values are combined in a fragment program to produce the final values for fragment, as shown in Table 15-19.

Variable	Type	Description
gl_FragColor	vec4	Final color of the fragment
gl_FragDepth	float	Final depth of the fragment
gl_FragData[n]	vec4	Data value written to the nth data buffer

Table 15-19　Fragment Shader Output Global Variables

`gl_FragColor` is the final color of the fragment. While writing to `gl_FragColor` isn't required output from a fragment program, the results of the final fragment color for writing into the color buffer are undefined.

`gl_FragDepth` is the final depth of the fragment and is utilized in the depth test. While you cannot modify the *(x, y)* coordinate of a fragment, the depth value can be modified.

Finally, additional data may be written from a fragment program. The `gl_FragData` array allows for the writing of various data into extra buffers, as described below.

Rendering to Multiple Output Buffers

A fragment shader may output values to multiple buffers simultaneously using the `gl_FragData` array. Writing a value into array element `gl_FragData[n]` will cause the color to be written into the appropriate fragment in the buffer in element *n* of the array passed to **glDrawBuffers()**.

A fragment shader may write to either `gl_FragColor` or `gl_FragData` in a shader, but not both.

User-Defined Fragment Shader Outputs

You might find that using relatively nondescript names such as `gl_FragColor` is not suitable for specifying the output of your shader. While GLSL doesn't care, the next programmer to look at your code (which you probably forgot to comment) might not immediately understand that your shader does not output a color, but rather the results of evaluating a Bessel function of the second kind (or some other mathematical archana).

With GLSL version 1.30, you can give more suitable names to the outputs from your fragment shaders, and you can control the mapping of those outputs to the various bound drawing buffers. You can either specify the mapping of fragment output name to a buffer *before* linking or query the program *after* linking to determine the layout of variables.

To use the first approach, call **glBindFragDataLocation()** before calling **glLinkProgram()**.

> void **glBindFragDataLocation**(GLuint *program*, GLuint *colorNumber*,
> const char **name*);

Specifies the output of fragment variable *name* should be written to color buffer *colorNumber* for GLSL *program*. This affects only programs that have not yet been linked.

A GL_INVALID_VALUE error is generated if *colorNumber* is less than zero or greater than the value returned when querying GL_MAX_DRAW_ BUFFERS. A GL_INVALID_OPERATION error is generated if *name* begins with gl_.

After linking, you can retrieve the mapping by calling **glGetFragDataLocation()**:

> GLint **glGetFragDataLocation**(GLuint *program*, const char **name*);

Returns the color buffer index associated with the output of *name* from GLSL *program*.

A GL_INVALID_OPERATION error is generated if *program* did not successfully link, and **glGetFragDataLocation()** is called. A value of –1 is returned if *name* is not a fragment program output associated with *program* or if another error occurred.

Basics of GLUT: The OpenGL Utility Toolkit

This appendix describes a subset of the OpenGL Utility Toolkit (GLUT) originally developed by Mark Kilgard. We use an open-source version of GLUT named freeglut (`http://freeglut.sourceforge.net/`) developed by Pawel W. Olszta, with contributions from Andreas Umbach and Steve Baker. GLUT has become a popular library for OpenGL programmers because it standardizes and simplifies window and event management. GLUT has been ported atop a variety of OpenGL implementations, including both the X Window System and Microsoft Windows.

This appendix has the following major sections:

- "Initializing and Creating a Window"
- "Handling Window and Input Events"
- "Loading the Color Map"
- "Initializing and Drawing Three-Dimensional Objects"
- "Managing a Background Process"
- "Running the Program"

(See "How to Obtain the Sample Code" on page xli for information about how to obtain the source code for GLUT.)

With GLUT, your application structures its event handling to use callback functions. (This method is similar to using the Xt Toolkit, also known as the X Intrinsics, with a widget set.) For example, first you open a window and register callback routines for specific events. Then you create a main loop without an exit. In that loop, if an event occurs, its registered callback functions are executed. On completion of the callback functions, flow of control is returned to the main loop.

Initializing and Creating a Window

Before you can open a window, you must specify its characteristics. Should it be single-buffered or double-buffered? Should it store colors as RGBA values or as color indices? Where should it appear on your display? To specify the answers to these questions, call **glutInit()**, **glutInitDisplayMode()**, **glutInitWindowSize()**, and **glutInitWindowPosition()** before you call **glutCreateWindow()** to open the window.

---

void **glutInit**(int *argc*, char ****argv*);

glutInit() should be called before any other GLUT routine, because it initializes the GLUT library. **glutInit()** will also process command line options, but the specific options are window system dependent. For the X Window System, -iconic, -geometry, and -display are examples of command line options, processed by **glutInit()**. (The parameters to **glutInit()** should be the same as those to **main()**.)

---

void **glutInitDisplayMode**(unsigned int *mode*);

Specifies a display mode (such as RGBA or color-index, or single- or double-buffered) for windows created when **glutCreateWindow()** is called. You can also specify that the window have an associated depth, stencil, and/or accumulation buffer. The *mask* argument is a bitwise ORed combination of GLUT_RGBA or GLUT_INDEX, GLUT_SINGLE or GLUT_DOUBLE, and any of the buffer-enabling flags: GLUT_DEPTH, GLUT_STENCIL, or GLUT_ACCUM. For example, for a double-buffered, RGBA-mode window with a depth and stencil buffer, use GLUT_DOUBLE | GLUT_RGBA | GLUT_DEPTH | GLUT_STENCIL. The default value is GLUT_RGBA | GLUT_SINGLE (an RGBA, single-buffered window).

void **glutInitContextVersion**(int *majorVersion*, int *minorVersion*);

Specifies the major and minor versions of the OpenGL implementation that you want a context created for. To use OpenGL Version 3.0 or greater, you need to call this routine before calling **glutCreateWindow**(), due to the different context creation semantics introduced by OpenGL Version 3.0.

void **glutInitWindowSize**(int *width*, int *height*);
void **glutInitWindowPosition**(int *x*, int *y*);

Requests windows created by **glutCreateWindow**() to have an initial size and position. The arguments (*x, y*) indicate the location of a corner of the window, relative to the entire display. *width* and *height* indicate the window's size (in pixels). The initial window size and position are hints and may be overridden by other requests.

int **glutCreateWindow**(char **name*);

Opens a window with previously set characteristics (display mode, width, height, and so on). The string *name* may appear in the title bar if your window system does that sort of thing. The window is not initially displayed until **glutMainLoop**() is entered, so do not render into the window until then.

The value returned is a unique integer identifier for the window. This identifier can be used for controlling and rendering to multiple windows (each with an OpenGL rendering context) from the same application.

Handling Window and Input Events

After the window is created, but before you enter the main loop, you should register callback functions using the following routines.

void **glutDisplayFunc**(void (**func*)(void));

Specifies the function that's called whenever the contents of the window need to be redrawn. The contents of the window may need to be redrawn when the window is initially opened, when the window is popped and window damage is exposed, and when **glutPostRedisplay**() is explicitly called.

void **glutReshapeFunc**(void (*func*)(int *width*, int *height*));

Specifies the function that's called whenever the window is resized or moved. The argument *func* is a pointer to a function that expects two arguments, the new width and height of the window. Typically, *func* calls **glViewport**(), so that the display is clipped to the new size, and it redefines the projection matrix so that the aspect ratio of the projected image matches the viewport, avoiding aspect ratio distortion. If **glutReshapeFunc**() isn't called or is deregistered by passing NULL, a default reshape function is called, which calls **glViewport**(*0, 0, width, height*).

void **glutKeyboardFunc**(void (*func*)(unsigned char *key*, int *x*, int *y*));

Specifies the function, *func*, that's called when a key that generates an ASCII character is pressed. The *key* callback parameter is the generated ASCII value. The *x* and *y* callback parameters indicate the location of the mouse (in window-relative coordinates) when the key was pressed.

void **glutMouseFunc**(void (*func*)(int *button*, int *state*, int *x*, int *y*));

Specifies the function, *func*, that's called when a mouse button is pressed or released. The *button* callback parameter is GLUT_LEFT_BUTTON, GLUT_MIDDLE_BUTTON, or GLUT_RIGHT_BUTTON. The *state* callback parameter is either GLUT_UP or GLUT_DOWN, depending on whether the mouse has been released or pressed. The *x* and *y* callback parameters indicate the location (in window-relative coordinates) of the mouse when the event occurred.

void **glutMotionFunc**(void (*func*)(int *x*, int *y*));

Specifies the function, *func*, that's called when the mouse pointer moves within the window while one or more mouse buttons are pressed. The *x* and *y* callback parameters indicate the location (in window-relative coordinates) of the mouse when the event occurred.

void **glutPostRedisplay**(void);

Marks the current window as needing to be redrawn. At the next opportunity, the callback function registered by **glutDisplayFunc**() will be called.

Loading the Color Map

If you're using color-index mode, you might be surprised to discover there's no OpenGL routine to load a color into a color-lookup table. This is because the process of loading a color map depends entirely on the window system. GLUT provides a generalized routine to load a single color index with an RGB value, **glutSetColor()**.

---

void **glutSetColor**(GLint *index*, GLfloat *red*, GLfloat *green*, GLfloat *blue*);

Loads the index in the color map, *index*, with the given *red*, *green*, and *blue* values. These values are normalized to lie in the range [0.0, 1.0].

Initializing and Drawing Three-Dimensional Objects

Many sample programs in this guide use three-dimensional models to illustrate various rendering properties. The following drawing routines are included in GLUT to avoid having to reproduce the code to draw these models in each program. The routines render all their graphics in immediate mode. Each three-dimensional model comes in two flavors: wireframe without surface normals, and solid with shading and surface normals. Use the solid version when you're applying lighting. Only the teapot generates texture coordinates.

---

void **glutWireSphere**(GLdouble *radius,* GLint *slices,* GLint *stacks*);
void **glutSolidSphere**(GLdouble *radius,* GLint *slices,* GLint *stacks*);

---

void **glutWireCube**(GLdouble *size*);
void **glutSolidCube**(GLdouble *size*);

---

void **glutWireTorus**(GLdouble *innerRadius,* GLdouble *outerRadius,*
                    GLint *nsides,* GLint *rings*);
void **glutSolidTorus**(GLdouble *innerRadius,* GLdouble *outerRadius,*
                    GLint *nsides,* GLint *rings*);

```
void glutWireIcosahedron(void);
void glutSolidIcosahedron(void);
```

```
void glutWireOctahedron(void);
void glutSolidOctahedron(void);
```

```
void glutWireTetrahedron(void);
void glutSolidTetrahedron(void);
```

```
void glutWireDodecahedron(GLdouble radius);
void glutSolidDodecahedron(GLdouble radius);
```

```
void glutWireCone(GLdouble radius, GLdouble height, GLint slices,
        GLint stacks);
void glutSolidCone(GLdouble radius, GLdouble height, GLint slices,
        GLint stacks);
```

```
void glutWireTeapot(GLdouble size);
void glutSolidTeapot(GLdouble size);
```

Managing a Background Process

You can specify a function that's to be executed if no other events are pending—for example, when the event loop would otherwise be idle—with **glutIdleFunc()**. This is particularly useful for continuous animation or other background processing.

```
void glutIdleFunc(void (*func)(void));
```

Specifies the function, *func*, to be executed if no other events are pending. If NULL (zero) is passed in, execution of *func* is disabled.

Running the Program

After all the setup is completed, GLUT programs enter an event processing loop, **glutMainLoop()**.

---

void **glutMainLoop**(void);

Enters the GLUT processing loop, never to return. Registered callback functions will be called when the corresponding events instigate them.

Appendix B

State Variables

This appendix lists the queryable OpenGL state variables, their default values, and the commands for obtaining the values of these variables, and contains the following major sections:

- "The Query Commands"
- "OpenGL State Variables"

The Query Commands

In addition to the basic commands to obtain the values of simple state variables (commands such as **glGetIntegerv**() and **glIsEnabled**(), which are described in "Basic State Management" in Chapter 2), there are other specialized commands to return more complex state variables. The prototypes for these specialized commands are listed here. Some of these routines, such as **glGetError**() and **glGetString**(), have been discussed in more detail elsewhere in the book.

To find out when you need to use these commands and their corresponding symbolic constants, use the tables in the next section, "OpenGL State Variables."

void **glGetActiveAttrib**(GLuint *program*, GLuint *index*, GLsizei *bufSize*, GLsizei **length*, GLint **size*, GLenum **type*, char **name*);

void **glGetActiveUniformBlockiv**(GLuint *program*, GLuint *uniformBlockIndex*, GLenum *pname*, GLint **params*);

GLint **glGetActiveUniformName**(GLuint *program*, GLuint *uniformIndex*, GLsizei *bufSize*, GLsizei **length*, char **uniformName*)

void **glGetActiveUniformsiv**(GLuint *program*, GLsizei *uniformCount*, const GLuint **uniformIndices*, GLenum *pname*, GLint **params*)

void **glGetAttachedShaders**(GLuint *program*, GLsizei *maxCount*, GLsizei **count*, GLuint **shaders*);

void **glGetBufferSubData**(GLenum *target*, GLintptr *offset*, GLsizeiptr *size*, GLvoid* *data*);

void **glGetBufferParameteriv**(GLenum *target*, GLenum *pname*, GLint **params*);

void **glGetBufferPointerv**(GLenum *target*, GLenum *pname*, GLvoid ***pointer*);

void **glGetClipPlane**(GLenum *plane*, GLdouble **equation*);

void **glGetColorTable**(GLenum *target*, GLenum *pname*, GLenum *type*, GLvoid **table*);

void **glGetColorTableParameter**{if}**v**(GLenum *target*, GLenum *pname*,
          *TYPE *params*);

void **glGetCompressedTexImage**(GLenum *target*, GLint *lod*,
          GLvoid **pixels*);

void **glGetConvolutionFilter**(GLenum *target*, GLenum *format*,
          GLenum *type*, GLvoid **image*);

void **glGetConvolutionParameter**{if}**v**(GLenum *target*, GLenum *pname*,
          *TYPE *params*);

GLenum **glGetError**(void);

void **glGetHistogram**(GLenum *target*, GLboolean reset, GLenum *format*,
          GLenum *type*, GLvoid **values*);

void **glGetHistogramParameter**{if}**v**(GLenum *target*, GLenum *pname*,
          *TYPE *params*);

void **glGetLight**{if}**v**(GLenum *light*, GLenum *pname*, TYPE **params*);

void **glGetMap**{ifd}**v**(GLenum *target*, GLenum *query*, TYPE **v*);

void **glGetMaterial**{if}**v**(GLenum *face*, GLenum *pname*, TYPE **params*);

void **glGetMinmax**(GLenum *target*, GLboolean reset, GLenum *format*,
          GLenum *type*, GLvoid **values*);

void **glGetMinmaxParameter**{if}**v** (GLenum *target*, GLenum *pname*,
          *TYPE *params*);

void **glGetPixelMap**{f ui us}**v**(GLenum *map*, TYPE **values*);

void **glGetPolygonStipple**(GLubyte **mask*);

void **glGetProgramInfoLog**(GLuint *program*, GLsizei *bufSize*,
          GLsizei **length*, GLchar **infoLog*);

void **glGetProgramiv**(GLuint *program*, GLenum *pname*, GLint **params*);

void **glGetQueryiv**(GLenum *target*, GLenum *pname*, GLint **params*);

void **glGetQueryObjectiv**(GLuint *id*, GLenum *pname*, GLint **params*);

void **glGetQueryObjectuiv**(GLuint *id*, GLenum *pname*, GLuint **params*);

void **glGetSeparableFilter**(GLenum *target*, GLenum *format*,
          GLenum *type*, GLvoid **row*, GLvoid **column*,
          GLvoid **span*);

void **glGetShaderInfoLog**(GLuint *shader*, GLsizei *bufSize*, GLsizei **length*, GLchar **infoLog*);

void **glGetShaderiv**(GLuint *shader*, GLenum *pname*, GLint **params*);

void **glGetShaderSource**(GLuint *shader*, GLsizei *bufSize*, GLsizei **length*, GLchar **source*);

const GLubyte * **glGetString**(GLenum *name*);

const GLubyte * **glGetStringi**(GLenum *name*, GLuint *index*);

void **glGetTexEnv**{if}**v**(GLenum *target*, GLenum *pname*, *TYPE *params*);

void **glGetTexGen**{ifd}**v**(GLenum *coord*, GLenum *pname*, *TYPE *params*);

void **glGetTexImage**(GLenum *target*, GLint *level*, GLenum *format*, GLenum *type*, GLvoid **pixels*);

void **glGetTexLevelParameter**{if}**v**(GLenum *target*, GLint *level*, GLenum *pname*, *TYPE *params*);

void **glGetTexParameter**{if}**v**(GLenum *target*, GLenum *pname*, *TYPE *params*);

void **glGetUniform**{if}**v**(GLuint *program*, GLint *location*, TYPE **params*);

void **glGetVertexAttrib**{ifd}**v**(GLuint *index*, GLenum *pname*, *TYPE *params*);

void **glGetVertexAttribPointerv**(GLuint *index*, GLenum *pname*, GLvoid ***pointer*);

GLboolean **glIsBuffer**(GLuint *buffer*);

GLboolean **glIsList**(GLuint *list*);

GLboolean **glIsProgram**(GLuint *program*);

GLboolean **glIsQuery**(GLuint *id*);

GLboolean **glIsShader**(GLuint *shader*);

GLboolean **glIsTexture**(GLuint *texObject*);

void **gluGetNurbsProperty**(GLUnurbsObj **nobj*, GLenum *property*, GLfloat **value*);

const GLubyte * **gluGetString**(GLenum *name*);

void **gluGetTessProperty**(GLUtesselator **tess*, GLenum *which*, GLdouble **data*);

OpenGL State Variables

The following pages contain tables that list the names of queryable state variables. For each variable, the tables list a description of it, its attribute group, its initial or minimum value, and the suggested **glGet*()** command to use for obtaining it. State variables that can be obtained using **glGetBooleanv()**, **glGetIntegerv()**, **glGetFloatv()**, or **glGetDoublev()** are listed with just one of these commands—the one that's most appropriate given the type of data to be returned. (Some vertex-array variables can be queried only with **glGetPointerv()**.) These state variables can't be obtained using **glIsEnabled()**. However, state variables for which **glIsEnabled()** is listed as the query command can also be obtained using **glGetBooleanv()**, **glGetIntegerv()**, **glGetFloatv()**, and **glGetDoublev()**. State variables for which any other command is listed as the query command can be obtained only by using that command.

Note: When querying texture state, such as GL_TEXTURE_MATRIX, in an implementation where the GL_ARB_multitexture extension is defined, the values returned reference the currently active texture unit only. See "Multitexturing" on page 467 for details.

If one or more attribute groups are listed, the state variable belongs to the listed group or groups. If no attribute group is listed, the variable doesn't belong to any group. **glPushAttrib()**, **glPushClientAttrib()**, **glPopAttrib()**, and **glPopClientAttrib()** may be used to save and restore all state values that belong to an attribute group (see "Attribute Groups" in Chapter 2 for more information).

All queryable state variables have initial values; however, those that are implementation-dependent may not have an initial value listed. If no initial value is listed, you need to consult the section where that variable is discussed.

More detail on all of the query functions and values is available online at
`http://www.opengl.org/sdk/docs/man`.

Current Values and Associated Data

State Variable	Description	Attribute Group	Initial Value	Get Command
GL_CURRENT_COLOR	Current color	current	(1, 1, 1, 1)	glGetIntegerv(), glGetFloatv()
GL_CURRENT_SECONDARY_COLOR	Current secondary color	current	(0, 0, 0, 1)	glGetIntegerv(), glGetFloatv()
GL_CURRENT_INDEX	Current color index	current	1	glGetIntegerv(), glGetFloatv()
GL_CURRENT_TEXTURE_COORDS	Current texture coordinates	current	(0, 0, 0, 1)	glGetFloatv()
GL_CURRENT_NORMAL	Current normal	current	(0, 0, 1)	glGetFloatv()
GL_CURRENT_FOG_COORD	Current fog coordinate	current	0	glGetIntegerv(), glGetFloatv()
GL_CURRENT_RASTER_POSITION	Current raster position	current	(0, 0, 0, 1)	glGetFloatv()
GL_CURRENT_RASTER_DISTANCE	Current raster distance	current	0	glGetFloatv()
GL_CURRENT_RASTER_COLOR	Color associated with raster position	current	(1, 1, 1, 1)	glGetIntegerv(), glGetFloatv()
GL_CURRENT_RASTER_SECONDARY_COLOR	Secondary color associated with raster position	current	(0, 0, 0, 1)	glGetIntegerv(), glGetFloatv()

Table B-1   State Variables for Current Values and Associated Data

State Variable	Description	Attribute Group	Initial Value	Get Command
GL_CURRENT_RASTER_INDEX	Color index associated with raster position	current	1	glGetIntegerv(), glGetFloatv()
GL_CURRENT_RASTER_TEXTURE_COORDS	Texture coordinates associated with raster position	current	(0, 0, 0, 1)	glGetFloatv()
GL_CURRENT_RASTER_POSITION_VALID	Raster position valid bit	current	GL_TRUE	glGetBooleanv()
GL_EDGE_FLAG	Edge flag	current	GL_TRUE	glGetBooleanv()

Table B-1 (continued)   State Variables for Current Values and Associated Data

Vertex Array Data State (Not Included in Vertex Array Object State)

State Variable	Description	Attribute Group	Initial Value	Get Command
GL_CLIENT_ACTIVE_TEXTURE	Active texture unit, for texture-coordinate array	vertex-array	GL_TEXTURE0	glGetIntegerv()
GL_ARRAY_BUFFER_BINDING	Current buffer binding	vertex-array	0	glGetIntegerv()
GL_PRIMITIVE_RESTART	Primitive restart enable	—	GL_FALSE	glIsEnabled()
GL_PRIMITIVE_RESTART_INDEX	Primitive restart index value	—	0	glGetIntegerv()

Table B-2   Vertex Array Data State Variables

Vertex Array Object State

State Variable	Description	Attribute Group	Initial Value	Get Command
GL_VERTEX_ARRAY	Vertex array enable	vertex-array	GL_FALSE	glIsEnabled()
GL_VERTEX_ARRAY_BINDING	Vertex array object binding	vertex-array	0	glGetIntegerv()
GL_VERTEX_ARRAY_SIZE	Coordinates per vertex	vertex-array	4	glGetIntegerv()
GL_VERTEX_ARRAY_TYPE	Type of vertex coordinates	vertex-array	GL_FLOAT	glGetIntegerv()

Table B-3   Vertex Array Object State Variables

State Variable	Description	Attribute Group	Initial Value	Get Command
GL_VERTEX_ARRAY_STRIDE	Stride between vertices	vertex-array	0	glGetIntegerv()
GL_VERTEX_ARRAY_POINTER	Pointer to the vertex array	vertex-array	NULL	glGetPointerv()
GL_NORMAL_ARRAY	Normal array enable	vertex-array	GL_FALSE	glIsEnabled()
GL_NORMAL_ARRAY_TYPE	Type of normal coordinates	vertex-array	GL_FLOAT	glGetIntegerv()
GL_NORMAL_ARRAY_STRIDE	Stride between normals	vertex-array	0	glGetIntegerv()
GL_NORMAL_ARRAY_POINTER	Pointer to the normal array	vertex-array	NULL	glGetPointerv()
GL_FOG_COORD_ARRAY	Fog coordinate array enable	vertex-array	GL_FALSE	glIsEnabled()
GL_FOG_COORD_ARRAY_TYPE	Type of fog coordinate components	vertex-array	GL_FLOAT	glGetIntegerv()
GL_FOG_COORD_ARRAY_STRIDE	Stride between fog coordinates	vertex-array	0	glGetIntegerv()
GL_FOG_COORD_ARRAY_POINTER	Pointer to the fog coordinate array	vertex-array	NULL	glGetPointerv()
GL_COLOR_ARRAY	RGBA color array enable	vertex-array	GL_FALSE	glIsEnabled()

Table B-3 (continued)   Vertex Array Object State Variables

State Variable	Description	Attribute Group	Initial Value	Get Command
GL_COLOR_ARRAY_SIZE	Color components per vertex	vertex-array	4	glGetIntegerv()
GL_COLOR_ARRAY_TYPE	Type of color components	vertex-array	GL_FLOAT	glGetIntegerv()
GL_COLOR_ARRAY_STRIDE	Stride between colors	vertex-array	0	glGetIntegerv()
GL_COLOR_ARRAY_POINTER	Pointer to the color array	vertex-array	NULL	glGetPointerv()
GL_SECONDARY_COLOR_ARRAY	Secondary color array enable	vertex-array	GL_FALSE	glIsEnabled()
GL_SECONDARY_COLOR_ARRAY_SIZE	Secondary color components per vertex	vertex-array	3	glGetIntegerv()
GL_SECONDARY_COLOR_ARRAY_TYPE	Type of secondary color components	vertex-array	GL_FLOAT	glGetIntegerv()
GL_SECONDARY_COLOR_ARRAY_STRIDE	Stride between secondary colors	vertex-array	0	glGetIntegerv()
GL_SECONDARY_COLOR_ARRAY_POINTER	Pointer to the secondary color array	vertex-array	NULL	glGetPointerv()
GL_INDEX_ARRAY	Color-index array enable	vertex-array	GL_FALSE	glIsEnabled()
GL_INDEX_ARRAY_TYPE	Type of color indices	vertex-array	GL_FLOAT	glGetIntegerv()

Table B-3 (continued)   Vertex Array Object State Variables

State Variable	Description	Attribute Group	Initial Value	Get Command
GL_INDEX_ARRAY_STRIDE	Stride between color indices	vertex-array	0	glGetIntegerv()
GL_INDEX_ARRAY_POINTER	Pointer to the index array	vertex-array	NULL	glGetPointerv()
GL_TEXTURE_COORD_ARRAY	Texture-coordinate array enable	vertex-array	GL_FALSE	glIsEnabled()
GL_TEXTURE_COORD_ARRAY_SIZE	Texture coordinates per element	vertex-array	4	glGetIntegerv()
GL_TEXTURE_COORD_ARRAY_TYPE	Type of texture coordinates	vertex-array	GL_FLOAT	glGetIntegerv()
GL_TEXTURE_COORD_ARRAY_STRIDE	Stride between texture coordinates	vertex-array	0	glGetIntegerv()
GL_TEXTURE_COORD_ARRAY_POINTER	Pointer to the texture-coordinate array	vertex-array	NULL	glGetPointerv()
GL_VERTEX_ATTRIB_ARRAY_ENABLED	Vertex attrib array enable	vertex-array	GL_FALSE	glGetVertexAttribiv()
GL_VERTEX_ATTRIB_ARRAY_SIZE	Vertex attrib array size	vertex-array	4	glGetVertexAttribiv()
GL_VERTEX_ATTRIB_ARRAY_STRIDE	Vertex attrib array stride	vertex-array	0	glGetVertexAttribiv()
GL_VERTEX_ATTRIB_ARRAY_TYPE	Vertex attrib array type	vertex-array	GL_FLOAT	glGetVertexAttribiv()

Table B-3 (continued)   Vertex Array Object State Variables

State Variable	Description	Attribute Group	Initial Value	Get Command
GL_VERTEX_ATTRIB_ARRAY_NORMALIZED	Vertex attrib array normalized	vertex-array	GL_FALSE	glGetVertexAttribiv()
GL_VERTEX_ATTRIB_ARRAY_INTEGER	Vertex attrib array has unconverted integer values	vertex-array	GL_FALSE	glGetVertexAttribiv()
GL_VERTEX_ATTRIB_ARRAY_POINTER	Vertex attrib array pointer	vertex-array	NULL	glGetVertexAttribPointer()
GL_EDGE_FLAG_ARRAY	Edge flag array enable	vertex-array	GL_FALSE	glIsEnabled()
GL_EDGE_FLAG_ARRAY_STRIDE	Stride between edge flags	vertex-array	0	glGetIntegerv()
GL_EDGE_FLAG_ARRAY_POINTER	Pointer to the edge-flag array	vertex-array	NULL	glGetPointerv()
GL_ARRAY_BUFFER_BINDING	Current buffer binding	vertex-array	0	glGetIntegerv()
GL_VERTEX_ARRAY_BUFFER_BINDING	Vertex array buffer binding	vertex-array	0	glGetIntegerv()
GL_NORMAL_ARRAY_BUFFER_BINDING	Normal array buffer binding	vertex-array	0	glGetIntegerv()
GL_COLOR_ARRAY_BUFFER_BINDING	Color array buffer binding	vertex-array	0	glGetIntegerv()
GL_INDEX_ARRAY_BUFFER_BINDING	Index array buffer binding	vertex-array	0	glGetIntegerv()

Table B-3 (continued)   Vertex Array Object State Variables

State Variable	Description	Attribute Group	Initial Value	Get Command
GL_TEXTURE_COORD_ARRAY_BUFFER_ BINDING	Texture-coordinate array buffer binding	vertex-array	0	glGetIntegerv()
GL_EDGE_FLAG_ARRAY_BUFFER_ BINDING	Edge flag array buffer binding	vertex-array	0	glGetIntegerv()
GL_SECONDARY_COLOR_ARRAY_ BUFFER_BINDING	Secondary color array buffer binding	vertex-array	0	glGetIntegerv()
GL_FOG_COORD_ARRAY_BUFFER_ BINDING	Fog-coordinate array buffer binding	vertex-array	0	glGetIntegerv()
GL_ELEMENT_ARRAY_BUFFER_BINDING	Element array buffer binding	vertex-array	0	glGetIntegerv()
GL_VERTEX_ATTRIB_ARRAY_BUFFER_ BINDING	Vertex attribute array buffer binding	vertex-array	0	glGetVertexAttribiv()
GL_VERTEX_ARRAY_BINDING	Current vertex array object binding	vertex-array	0	glGetIntegerv()

Table B-3 (continued)   Vertex Array Object State Variables

State Variable	Description	Attribute Group	Initial Value	Get Command
GL_BUFFER_SIZE	Buffer data size	—	0	glGetBufferParameteriv()
GL_BUFFER_USAGE	Buffer usage pattern	—	GL_STATIC_DRAW	glGetBufferParameteriv()
GL_BUFFER_ACCESS	Buffer access flag	—	GL_READ_WRITE	glGetBufferParameteriv()
GL_BUFFER_ACCESS_FLAGS	Extended buffer access flags	—	0	glGetBufferParameteriv()
GL_BUFFER_MAPPED	Buffer map flag	—	GL_FALSE	glGetBufferParameteriv()
GL_BUFFER_MAP_POINTER	Mapped buffer pointer	—	NULL	glGetBufferPointerv()
GL_BUFFER_MAP_OFFSET	Start of mapped buffer range	—	0	glGetBufferParameteriv()
GL_BUFFER_MAP_LENGTH	Size of mapped buffer range	—	0	glGetBufferParameteriv()

Table B-4   Vertex Buffer Object State Variables

Transformation

State Variable	Description	Attribute Group	Initial Value	Get Command
GL_COLOR_MATRIX	Color matrix stack	—	Identity	glGetFloatv()
GL_TRANSPOSE_COLOR_MATRIX	Stack of transposed color matrices	—	Identity	glGetFloatv()
GL_MODELVIEW_MATRIX	Modelview matrix stack	—	Identity	glGetFloatv()
GL_TRANSPOSE_MODELVIEW_MATRIX	Stack of transposed modelview matrices	—	Identity	glGetFloatv()
GL_PROJECTION_MATRIX	Projection matrix stack	—	Identity	glGetFloatv()
GL_TRANSPOSE_PROJECTION_MATRIX	Stack of transposed projection matrices	—	Identity	glGetFloatv()
GL_TEXTURE_MATRIX	Texture matrix stack	—	Identity	glGetFloatv()
GL_TRANSPOSE_TEXTURE_MATRIX	Stack of transposed texture matrices	—	Identity	glGetFloatv()
GL_VIEWPORT	Viewport origin and extent	viewport	—	glGetIntegerv()
GL_DEPTH_RANGE	Depth range near and far	viewport	0, 1	glGetFloatv()
GL_COLOR_MATRIX_STACK_DEPTH	Color matrix stack pointer	—	1	glGetIntegerv()

Table B-5   Transformation State Variables

State Variable	Description	Attribute Group	Initial Value	Get Command
GL_MODELVIEW_STACK_DEPTH	Modelview matrix stack pointer	—	1	glGetIntegerv()
GL_PROJECTION_STACK_DEPTH	Projection matrix stack pointer	—	1	glGetIntegerv()
GL_TEXTURE_STACK_DEPTH	Texture matrix stack pointer	—	1	glGetIntegerv()
GL_MATRIX_MODE	Current matrix mode	transform	GL_MODELVIEW	glGetIntegerv()
GL_NORMALIZE	Current normal normalization on/off	transform/ enable	GL_FALSE	glIsEnabled()
GL_RESCALE_NORMAL	Current normal rescaling on/off	transform/ enable	GL_FALSE	glIsEnabled()
GL_CLIP_DISTANCE*i* (replacing GL_ CLIP_PLANE*i* in Version 3.0 and greater)	User clipping-plane coefficients	transform	(0, 0, 0, 0)	glGetClipPlane()
GL_CLIP_DISTANCE*i* (replacing GL_ CLIP_PLANE*i* in Version 3.0 and greater)	*i*th user clipping plane enabled	transform/ enable	GL_FALSE	glIsEnabled()

Table B-5 (continued)   Transformation State Variables

Coloring

State Variable	Description	Attribute Group	Initial Value	Get Command
GL_FOG_COLOR	Fog color	fog	(0, 0, 0, 0)	glGetFloatv()
GL_FOG_INDEX	Fog index	fog	0	glGetFloatv()
GL_FOG_DENSITY	Exponential fog density	fog	1.0	glGetFloatv()
GL_FOG_START	Linear fog start	fog	0.0	glGetFloatv()
GL_FOG_END	Linear fog end	fog	1.0	glGetFloatv()
GL_FOG_MODE	Fog mode	fog	GL_EXP	glGetIntegerv()
GL_FOG	True if fog enabled	fog/enable	GL_FALSE	glIsEnabled()
GL_FOG_COORD_SRC	Source of coordinates for fog calculation	fog	GL_FRAGMENT_DEPTH	glGetIntegerv()
GL_COLOR_SUM	True if color sum is enabled	fog/enable	GL_FALSE	glIsEnabled()
GL_SHADE_MODEL	glShadeModel() setting	lighting	GL_SMOOTH	glGetIntegerv()
GL_CLAMP_VERTEX_COLOR	Vertex clamping color	lighting/enable	GL_TRUE	glGetIntegerv()
GL_CLAMP_FRAGMENT_COLOR	Fragment clamping color	color-buffer/enable	GL_FIXED_ONLY	glGetIntegerv()
GL_CLAMP_READ_COLOR	Read color clamping	color-buffer/enable	GL_FIXED_ONLY	glGetIntegerv()

Table B-6   Coloring State Variables

Lighting

See also Tables 5-1 and 5-3 for initial values.

State Variable	Description	Attribute Group	Initial Value	Get Command
GL_LIGHTING	True if lighting is enabled	lighting /enable	GL_FALSE	glIsEnabled()
GL_COLOR_MATERIAL	True if color tracking is enabled	lighting	GL_FALSE	glIsEnabled()
GL_COLOR_MATERIAL_PARAMETER	Material properties tracking current color	lighting	GL_AMBIENT_ AND_DIFFUSE	glGetIntegerv()
GL_COLOR_MATERIAL_FACE	Face(s) affected by color tracking	lighting	GL_FRONT_ AND_BACK	glGetIntegerv()
GL_AMBIENT	Ambient material color	lighting	(0.2, 0.2, 0.2, 1.0)	glGetMaterialfv()
GL_DIFFUSE	Diffuse material color	lighting	(0.8, 0.8, 0.8, 1.0)	glGetMaterialfv()
GL_SPECULAR	Specular material color	lighting	(0.0, 0.0, 0.0, 1.0)	glGetMaterialfv()
GL_EMISSION	Emissive material color	lighting	(0.0, 0.0, 0.0, 1.0)	glGetMaterialfv()
GL_SHININESS	Specular exponent of material	lighting	0.0	glGetMaterialfv()
GL_LIGHT_MODEL_AMBIENT	Ambient scene color	lighting	(0.2, 0.2, 0.2, 1.0)	glGetFloatv()
GL_LIGHT_MODEL_LOCAL_VIEWER	Viewer is local	lighting	GL_FALSE	glGetBooleanv()

Table B-7   Lighting State Variables

State Variable	Description	Attribute Group	Initial Value	Get Command
GL_LIGHT_MODEL_TWO_SIDE	Use two-sided lighting	lighting	GL_FALSE	glGetBooleanv()
GL_LIGHT_MODEL_COLOR_CONTROL	Color control	lighting	GL_SINGLE_COLOR	glGetIntegerv()
GL_AMBIENT	Ambient intensity of light i	lighting	(0.0, 0.0, 0.0, 1.0)	glGetLightfv()
GL_DIFFUSE	Diffuse intensity of light i	lighting	—	glGetLightfv()
GL_SPECULAR	Specular intensity of light i	lighting	—	glGetLightfv()
GL_POSITION	Position of light i	lighting	(0.0, 0.0, 1.0, 0.0)	glGetLightfv()
GL_CONSTANT_ATTENUATION	Constant attenuation factor	lighting	1.0	glGetLightfv()
GL_LINEAR_ATTENUATION	Linear attenuation factor	lighting	0.0	glGetLightfv()
GL_QUADRATIC_ATTENUATION	Quadratic attenuation factor	lighting	0.0	glGetLightfv()
GL_SPOT_DIRECTION	Spotlight direction of light i	lighting	(0.0, 0.0, −1.0)	glGetLightfv()
GL_SPOT_EXPONENT	Spotlight exponent of light i	lighting	0.0	glGetLightfv()
GL_SPOT_CUTOFF	Spotlight angle of light i	lighting	180.0	glGetLightfv()
GL_LIGHTi	True if light i enabled	lighting /enable	GL_FALSE	glIsEnabled()
GL_COLOR_INDEXES	c_a, c_d, and c_s for color-index lighting	lighting	0, 1, 1	glGetMaterialfv()

Table B-7 (continued)   Lighting State Variables

Rasterization

State Variable	Description	Attribute Group	Initial Value	Get Command
GL_POINT_SIZE	Point size	point	1.0	glGetFloatv()
GL_POINT_SMOOTH	Point antialiasing on	point/enable	GL_FALSE	glIsEnabled()
GL_POINT_SPRITE	Point sprite enable	point/enable	GL_FALSE	glIsEnabled()
GL_POINT_SIZE_MIN	Attenuated minimum point size	point	0.0	glGetFloatv()
GL_POINT_SIZE_MAX	Attenuated maximum point size	point	See Note a at end of table.	glGetFloatv()
GL_POINT_FADE_THRESHOLD_SIZE	Threshold for alpha attenuation	point	1.0	glGetFloatv()
GL_POINT_DISTANCE_ATTENUATION	Attenuation coefficients	point	1, 0, 0	glGetFloatv()
GL_POINT_SPRITE_COORD_ORIGIN	Origin orientation for point sprites	point	GL_UPPER_LEFT	glGetIntegerv()
GL_LINE_WIDTH	Line width	line	1.0	glGetFloatv()
GL_LINE_SMOOTH	Line antialiasing on	line/enable	GL_FALSE	glIsEnabled()
GL_LINE_STIPPLE_PATTERN	Line stipple	line	1's	glGetIntegerv()
GL_LINE_STIPPLE_REPEAT	Line stipple repeat	line	1	glGetIntegerv()

Table B-8   Rasterization State Variables

State Variable	Description	Attribute Group	Initial Value	Get Command
GL_LINE_STIPPLE	Line stipple enable	line/enable	GL_FALSE	glIsEnabled()
GL_CULL_FACE	Polygon culling enabled	polygon/enable	GL_FALSE	glIsEnabled()
GL_CULL_FACE_MODE	Cull front-/back-facing polygons	polygon	GL_BACK	glGetIntegerv()
GL_FRONT_FACE	Polygon front-face CW/CCW indicator	polygon	GL_CCW	glGetIntegerv()
GL_POLYGON_SMOOTH	Polygon antialiasing on	polygon/enable	GL_FALSE	glIsEnabled()
GL_POLYGON_MODE	Polygon rasterization mode (front and back)	polygon	GL_FILL	glGetIntegerv()
GL_POLYGON_OFFSET_FACTOR	Polygon offset factor	polygon	0	glGetFloatv()
GL_POLYGON_OFFSET_UNITS	Polygon offset units	polygon	0	glGetFloatv()
GL_POLYGON_OFFSET_POINT	Polygon offset enable for GL_POINT mode rasterization	polygon/enable	GL_FALSE	glIsEnabled()
GL_POLYGON_OFFSET_LINE	Polygon offset enable for GL_LINE mode rasterization	polygon/enable	GL_FALSE	glIsEnabled()
GL_POLYGON_OFFSET_FILL	Polygon offset enable for GL_FILL mode rasterization	polygon/enable	GL_FALSE	glIsEnabled()
GL_POLYGON_STIPPLE	Polygon stipple enable	polygon/enable	GL_FALSE	glIsEnabled()
—	Polygon stipple pattern	polygon-stipple	1's	glGetPolygon Stipple()

Table B-8 (continued)   Rasterization State Variables

a. The initial value of GL_POINT_SIZE_MAX is the maximum of GL_ALIASED_POINT_SIZE_RANGE and GL_SMOOTH_POINT_SIZE_RANGE.

Multisampling

State Variable	Description	Attribute Group	Initial Value	Get Command
GL_MULTISAMPLE	Multisample rasterization	multisample/ enable	GL_TRUE	glIsEnabled()
GL_SAMPLE_ALPHA_TO_COVERAGE	Modify coverage from alpha	multisample/ enable	GL_FALSE	glIsEnabled()
GL_SAMPLE_ALPHA_TO_ONE	Set alpha to maximum	multisample/ enable	GL_FALSE	glIsEnabled()
GL_SAMPLE_COVERAGE	Mask to modify coverage	multisample/ enable	GL_FALSE	glIsEnabled()
GL_SAMPLE_COVERAGE_VALUE	Coverage mask value	multisample	1	glGetFloatv()
GL_SAMPLE_COVERAGE_INVERT	Invert coverage mask value	multisample	GL_FALSE	glGetBooleanv()

Table B-9   Multisampling

Texturing

State Variable	Description	Attribute Group	Initial Value	Get Command
GL_COMPRESSED_TEXTURE_FORMATS	List of supported compressed texture formats	—	varies	glGetIntegerv()
GL_TEXTURE_x	True if x (dimensional) texturing is enabled (x is 1D, 2D, or 3D)	texture/enable	GL_FALSE	glIsEnabled()
GL_TEXTURE_x	x-D texture image at level of detail i (x is 1D, 2D, or 3D)	—	—	glGetTexImage()
GL_TEXTURE_1D_ARRAY	1D texture array image at row i	—	—	glGetTexImage()
GL_TEXTURE_2D_ARRAY	2D texture array image at slice i	—	—	glGetTexImage()
GL_TEXTURE_RECTANGLE	Rectangular texture image at LOD 0	—	—	glGetTexImage()
GL_TEXTURE_BINDING_x	Texture object bound to GL_TEXTURE_x (x is 1D, 2D, or 3D)	texture	0	glGetIntegerv()
GL_TEXTURE_BINDING_1D_ARRAY	Texture object bound to GL_TEXTURE_1D_ARRAY	texture	0	glGetIntegerv()
GL_TEXTURE_BINDING_2D_ARRAY	Texture object bound to GL_TEXTURE_2D_ARRAY	texture	0	glGetIntegerv()
GL_TEXTURE_BINDING_RECTANGLE	Texture object bound to GL_TEXTURE_RECTANGLE	—	0	glGetIntegerv()

Table B-10   Texturing State Variables

State Variable	Description	Attribute Group	Initial Value	Get Command
GL_TEXTURE_BINDING_CUBE_MAP	Texture object bound to GL_TEXTURE_CUBE_MAP	texture	0	glGetIntegerv()
GL_TEXTURE_BUFFER_DATA_STORE_BINDING	Buffer object bound as the data store for the active image unit's buffer texture	—	0	glGetTexLevelParameter()
GL_TEXTURE_COMPRESSED	True if texture map is stored internally in a compressed format	—	GL_FALSE	glGetTexLevelParameter*()
GL_TEXTURE_COMPRESSED_IMAGE_SIZE	Number of bytes in compressed texture image array	—	0	glGetTexLevelParameter*()
GL_TEXTURE_CUBE_MAP	True if cube map texturing is enabled	texture/enable	GL_FALSE	glIsEnabled()
GL_TEXTURE_CUBE_MAP_POSITIVE_X	+x face cube map texture image at level of detail i	—	—	glGetTexImage()
GL_TEXTURE_CUBE_MAP_NEGATIVE_X	-x face cube map texture image at level of detail i	—	—	glGetTexImage()
GL_TEXTURE_CUBE_MAP_POSITIVE_Y	+y face cube map texture image at level of detail i	—	—	glGetTexImage()
GL_TEXTURE_CUBE_MAP_NEGATIVE_Y	-y face cube map texture image at level of detail i	—	—	glGetTexImage()

Table B-10 (continued)   Texturing State Variables

State Variable	Description	Attribute Group	Initial Value	Get Command
GL_TEXTURE_CUBE_MAP_POSITIVE_Z	+z face cube map texture image at level of detail i	—	—	glGetTexImage()
GL_TEXTURE_CUBE_MAP_NEGATIVE_Z	-z face cube map texture image at level of detail i	—	—	glGetTexImage()
GL_TEXTURE_BORDER_COLOR	Texture border color	texture	(0, 0, 0, 0)	glGetTexParameter*()
GL_TEXTURE_MIN_FILTER	Texture minification function	texture	GL_NEAREST_MIPMAP_LINEAR	glGetTexParameter*()
GL_TEXTURE_MAG_FILTER	Texture magnification function	texture	GL_LINEAR	glGetTexParameter*()
GL_TEXTURE_WRAP_S	Texture coord S wrap mode	texture	GL_REPEAT	glGetTexParameter*()
GL_TEXTURE_WRAP_T	Texture coord T wrap mode (2D, 3D, cube map textures only)	texture	GL_REPEAT	glGetTexParameter*()
GL_TEXTURE_WRAP_R	Texture coord R wrap mode (3D textures only)	texture	GL_REPEAT	glGetTexParameter*()
GL_TEXTURE_PRIORITY	Texture object priority	texture	1	glGetTexParameter*()
GL_TEXTURE_RESIDENT	Texture residency	texture	varies	glGetTexParameteriv()
GL_TEXTURE_MIN_LOD	Minimum level of detail	texture	–1000	glGetTexParameterfv()
GL_TEXTURE_MAX_LOD	Maximum level of detail	texture	1000	glGetTexParameterfv()

Table B-10 (continued)   Texturing State Variables

OpenGL State Variables   **763**

State Variable	Description	Attribute Group	Initial Value	Get Command
GL_TEXTURE_BASE_LEVEL	Base texture array	texture	0	glGetTexParameterfv()
GL_TEXTURE_MAX_LEVEL	Maximum texture array level	texture	1000	glGetTexParameterfv()
GL_TEXTURE_LOD_BIAS	Texture level-of-detail bias	texture	0.0	glGetTexParameterfv()
GL_DEPTH_TEXTURE_MODE	Depth texture mode	texture	GL_LUMINANCE	glGetTexParameteriv()
GL_TEXTURE_COMPARE_MODE	Texture comparison mode	texture	GL_NONE	glGetTexParameteriv()
GL_TEXTURE_COMPARE_FUNC	Texture comparison function	texture	GL_LEQUAL	glGetTexParameteriv()
GL_GENERATE_MIPMAP	Automatic mipmap generation	texture	GL_FALSE	glGetTexParameter*()
GL_TEXTURE_WIDTH	Texture image i's width	—	0	glGetTexLevelParameter*()
GL_TEXTURE_HEIGHT	2D/3D texture image i's height	—	0	glGetTexLevelParameter*()
GL_TEXTURE_DEPTH	3D texture image i's depth	—	0	glGetTexLevelParameter*()
GL_TEXTURE_BORDER	Texture image i's border width	—	0	glGetTexLevelParameter*()
GL_TEXTURE_INTERNAL_FORMAT	Texture image i's internal image format	—	GL_RGBA or GL_R8	glGetTexLevelParameter*()
GL_TEXTURE_COMPONENTS	Texture image i's internal image format	—	1	glGetTexLevelParameter*()
GL_TEXTURE_RED_SIZE	Texture image i's red resolution	—	0	glGetTexLevelParameter*()

Table B-10 (continued)   Texturing State Variables

State Variable	Description	Attribute Group	Initial Value	Get Command
GL_TEXTURE_GREEN_SIZE	Texture image i's green resolution	—	0	glGetTexLevelParameter*()
GL_TEXTURE_BLUE_SIZE	Texture image i's blue resolution	—	0	glGetTexLevelParameter*()
GL_TEXTURE_ALPHA_SIZE	Texture image i's alpha resolution	—	0	glGetTexLevelParameter*()
GL_TEXTURE_LUMINANCE_SIZE	Texture image i's luminance resolution	—	0	glGetTexLevelParameter*()
GL_TEXTURE_INTENSITY_SIZE	Texture image i's intensity resolution	—	0	glGetTexLevelParameter*()
GL_TEXTURE_DEPTH_SIZE	Texture image i's depth resolution	—	0	glGetTexLevelParameter*()
GL_SHARED_SIZE	Shared exponent field resolution	—	0	glGetTexLevelParameter*()
GL_TEXTURE_RED_TYPE	Texture image i's red type	—	GL_NONE	glGetTexLevelParameter*()
GL_TEXTURE_GREEN_TYPE	Texture image i's green type	—	GL_NONE	glGetTexLevelParameter*()
GL_TEXTURE_BLUE_TYPE	Texture image i's blue type	—	GL_NONE	glGetTexLevelParameter*()
GL_TEXTURE_ALPHA_TYPE	Texture image i's alpha type	—	GL_NONE	glGetTexLevelParameter*()
GL_TEXTURE_LUMINANCE_TYPE	Texture image i's luminance type	—	GL_NONE	glGetTexLevelParameter*()
GL_TEXTURE_INTENSITY_TYPE	Texture image i's intensity type	—	GL_NONE	glGetTexLevelParameter*()
GL_TEXTURE_DEPTH_TYPE	Texture image i's depth type	—	GL_NONE	glGetTexLevelParameter*()

Table B-10 (continued)   Texturing State Variables

State Variable	Description	Attribute Group	Initial Value	Get Command
GL_TEXTURE_COMPRESSED	True, if texture image has a compressed internal format	—	GL_FALSE	glGetTexLevelParameter*()
GL_TEXTURE_COMPRESSED_ IMAGE_SIZE	Size (in GLubyte) of compressed texture image	—	0	glGetTexLevelParameter*()
GL_COORD_REPLACE	Coordinate replacement enable	point	GL_FALSE	glTexEnviv()
GL_ACTIVE_TEXTURE	Active texture unit	texture	GL_TEXTURE0	glGetIntegerv()
GL_TEXTURE_ENV_MODE	Texture application function	texture	GL_MODULATE	glGetTexEnviv()
GL_TEXTURE_ENV_COLOR	Texture environment color	texture	(0, 0, 0, 0)	glGetTexEnvfv()
GL_TEXTURE_LOD_BIAS	Texture level of detail bias	texture	0.0	glGetTexEnvfv()
GL_TEXTURE_GEN_x	Texgen enabled (x is S, T, R, or Q)	texture/ enable	GL_FALSE	glIsEnabled()
GL_EYE_PLANE	Texgen plane equation coefficients	texture	—	glGetTexGenfv()
GL_OBJECT_PLANE	Texgen object linear coefficients	texture	—	glGetTexGenfv()
GL_TEXTURE_GEN_MODE	Function used for texgen	texture	GL_EYE_ LINEAR	glGetTexGeniv()
GL_COMBINE_RGB	RGB combiner function	texture	GL_MODULATE	glGetTexEnviv()
GL_COMBINE_ALPHA	Alpha combiner function	texture	GL_MODULATE	glGetTexEnviv()

Table B-10 (continued)   Texturing State Variables

State Variable	Description	Attribute Group	Initial Value	Get Command
GL_SRC0_RGB	RGB source 0	texture	GL_TEXTURE	glGetTexEnviv()
GL_SRC1_RGB	RGB source 1	texture	GL_PREVIOUS	glGetTexEnviv()
GL_SRC2_RGB	RGB source 2	texture	GL_CONSTANT	glGetTexEnviv()
GL_SRC0_ALPHA	Alpha source 0	texture	GL_TEXTURE	glGetTexEnviv()
GL_SRC1_ALPHA	Alpha source 1	texture	GL_PREVIOUS	glGetTexEnviv()
GL_SRC2_ALPHA	Alpha source 2	texture	GL_CONSTANT	glGetTexEnviv()
GL_OPERAND0_RGB	RGB operand 0	texture	GL_SRC_COLOR	glGetTexEnviv()
GL_OPERAND1_RGB	RGB operand 1	texture	GL_SRC_COLOR	glGetTexEnviv()
GL_OPERAND2_RGB	RGB operand 2	texture	GL_SRC_ALPHA	glGetTexEnviv()
GL_OPERAND0_ALPHA	Alpha operand 0	texture	GL_SRC_ALPHA	glGetTexEnviv()
GL_OPERAND1_ALPHA	Alpha operand 1	texture	GL_SRC_ALPHA	glGetTexEnviv()
GL_OPERAND2_ALPHA	Alpha operand 2	texture	GL_SRC_ALPHA	glGetTexEnviv()
GL_RGB_SCALE	RGB post-combiner scaling	texture	1.0	glGetTexEnviv()
GL_ALPHA_SCALE	Alpha post-combiner scaling	texture	1.0	glGetTexEnviv()

Table B-10 (continued)   Texturing State Variables

Pixel Operations

State Variable	Description	Attribute Group	Initial Value	Get Command
GL_SCISSOR_TEST	Scissoring enabled	scissor/enable	GL_FALSE	glIsEnabled()
GL_SCISSOR_BOX	Scissor box	scissor	—	glGetIntegerv()
GL_ALPHA_TEST	Alpha test enabled	color-buffer/enable	GL_FALSE	glIsEnabled()
GL_ALPHA_TEST_FUNC	Alpha test function	color-buffer	GL_ALWAYS	glGetIntegerv()
GL_ALPHA_TEST_REF	Alpha test reference value	color-buffer	0	glGetIntegerv()
GL_STENCIL_TEST	Stenciling enabled	stencil-buffer/enable	GL_FALSE	glIsEnabled()
GL_STENCIL_FUNC	Stencil function	stencil-buffer	GL_ALWAYS	glGetIntegerv()
GL_STENCIL_VALUE_MASK	Stencil mask	stencil-buffer	1's	glGetIntegerv()
GL_STENCIL_REF	Stencil reference value	stencil-buffer	0	glGetIntegerv()
GL_STENCIL_FAIL	Stencil fail action	stencil-buffer	GL_KEEP	glGetIntegerv()
GL_STENCIL_PASS_DEPTH_FAIL	Stencil depth-buffer fail action	stencil-buffer	GL_KEEP	glGetIntegerv()
GL_STENCIL_PASS_DEPTH_PASS	Stencil depth-buffer pass action	stencil-buffer	GL_KEEP	glGetIntegerv()
GL_STENCIL_BACK_FUNC	Back stencil function	stencil-buffer	GL_ALWAYS	glGetIntegerv()

Table B-11   Pixel Operations

State Variable	Description	Attribute Group	Initial Value	Get Command
GL_STENCIL_BACK_VALUE_MASK	Back stencil mask	stencil-buffer	1's	glGetIntegerv()
GL_STENCIL_BACK_REF	Back stencil reference value	stencil-buffer	0	glGetIntegerv()
GL_STENCIL_BACK_FAIL	Back stencil fail action	stencil-buffer	GL_KEEP	glGetIntegerv()
GL_STENCIL_BACK_PASS_DEPTH_FAIL	Back stencil depth-buffer fail action	stencil-buffer	GL_KEEP	glGetIntegerv()
GL_STENCIL_BACK_PASS_DEPTH_PASS	Back stencil depth-buffer pass action	stencil-buffer	GL_KEEP	glGetIntegerv()
GL_DEPTH_TEST	Depth buffer enabled	depth-buffer/ enable	GL_FALSE	glIsEnabledi()
GL_DEPTH_FUNC	Depth-buffer test function	depth-buffer	GL_LESS	glGetIntegerv()
GL_BLEND	Blending enabled for draw buffer i	color-buffer/ enable	GL_FALSE	glIsEnabled()
GL_BLEND_SRC_RGB	Blending source RGB function	color-buffer	GL_ONE	glGetIntegerv()
GL_BLEND_SRC_ALPHA	Blending source alpha function	color-buffer	GL_ONE	glGetIntegerv()
GL_BLEND_DST_RGB	Blending destination RGB function	color-buffer	GL_ZERO	glGetIntegerv()
GL_BLEND_DST_ALPHA	Blending destination alpha function	color-buffer	GL_ZERO	glGetIntegerv()

Table B-11 (continued)   Pixel Operations

State Variable	Description	Attribute Group	Initial Value	Get Command
GL_BLEND_EQUATION_RGB	RGB blending equation	color-buffer	GL_FUNC_ADD	glGetIntegerv()
GL_BLEND_EQUATION_ALPHA	Alpha blending equation	color-buffer	GL_FUNC_ADD	glGetIntegerv()
GL_BLEND_COLOR	Constant blend color	color-buffer	(0, 0, 0, 0)	glGetFloatv()
GL_FRAMEBUFFER_SRGB	sRGB update and blending enabled	color-buffer/ enable	GL_FALSE	glIsEnabled()
GL_DITHER	Dithering enabled	color-buffer/ enable	GL_TRUE	glIsEnabled()
GL_INDEX_LOGIC_OP	Color index logical operation enabled	color-buffer/ enable	GL_FALSE	glIsEnabled()
GL_COLOR_LOGIC_OP	RGBA color logical operation enabled	color-buffer/ enable	GL_FALSE	glIsEnabled()
GL_LOGIC_OP_MODE	Logical operation function	color-buffer	GL_COPY	glGetIntegerv()

Table B-11 (continued)   Pixel Operations

Framebuffer Control

State Variable	Description	Attribute Group	Initial Value	Get Command
GL_DRAW_BUFFER*i*	Buffers selected for color *i*	color-buffer	—	glGetIntegerv()
GL_DRAW_BUFFER	Buffers selected for color 0	color-buffer	—	glGetIntegerv()
GL_INDEX_WRITEMASK	Color-index writemask	color-buffer	1's	glGetIntegerv()
GL_COLOR_WRITEMASK	Color write enabled; R, G, B, or A for draw buffer *i*	color-buffer	GL_TRUE	glGet Booleani_v()
GL_DEPTH_WRITEMASK	Depth buffer enabled for writing	depth-buffer	GL_TRUE	glGetBooleanv()
GL_STENCIL_WRITEMASK	Front stencil buffer writemask	stencil-buffer	1's	glGetIntegerv()
GL_STENCIL_BACK_ WRITEMASK	Back stencil buffer writemask	stencil-buffer	1's	glGetIntegerv()
GL_COLOR_CLEAR_VALUE	Color-buffer clear value (RGBA mode)	color-buffer	(0, 0, 0, 0)	glGetFloatv()
GL_INDEX_CLEAR_VALUE	Color-buffer clear value (color-index mode)	color-buffer	0	glGetFloatv()
GL_DEPTH_CLEAR_VALUE	Depth-buffer clear value	depth-buffer	1	glGetIntegerv()
GL_STENCIL_CLEAR_VALUE	Stencil-buffer clear value	stencil-buffer	0	glGetIntegerv()
GL_ACCUM_CLEAR_VALUE	Accumulation-buffer clear value	accum-buffer	0	glGetFloatv()

Table B-12   Framebuffer Control State Variables

Framebuffer Object State

State Variable	Description	Attribute Group	Initial Value	Get Command
GL_DRAW_FRAMEBUFFER_BINDING	Framebuffer object bound to GL_DRAW_FRAMEBUFFER	—	0	glGetIntegerv()
GL_READ_FRAMEBUFFER_BINDING	Framebuffer object bound to GL_READ_FRAMEBUFFER	—	0	glGetIntegerv()
GL_DRAW_BUFFERi	Draw buffer selected for color output i	color-buffer	—	glGetIntegerv()
GL_READ_BUFFER	Read source buffer	pixel	—	glGetIntegerv()
GL_FRAMEBUFFER_ATTACHMENT_OBJECT_TYPE	Type of image attached to framebuffer attachment point	—	GL_NONE	glGetFramebuffer Attachment Parameteriv()
GL_FRAMEBUFFER_ATTACHMENT_OBJECT_NAME	Name of object attached to framebuffer attachment point	—	0	glGetFramebuffer Attachment Parameteriv()
GL_FRAMEBUFFER_ATTACHMENT_TEXTURE_LEVEL	Mipmap level of texture image attached, if object attached is a texture	—	0	glGetFramebuffer Attachment Parameteriv()

Table B-13   Framebuffer Object State Variables

State Variable	Description	Attribute Group	Initial Value	Get Command
GL_FRAMEBUFFER_ ATTACHMENT_TEXTURE_ CUBE_MAP_FACE	Cubemap face of texture image attached, if object attached is a cubemap texture	—	GL_ TEXTURE_ CUBE_MAP_ POSITIVE_X	glGetFramebuffer Attachment Parameteriv()
GL_FRAMEBUFFER_ ATTACHMENT_TEXTURE_ LAYER	Layer of texture image attached, if attached object is a 3D texture	—	0	glGetFramebuffer Attachment Parameteriv()
GL_FRAMEBUFFER_ ATTACHMENT_COLOR_ ENCODING	Encoding of components in the attached image	—	—	glGetFramebuffer Attachment Parameteriv()
GL_FRAMEBUFFER_ ATTACHMENT_COMPONENT_ TYPE	Type of components in the attached image	—	—	glGetFramebuffer Attachment Parameteriv()
GL_FRAMEBUFFER_ ATTACHMENT_RED_SIZE	Size in bits of attached image's red component	—	GL_NONE	glGetFramebuffer Attachment Parameteriv()
GL_FRAMEBUFFER_ ATTACHMENT_GREEN_SIZE	Size in bits of attached image's green component	—	GL_NONE	glGetFramebuffer Attachment Parameteriv()
GL_FRAMEBUFFER_ ATTACHMENT_BLUE_SIZE	Size in bits of attached image's blue component	—	GL_NONE	glGetFramebuffer Attachment Parameteriv()

Table B-13 (continued)   Framebuffer Object State Variables

State Variable	Description	Attribute Group	Initial Value	Get Command
GL_FRAMEBUFFER_ ATTACHMENT_ALPHA_SIZE	Size in bits of attached image's alpha component	—	GL_NONE	glGetFramebuffer Attachment Parameteriv()
GL_FRAMEBUFFER_ ATTACHMENT_DEPTH_SIZE	Size in bits of attached image's depth component	—	GL_NONE	glGetFramebuffer Attachment Parameteriv()
GL_FRAMEBUFFER_ ATTACHMENT_STENCIL_SIZE	Size in bits of attached image's stencil component	—	GL_NONE	glGetFramebuffer Attachment Parameteriv()

Table B-13 (continued)   Framebuffer Object State Variables

Renderbuffer Object State

State Variable	Description	Attribute Group	Initial Value	Get Command
GL_RENDERBUFFER_BINDING	Renderbuffer object bound to GL_RENDERBUFFER	—	0	glGetIntegerv()
GL_RENDERBUFFER_WIDTH	Width of renderbuffer	—	0	glGetRenderbufferParameteriv()
GL_RENDERBUFFER_HEIGHT	Height of renderbuffer	—	0	glGetRenderbufferParameteriv()
GL_RENDERBUFFER_INTERNAL_FORMAT	Internal format of renderbuffer	—	GL_RGBA	glGetRenderbufferParameteriv()
GL_RENDERBUFFER_RED_SIZE	Size in bits of renderbuffer image's red component	—	0	glGetRenderbufferParameteriv()
GL_RENDERBUFFER_GREEN_SIZE	Size in bits of renderbuffer image's green component	—	0	glGetRenderbufferParameteriv()
GL_RENDERBUFFER_BLUE_SIZE	Size in bits of renderbuffer image's blue component	—	0	glGetRenderbufferParameteriv()
GL_RENDERBUFFER_ALPHA_SIZE	Size in bits of renderbuffer image's alpha component	—	0	glGetRenderbufferParameteriv()
GL_RENDERBUFFER_DEPTH_SIZE	Size in bits of renderbuffer image's depth component	—	0	glGetRenderbufferParameteriv()

Table B-14   Renderbuffer Object State Variables

State Variable	Description	Attribute Group	Initial Value	Get Command
GL_RENDERBUFFER_STENCIL_SIZE	Size in bits of renderbuffer image's stencil component	—	0	glGetRenderbufferParameteriv()
GL_RENDERBUFFER_SAMPLES	Number of samples	—	0	glGetRenderbufferParameteriv()

Table B-14 (continued)   Renderbuffer Object State Variables

Pixels

State Variable	Description	Attribute Group	Initial Value	Get Command
GL_UNPACK_SWAP_BYTES	Value of GL_UNPACK_SWAP_BYTES	pixel-store	GL_FALSE	glGetBooleanv()
GL_UNPACK_LSB_FIRST	Value of GL_UNPACK_LSB_FIRST	pixel-store	GL_FALSE	glGetBooleanv()
GL_UNPACK_IMAGE_HEIGHT	Value of GL_UNPACK_IMAGE_HEIGHT	pixel-store	0	glGetIntegerv()
GL_UNPACK_SKIP_IMAGES	Value of GL_UNPACK_SKIP_IMAGES	pixel-store	0	glGetIntegerv()
GL_UNPACK_ROW_LENGTH	Value of GL_UNPACK_ROW_LENGTH	pixel-store	0	glGetIntegerv()
GL_UNPACK_SKIP_ROWS	Value of GL_UNPACK_SKIP_ROWS	pixel-store	0	glGetIntegerv()
GL_UNPACK_SKIP_PIXELS	Value of GL_UNPACK_SKIP_PIXELS	pixel-store	0	glGetIntegerv()

Table B-15   Pixel State Variables

State Variable	Description	Attribute Group	Initial Value	Get Command
GL_UNPACK_ALIGNMENT	Value of GL_UNPACK_ALIGNMENT	pixel-store	4	glGetIntegerv()
GL_PIXEL_PACK_BUFFER_BINDING	Pixel pack buffer binding	pixel-store	0	glGetIntegerv()
GL_PIXEL_UNPACK_BUFFER_BINDING	Pixel unpack buffer binding	pixel-store	0	glGetIntegerv()
GL_PACK_SWAP_BYTES	Value of GL_PACK_SWAP_BYTES	pixel-store	GL_FALSE	glGetBooleanv()
GL_PACK_LSB_FIRST	Value of GL_PACK_LSB_FIRST	pixel-store	GL_FALSE	glGetBooleanv()
GL_PACK_IMAGE_HEIGHT	Value of GL_PACK_IMAGE_HEIGHT	pixel-store	0	glGetIntegerv()
GL_PACK_SKIP_IMAGES	Value of GL_PACK_SKIP_IMAGES	pixel-store	0	glGetIntegerv()
GL_PACK_ROW_LENGTH	Value of GL_PACK_ROW_LENGTH	pixel-store	0	glGetIntegerv()
GL_PACK_SKIP_ROWS	Value of GL_PACK_SKIP_ROWS	pixel-store	0	glGetIntegerv()
GL_PACK_SKIP_PIXELS	Value of GL_PACK_SKIP_PIXELS	pixel-store	0	glGetIntegerv()
GL_PACK_ALIGNMENT	Value of GL_PACK_ALIGNMENT	pixel-store	4	glGetIntegerv()
GL_MAP_COLOR	True if colors are mapped	pixel	GL_FALSE	glGetBooleanv()
GL_MAP_STENCIL	True if stencil values are mapped	pixel	GL_FALSE	glGetBooleanv()
GL_INDEX_SHIFT	Value of GL_INDEX_SHIFT	pixel	0	glGetIntegerv()

Table B-15 (continued)   Pixel State Variables

State Variable	Description	Attribute Group	Initial Value	Get Command
GL_INDEX_OFFSET	Value of GL_INDEX_OFFSET	pixel	0	glGetIntegerv()
GL_x_SCALE	Value of GL_x_SCALE; x is GL_RED, GL_GREEN, GL_BLUE, GL_ALPHA, or GL_DEPTH	pixel	1	glGetFloatv()
GL_x_BIAS	Value of GL_x_BIAS; x is GL_RED, GL_GREEN, GL_BLUE, GL_ALPHA, or GL_DEPTH	pixel	0	glGetFloatv()
GL_COLOR_TABLE	True if color table lookup is enabled	pixel/ enable	GL_FALSE	glIsEnabled()
GL_POST_CONVOLUTION_ COLOR_TABLE	True if post convolution color table lookup is enabled	pixel/ enable	GL_FALSE	glIsEnabled()
GL_POST_COLOR_MATRIX_ COLOR_TABLE	True if post color matrix color table lookup is enabled	pixel/ enable	GL_FALSE	glIsEnabled()
GL_COLOR_TABLE	Color tables	—	empty	glGetColorTable()
GL_COLOR_TABLE_FORMAT	Color tables' internal image format	—	GL_RGBA	glGetColorTable Parameteriv()
GL_COLOR_TABLE_WIDTH	Color tables' specified width	—	0	glGetColorTable Parameteriv()

Table B-15 (continued)   Pixel State Variables

State Variable	Description	Attribute Group	Initial Value	Get Command
GL_COLOR_TABLE_x_SIZE	Color table component resolution; x is RED, GREEN, BLUE, ALPHA, LUMINANCE, or INTENSITY	—	0	glGetColorTableParameteriv()
GL_COLOR_TABLE_SCALE	Scale factors applied to color table entries	pixel	(1, 1, 1, 1)	glGetColorTableParameterfv()
GL_COLOR_TABLE_BIAS	Bias values applied to color table entries	pixel	(0, 0, 0, 0)	glGetColorTableParameterfv()
GL_CONVOLUTION_1D	True if 1D convolution is enabled	pixel/enable	GL_FALSE	glIsEnabled()
GL_CONVOLUTION_2D	True if 2D convolution is enabled	pixel/enable	GL_FALSE	glIsEnabled()
GL_SEPARABLE_2D	True if separable 2D convolution is enabled	pixel/enable	GL_FALSE	glIsEnabled()
GL_CONVOLUTION_1D	1D convolution filter	—	empty	glGetConvolutionFilter()
GL_CONVOLUTION_2D	2D convolution filter	—	empty	glGetConvolutionFilter()
GL_SEPARABLE_2D	2D separable convolution filter	—	empty	glGetSeparableFilter()

Table B-15 (continued)   Pixel State Variables

State Variable	Description	Attribute Group	Initial Value	Get Command
GL_CONVOLUTION_ BORDER_COLOR	Convolution border color	pixel	(0, 0, 0, 0)	glGetConvolution Parameterfv()
GL_CONVOLUTION_ BORDER_MODE	Convolution border mode	pixel	GL_REDUCE	glGetConvolution Parameteriv()
GL_CONVOLUTION_ FILTER_SCALE	Scale factors applied to convolution filter entries	pixel	(1, 1, 1, 1)	glGetConvolution Parameterfv()
GL_CONVOLUTION_ FILTER_BIAS	Bias values applied to convolution filter entries	pixel	(0, 0, 0, 0)	glGetConvolution Parameterfv()
GL_CONVOLUTION_FORMAT	Convolution filter internal format	—	GL_RGBA	glGetConvolution Parameteriv()
GL_CONVOLUTION_WIDTH	Convolution filter width	—	0	glGetConvolution Parameteriv()
GL_CONVOLUTION_HEIGHT	Convolution filter height	—	0	glGetConvolution Parameteriv()
GL_POST_CONVOLUTION_ x_SCALE	Component scale factors after convolution; x is RED, GREEN, BLUE, or ALPHA	pixel	1	glGetFloatv()
GL_POST_CONVOLUTION_ x_BIAS	Component bias values after convolution; x is RED, GREEN, BLUE, or ALPHA	pixel	0	glGetFloatv()

Table B-15 (continued)   Pixel State Variables

State Variable	Description	Attribute Group	Initial Value	Get Command
GL_POST_COLOR_MATRIX_x_SCALE	Component scale factors after color matrix; x is RED, GREEN, BLUE, or ALPHA	pixel	1	glGetFloatv()
GL_POST_COLOR_MATRIX_x_BIAS	Component bias values after color matrix; x is RED, GREEN, BLUE, or ALPHA	pixel	0	glGetFloatv()
GL_HISTOGRAM	True if histogramming is enabled	pixel/enable	GL_FALSE	glIsEnabled()
GL_HISTOGRAM	Histogram table	—	empty	glGetHistogram()
GL_HISTOGRAM_WIDTH	Histogram table width	—	0	glGetHistogram Parameteriv()
GL_HISTOGRAM_FORMAT	Histogram table internal format	—	GL_RGBA	glGetHistogram Parameteriv()
GL_HISTOGRAM_x_SIZE	Histogram table component resolution; x is RED, GREEN, BLUE, ALPHA, or LUMINANCE	—	0	glGetHistogram Parameteriv()
GL_HISTOGRAM_SINK	True if histogramming consumes pixel groups	—	GL_FALSE	glGetHistogram Parameteriv()
GL_MINMAX	True if minmax is enabled	pixel/enable	GL_FALSE	glIsEnabled()

Table B-15 (continued)   Pixel State Variables

State Variable	Description	Attribute Group	Initial Value	Get Command
GL_MINMAX	Minmax table	—	See Note a at the end of table.	glGetMinmax()
GL_MINMAX_FORMAT	Minmax table internal format	—	GL_RGBA	glGetMinmax Parameteriv()
GL_MINMAX_SINK	True if minmax consumes pixel groups	—	GL_FALSE	glGetMinmax Parameteriv()
GL_ZOOM_X	x zoom factor	pixel	1.0	glGetFloatv()
GL_ZOOM_Y	y zoom factor	pixel	1.0	glGetFloatv()
GL_PIXEL_MAP_x	glPixelMap() translation tables; x is a map name from Table 8-1	—	0's	glGetPixelMap*()
GL_PIXEL_MAP_x_SIZE	Size of glPixelMap() translation table x	—	1	glGetIntegerv()
GL_READ_BUFFER	Read source buffer	pixel	—	glGetIntegerv()

Table B-15 (continued)   Pixel State Variables

a. Min table initially set to maximum representable values. Max table set to minimum representable values.

Evaluators

State Variable	Description	Attribute Group	Initial Value	Get Command
GL_ORDER	1D map order	—	1	glGetMapiv()
GL_ORDER	2D map orders	—	1, 1	glGetMapiv()
GL_COEFF	1D control points	—	—	glGetMapfv()
GL_COEFF	2D control points	—	—	glGetMapfv()
GL_DOMAIN	1D domain endpoints	—	—	glGetMapfv()
GL_DOMAIN	2D domain endpoints	—	—	glGetMapfv()
GL_MAP1_x	1D map enables: x is map type	eval/enable	GL_FALSE	glIsEnabled()
GL_MAP2_x	2D map enables: x is map type	eval/enable	GL_FALSE	glIsEnabled()
GL_MAP1_GRID_DOMAIN	1D grid endpoints	eval	0, 1	glGetFloatv()
GL_MAP2_GRID_DOMAIN	2D grid endpoints	eval	0, 1; 0, 1	glGetFloatv()
GL_MAP1_GRID_SEGMENTS	1D grid divisions	eval	1	glGetFloatv()
GL_MAP2_GRID_SEGMENTS	2D grid divisions	eval	1, 1	glGetFloatv()
GL_AUTO_NORMAL	True if automatic normal generation is enabled	eval/enable	GL_FALSE	glIsEnabled()

Table B-16   Evaluator State Variables

Shader Object State

State Variable	Description	Attribute Group	Initial Value	Get Command
GL_SHADER_TYPE	Type of shader (vertex or fragment)	—	—	glGetShaderiv()
GL_DELETE_STATUS	Shader flagged for deletion	—	GL_FALSE	glGetShaderiv()
GL_COMPILE_STATUS	Last compilation status	—	GL_FALSE	glGetShaderiv()
—	Information log for shader objects	—	empty string	glGetShaderInfoLog()
GL_INFO_LOG_LENGTH	String length of shader information log	—	0	glGetShaderiv()
—	Source code for a shader	—	empty string	glGetShaderSource()
GL_SHADER_SOURCE_LENGTH	String length of shader source code	—	0	glGetShaderiv()

Table B-17   Shader Object State Variables

Program Object State

State Variable	Description	Attribute Group	Initial Value	Get Command
GL_CURRENT_PROGRAM	Name of current program object	—	0	glGetIntegerv()
GL_DELETE_STATUS	Program object deleted	—	GL_FALSE	glGetProgramiv()
GL_LINK_STATUS	Last link attempt succeeded	—	GL_FALSE	glGetProgramiv()
GL_VALIDATE_STATUS	Last validate attempt succeeded	—	GL_FALSE	glGetProgramiv()
GL_ATTACHED_SHADERS	Number of attached shader objects	—	0	glGetProgramiv()
—	Shader objects attached	—	empty	glGetAttachedShaders()
—	Info log for program object	—	empty	glGetProgramInfoLog()
GL_INFO_LOG_LENGTH	Length of info log	—	0	glGetProgramiv()
GL_ACTIVE_UNIFORMS	Number of active uniforms	—	0	glGetProgramiv()
—	Location of active uniforms	—	—	glGetUniformLocation()
—	Size of active uniform	—	—	glGetActiveUniform()
—	Type of active uniform	—	—	glGetActiveUniform()
—	Name of active uniform	—	empty	glGetActiveUniform()
GL_ACTIVE_UNIFORM_MAX_LENGTH	Maximum active uniform name length	—	0	glGetProgramiv()

Table B-18   Program Object State Variables

State Variable	Description	Attribute Group	Initial Value	Get Command
—	Uniform value	—	0	glGetUniform()
GL_ACTIVE_ATTRIBUTES	Number of active attributes	—	0	glGetProgramiv()
—	Location of active generic attribute	—	—	glGetAttribLocation()
—	Size of active attribute	—	—	glGetActiveAttrib()
—	Type of active attribute	—	—	glGetActiveAttrib()
—	Name of active attribute	—	empty	glGetActiveAttrib()
GL_ACTIVE_ATTRIBUTE_MAX_LENGTH	Maximum active attribute name length	—	0	glGetProgramiv()
GL_TRANSFORM_FEEDBACK_BUFFER_MODE	Transform feedback mode for the program	—	GL_INTERLEAVED_ATTRIBS	glGetProgramiv()
GL_TRANSFORM_FEEDBACK_VARYINGS	Number of varyings to stream to buffer objects	—	0	glGetProgramiv()
GL_TRANSFORM_FEEDBACK_VARYING_MAX_LENGTH	Maximum transform feedback varying name length	—	0	glGetProgramiv()
—	Size of each transform feedback varying variable	—	—	glGetTransformFeedbackVarying()

Table B-18 (continued) Program Object State Variables

State Variable	Description	Attribute Group	Initial Value	Get Command
—	Type of each transform feedback varying variable	—	—	glGetTransformFeedbackVarying()
—	Name of each transform feedback varying variable	—	—	glGetTransformFeedbackVarying()
GL_UNIFORM_BUFFER_BINDING	Uniform buffer object bound to to the context	—	0	glGetIntegerv()
GL_UNIFORM_BUFFER_BINDING	Uniform buffer object bound to a specific context binding point	—	0	glGetIntegeri_v()
GL_ACTIVE_UNIFORM_BLOCKS	Number of active uniform blocks	—	0	glGetProgramiv()
GL_ACTIVE_UNIFORM_BLOCK_MAX_NAME_LENGTH	Length of longest active uniform block name	—	0	glGetProgramiv()
GL_UNIFORM_TYPE	Type of active uniform	—	—	glGetActiveUniformsiv()
GL_UNIFORM_SIZE	Size of active uniform	—	—	glGetActiveUniformsiv()
GL_UNIFORM_NAME_LENGTH	Uniform name length	—	—	glGetActiveUniformsiv()
GL_UNIFORM_BLOCK_INDEX	Uniform block index	—	—	glGetActiveUniformsiv()
GL_UNIFORM_OFFSET	Uniform buffer offset	—	—	glGetActiveUniformsiv()

Table B-18 **(continued)** Program Object State Variables

State Variable	Description	Attribute Group	Initial Value	Get Command
GL_UNIFORM_ARRAY_STRIDE	Uniform buffer array stride	—	—	glGetActiveUniformsiv()
GL_UNIFORM_MATRIX_STRIDE	Uniform buffer intra-matrix stride	—	—	glGetActiveUniformsiv()
GL_UNIFORM_IS_ROW_MAJOR	Is uniform a row-major matrix?	—	—	glGetActiveUniformsiv()
GL_UNIFORM_BLOCK_BINDING	Uniform buffer binding point associated with the specified uniform block	—	0	glGetActiveUniform Blockiv()
GL_UNIFORM_BLOCK_DATA_SIZE	Size of storage needed to hold uniform block's data	—	—	glGetActiveUniform Blockiv()
GL_UNIFORM_BLOCK_ACTIVE_UNIFORMS	Number of active uniforms in the specified uniform block	—	—	glGetActiveUniform Blockiv()
GL_UNIFORM_BLOCK_ACTIVE_UNIFORMS_INDICES	Array of active uniform indices of the specified uniform block	—	—	glGetActiveUniform Blockiv()
GL_UNIFORM_BLOCK_REFERENCED_BY_VERTEX_SHADER	True if uniform block is actively referenced by the vertex stage	—	0	glGetActiveUniform Blockiv()
GL_UNIFORM_BLOCK_REFERENCED_BY_FRAGMENT_SHADER	True if uniform block is actively referenced by the fragment stage	—	0	glGetActiveUniform Blockiv()

Table B-18   **(continued)**   Program Object State Variables

Query Object State

State Variable	Description	Attribute Group	Initial Value	Get Command
GL_QUERY_RESULT	Query object result	—	0	glGetQueryObject uiv()
GL_QUERY_RESULT_AVAILABLE	Is the query object's result available?	—	GL_FALSE	glGetQueryObject uiv()

Table B-19   Query Object State Variables

Transform Feedback State

State Variable	Description	Attribute Group	Initial Value	Get Command
GL_TRANSFORM_FEEDBACK_ BUFFER_BINDING	Buffer object bound to generic bind point for transform feedback	—	0	glGetIntegerv()
GL_TRANSFORM_FEEDBACK_ BUFFER_BINDING	Buffer object bound to each transform feedback attribute stream	—	0	glGetIntegeri_v()
GL_TRANSFORM_FEEDBACK_ BUFFER_START	Starting offset of range bound for each transform feedback attribute stream	—	0	glGetIntegeri_v()

Table B-20   Transform Feedback State Variables

State Variable	Description	Attribute Group	Initial Value	Get Command
GL_TRANSFORM_FEEDBACK_ BUFFER_SIZE	Size of range bound for each transform feedback attribute stream	—	0	glGetIntegeri_v()
GL_TRANSFORM_FEEDBACK_ INTERLEAVED_COMPONENTS	Maximum number of components to write to a single buffer in interleaved mode	—	64	glGetIntegerv()
GL_TRANSFORM_FEEDBACK_ SEPARATE_ATTRIBS	Maximum number of separate varying attributes that can be captured in transform feedback	—	4	glGetIntegerv()
GL_TRANSFORM_FEEDBACK_ SEPARATE_COMPONENTS	Maximum number of separate varying components in separate mode	—	4	glGetIntegerv()

Table B-20 (continued)   Transform Feedback State Variables

Vertex Shader State

State Variable	Description	Attribute Group	Initial Value	Get Command
GL_VERTEX_PROGRAM_TWO_SIDE	Two-sided color mode	enable	GL_FALSE	glIsEnabled()
GL_CURRENT_VERTEX_ATTRIB	Generic vertex attribute	current	(0, 0, 0, 1)	glGetVertexAttribfv()
GL_VERTEX_PROGRAM_POINT_SIZE	Point size mode	enable	GL_FALSE	glIsEnabled()

Table B-21   Vertex Shader State Variables

Hints

State Variable	Description	Attribute Group	Initial Value	Get Command
GL_PERSPECTIVE_CORRECTION_HINT	Perspective correction hint	hint	GL_DONT_CARE	glGetIntegerv()
GL_POINT_SMOOTH_HINT	Point smooth hint	hint	GL_DONT_CARE	glGetIntegerv()
GL_LINE_SMOOTH_HINT	Line smooth hint	hint	GL_DONT_CARE	glGetIntegerv()
GL_POLYGON_SMOOTH_HINT	Polygon smooth hint	hint	GL_DONT_CARE	glGetIntegerv()
GL_FOG_HINT	Fog hint	hint	GL_DONT_CARE	glGetIntegerv()
GL_GENERATE_MIPMAP_HINT	Mipmap generation hint	hint	GL_DONT_CARE	glGetIntegerv()

Table B-22   Hint State Variables

State Variable	Description	Attribute Group	Initial Value	Get Command
GL_TEXTURE_COMPRESSION_HINT	Texture compression hint	hint	GL_DONT_CARE	glGetIntegerv()
GL_FRAGMENT_SHADER_DERIVATIVE_HINT	Fragment shader derivative accuracy hint	hint	GL_DONT_CARE	glGetIntegerv()

Table B-22 (continued)   Hint State Variables

Implementation-Dependent Values

State Variable	Description	Attribute Group	Minimum Value	Get Command
GL_MAX_LIGHTS	Maximum number of lights	—	8	glGetIntegerv()
GL_MAX_CLIP_DISTANCES (which replaces GL_MAX_CLIP_PLANES in Version 3.0 and greater)	Maximum number of user clipping planes	—	6	glGetIntegerv()
GL_MAX_COLOR_MATRIX_STACK_DEPTH	Maximum color matrix stack depth	—	2	glGetIntegerv()
GL_MAX_MODELVIEW_STACK_DEPTH	Maximum modelview-matrix stack depth	—	32	glGetIntegerv()
GL_MAX_PROJECTION_STACK_DEPTH	Maximum projection-matrix stack depth	—	2	glGetIntegerv()

Table B-23   Implementation-Dependent State Variables

State Variable	Description	Attribute Group	Minimum Value	Get Command
GL_MAX_TEXTURE_STACK_DEPTH	Maximum depth of texture matrix stack	—	2	glGetIntegerv()
GL_SUBPIXEL_BITS	Number of bits of subpixel precision in x and y	—	4	glGetIntegerv()
GL_MAX_3D_TEXTURE_SIZE	See discussion in "Texture Proxy" in Chapter 9	—	16	glGetIntegerv()
GL_MAX_TEXTURE_SIZE	See discussion in "Texture Proxy" in Chapter 9	—	64	glGetIntegerv()
GL_MAX_ARRAY_TEXTURE_LAYERS	Maximum number of layers for texture arrays	—	256	glGetIntegerv()
GL_MAX_TEXTURE_LOD_BIAS	Maximum absolute texture level of detail bias	—	2.0	glGetFloatv()
GL_MAX_CUBE_MAP_TEXTURE_SIZE	Maximum cube map texture image dimension	—	16	glGetIntegerv()
GL_MAX_RENDERBUFFER_SIZE	Maximum width and height of renderbuffers	—	1024	glGetIntegerv()
GL_MAX_PIXEL_MAP_TABLE	Maximum size of a glPixelMap() translation table	—	32	glGetIntegerv()
GL_MAX_NAME_STACK_DEPTH	Maximum selection-name stack depth	—	64	glGetIntegerv()

Table B-23 (continued)   Implementation-Dependent State Variables

State Variable	Description	Attribute Group	Minimum Value	Get Command
GL_MAX_LIST_NESTING	Maximum display-list call nesting	—	64	glGetIntegerv()
GL_MAX_EVAL_ORDER	Maximum evaluator polynomial order	—	8	glGetIntegerv()
GL_MAX_VIEWPORT_DIMS	Maximum viewport dimensions	—	—	glGetIntegerv()
GL_MAX_ATTRIB_STACK_DEPTH	Maximum depth of the attribute stack	—	16	glGetIntegerv()
GL_MAX_CLIENT_ATTRIB_STACK_DEPTH	Maximum depth of the client attribute stack	—	16	glGetIntegerv()
GL_NUM_COMPRESSED_TEXTURE_FORMATS	Number of supported texture compression formats	—	—	glGetIntegerv()
GL_AUX_BUFFERS	Number of auxiliary buffers	—	0	glGetBooleanv()
GL_RGBA_MODE	True if color buffers store RGBA	—	—	glGetBooleanv()
GL_INDEX_MODE	True if color buffers store indices	—	—	glGetBooleanv()
GL_DOUBLEBUFFER	True if front and back buffers exist	—	—	glGetBooleanv()
GL_STEREO	True if left and right buffers exist	—	—	glGetBooleanv()
GL_ALIASED_POINT_SIZE_RANGE	Range (low to high) of aliased point sizes	—	1, 1	glGetFloatv()
GL_SMOOTH_POINT_SIZE_RANGE	Range (low to high) of antialiased point sizes	—	1, 1	glGetFloatv()

Table B-23 (continued)   Implementation-Dependent State Variables

State Variable	Description	Attribute Group	Minimum Value	Get Command
GL_SMOOTH_POINT_SIZE_GRANULARITY	Antialiased point-size granularity	—	—	glGetFloatv()
GL_ALIASED_LINE_WIDTH_RANGE	Range (low to high) of aliased line widths	—	1, 1	glGetFloatv()
GL_SMOOTH_LINE_WIDTH_RANGE	Range (low to high) of antialiased line widths	—	1, 1	glGetFloatv()
GL_SMOOTH_LINE_WIDTH_GRANULARITY	Antialiased line-width granularity	—	—	glGetFloatv()
GL_MAX_CONVOLUTION_WIDTH	Maximum width of convolution filter	—	3	glConvolution Parameteriv()
GL_MAX_CONVOLUTION_HEIGHT	Maximum height of convolution filter	—	3	glConvolution Parameteriv()
GL_MAX_ELEMENTS_INDICES	Recommended maximum number of glDrawRangeElements() indices	—	—	glGetIntegerv()
GL_MAX_ELEMENTS_VERTICES	Recommended maximum number of glDrawRangeElements() vertices	—	—	glGetIntegerv()
GL_MAX_TEXTURE_UNITS	Maximum number of texture units (not to exceed 32)	—	2	glGetIntegerv()
GL_SAMPLE_BUFFERS	Number of multisample buffers	—	0	glGetIntegerv()
GL_SAMPLES	Coverage mask size	—	0	glGetIntegerv()

Table B-23 (continued)   Implementation-Dependent State Variables

State Variable	Description	Attribute Group	Minimum Value	Get Command
GL_MAX_SAMPLES	Maximum number of multisample samples	—	4	glGetIntegerv()
GL_MAX_COLOR_ATTACHMENTS	Maximum number of framebuffer object color attachment points	—	8	glGetIntegerv()
GL_COMPRESSED_TEXTURE_FORMATS	Enumerated compressed texture formats	—	—	glGetIntegerv()
GL_NUM_COMPRESSED_TEXTURE_FORMATS	Number of enumerated compressed texture formats	—	0	glGetIntegerv()
GL_QUERY_COUNTER_BITS	Number of bits in the occlusion query counter	—	—	glGetQueryiv()
GL_EXTENSIONS	Supported extensions	—	—	glGetStringi()
GL_NUM_EXTENSIONS	Number of supported extensions	—	—	glGetIntegerv()
GL_MAJOR_VERSION	Major version number	—	—	glGetIntegerv()
GL_MINOR_VERSION	Minor version number	—	—	glGetIntegerv()
GL_CONTEXT_FLAGS	Value for full- or forward-compatible context flag	—	—	glGetIntegerv()
GL_RENDERER	Renderer string	—	—	glGetString()

Table B-23 (continued)   Implementation-Dependent State Variables

State Variable	Description	Attribute Group	Minimum Value	Get Command
GL_SHADING_LANGUAGE_VERSION	OpenGL Shading Language (GLSL) version	—	—	glGetString()
GL_VENDOR	Vendor string	—	—	glGetString()
GL_VERSION	Version string	—	—	glGetString()
GL_MAX_VERTEX_ATTRIBS	Number of active vertex attributes	—	16	glGetIntegerv()
GL_MAX_VERTEX_UNIFORM_COMPONENTS	Number of words for vertex shader uniform variables	—	512	glGetIntegerv()
GL_MAX_VARYING_COMPONENTS (which replaces GL_MAX_VARYING_FLOATS in Version 3.0 and greater)	Number of floats for varying variables	—	32	glGetIntegerv()
GL_MAX_COMBINED_TEXTURE_IMAGE_UNITS	Total number of texture units accessible by OpenGL	—	2	glGetIntegerv()
GL_MAX_VERTEX_TEXTURE_IMAGE_UNITS	Number of texture image units accessible by a vertex shader	—	0	glGetIntegerv()
GL_MAX_TEXTURE_IMAGE_UNITS	Number of texture image units accessible by fragment processing	—	2	glGetIntegerv()
GL_MAX_TEXTURE_COORDS	Number of texture-coordinate sets	—	2	glGetIntegerv()

Table B-23 (continued)   Implementation-Dependent State Variables

State Variable	Description	Attribute Group	Minimum Value	Get Command
GL_MAX_TEXTURE_BUFFER_SIZE	Number of addressable texels for buffer textures	—	65536	glGetIntegerv()
GL_MAX_RECTANGLE_TEXTURE_SIZE	Maximum width and height of rectangular textures	—	1024	glGetIntegerv()
GL_MAX_FRAGMENT_UNIFORM_COMPONENTS	Number of words for fragment shader uniform variables	—	64	glGetIntegerv()
GL_MIN_PROGRAM_TEXEL_OFFSET	Minimum texel offset allowed in texel lookup	—	−8	glGetIntegerv()
GL_MAX_PROGRAM_TEXEL_OFFSET	Maximum texel offset allowed in texel lookup	—	7	glGetIntegerv()
GL_MAX_DRAW_BUFFERS	Maximum number of active draw buffers	—	1+	glGetIntegerv()
GL_MAX_VERTEX_UNIFORM_BLOCKS	Maximum number of vertex uniform buffers per program	—	12	glGetIntegerv()
GL_MAX_FRAGMENT_UNIFORM_BLOCKS	Maximum number of fragment uniform buffers per program	—	12	glGetIntegerv()
GL_MAX_COMBINED_UNIFORM_BLOCKS	Maximum number of combined uniform buffers per program	—	24	glGetIntegerv()

Table B-23 (continued)   Implementation-Dependent State Variables

State Variable	Description	Attribute Group	Minimum Value	Get Command
GL_MAX_UNIFORM_BUFFER_BINDINGS	Maximum number of uniform buffer binding points per context	—	24	glGetIntegerv()
GL_MAX_UNIFORM_BLOCK_SIZE	Maximum size in machine units of a uniform block	—	16384	glGetIntegerv()
GL_UNIFORM_BUFFER_OFFSET_ALIGNMENT	Minimum required alignment for uniform buffer sizes and offsets	—	1	glGetIntegerv()
GL_MAX_VERTEX_UNIFORM_COMPONENTS	Number of words for vertex shader uniform variables in default uniform block	—	1	glGetIntegerv()
GL_MAX_FRAGMENT_UNIFORM_COMPONENTS	Number of words for fragment shader uniform variables in default uniform block	—	1	glGetIntegerv()
GL_MAX_COMBINED_VERTEX_UNIFORM_COMPONENTS	Number of words for vertex shader uniform variables in all uniform blocks (including the default uniform block)	—	1	glGetIntegerv()
GL_MAX_COMBINED_FRAGMENT_UNIFORM_COMPONENTS	Number of words for fragment shader uniform variables in all uniform blocks (including the default uniform block)	—	1	glGetIntegerv()

Table B-23 (continued)   Implementation-Dependent State Variables

Implementation-Dependent Pixel Depths

State Variable	Description	Attribute Group	Minimum Value	Get Command
GL_x_BITS	Number of bits in *x* color buffer component (*x* is one of RED, GREEN, BLUE, ALPHA, or INDEX)	—	—	glGetIntegerv()
GL_DEPTH_BITS	Number of depth-buffer bitplanes	—	—	glGetIntegerv()
GL_STENCIL_BITS	Number of stencil bitplanes	—	—	glGetIntegerv()
GL_ACCUM_x_BITS	Number of bits in *x* accumulation buffer component (*x* is one of RED, GREEN, BLUE, or ALPHA)	—	—	glGetIntegerv()

Table B-24   Implementation-Dependent Pixel-Depth State Variables

Miscellaneous

State Variable	Description	Attribute Group	Initial Value	Get Command
GL_LIST_BASE	Setting of glListBase()	list	0	glGetIntegerv()
GL_LIST_INDEX	Number of display list under construction; 0 if none	—	0	glGetIntegerv()
GL_LIST_MODE	Mode of display list under construction; undefined if none	—	0	glGetIntegerv()

Table B-25   Miscellaneous State Variables

State Variable	Description	Attribute Group	Initial Value	Get Command
GL_ATTRIB_STACK_DEPTH	Attribute stack pointer	—	0	glGetIntegerv()
GL_CLIENT_ATTRIB_STACK_DEPTH	Client attribute stack pointer	—	0	glGetIntegerv()
GL_NAME_STACK_DEPTH	Name stack depth	—	0	glGetIntegerv()
GL_RENDER_MODE	glRenderMode() setting	—	GL_RENDER	glGetIntegerv()
GL_SELECTION_BUFFER_POINTER	Pointer to selection buffer	select	0	glGetPointerv()
GL_SELECTION_BUFFER_SIZE	Size of selection buffer	select	0	glGetIntegerv()
GL_FEEDBACK_BUFFER_POINTER	Pointer to feedback buffer	feedback	0	glGetPointerv()
GL_FEEDBACK_BUFFER_SIZE	Size of feedback buffer	feedback	0	glGetIntegerv()
GL_FEEDBACK_BUFFER_TYPE	Type of feedback buffer	feedback	GL_2D	glGetIntegerv()
—	Current error code(s)	—	0	glGetError()
GL_CURRENT_QUERY	Active occlusion query ID	—	0	glGetQueryiv()
GL_COPY_READ_BUFFER	Buffer object bound to copy buffer "read" bind point	—	0	glGetIntegerv()
GL_COPY_WRITE_BUFFER	Buffer object bound to copy buffer "write" bind point	—	0	glGetIntegerv()
GL_TEXTURE_BUFFER	Buffer object bound to texture buffer bind point	—	0	glGetIntegerv()

Table B-25 (continued)   Miscellaneous State Variables

Appendix C

Homogeneous Coordinates and Transformation Matrices

This appendix presents a brief discussion of homogeneous coordinates. It also lists the forms of the transformation matrices used for rotation, scaling, translation, perspective projection, and orthographic projection. These topics are introduced and discussed in Chapter 3. For a more detailed discussion of these subjects, see almost any book on three-dimensional computer graphics—for example, *Computer Graphics: Principles and Practice,* by Foley, van Dam, Feiner, and Hughes (Addison-Wesley, 1990); or a text on projective geometry—for example, *The Real Projective Plane,* by H. S. M. Coxeter, 2nd ed. (Cambridge University Press, 1961). In the discussion that follows, the term *homogeneous coordinates* always means three-dimensional homogeneous coordinates, although projective geometries exist for all dimensions.

This appendix has the following major sections:

* "Homogeneous Coordinates"

* "Transformation Matrices"

Homogeneous Coordinates

OpenGL commands usually deal with two- and three-dimensional vertices, but in fact all are treated internally as three-dimensional homogeneous vertices comprising four coordinates. Every column vector $(x, y, z, w)^T$ represents a homogeneous vertex if at least one of its elements is nonzero. If the real number a is nonzero, then $(x, y, z, w)^T$ and $(ax, ay, az, aw)^T$ represent the same homogeneous vertex. (This is just like fractions: $x/y = (ax)/(ay)$.) A three-dimensional Euclidean space point $(x, y, z)^T$ becomes the homogeneous vertex with coordinates $(x, y, z, 1.0)^T$, and the two-dimensional Euclidean point $(x, y)^T$ becomes $(x, y, 0.0, 1.0)^T$.

As long as w is nonzero, the homogeneous vertex $(x, y, z, w)^T$ corresponds to the three-dimensional point $(x/w, y/w, z/w)^T$. If $w = 0.0$, it corresponds to no Euclidean point, but rather to some idealized "point at infinity." To understand this point at infinity, consider the point $(1, 2, 0, 0)$, and note that the sequence of points $(1, 2, 0, 1)$, $(1, 2, 0, 0.01)$, and $(1, 2.0, 0.0, 0.0001)$ corresponds to the Euclidean points $(1, 2)$, $(100, 200)$, and $(10,000, 20,000)$. This sequence represents points rapidly moving toward infinity along the line $2x = y$. Thus, you can think of $(1, 2, 0, 0)$ as the point at infinity in the direction of that line.

Note: OpenGL might not handle homogeneous clip coordinates with $w < 0$ correctly. To be sure that your code is portable to all OpenGL systems, use only non-negative w-values.

Transforming Vertices

Vertex transformations (such as rotations, translations, scaling, and shearing) and projections (such as perspective and orthographic) can all be represented by applying an appropriate 4×4 matrix to the coordinates representing the vertex. If $\mathbf{v}$ represents a homogeneous vertex and $\mathbf{M}$ is a 4×4 transformation matrix, then $\mathbf{Mv}$ is the image of $\mathbf{v}$ under the transformation by $\mathbf{M}$. (In computer-graphics applications, the transformations used are usually nonsingular—in other words, the matrix $\mathbf{M}$ can be inverted. This isn't required, but some problems arise with singular matrices.)

After transformation, all transformed vertices are clipped so that x, y, and z are in the range $[-w, w]$ (assuming $w > 0$). Note that this range corresponds in Euclidean space to $[-1.0, 1.0]$.

Transforming Normals

Normal vectors aren't transformed in the same way as vertices or position vectors are. Mathematically, it's better to think of normal vectors not as vectors, but as planes perpendicular to those vectors. Then, the transformation rules for normal vectors are described by the transformation rules for perpendicular planes.

A homogeneous plane is denoted by the row vector (a, b, c, d), where at least one of a, b, c, and d is nonzero. If q is a nonzero real number, then (a, b, c, d) and (qa, qb, qc, qd) represent the same plane. A point $(x, y, z, w)^T$ is on the plane (a, b, c, d) if $ax + by + cz + dw = 0$. (If $w = 1$, this is the standard description of a Euclidean plane.) In order for (a, b, c, d) to represent a Euclidean plane, at least one of a, b, or c must be nonzero. If they're all zero, then $(0, 0, 0, d)$ represents the "plane at infinity," which contains all the "points at infinity."

If $\mathbf{p}$ is a homogeneous plane and $\mathbf{v}$ is a homogeneous vertex, then the statement "$\mathbf{v}$ lies on plane $\mathbf{p}$" is written mathematically as $\mathbf{pv} = 0$, where $\mathbf{pv}$ is normal matrix multiplication. If $\mathbf{M}$ is a nonsingular vertex transformation (that is, a 4×4 matrix that has an inverse $\mathbf{M}^{-1}$), then $\mathbf{pv} = 0$ is equivalent to $\mathbf{pM}^{-1}\mathbf{Mv} = 0$, so $\mathbf{Mv}$ lies in the plane $\mathbf{pM}^{-1}$. Thus, $\mathbf{pM}^{-1}$ is the image of the plane under the vertex transformation $\mathbf{M}$.

If you like to think of normal vectors as vectors instead of as the planes perpendicular to them, let $\mathbf{v}$ and $\mathbf{n}$ be vectors such that $\mathbf{v}$ is perpendicular to $\mathbf{n}$. Then, $\mathbf{n}^T\mathbf{v} = 0$. Thus, for an arbitrary nonsingular transformation $\mathbf{M}$, $\mathbf{n}^T\mathbf{M}^{-1}\mathbf{Mv} = 0$, which means that $\mathbf{n}^T\mathbf{M}^{-1}$ is the transpose of the transformed normal vector. Thus, the transformed normal vector is $(\mathbf{M}^{-1})^T\mathbf{n}$. In other words, normal vectors are transformed by the inverse transpose of the transformation that transforms points. Whew!

Transformation Matrices

Although any nonsingular matrix $\mathbf{M}$ represents a valid projective transformation, a few special matrices are particularly useful. These matrices are listed in the following subsections.

Translation

The call **glTranslate***(x, y, z) generates **T**, where

$$\mathbf{T} = \begin{bmatrix} 1 & 0 & 0 & x \\ 0 & 1 & 0 & y \\ 0 & 0 & 1 & z \\ 0 & 0 & 0 & 1 \end{bmatrix} \text{ and } \mathbf{T}^{-1} = \begin{bmatrix} 1 & 0 & 0 & -x \\ 0 & 1 & 0 & -y \\ 0 & 0 & 1 & -z \\ 0 & 0 & 0 & 1 \end{bmatrix}$$

Scaling

The call **glScale***(x, y, z) generates **S**, where

$$\mathbf{S} = \begin{bmatrix} x & 0 & 0 & 0 \\ 0 & y & 0 & 0 \\ 0 & 0 & z & 0 \\ 0 & 0 & 0 & 1 \end{bmatrix} \text{ and } \mathbf{S}^{-1} = \begin{bmatrix} \frac{1}{x} & 0 & 0 & 0 \\ 0 & \frac{1}{y} & 0 & 0 \\ 0 & 0 & \frac{1}{z} & 0 \\ 0 & 0 & 0 & 1 \end{bmatrix}$$

Notice that $\mathbf{S}^{-1}$ is defined only if x, y, and z are all nonzero.

Rotation

The call **glRotate***(a, x, y, z) generates **R** as follows:

Let $\mathbf{v} = (x, y, z)^{\mathrm{T}}$, and $\mathbf{u} = \mathbf{v}/\|\mathbf{v}\| = (x', y', z')^{\mathrm{T}}$.

Also let

$$\mathbf{S} = \begin{bmatrix} 0 & -z' & y' \\ z' & 0 & -x' \\ -y' & x' & 0 \end{bmatrix} \text{ and } \mathbf{M} = \mathbf{u}\mathbf{u}^{\mathrm{T}} + (\cos a)(\mathbf{I} - \mathbf{u}\mathbf{u}^{\mathrm{T}}) + (\sin a)\,\mathbf{S}$$

Then

$$\mathbf{R} = \begin{bmatrix} m & m & m & 0 \\ m & m & m & 0 \\ m & m & m & 0 \\ 0 & 0 & 0 & 1 \end{bmatrix}$$

where *m* represent the elements from **M**, which is the 3 × 3 matrix defined on the preceding page. The **R** matrix is always defined. If $x = y = z = 0$, then **R** is the identity matrix. You can obtain the inverse of **R**, $\mathbf{R}^{-1}$, by substituting $-a$ for a, or by transposition.

The **glRotate*()** command generates a matrix for rotation about an arbitrary axis. Often, you're rotating about one of the coordinate axes; the corresponding matrices are as follows:

glRotate*(*a*, 1, 0, 0): $\begin{bmatrix} 1 & 0 & 0 & 0 \\ 0 & \cos a & -\sin a & 0 \\ 0 & \sin a & \cos a & 0 \\ 0 & 0 & 0 & 1 \end{bmatrix}$

glRotate*(*a*, 0, 1, 0): $\begin{bmatrix} \cos a & 0 & \sin a & 0 \\ 0 & 1 & 0 & 0 \\ -\sin a & 0 & \cos a & 0 \\ 0 & 0 & 0 & 1 \end{bmatrix}$

glRotate*(*a*, 0, 0, 1): $\begin{bmatrix} \cos a & -\sin a & 0 & 0 \\ \sin a & \cos a & 0 & 0 \\ 0 & 0 & 1 & 0 \\ 0 & 0 & 0 & 1 \end{bmatrix}$

As before, the inverses are obtained by transposition.

Perspective Projection

The call **glFrustum**(*l*, *r*, *b*, *t*, *n*, *f*) generates **R**, where

$$\mathbf{R} = \begin{bmatrix} \dfrac{2n}{r-l} & 0 & \dfrac{r+l}{r-l} & 0 \\ 0 & \dfrac{2n}{t-b} & \dfrac{t+b}{t-b} & 0 \\ 0 & 0 & \dfrac{-(f+n)}{f-n} & \dfrac{-2fn}{f-n} \\ 0 & 0 & -1 & 0 \end{bmatrix} \text{ and } \mathbf{R}^{-1} = \begin{bmatrix} \dfrac{r-l}{2n} & 0 & 0 & \dfrac{r+l}{2n} \\ 0 & \dfrac{t-b}{2n} & 0 & \dfrac{t+b}{2n} \\ 0 & 0 & 0 & -1 \\ 0 & 0 & \dfrac{-(f-n)}{2fn} & \dfrac{f+n}{2fn} \end{bmatrix}$$

R is defined as long as $l \neq r$, $t \neq b$, and $n \neq f$.

Orthographic Projection

The call **glOrtho(**l, r, b, t, n, f **)** generates **R**, where

$$\mathbf{R} = \begin{bmatrix} \dfrac{2}{r-l} & 0 & 0 & -\dfrac{r+l}{r-l} \\[2ex] 0 & \dfrac{2}{t-b} & 0 & -\dfrac{t+b}{t-b} \\[2ex] 0 & 0 & \dfrac{-2}{f-n} & \dfrac{f+n}{f-n} \\[2ex] 0 & 0 & 0 & 1 \end{bmatrix} \text{ and } \mathbf{R}^{-1} = \begin{bmatrix} \dfrac{r-l}{2} & 0 & 0 & \dfrac{r+l}{2} \\[2ex] 0 & \dfrac{t-b}{2} & 0 & \dfrac{t+b}{2} \\[2ex] 0 & 0 & \dfrac{f-n}{-2} & \dfrac{n+f}{2} \\[2ex] 0 & 0 & 0 & 1 \end{bmatrix}$$

R is defined as long as $l \neq r$, $t \neq b$, and $n \neq f$.

OpenGL and Window Systems

OpenGL is available on many different platforms and works with many different window systems. It is designed to complement window systems, not duplicate their functionality. Therefore, OpenGL performs geometric and image rendering in two and three dimensions, but it does not manage windows or handle input events.

However, the basic definitions of most window systems don't support a library as sophisticated as OpenGL, with its complex and diverse pixel formats, including depth, stencil, and accumulation buffers, as well as double-buffering. For most window systems, some routines are added to extend the window system to support OpenGL.

This appendix introduces the extensions defined for several window and operating systems: the X Window System, the Apple Mac OS, and Microsoft Windows. You need to have some knowledge of the window systems to fully understand this appendix.

This appendix has the following major sections:

- "Accessing New OpenGL Functions"

- "GLX: OpenGL Extension for the X Window System"

- "AGL: OpenGL Extensions for the Apple Macintosh"

- "WGL: OpenGL Extension for Microsoft Windows 95/98/NT/ME/2000/XP"

Accessing New OpenGL Functions

OpenGL is changing all the time. The manufacturers of OpenGL graphics hardware add new extensions and the Khronos OpenGL ARB Working Group approve those extensions and merge them into the core of OpenGL. Since each manufacturer needs to be able to update its version of OpenGL, the header files (like gl.h), and the library you use to compile (like opengl32.lib, on Microsoft Windows, for example) may be out of sync with the latest version. This would likely cause errors when compiling (or more specifically, linking) your application.

To help you work around this problem, a mechanism for accessing the new functions was added to each of the window system libraries. This method varies among the different window systems, but the idea is the same in all cases. You will need to retrieve function pointers for the functions that you want to use. You need to do this only if the function is not available explicitly from your library (you'll know when it isn't; you'll get a linker error).

Each window system has its own function for getting an OpenGL function pointer; check the respective section in this appendix for specifics.

Here is an example for Microsoft Windows:

```
#include <windows.h>   /* for wglGetProcAddress() */
#include "glext.h"

PFNGLBINDPROGRAMARBPROC  glBindProgramARB;

void
init(void)
{
   glBindProgramARB = (PFNGLBINDPROGRAMARB)
     wglGetProcAddress("glBindProgramARB");
   ...
}
```

The function pointer type—in this case, PFNGLBINDPROGRAMARBPROC—is defined in glext.h, as are all of the enumerants that you pass into OpenGL functions. If the returned value is zero (effectively a NULL pointer), the function is not available in the OpenGL implementation that your program is using.

GLUT includes a similar routine, **glutGetProcAddress()**, which simply wraps the window-system dependent routine.

It's not sufficient in all cases to merely retrieve a function pointer to determine if functionality is present. To verify that the extension the functionality is defined from is available, check the extension string (see "The Query Commands" in Appendix B for details).

GLEW: The OpenGL Extension Wrangler

To simplify both verifying extension support and dealing with the associated function pointers, we recommend using the open-source GLEW library (http://glew.sourceforge.net/) developed by Milan Ikits and Marcelo Magallon, which manages this process simply and elegantly.

To incorporate GLEW into your applications, follow these three simple steps:

1. Replace the OpenGL and glext.h header files with those of GLEW: glew.h

2. Initialize GLEW by calling **glewInit()** after you've created your window (or more specifically, your OpenGL context). This causes GLEW to query and retrieve all available function pointers from your implementation as well as to provide a convenient set of variables for determining whether a particular version or extension is supported.

3. Verify that the extension containing the functionality you want to use is available. GLEW provides a set of Boolean variables named after the extension (for example, GL_ARB_map_buffer_range is the variable name for the OpenGL map buffer range extension). If the variable's value is true, you can use the extension's functions.

Here's a short example using our **init()** routine, which is executed after calling **glutCreateWindow()**:

```
#include <GLEW.h>

void
init()
{
    GLuint vao;

    glewInit(); // Initialize the GLEW library

    if ( GLEW_VERSION_3_0 ) {
        // We know that we're using OpenGL Version 3.0, and
        // that vertex array objects are supported
```

```
        glGenVertexArrays( 1, &vao );
        glBindVertexArray( vao );
    }

    // Initialize and bind all other vertex arrays
    ...
}
```

We can use one of GLEW's variables, `GLEW_VERSION_3_0`, in this case to determine our OpenGL version and make decisions about use of features.

GLX: OpenGL Extension for the X Window System

In the X Window System, OpenGL rendering is made available as an extension to X in the formal X sense. GLX is an extension to the X protocol (and its associated API) for communicating OpenGL commands to an extended X server. Connection and authentication are accomplished with the normal X mechanisms.

As with other X extensions, there is a defined network protocol for OpenGL's rendering commands encapsulated within the X byte stream, so client-server OpenGL rendering is supported. Since performance is critical in three-dimensional rendering, the OpenGL extension to X allows OpenGL to bypass the X server's involvement in data encoding, copying, and interpretation, and instead render directly to the graphics pipeline.

GLX Version 1.3 introduces several sweeping changes, starting with the new GLXFBConfig data structure, which describes the GLX framebuffer configuration (including the depth of the color buffer components, and the types, quantities, and sizes of the depth, stencil, accumulation, and auxiliary buffers). The GLXFBConfig structure describes these framebuffer attributes for a GLXDrawable rendering surface. (In X, a rendering surface is called a *Drawable*.)

GLX 1.3 also provides for three types of GLXDrawable surfaces: GLXWindow, GLXPixmap, and GLXPbuffer. A GLXWindow is on-screen; a GLXPixmap or GLXPbuffer is off-screen. Because a GLXPixmap has an associated X pixmap, both X and GLX may render into a GLXPixmap. GLX may be the only way to render into a GLXPbuffer. The GLXPbuffer is intended to store pixel data in nonvisible framebuffer memory. (Off-screen rendering isn't guaranteed to be supported for direct renderers.)

GLX version 1.4 increased support for framebuffer configuration by adding drawable configuration options for number of buffers and samples for multisampled drawables.

The X Visual is an important data structure for maintaining pixel format information about an OpenGL window. A variable of data type XVisualInfo keeps track of pixel format information, including pixel type (RGBA or color-index), single- or double-buffering, resolution of colors, and presence of depth, stencil, and accumulation buffers. The standard X Visuals (for example, PseudoColor, and TrueColor) do not describe the pixel format details, so each implementation must extend the number of X Visuals supported.

In GLX 1.3, a GLXWindow has an X Visual, associated with its GLXFBConfig. For a GLXPixmap or a GLXPbuffer, there may or may not be a similar associated X Visual. Prior to GLX 1.3, all surfaces (windows or pixmaps) were associated with an X Visual. (Prior to 1.3, Pbuffers were not part of GLX.)

The GLX routines are discussed in more detail in the *OpenGL Reference Manual*. Integrating OpenGL applications with the X Window System and the Motif widget set is discussed in great detail in *OpenGL Programming for the X Window System* by Mark Kilgard (Addison-Wesley, 1996), which includes full source code examples. If you absolutely want to learn about the internals of GLX, you may want to read the GLX specification, which can be found at

```
http://www.opengl.org/developers/documentation/glx.html
```

Initialization

Use **glXQueryExtension()** and **glXQueryVersion()** to determine whether the GLX extension is defined for an X server and, if so, which version is present. **glXQueryExtensionsString()** returns extension information about the client-server connection. **glXGetClientString()** returns information about the client library, including extensions and version number. **glXQueryServerString()** returns similar information about the server.

glXChooseFBConfig() returns a pointer to an array of GLXFBConfig structures describing all GLX framebuffer configurations that meet the client's specified attributes. You may use **glXGetFBConfigAttrib()** to query a framebuffer configuration about its support of a particular GLX attribute. You may also call **glXGetVisualFromFBConfig()** to retrieve the X visual associated with a GLXFBConfig.

Creation of rendering areas varies slightly, depending on the type of drawable. For a GLXWindow, first create an X Window with an X visual that corresponds to the GLXFBConfig. Then use that X Window when calling **glXCreateWindow()**, which returns a GLXWindow. Similarly for a GLXPixmap, first create an X Pixmap with a pixel depth that matches the GLXFBConfig. Then use that Pixmap when calling **glXCreatePixmap()** to create a GLXPixmap. A GLXPbuffer does not require an X Window or an X Pixmap; just call **glXCreatePbuffer()** with the appropriate GLXFBConfig.

Note: If you are using GLX 1.2 or earlier, you do not have a GLXFBConfig structure. Instead, use **glXChooseVisual()**, which returns a pointer to an XVisualInfo structure describing the X visual that meets the client's specified attributes. You can query a visual about its support of a particular OpenGL attribute with **glXGetConfig()**. To render to an off-screen pixmap, you must use the earlier **glXCreateGLXPixmap()** routine.

Accessing OpenGL Functions

To access function pointers for extensions and new features in the X Window System, use the **glXGetProcAddress()** function. This function is defined in the glxext.h header file, which can be downloaded from the OpenGL Web site.

Controlling Rendering

Several GLX routines are provided for creating and managing an OpenGL rendering context. Routines are also provided for such tasks as handling GLX events, synchronizing execution between the X and OpenGL streams, swapping front and back buffers, and using an X font.

Managing an OpenGL Rendering Context

An OpenGL rendering context is created with either **glXCreateNewContext()** or **glXCreateContextAttribsARB()**, whose use is required in OpenGL Version 3.0 and greater. One of the arguments to these routines allows you to request a direct rendering context that bypasses the X server as described previously. (To perform direct rendering, the X server connection must be local, and the OpenGL implementation needs to support direct rendering.) Another argument also allows display-list and texture-object indices and definitions to be shared by multiple rendering contexts. You can determine whether a GLX context is direct with **glXIsDirect()**.

glXMakeContextCurrent() binds a rendering context to the current rendering thread and also establishes two current drawable surfaces. You can draw into one of the current drawable surfaces and read pixel data from the other drawable. In many situations, the *draw* and *read* drawables refer to the same GLXDrawable surface. **glXGetCurrentContext()** returns the current context. You can also obtain the current *draw* drawable with **glXGetCurrentDrawable()**, the current *read* drawable with **glXGetCurrentReadDrawable()**, and the current X Display with **glXGetCurrentDisplay()**. You can use **glXQueryContext()** to determine the current values for context attributes.

Only one context can be current for any thread at any one time. If you have multiple contexts, you can copy selected groups of OpenGL state variables from one context to another with **glXCopyContext()**. When you're finished with a particular context, destroy it with **glXDestroyContext()**.

Note: If you are using GLX 1.2 or earlier, use **glXCreateContext()** to create a rendering context and **glXMakeCurrent()** to make it current. You cannot declare a drawable as a separate *read* drawable, so you do not have **glXGetCurrentReadDrawable()**.

Handling GLX Events

GLX 1.3 introduces GLX events, which are returned in the event stream of standard X11 events. GLX event handling has been added specifically to deal with the uncertainty of the contents of a GLXPbuffer, which may be clobbered at any time. In GLX 1.3, you may use **glXSelectEvent()** to select only one event with GLX_PBUFFER_CLOBBER_MASK. With standard X event handling routines, you can now determine if a portion of a GLXPbuffer (or GLXWindow) has been damaged and then take steps, if desired, to recover. (Also, you can call **glXGetSelectedEvent()** to find out if you are already monitoring this GLX event.)

Synchronizing Execution

To prevent X requests from executing until any outstanding OpenGL rendering is completed, call **glXWaitGL()**. Then, any previously issued OpenGL commands are guaranteed to be executed before any X rendering calls made after **glXWaitGL()**. Although the same result can be achieved with **glFinish()**, **glXWaitGL()** doesn't require a round-trip to the server and thus is more efficient in cases where the client and server are on separate machines.

To prevent an OpenGL command sequence from executing until any out-standing X requests are completed, use **glXWaitX()**. This routine guarantees that previously issued X rendering calls are executed before any OpenGL calls made after **glXWaitX()**.

Swapping Buffers

For drawables that are double-buffered, the front and back buffers can be exchanged by calling **glXSwapBuffers()**. An implicit **glFlush()** is done as part of this routine.

Using an X Font

A shortcut for using X fonts in OpenGL is provided with the command **glXUseXFont()**. This routine builds display lists, each of which calls **glBitmap()** for each requested character from the specified font and font size.

Cleaning Up Drawables

Once rendering is completed, you can destroy the drawable surface with the appropriate call to **glXDestroyWindow()**, **glXDestroyPixmap()**, or **glXDestroyPbuffer()**. (These routines are not available prior to GLX 1.3, although there is **glXDestroyGLXPixmap()**, which is similar to **glXDestroyPixmap()**.)

GLX Prototypes

Initialization

Determine whether the GLX extension is defined on the X server:

> Bool **glXQueryExtension**(Display *dpy*, int *errorBase*,
>   int *eventBase*);

Query version and extension information for client and server:

> Bool **glXQueryVersion**(Display *dpy*, int *major*, int *minor*);
>
> const char* **glXGetClientString**(Display *dpy*, int *name*);
>
> const char* **glXQueryServerString**(Display *dpy*, int *screen*,
>   int *name*);
>
> const char* **glXQueryExtensionsString**(Display *dpy*, int *screen*);

Obtain available GLX framebuffer configurations:

> GLXFBConfig * **glXGetFBConfigs**(Display *dpy*, int *screen*,
>   int **nelements*);

> GLXFBConfig * **glXChooseFBConfig**(Display *dpy*, int *screen*,
>   const int *attribList*, int **nelements*);

Query a GLX framebuffer configuration for attribute or X Visual
information:

> int **glXGetFBConfigAttrib**(Display *dpy*, GLXFBConfig *config*,
>   int *attribute*, int **value*);

> XVisualInfo * **glXGetVisualFromFBConfig**(Display *dpy*,
>   GLXFBConfig *config*);

Create surfaces that support rendering (both on-screen and off-screen):

> GLXWindow **glXCreateWindow**(Display *dpy*,
>   GLXFBConfig *config*, Window *win*, const int **attribList*);

> GLXPixmap **glXCreatePixmap**(Display *dpy*, GLXFBConfig *config*,
>   Pixmap *pixmap*, const int **attribList*);

> GLXPbuffer **glXCreatePbuffer**(Display *dpy*, GLXFBConfig *config*,
>   const int **attribList*);

Obtain a pointer to an OpenGL function:

> __GLXextFuncPtr **glXGetProcAddress**(const char* *funcName*);

Controlling Rendering

Manage and query an OpenGL rendering context:

> GLXContext **glXCreateNewContext**(Display *dpy*,
>   GLXFBConfig *config*, int *renderType*, GLXContext *shareList*,
>   Bool *direct*);

> GLXContext **glXCreateContextAttribsARB** (Display *dpy*,
>   GLXFBConfig *config*, GLXContext *shareList*, Bool *direct*,
>   const int **attribs*);

> Bool **glXMakeContextCurrent**(Display *dpy*,
>   GLXDrawable *drawable*, GLXDrawable *read*, GLXContext *context*);

> void **glXCopyContext**(Display *dpy*, GLXContext *source*,
>   GLXContext *dest*, unsigned long *mask*);

Bool **glXIsDirect**(Display *dpy*, GLXContext *context*);

GLXContext **glXGetCurrentContext**(void);

Display* **glXGetCurrentDisplay**(void);

GLXDrawable **glXGetCurrentDrawable**(void);

GLXDrawable **glXGetCurrentReadDrawable**(void);

int **glXQueryContext**(Display *dpy*, GLXContext *context*,
  int *attribute*, int *value*);

void **glXDestroyContext**(Display *dpy*, GLXContext *context*);

Ask to receive and query GLX events:

int **glXSelectEvent**(Display *dpy*, GLXDrawable *drawable*,
  unsigned long *eventMask*);

int **glXGetSelectedEvent**(Display *dpy*, GLXDrawable *drawable*,
  unsigned long *eventMask*);

Synchronize execution:

void **glXWaitGL**(void);

void **glXWaitX**(void);

Exchange front and back buffers:

void **glXSwapBuffers**(Display *dpy*, GLXDrawable *drawable*);

Use an X font:

void **glXUseXFont**(Font *font*, int *first*, int *count*, int *listBase*);

Clean up drawables:

void **glXDestroyWindow**(Display *dpy*, GLXWindow *win*);

void **glXDestroyPixmap**(Display *dpy*, GLXPixmap *pixmap*);

void **glXDestroyPbuffer**(Display *dpy*, GLXPbuffer *pbuffer*);

Deprecated GLX Prototypes

The following routines have been deprecated in GLX 1.3. If you are using
GLX 1.2 or a predecessor, you may need to use several of these routines.

Obtain the desired visual:

XVisualInfo* **glXChooseVisual**(Display **dpy*, int *screen*,
int **attribList*);

int **glXGetConfig**(Display **dpy*, XVisualInfo **visual*, int *attrib*,
int **value*);

Manage an OpenGL rendering context:

GLXContext **glXCreateContext**(Display **dpy*, XVisualInfo **visual*,
GLXContext *shareList*, Bool *direct*);

Bool **glXMakeCurrent**(Display **dpy*, GLXDrawable *drawable*,
GLXContext *context*);

Perform off-screen rendering:

GLXPixmap **glXCreateGLXPixmap**(Display **dpy*,
XVisualInfo **visual*, Pixmap *pixmap*);

void **glXDestroyGLXPixmap**(Display **dpy*, GLXPixmap *pix*);

AGL: OpenGL Extensions for the Apple Macintosh

This section covers the routines defined as the OpenGL extension to the
Apple Macintosh (AGL). An understanding of the way the Macintosh
handles graphics rendering is required. The *OpenGL Programming Guide
for Mac OS X* contains a complete reference for using OpenGL within
Apple's Mac OS X operating system (accessible on the Internet at
`http://developer.apple.com/DOCUMENTATION/GraphicsImaging/`
`Conceptual/OpenGL-MacProgGuide/opengl_intro/opengl_intro.html`.)

In addition to AGL, Mac OS X supports other interfaces for OpenGL: CGL
(Core OpenGL API), which is a low-level interface to OpenGL contexts
(not recommended for novice users); and NSOpenGL* routines, which are
part of Cocoa, Apple's set of media APIs. We only describe AGL in this
appendix, and refer the interested reader to Apple's Developer Web site:
`http://developer.apple.com/`.

The data type AGLPixelFormat (the AGL equivalent to XVisualInfo)
maintains pixel information, including pixel type (RGBA or color index);
single- or double-buffering; resolution of colors; and presence of depth,
stencil, and accumulation buffers.

Initialization

Use **aglGetVersion()** to determine which version of AGL for the Macintosh is available.

The capabilities of underlying graphics devices and your requirements for rendering buffers are resolved using **aglChoosePixelFormat()**. It returns an AGLPixelFormat structure or NULL, depending on whether or not your requirements can be accommodated.

Rendering and Contexts

Several AGL routines are provided for creating and managing an OpenGL rendering context. You can use such a context to render into either a window or an off-screen graphics world. Routines are also provided that allow you to swap front and back rendering buffers; adjust buffers in response to a move, resize, or graphics device change event; and use Macintosh fonts. For software rendering (and, in some cases, hardware-accelerated rendering), the rendering buffers are created in the system memory space.

Managing an OpenGL Rendering Context

An OpenGL rendering context is created (at least one context per window being rendered into) with **aglCreateContext()**. This takes the pixel format you selected as a parameter and uses it to initialize the context.

Use **aglSetDrawable()** to attach the context to the drawable and then **aglSetCurrentContext()** to make a rendering context current. Only one context can be current for a thread of control at any time. This indicates which drawable is to be rendered into and which context to use with it. It's possible for more than one context to be used (not simultaneously) with a particular drawable. Two routines allow you to determine the current rendering context and drawable being rendered into: **aglGetCurrentContext()** and **aglGetDrawable()**.

If you have multiple contexts, you can copy selected groups of OpenGL state variables from one context to another with **aglCopyContext()**. When a particular context is no longer needed, it should be destroyed by calling **aglDestroyContext()**.

On-Screen Rendering

To render on-screen, first create a pixel format. Create a context based on this pixel format and attach the context to the window with **aglSetDrawable()**. The buffer rectangle can be modified by calling **aglSetInteger(AGL_BUFFER_RECT, ...)**.

Off-Screen Rendering

To render off-screen, create a pixel format with the AGL_OFFSCREEN attribute. Create a context based on this pixel format and attach the context to the screen with **aglSetOffScreen()**.

Full-Screen Rendering

To render full-screen, create a pixel format with the AGL_FULLSCREEN attribute. Create a context based on this pixel format and attach the context to the screen with **aglSetFullScreen()**.

Swapping Buffers

For drawables that are double-buffered (as per the pixel format of the current rendering context), call **aglSwapBuffers()** to exchange the front and back buffers. The swap rectangle can be modified by calling **aglSetInteger(AGL_SWAP_RECT, ...)**. An implicit **glFlush()** is performed as part of this routine.

Updating the Rendering Buffers

The Apple Macintosh toolbox requires you to perform your own event handling and does not provide a way for libraries to hook into the event stream automatically. So that the drawables maintained by OpenGL can adjust to changes in drawable size, position, and pixel depth, **aglUpdateContext()** is provided.

This routine must be called by your event processing code whenever one of these events occurs in the current drawable. Ideally, the scene should be re-rendered after an update call to take into account the changes made to the rendering buffers.

Using an Apple Macintosh Font

A shortcut for using Macintosh fonts is provided with **aglUseFont()**. This routine builds display lists, each of which calls **glBitmap()** for each requested character from the specified font and font size.

Error Handling

An error-handling mechanism is provided for the Apple Macintosh OpenGL extension. When an error occurs, you can call **aglGetError()** to get a more precise description of what caused the error.

AGL Prototypes

Initialization

Determine version information:

> void **aglGetVersion**(GLint *major*, GLint *minor*);

Determine available pixel formats:

> AGLPixelFormat **aglCreatePixelFormat**(const GLint *attribs*);
>
> AGLPixelFormat **aglChoosePixelFormat**(const AGLDevice *gdevs*, GLint *ndev*, const GLint *attribs*);
>
> GLboolean **aglDescribePixelFormat**(AGLPixelFormat *pix*, GLint *attrib*, GLint *value*);
>
> void **aglDestroyPixelFormat**(AGLPixelFormat *pix*);
>
> AGLPixelFormat **aglNextPixelFormat**(AGLPixelFormat *pix*);
>
> AGLDevice *__aglDevicesOfPixelFormat__(AGLPixelFormat *pix*, GLint *ndevs*);

Renderer information functions:

AGLRendererInfo **aglQueryRendererInfo**(const AGLDevice *gdevs,
GLint ndev);

void **aglDestroyRendererInfo**(AGLRendererInfo rend);

AGLRendererInfo **aglNextRendererInfo**(AGLRendererInfo rend);

GLboolean **aglDescribeRenderer**(AGLRendererInfo rend,
GLint prop, GLint *value);

Controlling Rendering

Manage OpenGL rendering contexts:

AGLContext **aglCreateContext**(AGLPixelFormat pix,
AGLContext share);

GLboolean **aglDestroyContext**(AGLContext ctx);

GLboolean **aglCopyContext**(AGLContext src, AGLContext dst,
GLuint mask);

GLboolean **aglUpdateContext**(AGLContext ctx);

Current state functions:

GLboolean **aglSetCurrentContext**(AGLContext ctx);

AGLContext **aglGetCurrentContext**(void);

Drawable functions:

GLboolean **aglSetDrawable**(AGLContext ctx, AGLDrawable draw);

GLboolean **aglSetOffScreen**(AGLContext ctx, GLsizei width,
GLsizei height, GLsizei rowbytes, GLvoid *baseaddr);

GLboolean **aglSetFullScreen**(AGLContext ctx, GLsizei width,
GLsizei height, GLsizei freq, GLint device);

AGLDrawable **aglGetDrawable**(AGLContext ctx);

Virtual screen functions:

GLboolean **aglSetVirtualScreen**(AGLContext ctx, GLint screen);

GLint **aglGetVirtualScreen**(AGLContext ctx);

Configure global library option:

>   GLboolean **aglConfigure**(GLenum *pname*, GLuint *param*);

Swap function:

>   void **aglSwapBuffers**(AGLContext *ctx*);

Per context options:

>   GLboolean **aglEnable**(AGLContext *ctx*, GLenum *pname*);
>
>   GLboolean **aglDisable**(AGLContext *ctx*, GLenum *pname*);
>
>   GLboolean **aglIsEnabled**(AGLContext *ctx*, GLenum *pname*);
>
>   GLboolean **aglSetInteger**(AGLContext *ctx*, GLenum *pname*,
>   const GLint **params*);
>
>   GLboolean **aglGetInteger**(AGLContext *ctx*, GLenum *pname*,
>   GLint **params*);

Font function:

>   GLboolean **aglUseFont**(AGLContext *ctx*, GLint *fontID*, Style *face*,
>   GLint *size*, GLint *first*, GLint *count*, GLint *base*);

Error functions:

>   GLenum **aglGetError**(void);
>
>   const GLubyte ***aglErrorString**(GLenum *code*);

Soft reset function:

>   void **aglResetLibrary**(void);

WGL: OpenGL Extension for Microsoft Windows 95/98/NT/ME/2000/XP

OpenGL rendering is supported on systems that run any modern version of Microsoft Windows (from Windows 95 and later). The functions and routines of the Win32 library are necessary to initialize the pixel format and control rendering, and for access to extensions for OpenGL. Some routines, which are prefixed by **wgl**, extend Win32 so that OpenGL can be fully supported.

For Win32/WGL, the PIXELFORMATDESCRIPTOR is the key data structure for maintaining pixel format information about the OpenGL window. A variable of data type PIXELFORMATDESCRIPTOR keeps track of pixel information, including pixel type (RGBA or color-index); single- or double-buffering; resolution of colors; and presence of depth, stencil, and accumulation buffers.

To get more information about WGL, you may want to start with technical articles available through the Microsoft Developer Network Web site.

Initialization

Use **GetVersion()** or the newer **GetVersionEx()** to determine version information. **ChoosePixelFormat()** tries to find a PIXELFORMAT DESCRIPTOR with specified attributes. If a good match for the requested pixel format is found, then **SetPixelFormat()** should be called for actual use of the pixel format. You should select a pixel format in the device context before creating a rendering context.

If you want to find out details about a given pixel format, use **DescribePixelFormat()** or, for overlays or underlays, **wglDescribeLayerPlane()**.

Accessing OpenGL Functions

To access function pointers for extensions and new features in Microsoft Windows, use the **wglGetProcAddress()** function. This function is defined in the wingdi.h header file, which is automatically included when you include windows.h in your application.

Controlling Rendering

Several WGL routines are provided for creating and managing an OpenGL rendering context, rendering to a bitmap, swapping front and back buffers, finding a color palette, and using either bitmap or outline fonts.

Managing an OpenGL Rendering Context

wglCreateContext() and **wglCreateContextAttribsARB()** (the latter for use with OpenGL Version 3.0 and greater) create an OpenGL rendering context for drawing on the device in the selected pixel format of the device context. (To create an OpenGL rendering context for overlay or underlay windows, use **wglCreateLayerContext()** instead.) To make a rendering context current, use **wglMakeCurrent()**; **wglGetCurrentContext()** returns the current context. You can also obtain the current device context with **wglGetCurrentDC()**. You can copy some OpenGL state variables from one context to another with **wglCopyContext()** or make two contexts share the same display lists and texture objects with **wglShareLists()**. When you're finished with a particular context, destroy it with **wglDestroyContext()**.

Accessing OpenGL Extensions

Use **wglGetProcAddress()** to access implementation-specific OpenGL extension procedure calls. To determine which extensions are supported by your implementation, use **glGetString(GL_EXTENSIONS)**. **wglGetProcAddress()**, when passed the exact name of the extension returned from **glGetString()**, returns a function pointer for the extension procedure call, or returns NULL if the extension is not supported.

OpenGL Rendering to a Bitmap

Win32 has a few routines for allocating (and deallocating) bitmaps, to which you can render OpenGL directly. **CreateDIBitmap()** creates a device-dependent bitmap (DDB) from a device-independent bitmap (DIB). **CreateDIBSection()** creates a device-independent bitmap (DIB) that applications can write to directly. When finished with your bitmap, you can use **DeleteObject()** to free it up.

Synchronizing Execution

If you want to combine GDI and OpenGL rendering, be aware that there are no equivalents to functions such as **glXWaitGL()**, **glXWaitX()**, and **pglWaitGL()** in Win32. Although **glXWaitGL()** has no equivalent in Win32, you can achieve the same effect by calling **glFinish()**, which waits until all pending OpenGL commands are executed, or by calling **GdiFlush()**, which waits until all GDI drawing has been completed.

Swapping Buffers

For windows that are double-buffered, the front and back buffers can be exchanged by calling **SwapBuffers()** or **wglSwapLayerBuffers()**; the latter is used for overlays and underlays.

Finding a Color Palette

To access the color palette for the standard (nonlayer) bitplanes, use the standard GDI functions to set the palette entries. For overlay or underlay layers, use **wglRealizeLayerPalette()**, which maps palette entries from a given color-index layer plane into the physical palette or initializes the palette of an RGBA layer plane. **wglGetLayerPaletteEntries()** and **wglSetLayerPaletteEntries()** are used to query and set the entries in palettes of layer planes.

Using a Bitmap or Outline Font

WGL has two routines, **wglUseFontBitmaps()** and **wglUseFontOutlines()**, for converting system fonts for use with OpenGL. Both routines build a display list for each requested character from the specified font and font size.

WGL Prototypes

Initialization

Determine version information:

> BOOL **GetVersion**(LPOSVERSIONINFO *lpVersionInformation*);

> BOOL **GetVersionEx**(LPOSVERSIONINFO *lpVersionInformation*);

Pixel format availability, selection, and capability:

> int **ChoosePixelFormat**(HDC *hdc*,
>   CONST PIXELFORMATDESCRIPTOR * *ppfd*);

> BOOL **SetPixelFormat**(HDC *hdc*, int *iPixelFormat*,
>   CONST PIXELFORMATDESCRIPTOR * *ppfd*);

> int **DescribePixelFormat**(HDC *hdc*, int *iPixelFormat*, UINT *nBytes*,
>   LPPIXELFORMATDESCRIPTOR *ppfd*);

> BOOL **wglDescribeLayerPlane**(HDC *hdc*, int *iPixelFormat*,
>   int *iLayerPlane*, UINT *nBytes*, LPLAYERPLANEDESCRIPTOR *plpd*);

Obtain a pointer to an OpenGL function:

> PROC **wglGetProcAddress**(LPCSTR *funcName*);

Controlling Rendering

Manage or query an OpenGL rendering context:

    HGLRC **wglCreateContext**(HDC *hdc*);

    HGLRC **wglCreateContextAttribsARB**(HDC *hdc*,
        HGLRC *hShareContext*, const int **attribList*)

    HGLRC **wglCreateLayerContext**(HDC *hdc*, int *iLayerPlane*);

    BOOL **wglShareLists**(HGLRC *hglrc1*, HGLRC *hglrc2*);

    BOOL **wglDeleteContext**(HGLRC *hglrc*);

    BOOL **wglCopyContext**(HGLRC *hglrcSource*, HGLRC *hlglrcDest*,
        UINT *mask*);

    BOOL **wglMakeCurrent**(HDC *hdc*, HGLRC *hglrc*);

    HGLRC **wglGetCurrentContext**(VOID);

    HDC **wglGetCurrentDC**(VOID);

Access implementation-dependent extension procedure calls:

    PROC **wglGetProcAddress**(LPCSTR *lpszProc*);

Access and release the bitmap of the front buffer:

    HBITMAP **CreateDIBitmap**(HDC *hdc*,
        CONST BITMAPINFOHEADER **lpbmih*, DWORD *fdwInit*,
        CONST VOID **lpbInit*, CONST BITMAPINFO **lpbmi*,
        UINT *fuUsage*);

    HBITMAP **CreateDIBSection**(HDC *hdc*, CONST BITMAPINFO **pbmi*,
        UINT *iUsage*, VOID **ppvBits*, HANDLE *hSection*,
        DWORD *dwOffset*);

    BOOL **DeleteObject**(HGDIOBJ *hObject*);

Exchange front and back buffers:

    BOOL **SwapBuffers**(HDC *hdc*);

    BOOL **wglSwapLayerBuffers**(HDC *hdc*, UINT *fuPlanes*);

Find a color palette for overlay or underlay layers:

> int **wglGetLayerPaletteEntries**(HDC *hdc*, int *iLayerPlane*,
>   int *iStart*, int *cEntries*, CONST COLORREF **pcr*);

> int **wglSetLayerPaletteEntries**(HDC *hdc*, int *iLayerPlane*, int *iStart*
>   int *cEntries*, CONST COLORREF **pcr*);

> BOOL **wglRealizeLayerPalette**(HDC *hdc*, int *iLayerPlane*,
>   BOOL *bRealize*);

Use a bitmap or an outline font:

> BOOL **wglUseFontBitmaps**(HDC *hdc*, DWORD *first*, DWORD *count*,
>   DWORD *listBase*);

> BOOL **wglUseFontOutlines**(HDC *hdc*, DWORD *first*, DWORD *count*,
>   DWORD *listBase*, FLOAT *deviation*, FLOAT *extrusion*, int *format*,
>   LPGLYPHMETRICSFLOAT *lpgmf*);

Glossary

API

An abbreviation of "application-programming interface."

accumulation buffer

Memory (bitplanes) that is used to accumulate a series of images generated in the color buffer. Using the accumulation buffer may significantly improve the quality of the image, but also take correspondingly longer to render. The accumulation buffer is used for effects such as depth of field, motion blur, and full-scene antialiasing.

aliasing

A rendering technique that assigns to pixels the color of the primitive being rendered, regardless of whether that primitive covers all or only a portion of the pixel's area. This results in jagged edges, or jaggies.

alpha

A fourth color component. The alpha component is never displayed directly and is typically used to control color blending. By convention, OpenGL alpha corresponds to the notion of opacity, rather than transparency, meaning that an alpha value of 1.0 implies complete opacity, and an alpha value of 0.0 complete transparency.

ambient

Ambient light is nondirectional and distributed uniformly throughout space. Ambient light falling upon a surface approaches from all directions. The light is reflected from the object independent of surface location and orientation, with equal intensity in all directions.

animation

Generating repeated renderings of a scene, with smoothly changing view-point and/or object positions, quickly enough so that the illusion of motion is achieved. OpenGL animation is almost always done using double-buffering.

antialiasing

A rendering technique that assigns pixel colors based on the fraction of the pixel's area that's covered by the primitive being rendered. Antialiased rendering reduces or eliminates the jaggies that result from aliased rendering.

application-specific clipping

Clipping of primitives against planes in eye coordinates; the planes are specified by the application using **glClipPlane()**.

ARB Imaging Subset

The collection of OpenGL extensions for processing pixel rectangles. Imaging Subset operations include color table lookups, color matrix transformations, image convolutions, and image statistics.

attenuation

The property of light that describes how a light's intensity diminishes over distance.

attribute group

A set of related state variables, which OpenGL can save or restore together at one time.

back faces

See *faces*.

bit

Binary digit. A state variable having only two possible values: 0 or 1. Binary numbers are constructions of one or more bits.

bitmap

A rectangular array of bits. Also, the primitive rendered by the **glBitmap()** command, which uses its *bitmap* parameter as a mask.

bitplane

A rectangular array of bits mapped one-to-one with pixels. The framebuffer is a stack of bitplanes.

blending

Reduction of two color components to one component, usually as a linear interpolation between the two components.

buffer

A group of bitplanes that store a single component (such as depth or green) or a single index (such as the color index or the stencil index). Sometimes the red, green, blue, and alpha buffers together are referred to as the color buffer, rather than the color buffers.

buffer object

A vertex array located in the GL's server memory, as opposed to the client application's memory. Vertex data and indices stored in buffer objects may render considerably faster than the equivalent client-side versions.

byte swapping

The process of exchanging the ordering of bytes in a (usually integer) variable type (i.e., `int`, `short`, etc.)

C

God's programming language.

C++

The object-oriented programming language of a pagan deity.

client

The computer from which OpenGL commands are issued. The computer that issues OpenGL commands can be connected via a network to a different computer that executes the commands, or commands can be issued and executed on the same computer. See also *server*.

client memory

The main memory (where program variables are stored) of the client computer.

clip coordinates

The coordinate system that follows transformation by the projection matrix and precedes perspective division. View-volume clipping is done in clip coordinates, but application-specific clipping is not.

clipping

Elimination of the portion of a geometric primitive that's outside the half-space defined by a clipping plane. Points are simply rejected if outside. The portion of a line or polygon that's outside the half-space is eliminated, and additional vertices are generated as necessary to complete the primitive within the clipping half-space. Geometric primitives and the current raster position (when specified) are always clipped against the six half-spaces defined by the left, right, bottom, top, near, and far planes of the view volume. Applications can specify optional application-specific clipping planes to be applied in eye coordinates.

color index

A single value that represents a color by name, rather than by value. OpenGL color indices are treated as continuous values (for example, floating-point numbers), while operations such as interpolation and dithering are performed on them. Color indices stored in the framebuffer are always integer values, however. Floating-point indices are converted to integers by rounding to the nearest integer value.

color-index mode

An OpenGL context is in color-index mode if its color buffers store color indices, rather than red, green, blue, and alpha color components.

color-lookup table

A one-dimensional image used to substitute RGBA color components in an image pixel.

color map

A table of index-to-RGB mappings that's accessed by the display hardware. Each color index is read from the color buffer, converted to an RGB triple by lookup in the color map, and sent to the monitor.

color matrix

The 4×4 matrix used to transform RGBA pixel values when passed into the Imaging Subset. Color matrices are particularly useful in color space conversions.

components

Single, continuous (for example, floating-point) values that represent
intensities or quantities. Usually, a component value of zero represents the
minimum value or intensity, and a component value of one represents the
maximum value or intensity, although other ranges are sometimes used.
Because component values are interpreted in a normalized range, they
are specified independent of actual resolution. For example, the RGB
triple (1, 1, 1) is white, regardless of whether the color buffers store 4, 8,
or 12 bits each.

Out-of-range components are typically clamped to the normalized range,
not truncated or otherwise interpreted. For example, the RGB triple
(1.4, 1.5, 0.9) is clamped to (1.0, 1.0, 0.9) before it's used to update the color
buffer. Red, green, blue, alpha, and depth are always treated as components,
never as indices.

concave

A polygon that is not convex. See *convex*.

context

A complete set of OpenGL state variables. Note that framebuffer contents are
not part of OpenGL state, but that the configuration of the framebuffer (and
any associated renderbuffers) is.

convex

A polygon is convex if no straight line in the plane of the polygon intersects
the polygon more than twice.

convex hull

The smallest convex region enclosing a specified group of points. In two
dimensions, the convex hull is found conceptually by stretching a rubber
band around the points so that all of the points lie within the band.

convolution filter

One- or two-dimensional images that are used for computing the weighted
average of pixel images.

convolution kernel

See *convolution filter*.

coordinate system

In *n*-dimensional space, a set of *n* linearly independent vectors anchored to a point (called the origin). A group of coordinates specifies a point in space (or a vector from the origin) by indicating how far to travel along each vector to reach the point (or tip of the vector).

culling

The process of eliminating a front face or back face of a polygon so that it isn't drawn.

current matrix

A matrix that transforms coordinates in one coordinate system to coordinates of another system. There are three current matrices in OpenGL: The modelview matrix transforms object coordinates (coordinates specified by the programmer) to eye coordinates; the perspective matrix transforms eye coordinates to clip coordinates; the texture matrix transforms specified or generated texture coordinates as described by the matrix. Each current matrix is the top element on a stack of matrices. Each of the three stacks can be manipulated with OpenGL matrix-manipulation commands.

current raster position

A window coordinate position that specifies the placement of an image primitive when it's rasterized. The current raster position and other current raster parameters are updated when **glRasterPos()** is called.

decal

A method of calculating color values during texture application, where the texture colors replace the fragment colors or, if alpha blending is enabled, the texture colors are blended with the fragment colors, using only the alpha value.

deprecated

The identification of a function entry point, or feature exposed as a token passed into a function call, that is slated for potential removal in future versions of the API.

depreciation model

The plan used for the identification and potential removal of features from the OpenGL library. The depreciation model was introduced with OpenGL Version 3.0, and the first features were removed from the API in Version 3.1.

depth

Generally refers to the *z* window coordinate.

depth buffer

Memory that stores the depth value at every pixel. To perform hidden-surface removal, the depth buffer records the depth value of the object that lies closest to the observer at every pixel. The depth value of every new fragment uses the recorded value for depth comparison and must pass the comparison test before being rendered.

depth-cuing

A rendering technique that assigns color based on distance from the viewpoint.

diffuse

Diffuse lighting and reflection accounts for the direction of a light source. The intensity of light striking a surface varies with the angle between the orientation of the object and the direction of the light source. A diffuse material scatters that light evenly in all directions.

directional light source

See *infinite light source.*

display list

A named list of OpenGL commands. Display lists are always stored on the server, so display lists can be used to reduce network traffic in client-server environments. The contents of a display list may be preprocessed and might therefore execute more efficiently than the same set of OpenGL commands executed in immediate mode. Such preprocessing is especially important for computing intensive commands such as NURBS or polygon tessellation.

dithering

A technique for increasing the perceived range of colors in an image at the cost of spatial resolution. Adjacent pixels are assigned differing color values; when viewed from a distance, these colors seem to blend into a single intermediate color. The technique is similar to the halftoning used in black-and-white publications to achieve shades of gray.

double-buffering

OpenGL contexts with both front and back color buffers are double-buffered. Smooth animation is accomplished by rendering into only the back buffer (which isn't displayed), and then causing the front and back buffers to be swapped. See **glutSwapBuffers()** in "Motion = Redraw + Swap" in Chapter 1Appendix A.

edge flag

A Boolean value at a vertex that marks whether that vertex precedes a boundary edge. **glEdgeFlag*()** may be used to mark an edge as not on the boundary. When a polygon is drawn in GL_LINE mode, only boundary edges are drawn.

element

A single component or index.

emission

The color of an object that is self-illuminating or self-radiating. The intensity of an emissive material is not attributed to any external light source.

evaluated

The OpenGL process of generating object-coordinate vertices and parameters from previously specified Bézier equations.

execute

An OpenGL command is executed when it's called in immediate mode or when the display list that it's a part of is called.

extension

A new feature of OpenGL that hasn't been added into the core of OpenGL. An extension does not have to be supported by every OpenGL implementation, as compared to core OpenGL functions, which are supported for every OpenGL implementation. There are different types of extensions, based upon how broadly supported the functionality is. Generally, extensions supported only by a single company's OpenGL implementation will have a name that includes an abbreviation of the company name. If more companies adopt the extension, its name will change from the abbreviation to a string that includes the letters, EXT; for example, GL_EXT_polygon_offset. If OpenGL's governing body, the Khronos OpenGL ARB Working Group (or ARB, for short) reviews and approves the extension, its name will change once again. For example, a reviewed extension that was approved by the ARB is GL_ARB_multitexture.

eye coordinates

The coordinate system that follows transformation by the modelview matrix and precedes transformation by the projection matrix. Lighting and application-specific clipping are done in eye coordinates.

faces

The sides of a polygon. Each polygon has two faces: a front face and a back face. Only one face or the other is ever visible in the window. Whether the back or front face is visible is effectively determined after the polygon is projected onto the window. After this projection, if the polygon's edges are directed clockwise, one of the faces is visible; if directed counterclockwise, the other face is visible. Whether clockwise corresponds to front or back (and counterclockwise corresponds to back or front) is determined by the OpenGL programmer.

feedback

OpenGL's mechanism for allowing an application to retrieve information about which geometric and imaging primitives that would have rasterized to the window. No pixels are updated in feedback mode.

filtering

The process of combining pixels or texels to obtain a higher or lower resolution version of an input image or texture.

fixed-function pipeline

The processing model where the order of operations that OpenGL uses on vertices and fragments is fixed by the implementation. A programmer's control over its operation is limited by setting state values and enabling or disabling operations. See *programmable graphics pipeline.*

flat shading

Refers to a primitive colored with a single, constant color across its extent, rather than smoothly interpolated colors across the primitive. See *Gouraud shading.*

fog

A rendering technique that can be used to simulate atmospheric effects such as haze, fog, and smog by fading object colors to a background color based on distance from the viewer. Fog also aids in the perception of distance from the viewer, giving a depth cue.

fonts

Groups of graphical character representations generally used to display strings of text. The characters may be roman letters, mathematical symbols, Asian ideograms, Egyptian hieroglyphics, and so on.

fragment

Fragments are generated by the rasterization of primitives. Each fragment corresponds to a single pixel and includes color, depth, and sometimes texture-coordinate values.

framebuffer

All the buffers of a given window or context. Sometimes includes all the pixel memory of the graphics hardware accelerator.

framebuffer attachment

A connection point in a framebuffer object that makes an association between allocated image storage (which might be a texture map level, a *renderbuffer*, pixel buffer object, or any of the other types of object storage in OpenGL), and a rendering target, such as a color buffer, the depth buffer, or the stencil buffer.

front faces

See *faces*.

frustum

The view volume warped by perspective division.

gamma correction

A function applied to colors stored in the framebuffer to correct for the nonlinear response of the eye (and sometimes of the monitor) to linear changes in color-intensity values.

geometric model

The object-coordinate vertices and parameters that describe an object. Note that OpenGL doesn't define a syntax for geometric models, but rather a syntax and semantics for the rendering of geometric models.

geometric object

See *geometric model*.

geometric primitive

A point, a line, or a polygon.

GLSL

The short name for *The OpenGL Shading Language*.

GLX

The window system interface for OpenGL on the X Window System.

GPU

The abbreviation for Graphics Processing Unit.

GPGPU

The short name for General-Purpose computing on GPUs, which is the field of techniques attempting to do general computation (algorithms that you would normally execute on a CPU) on graphics processors.

Gouraud shading

Smooth interpolation of colors across a polygon or line segment. Colors are assigned at vertices and linearly interpolated across the primitive to produce a relatively smooth variation in color. Also called *smooth shading*.

group

Each pixel of an image in client memory is represented by a group of one, two, three, or four elements. Thus, in the context of a client memory image, a group and a pixel are the same thing.

half-spaces

A plane divides space into two half-spaces.

hidden-line removal

A technique to determine which portions of a wireframe object should be visible. The lines that comprise the wireframe are considered to be edges of opaque surfaces, which may obscure other edges that are farther away from the viewer.

hidden-surface removal

A technique to determine which portions of an opaque, shaded object should be visible and which portions should be obscured. A test of the depth coordinate, using the depth buffer for storage, is a common method of hidden-surface removal.

histogram

A database of the distribution of pixel values in an image. The results of the histogram process are counts of unique pixel values.

homogeneous coordinates

A set of $n+1$ coordinates used to represent points in n-dimensional projective space. Points in projective space can be thought of as points in Euclidean space together with some points at infinity. The coordinates are homogeneous because a scaling of each of the coordinates by the same nonzero constant doesn't alter the point that the coordinates refer to. Homogeneous coordinates are useful in the calculations of projective geometry, and thus in computer graphics, where scenes must be projected onto a window.

image

A rectangular array of pixels, either in client memory or in the framebuffer.

image primitive

A bitmap or an image.

immediate mode

Execution of OpenGL commands when they're called, rather than from a display list. No immediate-mode bit exists; the mode in immediate mode refers to use of OpenGL, rather than to a specific bit of OpenGL state.

index

A single value that's interpreted as an absolute value rather than as a normalized value in a specified range (as is a component). Color indices are the names of colors, which are dereferenced by the display hardware using the color map. Indices are typically masked, rather than clamped when out of range. For example, the index 0xf7 is masked to 0x7 when written to a 4-bit buffer (color or stencil). Color indices and stencil indices are always treated as indices, never as components.

indices

Preferred plural of index. (The choice between the plural forms indices or indexes—as well as matrices or matrixes and vertices or vertexes—has engendered much debate between the authors and principal reviewers of this guide. The authors' compromise solution is to use the -ices form, but to state clearly for the record that the use of indice [*sic*], matrice [*sic*], and vertice [*sic*] for the singular forms is an abomination.)

infinite light source

A directional source of illumination. The radiating light from an infinite light source strikes all objects as parallel rays.

instance id

A identifier available in vertex shaders for identifying a unique group of primitives. In GLSL, the instance id is provided in the monotonically increasing variable `gl_InstanceID`.

instanced rendering

Drawing multiple copies of the same set of geometry, varying a unique identifier for each copy of the geometry. See *instance id*.

interleaved

A method of storing vertex arrays whereby heterogeneous types of data (i.e., vertex, normals, texture coordinates, etc.) are grouped together for faster retrieval.

interpolation

Calculation of values (such as color or depth) for interior pixels, given the values at the boundaries (such as at the vertices of a polygon or a line).

IRIS GL

Silicon Graphics' proprietary graphics library, developed from 1982 through 1992. OpenGL was designed with IRIS GL as a starting point.

jaggies

Artifacts of aliased rendering. The edges of primitives that are rendered with aliasing are jagged, rather than smooth. A near-horizontal aliased line, for example, is rendered as a set of horizontal lines on adjacent pixel rows, rather than as a smooth, continuous line.

jittering

A pseudo-random displacement (shaking) of the objects in a scene, used in conjunction with the accumulation buffer to achieve special effects.

kernel

See *convolution kernel*.

level of detail

The process of creating multiple copies of an object or image with different levels of resolution. See also *mipmap*.

lighting

The process of computing the color of a vertex based on current lights, material properties, and lighting-model modes.

line

A straight region of finite width between two vertices. (Unlike mathematical lines, OpenGL lines have finite width and length.) Each segment of a strip of lines is itself a line.

local light source

A source of illumination that has an exact position. The radiating light from a local light source emanates from that position. Other names for a local light source are *point light source* or *positional light source*. A *spotlight* is a special kind of local light source.

local viewer mode

An OpenGL light model mode that accurately computes the vector from a vertex to the eye. For performance reasons, *local viewer mode* is not enabled, and an approximation to the real vector is used for lighting computations.

logical operation

Boolean mathematical operations between the incoming fragment's RGBA color or color-index values and the RGBA color or color-index values already stored at the corresponding location in the framebuffer. Examples of logical operations include AND, OR, XOR, NAND, and INVERT.

luminance

The perceived brightness of a surface. Often refers to a weighted average of red, green, and blue color values that indicates the perceived brightness of the combination.

material

A surface property used in computing the illumination of a surface.

matrices

Preferred plural of matrix. See *indices*.

matrix

A two-dimensional array of values. OpenGL matrices are all 4×4, though when stored in client memory they're treated as 1×16 single-dimension arrays.

minmax

The process of computing the minimum and maximum pixel values in an image using the Imaging Subset.

mipmap

A reduced resolution version of a texture map, used to texture a geometric primitive whose screen resolution differs from the resolution of the source texture map.

modelview matrix

The 4×4 matrix that transforms points, lines, polygons, and raster positions from object coordinates to eye coordinates.

modulate

A method of calculating color values during texture application whereby the texture and the fragment colors are combined.

monitor

The device that displays the image in the framebuffer.

motion blurring

A technique that uses the accumulation buffer to simulate what appears on film when you take a picture of a moving object or when you move the camera while taking a picture of a stationary object. In animations without motion blur, moving objects can appear jerky.

multitexturing

The process of applying several texture images to a single primitive. The images are applied one after another, in a pipeline of texturing operations.

network

A connection between two or more computers that enables each to transfer data to and from the others.

nonconvex

A polygon is nonconvex if a line exists in the plane of the polygon that intersects the polygon more than twice.

normal

A three-component plane equation that defines the angular orientation, but not position, of a plane or surface.

normal vectors

See *normal*.

normalized

To normalize a normal vector, divide each of the components by the square root of the sum of their squares. Then, if the normal is thought of as a vector from the origin to the point (nx', ny', nz'), this vector has unit length.

factor = sqrt$(nx^2 + ny^2 + nz^2)$

$nx' = nx$ / factor

$ny' = ny$ / factor

$nz' = nz$ / factor

NURBS

Non-Uniform Rational B-Spline. A common way to specify parametric curves and surfaces. (See GLU NURBS routines in Chapter 12.)

object

An object-coordinate model that's rendered as a collection of primitives.

object coordinates

Coordinate system prior to any OpenGL transformation.

off-screen rendering

The process of drawing into a framebuffer that is not directly displayed to the visible screen.

The OpenGL Shading Language

The language used for authoring *shader program*. Also commonly known as the *GLSL*.

orthographic

Nonperspective (or parallel) projection, as in some engineering drawings, with no foreshortening.

outer product

A process that produces a matrix from two vectors. For the matrix A, which is the outer product of the vectors u and v, $A_{ij} = u_i v_j$.

pack

The process of converting pixel colors from a buffer into the format requested by the application.

parameters

Values passed as arguments to OpenGL commands. Sometimes parameters are passed by reference to an OpenGL command.

perspective correction

An additional calculation for texture coordinates to fix texturing artifacts for a textured geometric rendered in a perspective projection.

perspective division

The division of x, y, and z by w, carried out in clip coordinates.

picking

A form of *selection* that uses a rectangular region (usually near the cursor location) to determine which primitives to select.

ping-pong buffers

A *GPGPU* technique of writing values to a buffer (usually a texture map) that is immediately rebound as a texture map to be read from to do a subsequent computation. Effectively, you can consider the buffer written-to, and subsequently read-from as being a collection of temporary values. Ping-ponging buffers is usually done using *framebuffer objects*.

pixel

Picture element. The bits at location (x, y) of all the bitplanes in the frame-buffer constitute the single pixel (x, y). In an image in client memory, a pixel is one group of elements. In OpenGL window coordinates, each pixel corresponds to a 1.0×1.0 screen area. The coordinates of the lower left corner of the pixel are (x, y), and of the upper right corner are $(x + 1, y + 1)$.

point

An exact location in space, which is rendered as a finite-diameter dot.

point light source

See *local light source*.

polygon

A near-planar surface bounded by edges specified by vertices. Each triangle of a triangle mesh is a polygon, as is each quadrilateral of a quadrilateral mesh. The rectangle specified by **glRect*()** is also a polygon.

polygon offset

A technique to modify depth-buffer values of a polygon when additional geometric primitives are drawn with identical geometric coordinates.

positional light source

See *local light source*.

primitive

A point, a line, a polygon, a bitmap, or an image. (Note: Not just a point, a line, or a polygon!)

projection matrix

The 4 × 4 matrix that transforms points, lines, polygons, and raster positions from eye coordinates to clip coordinates.

proxy texture

A placeholder for a texture image, which is used to determine if there are enough resources to support a texture image of a given size and internal format resolution.

programmable graphics pipeline

The mode of operation where the processing of *vertices*, *fragments*, and their associated data (texture coordinates, for example) is under the control of *shader programs* specified by the programmer.

quadrilateral

A polygon with four edges.

rasterization

Converts a projected point, line, or polygon, or the pixels of a bitmap or image, to fragments, each corresponding to a pixel in the framebuffer. Note that all primitives are rasterized, not just points, lines, and polygons.

rectangle

A quadrilateral whose alternate edges are parallel to each other in object coordinates. Polygons specified with **glRect*()** are always rectangles; other quadrilaterals might be rectangles.

rendering

Conversion of primitives specified in object coordinates to an image in the framebuffer. Rendering is the primary operation of OpenGL—it's what OpenGL does.

render-to-texture

A technique where the storage for a texture map is used as a destination for rendering (i.e., a renderbuffer). Render-to-texture enables a more efficient method for updating texture maps than rendering into the color buffer, and copy the results into texture memory, saving the copy operation.

renderbuffer

An allocation of memory in the OpenGL server for the storage of pixel values. Renderbuffers are used as a destination for rendering, as well as able to be as texture maps without requiring a copy of the renderbuffer's data.

resident texture

A texture image that is cached in special, high-performance texture memory. If an OpenGL implementation does not have special, high-performance texture memory, then all texture images are deemed resident textures.

RGBA

Red, green, blue, alpha.

RGBA mode

An OpenGL context is in RGBA mode if its color buffers store red, green, blue, and alpha color components, rather than color indices.

scissoring

A fragment clipping test. Fragments outside of a rectangular scissor region are rejected.

selection

The process of determining which primitives intersect a 2D region or 3D volume defined by matrix transformations.

separable filter

A form of 2D *convolution filter* that can be represented by two 1D vectors. The 2D separable filter is determined by computing the *outer product* of the two vectors.

server

The computer on which OpenGL commands are executed. This might differ from the computer from which commands are issued. See *client*.

shader program

A set of instructions written in a graphics shading language (The OpenGL Shading Language, also called GLSL) that control the processing of graphics primitives.

shading

The process of interpolating color within the interior of a polygon, or between the vertices of a line, during rasterization.

shininess

The exponent associated with *specular* reflection and lighting. Shininess controls the degree with which the specular highlight decays.

single-buffering

OpenGL contexts that don't have back color buffers are single-buffered. You can use these contexts for animation, but take care to avoid visually disturbing flashes when rendering.

singular matrix

A matrix that has no inverse. Geometrically, such a matrix represents a transformation that collapses points along at least one line to a single point.

smooth shading

See *Gouraud shading*.

specular

Specular lighting and reflection incorporates reflection off shiny objects and the position of the viewer. Maximum specular reflectance occurs when the angle between the viewer and the direction of the reflected light is zero. A specular material scatters light with greatest intensity in the direction of the reflection, and its brightness decays, based upon the exponential value *shininess*.

spotlight

A special type of local light source that has a direction (where it points to) as well as a position. A spotlight simulates a cone of light, which may have a fall-off in intensity, based upon distance from the center of the cone.

sprite

A screen-aligned graphics primitive. Sprites are usually represented as either a single vertex that is expanded to cover many pixels around the transformed vertex, or as a quadrilateral its vertices specified so that it is perpendicular to the viewing direction (or put another way, parallel to the image plane).

sRGB color space

An RGB color space standard specified by the International Electrotechnical Commission (IEC) that matches the color intensity outputs of monitors and printers better than a linear RGB space. The sRGB approximately corresponds to gamma correcting RGB (but not alpha) values using a gamma value of 2.2. See IEC standard 61966-2-1 for all of the gory details.

stencil buffer

Memory (bitplanes) that is used for additional per-fragment testing, along with the *depth buffer*. The stencil test may be used for masking regions, capping solid geometry, and overlapping translucent polygons.

stereo

Enhanced three-dimensional perception of a rendered image by computing separate images for each eye. Stereo requires special hardware, such as two synchronized monitors or special glasses, to alternate viewed frames for each eye. Some implementations of OpenGL support stereo by including both left and right buffers for color data.

stipple

A one- or two-dimensional binary pattern that defeats the generation of fragments where its value is zero. Line stipples are one-dimensional and are applied relative to the start of a line. Polygon stipples are two-dimensional and are applied with a fixed orientation to the window.

tessellation

Reduction of a portion of an analytic surface to a mesh of polygons, or of a portion of an analytic curve to a sequence of lines.

texel

A texture element. A texel is obtained from texture memory and represents the color of the texture to be applied to a corresponding fragment.

texture mapping

The process of applying an image (the texture) to a primitive. Texture mapping is often used to add realism to a scene. For example, you can apply a picture of a building facade to a polygon representing a wall.

texture matrix

The 4 × 4 matrix that transforms texture coordinates from the coordinates in which they're specified to the coordinates that are used for interpolation and texture lookup.

texture object

A named cache that stores texture data, such as the image array, associated mipmaps, and associated texture parameter values: width, height, border width, internal format, resolution of components, minification and magnification filters, wrapping modes, border color, and texture priority.

textures

One- or two-dimensional images that are used to modify the color of fragments produced by rasterization.

texture unit

When multitexturing, as part of an overall multiple pass application of texture images, a texture unit controls one processing step for a single texture image. A texture unit maintains the texturing state for one texturing pass, including the texture image, filter, environment, coordinate generation, and matrix stack. Multitexturing consists of a chain of texture units.

transformations

The warping of spaces. In OpenGL, transformations are limited to projective transformations that include anything that can be represented by a 4×4 matrix. Such transformations include rotations, translations, (non-uniform) scalings along the coordinate axes, perspective transformations, and combinations of these.

triangle

A polygon with three edges. Triangles are always convex.

uniform variable

A type of variable used in vertex or fragment shaders that doesn't change its value across a set of primitives (either a single primitive, or the collection of primitives specified by a single draw call).

uniform buffer object

A type of buffer object that encapsulates a set of uniform variables, making access and update of that collection of uniform variables much faster with less function call overhead.

unpack

The process of converting pixels supplied by an application to OpenGL's internal format.

vertex

A point in three-dimensional space.

vertex array

A block of vertex data (vertex coordinates, texture coordinates, surface normals, RGBA colors, color indices, and edge flags) may be stored in an array and then used to specify multiple geometric primitives through the execution of a single OpenGL command.

vertices

Preferred plural of vertex. See *indices*.

viewpoint

The origin of either the eye- or the clip-coordinate system, depending on context. (For example, when discussing lighting, the viewpoint is the origin of the eye-coordinate system. When discussing projection, the viewpoint is the origin of the clip-coordinate system.) With a typical projection matrix, the eye-coordinate and clip-coordinate origins are at the same location.

view volume

The volume in clip coordinates whose coordinates satisfy the following three conditions:

$-w \leq x \leq w$

$-w \leq y \leq w$

$-w \leq z \leq w$

Geometric primitives that extend outside this volume are clipped.

VRML

VRML stands for Virtual Reality Modeling Language, which is (according to the VRML Mission Statement) "a universal description language for multi-participant simulations." VRML is specifically designed to allow people to navigate through three-dimensional worlds that are placed on the World Wide Web. The first versions of VRML are subsets of the Open Inventor file format with additions to allow hyperlinking to the Web (to URLs—Universal Resource Locators).

window

A subregion of the framebuffer, usually rectangular, whose pixels all have the same buffer configuration. An OpenGL context renders to a single window at a time.

window-aligned

When referring to line segments or polygon edges, implies that these are parallel to the window boundaries. (In OpenGL, the window is rectangular, with horizontal and vertical edges.) When referring to a polygon pattern, implies that the pattern is fixed relative to the window origin.

window coordinates

The coordinate system of a window. It's important to distinguish between the names of pixels, which are discrete, and the window-coordinate system, which is continuous. For example, the pixel at the lower left corner of a window is pixel (0, 0); the window coordinates of the center of this pixel are (0.5, 0.5, z). Note that window coordinates include a depth, or z, component, and that this component is continuous as well.

wireframe

A representation of an object that contains line segments only. Typically, the line segments indicate polygon edges.

working set

On machines with special hardware that increases texture performance, this is the group of texture objects that are currently resident. The performance of textures within the working set outperforms the textures outside the working set.

X Window System

A window system used by many of the machines on which OpenGL is implemented. GLX is the name of the OpenGL extension to the X Window System. (See Appendix D.)

Index

drawing
  clearing the window, 34
  forcing completion of, 38
  icosahedron, 115
  points, 48
  polygons, 48, 61
  preparing for, 34
  rectangles, 45
  spheres, cylinders, and disks, 559–567
drawing pixel data, *see* pixel data
Duff, Tom, 259

E

edge flags, 67–68
  tessellated polygons generate, 546
  vertex arrays, specifying values with, 74
emission, 208, 234, 241
enabling
  alpha test, 502
  antialiasing of points or lines, 269
  antialiasing polygons, 280
  blending, 255
  color material properties mode, 237
  color sum mode, 478
  culling, 62
  depth test, 510
  dithering, 193, 517
  evaluators, 575, 579
  fog, 281
  lighting, 231
  line stippling, 57
  logical operations, 517
  multisampling, 276
  normal vectors for evaluated surfaces,
    automatic generation of, 579, 587
  polygon offset, 294
  polygon stippling, 63
  rescaling normals, 70, 212
  stencil test, 504

texture coordinate generation, 462
texturing, 396, 399
unit length normal vectors ensured, 70,
    212
endianness, 349
environment mapping, 463, 465
errata, xlii
error handling, 637–639
  error string description, 639
evaluators, 572–586
  basis functions, 571, 575
  evenly spaced values, 577, 581
  one-dimensional, 572
  rendering pipeline stage, 11
  sample program using mesh for 2D Bézier
    surface, 582
  sample program which draws 1D Bézier
    curve, 573
  sample program which draws 2D Bézier
    surface, 580
  sample program which generates texture
    coordinates, 584
  texture coordinates, generating, 584
  two-dimensional, 580
event management, using GLUT, 21
extensions
  Microsoft Windows and
    wglGetProcAddress(), 643
  vendor-specific, 641
eye coordinates, 128, 170
  texture coordinate generation, 458, 462

F

fade effect, 645
Farin, Gerald E., 571
feedback, 627–634
  array contents, 633
  pass-through markers, 630
  querying current rendering mode, 608
  returned data, 629

X

X Window System, 15, 813
  client-server rendering, 5
  minimum framebuffer configuration, 492
  X Visual, 196, 813

Z

z buffer, *see* depth buffer
z coordinates, *see* depth coordinates
zooming images, 356
  filtered, 666